A DICTIONARY OF
CHINESE BUDDHIST TERMS

A DICTIONARY OF

CHINESE BUDDHIST TERMS

WITH SANSKRIT AND ENGLISH EQUIVALENTS
AND A SANSKRIT-PALI INDEX

Compiled by

WILLIAM EDWARD SOOTHILL

M.A. OXON, HON. M.A. CANTAB.

Late Professor of Chinese Language and Literature, Oxford University

LEWIS HODOUS

Late Professor of the Philosophy of Religion,
Hartford Seminary Foundation, Hartford, Conn.

MOTILAL BANARSIDASS PUBLISHERS
PRIVATE LIMITED • DELHI

Reprint: Delhi, 1977, 1987, 1994, 1997, 2000, 2003

First Edition: London, 1937

(By arrangement with M/s. Kegan Paul, Trench, Trubner and Co. Ltd. London)

ISBN: 81-208-0319-1

Also available at:

MOTILAL BANARSIDASS

41 U.A. Bungalow Road, Jawahar Nagar, Delhi 110 007
8 Mahalaxmi Chambers, 22 Bhulabhai Desai Road, Mumbai 400 026
236, 9th Main III Block, Jayanagar, Bangalore 560 011
120 Royapettah High Road, Mylapore, Chennai 600 004
Sanas Plaza, 1302 Baji Rao Road, Pune 411 002
8 Camac Street, Kolkata 700 017
Ashok Rajpath, Patna 800 004
Chowk, Varanasi 221 001

Printed in India

BY JAINENDRA PRAKASH JAIN AT SHRI JAINENDRA PRESS,
A-45 NARAINA, PHASE-I, NEW DELHI 110 028
AND PUBLISHED BY NARENDRA PRAKASH JAIN FOR
MOTILAL BANARSIDASS PUBLISHERS PRIVATE LIMITED,
BUNGALOW ROAD, DELHI 110 007

TABLE OF CONTENTS

PROFESSOR SOOTHILL'S PREFACE

As compilers of the first Dictionary of Chinese Mahayana Terms, we are far from considering our attempt as final. Our desire has been to provide a key for the student with which to unlock a closed door. If it serves to reveal the riches of the great Buddhist thesaurus in China, we will gladly leave to others the correction and perfecting of our instrument. It was Dr. E. J. Eitel, of the London Missionary Society, who over sixty years ago, in 1870, provided the first means in English of studying Chinese Buddhist texts by his *Handbook for the Student of Chinese Buddhism*. It has been of great service; but it did not deal with Chinese Buddhist terminology in general. In form it was Sanskrit-Chinese-English, and the second edition unhappily omitted the Chinese-Sanskrit Index which was essential for the student reading the Chinese Sutras.[1]

Lacking a dictionary of Chinese Buddhist terms, it was small wonder that the translation of Chinese texts has made little progress, important though these are to the understanding of Mahayana Buddhism, especially in its Far Eastern development. Two main difficulties present themselves: first of all, the special and peculiar use of numerous ordinary Chinese terms; and, secondly, the large number of transliterated phrases.

In regard to the first difficulty, those who have endeavoured to read Chinese texts apart from the apprehension of a Sanskrit background have generally made a fallacious interpretation, for the Buddhist canon is basically translation, or analogous to translation. In consequence, a large number of terms existing are employed approximately to connote imported ideas, as the various Chinese translators understood those ideas. Various translators invented different terms; and, even when the same term was finally adopted, its connotation varied, sometimes widely, from the Chinese term or phrase as normally used by the Chinese. For instance, *kleśa* undoubtedly has a meaning in Sanskrit similar to that of 煩 惱, i.e. affliction, distress, trouble. In Buddhism affliction (or, as it may be understood from Chinese, the afflicters, distressers, troublers) means the passions and illusions; and consequently *fan-nao* in Buddhist phraseology has acquired this technical connotation of the passions and illusions. Many terms of a similar character will be noted in the body of this work. Consequent partly on this use of ordinary terms, even a well-educated Chinese without a knowledge of the technical equivalents finds himself unable to understand their implications.

[1] A reprint of the second edition, incorporating a Chinese Index, was published in Japan in 1904, but is very scarce.

A difficulty equally serious is the transliteration of Sanskrit, a difficulty rendered far greater by the varied versions of many translators. Take, for instance, the word "Buddha" and its transliteration as 佛；佛陀；浮陀，浮圖，浮頭，勃陀，勃馱，部陀，母陀，沒馱，and so on. The pages of the Chinese canon are peppered with such transliterations as these from the Sanskrit, in regrettable variety. The position resembles that of Chinese terminology in Modern Science, which was often transliteration twenty or thirty years ago, when I drew the attention of the Board of Education in Peking to the need of a regulated terminology for Science. Similarly, in pages devoid of capitals, quotation-marks, or punctuation, transliterated Sanskrit-into-Chinese may well seem to the uninitiated, whether Chinese or foreign, to be ordinary phrases out of which no meaning can be drawn.

Convinced, therefore, that until an adequate dictionary was in existence, the study of Far Eastern Buddhist texts could make little progress amongst foreign students in China, I began the formation of such a work. In 1921 I discovered in Bodley's Library, Oxford, an excellent version of the 翻譯名義集 *Fan I Ming I Chi*, i.e. Translation of Terms and Meanings, composed by 法雲 Fa-yün, *circa* the tenth century A.D. At the head of each entry in the volume I examined, some one, I know not whom, had written the Sanskrit equivalent in Sanskrit letters. These terms were at once added to my own card index. Unhappily the writer had desisted from his charitable work at the end of the third volume, and the remaining seven volumes I had laboriously to decipher with the aid of Stanislas Julien's *Méthode pour déchiffrer et transcrire les noms sanscrits qui se rencontrent dans les livres chinois*, 1861, and various dictionaries, notably that of Monier Williams. Not then possessed of the first edition of Eitel's Handbook, I also perforce made an index of the whole of his book. Later there came to my knowledge the admirable work of the Japanese 織田得能 Oda Tokunō in his 佛教大辭典; and also the Chinese version based upon it of 丁福保 Ting Fu-pao, called the 佛學大辭典 in sixteen volumes; also the 佛學小辭典 in one volume. Apart from these, it would have been difficult for Dr. Hodous and myself to have collaborated in the production of this work. Other dictionaries and vocabularies have since appeared, not least the first three fascicules of the *Hôbôgirin*, the Japanese-Sanskrit-French Dictionary of Buddhism.

When my work had made considerable progress, Dr. Y. Y. Tsu called upon me and in the course of conversation mentioned that Dr. Hodous, of Hartford Theological Seminary, Connecticut, U.S.A., who had spent many years in South China and studied its religions, was also engaged on a Buddhist Dictionary. After some delay and correspondence, an arrangement was made by which the work was divided between us, the final editing and publishing being allotted to me. Lack of time and funds has prevented our studying the Canon, especially historically, or engaging a staff of competent Chinese Buddhist scholars to study it for the purpose. We are consequently all too well aware that the Dictionary is not as perfect or complete as it might be.

Nevertheless, it seems better to encourage the study of Chinese Buddhism as early as possible by the provision of a working dictionary rather than delay the publication perhaps for years, until our ideals are satisfied—a condition which might never be attained.

We therefore issue this Compendium—for it is in reality more than a Dictionary—in the hope that many will be stimulated to devote time to a subject which presents so fascinating a study in the development of religion.

My colleague and collaborator, Dr. Hodous, took an invaluable share in the draft of this work, and since its completion has carefully read over the whole of the typed pages. It may, therefore, be considered as the common work of both of us, for which we accept a common responsibility. It seemed scarcely possible for two men living outside China, separated by 2,000 miles of ocean, and with different mentalities and forms of expression, to work together to a successful conclusion. The risky experiment was hesitatingly undertaken on both sides, but we have been altogether happy in our mutual relations.

To Dr. F. W. Thomas, Boden Professor of Sanskrit, Oxford University, I am deeply indebted for his great kindness in checking the Sanskrit terminology. He is in no way responsible for the translation from the Chinese; but his comments have led to certain corrections, and his help in the revision of the proper spelling of the Sanskrit words has been of very great importance. In the midst of a busy life, he has spared time, at much sacrifice, to consider the Sanskrit phrases throughout the entire work, except certain additional words that have since come to my notice. As an outstanding authority, not only on the Sanskrit language, but on Tibetan Buddhism and the Tibetan language, his aid has been doubly welcome. Similarly, Dr. Hodous wishes specially to thank his colleague at Trinity College, Hartford, Conn., Dr. LeRoy Carr Barret, for the generous assistance he rendered in revising the Sanskrit terms in his section of our joint work, and for his well-considered and acceptable comments and suggestions.

Dr. Lionel Giles, Keeper of the Department of Oriental Printed Books and MSS., British Museum, illustrious son of an illustrious parent, has also our special appreciation, for he magnanimously undertook to read the proofs. He brings his own ripe scholarship and experienced judgment to this long labour; and the value and precision of the Dictionary will undoubtedly be enhanced through his accurate and friendly supervision.

Next, we would most gratefully acknowledge the gift of Mrs. Paul de Witt Twinem, of Trenton, New Jersey, U.S.A. She has subscribed a sum of money which has made the publication of our work possible. To this must be added further aid in a very welcome subvention from the Prize Publication Fund of the Royal Asiatic Society. Such a practical expression of encouragement by fellow-orientalists is a matter of particular gratification.

Our thanks are due to Mr. Zu-liang Yih 葉樹梁, who with accuracy, zeal, and faithfulness has written the large number of Chinese characters needed. To the Hon. Mrs. Wood I am grateful for help in the exacting task of transcribing. As to my daughter, Lady Hosie, I have no words to express my personal indebtedness to her. Without her loving and unflagging aid as amanuensis, I should have been unable to finish my part in this work, which—so the authors hope—will once again demonstrate the implicit and universal need of the human spirit for religion, and its aspirations towards the Light that " lighteth every man that cometh into the world ".

W. E. SOOTHILL.

Oxford, England, 1934.

PROFESSOR HODOUS'S PREFACE

AFTER the Dictionary went to press, Professor Soothill died. The work on the Dictionary, however, was completed. For ten years we worked together, he at Oxford and I at Hartford, and the manuscript crossed the Atlantic four times. During his semester in New York as Visiting Professor in Columbia University and on my brief visit to Oxford, we had opportunity to consult together on some outstanding problems. The work of organizing the material and harmonizing the differences was done by Professor Soothill. He was well equipped to undertake the task of producing a Buddhist Dictionary, having a thorough knowledge of the Chinese language. His Pocket Chinese Dictionary is still in use. He knew Chinese culture and religion. He possessed a keen sense for the significant and a rare ability to translate abstruse terms into terse English. But even more valuable was his profound insight into and deep sympathy with the religious life and thought of another people.

The text and the indexes were again finally revised during his last long illness by Lady Hosie under his supervision. He was able also to appreciate the kind collaboration of Dr. Lionel Giles on the earlier proof-sheets. But his death meant a vastly increased amount of work for Dr. Giles who, on the other side of the Atlantic from myself, has had to assume a responsibility quite unexpected by himself and by us. For two to three years, with unfailing courtesy and patience, he has considered and corrected the very trying pages of the proofs, while the Dictionary was being printed. He gave chivalrously of his long knowledge both of Buddhism and of the Chinese literary characters. He adds yet another laurel to the cause of Chinese learning and research. And in the same way Professor F. W. Thomas bore the brunt of the Sanskrit proof-reading. We have indeed been fortunate to have had our work checked *in extenso* by such exacting scholars.

To Sir E. Denison Ross, who kindly looked over the proofs, and added certain welcome corrections, our thanks are due. Also we would wish to acknowledge the help of Mr. L. M. Chefdeville, who, putting his experience of various Oriental languages at our disposal, made many helpful suggestions, especially as regards the Indexes. Nor do we forget the fidelity and careful work of the printers, Messrs. Stephen Austin and Sons, who collaborated with us in every way in our desire to produce a volume a little worthy of its notable subject.

Our object is well expressed by my late colleague. The difficulties in the production of the book were not small. Buddhism has a long history. Its concepts were impregnated by different cultures, and expressed in different languages. For about a thousand years

Buddhism dominated the thought of China, and her first-rate minds were occupied with Buddhist philosophy. For a period it lagged ; but to-day is in a different position from what it was a generation ago. Buddhism is no longer a decadent religion and in certain countries it is making considerable progress. It is therefore to be hoped that this Dictionary will help to interpret Chinese culture both through the ages and to-day.

LEWIS HODOUS.

Hartford, Connecticut, 1937.

METHOD AND NOTES

1. The rule adopted has been to arrange the terms, first, by strokes, then by radicals, i.e. :—

(*a*) By the number of strokes in the initial character of a term ; then,

(*b*) According to its radical.

Thus 佛 will be found under seven strokes and under the 亻 radical ; 法 under eight strokes and the radical ; 愛 under thirteen strokes and the 心 radical. A page index is provided showing where changes in the number of strokes occur.

2. A list of difficult characters is provided.

3. An index of the Sanskrit terms is given with references to the Chinese text.

4. A limited number of abbreviations have been used, which are self-evident, e.g. tr. for translation, translator, etc. ; translit. for transliteration, transliterate, etc. ; abbrev. for abbreviation ; intp. for interpreted or interpretation ; u.f. for used for. " Eitel " refers to Dr. Eitel's *Handbook of Chinese Buddhism* ; " M.W." to Monier-Williams' *Sanskrit-English Dictionary* ; " Keith " to Professor A. Berriedale Keith's *Buddhist Philosophy* ; " Getty " to Miss Alice Getty's *The Gods of Northern Buddhism* ; B.D. to the 佛 學 大 辭 典 ; B.N. to Bunyiu Nanjio's Catalogue.

5. Where characters are followed by others in brackets, they are used alone or in combination ; e.g. in 十 善 (正 法) the term 十 善 may be used alone or in full 十 善 正 法.

6. In the text a few variations occur in the romanization of Sanskrit and other non-Chinese words. These have been corrected in the Sanskrit index, which should be taken as giving the correct forms.

In this Dictionary it was not possible to follow the principle of inserting hyphens between the members of Sanskrit compound words.

INDEX OF CLASSIFICATION BY STROKES

LIST OF RADICALS

One Stroke

1. 一
2. 丨
3. 丶
4. 丿
5. 乙
,, 乚
6. 亅

Two Strokes

7. 二
8. 亠
9. 人
,, 亻
10. 儿
11. 入
12. 八
13. 冂
14. 冖
15. 冫
16. 几
17. 凵
18. 刀
,, 刂
19. 力
20. 勹
21. 匕
22. 匚
23. 匸
24. 十
25. 卜
26. 卩
,, 㔾
27. 厂
28. 厶
29. 又

Three Strokes

30. 口
31. 囗
32. 土
,, 土
33. 士
34. 夂
35. 夊
36. 夕
37. 大
38. 女
39. 子
40. 宀
41. 寸
42. 小
43. 尢
,, 兀
,, 尣
44. 尸
45. 屮
46. 山
47. 川
,, 巛
,, 巜
48. 工
49. 己
50. 巾
51. 干
52. 幺
53. 广
54. 廴
55. 廾
56. 弋
57. 弓
58. 彐
,, ⺕
,, 彑
59. 彡
60. 彳

Four Strokes

61. 心
,, 忄
,, ⺗
62. 戈
63. 戶
64. 手
,, 扌
65. 支
66. 攴
,, 攵
67. 文
68. 斗
69. 斤
70. 方
71. 无
72. 日
73. 曰
74. 月
75. 木
76. 欠
77. 止
78. 歹
,, 歺
79. 殳
80. 毋
81. 比
82. 毛
83. 氏
84. 气
85. 水
,, 氺
,, 氵
86. 火
,, 灬
87. 爪
,, 爫
88. 父
89. 爻
90. 爿
91. 片
92. 牙
93. 牛
94. 犬
,, 犭

Five Strokes

95. 玄
96. 玉
,, 王
97. 瓜
98. 瓦
99. 甘
100. 生
101. 用
102. 田
103. 疋
104. 疒
105. 癶
106. 白
107. 皮
108. 皿
109. 目
,, 罒
110. 矛
111. 矢

112. 石
113. 示
,, 礻
,, 礻
114. 禸
115. 禾
116. 穴
117. 立

SIX STROKES

118. 竹
,, ⺮
119. 米
120. 糸
121. 缶
,, 缶
122. 网
,, ⺳
,, 罒
,, ⺲
123. 羊
124. 羽
125. 老
,, 耂
126. 而
127. 耒
128. 耳
129. 聿
130. 肉
,, ⺼
,, 月
131. 臣
132. 自
133. 至
134. 臼
135. 舌
136. 舛
137. 舟
138. 艮
139. 色
140. 艸
,, ⺾
,, 艹
141. 虍
142. 虫
143. 血
144. 行
145. 衣
,, 衤
146. 襾
,, 覀

SEVEN STROKES

147. 見
148. 角
149. 言
150. 谷
151. 豆
152. 豕
153. 豸
154. 貝
155. 赤
156. 走
157. 足
158. 身
159. 車
160. 辛
161. 辰
162. 辵
,, 辶
163. 邑
163. 阝 (R)
164. 酉
165. 釆
166. 里

EIGHT STROKES

167. 金
168. 長
,, 镸
169. 門
170. 阜
,, 阝 (L)
171. 隶
172. 隹
173. 雨
,, ⻗
174. 靑
175. 非

NINE STROKES

176. 面
177. 革
178. 韋
179. 韭
180. 音
181. 頁
182. 風
183. 飛
184. 食
,, 飠
185. 首
186. 香

TEN STROKES

187. 馬
188. 骨
189. 高
190. 髟
191. 鬥
192. 鬯
193. 鬲
194. 鬼

ELEVEN STROKES

195. 魚
196. 鳥
197. 鹵
198. 鹿
199. 麥
200. 麻

TWELVE STROKES

201. 黃
202. 黍
203. 黑
204. 黹

THIRTEEN STROKES

205. 黽
206. 鼎
207. 鼓
208. 鼠

FOURTEEN STROKES

209. 鼻
210. 齊

FIFTEEN STROKES

211. 齒

SIXTEEN STROKES

212. 龍
213. 龜

SEVENTEEN STROKES

214. 龠

CHARACTERS WITH RADICALS NOT EASILY IDENTIFIED

ARRANGED ACCORDING TO THE NUMBER OF STROKES

Strokes		Radical	Page
2.	七	1	10a
	九	5	20a
	了	6	20a
3.	久	4	80b
	乞	5	80b
	于	7	81a
	凡	16	81a
	叉	29	82a
4.	不	1	103a
	丹	3	112a
	井	7	112a
	互	7	112a
	云	7	112a
	午	10	143a
	屯	45	148b
	巴	49	148b
5.	丙	1	164a
	且	1	164a
	丘	1	164a
	乏	4	165b
	出	17	166b
	北	21	168a
	占	25	168b
	去	28	168b
	失	37	184b
	央	37	184b
	巨	48	186a
	市	50	186a
	平	51	187b
	弗	57	187b
	由	102	197b
	甲	102	197b
5.	申	102	197b
6.	亦	8	199a
	交	8	199b
	兆	10	201b
	先	10	201b
	全	11	202b
	共	12	202b
	再	13	203a
	卍	24	203a
	危	26	203a
	年	51	212b
	求	85	241b
7.	免	10	230a
	兎	10	230a
	初	18	251a
	卵	26	233a
	君	30	233b
	弟	57	236b
	每	80	241a
8.	事	6	248a
	亟	7	249a
	亞	7	249a
	兩	11	250a
	函	17	250b
	夜	36	253b
	奉	38	253b
	承	64	260a
	明	72	262a
	東	75	263b
	秉	115	276a
	育	130	278a
	肩	130	278a
8.	表	145	280a
9.	冐	13	297a
	南	24	297b
	威	38	299b
	帝	50	300b
	幽	52	301a
	拜	64	302b
	曷	73	304a
	甚	99	308b
	禺	114	311a
	背	130	311b
10.	乘	4	320a
	兼	12	322a
	冥	14	322b
	夏	35	323a
	秦	115	335a
	能	130	336b
11.	乾	5	341a
	執	32	345a
	堂	32	345a
	常	50	349a
	曹	73	352b
	曼	73	352b
	牽	93	358b
	率	95	359b
	畢	102	361a
	罣	122	362b
12.	勝	19	367b
	博	24	368a
	喪	30	368a
	報	32	369b
	斑	67	374a
12.	普	72	374a
	棄	75	376b
	爲	87	383b
	疏	103	383b
	舜	136	387a
	華	140	387a
	衆	143	390a
	量	166	392b
13.	亂	5	395a
	募	19	395b
	勢	19	396a
	嗣	30	396a
	會	73	402b
	業	75	403a
	楚	75	402b
	聖	128	410a
14.	嘉	30	421b
	壽	33	422a
	夢	36	422b
	截	62	424a
	斡	68	424a
	朅	73	424a
	爾	89	425b
	疑	103	425b
	與	134	428a
	舞	136	428a
	蒙	140	428a
	鳴	196	430b
15.	弊	55	432a
	慶	61	432b
	慕	61	432b
	憂	61	433a

Strokes		Radical	Page	Strokes		Radical	Page	Strokes		Radical	Page	Strokes		Radical	Page
15.	摩	64	434b	16.	賴	154	451a	18.	叢	29	464a	20.	釋	165	481b
	暫	72	438b		龜	213	455b		歸	77	465a		騰	187	483b
	養	184	446a	17.	罽	122	461b		舊	134	467a	21.	竈	116	484a
	黎	202	446a		舉	134	467a	19.	攀	64	471a	22.	囊	30	486a
16.	學	39	446b		賽	154	463a		瓣	97	471b		懿	61	478b
	歷	77	448a		蹇	157	463a		辭	160	474b	23.	變	149	488a
	興	134	449b		隸	171	463b	20.	嚴	30	476a	24.	鹽	197	489b
	蕭	140	449b		齋	210	464b		競	117	478b	29.	鬱	192	491a

CORRIGENDA

p. 1b, l. 15. Place comma after 華.

p. 3a, last line. Add 佛 after 成.

p. 3b, l. 2. For 皆 悉 read 悉 皆.

p. 3b, l. 30. Add 法 after 萬.

p. 4b, l. 15. For Shinron read Shinran.

p. 52a, l. 29. Before 切 insert 一.

p. 95b, l. 20. For Kele-yin iikin tegri read Kele-yin űkin tegri.

p. 106a, l. 11. For Abrahamacaryā-veramaṇī read Abrahamararyād vairamaṇī.

p. 194b, l. 6. Add 玄 before 應.

p. 216a, l. 40. 污, 6 strokes, reappears p. 241b, 7 strokes.

p. 251a, l. 8. 初, 7 strokes, in 8 by error.

p. 260a, last line. For 折 read 拆.

p. 267b, l. 25. 法 Dharma; (1) thing, object, appearance; (2) characteristic, attribute, predicate; (3) the substantial bearer of the transcendent substratum of the simple element of conscious life; (4) element of conscious life; (5) nirvāṇa, i.e. dharma *par excellence*; (6) the absolute, the truly real; (7) the teaching, the religion of Buddha.

p. 363a, l. 10. 皐, 12 strokes, in 11 by error.

p. 402a, l. 13. Transpose 身 and 愛.

p. 446a, l. 33. 劍, 15 strokes, in 16 by error.

p. 456b, l. 3 from bottom. For 邪 read 耶.

p. 467a, l. 8. 舉, 17 strokes, in 18 by error.

NOTE

p. 15b, l. 34. Char. 乃, sometimes counted 3 strokes, to be found in 2 strokes.

p. 363a, l. 16. Char. 莽, sometimes counted 12 strokes, to be found in 11 strokes.

A DICTIONARY OF CHINESE-BUDDHIST TERMS

1. ONE STROKE

一 Eka. One, unity, monad, once, the same; immediately on (seeing, hearing, etc.). 一 一 One by one, each, every one, severally.

一丈六像 Sixteen "feet" form, or image, said to be the height of the Buddha's body, or "transformation" body; v. 丈六金身.

一三昧 Ekāgra, aikāgrya. Undeflected concentration, meditation on one object; v. 一行三昧.

一中 A hall of spread tables; idem 一普.

一中一切中 One being recognized as "mean" then all is of "the mean"; the three aspects of reality, noumenon, phenomenon, and madhya, are identical in essence; v. 止觀 5.

一乘 Ekayāna, One Yāna, the One Yāna, the vehicle of one-ness. 一佛乘 The one Buddha-Yāna. The One Vehicle, i.e. Mahāyāna, which contains the final or complete law of the Buddha and not merely a part, or preliminary stage, as in Hīnayāna. Mahāyānists claim it as the perfect and only way to the shore of parinirvāṇa. It is especially the doctrine of the 法華經 Lotus Sūtra; v. 大乘. | | 之珠 The pearl of the One Yāna, i.e. The Lotus Scripture. | | 圓宗. The T'ien-t'ai, or Lotus School of the perfect teaching, or the one vehicle; v. 天台宗. | | 家 The one-vehicle family or sect, especially the T'ien-t'ai or Lotus School. | | 法 (門) The one-vehicle method as revealed in the Lotus Sūtra. | | 究竟教 The One Vehicle in its final teaching, especially as found in the Lotus Sūtra. | | 經; | | 妙典 (or 文) Another name for the Lotus Sūtra, so called because it declares the one way of salvation, the perfect Mahāyāna. | | 菩提 The one-vehicle enlightenment. | | 顯性教 One of the five divisions made by 圭峯 Kuei-fêng of the Hua-yen 華嚴 or Avataṁsaka School; v. 五教.

一九 A Shingon term for Amitābha. | | 之生 Future life in the Amitābha Pure Land.

一人作虛萬人傳實 One man's untruth is propagated by a myriad men as truth; famae mendacia.

一代 A human lifetime; especially the lifetime of Śākyamuni on earth. | | 三段 The three sections, divisions, or periods of Buddha's teaching in his lifetime, known as 序分, i.e. the 華嚴, 阿含, 方等, and 般若 sūtras; 正宗分, i.e. 無量義, 法華, and 普賢觀 sūtras; and 流通分, i.e. the 涅槃經; they are known as introductory, main discourse, and final application. There are other definitions. | | 五時佛法 The five periods of Buddha's teachings, as stated by Chih-i 智顗 of the T'ien-t'ai School. The five are 華嚴, 阿含, 方等, 般若, 法華涅槃, the last two being the final period. | | 教 The whole of the Buddha's teaching from his enlightenment to his nirvāṇa, including Hīnayāna and Mahāyāna teaching.

一位一切位 idem 一門普門.

一佛世界 A Buddha-cosmos; a world undergoing transformation by a Buddha. | | 乘 The Mahāyāna, or one-Buddha vehicle, especially the teaching of the Lotus Sūtra. | | (國) 土; idem | | 世界 A Buddha-domain; or a one-Buddha region; also the Pure Land. | | 多佛 One Buddha or many Buddhas, i.e. some Hīnayāna Schools say only one Buddha exists in the same æon; Mahāyāna says many Buddhas appear in the same æon in many worlds. | | 淨土 A Buddha's Pure Land, especially that of Amitābha.

一來 (向) Sakṛdāgāmin. Only one more return to mortality, v. 斯 and 四向. | | 果 v. 四果.

一個半個 A particle, the very least.

一光三尊 Three honoured ones in one light or halo—Amitābha, Avalokiteśvara, and Mahāsthāmaprāpta; or Śākyamuni, Bhaiṣajya the 藥王 and 藥上 his younger brother.

一兎毛塵 An atom of dust on a hare's down (śaśorṇa). A measure, the 22,588,608,000th part of a yojana.

一回忌 The first anniversary of a death; any such anniversary; also 一周|.

一刀三禮 In carving an image of Buddha, at each cut thrice to pay homage to the Triratna. 一筆三禮 and 一字三禮 indicate a similar rule for the painter and the writer.

一分家 A school founded by 安慧 An-hui, teaching 心識之一分說 that cognition is subjective.

一分菩薩 A one-tenth bodhisattva, or disciple; one who keeps one-tenth of the commandments.

一切 Sarva. All, the whole; 普, 遍, 具.

一切一心識 That all things are mind, or mental.

一切世尊最尊特身 The most honoured of all the world-honoured; a title of Vairocana; v. 毘.

一切人中尊 The most honoured among men, especially Vairocana; v. 毘.

一切佛心印 Trikoṇa. The sign on a Buddha's breast, especially that on Vairocana's; the sign of the Buddha-mind; it is a triangle of flame pointing downwards to indicate power over all temptations; it is also 一切徧智印 the sign of omniscience.

一切佛會 The assembly of all the Buddhas, a term for the two maṇḍalas, or circles; v. 胎藏界 and 金剛界, i.e. the Garbhadhātu and the Vajradhātu.

一切即一 v. 一即一切.

一切如來 Sarvatathāgata, all Tathāgatas, all the Buddhas.

一切如來定 The highest of the 108 degrees of samādhi practised by bodhisattvas, also called 大空三昧 Śūnyasamādhi, i.e. of the great void, or immateriality, and 金剛三昧 Vajrasamādhi, Diamond samādhi. A samādhi on the idea that all things are of the (same) Buddha-nature.

一切如來寶 The talismanic pearl of all Buddhas, especially one in the Garbhadhātu maṇdala who holds a lotus in his left hand and the talismanic pearl in his right.

一切如來必定印 The sign of the assurance of attaining Buddhahood.

一切如來智印 A sign of the wisdom of all buddhas, a triangle on a lotus in the Garbhadhātu group.

一切如來眼色如明照三摩地 A Vairocana-samādhi, in which the light of the Tathāgata-eye streams forth radiance. Vairocana by reason of this samādhi is accredited with delivering the "true word" which sums up all the principles and practices of the masters.

一切如來諸法本性清淨蓮華三昧 A lotus-samādhi of Vairocana from which Amitābha was born. It is a Tathāgata meditation, that the fundamental nature of all existence is pure like the lotus.

一切如來金剛誓誡 The original oath of every Tathāgata, when as with the roar of a lion he declares that all creatures shall become as himself.

一切智 Sarvajña; v. 薩, i.e. 佛智 Buddha-wisdom, perfect knowledge, omniscience. |||地 The state or place of such wisdom. |||藏 Its thesaurus; Buddha. |||人 or 者 Buddha. |||舟 or 船 Its vehicle (Mahāyāna), which carries men to the |||地. |||相 Sarvajñatā, omniscience, or the state or condition of such wisdom. |||經 The 59th chapter of the 中阿含經. |||智 The wisdom of all wisdom, Buddha's wisdom, including bodhi, perfect enlightenment and purity; 大悲 great pity (for mortals); and 方便 tact or skill in teaching according to receptivity. |||句 The state or abode of all wisdom, i.e. of Buddha; 句 is 住處. |||天; 薩婆愼若提婆 Sarvajñadeva, the deva (i.e. Buddha) of universal wisdom. 丨丨丨心 The Buddha-wisdom mind. 丨丨丨慧者 The all-wise one, a title of Vairocana; v. 毘.

一切普門身 The one who completely fills all the "four realms" (dharmadhātu), a doctrine of the 華嚴 School.

一切有 Sarvabhāva. All things or beings; tr. of the name of Viśvabhū; v. 毘. 丨丨有情; 丨丨衆生 All sentient beings. 丨丨丨根本 The Mūlasarvāstivādaḥ, a branch of the Sarvāstivādin sect, which asserted the reality of things. 丨丨有爲 All phenomena, the phenomenal; all that is produced by causative action; everything that is dynamic and not static. 丨丨丨部 The realistic School, Sarvāstivādaḥ, a branch of the Vaibhāṣika, claiming Rāhula as founder, asserting the reality of all phenomena: 說一切有部; 薩婆多部; 薩婆阿私底婆拖部; 一切語言部. It divided, and the following seven schools are recorded, but the list is doubtful:—Mūlasarvāstivādaḥ 一切有根本部. Kāṣyapīyāḥ 迦葉毘維, also known as Suvarṣakāḥ 蘇跋梨柯部; 遊梨沙部; 蘇梨沙部; and 善歲部. Dharmaguptāḥ 法密部; 法藏部; 法護部. Mahīśāsakāḥ or Mahīśāsikāḥ 摩醯奢娑迦部; 彌喜捨婆阿部; 彌沙塞部; 化地部; 正地部. Tāmraṣāṭīyāḥ. Vibhajyavādinaḥ 分別說部. Bahuśrutīyāḥ 婆收婁多柯 or 多聞部.

一切施 Sarvadā. 薩縛達 One who gives his all; all-bestowing.

一切法; 丨丨萬法; 丨丨諸法 Sarvadharma. All things; all laws, existences, or beings. 丨丨丨界生印 One of the three signs in the maṇḍala of the Shingon School—the sign of producing all things or realms. 丨丨丨界決定智印 The "true word" of assurance of Vairocana and of all the eight classes of beings, as the symbol through which all may attain the sure Buddha-wisdom. 丨丨丨界自身表 Buddha's self-manifestation to all creation. 丨丨丨空 Sarvadharma-śūnyatā, the emptiness or unreality of all things.

一切無障法印明 A sign for overcoming all hindrances, i.e. by making the sign of a sword through lifting both hands, palms outward and thumbs joined, saying Hail! Bhagavat! Bhagavat svāhā! 丨丨丨丨礙 Absolutely free or unhindered, e.g. like air; illimitable, universal.

一切皆成 All beings become Buddhas, for all have the Buddha-nature and must ultimately become enlightened, i.e. 一切衆生皆悉成佛. This is the doctrine of developed Mahāyāna, or Universalism, as opposed to the limited salvation of Hīnayāna and of undeveloped Mahāyāna; 法華經方便品; 若有聞法者無一不成佛 if there be any who hear the dharma, not one will fail to become Buddha. 丨丨丨空宗 The sects which maintain the unreality of all things; v. 十宗.

一切眞言主 All the "true word" rulers, shown in the Garbhadhātu and Vajradhātu groups. 丨丨丨丨心 The first Sanskrit letter "a"; it is pronounced "an" by the Shingon School and emphasized as the heart of all wisdom. In India "a" is the "name of Vishṇu (especially as the first of the three sounds in the sacred syllable *om* or *aum*), also of Brahmā, Śiva, and Vaiśvānara (Agni)" M. W.

一切種妙三昧 The samādhi, or trance, which brings every kind of merit for one's adornment. 丨丨種智, see 三智. 丨丨種識 The 8th of the 八識 q.v.

一切經 The Tripiṭaka 大藏經 or 藏經, i.e. the whole of the Buddhist Canon. The collection was first made in China in the first year of 開皇 A.D. 581. See B. N.

一切義成 Sarvārthasiddha, or Siddhārtha; all wishes realized, name given to Śākyamuni at his birth; v. 悉, 薩.

一切萬; 丨丨諸法; 丨丨物 All things, idem 丨丨法.

一切處 Samanta. Everywhere, universal; a universal dhyāna. 丨丨丨無不相應眞言 The Shingon or "True word" that responds everywhere.

一切衆生之父 The Father of all the living, Brahmā 梵王. 丨丨丨丨喜見佛 Sarvasattva-priya-darśana. The Buddha at whose appearance all beings rejoice. (1) A fabulous Bodhisattva who destroyed himself by fire and when reborn burned both arms to cinders, an act described in the Lotus Sūtra as the highest form of sacrifice. Reborn as Bhaiṣajyarāja 藥王. (2) The name under which Buddha's aunt, Mahāprajāpatī, is to be reborn as Buddha. 丨丨丨丨精氣 Sarvasattvāujohārī. Lit. subtle vitality of all beings; the quintessence or energy of all living beings. A certain Rākṣasī, wife of a demon. | | | | 離諸惡趣 Sarvasattva-pāpa-prahāṇa. A samādhi on a world free from all the evil destinies.

一切語言部 idem 一切有部.

一切諸佛 All Buddhas.

一切遍智印 Trikoṇa. A triangle above a white lotus, apex downward, of pure white colour, representing wisdom as a flame which burns up all passion and overcomes all opposition; the symbol of every Tathāgata. It is specially connected with Vairocana. Also 一切佛心印; 諸佛心印.

一刹 v. 掣. A kṣetra, a land, a Buddha-realm or chiliocosm. | | 那 A kṣaṇa, the shortest space of time, a moment, the 90th part of a thought, and 4,500th part of a minute, during which 90 or 100 are born and as many die.

一化 The teaching and influence of a Buddha during one Buddha-period; also the teaching of the whole truth at once; also an instantaneous reform. | | 五味之教 The Five Tastes or periods of the Buddha's teaching as defined by the T'ien-t'ai School, i.e. the 華嚴; 阿含; 方等; 般若 and 法華涅槃 q.v. and v. 五味.

一千 Sahasra; a thousand. | | 二百 1,200. | | | | 功德 The 1,200 merits or powers of the organs of eye, tongue, and mind predicted in the Lotus Sūtra, but, generally, the merits therein predicted to all six organs.

一印 A seal, sign, symbol. | | 會 the sixth of the nine Vajradhātu groups.

一即一切一切即一 "One is all and all is one." Expressing the essential unity of all things; a tenet of the Hua-yen and T'ien-t'ai schools. | | 三 One is (or includes) three; especially the one Yāna (the Buddha vehicle) is, or includes the three vehicles, i.e. bodhisattva, pratyekabuddha, and śrāvaka. | | 十 One is ten, or, if one then ten, one being the root or seed of numbers, and containing all the rest. There are many other forms, e.g. 一心即一切心 and so on.

一叉鳩王 Ikṣvāku Virūḍhaka or Videhaka, translated by 甘蔗王 Sugar-cane king, also 日種善生 Sūryavaṁśa, an ancient king of Potala and ancestor of the Śākya line.

一句 A word, or sentence; 一句子 a subordinate or explanatory word or sentence; 句 is also used for 處. | | 投火 For but one sentence of the Truth willingly to cast oneself into the fire. | | 道盡 With one word to make clear the whole Law.

一合相 An organism, a cosmos, or any combined form, e.g. a man, a world.

一向 One direction, each direction; with single mind, the mind fixed in one direction, undistracted; e.g. 一向清淨無有女人 (The land of that Buddha is) everywhere pure; no women are there. | | 宗 The 眞宗 Shin or Pure-land Shin Sect founded by Shinron, in Japan, whose chief tenet is unwavering reflection on Amida (by repeating his name). | | 小乘寺 A monastery wholly Hīnayāna. | | 大乘寺 A monastery wholly Mahāyāna. | | 記 A confirmatory reply to a question, e.g. Do not all die? All die.

一吹 v. 一唾.

一味 One, or the same flavour, kind or character, i.e. the Buddha's teaching. 一味瀉瓶 Completely, exhaustively, e.g. as water can be poured from one bottle to another without loss, so should be a master's pouring of the Law into the minds of his disciples.

一品(經) Varga 跋渠; a chapter, or division (of a sūtra).

一周忌 Anniversary of a death; also | | 關 and | 回忌.

一唾一吹 A spit or a puff, i.e. as futile as thinking that a man could puff out a burning world and blow it again into complete existence, or could with a spit or a puff put it out.

一喝 A call, shout, deafening shout.

一四句偈 A four-character line of a gāthā, or verse. | | 天下 A world of four great continents surrounding a Mt. Sumeru.

一因 A cause; the cause from which the Buddha-law arises.

一地 The one ground; the same ground; the Buddha-nature of all living beings, i.e. as all the plants grow out of the one ground, so all good character and works grow from the one Buddha-nature.

一坐食 One meal a day taken before noon and without rising from the seat; it is the 5th of the 12 dhūtas.

一境 One region, realm, order, or category. 丨丨三諦 The three axioms in the one category; the three are 空, 假, and 中, which exist in every universe; v. 三諦. It is a principle of the T'ien-t'ai 圓敎. 丨丨四心 Four different ways of looking at the same thing. Similar to 一水四見, i.e. one and the same reality though seen from different aspects.

一塵 A grain of dust, an atom, a particle. 丨丨法界 The whole in an atom, a universe in a grain of dust, one grain of dust is a microcosm of the universal whole.

一增一減 A kalpa during which a human lifetime increases from ten years to 80,000 years and then decreases back to ten. At the end of the first century the increase is to 11 years; at the end of the second century to 12 years, and so on till a lifetime lasts 80,000 years; then decrease follows in the same ratio till 10 is reached. The whole period of accretion and declension covers a small kalpa, i.e. 16,800,000 years; also called 中劫.

一壇構 The setting up of altars before the Vajradhātu and Garbhadhātu maṇḍalas, each erected and worshipped separately; also 丨檀丨.

一夏 The summer retreat in India of 90 days, from the 16th of the 4th moon to the 15th of the 7th; v. 雨.

一大三千世界 A great chiliocosmos or universe of the three kinds of thousands of worlds. The three 千 are termed 一千; 中千; 大千. A great chiliocosmos is also termed 三千大千世界 q.v. Each world consists of its central mountain Sumeru, surrounded by four continents, its seas being surrounded by a girdle or wall of iron; 1,000 such worlds make a small chiliocosmos; 1,000 of these make a medium chiliocosmos; 1,000 of these make a great chiliocosmos, or 1,000,000,000 worlds. Later Buddhists increased this number to a figure with 4,456,489 digits. It is a Buddha-universe.

一大宅 The great house, i.e. the burning house (of the world) in the Lotus Sūtra; also 火宅. 丨丨車 The one great salvation vehicle of the Lotus Sūtra, the Mahāyāna. 丨丨事 The one great work of a Buddha, universal enlightenment and release; also a life, or lifetime.

一如 The one Ju, i.e. the bhūtatathatā, or absolute, as the norm and essence of life. The 眞如 true suchness, or true character, or reality; the 法性 nature of things or beings. The whole of things as they are, or seem; a cosmos; a species; things of the same order. Name of a celebrated monk, I-ju. V. 一眞; 一實. 丨丨觀音 One of the 33 representations of Kuan-yin, ascending on the clouds. 丨丨頓證 Immediate experiential enlightenment by the Tathāgata truth; the immediate realization that all is 眞如 bhūtatathatā.

一字 One word; a magic or esoteric word. 丨丨三禮 Three homages at every word one copies of the sūtras. 丨丨文殊 The "Single-word Mañjuśrī", the magic word is 齒臨; or 體哩呬淫; or 叱洛呬演, and is used to avoid difficult parturition and to heal arrow-wounds. The image used is of a youthful smiling Mañjuśrī, wearing the felicitous pearl, with one tress on his head, hence also called 一髻文殊. 丨丨禪 A cryptic single-word reply to a question, requiring meditation for its apprehension; it is a Ch'an or Zen method. 丨丨金輪(頂)法 The one word golden-wheel magical method (Shingon), the one word is Bhrūṁ; also 丨丨丨丨佛頂法.

一家宴 A monasterial family party, i.e. when a monk, on becoming head of a monastery, invites its inmates to a feast.

一寧 I-ning, a monk who went to Japan in 1299; v. 一山.

一實 The one reality; the bhūtatathatā; idem 一如, 一眞. 丨丨乘 The one method of salvation, the 一實 School. 丨丨圓乘 The Tathāgata's perfect vehicle, i.e. that of the Lotus Scripture. 丨丨圓宗 The one real and perfect school, i.e. the T'ien-t'ai or Lotus School. 丨丨境界 The state or realm of 一實; the realization of the spirituality of all things; it is the 如來法身 the Tathāgata-dharmakāya. 丨丨相 The state of bhūtatathatā, above all differentiation, immutable; it implies the Buddha-nature, or the immateriality and unity of all things; 眞如之理無二無別, 離諸虛妄

之相; it is undivided unity apart from all phenomena. ||無相 The one reality being indivisible is apart from all transient (or empty) forms, and is therefore styled the formless, e.g. the invisible.

一寶 The one precious thing, the spirit, or intelligent nature; the intelligent mind (behind all things).

一小劫 A small kalpa; a period of the growth and decay of a universe. See 一增一減 and 劫.

一山 A hill; a monastery; I-shan, the name of a Chinese monk who voyaged to Japan in A.D. 1299 and who was also styled 一寧 I-ning.

一形 An appearance, a lifetime, the period of an individual existence, also 一期 and 一生涯.

一往 One passage, or time, once; on one superficial going.

一微塵 A particle of dust; an atom, the smallest particle, a microcosm of the universe.

一心 With the whole mind or heart; one mind or heart; also the bhūtatathatā, or the whole of things; the universe as one mind, or a spiritual unity. ||稱名 With undivided mind to call on the name (of Kuan-yin). ||三惑; 同體三惑 The T'ien-t'ai "three doubts" in the mind of a bodhisattva, producing fear of illusion, confusion through multiplicity of duties, and ignorance, i.e. 見思; 塵沙 and 無明 q.v. ||三智 One mind and three aspects of knowledge. The 別教 separates the three aspects into 空, 假, and 中 q.v.; T'ien-t'ai unifies them into one immediate vision, or regards the three as aspects of the one mind. ||三觀 The above T'ien-t'ai insight; also simultaneous vision of past, present, and future; also called 圓融三觀; 不可思議三觀. ||金剛寶戒; 圓頓戒 The infrangible-diamond rules of all bodhisattvas and Buddhas, a term of the T'ien-t'ai School, founded on the 梵網經.

一念 A kṣaṇa, or thought; a concentration of mind; a moment; the time of a thought, of which there are varying measurements from 60 kṣaṇa upwards; the Fan-i-ming-i makes it one kṣaṇa. A reading. A repetition (especially of Amitābha's name). The Pure-land sect identify the thought of Buddha with Amitābha's vow, hence it is an assurance of salvation. ||不生 Not a thought arising; beyond the necessity of thinking, as in the case of a Buddha. ||三千 In one thought to survey or embrace the 3,000 worlds, or a chiliocosmos with all its forms of existence; to see the universe as a thought; it is a T'ien-t'ai mode of meditation. ||業成 At one thought the work completed; karma complete in one thought. One repetition, or sincere thought of or faith in Amitābha's vow, and entrance into the Pure Land is assured. ||萬年 In a moment's thought to obtain a myriad years and no return to mortality.

一性宗 Monophysitic or "pantheistic" sects of Mahāyāna, which assert that all beings have one and the same nature with Buddha.

一息 A breath, i.e. inspiration-cum-expiration; a rest, or cessation. ||半步 half a step at a breathing on arising from meditation.

一恒(河沙) As one Ganges, i.e. as the sands of one Ganges river.

一成一切成 The Hua-yen doctrine that the law of the universal runs through the phenomenal, therefore a speck of dust is a microcosmos; also that with the Tathāgata's enlightenment all beings were enlightened in him; in the perfection of one all are perfected; one deed includes all.

一持 Adherence to one Buddha and one sūtra.

一拶 A sudden remark, or question, by a monk or master to test a disciple, a Ch'an (Zen) method.

一指頭禪 The one finger-tip contemplation used by a certain monk to bring to another a conception of the universe. Also a parable in the 楞伽經 Laṅkāvatāra-sūtra. The Ch'an or Zen sect 禪宗 regard the sūtras merely as indicators, i.e. pointing fingers, their real object being only attained through personal meditation.

一揣食 A ball (or handful) of food; one helping; a frugal meal, the sixth of the 12 dhūtas; also called 節量食 and 一摶食.

一日 A sun, or day from sunrise to sunset. ||一夜 Ahorātra. One day one night, a day and night, a division of time. ||三時 The three divisions of a day, morning, noon, evening. | | 佛 A one-day Buddha, i.e. he who lives a whole day purely. | | 經 A sūtra copied in one day (perhaps by many hands); also styled 頓 寫.

一明 Ming (i.e. bright, clear, illuminating) is the Shingon word for a dhāraṇī, or magical formula; especially applied to magical acts.

一時 Ekasmin samaye (Pali: ekaṃ samayaṃ); "on one occasion," part of the usual opening phrase of a sūtra—"Thus have I heard, once," etc. A period, e.g. a session of expounding a sūtra.

一普 A company; a general assembly of monks in a monastery.

一月三舟 The one moon represents Buddha, the three boats represent varying ways of viewing him, e.g. according as those in an anchored boat and those in two others sailing in opposite directions see different aspects of the moon, so is it in regard to the Buddha. | | 三身 The allegorical trikāya or three bodies of the moon, i.e. its form as 法身, its light as 報身, its reflection as 應身; the Buddha-truth 法 has also its 體 body, its light of wisdom 智, and its application or use 用, but all three are one, or a trinity; see Trikāya, 三身.

一期 A date, fixed time; a lifetime.

一極 The one ultimate, or finality; ultimate enlightenment; the one final truth or way; the 一實 or Absolute.

一業 A karma; a 業因 karma-cause, causative of the next form of existence.

一機一境 The 機 is subjective; the 境 is objective, e.g. smoke is the objective phenomenon, fire the subjective inference.

一段事 The unity or continuity in the unbroken processes of nature; all nature, all being is but one continuous process.

一殺多生 To kill one that many may live.

一毛端 A hair's tip; the smallest division (of space or time).

一水四見 The same water may be viewed in four ways—devas see it as bejewelled land, men as water, hungry ghosts as pus and blood, fish as a place to live in. Cf. 一境四心.

一法 A dharma, or law; an ordered something, a thing, a matter. | | 印 The seal or assurance of the one truth or law, see 一如 and 一實; the criterion of Mahāyāna doctrine, that all is bhūtatathatā, as contrasted with the Hīnayāna criteria of impermanence, non-personality, and nirvāṇa. | | 句 The one-law abode, i.e. the sum of the 29 particular 句 or states of perfection in the Pure-land śāstra of Vasubandhu. | | 界 The bhūtatathatā considered in terms of mind and as a whole; a law-realm; a spiritual realm; a universe. | | | 心 A mind universal, above limitations of existence or differentiation.

一浮漚 A floating bubble (on the ocean), a man's life, or body.

一流 In one, or the same flow; of the same class.

一炷 One burning of incense; a candle, or lamp.

一無礙道 The one way without barrier, i.e. the end of reincarnations in nirvāṇa; a meditation on it.

一物不將來 A Ch'an sect idea—not a thing to bring or carry away, empty-handed, i.e. nothingness.

一生 All one's life, a whole lifetime. | | 不犯 Life-long innocence—especially sexual. | | 入妙覺 A T'ien-t'ai doctrine that Buddha-enlightenment can be attained by any in one lifetime, i.e. the present life. | | 所繫菩薩 idem 一生補處菩薩. | | 果遂 In this one life to accomplish the three stages for final entry; it is associated with the 20th vow of Amitābha; cf. 三生果遂. | | 補處 Eka-jāti-prati-baddha; a name for Maitreya, who is to be the next Buddha in this world. Another definition is—from one enlightenment to attain to Buddhahood. | | | | 菩薩像 A 30-armed image of Maitreya.

一異 Unity-cum-differentiation; monism and pluralism; one and many; ekatva-anyatva, oneness and otherness.

一白三羯磨 One announcement, or reading, and three responses, or promises of performance (karman); it is the mode of ordaining monks, three responses to the one call of the abbot. Also 白四(羯磨).

一百 Śata. A hundred. 丨丨八; 百八 Aṣṭaśatam. The 108 kleśa, distresses, disturbing passions, or illusions 煩惱 of mankind, hence the 108 beads on a rosary, repetitions of the Buddha's name, strokes of a bell, etc., one for each distress. Also, one of the Mahārājas, with 108 hands, each holding a different implement.

一目多伽 Itivṛttaka; stories of the lives of saints, part of the canon; also 丨曰丨丨.

一相 Lakṣana. One aspect, form, or side; ekatva, unity as contrasted with diversity; monism; the bhūtatathatā; the one mind in all things; cf. 一異. 丨丨一味 The term 一相 is defined as the common mind in all beings, or the universal mind; the 一味 is the Buddha's Mahāyāna teaching; the former is symbolized by the land, the latter by the rain fertilizing it. 丨丨三昧 A state of samādhi in which are repressed hate and love, accepting and rejecting, etc., and in which the mind reaches an undivided state, being anchored in calm and quiet. 丨丨智 The wisdom that all is bhūtatathatā and a unity. 丨丨法門 The unitary or monistic method is interpreted in more than a dozen ways; in general it means to reach a stage beyond differentiation where all is seen as a unity. 丨丨無相 One-ness means none-ness; in ultimate unity, or the unity of the absolute, there is no diversity.

一眞 The whole of reality, the universe, the all, idem 眞如; cf. 一如, 一實 bhūtatathatā. 丨丨地 The state of meditation on the absolute. 丨丨法界 The dharma realm of the one reality, i.e. of the bhūtatathatā, complete in a speck of dust as in a universe; such is the dharmakāya, or spiritual body of all Buddhas, eternal, above terms of being, undefinable, neither immanent nor transcendent, yet the one reality, though beyond thought. It is the fundamental doctrine of the 華嚴宗. The 法界 is 諸佛平等法身, 從本以來不生不滅, 非空非有, 離名離相, 無內無外, 惟一眞實, 不可思議, 是名一眞法界; see 三藏法數 4. 丨丨無爲 The 一眞法界 one reality, or undivided absolute, is static, not phenomenal, it is effortless, just as it is 自然 self-existing.

一眼之龜 A sea turtle with only one eye, and that underneath, entered a hollow in a floating log; the log, tossed by the waves, happened to roll over, whereupon the turtle momentarily saw the sun and moon; an illustration of the rareness of the appearance of a Buddha; also of the difficulty of being reborn as a man.

一禿乘 A bald-pated "vehicle"—an unproductive monk or disciple.

一空 All is empty, or of the void, non-material.

一等 Equal, all equal; of the first stage; a grade, rank, step.

一筆三禮 Three salutations at each (use of the) pen, on painting a picture of the Buddha, or copying a scripture; cf. 一刀三禮. 丨丨勾(銷) "Crossed out" with a stroke of the pen; expunged; forgiven.

一篋四蛇 Four snakes in one basket, i.e. the four passions in one body; cf. 四大.

一箭道 An arrow's flight, two li.

一縷一觸 "A thread, a butt"; the dragon which snatched a thread of a monk's robe and was consequently protected from a dangerous bird; the ox which butted a monk's robe and became a monk at its next transmigration; e.g. the virtue of the robe.

一翳 A film on the eye; a hindrance to enlightenment.

一臈; 一臘 The end of the monastic year at the summer retreat; a monastic year; also called 法丨 or 法歲, the religious year; cf. 一夏.

一色 A colour, the same colour; the same; especially a thing, or a form, v. rūpa 色; minute, trifling, an atom. 丨丨一香無非中道 An atom or an odour is a complete microcosm of the 中道 middle way or golden mean; the Mean is found in all things.

一莖草 A blade of grass—may represent the Buddha, as does his image; it is a Buddha-centre.

一葉 A leaf; a palm-leaf or page of a sūtra.

| | 觀音 One of the 33 forms of Kuan-yin, standing on a lotus leaf.

一蓮 The Lotus-flower of the Pure-land of Amitābha, idem 蓮臺. | | 之實 The certainty of being born in the Pure-land. | | 托生 One lotus bearing all the living, i.e. the Pure-land of Amitābha.

一蟣 A likṣā, a nit, the 131,712,000th part of a yojana, seven times the smallest atom.

一行 One act (of body, mouth, or mind); holding to one course; devoted. I-hsing, A.D. 672–717, a celebrated monk whose secular name was 張遂 Chang Sui, posthumous title 大慧禪師; he was versed in mathematics and astronomy, a reformer of the Chinese calendar, and author of several works. | | 一切行 In one act to do all other acts; the act which includes all other acts, e.g. the first step; the one discipline which embraces all discipline; the fourth degree of a samādhi. | | 三昧, 眞如三昧, 一相三昧 A samādhi for realizing that the nature of all Buddhas is the same; the 起信論 says all Buddhas and all beings. Another meaning is entire concentration of the mind on Buddha.

一角仙人 Ekaśṛṅga ṛṣi; also 獨 | | | The unicorn ṛṣi, an ascetic born of a deer; ensnared by a woman, he lost his power, and became a minister of state; he is one of the previous incarnations of Śākyamuni.

一觸 See 一縷.

一訶子 Harītakī. A fruit of the yellow myrobolan. Also 阿 (or 訶) 黎勒果.

一說部 Ekavyāvahārika 猗柯毘與婆訶利柯 or (Pali) Ekabyohāra 鞞婆訶羅 One of the 20 Hīnayāna schools, a nominalistic school, which considered things as nominal, i.e. names without any underlying reality; also styled 諸法但名宗 that things are but names.

一諦 The doctrine of fundamental unity; an abbrev. for 一實諦 the Mādhyamika fundamental doctrine; also, generally, in the sense of an axiom, or fundamental truth; there are varying definitions of the one fundamental truth.

一識 One sense or perception; the one individual intelligence or soul which uses the various senses, likened to a monkey which climbs in and out of the various windows of a house—a Satyasiddhi and Sautrāntika doctrine. Also, a Vairocana maṇḍala. | | 外道 Followers of the above heretical view.

一轉語 A turning word; a fateful word.

一遍 Once, one recital of Buddha's name, or of a sūtra, or magic formula; style of 智眞 Chih-chên, founder of the 時宗 Ji-shū (Japan).

一道 One way, the one way; the way of deliverance from mortality, the Mahāyāna. I-tao, a learned monk of the Pure-land sect. | | 法門 The 阿 "A" school (Shingon) which takes A as the alpha (and even omega) of all wisdom; the way by which all escape mortality. | | 無爲心 Mind apart from all ideas of activity or inactivity. Also styled, or explained, by 如實一道心, 如實知自心, 空性無境心, 一如本淨心. The third of the ten mental resting places of the esoteric school. | | 神光 Inner light; intuitive wisdom.

一門 The one door out of mortality into Nirvāṇa, i.e. the Pure-land door. | | 普門 The one door is the all-door; by entering the one door all doors of the faith are opened.

一間 Ekavīcika 翳迦鼻致迦 Still one final stage of mortality before nirvāṇa. Also wrongly styled Bījaka 鼻致迦, a seed 一種 which leads to one more reincarnation. | | 聖者 The holy ones who have only one interval, or stage of mortality before nirvāṇa.

一闡提(迦) Icchantika. Also 一顚迦, 阿闡底迦 One without desire for Buddha-enlightenment; an unbeliever; shameless, an enemy of the good; full of desires; 斷善根者 one who has cut off his roots of goodness; it is applied also to a bodhisattva who has made a vow not to become a Buddha until all beings are saved. This is called 大悲闡提 the icchantika of great mercy.

一際 Of the same realm or boundary, i.e. the world and nirvāṇa are one.

一雨 A rain, i.e. a lesson from the Buddha, or his teaching, see Lotus V.

一音教 The one-sound teaching, i.e. the totality of the Buddha's doctrine; a school founded by Kumārajīva and Bodhiruci.

一願建立 The one vow, i.e. the 18th of the 48 vows of Amitābha, on which his sect is established.

一顛迦 idem 一闡提迦.

一食 A meal a day, one of the twelve dhūtas.

一體 Though externally differing, in nature the same; the fundamental unity of the universe. 天地與我同根, 萬物與我一體 Heaven, earth, and myself have the same root; all things are one corpus with me. | | 三分 The trinity of 摩醯首羅 Maheśvara (Śiva), 那羅延 Nārāyaṇa (Viṣṇu), and 梵天 Brahmā. One being in three manifestations. | | 三寶 In the one body of the Saṅgha is the whole Triratna, Buddha, Dharma, and Saṅgha. Also, Mind, Buddha, and the living, these three are without differentiation, 心佛與衆生是三無差別, i.e. are all one. | | 三身自性佛 In one's own body to have the Trikāya of the self-natured Buddha, i.e. by personal surrender to the Buddha. | | 速疾力三昧 A samādhi in which instantaneous powers are acquired.

一髻 A topknot. | | 文殊 The one topknot Mañjuśrī; there are other representations with 5 and 8; cf. 一字文殊. | | 羅刹女 The female rakṣaḥ styled "Single top-knot", wife of a great rakṣaḥ who dwells by a great ocean; on scenting blood, she can fly to it in a night 80,000 yojanas. | | | | 王菩薩 The four-handed, dark-blue rakṣaḥ with the flame of fire coming out of his head, a bodhisattva in the Garbhadhātu maṇḍala.

一麻一米 A hempseed and a grain of rice a day, the scanty diet to which Śākyamuni reduced himself before his enlightenment.

一魔萬箭 One demon a myriad arrows, i.e. to listen to one Māra-temptation opens the way for a myriad Māra-arrows.

2. TWO STROKES

七 Sapta, seven.

七七 The period of forty-nine days after death, when masses are said every seventh day till the seventh seventh day. | | 忌 The seventh seventh day of the masses for the dead. | | 齋 Masses for the dead on every seventh day for seven times. During this period the deceased is in the antarābhava or intermediate state, known as 中有 and 中陰; at the end of forty-nine days, judgment having been made, he enters upon his next state. By observing the proper rites, his family may aid him in overcoming his perils and attaining to a happy destiny.

七丈夫, also 七士夫趣; v. 七賢七聖.

七不可避 The seven unavoidables—rebirth, old age, sickness, death, punishment (for sin), happiness (for goodness), consequences (cause and effect 因緣).

七事隨身 The seven appurtenances of a monk—the three garments, bowl, censer, duster (or fly-brush), stool (*niṣīdana*), paper, and material for washing.

七佛 Sapta Buddha. The seven ancient Buddhas, viz. Vipaśyin 毘婆尸, Śikhin 尸棄, Viśvabhū 毘舍婆, Krakucchanda 拘樓孫, Kanakamuni 倶那含牟尼 or 拘那含, Kāśyapa 迦葉, and Śākyamuni 釋迦. The last four are said to be of the present kalpa. | | 藥師 The seven healing Buddhas, also | 躬醫王, of whom there are two descriptions, one representing them as at various places in the eastern regions of space; another gives five in the east and two in the south.

七使 The seven messengers, agents, or kleśas—desire 欲愛; anger, or hate 瞋恚; attachment, or clinging 有愛; pride, or arrogance 慢; ignorance, or unenlightenment 無明; false views 見; and doubt 疑.

七例句 v. 七轉九例.

七倶胝佛母尊 Saptakoṭibuddha-mātṛ. The fabulous mother of seven koṭis of Buddhas; i.e. Marīci 摩利支; also 準提 Cundī, or Cundā; or 準提觀音 Cundī-Kuanyin, q.v., who is represented as of whitish colour, with eighteen hands and three eyes.

七條 (衣 or 袈裟) The outer mantle, or toga, of a monk, composed of seven pieces; the Uttarā-saṅga, v. 鬱.

七僧 A monastery is supposed to possess the following seven monks: 咒願師 invoker; 導師 leader; 唄師 intoner, or leader of the chanting; 散花師 flower-scatterer; 梵音師 master of sacred words, or Sanskrit; 錫杖師 shaker of the rings on the metal staff, or crozier; 堂達 distributor of missals, etc. Another division is 講師 expounder; 讀師 reader; 咒願師; 三禮師 director of the three ceremonies; 唄師; 散花師; and 堂達. | | 法會 An assembly of a monasterial fraternity. | | 齋 A "western" term meaning an endowment for a complete monastic fraternity of seven monks.

七八行 The practice of the seven bodhyaṅga 七菩提分, and the 八正道 eight mārga or noble paths.

七加行 idem 七方便.

七勝事 The seven surpassing qualities of a Buddha; v. also 七種無上; they are his body, or person, his universal law, wisdom, perfection, destination (nirvāṇa), ineffable truth, and deliverance.

七十 Saptati, seventy. | | 三尊 The "Diamond world" maṇḍala, or pantheon, of the esoteric sect, containing seventy-three honoured ones.

七十二天 The seventy-two devas, namely, sixty-nine devas, the lord of T'ai Shan, the god of the five roads, and 大吉祥天 Mahāśrī. | | | 字 Brahmā obtained seventy-two words with which to save the world, but failing he swallowed seventy, leaving one at each side of his mouth 阿 and 漚, i.e. 無 and 有 things are, things are not, being and non-being. | | | 歲 The age, 72, at which Buddha is reputed to have preached the Lotus Sūtra.

七十五 Pañcasaptati; 75.

七十五法 The seventy-five dharmas of the Abhidharma Kośa, which classifies all phenomena under seventy-five categories or elements, divided into five groups; cf. 五根, 五境, 無表色. (1) Material 色法 Rūpāṇi, 11. (2) Mind 心法 Cittam, 1. (3) Mental qualities 心所有法 Citta-samprayuktasaṁskārāḥ, 46. (4) Non-mental 心不相應行法 Cittaviprayuktasaṁskārāḥ, 14. These are the seventy-two Sarvāstivādin divisions (v. Keith, B.I., p. 201). (5) In addition there are three unconditioned or non-phenomenal elements 無爲法 Asaṁskṛta dharma, 3 (v. Keith, p. 160).

七善 The seven excellences claimed for the Buddha's teaching—good in its 時 timing or seasonableness, 義 meaning, 語 expression, 獨法 uniqueness, 具足 completeness, 清淨調柔 pure adaptability, and 梵行 its noble objective, nirvāṇa. There are other similar groups.

七喩 The seven parables of the Lotus Sūtra.

七垢 The seven defilements—desire 欲, false views 見, doubt 疑, pride 慢, arrogance 憍, torpor 隨眠, and 慳 stinginess; cf. 七使.

七夢 (經) Ānanda's seven dreams, and the account of them.

七大 Earth, water, fire, wind, space (or ether), sight, and perception 地, 水, 火, 風, 空, 見, 識; cf. 大, 五大 and 六境; 見大 and 六根; 識大 and 六識.

七如來 Sapta Tathāgatāḥ. The seven Tathāgatas whose names are inscribed on a heptagonal pillar (七如來寶塔) in some Buddhist temples. One list is 阿彌陀, 甘露飯王, 觀音, 毘耶婆, 妙色身, 羅担納担羅耶 and 寶勝. Another list gives Amitābha, Kan-lu-wang, 離怖畏, 廣博身, Miao-sê-shên, Pao-shêng (Ratnasaṁbhava) and 多寶 (Prabhūtaratna).

七子 The parable in the Nirvāṇa Sūtra of the sick son whose parents, though they love all their sons equally, devote themselves to him. So does the Buddha specially care for sinners. The seven sons are likened to mankind, devas, śrāvakas, pratyeka-buddhas, and the three kinds of bodhisattvas of the 藏, 通 and 別敎.

七宗 The seven Japanese sects of 律 Ritsu (or Risshū), 法相 Hossō, 三論 Sanron, 華嚴 Kegon, 天台 Tendai, 眞言 Shingon, and 禪 Zen.

七寶 Sapta ratna 薩不荅羅的捺 The

seven treasures, or precious things, of which there are varying descriptions, e.g. 金 *suvarṇa*, gold; 銀 *rūpya*, silver; 瑠璃 *vaidūrya*, lapis lazuli; 玻瓈 *sphaṭika*, crystal; 硨磲 *musāragalva*, agate; 赤珠 *rohita-mukta*, rubies or red pearls; 瑪瑙 *aśmagarbha*, cornelian. Also the seven royal (*cakravartin*) treasures—the golden wheel; elephants; dark swift horses; the divine pearl, or beautiful pearls; able ministers of the Treasury; jewels of women; and loyal generals. | | 樹林 The grove of jewel trees, or trees of the seven precious things—a part of the "Pure-land", or Paradise.

七微 The seven atoms composing an aṇu 阿耨, 阿拏, 阿菟色 Eitel's definition is seven atoms of dust, but the definition is doubtful. This molecule is larger than an "atom", and according to the Sarvāstivāda it is the smallest visible particle. It is also a division of a yojana.

七心界 The seven realms of vijñāna, or perception, produced by eye, ear, nose, tongue, body, mind, to which is added thought, 意根 q.v.

七情 The seven emotions: pleasure, anger, sorrow, joy, love, hate, desire.

七慢 The seven pretensions or arrogances—慢 asserting superiority over inferiors and equality with equals, 過 | superiority over equals and equality with superiors, | 過 | superiority over manifest superiors, 我 | egotism or overweening pride, 增上 | vaunting assertion of possessing the Truth, 卑 | vaunting one's inferiority (or false humility), and 邪 | vaunting lack of virtue for virtue.

七摩怛里 Saptamātṛ. The seven "divine mothers, or personified energies of the principal deities"; they are associated "with the worship of the god Śiva", and attend on "his son Skanda or Kārttikeya, to whom at first only seven Mātṛs were assigned, but in the later mythology an innumerable number, who are sometimes represented as having displaced the original divine mothers" M.W. Their names are given as (1) Cāmuṇḍā 遮文荼 or 左問拏; (2) Gaurī 嬌吠哩; (3) Vaiṣṇavī 吠瑟拏微; (4) Kaumārī 嬌麽哩; (5) Indrāṇī, Aindrī, or Māhendrī 燕捺利 or 印捺哩; (6) Raudrī 勞捺哩; and (7) Vārāhī 末羅呬弭; cf. 七母天.

七支 The seven (spreading) branches—three sins of the body and four of speech, 身三 killing, robbing, adultery; 口四 lying, slander, abuse, double-tongue (or vain conversation). These are the first seven of the ten evils 十惡. | | 念誦 A method of invocation in which only seven kinds of signs and magical words are required. It is explained in the | | | | 隨行法 part of the Vairocana sūtra. | | 業 The karma resulting from the above seven sins.

七方便(位) (1) The seven "expedient" or temporary attainments or positions of Hīnayāna, superseded in Mahāyāna by the 七賢(位) or 七加行(位) all preparatory to the 七聖(位). (2) The seven vehicles, i.e. those of ordinary human beings, of devas, of śrāvakas, of pratyekabuddhas, and of the three bodhisattvas of the three teachings 藏, 通 and 別. (3) Also, 藏敎之聲緣二人, 通敎之聲緣菩三人, 別敎 and 圓敎之二菩薩; (2) and (3) are T'ien-t'ai groups.

七星 Ursa major; it is worshipped in Japan as 妙見菩薩 q.v. Wonderful Sight Bodhisattva who protects this world.

七曇 Siddham, idem 悉曇.

七曜 The seven brilliant ones—the sun and moon, together with the five planets which are connected with fire, water, wood, metal, and earth. Their essence shines in the sky, but their spirits are over men as judges of their good and evil, and as rulers over good and evil fortune. The following table shows their names in

Chinese	*Sanskrit*
Sun 日, 太陽	Āditya 阿彌底耶
Moon 月, 太陰	Soma 蘇摩
Mars 火星, 勞惑	Aṅgāraka 盎哦囉迦
Mercury 水 |, 辰星	Budha 部陀
Jupiter 木 |, 歲星	Bṛhaspati 勿哩訶娑跛底
Venus 金 |, 太白	Śukra 戍羯羅
Saturn 土 |, 鎮星	Śanaiścara 賒乃以室折羅

七最勝 The seven perfections, see 唯識論 9. 安住最勝 Perfect rest in the bodhisattva nature. 依止 | | Perfect reliance on, or holding fast to the great bodhi (or, awakened mind). 意果 | | Perfect resultant aim—in pity for all. 事業 | | Perfect in constant performance. 巧便 | | Perfect in able device (for spiritual presentation). 廻向 | | Perfect direction towards the highest bodhi. 清淨 | | Perfect purity and peace.

七有; 七生 The seven stages of existence in a human world, or in any 欲界 desire-world. Also (1) in the hells, (2) as animals, (3) hungry ghosts, (4) gods, (5) men, (6) karma 業, and (7) in the intermediate stage.

七有依福業 The seven grounds for a happy karma through benevolence to the needy—almsgiving to visitors, to travellers, to the sick, to their nurses, gifts of gardens and groves to monasteries, etc., regular provision of food for them, and seasonable clothing and food for their occupants.

七步蛇 A snake whose bite brings death before seven steps can be taken.

七母天; 七姉妹 The seven divine mothers, also styled the seven sisters; v. 七摩怛里.

七毘尼 The seven vinaya, v. 七滅諍法.

七治 Seven forms of punishment for monks, v. 七羯磨.

七法 The seven (unavoidable) things, v. 七不可避.

七法財 The seven riches, or seven ways of becoming rich in the Law: 信 faith, 進 zeal, 戒 moral restraint, 慚愧 shame, 聞 obedient hearing (of the Law), 捨 abnegation, and 定慧 wisdom arising from meditation.

七淨華 see 七華.

七滅諍法 Saptādhikaraṇa - śamatha. Seven rules given in the Vinaya for settling disputes among the monks. Disputes arise from four causes: from arguments; from discovery of misconduct; judgment and punishment of such; the correctness or otherwise of a religious observance. The seven rules are:—現前毘尼 Saṁmukha-vinaya, face to face evidence, or appeal to the law; 憶念 | | Smṛti-v., witness or proof; 不痴 | | Amūḍha-v., irresponsibility, e.g. lunacy; 自言 | | Tatsvabhavaiṣīya-v., voluntary confession; 多語 | | Pratijñākāraka-v., decision by majority vote; 罪處所 | | Yadbhūyasikīya-v., condemnation of unconfessed sin by the 白四 or jñapticaturthin method, i.e. to make a statement and ask thrice for judgment; 草覆地 | | Tṛṇastāraka-v., i.e. covering the mud with straw, i.e. in protracted disputes the appointment by each side of an elder to spread the straw of the law over the mud of the dispute.

七災難 v. 七難.

七無上道 idem 七種無上.

七珍 idem 七寶.

七生 idem 七有.

七百賢聖 The 700 disciples who met in the second synod at Vaiśālī; also | | 結集.

七眞如 The seven aspects of the bhūtatathatā, v. 眞如. One list is 流轉 | |, 實相 | |, 唯識 | |, 安立 | |, 邪行 | |, 清淨 | |, and 正行 | |. Cf. 唯識論 8.

七知 The seven knowings — to know the Law, its meaning, the times for all duties, moderation, oneself, the different classes of people, and people as individuals.

七祖 The seven founders of the (1) 華嚴 Hua-yen or Kegon School, whose names are given as 馬鳴 Aśvaghoṣa, 龍樹 Nāgārjuna, 杜順 (i.e. 法順), 智儼, 法藏, 澄觀 and 宗密; (2) of the 禪 Ch'an or Zen School, i.e. 達磨 or 菩提 | | Bodhidharma; 慧可, 僧璨, 道信, 弘忍, 慧能 and 荷澤 (or 神會); (3) of the 淨土 Ching-t'u (Jōdo) or Pure-land School, i.e. Nāgārjuna, 天親 or 世親 Vasubandhu, 曇鸞, 道綽, 善導, 源信 and 源空 (or 法然), whose teaching is contained in the 七祖聖教.

七種不淨 The seven kinds of uncleanness, derived from the parental seed, parental intercourse, the womb, the pre-natal blood of the mother, birth, one's own flesh, one's own putrid corpse. | | 布施 The seven kinds of almsgiving—to callers, travellers, the sick, their nurses, monasteries, regular food (to monks), general alms; v. 七有, etc. | | 懺悔心 The seven mental attitudes in penitential meditation or worship: shame, at not yet being free from mortality; fear, of the pains of hell, etc.; turning from the evil world; desire for enlightenment and complete renunciation; impartiality in love to all; gratitude to the Buddha; meditation on the unreality of the sin-nature, that sin arises from perversion and that it has no real existence. 丨丨捨 Seven abandonments or riddances—cherishing none and nothing, no relations with others, riddance of love and hate, of anxiety about the salvation of others, of form, giving to others (e.g. supererogation), benefiting others without hope of return. Another form is—cherishing nothing, riddance of love and hate, of desire, anger, etc., of anxiety about, etc., as above. 丨丨無上 The seven peerless qualities of a Buddha :—his body 身 with its thirty-two signs and eighty-four marks; his way 道 of universal mercy; his perfect insight or doctrine 見; his wisdom 智; his supernatural power 神力; his ability to overcome hindrances 斷障, e.g. illusion, karma, and suffering; and his abiding place 住, i.e. Nirvāṇa. Cf. 七勝事. 丨丨無常 Sapta-anitya. The seven impermanences, a non-Buddhist nihilistic doctrine discussed in the 楞伽經 4. 丨丨生死 The seven kinds of mortality, chiefly relating to bodhisattva incarnation. 丨丨禮佛 Seven degrees of worshipping Buddha, ranging from the merely external to the highest grade. 丨丨自性 The seven characteristics of a Buddha's nature, v. 自性. 丨丨般 v. 不還. 丨丨衣 The seven kinds of clothing, i.e. of hair, hemp, linen, felt, fine linen, wool, or silk. 丨丨語 Buddha's seven modes of discourse: 因語 from present cause to future effect; 果丨 from present effect to past cause; 因果丨 inherent cause and effect; 喩丨 illustrative or figurative; 不應說丨 spontaneous or parabolic; 世界流丨 ordinary or popular; 如意丨 unreserved, or as he really thought, e.g. as when he said that all things have the Buddha-nature. 丨丨辯 The seven rhetorical powers or methods of bodhisattvas :—direct and unimpeded; acute and deep; unlimited in scope; irrefutable; appropriate, or according to receptivity; purposive or objective (i.e. nirvāṇa); proving the universal supreme method of attainment, i.e. Mahāyāna. 丨丨食 The seven kinds of food or āhāra, sustenance :—sleep for eyes, sound for ears, fragrance for nose, taste for tongue, fine smooth things for the body, the Law for the mind, and freedom from laxness for nirvāṇa.

七空 The seven unrealities or illusions, v. 空. There are two lists: (1) 相空, 性自性丨, 行丨, 無行丨, 一切法離言說丨, 第一義聖智大空 and 彼彼丨; v. Laṅkāvatāra-sūtra 1. (2) 性丨, 自相丨, 諸法丨, 不可得丨, 無法丨, 有法丨 and 無法有法丨; v. 智度論 36.

七等覺支 v. 七菩提分.

七羯磨 Karmavācā. 七治 The seven punishments of a monk.

七聖 v. 七賢丨丨. 丨丨財 Saptadhana. The seven sacred graces, variously defined, e.g. 信 faith, 戒 observance of the commandments, 聞 hearing instruction, 慙 shame (for self), 愧 shame (for others); 捨 renunciation; and 慧 wisdom. 丨丨覺 v. 七菩提分.

七聲 v. 七轉九例.

七菩提分 Saptabodhyaṅga, also 丨丨丨寶, 七覺分, 七覺支, 七等覺支. Seven characteristics of bodhi; the sixth of the 七科道品 in the thirty-seven categories of the bodhipakṣika dharma, v. 三十七丨丨丨. It represents seven grades in bodhi, viz. (1) 擇法覺支 (or 丨丨菩提分 and so throughout), dharma-pravicaya-saṁbodhyaṅga, discrimination of the true and the false; (2) 精進 vīrya-saṁ., zeal, or undeflected progress; (3) 喜 prīti-s., joy, delight; (4) 輕安 or 除 praśrabdhi-s., riddance of all grossness or weight of body or mind, so that they may be light, free, and at ease; (5) 念 smṛti-s., power of remembering the various states passed through in contemplation; (6) 定 samādhi-s., power to keep the mind in a given realm undiverted; (7) 行捨 or 捨 upekṣā-s., or upekṣaka, complete abandonment, auto-hypnosis, or indifference to all disturbances of the sub-conscious or ecstatic mind.

七華 The seven flowers of enlightenment, idem 七菩提分. Another version is pure in the commandments, in heart, in views, in doubt-discrimination, in judgment, in conduct, and in nirvāṇa.

七葉巖 The crag at Rājagṛha on which the "seven-leaf tree" grew, in the cave beneath which the first "synod" is said to have been held after the Buddha's death, to recall and determine his teaching.

七處八會 The eight assemblies in seven different places, at which the sixty sections of the 華嚴經 Avataṁsaka Sūtra are said to have been preached; the same sūtra in eighty sections is accredited to the 丨丨九會. 丨丨平滿相 One of the thirty-two signs on the Buddha's body—the perfection of feet, hands, shoulders, and head.

七衆 The seven classes of disciples :—(1) 比丘 bhikṣu, monk; (2) 丨丨尼 bhikṣuṇī, a female observer of all the commandments; (3) 式叉摩那

śikṣamāṇa, a novice, or observer of the six commandments; (4) 沙彌 śrāmaṇera, and (5) 沙彌尼 śrāmanerikā, male and female observers of the minor commandments; (6) 優婆塞 upāsaka, male observers of the five commandments; and (7) 優婆夷 upāsikā, female ditto. The first five have left home, the last two remain at home. T'ien-t'ai makes nine groups by dividing the last two into four, two remaining at home, two leaving home and keeping the eight commandments. Others make four groups, i.e. (1), (2), (6), and (7) of the above. T'ien-t'ai also has a four-group.

七衆溺水 The seven types who fall into the waters of this life—the first is drowned, the seventh is a Buddha; the seven are icchantika, men and devas, ordinary believers, śrāvakas, pratyekabuddhas, bodhisattvas, and Buddhas; also called 丨丨人.

七見 The seven heretical views, v. 見. They are 邪丨, 我丨, 常丨, 斷丨, 戒盜丨, 果盜丨, and 疑丨.

七覺分 or 支, v. 七菩提分.

七證(師) v. 三師七證.

七識住 v. 九有情居.

七識十名 The ten names of the seventh vijñāna, v. manas 末那識.

七財 v. 七法財.

七賢(位) Also 七方便位, 七加行位 The seven grades or steps in virtue preceding the entry into 見道 faultless wisdom, or faultlessness in its first realization. These seven are preliminary to the 七聖(位). Both are grades of the 俱舍 Kośa school of Hīnayāna. 丨丨七聖 The 七聖 are seven developments of holiness, which follow the above. In the Hua-yen 華嚴 school they are called 七士夫, 七大夫 or 七聖人. Cf. 俱舍論 25.

七趣 The seven gati or states of sentient beings—*nārakagati*, in hell; *preta*, hungry ghost; *tiryagyoni*, animal; *manuṣya*, man; *ṛṣi*, a genius or higher spiritual being; *deva*, god; *asura*, demon of the higher order.

七躬醫王 v. 七佛藥師.

七轉九例 The seven Sanskrit cases and nine conjugations. The former are also styled 七聲 and 七例 subanta 蘇漫 (or 槃多); sometimes with the Vocative called 八轉聲. The 九例 or tiṅanta 丁彥多 are also styled 二九韻, i.e. nine parasmai and nine ātmane.

七逆(罪) The seven rebellious acts, or deadly sins—shedding a Buddha's blood, killing father, mother, monk, teacher, subverting or disrupting monks, killing an arhat. v. 梵網經下.

七遮罪 Concealing, or non-confession of, any one of the seven deadly sins 七逆, for which it is also used.

七重行樹 The seven avenues of gem trees in Paradise.

七金山 The seven concentric mountain ranges which surround Sumeru, the central mountain of a universe, each range separated from the others by a sea; see 九山八海. Their names are 持雙, 持軸, 擔木(樹), 善見, 馬耳, 障礙 (or 象鼻), 持地 (or 邊) 山.

七難 The seven calamities in the 仁王經受持品 during which that sūtra should be recited: sun and moon losing their order (eclipses), constellations irregular, fire, flood, wind-storms, drought, brigands. Another set is — pestilence, invasion, rebellion, unlucky stars, eclipses, too early monsoon, too late monsoon. Another is—fire, flood, rakṣas, misrule, evil spirits, cangue and prison, and robbers.

七顚倒 v. 顚倒; viparyaya, the seven inversions, or upside-downs, i.e. contrary or false positions—想, 見, 心, 常無常, 苦樂, 淨不淨, 我無我.

乃至 (1) A translation of antaśas meaning "at least"; and (2) of yāvat, as far as. 丨丨一念 Even, or at least, a thought. 乃往 As far as the past (is concerned).

九 Navan; nava. Nine.

九上緣惑 The nine kinds of error or illusion in 見, i.e. views or mental processes, found also in higher conditions of development.

九世 In past, present, and future worlds, each

has its own past, present, and future, hence nine worlds or ages. 丨丨間 The nine lower of the ten worlds, the highest or tenth being the Buddha-world; the nine are always subject to illusion, confused by the senses.

九住心 Nine stages of mental concentration when in dhyāna meditation, viz. 安, 攝, 解, 轉, 伏, 息, 滅, 性, and 持 (住心).

九條衣; 丨丨袈裟 The lowest rank of the patch-robe, v. 九品大衣.

九儀 The nine "Indian" ways of showing respect, according to Hsüan-tsang—asking about welfare; bowing the head; holding high the hands; bowing with folded hands; bending the knee; kneeling; hands and knees on the ground; elbows and knees ditto; the whole body prostrate.

九入 v. 九孔.

九劫 The nine kalpas; though Śākyamuni and Maitreya started together, the zeal of the first enabled him to become Buddha nine kalpas sooner; see 大寶積經 111.

九十六術 Also 丨丨丨種外道. Ninety-six classes of non-Buddhists or heretics and their practices, i.e. their six founders and each of them with fifteen schools of disciples; some say 九十五種外道.

九十八使 Also 丨丨丨隨眠 The Hīnayāna ninety-eight tempters, or temptations, that follow men with all subtlety to induce laxity. They are the ninety-eight kleśas, or moral temptations in the realm of 見思 view and thought, or external and internal ideas.

九句因 A term in Buddhist logic; the nine possible combinations of like and unlike examples in a syllogism.

九品 Nine classes, or grades, i.e. 上上, 上中, 上下 upper superior, middle superior, lower superior, and so on with 中 and 下. They are applied in many ways, e.g. 上品上生, the highest type of incarnate being, to 下品下生, the lowest, with corresponding karma; see 九品淨土. Each grade may also be subdivided into nine, thus making a list of eighty-one grades, with similar further subdivision *ad infinitum*. 丨丨上 An abbreviation for 上品上生, the highest grade in the Pure Land, see 丨丨淨土. 丨丨大衣 The 僧伽梨 saṅghāṭī. There are nine grades of the monk's patch robe; the three lowest ranks have 9, 11, and 13 patches, two long patches to one short one; the three middle 15, 17, 19, three long to one short; and the three superior 21, 23, 25, four long to one short. 丨丨安養之化生 Those born by transformation from the (heavenly) lotus into the ninefold 安養 Paradise, idem 丨丨淨土. 丨丨彌陀 The nine forms of Amitābha, corresponding to the nine departments of the Pure Land; chiefly used with reference to the manual signs of his images. 丨丨往生 The ninefold future life, in the Pure Land, v. 丨丨淨土. It is detailed in the sūtra of this name whose full title is 阿彌陀三摩地集陀羅尼經. 丨丨惑 Also 丨丨煩惱 The four 修惑, i.e. illusions or trials in the practice of religion, i.e. desire, anger, pride, ignorance; these are divided each into 九品 q.v.; hence desire has all the nine grades, and so on with the other three. 丨丨淨土, also 丨丨丨刹, 丨丨安養, 丨丨蓮臺, 丨丨往生 The nine grades, or rewards, of the Pure Land, corresponding to the nine grades of development in the previous life, upon which depends, in the next life, one's distance from Amitābha, the consequent æons that are needed to approach him, and whether one's lotus will open early or late. 丨丨行業 The nine karma to be attained by the conduct or practice through which one may be born into the above Pure Land. 丨丨覺王 The king or lord of the bodhi of the Pure Land, Amitābha.

九喩 The nine similes: stars, eye-film, lamp, prestidigitation, dew, bubble, dream, lightning, cloud. There is also another group.

九因一果 Nine of the 十界 ten dhātu or regions are causative, the tenth is the effect or resultant.

九地 The nine lands, i.e. the 欲界 realm of desire or sensuous realm; the four 色界 realms of form or material forms; and the four 無色界 formless realms, or realms beyond form; v. 九有, 九有情居, 禪 and 定. The nine realms are:—(1) 欲界五趣地, the desire-realm with its five gati, i.e. hells, hungry ghosts, animals, men, and devas. In the four form-realms are:—(2) 離生喜樂地 Paradise after earthly life; this is also the first dhyāna, or subject of meditation, 初禪. (3) 定生喜樂地 Paradise of cessation of rebirth, 二禪. (4) 離喜妙樂地 Land of wondrous joy after the previous joys, 三禪.

(5) 捨念清淨地 The Pure Land of abandonment of thought, or recollection (of past delights), 四禪. The four formless, or infinite realms, catur arūpa dhātu, are:—(6) 空無邊處地 ākāśānantyāyatanam, the land of infinite space; also the first samādhi, 第一定. (7) 識無邊處地 vijñānānantyāyatanam, the land of omniscience, or infinite perception, 二定. (8) 無所有處地 ākiñcanyāyatana, the land of nothingness, 三定. (9) 非想非非想處地 naivasaṁjñānā-saṁjñāyatana, the land (of knowledge) without thinking or not thinking, or where there is neither consciousness nor unconsciousness, i.e. above either; this is the 四定. Eitel says that in the last four, "Life lasts 20,000 great kalpas in the 1st, 40,000 in the 2nd, 60,000 in the 3rd, and 80,000 great kalpas in the 4th of these heavens." ||九品思惑 v. 八十一品思惑.

九域 idem 九地 and 九界.

九執 The nine graha, i.e. "seizers" or upholders, i.e. luminaries or planets, idem 九曜.

九士生地 idem Kuśinagara; v. 拘.

九孔 Also 九入, 九竅, 九漏, 九流, 九瘡 the nine orifices, cavities, entrances, leakages, or suppurations, i.e. the two eyes, two ears, two nostrils, mouth, and two lower organs.

九字 The nine magical characters 臨兵鬪者皆陳列在前 implying that the armed forces are arrayed against the powers of evil. After reciting these words, four vertical and five horizontal lines, forming a grid, are drawn in the air to show that the forces are arrayed. It was used among Taoists and soldiers, and is still used in Japan, especially when going into the mountains. ||曼荼羅 The nine character maṇḍala, i.e. the lotus, with its eight petals and its centre; Avalokiteśvara may be placed in the heart and Amitābha on each petal, generally in the shape of the Sanskrit "seed" letter, or alphabetic letter.

九宗 The eight sects 八| (q.v.) plus the 禪 Ch'an or Zen, or the Pure-land or Jōdo sect.

九尊 The nine honoured ones in the eight-petalled hall of the Garbhadhātu, i.e. Vairocana in the centre of the lotus, with four Buddhas and four bodhisattvas on the petals, the lotus representing the human heart; v. 五佛.

九居 v. 九有情居.

九山八海 The nine cakravāla, or concentric mountain ranges or continents, separated by eight seas, of a universe. The central mountain of the nine is Sumeru 須彌 and around it are the ranges Khadiraka 佉提羅, Īṣādhara 伊沙陀羅, Yugaṁdhara 遊乾陀羅, Sudarśana 蘇達梨舍那, Aśvakarṇa 安濕縛竭拏, Nemiṁdhara 尼民陀羅, Vinataka 毘那多迦, Cakravāḍa 斫迦羅; v. 七金山. The Abhidharma Kośa gives a different order:—Sumeru, Yugaṁdhara, Īṣādhara, Khadiraka, Sudarśana, Aśvakarṇa, Vinataka, Nemiṁdhara, with an "iron-wheel" mountain encompassing all; there are also differences in the detail.

九參上堂 The nine monthly visits or ascents to the hall for worship, every third day.

九徧知 The nine forms of complete knowledge of the four axioms and the cutting off of passion, delusion, etc., in the processes of 見 and 修, as distinct from 無學.

九徹 The nine penetrating flames of the sword of Acala, 不動明王, emblem of the destruction of illusions and hindrances in the nine realms, v. 九地; also used for the 九尊 q.v.

九心輪 The nine evolutions, or movements of the mind in perception.

九想(觀) or |相 Navasaṁjñā. Meditation on a corpse in order to curb desire; one of the meditations on the unclean:—*vyādhmātakasaṁjñā*, its tumefaction; *vinīlakas.*, its blue, mottled colour; *vipaḍumakas.*, its decay; *vilohitakas.*, its mess of blood, etc.; *vipūyakas.*, its discharges and rotten flesh; *vikhāditakas.*, its being devoured by birds and beasts; *vikṣiptakas.*, its dismembering; *asthis.*, its bones; *vidagdhakas.*, their being burnt and returning to dust.

九惱; also |難, |橫, |罪報 The nine distresses borne by the Buddha while in the flesh, i.e. the two women Sundarā and Cañcā; others from Devadatta, Ajātaśatru, etc.; v. 智度論 9.

九慢 The nine forms of pride—that I surpass, am equal to, not so bad as others; that others surpass, are as bad as, are inferior to me; that none surpass, are equal to, or worse than me.

九方便 The nine suitable stages in religious service; cf. 大日經, 7; 作禮 salutation to the universal Triratna; 出罪 repentance and confession; 歸依 trust (in the Triratna); 施身 giving of self (to the Tathāgata); 發菩提心 vowing to devote the mind to bodhi; 隨喜 rejoicing (in all good); 勸請 beseeching (all Tathāgatas to rain down the saving law); 奉請法身 praying for the Buddha-nature in self and others for entry in the Pure Land; 迴向 demitting the good produced by the above eight methods, to others, universally, past, present, and future. This form of service is generally performed before engaging in esoteric observances. The verses in which these nine stages are presented are of a commendably devotional character. | | | 十波羅蜜菩薩 Of the ten pāramitā bodhisattvas, q.v., in the tenth or empyrean court of the Garbhadhātu, the first nine are associated with the above nine progressive steps, the tenth is associated with the last four of the nine.

九會(曼陀羅) The nine groups in the diamond-realm maṇḍala. 九會(說) The Hua-yen 華嚴 sūtra in its older sixty chüan version is said to have been delivered at eight assemblies in seven places; the newer eighty chüan at nine assemblies in seven places; cf. | 處.

九曜; 九執 q.v. Navagraha. The nine luminaries: 日 Āditya, the sun; 月 Sōma, the moon; the five planets, i.e. 火星 Aṅgāraka, Mars; 水 Budha, Mercury; 木 Bṛhaspati, Jupiter; 金 Śukra, Venus; and 土 Śanaiścara, Saturn; also 羅睺 Rāhu, the spirit that causes eclipses; and 計都 Ketu, a comet. Each is associated with a region of the sky and also with a bodhisattva, etc., e.g. the sun with Kuan-yin, Venus with Amitābha, etc.

九有 The nine realities, states, or conditions in which sentient beings enjoy to dwell, v. next. | | 情居 (or 處), | 衆生居, | 居, | 門, see also | 有, | 地, 禪 and 定; the nine happy abodes or states of sentient beings of the 長阿含經 9; they are the 七識住 seven abodes or stages of perception or consciousness to which are added the fifth and ninth below:—(1) 欲界之人天 the world and the six deva-heavens of desire in which there is variety of bodies (or personalities) and thinking (or ideas); (2) 梵衆天 the three brahma-heavens where bodies differ but thinking is the same, the first dhyāna heaven; (3) 極光淨天 the three bright and pure heavens where bodies are identical but thinking differs, the second dhyāna heaven; (4) 遍淨天 the three universally pure heavens where bodies and thinking are the same, the third dhyāna heaven; (5) 無想天 the no-thinking or no-thought heaven, the highest of the four dhyāna heavens; (6) 空無邊處 limitless space, the first of the formless realms; (7) 識無邊處 limitless perception, the second ditto; (8) 無所有處 nothingness, the place beyond things, the third ditto; and (9) 非想非非想 beyond thought or non-thought, the fourth ditto.

九梵 The nine heavens of the fourth dhyāna heaven.

九業 The nine kinds of karma, i.e. the desire realm and the form realm each has conduct that causes karma, does not cause karma, or is neutral, making 6; in the formless realm there are non-causative deeds, neutrality, and immortality, making 9; 成實論 8.

九橫(死) The nine kinds of irregular death; there are two groups, one connected with improper food or meals, another with improper medical treatment, law-breaking, drowning, etc. See also 九惱. | | 經 A sūtra translated in the later Han dynasty by 安世高 An Shih-kao.

九次第定 The samādhi of the nine degrees, i.e. the four dhyānas 四禪, the four realms beyond form 四無色, and the samādhi beyond sensation and thought 滅受想定; see 九有情居 and 九地.

九流; 九漏 idem | 孔.

九無學 The nine grades (of arhats) who are no longer learning, having attained their goal. | | 爲 The nine kinds of, and meditations on, 無爲 q.v. There are two somewhat different groups; one has 擇滅, 非擇滅, 虛空, 空無邊處, 識無邊處, 無所有處, 非想非非想處 (v. 九有情處), 緣起支性, and 聖道支性. | | 間道 In every universe there are nine realms, in every realm there are nine illusions in practice 修, and nine ways of relief; hence the nine ways of overcoming hindrances; also there are nine uninterrupted ways of advance from one stage to another of the nine stages of the 三界 trailokya, by the wisdom of overcoming delusion in each stage; also | | 礙 |; and cf. 九解脫道.

九界(情執) The nine realms of error, or subjection to the passions, i.e. all the realms of the living except the tenth and highest, the Buddha-realm.

九瘡 idem 九孔.

九祖(相承) The succession of nine founders of the T'ien-t'ai School; v. 天台九宗.

九禪 v. next.

九種大禪 The nine kinds of Mahāyāna dhyāna for bodhisattvas, given in the 菩薩地持經 6 and in other works; they are associated with the patience 忍 pāramitā and with the dhyāna of the super-realms. The nine are meditations—(1) 自性禪 on the original nature of things, or mind as the real nature, from which all things derive; (2) 一切 | on achieving the development of self and all others to the utmost; (3) 難 | on the difficulties of certain dhyāna conditions; (4) 一切門 | on the entrance to all the (superior) dhyāna conditions; (5) 善人 | on the good; (6) 一切行 | on all Mahāyāna practices and actions; (7) 除煩惱 | on ridding all sufferers from the miseries of passion and delusion; (8) 此世他世樂 | on the way to bring joy to all people both in this life and hereafter; (9) 清淨淨 | on perfect purity in the termination of all delusion and distress and the obtaining of perfect enlightenment.

九竅 v. 九孔.

九結 The nine bonds that bind men to mortality:—love, hate, pride, ignorance, (wrong) views, possessions (or grasping), doubt, envy, meanness (or selfishness). They are the 六隨眠 plus grasping, envy, and meanness.

九經 idem | 部 |.

九縛一脫 The nine states of bondage and the one state of liberation. The nine states are the hells of fire, of blood, of swords; asuras, men, devas, māras, nirgranthas, form and formless states; these are all saṁsāra states, i.e. of reincarnation. The one state of freedom, or for obtaining freedom, is nirvāṇa.

九罪報 v. 九惱.

九蓮 The paradise of Amitābha, i.e. 九品蓮臺.

九華山 Formerly called 九子山, which was changed by the T'ang poet Li Po to the above; it is one of the four sacred mountains of Buddhism, situated in Anhui, and its patron Bodhisattva is Ti-tsang, 地藏.

九衆 The 七 | q.v. plus junior monks and nuns, i.e. novices who have received the eight commandments. | | 生居 v. 九有情居.

九解脫道 In the nine stages of the trailokya 三界 each has its possible delusions and erroneous performances; the latter are overcome by the 九無間道 q.v.

九諦 The nine truths, or postulates: impermanence; suffering; voidness (or unreality of things); no permanent ego, or soul; love of existence or possessions, resulting in suffering; the opposite (or fear of being without them), also resulting in suffering; the cutting off of suffering and its cause; nirvāṇa with remainder still to be worked out; complete nirvāṇa.

九識 The nine kinds of cognition or consciousness (vijñāna); those of sight, hearing, smell, taste, touch, mind, manas (or 阿陀那 | ādāna), i.e. mental perception; 阿賴耶 | ālaya, bodhi-consciousness, and 阿摩羅 | amala, purified or Buddha-consciousness. There is considerable difference as to the meaning of the last three.

九輪 The nine wheels or circles on the top of a pagoda, also called 空輪 the wheels in space; the nine should only be on the stūpa of a Buddha, others are entitled to as many as eight and as few as one.

九轍 Kumārajīva's nine divisions of the meaning of the Lotus Sūtra, whence he was styled the | | 法師.

九道 idem 九有情居.

九部(經) Nine of the Hīnayāna twelve classes of sūtras, that is, all except the 方廣, 授記 and 無問自說. Generally the term is thus interpreted, but there is also a Mahāyāna division of nine of the twelve sūtras, i.e. all except the 緣起, 譬喩, and 論議. These are: sūtras, the Buddha's sermons; geyas, metrical pieces; vyākaraṇas, prophecies; gāthās, chants or poems; udānas, impromptu or unsolicited addresses; ityuktas, or itivṛttakas, narratives; jātakas, stories of former lives of Buddha, etc.; vaipulyas, expanded sūtras, etc.; adbhuta-dharmas, miracles, etc.; v. 十二部經.

九門 v. 九有情居.

九難 v 九惱.

九類生 The nine kinds of birth; the four from the womb, egg, moisture, transformation are common to devas, earth, and the hells; the five others are birth into the heavens of form, of non-form, of thought, of non-thought, and of neither (i.e. beyond either).

九鬼 The nine classes of ghosts are of three kinds: without means, small means, rich. The first group have 炬口 burning torch-like mouths, or 鍼口 narrow needle mouths, or 臭口 stinking mouths; the second group have hair like needles, or stinking hair, or tumours; the rich ghosts haunt sacrifices to the dead, or eat human leavings, or live truculently.

九陰 The five elements together with time, space, mind (*manas*), and soul (*ātman*) according to the teaching of the "heretical" Vaiśeṣika sect; v. 鞞.

九齋日 The nine kinds of days of abstinence on which no food is eaten after twelve o'clock noon and the commands are observed. They are: Every day of the first month, of the fifth month, of the ninth month, and the following six days of each month, 8th, 14th, 15th, 23rd, 29th, and 30th. On these days Indra and the four deva-kings investigate the conduct of men.

了 To end, see through, understand, thoroughly know, make clear, thoroughly, completely, final.

了了見 The complete vision obtained when the body is in complete rest and the mind freed from phenomenal disturbance.

了因 A revealing cause, v. 二因, i.e. 生| a producing or direct cause, e.g. a seed; and 了| a revealing "cause", e.g. a light, as indicating the effect; knowledge or wisdom. ||佛性 The second of the three Buddha-nature "causes", i.e. 正因佛性 is the 眞如 as direct cause of attaining the perfect Buddha-nature, associated with the 法身; 了因佛性 is the revealing or enlightening cause, associated with the Buddha-wisdom; 緣因佛性 is the environing cause, e.g. his goodness and merits which result in deliverance, or salvation.

了徹禪定 The mastery of abstract contemplation.

了悟 Complete enlightenment, or clear apprehension.

了教 A noted disciple named Ajñāta-Kauṇḍinya, v. 阿, also known as 拘鄰隣, 了本際 and 知本際. He is described as "a prince of Magadha, maternal uncle of Śākyamuni, whose first disciple he became". He is "to be reborn as Buddha under the name of Samanta-Prabhāsa". Eitel.

了知 Parijñā, thorough knowledge.

了義 Revelation of the whole meaning, or truth, as 不|| is partial revelation adapted (方便) to the capacity of the hearers. ||教 Teaching of the whole truth. ||經 The sūtras containing it. Mahāyāna counts all Hīnayāna sūtras as 不|||; Mahāyāna sūtras are divided into both kinds according to different schools.

了達 Thorough penetration, clear understanding.

二 Dvā, dvau. Two; dvitīya, second.

二三 The six non-Buddhist philosophers, ||邪徒.

二世 This life and the hereafter. ||尊 Śākyamuni and Prabhūtaratna, the Buddha 多寶 in the eleventh chapter of the Lotus Sūtra; see also 二尊. ||間 The two realms of conscious or sentient beings 有情世間, and unconscious or material things 器世間.

二乘 Dviyāna. The two vehicles conveying to the final goal. There are several definitions:—(1) Mahāyāna and Hīnayāna. (2) 聲聞 and 緣覺 or 聲覺||. Śrāvaka and Pratyekabuddha. (3) ||作佛 The Lotus Sūtra teaches that śrāvakas and pratyekas also become Buddhas. (4) 三一|| The "two vehicles" of "three" and "one", the three being the pre-Lotus ideas of śrāvaka, pratyeka, and bodhisattva, the one being the doctrine of the Lotus Sūtra which combined all three in one.

二九五部 The eighteen Hīnayāna sects and the five Vinaya 律 sects. ||韻 The eighteen

丁岸哆 tiṅanta, personal endings of the Sanskrit verb.

二二合緣 A method of meditation by coupling 法 with 身, 受, 心 respectively. Cf. 四念處觀.

二五食 The two groups of food, each of five kinds: *bhojanīya*, v. 蒲 cereals, fish, and flesh; and *khādanīya*, v. 佉 fruits and sweetmeats.

二佛並坐 The two Buddhas sitting together, v. 二世尊. ||中門 The period between the nirvāṇa of Śākyamuni and the future advent of Maitreya, i.e. the present period. ||性 Dual aspects of the Buddha-nature, i.e. 理佛性 the Buddha-nature which is fundamentally in all sentient beings, and 行佛性 the functioning Buddha-nature active and effective in some, but not in others, a doctrine of the 法相 school. ||身 v. 二身.

二修 Two kinds of devotion or practice, 專 and 雜 sole or single-minded, and miscellaneous or varied, defined as (1) chief or sole duty, and (2) aids thereto or adjunctive observances. Also 緣 | causative devotion of a bodhisattva in former life, and 眞 | its actual manifestation here.

二俱犯過 or 二人俱犯 A term applied by T'ien-t'ai in criticism of Hua-yen, which while it is a 圓教 perfect or complete doctrine, yet has the "crudities" of the 別教 and comes short of the really perfect Lotus doctrine.

二假 Two hypotheses in the 唯識論 1:—(1) 無體隨情假 the non-substantial hypothesis, that there is no substantial entity or individuality, i.e. no 見分 and 相分, no 實我 and 實法, no real subject and object, but that all is transient emotion; (2) 有體施設假 the factual hypothesis, that there is entity or individuality, subject and object, etc.

二光 The dual lights, i.e. 色 | the halo from a Buddha's body and 心光 the light from his mind. Also 常光 the constant halo from the bodies of Buddhas and 神通 | the supernatural light sent out by a Buddha (e.g. from between his eyebrows) to illuminate a distant world.

二入 The two ways of entering the truth:—理入 by conviction intellectually, 行入 by (proving it in) practice.

二八 The sixteen 觀 or meditations. V. 十六觀.

二六 Twelve. ||之緣 idem 十二因緣. ||之願 the twelve vows of 藥師. ||時中 during the twelve (= twenty-four) hours of the day.

二凡 The two external and internal, or ordinary ranks, 外凡 and 內凡, in the first forty of the fifty-two stages 位; the 外 | are ordinary believers who pursue the stages of 十信; the 內 | are the zealous, who are advancing through the next three groups of stages up to the fortieth.

二出 The two modes of escape from mortality, 竪 | the long way called the 聖道門 or 自力教, i.e. working out one's own salvation; and 橫 the across or short way of the Pure-land sect or 他力教 faith in or invocation of another, i.e. Amitābha.

二利 The dual benefits, or profits: benefiting or developing oneself and others; 自利 in seeking enlightenment in bodhisattvahood, 利他 in saving the multitude. Hīnayāna "seeks only one's own benefit"; the bodhisattva rule seeks both one's own benefit and that of others, or personal improvement for the improving of others.

二力 Dual powers; there are three definitions:—(1) 自力 one's own strength, or endeavours, i.e. salvation by cultivating 戒, 定, and 慧; 他力 another's strength, e.g. the saving power of Amitābha. (2) 思擇 | Power of thought in choosing (right principles); 修習力 power of practice and performance. (3) 有 | and 無 | positive and negative forces; dominant and subordinate; active and inert energy.

二加 The dual aid bestowed by the Buddha, 顯 | manifest or external, in the blessings and powers of this life; 冥 | invisible, in getting rid of sins, increasing virtue, etc.

二勝果 The two surpassing fruits, or rewards given by Buddha, i.e. final nirvāṇa and perfect enlightenment.

二十 Viṁśati. Twenty.

二十二品 Twenty-two of the 三十七道品 q.v.; they are 四念處、四正勤、四如意、足五根 and 五力. |||根 The twenty-two roots, organs, or powers, v. 根. They are :—(1) 眼 | eye, *cakṣurindriya*; (2) 耳 | ear, *śrotrendriya*; (3) 鼻 | nose, *ghrāṇendriya*; (4) 舌 | tongue, *jihvendriya*; (5) 身 | body, *kāyendriya*; (6) 意 | mind, *manaïndriya* (the above are the 六根); (7) 女 | female organ, *strīndriya*; (8) 男 | male organ, *puruṣendriya*; (9) 命 | life, *jīvitendriya*; (10) 苦 | suffering (or pain), *duḥkhendriya*; (11) 樂 | pleasure, *sukhendriya*; (12) 憂 | sorrow, *daurmanasyendriya*; (13) 喜 | joy, *saumanasyendriya*; (14) 捨 | abandoning, *upekṣendriya* (from 10 to 14 they are the 五受); (15) 信 | faith, *śraddhendriya*; (16) 精進 | zeal, *vīryendriya*; (17) 念 | memory, *smṛtīndriya*; (18) 定 | meditation, or trance, *samādhīndriya*; (19) 慧 | wisdom, *prajñendriya* (these are the 信等之五根); (20) 未知當知 | the power for learning (the Four Noble Truths) *anājñātamājñāsyāmīndriya*; (21) 已知根 the power of having learned (them), *ājñendriya*; (22) 具知 | the power of perfect knowledge (of them), *ājñātāvīndriya* (these three are called the 無漏根). | | | 門 The Abhidharma Kośa divides the eighteen realms 十八界 into twenty-two categories. Also, there are twenty-two modes or processes in the perfect development of a Buddha and his works.

二十五條 The monk's twenty-five-patch garment, v. 袈. | | | 圓通 The twenty-five kinds of perfect understanding of the truth; they refer to the 六塵, 六根, 六識, and 七大; disciples of the Buddha are said each to have acquired a special knowledge of one of these twenty-five and to have been recognized as its authority, e.g. Kuan-yin of the ear, Dignāga of sound, etc. | | | 方便 T'ien-t'ai's twenty-five aids to meditation, v. 止觀. | | | 有 The twenty-five forms of existence, fourteen in the desire realms 欲界, seven in the realms of form 色界, and four in the formless realms 無色界, v. 有. | | | 神 The twenty-five guardian deities who protect any keeper of the commandments, i.e. five for each of the commandments against killing, robbing, adultery, lying, and drinking. | | | 菩薩 The twenty-five bodhisattvas who protect all who call on Amitābha, i.e. 觀音, 大勢至, 藥王, 藥上, 普賢, 法自在, 師子吼, 陀羅尼, 虛空藏, 佛藏, 菩藏, 金藏, 金剛藏, 山海慧, 光明王, 華嚴王, 衆寶王, 月光王, 日照王, 三昧王, 定自在王, 大自在王, 白象王, 大威德王 and 無邊身菩薩. | | | 點 Each of the five 更 night watches is divided into five, making twenty-five tien.

二十億耳 Śroṇakoṭīviṁśa. Defined as the most zealous of Śākyamuni's disciples, who became an arhat. Having lived in a heaven for ninety-one kalpas, where his feet did not touch the ground, he was born with hair on his soles two inches long, an omen which led his father and brothers to endow him with twenty koṭīs of ounces of gold, hence this name. v. 智度論 22.

二十八天 The twenty-eight heavens, or devalokas: six of the desire-world 欲界, eighteen of the form-world 色界, and four arūpa or formless heavens 無色界. The heavens of the world of form are sixteen according to the 薩婆多部 Sarvāstivāda School, seventeen according to 經部 Sūtra School, and eighteen according to the 上座部 Sthavirāḥ. | | | 宿 The twenty-eight nakṣatras or constellations, divided into four mansions of seven each, referred to East, or Spring; South, Summer; West, Autumn; and North, Winter. The month-names derived from them differ slightly in form. E.: 角 Citrā, 亢 Niṣṭyā (or Svāti), 氐 Viśākhā, 房 Anurādhā, 心 Rohiṇī, Jyeṣṭhaghnī (or Jyeṣṭhā), 尾 Mūlabarhaṇī (or Mūla), 箕 Pūrva-Aṣādhā. N.: 斗 Uttara-Aṣāḍhā, 牛 Abhijit, 女 Śravaṇā, 虛 Śraviṣṭhā (or Dhaniṣṭhā), 危 Śatabhiṣā, 室 Pūrva-Proṣṭhapada, 壁 Uttara-Proṣṭhapada. W.: 奎 Revatī, 婁 Aśvayuj (or Aśvinī), 胃 Apabharaṇī (or Bharaṇī), 昴 Kṛttikā, 畢 Rohiṇī, 觜 Invakā (or Mṛgaśiras), 參 Bāhu (or Ārdrā). S.: 井 Punarvasu, 鬼 Tiṣya (or Puṣya), 柳 Aśleṣā, 星 Maghā, 張 Pūrva-Phalgunī, 翼 Uttara-Phalgunī, 軫 Hastā. | | | 有 or 生 The twenty-eight forms of existence, or birth. 二十九有 the twenty-ninth is the non-existent; v. 有. | | | 祖 The twenty-eight Buddhist patriarchs as stated by the Mahāyānists. The T'ien-t'ai school reckons twenty-three, or twenty-four, with the addition of Śāṇakavāsa, contemporary with his predecessors, but the Ch'an school reckons twenty-eight:—(1) Mahākāśyapa, 摩訶迦葉(波); (2) Ānanda, 阿難; (3) Śāṇakavāsa, 商那和修; (4) Upagupta, 優婆毱多; (5) Dhṛṭaka, 提多迦; (6) Mikkaka, or Miccaka, or Micchaka, 彌遮迦; (7) Vasumitra, 婆須蜜; (8) Buddhanandi, 佛陀難提; (9) Buddhamitra, 伏馱密多; (10) Pārśva, or Pārśvika, 波栗溼縛 or 脇尊者; (11) Puṇyayaśas, 富那耶舍; (12) Aśvaghoṣa, 馬鳴大士; (13) Kapimala, 迦毘摩羅; (14) Nāgārjuna, 龍樹; (15) Kāṇadeva, 迦那提婆; (16) Rāhulata, 羅睺羅多; (17) Saṅghanandi, 僧伽難提; (18) Gayāśata, 伽耶舍多; (19) Kumārata, 鳩摩羅多; (20) Jayata, 闍夜多; (21) Vasubandhu, 婆修盤頭; (22) Manorhita, 摩拏羅; (23) Haklena, 鶴勒那; (24) Āryasiṁha, 師子尊者; (25) Basiasita, 婆舍斯多; (26) Puṇyamitra, 不如密多; (27) Prajñātāra, 般若多羅; (28) Bodhidharma, 菩提達磨. | | | 藥叉 the twenty-eight yakṣas. | | | 部衆 The thousand-hand Kuan-yin has twenty-eight groups of 大仙衆 great ṛṣis or genii, under the direction of the 孔雀王 Peacock king, Mayūrarāja; also each of the 四天王 mahārājas, or guardians of the four regions, has the same provision of demons, known as 鬼神衆 company of spirits.

二十唯識 The name of the 唯識二十論.

二十天 The twenty devas. (1) 大梵天王 (Mahābrahman), (2) 帝釋尊天 (Śakra devānām Indra), (3) 多聞天王 (Vaiśravaṇa, 毘沙門, or Dhanada), (4) 持國天王 (Dhṛtarāṣṭra), (5) 增長天王 (Virūḍhaka), (6) 廣目天王 (Virūpākṣa), (7) 金剛密迹 (? Guhyapati), (8) 摩醯首羅 (Maheśvara), (9) 散脂 (迦) 大將 (Pañcika), (10) 大辯才天 (Sarasvatī), (11) 大功德天 (Lakṣmī), (12) 韋駄天神 (Skanda), (13) 堅牢地神 (Pṛthivī), (14) 菩提樹神 (Bodhidruma, or Bodhivṛkṣa), (15) 鬼子母神 (Hāritī), (16) 摩利支天 (Marīci), (17) 日宮天子 (Sūrya) (18) 月宮天子 (Candra, etc. There are many different names), (19) 娑竭龍王 (Sāgara), (20) 閻摩羅王 (Yama-rāja).

二十智 The twenty kinds of wisdom or knowledge as defined by T'ien-t'ai, i.e. the Hīnayāna (or 三藏) with seven kinds, 通教 five, 別教 four, and 圓教 four; cf. 智. | | 犍度 The twenty skandhas, intp. as 章篇 sections or chapters, i.e. the thirty-one to the fifty-three chüan of the 四分律, beginning with 受戒 | | and ending with 雜 | |; they are twenty sections containing rules for the monastic life and intercourse. | | 部 The eighteen Hīnayāna sects, together with the two original assemblies of elders.

二受 The dual receptivity or karma of pleasure and pain, the physical and the mental, i.e. 身 and 心.

二吉羅 The two duṣkṛta, doing evil and speaking evil; v. 突 | |.

二和 The double harmony or unity, i.e. 理 and 事, indicating those who are united in doctrine and practice, or the saṅgha.

二善 The two good things, 定 | the good character that arises from meditation or contemplation—especially of the Pure Land; 散 | the good character attainable when, though not in meditation, one controls oneself in thought, word, and deed. Also 未生 | and 已生 | the good character not yet and that already evolved. Also 事理 | goodness in theory and practice.

二因 Two causes, of which there are various definitions: (1) 生 | The producing cause (of all good things); and 了 | the revealing or illuminating cause, i.e. knowledge, or wisdom. (2) 能生 | The 8th 識 q.v.: the cause that is able to produce all sense and perceptions, also all good and evil; and 方便 | the environmental or adaptive cause, which aids the 8th 識, as water or earth does the seed, etc. (3) 習 | or 同類 | Practice or habit as cause, e.g. desire causing desire; and 報 | or 果熟 | the rewarding-cause, or fruit-ripening cause, e.g. pleasure or pain caused by good or evil deeds. (4) 正 | Correct or direct cause, i.e. the Buddha-nature of all beings; and 緣 | the contributory cause, or enlightenment (see 了 | above) which evolves the 正 | or Buddha-nature by good works. (5) 近 | Immediate or direct cause and 遠 | distant or indirect cause or causes.

二圓 The two perfect doctrines, a term of the T'ien-t'ai School, called 今 | (also 開顯 | and 絕待 |) and 昔 | (also 相待 |). 今 | is the present really perfect 一實 doctrine arising from the Lotus Sūtra; 昔 | the older, or 相待 comparatively speaking perfect doctrine of the pre-Lotus teaching, that of the 藏, 通, and 別 schools; but the older was for limited salvation and not universal like the 今 |; these two are also termed 部 | and 教 |. The Hua-yen school has a division of the two perfections into 漸 | and 頓 | gradual and immediate perfection.

二嚴 The dual adornment, that of 智慧 wisdom and that of 福德, good deeds, 涅槃經 27.

二土 There are three groups: 性 | and 相 |: the former is the ubiquitous, unadulterated or innocent 法性之理 dharma-nature, or essence of things; the latter is the form-nature, or formal existence of the dharma, pure or impure according to the mind and action of the living. The 淨 | and 穢 | are Pure-land or Paradise; and impure land, e.g. the present world. In the Pure-land there are also 報 |, the land in which a Buddha himself dwells and 化土 in which all beings are transformed. There are other definitions, e.g. the former is Buddha's Paradise, the latter the world in which he dwells and which he is transforming, e.g. this Sahā-world.

二執 The two (erroneous) tenets, or attachments: (1) 我執 or 人執 that of the reality of the ego, permanent personality, the ātman, soul or self. (2) 法執 that of the reality of dharma, things or phenomena. Both are illusions. "All illusion arises from holding to the reality of the ego and of things."

二報 The dual reward. (1) 依報 or 依果 The material environment on which a person depends, resulting from former karma, e.g. country, house, property, etc. (2) 正報 or 正果 his direct reward, i.e. his body, or person.

二增菩薩 The two superior kinds of bodhisattvas, 智增||| superior in wisdom (chiefly beneficial to self); 悲增||| superior in pity for others and devotion to their salvation.

二天 The two devas. (1) 日天 and 月天 Sun-deva and Moon-deva. (2) 同生天 A deva born simultaneously with the individual, and 同名天 a deva with the same name as the individual; both devas have the duty of watching over the individual. (3) 梵天 and 帝釋天 Brahmā and Indra. ||三仙 The two devas are Maheśvara and Viṣṇu; the three ṛṣi are Kapila, Ulūka, and Ṛṣabha; v. 迦, 優, and 勒.

二女 The two sisters, one the deva 功德 "merit" or "achieving", who causes people to acquire wealth; the other, 黑闇女 the "dark" one, who causes them to spend and waste; these sisters always accompany each other.

二如 There are various definitions of the two aspects of the 眞如 bhūtatathatā. (1) (*a*) 不變眞如 The changeless essence or substance, e.g. the sea; (*b*) 隨緣眞如 its conditioned or ever-changing forms, as in the phenomenal world, e.g. the waves. (2) (*a*) 離言眞如 The inexpressible absolute, only mentally conceivable; (*b*) 依言眞如 aspects of it expressible in words, its ideal reflex. (3) (*a*) 空眞如 The absolute as the void, e.g. as space, the sky, a clear mirror; (*b*) 不空眞如 the absolute in manifestation, or phenomenal, e.g. images in the mirror; the womb of the universe in which are all potentialities. (4) (*a*) 在纏眞如 The Buddha-nature in bonds, i.e. all beings in suffering; (*b*) 出纏眞如 the Buddha-nature set free by the manifestation of the Buddha and bodhisattvas. (5) (*a*) 有垢眞如 The Buddha-nature defiled, as in unenlightened man, etc., e.g. the water-lily with its roots in the mud; (*b*) 無垢眞如 the pure Buddha-nature, purified or bright as the full moon. (6) 安立 and 非安立眞如 similar to the first definition given above.

二妙 The dual "marvel" of the Lotus sūtra, the 相待| or comparative view, i.e. compared with all previous teaching, which is the rough groundwork; and the 絕待| or view of it as the perfection of teaching; hence it is "wonderful" in comparison with all previous doctrine, and absolutely "wonderful" in itself; cf. 二圓.

二始 The two beginnings, i.e. of Hīnayāna, by the preaching of the 阿含 Āgama sūtras; and of Mahāyāna by the preaching of the 華嚴 Avataṁsaka sūtra.

二字 Double-letters, i.e. a monk—because a monk's name consists of two characters. ||文殊 The two-character Mañjuśrī.

二學 The two kinds of study or learning: (*a*) reading and reciting, (*b*) meditation and thought.

二宗 Two theories or schools stated by the Hua-yen (Kegon) school as 法相宗 and 法性宗 q.v., known also as 相宗 and 性宗. There are ten points of difference between them. Another division is the 空宗 and 性宗 q.v.

二密 The two esoteric aspects, i.e. 理| and 事|, the former referring to the doctrine, the latter to the esoteric acts of a Tathāgata.

二尊 The two honoured ones, Śākyamuni and Amitābha. ||一敎 (or 致) The two as one in teaching. ||二敎 The two as teacher and saviour, with reference to the teaching of the way of salvation of the first, and the consequent saving vows of the second; cf. 二世尊.

二師 The two sages, or preceptors in the Lotus Sūtra, Śākyamuni and Prabhūtaratna. Also sages and ordinary preceptors.

二序 The two kinds of introductory phrase: (*a*) the ordinary opening phrase of a sūtra—"Thus have I heard"; and (*b*) specific openings referring to the circumstances in which the sūtra was produced.

二往 and 再往 Twice over, a second time.

二德 The two kinds of power or virtue are 智| and 斷|; also 悲| and 智|; also 性| and 修| q.v. and v. 德.

二心 The two minds, 眞心 the original,

simple, pure, natural mind of all creatures, the Buddha-mind, i.e. 如來藏心; and 妄心 the illusion-mind, which results in complexity and confusion. Also 定心 the meditative mind, or mind fixed on goodness; and the 散心 the scattered, inattentive mind, or mind that is only good at intervals.

二忍 The two patiences or endurances: 衆生 | patience towards all under all circumstances; 無生(法) | calm rest, as a bodhisattva, in the assurance of no (re-)birth, i.e. in immortality. Also 安受苦 | patience under suffering, and 觀察法 | imperturbable examination of or meditation in the law or of all things. Also, physical and mental patience, or endurance.

二悟 The two awakenings, or kinds of entry into bodhisattvahood, i.e. 頓 immediate and 漸 gradual.

二惑 The two aspects of illusion: 見 | perplexities or illusions and temptations arise from false views or theories. 思 | or 修 |, ditto from thoughts arising through contact with the world, or by habit, such as desire, anger, infatuation, etc. They are also styled 理 | illusions connected with principles and 事 | illusions arising in practice; v. 見思.

二愛 The two kinds of love, 欲 | ordinary human love springing from desire; 法 | bodhisattva or religious love, i.e. desiring to save all creatures.

二應身 The two kinds of transformation-body of a Buddha, i.e. 勝 | | his surpassing body as seen by bodhisattvas, and 劣 | | his inferior human body as seen by ordinary people.

二戒 The two grades of commandments, or prohibitions, e.g. 十戒 and 具足戒 for monks; 五戒 and 八戒 for the laity; 邪 | and 正 |, heretical rules and correct rules; and numerous other pairs.

二我(見) The two erroneous views of individualism: (*a*) 人我見 The erroneous view that there is an independent human personality or soul, and (*b*) 法我見 the like view that anything exists with an independent nature. | | 執 The two reasons for clinging to the idea of the self: (*a*) 具生我執 the natural, or instinctive cleaving to the idea of a self, or soul; (*b*) 分別我執 the same idea developed as the result of (erroneous) reasoning. Cf. 二法執.

二持 The two values of the commandments: (*a*) 止持 prohibitive, restraining from evil; (*b*) 作持 constructive, constraining to goodness.

二教 Dual division of the Buddha's teaching. There are various definitions: (1) T'ien-t'ai has (*a*) 顯 | exoteric or public teaching to the visible audience, and (*b*) 密 | at the same time esoteric teaching to an audience invisible to the other assembly. (2) The 眞言 Shingon School by "exoteric" means all the Buddha's preaching, save that of the 大日經 which it counts esoteric. (3) (*a*) 漸 | and (*b*) 頓 | graduated and immediate teaching, terms with various uses, e.g. salvation by works, Hīnayāna, and by faith, Mahāyāna, etc.; they are applied to the Buddha's method, to the receptivity of hearers and to the teaching itself. (4) T'ien-t'ai has (*a*) 界内 | and (*b*) 界外 | teachings relating to the 三界 or realms of mortality and teachings relating to immortal realms. (5) (*a*) 半字 | and (*b*) 滿字 | Terms used in the **Nirvāṇa** sūtra, meaning incomplete word, or letter, teaching and complete-word teaching, i.e. partial and complete, likened to Hīnayāna and Mahāyāna. (6) (*a*) 捃收 | and (*b*) 扶律談常 | of the Nirvāṇa sūtra, (*a*) completing those who failed to hear the Lotus; (*b*) "supporting the law, while discoursing on immortality," i.e. that the keeping of the law is also necessary to salvation. (7) T'ien-t'ai's division of (*a*) 偏 | and (*b*) 圓 | the partial teaching of the 藏, 通, and 別 schools as contrasted with the perfect teaching of the 圓 school. (8) T'ien-t'ai's division of (*a*) 權 | and (*b*) 實 | temporary and permanent, similar to the last two. (9) (*a*) 世間教 The ordinary teaching of a moral life here; (*b*) 出 | | | the teaching of Buddha-truth of other-worldly happiness in escape from mortality. (10) (*a*) 了義 | the Mahāyāna perfect or complete teaching, and (*b*) 不 | | | Hīnayāna incompleteness. (11) The Hua-yen division of (*a*) 屈曲 | indirect or uneven teaching as in the Lotus and Nirvāṇa sūtras, and (*b*) 平道 | direct or levelled up teaching as in the Hua-yen sūtra. (12) The Hua-yen division of (*a*) 化 | all the Buddha's teaching for conversion and general instruction, and (*b*) 制 | his rules and commandments for the control and development of his order.

二時 The two times or periods—morning and evening. Also 迦羅 kāla, a regular or fixed hour for meals, and 三昧耶 samaya, irregular or unfixed hours or times.

二智 The two kinds of wisdom; there are various pairs. The Hua-yen school uses 如理 and 如量; the Fa-hsiang (法相) uses 根本 and

後得; the T'ien-t'ai uses 權智 and 實智. (1) (*a*) 如理 | or 根本 |, 無分別 |, 正體 |, 眞 |, 實 | is Buddha-wisdom, or Bodhisattva real wisdom; (*b*) 如量 | or 後得 |, 有分別 |, 俗 |, 偏 |, the same wisdom in its limitation and relation to ordinary human affairs. (2) (*a*) 實 | Absolute wisdom and (*b*) 權 | or 方便 | relative or temporal wisdom. (3) (*a*) 一切 | wisdom of the all, (*b*) 一切種 | wisdom of all the particulars. | | 圓滿 The two kinds of Tathāgata-wisdom, 實 and 權 absolute and functional (or relative), both perfect and complete.

二果 Sakṛdāgāmin; v. 娑 and 斯. The second "fruit" of the four kinds of Hīnayāna arhats, who have only once more to return to mortality. Also the two kinds of fruit or karma: (*a*) 習氣果 The good or evil characteristics resulting from habit or practice in a former existence; (*b*) 報果 the pain or pleasure resulting (in this life) from the practices of a previous life.

二根 The two "roots", or natural powers. (1) (*a*) 利根 keen, able (in the religion); (*b*) 鈍根 dull. (2) (*a*) 正根; 勝義根 The power or ability which uses the sense organs to discern the truth; (*b*) 扶根; 扶 (or 浮) 塵根 the sense organs as aids. (3) The male and female sexual organs.

二業 Two classes of karma. (1) (*a*) 引 | leads to the 總報, i.e. the award as to the species into which one is to be born, e.g. men, gods, etc.; (*b*) 滿 | is the 別報 or fulfilment in detail, i.e. the kind or quality of being, e.g. clever or stupid, happy or unhappy, etc. (2) (*a*) 善 | and (*b*) 惡 | Good and evil karma, resulting in happiness or misery. (3) (*a*) 助 | Aids to the karma of being reborn in Amitābha's Pure-land, e.g. offerings, chantings, etc.; (*b*) 正 | thought and invocation of Amitābha with undivided mind, as the direct method.

二檀 The two dāna 檀那, i.e. kinds of donating, or almsgiving: (*a*) 世間 | ordinary alms, and (*b*) 出世間 | spiritual, or other-worldly gifts.

二求 The two kinds of seeking: 得 | seeking to get (e.g. pleasure) and 命 | seeking long life.

二法執 The two tenets in regard to things; cf. 二我執, i.e. 俱生 | | the common or natural tendency to consider them as real; 分別 | | the tenet of their reality as the result of false reasoning and teaching. | | 身 Contrasted types of the Dharmakāya; five pairs are given, 理 and 智法身; 果極 and 應化 | |; 自性 and 應化 | |; 法性 and 方便 | |; 理 and 事 | |; cf. 法身.

二河白道 The two rivers and the white path, i.e. the path leading to life between the rivers of desire and hatred, which are compared to water and fire.

二流 The two ways in the current of transmigration: 順 | to flow with it in continual re-incarnation; 逆 | resist it and seek a way of escape by getting rid of life's delusions, as in the case of the saints.

二涅槃 Two Nirvāṇas, v. 二種 | |.

二漏 The two conditions relating to the passions and delusions: 有 | the condition in which they can prevail; 無 | that in which they cannot prevail.

二無常 Two kinds of impermanence, immediate and delayed. 念念 | | things in motion, manifestly transient; 相續 | | things that have the semblance of continuity, but are also transient, as life ending in death, or a candle in extinction.

二無我 The two categories of anātman:—人 | | no (permanent) human ego, or soul; 法 | | no (permanent) individuality in or independence of things, the latter is a Mahāyāna extension of the former, and takes the form of the unreality of the self or of things. | | | 智 The wisdom that recognizes the above laws, v. 四諦.

二無記 The two neutrals, or indeterminates which cannot be noted as good or evil.

二煩惱 The two kinds of kleśa, i.e. passions, delusions, temptations, or trials. (1) (*a*) 根本 | | The six fundamental kleśas arising from the six senses; (*b*) 隨 | | the twenty consequent kleśas arising out of the six. (2) (*a*) 分別起 | | Kleśa arising from false reasoning; (*b*) 俱生起 | | that which is natural to all. (3) (*a*) 大 | | 地法 The six great, e.g. extravagance, and (*b*) 小 | | | | ten minor afflictions, e.g. irritability. (4) (*a*) 數行 | | Ordinary passions, or temptations, (*b*) 猛利 | | fierce, sudden, or violent ditto.

二犯 The two kinds of sin, 止 | and 作 |

preventing good and doing evil; also, sins of omission and commission.

二王 The two guardian spirits represented on the temple gates, styled Vajrayakṣa 金剛夜叉 or 神, or 夜叉神.

二現 The two kinds of manifestation, or appearance, 須| and 不須|, the necessary appearance in the flesh of the Buddha for ordinary people, and the non-necessity for this to those of spiritual vision.

二百五十戒 The 250 commandments, or 具足| perfect or complete commandments, which are obligatory on monks and nuns. They are 四波羅夷 or 四根本極惡 the four pārājika; 十三殘 thirteen saṅghāvaśeṣa; 二不定法 two aniyata; 三十捨隨 thirty naiḥsargikāḥ-pāyattikāḥ; 九十波逸提 ninety prāyaścittikāḥ; 四提舍尼 four pratideśanīya; 百衆學 hundred śikṣākaraṇīya, and 七滅諍 seven kinds of vinaya for ending disputes.

二益 The dual advantages or benefits: profitable to the life which now is, and that which is to come.

二相 The two forms, or characteristics, of the bhūtatathatā, universal and particular. The 起信論 gives (*a*) 淨智相 pure wisdom, cf. ālaya-vijñāna, out of whose primary condition arise (*b*) 不思議用相 inconceivable, beneficial functions and uses. The same śāstra gives also a definition of the 眞如 as (*a*) 同相 that all things, pure or impure, are fundamentally of the same universal, e.g. clay which is made into tiles; (*b*) 異相 but display particular qualities, as affected by pure or impure causes, e.g. the tiles. Another definition, of the 智度論 31, is (*a*) 總相 universals, as impermanence; (*b*) 別相 particulars, for though all things have the universal basis of impermanence they have particular qualities, e.g. earth-solidity, heat of fire, etc.

二眞如 v. 二如 and 眞如.

二礙 idem 二障.

二祖(斷臂) The second patriarch in China 慧可 Hui-k'o of the 禪 Ch'an (Zen) school who, to induce Bodhidharma to receive him, is said to have cut off his left arm in the snow in order to prove his firmness and determination.

二福 The bliss of the gods, and the bliss of the saints 聖; v. also 福. ||田 The two fields for the cultivation of happiness: (*a*) 學人田 the eighteen Hīnayāna classes of those under training in religion; (*b*) 無學人田 the nine divisions of those no longer in training, i.e. who have completed their course. Also (*a*) 悲田 the pitiable, or poor and needy, as the field or opportunity for charity; (*b*) 敬田 the field of religion and reverence of the Buddhas, the saints, the priesthood.

二種 Two kinds or classes. For those not given below see under 二, etc., as for instance 二種世間 see under 二世間.

二種佛境 The two Buddha-domains: (*a*) 證境 his domain or state of absolute enlightenment; (*b*) 化境 the domain that he is transforming.

二種供養 The two forms of service, or offerings: (1) (*a*) 出纏供養 to those who have escaped from the toils, e.g. Buddhas; (*b*) 在纏供養 to those still living in the toils. (2) (*a*) 財供養 offerings of goods; (*b*) 法供養 of the Buddha-truth.

二種光明 The two kinds of light:—(1) (*a*) 色光明 physical light; (*b*) 智(慧)光明 or 心光明 wisdom or mental light. (2) (*a*) 魔光 Māra's delusive light; (*b*) 佛光 the true light of the Buddha. (3) (*a*) 常光 The constant or eternal light; (*b*) 現起光 the light in temporary manifestations.

二種因果 Two aspects of cause and effect, a division of the 四諦 "four noble truths": (*a*) 世間因果 in the present life, the 苦諦 being the effect, and the 集諦 the cause; (*b*) 出世間因果 in the future life, the 滅諦, extinction (of passion, or mortality) being the fruit, and the 道諦 the "eightfold noble path" the cause.

二種子 Two kinds of seed: (1) (*a*) 本有種子 the seed or latent undivided (moral) force immanent in the highest of the eight 識, i.e. the ālaya-vijñāna; (*b*) 新熏種子 the newly influenced, or active seed when acted upon by the seven other 識, thus becoming productive. (2) (*a*) 名言種子 The so-called seed which causes moral action similar to 本有種子, e.g. good or evil seed producing good or evil deeds; (*b*) 業種子 karma seed, the sixth 識 acting with the eighth.

二種寂靜 Two kinds of seclusion, or retirement from the world: Bodily withdrawal into seclusion. Spiritual withdrawal from all evil, and into meditation.

二種(布)施 Two kinds of charity: (1) (*a*) goods; (*b*) the saving truth. (2) (*a*) 淨施 Pure charity, expecting no return; (*b*) the opposite.

二種心相 Two kinds of mind: mind in its inner character and influence; in its outer manifestations.

二種忍辱 Two kinds of patience, or endurance: (*a*) of the assaults of nature, heat, cold, etc.; (*b*) of human assaults and insults.

二種性 Two kinds of seed-nature, the character of the ālaya seed and its development: (1) (*a*) 性種子 The original good seed-nature; (*b*) 習種子 the seed-nature in practice or development. (2) (*a*) 本性住種性 The immanent abiding original good seed-nature; (*b*) 習所成種性 the seed productive according to its ground. (3) (*a*) 聖種性 The seed-nature of the saints, by which they attain nirvāṇa; (*b*) 愚夫種性 the seed-nature in the foolish and ignorant.

二種授記 Two classes of Buddha's predictions of a disciple's destiny, 無餘授記 prediction in finality, or complete detail; 有餘授記 partial, or incomplete prediction.

二種施 v. ||布|.

二種死 The two kinds of death, 命盡| natural, and 外緣 | violent death, or from external cause.

二種比丘 Two classes of monks: 多聞|| those who hear and repeat many sūtras, but are not devoted doers; 寡淺|| those who read and repeat few sūtras but are devoted in their lives.

二種清淨 Two kinds of purity, according to the Hua-yen sūtra; 自性淸淨 natural purity, i.e. the natural 眞如 purity; and 離垢淸淨 acquired purity through avoiding pollution.

二種涅槃 Two nirvāṇas: (1) 有餘涅槃 also 有餘依 That with a remnant; the cause 因 has been annihilated, but the remnant of the effect 果 still remains, so that a saint may enter this nirvāṇa during life, but have to continue to live in this mortal realm till the death of his body. (2) 無餘涅槃 or 無餘依 Remnantless nirvāṇa, without cause and effect, the connection with the chain of mortal life being ended, so that the saint enters upon perfect nirvāṇa on the death of the body; cf. 智度論 31. Another definition is that Hīnayāna has further transmigration, while Mahāyāna maintains final nirvāṇa. "Nothing remaining" is differently interpreted in different schools, by some literally, but in Mahāyāna generally as meaning no further mortal suffering, i.e. final nirvāṇa.

二種灌頂 Two forms of esoteric baptism, v. 灌.

二種舍利 Two kinds of relics—the whole body, or parts of it. Also, the Buddha's physical remains or relics, and the sūtras, which form his spiritual (dharmakāya) remains.

二種菩薩 Monastic and lay bodhisattvas. ||菩薩身 A bodhisattva's mortal and immortal bodies.

二種病 Two kinds of sickness: physical and mental or spiritual.

二種聖 Two classes of saints or preachers: those who preach and those who preach without words.

二種資糧 The two kinds of (spiritual) provender: charity and wisdom.

二種邪見 The two false views, one that of a nihilistic school which denied that earthly happiness is dependent on a moral life; the other a materialistic school which maintained the moral life in the interests of self, sought earthly happiness, and failed to apprehend nirvāṇa.

二種(一)闡提 Two kinds of icchantika, q.v.: (*a*) the utterly depraved, abandoned, and blasphemers of Buddha-truth; (*b*) bodhisattvas who refuse to enter upon their Buddhahood in order to save all beings.

二空 The two voids, unrealities, or immaterialities; v. 空. There are several antitheses:

(1) (*a*) 人空；我空 The non-reality of the ātman, the soul, the person; (*b*) 法空 the non-reality of things. (2) (*a*) 性空 The T'ien-t'ai division that nothing has a nature of its own; (*b*) 相空 therefore its form is unreal, i.e. forms are temporary names. (3) (*a*) 但空 T'ien-t'ai says the 藏 and 通 know only the 空; (*b*) 不但空 the 別 and 圓 have 空, 假, and 中 q.v. (4) (*a*) 如實空 The division of the 起信論 that the 眞如 is devoid of all impurity; (*b*) 如實不空 and full of all merit, or achievement. | | 觀 Two kinds of meditation on the "void", or unreality: (*a*) 無生觀 the meditation that things are unproduced, having no individual or separate natures, i.e. that all things are void and unreal; cf. 性空; (*b*) 無相觀 that they are therefore formless, cf. 相空. Also 人 and 法空觀 see above.

二答 Two kinds of reply, one by words, the other by signs.

二經體 The two bodies or elements in a sūtra: 文 and 義 the words and the meaning, or ideas.

二罪 The two classes of offence: (*a*) 性 | that which is wrong in itself, e.g. murder, etc.; (*b*) 遮 | not wrong in itself, e.g. taking alcohol, but forbidden by the Buddha for the sake of the other commandments; transgression of this is therefore a sin against the Buddha.

二美 Two excellent things, i.e. meditation and wisdom.

二義 The two meanings or teachings, partial and complete; v. 二教.

二翼 A pair of wings: charity and wisdom.

二聖 Śākyamuni and Prabhūtaratna 多寶.

二脇士；二挾侍 The two attendants by the side of Amitābha, i.e. 觀音 Kuanyin and 大勢至 Mahāsthāmaprāpta; also the two by Yao Shih, the Master of Medicine, i.e. 日光 sunlight and 月光 moonlight; also the two by Śākyamuni, i.e. 文殊 Mañjuśrī and 普賢 Samantabhadra.

二般若 Two kinds of prajñā, or wisdom. (1) (*a*) 共 | | That of the three stages of śrāvaka, pratyekabuddha, and imperfect Bodhisattva schools; (*b*) 不共 | | that of the perfect Bodhisattva teaching—a T'ien-t'ai division. (2) (*a*) 世間 | | Temporal; (*b*) 出世間 | | supernatural. (3) (*a*) 實相 | | The first part of the Prajñāpāramitā; (*b*) 觀照 | | the second part.

二色身 The two rūpakāya or incarnation-bodies of a Buddha, his 報 | and 應 | or sambhogakāya and nirmāṇakāya, as distinguished from 法 | the dharmakāya.

二處三會 The two places from which the Buddha is supposed to have preached the Lotus Sūtra, i.e. the Vulture Peak, the sky, and again the Vulture Peak; the three assemblies are (1) those he addressed from the Peak, chapters 1 to the middle of the eleventh chapter; (2) those addressed from the sky, to the end of the twenty-second chapter; and (3) again those on the Vulture Peak, from the twenty-third chapter to the end.

二苦 Two kinds of suffering: within, e.g. sickness, sorrow; from without, e.g. calamities.

二藏 The two piṭakas, or tripiṭakas, i.e. the Buddhist canon: (*a*) 聲聞 | the Śrāvaka, or Hīnayāna canon; (*b*) 菩薩 | the Bodhisattva, or Mahāyāna canon.

二衆 The two groups: the monks, or clergy; the laity who observe the five and the eight commands.

二行 Two classes of conduct: following wrong views; following wrong desires, or emotions. There are other pairs.

二衣 The two kinds of clothing: (*a*) 制 | the regulation three robes for monks and five for nuns, which must be worn; (*b*) 聽 | optional garments.

二見 Two (wrong) views: (1) Looking on people grudgingly with regard to almsgiving and preaching the Buddha-truth. (2) (*a*) 有見 Holding to the real existence of (material) things; (*b*) 無見 holding to their entire unreality. (3) (*a*) 斷見 Holding to the view of total annihilation; (*b*) 常見 to that of permanence or immortality.

二覺 The two enlightenments: (1) The 起信論 has two—(*a*) 本 | the immanent mind in all things, e.g. "which lighteth every man that cometh into the world", also defined as the 法身 dharmakāya; (*b*) 始| initial enlightenment or beginning of illumination; this initiation leads on to Buddhahood, or full enlightenment. (2) (*a*) 等| The fifty-first stage of a bodhisattva's 行位 practice; (*b*) 妙| the fifty-second stage, or enlightenment of Buddhahood. (3) (*a*) 自| A Buddha's own or natural enlightenment; (*b*) |他 his enlightening of all others.

二觀 The two univeral bases of meditation: 事| the external forms, or the phenomenal, and 理| the real or underlying nature, i.e. practice and theory.

二解脫 Two kinds of deliverance, mukti or mokṣa: (1) (*a*) 有爲|| Active or earthly deliverance to arhatship; (*b*) 無爲|| nirvāṇa-deliverance. (2) (*a*) 性淨|| The pure, original freedom or innocence; (*b*) 障盡|| deliverance acquired by the ending of all hindrances (to salvation). (3) (*a*) 慧|| The arhat's deliverance from hindrances to wisdom; (*b*) 具|| his complete deliverance in regard to both wisdom and vision 慧 and 定. (4) (*a*) 時|| The dull who take time or are slow in attaining to 定 vision; (*b*) 不時|| the quick or clever who take "no time". (5) (*a*) 心|| A heart or mind delivered from desires; (*b*) 慧|| a mind delivered from ignorance by wisdom.

二詮 Two kinds of statement, or definition: 遮 latent or negative and 表 patent or positive; e.g. 不生不滅 is a negative statement, 知見覺照 is a positive statement.

二語 Double-tongued; also 二舌.

二諦 Two forms of statement: (*a*) 俗| Saṁvṛti-satya, also called 世|, 世俗|, 覆俗|, 覆|, meaning common or ordinary statement, as if phenomena were real; (*b*) 眞| paramārtha-satya, also called 第一|, 勝義|, meaning the correct dogma or averment of the enlightened. Another definition is 王法 and 佛法, royal law and Buddha law.

二識 Ālaya-vijñāna and mano-vijñāna; i.e. 阿梨耶| and 分別事|; v. 識.

二護 The two protectors: the inner, oneself, by studying and following the Law; the outer, those who supply what is needful for one's body and mind, e.g. supporters.

二貧 The two kinds of poverty: of goods, and of the religion.

二超 Two ways of passing over (to bliss): 豎 the lengthwise, or long way (of Hīnayāna); and 橫 the crosswise, or short way of Mahāyāna.

二足 A man's two legs, compared to goodness and wisdom, 福 being counted as the first five of the pāramitās, 智 as the sixth; v. 六度. ||尊 The honoured one among bipeds or men, i.e. a Buddha; cf. 兩|.

二身 Two forms of body; there are numerous pairs, e.g. (1) (*a*) 分段身 The varied forms of the karmaic or ordinary mortal body, or being; (*b*) 變易身 the transformable, or spiritual body. (2) (*a*) 生身 The earthly body of the Buddha; (*b*) 化身 his nirmāṇakāya, which may take any form at will. (3) (*a*) 生身 his earthly body; (*b*) 法身 his moral and mental nature—a Hīnayāna definition, but Mahāyāna takes his earthly nirmāṇakāya as the 生身 and his dharmakāya or that and his saṁbhogakāya as 法身. (4) 眞應二身 The dharmakāya and nirmāṇakāya. (5) (*a*) 實相身 The absolute truth, or light, of the Buddha, i.e. the dharmakāya; (*b*) 爲物身 the functioning or temporal body. (6) (*a*) 眞身 the dharmakāya and saṁbhogakāya; (*b*) 化身 the nirmāṇakāya. (7) (*a*) 常身 his permanent or eternal body; (*b*) 無常身 his temporal body. (8) (*a*) 實身 and 化身 idem 二色身.

二輪 The two wheels of a cart compared by the T'ien-t'ai school to 定 (or to its T'ien-t'ai form 止觀) and 慧 meditation and wisdom; see 止觀 5. Also 食 food and 法 the doctrine, i.e. food physical and spiritual.

二道 The two Ways: (1) (*a*) 無礙道 or 無間道 The open or unhindered way, or the way of removing all obstacles or intervention, i.e. all delusion; (*b*) 解脫| the way of release, by realization of truth. (2) (*a*) 難行道 The hard way of "works", i.e. by the six pāramitā and the disciplines. (*b*) 易行| the easy way of salvation, by the invocation of Amitābha. (3) (*a*) 有漏道 The way of reincarnation or mortality; (*b*) 無漏| the enlightened way of escape from the miseries of transmigration. (4) (*a*) 教道 The way of instruction; (*b*) 證| the way of realization. (5) The two lower excretory organs.

二邊 The two sides, extremes, or antitheses.

(1) (*a*) 有 | That things exist; (*b*) 無邊 that since nothing is self-existent, things cannot be said to exist. (2) (*a*) 增益 | The plus side, the common belief in a soul and permanence; (*b*) 損減 | the minus side, that nothing exists even of karma. (3) (*a*) 斷 | 見 and (*b*) 常 | 見 annihilation and immortality; v. 見.

二部五部 The two are the divisions which took place immediately after the Buddha's death into (*a*) the elder monks or intimate disciples, and (*b*) the general body of disciples, styled respectively 上座 and 大衆 q.v.; the five are the divisions, which are said to have occurred a century later, into Dharmaguptāḥ 曇無德, Mūlasarvāstivādāḥ 薩婆多, Mahīśāsakāḥ 彌沙塞, Kāśyapīyāḥ 迦葉遺, and Vātsīputrīyāḥ 婆麤富羅.

二量 The two "measurings", or parts of a syllogism: (*a*) 現 | appearance, e.g. smoke; (*b*) 比 | inference, e.g. fire from smoke.

二門 Two doors, entrances, schools, etc. There are many such pairs.

二際 The two borders, or states: according to Hīnayāna, nirvāṇa and mortality; according to Mahāyāna the two are one.

二障 The two hindrances: (1) (*a*) 煩惱 | The passions and delusion which aid rebirth and hinder entrance into nirvāṇa; (*b*) 智 | or 所知 |, worldly wisdom, e.g. accounting the seeming as real, a hindrance to true wisdom. (2) (*a*) 煩惱 | as above; (*b*) 解脫 | hindrances to deliverance. (3) (*a*) 理 | hindrances to truth; (*b*) 事 | hindrances of the passions, etc.

二頓 The two immediate or direct ways to perfection, as defined by 荊溪 Ching-ch'i of the Hua-yen school; the gradual direct way of the Lotus; the direct way of the Hua-yen sūtra, which is called the 頓頓頓圓, while that of the Lotus is called the 漸頓漸圓.

二類各生 The Pure Land will not be limited to those who repeat the name of Amitābha according to his eighteenth vow; but includes those who adopt other ways (as shown in his nineteenth and twentieth vows). | | 種子 v. 二種子.

二食 The two kinds of food: (1) (*a*) The joy of the Law; (*b*) the bliss of meditation. (2) (*a*) The right kind of monk's livelihood—by mendicancy; (*b*) the wrong kind—by any other means.

二餘 see 餘.

二鳥 The drake and hen of the mandarin duck who are always together, typifying various contrasted theories and ideas, e.g. permanence and impermanence, joy and sorrow, emptiness and non-emptiness, etc.

二鼠 The black and white rats—night and day.

人 Manuṣya; nara; puruṣa; pudgala. Man, the sentient thinking being in the desire-realm, whose past deeds affect his present condition.

人(中)尊 The Honoured One among or of men, the Buddha. | (|) 分陀利華 A Lotus among men, a Buddha, also applied to all who invoke Amitābha. | (|) 師子; 人師 (or 獅) 子; 人雄師子 A Lion among men, a Buddha. | (|) 樹 The Tree among men, giving shelter as the bodhi-tree, a Buddha. | | 牛王 The Lord of the herd. These and other similar terms are applied to the Buddha. | | 三惡 The three most wicked among men: the Icchantika; v. 一闡提: the slanderers of Mahāyāna, and those who break the four great commandments.

人乘 One of the five vehicles, v. 五 |, that of the five commandments, the keeping of which ensures rebirth in the world of men.

人人本具 Every man has by origin the perfect Buddha-nature.

人仙 The ṛṣi jina, or immortal among men, i.e. the Buddha; also a name for Bimbisāra in his reincarnation.

人伽藍 This is given by Eitel as "Narasaṁghārāma". "An ancient monastery close to the capital of Kapiśā." But this is doubtful.

人吉蔗 Mānuṣa-kṛtya; demons shaped like men; domestic slaves, introduced into Kashmir by Madhyāntika; also intp. as "work to be done by men".

人因 The causative influences for being reborn

as a human being, i.e. a good life. Those in positions of honour have obtained them by former deeds of benevolence, reverence to Buddhas and monks, patience, humility, devotion to the sūtras, charity, morality, zeal and exhortation, obedience, loyalty—hence they have obtained affluence, long life, and are held in high regard. Those in mean condition are thus born because of the opposite characteristics in previous incarnation.

人執 The (false) tenet of a soul, or ego, or permanent individual, i.e. that the individual is real, the ego an independent unit and not a mere combination of the five skandhas produced by cause and in effect disintegrating; v. 我執.

人天 Men and devas. | | 乘 Two of the 五乘 q.v. | | 教 Two of the 五教 q.v. | | 眼目 A summary of the teaching of the 禪 Ch'an (Zen) sect by 智照 Chih-chao of the Sung dynasty. | | 勝妙善果 The highest forms of reincarnation, i.e. those of devas and men.

人定 The third beat of the first watch, 9–11 p.m., when men are settled for the night.

人寶 The treasure of men, Buddha.

人尊 idem 人中尊.

人師 A leader or teacher of men. | | (or 獅) 子 Nṛsiṁha. The Lion of men, Buddha as leader and commander.

人我 Personality, the human soul, i.e. the false view, | | 見 that every man has a permanent lord within, 常一主宰, which he calls the ātman, soul, or permanent self, a view which forms the basis of all erroneous doctrine. Also styled 人見; 我見; 人執; cf. 二我.

人有 Human bhāva or existence, one of the 七有.

人法 Men and things; also, men and the Buddha's law, or teaching.

人無我 Man as without ego, or permanent soul; cf. 人我 and 二無我. Other similar terms are 衆生無我; 生空; 人空 and 我空. | | | 智 The knowledge, or wisdom, of anātman, cf. above.

人空 Man is only a temporary combination formed by the five skandhas and the twelve nidānas, being the product of previous causes, and without a real self or permanent soul. Hīnayāna is said to end these causes and consequent reincarnation by discipline in subjection of the passions and entry into nirvāṇa by the emptying of the self. Mahāyāna fills the "void" with the Absolute, declaring that when man has emptied himself of the ego he realizes his nature to be that of the absolute, bhūtatathatā; v. 二空. | | 觀 The meditation on, or insight into the above.

人莽娑; 人摩娑 Human māṁsa or flesh.

人藥王子 Human-touch healing prince, i.e. Śākyamuni in a previous incarnation, whose touch healed all diseases, as did the application of his powdered bones after his decease in that incarnation.

人趣; 人道 The human stage of the six gati, or states of existence.

人身 The human body, or person. | | 牛 Cattle in human shape, stupid, ignorant, heedless.

人雄師子 idem 人中師子.

人非人 A being resembling but not a human being, i.e. a kinnara.

人頭幢 A human head at the top of a daṇḍa or flagpole, used as one of Yama's symbols; v. 檀茶 (or 拏).

人鬼 Men and disembodied spirits, or demons; disembodied ghosts

入 To enter, entry, entrance; come, bring or take in; at home; awaken to the truth; begin to understand; to relate the mind to reality and thus evolve knowledge. The "six entries" 六 | ṣaḍāyatana, which form one of the links in the chain of causation, v. 十二因緣, the preceding link being 觸 contact, and the succeeding link 識 perception. The six are the qualities and effects of the six organs of sense producing sight, hearing, smell, taste, touch, and thought (or mental presentations). v. also 二 |.

入不二門 To enter the school of monism, i.e. that the 一實 one great reality is universal and absolute without differentiation.

入住出三心 Entrance, stay, exit; v. 入心.

入佛 The bringing in of an image of a Buddha. 丨丨供養 The ceremony of bringing in a Buddha's image. 丨丨平等戒 The Buddha-law by which all may attain to Buddhahood.

入信 To believe, or enter into belief.

入出二門 The two doors of ingress and egress, i.e. enter the gate of self-purification and adornment, then go forth 出 to benefit and save others.

入嚩羅 Jvāla. Flaming, blazing, glowing.

入堂(五法) v. 入衆.

入塔 To inter the bones or body of a monk in a dagoba; v. 入骨.

入壇 To go to the altar (for baptism, in the esoteric sect).

入定 To enter into meditation by tranquillizing the body, mouth (i.e. lips), and mind, 身口意.

入室 To enter the master's study for examination or instruction; to enter the status of a disciple, but strictly of an advanced disciple. To receive consecration.

入寂 To enter into rest, or nirvāṇa; also, to die. Also 入滅 or 入寂滅.

入唐八家 The eight Japanese who came to China in the T'ang dynasty and studied the 密教 esoteric doctrine.

入心 To enter the heart, or mind; also used for 入地 entering a particular state, its three stages being 入住出 entry, stay, and exit.

入我我入 He in me and I in him, i.e. the indwelling of the Buddha, any Buddha, or the Buddhas.

入文解釋 The method in expounding scriptures of giving the main idea before proceeding to detailed exposition.

入流 Srota-āpanna, v. 須陀洹.

入滅 idem 入寂.

入王宮聚落衣 The monk's robe, worn equally for a palace, or for begging in town or hamlet.

入重玄門 To enter again through the dark gate into mortality, e.g. as a bodhisattva does, even into the hells, to save the suffering. Another interpretation is the return of a bodhisattva to common life for further enlightenment.

入聖 To become an arhat.

入衆 To enter the assembly (of monks); also 交衆. 丨丨五法 Five rules for the entrant—submission, kindness, respect, recognition of rank or order, and none but religious conversation.

入觀 To enter into meditation; it differs from 入定 as 定 means 自心之寂靜 complete stillness of the mind, while 觀 means 自觀照理 thought and study for enlightenment in regard to truth.

入道 To become a monk, 出家入道 to leave home and enter the Way.

入骨 To inter the bones (of a monk) in a stūpa, or a grave.

入龕 Entering, or putting into the casket (for cremation); i.e. encoffining a dead monk.

八 Aṣṭa, eight. 丨不(中道) The eight negations of Nāgārjuna, founder of the Mādhyamika or Middle School 三論宗. The four pairs are "neither birth nor death, neither end nor permanence, neither identity nor difference, neither coming nor going". These are the eight negations; add "neither cause nor effect" and there are the 十不 ten negations; v. 八迷. 丨丨正(or 中)觀 Meditation on the above eight negations. These eight, birth, death, etc., are the 八迷 eight misleading ideas, or 八計 eight wrong calculations. No objection is made to the terms in the apparent, or relative, sense 俗諦, but in the real or absolute sense 眞諦 these eight ideas are incorrect, and the truth lies between them; in the relative, mortality need not be denied, but in the absolute we cannot speak of mortality or immortality. In regard to the relative view, beings have apparent birth and apparent death from various causes, but are not really born and do not really die, i.e. there is the difference of appearance and reality. In the absolute there is no apparent birth and apparent death. The other three pairs are similarly studied. 丨丨可越 idem 八敬戒. 丨丨思議 The eight inexpressibles, or things surpassing thought, i.e. eight qualities of the ocean (depth, extent, etc.) in illustration of nirvāṇa; v. 大海. 丨丨正見 The teaching of the 大集經 26, on the eight incorrect views in regard to (1) 我見 the existence of a permanent ego; (2) 衆生見 the five skandhas as not the constituents of the living; (3) 壽命見 fate, or determination of length of life; (4) 士夫見 a creator; (5) 常見 permanence; (6) 斷見 annihilation; (7) 有見 the reality of things; (8) 無見 their unreality. 丨丨淨 The eight things "unclean" to monks, of which there are different groups. One group is—to keep gold, silver, male slaves, female slaves, cattle, stores, or to trade or farm. Another is—to own cultivated lands, to farm, keep supplies of grain and silk, servants, animals or birds, money, cushions and pans, and furniture and gilded beds. 丨丨顯實 By the eight negations of the Mādhyamika doctrine, the true reality of things is shown.

八中洲 Each of the "four continents" has two other continents, i.e. Jambudvīpa has Cāmara and Varacāmara; Pūrvavideha has Deha and Videha; Aparagodānīya has Śāṭhā and Uttaramantriṇaḥ; and Uttarakuru has Kuravaḥ and Kaurava; v. 四洲.

八乾 The eight skandhas, or sections of the Abhidharma, v. 八犍度.

八事隨身 The eight appurtenances of a monk—three garments, bowl, stool, filter, needle and thread, and chopper.

八五三二 The four special characteristics of the 法相 Dharmalakṣaṇa sect, i.e. 八識, 五法, 三性, and 二無我 q.v.

八交道 The eight roads in the eight directions, bounded with golden cords, mentioned in the Lotus Sūtra as in certain Buddha-realms.

八佛 Eight Buddhas of the eastern quarter.

八位 The classification or grades of disciples according to the T'ien-t'ai 圓教 perfect teaching, i.e. (1) 觀行卽 grade of the five classes, or stages, of lay disciples; (2) 相似卽 grade of the ten classes of ordinary monks and nuns; above these are the 分眞卽 bodhisattva stages of those progressing towards Buddhahood, i.e. (3) 十住, (4) 十行, (5) 十廻向, (6) 十地, (7) 等覺, and (8) the perfect or Buddha stage 究竟卽, i.e. 妙覺. Cf. 六卽. 丨丨胎藏 The eight stages of the human fœtus: 羯羅藍 kalala, the appearance after the first week from conception; 頞部曇 arbuda, at end of second week; 閉尸 peśī, third; 健南 ghana, fourth; 鉢羅奢佉 praśākhā, limbs formed during fifth week; sixth, hair, nails, and teeth; seventh, the organs of sense, eyes, ears, nose, and tongue; and eighth, complete formation.

八倒 v. 丨顚丨.

八億四千萬念 The myriads of "thoughts", or moments in a single day and night, each with its consequences of good and evil; probably 8,400,000,000 is meant.

八勝處 The eight victorious stages, or degrees, in meditation for overcoming desire, or attachment to the world of sense; v. 八解脫.

八十 Aśīti, eighty. 丨丨一品思惑 The eighty-one kinds of illusion, or misleading thoughts, arising out of desire, anger, foolishness, and pride—nine grades in each of the nine realms of desire, of form and beyond form. 丨丨丨法 The eighty-one divisions in the Prajñā-pāramitā sūtra 大般若經 comprising form 色; mind 心; the five skandhas 五陰; twelve means of sensation 入; eighteen realms 界; four axioms 諦; twelve nidānas 因緣; eighteen śūnya 空; six pāramitā 度, and four jñāna 智. Also 丨丨丨科. 丨丨種好; 丨丨隨形好 The eighty notable physical characteristics of Buddha; cf. 三十二相. 丨丨華嚴經 The translation of the Hua-yen 華嚴經 in eighty chüan, made by Śikṣānanda in the T'ang dynasty. 丨丨誦律 The original Vinaya recited by the Buddha's disciple Upāli eighty times during the summer retreat, while the Tripiṭaka was being composed after the Buddha's death.

八句義 The eight fundamental principles, intuitional or relating to direct mental vision, of the Ch'an (Zen) School, 禪宗 q.v.; they are 正法眼藏; 涅槃妙心; 實相無相; 微妙

法門；不立文字；敎外別傳；直指人心；見性成佛.

八味 The eight savours (or pleasures) of the Buddha's nirvāṇa: 常住 perpetual abode, 寂滅 extinction (of distress, etc.), 不老 eternal youth, 不死 immortality, 清淨 purity, 虛通 absolute freedom (as space), 不動 imperturbility, and 快樂 joy.

八囀(聲) The eight cases of nouns in Sanskrit, termed Subanta, 蘇漫多, i.e. nirdeśa, upadeśana, kartṛkaraṇa, sampradāna, apādāna, svāmivacana, saṃnidhānārtha, āmantraṇa.

八圓 Eight fundamental characteristics of a 圓敎 complete or perfect school of teaching, which must perfectly express 敎, 理, 智, 斷, 行, 位, 因, and 果.

八塔 idem 八大靈塔.

八墮 idem 八波羅夷.

八多羅樹 As high as eight tāla (palmyra) trees, very high.

八大(地獄) The eight great naraka, or hot hells: (1) sañjīva 等活 hell of rebirth into (2) kālasūtra 黑繩, i.e. the hell of black cords or chains; (3) saṅghāta 衆合, in which all are squeezed into a mass between two mountains falling together; (4) raurava 號叫 hell of crying and wailing; (5) mahāraurava 大號叫 hell of great crying; (6) tapana 炎熱 hell of burning; (7) pratāpana 大熱 hell of fierce heat; (8) avīci 無間 unintermitted rebirth into its sufferings with no respite. v. 地獄 and 八寒地獄.

八大明王 The eight diamond-kings, or bodhisattvas, in their representations as fierce guardians of Vairocana 大日; 金剛手 is represented as 降三世; 妙吉祥 as 大威德; 虛空藏 as 大笑; 慈氏 as 大輪; 觀自在 as 馬頭; 地藏 as 無能勝明; 除蓋障 as 不動尊; and 普賢 as 步擲.

八大自在我 The eight great powers of personality or sovereign independence, as one of the four qualities 常樂我淨 of nirvāṇa: powers of self-manifolding, infinite expansion, levitation and transportation, manifesting countless forms permanently in one and the same place, use of one physical organ in place of another, obtaining all things as if nothing, expounding a stanza through countless kalpas, ability to traverse the solid as space. v. 涅槃經 23.

八大菩薩 see 八大明王. Another group is given in the ｜｜｜｜曼荼羅經; another in the 藥師經 translated by I-ching; another in the ｜｜｜｜經 translated by Fa-hsien; and there are other groups.

八大觀音 The eight Shingon representations of Kuan-yin: as one of the above 八大明王, as the white-robed one, as a rākṣasī, as with four faces, as with a horse's head, as Mahāsthāmaprāpta 大勢至, and as Tārā 陀羅.

八大辛苦 idem 八苦.

八大童子 The eight messengers of 不動明王, also known as ｜｜金剛｜｜; Mañjuśrī also has eight.

八大金剛明王 or ｜｜｜｜童子 The eight attendants on 不動明王 (cf. 八大明王). They are 慧光, 慧喜, 阿耨達多, 指德, 烏俱婆迦, 淸德, 矜羯羅, and 制吒迦.

八大靈塔 The eight great "spirit" or sacred stūpas erected at (1) Kapilavastu, Buddha's birthplace; (2) Magadha, where he was first enlightened; (3) the deer-park Benares, where he first preached; (4) Jetavana, where he revealed his supernatural powers; (5) Kanyākubja (Kanauj), where he descended from Indra's heavens; (6) Rājagṛha, where Devadatta was destroyed and the Saṅgha purified; (7) Vaiśālī, where he announced his speedy nirvāṇa; (8) Kuśinagara, where he entered nirvāṇa. There is another slightly variant list.

八字 The eight leading characters of the 聖行 chapter in the Nirvāṇa sūtra 生滅滅已寂滅爲樂, the teaching of the sūtra is death, or nirvāṇa, as entry into joy. ｜｜布字 The eight magic words to be placed on eight parts of the body. ｜｜文殊法 The eight-word dhāraṇī, esoteric methods connected with Vairocana and Mañjuśrī.

八天 The eight devalokas, i.e. four dhyāna

devalokas of the region of form, and four arūpalokas; 四禪天 and 四空處.

八定 The eight degrees of fixed abstraction, i.e. the four dhyānas corresponding to the four divisions in the heavens of form, and the four degrees of absolute fixed abstraction on the 空 or immaterial, corresponding to the arūpadhātu, i.e. heavens of formlessness.

八宗 or 八家 Eight of the early Japanese sects: 倶舍 Kusha, 成實 Jōjitsu, 律 Ritsu, 法相 Hossō, 三論 Sanron, 華嚴 Kegon, 天台 Tendai, 眞言 Shingon. | | 九宗; 八家九宗 The above eight with the Zen 禪 school added. The first four are almost or entirely extinct.

八寒八熱 The eight cold and eight hot hells.

八寒(冰)地獄 The eight cold narakas, or hells: (1) 頞浮陀 arbuda, tumours, blains; (2) 泥羅浮陀 nirarbuda, enlarged ditto; 疱裂 bursting blains; (3) 阿吒吒 aṭaṭa, chattering (teeth); (4) 阿波波 hahava, or ababa, the only sound possible to frozen tongues; (5) 嘔侯侯 ahaha, or hahava, ditto to frozen throats; (6) 優鉢羅 utpala, blue lotus flower, the flesh being covered with sores resembling it; (7) 波頭摩 padma, red lotus flower, ditto; (8) 分陀利 puṇḍarīka, the great lotus, ditto. v. 地獄 and 八大地獄.

八尊重法 idem 八敬戒.

八師 The eight teachers—murder, robbery, adultery, lying, drinking, age, sickness, and death; v. | | 經.

八忍 The eight kṣānti, or powers of patient endurance, in the desire-realm and the two realms above it, necessary to acquire the full realization of the truth of the Four Axioms, 四諦; these four give rise to the 四法忍, i.e. 苦, 集, 滅, 道法忍, the endurance or patient pursuit that results in their realization. In the realm of form and the formless, they are called the 四類忍. By patient meditation the 見惑 false or perplexed views will cease, and the 八智 eight kinds of jñāna or gnosis be acquired; therefore 智 results from 忍 and the sixteen, 八忍八智 (or 觀), are called the 十六心, i.e. the sixteen mental conditions during the stage of 見道, when 惑 illusions or perplexities of view are destroyed. Such is the teaching of the 唯識宗. The 八智 are 苦, 集, 滅, 道法智 and 苦, etc. 類智.

八念 (法 or 門). Eight lines of thought, in the 智度論 21, for resisting Māra-attacks and evil promptings during the meditation on impurity, etc.; i.e. thought of the Buddha, of the Law (or Truth), the fraternity, the commandments, alms-giving, the devas, breathing, and death. There are also the 大人 | |, i.e. that truth 道 is obtained through absence of desire, contentment, aloneness, zeal, correct thinking, a fixed mind, wisdom, and inner joy. v. 八念經.

八(or 發)思巴 Bashpa, Phagspa, Baghcheba, Blo-gros-rgyal-mtshan. A śramaṇa of Tibet, teacher and confidential adviser of Kublai Khan, who appointed him head of the Buddhist church of Tibet A.D. 1260. He is the author of a manual of Buddhist terminology 彰所知論 and translated another work into Chinese. In A.D. 1269 he constructed an alphabet for the Mongol language, "adapted from the Tibetan and written vertically," and a syllabary borrowed from Tibetan, known by the name of Ḫkhor-yig, for which, however, the Lama Chos-kyi-ḥod-zer 1307–1311 substituted another alphabet based on that of Śākya-paṇḍita.

八慢 The eight kinds of pride, māna, arrogance, or self-conceit, 如慢 though inferior, to think oneself equal to others (in religion); 慢慢 to think oneself superior among manifest superiors; 不如 | to think oneself not so much inferior among manifest superiors; 增上 | to think one has attained more than is the fact, or when it is not the fact; 我 | self-superiority, or self-sufficiency; 邪 | pride in false views, or doings; 憍 | arrogance; 大 | extreme arrogance.

八憍 The eight kinds of pride, or arrogance, resulting in domineering: because of strength; of clan, or name; of wealth; of independence, or position; of years, or age; of cleverness, or wisdom; of good or charitable deeds; of good looks. Of these, eight birds are named as types: 鴟梟 two kinds of owl, eagle, vulture, crow, magpie, pigeon, wagtail.

八成 idem 八相成道. | | 立因 The eight factors of a Buddhist syllogism.

八戒(齋) The first eight of the ten commandments, see 戒; not to kill; not to take things not given; no ignoble (i.e. sexual) conduct; not to speak falsely; not to drink wine; not to indulge in cosmetics, personal adornments, dancing, or music; not to sleep on fine beds, but on a mat on the ground; and not to eat out of regulation hours, i.e. after noon. Another group divides the sixth into two—against cosmetics and adornments and against dancing and music; the first eight are then called the eight prohibitory commands and the last the 齋 or fasting commandment. Also | 齋 戒; | 關 (or 支) 齋; cf. 八 種 勝 法.

八 教 The eight T'ien-t'ai classifications of Śākyamuni's teaching, from the Avataṁsaka to the Lotus and Nirvāṇa sūtras, divided into the two sections (1) 化 法 四 教 his four kinds of teaching of the content of the Truth accommodated to the capacity of his disciples; (2) 化 儀 四 教 his four modes of instruction. (1) The four 化 法 教 are: (a) 三 藏 教 The Tripiṭaka or Hīnayāna teaching, for śrāvakas and pratyekabuddhas, the bodhisattva doctrine being subordinate; it also included the primitive śūnya doctrine as developed in the Satyasiddhi śāstra. (b) 通 教 His later "intermediate" teaching which contained Hīnayāna and Mahāyāna doctrine for śrāvaka, pratyekabuddha, and bodhisattva, to which are attributed the doctrines of the Dharmalakṣaṇa or Yogācārya and Mādhyamika schools. (c) 別 教 His differentiated, or separated, bodhisattva teaching, definitely Mahāyāna. (d) 圓 教 His final, perfect, bodhisattva, universal teaching as preached, e.g. in the Lotus and Nirvāṇa sūtras. (2) The four methods of instruction 化 儀 are: (a) 頓 教 Direct teaching without reserve of the whole truth, e.g. the 華 嚴 sūtra. (b) 漸 教 Gradual or graded, e.g. the 阿 含, 方 等, and 般 若 sūtras; all the four 化 法 are also included under this heading. (c) 秘 密 教 Esoteric teaching, only understood by special members of the assembly. (d) 不 定 | General or indeterminate teaching, from which each hearer would derive benefit according to his interpretation.

八 敬 戒 The eight commands given by the Buddha to his foster-mother, i.e. aunt, when she was admitted to the order, and which remain as commands to nuns: (1) even though a hundred years old a nun must pay respect to a monk, however young, and offer her seat to him; (2) must never scold a monk; (3) never accuse, or speak of his misdeeds; but a monk may speak of hers; (4) at his hands obtain reception into the order; (5) confess sin (sexual or other) before the assembly of monks and nuns; (6) ask the fraternity for a monk as preceptor; (7) never share the same summer resort with monks; (8) after the summer retreat she must report and ask for a responsible confessor. Also | | 法; | 不 可 越 (or 過) 法; | 尊 重 法; v. 四 分 律 48.

八 支 idem 八 正 道; also the eight sections of the 八 支 śāstra; also a term for the first eight commandments.

八 方 上 下 The four quarters, the four 維 half-quarters and above and below, i.e. the universe in all directions. | | 天 The eight heavens and devas at the eight points of the compass: E., the Indra, or Śakra heaven; S., the Yama heaven; W., the Varuṇa, or water heaven; N., the Vaiśramaṇa, or Pluto heaven; N.E., the Īśāna, or Śiva heaven; S.E., the Homa, or fire heaven; S.W., the Nirṛti, or Rakṣaḥ heaven; N.W., the Vāyu, or wind heaven. All these may be considered as devalokas or heavens.

八 時 An Indian division of the day into eight "hours", four for day and four for night.

八 智 The 四 法 智 and 四 類 智; see 八 忍.

八 會 The 華 嚴 經 Hua-yen sūtra, as delivered at eight assemblies.

八 棄 idem 八 波 羅 夷.

八 正 道 (分) Āryamārga. The eight right or correct ways, the "eightfold noble path" for the arhat to nirvāṇa; also styled 八 道 船, 八 正 門, 八 由 行, 八 遊 行, 八 聖 道 支, 八 道 行, 八 直 行, 八 直 道. The eight are: (1) 正 見 Samyag-dṛṣṭi, correct views in regard to the Four Axioms, and freedom from the common delusion. (2) 正 思 Samyak-saṁkalpa, correct thought and purpose. (3) 正 語 Samyag-vāc, correct speech, avoidance of false and idle talk. (4) 正 業 Samyak-karmānta, correct deed, or conduct, getting rid of all improper action so as to dwell in purity. (5) 正 命 Samyag-ājīva, correct livelihood or occupation, avoiding the five immoral occupations. (6) 正 精 進 Samyag-vyāyāma, correct zeal, or energy in uninterrupted progress in the way of nirvāṇa. (7) 正 念 Samyak-smṛti, correct remembrance, or memory, which retains the true and excludes the false. (8) 正 定 Samyak-samādhi, correct meditation, absorption, or abstraction. The 正 means of course Buddhist orthodoxy, anything contrary to this being 邪 or heterodox, and wrong. | | | 經 Buddha-bhāṣita-aṣṭāṅga-samyaṅ-mārga-sūtra. Tr. by

An Shih-kao of the Eastern Han. B.N. 659; being an earlier translation of the Samyuktāgama 雜阿含經.

八水 Eight rivers of India—Ganges, Jumna, 薩羅? Sarasvatī, Hiraṇyavatī or Ajiravatī, 摩河? Mahī, Indus, Oxus, and Sītā.

八法 The eight dharmas, things, or methods. There are three groups: (1) idem 八風 q.v. (2) 四大 and 四微 q.v. (3) The eight essential things, i.e. 教 instruction, 理 doctrine, 智 knowledge or wisdom attained, 斷 cutting away of delusion, 行 practice of the religious life, 位 progressive status, 因 producing 果 the fruit of saintliness. Of these 教理行果 are known as the 四法.

八波羅夷 or 八重罪 The eight pārājika, in relation to the sins of a nun; for the first four see 四||| ; (5) libidinous contact with a male; (6) any sort of improper association (leading to adultery); (7) concealing the misbehaviour (of an equal, or inferior); (8) improper dealings with a monk.

八海 v. 九山八海.

八無暇 The eight conditions of no leisure or time to hear a Buddha or his truth, idem 八難. ||礙 The eight universalized powers of the 六識 six senses, 意根 the mind and the 法界 dharmadhātu.

八熱地獄 v. 八大地獄.

八犍度 The eight skandhas or sections of the Abhidharma, i.e. miscellaneous; concerning bondage to the passions, etc.; wisdom; practice; the four fundamentals, or elements; the roots, or organs; meditation; and views. The ||論 in thirty sections, attributed to Kātyāyana, is in the Abhidharma.

八王子 The eight sons of the last of the 20,000 shining Buddhas 燈明佛 born before he left home to become a monk; their names are given in the first chapter of the Lotus sūtra. In Japan there are also eight sons of a Shinto deity, reincarnated as one of the six Kuan-yin. ||日 The eight royal days, i.e. the solstices, the equinoxes, and the first day of each of the four seasons.

八由行, also 八直行 (or 道) idem |正道.

八相(成道) also 八相示現 Eight aspects of the Buddha's life, which the 起信論 gives as: (1) descent into and abode in the Tuṣita heaven; (2) entry into his mother's womb; (3) abode there visibly preaching to the devas; (4) birth from mother's side in Lumbinī; (5) leaving home at 19 (or 25) as a hermit; (6) after six years' suffering attaining enlightenment; (7) rolling the Law-wheel, or preaching; (8) at 80 entering nirvāṇa. The 四教義 group of T'ien-t'ai is slightly different—descent from Tuṣita, entry into womb, birth, leaving home, subjection of Māra, attaining perfect wisdom, preaching, nirvāṇa. See also the two 四相, i.e. 四本| and 四隨|.

八神變 idem 八變化.

八祖相承 The succession of the eight founders of the esoteric sect, 眞言 or Shingon, i.e. 大日, 金剛, 龍猛, 龍智, 金剛智, 不空, 惠果 and the Japanese 弘法.

八禁 idem 八戒.

八福生處 The eight happy conditions in which he may be reborn who keeps the five commands and the ten good ways and bestows alms: (1) rich and honourable among men; (2) in the heavens of the four deva kings; (3) the Indra heavens; (4) Suyāma heavens; (5) Tuṣita heaven; (6) 化樂 nirmāṇarati heaven, i.e. the fifth devaloka; (7) 他化 paranirmita-vaśavartin, i.e. the sixth devaloka heaven; (8) the brahma-heavens. ||田 The eight fields for cultivating blessedness: Buddhas; arhats (or saints); preaching monks (upādhyāya); teachers (ācārya); friars; father; mother; the sick. Buddhas, arhats, and friars (or monks in general) are termed 敬田 reverence-fields; the sick are 悲田 compassion-fields; the rest are 恩田 grace- or gratitude-fields. Another group is: to make roads and wells; canals and bridges; repair dangerous roads; be dutiful to parents; support monks; tend the sick; save from disaster or distress; provide for a quinquennial assembly. Another: serving the Three Precious Ones, i.e. the Buddha; the Law; the Order; parents; the monks as teachers; the poor; the sick; animals.

八種別解脫戒 Differentiated rules of liberation for the eight orders—monks; nuns; mendicants; novices male; and female; disciples male; and female; and the laity who observe the first eight commandments. ||勝法 The eight kinds of surpassing things, i.e. those who keep the first eight commandments receive the eight kinds of reward—they escape from falling into the hells; becoming pretas; or animals; or asuras; they will be born among men, become monks, and obtain the truth; in the heavens of desire; in the brahma-heaven, or meet a Buddha; and obtain perfect enlightenment. | | 粥 The eight kinds of congee, or gruel, served by the citizens to the Buddha and his disciples when in retreat in the bamboo grove of Kāśī; they were of butter, or fats, or hempseed, milk, peas, beans, sesamum, or plain gruel. | | (布) 施 Eight causes of giving—convenience; fear; gratitude; reward-seeking; traditional (or customary); hoping for heaven; name and fame; personal virtue. | | 授 記 The eight kinds of prediction—made known to self, not to others; to others not to self; to self and others; unknown to self or others; the near made known but the remote not; the remote made known but not the intermediate steps; near and remote both made known; near and remote both not made known. | | 法 idem | 戒; also eight divisions of the 五 十 法 q.v. | | 清 風 Pleasant breezes from the eight directions of the compass.

八穢 Eight things unclean to a monk: buying land for self, not for Buddha or the fraternity; ditto cultivating; ditto laying by or storing up; ditto keeping servants (or slaves); keeping animals (for slaughter); treasuring up gold, etc.; ivory and ornaments; utensils for private use.

八童子 idem 八大金剛童子.

八筏 The eight rafts, idem 八正道 The eightfold noble path.

八纏 The eight entanglements, or evils: to be without shame; without a blush; envious; mean; unregretful; sleepy (or indolent); ambitious; stupid (or depressed).

八聖 The 四向 and 四果 of śrāvakas. | | (道支) idem 八正道.

八背捨 idem 八解脫.

八臂天 The eight-arm deva; an epithet of Brahma as Nārāyaṇadeva 那羅延天 creator of men.

八自在 idem | 變化 and | 大自在.

八色幡 The Amitābha eight pennons of various colours, indicating the eight directions of space.

八苦 The eight distresses—birth, age, sickness, death, parting with what we love, meeting with what we hate, unattained aims, and all the ills of the five skandhas.

八菩薩 idem 八大菩薩.

八萬 An abbreviation for 八萬四(千) The number of atoms in the human body is supposed to be 84,000. Hence the term is used for a number of things, often in the general sense of a great number. It is also the age apex of life in each human world. There are the 84,000 stūpas erected by Aśoka, each to accommodate one of the 84,000 relics of the Buddha's body; also the 84,000 forms of illumination shed by Amitābha; the 84,000 excellent physical signs of a Buddha; the 84,000 mortal distresses, i.e. 84,000 煩惱 or 塵勞; also the cure found in the 84,000 methods, i.e. 法藏, 法蘊, 法門, or 敎門. | | 十二 An abbreviation for 八萬四千法藏 the 84,000 teachings or lessons credited to the Buddha for the cure of all sufferings, and the 十二部經 12 sūtras in which they are contained. | | 威儀 The bodhisattva's 80,000 duties.

八葉 The eight lotus-petals, a name for Sumeru. | | 院 is the central court of the 胎藏界 with Vairocana as its central figure, also termed | | 蓮臺 or 座 An esoteric name for the heart is the eight-petal fleshly heart, and being the seat of meditation it gives rise to the term eight-leaf lotus meditation.

八覺 The eight (wrong) perceptions or thoughts, i.e. desire; hate; vexation (with others); 親里 home-sickness; patriotism (or thoughts of the country's welfare); dislike of death; ambition for one's clan or family; slighting or being rude to others. 華嚴經 13.

八解脫 Aṣṭa-vimokṣa, mokṣa, vimukti, mukti. Liberation, deliverance, freedom, emancipation, escape, release—in eight forms; also 八背捨 and cf. 解脫 and 八勝處. The eight are stages of mental concentration: (1) 內有色想觀外色解脫 Liberation, when subjective desire arises, by examination of the object, or of all things and realization of their filthiness. (2) 內無色想觀外色解脫 Liberation, when no subjective desire arises, by still meditating as above. These two are deliverance by meditation on impurity, the next on purity. (3) 淨身作證具足住解脫 Liberation by concentration on the pure to the realization of a permanent state of freedom from all desire. The above three "correspond to the four Dhyānas". (Eitel.) (4) 空無邊處解脫 Liberation in realization of the infinity of space, or the immaterial. (5) 識無邊處解脫 Liberation in realization of infinite knowledge. (6) 無所有處解脫 Liberation in realization of nothingness, or nowhereness. (7) 非想非非想處解脫 Liberation in the state of mind where there is neither thought nor absence of thought. These four arise out of abstract meditation in regard to desire and form, and are associated with the 四空天. (8) 滅受想定解脫 Liberation by means of a state of mind in which there is final extinction, nirvāṇa, of both sensation, vedanā, and consciousness, saṁjñā.

八觸 Eight physical sensations which hinder meditation in its early stages: restlessness, itching, buoyancy, heaviness, coldness, heat, roughness, smoothness. 止觀 8.

八論 The eight śāstras; there are three lists of eight; one non-Buddhist; one by 無着 Asaṅga, founder of the Yoga School; a third by 陳那 Jina Dinnāga. Details are given in the 寄歸傳 4 and 解纜鈔 4.

八諦 The eight truths, postulates, or judgments of the 法相 Dharmalakṣaṇa school, i.e. four common or mundane, and four of higher meaning. The first four are (1) common postulates on reality, considering the nominal as real, e.g. a pot; (2) common doctrinal postulates, e.g. the five skandhas; (3) abstract postulates, e.g. the four noble truths 四諦; and (4) temporal postulates in regard to the spiritual in the material. The second abstract or philosophical four are (5) postulates on constitution and function, e.g. of the skandhas; (6) on cause and effect, e.g. the 四諦; (7) on the void, the immaterial, or reality; and (8) on the pure inexpressible ultimate or absolute.

八識 The eight parijñāna, or kinds of cognition, perception, or consciousness. They are the five senses of cakṣur-vijñāna, śrotra-v., ghrāṇa-v., jihvā-v., and kāya-v., i.e. seeing, hearing, smelling, tasting, and touch. The sixth is mano-vijñāna, the mental sense, or intellect, v. 末那. It is defined as 意 mentality, apprehension, or by some as will. The seventh is styled kliṣṭa-mano-vijñāna 末那 | discriminated from the last as 思量 pondering, calculating; it is the discriminating and constructive sense, more than the intellectually perceptive; as infected by the ālaya-v., or receiving "seeds" from it, it is considered as the cause of all egoism and individualizing, i.e. of men and things, therefore of all illusion arising from assuming the seeming as the real. The eighth is the ālaya-vijñāna, 阿賴耶 | which is the storehouse, or basis from which come all "seeds" of consciousness. The seventh is also defined as the ādāna 阿陀那 | or "laying hold of" or "holding on to" consciousness. | | 心王 The eight fundamental powers of the | | and | | 心所 the eight powers functioning, or the concomitant sensations. | | 體一 The eight perceptions are fundamentally a unity, opposed by the 唯識 school with the doctrine | | 體別 that they are fundamentally discrete.

八辯 Eight characteristics of a Buddha's speaking: never hectoring; never misleading or confused; fearless; never haughty; perfect in meaning; and in flavour; free from harshness; seasonable (or, suited to the occasion).

八變化 Eight supernatural powers of transformation, characteristics of every Buddha: (1) to shrink self or others, or the world and all things to an atom; (2) to enlarge ditto to fill all space; (3) to make the same light as a feather; (4) to make the same any size or anywhere at will; (5) everywhere and in everything to be omnipotent; (6) to be anywhere at will, either by self-transportation, or bringing the destination to himself, etc.; (7) to shake all things (in the six, or eighteen ways); (8) to be one or many and at will pass through the solid or through space, or through fire or water, or transform the four elements at will, e.g. turn earth into water. Also | 神變; | 自在.

八輪 The eight (spoke) wheel, idem 八正道.

八輩 The eight grades, i.e. those who have attained the 四向 and 四果.

八迷 The eight misleading terms, which form the basis of the logic of the 中論, i.e. 生 birth, 滅 death, 去 past, 來 future, 一 identity, 異 difference, 斷 annihilation, 常 perpetuity (or eternity). The 三論宗 regard these as unreal; v. 八不中道.

八遊行 idem 八正道.

八道 (支 or 船 or 行) idem 八正道.

八遮 A 三論 term for 八不中道 q.v.

八邪 The eight heterodox or improper practices, the opposite of the eight correct paths 八正道.

八部(衆) The eight classes of supernatural beings in the Lotus sūtra: 天 deva, 龍 nāga, 夜叉 yakṣa, 乾闥婆 gandharva, 阿修羅 asura, 迦樓羅 garuḍa, 緊那羅 kinnara, 摩睺羅迦 mahoraga. Also called 天龍八部 and 龍神八部. 丨丨鬼衆 The eight groups of demon-followers of the four mahārājas, i.e. gandharvas, piśācas, kumbhāṇḍas, pretas, nāgas, pūtanas, yakṣas, and rākṣasas.

八重眞寶 The eight weighty and truly precious things, i.e. the eight metals, which depend for evaluation on gold, the highest and greatest, used to illustrate the Buddha as supreme and the other classes in grades beneath him. Also 丨丨無價, i.e. the eight priceless things.

八門 (二悟 or 兩益) Eight kinds of syllogisms in Buddhist logic; v. 因明八正理論. (1) 能立 a valid proposition; (2) 能破 an invalid proposition; (3) 似能立 doubtful, or seemingly valid but faulty; (4) 似能破 seemingly invalid, and assailable; (5) 現量 manifest, or evidential; (6) 比量 inferential; (7) 似現量 seemingly evidential; (8) 似比量 seemingly inferential.

八關齋 idem 八戒齋.

八難 The eight conditions in which it is difficult to see a Buddha or hear his dharma: in the hells; as hungry ghosts; as animals; in Uttarakuru (the northern continent where all is pleasant); in the long-life heavens (where life is long and easy); as deaf, blind, and dumb; as a worldly philosopher; in the intermediate period between a Buddha and his successor. Also 丨無暇.

八音 The eight tones of a Buddha's voice—beautiful, flexible, harmonious, respect-producing, not effeminate (i.e. manly), unerring, deep and resonant.

八顚倒 The eight upside-down views: heretics believe in 常樂我淨 permanence, pleasure, personality, and purity; the two Hīnayāna vehicles deny these both now and in nirvāṇa. Mahāyāna denies them now, but asserts them in nirvāṇa. Also 丨倒.

八風 The eight winds, or influences which fan the passions, i.e. gain, loss; defamation, eulogy; praise, ridicule; sorrow, joy. Also 丨法.

八魔 The eight Māras, or destroyers: 煩惱丨 the māras of the passions; 陰丨 the skandha-māras, v. 五陰; 死丨 death-māra; 他化自在天丨 the māra-king. The above four are ordinarily termed the four māras; the other four are the four Hīnayāna delusions of śrāvakas and pratyekabuddhas, i.e. 無常 impermanence; 無樂 joylessness; 無我 impersonality; 無淨 impurity; cf. 丨顚倒.

八齋(戒) idem 八戒齋.

刀山 The hill of swords in one of the hells.

刀途 The gati or path of rebirth as an animal, so called because animals are subjects of the butcher's knife.

刀風 The wind that cuts all living beings to pieces—at the approach of a world-kalpa's end; also described as the disintegrating force at death.

力 Bala; power, strength, of which there are several categories: 二丨 power of choice and of practice; 三丨 the power of Buddha; of meditation (samādhi) and of practice. 五丨 Pañcabala, the five powers of faith, zeal, memory (or remembering), meditation, and wisdom. 六丨 A child's power is in crying; a woman's in resentment; a king's in domineering; an arhat's in zeal (or progress); a Buddha's in mercy; and a bhikṣu's in endurance (of despite). 十丨 q.v. The ten powers of Buddhas and bodhisattvas.

力士; 力者 Vīra. A strong or mighty man, hero, demigod. Used for the Licchavi, also 離車; 梨 (or 黎) 車; 栗呫嫛. The terms 力士城 and 力士生地 are defined as Kuśinagara.

力者(法師) A monk who degrades himself by becoming a fighter (e.g. boxer), or a slave.

力波羅蜜 The vīrya-pāramitā. 丨丨丨丨菩薩 One of the twenty-eight honoured ones in the Garbhadhātu group.

力無(所)畏 The 力 is intp. as the ten powers of a Buddha, the 無所畏 are his four qualities of fearlessness.

力生 Power-born; one who is born from the Truth, a monk.

十 Daśa, ten, the perfect number.

十一 Ekādaśa, eleven. |一切處 Ten universals, or modes of contemplating the universe from ten aspects, i.e. from the viewpoint of earth, water, fire, wind, blue, yellow, red, white, space, or mind. For example, contemplated under the aspect of water, then the universe is regarded as in flux and change. Also called 十禪支, 十遍處定. It is one of the 三法. ||面觀音 The eleven-faced Kuan-yin, especially connected with tantric performances, ekādaśamukha; there are three or more sūtras on the subject.

十三 Trayodaśa; thirteen. ||佛 The thirteen Shingon rulers of the dead during the forty-nine days and until the thirty-third commemoration. The thirteen are 不動明王, 釋迦, 文殊, 普賢, 地藏, 彌勒, 藥師, 觀音, 勢至, 阿彌陀, 阿閦, 大日 and 虛空藏; each has his place, duties, magical letter, signs, etc. ||力 The thirteen powers or bodhisattva balas of the Pure-land school: 因|, 緣|, 意|, 願|, 方便|, 常|, 善|, 定|, 慧|, 多聞|, 持戒忍辱精進禪定|, 正念正觀諸通明|, and 如法調伏諸衆生|. ||宗 The thirteen Buddhist schools of China, v. 宗派.

十不二門 The school of the ten pairs of unified opposites founded by 荊溪 Ching-ch'i on the teaching of the Lotus sūtra. There are several books bearing the name. The unifying principle is that of the identity of contraries, and the ten apparent contraries are matter and mind, internal and external, 修證 practice and proof (or realization), cause and effect, impurity and purity, objective and subjective, self and other, 三業 action, speech, and thought, 權實 relative and absolute, the fertilized and the fertilizer (i.e. receiver and giver). There are several treatises on the subject in the Canon. ||善業 (or 道) idem 十惡(業). ||悔戒 The ten rules which produce no regrets—not to kill, steal, fornicate, lie, tell of a fellow-Buddhist's sins, deal in wine, praise oneself and discredit others, be mean, be angry, defame the Triratna (Buddha, Law, Fraternity).

十乘(觀) A T'ien-t'ai mode of meditation in ten "vehicles" or stages, for the attainment of bodhi. ||床 The comfort or ease of progress produced by the above is compared to a couch or divan. ||風 The above method like a breeze blows away error and falsity as dust.

十事功德 The bodhisattva-merit resulting from the attainment of the ten groups of excellences in the southern version of the Nirvāṇa Sūtra 南本涅槃經 19–24. There is an unimportant 十事經 not connected with the above. ||非法 Ten unlawful things said to have been advocated by the Vaiśālī monks, which led to the calling of the second Council.

十二 Dvādaśa, twelve.

十二不律儀 idem 十二惡律儀.

十二佛 The twelve Buddhas of the esoteric sect placed three on the east, one in each of the other seven directions, and one each for zenith and nadir.

十二光佛 Amitābha's twelve titles of light. The 無量壽經上 gives them as 無量光佛, etc., i.e. the Buddha of light that is immeasurable, boundless, irresistible, incomparable, yama (or flaming), pure, joy, wisdom, unceasing, surpassing thought, ineffable, surpassing sun and moon. Another list is given in the 九品往生阿彌陀...經.

十二分經 (or 教) idem 十二部經.

十二因緣 Dvādaśāṅga pratītyasamutpāda; the twelve nidānas; v. 尼 and 因; also 十二緣起; ||(有)支; ||牽連; ||棘園; ||輪; ||重城; 因緣觀; 支佛觀. They are the twelve links in the chain of existence: (1) 無明 avidyā, ignorance, or unenlightenment; (2) 行 saṁskāra, action, activity, conception, "dispositions," Keith; (3) 識 vijñāna, consciousness; (4) 名色 nāmarūpa, name and form; (5) 六入 ṣaḍāyatana, the six sense organs, i.e. eye, ear, nose, tongue, body, and mind; (6) 觸 sparśa, contact, touch; (7) 受 vedanā, sensation, feeling; (8) 愛 tṛṣṇā, thirst, desire, craving; (9) 取 upādāna, laying hold of, grasping; (10) 有 bhava, being, existing; (11) 生 jāti, birth; (12) 老死 jarāmaraṇa, old age, death. The "classical formula" reads "By reason of ignorance dispositions; by reason of dispositions consciousness ", etc. A further application of the twelve nidānas is made in regard to their causation of rebirth : (1) ignorance, as inherited passion from the beginningless past ; (2) karma, good and evil, of past lives ; (3) conception as a form of perception ; (4) nāmarūpa, or body and mind evolving (in the womb) ; (5) the six organs on the verge of birth ; (6) childhood whose intelligence is limited to sparśa, contact or touch ; (7) receptivity or budding intelligence and discrimination from 6 or 7 years ; (8) thirst, desire, or love, age of puberty ; (9) the urge of sensuous existence ; (10) forming the substance, bhava, of future karma ; (11) the completed karma ready for rebirth ; (12) old age and death. The two first are associated with the previous life, the other ten with the present. The theory is equally applicable to all realms of reincarnation. The twelve links are also represented in a chart, at the centre of which are the serpent (anger), boar (ignorance, or stupidity), and dove (lust) representing the fundamental sins. Each catches the other by the tail, typifying the train of sins producing the wheel of life. In another circle the twelve links are represented as follows : (1) ignorance, a blind woman ; (2) action, a potter at work, or a man gathering fruit ; (3) consciousness, a restless monkey ; (4) name and form, a boat ; (5) sense organs, a house ; (6) contact, a man and woman sitting together ; (7) sensation, a man pierced by an arrow ; (8) desire, a man drinking wine ; (9) craving, a couple in union ; (10) existence through childbirth ; (11) birth, a man carrying a corpse ; (12) disease, old age, death, an old woman leaning on a stick. v. 十 二 因 緣 論 Pratītya-samutpāda śāstra.

十 二 地 To the 十 地 add 等 覺 and 妙 覺 q.v.

十 二 (大 or 上) 願 The twelve vows of the Master of Healing ; v. 藥 師.

十 二 天 The twelve devas (especially of the Shingon sect) : Brahmā ; the deva of earth ; of the moon ; of the sun ; Indra ; of fire ; Yama ; of the rakṣas (or demons) ; of water ; of wind ; Vaiśramaṇa (wealth) ; and Maheśvara (Śiva). Also | | 大 天 衆.

十 二 宮 The twelve zodiacal mansions : east—gemini 夫 婦 or 雙 女 ; aries 羊 ; taurus 牛 ; west—libra 秤 ; scorpio 蝎 ; sagittarius 弓 or 人 馬 ; south—aquarius 瓶 ; pisces 魚 ; capricornus 密 牛 ; north—cancer 螃 蟹 ; leo 獅 子 ; virgo (or twin maidens 雙 女). They are used in the vajradhātu group of the Garbhadhātu maṇḍala, E. W. S. N.

十 二 惡 律 儀 The twelve bad occupations : sheep-butcher ; poulterer (or hen-breeder) ; pork butcher ; fowler ; fisherman ; hunter ; thief ; executioner ; jailer ; juggler ; dog-butcher ; beater (i.e. hunt servant).

十 二 法 人 Those who follow the twelve practices of the ascetics : (1) live in a hermitage ; (2) always beg for food ; (3) take turns at begging food ; (4) one meal a day ; (5) reduce amount of food ; (6) do not take a drink made of fruit or honey after midday ; (7) wear dust-heap garments ; (8) wear only the three clerical garments ; (9) dwell among graves ; (10) stay under a tree ; (11) on the dewy ground ; (12) sit and never lie.

十 二 火 天 The homa-, or fire-spirits ; whose representations, colours, magic words, signs, symbols, and mode of worship are given in the 大 日 經 疏 20. Also | | | 尊 ; | | 種 火 法. The twelve fire-spirits are : (1) Indra or Vairocana, the discoverer or source of fire, symbolizing 智 knowledge ; (2) the moon 行 滿 which progresses to fullness, with mercy as root and enlightenment as fruit, i.e. Buddha ; (3) the wind, represented as a half-moon, fanner of flame, of zeal, and by driving away dark clouds, of enlightenment ; (4) the red rays of the rising sun, rohitaka, his swords (or rays) indicating 慧 wisdom ; (5) 沒 嘌 拏 a form half stern, half smiling, sternly driving away the passions and trials ; (6) 忿 怒 irate, bellowing with open mouth, showing four teeth, flowing locks, one eye closed ; (7) 闍 吒 羅 fire burning within, i.e. the inner witness, or realization ; (8) 迄 灑 耶 the waster, or destroyer of waste and injurious products within, i.e. inner purification ; (9) 意 生 the producer at will, capable of all variety, resembling Viśvakarman, the Brahmanic Vulcan ; (10) 羯 羅 微 the fire-eater ; (11) untraceable ; (12) 謨 賀 那 the completer, also the subduer of demons.

十 二 無 爲 v. 十 二 眞 如.

十 二 燈 The twelve lamps used in the cult of the Master of Healing 藥 師.

十 二 獸 The twelve animals for the " twelve horary branches " with their names, hours, and the Chinese transliterations of their Sanskrit equivalents ; v. 大 集 經 23 and 56. There are also the thirty-six animals, three for each hour. The twelve are : Serpent 蛇 巳, 9–11 a.m. 迦 若 ; Horse

馬 午, 11–1 noon 兜 羅; Sheep 羊 未, 1–3 p.m. 毘 梨 支 迦; Monkey 猴 申, 3–5 p.m. 檀 尼 毘; Cock 鷄 酉, 5–7 p.m. 摩 迦 羅; Dog 犬 戌, 7–9 p.m. 鳩 槃; Boar 豕 亥, 9–11 p.m. 彌 那; Rat 鼠 子, 11–1 midnight 彌 沙; Ox 牛 丑, 1–3 a.m. 毘 利 沙; Tiger (or Lion) 虎 寅, 3–5 a.m. 彌 偷 那; Hare 兎 卯, 5–7 a.m. 羯 迦 吒 迦; Dragon 龍 辰, 7–9 a.m. 絲 阿.

十二眞如 The twelve aspects of the bhūtatathatā or the ultimate, which is also styled the | | 無 爲 "inactive" or nirvāṇa-like: and the | | 空 "void" or immaterial: (1) The *chên ju* itself; (2) 法 界 as the medium of all things; (3) 法 性 as the nature of all things; (4) 不 虛 妄 性 its reality contra the unreality of phenomena; (5) 不 變 異 性 its immutability contra mortality and phenomenal variation; (6) 平 等 性 as universal or undifferentiated; (7) 離 生 性 as immortal, i.e. apart from birth and death, or creation and destruction; (8) 法 定 as eternal, its nature ever sure; (9) 法 住 as the abode of all things; (10) 實 際 as the bounds of all reality; (11) 虛 空 界 as the realm of space, the void, or immateriality; (12) 不 思 議 界 as the realm beyond thought or expression.

十二神(明王) The twelve spirits connected with the cult of 藥 師 the Master of Healing. Also | | 神 將. They are associated with the twelve hours of the day, of which they are guardian spirits. Their names are as follows: 宮 (or 金) 毘 羅 Kumbhīra; 伐 折 羅 Vajra; 迷 企 羅 Mihira; 安 底 羅 Aṇḍīra; 頞 儞 羅 Anila; 珊 底 羅 Śaṇḍila; 因 陀 羅 Indra; 波 夷 羅 Pajra; 摩 虎 羅 Mahoraga; 眞 達 羅 Kinnara 招 杜 羅 Catura; and 毘 羯 羅 Vikarāla.

十二禽 idem 十 二 獸.

十二種火法 v. 十 二 火 天.

十二空 v. 十 二 眞 如.

十二緣起; | | 輪; | | 門; idem 十 二 因 緣.

十二藥叉大將 idem 十 二 神.

十二部經 Twelve divisions of the Mahāyāna canon: (1) 修 多 羅 sūtra; (2) 祇 夜 geya; (3) 伽 陀 gāthā; (4) 尼 陀 那 nidāna, also 因 緣; (5) 伊 帝 目 多 itivṛttaka; (6) 闍 多 伽 jātaka; (7) 阿 浮 達 摩 adbhuta-dharma, i.e. the 阿 毘 達 摩 abhidharma; (8) 阿 波 陀 那 avadāna; (9) 優 婆 提 舍 upadeśa; (10) 優 陀 那 udāna; (11) 毘 佛 略 vaipulya; (12) 和 伽 羅 vyākaraṇa. Cf. 九 部 經.

十二遊經 Dvādaśaviharaṇa sūtra. The life of Śākyamuni to his twelfth year, translated by Kālodaka A.D. 392.

十二門 idem | | 因 緣. | | | 論 Dvādaśanikāya Śāstra. One of the 三 論, composed by Nāgārjuna, translated by Kumārajīva A.D. 408. There are several works on it.

十二願王 The twelve-vow king, i.e. Yao Shih 藥 師, the Master of Healing.

十五 Pañcadaśa, fifteen. | | 尊 The fifteen honoured ones, with whom certain 眞 言 Shingon devotees seek by yoga to become united; of the fifteen, each represents a part of the whole, e.g. the eyes, ears, mouth, hands, feet, etc. v. 瑜 祇 經 in its 金 剛 薩 埵, etc., chapter. | | 尊 觀 音 The fifteen kinds of Kuan-yin's images—normal face, with thousand hands, horse's head, eleven faces, as Cundā (Marīci), with the 如 意 talismanic wheel, net, white robe, leaf robe, moon, willow, fruit, as Tārā, with azure neck, and as Gandharāja. | | 智 斷 The fifteen days of the waxing moon are likened to the fifteen kinds of increasing wisdom 智, and the fifteen waning days to the fifteen kinds of deliverance from evil 斷.

十住 The ten stages, or periods, in bodhisattva-wisdom, prajñā 般 若, are the 十 住; the merits or character attained are the 十 地 q.v. Two interpretations may be given. In the first of these, the first four stages are likened to entry into the holy womb, the next four to the period of gestation, the ninth to birth, and the tenth to the washing or baptism with the water of wisdom, e.g. the baptism of a Kṣatriya prince. The ten stages are (1) 發 心 | the purposive stage, the mind set upon Buddhahood; (2) 治 地 | clear understanding and mental control; (3) 修 行 | unhampered liberty in every direction; (4) 生 貴 | acquiring the Tathāgata nature or seed; (5) 方 便 具 足 | perfect adaptability and resemblance in self-development and development of others; (6) 正 心 | the whole mind becoming Buddha-like; (7) 不 退 | no retrogression, perfect unity and constant progress; (8) 童 眞 | as a Buddha-son now complete; (9) 法 王 子 | as prince of the law; (10) 灌 頂 | baptism as such, e.g. the consecration of kings. Another interpretation of the above is:

(1) spiritual resolve, stage of śrota-āpanna ; (2) submission to rule, preparation for Sakṛdāgāmin stage ; (3) cultivation of virtue, attainment of Sakṛdāgāmin stage ; (4) noble birth, preparation for the anāgāmin stage ; (5) perfect means, attainment of anāgāmin stage ; (6) right mind, preparation for arhatship ; (7) no-retrogradation, the attainment of arhatship ; (8) immortal youth, pratyekabuddhahood ; (9) son of the law-king, the conception of bodhisattvahood ; (10) baptism as the summit of attainment, the conception of Buddhahood. | | 心 Ten stages of mental or spiritual development in the 眞 言 Shingon sect, beginning with the human animal and ending with perfect enlightenment ; a category by the Japanese monk 弘 法 Kōhō, founded on the 大 日 經 十 心 品. | | 毘 婆 沙 論 Daśabhūmivibhāṣā śāstra. A commentary by Nāgārjuna on the 十 住 經 and the 十 地 經, said to contain the earliest teaching regarding Amitābha ; translated by Kumārajīva *circa* A.D. 405.

十 佛 There are several groups ; that of the Hua-yen sūtra is Kāśyapa, Kanakamuni, Krakucchanda, Viśvabhū, Śikhin, Vipaśyi, Tiṣya (or Puṣya), Tissa, ? Padma, and Dīpaṅkara. Another group is that of the Amitābha cult, one for each of the ten directions. There are other groups.

十 來 (偈) The ten rhymes in "lai", a verse which expresses the Buddhist doctrine of moral determinism, i.e. that the position anyone now occupies is solely the result of his character in past lives ; heredity and environment having nothing to do with his present condition, for, whether in prince or beggar, it is the reward of past deeds.

The upright from the forbearing come,
The poor from the mean and greedy come,
Those of high rank from worshippers come,
The low and common from the prideful come,
Those who are dumb from slanderers come,
The blind and deaf from unbelievers come,
The long-lived from the merciful come,
The short-lived from life-takers come,
The deficient in faculties from command-breakers come,
The complete in faculties from command-keepers come.

端正者忍辱中來。
貧窮者慳貪中來。
高位者禮拜中來。
下賤者憍慢中來。
瘖啞者誹謗中來。
盲聾者不信中來。
長壽者慈悲中來。
短命者殺生中來。
諸根不具者破戒中來。
六根具足者持戒中來。

十使 ; 十大惑 ; 十根本煩惱 The ten messengers, deluders, fundamental passions ; they are divided into five sharp and five dull ; the five 鈍 使 dull ones are desire, hate, stupidity, pride, and doubt ; the five sharp 利 使 are 身 見, 邊 見, 邪 見, 見 取 見, 戒 禁 見, v. 見.

十 信 The ten grades of bodhisattva faith, i.e. the first ten 位 in the fifty-two bodhisattva positions : (1) 信 faith (which destroys illusion and results in) (2) 念 remembrance, or unforgetfulness ; (3) 精 進 zealous progress ; (4) 慧 wisdom ; (5) 定 settled firmness in concentration ; (6) 不 退 non-retrogression ; (7) 護 法 protection of the Truth ; (8) 廻 向 reflexive powers, e.g. for reflecting the Truth ; (9) 戒 the nirvāṇa mind in 無 爲 effortlessness ; (10) 願 action at will in anything and everywhere.

十 八 Aṣṭādaśa, eighteen. | | 不 共 法 Āveṇikadharma, or buddhadharma, the eighteen different characteristics of a Buddha as compared with bodhisattvas, i.e. his perfection of body (or person), mouth (or speech), memory, impartiality to all, serenity, self-sacrifice, unceasing desire to save, unflagging zeal therein, unfailing thought thereto, wisdom in it, powers of deliverance, the principles of it, revealing perfect wisdom in deed, in word, in thought, perfect knowledge of past, future, and present. v. 智 度 論 26. | | 圓 淨 The eighteen perfections of a buddha's sambhogakāya, v. 三 身. Also | | | 滿. | | 天 Brahmaloka, the eighteen heavens of form, rūpadhātu, three of the first dhyāna, 梵 衆 | ; 梵 輔 | ; 大 梵 | ; three of the second, 少 光 | ; 無 量 光 | ; 光 音 | ; three of the third, 少 淨 | ; 無 量 淨 | ; 徧 淨 | ; and nine of the fourth, 無 雲 | ; 福 生 | ; 廣 果 | ; 無 想 | ; 無 煩 | ; 無 熱 | ; 善 見 | ; 善 現 | ; 色 究 竟 |. "Southern Buddhism knows only sixteen. Those two which Northern Buddhists added are Punya-prasava 福 生 and Anabhraka 無 雲." Eitel. | | 宗 The eighteen Japanese Buddhist sects, i.e. 三 論 ; 法 相 ; 華 嚴 ; 律 ; 俱 舍 ; 成 實 ; 天 台 ; 眞 言 ; 融 通 念 佛 ; 淨 土 ; 眞 ; 日 蓮 ; 時 ; 臨 濟 ; 曹 洞 ; 黃 檗 ; 普 化 ; and 修 驗 宗. | | 應 眞 The eighteen arhats. | | 物 The eighteen things a monk should carry in the performance of his duties—willow twigs, soap, the three garments, a water-bottle, a begging-bowl, mat, staff, censer, filter, handkerchief, knife, fire-producer, pincers, hammock, sūtra, the vinaya, the Buddha's image, and bodhisattva image or images ; cf. 梵 網 經 37. | | 生 處 The eighteen Brahmalokas, where rebirth is necessary, i.e. where mortality still exists. | | 界 The eighteen dhātu, or realms of sense, i.e.

六根, 六境, 六識 the six organs, their objects or conditions, and their perceptions. | | (大) 經; | | 明處 The eighteen Indian non-Buddhist classics, i.e. the four vedas, six śāstras, and eight śāstras. | | 賢 (聖 or 衆); | | 境界; | | 有學 v. 有學. | | 部 The eighteen schools of Hīnayāna as formerly existing in India; v. 小乘. | | 重地獄 The eighteen layers of hells, which are described by one writer as the conditions in which the six sense organs, their six objects, and the six perceptions do not harmonize. Another says the eighteen are the hell of knives, the boiling sands, the boiling excrement, the fiery carriage, the boiling cauldron, the iron bed, etc. | | 道 In the two maṇḍalas, Vajradhātu and Garbhadhātu, each has nine central objects of worship. The Shingon disciple devotes himself to meditation on one of these eighteen each day.

十六 Ṣoḍaśa. Sixteen is the esoteric (Shingon) perfect number, just as ten is the perfect number in the Hua-yen sūtra and generally, see 大日經疏 5. | | 心, i.e. the 八忍 and 八智. | | (大) 天 The sixteen devas are E. Indra and his wife; S.E. the fire deva and his wife; S. Yama and his wife; S.W. Yakṣa-rāja (Kuvera) and wife; W. the water deva and his nāga wife (Śakti); N.W. the wind deva and wife; N. Vaiśramaṇa and wife; N.E. Īśāna and wife. | | 師 The sixteen non-Buddhist "heretical" Indian philosophers. | | 會 The sixteen lessons of the Prajña-pāramitā. | | (心) 行; | | 諦觀 idem | | 行相. The sixteen 行相 of the Four Axioms 四諦, i.e. four forms of considering each of the axioms, associated with 見道. | | 善神 Two lists are given, one of sixteen 大將 mahārājas; another of sixteen 善神 good spirits or gods; all of them are guardians of the good and enemies of evil. | | 國王; | | 大國 The sixteen ancient kingdoms of India whose kings are addressed in the 仁王經 2; i.e. Vaiśālī, Kośala, Śrāvastī, Magadha, Bārāṇasi, Kapilavastu, Kuśinagara, Kauśāmbī, Pañcāla, Pāṭaliputra, Mathurā, Uṣa (Uśīra), Puṇyavardhana, Devāvatāra, Kāśī, and Campā. | | 大力 The sixteen great powers obtainable by a bodhisattva, i.e. of will, mind, action, shame (to do evil), energy, firmness, wisdom, virtue, reasoning, personal appearance, physical powers, wealth, spirit, magic, spreading the truth, subduing demons. | | 想觀 idem 十六觀. | | 王子 (佛); | | 沙彌 The sixteen princes in the Lotus Sūtra who became Buddhas after hearing their father preach it. | | 知見; | | 神我 The sixteen heretical views on me and mine, i.e. the ego in self and others, determinism or fate, immortality, etc.; v. 智度論 25. | | 菩薩; | | 大 (or 正) 士 The sixteen bodhisattvas; there are two groups, one of the 顯敎 exoteric, one of the 密敎 esoteric cults; the exoteric list is indefinite; the esoteric has two lists, one is of four bodhisattvas to each of the Buddhas of the four quarters of the Diamond Realm; the other is of the sixteen who represent the body of bodhisattvas in a 賢 kalpa, such as the present: E. 彌勒, 不空, 除憂, 除惡; S. 香象, 大精進, 虛空藏, 智幢; W. 無量光, 賢護, 網明, 月光; N. 無量意 (文殊), 辨積, 金剛藏, 普賢. | | 觀 The sixteen meditations of Amitābha on the setting sun, water (as ice, crystal, etc.), the earth, and so on. | | 資具 Sixteen necessaries of a strict observer of ascetic rules, ranging from garments made of rags collected from the dust heap to sleeping among graves.

十利 There are many groups of ten profitable things or advantages, e.g. ten in regard to edibles, ten to congee, to learning, to study of the Scriptures, to wisdom, to zeal, etc.

十力 Daśabala. The ten powers of a Buddha, giving complete knowledge of: (1) what is right or wrong in every condition; (2) what is the karma of every being, past, present, and future; (3) all stages of dhyāna liberation, and samādhi; (4) the powers and faculties of all beings; (5) the desires, or moral direction of every being; (6) the actual condition of every individual; (7) the direction and consequence of all laws; (8) all causes of mortality and of good and evil in their reality; (9) the end of all beings and nirvāṇa; (10) the destruction of all illusion of every kind. See the 智度論 25 and the 俱舍論 29. | | 敎 The religion of Him who has the ten powers, i.e. Buddhism. | | (無等) 尊 The honoured (unequalled) possessor of the ten powers, Buddha. | | 迦葉 Daśabala-Kāśyapa, one of the first five disciples. | | 明 The ten powers and ten understandings of a Buddha.

十功德 (論) Ten merits (or powers) commended by the Buddha to his bhikṣus—zealous progress, contentment with few desires, courage, learning (so as to teach), fearlessness, perfect observance of the commands and the fraternity's regulations, perfect meditation, perfect wisdom, perfect liberation, and perfect understanding of it.

十劫 The ten kalpas that have expired since Amitābha made his forty-eight vows, or | | 正覺 attained complete bodhi, hence he is styled 十劫彌陀. These ten kalpas as seen by P'u-hsien are 十劫須臾 but as a moment.

十勝行 The ten pāramitās observed by bodhisattvas, see 十地 and 十住. Hīnayāna has another group, adding to the four 梵福 q.v. the six of sacrificing one's life to save mother; or father; or a Buddha; to become a monk; to induce another to become a monk; to obtain authority to preach.

十名 idem 十號.

十問 The ten questions to the Buddha, put into the mouth of Vajrapāṇi, which, with the answers given, form the basis of the 大日經. What is (or are) (1) the nature of the bodhi-mind? (2) its form or forms? (3) the mental stages requisite to attainment? (4) the difference between them? (5) the time required? (6) the character of the merits attained? (7) the activities or practices necessary? (8) the way of such practices? (9) the condition of the uncultivated and cultivated mind? (10) the difference between it and that of the follower of Yoga?

十善(正法) The ten good characteristics, or virtues, defined as the non-committal of the 十惡 ten evils, q.v. T'ien-t'ai has two groups, one of ceasing 止 to do evil, the other of learning to do well 行. ||位; ||戒力; ||王 The position, or power, attained in the next life by observing the ten commandments here, to be born in the heavens, or as rulers of men. ||巧 The ten good crafts, or meditations of pratyeka-buddhas, i.e. on the five skandhas, twelve 處, eighteen 界, twelve 因緣, etc. ||戒 The ten commandments (as observed by the laity). ||業(道) The excellent karma resulting from practice of the ten commandments. ||菩薩 The bodhisattvas of the 十信位 q.v.

十四 Caturdaśa, fourteen. ||佛國往生 The fourteen other-world realms of fourteen Buddhas, i.e. this realm of Śākyamuni and thirteen others. ||神九王 The fourteen devas and nine dragon and other kings, who went in the train of Mañjuśrī to thank the Buddha at the last of his Hua-yen addresses; for list see 唐華嚴經 61. ||變化 The fourteen transformations that are connected with the four dhyāna heavens. ||難 The fourteen difficult questions of the "heretics" to which the Buddha made no reply, for, as it is said, the questions were no more properly put than if one asked "How much milk can you get from a cow's horn?" They are forms of: All is permanent, impermanent, both or neither; all changes, changes not, both, neither; at death a spirit departs, does not, both, neither; after death we have the same body (or personality) and spirit, or body and spirit are different.

十地 Daśabhūmi; v. |住. The "ten stages" in the fifty-two sections of the development of a bodhisattva into a Buddha. After completing the 十四向 he proceeds to the 十地. There are several groups. I. The ten stages common to the Three Vehicles 三乘 are: (1) 乾慧地 dry wisdom stage, i.e. unfertilized by Buddha-truth, worldly wisdom; (2) 性| the embryo-stage of the nature of Buddha-truth, the 四善根; (3) 八人 (or 忍) |, the stage of the eight patient endurances; (4) 見| of freedom from wrong views; (5) 薄| of freedom from the first six of the nine delusions in practice; (6) 離欲| of freedom from the remaining three; (7) 已辨| complete discrimination in regard to wrong views and thoughts, the stage of an arhat; (8) (辟)支佛| pratyekabuddhahood, only the dead ashes of the past left to sift; (9) 菩薩| bodhisattvahood; (10) 佛| Buddhahood. v. 智度論 78. II. 大乘菩薩十地 The ten stages of Mahāyāna bodhisattva development are: (1) 歡喜| Pramuditā, joy at having overcome the former difficulties and now entering on the path to Buddhahood; (2) 離垢| Vimalā, freedom from all possible defilement, the stage of purity; (3) 發光| Prabhākarī, stage of further enlightenment; (4) 焰慧| Arciṣmatī, of glowing wisdom; (5) 極難勝| Sudurjayā, mastery of utmost or final difficulties; (6) 現前| Abhimukhī, the open way of wisdom above definitions of impurity and purity; (7) 遠行| Dūraṁgamā, proceeding afar, getting above ideas of self in order to save others; (8) 不動| Acalā, attainment of calm unperturbedness; (9) 善慧| Sādhumatī, of the finest discriminatory wisdom, knowing where and how to save, and possessed of the 十力 ten powers; (10) 法雲| Dharmamegha, attaining to the fertilizing powers of the law-cloud. Each of the ten stages is connected with each of the ten pāramitās, v. 波. Each of the 四乘 or four vehicles has a division of ten. III. The 聲聞乘十地 ten Śrāvaka stages are: (1) 受三歸| initiation as a disciple by receiving the three refuges, in the Buddha, Dharma, and Saṅgha; (2) 信| belief, or the faith-root; (3) 信法| belief in the four truths; (4) 內凡夫| ordinary disciples who observe the 五停心觀, etc.; (5) 學信戒 those who pursue the 三學 three studies; (6) 八人 (i.e. 忍) | the stage of 見道 seeing the true Way; (7) 須陀洹| śrota-āpanna, now definitely in the stream and assured of nirvāṇa; (8) 斯陀含| sakṛdāgāmin, only one more rebirth; (9) 阿那含| anāgāmin, no rebirth; and (10) 阿羅漢| arhatship. IV. The ten stages of the pratyekabuddha 緣覺乘|| are (1) perfect asceticism; (2)

mastery of the twelve links of causation; (3) of the four noble truths; (4) of the deeper knowledge; (5) of the eightfold noble path; (6) of the three realms 三法界; (7) of the nirvāṇa state; (8) of the six supernatural powers; (9) arrival at the intuitive stage; (10) mastery of the remaining influence of former habits. V. 佛乘||The ten stages, or characteristics of a Buddha, are those of the sovereign or perfect attainment of wisdom, exposition, discrimination, māra-subjugation, suppression of evil, the six transcendent faculties, manifestation of all bodhisattva enlightenment, powers of prediction, of adaptability, of powers to reveal the bodhisattva Truth. VI. The Shingon has its own elaborate ten stages, and also a group 十地十心, see 十心; and there are other groups. ||品 The twenty-second chapter of the sixty-chapter version of the 華嚴經, the twenty-sixth of the eighty-chapter version. ||願行 The vow of bodhisattvas to attain the 十地 by fulfilling the ten pāramitās, v. 十波. ||心 Ten stages of mind, or mental development, i.e. (1) 四無量心 the four kinds of boundless mind; (2) 十善心 the mind of the ten good qualities; (3) 明光心 the illuminated mind; (4) 焰慧心 the mind of glowing wisdom; (5) 大勝心 the mind of mastery; (6) 現前心 the mind of the open way (above normal definitions); (7) 無生心 the mind of no rebirth; (8) 不思議心 the mind of the inexpressible; (9) 慧光心 the mind of wisdom-radiance; (10) 受位心 the mind of perfect receptivity. v. also 十心.

十境 Ten objects of or stages in meditation 觀 in the T'ien-t'ai school, i.e. 陰| the five skandhas; 煩惱| life's distresses and delusion; 病患| sickness, or duḥkha, its cause and cure; 業相| age-long karmaic influences; 魔事| Māra affairs, how to overthrow their rule; 禪定| the conditions of dhyāna and samādhi; 諸見| various views and doubts that arise; 慢| pride in progress and the delusion that one has attained nirvāṇa; 二乘| temptation to be content with the lower nirvāṇa, instead of going on to the greater reward; 菩薩| bodhisattvahood; see the 止觀 5.

十夜(念佛) The ten nights (and days) from the sixth to the fifteenth of the tenth moon, when the Pure-land sect intones sūtras.

十大弟子 The ten chief disciples of Śākyamuni, each of whom was master of one power or gift. Śāriputra of wisdom; Maudgalyāyana of supernatural powers; Mahākāśyapa of discipline; Aniruddha of 天眼 deva vision; Subhūti of explaining the void or immaterial; Pūrṇa of expounding the law; Kātyāyana of its fundamental principles; Upāli of maintaining the rules; Rāhula of the esoteric; and Ānanda of hearing and remembering. ||惑 idem 十使. ||願 The ten vows of P'u Hsien 普賢, or Samantabhadra.

十如(是) The ten essential qualities, or characteristics, of a thing, according to the 方便 chapter of the Lotus sūtra: 相如 form; 性| nature; 體| corpus or embodiment; 力| powers; 作| function; 因| primary cause; 緣| environmental cause; 果| effect; 報| karmaic reward; 本末究竟等 the inseparability, or inevitability of them all.

十如來地 v. 十地.

十妙 The ten wonders, or incomprehensibles; there are two groups, the 迹 traceable or manifested and 本門 the fundamental. The 迹門|| are the wonder of: (1) 境妙 the universe, sphere, or whole, embracing mind, Buddha, and all things as a unity; (2) 智| a Buddha's all-embracing knowledge arising from such universe; (3) 行| his deeds, expressive of his wisdom; (4) 位| his attainment of all the various Buddha stages, i.e. 十住 and 十地; (5) 三法| his three laws of 理, 慧, and 定 truth, wisdom, and vision; (6) 感應| his response to appeal, i.e. his (spiritual) response or relation to humanity, for "all beings are my children"; (7) 神通| his supernatural powers; (8) 說法| his preaching; (9) 眷屬| his supernatural retinue; (10) 利益| the blessings derived through universal elevation into Buddhahood. The 本門|| are the wonder of (1) 本因 the initial impulse or causative stage of Buddhahood; (2) 本果| its fruit or result in eternity, joy, and purity; (3) 國土| his (Buddha) realm; (4) 感應| his response (to human needs); (5) 神通| his supernatural powers; (6) 說法| his preaching; (7) 眷屬| his supernatural retinue; (8) 涅槃| his nirvāṇa; (9) 壽命| his (eternal) life; (10) his blessings as above. Both groups are further defined as progressive stages in a Buddha's career. These "wonders" are derived from the Lotus sūtra.

十宗 The ten schools of Chinese Buddhism: I. The (1) 律| Vinaya-discipline, or 南山|; (2) 俱舍 Kośa, Abhidharma, or Reality (Sarvāstivādin) 有|; (3) 成實| Satya-siddhi sect founded on this śāstra by Harivarman; (4) 三論| Mādhyamika or 性空|; (5) 法華| Lotus, "Law-flower" or T'ien-t'ai 天台|; (6) 華嚴| Hua-yen or 法性 or 賢首|; (7) 法相| Dharmalakṣaṇa or 慈恩| founded on the 唯識論; (8) 心| Ch'an or Zen, mind-only or intuitive, v. 禪 |; (9) 眞言 | (Jap. Shingon) or esoteric 密 |; (10) 蓮 | Amitābha-lotus or Pure Land (Jap. Jōdo) 淨土 |. The 2nd, 3rd, 4th, and 9th are found in Japan rather than in China, where they have ceased to be of importance. II. The Hua-yen has also ten divisions into ten schools of thought: (1) 我法俱有 the reality of self (or soul) and things, e.g. mind and matter; (2) 法有我無 the reality of things but not of soul; (3) 法無去來 things have neither creation nor destruction; (4) 現通假實 present things are both apparent and real; (5) 俗妄眞實 common or phenomenal ideas are wrong, fundamental reality is the only truth; (6) things are merely names; (7) all things are unreal 空; (8) the bhūtatathatā is not unreal; (9) phenomena and their perception are to be got rid of; (10) the perfect, all-inclusive, and complete teaching of the One Vehicle. III. There are two old Japanese divisions: 大乘律宗, 俱舍 |, 成實 |, 法相 |, 三論 |, 天台 |, 華嚴 |, 眞言 |, 小乘律 |, and 淨土 |; the second list adds 禪 | and omits 大乘律宗. They are the Ritsu, Kusha, Jōjitsu, Hossō, Sanron, Tendai, Kegon, Shingon, (Hīnayāna) Ritsu, and Jōdo; the addition being Zen.

十寶 The ten precious things; 十寶山 the ten precious mountains, or mountain of ten precious things; v. 十善 and 十善王.

十山王 The spirit king of each of the ten mountains—Himālaya, Gandhamādana, Vaidharī, 神仙山, Yugaṁdhara, Aśvakarṇa, Nemindhara, Cakravāḍa, Ketumatī, and Sumeru.

十師 The ten monks necessary for a full ordination of a monk, i.e. 三師七證 three leaders and seven witnesses.

十度 The ten pāramitās or virtues transporting to nirvāṇa; idem 十波羅蜜 q.v. | | 三行 each of the pāramitās has three forms of observance, e.g. the first, 施 dāna or giving has 財施 alms-giving, 法施 truth-giving, and 無畏施 courage-giving. The three forms differ with each pāramitā.

十弟子 The ten acolytes or attendants on an ācārya, or superior religious teacher, in his ceremonial offices, following the pattern of the ten principal disciples of Śākyamuni.

十德 The ten virtues, powers, or qualities, of which there are several groups, e.g. in the 華嚴經十地品 there are 法師十德 the ten virtues of a teacher of the Law, i.e. he should be well versed in its meaning; able widely to publish it; not be nervous before an audience; be untiring in argument; adaptable; orderly so that his teaching can be easily followed; serious and dignified; bold and zealous; unwearied; and enduring (able to bear insult, etc.). The 弟子十德 ten virtues or qualities of a disciple according to the 大日經疏 4, are faith; sincerity; devotion to the trikāya; (seeking the) adornment of true wisdom; perseverance; moral purity; patience (or bearing shame); generosity in giving; courage; resoluteness.

十心 The ten kinds of heart or mind; there are three groups. One is from the 止觀 4, minds ignorant and dark; affected by evil companions; not following the good; doing evil in thought, word, deed; spreading evil abroad; unceasingly wicked; secret sin; open crime; utterly shameless; denying cause and effect (retribution)—all such must remain in the flow 流 of reincarnation. The second group (from the same book) is the 逆流 the mind striving against the stream of perpetual reincarnation; it shows itself in devout faith, shame (for sin), fear (of wrong-doing), repentance and confession, reform, bodhi (i.e. the bodhisattva mind), doing good, maintaining the right law, thinking on all the Buddhas, meditating on the void (or, the unreality of sin). The third is the 眞言 group from the 大日經疏 3; the "seed" heart (i.e. the original good desire), the sprout (under Buddhist religious influence), the bud, leaf, flower, fruit, its serviceableness; the child-heart, the discriminating heart, the heart of settled judgment (or resolve).

十快 The ten inexpressible joys of the Pure-land; also 十樂.

十念 The ten repetitions of an invocation, e.g. Namo Amitābha. | | 往生 These ten invocations will carry a dying man with an evil karma into the Pure-land. | | 成就 Similar to the last, but cf. 十聲. | | 處 A bodhisattva's ten objects of thought or meditation, i.e. body, the senses, mind, things, environment, monastery, city (or district), good name, Buddha-learning, riddance of all passion and delusion. | | 血脉 The arteries of the "ten invocations", i.e. the teacher's giving and the disciple's receiving of the law.

十忿怒明王 The ten irate rājas, or protectors, whose huge images with many heads and limbs are seen in temples; perhaps the ten krodha gods of the Tibetans (Khro-bo); their names are 焰鬘得迦 Yamāntaka; 無能勝 Ajita; 鉢納

鬘得迦 ? Padmāntaka; 尾覲那得迦 Vighnāntaka; 不動尊 Acala; 吒枳 ? Ḍākinī; 㑩羅難拏 ? Nīladaṇḍa; 大力, 逡婆 Śambara; and 縛日羅播多羅 Vīrabhadra.

十恩 Ten kinds of the Buddha's grace: his (1) initial resolve to universalize (his salvation); (2) self-sacrifice (in previous lives); (3) complete altruism; (4) his descent into all the six states of existence for their salvation; (5) relief of the living from distress and mortality; (6) profound pity; (7) revelation of himself in human and glorified form; (8) teaching in accordance with the capacity of his hearers, first hīnayāna, then mahāyāna doctrine; (9) revealing his nirvāṇa to stimulate his disciples; (10) pitying thought for all creatures, in that dying at 80 instead of at 100 he left twenty years of his own happiness to his disciples; and also the tripiṭaka for universal salvation.

十惑 idem 十使.

十悪 Daśākuśala. The ten "not right" or evil things are killing, stealing, adultery, lying, double-tongue, coarse language, filthy language, covetousness, anger, perverted views; these produce the ten resultant evils | | 業 (道). Cf. 十善; 十戒.

十惱亂 The ten disturbers of the religious life: a domineering (spirit); heretical ways; dangerous amusements; a butcher's or other low occupation; asceticism (or selfish hīnayāna salvation); (the condition of a) eunuch; lust; endangering (the character by improper intimacy); contempt; breeding animals, etc. (for slaughter).

十成 Entirely completed, perfect.

十戒 Śikṣāpada. The ten prohibitions (in Pāli form) consist of five commandments for the layman: (1) not to destroy life 不殺生 pāṇātipātāveramaṇi; (2) not to steal 不偸盜 adinnādānāver.; (3) not to commit adultery 不婬慾 abrahmacaryāver.; (4) not to lie 不妄語 musāvādāver.; (5) not to take intoxicating liquor 不飲酒 suramereyya-majjapamādaṭṭhānāver. Eight special commandments for laymen consist of the preceding five plus: (6) not to eat food out of regulated hours 不非時食 vikāla-bhojanāver.; (7) not to use garlands or perfumes 不著華鬘好香塗身 mālā-gandha-vilepana-dhāraṇa-maṇḍana-vibhūṣanaṭṭhānā; (8) not to sleep on high or broad beds (chastity) 不坐高廣大牀 uccāsayanā-mahāsayanā. The ten commandments for the monk are the preceding eight plus: (9) not to take part in singing, dancing, musical or theatrical performances, not to see or listen to such 不歌舞倡伎不往觀聽 nacca-gīta-vādita-visūkadassanāver.; (10) to refrain from acquiring uncoined or coined gold, or silver, or jewels 不得捉錢金銀寶物 jātarūpa-rajata-paṭiggahaṇāver. Under the Mahāyāna these ten commands for the monk were changed, to accord with the new environment of the monk, to the following: not to kill, not to steal, to avoid all unchastity, not to lie, not to slander, not to insult, not to chatter, not to covet, not to give way to anger, to harbour no scepticism.

十支論 The ten Yoga books, the foundation work being the 瑜伽 |, the other ten are 百法 |, 五蘊 |, 顯揚 |, 攝大乘 |, 雜集 |, 辨中邊 |, 二十唯識 |, 三十唯識 |, 大莊嚴 |, and 分別瑜伽 |.

十教 v. 十宗.

十方 The ten directions of space, i.e. the eight points of the compass and the nadir and zenith. There is a Buddha for each direction 十方十佛. | | 世界 The worlds in all directions. | | 佛土 A Buddha-realm, idem 大千世界. | | 常住僧物; | | 現前僧物 see 四種僧物.

十普門 The ten universals of a bodhisattva: 慈悲普 universal pity; 弘誓 | vow of universal salvation; 修行 | accordant action; 斷惑 | universal cutting off of delusions; 入法門 | freedom of entry into all forms of truth; 神通 | universal superhuman powers; 方便 | universal accordance with conditions of the receptivity of others; 說法 | powers of universal explication of the truth; 供養諸佛 | power of universal service of all Buddhas; 成就衆生 | the perfecting of all beings universally.

十智 The ten forms of understanding. I. Hīnayāna: (1) 世俗智 common understanding; (2) 法 | enlightened understanding, i.e. on the Four Truths in this life; (3) 類 | ditto, applied to the two upper realms 上二界; (4), (5), (6), (7) understanding *re* each of the Four Truths separately, both in the upper and lower realms, e.g. 苦智; (8) 他心 | understanding of the minds of others; (9) 盡 | the understanding that puts an end to all previous faith in or for self, i.e. 自信智; (10) 無生 | nirvāṇa wisdom; v. 俱舍論 26. II.

Mahāyāna. A Tathāgata's ten powers of understanding or wisdom: (1) 三世 | perfect understanding of past, present, and future; (2) ditto of Buddha Law; (3) 法界無礙 | unimpeded understanding of the whole Buddha-realm; (4) 法界無邊 | unlimited, or infinite ditto; (5) 充滿一切 | of ubiquity; (6) 普照一切世間 | of universal enlightenment; (7) 住持一切世界 | of omnipotence, or universal control; (8) 知一切衆生 | of omniscience *re* all living beings; (9) 知一切法 | of omniscience *re* the laws of universal salvation; (10) 知無邊諸佛 | of omniscience *re* all Buddha wisdom. v. 華嚴經 16. There are also his ten forms of understanding of the "Five Seas" 五海 of worlds, living beings, karma, passions, and Buddhas.

十根本煩惱 idem 十使.

十樂 v. 十快.

十殊勝語 The ten rare or surpassing terms connected with the ten surpassing laws; they are given in Hsüan-tsang's translation of Vasubandhu's 攝論釋.

十殿閻王 The ten Yama courts, cf. 十王.

十法 The ten 成就 perfect or perfecting Mahāyāna rules; i.e. in (1) right belief; (2) conduct; (3) spirit; (4) the joy of the bodhi mind; (5) joy in the dharma; (6) joy in meditation in it; (7) pursuing the correct dharma; (8) obedience to, or accordance with it; (9) departing from pride, etc.; (10) comprehending the inner teaching of Buddha and taking no pleasure in that of the śrāvaka and pratyeka-buddha order. | | 界 The ten dharma-worlds, or states of existence, i.e. the hells (or purgatories), pretas, animals, asuras, men, devas, śrāvakas, pratyeka-buddhas, bodhisattvas, Buddhas. In the esoteric teaching there is a series of hells, pretas, animals, asuras, men, devas, śrāvakas, bodhisattvas, 權佛 relative Buddhas, 實佛 absolute Buddhas. | | 行 Ten ways of devotion to the Buddhist sūtras: to copy them; serve the places where they are kept, as if serving the Buddha's shrine; preach or give them to others; listen attentively to their exposition; read; maintain; discourse on them to others; intone them; ponder over them; observe their lessons.

十波羅夷 The ten pārājikas, or sins unpardonable in a monk involving his exclusion from the community; v. 十重禁戒. | | | 蜜 (or 密多) The ten are the six pāramitās with four added. The six are charity (or almsgiving), purity (or morality), patience, zealous progress, meditation, wisdom; i.e. 施, 戒, 忍辱, 精進, 禪, 慧. The four additions are 方便; 願; 力 and 智 upāya, adaptability (or, teaching as suited to the occasion and hearer); praṇidhāna, vows; bala, force of purpose; and jñāna, knowledge. Also 十度.

十無二 Ten powers only possessed by Buddhas: (1) prediction; (2) knowing and fulfilling the desires of the living; (3)–(10) are various forms of omniscience, i.e. (3) of all Buddha-realms and their inhabitants; (4) their natures; (5) good roots; (6) laws; (7) wisdom; (8) every moment; (9) evolving domains, or conditions; (10) language, words, and discussions. v. 宗鏡錄 99. | | 盡戒 idem | 重(禁) |. | | 盡藏 The ten boundless treasuries of a bodhisattva: (1) 信 belief and faith; (2) 戒 the commandments; (3) 慚 shame of past misdeeds; (4) 愧 blushing over the misdeeds of others; (5) hearing and knowledge of the truth; (6) giving; (7) wisdom; (8) memory; (9) keeping and guarding the sūtras; (10) powers of expounding them. 華嚴經 20. | | 礙 The ten unhindered transformations and ubiquitous powers of a Buddha.

十牛圖(序) The ten ox-pictures, the first, a man looking for an ox, then seeing its tracks, then seeing the ox, catching it, feeding it, riding it home, ox dies man lives, both dead, return whence they came, and enter the dust.

十玄(緣起); 十玄門 The ten philosophic ideas expressed in two metrical versions, each line ending with 門. v. 玄門.

十王 The ten kings presiding over the ten departments of purgatory.

十甘露王 The king of the ten sweet dews, i.e. Amitābha.

十界 idem 十法界. | | 皆成佛 The teaching of the Lotus sūtra of universalism, that all become Buddha. | | 能化菩薩 Bodhisattvas, above the 初地, who have reached the stage of transforming beings in all the ten kinds of realms.

十發趣心 The ten directional decisions: (1) renouncement of the world; (2) observance of the commandments; (3) patience or endurance; (4) zealous progress; (5) meditation; (6) wisdom or understanding; (7) 願心 the will for good for oneself and others; (8) 護 | protection (of Buddha, Dharma, Saṅgha); (9) 喜 | joy; (10) 頂 | highest wisdom. v. 梵網經心地品.

十眞如 The ten aspects of the bhūtatathatā or reality attained by a bodhisattva during his fifty-two stages of development, cf. 十地 and 十障, each of which is associated with one of these *chên-ju*: (1) 遍行 | | the universality of the *chên-ju*; (2) 最勝 | | its superiority over all else; (3) 勝流 | | its ubiquity; (4) 無攝受 | | its independence or self-containedness; (5) 無別 | | subjective indifferentiation; (6) 無染淨 | | above differences of impurity and purity; (7) 法無別 | | objective indifferentiation; (8) 不增減 | | invariable, i.e. can be neither added to nor taken from; (9) 智自在所依 the basis of all wisdom; (10) 業自在等所依 | | and of all power. The above are the 別教 group from the 唯識論 10. Another group, of the 圓教, is the same as the 十如是 q.v.

十眼 The ten kinds of eyes: (1) 肉眼 eyes of flesh; (2) 天 | deva eyes; (3) 慧 | wisdom eyes; (4) 法 | dharma eyes; (5) 佛 | Buddha eyes; (6) 智 | eyes of judgment; (7) 光明 | eyes shining with Buddha-light; (8) 出生死 | immortal eyes; (9) 無碍 | unhindered eyes; (10) 一切智 | omniscient eyes.

十禪支 v. 十一切處.

十科; 十條 The ten rules for translation. v. 翻譯名義集 3.

十種不淨 The deluded, e.g. the hīnayānists, because of their refusal to follow the higher truth, remain in the condition of reincarnation and are impure in ten ways: in body, mouth, mind, deed, state, sitting, sleeping, practice, converting others, their expectations. | | 所觀法 Ten meditations on each of the 十住, 十行, 十廻向, 十地 and 等覺. | | 方便 Ten kinds of suitable aids to religious success: almsgiving (or self-sacrifice); keeping the commandments; forbearance; zealous progress; meditation; wisdom; great kindness; great pity; awaking and stimulating others; preaching (or revolving) the never receding wheel of the Law. | | 智力 The ten kinds of wisdom and power, v. 十智 and 十力. | | 智明 Ten kinds of bodhisattva wisdom, or omniscience, for the understanding of all things relating to all beings, in order to save them from the sufferings of mortality and bring them to true bodhi. The ten are detailed in the Hua-yen 華嚴 sūtra in two groups, one in the 十明品 and one in the 離世間品. | | 行願 The ten vows of P'u Hsien 普賢. | | 觀法 idem 十乘觀法. | | 魔軍 idem 十軍.

十緣生句 Ten illusions arising from environmental conditions: sleight of hand; mirage; dreams; reflections or shadows; gandharva cities (or cities of the sirens, seen in the sea-mist); echoes; the moon reflected in water; floating bubbles; motes (*muscæ volitantes*); fire-wheel (made by revolving a flare). | | 觀; 十喩觀 A meditation, or reflection on these ten illusions.

十纏 The ten bonds that bind men to mortality —to be shameless, unblushing, envious, mean, regretful, torpid, busy, absorbed, angry, secretive (of sin).

十羅刹女 The ten rākṣasī, or demonesses mentioned in the Lotus Sūtra 陀羅尼品. They are now represented in the temples, each as an attendant on a Buddha or bodhisattva, and are chiefly connected with sorcery. They are said to be previous incarnations of the Buddhas and bodhisattvas with whom they are associated. In their evil state they were enemies of the living, converted they are enemies of evil. There are other definitions. Their names are: (1) 藍婆 Lambā, who is associated with Śākyamuni; (2) 毘藍婆 Vilambā, ditto with Amitābha; (3) 曲齒 Kūṭadantī, with 藥師 Bhaiṣajya; (4) 華齒 Puṣpadantī, with 多寳 Prabhūtaratna; (5) 黑齒 Makuṭadantī, with 大日 Vairocana; (6) 多髮 Keśinī, with 普賢 Samantabhadra; (7) 無厭足 ? Acalā, with 文殊 Mañjuśrī; (8) 持瓔珞 Mālādharī, with 彌勒 Maitreya; (9) 皐帝 Kuntī, with 觀音 Avalokiteśvara; (10) 奪一切衆生精氣 Sarvasattvaujohārī, with 地藏 Kṣitigarbha.

十萬 A lakh, i.e. an 億 or 洛叉. | | 億佛土 The Happy Land i.e. Amitābha's Paradise in the West, beyond ten thousand million Buddha-realms.

十號 Ten titles of a Buddha: 如來 Tathāgata; 應供 Arhat; 正徧知 Samyak-saṁbuddha; 明行足 Vidyācaraṇa-sampanna; 善逝 Sugata; 世間解 Lokavid; 無上士 Anuttara; 調御丈夫 Puruṣa-damya-sārathi; 天人師 Śāstā deva-manuṣyāṇām; 佛世尊 Buddha-lokanātha, or Bhagavān.

十 行 The ten necessary activities in the fifty-two stages of a bodhisattva, following on the 十 信 and 十 住; the two latter indicate personal development 自 利. These ten lines of action are for the universal welfare of others 利 他. They are: joyful service; beneficial service; never resenting; without limit; never out of order; appearing in any form at will; unimpeded; exalting the pāramitās amongst all beings; perfecting the Buddha-law by complete virtue; manifesting in all things the pure, final, true reality.

十 見 The ten (wrong) views; see 五 | and add 貪, 恚, 慢, 無 明 and 疑 見 desire, hate, pride, ignorance, and doubt.

十 誡 idem 十 戒.

十 護 The ten guardians of the law, assistants to the 十 大 明 王.

十 身 Ten aspects of the Buddhakāya 佛 身 q.v.

十 軍 The ten armies of Māra, which the Buddha attacks and destroys; the armies are desire, anxiety, hunger and thirst, longing, torpidity, fear, doubt, poison, gain, haughtiness (i.e. disdaining monks).

十 輪 idem | 種 智 力; v. 十 力.

十 通 Ten supernatural powers, e.g. of seeing, hearing, appearance, etc.; cf. 五 神 通.

十 進 九 退 The Buddha's teaching is so difficult that of ten who enter it nine fall away.

十 道 The ten (good) ways for deliverance from mortality—not to kill, steal, act wrongly, lie, be double-tongued, be of evil speech, slander, covet, be angry, look wrongly (or wrong views).

十 過 Ten faults in eating flesh, and ten in drinking intoxicants.

十 遍 處 定 v. 十 一 切 處.

十 重 (禁) 戒 The ten pārājika, or a monk's most serious sins; also 十 波 羅 夷; 波 羅 闍 巳 迦. They are killing, stealing, adultery, lying, selling wine, talking of a monk's misdeeds, self-praise for degrading others, meanness, anger at rebuke, vilifying the Triratna. The esoteric sect has a group in regard to giving up the mind of enlightenment, renouncing the Triratna and going to heretical sects, slandering the Triratna, etc. Another group of ten is in the 大 日 經 9 and 17; cf. 十 波 羅 夷.

十 重 罪 idem 十 惡, 十 不 善.

十 重 障 The ten weighty bodhisattva hindrances, according to the 別 敎, which are respectively overcome by entry into the 十 地; v. 成 唯 識 論 9; the first is 異 生 性 the natural heart hindering the 聖 性 holy heart, etc.; v. 十 障.

十 金 剛 心 Ten characteristics of the "diamond heart" as developed by a bodhisattva: (1) complete insight into all truth; (2) saving of all creatures; (3) the glorifying of all Buddha-worlds; (4) supererogation of his good deeds; (5) service of all Buddhas; (6) realization of the truth of all Buddha-laws; (7) manifestation of all patience and endurance; (8) unflagging devotion to his vocation; (9) perfection of his work; (10) aiding all to fulfil their vows and accomplish their spiritual ends. 華 嚴 經 55. | | | | 向 果 Ten "fruits" that accrue to the resolute "diamond-heart" of a bodhisattva: faith; meditation; reflection on the doctrine; thoroughness in contemplation; straightforward progress to Buddhahood; no retrogression; the Mahāyāna spirit (of universal salvation); freedom from externals (or impressions); wisdom; firm establishment; v. 梵 網 經 心 地 品.

十 長 養 心 The ten kinds of well-nourished heart, essential to entry into the cult of the higher patience and endurance: a heart of kindness; of pity; of joy (in progress toward salvation of others); renunciation; almsgiving; delight in telling the doctrine; benefiting or aiding others to salvation; unity, or amity; concentration in meditation; wisdom; v. 梵 網 經 心 地 品.

十 門 The ten "doors" or connections between 事 and 理; 事 is defined as 現 象 form and 理 as 本 體 substance; the common illustration of wave and water indicates the idea thus expressed. The 理 事 無 礙 十 門 means that in ten ways form and substance are not separate, unconnected entities. (1) *li* the substance is always present with *shih* the phenomena; (2) *shih* is always present with *li*; (3) *shih* depends on *li* for its existence; (4) the *shih* can reveal the *li*; (5) the *shih* (mere form, which is unreal) can disappear in the *li*; (6) the *shih* can conceal the *li*; (7) the true *li* is the *shih*; (8) the *shih* is *li*; (9) the true *li* (or reality) is not the *shih*; (10) the *shih* is not the (whole) *li*; v. 華嚴大疏 2. 周遍含容觀十門 The fifth of the five 觀 meditations of the 華嚴宗, i.e. on *li* and *shih*, e.g. (1) the *li* is as the *shih*; (2) the *shih* is as the *li*; 理如事, 事如理 and so on. The 止觀十門 in the 宗鏡錄 35, also deals with *li* and *shih* chiefly for purposes of meditation. Another group, the 華嚴釋經十門, treats of the Canon and the schools.

十障 Ten hindrances; bodhisattvas in the stage of 十地 overcome these ten hindrances and realize the 十眞如 q.v. The hindrances are: (1) 異生性 | the common illusions of the unenlightened, taking the seeming for real; (2) 邪行 | common unenlightened conduct; (3) 暗鈍 | ignorant and dull ideas; (4) 細惑現行 | the illusion that things are real and have independent existence; (5) 下乘涅槃 | the lower ideals in Hīnayāna of nirvāṇa; (6) 粗相現行 | the ordinary ideas of the pure and impure; (7) 細相現行 | the idea of reincarnation; (8) 無相加行 | the continuance of activity even in the formless world; (9) 不欲行 | no desire to act for the salvation of others; (10) 法未自在 | non-attainment of complete mastery of all things. v. 唯識論 10.

十願王 The king of the ten vows, P'u Hsien 普賢, or Samantabhadra.

十齋(日) The ten "fast" days of a month are 1, 8, 14, 15, 18, 23, 24, 28, 29, and 30. In certain periods flesh was forbidden on these days, also all killing, hunting, fishing, executions, etc. | | (|) 佛 The ten Buddhas or bodhisattvas connected with these days who in turn are 定光, 藥師, 普賢, 阿彌陀, 觀音, 勢至, 地藏, 毘盧遮那, 藥王, 釋迦.

卜 To divine, foretell.

卜羯娑 Pukkaśa; also 補 | | A degraded caste of sweepers, or scavengers, and bearers of corpses.

3. THREE STROKES

丈 Ten feet; an elder; a wife's parents; a husband. | 六 Sixteen "feet", the normal height of a Buddha in his "transformation body" 化身 nirmāṇa-kāya; said to be the height of the Buddha when he was on earth. | | 金身 Ditto; also a metal or golden image of the Buddha 16 feet high mentioned in the 北史 Northern History. | 夫 A virile, zealous disciple, a man who presses forward unceasingly. | | 志幹 A firm-willed man, especially used of a bodhisattva who dauntlessly presses forward. | | 國 The country of virile men, Puruṣapura 富婁沙富羅, ancient capital of Gandhāra, the modern Peshawar; birthplace of 天親 Vasubandhu.

下 Hīna, adhara. Below, lower, inferior, low; to descend, let down, put down.

下三途 The three lower paths of the six destinations (gati) 六道, i.e. beings in hell, pretas, and animals.

下乘 The lower yāna, i.e. Hīnayāna; likened to an old worn-out horse. To alight from (a vehicle, horse, etc.).

下八地 The regions in the nine divisions of the trailokya below the 無所有處地 of the arūpadhātu, v. 九地.

下劣乘 The inferior, mean yāna, a scornful term for Hīnayāna.

下化(衆生) Below, to transform all beings, one of the great vows of a bodhisattva. 上求菩提 above, to seek bodhi. Also 下濟衆生.

下口食 One of the 四邪命食 four heterodox means of living, i.e. for a monk to earn his livelihood by bending down to cultivate the land, collect herbs, etc.; opposite of 仰口食, i.e. making a heterodox living by looking up, as in astrology, fortune-telling, etc. 智度論 3.

下品 The three lowest of the nine classes born

in the Amitābha Pure Land, v. 無量壽經. These three lowest grades are (1) | | 上生 The highest of the three lowest classes who enter the Pure Land of Amitābha, i.e. those who have committed all sins except dishonouring the sūtras. If at the end of life the sinner clasps hands and says "Namo Amitābha", such a one will be born in His precious lake. (2) | | 中生 The middle class consists of those who have broken all the commandments, even stolen from monks and abused the law. If at death such a one hears of the great power of Amitābha, and assents with but a thought, he will be received into paradise. (3) | | 下生 The lowest class, because of their sins, should have fallen into the lowest gati, but by invoking the name of Amitābha, they can escape countless ages of reincarnation and suffering and on dying will behold a lotus flower like the sun, and, by the response of a single thought, will enter the Pure Land of Amitābha.

下地 The lower regions of the 九地 q.v.; also the lower half of the 十地 in the fifty-two grades of bodhisattva development. | | 麤苦障 To see the lower grade out of which one has migrated, as rough, wretched, and a hindrance; a brahman form of meditation.

下堂 To descend from the hall, especially after the morning congee.

下塵 The lower gati, the hells, hungry ghosts, animals.

下根 Those (born) with base character, or of low capacity.

下棒 To lay on the cudgel, beat; syn. for the 德山 Tê Shan monastery, whose Ch'an sect abbot instilled intelligence with his staff.

下火; 下炬 To apply the torch; syn. for setting alight the funeral pyre of a monk.

下生經 idem 彌勒下生經.

下界 The lower, or human world 人界.

下種 To sow the seed; to preach, or teach. T'ien-t'ai defines three periods: (1) 種 when the seed of Buddha's teaching is sown in the heart; (2) 熟 when it ripens; (3) 脫 when it is stripped or harvested, i.e when one abandons all things.

下蠟 Inferior candles. The 上 and 下 | superior and inferior candles are senior and junior monks; those of longer and shorter service; but see 上臈.

下衆 The seven lower orders of disciples, who with the monks and nuns in full orders make the 九衆.

下衣 The lowest order of a monk's robes, that of five patches; lower garments.

下語 To give instruction; to state a case (as at law).

下輩觀 A meditation of the Amitābha sect on the 下品 q.v.; it is the last of sixteen contemplations, and deals with those who have committed the five rebellious acts 五逆 and the ten evils 十惡, but who still can obtain salvation; v. 無量壽經. | | 下生觀 idem.

下轉 The downward turn, in transmigration. Primal ignorance or unenlightenment 無明 acting against the primal, true, or Buddha-nature causes transmigration. The opposite is 上轉 when the good prevails over the evil. 下轉 is sometimes used for 下化 to save those below.

下間 The inferior rooms of a monastery, on the left as one enters.

上 Uttara 嗢呾羅; above, upper, superior; on; former. To ascend, offer to a superior.

上中下法 The three dharmas, systems, or vehicles, 菩薩, 緣覺, and 聲聞 bodhisattva, pratyeka-buddha, and śrāvaka.

上乘 Mahāyāna; also 上衍, 大乘 q.v. | | 密宗 The Mahāyāna esoteric school, especially the 眞言 Shingon. | | 瑜伽 Mahāyāna-yoga, chiefly associated with the last. | | 禪 The Mahāyāna Ch'an (Zen) School, which considers that it alone attains the highest realization of Mahāyāna truth. Hīnayāna philosophy is said only to realize the unreality of the ego and not the unreality of all things. The Mahāyāna realizes the unreality of the ego and of all things. But the Ch'an school is pure idealism, all being mind. This mind is Buddha, and is the universal fundamental mind.

上元燒燈 The lantern festival at the first full moon of the year.

上人 A man of superior wisdom, virtue, and conduct, a term applied to monks during the T'ang dynasty. 上上人 A term used in the Pure-land sect for a worshipper of Amitābha.

上供 To offer up an offering to Buddha, or to ancestors.

上品 Superior order, grade, or class. 丨丨上生; 丨丨中生; 丨丨下生 The three highest of the nine stages of birth in the Pure Land, v. 中, 下 and 九品. 丨丨蓮臺 The highest stages in the Pure Land where the best appear as lotus flowers on the pool of the seven precious things; when the lotuses open they are transformed into beings of the Pure Land.

上堂 To go into the hall to expound the doctrine; to go to a temple for the purpose of worship, or bearing presents to the monks; to go to the refectory for meals. 丨丨牌 The tablet announcing the time of worship at a temple or monastery.

上士 The superior disciple, who becomes perfect in (spiritually) profiting himself and others. The 中士 profits self but not others; the 下士 neither.

上座 Sthavira; or Mahāsthavira. Old man, or elder; head monk, president, or abbot; the first Buddhist fathers; a title of Mahākāśyapa; also of monks of twenty to forty-nine years standing, as 中座 are from ten to nineteen and 下座 under ten. The 釋氏要覽 divides presiding elders into four classes, those presiding over monasteries, over assemblies of monks, over sects, and laymen presiding over feasts to monks. 丨丨部; 他毘梨輿部; 他鞞羅部 Sthavirāḥ; Sthaviranikāya; or Āryasthāvirāḥ. The school of the presiding elder, or elders. The two earliest sections of Buddhism were this (which developed into the Mahāsthavirāḥ) and the Mahāsāṅghikāḥ or 大衆部. At first they were not considered to be different schools, the 上座部 merely representing the intimate and older disciples of Śākyamuni and the 大衆 being the rest. It is said that a century later under Mahādeva 大天 a difference of opinion arose on certain doctrines. Three divisions are named as resulting, viz. Mahāvihāravāsinaḥ, Jetavanīyāḥ, and Abhayagiri-vāsinaḥ. These were in Ceylon. In course of time the eighteen Hīnayāna sects were developed. From the time of Aśoka four principal schools are counted as prevailing: Mahāsāṅghika, Sthavira, Mūlasarvāstivāda, and Saṁmitīya. The following is a list of the eleven sects reckoned as of the 上座部: 說一切有部; 雪山; 犢子; 法上; 賢胄; 正量; 密林山; 化地; 法藏; 飲光; and 經量部. The Sthaviravādin is reputed as nearest to early Buddhism in its tenets, though it is said to have changed the basis of Buddhism from an agnostic system to a realistic philosophy.

上方; 上手 An abbot. 上方 originally meant a mountain monastery.

上根 A man of superior character or capacity, e.g. with superior organs of sight, hearing, etc.

上求本來 Similar to the first half of 上求菩提下化衆生 Above to seek bodhi, below to save all. 本來 means the original or Buddha-nature, which is the real nature of all beings.

上流(般) Ūrdhvasrotas. The flow upwards, or to go upwards against the stream of transmigration to parinirvāṇa. Also 丨丨般涅槃.

上煩惱 The severe fundamental trials arising out of the ten great delusions; also the trials or distresses of present delusions.

上界天 The devas of the regions of form and formlessness. v. 色.

上祭 To place offerings on an altar; also 下祭.

上綱 The "higher bond" or superior, the 上座 or Sthavira, among the three directors of a monastery. v. 三綱.

上著衣 A monk's outer robe, uttarā saṁghāṭī, worn over the shirt or antara-vāsaka.

上肩 Upper shoulder, i.e. the left or superior; one worthy of respect. 丨丨順轉 Circumambulation with the superior shoulder to the image; the left was formerly considered the superior side; but this is uncertain.

上臘 The "la" is the end of a summer's retreat, which ends the monastic year, hence 丨丨 are senior, 下臘 junior monks.

上茅(宮)城 Kuśāgrapura, 矩奢揭羅補羅 city of Kuśa-grass palaces, or 山城 the mountain city. v. 吉祥茅國.

上行菩薩 Viśiṣṭa-cāritra Bodhisattva, who suddenly rose out of the earth as Buddha was concluding one of his Lotus sermons; v. Lotus sūtra 15 and 21. He is supposed to have been a convert of the Buddha in long past ages and to come to the world in its days of evil. Nichiren in Japan believed himself to be this Bodhisattva's reincarnation, and the Nichiren trinity is the Buddha, i.e. the eternal Śākyamuni Buddha; the Law, i.e. the Lotus Truth; and the Saṅgha, i.e. this Bodhisattva, in other words Nichiren himself as the head of all living beings, or eldest son of the Buddha.

上衍 Mahāyāna, 上乘; v. 大乘.

上衣 The superior or outer robe described as of twenty-five patches, and styled the uttarā saṁghāṭī.

上趣 The higher gati, directions, or transmigrations.

上足 A superior disciple or follower.

上輩 Superior, or highest class, idem 上品. | | 觀 The fourteenth of the sixteen contemplations of the Amitābha school, with reference to those who seek the Pure Land with sincere, profound, and altruistic hearts.

上轉 The upward turn: (1) progress upward, especially in transmigration; (2) increase in enlightenment for self, while 下轉 q.v. is for others.

上間 The superior rooms, i.e. on the right as one enters a monastery, the 下間 are on the left.

上首 President, or presiding elders.

三 Tri, trayas; three. 三一 Trinity; also 31.

三七日思惟 The twenty-one days spent by the Buddha, after his enlightenment, in walking round the bō-tree and considering how to carry his Mahāyāna way of salvation to the world; v. 法華經方便品.

三三昧(地) The three samādhis, or the samādhi on three subjects; 三三摩(地); 三定, 三等持; 三空; 三治; 解脫門, 三重三昧; 三重等持. There are two forms of such meditation, that of 有漏 reincarnational, or temporal, called 三三昧; and that of 無漏 liberation, or nirvāṇa, called 三解脫. The three subjects and objects of the meditation are (1) 空 to empty the mind of the ideas of me and mine and suffering, which are unreal; (2) 無相 to get rid of the idea of form, or externals, i.e. the 十相 which are the five senses, and male and female, and the three 有; (3) 無願 to get rid of all wish or desire, also termed 無作 and 無起. A more advanced meditation is called the Double Three Samādhi 重三三昧 in which each term is doubled 空空, 無相無相, 無願無願. The esoteric sect has also a group of its own.

三不三信 This refers to the state of faith in the worshipper; the three 不 are impure, not single, not constant; the three 信 are the opposite. | | 善根 Three bad roots, or qualities—desire, anger, and stupidity 貪, 瞋, 痴, v. 三毒. | | 堅法 Three unstable things—the body, length of life, wealth. | | 失 The three never lost, idem | | 護. | | 淨肉 The three kinds of flesh unclean to a monk, i.e. when he has seen or heard the animal killed or has doubt about it; v. 三淨肉. | | 能 v. 三能. | | 護 The three that need no guarding, i.e. the 三業 of a Buddha, his body, mouth (or lips), and mind, which he does not need to guard as they are above error. | | 退 The three non-backslidings, i.e. from position attained, from line of action pursued, and in dhyāna.

三世 The three periods, 過去, 現在, 未來 or 過, 現, 未, past, present, and future. The universe is described as eternally in motion, like a flowing stream. Also 未生, 已生, 後滅, or 未, 現, 過 unborn, born, dead. The 華嚴經 Hua-yen sūtra has a division of ten kinds of past, present, and future, i.e. the past spoken of as past, present, and future, the present spoken of in like manner, the future also, with the addition of the present as the three periods in one instant. Also 三際. | | 三千佛 The thousand Buddhas of each of the three kalpas—of the past, called 莊嚴 kalpa, the present 賢, and the future 星宿. Their names are variously given in several sūtras; a complete list is in the 三千佛名經. | | 不可得 Everything past, present, future, whether mental or material, is intangible, fleeting, and cannot be held; v. | | 心. | | 了達 A Buddha's perfect knowledge of past, present, and future. | | 佛 The Buddhas of the past, present, and future, i.e. Kāśyapa, Śākyamuni, and Maitreya. | | 假實 The reality or otherwise of things or events past, present, and future. Some Hīnayāna schools admit the reality of the present but dispute the reality of the past 已有 and the future 當有. Others take different views, all of which have been exhaustively discussed. See Vibhāśā śāstra 婆沙論 77, or 俱舍論 20. | | 實有法體恒有 The Sarvāstivādaḥ school maintains that as the three states (past, present, future) are real, so the substance of all things is permanent; i.e. time is real, matter is eternal. | | 心 Mind, or thought, past, present or future, is momentary, always moving, unreal and cannot be laid hold of. | | 成佛 idem 三生. | | 智 One of a Tathāgata's ten kinds of wisdom, i.e. knowledge of past, present, and future. | | 無障礙智戒 The wisdom-law or moral law that frees from all impediments, past, present, and future. Also styled 三昧耶戒; 自性本源戒; 三平等戒; 菩提心戒; 無爲戒 and 眞法戒. | | 覺母 A name for Mañjuśrī 文殊; as guardian of the wisdom of Vairocana he is the bodhi-mother of all Buddhas past, present, and future. | | 間 There are two definitions: (1) The realms of 器 matter, of 衆生 life, and 智正覺 mind, especially the Buddha's mind. (2) The 五陰 psychological realm (mind), 衆生 realm of life, and 國土 or 器 material realm.

三乘 Triyāna, the three vehicles, or conveyances which carry living beings across saṁsāra or mortality (births-and-deaths) to the shores of nirvāṇa. The three are styled 小, 中, and 大. Sometimes the three vehicles are defined as 聲聞 Śrāvaka, that of the hearer or obedient disciple; 緣覺 Pratyeka-buddha, that of the enlightened for self; these are described as 小乘 because the objective of both is personal salvation; the third is 菩薩 Bodhisattva, or 大乘 Mahāyāna, because the objective is the salvation of all the living. The three are also depicted as 三車 three wains, drawn by a goat, a deer, an ox. The Lotus declares that the three are really the One Buddha-vehicle, which has been revealed in three expedient forms suited to his disciples' capacity, the Lotus Sūtra being the unifying, complete, and final exposition. The Three Vehicles are differently explained by different exponents, e.g. (1) Mahāyāna recognizes (*a*) Śrāvaka, called Hīnayāna, leading in longer or shorter periods to arhatship; (*b*) Pratyeka-buddha, called Madhyamayāna, leading after still longer or shorter periods to a Buddhahood ascetically attained and for self; (*c*) Bodhisattva, called Mahāyāna, leading after countless ages of self-sacrifice in saving others and progressive enlightenment to ultimate Buddhahood. (2) Hīnayāna is also described as possessing three vehicles 聲, 緣, 菩 or 小, 中, 大, the 小 and 中 conveying to personal salvation their devotees in ascetic dust and ashes and mental annihilation, the 大 leading to bodhi, or perfect enlightenment, and the Buddha's way. Further definitions of the Triyāna are: (3) True bodhisattva teaching for the 大; pratyeka-buddha without ignorant asceticism for the 中; and śrāvaka with ignorant asceticism for the 小. (4) (*a*) 一乘 The One-Vehicle which carries all to Buddhahood; of this the 華嚴 Hua-yen and 法華 Fa-hua are typical exponents; (*b*) 三乘法 the three-vehicle, containing practitioners of all three systems, as expounded in books of the 深密般若; (*c*) 小乘 the Hīnayāna pure and simple as seen in the 四阿含經 Four Āgamas. Śrāvakas are also described as hearers of the Four Truths and limited to that degree of development; they hear from the pratyeka-buddhas, who are enlightened in the Twelve Nidānas 因緣; the bodhisattvas make the 六度 or six forms of transmigration their field of sacrificial saving work, and of enlightenment. The Lotus Sūtra really treats the 三乘 Three Vehicles as 方便 or expedient ways, and offers a 佛乘 Buddha Vehicle as the inclusive and final vehicle. | | 家 The Dharmalakṣaṇa School of the Three Vehicles, led by the 法相宗. | | 眞實一乘方便 The 三乘家 consider the Triyāna as real, and the "one vehicle" of the Lotus School as merely tactical, or an expedient form of expression.

三事戒 The commands relating to body, speech, and mind 身, 口, 意. | | 練磨 v. 三退屈. | | 衲 (or 衣) A term for a monk's robe of five, seven, or nine patches.

三仙二天 The three ṛṣis or wise men and the two devas, i.e. 迦毘羅 Kapila, founder of the Sāṁkhya philosophy; 休鶹鶹 or 優樓佉 Ulūka or Kaṇāda, founder of the 勝論宗 or Vaiśeṣika philosophy; and 勒沙婆 Ṛṣabha, founder of the Nirgranthas; with Śiva and Viṣṇu as the two deities.

三伐持 Saṁvaji; the heretical people of Vṛji, an ancient kingdom north of the Ganges, south-east of Nepāl. (Eitel.)

三佛 Trikāya, v. 三身. Also the three 岐 or founders of the 楊岐 branch of the Ch'an (Zen) School, i.e. 慧勤 Hui-ch'in, 淸遠 Ch'ing-yüan, and 克勤 K'o-ch'in. | | 土 The three Buddha-lands, realms, or environment, corresponding to the Trikāya; v. 三身 and 佛土. | | 子 All the living are Buddha-sons, but they are of three kinds —the commonalty are 外子 external sons; the followers of the two inferior Buddhist vehicles, 小 and 中乘, are 庶子 secondary sons (i.e. of concubines); the bodhisattvas (i.e. mahāyānists) are 道子 true sons, or sons in the truth. | | 性 The three kinds of Buddha-nature: (1) 自性住佛性 the Buddha-nature which is in all living beings, even those in the three evil paths (gati). (2) 引出佛性 the Buddha-nature developed by the right discipline. (3) 至得果佛性 the final or perfected Buddha-nature resulting from the development of the original potentiality. | | 栗底 Saṁvṛti, which means concealed, not apparent, is intp. as common ideas 世俗諦 or phenomenal truth; it is also intp. as that which hides reality, or seems to be real, the seeming. | | 菩提 The bodhi, or wisdom, of each of the Trikāya, 三身, i.e. that under the bodhi tree, that of parinirvāṇa, that of tathāgata-garbha in its eternal nirvāṇa aspect. | | 語 The Buddha's three modes of discourse—unqualified, i.e. out of the fullness of his nature; qualified to suit the intelligence of his hearers; and both. | | 身 idem 三身. | | 陀 Saṁbuddha; the truly enlightened one, or correct enlightenment.

三使 The three (divine) messengers—birth, sickness, death; v. 使. Also | 天 |.

三修 The three ways of discipline, i.e. three śrāvaka and three bodhisattva ways. The three śrāvaka ways are 無常修 no realization of the eternal, seeing everything as transient; 非樂修 joyless, through only contemplating misery and not realizing the ultimate nirvāṇa-joy; 無我修 non-ego discipline, seeing only the perishing self and not realizing the immortal self. The bodhisattva three are the opposite of these.

三倒 idem 三顛倒.

三條椽下 Under three rafters—the regulation space for a monk's bed or seat; in meditation.

三假 Prajñapti. The word 假 q.v. in Buddhist terminology means that everything is merely phenomenal, and consists of derived elements; nothing therefore has real existence, but all is empty and unreal, 虛妄不實. The three 假 are 法 things, 受 sensations, and 名 names. | | 施設; 三攝提 The three fallacious postulates in regard to 法, 受, and 名. | | 觀 The meditations on the above.

三僧祇 idem 三阿僧祇劫.

三偿 The three misleading things: 貪 desire, 瞋 ire, and 邪 perverted views. 偿 = 愆.

三僞一眞 The three half-true, or partial revelations of the 小, 中 and 大乘, and the true one of the Lotus Sūtra.

三億家 The 300,000 families of Śrāvastī city who had never heard of the Buddha's epiphany—though he was often among them.

三光(天) Sun, moon, and stars. Also, in the second dhyāna of the form-world there are the two deva regions 少光天, 無量光天, and 光音天 q.v. Also 觀音 Avalokiteśvara is styled 日天子 sun-prince, or divine son of the sun, 大勢至 Mahāsthāmaprāpta is styled 月天子 divine son of the moon, and 虛空藏菩薩 the bodhisattva of the empyrean, is styled 明星天子 divine son of the bright stars.

三八日 The eighth, eighteenth, and twenty-eighth days of a moon.

三六 Eighteen, especially referring to the eighteen sects of Hīnayāna.

三六九 An esoteric objection to three, six, or nine persons worshipping together.

三具足 The three essential articles for worship: flower-vase, candlestick, and censer.

三力 The three powers, of which there are various groups: (1) (*a*) personal power; (*b*) tathāgata-power; (*c*) power of the Buddha-nature within. (2) (*a*) power of a wise eye to see the Buddha-medicine (for evil); (*b*) of diagnosis of the ailment; (*c*) of suiting and applying the medicine to the disease. (3) (*a*) the power of Buddha; (*b*) of samādhi; (*c*) of personal achievement or merit. | | 偈 The triple-power verse:—

以我功德力 In the power of my virtue,
如來加持力 And the aiding power of the Tathāgata,
及與法界力 And the power of the spiritual realm,
周遍衆生界 I can go anywhere in the land of the living.

三分科經 The three divisions of a treatise on a sūtra, i.e. 序分 introduction, 正宗分 discussion of the subject, 流通分 application.

三劫 The three asaṅkhyeya kalpas, the three countless æons, the period of a bodhisattva's development; also the past 莊嚴 |, the present 賢 |, and the future 星宿 | kalpas. There are other groups. | | 三千佛 The thousand Buddhas in each of the three kalpas.

三十 Tridaśa. Thirty; abbreviation for the thirty-three deities, heavens, etc.

三十二 Dvātriṁśa. Thirty-two. | | | 應 (or 身) The thirty-two forms of Kuan-yin, and of P'u-hsien, ranging from that of a Buddha to that of a man, a maid, a rakṣas; similar to the thirty-three forms named in the Lotus Sūtra. | | | 相; | | | 大人相 Dvātriṁśadvaralakṣaṇa. The thirty-two lakṣaṇas, or physical marks of a cakravartī, or "wheel-king", especially of the Buddha, i.e. level feet, thousand-spoke wheel-sign on feet, long slender fingers, pliant hands and feet, toes and fingers finely webbed, full-sized heels, arched insteps, thighs like a royal stag, hands reaching below the knees, well-retracted male organ, height and stretch of arms equal, every hair-root dark coloured, body hair graceful and curly, golden-hued body, a 10 ft. halo around him, soft smooth skin, the 七處, i.e. two soles, two palms, two shoulders, and crown well rounded, below the armpits well-filled, lion-shaped body, erect, full shoulders, forty teeth, teeth white even and close, the four canine teeth pure white, lion-jawed, saliva improving the taste of all food, tongue long and broad, voice deep and resonant, eyes deep blue, eyelashes like a royal bull, a white ūrṇā or curl between the eyebrows emitting light, an uṣṇīṣa or fleshy protuberance on the crown. These are from the 三藏法數 48, with which the 智度論 4, 涅槃經 28, 中阿含經, 三十二相經 generally agree. The 無量義經 has a different list. | | | | 經 The eleventh chapter of the 阿含經. | | | | 經願 The twenty-first of Amitābha's vows, v. 無量壽經.

三十三 Trayastriṁśat. Thirty-three. | | | 天; 忉利天; 怛梨天, 多羅夜登陵舍; 怛利夜登陵奢; 怛利耶怛利奢 Trayastriṁśās. The Indra heaven, the second of the six heavens of form. Its capital is situated on the summit of Mt. Sumeru, where Indra rules over his thirty-two devas, who reside on thirty-two peaks of Sumeru, eight in each of the four directions. Indra's capital is called 殊勝 Sudarśana, 喜見城 Joy-view city. Its people are a yojana in height, each one's clothing weighs 六銖 ($\frac{1}{4}$ oz.), and they live 1,000 years, a day and night being equal to 100 earthly years. Eitel says Indra's heaven "tallies in all its details with the Svarga of Brahminic mythology" and suggests that "the whole myth may have an astronomical meaning", or be connected with "the atmosphere with its phenomena, which strengthens Koeppen's hypothesis explaining the number thirty-three as referring to the eight Vasus, eleven Rudras, twelve Ādityas, and two Aśvins of Vedic mythology". In his palace called Vaijayanta "Indra is enthroned with 1,000 eyes with four arms grasping the vajra. There he revels in numberless sensual pleasures together with his wife Śacī . . . and with 119,000 concubines with whom he associates by means of transformation". | | | (尊) 觀音 The thirty-three forms in which Kuan-yin is represented: with willow, dragon, sūtra, halo, as strolling, with white robe, as lotus-sleeping, with fishing-creel, as medicine-bestowing, with folded hands, holding a lotus, pouring water, etc. | | | 過 The thirty-three possible fallacies in the statement of a syllogism, nine in the proposition 宗 pratijñā, fourteen in the reason 因 hetu, and ten in the example 喩 udāharaṇa. | | | 身 The thirty-three forms in which Avalokiteśvara (Kuan-yin) is said to have presented himself, from that of a Buddha to that of a woman or a rakṣas. Cf. Lotus Sūtra 普門 chapter.

三十五佛 The thirty-five Buddhas before whom those who have committed sins involving interminable suffering should heartily repent. There are different lists.

三十六物 The thirty-six physical parts and excretions of the human body, all being unclean, i.e. the vile body.

三十六(部)神 The thirty-six departmental guardian divinities given in the 灌頂 . . . 咒經. Each is styled 彌栗頭 mṛdu, benign, kindly, for which 善 is used. Their Sanskrit and Chinese names are given in Chinese as follows: (1) 不羅婆 or 善光 kindly light, has to do with attacks of disease; (2) 婆呵婆 or 善明 headaches; (3) 婆邏婆 or | 力 fevers; (4) 抗陀羅 or | 月 disorders of the stomach; (5) 陀利奢 or | 見 tumours; (6) 阿婁呵 or | 供 madness; (7) 伽婆帝 or | 捨 stupidity; (8) 悉抵哆 or | 寂 irascibility; (9) 菩提薩 or | 覺 lust; (10) 提婆羅 or | 天 devils; (11) 呵婆帝 or | 住 deadly injuries; (12) 不若羅 or | 福 graves; (13) 苾闍伽 or | 術

the four quarters; (14) 迦隸婆 or ｜帝 enemies; (15) 羅闍遮 or ｜主 robbers; (16) 須乾陀 or ｜香 creditors; (17) 檀那波 or ｜施 thieves; (18) 支多那 or ｜意 pestilence; (19) 羅婆那 or ｜吉 the five plagues (? typhoid); (20) 鉢婆馱 or ｜山 corpse worms; (21) 三摩提 or ｜調 continuous concentration; (22) 戾禘馱 or ｜備 restlessness; (23) 波利陀 or ｜敬 attraction; (24) 波利那 or ｜淨 evil cabals; (25) 度伽地 or ｜品 deadly poison; (26) 毘梨馱 or ｜結 fear; (27) 支陀那 or ｜壽 calamities; (28) 伽林摩 or ｜逝 childbirth and nursing; (29) 阿留伽 or ｜願 the district magistracy; (30) 闍利馱 or ｜固 altercations; (31) 阿伽馱 or ｜照 anxieties and distresses; (32) 阿訶婆 or ｜生 uneasiness; (33) 婆和邏 or ｜思 supernatural manifestations; (34) 波利那 or ｜藏 jealousy; (35) 固陀那 or ｜音 curses; (36) 韋陀羅 or ｜妙 exorcism. They have innumerable assistants. He who writes their names and carries them with him can be free from all fear.

三十七(助)道品 Bodhipakṣika dharma. 三十七(菩提)分法, 三十七品 The thirty-seven conditions leading to bodhi, or Buddhahood, i.e. 四念處 smṛtyupasthāna, four states of memory, or subjects of reflection; 四正勤 samyakprahāṇa, four proper lines of exertion; 四如意足 ṛddhipāda, four steps towards supernatural power; 五根 pañca indriyāṇi, five spiritual faculties; 五力 pañca balāni, their five powers; 七覺支 sapta bodhyaṅga, seven degrees of enlightenment, or intelligence; and 八正道 aṣṭa-mārga, the eightfold noble path. ｜｜｜尊 The thirty-seven heads in the Vajradhātu or Diamond-realm maṇḍala. ｜｜｜｜四大輪 The four large circles in each of which the thirty-seven are represented, in one all hold the diamond-realm symbol, the vajra; in another, the symbol relating to the triple realm of time, past, present, future; in another, the Kuan-yin symbol; and in another, the symbol of infinite space.

三十捨墮 idem 尼薩耆波逸提.

三十生 In each of the 十地 ten states there are three conditions, 入, 住, 出, entry, stay, exit, hence the "thirty lives".

三千 Trisahasra, three thousand; a term used by the T'ien-t'ai School for 一切諸法, i.e. all things, everything in a chiliocosm, or Buddha-world; v. 三千大千世界. ｜｜佛 idem 三世. ｜｜塵點劫 The kalpa of the ancient Buddha Mahābhijñābhibhū (大通智; 勝佛), mentioned in the Lotus Sūtra, i.e. a kalpa of incalculable antiquity, e.g. surpassing the number of the particles of a chiliocosm which has been ground to powder, turned into ink, and dropped, drop by drop, at vast distances throughout boundless space. ｜｜大千世界 Tri-sahasra-mahā-sahasra-loka-dhātu, a great chiliocosm; 三千; 三千(世)界. Mt. Sumeru and its seven surrounding continents, eight seas and ring of iron mountains form one small world; 1,000 of these form a small chiliocosm 小千世界; 1,000 of these small chiliocosms form a medium chiliocosm 中千世界; a thousand of these form a great chiliocosm 大千世界, which thus consists of 1,000,000,000 small worlds. The 三千 indicates the above three kinds of thousands, therefore 三千大千世界 is the same as 大千世界, which is one Buddha-world. ｜｜實相 The reality at the basis of all things, a T'ien-t'ai doctrine, i.e. the 眞如 or 法性 idem 諸法實相. ｜｜年一現 The udumbara flower which flowers but once in 3,000 years; v. 優. ｜｜威儀 A bhikṣu's regulations amount to about 250; these are multiplied by four for the conditions of walking, standing, sitting, and sleeping and thus make 1,000; again multiplied by three for past, present, and future, they become 3,000 regulations. ｜｜｜｜經 The sūtra of this name.

三印 The three signs or proofs of a Hīnayāna sūtra—non-permanence, non-personality, nirvāṇa; without these the sūtra is spurious and the doctrine is of Māra; the proof of a Mahāyāna sūtra is the doctrine of 一實 ultimate reality, q.v. Also ｜法｜.

三即一 The three vehicles (Hīnayāna, Madhyamayāna, Mahāyāna) are one, i.e. the three lead to bodhisattvaship and Buddhahood for all.

三受 The three states of Vedanā, i.e. sensation, are divided into painful, pleasurable, and freedom from both 苦, 樂, 捨. When things are opposed to desire, pain arises; when accordant, there is pleasure and a desire for their continuance; when neither, one is detached or free. 倶舍論 1. ｜｜業 The karma or results arising from the pursuit of courses that produce pain, pleasure, or freedom from both.

三句 Three cryptic questions of 雲門 Yün-mên, founder of the Yün-mên Ch'an School. They are: (1) 截斷衆流 What is it that stops all flow (of reincarnation)? The reply from the 起信論 is 一心, i.e. the realization of the oneness of mind, or that all is mind. (2) 函蓋乾坤 What contains and includes the universe? The 眞如. (3) 隨波逐浪 One wave following another—what is this? Birth and death 生死, or transmigration, phenomenal existence.

三味 The three flavours, or pleasant savours: the monastic life, reading the scriptures, meditation.

三和 The union of the three, i.e. 根 indriya, 境 ālambana, and 識 vijñāna, i.e. organ, object, and cognition.

三品 The general meaning is 上, 中, 下 superior, medium, inferior. | | 悉地 The three esoteric kinds of siddhi, i.e. complete attainment, supreme felicity. They are 上 superior, to be born in the 密嚴國 Vairocana Pure-land; 中 in one of the other Pure-lands among which is the Western Paradise; and 下 in the 修羅宮 Sun Palaces among the devas. Also styled | | 成就. | | 沙彌 The three grades of śrāmaṇera, i.e. 7–13 years old styled 駈烏 | |; 14–19 應法 | |; and 20 and upwards 名字 | |. | | 聽法 The three grades of hearers, i.e. 上 with the 神 spirit; 中 with the 心 mind; 下 with the 耳 ear.

三善 idem 三時教 and 三善根. | | 根 The three good "roots", the foundation of all moral development, i.e. 無貪, 無瞋, 無痴 no lust (or selfish desire), no ire, no stupidity (or unwillingness to learn). Also, 施, 慈, 慧 giving, kindness, moral wisdom; v. 三毒 the three poisons for which these are a cure. | | 知識 The three types of friends with whom to be intimate, i.e. a teacher (of the Way), a fellow-endeavourer and encourager, and a patron who supports by gifts (dānapati). | | 道 (or 趣) The three good or upward directions or states of existence: 天 the highest class of goodness rewarded with the deva life, or heaven; 人 the middle class of goodness with a return to human life; 阿修羅 the inferior class of goodness with the asura state. Cf. 三惡道; v. 智度論 30.

三因 The six "causes" of the Abhidharma Kośa 俱舍論 as reduced to three in the Satyasiddhi śāstra 成實論, i.e. 生 | producing cause, as good or evil deeds cause good or evil karma; 習 | habit cause, e.g. lust breeding lust; 依 | dependent or hypostatic cause, e.g. the six organs 六根 and their objects 六境 causing the cognitions 六識. | | 三果 The three causes produce their three effects: (1) 異熟因異熟果 differently ripening causes produce differently ripening effects, i.e. every developed cause produces its developed effect, especially the effect of the present causes in the next transmigration; (2) 福因福報 blessed deeds produce blessed rewards, now and hereafter; (3) 智因智果 wisdom (now) produces wisdom-fruit (hereafter).

三國土 idem 四土 omitting 寂光土.

三土 idem 三佛土.

三垢 The three defilers—desire, hate, stupidity (or ignorance), idem 三毒.

三堅 The three sure or certain things are 身, 命 and 財, i.e. the reward of the true disciple is an infinite body or personality, an endless life, and boundless (spiritual) possessions, 無極之身, 無窮之命, 無盡之財, v. 維摩經菩薩品.

三報 The three recompenses, i.e. 現 | in the present life for deeds now done; 生 | in the next rebirth for deeds now done; and 後 | in subsequent lives.

三境 v. 三類境.

三塗 The 塗 mire is intp. by 途 a road, i.e. the three unhappy gati or ways; (*a*) 火 | to the fires of hell; (*b*) 血 | to the hell of blood, where as animals they devour each other; (*c*) 刀 | the asipattra hell of swords, where the leaves and grasses are sharp-edged swords. Cf. 三惡趣.

三多 Much intercourse with good friends, much hearing of the Law, much meditation on the impure. Also, much worship, much service of good friends, much inquiry on important doctrines. There are other groups.

三大 The three great characteristics of the 眞如 in the 起信論 Awakening of Faith: (1) 體大 The greatness of the bhūtatathatā in its essence or substance; it is 衆生心之體性 the embodied nature of the mind of all the living, universal, immortal, immutable, eternal; (2) 相大 the greatness of its attributes or manifestations, perfect in wisdom and mercy, and every achievement; (3) 用大 the greatness of its functions and operations within and without, perfectly transforming all the living to good works and good karma now and hereafter. There are other groups, e.g. 體, 宗, and 用. | | 部 Three authoritative works of the T'ien-t'ai School, i.e. the 玄義, 文句, and 止觀, each of ten chüan.

三天 The trimūrti—Śiva, Viṣṇu, and Brahmā. | | 使 v. 三使. | | 四仙 v. 二天三仙 and add 鳩摩羅 Kuveradeva and 若提子 Nirgrantha, son of Jñātṛ, i.e. of the Jñātṛ clan.

三契 Three repetitions (of a verse).

三妙行 A muni, recluse, or monk, who controls his body, mouth, and mind 身, 口, 意. Also 三牟尼.

三子 The three sons, one filial, wise, and competent; one unfilial but clever and competent; one unfilial, stupid, and incompetent; types respectively of bodhisattvas, śrāvakas, and icchantikas, 涅槃經 33.

三季 The "three seasons" of an Indian year—spring, summer, and winter; a year.

三學 The "three studies" or vehicles of learning—discipline, meditation, wisdom: (*a*) 戒 | learning by the commandments, or prohibitions, so as to guard against the evil consequences of error by mouth, body, or mind, i.e. word, deed, or thought; (*b*) 定 | by dhyāna, or quietist meditation; (*c*) 慧 | by philosophy, i.e. study of principles and solving of doubts. Also the Tripiṭaka; the 戒 being referred to the 律 vinaya, the 定 to the 經 sūtras, and the 慧 to the 論 śāstras.

三安居 The three months of summer retreat, varṣāḥ; v. 跋.

三字 The "three characters", a term for 阿彌陀 Amitābha.

三宗 The three Schools of 法相 |, 破相 |, and 法性 | q.v., representing the ideas of 空, 假, and 不空假, i.e. unreality, temporary reality, and neither; or absolute, relative, and neither.

三定聚 idem 三聚.

三密 The three mystic things: the body, mouth (i.e. voice), and mind of the Tathāgata, which are universal, all things being this mystic body, all sound this mystic voice, and all thought this mystic mind. All creatures in body, voice, and mind are only individualized parts of the Tathāgata, but illusion hides their Tathāgata nature from them. The esoterics seek to realize their Tathāgata nature by physical signs and postures, by voicing of 眞言 dhāraṇī and by meditations, so that 入我我入 He may enter me and I Him, which is the perfection of siddhi 悉地; v. 大日經疏 1. 菩提心論. | | 六大 The three mystic things associated with the six elements, i.e. the mystic body is associated with earth, water, and fire; the mystic words with wind and space; the mystic mind with 識 cognition. | | 栗底尼迦耶, v. 三彌底 Sammitīya-nikāya. | | 相應 The three mystic things, body, mouth, and mind, of the Tathāgata are identical with those of all the living, so that even the fleshly body born of parents is the dharmakāya, or body of Buddha: 父母所生之肉身卽爲佛身也.

三寶 Triratna, or Ratnatraya, i.e. the Three Precious Ones: 佛 Buddha, 法 Dharma, 僧 Saṅgha, i.e. Buddha, the Law, the Ecclesia or Order. Eitel suggests this trinity may be adapted from the Trimūrti, i.e. Brahmā, Viṣṇu, and Śiva. The Triratna takes many forms, e.g. the Trikāya 三身 q.v. There is also the Nepalese idea of a triple existence of each Buddha as a Nirvāṇa-Buddha, Dhyāni-Buddha, and Mānuṣi-Buddha; also the Tāntric trinity of Vairocana as Nirvāṇa-Buddha, Locana according to Eitel "existing in reflex in the world of forms", and the human Buddha, Śākyamuni. There are other elaborated details known as the four and the six kinds of triratna 四 and 六種三寶, e.g. that the Triratna exists in each member of the trinity. The term has also been applied to the 三仙 q.v. Popularly the 三寶 are referred to the three images in the main hall of monasteries. The centre one is Śākyamuni, on his left Bhaiṣajya 藥師 and on his right Amitābha. There are other explanations, e.g. in some temples Amitābha is in the centre, Avalokiteśvara on his left, and Mahāsthāmaprāpta or Mañjuśrī on his right. Table of Triratna, Trikāya, and Trailokya:—

Dharma	Saṅgha	Buddha
Essential Bodhi	Reflected Bodhi	Practical Bodhi
Dhyāni Buddha	Dhyāni Bodhisattva	Mānuṣī Buddha
Dharmakāya	Sambhogakāya	Nirmāṇakāya
Purity	Completeness	Transformations
4th Buddha-kṣetra	3rd Buddha-kṣetra	1st and 2nd Buddha-kṣetra
Arūpadhātu	Rūpadhātu	Kāmadhātu

| | 物 The things appertaining to the Triratna, i.e. to the Buddha—temples and images, etc.; to the Dharma—the scriptures; to the Saṅgha—cassock, bowl, etc. | | 藏 The Tritratna as the treasury of all virtue and merit; also the Tripiṭaka, sūtras 經, vinaya 律, abhidharma 論; also śrāvakas, pratyeka-buddhas, and bodhisattvas. | | 衣 idem 三衣. | | 身 v. 三身.

三尊 The three honoured ones: Buddha, the Law, the Ecclesia or Order. Others are: Amitābha, Avalokiteśvara, and Mahāsthāmaprāpta, who, according to the Pure-land sect, come to welcome the dying invoker. Another group is Bhaiṣajya, Vairocana, and Candraprabha; and another, Śākyamuni, Mañjuśrī, and Samantabhadra. | | 佛 The three honoured Buddhas of the West: Amitābha, Avalokiteśvara, Mahāsthāmaprāpta. Though bodhisattvas, the two latter are called Buddhas when thus associated with Amitābha. | | 來迎 Amitābha, Avalokiteśvara, Mahāsthāmaprāpta, receive into the western paradise the believer who calls on Amitābha.

三市 The thrice repeated procession around an image; there is dispute as to which shoulder should be next to the image, v. 右繞.

三師七證 The three superior monks and a minimum of seven witnesses required for an ordination to full orders; except in outlandish places, when two witnesses are valid.

三平等 The esoteric doctrine that the three —body, mouth, and mind—are one and universal. Thus in samādhi the Buddha "body" is found everywhere and in everything (pan-Buddha), every sound becomes a "true word", dhāraṇī or potent phrase, and these are summed up in mind, which being universal is my mind and my mind it, 入我我入 it in me and I in it. Other definitions of the three are 佛, 法, 僧 the Triratna; and 心, 佛, 衆生 mind, Buddha, and the living. Also 三三昧. Cf. 三密. v. 大日經 1. | | | 地 The three universal positions or stages, i.e. the three states expressed by 空, 無相, and 無願; v. 三三昧地. | | | 戒 idem 三昧耶戒 and 三世無障礙智戒. | | | 觀 idem 三三昧觀. | | | 護摩壇 The three equal essentials of the fire sacrifice, i.e. the individual as offerer, the object of worship, and the altar.

三彌叉 Samīkṣā, 觀察 investigation, i.e. the Sāṁkhya, a system of philosophy, wrongly ascribed by Buddhists to 闍提首那 Jātisena, or 闍耶犀那 Jayasena, who debated the twenty-five Sāṁkhya principles (tattvas) with Śākyamuni, but succumbed, shaved his head and became a disciple, according to the 涅槃經 39. | | 底; 彌底; 彌離底; 三密 (or 蜜) 栗底尼迦耶; 三眉底與量弟子 Saṁmatīyanikāya, Saṁmata, or Saṁmitīyas. A Hīnayāna sect, the 正量部 correctly commensurate or logical school, very numerous and widely spread during the early centuries of our era. The 三彌底部論 is in the Tripiṭaka. It taught "that a soul exists in the highest and truest sense", "that an arhat can fall from arhatship, that a god can enter the paths of the Order, and that even an unconverted man can get rid of all lust and ill-will" (Eliot, i, 260). It split into the three branches of Kaurukullakāḥ, Āvantikāḥ, and Vātsīputrīyāḥ. | | 提 Saṁmiti is a saint mentioned in the 阿含經.

三形 idem 三昧耶形.

三從 A woman's three subordinations, to father, husband, and son; stated in several sūtras, e.g. 四十華嚴經 28.

三德 The three virtues or powers, of which three groups are given below. (1) (*a*) 法身 | The virtue, or potency of the Buddha's eternal, spiritual body, the dharmakāya; (*b*) 般若 | of his prājñā, or wisdom, knowing all things in their reality; (*c*) 解脫 | of his freeedom from all bonds and his sovereign liberty. Each of these has the four qualities of 常, 樂, 我, 淨 eternity, joy, personality, and purity; v. 涅槃經. (2) (*a*) 智 | The potency of his perfect knowledge; (*b*) 斷 | of his cutting off all illusion and perfecting of supreme nirvāṇa; the above two are 自利 for his own advantage; (*c*) 恩 | of his universal grace and salvation, which 利他 bestows the benefits he has acquired on others. (3) (*a*) 因圓 | The perfection of his causative or karmaic works during his three great kalpas of preparation; (*b*) 果圓 | the perfection of the fruit, or results in his own character and wisdom; (*c*) 恩圓 | the perfection of his grace in the salvation of others.

三心 The three minds, or hearts; various groups are given: (1) Three assured ways of reaching the Pure Land, by (*a*) 至誠 | perfect sincerity; (*b*) 深 | profound resolve for it; (*c*) 廻向發願 | resolve on demitting one's merits to others. (2) (*a*) 根本 | The 8th or ālaya-vijñāna mind, the store-house, or source of all seeds of good or evil; (*b*) 依本 | the 7th or mano-vijñāna mind, the mediating cause of all taint; (*c*) 起事 | the ṣaḍāyatana-vijñāna mind, the immediate influence of the six senses. (3) (*a*) 入 | (*b*) 住 | (*c*) 出 | The mind entering into a condition, staying there, departing. (4) A pure, a single, and an undistracted mind. There are other groups.

三忍 The three forms of kṣānti, i.e. patience (or endurance, tolerance). One of the groups is patience under hatred, under physical hardship, and in pursuit of the faith. Another is patience of the blessed in the Pure Land in understanding the truth they hear, patience in obeying the truth, patience in attaining absolute reality; v. 無量壽經. Another is patience in the joy of remembering Amitābha, patience in meditation on his truth, and patience in constant faith in him. Another is the patience of submission, of faith, and of obedience.

三念住 (or 處). Whether all creatures believe, do not believe, or part believe and part do not believe, the Buddha neither rejoices, nor grieves, but rests in his proper mind and wisdom, i.e. though full of pity, his far-seeing wisdom 正念正智 keeps him above the disturbances of joy and sorrow. 俱舍論 27.

三性 The three types of character 善, 惡, 無記 good, bad and undefinable, or neutral; v. 唯識論 5. Also, 徧依圓三性 the three aspects of the nature of a thing—partial, as when a rope is mistaken for a snake; only partly reliable, i.e. incomplete inference, as when it is considered as mere hemp; all round, or perfect, when content, form, etc., are all considered. | | 分別 The differentiation of the three conditions of good, evil, and neutral.

三思 All action and speech have three mental conditions—reflection, judgment, decision.

三惑 A T'ien-t'ai classification of the three delusions, also styled 三煩惱; 三漏; 三垢; 三結; trials or temptations, leakages, uncleannesses, and bonds. The first of the following three is common to all disciples, the two last to bodhisattvas. They arise from (*a*) 見, 思, 惑 things seen and thought, i.e. illusions from imperfect perception, with temptation to love, hate, etc.; to be rid of these false views and temptations is the discipline and nirvāṇa of ascetic or Hīnayāna Buddhists. Mahāyāna proceeds further in and by its bodhisattva aims, which produce their own difficulties, i.e. (*b*) 塵沙惑 illusion and temptation through the immense variety of duties in saving men; and (*c*) 無明惑 the illusions and temptations that arise from failure philosophically to understand things in their reality.

三惡 The three evil gati, or paths of transmigration; also 三惡道, 三惡趣 the hells, hungry ghosts, animals. | | 覺 The three evil mental states: 欲 desire, 瞋 hate (or anger), 害 malevolence.

三想 The three evil thoughts are the last, desire, hate, malevolence; the three good thoughts are 怨 | thoughts of (love to) enemies, 親 | the same to family and friends, 中人 | the same to those who are neither enemies nor friends, i.e. to all; v. 智度論 72.

三慈 v. 三種慈悲.

三慕達羅 Samudra, the sea, an ocean; also 三母捺羅娑誐羅 samudra-sāgara. Samudra and sāgara are synonyms.

三慧 The three modes of attaining moral wisdom: 聞 | from reading, hearing, instruction; 思 | from reflection, etc.; 修 | from practice (of abstract meditation).

三應供養 The three who should be served, or worshipped—a Buddha, an arhat, and a cakravartī king.

三懺 idem 三種悔法.

三戒 The three sets of commandments, i.e. the ten for the ordained who have left home, the eight for the devout at home, and the five for the ordinary laity.

三拔諦 idem 三跋致.

三摩 Sama, level, equal, same, etc.; cf. 三昧(耶) and 平等. | | 半那 Samāpanna, in the state of samādhi. | | 呬多 Samāhita; steadfast, tranquil. A degree of meditation. | | 呾吒 Samataṭa, an ancient kingdom on the left bank of the Ganges, near its mouths, extending to the Hooghly, over 3,000 li in circuit, low and damp, with a hardy people, short and dark. Eitel says: "close to the sea at the mouth of the Brahmaputra." Eliot says: "In the east of Bengal and not far from the modern

Burmese frontier." | | 地 (or 提, 帝, 底 or 胝) Samādhi; idem 三 昧. | | | 念 誦 Silent or meditative repetition of the name of Buddha. | | 娑 Samāsa. 殺 三 摩 娑 Ṣaṭ-samāsa, v. 六 離 合 釋. | | 婆 夜 Samavāya, coming together, combination; 利 合 advantageous union. | | 皮 陀; 縒 摩 吠 陀; 沙 磨; 平 論; 歌 詠 Sāma-veda-saṁhitā. A collection of verses sung at sacrifices, etc. The third of the three Vedas, or four if Atharva Veda is counted, as it was later; the verses are taken almost wholly from the Ṛgveda. | | 竭 Sumāgadhā, said to be a daughter of Anāthapiṇḍada of Śrāvāstī, who married the ruler of 難 國 and converted the ruler and people. | | 耶 (or 曳) idem 三 昧 耶; but 三 摩 耶 is also explained as a short period, a season of the year. | | 耶 道 A term among the esoterics for the 三 平 等 q.v. | | 若 Sāmānya, generality; in common; inclusive; v. 共. | | 越 idem | | 鉢 底. | | 近 離 The public gathering for a festival, lay and cleric, before parting at the end of the summer retreat. | | 鉢 底 (or 提); | | 拔 (or 跋) 提; | | 越 Samāpatti, attainment, arrival; defined by 等 至 and 等 持, which is intp. as complete dhyāna; similar to 三 摩 半 那 Samāpanna, attainment. Eitel says: "a degree of abstract ecstatic meditation preparatory to the final attainment of samādhi." Clough speaks of eight samāpattis, i.e. attainments —"eight successive states induced by the ecstatic meditation." v. also 三 摩 越. | | 難 呾 囉 Samanantaram, immediately following or contiguous; 等 無 間 緣, i.e. one of the four 緣 q.v.; it means without interval, i.e. an immediate cause.

三 攝 提 The three prajñapti, v. 三 假 施 設; they are the 受 and 法 and 名 假 施 設.

三 支 (比 量) Three members of a syllogism: pratijñā 宗 the proposition, hetu 因 the reason, udāharaṇa 喩 the example; cf. 因 明.

三 教 The three teachings, i.e. 儒, 佛 (or 釋), and 道 Confucianism, Buddhism, and Taoism; or 孔, 老, 釋 Confucianism, Taoism (also known as 神 |), and Buddhism. In Japan they are Shinto, Confucianism, and Buddhism. In Buddhism the term is applied to the three periods of Śākyamuni's own teaching, of which there are several definitions: (1) The Kiang-nan 南 中 School describe his teaching as (*a*) 漸 progressive or gradual; (*b*) 頓 immediate, i.e. as one whole, especially in the 華 嚴 經; and (*c*) 不 定 or indeterminate. (2) 光 統 Kuang-t'ung, a writer of the later Wei dynasty, describes the three as (*a*) 漸 progressive for beginners, i.e. from impermanence to permanence, from the void to reality, etc.; (*b*) 頓 immediate for the more advanced; and (*c*) 圓 complete, to the most advanced, i.e. the Hua-yen as above. (3) The 三 時 教 q.v. (4) The 南 山 Southern school deals with (*a*) the 性 空 of Hīnayāna; (*b*) 相 空 of Mahāyāna; and (*c*) 唯 識 圓 the perfect idealism. v. 行 事 鈔 中 4. T'ien-t'ai accepts the division of 漸, 頓, and 不 定 for pre-Lotus teaching, but adopts 漸 gradual, 頓 immediate, and 圓 perfect, with the Lotus as the perfect teaching; it also has the division of 三 藏 |, 通 |, and 別 | q.v. | | 法 師 Master of the Tripiṭaka; a title of Hsüan-tsang 玄 奘.

三 斷 The three cuttings off or excisions (of 惑 beguiling delusions, or perplexities). (1) (*a*) 見 所 斷 to cut off delusions of view, of which Hīnayāna has eighty-eight kinds; (*b*) 修 所 斷 in practice, eighty-one kinds; (*c*) 非 所 斷 nothing left to cut off, perfect. v. 俱 舍 論 2. (2) (*a*) 自 性 | to cut off the nature or root (of delusion); (*b*) 緣 縛 | to cut off the external bonds, or objective causes (of delusions); (*c*) 不 生 斷 (delusion) no longer arising, therefore nothing produced to cut off. The third stage in both groups is that of an arhat.

三 方 便 A term of the esoterics for body, mouth (speech), and mind, their control, and the entry into the 三 密 q.v. 大 日 經 疏 1.

三 施 The three forms of giving: (1) (*a*) one's goods; (*b*) the Law or Truth; (*c*) courage, or confidence: 智 度 論 11. (2) (*a*) goods; (*b*) worship; (*c*) preaching. (3) (*a*) food; (*b*) valuables; (*c*) life.

三 日 齋 The third day's ceremonies after a death, to gain Yama's favour as the deceased appears before him.

三 明 The three insights; also 三 達. Applied to Buddhas they are called 三 達, to arhats 三 明. (*a*) 宿 命 明 Insight into the mortal conditions of self and others in previous lives; (*b*) 天 眼 明 supernatural insight into future mortal conditions; (*c*) 漏 盡 明 nirvāṇa insight, i.e. into present mortal sufferings so as to overcome all passions or temptations. In the 俱 舍 論 27 the three are termed 宿 住 智 證 明; 死 生 | | | and 漏 盡 | | |. For 三 明 經 v. 長 阿 含 16. | | (智) Trividyā. The three clear conceptions that (1) all is impermanent 無 常 anitya; (2) all is sorrowful 苦 duḥkha; (3) all is devoid of a self 無 我 anātman.

三 昧 (地) Samādhi, "putting together, composing the mind, intent contemplation, perfect absorption, union of the meditator with the object of meditation." (M. W.) Also 三摩地 (提, 帝, 底 or 胝). Interpreted by 定 or 正定, the mind fixed and undisturbed; by 正受 correct sensation of the object contemplated; by 調直定 ordering and fixing the mind; by 正心行處 the condition when the motions of the mind are steadied and harmonized with the object; by 息慮凝心 the cessation of distraction and the fixation of the mind; by 等持 the mind held in equilibrium; by 奢摩他, i.e. 止息 to stay the breathing. It is described as concentration of the mind (upon an object). The aim is 解脫, mukti, deliverance from all the trammels of life, the bondage of the passions and reincarnations. It may pass from abstraction to ecstasy, or rapture, or trance. Dhyāna 定 represents a simpler form of contemplation; samāpatti 三摩鉢底 a stage further advanced; and samādhi the highest stage of the Buddhist equivalent for Yoga, though Yoga is considered by some as a Buddhist development differing from samādhi. The 翻譯名義 says: 思專 when the mind has been concentrated, then 志一不分 the will is undivided; when 想寂 active thought has been put to rest, then 氣虛神朗 the material becomes etherealized and the spirit liberated, on which 智 knowledge, or the power to know, has free course, and there is no mystery into which it cannot probe. Cf. 智度論 5, 20, 23, 28; 止觀 2; 大乘義章 2, 9, 13, 20, etc. There are numerous kinds and degrees of samādhi. | | 佛 Samādhi Buddha, one of the ten Buddhas mentioned in the 華嚴經. | | 月輪相; 月輪三昧 The candra-maṇḍala, i.e. moon-wheel or disc samādhi; Nāgārjuna is said to have entered it and taken his departure as a cicada after delivering the Law (or patriarchate) to Kāṇadeva. | | 火 Fire of samādhi, the fire that consumed the body of Buddha when he entered nirvāṇa. | | 相應 The symbols or offerings should tally with the object worshipped, e.g. a white flower with a merciful or a white image. | | 門 The different stages of a bodhisattva's samādhi; cf. 智度論 28. | | 魔 Samādhimāra, one of the ten māras, who lurks in the heart and hinders progress in meditation, obstructs the truth and destroys wisdom.

三昧 (耶) Samaya is variously defined as 會 coming together, meeting, convention; 時 timely; 宗 in agreement, of the same class; 平等 equal, equalized; 驚覺 aroused, warned; 除垢障 riddance of unclean hindrances. Especially it is used as indicating the vows made by Buddhas and bodhisattvas, hence as a tally, symbol, or emblem of the spiritual quality of a Buddha or bodhisattva. | | | 形 The distinguishing symbol of a Buddha or bodhisattva, e.g. the Lotus of Kuan-yin; also used for | | | 身 q.v. | | | 戒 Samaya commandments: the rules to be strictly observed before full ordination in the esoteric sects. | | | 曼荼羅 Samaya-maṇḍala. One of the four kinds of magic circles in which the saints are represented by the symbols of their power, e.g. pagoda, jewel, lotus, sword. | | | 智 Samaya wisdom. In esoteric teaching, the characteristic of a Buddha's or bodhisattva's wisdom, as shown in the maṇḍala. | | | 會 The Samaya assembly, i.e. the second of the nine maṇḍalas, consisting of seventy-three saints represented by the symbols of their power. | | | 界 Samaya world, a general name for the esoteric sect. | | | 身 (or 形) The embodiment of Samaya, a term of the esoteric sect; i.e. the symbol of a Buddha or bodhisattva which expresses his inner nature, e.g. the stūpa as one of the symbols of Vairocana 大日; the lotus of Kuan-yin, etc. 身 is used for a Buddha, 形 for a bodhisattva. The exoteric sects associate the term with the 報身 saṁbhogakāya.

三時 The three divisions of the day, i.e. dawn, daylight, and sunset; or morning, noon, and evening; also the three periods, after his nirvāṇa, of every Buddha's teaching, viz., 正 correct, or the period of orthodoxy and vigour, 像 semblance, or the period of scholasticism, and 末 end, the period of decline and termination. | | 坐禪 The thrice a day meditation—about 10 a.m. and 4 and 8 p.m. | | 年限 The three periods of Buddhism—1,000 years of 正法 pure or orthodox doctrine, 1,000 years of 像法 resemblance to purity, and 10,000 years of 末法 decay. Other definitions are 正 and 像 500 years each, or 正 1,000 and 像 500, or 正 500 and 像 1,000. | | 性 i.e. 徧依圓三性 v. 三性. | | 敎 (判) The three periods and characteristics of Buddha's teaching, as defined by the Dharmalakṣana school 法相宗. They are: (1) 有, when he taught the 實有 reality of the skandhas and elements, but denied the common belief in 實我 real personality or a permanent soul; this period is represented by the four 阿含經 āgamas and other Hīnayāna sūtras. (2) 空 Śūnya, when he negatived the idea of 實法 the reality of things and advocated that all was 空 unreal; the period of the 般若經 prajñā sūtras. (3) 中 Madhyama, the mean, that mind or spirit is real, while things are unreal; the period of this school's specific sūtra the 解深密經, also the 法華 and later sūtras. In the two earlier periods he is said to have 方便 adapted his teaching to the development of his hearers; in the third to have delivered his complete and perfect doctrine. Another division by the 空宗 is (1) as above; (2) the early period of the Mahāyāna represented by the 深密經; (3) the higher Mahāyāna as in the 般若經. v. also 三敎. | | 業 The three stages of karma—in the present life because of present deeds; in the next life because of present actions; and in future lives because of present actions.

三智 The three kinds of wisdom: (1) (*a*) 一切｜śrāvaka and pratyeka-buddha knowledge that all the dharma or laws are 空 void and unreal; (*b*) 道種｜bodhisattva-knowledge of all things in their proper discrimination; (*c*) 一切種｜Buddha-knowledge, or perfect knowledge of all things in their every aspect and relationship past, present, and future. T'ien-t'ai associates the above with 空, 假, 中. (2) (*a*) 世間｜earthly or ordinary wisdom; (*b*) 出世間｜supra-mundane, or spiritual (śrāvaka and pratyeka-buddha) wisdom; (*c*) 出世間上上｜supreme wisdom of bodhisattvas and Buddhas. v. 智度論 27, 止觀 3, and 楞伽經 3. Cf. 一心三智.

三暮多 God of the wind, which is Vāta in Sanskrit.

三曼多 Samanta; tr. by 等, 普, 遍 universal, everywhere; also ｜｜陀, 三滿多. ｜｜(or 萬) 陀犍陀 (or 提) Samantagandha, 普熏 universally fragrant. A tree in Paradise; a title of a Buddha. ｜｜(陀) 颰陀 (羅); ｜｜跋陀 Samantabhadra, 普賢 P'u-hsien; v. 三滿.

三有 The three kinds of bhava, or existence; idem 三界 q.v. The three states of mortal existence in the trailokya, i.e. in the realms of desire, of form, and beyond form. Another definition is 現有 present existence, or the present body and mind; 當有 in a future state; 中有 antarā-bhava, in the intermediate state. ｜｜對 The three sets of limitation on freedom: (*a*) direct resistance or opposition; (*b*) environment or condition; (*c*) attachment. ｜｜爲法 The three active or functioning dharmas: (1) pratigha, matter or form, i.e. that which has "substantial resistance"; (2) mind; and (3) 非色非心 entities neither of matter nor mind; cf. 七十五法. ｜｜爲相 The three forms of all phenomena, birth, stay (i.e. life), death; utpāda, sthiti, and nirvāṇa.

三末多 Sammata, intp. as 共許 "unanimously accorded"; i.e. name of the first king (elected) at the beginning of each world-kalpa.

三果 The third of the Hīnayāna 四果 four fruits or results, i.e. non-return to mortality.

三株 The three tree-trunks, or main stems—desire, hate, stupidity; v. 三毒.

三根 The three (evil) "roots"—desire, hate, stupidity, idem 三毒. Another group is the three grades of good "roots", or abilities 上, 中, 下 superior, medium, and inferior. Another is the three grades of faultlessness 三無漏根.

三梵 The three Brahma heavens of the first dhyāna: that of 梵衆 Brahma-pāriṣadya, the assembly of Brahmā; 梵輔 Brahma-purohitas, his attendants; 大梵 Mahābrahmā, Great Brahmā.

三極少 The three smallest things, i.e. an atom as the smallest particle of matter; a letter as the shortest possible name; a kṣaṇa, as the shortest period of time.

三業 Trividha-dvāra. The three conditions, inheritances, or karma, of which there are several groups. (1) Deed, word, thought, 身, 口, 意. (2) (*a*) Present-life happy karma; (*b*) present-life unhappy karma; (*c*) 不動 karma of an imperturbable nature. (3) (*a*) Good; (*b*) evil; (*c*) neutral karma. (4) (*a*) 漏｜Karma of ordinary rebirth; (*b*) 無漏｜karma of Hīnayāna nirvāṇa; (*c*) 非漏非無漏 karma of neither, independent of both, Mahāyāna nirvāṇa. (5) (*a*) Present deeds and their consequences in this life; (*b*) present deeds and their next life consequences; (*c*) present deeds and consequences after the next life. There are other groups of three. ｜｜供養; ｜｜相應 To serve or worship with perfect sincerity of body, mouth, and mind; the second form means that in worship all three correspond.

三樂 The three joys—the joy of being born a deva, the joy of meditation, the joy of nirvāṇa.

三機 v. 三聚.

三檀 The three kinds of dāna, i.e. charity; giving of goods, of the dharma, of abhaya, or fearlessness. Idem 三施.

三權一實 The T'ien-t'ai division of the Schools of Buddhism into four, three termed 權 temporary, i.e. 藏, 通, and 別 q.v., the fourth is the 實 or 圓 real or perfect School of Salvation by faith to Buddhahood, especially as revealed in the Lotus Sūtra, see 一實.

三欲 The three lusts, i.e. for 形貌 form, 姿態 carriage or beauty, and 細觸 refinement, or softness to the touch.

三武 The three emperors Wu who persecuted Buddhism: 太武 of the Wei dynasty A.D. 424–452; 武帝 of the Chou A.D. 561–578; 武宗 of the T'ang A.D. 841–7.

三歸 Triśaraṇa, or Śaraṇa-gamana. The three surrenders to, or "formulas of refuge" in, the Three Precious Ones 三寶, i.e. to the Buddha 佛, the Dharma 法, the Saṅgha 僧. The three formulas are 歸依佛 Buddhaṁ śaraṇaṁ gacchāmi, 歸依法 Dharmaṁ śaraṇaṁ gacchāmi, 歸依僧 Saṅghaṁ śaraṇaṁ gacchāmi. It is "the most primitive formula fidei of the early Buddhists". The surrender is to the Buddha as teacher 師, the Law as medicine 藥, the Ecclesia as friends 友. These are known as the 三歸依. | | 受法 The receiving of the Law, or admission of a lay disciple, after recantation of his previous wrong belief and sincere repetition to the abbot or monk of the above three surrenders. | | (五) 戒 The ceremony which makes the recipient a 優婆塞 or 優婆夷 upāsaka or upāsikā, male or female disciple, accepting the five commandments. There are 五種三歸 five stages of san-kuei; the first two are as above, at the third the eight commandments are accepted, at the fourth the ten, at the fifth all the commandments. 三歸 is also a general term for a Buddhist.

三毒 The three poisons, also styled 三根; 三株; they are 貪 concupiscence, or wrong desire, 瞋 anger, hate, or resentment, and 痴 stupidity, ignorance, unintelligence, or unwillingness to accept Buddha-truth; these three are the source of all the passions and delusions. They represent in part the ideas of love, hate, and moral inertia. v. 智度論 19, 31. | | 尸利 The Śrī (i.e. goddess of Fortune) of the three poisons, a title of Mañjuśrī.

三治 idem 三三昧門 v. 三解脫.

三法 The three dharma, i.e. 敎 | the Buddha's teaching; 行 | the practice of it; 證 | realization or experiential proof of it in bodhi and nirvāṇa. | | 印 idem 三印. | | 忍 idem 三忍. For | | 妙 v. 三軌.

三法無差 idem 三無差別 q.v. | | 輪 The three law-wheels, or periods of the Buddha's preaching, according to Paramārtha, to 嘉祥 Chia-hsiang of the 三論 school, and to 玄奘 Hsüan-tsang of the 法相 school.

三波多 Samāpta; finished, ended, perfect; a term used at the conclusion of Homa or Fire-worship. | | 羅扇提 The three prajñāpti, 三假 q.v. | | 訶 Sampaha, according to Eitel, Malasa, a valley in the upper Punjab; but perhaps Śāmbī, a state north of Citral in the Hindukush.

三涅槃門 The three gates to the city of nirvāṇa, i.e. 空, 無相, and 無作 the void (or the immaterial), formlessness, and inactivity; idem 三解脫門.

三淨肉 The three kinds of "clean" flesh—when a monk has not seen the creature killed, has not heard of its being killed for him, and has no doubt thereon.

三滿多跋捺囉 Samantabhadra, interpreted 普賢 P'u-hsien, pervading goodness, or "all gracious", Eliot; also 徧吉 universal fortune; also styled Viśvabhadra. The principal Bodhisattva of O-mei shan. He is the special patron of followers of the Lotus Sūtra. He is usually seated on a white elephant, and his abode is said to be in the East. He is one of the four Bodhisattvas of the Yoga school. v. 三曼.

三漸 The three progressive developments of the Buddha's teaching according to the Prajñā school: (*a*) the 鹿苑 initial stage in the Lumbinī deer park; (*b*) the 方等 period of the eight succeeding years; (*c*) the 般若 prajñā or wisdom period which succeeded.

三漏 The three affluents that feed the stream of mortality, or transmigration: 欲 desire; 有 (material, or phenomenal) existence; 無明 ignorance (of the way of escape). 涅槃經 22.

三火 The three fires—desire, hate, and stupidity; v. 三毒.

三災 The three calamities; they are of two kinds, minor and major. The minor, appearing during a decadent world-period, are sword, pestilence, and famine; the major, for world-destruction, are fire, water, and wind. 俱舍論 12.

三煩惱 v. 三惑.

三熱 The three distresses of which dragons and dragon-kings are afraid—fiery heat, fierce wind, and the garuḍa bird which preys on them for food.

三無差(別) The three that are without (essential) difference, i.e. are of the same nature: (*a*) 心 The nature of mind is the same in Buddhas, and men, and all the living; (*b*) 佛 the nature and enlightenment of all Buddhas is the same; (*c*) 衆生 the nature and enlightenment of all the living is the same. The 華嚴經 says 心佛及衆生,是三無差別. | | 性 The three things without a nature or separate existence of their own: (*a*) 相無性 form, appearance or seeming, is unreal, e.g. a rope appearing like a snake; (*b*) 生無性 life ditto, for it is like the rope, which is derived from constituent materials; (*c*) 勝義無性 the 勝義, concept of the 眞如 or bhūtatathatā is unreal, e.g. the hemp of which the rope is made; the bhūtatathatā is perfect and eternal. Every representation of it is abstract and unreal. The three are also known as 相無性, 無自然性, 法無性; v. 唯識論 9. | | 漏學 The three studies, or endeavours, after the passionless life and escape from transmigration: (*a*) 戒 Moral discipline; (*b*) 定 meditation, or trance; (*c*) 慧 the resulting wisdom. | | 漏根 The three roots for the passionless life and final escape from transmigration, i.e. the last three of the 二十二根 q.v. An older group was 未知欲知根; 知根; 知已根 v. 倶舍論 3. 智度論 23. | | 盡莊嚴藏 The treasury of the three inexhaustible adornments or glories, i.e. the 身, 口, 意, deeds, words, and thoughts of a Buddha.

三照 The three shinings; the sun first shining on the hill-tops, then the valleys and plains. So, according to T'ien-t'ai teaching of the Hua-yen sūtra, the Buddha's doctrine had three periods of such shining: (*a*) first, he taught the Hua-yen sūtra, transforming his chief disciples into bodhisattvas; (*b*) second, the Hīnayāna sūtras in general to śrāvakas and pratyeka-buddhas in the Lumbinī garden; (*c*) third, the 方等 sūtras down to the 涅槃經 for all the living. See the 六十華嚴經 35, where the order is five, i.e. bodhisattvas, pratyeka-buddhas, śrāvakas, lay disciples, and all creatures.

三牟提耶 Samudaya, gather together, accumulate, the 聚 or 集諦, i.e. the second of the Four Truths, the aggregation of suffering.

三猿 The three monkeys, one guarding its eyes, another its ears, a third its mouth.

三獸 The three animals—hare, horse, elephant—crossing a stream. The śrāvaka is like the hare who crosses by swimming on the surface; the pratyeka-buddha is like the horse who crosses deeper than the hare; the bodhisattva is like the elephant who walks across on the bottom. Also likened to the triyāna. 涅槃經 23, 27.

三甜 The three sweet things—cream, honey, curd.

三生 The three births, or reincarnations, past, present, future. T'ien-t'ai has (*a*) 種 planting the seed; (*b*) 熟 ripening; (*c*) 脫 liberating, stripping, or harvesting, i.e. beginning, development, and reward of bodhi, a process either gradual or instantaneous. Hua-yen has (*a*) 見聞生 a past life of seeing and hearing Buddha-truth; (*b*) 解行生 liberation in the present life; (*c*) 證入生 realization of life in Buddhahood. This is also called 三生成佛, Buddhahood in the course of three lives. There is also a definition of three rebirths as the shortest term for arhatship, sixty kalpas being the longest. There are other definitions.

三田 The three "fields" of varying qualities of fertility, i.e. bodhisattvas, śrāvakas, and icchantis, respectively producing a hundred-fold, fifty-fold, one-fold. 涅槃經 33.

三界 Trailokya or Triloka; the three realms; also 三有. It is the Buddhist metaphysical equivalent for the Brahmanic cosmological bhuvanatraya, or triple world of bhūr, bhuvaḥ, and svar, earth, atmosphere, and heaven. The Buddhist three are 欲, 色, and 無色界, i.e. world of sensuous desire, form, and formless world of pure spirit. (*a*) 欲 | Kāmadhātu is the realm of sensuous desire, of 婬 and 食 sex and food; it includes the six heavens of desire, the human world, and the hells. (*b*) 色界 Rūpadhātu is the realm of form, meaning 質礙 that which is substantial and resistant; it is above the lust-world and contains (so to speak) bodies, palaces, things, all mystic and wonderful—a semi-material conception like that in Revelation; it is represented in the 四禪天, or Brahmalokas. (*c*) 無色界 Arūpadhātu, or ārūpyadhātu, is the formless realm of pure spirit, where there are no bodies, places, things, at any rate none to which human terms would apply, but where the mind dwells in mystic contemplation; its extent is indefinable, but it is conceived of in four stages, i.e. 四空處 the four "empty" regions, or regions of space in the immaterial world, which are 四無色 the four "formless" realms, or realms beyond form; being above the realm of form, their bounds cannot be defined. v. 倶舍論世間品. | | 九地 v. 九地. | | 唯一心 The triple world is but one mind; from a verse of the 華嚴 sūtra; it proceeds 心外無別法,

心佛及衆生，是三無差別 "outside mind there is no other thing; mind, Buddha, and all the living, these three are not different"; in other words, there is no differentiating between these three, for all is mind. | | 尊 The honoured one of the three worlds, i.e. Buddha. | | 慈父 The kindly father of the triple world—Buddha. | | 火宅 The burning house of the triple world, as in the Lotus Sūtra parable. | | 牀 The sick-bed of the trailokya, especially this world of suffering. | | 眼 The trailokya eye, i.e. Buddha, who sees all the realms and the way of universal escape. | | 萬靈牌 The tablet used at the annual ceremonial offerings to "all souls", v. 盂蘭. | | 藏 The trailokya-garbha, the womb or storehouse of all the transmigrational. | | 雄 The hero of the trailokya—Buddha.

三疑 The three doubts—of self, of teacher, of the dharma-truth.

三病 The three ailments: (1) (*a*) 貪 lust, for which the 不淨觀 meditation on uncleanness is the remedy; (*b*) 瞋 anger, or hate, remedy 慈悲觀 meditation on kindness and pity; (*c*) 癡 stupidity, or ignorance, remedy 因緣觀 meditation on causality. (2) (*a*) 謗 Slander of Mahāyāna; (*b*) 五逆罪 the five gross sins; (*c*) to be a "heathen" or outsider; the forms recorded seem to be icchantika, ecchantika, and aicchantika. Cf. 三毒.

三發心 The three resolves of the 起信論 Awakening of Faith: (*a*) 信成就 | | to perfect the bodhi of faith, i.e. in the stage of faith; (*b*) 解行 | | to understand and carry into practice this wisdom; (*c*) 證 | | the realization, or proof of or union with bodhi.

三白食 The three white foods—milk, cream (or curd), and rice (especially upland rice); | | 法 is the rule of these three.

三百四十八 (or 一) 戒 The 348 or 341 rules for a nun; there are also groups of 250 and 500 such rules. | | 六十會 The reputed and disputed number (360) of Śākyamuni's assemblies for preaching. | | 由旬 The 300 yojanas parable of the Magic City, erected by a leader who feared that his people would become weary and return; i.e. Hīnayāna nirvāṇa, a temporary rest on the way to the real land of precious things, or true nirvāṇa; v. 法華化城品.

三皈 idem 三歸.

三監 idem 三從.

三目 The three-eyed, a term for Śiva, i.e. Maheśvara; simile for the dharmakāya, or spiritual body, prajñā, or wisdom, and nirvāṇa emancipation.

三相 The three forms or positions: 解脫相 nirvāṇa; 離相 no nirvāṇa; 滅相 or 非有非無之中道 absence of both, or the "middle way" of neither. | | 續 The three links, or consequences: (*a*) the worlds with their kingdoms, which arise from the karma of existence; (*b*) all beings, who arise out of the five skandhas; (*c*) rewards and punishments, which arise out of moral karma causes.

三眞如 Three aspects of the bhūtatathatā, implying that it is above the limitations of form, creation, or a soul. (1) (*a*) 無相 | | without form; (*b*) 無生 | | without creation; (*c*) 無性 | | without anything that can be called a nature for comparison; e.g. chaos, or primal matter. (2) (*a*) 善法 | | The bhūtatathatā as good; (*b*) 不善法 | | as evil; (*c*) 無記法 | | as neutral, or neither good nor evil.

三眉底與部 Saṁmatīya, v. 三彌底.

三祇百(大)劫 The period necessary for a bodhisattva to become a Buddha, i.e. three asaṅkhyeyas 阿僧祇 to attain the 六度, and 100 kalpas to acquire the thirty-two 相 or characteristic marks of a Buddha; cf. 三阿.

三福 The three (sources of) felicity: (1) The 無量壽經 has the felicity of (*a*) 世 | filial piety, regard for elders, keeping the ten commandments; (*b*) 戒 | of keeping the other commandments; (*c*) 行 | of resolve on complete bodhi and the pursuit of the Buddha-way. (2) The 俱舍論 18, has the blessedness of (*a*) 施類 | almsgiving, in evoking resultant wealth; (*b*) 戒類 | observance of the 性戒 (against killing, stealing, adultery, lying) and the 遮戒 (against alcohol, etc.), in obtaining a happy lot in the heavens; (*c*) 修類 | observance of meditation in obtaining final escape from the mortal round. Cf. 三種淨業. | | 業 The three things that bring a happy lot—almsgiving, impartial kindness and love, pondering over the demands of the life beyond.

三禪 The third dhyāna heaven of form, the highest paradise of form.

三禮 Worship with 身, 口, 意, body, mouth, and mind.

三科 The three categories of 五蘊, 十二處 or 入, and eighteen 界.

三秘密 The three mysteries, a term of the esoteric school for 身, 口, and 意; i.e. the symbol; the mystic word, or sound; the meditation of the mind. The | | | 身 is a term for the mystic letter, the mystic symbol, and the image.

三種 Three kinds, sorts, classes, categories, etc.

三種三世 Three kinds of past, present, and future as intp. according to 道理, 神通, and 唯識.

三種三觀 The three types of meditation on the principles of the 三諦 q.v., i.e. the dogmas of 空, 假, 中.

三種世間 v. 三世間.

三種供養 Three modes of serving (the Buddha, etc.): (*a*) offerings of incense, flowers, food, etc.; (*b*) of praise and reverence; (*c*) of right conduct.

三種光明 The three kinds of light: (*a*) external—sun, moon, stars, lamps, etc.; (*b*) dharma, or the light of right teaching and conduct; (*c*) the effulgence or bodily halo emitted by Buddhas, bodhisattvas, devas.

三種善根 The three kinds of good roots—almsgiving, mercy, and wisdom.

三種圓融 Three kinds of unity or identity of (*a*) 事理 phenomena with "substance", e.g. waves and the water; (*b*) 事事 phenomena with phenomena, e.g. wave with wave; (*c*) 理理 substance with substance, e.g. water with water.

三種地獄 The three kinds of hells—hot, cold, and solitary.

三種大智 The three major kinds of wisdom: (*a*) self-acquired, no master needed; (*b*) unacquired and natural; (*c*) universal.

三種天 Three definitions of heaven: (*a*) as a name or title, e.g. divine king, son of Heaven, etc.; (*b*) as a place for rebirth, the heavens of the gods; (*c*) the pure Buddha-land.

三種常 A Buddha in his three eternal qualities: (*a*) 本性 | in his nature or dharmakāya; (*b*) 不斷 | in his unbroken eternity, saṁbhogakāya; (*c*) 相續 | in his continuous and eternally varied forms, nirmāṇakāya.

三種心苦 The three kinds of mental distress: desire, anger, stupidity, idem 三毒.

三種忍行 Patience or forbearance of body, mouth, and mind.

三種悔(or 懺)法 Three modes of repentance: (*a*) 無生 | to meditate on the way to prevent wrong thoughts and delusions; (*b*) 取相 | to seek the presence of the Buddha to rid one of sinful thoughts and passions; (*c*) 作法懺 in proper form to confess one's breach of the rules before the Buddha and seek remission.

三種慈悲 (or 緣慈) The three reasons of a bodhisattva's pity—because all beings are like helpless infants; because of his knowledge of all laws and their consequences; without external cause, i.e. because of his own nature.

三種教相 The three modes of the Buddha's teaching of the Southern Sects: 頓 immediate, 漸 gradual or progressive, and 不定 indeterminate.

三種斷 The three kinds of uccheda—cutting-off, excision, or bringing to an end: (1) (*a*) 自性 | with the incoming of wisdom, passion or illusion ceases of itself; (*b*) 不生 | with realization of the doctrine that all is 空 unreal, evil karma ceases to arise; (*c*) 緣縛 | illusion being ended, the causal nexus of the passions disappears and the attraction of the external ceases. (2) The three śrāvaka or ascetic stages are (*a*) 見所 | ending the condition of false views; (*b*) 修行 | getting rid of desire and illusion in practice; (*c*) 非所 | no more illusion or desire to be cut off.

三種智 The wisdom of common men, of the heterodox, and of Buddhism; i.e. (*a*) 世間 | normal, worldly knowledge or ideas; (*b*) 出世間 | other-worldly wisdom, e.g. of Hīnayāna; (*c*) 出世間上上 |

the highest other-worldly wisdom, of Mahāyāna; cf. | | 波羅蜜.

三種有 Three kinds of existence: (*a*) 相待 | that of qualities, as of opposites, e.g. length and shortness; (*b*) 假名 | that of phenomenal things so-called, e.g. a jar, a man; (*c*) 法 | that of the noumenal, or imaginary, understood as facts and not as illusions, such as a "hare's horns" or a "turtle's fur".

三種欲 Three kinds of desire—food, sleep, sex.

三種止觀 Three T'ien-t'ai modes of entering dhyāna: (*a*) 漸次 gradual, from the shallow to the deep, the simple to the complex; (*b*) 不定 irregular, simple, and complex mixed; (*c*) 圓頓 immediate and whole.

三種法輪 v. 三輪敎.

三種波羅蜜 The three kinds of pāramitā ideals, or methods of perfection: (*a*) 世間 | | | that of people in general relating to this world; (*b*) 出世間 | | | that of śrāvakas and pratyekabuddhas relating to the future life for themselves; (*c*) 出世間上上 | | | the supreme one of bodhisattvas, relating to the future life for all; cf. | | 智.

三種淨業 The threefold way of obtaining a pure karma, idem 三福.

三種淸淨 The three purities of a bodhisattva—a mind free from all impurity, a body pure because never to be reborn save by transformation, an appearance 相 perfectly pure and adorned.

三種灌頂 Three kinds of baptism: (1) (*a*) 摩頂灌頂 Every Buddha baptizes a disciple by laying a hand on his head; (*b*) 授記 | | by predicting Buddhahood to him; (*c*) 放光 | | by revealing his glory to him to his profit. (2) Shingon has (*a*) baptism on acquiring the mystic word; (*b*) on remission of sin and prayer for blessing and protection; (*c*) on seeking for reward in the next life.

三種生 The three sources, or causes of the rise of the passions and illusions: (*a*) 想 | the mind, or active thought; (*b*) 相 | the objective world; (*c*) 流注 | their constant interaction, or the continuous stream of latent predispositions.

三種相 The three kinds of appearance: (1) In logic, the three kinds of percepts: (*a*) 標相 inferential, as fire is inferred from smoke; (*b*) 形相 formal or spatial, as length, breadth, etc.; (*c*) 體 | qualitative, as heat is in fire, etc. (2) (*a*) 假名相 names, which are merely indications of the temporal; (*b*) 法相 dharmas, or "things"; (*c*) 無相相 the formless—all three are incorrect positions.

三種示導 Three ways in which bodhisattvas manifest themselves for saving those suffering the pains of hell, i.e. 身 physically, by supernatural powers, change of form, etc.; 意 mentally, through powers of memory and enlightenment; 口 orally, by moral exhortation.

三種色 Three kinds of rūpa, i.e. appearance or object: (1) (*a*) visible objects; (*b*) invisible objects, e.g. sound; (*c*) invisible, immaterial, or abstract objects. (2) (*a*) colour, (*b*) shape, (*c*) quality.

三種見惑 Three classes of delusive views, or illusions—those common to humanity; those of the inquiring mind; and those of the learned and settled mind.

三種身 The T'ien-t'ai School has a definition of 色 | the physical body of the Buddha; 法門 | his psychological body with its vast variety; 實相 | his real body, or dharmakāya. The esoteric sect ascribes a trikāya to each of its honoured ones. v. 三身. | | | 苦 The three duḥkha or afflictions of the body—old age, sickness, death.

三種闡提 The three kinds of icchantika: (*a*) 一闡提迦 the wicked; (*b*) 阿闡提迦 called 大悲闡提 bodhisattvas who become icchantika to save all beings; (*c*) 阿顚底迦 otherwise 無性闡提 those without a nature for final nirvāṇa. Cf. 三病.

三種香 Three kinds of scent, or incense, i.e. from root, branch, or flower.

三空 The three voids or immaterialities. The first set of three is (*a*) 空, (*b*) 無相, (*c*) 無願, v. 三三昧. The second, (*a*) 我 |, (*b*) 法 |, (*c*) 俱 | the self, things, all phenomena as "empty" or immaterial. The third relates to charity: (*a*) giver, (*b*) receiver, (*c*) gift, all are "empty". | | (觀) 門 idem 三解脫門.

三等 The three equal and universal characteristics of the one Tathāgata, an esoteric definition: (1) (*a*) his 身 body, (*b*) 語 discourse, (*c*) 意 mind. (2) (*a*) his life or works 修行; (*b*) spiritual body 法身; (*c*) salvation 度生; in their equal values and universality. | | 流 Three equal or universal currents or consequences, i.e. 眞等 | the certain consequences that follow on a good, evil, or neutral kind of nature, respectively; 假 | | the temporal or particular fate derived from a previous life's ill deeds, e.g. shortened life from taking life; 分位 | | each organ as reincarnated according to its previous deeds, hence the blind.

三篋 idem 三藏 tripiṭaka.

三節 The three divisions of the 十二因緣 twelve nidānas, q.v.: (*a*) past, i.e. the first two; (*b*) present—the next eight; (*c*) future—the last two.

三精氣 The three auras of earth, of the animate, and of the inanimate invoked against demon influences.

三細 The three refined, or subtle conceptions, in contrast with the 六麤 cruder or common concepts, in the Awakening of Faith 起信論. The three are 無明業相 "ignorance", or the unenlightened condition, considered as in primal action, the stirring of the perceptive faculty; 能見相 ability to perceive phenomena; perceptive faculties; 境界相 the object perceived, or the empirical world. The first is associated with the 體 corpus or substance, the second and third with function, but both must have co-existence, e.g. water and waves. v. 六麤.

三結 The three ties: (*a*) 見 |, the tie of false views, e.g. of a permanent ego; (*b*) 戒取 | of discipline; (*c*) 疑 | of doubt. The three are also parts of 見惑 and used for it.

三經一論 The three sūtras and one śāstra on which the Pure Land sect bases its teaching: 佛說無量壽經; 佛說觀無量壽經; 佛說阿彌陀經; 天親淨土論.

三綱 The three bonds, i.e. directors of a monastery: (*a*) 上座 sthavira, elder, president; (*b*) 寺主 vihārasvāmin, v. 毘 the abbot who directs the temporal affairs; (*c*) 維那 karmadāna, v. 羯 who directs the monks. Another meaning: (*a*) 上座; (*b*) 維那; (*c*) 典座 vihārapāla, v. 毘 director of worship. The three vary in different countries.

三練磨 v. 三退屈.

三縛 The three bonds—desire, anger, stupidity; idem 三毒.

三緣 The three nidānas or links with the Buddha resulting from calling upon him, a term of the Pure Land sect: (*a*) 親 | that he hears those who call his name, sees their worship, knows their hearts and is one with them; (*b*) 近 | that he shows himself to those who desire to see him; (*c*) 增上 | that at every invocation æons of sin are blotted out, and he and his sacred host receive such a disciple at death.

三罰業 The three things that work for punishment—body, mouth, and mind.

三耶三佛(檀) v. 三藐三佛陀. | | | 菩 v. 三藐三菩提.

三聖 The three sages, or holy ones, of whom there are several groups. The 華嚴 Hua-yen have Vairocana in the centre with Mañjuśrī on his left and Samantabhadra on his right. The 彌陀 Mi-t'o, or Pure-land sect, have Amitābha in the centre, with Avalokiteśvara on his left and Mahāsthāmaprāpta on his right. The T'ien-t'ai use the term for the 藏, 別, and 圓 教, v. 三教.

三聚 The three groups, i.e. 正定 | Those decided for the truth; 邪定 | those who are decided for heresy; 不定 | the undecided. Definitions vary in different schools. | | (淨) 戒 The three cumulative commandments: (*a*) the formal 5, 8, or 10, and the rest; (*b*) whatever works for goodness; (*c*) whatever works for the welfare or salvation of living, sentient beings. 三聚圓戒 interprets the above three as implicit in each of the ten commandments, e.g. (*a*) not to kill implies (*b*) mercy and (*c*) protection or salvation.

三能三不能 The three things possible and impossible to a Buddha. He can (*a*) have perfect knowledge of all things; (*b*) know all the natures of all beings, and fathom the affairs of countless ages; (*c*) save countless beings. But he cannot (*a*) annihilate causality, i.e. karma; (*b*) save unconditionally; (*c*) end the realm of the living.

三脫門 v. 三解脫(門), but the former is only associated with 無漏, or nirvāṇa.

三自 Three divisions of the eight-fold noble path, the first to the third 自調 self-control, the fourth and fifth 自淨 self-purification, the last three 自度 self-development in the religious life and in wisdom. Also 自體, 自相, 自用, substance, form, and function.

三舉 The three exposures, i.e. the three sins of a monk each entailing his unfrocking—wilful non-confession of sin, unwillingness to repent, claiming that lust is not contrary to the doctrine.

三舟觀月 v. 一月三舟.

三般若 The three prajñās, or perfect enlightenments: (*a*) 實相 | | wisdom in its essence or reality; (*b*) 觀照 | | the wisdom of perceiving the real meaning of the last; (*c*) 方便 | | or 文字 | | the wisdom of knowing things in their temporary and changing condition.

三色 The three kinds of rūpa, or form-realms: the five organs (of sense), their objects, and invisible perceptions, or ideas. Cf. 三種色.

三苦 The three kinds of duḥkha, pain, or suffering: 苦苦 that produced by direct causes; 壞 | by loss or deprivation; 行 | by the passing or impermanency of all things.

三草二木 A parable in the Lotus Sūtra; the small plants representing ordinary men and devas, medium sized plants śrāvakas and pratyeka-buddhas, and 大草, 小樹 and 大樹 tall plants and small and large trees three grades of bodhisattvas. Another definition applies the term to the 五乘 five "vehicles". There are also others.

三莊嚴 The three adornments, or glories, of a country: material attractions; religion and learning; men, i.e. religious men and bodhisattvas.

三菩伽 Sambhoga or Saṁbhūta. An ancient ṛṣi of Mathurā. | | | 迦耶 Sambhogakāya. (1) The "body of enjoyment" or recompense-body of a Buddha; his 報身 or reward-body, one of the Trikāya, 三身. (2) The third of the buddhakṣetra 佛土, the domain in which all respond perfectly to their Buddha.

三菩提 Sambodhi, 糝帽地 intp. 正等覺. Perfect universal awareness, perfectly enlightened; v. 菩提.

三落叉 The three lakṣa; a lakṣa is a mark, sign, token, aim, object; it is also 100,000, i.e. an 億. The three lakṣa of the esoteric sects are the 字 or magic word, the 印 symbol and the 本尊 object worshipped. Other such threes are body, mouth, and mind; morning, noon, and evening; cold, heat, and rain, etc.

三藏 v. 藏. | | 教 A T'ien-t'ai name for Hīnayāna, whose tripiṭaka is ascribed to Mahākāśyapa. | | 學者 A student of Hīnayāna. | | 法師 A teacher of the Law; especially 玄奘 Hsüan-tsang of the T'ang dynasty; and cf. 般若.

三藐三佛陀 Samyaksaṁbuddha 三耶三佛 (檀). The third of the ten titles of a Buddha, defined as 正徧知 (or 覺), or 正等覺, etc., one who has perfect universal knowledge or understanding; omniscient. | | | 菩提; 三貌糝帽地; 三耶三菩 Samyak-saṁbodhi. Correct universal intelligence, 正徧知(道). Correct equal or universal enlightenment (正等覺). Correct universal perfect enlightenment (正等正覺). An epithet of every Buddha. The full term is anuttara-samyak-saṁbodhi, perfect universal enlightenment, knowledge, or understanding; omniscience.

三蘊 The three kinds of skandhas, aggregations, or combinations, into which all life may be expressed according to the 化地 or Mahīśāsakāḥ school: 一念 | combination for a moment, momentary existence; 一期 | combination for a period, e.g. a single human lifetime; 窮生死 | the total existence of all beings.

三處傳心 The three places where Śākyamuni is said to have transmitted his mind or thought direct and without speech to Kāśyapa: at the 靈山 by a smile when plucking a flower; at the 多子塔 when he shared his seat with him; finally by putting his foot out of his coffin. | | 木叉 The mokṣa of the three places, i.e. moral control over body, mouth, and mind. | | 阿蘭若 Three classes of āraṇyakāḥ or ascetics distinguished by their three kinds of abode —those who dwell in retired places, as in forests; among tombs; in deserts; v. 阿蘭若.

三行 Three lines of action that affect karma, i.e. the ten good deeds that cause happy karma; the ten evil deeds that cause unhappy karma; 不動業 or 無動行 karma arising without activity, e.g. meditation on error and its remedy.

三衍 The three yāna, or vehicles to nirvāṇa,

i.e. śrāvaka, pratyekabuddha, and bodhisattva, v. 三乘.

三術 Three devices in meditation for getting rid of Māra-hindrances: within, to get rid of passion and delusion; without, to refuse or to withdraw from external temptation.

三衣 The three regulation garments of a monk, 袈裟 kāṣāya, i.e. 僧伽梨 saṅghāṭī, assembly robe; 鬱多羅僧 uttarāsaṅga, upper garment worn over the 安陀會 antarvāsaka, vest or shirt. 單 | | The only proper garments of a monk.

三衰 The three deteriorators, idem 三毒.

三補吒 Sampuṭa. One of the twelve ways of putting the hands together in worship, i.e. bringing the hands together without the palms touching.

三覆八校 The three reports and eight investigations. 三 | denote a day in each of the first, fifth, and ninth months when the recording angels of the four Lokapālas report on the conduct of each individual; 八 | are the opening days of the four seasons and the two solstices and two equinoxes during which similar investigations are made. Two angels, 同生 and 同名, observe each individual, the first a female at his right shoulder noting the evil deeds; the second, a male, at his left shoulder noting the good deeds; both report on high and in hades six times a month. Thus in each month there are 六齋 and in each year 三覆 and 八校.

三覺 The three kinds of enlightenment: (1) (*a*) 自覺 Enlightenment for self; (*b*) 覺他 for others; (*c*) 覺行圓 (or 窮) 滿 perfect enlightenment and accomplishment; the first is an arhat's, the first and second a bodhisattva's, all three a Buddha's. (2) From the Awakening of Faith 起信論 (*a*) 本 | inherent, potential enlightenment or intelligence of every being; (*b*) 始 |, initial, or early stages of such enlightenment, brought about through the external perfuming or influence of teaching, working on the internal perfuming of subconscious intelligence; (*c*) 究竟 | completion of enlightenment, the subjective mind in perfect accord with the subconscious (or superconscious) mind, or the inherent intelligence.

三觀 The three studies, meditations, or insights. The most general group is that of T'ien-t'ai: (*a*) 空 | study of all as void, or immaterial; (*b*) 假 | of all as unreal, transient, or temporal; (*c*) 中 | as the *via media* inclusive of both. The Hua-yen group is 眞空 |, 理事無礙 | and 周遍含容 |, see 華嚴經法界觀. The 南山 group is 性空 |, 相空 |, and 唯識 |. The 慈恩 group is 有 |, 空 | and 中 |.

三角壇 A three-cornered altar in the fire-worship of Shingon, connected with exorcism.

三解脫(門) The three emancipations, idem 三空 and 三三昧 q.v. They are 空解脫, 無相 | | and 無作 | |. Cf. 三涅槃門.

三語 Buddha's three modes of discourse, i.e. without reserve, or the whole truth; tactical or partial, adapting truth to the capacity of his hearers; and a combination of both.

三論 The three śastras translated by Kumārajīva, on which the 三論宗 Three Śāstra School (Mādhyamika) bases its doctrines, i.e. 中論 Madhyamaka-śāstra, on "the Mean", A.D. 409; 十二門論 Dvādaśanikāya-śāstra, on the twelve points, A.D. 408; 百論 Śata-śāstra, the hundred verses, A.D. 404. | | 宗 The San-lun, Mādhyamika, or Middle School, founded in India by Nāgārjuna, in China by 嘉祥 Chia-hsiang during the reign of 安帝 An Ti, Eastern Tsin, A.D. 397–419. It flourished up to the latter part of the T'ang dynasty. In 625 it was carried to Japan as Sanron. After the death of Chia-hsiang, who wrote the 三論玄義, a northern and southern division took place. While the Mādhyamika denied the reality of all phenomenal existence, and defined the noumenal world in negative terms, its aim seems not to have been nihilistic, but the advocacy of a reality beyond human conception and expression, which in our terminology may be termed a spiritual realm.

三請 A request thrice repeated — implying earnest desire.

三諦 The three dogmas. The "middle" school of T'ien-t'ai says 即空, 即假, 即中, i.e. 就是空, 假, 中; (*a*) by 空 śūnya is meant that things causally produced are in their essential nature unreal (or immaterial) 實空無; (*b*) 假, though things are unreal in their essential nature their derived forms are real; (*c*) 中; but both are one, being of the one 如 or reality. These three dogmas are founded on a verse of Nāgārjuna's—

因緣所生法、我說即是空、
亦爲是假名、亦是中道義.

"All causally produced phenomena, I say, are unreal,
Are but a passing name, and indicate the 'mean'."
There are other explanations—the 圓 敎 interprets the 空 and 假 as 中; the 別 敎 makes 中 independent. 空 is the all, i.e. the totality of all things, and is spoken of as the 眞 or 實 true, or real; 假 is the differentiation of all things and is spoken of as 俗 common, i.e. things as commonly named; 中 is the connecting idea which makes a unity of both, e.g. "all are but parts of one stupendous whole." The 中 makes all and the all into one whole, unifying the whole and its parts. 空 may be taken as the immaterial, the undifferentiated all, the sum of existences, by some as the Tathāgata-garbha 如來藏; 假 as the unreal, or impermanent, the material or transient form, the temporal that can be named, the relative or discrete; 中 as the unifier, which places each in the other and all in all. The "shallower" 山外 school associated 空 and 中 with the noumenal universe as opposed to the phenomenal and illusory existence represented by 假. The "profounder" 山內 school teaches that all three are aspects of the same. | | 相 卽 The unity of 空, 假, 中, three aspects of the same reality, taught by the 圓 敎 as distinguished from the 別 敎 which separates them.

三 識 The three states of mind or consciousness: 眞 | the original unsullied consciousness or Mind, the Tathāgata-garbha, the eighth or ālaya |; 現 | mind or consciousness diversified in contact with or producing phenomena, good and evil; 分 別 | consciousness discriminating and evolving the objects of the five senses. Also 意 | manas, 心 | ālaya, and 無 垢 | amala, v. 識.

三 變 (土 田) The three transformations of his Buddha-realm made by Śākyamuni on the Vulture Peak—first, his revelation of this world, then its vast extension, and again its still vaster extension. See Lotus Sūtra.

三 賢 十 聖 (or 地). The three virtuous positions, or states, of a bodhisattva are 十 住, 十 行 and 十 廻 向. The ten excellent characteristics of a 聖 saint or holy one are the whole of the 十 地.

三 跋 致 (or 諦) Saṁpatti. To turn out well, prosper, be on the path of success.

三 跋 羅 Saṁvara. 三 婆 (or 嚩) 羅 To hinder, ward off, protect from falling into the three inferior transmigrations; a divine being that fills this office worshipped by the Tantra School. The sixth vijñāna, v. 八 識.

三 身 Trikāya. 三 寶 身 The threefold body or nature of a Buddha, i.e. the 法, 報, and 化 身, or Dharmakāya, Sambhogakāya, and Nirmāṇakāya. The three are defined as 自 性, 受 用, and 變 化, the Buddha-body *per se*, or in its essential nature; his body of bliss, which he "receives" for his own "use" and enjoyment; and his body of transformation, by which he can appear in any form; i.e. spiritual, or essential; glorified; revealed. While the doctrine of the Trikāya is a Mahāyāna concept, it partly results from the Hīnayāna idealization of the earthly Buddha with his thirty-two signs, eighty physical marks, clairvoyance, clairaudience, holiness, purity, wisdom, pity, etc. Mahāyāna, however, proceeded to conceive of Buddha as the Universal, the All, with infinity of forms, yet above all our concepts of unity or diversity. To every Buddha Mahāyāna attributed a three-fold body: that of essential Buddha; that of joy or enjoyment of the fruits of his past saving labours; that of power to transform himself at will to any shape for omnipresent salvation of those who need him. The trinity finds different methods of expression, e.g. Vairocana is entitled 法 身, the embodiment of the Law, shining everywhere, enlightening all; Locana is 報 身; cf. 三 寶, the embodiment of purity and bliss; Śākyamuni is 化 身 or Buddha revealed. In the esoteric sect they are 法 Vairocana, 報 Amitābha, and 化 Śākyamuni. The 三 寶 are also 法 Dharma, 報 Saṅgha, 化 Buddha. Nevertheless, the three are considered as a trinity, the three being essentially one, each in the other. (1) 法 身 Dharmakāya in its earliest conception was that of the body of the dharma, or truth, as preached by Śākyamuni; later it became his mind or soul in contrast with his material body. In Mādhyamika, the dharmakāya was the only reality, i.e. the void, or the immaterial, the ground of all phenomena; in other words, the 眞 如, the Tathāgata-garbha, the bhūtatathatā. According to the Hua-yen (Kegon) School it is the 理 or noumenon, while the other two are 氣 or phenomenal aspects. "For the Vijñānavāda . . . the body of the law as highest reality is the void intelligence, whose infection (saṁkleça) results in the process of birth and death, whilst its purification brings about Nirvāṇa, or its restoration to its primitive transparence" (Keith). The "body of the law is the true reality of everything". Nevertheless, in Mahāyāna every Buddha has his own 法 身; e.g. in the dharmakāya aspect we have the designation Amitābha, who in his saṁbhogakāya aspect is styled Amitāyus. (2) 報 身 Sambhogakāya, a Buddha's reward body, or body of enjoyment of the merits he attained as a bodhisattva; in other words, a Buddha in glory in his heaven. This is the form of Buddha as an object of worship. It is defined in two aspects, (a) 自受用身 for his own bliss, and (b) 他受用身 for the sake of others, revealing himself in his glory to bodhisattvas, enlightening and inspiring them. By wisdom a Buddha's dharmakāya is attained, by bodhisattva-merits his saṁbhogakāya. Not only has every Buddha all the three bodies or aspects, but as all men are of the same essence, or nature, as Buddhas, they are therefore potential Buddhas and are in and of the Trikāya. Moreover, Trikāya is not divided, for a Buddha in his 化身 is still one with his 法身 and 報身, all three bodies being co-existent. (3) 化身; 應身; 應化身 Nirmāṇakāya, a Buddha's transformation, or miraculous body, in which he appears at will and in any form outside his heaven, e.g. as Śākyamuni among men. | | 三德 The 三身 are as above the 法報應; the 三德 are 法, 般, and 解, i.e. the virtue, or merit, of the (a) 法身 being absolute independence, reality; of (b) 報身, being 般若 prajñā or wisdom; and of (c) 應身, being 解脫德 liberation, or Nirvāṇa. | | 佛性 v. 三身. | | 如來 v. 三身. | | 業 The three physical wrong deeds—killing, robbing, adultery.

三車 Triyāna. 三乘 or 三乘法門 (1) The three vehicles across saṁsāra into nirvāṇa, i.e. the carts offered by the father in the Lotus Sūtra to lure his children out of the burning house: (a) goat carts, representing śrāvakas; (b) deer carts, pratyekabuddhas; (c) bullock carts, bodhisattvas. (2) The three principal schools of Buddhism—Hīnayāna, Madhyamayāna, Mahāyāna. | | 家 idem 三乘家.

三軌 The three rules 三法 (妙) of the T'ien-t'ai Lotus School: (a) 眞性 | The absolute and real, the 眞如 or bhūtatathatā; (b) 觀照 | meditation upon and understanding of it; (c) 資成 | the extension of this understanding to all its workings. In the 三軌弘經 the three are traced to the 法師品 of the Lotus Sūtra and are developed as: (a) 慈悲室 the abode of mercy, or to dwell in mercy; (b) 忍辱衣 the garment of endurance, or patience under opposition; (c) 法空座 the throne of immateriality (or spirituality), a state of nirvāṇa tranquillity. Mercy to all is an extension of 資成 |, patience of 觀照 | and nirvāṇa tranquillity of 眞性 |.

三輩 The three ranks of those who reach the Pure Land of Amitābha: superior, i.e. monks and nuns who become enlightened and devote themselves to invocation of the Buddha of boundless age; medium, i.e. laymen of similar character who do pious deeds; inferior, i.e. laymen less perfect than the last.

三輪 The three wheels: (1) The Buddha's (a) 身 body or deeds; (b) 口 mouth, or discourses; (c) 意 mind or ideas. (2) (a) 神通 (or 變) His supernatural powers, or powers of (bodily) self-transformation, associated with 身 body; (b) 記心 | his discriminating understanding of others, associated with 意 mind; (c) 教誡 | or 正教 | his (oral) powers of teaching, associated with 口. (3) Similarly (a) 神足 |; (b) 說法 |; (c) 憶念 |. (4) 惑, 業, and 苦. The wheel of illusion produces karma, that of karma sets rolling that of suffering, which in turn sets rolling the wheel of illusion. (5) (a) Impermanence; (b) uncleanness; (c) suffering. Cf. 三道. | | 世界 The three-wheel world, i.e. 風, 水, and 金輪. Every world is founded on a wheel of whirling wind; above this is one of water; above this is one of metal, on which its nine mountains and eight seas are formed. | | 化導 idem 三種示導. | | 教 The three periods of the Buddha's teaching as defined by Paramārtha: (a) 轉法輪 the first rolling onwards of the Law-wheel, the first seven years' teaching of Hīnayāna, i.e. the 四諦 four axioms and 空 unreality; (b) 照法輪 illuminating or explaining the law-wheel, the thirty years' teaching of the 般若 prajñā or wisdom sūtras, illuminating 空 and by 空 illuminating 有 reality; (c) 持法輪 maintaining the law-wheel, i.e. the remaining years of teaching of the deeper truths of 空有 both unreality and reality. Also the three-fold group of the Lotus School: (a) 根本法輪 radical, or fundamental, as found in the 華嚴 sūtra; (b) 枝末法輪 branch and leaf, i.e. all other teaching; until (c) 攝末歸本法輪 branches and leaves are reunited with the root in the Lotus Sūtra, 法華經. | | 相 The three-wheel condition—giver, receiver, gift.

三轉(法輪) The three turns of the law-wheel when the Buddha preached in the Deer Park: (a) 示轉 indicative, i.e. postulation and definition of the 四諦; (b) 勸轉 hortative, e.g. 苦當知 suffering should be diagnosed; (c) 證轉 evidential, e.g. I have overcome suffering, etc. | | | | 十二行 (相) The twelve 行 processes are the application of the above 示, 勸, and 證 to each of the four postulates. The three "turns" are also applied to the four kinds of knowledge, i.e. 眼, 智, 明, and 覺.

三迦葉 Three brothers Kāśyapa, all three said to be disciples of the Buddha.

三逆 The three unpardonable sins of Devadatta,

which sent him to the Avīci hell—schism, stoning the Buddha to the shedding of his blood, killing a nun.

三迷 Sama, 等, equal, like, same as.

三退屈 The three feelings of oppression that make for a bodhisattva's recreancy—the vastness of bodhi; the unlimited call to sacrifice; the uncertainty of final perseverance. There are 三事練磨 three modes of training against them.

三通力 idem 三達 and 三明.

三道 (1) The three paths all have to tread; 輪廻三道, 三輪, i.e. (a) 煩惱 丨; 惑 丨; the path of misery, illusion, mortality; (b) 業 丨 the path of works, action, or doing, productive of karma; (c) 苦 丨 the resultant path of suffering. As ever recurring they are called the three wheels. (2) 聲, 緣, 菩 Śrāvakas, pratyeka-buddhas, bodhisattvas, cf. 三乘. 丨丨眞言 Three magical "true words" or terms of Shingon for self-purification, i.e. 吽嚂嗒 which is the "true word" for 身 the body; 訶囉鶴 for 語 the mouth or speech; and 嚂嗒 for 意 the mind.

三過 Transgressions of body, mouth, mind, i.e. thought, word, deed.

三達 Three aspects of the omniscience of Buddha: knowledge of future karma, of past karma, of present illusion and liberation; v. 三明.

三那三佛 idem 三藐三佛陀.

三部(大法) (1) The Garbhadhātu maṇḍala, or pantheon, has the three divisions of 佛, 蓮, 金, i.e. Vairocana, Lotus, and Diamond or Vajra. (2) The teaching of the 胎藏界, 金剛界, and 蘇悉地法 is said to cover the whole of esoteric Buddhism. 丨丨主色 the colours of the three divisions: Vairocana, white; 觀世音 (as representing) Amitābha, yellow; and the Diamond Ruler, Śākyamuni, a ruddy yellow. 丨丨經 There are several groups: (1) The Amitābha group, also styled 淨土三部, is 無量壽經, 觀無量壽經 and 阿彌陀經. (2) The Vairocana group is 大日經, 金剛頂經 and 蘇悉地經; also called 丨丨秘經. (3) The Lotus group is the 無量義經, 妙法蓮華經 and 觀普賢菩薩行法經. (4) The Maitreya group is 觀彌勒菩薩上生兜率天經, 彌勒下生經 and 彌勒大成佛經.

三醫 The three modes of diagnosis: the superior, 聽聲 listening to the voice; the medium, 相色 observing the external appearance; the inferior, 診脈 testing the pulse.

三重三昧 (or 等持) idem 三三昧. 丨丨法界 The three meditations, on the relationship of the noumenal and phenomenal, of the 華嚴宗 Hua Yen School: (a) 理法界 the universe as law or mind, that all things are 眞如, i.e. all things or phenomena are of the same Buddha-nature, or the Absolute; (b) 理事無礙法界 that the Buddha-nature and the thing, or the Absolute and phenomena are not mutually exclusive; (c) 事事無礙法界 that phenomena are not mutually exclusive, but in a common harmony as parts of the whole.

三金 The three metals, gold, silver, copper. The esoterics have (a) earth, water, fire, representing the 身密 mystic body; (b) space and wind, the 語密 mystic mouth or speech; (c) 識 cognition, the 意密 mystic mind.

三鉢羅佉哆 Samprāpta, intp. by 善至, 正至, or 時至 well, properly, or timely arrived. Also written 僧跋 intp. 等施 bestowed equally or universally. It is a word spoken authoritatively, some say before, some say after a common meal; a "blessing" to ward off evil from the food.

三鈷 A trident; emblem of the Garbhadhātu 三部; and of the 三智, 三觀 等, and 三軌. Also written 丨古; 丨胡; 丨股.

三銖 Three twenty-fourths of a tael, the weight of a deva's garments, e.g. featherweight.

三長(齋)月 The three whole months of abstinence, the first, fifth, and ninth months, when no food should be taken after noon. The four deva-kings are on tours of inspection during these months.

三門 Trividha-dvāra, the three gates; a monastery; purity of body, speech, and thought; idem 三解脫門 also 三業. 丨丨三大侍者 The three officiators in a monastery—for incense, for writing, and for acting as host.

三阿僧祇刼 The three great asaṁkhyeya (i.e. beyond number) kalpas—the three timeless periods of a bodhisattva's progress to Buddhahood.

三陀羅尼 The three dhāraṇī, which word from dhāra, "maintaining," "preserving," is defined as the power maintaining wisdom or knowledge. Dhāraṇī are "spells chiefly for personal use" (Eliot), as compared with mantra, which are associated with religious services. The T'ien-t'ai School interprets the "three dhāraṇī" of the Lotus Sūtra on the lines of the 三諦, i.e. 空, 假, and 中. Another group is 聞持｜｜｜ the power to retain all the teaching one hears; 分別｜｜｜ unerring powers of discrimination; 入音聲｜｜｜ power to rise superior to external praise or blame.

三階(佛)法 The Three Stages School founded by the monk 信行 Hsin-hsing in the Sui dynasty; it was proscribed in A.D. 600 and again finally in A.D. 725; also styled ｜｜院; ｜｜敎.

三際 Past, present, future, idem 三世. ｜｜時 The three Indian seasons, spring, summer, and winter, also styled 熱, 雨, 寒際時, the hot, rainy, and cold seasons.

三障 The three vighna, i.e. hinderers or barriers, of which three groups are given: (1) (*a*) 煩惱｜ the passions, i.e. 三毒 desire, hate, stupidity; (*b*) 業｜ the deeds done; (*c*) 報｜ the retributions. (2) (*a*) 皮煩惱｜; (*b*) 肉｜｜｜; (*c*) 心｜｜｜ skin, flesh, and heart (or mind) troublers, i.e. delusions from external objects, internal views, and mental ignorance. (3) 三重障 the three weighty obstructions: (*a*) self-importance, 我慢; (*b*) envy, 嫉妬; (*c*) desire, 貪欲.

三雜染 The three kaṣāya, i.e. "mixed dyes" or infections: the passions; their karma; reincarnation; or illusion, karma, and suffering.

三難 The three hardships, or sufferings in the three lower paths of transmigration, v. 三惡道.

三面大黑 The three-faced great black deva, Mahākāla v. 摩, with angry mien, a form of Maheśvara, or Śiva, as destroyer. Another interpretation says he is a union of Mahākāla, Vaiśravaṇa, and a Gandharva.

三顚倒 The three subversions or subverters: (evil) thoughts, (false) views, and (a deluded) mind.

三餘 The three after death remainders, or continued mortal experiences, of śrāvakas and pratyekabuddhas, who mistakenly think they are going to 無餘涅槃 final nirvāṇa, but will still find 煩惱｜ further passion and illusion, 業｜ further karma, and 果｜ continued rebirth, in realms beyond the 三界 trailokya.

三馬 The three horses, one young, strong, and tractable; another similar but not tractable; a third old and intractable, i.e. bodhisattvas (or bodhisattva-monks), śrāvakas, and icchantis.

三魔 The three kinds of evil spirits, of which three groups are given: (1) 煩惱｜, 陰｜, and 他化自在天子｜; (2) 煩惱｜, 天｜, and 死｜; (3) 善知識｜, 三昧｜, and 菩提心｜.

三默堂 The three halls of silence where talk and laughter are prohibited: the bathroom, the sleeping apartment, the privy.

三點 See 伊字三點.

三齋月 See 三長(｜)｜.

丸香 Incense balls made of various kinds of ingredients; typifying the aggregation of mortal suffering, and its destruction by the fires of wisdom.

久 Long, for long, long ago; also ｜遠. ｜住者 One who has spent many years in monastic life, or in a particular monastery. ｜成正覺 Perfect enlightenment long acquired; Śākya-Tathāgata in ancient kalpas having achieved complete bodhi, transmitted it to Mañjuśrī, Avalokiteśvara, and others, i.e. their enlightenment is the fruit of his enlightenment. 法華經壽量品. ｜遠實成 The perfect enlightenment achieved by the Buddha in remote kalpas.

乞 To beg; ｜丐 a beggar. ｜士 A bhikṣu, mendicant monk, or almsman. ｜嘌雙提贊 Khri-srong-lde-btsan, king of Tibet (A.D. 743–798). In 747 he brought to Tibet "the real founder of Lamaism" (Eliot), Padmasaṁbhava 蓮華生上師, a Buddhist of Swat (Urgyan), who introduced a system of magic and mysticism (saturated with Śivaism) which found its way into Mongolia and China. The king was converted to Buddhism by his mother, a Chinese princess, and became a powerful supporter of it. He encouraged the translation of the Buddhist canon which was completed by his successors. He is worshipped as an incarnation of Mañjuśrī. ｜灑; ｜察; ｜叉; 吃灑; 葛叉; 訖灑; 差; 叉; 剎; Kṣaya, used in the sense of omega, implying finality, or nirvāṇa. |眼婆羅門 The Brahman who begged one of Śāriputra's eyes in a former incarnation, then trampled on it, causing Śāriputra to give up his efforts to become a bodhisattva and turn back to the Hīnayāna. |食 To beg for food, one of the twelve dhūtas prescribing outward conduct of the monk; mendicancy is the 正命 right livelihood of a monk, to work for a living is 邪命 an improper life; mendicancy keeps a monk humble, frees him from the cares of life, and offers the donors a field of blessedness; but he may not ask for food. |食四分 The four divisions of the mendicant's dole; to provide for (1) fellow religionists, (2) the poor, (3) the spirits, (4) self.

于 Yü, a preposition, in, at, etc., similar to 於. In |遮那摩羅 and the next it is used in error for 干 kan; Kāñcana-mālā, a hair circlet or ornament of pure gold; name of the wife of Kuṇāla, noted for fidelity to her husband when he had been disgraced. |闍那; |闍羅 Kuñjara. Name of a tree. |闐; |遁; |殿; |塡; 谿丹; 屈丹; 和闐; 澳那; 瞿薩怛那 Kustana, or Khotan, in Turkestan, the principal centre of Central Asian Buddhism until the Moslem invasion. Buddhism was introduced there about 200 B.C. or earlier. It was the centre from which is credited the spread of Mahāyānism, v. 西域記 12.

亡 Gone, lost, dead, ruined; not. |五衆物 The things left behind at death by any one of the five orders of monks or nuns; clothing, etc., being divided among the other monks or nuns; valuables and land, etc., going to the establishment. |者 Dead; the dead. |魂 The soul of the dead.

凡 All, everybody, common, ordinary. |僧 The ordinary practising monk as contrasted with the 聖僧 the holy monk who has achieved higher merit. |夫; 波羅; 婆羅必栗託佐那; 婆羅必利他伽闍那 Bālapṛthagjana. Everyman, the worldly man, the sinner. Explained by 異生 or 愚異生 one who is born different, or outside the Law of the Buddha, because of his karma. |夫十重妄 The serious misfortunes of the sinful man in whom the Ālaya-vijñāna, the fundamental intelligence, or life force, of everyman, is still unenlightened; they are compared to ten progressive stages of a dream in which a rich man sees himself become poor and in prison. |(夫)性 The common underlying nature of all men; also called 異生性. |小 Common men, or sinners, also believers in Hīnayāna; also the unenlightened in general. |小八倒 The eight subverted views of common men and Hīnayānists—counting the impermanent as permanent, the non-joy as joy, the non-ego as ego, the impure as pure; the really permanent as impermanent, the real joy, the true ego, the real purity as non-joy, non-ego, impurity; cf. 四德. |師 Ordinary, or worldly teachers unenlightened by Buddhist truth. |情 Desires or passions of the unconverted. |愚 Common, ignorant, or unconverted men. |慮 The anxieties of common or unconverted men. |福 The ordinary blessedness of devas and men as compared with that of the converted. |種 Common seed, ordinary people. |習 The practices, good and evil, of common, or unconverted men. |聖 Sinners and saints. ||一如; ||不二 Sinners and saints are of the same fundamental nature. ||同居土 This world, where saints and sinners dwell together; one of the T'ien-t'ai 四土. |識 Ordinary knowledge, worldly knowledge, that of the unenlightened by Buddha. |身 The common mortal body, the ordinary individual.

刃 A blade, a sword; to kill. |(or 劍)葉林 Asipattravana; the forest of swords, where every leaf is a sharp sword, v. 地獄.

千 Sahasra. A thousand. |二百五十人 The 1,250, i.e. the immediate disciples of Buddha's disciples, all former heretics converted to Buddha's truth. |二百舌 (or 耳, or 意) 功德 The 1,200 merits of tongue, ear, or mind, in the Lotus Sūtra. |佛 The thousand Buddhas. Each of the past, present, and future kalpas has a thousand Buddhas; Śākyamuni is the "fourth" Buddha in the present kalpa. The ||名經 professes to give their names. |化 The thousand-petalled lotus on which sits Locana Buddha, each petal a transformation of Śākyamuni; Locana represents also the Saṅgha, as Vairocana represents the Dharma. |如是 The thousand "suchnesses" or characteristics, a term of the T'ien-t'ai sect. In each of the ten realms 十界, from Buddha to purgatory, the ten are present, totalling one hundred. These multiplied by the ten categories of existence make a thousand, and multiplied by the three categories of group existence make 3,000. |手(千眼); 千手千眼大慈大悲觀音菩薩 The thousand-hand Kuan-yin, see below. There are various sūtras associated with this title, e.g. ||經, an abbreviation of ||千眼觀世音菩薩大...陀羅尼經; also ||軌 or 軌經 an abbreviation of 金剛頂瑜伽 ||...儀軌經; it is also called ||陀羅尼 and ||千眼儀軌經; there are many others, e.g. ||||觀世音菩薩姥陀羅尼身經 and ||||廣大圓滿無礙大悲心陀羅尼經 both idem ||千臂陀羅尼神咒, which is the Avalokiteśvara-padma-jāla-mūla-tantra-nāma-dhāraṇī. 丨手觀音; 千手千眼觀音; 千眼千臂觀世音 Sahasrabhuja-sahasranetra. One of the six forms of Kuan-yin with a thousand arms and a thousand eyes. The image usually has forty arms, one eye in each hand; and forty multiplied by twenty-five is the number of regions in this universe. For the 二十八部 or retinue, the maṇḍala and signs v. 千手經. 丨法明門 The gate of understanding of the thousand laws—the second stage of a bodhisattva's study and attainment. 丨泉 Bingheul. 屏律 Mingbulak. A lake country 30 li E. of Talas. 丨百億身 The Buddha Locana seated on a lotus of a thousand petals, each containing myriads of worlds; in each world is Śākyamuni seated under a bodhi-tree, all such worlds attaining bodhi at the same instant; see above. 丨眼天 The Deva with 1,000 eyes, epithet of Indra, 帝釋. 丨葉臺 The throne of a thousand petals, i.e. that of Locana Buddha; see above. 丨輻輪相 Sahasrāra; the thousand-spoked wheel sign, i.e. the wrinkles on the soles of a cakravarti, or Buddha. 丨部論師 (or 主) Master of a thousand śāstras—a title of Nāgārjuna and of Vasubandhu. 丨里駒 The thousand-li colt, a name for Hsüan-tsang.

叉 A fork, forked; to fold, folded. 丨手 The palms of the hands together with the fingers crossed forming ten. Also, the palms together with the middle fingers crossing each other, an old Indian form of greeting. In China anciently the left hand was folded over the right, but with women the right hand was over the left. In mourning salutations the order was reversed. 丨拏 Kṣaṇa, an instant, a moment; also 刹丨. 丨磨 Kṣamā, v. 懺悔. 丨耶 Kṣaya, diminish, decay, end; v. 乞.

口 Mukha, the mouth, especially as the organ of speech. 身, 口, 意 are the three media of corruption, body or deed, mouth or word, and mind or thought. 丨傳; 丨授 Oral transmission. 丨力外道 One of the eleven heretical sects of India, which is said to have compared the mouth to the great void out of which all things were produced. The great void produced the four elements, these produced herbs, and these in turn all the living; or more in detail the void produced wind, wind fire, fire warmth, warmth water, water congealed and formed earth which produced herbs, herbs cereals and life, hence life is food; ultimately all returns to the void, which is nirvāṇa. 丨丨論師; 因力論師 Exponents of the above doctrine. 丨印 The mouth sign, one of the fourteen symbols of 不重尊 q.v. 丨和 Harmony of mouths or voices, unanimous approval. 丨四 The four evils of the mouth, lying, double tongue, ill words, and exaggeration; cf. 十惡. 丨密; 語密 One of the 三密. Secret or magical words, either definite formulas of the Buddha or secret words from his dharmakāya, or spirit. 丨忍 Patience of the mouth, uttering no rebuke under insult or persecution; there are similarly 身丨 and 意丨. 丨業; 語業 One of the 三業. (1) The work of the mouth, i.e. talk, speech. (2) The evil karma produced by the mouth, especially from lying, double-tongue, ill words, and exaggeration. 丨業供養 The offering of the praise or worship of the lips; also 身丨丨丨 and 意丨丨丨. 丨疏; 奥疏 Esoteric commentary or explanation of two kinds, one general, the other only imparted to the initiated. 丨稱 Invocation. 丨丨三昧 The samādhi in which with a quiet heart the individual repeats the name of Buddha, or the samādhi attained by such repetition. 丨訣 Orally transmitted decisions or instructions. 丨輪; 正教輪 One of the 三輪. The wheel of the mouth, or the wheel of the true teaching; Buddha's teaching rolling on everywhere, like a chariot-wheel, destroying misery. 丨頭禪 Mouth meditation, i.e. dependence on the leading of others, inability to enter into personal meditation.

土 Bhū; bhūmi; pṛthivī. Earth, locality, local, vulgar. 丨地神 The local guardian deity of the soil or locality, deus loci; in the classics and government sacrifices known as 社; as guardian deity of the grave 后土. The 土地堂 is the shrine of this deity as ruler of the site of a monastery, and is usually east of the main hall. On the 2nd and 16th of each month a 土地諷經 or reading of a sūtra should be done at the shrine. 丨星; 賒乃以室拆羅 Śanaiścara. Saturn. Śani, the Hindu ruler of the planet, was "identified with the planet itself". [Eitel.] 丨波 Tibet. 丨砂供養; 丨丨加持 The putting of earth on the grave 108 times by the Shingon sect; they also put it on the deceased's body, and even on the sick, as a kind of baptism for sin, to save the deceased from the hells and base reincarnations, and bring them to the Pure Land. 丨羅遮; 偸蘭遮 Sthūlātyaya. Serious sin. 丨饅頭 An earthen loaf, i.e. a grave; but v. 土饅頭. 丨麨 Aśoka is said to have become king as a reward for offering, when a child in a previous incarnation, a double-handful of sand as wheat or food to the Buddha.

士 A gentleman, scholar, officer. 丨夫 v. 補盧沙 Puruṣa. 丨夫見 One of the eight heterodox views, i.e. the pride arising from belief in a puruṣa, 補盧沙 q.v. 丨饅頭 Śmaśāna. A crematory; a burial place for remains from cremation. A grave; v. 土饅頭. The form is doubtful.

夕 Evening. 丨座 The evening service, as 朝座 is the morning service.

大 Mahā. 摩訶; 麼賀. Great, large, big; all-pervading, all-embracing; numerous 多; surpassing 勝; mysterious 妙; beyond comprehension 不可思議; omnipresent 體無不在. The elements, or essential things, i.e. (*a*) 三大 The three all-pervasive qualities of the 眞如 q.v.: its 體, 相, 用 substance, form, and functions, v. 起信論. (*b*) 四大 The four tanmātra or elements, earth, water, fire, air (or wind) of the 俱舍論. (*c*) 五大 The five, i.e. the last four and space 空, v. 大日經. (*d*) 六大 The six elements, earth, water, fire, wind, space (or ether), mind 識. Hīnayāna, emphasizing impersonality 人空, considers these six as the elements of all sentient beings; Mahāyāna, emphasizing the unreality of all things 法空, counts them as elements, but fluid in a flowing stream of life, with mind 識 dominant; the esoteric sect emphasizing non-production, or non-creation, regards them as universal and as the Absolute in differentiation. (*e*) 七大 The 楞嚴經 adds 見 perception, to the six above named to cover the perceptions of the six organs 根.

大三末多 Mahāsaṁmata. The first of the five kings of the Vivarta kalpa (成劫五王), one of the ancestors of the Śākya clan.

大不可棄子部 Āvantikās. The great school of the son who "could not be abandoned" (a subdivision of the Saṁmatīyas 三彌底), whose founder when a newborn babe was abandoned by his parents.

大不善地法 The two great characteristics of the evil state, 無慚無愧 no sense of shame or disgrace, shameless.

大乘 Mahāyāna; also called 上丨; 妙丨; 勝丨; 無上丨; 無上上丨; 不惡丨; 無等丨; 無等等丨; 摩訶衍 The great yāna, wain, or conveyance, or the greater vehicle in comparison with the 小丨 Hīnayāna. It indicates Universalism, or Salvation for all, for all are Buddha and will attain bodhi. It is the form of Buddhism prevalent in Tibet, Mongolia, China, Korea, Japan, and in other places in the Far East. It is also called Northern Buddhism. It is interpreted as 大敎 the greater teaching as compared with 小敎 the smaller, or inferior. Hīnayāna, which is undoubtedly nearer to the original teaching of the Buddha, is unfairly described as an endeavour to seek nirvāṇa through an ash-covered body, an extinguished intellect, and solitariness; its followers are śrāvakas and pratyeka-buddhas (i.e. those who are striving for their own deliverance through ascetic works). Mahāyāna, on the other hand, is described as seeking to find and extend all knowledge, and, in certain schools, to lead all to Buddhahood. It has a conception of an Eternal Buddha, or Buddhahood as Eternal (Ādi-Buddha), but its especial doctrines are, *inter alia*, (*a*) the bodhisattvas 菩薩, i.e. beings who deny themselves final Nirvāṇa until, according to their vows, they have first saved all the living; (*b*) salvation by faith in, or invocation of the Buddhas or bodhisattvas; (*c*) Paradise as a nirvāṇa of bliss in the company of Buddhas, bodhisattvas, saints, and believers. Hīnayāna is sometimes described as 自利 self-benefiting, and Mahāyāna as 自利利他 self-benefit for the benefit of others, unlimited altruism and pity being the theory of Mahāyāna. There is a further division into one-yāna and three-yānas; the triyāna may be śrāvaka, pratyeka-buddha, and bodhisattva, represented by a goat, deer, or bullock cart; the one-yāna is that represented by the Lotus School as the one doctrine of the Buddha, which had been variously taught by him according to the capacity of his hearers, v. 方便. Though Mahāyāna tendencies are seen in later forms of the older Buddhism, the foundation of Mahāyāna has been attributed to Nāgārjuna 龍樹. "The characteristics of this system are an excess of transcendental speculation tending to abstract nihilism, and the substitution of fanciful degrees of meditation and contemplation (v. Samādhi and Dhyāna) in place of the practical asceticism of the Hīnayāna school." [Eitel 68–9.] Two of its foundation books are the 起信論 and the 妙法蓮華經, but a large number of Mahāyāna sūtras are ascribed to the Buddha.

大乘二種成佛 The two Mahāyāna kinds of Buddhahood: (1) that of natural purity, for every one has the inherent nature; (2) that attained by practice.

大乘善根界 The Mahāyāna good roots realm, a name for the Amitābha Pure-land of the West.

大乘四果 The four fruits, or bodhisattva stages in Mahāyāna, the fourth being that of a Buddha: 須陀洹 srota-āpanna, 斯陀含 sakṛdāgāmin, 阿那含 anāgāmin, and 阿羅漢 arhan. This is a 通敎 category.

大乘因 Mahāyāna "cause" is variously described as the mind of enlightenment 菩提心; or the reality behind all things 諸法實相.

大乘基 "Mahāyāna-fundament", title of 窺基 K'uei-chi, a noted disciple of Hsüan-tsang; known also as 大乘法師.

大乘妙經 idem 法華經 the Lotus sūtra.

大乘天 "Mahāyāna-deva", a title given to 玄奘 Hsüan-tsang, who was also styled 木叉提婆 Mokṣa-deva.

大乘宗 The school of Mahāyāna, attributed to the rise in India of the Mādhyamika, i.e. the 中觀 or 三論 school ascribed to Nāgārjuna, and the Yoga 瑜伽 or Dharmalakṣana 法相 school, the other schools being Hīnayāna. In China and Japan the 倶舍 and 成實 are classed as Hīnayāna, the rest being Mahāyāna, of which the principal schools are 律, 法相, 三論, 華嚴, 天台, 眞言, 淨土, 禪 q.v.

大乘心 The mind or heart of the Mahāyāna; seeking the mind of Buddha by means of Mahāyāna.

大乘戒 The commands or prohibitions for bodhisattvas and monks, also styled 菩薩|; 三聚淨|; 圓頓| and other titles according to the school. The 梵網經 gives ten weighty prohibitions and forty-eight lighter ones; v. also |||經.

大乘教 v. 大乘; for ||| 九部 v. 九部.

大乘方等經典 The sūtras and scriptures of the Mahāyāna, their doctrines being 方正 square and correct and 平等 for all equally, or universal.

大乘楞伽經唯識論 Viṁśatikāvijñaptimātratāsiddhi-śāstra. A title of one of three treatises by Vasubandhu, tr. A.D. 508-535, 大乘唯識論 tr. 557-569, and 唯識二十論 tr. by Hsüan-tsang in 661 being the other two.

大乘法師 a title for 窺基 v. ||基.

大乘法相教 and || 破相敎 v. 法相敎.

大乘無上法 The supreme Mahāyāna truth, according to the 楞伽經, is that of ultimate reality in contrast with the temporary and apparent; also reliance on the power of the vow of the bodhisattva.

大乘無作大戒 The Mahāyāna great moral law involving no external action; a T'ien-t'ai expression for the inner change which occurs in the recipient of ordination; it is the activity within; also |||| 圓頓戒; 無表大戒.

大乘純界 The lands wholly devoted to Mahāyāna, i.e. China and Japan, where in practice there is no Hīnayāna.

大乘經 Mahāyāna sūtras, the Sūtra-piṭaka. Discourses ascribed to the Buddha, presumed to be written in India and translated into Chinese. These are divided into five classes corresponding to the Mahāyāna theory of the Buddha's life: (1) Avataṁsaka, 華嚴, the sermons first preached by Śākyamuni after enlightenment; (2) Vaipulya, 方等; (3) Prajñā Pāramitā, 般若; (4) Saddharma Puṇḍarīka, 法華; and last (5) Mahāparinirvāṇa, 涅槃. Another list of Mahāyāna sūtras is 般若; 寶積; 大集; 華嚴 and 涅槃. The sūtras of Hīnayāna are given as the Āgamas 阿含, etc.

大乘莊嚴經論 Mahāyānasūtrālaṁkāra-ṭīkā. An exposition of the teachings of the Vijñāna-vāda School, by Asaṅga, tr. A.D. 630-3 by Prabhākaramitra. 13 chüan.

大乘起信論 Mahāyāna-śraddhotpāda-śāstra, attributed to Aśvaghoṣa 馬鳴 (without sufficient evidence), tr. by Paramārtha A.D. 553 and Śikṣānanda between 695-700; there are nineteen commentaries on it. It is described as the foundation work of the Mahāyāna. Tr. into English by Timothy Richard and more correctly by T. Suzuki as *The Awakening of Faith.*

大乘論 Abhidharma of the Mahāyāna, the collection of discourses on metaphysics and doctrines.

大乘頂王經 Vimalakīrti-nirdeśa-sūtra, is the Sanskrit title of a work of which there exist six translations, one made by Upaśūnya A.D. 502-557.

大事(因緣) For the sake of a great cause, or because of a great matter—the Buddha appeared, i.e. for changing illusion into enlightenment. The Lotus interprets it as enlightenment; the Nirvāṇa as the Buddha-nature; the 無量壽經 as the joy of Paradise.

大人相印 Sealed with the sign of manhood, i.e. of the religious life.

大仙 Maharṣi. Great sages, applied to Buddhist saints as superior to ordinary "immortals"; also to śrāvakas, and especially to Buddha; | | 戒 are the Buddha's laws or commands. Vasiṣṭha 婆私瑟侘 was one of the seven ṛṣis 大仙 of Brahmanic mythology.

大佛頂 A title of the esoteric sect for their form of Buddha, or Buddhas, especially of Vairocana of the Vajradhātu and Śākyamuni of the Garbhadhātu groups. Also, an abbreviation of a dhāraṇī as is | | | 經 of a sūtra, and there are other | | | scriptures.

大休歇底 Ended, finished; dead to the world; also | 死底.

大信(心) Great or firm faith in, or surrender to Buddha, especially to Amitābha. | | | 海 A heart of faith great as the ocean.

大僧 A fully ordained monk, i.e. a bhikṣu as contrasted with the śramaṇa. | | 正 The Director or Pope of monks; an office under Wu-ti, A.D. 502–550, of the Liang dynasty, for the control of the monks. Wên Ti, 560–7, of the Ch'ên dynasty appointed a | | 統 or Director over the monks in his capital.

大元帥明王 The great commander, one of the sixteen 明王 q.v., named Āṭavika 阿吒薄迦 (or 俱 or 皆). There are four sūtras, chiefly spells connected with his cult.

大光明王 The Great-Light Ming-wang, Śākyamuni in a previous existence, when king of Jambudvīpa, at Benares. There his white elephant, stirred by the sight of a female elephant, ran away with him into the forest, where he rebuked his mahout, who replied, "I can only control the body not the mind, only a Buddha can control the mind." Thereupon the royal rider made his resolve to attain bodhi and become a Buddha. Later, he gave to all that asked, finally even his own head to a Brahman who demanded it, at the instigation of an enemy king. | | 音天 Ābhāsvara. The third of the celestial regions in the second dhyāna heaven of the form realm; v. 四禪天. | | 普照 The great light shining everywhere, especially the ray of light that streamed from between the Buddha's eyebrows, referred to in the Lotus sūtra. | | | | 觀音 One of the six forms of Kuan-yin.

大准提 Mahā-cundī, a form of Kuan-yin. There are dhāraṇīs beginning with the name Cundī.

大刧 Mahākalpa. The great kalpa, from the beginning of a universe till it is destroyed and another begins in its place. It has four kalpas or periods known as vivarta 成 | the creation period; vivarta-siddha 住 | the appearance of sun and moon, i.e. light, and the period of life, human and general; saṁvarta 壞 | or 滅 | destruction first by fire, then water, then fire, then deluge, then a great wind, i.e. water during seven small kalpas, fire during 56 and wind one, in all 64; saṁvartatthāhi 增滅 | total destruction gradually reaching the void. A great kalpa is calculated as eighty small kalpas and to last 1,347,000,000 years. | | 賓寧 Kapphiṇa or Mahākapphiṇa v. 刼賓那.

大力王 King Powerful, noted for his unstinted generosity. Indra to test him appeared as a Brahman and asked for his flesh; the king ungrudgingly cut off and gave him his arm. Indra was then Devadatta, King Powerful was Śākyamuni; v. 菩薩藏經下. | | 金剛 The mighty "diamond" or Vajra-mahārāja in the Garbhadhātu group, a fierce guardian and servant of Buddhism, see below.

大勇 Āryaśūra. Also 聖勇. The great brave, or Ārya the brave. An Indian Buddhist author of several works. | | 猛菩薩 A guardian ruler in the Garbhadhātu group called Mahānīla, the Great Blue Pearl, or perhaps sapphire, which in some way is associated with him.

大勝金剛 Another name for 金輪佛頂, one of the incarnations of Vairocana represented with twelve arms, each hand holding one of his symbols. Also 大轉輪王; 金剛手.

大勢(至菩薩) Mahāsthāma or Mahāsthāmaprāpta 摩訶那鉢. A Bodhisattva representing the Buddha-wisdom of Amitābha; he is on Amitābha's right, with Avalokiteśvara on the left.

They are called the three holy ones of the western region. He has been doubtfully identified with Maudgalyāyana. Also 勢至. ||佛 The Buddha of mighty power (to heal and save), a Buddha's title.

大勤勇 Greatly zealous and bold—a title of Vairocana.

大化 The transforming teaching and work of a Buddha in one lifetime.

大千(世界) A major chiliocosm, or universe, of 3,000 great chiliocosms, v. 三千大千.

大召 A temple and its great bell in Lhasa, Tibet, styled 老木郎, built when the T'ang princess became the wife of the Tibetan king Ts'an-po and converted Tibet to Buddhism.

大吉祥天 The good-fortune devīs, and also devas, also called 功德天, concerning whom there are several sūtras. |||金剛 idem 金剛手. |||明菩薩 The sixth bodhisattva in the second row of the Garbhadhātu Kuan-yin group. ||大明菩薩 The fifth ditto. |||變菩薩 The sixth in the third row.

大叫喚地獄 Mahāraurava. The hell of great wailing, the fifth of the eight hot hells. Also 大呌; 大號呌; 大呼.

大和尙 Great monk, senior monk, abbot; a monk of great virtue and old age. Buddhoṣingha, 佛圖澄 Fo-t'u-ch'êng, who came to China A.D. 310, was so styled by his Chinese disciple 石子龍 Shih-tzŭ-lung. ||竭羅 Dīpaṁkara. The Buddha of burning light, the twenty-fourth predecessor of Śākyamuni, a disciple of Varaprabha; v. 燃 and 提. In the Lotus sūtra he appears from his nirvāṇa on the Vulture Peak with Śākyamuni, manifesting that the nirvāṇa state is one of continued existence.

大命 The great order, command, destiny, or fate, i.e. life-and-death, mortality, reincarnation.

大周刋定衆經目錄 The catalogue in 14 chüan of the Buddhist scriptures made under the Empress Wu of the T'ang dynasty, the name of which she changed to Chou.

大品(經) The larger, or fuller edition of a canonical work, especially of the next. ||般若經; 摩訶般若波羅蜜經 The Mahāprajñāpāramitā sūtra as tr. by Kumārajīva in 27 chüan, in contrast with the 10 chüan edition.

大哉解脫服 Great! the robe of deliverance—verses in praise of the cassock, from the 善見論, sung on initiation into the order.

大唐內典錄 A catalogue of the Buddhist library in the T'ang dynasty A.D. 664. ||西域記 The Record of Western Countries by Hsüan-tsang of the T'ang dynasty; v. 西.

大善利 The great benefit that results from goodness, also expressed as ||大利 implying the better one is the greater the resulting benefit. ||地法 The ten mental conditions for cultivation of goodness, being a part of the forty-six methods mentioned in the 俱舍論 4; faith, zeal, renunciation, shame (for one's own sin), shame (for another's sin), no desire, no dislike, no harm, calmness, self-control. v. 大地法. ||知識 Well acquainted with the good; great friends.

大嚫 Dakṣiṇā, v. 達嚫.

大因陀羅座 The throne of Indra, whose throne is four-square to the universe; also 金剛輪座. ||||壇 Indra-altar of square shape. He is worshipped as the mind-king of the universe, all things depending on him.

大圓覺 Great and perfect enlightenment, Buddha-wisdom. ||鏡智 Great perfect mirror wisdom, i.e. perfect all-reflecting Buddha-wisdom. ||||觀 A meditation on the reflection of the perfect Buddha-wisdom in every being, that as an image may enter into any number of reflectors, so the Buddha can enter into me and I into him 入我我入.

大地 Great earth, the whole earth, everywhere, all the land, etc. ||(法) Ten bodhisattva bhūmi, or stages above that of 見道 in the 俱舍論 4, and the mental conditions connected with them. 大地 is also defined as good and evil, the association of mind with them being by the ten methods of 受, 想, 思, 觸, 欲, 慧, 念, 作意, 勝解, 三摩地.

大域龍 Dignāga, or Mahā-Dignāga, also known as 陳那 Jina, founder of the medieval school of Buddhist logic about the fifth century A.D. His works are known only in Tibetan translations. [Winternitz.]

大壇 A great altar, the chief altar.

大士 Mahāsattva. 開士 A great being, noble, a leader of men, a bodhisattva; also a śrāvaka, a Buddha; especially one who 自利利他 benefits himself to help others. ||籤 Bamboo slips used before Kuan-yin when the latter is consulted as an oracle.

大夜 The great night, i.e. that before the funeral pyre of a monk is lighted; also 迨|; 宿|.

大夢 The great dream, "the dream of life," this life, the world.

大天 Mahādeva. 摩訶提婆. (1) A former incarnation of Śākyamuni as a Cakravartī. (2) A title of Maheśvara. (3) An able supporter of the Mahāsāṅghikāḥ, whose date is given as about a hundred years after the Buddha's death, but he is also described as a favourite of Aśoka, with whom he is associated as persecutor of the Sthavirāḥ, the head of which escaped into Kashmir. If from the latter school sprang the Mahāyāna, it may account for the detestation in which Mahādeva is held by the Mahāyānists. An account of his wickedness and heresies is given in 西域記 3 and in 婆沙論 99.

大秦寺 (1) A monastery of the Manichæan sect, erected in Ch'ang-an during the T'ang dynasty by order of the emperor T'ai Tsung A.D. 627–650; also 波斯寺. (2) A Nestorian monastery mentioned in the Christian monument at Sianfu.

大姉 Elder sister, a courtesy title for a lay female devotee, or a nun.

大威德 Mahātejas. Of awe-inspiring power, or virtue, able to suppress evil-doers and protect the good. A king of garuḍas, v. 迦. Title of a 明王 protector of Buddhism styled |||者; |||尊; |||明王; 百光扁照王; there are symbols, spells, esoteric words, sūtras, etc., connected with this title.

大婆羅門 The great Brāhmaṇa, applied to the Buddha, who though not of Brahman caste was the embodiment of Brahman virtues. ||||經 A sūtra dealing with this aspect. 大堅固||| The great reliable Brāhmaṇa, i.e. Śākyamuni in a previous life when minister of a country; there is a sūtra of this name.

大孔雀王 The mayūra, or "peacock" 明王, v. 孔雀王. There are seven sets of spells connected with him.

大安達羅 Mahendra, or Mahendrī, or Rājamahendrī. A city near the mouth of the Godavery, the present Rājamundry. ||慰 The great comforter, or pacifier—a Buddha's title.

大定智悲 Great insight, great wisdom, great pity, the three virtues 三德 of a Buddha by which he achieves enlightenment and wisdom and saves all beings.

大寂定 The samādhi which the Tathāgata enters, of perfect tranquillity and concentration with total absence of any perturbing element; also parinirvāṇa. Also ||室三昧; ||靜三摩地. ||法王 The great tranquil or nirvāṇa dharma-king, i.e. Vairocana. ||滅 Parinirvāṇa; the great nirvāṇa.

大寒林 The grove of great cold, śītavana, i.e. burial stūpas, the graveyard.

大寶 Great Jewel, most precious thing, i.e. the Dharma or Buddha-law; the bodhisattva; the fire-altar of the esoteric cult. ||坊 The "great precious region", described in the 大集 sūtra as situated between the world of desire and the world of form. ||摩尼 The great precious maṇi, or pure pearl, the Buddha-truth. ||法王 Mahāratna-dharma-rāja. Title of the reformer of the Tibetan church, founder of the Yellow sect, b. A.D. 1417, worshipped as an incarnation of Amitābha, now incarnate in every Bogdo gegen Hutuktu reigning in Mongolia. He received this title in A.D. 1426. v. 宗客巴 Tsong-kha-pa. ||海 The "great precious ocean" (of the merit of Amitābha). ||積經 Mahāratnakūṭa-sūtra. Collection of forty-nine sūtras, of which thirty-six were translated by Bodhiruci and collated by him with various previous translations. ||華 The great precious flower, a lotus made of pearls. |||王 King of jewel-lotuses, i.e. the finest of such gem-flowers. ||||座 A throne of such. ||藏 The great precious treasury, containing the gems of the Buddha-truth.

大寺 Mahāvihāra. The Great Monastery, especially that in Ceylon visited by Fa-hsien about A.D. 400, when it had 3,000 inmates; v. 毘訶羅.

大導師 The great guide, i.e. Buddha, or a Bodhisattva.

大小二乘 The two vehicles, Mahāyāna and Hīnayāna; v. 大乘 and 小乘.

大師 Great teacher, or leader, one of the ten titles of a Buddha.

大幻師 Great magician, a title given to a Buddha.

大度師 Great leader across mortality to nirvāṇa, i.e. Buddha, or Bodhisattva.

大廣智三藏 He of great, wide wisdom in the Tripiṭaka, a title of Amogha 阿目佉.

大德 Bhadanta. 婆檀陀 Most virtuous, a title of honour of a Buddha; in the Vinaya applied to monks.

大心力 The great mind and power, or wisdom and activity of Buddha. | | 海 Great mind ocean, i.e. omniscience.

大念(佛) Invoking Buddha with a loud voice; meditating on Buddha with continuous concentration.

大志焚身 The monk Ta-chih who sacrificed himself on the pyre, and thus caused Yang Ti of the Sui dynasty to withdraw his order for dispersing the monks.

大忍法界 The great realm for learning patience, i.e. the present world.

大恩教主 The Lord of great grace and teacher of men, Buddha.

大惡象 The great wild elephant, i.e. the untamed heart.

大悲 Mahākaruṇā, "great pity"; i.e. greatly pitiful, a heart that seeks to save the suffering; applied to all Buddhas and bodhisattvas; especially to Kuan-yin. | | 三昧 The samādhi of great pity, in which Buddhas and bodhisattvas develop their great pity. | | 代受苦 Vicarious suffering (in purgatory) for all beings, the work of bodhisattvas. The same idea in regard to Kuan-yin is conveyed in | | 千手(地)獄. | | 咒 Another name of the 千手經 or 千手陀羅尼 containing a spell against lust. | | 壇 The altar of pity, a term for the Garbhadhātu maṇḍala, or for the Śākyamuni group. | | 弓 The bow of great pity. Pity, a bow in the left hand; wisdom 智, an arrow in the right hand. | | 四八之應 The thirty-two or thirty-three manifestations of the All-pitiful Kuan-yin responding to every need. | | 普現 Great pity universally manifested, i.e. Kuan-yin, who in thirty-three manifestations meets every need. | | 生心三昧耶 The samādhi of Maitreya. | | 經 Mahākaruṇā-puṇḍarīka sūtra, tr. by Narendrayaśas and Dharmaprajña A.D. 552, five books. | | 者 The great pitiful one, Kuan-yin. | | 胎藏 The womb—store of great pity, the fundamental heart of bodhi in all; this womb is likened to a heart opening as an eight-leaved lotus, in the centre being Vairocana, the source of pity. | | (| |) 曼荼羅 The maṇḍala of the above. | | | | 三昧 The samādhi in which Vairocana evolves the group, and it is described as the "mother of all Buddha-sons". | | 菩薩 Kuan-yin, the Bodhisattva of great pity. | | 觀(世)音 Kuan-yin, the greatly pitiful regarder of (earth's) cries. | | 鎧冑門 A degree of samādhi in which Vairocana produced the Bodhisattva Vajrapāla 金剛護菩薩 who protects men like a helmet and surrounds them like mail by his great pity. | | 闡提 The greatly pitiful icchantikaḥ, who cannot become a Buddha till his saving work is done, i.e. Kuan-yin, Ti-tsang.

大慈 Great mercy, or compassion. | | 大悲 Great mercy and great pity, characteristics of Buddhas and bodhisattvas, i.e. kindness in giving joy and compassion in saving from suffering. It is especially applied to Kuan-yin. | | 尊 The honoured one of great kindness, Maitreya. | | 恩寺 The monastery of "Great Kindness and Grace", built in Ch'ang-an by the crown prince of T'ai Tsung A.D. 648, where Hsüan-tsang lived and worked and to which in 652 he added its pagoda, said to be 200 feet high, for storing the scriptures and relics he had brought from India. | | | | 三藏 "Tripiṭaka of the Ta T'zŭ En Ssŭ" is one of his titles.

大慈生菩薩 The director or fosterer of pity among all the living, i.e. the fifth in the 除蓋障 court of the Garbhadhātu group. Also 大慈起; 慈發生; 慈愍慧; 慈念金剛. His Sanskrit name is translit. 昧怛利也毘庾拏蘖多.

大意 The general meaning or summary of a sūtra or śāstra. Also, the name of a youth, a former incarnation of the Buddha; to save his nation from their poverty, he plunged into the sea to obtain a valuable pearl from the sea-god who, alarmed by the aid rendered by Indra, gave up the pearl; v. | | 經 tr. by Guṇabhadra of the Liu Sung dynasty, 1 chüan.

大愛道 Mahāprajāpatī, 摩訶波闍波提 Gautama's aunt and foster-mother, also styled Gotamī or Gautamī, the first woman received into the order. There are sūtras known by her name. 大愛 is also a name for the sea-god.

大應供 The great worshipful—one of the ten titles of a Buddha.

大會 A general assembly. | | 衆 The general assembly (of the saints).

大愚 The "greatly ignorant", name of a monastery and title of its patriarch, of the Ch'an (Zen) or intuitive school.

大慧 Mahāmati 摩訶摩底. (1) Great wisdom, the leading bodhisattva of the Laṅkāvatāra sūtra. (2) Name of a Hangchow master of the Ch'an school, 宗杲 Tsung-kao of the Sung dynasty, whose works are the | | 書. (3) Posthumous title of 一行 I-hsing, a master of the Ch'an school, T'ang dynasty. | | 刀印 The sign of the great wisdom sword, the same esoteric sign as the 寶瓶印 and 塔印. There are two books, the abbreviated titles of which are | | 語錄 and its supplement the | | 武庫.

大成 Mahāsaṁbhava. Great completion. The imaginary realm in which (in turn) appeared 20,000 koṭis of Buddhas all of the same title, Bhīṣmagarjitaghoṣasvararāja.

大戒 The complete commandments of Hīnayāna and Mahāyāna, especially of the latter.

大我 The greater self, or the true personality 眞我. Hīnayāna is accused of only knowing and denying the common idea of a self, or soul, whereas there is a greater self, which is a nirvāṇa self. It especially refers to the Great Ego, the Buddha, but also to any Buddha; v. 大日經 1, etc., and 涅槃經 23.

大拘絺那 Mahākauṣṭhila, 摩訶俱絺 (or 祉) 羅, an eminent disciple of Śākyamuni, maternal uncle of Śāriputra, reputed author of the Saṁgītiparyāya śāstra.

大拏 Sudāna, 須達 (or 大) 拏; 蘇達拏; i.e. Śākyamuni as a prince in a former life, when he forfeited the throne by his generosity.

大攝受 The great all-embracing receiver—a title of a Buddha, especially Amitābha.

大教 The great teaching. (1) That of the Buddha. (2) Tantrayāna. The mahātantra, yoga, yogācārya, or tantra school which claims Samantabhadra as its founder. It aims at ecstatic union of the individual soul with the world soul, Īśvara. From this result the eight great powers of Siddhi (Aṣṭa-mahāsiddhi), namely, ability to (1) make one's body lighter (laghiman); (2) heavier (gariman); (3) smaller (aṇiman); (4) larger (mahiman) than anything in the world; (5) reach any place (prāpti); (6) assume any shape (prākāmya); (7) control all natural laws (īśitva); (8) make everything depend upon oneself (vaśitva); all at will (v. 如意身 and 神足). By means of mystic formulas (tantras or dhāraṇīs), or spells (mantras), accompanied by music and manipulation of the hands (mudrā), a state of mental fixity characterized neither by thought nor the annihilation of thought, can be reached. This consists of six-fold bodily and mental happiness (yoga), and from this results power to work miracles. Asaṅga compiled his mystic doctrines *circa* A.D. 500. The system was introduced into China A.D. 647 by Hsüan-tsang's translation of the Yogācārya-bhūmi-śāstra 瑜伽師地論; v. 瑜. On the basis of this, Amoghavajra established the Chinese branch of the school A.D. 720; v. 阿目. This was popularized by the labours of Vajrabodhi A.D. 732; v. 金剛智. | | 經 idem 大金剛頂經. | | 網 The net of the great teaching, which saves men from the sea of mortal life.

大方便 Mahopāya; the great appropriate means, or expedient method of teaching by buddhas and bodhisattvas; v. 方便.

大方廣 Mahāvaipulya; cf. | | 等 The great Vaipulyas, or sūtras of Mahāyāna. 方廣 and 方等 are similar in meaning. Vaipulya is extension, spaciousness, widespread, and this is the idea expressed both in 廣 broad, widespread, as opposed to narrow, restricted, and in 等 levelled up, equal everywhere, universal. These terms suggest the broadening of the basis of Buddhism, as is found in Mahāyāna. The Vaipulya works are styled sūtras, for the broad doctrine of universalism, very different from the traditional account of his discourses, is put into the mouth of the Buddha in wider, or universal aspect. These sūtras are those of universalism, of which the Lotus 法華 is an outstanding example. The form Vaitulya instead of Vaipulya is found in some Kashgar MSS. of the Lotus, suggesting that in the Vetulla sect lies the origin of the Vaipulyas, and with them of Mahāyāna, but the evidence is inadequate. ｜｜｜佛 The 本尊 fundamental honoured one of the 華嚴經, described as the Buddha who has realized the universal law. ｜｜｜｜華嚴經 Buddhāvataṁsaka-mahāvaipulya-sūtra; the Avataṁsaka, Hua-yen, or Kegon sūtra; tr. by Buddhabhadra and others A.D. 418–420. The various translations are in 60, 80, and 40 chüan, v. 華嚴經. ｜｜｜如來秘密藏經 Tathāgata-garbha-sūtra, tr. A.D. 350–431, idem 大方等如來藏經, tr. by Buddhabhadra A.D. 417–420, 1 chüan.

大方等 Mahāvaipulya or Vaipulya 大方廣; 毗佛畧. They are called 無量義經 sūtras of infinite meaning, or of the infinite; first introduced into China by Dharmarakṣa (A.D. 266–317). The name is common to Hīnayāna and Mahāyāna, but chiefly claimed by the latter for its special sūtras as extending and universalizing the Buddha's earlier preliminary teaching. v. 大方廣 and 方等. ｜｜｜大集經 Mahāvaipulya-mahāsaṃnipāta-sūtra, tr. A.D. 397–439, said to have been preached by the Buddha "from the age of 45 to 49 . . . to Buddhas and bodhisattvas assembled from every region, by a great staircase made between the world of desire and that of form". B.N. Another version was made by Jñānagupta and others in A.D. 594 called ｜｜｜｜｜賢護經. ｜｜｜頂王說經 Vimalakīrtti-nirdeśa-sūtra, tr. by Dharmarakṣa A.D. 265–316.

大族王 Mihirakula 摩醯羅矩羅, an ancient Hūna king in the Punjab *circa* A.D. 520 who persecuted Buddhism; v. 西域記 4.

大施太子 (or 菩薩). The great princely almsgiver, i.e. Śākyamuni in a previous life; also 能施｜｜(or ｜｜). ｜｜會; 無遮大會 Mokṣa-mahā-pariṣad; a great gathering for almsgiving to all, rich and poor, nominally quinquennial.

大日 Vairocana, or Mahāvairocana 大日如來; 遍照如來; (摩訶) 毘盧遮那; 大日覺王 The sun, "shining everywhere." The chief object of worship of the Shingon sect in Japan, "represented by the gigantic image in the temple at Nara." (Eliot.) There he is known as Dai-nichi-nyorai. He is counted as the first, and according to some, the origin of the five celestial Buddhas (dhyāni-buddhas, or jinas). He dwells quiescent in Arūpa-dhātu, the Heaven beyond form, and is the essence of wisdom (bodhi) and of absolute purity. Samanta-bhadra (P'u-hsien) is his dhyāni-bodhisattva. The ｜｜經 "teaches that Vairocana is the whole world, which is divided into Garbhadhātu (material) and Vajradhātu (indestructible), the two together forming Dharmadhātu. The manifestations of Vairocana's body to himself—that is, Buddhas and Bodhisattvas—are represented symbolically by diagrams of several circles". Eliot. In the 金剛界 or Vajradhātu maṇḍala he is the centre of the five groups. In the 胎藏界 or Garbhadhātu he is the centre of the eight-leaf (lotus) court. His appearance, symbols, esoteric word, differ according to the two above distinctions. Generally he is considered as an embodiment of the Truth 法, both in the sense of Dharmakāya 法身 and Dharmaratna 法寶. Some hold Vairocana to be the dharmakāya of Śākyamuni 大日與釋迦同一佛 but the esoteric school denies this identity. Also known as 最高顯廣眼藏如來, the Tathāgata who, in the highest, reveals the far-reaching treasure of his eye, i.e. the sun. 大日大聖不動明王 is described as one of his transformations. Also, a śramaṇa of Kashmir (contemporary of Padma-saṁbhava); he is credited with introducing Buddhism into Khotan and being an incarnation of Mañjuśrī; the king Vijaya Saṁbhava built a monastery for him. ｜｜供 A meeting for the worship of Vairocana. ｜｜宗 The cult of Vairocana especially associated with the 胎藏界 Garbhakośadhātu, or phenomenal world. ｜｜經 The Vairocana sūtra, styled in full 毘盧遮那成佛神變加持經, tr. in the T'ang dynasty by Śubhakarasiṁha 善無畏 in 7 chüan, of which the first six are the text and the seventh instructions for worship. It is one of the three sūtras of the esoteric school. Its teaching pairs with that of the 金剛頂經. There are two versions of notes and comments on the text, the ｜｜｜疏 20 chüan, and ｜｜｜義疏 14 chüan; and other works, e.g. ｜｜｜義釋; ｜｜｜不思議疏; ｜｜｜義軌 in four versions with different titles. The cult has its chief vogue in Japan. ｜｜覺王 Vairocana, the king of bodhi.

大明王 The angels or messengers of Vairocana, v. 明王. ｜｜三藏聖敎目錄 The "Great Ming" dynasty catalogue of the Tripiṭaka, made during the reign of the emperor Yung Lo; it is the catalogue of the northern collection. ｜｜白身菩薩

The great bright white-bodied bodhisattva, sixth in the first row of the Garbhadhātu Kuan-yin group. | | 續入藏諸集 Supplementary miscellaneous collection of Buddhist books, made under the Ming dynasty A.D. 1368–1644.

大智 Mahāmati; cf. 大慧; Great Wisdom, Buddha-wisdom, omniscience; a title of Mañjuśrī, as the apotheosis of transcendental wisdom. | | 度論 A śāstra ascribed to Nāgārjuna on the greater Prajñā-pāramitā sūtra; the śāstra was tr. by Kumārajīva, A.D. 397–415, in 100 chüan. | | 慧門 The Buddha-door of great wisdom, as contrasted with that of his 大悲 great compassion. | | 灌頂地 The stage of the Great Wisdom chrism, or anointing of a Buddha, as having attained to the Great Wisdom, or omniscience; it is the eleventh stage. | | 藏 The Buddha-wisdom store.

大曼(荼羅) The great maṇḍala; one of four groups of Buddhas and bodhisattvas of the esoteric school. The esoteric word 阿 "a" is styled the great maṇḍala-king.

大本 The great, chief, or fundamental book or text. T'ien-t'ai takes the 無量壽經 as the major of the three Pure-land sūtras, and the 阿彌陀經 as the 小本 minor.

大林寺 Mahāvana-saṅghārāma 摩訶伐那伽藍摩 "The monastery of the great forest", S. of Mongali. | | 精舍 The Veṇuvana monastery, called 竹林 | | or 寺, and 竹苑, Veṇuvana vihāra, in the Karaṇḍa veṇuvana, near Rājagṛha, a favourite resort of Śākyamuni.

大相 Mahārūpa; great form. The kalpa of Mahābhijñā-jñānābhibhu, who is to appear as Buddha in a realm called Saṁbhava.

大染法 The great taint, or dharma of defilement, sex-attraction, associated with 愛染明王 Eros, the god of love.

大梵 Mahābrahmāṇas; the third Brahmaloka, the third region of the first dhyāna. Mahābrahman; the great Brahma, | | 天; it is also a title of one of the six Kuan-yin of the T'ien-t'ai sect.

大梵天 Mahābrahman; Brahmā;. 跋羅吸摩; 波羅賀磨; 梵覽摩; 梵天王; 梵王; 梵. Eitel says: "The first person of the Brahminical Trimūrti, adopted by Buddhism, but placed in an inferior position, being looked upon not as Creator, but as a transitory devatā whom every Buddhistic saint surpasses on obtaining bodhi. Notwithstanding this, the Saddharma-puṇḍarīka calls Brahmā 'the father of all living beings'" 一切衆生之父. Mahābrahman is the unborn or uncreated ruler over all, especially according to Buddhism over all the heavens of form, i.e. of mortality. He rules over these heavens, which are of threefold form: (*a*) Brahmā (lord), (*b*) Brahma-purohitas (ministers), and (*c*) Brahma-pāriṣadyāḥ (people). His heavens are also known as the middle dhyāna heavens, i.e. between the first and second dhyānas. He is often represented on the right of the Buddha. According to Chinese accounts the Hindus speak of him (1) as born of Nārāyaṇa, from Brahmā's mouth sprang the brahmans, from his arms the kṣatriyas, from his thighs the vaiśyas, and from his feet the śūdras; (2) as born from Viṣṇu; (3) as a trimūrti, evidently that of Brahmā, Viṣṇu, and Śiva, but Buddhists define Mahābrahmā's dharmakāya as Maheśvara (Śiva), his saṁbhogakāya as Nārāyaṇa, and his nirmāṇakāya as Brahmā. He is depicted as riding on a swan, or drawn by swans. | | 如意天 idem | | 天 The term is incorrectly said by Chinese interpreters to mean freedom from sexual desire. He is associated with Vairocana, and with fire. v. also 尸棄. | | 天王 Mahābrahmā devarāja, king of the eighteen Brahmalokas.

大樂說 Mahāpratibhāna. A bodhisattva in the Lotus sūtra, noted for pleasant discourse. | | 不空; | | 金剛(薩埵) "Unceasing great joy", a Shingon name for the second of its eight patriarchs, P'u-hsien, v. 金剛薩埵. There are works under this title.

大樓炭經 A sūtra, also called 起世經, on Buddhist cosmology, 6 chüan, tr. by 法立 Fa-li and others; 樓炭 is a Sanskrit term meaning 成敗 creation and destruction.

大機 The great opportunity, or Mahāyāna method of becoming a bodhisattva.

大樹 Great trees, i.e. bodhisattvas, cf. 三草. | | 仙人 Mahāvṛkṣa ṛṣi, the ascetic Vāyu, who meditated so long that a big tree grew out of his shoulders. Seeing a hundred beautiful princesses he desired them; being spurned, he was filled with hatred, and with a spell turned them into hunchbacks; hence Kanyākubja, v. 羯 or 罽 the city of hump-backed maidens; its king was ? Brahmadatta. v. 西域記 5. | | 緊那羅 The King of the mahādruma Kinnaras, Indra's musicians, who lives on Gandha-mādana.

His sūtra is | | | | | 王所問經, 4 chüan, tr. by Kumārajīva.

大權 The great potentiality; or the great power of Buddhas and bodhisattvas to transform themselves into others, by which e.g. Māyā becomes the mother of 1,000 Buddhas, Rāhula the son of 1,000 Buddhas, and all beings are within the potency of the dharmakāya. | | 善經 is an abbreviation of 慧上菩薩問 | | | |. | | 修利菩薩 A bodhisattva—protector of monasteries, depicted as shading his eyes with his hand and looking afar, said to have been a Warden of the Coast under the emperor Aśoka.

大死底人 One who has swept away completely all illusions, or all consciousness; also 大休歇底.

大比丘 Great bhikṣu, i.e. one of virtue and old age; similar to 大和尙.

大毘盧遮那 Mahāvairocana, v. 大日.

大水火(災) Mahāpralaya; the final and utter destruction of a universe by (wind), flood, and fire.

大紅蓮 Great red lotuses—name of a cold hell where the skin is covered with chaps like lotuses.

大沙門 Mahāśramaṇa. The great shaman, i.e. Buddha; also any bhikṣu in full orders. | | | 統 A director of the order appointed by Wên Ti of the Sui dynasty, A.D. 581–618.

大法 The great Dharma, or Law (of Mahāyāna salvation). | | 慢 Intellectual pride, arrogance through possession of the Truth. | | 王 Sudharma-rāja, King of the Sudharma Kinnaras, the horse-headed human-bodied musicians of Kuvera. | | 螺 The Great Law conch, or Mahāyāna bugle. | | 鼓 The Great Law drum; v. | | | 經 Mahābherī-hāraka-parivarta; tr. by Guṇabhadra A.D. 420–479. | | 雨 The raining, i.e. preaching, of the Mahāyāna.

大波羅蜜 The great pāramitās, or perfections, of bodhisattvas, i.e. the ten pāramitās above the 八地.

大洲 A great continent; one of the four great continents of a world; v. 四洲.

大海 Mahāsamudra-sāgara 摩訶三母捺羅娑誐羅 The Ocean. | | 八不思議 The eight marvellous characteristics of the ocean—its gradually increasing depth, its unfathomableness, its universal saltness, its punctual tides, its stores of precious things, its enormous creatures, its objection to corpses, its unvarying level despite all that pours into it. | | 十相 The ten aspects of the ocean, the Hua-yen sūtra adds two more to the above eight, i.e. all other waters lose their names in it; its vastness of expanse. | | 印 The ocean symbol, i.e. as the face of the sea reflects all forms, so the samādhi of a bodhisattva reflects to him all truths; it is also termed 海印三昧. | | 衆 The great ocean congregation; as all waters flowing into the sea become salty, so all ranks flowing into the saṅgha become of one flavour and lose old differentiations.

大滅諦金剛智 The first two of the 三德 three Buddha-powers; they are (*a*) his principle of nirvāṇa, i.e. the extinction of suffering, and (*b*) his supreme or vajra wisdom.

大滿 Great, full, or complete; tr. of mahā-pūrṇa, king of monster birds or garuḍas who are enemies of the nāgas or serpents; he is the vehicle of Viṣṇu in Brahmanism. | | 願義 One of the sixteen bodhisattvas of the southern quarter, born by the will of Vairocana.

大灌頂 The greater baptism, used on special occasions by the Shingon sect, for washing away sin and evil and entering into virtue; v. 灌頂經.

大炎熱 Pratāpana or Mahātāpana; the hell of great heat, the seventh of the eight hot hells.

大無量壽經 idem 大經 q.v.

大煩惱地法 The six things or mental conditions producing passion and delusion: stupidity, excess, laziness, unbelief, confusion, discontent (or ambition); v. 俱舍論 4.

大燒炙獄 v. 大炎熱 Pratāpana, above.

大熾盛光 The great blazing perfect light, a title of 金輪佛頂尊.

大牛車 The great ox cart in the Lotus sūtra parable of the burning house, i.e. Mahāyāna. | | 音 Krośa; the distance of the lowing of a great ox, the "eighth" (more correctly fourth) part of a yojana; v. 拘盧.

大王 Mahārāja 摩賀羅惹. Applied to the four guardians of the universe, 四大天王.

大生主 Mahāprajāpatī 摩訶波闍婆提, great "lady of the living", the older translation being 大愛道 the great way (or exemplar) of love; also 衆主 head of the community (of nuns), i.e. Gautamī, the aunt and nurse of Śākyamuni, the first nun. She is to be reborn as a Buddha named Sarvasattvapriyadarśanā.

大界 The area of a vihāra or monastic establishment. ||外相 Four characters often placed on the boundary stones of monasterial grounds.

大白傘蓋佛母 The "mother of Buddhas" with her great snow-white (radiant) umbrella, emblem of her protection of all beings; there are two dhāraṇī-sūtras that bear this name and give her description, 佛頂|||| and 佛說||||總持陀羅尼經. ||光神; 鬱多羅迦神 ? Uttaraka. The deva of the Himālayas, one of the retinue of the 十二神. ||牛車 The great white-bullock cart of the Lotus sūtra, the Mahāyāna, as contrasted with the deer-cart and goat-cart of śrāvakas and pratyeka-buddhas, i.e. of Hīnayāna. ||華 The great mandāra 曼陀羅 flower, also called ||團|. ||衣 Pāṇḍaravāsinī, the great white-robed one, a form of Kuan-yin all in white, with white lotus, throne, etc., also called 白衣 or 白處觀音.

大目乾連 Mahāmaudgalyāyana; v. 摩訶目犍連.

大相國寺 The great aid-the-dynasty monastery at Kaifeng, Honan, founded in A.D. 555, first named 建國, changed *circa* 700 to the above; rebuilt 996, repaired by the Kin, the Yüan, and Ming emperors, swept away in a Yellow River flood, rebuilt under Shun Chih, restored under Ch'ien Lung. ||看 The reception by an abbot of all his monks on the first day of the tenth moon.

大神力 Supernatural or magical powers. ||咒 are dhāraṇī spells or magical formulæ connected with these powers. ||王 The great deva-king, Mahākāla, the great black one, (1) title of Maheśvara, i.e. Śiva; (2) a guardian of monasteries, with black face, in the dining hall; he is said to have been a disciple of Mahādeva, a former incarnation of Śākyamuni.

大祥忌 The great propitious anniversary, i.e. a sacrifice every third year.

大種 The four great seeds, or elements (四大) which enter into all things, i.e. earth, water, fire, and wind, from which, as from seed, all things spring.

大空 The great void, or the Mahāyāna parinirvāṇa, as being more complete and final than the nirvāṇa of Hīnayāna. It is used in the Shingon sect for the great immaterial or spiritual wisdom, with its esoteric symbols; its weapons, such as the vajra; its samādhis; its sacred circles, or maṇḍalas, etc. It is used also for space, in which there is neither east, west, north, nor south.

大笑(明王) ? Vajrahāsa 跋折羅吒訶婆 The great laughing Ming-wang, v. 明王.

大弟子 Sthavira, a chief disciple, the Fathers of the Buddhist church; an elder; an abbot; a priest licensed to preach and become an abbot; also 上坐.

大精進菩薩 Śūra, a hero bodhisattva, one of the sixteen in the southern external part of the 金剛界 group.

大統 The head of the order, an office instituted by Wên Ti of the Sui dynasty; cf. 大僧正.

大經 The great sūtra, i.e. the 2-chüan 佛說無量壽經, so called by the Pure-land sect and by T'ien-t'ai, the Amida sūtra being the 小本 smaller sūtra; cf. 大本 and 大日經. ||卷 A term for the heart.

大綱 The main principles of Buddhism, likened to the great ropes of a net.

大總相法門 The Bhūtatathatā as the totality of things, and Mind 心眞如 as the Absolute, v. 起信論.

大義王 (or 城) The king, or city, of all ideas, or aims, i.e. the heart as mind.

大聖 The great sage or saint, a title of a Buddha,

or a bodhisattva of high rank; as also are | | 世尊 and | | 主 the great holy honoured one, or lord. For | | 天 idem | | 歡喜天 v. 歡喜天, on whom there are three works. | | 金剛夜叉 one of the five 大明王. For | | 妙吉祥 and | | 曼殊室利 see Mañjuśrī; there are two works under the first of these titles, one under the second, and one under | | 文殊.

大自在 Īśvara, self-existent, sovereign, independent, absolute, used of Buddhas and bodhisattvas. | | | 天 Maheśvara, 摩醯首濕伐羅 or Śiva, lord of the present chiliocosm, or universe; he is described under two forms, one as the prince of demons, the other as divine, i.e. 毘舍闍 Piśāca-maheśvara and 淨居 Śuddhāvāsa- or Śuddhodana-maheśvara. As Piśāca, head of the demons, he is represented with three eyes and eight arms, and riding on a white bull; a bull or a liṅga being his symbol. The esoteric school takes him for the transformation body of Vairocana, and as appearing in many forms, e.g. Viṣṇu, Nārāyaṇa (i.e. Brahmā), etc. His wife (śakti) is Bhīmā, or | | | | 婦. As Śuddhāvāsa, or Pure dwelling, he is described as a bodhisattva of the tenth or highest degree, on the point of entering Buddhahood. There is dispute as to whether both are the same being, or entirely different. The term also means the sixth or highest of the six desire-heavens. | | | 宮 The abode of Maheśvara at the apex of the Form-realm. Also, the condition or place from which the highest type of bodhisattva proceeds to Buddhahood, whence it is also styled 淨居天 the pure abode heaven.

大興善寺 The great goodness-promoting monastery, one of the ten great T'ang monasteries at Ch'ang-an, commenced in the Sui dynasty.

大船 The great ship of salvation—Mahāyāna. | | 師 Its captain, Buddha.

大般涅槃 Mahāparinirvāṇa, explained by 大入滅息 the great, or final entrance into extinction and cessation; or 大圓寂入 great entrance into perfect rest; 大滅度 great extinction and passing over (from mortality). It is interpreted in Mahāyāna as meaning the cessation or extinction of passion and delusion, of mortality, and of all activities, and deliverance into a state beyond these concepts. In Mahāyāna it is not understood as the annihilation, or cessation of existence; the reappearance of Dīpaṁkara 然燈 (who had long entered nirvāṇa) along with Śākyamuni on the Vulture Peak supports this view. It is a state above all terms of human expression. See the Lotus sūtra and the Nirvāṇa sūtra. | | | | 經 The Mahā-parinirvāṇa sūtras, commonly called the 涅槃經 Nirvāṇa sūtras, said to have been delivered by Śākyamuni just before his death. The two Hīnayāna versions are found in the 長阿含遊行經. The Mahāyāna has two Chinese versions, the northern in 40 chüan, and the southern, a revision of the northern version, in 36 chüan. Fa-hsien's version is styled | | 泥洹經 6 chüan. Treatises on the sūtra are | | | | | 後分 2 chüan tr. by Jñānabhadra; | | | | | 疏 33 chüan; | | | | | 論 1 chüan by Vasubandhu, tr. by Bodhidharma.

大般若(經) The Mahā-prajñā-pāramitā sūtra. | | | 供養 The worship of a new copy of the sūtra when finished, an act first attributed to Hsüan-tsang. | | | (波羅蜜多) 經 Mahā-prājñā-pāramitā sūtra, said to have been delivered by Śākyamuni in four places at sixteen assemblies, i.e. Gṛidhrakūṭa near Rājagṛha (Vulture Peak); Śrāvastī; Paranirmitavaśavartin, and Veluvana near Rājagṛha (Bamboo Garden). It consists of 600 chüan as translated by Hsüan-tsang. Parts of it were translated by others under various titles and considerable differences are found in them. It is the fundamental philosophical work of the Mahāyāna school, the formulation of wisdom, which is the sixth pāramitā.

大苦海 The great bitter sea, or great sea of suffering, i.e. of mortality in the six gati, or ways of incarnate existence.

大莊嚴 Mahāvyūha; great fabric; greatly adorned, the kalpa or Buddha-æon of Mahākāśyapa. | | | 世界 The great ornate world; i.e. the universe of Ākāśagarbha Bodhisattva 虛空藏菩薩; it is placed in the west by the sūtra of that name, in the east by the 大集經 12. | | | 經 Vaipulya-mahāvyūha-sūtra, tr. by Divākara, T'ang dynasty, 12 chüan; in which the Buddha describes his life in the Tuṣita heaven and his descent to save the world. | | | 經論 or 論經. Sūtrālaṅkāra-śāstra. A work by Aśvaghoṣa, tr. by Kumārajīva A.D. 405, 15 chüan.

大菩提(心) The great bodhi, i.e. Mahāyāna- or Buddha-enlightenment, as contrasted with the inferior bodhi of the śrāvaka and pratyeka-buddha. | | | 幢 The banner of great bodhi, an esoteric symbol of Buddha-enlightenment.

大菩薩 Bodhisattva-mahāsattva, a great Bodhisattva.

大蓮華 Puṇḍarīka, 分陀利; 芬利; 奔荼 the great white lotus; the last of the eight cold hells is so called. 丨丨丨法藏界 The great Lotus heaven in the Paradise of the West. 丨丨丨智慧三摩地智 The wisdom of the great lotus, samādhi-wisdom, the penetrating wisdom of Amitābha.

大薩遮尼犍子 Mahāsatya-nirgrantha. An ascetic who is said to have become a disciple of the Buddha.

大藏(經) The Tripiṭaka; the Buddhist canon. 丨丨一覽 "The Tripiṭaka at a Glance" in 10 chüan by 陳實 Ch'ên Shih of the Ming dynasty. 丨丨目錄 A catalogue of the Korean canon in 3 chüan.

大號叫 Mahāraurava 大叫; 大呼 The hell of great wailing, the fifth of the eight hot hells.

大衆 Mahāsaṅgha. The great assembly, any assembly, all present, everybody. 丨丨印 The seal of a monastery. 丨丨威德畏 Stage-struck, awed by an assembly, one of the five 怖畏. 丨丨部; 摩訶僧祇部 Mahāsāṅghikāḥ, the school of the community, or majority; one of the chief early divisions, cf. 上坐部 Mahāsthavirāḥ or Sthavirāḥ, i.e. the elders. There are two usages of the term, first, when the sthavira, or older disciples assembled in the cave after the Buddha's death, and the others, the 大衆, assembled outside. As sects, the principal division was that which took place later. The Chinese attribute this division to the influence of 大天 Mahādeva, a century after the Nirvāṇa, and its subsequent five subdivisions are also associated with his name; they are Pūrvaśailāḥ, Avaraśailāḥ, Haimavatāḥ, Lokottara-vādinaḥ, and Prajñapti-vādinaḥ; v. 小乘.

大衣 The monk's patch-robe, made in varying grades from nine to twenty-five patches.

大覺 The supreme bodhi, or enlightenment, and the enlightening power of a Buddha. 丨丨世尊 The World-honoured One of the great enlightenment, an appellation of the Buddha. 丨丨母 The mother of the great enlightenment, an appellation of Mañjuśrī. 丨丨金仙 The great enlightened golden ṛṣi, a name given to Buddha in the Sung dynasty.

大論 idem 丨智度丨. 丨丨師 Mahāvādin, Doctor of the Śāstras, a title given to eminent teachers, especially of the Sāṅkhya and Vaiseṣika schools.

大辯天 Sarasvatī 丨丨才天(女); 丨丨(才)功德天; 薩羅娑縛底; 薩羅酸底 A river, "the modern Sursooty"; the goddess of it, who "was persuaded to descend from heaven and confer her invention of language and letters on the human race by the sage Bhārata, whence one of her names is Bhāratī"; sometimes assumes the form of a swan; eloquence, or literary elegance is associated with her. Cf. M.W. Known as the mother of speech, eloquence, letters, and music. Chinese texts describe this deity sometimes as male, but generally as female, and under several forms. As "goddess of music and poetry" she is styled 妙(or 美)音天; 妙音樂天; 妙音佛母. She is represented in two forms, one with two arms and a lute, another with eight arms. Sister of Yama. "A consort of both Brahmā and Mañjuśrī," Getty. In Japan, when with a lute, Benten is a form of Saravastī, colour white, and riding a peacock. Tib. sbyaṅs-can-ma, or ṅag-gi-lha-mo; M. kele-yin iikin tegri; J. ben-zai-ten, or benten.

大護印 The great protective sign, a manual sign, accompanied with a transliterated repetition of "Namaḥ sarva-tathāgatebhyaḥ; Sarvathā Haṁ Khaṁ Rākṣasī mahābali; Sarva-tathāgata-puṇyo nirjāti; Hūṁ Hūṁ Trāta Trāta apratihati svāhā".

大象藏 Great elephant (or nāga) treasure, an incense supposed to be produced by nāgas or dragons fighting.

大賢 Ta-hsien (Jap. Daiken), a Korean monk who lived in China during the T'ang dynasty, of the 法相 Dharmalakṣaṇa school, noted for his annotations on the sūtras and styled 古迹記 the archæologist.

大寶積經 The sūtra of this name (Mahāratnakūṭa) tr. by Bodhiruci (in abridged form) and others.

大赤華 Mahāmañjūṣaka 摩訶曼珠沙 or rubia cordifolia, from which madder is made.

大路邊生 Born by the highway side, v. 周那 Cunda; also 純陀.

大身 The great body, i.e. the nirmāṇakāya, or transformable body 化身 of a Buddha. Also, Mahākāya, a king of garuḍas.

大車 The great bullock-cart in the parable of the burning house, i.e. Mahāyāna, v. Lotus sūtra.

大輪金剛 One of the thirty-three bodhisattvas in the 金剛手 court of the Garbhadhātu group, destroyer of delusion. Also 丨丨明王.

大轉輪王 v. 大勝金剛. 丨丨丨佛頂 idem 佛頂尊.

大迦多衍那 Mahākātyāyana or Kātyāyana 摩訶迦旃延; 迦延, v. 摩 and 迦. (1) A disciple of Śākyamuni. (2) Name of many persons. 丨丨葉 Mahākāśyapa, v. 摩訶丨丨.

大通(智勝) Mahābhijñā Jñānābhibhu. The great Buddha of supreme penetration and wisdom. "A fabulous Buddha whose realm was Saṁbhava, his kalpa Mahārūpa. Having spent ten middling kalpas in ecstatic meditation he became a Buddha, and retired again in meditation for 84,000 kalpas, during which his sixteen sons continued (as Buddhas) his preaching. Incarnations of his sons are," Akṣobhya, Merukūṭa, Siṁhaghoṣa, Siṁhadhvaja, Ākāśapratiṣṭhita, Nityaparivṛtta, Indradhvaja, Brahmadhvaja, Amitābha, Sarvalokadhātūpadravodvegapratyuttīrṇa, Tamāla-patra-candanagandha, Merukalpa, Meghasvara, Meghasvararāja, Sarvaloka-bhayastambhitatva-vidhvaṁsanakāra, and Śākyamuni; v. Eitel. He is said to have lived in a kalpa earlier than the present by kalpas as numerous as the atoms of a chiliocosm. Amitābha is his ninth son, Śākyamuni his sixteenth, and the present 大衆 or assembly of believers are said to be the reincarnation of those who were his disciples in that former æon; v. Lotus Sūtra, chapter 7. 丨丨和尙 Title of 神秀 Shên-hsiu, a disciple of the fifth patriarch.

大道心 One who has the mind of or for supreme enlightenment, e.g. a bodhisattva-mahāsattva.

大醫王 Great Lord of healing, an epithet of Buddhas and bodhisattvas.

大鐘 The great bell in the bell tower of a large monastery.

大鐵圍(山) Mahācakravāla. The great circular "iron" enclosure; the higher of the double circle of mountains forming the outer periphery of every world, concentric to the seven circles around Sumeru.

大鑑(禪師) The great mirror, posthumous title of the sixth 禪 Ch'an (Zen) patriarch, 慧能 Hui-nêng, imperially bestowed in A.D. 815.

大陰界入 Four fundamentals, i.e. the 四大, 五陰, 十八界, and 十二入 q.v.

大雄 The great hero—a Buddha's title, indicating his power over demons. 丨丨峯 Great cock peak, any outstanding peak.

大集經 Mahāsaṁghāta-sūtra 大方等大集經 The sūtra of the great assembly of Bodhisattvas from 十方 every direction, and of the apocalyptic sermons delivered to them by the Buddha; 60 chüan, tr. in parts at various times by various translators. There are several works connected with it and others independent, e.g. 丨丨須彌藏經, 丨丨日 (and 月) 藏經, 丨丨(經)寶護, 丨丨會正法經, 丨丨譬喩王經, etc. 丨丨部 Mahāsaṁnipāta. A division of the sūtrapiṭaka containing avadānas, i.e. comparisons, metaphors, parables, and stories illustrating the doctrines.

大雲光明寺 A monastery for Uigur Manichæans, ordered to be built by 代宗 A.D. 765.

大靑珠 Mahānīla. 摩訶尼羅 A precious stone, large and blue, perhaps identical with Indranīla-muktā, i.e. the Indra of precious stones, a "sapphire" (M. W.).

大願 The great vow, of a Buddha, or bodhisattva, to save all the living and bring them to Buddhahood. 丨丨業力 The forty-eight vows and the great meritorious power of Amitābha, or the efficacy of his vows. 丨丨淸淨報土 The Pure Reward-Land of Amitābha, the reward resulting from his vows. 丨丨船 The great vow boat, i.e. that of Amitābha, which ferries the believer over the sea of mortality to the Pure Land.

大顚 Ta Tien, the appellation of a famous monk and writer, named 寶通 Pao-t'ung, whom tigers followed; he died at 93 years of age in A.D. 824; author of 般若波羅蜜多心經 and 金剛經釋義.

大風災 Great Storms, the third of the three destructive calamities to end the world.

大飲光 Mahākāśyapa q.v., he who "drank in light" (with his mother's milk), she having become radiant with golden-hued light through obtaining a golden-coloured pearl, a relic of Vipaśyin, the first of the seven former Buddhas; it is a false etymology.

大高王 Abhyudgata-rāja. Great august monarch, name of the kalpa in which Śubha-vyūha 妙莊嚴王, who is not known in the older literature, is to be reborn as a Buddha.

大魚 Makara 摩竭 (羅) a monster fish.

大黑天 Mahākāla 摩訶迦 (or 謌) 羅 the great black deva | | 神. Two interpretations are given. The esoteric cult describes the deva as the masculine form of Kālī, i.e. Durgā, the wife of Śiva; with one face and eight arms, or three faces and six arms, a necklace of skulls, etc. He is worshipped as giving warlike power, and fierceness; said also to be an incarnation of Vairocana for the purpose of destroying the demons; and is described as 大時 the "great time" (-keeper) which seems to indicate Vairocana, the sun. The exoteric cult interprets him as a beneficent deva, a Pluto, or god of wealth. Consequently he is represented in two forms, by the one school as a fierce deva, by the other as a kindly happy deva. He is shown as one of the eight fierce guardians with trident, generally blue-black but sometimes white; he may have two elephants underfoot. Six arms and hands hold jewel, skull cup, chopper, drum, trident, elephant-goad. He is the tutelary god of Mongolian Buddhism. Six forms of Mahākāla are noted: (1) 比丘大黑 A black-faced disciple of the Buddha, said to be the Buddha as Mahādeva in a previous incarnation, now guardian of the refectory. (2) 摩訶迦羅大黑女 Kālī, the wife of Śiva. (3) 王子迦羅大黑 The son of Śiva. (4) 眞陀大黑 Cintā-maṇi, with the talismanic pearl, symbol of bestowing fortune. (5) 夜叉大黑 Subduer of demons. (6) 摩迦羅大黑 Mahākāla, who carries a bag on his back and holds a hammer in his right hand. J., Daikoku; M., Yeke-gara; T., Nag-po c'en-po. | | 飛礫法 The black deva's flying shard magic: take the twig of a 榎 *chia* tree (Catalpa Bungei), the twig pointing north-west; twist it to the shape of a buckwheat grain, write the Sanskrit letter भ on each of its three faces, place it before the deva, recite his spell a thousand times, then cast the charm into the house of a prosperous person, saying may his wealth come to me.

大齋(會) A feast given to monks.

大龍權現 The Bodhisattva who, having attained the 大地 stage, by the power of his vow transformed himself into a dragon-king, 西域記 1.

女 Women, female; u.f. 汝 thou, you.

女人 Woman, described in the Nirvāṇa sūtra 涅槃經 9 as the "abode of all evil", 一切女人皆是衆惡之所住處. The 智度論 14 says: 大火燒人是猶可近, 清風無形是亦可捉, 蚖蛇含毒猶亦可觸, 女人之心不可得實 "Fierce fire that would burn men may yet be approached, clear breezes without form may yet be grasped, cobras that harbour poison may yet be touched, but a woman's heart is never to be relied upon." The Buddha ordered Ānanda: "Do not look at a woman; if you must, then do not talk with her; if you must, then call on the Buddha with all your mind"—an evidently apocryphal statement of 文句 8. | | 六欲 The six feminine attractions; eight are given, but the sixth and eighth are considered to be included in the others: colour, looks, style, carriage, talk, voice, refinement, and appearance. | | 定 v. 女子出定. | | 往生願 The thirty-fifth vow of Amitābha that he will refuse to enter into his final joy until every woman who calls on his name rejoices in enlightenment and who, hating her woman's body, has ceased to be reborn as a woman; also | | 成佛願. | | 拜 A woman's salutation, greeting, or obeisance, performed by standing and bending the knees, or putting hands together before the breast and bending the body. | | 禁制 "Women forbidden to approach," a sign placed on certain altars. | | 眷屬論師 One of the twenty heretical sects, who held that Maheśvara created the first woman, who begot all creatures.

女僧 A nun, or 比丘尼 bhikṣuṇī, which is abbreviated to 尼. The first nunnery in China is said to have been established in the Han dynasty.

女國 The woman-kingdom, where matriarchal government is said to have prevailed, e.g. Brahmapura, v. 婆, and Suvarṇagotra, v. 蘇.

女天 Female devas in the desire-realm. In and above the Brahmalokas 色界 they do not exist.

女子出定 The story of a woman named Li-i 離意 who was so deeply in samādhi before the Buddha that Mañjuśrī could not arouse her; she could only be aroused by a bodhisattva who has sloughed off the skandhas and attained enlightenment.

女居士 A lay woman who devotes herself to Buddhism.

女德 A woman of virtue, i.e. a nun, or bhikṣuṇī. The emperor Hui Tsung of the Sung dynasty (A.D. 1101–1126) changed the term 尼 to 女德.

女情 Sexual desire.

女根 Yoni. The female sex-organ.

女犯 The woman offence, i.e. sexual immorality on the part of a monk.

女病 Woman as a disease; feminine disease.

女色 Female beauty—is a chain, a serious delusion, a grievous calamity. The 智度論 14 says it is better to burn out the eyes with a red-hot iron than behold woman with unsteady heart.

女賊 Woman the robber, as the cause of sexual passion, stealing away the riches of religion, v. 智度論 14.

女鏁 Woman as chain, or lock, the binding power of sex. 智度論 14.

子 Kumāra; son; seed; sir; 11–1 midnight.

子合國 Kukyar, Kokyar, or Kukejar, a country west of Khotan, 1,000 li from Kashgar, perhaps Yarkand.

子斷 The seed 種子 cut off, i.e. the seed which produces the miseries of transmigration.

子果 Seed and fruit; seed-produced fruit is 子果, fruit-produced seed is 果子. The fruit produced by illusion in former incarnation is 子果, which the Hīnayāna arhat has not yet finally cut off. It is necessary to enter Nirvāṇa without remnant of mortality to be free from its "fruit", or karma.

子滿果 The fruit full of seeds, the pomegranate.

子璿 A famous learned monk Tzŭ-hsüan, of the Sung dynasty whose style was 長水 Ch'ang-shui, the name of his district; he had a large following; at first he specialized on the Śūraṁgama 楞嚴經; later he adopted the teaching of 賢首 Hsien-shou of the 華嚴 Hua-yen school.

子縛 The seed bond, or delusion of the mind, which keeps men in bondage.

子院 Small courts and buildings attached to a central monastery.

寸 An inch.

寸絲不掛 Questioned as to what he did with his day, 陸亘日 Lu Hsüan-jih replied "one does not hang things on an inch of thread".

小 Small, little; mean, petty; inferior.

小乘 Hīnayāna 希那衍. The small, or inferior wain, or vehicle; the form of Buddhism which developed after Śākyamuni's death to about the beginning of the Christian era, when Mahāyāna doctrines were introduced. It is the orthodox school and more in direct line with the Buddhist succession than Mahāyānism which developed on lines fundamentally different. The Buddha was a spiritual doctor, less interested in philosophy than in the remedy for human misery and perpetual transmigration. He "turned aside from idle metaphysical speculations; if he held views on such topics, he deemed them valueless for the purposes of salvation, which was his goal" (Keith). Metaphysical speculations arose after his death, and naturally developed into a variety of Hīnayāna schools before and after the separation of a distinct school of Mahāyāna. Hīnayāna remains the form in Ceylon, Burma, and Siam, hence is known as Southern Buddhism in contrast with Northern Buddhism or Mahāyāna, the form chiefly prevalent from Nepal to Japan. Another rough division is that of Pali and Sanskrit, Pali being the general literary language of the surviving form of Hīnayāna, Sanskrit of Mahāyāna. The term Hīnayāna is of Mahāyānist origination to emphasize the universalism and altruism of Mahāyāna over the narrower personal salvation of its rival. According to Mahāyāna teaching its own aim is universal Buddhahood, which means the utmost development of wisdom and the perfect transformation of all the living in the future state; it declares that Hīnayāna, aiming at arhatship and pratyeka-buddhahoood, seeks the destruction of body and mind and extinction in nirvāṇa. For arhatship the 四諦 Four Noble Truths are the foundation teaching, for pratyeka-buddhahood the 十二因緣 twelve-nidānas, and these two are therefore sometimes styled the two vehicles 二乘. T'ien-t'ai sometimes calls them the (Hīnayāna) Tripiṭaka school. Three of the eighteen Hīnayāna schools were transported to China: 俱舍 (Abhidharma) Kośa; 成實 Satyasiddhi; and the school of Harivarman, the 律 Vinaya school. These are described by Mahāyānists as the Buddha's adaptable way of meeting the questions and capacity of his hearers, though his own mind is spoken of as always being in the absolute Mahāyāna all-embracing realm. Such is the Mahāyāna view of Hīnayāna, and if the Vaipulya sūtras and special scriptures of their school, which are repudiated by Hīnayāna, are apocryphal, of which there seems no doubt, then Mahāyāna in condemning Hīnayāna must find other support for its claim to orthodoxy. The sūtras on which it chiefly relies, as regards the Buddha, have no authenticity; while those of Hīnayāna cannot be accepted as his veritable teaching in the absence of fundamental research. Hīnayāna is said to have first been divided into minority and majority sections immediately after the death of Śākyamuni, when the sthāvira, or older disciples, remained in what is spoken of as "the cave", some place at Rājagṛha, to settle the future of the order, and the general body of disciples remained outside: these two are the first 上坐部 and 大衆部 q.v. The first doctrinal division is reported to have taken place under the leadership of the monk 大天 Mahādeva (q.v.) a hundred years after the Buddha's nirvāṇa and during the reign of Aśoka; his reign, however, has been placed later than this by historians. Mahādeva's sect became the Mahāsāṅghikā, the other the Sthāvira. In time the two are said to have divided into eighteen, which with the two originals are the so-called "twenty sects" of Hīnayāna. Another division of four sects, referred to by I-ching, is that of the 大衆部 (Arya) Mahāsaṅghanikāya, 上座部 Āryasthavirāḥ, 根本說一切有部 Mūlasarvāstivādaḥ, and 正量部 Saṁmatīyāḥ. There is still another division of five sects, 五部律. For the eighteen Hīnayāna sects see below.

小乘三印 The three characteristic marks of all Hīnayāna sūtras: the impermanence of phenomena, the unreality of the ego, and nirvāṇa.

小乘九部 The nine classes of works belonging to the Hīnayāna, i.e. the whole of the twelve classes, v. 十二部, less the Udāna or Voluntary discourses; the Vaipulya, or broader teaching; and the Vyākaraṇa, or prophesies.

小乘二部 The 上座部 Sthaviravādin, School of Presbyters, and 大衆部 Sarvāstivādin, q.v.

小乘偏漸戒 The Hīnayāna partial and gradual method of obeying laws and commandments, as compared with the full and immediate salvation of Mahāyāna.

小乘十八部 A Chinese list of the "eighteen" sects of the Hīnayāna, omitting Mahāsāṅghikāḥ, Sthavira, and Sarvāstivādaḥ as generic schools: I. 大衆部 The Mahāsāṅghikāḥ is divided into eight schools as follows: (1) 一說部 Ekavyavahārikāḥ; (2) 說出世部 Lokottaravādinaḥ; (3) 雞胤部 Kaukkuṭikāḥ (Gokulikā); (4) 多聞部 Bahuśrutīyāḥ; (5) 說假部 Prajñāptivadinaḥ; (6) 制多山部 Jetavaniyāḥ, or Caityaśailāḥ; (7) 西山住部 Aparaśailāḥ; (8) 北山住部 Uttaraśailāḥ. II. 上坐部 Āryasthavirāḥ, or Sthāviravādin, divided into eight schools: (1) 雪山部 Haimavatāḥ. The 說一切有部 Sarvāstivādaḥ gave rise to (2) 犢子部 Vātsīputrīyāḥ, which gave rise to (3) 法上部 Dharmottarīyāḥ; (4) 賢胄部 Bhadrayānīyāḥ; (5) 正量部 Saṁmatīyāḥ; and (6) 密林山部 Saṇṇagarikāḥ; (7) 化地部 Mahīśāsakāḥ produced (8) 法藏部 Dharmaguptāḥ. From the Sarvāstivādins arose also (9) 飲光部 Kāśyaḥpīyā and (10) 經量部 Sautrāntikāḥ. v. 宗輪論. Cf. Keith, 149–150. The division of the two schools is ascribed to Mahādeva a century after the Nirvāṇa. Under I the first five are stated as arising two centuries after the Nirvāṇa, and the remaining three a century later, dates which are unreliable. Under II, the Haimavatāḥ and the Sarvāstivādaḥ are dated some 200 years after the Nirvāṇa; from the Sarvāstivādins soon arose the Vātsīputrīyas, from whom soon sprang the third, fourth, fifth, and sixth; then from the Sarvāstivādins there arose the seventh which gave rise to the eighth, and again, nearing the 400th year, the Sarvāstivādins gave rise to the ninth and soon after the tenth. In the list of eighteen the Sarvāstivādaḥ is not counted, as it split into all the rest.

小乘四門 T'ien-t'ai's division of Hīnayāna into four schools or doctrines: (1) 有門 Of reality, the existence of all phenomena, the doctrine of being (cf. 發智六足論, etc.); (2) 空門 of unreality, or non-existence (cf. 成實論); (3) 亦有亦空門 of both, or relativity of existence and non-existence (cf. 毘勒論); (4) 非有非空 of neither, or transcending existence and non-existence (cf. 迦旃延經).

小乘外道 Hīnayāna and the heretical sects; also, Hīnayāna is a heretical sect.

小乘戒 The commandments of the Hīnayāna, also recognized by the Mahāyāna: the five, eight, and ten commandments, the 250 for the monks, and the 348 for the nuns.

小乘經 The Hīnayāna sūtras, the four sections of the Āgamas 阿含經, v. 小乘九部.

小乘論 The Hīnayāna śāstras or Abhidharma | | 阿毗達磨 The philosophical canon of the Hīnayāna, now supposed to consist of some thirty-seven works, the earliest of which is said to be the Guṇanirdeśa śāstra, tr. as 分別功德論 before A.D. 220. "The date of the Abhidharma" is "unknown to us" (Keith).

小五條 The robe of five patches worn by some monks in China and by the 淨土宗 Jōdo sect of Japan; v. 掛.

小使 To urinate; also 小行. Buddhist monks are enjoined to urinate only in one fixed spot.

小劫 Antarā-kalpa, or intermediate kalpa; according to the 倶舍論 it is the period in which human life increases by one year a century till it reaches 84,000 with men 8,400 feet high; then it is reduced at the same rate till the life-period reaches ten years with men a foot high; these two are each a small kalpa; the 智度論 reckons the two together as one kalpa; and there are other definitions.

小千(世界) A small chiliocosm, consisting of a thousand worlds each with its Mt. Sumeru, continents, seas, and ring of iron mountains; v. 三千大千世界.

小參 Small group, a class for instruction outside the regular morning or evening services; also a class in a household; the leader is called | | 頭.

小品 A summarized version. | | (般若波羅蜜) 經 Kumārajīva's abbreviated version, in ten chüan, of the Mahā-prājñā-pāramitā-sūtra.

小宗 The sects of Hīnayāna.

小師 A junior monk of less than ten years full ordination, also a courtesy title for a disciple; and a self-depreciatory title of any monk; v. 鐸 dahara.

小律儀 The rules and regulations for monks and nuns in Hīnayāna.

小念 To repeat Buddha's name in a quiet voice, opposite of 大 |.

小本 A small volume; T'ien-t'ai's term for the (小) 阿彌陀經; the large sūtra being the 無量壽經.

小根; 小機 Having a mind fit only for Hīnayāna doctrine.

小樹 Small trees, bodhisattvas in the lower stages, v. 三草二木.

小水穿石 A little water or "dripping water penetrates stone"; the reward of the religious life, though difficult to attain, yields to persistent effort.

小法 The laws or methods of Hīnayāna.

小煩惱地法 Upakleśabhūmikāḥ. The ten lesser evils or illusions, or temptations, one of the five groups of mental conditions of the seventy-five Hīnayāna elements. They are the minor moral defects arising from 無明 unenlightenment; i.e. 忿 anger, 覆 hidden sin, 慳 stinginess, 嫉 envy, 惱 vexation, 害 ill-will, 恨 hate, 諂 adulation, 誑 deceit, 憍 pride.

小王 The small rājās, called 粟散王 millet-scattering kings.

小界 A small assembly of monks for ceremonial purposes.

小白華 One of the four divine flowers, the mandāra-flower, v. 曼.

小目連 The small Maudgalyāyana, one of six of that name, v. 目.

小祥忌 An anniversary (sacrifice).

小空 The Hīnayāna doctrine of the void, as contrasted with that of Mahāyāna.

小經 v. | 本; also styled | 彌 |.

小聖 The Hīnayāna saint, or arhat. The inferior saint, or bodhisattva, as compared with the Buddha.

小草 Smaller herbs, those who keep the five commandments and do the ten good deeds, thereby attaining to rebirth as men or devas, v. 三草二木.

小行 The practice, or discipline of Hīnayāna; also, urination.

小赤華 Mañjūṣaka. 曼殊沙華; 曼殊顏 Explained by 柔軟 pliable. Rubia cordifolia, yielding the madder (munjeeth) of Bengal.

小遠 The monk 慧遠 Hui-yüan of the Sui dynasty. There was a 晉 Chin dynasty monk of the same name.

小阿師 A junior monk ordained less than ten years.

小院 A junior teacher.

小食 The small meal, breakfast, also called 點心.

尸 A corpse; to manage; u.f. 尸羅.

尸利 Śrī. 師利; 室利; 室離; 室哩; 修利; 昔哩; 悉利 (1) Fortune, prosperity; high rank, success, good fortune, virtues, these four are named as its connotation. (2) The wife of Viṣṇu. (3) An honorific prefix or affix to names of gods, great men, and books. (4) An exclamation at the head of liturgies. (5) An abbreviation for Mañjuśrī. 丨丨佛逝 Śrībhuja, i.e. Malaya. 丨丨夜 Śrīyaśas, a god who bestows good luck. 丨丨沙; 丨丨灑; 舍利沙; 夜合樹 Śirīṣa. Acacia sirissa. The marriage tree 合婚樹. The 丨丨沙 is described as with large leaves and fruit; another kind the 丨丨駛 with small leaves and fruit. Also called 沙羅樹. 丨丨沙迦 Śirīṣaka. Name of a monk. 丨丨毱多; 丨丨崛多; 室利毱多 Śrīgupta, an elder in Rājagṛha, who tried to kill the Buddha with fire and poison; v. 丨丨丨丨長者經. 丨丨蜜多羅; 屍黎密 Śrīmitra, an Indian prince who resigned his throne to his younger brother, became a monk, came to China, translated the 灌頂 and other books.

尸半尸 To kill a person by the 毘陀羅 vetāla method of obtaining magic power by incantations on a dead body; when a headless corpse, or some part of the body, is used it is 半尸; when the whole corpse it is 尸.

尸城 Kuśinagara or Kuśigrāmaka. 拘尸那城; 拘尸那揭羅; 拘夷那竭; 拘尸城 Explained by 九士生地 the birthplace of nine scholars. An ancient kingdom and city, near Kasiah, 180 miles north of Patna; the place where Śākyamuni died.

尸多婆那 Śītavana, v. 尸陀林.

尸摩舍(or 賒)那 Śmaśāna, Aśmaśāyana, a cemetery, idem 尸陀林.

尸梨伽那 Śrīguṇa, 厚德 abundantly virtuous, a title of a Buddha.

尸棄 Śikhin, 式棄; 式詰; 尸棄那 (or 佛); 罽那尸棄; crested, or a flame; explained by 火 fire; 刺那尸棄 Ratnaśikhin occurs in the Abhidharma. In the 本行經 it is 螺髻 a shell like tuft of hair. (1) The 999th Buddha of the last kalpa, whom Śākyamuni is said to have met. (2) The second of the seven Buddhas of antiquity, born in Prabhadvaja 光相城 as a Kṣatriya. (3) A Mahābrahmā, whose name Śikhin is defined as 頂髻 or 火災頂 having a flaming tuft on his head; connected with the world-destruction by fire. The Fan-i ming-i describes Śikhin as 火 or 火首 flame, or a flaming head and as the god of fire, styled also 樹提 Śuddha, pure; he observed the 火定 Fire Dhyāna, broke the lures of the realm of desire, and followed virtue. 丨丨毘 A deva of music located in the East.

尸毘迦 Śivi, 丨丨伽; 丨丨略; also wrongly 濕鞞; one of Śākyamuni's former incarnations, when to save the life of a dove he cut off and gave his own flesh to an eagle which pursued it, which eagle was Śiva transformed in order to test him. 智度論 35.

尸羅 Śīla, 尸; 尸怛羅 intp. by 清涼 pure and cool, i.e. chaste; also by 戒 restraint, or keeping the commandments; also by 性善 of good disposition. It is the second pāramitā, moral purity, i.e. of thought, word, and deed. The four conditions of śīla are chaste, calm, quiet, extinguished, i.e. no longer perturbed by the passions. Also, perhaps śilā, a stone, i.e. a precious stone, pearl, or coral. For the ten śīlas or commandments v. 十戒, the first five, or pañca-śīla, are for all Buddhists. 丨丨不清凈 If the śīla, or moral state, is not pure, none can enter samādhi. 丨丨婆羅蜜 Śīlapāramitā. Morality, the second of the pāramitās. 丨丨幢 A curtain made of chaste precious stones. 丨丨拔

陀提; 戒賢 Śīlabhadra, a prince mentioned in 賢愚經 6. ｜｜清浄 Moral purity, essential to enter into samādhi. ｜｜跋提 Śrāvastī, idem 舍衛. ｜｜跋陀羅 Śīlabhadra. A learned monk of Nālanda, teacher of Hsüan-tsang, A.D. 625. ｜｜達磨 Śīladharma, a śramaṇa of Khotan. ｜｜鉢頗 Śīlaprabha, the Sanskrit name of a learned monk. ｜｜阿迭多 Śīlāditya, son of Pratāpāditya and brother of Rājyavardhana. Under the spiritual auspices of Avalokiteśvara, he became king of Kanyākubja A.D. 606 and conquered India and the Punjab. He was merciful to all creatures, strained drinking water for horses and elephants, was a most liberal patron of Buddhism, re-established the great quinquennial assembly, built many stūpas, showed special favour to Śīlabhadra and Hsüan-tsang, and composed the 八大靈塔梵讚 Aṣṭama-hāśrī-caitya-saṁskṛta-stotra. He reigned about forty years.

尸棄尼 Also 識 (or 瑟 or 式) 匿. Chavannes accepts the identification with Chighnān, a region of the Pamirs (*Documents sur les Tou-kiue Occidentaux*, p. 162).

尸賴拏伐底 Hiraṇyavatī, 吚離剌拏伐底; 阿利羅伐底; the gold river, a river of Nepal, now called the Gaṇḍakī, near which Śākyamuni is said to have entered nirvāṇa. The river is identified with the Ajitavatī.

尸迦羅越 Said to be Sujāta, son of an elder of Rājagṛha and the same as 須闍陀.

尸陀(林) Śītavana, 尸林; 尸陀婆; 尸多婆那; 屍陀 cold grove 寒林, i.e. a place for exposing corpses, a cemetery. It is also styled 恐畏林, 安陀林, 晝暗林; also v. 尸摩賒那 or 深摩舍那 śmaśāna.

山 A hill, mountain; a monastery.

山世 "Mountain world," i.e. monasteries.

山僧 (1) "Hill monk", self-deprecatory term used by monks. (2) A monk dwelling apart from monasteries.

山外宗 A branch of the T'ien-t'ai School founded by 晤恩 Wu Ên (d. A.D. 986) giving the "shallower" interpretation of the teaching of this sect; called Shan-wai because it was developed in temples away from the T'ien-t'ai mountain. The "profounder" sect was developed at T'ien-t'ai and is known as 山家宗 "the sect of the mountain family", or home sect.

山家 The "mountain school", the "profounder" interpretation of T'ien-t'ai doctrines developed by 四明 Ssŭ-ming; v. last entry.

山斤 The weight of a mountain, or of Sumeru—may be more readily ascertained than the eternity of the Buddha.

山毫 Writing brushes as numerous as mountains, or as the trees on the mountains (and ink as vast as the ocean).

山水衲 "Mountain and water robe," the name of a monastic garment during the Sung dynasty; later this was the name given to a richly embroidered dress.

山海如來 Sāgara-varadhara-buddhi-vikrīḍitābhijña. 山海慧 (or 惠) 自在通王如來. The name under which Ānanda is to reappear as Buddha, in Anavanāmita-vaijayanta, during the kalpa Manojña-śabdābhigarjita, v. 法華經. ｜｜空市 "Mountains, seas, the sky, the (busy) market place" cannot conceal one from the eye of 無常 Impermanence, the messenger of death, a phrase summing up a story of four brothers who tried to use their miraculous power to escape death by hiding in the mountains, seas, sky, and market places. The one in the market place was the first to be reported as dead, 法句經 2.

山王 The king of the mountains, i.e. the highest peak.

山門 The gate of a monastery; a monastery.

川 A stream, a mountain stream; Ssŭ-ch'uan province. ｜施餓鬼 Making offerings at the streams to the ghosts of the drowned.

工 Work, a period of work, a job. ｜夫 Time, work, a term for meditation; also 功夫. ｜巧明 Śilpasthāna-vidyā. 巧業明 One of the five departments of knowledge dealing with the arts, e.g. the various crafts, mechanics, natural science (yin-yang), calculations (especially for the calendar and astrology), etc. ｜伎兒 Naṭa, a dancer; the skilful or wily one, i.e. the heart or mind.

己 Self, personal, own. ｜利 Personal advantage, or profit. ｜心 One's own heart. ｜心法門;

| 心中所行法門 The method of the self-realization of truth, the intuitive method of meditation, 止觀 1. | 界 The Buddhakāya, or realm of Buddha in contrast with the realm of ordinary beings. | 證, 自證 Self-attained assurance of the truth, such as that of the Buddha. | 身彌陀唯心淨土 Myself (is) Amitābha, my mind (is) the Pure Land. All things are but the one Mind, so that outside existing beings there is no Buddha and no Pure Land. Thus Amitābha is the Amitābha within and the Pure Land is the Pure Land of the mind. It is an expression of Buddhist pantheism, that all is Buddha and Buddha is all.

已 Already, past; end, cease. | 今當 Past, present, future, 過去, 現在, 未來. | 今當往生 Those born into the "future life" (of the Pure Land) in the past, in the present, and to be born in the future. | 生; 部多 Bhūta. Become, the moment just come into existence, the present moment; being, existing; a being, ghost, demon; a fact; an element, of which the Hindus have five—earth, water, fire, air, ether; the past. | 知根 Ājñendriya. The second of the 三無漏根 q.v. One who already knows the indriya or roots that arise from the practical stage associated with the Four Dogmas, i.e. purpose, joy, pleasure, renunciation, faith, zeal, memory, abstract meditation, wisdom. | 達大德 A monk far advanced in religion; an arhat. | 還 Already returned, or, begun again, e.g. the recommencement of a cycle, or course. | 離欲者 Those who have abandoned the desire-realm; divided into two classes, 異生 ordinary people who have left desire, but will be born into the six gati; 聖者 the saints, who will not be reborn into the desire-realm; e.g. non-Buddhists and Buddhists.

干 A shield; a stem, or pole; to offend; to concern; to seek. | 栗馱; | 栗太; 乾栗馱; 訖利多 Hrd, hrdaya, the physical heart. | 闍那; 建折那 Kāñcana, golden; i.e. a tree, a shrub of the same type, with golden hue, described as of the leguminous order; perhaps the Kuñjara. Wrongly written 于 (or 那) 闍羅 and 千闍那.

弓 Dhanus. A bow; a bow's length, i.e. the 4,000th part of a yojana. Seven grains of wheat 麥 make 1 finger-joint 指節; 24 finger-joints make 1 elbow or cubit 肘; 4 cubits make 1 bow; or 1 foot 5 inches make 1 elbow or cubit; 4 cubits make 1 bow; 300 bows make 1 li; but the measures are variously given. | 槃茶 Kumbhāṇḍa demons, v. 鳩.

4. FOUR STROKES

不 No, not, none. (Sanskrit *a*, *an*.)

不一不異 Neither unity nor diversity, or doctrine of the 中論, v. 八不.

不久 Not long (in time). | | 詣道場 Not long before he visits the place of enlightenment or of Truth, i.e. soon will become a Buddha.

不了 Not to bring to a finish, not to make plain, not plain, not to understand, incomprehensible. | | 義經 Texts that do not make plain the Buddha's whole truth, such as Hīnayāna and 通教 or intermediate Mahāyāna texts. | | 佛智 The incomprehensible wisdom of Buddha.

不二 Advaya. No second, non-duality, the one and undivided, the unity of all things, the one reality, the universal Buddha-nature. There are numerous combinations, e.g. 善惡不二 good and evil are not a dualism; nor are 有 and 空 the material and immaterial, nor are 迷 and 悟 delusion and awareness—all these are of the one Buddha-nature. 不二不異 neither plural nor diverse, e.g. neither two kinds of nature nor difference in form. | | 之法 The one undivided truth, the Buddha-truth. Also, the unity of the Buddha-nature. | | 法門 is similar; also the cult of the monistic doctrine; and the immediacy of entering into the truth.

不但空 "Not only the void"; or, non-void; śrāvakas and pratyeka-buddhas see only the "void", bodhisattvas see also the non-void, hence | | | is the 中道空 the "void" of the "mean". It is a term of the 通教 Intermediate school.

不來 Not coming (back to mortality), an explanation of 阿那含 anāgāmin. | | 不去 Anāgamananirgama. Neither coming into nor going out of existence, i.e. the original constituents of all 法 things are eternal; the eternal conservation of energy, or of the primal substance. | | 迎 Without being called he comes to welcome; the Pure-land sect believes that Amitābha himself comes to welcome departing souls of his followers on their calling upon him, but the 淨土眞宗 (Jōdo Shin-shu sect) teaches that belief in him at any time ensures rebirth in the Pure Land, independently of calling on him at death.

不修外道 One of the ten kinds of "heresies" founded by Sañjayin Vairāṭīputra, v. 删, who taught that there is no need to 求道 seek the right path, as when the necessary kalpas have passed, mortality ends and nirvāṇa naturally follows.

不偷盜 Adinnādāna-veramaṇī; the second of the ten commandments, Thou shalt not steal.

不共 Not in the same class, dissimilar, distinctive, each its own. | | 三昧 Asakṛt-samādhi; a samādhi in more than one formula, or mode. | | 不定 One of the six 不定因 indefinite statements of a syllogism, where proposition and example do not agree. | | 中共 The general among the particulars, the whole in the parts. | | 業 Varied, or individual karma; each causing and receiving his own recompense. | | 法 Āveṇika-buddhadharma. The characteristics, achievements, and doctrine of Buddha which distinguish him from all others. 十八 | | | the eighteen distinctive characteristics as defined by Hīnayāna are his 十力, 四無畏, 三念住 and his 大悲; the Mahāyāna eighteen are perfection of body; of speech; of memory; impartiality or universality; ever in samādhi; entire self-abnegation; never diminishing will (to save); zeal; thought; wisdom; salvation; insight into salvation; deeds and mind accordant with wisdom; also his speech; also his mind; omniscience in regard to the past; also to the present; and to the future. | | 無明 Distinctive kinds of unenlightenment, one of the two kinds of ignorance, also styled 獨頭無明; particular results arising from particular evils. | | 相 Dissimilarity, singularity, *sui generis*. | | 般若 The things special to bodhisattvas in the 般若經 in contrast with the things they have in common with śrāvakas and pratyeka-buddhas. | | 變 Varied, or individual conditions resulting from karma; every one is his own transmigration; one of the 四變.

不分別 The indivisible, or middle way 中道.

不動 Acala; niścala; dhruva. The unmoved, immobile, or motionless; also 無動 the term is used for the unvarying or unchanging, for the pole-star, for fearlessness, for indifference to passion or temptation. It is a special term of Shingon 眞言 applied to its most important Bodhisattva, the | | 明王 q.v. | | 佛; 不動如來; 阿閦(鞞 or 婆) Akṣobhya, one of the 五智如來 Five Wisdom, or Dhyāni-Buddhas, viz., Vairocana, Akṣobhya, Ratnasambhava, Amitābha, and Amoghasiddhi. He is especially worshipped by the Shingon sect, as a disciple of Vairocana. As Amitābha is Buddha in the western heavens, so Akṣobhya is Buddha in the eastern heaven of Abhirati, the realm of joy, hence he is styled 善快 or 妙喜, also 無瞋恚 free from anger. His cult has existed since the Han dynasty, see the Akṣobhya-tathāgatasya-vyūha. He is first mentioned in the Prajñāpāramitā sūtra, then in the Lotus, where he is the first of the sixteen sons of Mahābhijña-jñānābhibhu. His dhyāni-bodhisattva is Vajrapāṇi. His appearance is variously described, but he generally sits on a lotus, feet crossed, soles upward, left hand closed holding robe, right hand fingers extended touching ground calling it as witness; he is seated above a blue elephant; his colour is pale gold, some say blue; a vajra is before him. His esoteric word is Hūṁ; his element the air, his human form Kanakamuni, v. 拘. Jap. Ashuku, Fudo, and Mudo; Tib. mi-bskyod-pa, mi-'khrugs-pa (mintug-pa); Mong. ülü küdelükci. v. 不動明王 | | 供 Offerings to | | 明王. | | 使者 His messengers. | | 咒; | | 慈救咒; | | 慈護咒; | | 陀羅尼; | | 使者(陀羅尼)秘密法. Prayers and spells associated with him and his messengers. | | 地 The eighth of the ten stages in a Buddha's advance to perfection. | | 安鎭法 Prayers to | | 明王 to protect the house. | | 定 The samādhi, or abstract meditation, in which he abides. | | 明王; | | 尊 Āryācalanātha 阿奢羅曩 tr. 不動尊 and 無動尊 and Acalaceṭa, 阿奢囉逝吒 tr. 不動使者. The mouthpiece or messenger, e.g. the Mercury, of the Buddhas; and the chief of the five Ming Wang. He is regarded as the third person in the Vairocana trinity. He has a fierce mien overawing all evil spirits. He is said to have attained to Buddhahood, but also still to retain his position with Vairocana. He has many descriptive titles, e.g. 無量力神通無動者; 不動忿怒王, etc. Five different verbal signs are given to him. He carries a sharp wisdom-sword, a noose, a thunder-bolt. The colour of his images is various—black, blue, purple. He has a youthful appearance; his hair falls over his left shoulder; he stands or sits on a rock; left eye closed; mouth shut, teeth gripping upper lip, wrinkled forehead, seven locks of hair, full-bodied. A second representation is with four faces and four arms, angry mien, protruding teeth, with flames around him. A third with necklaces. A fourth, red, seated on a rock, flames, trident, etc. There are other forms. He has fourteen distinguishing symbols, and many dhāraṇīs associated with the realm of fire, of saving those in distress, and of wisdom. He has two messengers 二童子 Kiṁkara 矜羯羅 and Ceṭaka 制吒迦, and, including these, a group of eight messengers 八大童子 each with image, symbol, word-sign, etc. Cf. 不動佛. | | 法 Prayer for the aid of | | 明王 to end calamity and cause prosperity. | | 無爲 One of the six 無爲 kinds of inaction, or *laissez-aller*, the state of being unmoved by pleasure or pain. Similarly | | 解脫 liberation from being disturbed (by the illusions of life); and | | 阿羅漢 an arhat who has attained to this state. | | 生死 Immortality, nirvāṇa. | | 義 Immobility, one of the ten meanings of the void. | | 講 An assembly for preaching and praising the virtues of | | 尊. | | 金剛明王 The | | 尊 as the vajra representative, or embodiment, of Vairocana for saving all sentient beings.

不卽不離 Neither the thing itself nor something apart, e.g. the water and the wave; similar to 不一不異.

不取正覺願 Amitābha's vow of not taking up his Buddhahood till each of his forty-eight vows is fulfilled, an affix to each of the vows.

不受一切法 Free from the receptivity, or sensation, of things, emancipated from desire. | | 三昧 In the Lotus sūtra, cap. 25, the bodhisattva 無盡意 obeying the Buddha's command, offered Kuan-yin a jewel-garland, which the latter refused saying he had not received the Buddha's command to accept it. This attitude is attributed to his 不受 samādhi, the samādhi of 畢竟空 utter "voidness", or spirituality.

不可 May not, can not; unpermissible, forbidden; unable. | | 得 Anupalabhya; Alabhya. Beyond laying hold of, unobtainable, unknowable, unreal, another name for 空 the void. 三世心不可得 The mind or thought, past, present, future, cannot be held fast; the past is gone, the future not arrived, the present does not stay. | | 得空 One of the eighteen 空; it is the 言亡慮絕之空, the "void" that is beyond words or thought. | | 思議 Beyond thought or description, v. 不思議. Pu-k'o, the name of a monk of the 靈妙寺 Ling Miao monastery in the T'ang dynasty, a disciple of Śubhakarasiṁha, and one of the founders of 眞言 Shingon. The four indescribables, v. 增一阿含經 18, are the worlds; living beings; dragons (nāgas); and the size of the Buddha-lands. The five, of the 智度論 30, are: The number of living beings; all the consequences of karma; the powers of a state of dhyāna; the powers of nāgas; the powers of the Buddhas. | | | | 尊; | | | | 光如來 The ineffable Honoured One; the Tathāgata of ineffable light; titles of Amitābha. | | | | (解脫)經 A name for the 華嚴經 Hua-yen sūtra. The full title is also a name for the 維摩經 Vimalakīrtti sūtra. | | | | 解脫法門 The samādhi, or liberation of mind, that ensures a vision of the ineffable. | | 有 The existence of those who do the 不可, or forbidden, i.e. the hells. | | 棄 Not to be cast-away—said to be the name of the founder of the Mahīśāsikaḥ, or 化地 school, cast into a well at birth by his mother, saved by his father, at first a brahman, afterwards a Buddhist; v. 文殊問經, but probably apocryphal. | | 稱智 The Buddha-wisdom that in its variety is beyond description. | | 見有對色; | | 見無對色 The first refers to invisible, perceptible, or material things, e.g. sound, smell, etc.; the second to invisible, imperceptible, or immaterial things. | | 說 Unmentionable, indefinable; truth that can be thought but not expressed. | | | 佛 Gaṇendra; the 733rd of the Buddhas of the present kalpa 賢劫, in which 1,000 Buddhas are to appear, of whom four have appeared. | | 越守護 Two guardians of the Law on the right of Mañjuśrī in the Garbhadhātu maṇḍala, named 難持 and 難勝.

不和合性 Unharmonizing natures, one of the 五法.

不善 Not good; contrary to the right and harmful to present and future life, e.g. 五逆十惡. | | 律儀 idem 非律儀, i.e. 不法 or 非善戒.

不唧嚁 Ignorant, rustic; immature or ignorant.

不坐高廣大牀 Anuccaśayanāmahāśayana. Not to sit on a high, broad, large bed, the ninth of the ten commandments.

不增不減 Neither adding nor subtracting; nothing can be added or taken away. In reference to the absolute 實相之空理 nothing can be added or taken away; vice versa with the relative. | | 減眞如 the unvarying 眞如 Bhūtatathatā, one of the ten 眞如; also the eighth of the 十地.

不壞 Avināśya; indestructible, never decaying, eternal. | | 句 A term in 眞言 Shingon for the magic word 阿 "a", the indestructible embodiment of Vairocana. | | 四禪 The four dhyāna heavens, where the samādhi mind of meditation is indestructible, and the external world is indestructible by the three final catastrophes. | | 法 Two kinds of arhats practise the 白骨觀 skull meditation, the dull who consider the dead as ashes, the intelligent who do not, but derive supernatural powers from the meditation. | | 金剛 Vairocana the indestructible, or eternal. | | | | 光明心殿 The luminous mind-temple of the eternal 大日 Vairocana, the place in the Vajradhātu, or Diamond-realm, of Vairocana as teacher.

不如蜜多 The twenty-sixth patriarch, said to be Puryamitra (Eitel), son of a king in Southern India, laboured in eastern India, d. A.D. 388 by samādhi.

不妄語 Musāvādā-veramaṇī, the fourth commandment, thou shalt not lie; no false speaking.

不婬慾 Abrahamacaryā-veramaṇī, the third commandment, thou shalt not commit adultery, i.e. against fornication and adultery for the lay, and against all unchastity for the clerics.

不學 Aśāikṣa; no longer studying, graduated, one who has attained.

不定 Unfixed, unsettled, undetermined, uncertain. | | 受業 One of the "four karma"—aniyata or indefinite karma; opposite of 定業. | | 地法 One of the six mental conditions, that of undetermined character, open to any influence good or evil. | | (種) 性 Of indeterminate nature. The 法相宗 Dharmalakṣana school divides all beings into five classes according to their potentialities. This is one of the divisions and contains four combinations: (1) Bodhisattva-cum-śrāvaka, with uncertain result depending on the more dominant of the two; (2) bodhisattva-cum-pratyeka-buddha; (3) śrāvaka-cum-pratyeka-buddha; (4) the characteristics of all three vehicles intermingled with uncertain results; the third cannot attain Buddhahood, the rest may. | | 性聚; | | 聚 One of the three T'ien-t'ai groups of humanity, the indeterminate normal class of people, as contrasted with sages 正定性聚 whose natures are determined for goodness, and the wicked 邪定性聚 whose natures are determined for evil. | | 敎 Indeterminate teaching. T'ien-t'ai divides the Buddha's mode of teaching into four; this one means that Buddha, by his extraordinary powers of 方便 upāya-kauśalya, or adaptability, could confer Mahāyāna benefits on his hearers out of his Hīnayāna teaching and vice versa, dependent on the capacity of his hearers. | | (止) 觀 Direct insight without any gradual process of samādhi; one of three forms of T'ien-t'ai meditation.

不害 Ahiṁsā. Harmlessness, not injuring, doing harm to none.

不審 A term of greeting between monks, i.e. I do not take the liberty of inquiring into your condition.

不廻 Anāgāmin. He who does not return; one exempt from transmigration.

不律儀 Practices not in accord with the rule; immoral or subverted rules, i.e. to do evil, or prevent good; heretical rules and practices.

不忘禪 The meditation against forgetfulness.

不思議 Acintya. 阿軫帝也 Beyond thought and words, beyond conception, baffling description, amazing. | | | 乘 The ineffable vehicle, Buddhism. | | | 慧童子 The youth of ineffable wisdom, one of the eight youths in the Mañjuśrī court of the Garbhadhātu. | | | 智 Acintya-jñāna, inconceivable wisdom, the indescribable Buddha-wisdom. | | | 業相 Inexpressible karma-merit always working for the benefit of the living. | | | 界 Acintyadhātu. The realm beyond thought and words, another name for the Bhūtatathatā, 眞如. | | | 眞言相道法 The practice of the presence of the invisible Dharmakāya in the esoteric word. | | | 空; 第一義空 The Void beyond thought or discussion, a conception of the void, or that which is beyond the material, only attained by Buddhas and bodhisattvas. | | | | 智 The wisdom thus attained which removes all distresses and illusions. | | | (解脫) 經 The 華嚴經 Hua-yen sūtra. | | | 薰 The indescribable vāsanā, i.e. suffusion, or "fuming", or influence of primal 無明 ignorance, on the 眞如 bhūtatathatā, producing all illusion. v. 起信論 Awakening of Faith. | | | 變 The indescribable changes of the bhūtatathatā in the multitudinous forms of all things. | | | | 易生死 Ineffable changes and transmigrations, i.e. to the higher stages of mortality above the traidhātuka or trailokya 三界.

不悅 Unhappy, uneasy, the disturbing influence of desire.

不惜身命 The bodhisattva virtue of not sparing one's life (for the sake of bodhi).

不懺擧 The excommunication of an unrepentant monk; one of the 三擧.

不才淨 Neither clever nor pure—a term of rebuke.

不拜 Lay Buddhists may not pay homage to the gods or demons of other religions; monks and nuns may not pay homage to kings or parents.

不捉持生像金銀寶物 Jātarūpa-rajata-pratigrahaṇād vairamaṇī (virati). The tenth commandment, not to take or possess uncoined or coined gold and silver, or jewels.

不捨誓約 Amitābha's vow of non-abandonment, not to enter Buddhahood till all were born into his Paradise.

不放逸 No slackness or looseness; concentration of mind and will on the good.

不斷 Without ceasing, unceasing. | | 光 The unceasing light (or glory) of Amitābha. | | 光佛 One of the twelve shining Buddhas. | | 常 Unceasing continuity. | | 念佛 Unceasing remembrance, or invocation of the Buddha. | | 相應染 One of the 六染心. | | (讀) 經 Unceasing reading of the sūtras. | | 輪 Unceasing turning of the wheel, as in a monastery by relays of prayer and meditation.

不時解脫 The sixth, or highest of the six types of arhats; the other five groups have to bide their time and opportunity 時解脫 for liberation in samādhi, the sixth can enter immediately.

不更惡趣願 The second of Amitābha's forty-eight vows, that those born in his kingdom should never again enter the three evil lower paths of transmigration.

不染世間法 Unsullied by the things of the world (e.g. the lotus). | | 汚無知 Uncontaminated ignorance. | | 著諸法三昧 The samādhi which is uncontaminated by any (evil) thing, the samādhi of purity; i.e. Mañjuśrī in samādhi holding as symbol of it a blue lotus in his left hand.

不歌舞倡伎不往觀聽 Nātya-gīta-vāditra-viśūkadarśanād vairamaṇī (virati). The seventh commandment against taking part in singing, dancing, plays, or going to watch and hear them.

不正食 Not strict food, not exactly food, things that do not count as a meal, e.g. fruit and nuts.

不死 Undying, immortal. | | 甘露 Sweet dew of immortality, a baptismal water of 眞言 Shingon. | | 藥 Medicine of immortality, called 娑訶 So-ho, which grows on 雪山 the Himalayas and bestows on anyone seeing it endless and painless life. | | 覺 One of the eight 覺, the desire for long life. | | 門 The gate of immortality or nirvāṇa, i.e. mahāyāna.

不殺生 Prāṇātipātād vairamaṇī (virati). The first commandment, Thou shalt not kill the living.

不法 Not in acccordance with the Buddha-law, wrong, improper, unlawful.

不活畏 The fear of giving all and having nothing to keep one alive; one of the five fears.

不滅 Anirodha, not destroyed, not subject to annihilation. | | 不生 Anirodhānupāda, neither dying nor being reborn, immortal, v. 不生.

不淨 Unclean, common, vile. | | 忿怒; | | 金剛; 烏樞 (or 芻) 沙摩明王; 觸金剛 Ucchuṣma, a bodhisattva connected with 不動明王 who controls unclean demons. | | 施 "Unclean" almsgiving, i.e. looking for its reward in this or the next life. | | 肉 "Unclean" flesh, i.e. that of animals, fishes, etc., seen being killed, heard being killed, or suspected of being killed; Hīnayāna forbids these, Mahāyāna forbids all flesh. | | 行; 非梵行 Ignoble or impure deeds, sexual immorality. | | 觀 The meditation on the uncleanness of the human body of self and others, e.g. the nine stages of disintegration of the dead body 九想 q.v.; it is a meditation to destroy 貪 desire; other details are: parental seed, womb, the nine excretory passages, the body's component parts, worm-devoured corpse—all unclean. | | | 經 A sūtra of Dharmatrāta. | | 說法; 邪命說法 "Unclean" preaching, i.e. to preach, whether rightly or wrongly, from an impure motive, e.g. for making a living. | | 輪 One of the three 輪: impermanence, impurity, distress 無常, 不淨, 苦.

不生 Anutpatti; anutpāda. Non-birth; not to be reborn, exempt from rebirth; arhan is mistakenly interpreted as "not born", meaning not born again into mortal worlds. The "nir" in nirvāṇa is also erroneously said to mean "not born"; certain schools say that nothing ever has been born, or created, for all is eternal. The Shingon word 阿 "a" is interpreted as symbolizing the uncreated.

The unborn or uncreated is a name for the Tathāgata, who is not born, but eternal; hence by implication the term means "eternal". Ādi, which means "at first", "beginning", "primary", is also interpreted as 不生 uncreated. | | 斷 One of the 三斷, when illusion no longer arises the sufferings of being reborn in the evil paths are ended. | | 不滅 v. 不滅 "Neither (to be) born nor ended" is another term for 常住 permanent, eternal; nothing having been created nothing can be destroyed; Hīnayāna limits the meaning to the state of nirvāṇa, no more births and deaths; Mahāyāna in its Mādhyamika form extends it universally, no birth and death, no creation and annihilation, see 中論. The 四 | | are that nothing is produced (1) of itself; (2) of another, i.e. of a cause without itself; (3) of both; (4) of no-cause.

不疑殺 Not in doubt that the creature has been killed to feed me, v. 不淨肉.

不相應心 The non-interrelated mind, see 起信論. | | | 行 Actions non-interrelated (with mind).

不空 Amogha, Amoghavajra. 不空三藏; 智藏; 阿目佉跋折羅 Not empty (or not in vain) vajra. The famous head of the Yogācāra school in China. A Singhalese of northern brahmanic descent, having lost his father, he came at the age of 15 with his uncle to 東海, the eastern sea, or China, where in 718 he became a disciple of 金剛智 Vajrabodhi. After the latter's death in 732, and at his wish, Eliot says in 741, he went to India and Ceylon in search of esoteric or tantric writings, and returned in 746, when he baptized the emperor Hsüan Tsung. He was especially noted for rain-making and stilling storms. In 749 he received permission to return home, but was stopped by imperial orders when in the south of China. In ? 756 under Su Tsung he was recalled to the capital. His time until 771 was spent translating and editing tantric books in 120 volumes, and the Yogācāra 密教 rose to its peak of prosperity. He died greatly honoured at 70 years of age, in 774, the twelfth year of Tai Tsung, the third emperor under whom he had served. The festival of feeding the hungry spirits 盂蘭勝會 is attributed to him. His titles of 智藏 and | | 三藏 are Thesaurus of Wisdom and Amogha Tripiṭaka. | | 供養菩薩 Āryāmogha-pūrṇamaṇi, also styled 如意金剛 "At will vajra"; in the Garbhadhātu maṇḍala, the fifth on the south of the 悉地 court. | | 如來藏; | | 眞如 The realm of phenomena; in contrast with the universal 眞如 or 法身 dharmakāya, unmingled with the illusion of phenomena. | | 成就如來 Amoghasiddhi. The Tathāgata of unerring performance, the fifth of the five wisdom or dhyāni-buddhas of the diamond-realm. He is placed in the north; his image is gold-coloured, left hand clenched, right fingers extended pointing to breast. Also, "He is seated in 'adamantine' pose (legs closely locked)" (Getty), soles apparent, left hand in lap, palm upwards, may balance a double vajra, or sword; right hand erect in blessing, fingers extended. Symbol, double vajra; colour, green (Getty); word, aḥ!; blue-green lotus; element, earth; animal, garuḍa; Śakti (female personification), Tārā; Mānuṣi-Buddha (human or saviour Buddha), Maitreya. T., don-grub; J., Fukū jō-jū. | | 羂索 (觀音 or 王 or 菩薩); Amoghapāśa 阿牟伽皤賒. Not empty (or unerring) net, or lasso. One of the six forms of Kuan-yin in the Garbhadhātu group, catching deva and human fish for the bodhi-shore. The image has three faces, each with three eyes and six arms, but other forms have existed, one with three heads and ten arms, one with one head and four arms. The hands hold a net, lotus, trident, halberd, the gift of courage, and a plenipotentiary staff; sometimes accompanied by "the green Tārā, Sudhana-Kumāra, Hayagrīva and Bhṛkuṭī" (Getty). There are numerous sūtras, etc. | | 見菩薩 Amoghadarśin, the unerringly seeing Bodhisattva, shown in the upper second place of Ti-tsang's court in the Garbhadhātu; also 普觀金剛. | | 金剛菩薩 Amoghavajra. 阿目佉跋折羅 A Bodhisattva in the 蘇悉地 court of the Garbhadhātu. | | 鉤觀音 Amoghāṅkuśa. 央俱捨 Kuan-yin of the "Unerring hook", similar to | | 羂索 | |; also styled 淸淨蓮華明王央俱捨; in the court of the empyrean.

不立文字(教) The 禪 Ch'an or intuitive School does "not set up scriptures"; it lays stress on meditation and intuition rather than on books and other external aids; cf. Laṅkāvatāra sūtra.

不輕 Never Despise, 常 | | 菩薩 a previous incarnation of the Buddha, as a monk whose constant greeting to all he met, that they were destined for Buddhahood, brought him much persecution; see the chapter of this title in the Lotus sūtra. | | 行 The practice of "Never Despise".

不綺語 Unrefined, indecent, improper, or smart speech.

不著香華鬘不香塗身 Mālā-gandha-vilepana-dhāraṇa-maṇḍana-vibhūṣana-sthānād vairamaṇī (virati). The eighth commandment against adorning the body with wreaths of fragrant flowers, or using fragrant unguents.

不聞惡名願 The sixteenth of Amitābha's forty-eight vows, that he would not enter final Buddhahood as long as anyone of evil repute existed.

不臘(or 臈)次 Not in order of age, i.e. clerical age; disorderly sitting; taking a seat to which one is not entitled.

不自在 Not independent, not one's own master, under governance.

不與取 Adattādāna. Taking that which is not given, i.e. theft; against this is the second commandment.

不苦不樂受 One of the 三受, the state of experiencing neither pain nor pleasure, i.e. above them. Also styled 捨受 the state in which one has abandoned both.

不蘭迦葉 Pūraṇa-kāśyapa. 富蘭那迦葉 One of the six heretics, or Tīrthyas, opposed to Śākyamuni.

不虛妄性 Not of false or untrue nature; true, sincere; also 眞實性.

不行而行 Without doing yet to do, e.g. 無爲而爲.

不覺 Unenlightened, uncomprehending, without "spiritual" insight, the condition of people in general, who mistake the phenomenal for the real, and by ignorance beget karma, reaping its results in the mortal round of transmigration; i.e. people generally. | | 現行位 The first two of the 十地 of the saint, in which the illusion of mistaking the phenomenal for the real still arises.

不說四衆過罪戒 The prohibition of mentioning the errors and sins of other disciples, cleric or lay.

不請 Not to request; uninvited; voluntary. | | 之友 The uninvited friend, i.e. the Bodhisattva. | | 法 Uninvited preaching or offering of the Law, i.e. voluntarily bestowing its benefits.

不變易性 Unchanging nature, immutable, i.e. the bhūtatathatā. | | 眞如 The immutable bhūtatathatā in the absolute, as compared with 隨緣眞如, i.e. in relative or phenomenal conditions. | | 隨緣 The conditioned immutable, i.e. immutable as a whole, but not in its parts, i.e. its phenomenal activity.

不起法忍 The stage of endurance, or patient meditation, that has reached the state where phenomenal illusion ceases to arise, through entry into the realization of the Void, or noumenal; also 無生(or 起)法忍.

不退(轉) Avaivartika, or avinivartanīya. Never receding, always progressing, not backsliding, or losing ground; never retreating but going straight to nirvāṇa; an epithet of every Buddha. The 三 | | are never receding from 位 position attained; from a right course of 行 action; from pursuing a right line of 念 thought, or mental discipline. These are duties of every bodhisattva, and have numerous interpretations. 四 | | The Pure Land sect add another 處 place or abode to the above three, i.e. that those who reach the Pure Land never fall away, for which five reasons are given termed 五種 | | (|). The 法相 Dharmalakṣaṇa sect make their four 信, 位, 證, and 行, faith, position attained, realization, and accordant procedure. | | 住 The seventh of the 十住, the stage of never receding, or continuous progress. | | 土 The Pure Land, from which there is no falling away. | | 地 The first of a bodhisattva's 十地; it is also interpreted by right action and right thought. | | 相 One of the nine 無學 aśaikṣa, i.e. the stage beyond study, where intuition rules. Name of one of the twenty-seven sages. | | 菩薩 A never-receding bodhisattva, who aims at perfect enlightenment. | | (轉法)輪 The never-receding Buddha-vehicle, of universal salvation.

不還 Not to return, never returning. Cf. 不退. | | 向 The third of the 四向 four directions or aims, see 阿那含 anāgāmin, not returning to the desire-world, but rising above it to the 色界 or the 無色界 form-realm, or even formless realm. | | 果 The fruits, fruition, or rewards of the last. Various stages in the final life of parinirvāṇa are named, i.e. five, six, seven, eight, nine, or eleven kinds.

不釐務侍者 A nominal assistant or attendant, an attendant who has no responsibilities.

不非時食 Vikāla-bhojanād vairamaṇī (virati); part of the sixth of the ten commandments, i.e. against eating out of regulation hours, v. 不食肉.

不顧論宗 One of the 因明四宗, a philosophical school, whose rule was self-gratification, "not caring for" others.

不飲酒 Surā-maireya-madya-pramādasthānād vairamaṇī (virati). The fifth of the ten commandments, i.e. against alcohol.

不食肉 Vikālabhojana; part of the sixth of the ten commandments, i.e. against eating flesh; v. 不非時食.

中 Madhya. Middle, central, medium, the mean, within; to hit the centre. v. also 三諦.

中乘 The middle vehicle to nirvāṇa, includes all intermediate or medial systems between Hīnayāna and Mahāyāna. It also corresponds with the state of a pratyeka-buddha, who lives chiefly for his own salvation but partly for others, like a man sitting in the middle of a vehicle, leaving scarcely room for others. It is a definition made by Mahāyānists unknown to Hīnayāna.

中價衣 Another name for the uttarā saṅghāṭī, the middle garment of price, or esteem.

中元 The fifteenth of the seventh moon; the 上 | and 下 | are the fifteenth of the first and tenth moons respectively; cf. 盂蘭盆.

中劫 Middling kalpa, a period of 336,000,000 years.

中千(世)界 A middling chiliocosm, see 三千大千世界.

中印 Central India, i.e. of the 五印 Five Indies, as mentioned by Hsüan-tsang in the 西域記.

中含 The middle Āgama 阿含經.

中品 Middle rank or class.

中唄 Chanting of 梵唄 Buddhist hymns is divided into three kinds 初, 中, and 後.

中因 An arrangement by the esoteric sect of the Five Dhyāni-Buddhas, Vairocana being the first in position, Akṣobhya east, and so on.

中國 Madhyadeśa. 中天(竺); 中梵 The middle kingdom, i.e. Central North India, v. 中印.

中士 Medium disciples, i.e. śrāvakas and pratyeka-buddhas, who can gain emancipation for themselves, but cannot confer it on others; cf. 下士 and 上士.

中天(竺) Central North India, idem 中國. | | | 寺 A monastery on the 飛來 Fei-lai peak at Hangchow.

中宗 The school or principle of the mean, represented by the 法相宗 Dharmalakṣaṇa school, which divides the Buddha's teaching into three periods, the first in which he preached 有 existence, the second 空 non-existence, the third 中 neither, something "between" or above them, e.g. a realm of pure spirit, vide the 深密經 Sandhinirmocana sūtra and the Lotus sūtra.

中宿衣 A monk's inner garment, i.e. the five-patch garment; also | 着 |.

中實 idem 中道實相.

中尊 The central honoured one—in any group of Buddhas, e.g. 不動尊 among the five 明王.

中心經 idem 忠心經.

中悔 Repenting or recanting midway, i.e. doubting and falling away.

中有 One of the 四有, i.e. the antarā-bhava or intermediate state of existence between death and reincarnation; hence | | 之旅 is an unsettled being in search of a new habitat or reincarnation; v. | 陰.

中根 Medium capacity, neither clever nor dull, of each of the six organs 六根; there are three powers of each organ 上, 中, and 下.

中梵 Central North India, idem | 國.

中洲 Each of the four great continents at the foot of Mount Sumeru has two middling continents.

中流 In the midst of the stream, i.e. of 生死 mortality, or reincarnations.

中胎(藏) The central figure of the eight-petalled group of the Garbhadhātu maṇḍala; i.e. the phenomenal Vairocana who has around him four Buddhas and four bodhisattvas, each on a petal. From this maṇḍala spring the four other great maṇḍalas.

中臺 The name of a Buddha in the centre of a lotus. 丨丨八葉院 The Court of the eight-petalled lotus in the middle of the Garbhadhātu, with Vairocana in its centre and four Buddhas and four bodhisattvas on the eight petals. The lotus is likened to the human heart, with the Sun-Buddha 大日 at its centre. The four Buddhas are E. Akṣobhya, S. Ratnasaṁbhava, W. Amitābha, N. Amoghasiddhi; the four bodhisattvas are S.E. Samantabhadra, S.W. Mañjuśrī, N.W. Avalokiteśvara, and N.E. Maitreya.

中般 One of the five kinds of those who never recede but go on to parinirvāṇa, cf. 不還.

中草 Medium-sized herbs, medium capacity, v. 三草.

中觀 Meditation on the Mean, one of the 三觀; also meditation on the absolute which unites all opposites. There are various forms of such meditation, that of the 法相宗, the 三論宗, the 天台宗. v. next.

中論; 中觀論 Prāññyāya-mūla-śāstra-ṭīkā, or Prāṇyamūla-śāstra-ṭīkā; the Mādhyamika śāstra, attributed to the bodhisattvas Nāgārjuna as creator, and Nīlacakṣus as compiler; tr. by Kumārajīva A.D. 409. It is the principal work of the Mādhyamika, or Middle School, attributed to Nāgārjuna. Versions only exist in Chinese and Tibetan; an English translation by Miyamoto exists and publication is promised; a German version is by Walleser. The 中論 is the first and most important of the 三論 q.v. The teaching of this School is found additionally in the 順中論; 般若燈論釋大乘中觀釋論 and 中論疏. Cf. 中道. The doctrine opposes the rigid categories of existence and non-existence 假 and 空, and denies the two extremes of production (or creation) and non-production and other antitheses, in the interests of a middle or superior way.

中論性教 The Mādhyamika school, which has been described as a system of sophistic nihilism, dissolving every proposition into a thesis and its antithesis, and refuting both; but it is considered by some that the refuting of both is in the interests of a third, the 中 which transcends both.

中諦 The third of the 三諦 three postulates of the T'ien-t'ai school, i.e. 空, 假, and 中 q.v.

中輩 The middle stage of the 三輩 referred to in the 無量壽經, i.e. the middle class of those in the next life; also 丨丨生; the 丨丨觀 is the meditation on this condition.

中道 The "mean" has various interpretations. In general it denotes the mean between two extremes, and has special reference to the mean between realism and nihilism, or eternal substantial existence and annihilation; this "mean" is found in a third principle between the two, suggesting the idea of a realm of mind or spirit beyond the terminology of 有 or 無, substance or nothing, or, that which has form, and is therefore measurable and ponderable, and its opposite of total non-existence. See 中論. The following four Schools define the term according to their several scriptures: the 法相 School describes it as the 唯識, v. 唯識中道; the 三論 School as the 八不 eight negations, v. 三論; the T'ien-t'ai as 實相 the true reality; and the Hua-yen as the 法界 dharmadhātu. Four forms of the Mean are given by the 三論玄義. 丨丨即法界 The doctrine of the "mean" is the dharmadhātu, or "spiritual" universe.

中道宗 The third period of the Buddha's teaching, according to the 法相宗, giving the via media between the two extremes, the absolute as not confined to the phenomenal or the noumenal; also called 中道教. 丨丨實相 The reality of the "mean" is neither 有 substance or existent, nor 空 void or non-existent, but a reality which is neither, or a mean between the two extremes of materialism and nihilism; also 丨實. 丨丨應本 The "mean" as the basic principle in the 別 and 圓 Schools of the doctrine of the 應化身 "transformation body". 丨丨第一義 The "mean" is the first and chief of all principles, nothing is outside it. 丨丨觀 One of the T'ien-t'ai 三觀 three meditations, i.e. on the doctrine of the Mean to get rid of the illusion of phenomena.

中邊論 A treatise by Vasubandhu, translated by Hsüan-tsang in three chüan and by 陳眞諦

Ch'ên Chên-ti in two chüan. It is an explanation of the 辨｜｜｜頌 Madhyānta-vibhāga-śāstra, said to have been given by Maitreya to Asaṅga.

中間定 An intermediate dhyāna stage between two dhyāna-heavens; also ｜｜三昧; ｜｜禪; ｜｜靜慮.

中陰 The intermediate existence between death and reincarnation, a stage varying from seven to forty-nine days, when the karma-body will certainly be reborn; v. ｜有. ｜｜法事 The means used (by the deceased's family) for ensuring a favourable reincarnation during the intermediate stage, between death and reincarnation.

中食 The midday meal, after which nothing whatever may be eaten.

中體 The central Buddha in a group.

丹 Red, cinnabar colour; a remedy, drug, elixir. ｜田 The pubic region, 2½ inches below the navel.

云 To say, speak. ｜云 Continuing to speak; they say, people say; as follows, and so on, etc. ｜何 Why? ｜｜唄 The opening stanza of the Nirvāṇa sūtra 3.

互 Interlock, dovetail, mutual. ｜用罪 The fault of transferring from one object of worship over to another a gift, or duty, e.g. using gilt given for an image of Śākyamuni to make one for Maitreya; or "robbing Peter to pay Paul". ｜跪 Kneeling with both knees at once, as in India; in China the left knee is first placed on the ground; also 胡跪. ｜娑伽藍 Haṁsa saṁghārāma, "Wild goose monastery," on Mount Indraśailaguhā, whose inmates were once saved from starving by the self-sacrifice of a wild goose; also 僧娑 (or 鷹) 伽藍.

井 A well. ｜中撈月 Like ladling the moon out of the well; the parable of the monkeys who saw the moon fallen into a well, and fearing there would be no more moonlight, sought to save it; the monkey-king hung on to a branch, one hung on to his tail and so on, but the branch broke and all were drowned. ｜河 "Like the well and the river", indicating the impermanence of life. The "well" refers to the legend of the man who running away from a mad elephant fell into a well; the "river" to a great tree growing on the river bank yet blown over by the wind. ｜華 The flower of the water, i.e. that drawn from the well in the last watch of the night, at which time the water is supposed not to produce animal life.

五 Pañca, five.

五三八二 Five, three, eight, two, a summary of the tenets of the 法相 school, 五法, 三性, 八識, and 二無我 q.v.

五上分結 The five higher bonds of desire still existing in the upper realms, i.e. in both the form and formless realms.

五下分結 The five bonds in the lower desire-realms, i.e. desire, dislike, self, heretical ideals, doubt 貪, 瞋, 我, 邪戒, 疑.

五不可思議 The five inconceivable, or thought-surpassing things. v. 不可思議. ｜｜正食 Five improper things for a monk to eat—twigs, leaves, flowers, fruit, powders. ｜｜還天 idem 五淨居天. ｜｜｜果 idem 五種阿那含.

五乘 The five vehicles conveying to the karma-reward which differs according to the vehicle: they are generally summed up as (1) 人乘 rebirth among men conveyed by observing the five commandments; (2) 天乘 among the devas by the ten forms of good action; (3) 聲聞｜among the śrāvakas by the four noble truths; (4) 緣覺｜among pratyeka-buddhas by the twelve nidānas; (5) 菩薩｜among the Buddhas and bodhisattvas by the six pāramitās 六度 q.v. Another division is the various vehicles of bodhisattvas; pratyeka-buddhas; śrāvakas; general; and devas-and-men. Another is Hīnayāna Buddha, pratyeka-buddhas, śrāvakas, the gods of the Brahma-heavens, and those of the desire-realm. Another is Hīnayāna ordinary disciples; śrāvakas; pratyeka-buddhas; bodhisattvas; and the one all-inclusive vehicle. And a sixth, of T'ien-t'ai, is for men; devas; śrāvakas-cum-pratyeka-buddhas; bodhisattvas; and the Buddha-vehicle. The esoteric cult has: men, corresponding with earth; devas, with water; śrāvakas, with fire; pratyeka-buddhas, with wind; and bodhisattvas, with 空 the "void". ｜｜齊入 All the different classes will obtain an entrance into the Pure Land by the vow of Amitābha.

五事妄語 The five things fallaciously explained by Mahādeva, as stated in the Kathāvatthu.

五五百年 The five periods each of 500

years. In the tenth chapter of the 大集月藏經 the Buddha is reported as saying that after his death there would be five successive periods each of 500 years, strong consecutively in power (1) of salvation, (2) of meditation, (3) of learning, (4) of stūpa and temple building, and finally (5) of dissension. ||菩薩 The twenty-five Bodhisattvas 二十五||.

五人說經 v. 五種說人.

五住(地) The five fundamental conditions of 煩惱 the passions and delusions: wrong views which are common to the trailokya; clinging, or attachment, in the desire-realm; clinging, or attachment, in the form-realm; clinging, or attachment, in the formless realm which is still mortal; the state of unenlightenment or ignorance in the trailokya 三界 which is the root-cause of all distressful delusion. Also |||惑.

五佛 The Five Dhyāni-Buddhas of the Vajradhātu and Garbhadhātu; v. 五智如來. ||五身 A Shingon term for the five Buddhas in their five manifestations: Vairocana as eternal and pure dharmakāya; Akṣobhya as immutable and sovereign; Ratnasaṁbhava as bliss and glory; Amitābha as wisdom in action; Śākyamuni as incarnation and nirmāṇakāya. ||子 Five classes of Buddhists; also idem 五比丘 q.v. ||寶冠; ||冠; 五智(寶)冠; 五寶天冠; 寶冠 A Buddha-crown containing the Five Dhyāni-Buddhas. The five Buddhas "are always crowned when holding the śakti, and hence are called by the Tibetans the 'crowned Buddhas'" (Getty). Vairocana in the Vajradhātu wears a crown with five points indicative of the five qualities of perfect wisdom, etc., as represented by the Five Dhyāni-Buddhas. ||性 The five characteristics of a Buddha's nature; the first three are the 三因佛性 q.v., the fourth is 果佛性 the fruition of perfect enlightenment, and the fifth 果果佛性 the fruition of that fruition, or the revelation of parinirvāṇa. The first three are natural attributes, the two last are acquired. ||羯磨印 The manual signs by which the characteristic of each of the Five Dhyāni-Buddhas is shown in the Diamond-realm group, i.e. Vairocana, the closed hand of wisdom; Akṣobhya, right fingers touching the ground, firm wisdom; Ratnasaṁbhava, right hand open uplifted, vow-making sign; Amitābha, samādhi sign, right fingers in left palm, preaching and ending doubts; and Amoghasiddhi, i.e. Śākyamuni, the karma sign, i.e. final nirvāṇa. These mudrā, or manual signs, are from the 瑜祇經 but other forms are common. ||頂(尊); 五頂輪王 Five bodhisattvas sometimes placed on the left of Śākyamuni, indicative of five forms of wisdom: (1) 白傘(蓋)佛頂輪王; 白繖佛頂, Sitātapatra, with white parasol, symbol of pure mercy, one of the titles of Avalokiteśvara; (2) (殊)勝佛頂 Jaya, with sword symbol of wisdom, or discretion; (3) (一字) 最勝佛頂(輪王); (最勝)金輪佛頂; 轉輪王佛頂 Vijaya, with golden wheel symbol of unexcelled power of preaching; (4) 火聚佛頂; 光聚 (or 放光 or 火光) 佛頂; 高佛頂 Tejorāśi, collected brilliance, with insignia of authority 如意寶 or a flame; (5) 捨除佛頂; 除障||; 摧碎||; 除業||; 除蓋障||; 尊勝, etc. Vikīrṇa, scattering and destroying all distressing delusion, with a hook as symbol. ||頂法 The forms, colours, symbols, etc., of the above. ||頂經 Abbreviation for 一字佛頂輪王經. There is also a ||頂三昧陀羅尼經 translated by Bodhiruci circa A.D. 503. ||灌頂 Baptism with five vases of perfumed water, symbol of Buddha-wisdom in its five forms.

五作業根 The five working organs: the mouth, hands, feet, sex organ, and anus.

五位 The five categories, or divisions; there are several groups, e.g. (1) Hīnayāna and Mahāyāna have groupings of all phenomena under five heads, i.e. Hīnayāna has 75 法 which are 11 色法, 1 心法, 46 心所法, 14 不相離法, and 3 無爲法; Mahāyāna has 100 法 which are 8 心, 51 心所, 11 色, 24 不相因, and 6 無爲法. (2) The five divisions of 唯識 are 資糧位, 加行|, 通達|, 修習|, and 究竟 or 佛|. (3) The five evolutions in the womb are: kalalaṁ, embryo-initiation; arbudaṁ, after 27 days; peśī, 37; ghana, 47; praśākha, 57 days when form and organs are all complete. (4) Certain combinations of the 八卦 Eight Diagrams are sometimes styled ||君臣 five positions of prince and minister. ||三昧; 五種三昧 The five kinds of samādhi: (1) On mortality, the four 禪 and eight 定; (2) śrāvaka on the four axioms; (3) pratyeka-buddha on the twelve nidānas; (4) bodhisattva on the six 度 and the 萬行; (5) Buddha on the one Buddha-vehicle, which includes all others; v. 五乘.

五供養 The five kinds of offerings—unguents, chaplets, incense, food, and lamps (or candles).

五使者 The five messengers of Mañjuśrī, 文殊|||, 五種金剛使; they are shown on his left in his court in the Garbhadhātu group; their names are (1) Keśinī 髻 (or 計) 設尼; 繼室尼. (2) Upakeśinī 鄔波髻設尼; 烏波髻施儞 (or 尼); 優婆計設尼. (3) Citrā 質多

(or 怛) 羅. (4) Vasumatī, tr. 慧 and 財 慧; 嚩 蘇 摩 底. (5) Ākarṣaṇī, tr. 請 召, 鈎 召 and 招 召; 阿 羯 沙 尼.

五 俱 倫 The five comrades, i.e. Śākyamuni's five old companions in asceticism and first converts, v. 五 比 丘. Also | 拘 隣.

五 條 (袈 裟) The monk's robe of five patches or lengths, also termed 下 衣 as the lowest of the grades of patch-robes. It is styled 院 內 道 行 雜 作 衣 the garment ordinarily worn in the monastery, when abroad and for general purposes.

五 停 四 念 idem 五 停 心 觀 and 四 念 處 i.e. the five meditations for settling the mind and ridding it of the five errors of desire, hate, ignorance, the self, and a wayward or confused mind; the five meditations are 不 淨 |, 慈 悲 |, 因 緣 |, 界 分 別 | and 數 息 i.e. the vileness of all things, pity for all, causality, right discrimination, breathing; some substitute meditation on the Buddha in place of the fourth; another division puts breathing first, and there are other differences.

五 八 Five eights, i.e. forty. | | 十 具 All the five, eight, and ten commandments, i.e. the three groups of disciples, laity who keep the five and eight and monks who keep the ten. | | 尊 The forty forms of Kuan-yin, or the Kuan-yin with forty hands; the forty forms multiplied by the twenty-five 有 things make 1,000, hence Kuan-yin with the thousand hands. | | 識 The five sense perceptions and the eighth or Ālaya vijñāna, the fecundating principle of consciousness in man.

五 具 足 The five complete utensils for worship—two flower vases, two candlesticks, and a censer.

五 刀 The "five swords" or slayers who were sent in pursuit of a man who fled from his king, e.g. the five skandhas.

五 分 idem 五 分 法 身 and 五 部 大 論. | | 律; | | 戒 本 The Mahīśāsaka Vinaya, or five divisions of the law according to that school. | | 法 身 Pañca-dharmakāya, the five attributes of the dharmakāya or "spiritual" body of the Tathāgata, i.e. 戒 that he is above all moral conditions; 定 tranquil and apart from all false ideas; 慧 wise and omniscient; 解 脫 free, unlimited, unconditioned, which is the state of nirvāṇa; 解 脫 知 見 that he has perfect knowledge of this state. These five attributes surpass all conditions of form, or the five skandhas; Eitel interprets this by exemption from all materiality (rūpa); all sensations (vēdanā); all consciousness (saṁjñā); all moral activity (karman); all knowledge (vijñāna). The esoteric sect has its own group. See also 五 種 法 身. | | 香 The five kinds of incense, or fragrance, corresponding with the 五 分 法 身, i.e. the fragrance of 戒 香, 定 香, etc., as above.

五 利 使 Five of the ten "runners" or lictors, i.e. delusions; the ten are divided into five 鈍 dull, or stupid, and five 利 sharp or keen, appealing to the intellect; the latter are 身 見, 邊 見, 邪 見, 見 取 見, 戒 禁 取 見.

五 刧 思 惟 The five kalpas spent by Amitābha thinking out and preparing for his vows.

五 力 Pañcabalāni, the five powers or faculties —one of the categories of the thirty-seven bodhipakṣika dharma 三 十 七 助 道 品; they destroy the 五 障 five obstacles, each by each, and are: 信 | śraddhābala, faith (destroying doubt); 精 進 | vīryabala, zeal (destroying remissness); 念 or 勤 念 smṛtībala, memory or thought (destroying falsity); 正 定 samādhibala, concentration of mind, or meditation (destroying confused or wandering thoughts); and 慧 | prajñābala, wisdom (destroying all illusion and delusion). Also the five transcendent powers, i.e. 定 | the power of meditation; 通 | the resulting supernatural powers; 借 識 | adaptability, or powers of "borrowing" or evolving any required organ of sense, or knowledge, i.e. by beings above the second dhyāna heavens; 大 願 | the power of accomplishing a vow by a Buddha or bodhisattva; and 法 威 德 | the august power of Dharma. Also, the five kinds of Māra powers exerted on sight, hearing, smell, taste, and touch. | | 明 王 idem 五 大 明 王.

五 功 德 門 The five effective or meritorious gates to Amitābha's Pure Land, i.e. worship of him, praise of him, vows to him, meditation on him, willingness to suffer for universal salvation.

五 十 三 佛 Fifty-three past Buddhas, of which the lists vary. | | | 尊 The fifty-three honoured ones of the Diamond group, i.e. the thirty-seven plus sixteen bodhisattvas of the present kalpa. | | | 智 識; | | | 參 The fifty-three wise ones mentioned in the 入 法 界 chapter of the Hua-yen Sūtra.

五十二位 The fifty-two stages in the process of becoming a Buddha; of these fifty-one are to bodhisattvahood, the fifty-second to Buddhahood. They are: Ten 信 or stages of faith; thirty of the 三賢 or three grades of virtue, i.e. ten 住, ten 行, and ten 廻向; and twelve of the three grades of 聖 holiness, or sainthood, i.e. ten 地, plus 等覺 and 妙覺. These are the T'ien-t'ai stages; there are others, and the number and character of the stages vary in different schools. |||衆; |||類 The fifty-two groups of living beings, human and not-human, who, according to the Nirvāṇa-sūtra, assembled at the nirvāṇa of the Buddha. |||種供物 The fifty-two kinds of offerings of the |||衆. |||身像 The maṇḍala of Amitābha with his fifty-two attendant Bodhisattvas and Buddhas. Also known as 阿彌陀佛五十菩薩像 or 五十二尊 or 五通曼荼羅; said to have been communicated to 五通菩薩 in India at the 鷄頭摩寺.

五十五善知識 similar to 五十三智識.

五十八戒 The ten primary commands and the forty-eight secondary commands of the 梵網經.

五十六億七千萬歲 The period to elapse between Śākyamuni's nirvāṇa and the advent of Maitreya, 56,070,000,000 years.

五十天供 The fifty (or fifty-two) objects of worship for suppressing demons and pestilences, and producing peace, good harvests, etc.; the lists differ.

五十字門 The Sanskrit alphabet given as of fifty letters.

五十小劫 The fifty minor kalpas which, in the 涌出 chapter of the Lotus, are supernaturally made to seem as but half a day.

五十展轉 The fiftieth turn, i.e. the greatness of the bliss of one who hears the Lotus sūtra even at fiftieth hand; how much greater that of him who hears at first hand!

五十功德 idem 五十展轉 and 五十轉.

五十惡 The fifty evils produced by the five skandhas, i.e. 色 seventeen, 受 eight, 想 eight, 行 nine, 識 eight.

五十法 Fifty modes of meditation mentioned in the 大品般若; i.e. the 三十七品 bodhi pakṣika dharma, the 三三昧, four 禪, four 無量心, four 無色定, eight 背捨, eight 勝處, nine 次第定, and eleven 切處.

五千上慢 The five thousand supremely arrogant (i.e. Hīnayāna) monks who left the great assembly, refusing to hear the Buddha preach the new doctrine of the Lotus sūtra; see its 方便 chapter.

五印(度) The five Indias, or five regions of India, idem 五天竺 q.v.

五參日 Worship on the four fives, i.e. the fifth, tenth, twentieth, and twenty-fifth days of the month; also ||上堂.

五叉地獄 The hell in which the sufferers are dismembered with five-pronged forks.

五取蘊 The five tenacious bonds, or skandhas, attaching to mortality.

五受 The five vedanās, or sensations; i.e. of sorrow, of joy; of pain, of pleasure; of freedom from them all; the first two are limited to mental emotions, the two next are of the senses, and the fifth of both; v. 唯識論 5.

五同緣意識 One of the four kinds of 意識 q.v.; the mental concept of the perceptions of the five senses.

五味 The five flavours, or stages of making ghee, which is said to be a cure for all ailments; it is a T'ien-t'ai illustration of the five periods of the Buddha's teaching: (1) 乳| kṣīra, fresh milk, his first preaching, i.e. that of the 華嚴經 Avataṁsaka, for śrāvakas and pratyeka-buddhas; (2) 酪| dadhi, coagulated milk, cream, the 阿含經 Āgamas, for Hīnayāna generally; (3) 生酥| navanīta, curdled, the 方等經 Vaipulyas, for the Mahāyāna 通教; (4) 熟酥| ghola, butter, the 般若經 Prajñā, for the Mahāyāna 別教; (5) 醍醐| sarpirmaṇḍa, clarified butter, ghee, the 法華 Lotus and 涅槃經 Nirvāṇa sūtras, for the Mahāyāna 圓教; see also 五時教, and v. 涅槃經 14. Also, the ordinary five flavours—sour, bitter, sweet, pungent, and salty. | | 禪 Five kinds of concentration, i.e. that of heretics, ordinary people, Hīnayāna, Mahāyāna, and 最上乘 the supreme vehicle, or that of believers in the fundamental Buddha-nature of all things; this is styled 如來清淨禪; 一行三昧; 眞如三昧. | | 粥 The porridge of five flavours made on the eighth day of the twelfth moon, the anniversary of the Buddha's enlightenment.

五周因果 The five circuits or areas of cause and effect, i.e. the five main subjects of the Hua-yen sūtra.

五品 A division of the disciples, in the Lotus sūtra, into five grades—those who hear and rejoice; read and repeat; preach; observe and meditate; and transform self and others.

五唯(量) Pañcatanmātrāṇi, the five subtle or rudimentary elements out of which rise the five sensations of sound, touch, form, taste, and smell. They are the fourth of the twenty-five 諦.

五善 The five good (things), i.e. the first five commandments.

五因 The five causes, v. 俱舍論 7. i.e. (1) 生因 producing cause; (2) 依 | supporting cause; (3) 立 | upholding or establishing cause; (4) 持 | maintaining cause; (5) 養 | nourishing or strengthening cause. These all refer to the four elements, earth, water, fire, wind, for they are the 因 causers or producers and maintainers of the 果 infinite forms of nature. Another list from the Nirvāṇa-Sūtra 21 is (1) 生因 cause of rebirth, i.e. previous delusion; (2) 和合 | intermingling cause, i.e. good with good, bad with bad, neutral with neutral; (3) 住 | cause of abiding in the present condition, i.e. the self in its attachments; (4) 增長 | causes of development, e.g. food, clothing, etc.; (5) 遠 | remoter cause, the parental seed.

五堅固 idem 五五百年.

五執 The five planets, see 五星.

五境 The objects of the five senses, corresponding to the senses of form, sound, smell, taste, and touch.

五塵 The objects of the five senses, which being dusty or earthly things can taint the true nature; idem 五境.

五壇法 The ceremonies before the 五大明王.

五夢 The five bad dreams of King Ajātaśatru on the night that Buddha entered nirvāṇa—as the moon sank the sun arose from the earth, the stars fell like rain, seven comets appeared, and a great conflagration filling the sky fell on the earth.

五大 The five elements—earth, water, fire, wind, and space. v. also 五行 the five agents. In the esoteric cult the five are the physical manifestation, or garbhadhātu, v. 胎; as being in all phenomena they are called 五輪 the five evolvers; their phonetic embryos 種子 are those of the Five Dhyāni-Buddhas of the five directions, v. 五佛. | | 使者; | 天使者 The five dūta, i.e. great lictors, or deva-messengers—birth, old age, disease, death, earthly laws and punishments—said to be sent by Māra as warnings. | | 力菩薩 The five powerful Bodhisattvas, guardians of the four quarters and the centre. | | 尊 idem | | 明王. | | 形 The symbols of the five elements—earth as square, water round, fire triangular, wind half-moon, and space a combination of the other four. | | 施 The five great gifts, i.e. ability to keep the five commandments. | | 明王 The five Dharmapālas, or Law-guardians of the Five Dhyāni-Buddhas, of whom they are emanations or embodiments in two forms, compassionate and minatory. The five kings are the fierce aspect, e.g. Yamāntaka, or the 六足尊金剛 Six-legged Honoured One is an emanation of Mañjuśrī, who is an emanation of Amitābha. The five kings are 不動, 降三世, 軍荼梨, 六足尊, and 淨身, all vajra-kings. | | 色 The five chief colours—yellow for earth, white for water, red for fire, black for wind, azure for space (or the sky). Some say white for wind and black for water. | | 觀 The meditation on the 五大. | | 院 The fifth of the thirteen great courts of the Garbhadhātu-maṇḍala, named 持明院, the court of the five Dharmapālas. | | 龍王; 五類龍王 The five great dragon-kings of India.

五天(子) Five devas in the Garbhadhātu-maṇḍala located in the north-east. Also | 淨居天 (or 衆); | 那含天子. | 天竺; 五天 The five regions of India, north, south, east, west, and central; v. 西域記.

五如來 The five Tathāgatas, or Dhyāni-Buddhas, in their special capacity of relieving the lot of hungry ghosts; i.e. Ratnasaṁbhava, Akṣobhya, Amoghasiddhi, Vairocana, and Śākyamuni; v. 五智如來.

五妙 The five wonders, i.e. of purified or transcendental sight, sound, taste, smell, and touch in the Pure-land. | | 境界樂 The joys in the Pureland as above. | | (欲) The five creature desires stimulated by the objects of the five earthly senses.

五學處 idem 五戒.

五官 The five controlling powers, v. | 大使, birth, old age, sickness, death, and the (imperial) magistrate. | | 王 The fourth of the 十王 judges of the dead, who registers the weight of the sins of the deceased.

五宗 The five great schools of Mahāyāna, i.e. 天台, 華嚴, 法相, 三論, and 律宗. There are other classes, or groups.

五家(七宗) Divisions in China of the 禪 Ch'an, Intuitive or Meditative School. It divided into northern and southern schools under 神秀 Shên-hsiu and 慧能 Hui-nêng respectively. The northern schoool continued as a unit, the southern divided into five or seven 宗, viz. 潙仰宗, 臨濟 |, 曹洞 |, 雲門 |, and 法眼 |; the two others are 黃龍 and 揚岐. | | 所共 What the five classes, i.e. rulers, thieves, water, fire, and prodigal sons, have as their common prey, the wealth struggled for by others.

五寶 The five precious things, syn. all the precious things. There are several groups, e.g.—gold, silver, pearls, cowries, and rubies; or, coral, crystal, gold, silver, and cowries; or, gold, silver, pearls, coral, and amber; etc.

五專 The five special things, or five devotions, observance of any one of which, according to the Japanese 眞 Shin sect, ensures rebirth in the Pureland; they are 專禮, | 讀, | 觀, | 名, or | 讚嘆 either worship, reading, meditation, invocation, or praise.

五居 idem 五淨居天.

五山 Five mountains and monasteries: (1) in India, sacred because of their connection with the Buddha: 鞞婆羅跋怒 Vaibhāra-vana; 薩多般那求呵 Saptaparṇaguhā; 因陀羅勢羅求呵 Indraśailaguhā; 薩簸恕魂直迦鉢婆羅 Sarpiṣkuṇḍikā-prāgbhāra; 耆闍崛 Gṛdhrakūṭa; (2) in China, established during the Five Dynasties and the Southern Sung dynasty, on the analogy of those in India; three at Hangchow at 徑山 Ching Shan, 北山 Pei Shan, and 南山 Nan Shan and two at Ningpo at 阿育王山 King Aśoka Shan and 太白山 T'ai Po Shan. Later the Yüan dynasty established one at 金陵 Chin Ling, the 天界大龍翔集慶寺 which became chief of these under the Ming dynasty.

五師 The five masters or teachers, i.e. respectively of the sūtras, the vinaya, the śāstras, the abhidharma, and meditation. A further division is made of 異世 | | and 同世 | |. The first, i.e. of different periods, are Mahākāśyapa, Ānanda, Madhyāntika, Śāṇavāsa, and Upagupta; another group connected with the Vinaya is Upāli, Dāsaka, Sonaka, Siggava, and Moggaliputra Tissa. The 同世 or five of the same period are variously stated; the Sarvāstivādins say they were the five immediate disciples of Upagupta, i.e. Dharmagupta, etc.; see 五部. | | 子 The five lions that sprang from the Buddha's five fingers; 涅槃經 16.

五年大會 Pañca(vārṣika) pariṣad, or mokṣa mahā pariṣad, v. 般. The ancient quinquennial assembly for confession and exhortation, ascribed by some to Aśoka.

五度 The five means of transportation over the sea of mortality to salvation; they are the five pāramitās 五波羅蜜—almsgiving, commandment-keeping, patience under provocation, zeal, and meditation.

五律 The doctrines of the 五部 q.v.

五德 The five virtues, of which there are various definitions. The five virtues required in a confessor at the annual confessional ending the rainy retreat are: freedom from predilections, from anger, from fear, not easily deceived, discernment of shirkers of confession. Another group is the five virtues for a nurse of the sick, and there are others.

五心 The five conditions of mind produced by objective perception: 卒爾 | immediate or instantaneous, the first impression; 尋求 | attention, or inquiry; 決定 | conclusion, decision; 染淨 | the effect, evil or good; 等流 | the production therefrom of other causations.

五忍 The five stages of bodhisattva-kṣānti, patience or endurance according to the 別教: (1) 伏 | the causes of passion and illusion controlled but not finally cut off, the condition of 十住, 十行, and 十廻向; (2) 信 | firm belief, i.e. from the 初地 to the 三地; (3) 順 | patient progress towards the end of all mortality, i.e. 四 to 六地; (4) 無生 | patience for full apprehension of the truth of no rebirth, 七 to 九地; and (5) 寂滅 | the patience that leads to complete nirvāṇa, 十地 to 妙覺; cf. 五位.

五忿怒 The five angry ones, idem 五大明王.

五念門 The five devotional gates of the Pure-land sect: (1) worship of Amitābha with the 身 body; (2) invocation with the 口 mouth; (3) resolve with the 意 mind to be reborn in the Pure-land; (4) meditation on the glories of that land, etc.; (5) resolve to bestow one's merits, e.g. works of supererogation, on all creatures.

五性 The five different natures as grouped by the 法相宗 Dharmalakṣaṇa sect; of these the first and second, while able to attain to non-return to mortality, are unable to reach Buddhahood; of the fourth some may, others may not reach it; the fifth will be reborn as devas or men: (1) śrāvakas for arhats; (2) pratyeka-buddhas for pratyeka-buddhahood; (3) bodhisattvas for Buddhahood; (4) indefinite; (5) outsiders who have not the Buddha-mind. The 圓覺經 has another group, i.e. the natures of (1) ordinary good people; (2) śrāvakas and pratyeka-buddhas; (3) bodhisattvas; (4) indefinite; (5) heretics. | | 宗 idem 法相宗.

五(怖)畏 The five fears of beginners in the bodhisattva-way: fear of (1) giving away all lest they should have no means of livelihood; (2) sacrificing their reputation; (3) sacrificing themselves through dread of dying; (4) falling into evil; (5) addressing an assembly, especially of men of position.

五悔 The five stages in a penitential service. T'ien-t'ai gives: (1) confession of past sins and forbidding them for the future; (2) appeal to the universal Buddhas to keep the law-wheel rolling; (3) rejoicing over the good in self and others; (4) 廻向 offering all one's goodness to all the living and to the Buddha-way; (5) resolve, or vows, i.e. the 四弘誓. The 眞言 Shingon sect divides the ten great vows of 普賢 Samantabhadra into five 悔, the first three vows being included under 歸命 or submission; the fourth is repentance; the fifth rejoicing; the sixth, seventh, and eighth appeal to the Buddhas; the ninth and tenth, bestowal of acquired merit.

五惑 The five delusions, idem 五鈍使.

五情 The feelings, or passions, which are stirred by the 五根 five senses.

五惡 The five sins—killing, stealing, adultery, lying, drinking intoxicants. Cf. 五戒. | | 見 idem 五見. | | 趣 idem 五趣 and 五道.

五慳 The five kinds of selfishness, or meanness: monopolizing (1) an abode; (2) an almsgiving household; (3) alms received; (4) praise; (5) knowledge of the truth, e.g. of a sūtra.

五戒(法) Pañca veramaṇī; the first five of the ten commandments, against killing, stealing, adultery, lying, and intoxicating liquors. 不殺生; 不偸盜; 不邪婬; 不妄語; 不飮酒 They are binding on laity, male and female, as well as on monks and nuns. The observance of these five ensures rebirth in the human realm. Each command has five spirits to guard its observer 五戒二十五神.

五所依土 The five Buddha-kṣetra, or dependencies, the realms, or conditions of a Buddha. They are: (1) 法性土 his dharmakāya-kṣetra, or realm of his "spiritual nature", dependent on and yet identical with the 眞如 bhūtatathatā; (2) 實報土, i.e. his 自受用土 or saṁbhogakāya realm with its five immortal skandhas, i.e. his glorified body for his own enjoyment; (3) 色相土 the land or condition of his self-expression as wisdom; (4) 他受用土 his saṁbhogakāya realm for the joy of others; (5) 變化土 the realm on which his nirmāṇakāya depends, that of the wisdom of perfect service of all, which results in his relation to every kind of condition.

五扇提羅 idem 五闡提羅.

五拔刀賊 The five skandhas, idem 五刀.

五攝論 A śāstra of Asaṅga 無着, also tr. as the 攝大乘論, giving a description of Mahāyāna doctrine; Vasubandhu prepared a summary of it; tr. by 無性 Wu-hsing. Translations were also made by Paramārtha and Hsüan-tsang; other versions and treatises under various names exist.

五支(or 分)作法 The five parts (avayava) of a syllogism: 立宗 pratijñā, the proposition; 辯因 hetu, the reason; 引喩 udāharaṇa, the example; 合 upanaya, the application; and 結 nigamana, the summing up, or conclusion. These are also expressed in other terms, e.g. 立義; 因; 譬如; 合譬; and 決定. ||戒 The five moral laws or principles arising out of the idea of the mahā-nirvāṇa in the 大涅槃經 11.

五教 The five divisions of Buddhism according to the Hua-yen School, of which there are two groups. That of 杜順 Tu-shun down to 賢首 Hsien-shou is (1) 小乘| Hīnayāna which interprets nirvāṇa as annihilation; (2) 大乘始| the primary stage of Mahāyāna, with two sections the 相始| and 空始| or realistic and idealistic; (3) 大乘終| Mahāyāna in its final stage, teaching the 眞如 and universal Buddhahood; (4) 頓| the immediate, direct, or intuitive school, e.g. by right concentration of thought, or faith, apart from "works"; (5) 圓| the complete or perfect teaching of the Hua-yen, combining all the rest into one all-embracing vehicle. The five are now differentiated into 十宗 ten schools. The other division, by 圭峯 Kuei-fêng of the same school, is (1) 人天| rebirth as human beings for those who keep the five commandments and as devas those who keep the 十善 q.v.; (2) 小乘| as above; (3) 大乘法相| as 相始| above; (4) 大乘破相| as 空始| above; and (5) 一乘顯性| the one vehicle which reveals the universal Buddha-nature; it includes (3), (4), and (5) of the first group. See also 五時敎. ||章 The work in three chüan by 法藏 Fa-tsang of the T'ang dynasty, explaining the doctrines of the Five Schools.

五方五智 The five Dhyāni-Buddhas of the five regions; see the esoteric 五大. ||便 An abbreviation for 五五才便, i.e. 二十五||; also the T'ien-t'ai |||念佛門.

五族如來 The five Dhyāni-Buddhas of the Vajradhātu.

五旬 Pañcābhijñā. The five supernatural or magical powers; six is the more common number in Chinese texts, five is the number in Ceylon; v. |神通.

五更 The five night watches; also the fifth watch.

五明 Pañcavidyā, the five sciences or studies of India: (1) śabda, grammar and composition; śilpakarmasthāna, the arts and mathematics; cikitsā, medicine; hetu, logic; adhyātma, philosophy, which Monier Williams says is the "knowledge of the supreme spirit, or of ātman", the basis of the four Vedas; the Buddhists reckon the Tripiṭaka and the 十二部敎 as their 內明, i.e. their inner or special philosophy.

五星 The five planets, Jupiter, Mars, Saturn, Venus, and Mercury; also 五執.

五時八敎 A T'ien-t'ai classification of the Buddha's teaching into five periods and eight kinds of doctrine, which eight are subdivided into two groups of four each, 化儀四敎 and 化法四敎. ||(敎) The five periods or divisions of Śākyamuni's teaching. According to T'ien-t'ai they are (1) 華嚴時 the Avataṁsaka or first period in three divisions each of seven days, after his enlightenment, when he preached the contents of this sūtra; (2) 鹿苑時 the twelve years of his preaching the āgamas 阿含 in the deer park; (3) 方等時 the eight years of preaching mahāyāna-cum-hīnayāna doctrines, the vaipulya period; (4) 般若時 the twenty-two years of his preaching the prajñā or wisdom sūtras; (5) 法華涅槃時 the eight years of his preaching the Lotus sūtra and, in a day and a night, the Nirvāṇa sūtra. According to the Nirvāṇa School (now part of the T'ien-t'ai) they are (1) 三乘別敎 the period when the differentiated teaching began and the distinction of the three vehicles, as represented by the 四諦 Four Noble Truths for śrāvakas, the 十二因緣 Twelve Nidānas for pratyeka-buddhas, and the 六度 Six Pāramitās for bodhisattvas; (2) 三乘通敎 the teaching common to all three vehicles, as seen in the 般若經; (3) 抑揚敎 the teaching of the 維摩經, the 思益梵天所問經, and other sūtras extolling the bodhisattva teaching at the expense of that for śrāvakas; (4) 同歸敎 the common objective teaching calling all three vehicles, through the Lotus, to union in the one vehicle; (5) 常住敎 the teaching of eternal life, i.e. the revelation through the Nirvāṇa sūtra of the eternity of Buddhahood; these five are also called 有相; 無相; 抑揚; 會三歸一; and 圓常. According to 劉虬 Liu Ch'iu of the 晉 Chin dynasty, the teaching is divided into 頓 immediate and 漸 gradual attainment, the latter having five divisions called 五時敎 similar to those of the T'ien-t'ai group. According to 法寶 Fa-pao of the T'ang dynasty the five are (1) 小乘; (2) 般若 or 大乘; (3) 深密 or 三乘; (4) 法華 or 一乘; (5) 涅槃 or 佛性敎.

五智 The five kinds of wisdom of the 眞言 Shingon School. Of the six elements 六大 earth, water, fire, air (or wind), ether (or space) 空, and consciousness (or mind 識), the first five form the phenomenal world, or Garbhadhātu, the womb of all things 胎藏界, the sixth is the conscious, or perceptive, or wisdom world, the Vajradhātu 金剛界, sometimes called the Diamond realm. The two realms are not originally apart, but one, and there is no consciousness without the other five elements. The sixth element, vijñāna, is further subdivided into five called the 五智 Five Wisdoms: (1) 法界體性智 Dharmadhātu-prakṛti-jñāna, derived from the amala-vijñāna, or pure 識; it is the wisdom of the embodied nature of the dharmadhātu, defined as the six elements, and is associated with Vairocana 大日, in the centre, who abides in this samādhi; it also corresponds to the ether 空 element. (2) 大圓鏡智 Ādarśana-jñāna, the great round mirror wisdom, derived from the ālaya-vijñāna, reflecting all things; corresponds to earth, and is associated with Akṣobhya and the east. (3) 平等性智 Samatā-jñāna, derived from manovijñāna, wisdom in regard to all things equally and universally; corresponds to fire, and is associated with Ratnasambhava and the south. (4) 妙觀察智 Pratyavekṣaṇa-jñāna, derived from 意識, wisdom of profound insight, or discrimination, for exposition and doubt-destruction; corresponds to water, and is associated with Amitābha and the west. (5) 成所作智 Kṛtyānuṣṭhāna-jñāna, derived from the five senses, the wisdom of perfecting the double work of self-welfare and the welfare of others; corresponds to air 風 and is associated with Amoghasiddhi and the north. These five Dhyāni-Buddhas are the 五智如來. The five kinds of wisdom are the four belonging to every Buddha, of the exoteric cult, to which the esoteric cult adds the first, pure, all-reflecting, universal, all-discerning, and all-perfecting. ||如來; ||五佛; 五佛; 五如來 The five Dhyāni-Buddhas, or Wisdom-Tathāgatas of the Vajradhātu 金剛界, idealizations of five aspects of wisdom; possibly of Nepalese origin. The Wisdom-Buddha represents the dharmakāya or Buddha-mind, also the Dharma of the triratna, or trinity. Each evolves one of the five colours, one of the five senses, a Dhyāni-bodhisattva in two forms (one gracious, the other fierce), and a Mānuṣi-Buddha; each has his own śakti, i.e. feminine energy or complement; also his own bīja, or germ-sound 種子 or 印 seal, i.e. 眞言 real or substantive word, the five being for 大日 aṁ, for 阿閦 hūṁ, for 寶生 ? hrīḥ, for 彌陀 ? aḥ, for 不空 ? āḥ. The five are also described as the emanations or forms of an Ādi-Buddha, Vajrasattva; the four are considered by others to be emanations or forms of Vairocana as the Supreme Buddha. The five are not always described as the same, e.g. they may be 藥師 (or 王) Bhaiṣajya, 多寶 Prabhūtaratna, Vairocana, Akṣobhya, and either Amoghasiddhi or Śākyamuni. Below is a classified list of the generally accepted five with certain particulars connected with them, but these differ in different places, and the list can only be a general guide. As to the Dhyāni-bodhisattvas, each Buddha evolves three forms 五佛生五菩薩, 五金剛, 五忿怒, i.e. (1) a bodhisattva who represents the Buddha's dharmakāya, or spiritual body; (2) a vajra or diamond form who represents his wisdom in graciousness; and (3) a fierce or angry form, the 明王 who represents his power against evil. (1) Vairocana appears in the three forms of 轉法輪菩薩 Vajra-pāramitā Bodhisattva, 遍照金剛 Universally Shining Vajrasattva, and 不動明王 Ārya-Acalanātha Rāja; (2) Akṣobhya's three forms are 虛空藏 Ākāśagarbha, 如意 complete power, and 軍荼利明王 Kuṇḍali-rāja; (3) Ratnasambhava's are 普賢 Samantabhadra, 薩埵 Sattvavajra, and 孫婆 or 降三世明王 Trailokyavijaya-rāja; (4) Amitābha's are 觀世音 Avalokiteśvara, 法金剛 Dharmarāja, and 馬頭明王 Hayagrīva, the horse-head Dharmapāla; (5) Amoghasiddhi's are 彌勒 Maitreya, 業金剛 Karmavajra, and 金剛夜叉 Vajrayakṣa. The above Bodhisattvas differ from those in the following list:—

		Position.	*Element.*	*Sense.*	*Colour.*
Vairocana	大日	centre	ether	sight	white
Akṣobhya	阿閦	east	earth	sound	blue
Ratnasambhava	寶生	south	fire	smell	yellow
Amitābha	彌陀	west	water	taste	red
Amoghasiddhi	不空	north	air	touch	green

Germ.	*Animal.*	*Dhyani-Bodhisattva.*	*Buddha.*
aṁ	lion	Samantabhadra 普賢	Krakucchanda
hūṁ	elephant	Vajrapāṇi 金剛力士	Kanakamuni
? aḥ	horse	Ratnapāṇi 寶手	Kāśyapa
? hrīḥ	goose or peacock	Avalokiteśvara 觀音	Śākyamuni
? āḥ	garuḍa	Viśvapāṇi ?	Maitreya

||寶冠 idem 五佛寶冠. ||所生三身 Each of the Five Dhyāni-Buddhas is accredited with the three forms which represent his 身業 body, 口業 speech, and 意業 mind, e.g. the embodiment of Wisdom is Vairocana, his preaching form is 普賢, and his will form is 不動明王; the embodiment 身 of the mirror is Akṣobhya, his 口 is Mañjuśrī, his 意 is 降三世金剛; and so on; v. above.

五會念佛 Five ways of intoning "Amitābha" established by 法照 Fa-chao of the T'ang dynasty, known as 五會法師 from his brochure 五會法事讚.

五果 The five fruits, or effects; there are various groups, e.g. I. (1) 異熟果 fruit ripening divergently, e.g. pleasure and goodness are in different categories; present organs accord in pain or pleasure with their past good or evil deeds; (2) 等流果

fruit of the same order, e.g. goodness reborn from previous goodness; (3) 士用果 present position and function fruit, the rewards of moral merit in previous lives; (4) 增上果 superior fruit, or position arising from previous earnest endeavour and superior capacity; (5) 離繫果 fruit of freedom from all bonds, nirvāṇa fruit. II. Fruit, or rebirth: (1) 識 conception (viewed psychologically); (2) 名色 formation mental and physical; (3) 六處 the six organs of perception complete; (4) 觸 their birth and contact with the world; (5) 受 consciousness. III. Five orders of fruit, with stones, pips, shells (as nuts), chaff-like (as pine seeds), and with pods.

五根 Pañcendriyāṇi. (1) The five roots, i.e. the five organs of the senses: eyes, ears, nose, tongue, and body as roots of knowing. (2) The five spiritual organs or positive agents: 信 faith, 精進 energy, 念 memory, 定 visionary meditation, 慧 wisdom. The 五力 q.v. are regarded as negative agents. For ||色 see 五色. ||本 They are the six great kleśa, i.e. passions, or disturbers, minus 見 views, or delusions; i.e. desire, anger, stupidity (or ignorance), pride, and doubt.

五業 The five kinds of karma: of which the groups are numerous and differ.

五樂 The pleasures of the five senses, v. next.

五欲 The five desires, arising from the objects of the five senses, things seen, heard, smelt, tasted, or touched. Also, the five desires of wealth, sex, food-and-drink, fame, and sleep.

五正色 idem 五色. ||行; |種|| The five proper courses to ensure the bliss of the Pure Land: (1) Intone the three sūtras 無量壽經, 觀無量壽經, and 阿彌陀經; (2) meditate on the Pure Land; (3) worship solely Amitābha; (4) invoke his name; (5) extol and make offerings to him. Service of other Buddhas, etc., is styled 五(種)雜行. ||食; 半者蒲膳尼 Pañcabhojanīya. The five foods considered proper for monks in early Buddhism: boiled rice, boiled grain or pease, parched grain, flesh, cakes.

五股(杵 or 金剛); also 五鈷, |古, or |貼 The five-pronged vajra or thunderbolt emblem of the 五部 five groups and 五智 five wisdom powers of the vajradhātu; doubled it is an emblem of the ten pāramitās. In the esoteric cult the 五股印 five-pronged vajra is the symbol of the 五智 five wisdom powers and the 五佛 five Buddhas, and has several names 五大印, 五智印, 五峯印; 金剛慧印, 大羯印, and 大率都婆印, and has many definitions.

五比丘 The first five of Buddha's converts, also called 五佛子, Ājñāta-Kauṇḍinya, Aśvajit, Bhadrika, Daśabala-Kāśyapa, and Mahānāma-Kulika, i.e. 憍陳如; 額鞞; 拔提; 十力迦葉; 摩男拘利; but there are numerous other forms of their names.

五法 Pañcadharma. The five laws or categories, of which four groups are as follows: I. 相名五法 The five categories of form and name: (1) 相 appearances, or phenomena; (2) 名 their names; (3) 分別 sometimes called 妄想 ordinary mental discrimination of them—(1) and (2) are objective, (3) subjective; (4) 正智 corrective wisdom, which corrects the deficiencies and errors of the last; (5) 如如 the 眞如 Bhūtatathatā or absolute wisdom, reached through the 如理智 understanding of the law of the absolute, or ultimate truth. II. 事理五法 The five categories into which things and their principles are divided: (1) 心法 mind; (2) 心所| mental conditions or activities; (3) 色| the actual states or categories as conceived; (4) 不相應| hypothetic categories, 唯識 has twenty-four, the Abhidharma fourteen; (5) 無爲| the state of rest, or the inactive principle pervading all things; the first four are the 事 and the last the 理. III. 理智五法 cf. 五智; the five categories of essential wisdom: (1) 眞如 the absolute; (2) 大圓鏡智 wisdom as the great perfect mirror reflecting all things; (3) 平等性| wisdom of the equal Buddha-nature of all beings; (4) 妙觀察| wisdom of mystic insight into all things and removal of ignorance and doubt; (5) 成所作| wisdom perfect in action and bringing blessing to self and others. IV. 提婆五法 The five obnoxious rules of Devadatta: not to take milk in any form, nor meat, nor salt; to wear unshaped garments, and to live apart. Another set is: to wear cast-off rags, beg food, have only one set meal a day, dwell in the open, and abstain from all kinds of flesh, milk, etc. ||人 Followers of the five ascetic rules of Devadatta, the enemy of the Buddha. ||成身 idem |相||. ||身 idem |分||.

五波羅密 The five pāramitās (omitting the sixth, wisdom), i.e. dāna, almsgiving; śīla, commandment-keeping; kṣānti, patience (under provocation); vīrya, zeal; and dhyāna, meditation.

五海 The five "seas" or infinities seen in a vision by P'u-hsien, v. 舊華嚴經 3, viz., (1) all worlds, (2) all the living, (3) universal karma, (4) the roots of desire and pleasure of all the living, (5) all the Buddhas, past, present, and future.

五淨 The five "clean" products of the cow, its pañca-gavya, i.e. urine, dung, milk, cream (or sour milk), and cheese (or butter); cf. M. W. | | (居天), 五不還天 Cf. 色界. The five pure-dwelling heavens in the fourth dhyāna heaven, into which arhats are finally born: 無煩天 Avṛhās, the heaven free from all trouble; 無熱 | Atapās, of no heat or distress; 善現 | Sudṛśās, of beautiful presentation; 善見 | Sudarśanās, beautiful; and 色究竟天 Akaniṣṭhās, the highest heaven of the form-realm. | | 食, | 種 | | idem 五正食.

五濁; | 滓; | 渾 The five kaṣāya periods of turbidity, impurity, or chaos, i.e. of decay; they are accredited to the 住 kalpa, see 四劫, and commence when human life begins to decrease below 20,000 years. (1) 劫 | the kalpa in decay, when it suffers deterioration and gives rise to the ensuing form; (2) 見 | deterioration of view, egoism, etc., arising; (3) 煩惱 | the passions and delusions of desire, anger, stupidity, pride, and doubt prevail; (4) 衆生 | in consequence human miseries increase and happiness decreases; (5) 命 | human lifetime gradually diminishes to ten years. The second and third are described as the 濁 itself and the fourth and fifth its results. | | 増時 The above period of increasing turbidity or decay.

五燒 The five burnings, or 五痛 five pains, i.e. infraction of the first five commandments leads to state punishment in this life and the hells in the next.

五無量 The five infinites, or immeasurables —body, mind, wisdom, space, and all the living— as represented respectively by the five Dhyāni-Buddhas, i.e. 寶生, 阿閦, 無量壽, 大日, and 不空. | | 間 The uninterrupted, or no-interval hell, i.e. avīci hell, the worst, or eighth of the eight hells. It is ceaseless in five respects—karma and its effects are an endless chain with no escape; its sufferings are ceaseless; it is timeless; its fate or life is endless; it is ceaselessly full. Another interpretation takes the second, third, and fifth of the above and adds that it is packed with 罪器 implements of torture, and that it is full of all kinds of living beings. | | | 業 or 罪 The five karma, or sins, leading to the avīci hell, v. 五逆.

五燈錄 The five Têng-lu are (1) 傳燈錄 A.D. 1004–8; (2) 廣 | |; (3) 續 | |; (4) 聯 | |, and (5) 普 | |; the | | 會元 and | | 嚴統 are later collections.

五瓶 The five vases used by the esoteric school for offering flowers to their Buddha, the flowers are stuck in a mixture of the five precious things, the five grains and the five medicines mingled with scented water. | | 智水 The five vases are emblems of the five departments of the Vajradhātu, and the fragrant water the wisdom of the five Wisdom-Buddhas. | | 灌頂 Baptism with water of the five vases representing the wisdom of these five Buddhas.

五生 Five rebirths, i.e. five states, or conditions of a bodhisattva's rebirth: (1) to stay calamities, e.g. by sacrificing himself; (2) in any class that may need him; (3) in superior condition, handsome, wealthy, or noble; (4) in various grades of kingship; (5) final rebirth before Buddhahood; v. 瑜伽論 4.

五畏 idem 五怖畏.

五痛 idem | 燒.

五百 Pañcaśata. Five hundred, of which there are numerous instances, e.g. 500 former existences; the 500 disciples, etc. | | 世 or 生 500 generations. | | | 無手 A disciple who even passes the wine decanter to another person will be reborn without hands for 500 generations; v. 梵網經下. | | (大) 羅漢 500 great arhats who formed the synod under Kaniṣka and are the supposed compilers of the Abhidharma-mahāvibhāṣā-śāstra, 400 years after Buddha entered nirvāṇa (阿毗達磨大毗婆娑論), tr. by Hsüan-tsang (A.D. 656–9). The 500 Lohans found in some monasteries have various definitions. | | 戒 The "five hundred" rules for nuns, really 348, viz. 8 波羅夷, 17 僧殘, 30 捨墮, 178 單提, 8 提捨尼, 100 衆學, and 7 滅諍. | | 生 idem | | 世. | | 部; | | 小乘; | | 異部 The 500 sects according to the 500 years after the Buddha's death; 智度論 63. | | 問 (事) The 500 questions of Mahāmaudgalyāyana to the Buddha on discipline. | | 由旬 The 500 yojanas of difficult and perilous journey to the Land of Treasures; v. the Lotus Sūtra.

五盛陰苦 The mental and physical sufferings arising from the full-orbed activities of the skandhas 五陰, one of the eight sufferings; also 五陰盛(苦).

五眼 The five kinds of eyes or vision: human; deva (attainable by men in dhyāna); Hīnayāna wisdom; bodhisattva truth; and Buddha-vision or omniscience. There are five more related to omniscience making 十眼 ten kinds of eyes or vision.

五相 idem 丨丨成身 and 五衰. 丨丨成身(觀) A contemplation of the five stages in Vairocana Buddhahood—entry into the bodhi-mind; maintenance of it; attainment of the diamond mind; realization of the diamond embodiment; and perfect attainment of Buddhahood. It refers also to the 五智 of the Vairocana group; also 丨轉 (or 法) 成身.

五知根 The five indriyas or organs of perception—eyes, ears, nose, tongue, and skin. v. 五根.

五礙 idem 五障.

五神通 (or 變) Pañcābhijñā; also 五通(力) the five supernatural powers. (1) 天眼(智證)通 divyacakṣus; deva-vision, instantaneous view of anything anywhere in the form-realm. (2) 天耳(智證)通 divyaśrotra, ability to hear any sound anywhere. (3) 他心(智證)通 paracitta-jñāna, ability to know the thoughts of all other minds. (4) 宿命(智證)通 pūrvanivāsānusmṛti-jñāna, knowledge of all former existences of self and others. (5) 神通(智證)通; 神足通; 神如意通 ṛddhi-sākṣātkrīyā, power to be anywhere or do anything at will. See 智度論 5. Powers similar to these are also attainable by meditation, incantations, and drugs, hence heterodox teachers also may possess them.

五祖 The five patriarchs. Those of the Hua-yen (Kegon) sect are 終南杜順; 雲華智儼; 賢首法藏; 清涼澄觀, and 圭峯宗密. The Pure-land sect five patriarchs are 曇鸞; 道綽; 善導; 懷感, and 少康. The (白)蓮社 Lien-shê sect has 善導; 法照; 少康; 省常, and 宗賾.

五禁 idem 五戒.

五秘(密) The five esoteric or occult ones, i.e. the five bodhisattvas of the diamond realm, known as Vajrasattva in the middle; 欲 desire on the east; 觸 contact, south; 愛 love, west; and 慢 pride, north. Vajrasattva represents the six fundamental elements of sentient existence and here indicates the birth of bodhisattva sentience; desire is that of bodhi and the salvation of all; contact with the needy world for its salvation follows; love of all the living comes next; pride or the power of nirvāṇa succeeds. 丨丨丨曼荼羅 or 十七尊曼荼羅 The maṇḍala of this group contains seventeen figures representing the five above named, with their twelve subordinates.

五種 The five kinds; but frequently the 種 is omitted, e.g. for 丨丨正食 see 五正食.

五種三歸 The five modes of triśaraṇa, or formulas of trust in the Triratna, taken by those who (1) 翻邪 turn from heresy; (2) take the five commandments; (3) the eight commandments; (4) the ten commandments; (5) the complete commandments.

五種不女 The five kinds of sexually incomplete females, 螺, 筋, 鼓, 角, and 脉. v. 大藏法數 32.

五種不男 The five kinds of 般荼迦 paṇḍakas, i.e. eunuchs, or impotent males: by birth; emasculation; uncontrollable emission; hermaphrodite; impotent for half the month; they are known as 扇搋 Ṣaṇḍha; 留拏 ? Ruṇḍa; 伊梨沙掌拏 Īrṣyāpaṇḍaka; 半擇迦 Paṇḍaka; 博叉 Pakṣapaṇḍaka; there are numerous subdivisions.

五種不翻 The five kinds of terms which Hsüan-tsang did not translate but transliterated—the esoteric; those with several meanings; those without equivalent in China; old-established terms; and those which would be less impressive when translated.

五種不還 The five kinds of anāgāmins 那含, who never return to the desire-realm: (1) 中般 the anāgāmin who enters on the intermediate stage between the realm of desire and the higher realm of form; (2) 生般 who is born into the form-world and soon overcomes the remains of illusion; (3) 有行般 who diligently works his way through the final stages; (4) 無行般 whose final departure is delayed through lack of aid and slackness; (5) 上流般 who proceeds from lower to higher heavens into nirvāṇa. Also 丨丨那含 and 丨丨般, the 般 being "parinirvāṇa".

五種修法 Five kinds of esoteric ceremonial, i.e. (1) 扇底迦 śāntika, for stopping calamities; (2) 布 or 補瑟徵迦 pauṣṭika, for success or prosperity; (3) 阿畏遮嚕迦 abhicāraka, for suppressing, or exorcising; (4) 阿羯沙尼 ākarṣaṇī, for calling, or attracting (good beings, or aid); (5) 伐施迦囉軌 vaśīkaraṇa, for seeking the aid of Buddhas and bodhisattvas; also 五部尊法 and cf. 五種灌頂.

五種印 The signs of the five kinds of vision, v. 五眼.

五種唯識 The five kinds of wei-shih, or idealistic representation in the sūtras and śāstras as summed up by Tzŭ-ên 慈恩 of the 法相宗 Dharmalakṣaṇa school: (1) 境唯識 wisdom or insight in objective conditions; (2) 敎 | | in interpretation; (3) 理 | | in principles; (4) 行 | | in meditation and practice; (5) 果 | | in the fruits or results of Buddhahood. The first four are objective, the fifth subjective.

五種壇法 The five kinds of maṇḍala ceremonials, v. 五部尊法.

五(種)增上緣; 五緣 Five excellent causes, e.g. of blessedness: keeping the commandments; sufficient food and clothing; a secluded abode; cessation of worry; good friendship. Another group is: riddance of sin; protection through long life; vision of Buddha (or Amitābha, etc.); universal salvation (by Amitābha); assurance of Amitābha's heaven.

五種布施 The five kinds of almsgiving or dānas—to those from afar, to those going afar, to the sick, the hungry, and those wise in Buddhist doctrine.

五種性 The five germ-natures, or roots of bodhisattva development: (1) 習 | | the germ-nature of study of the 空 void (or immaterial), which corrects all illusions of time and space; it corresponds to the 十住 stage; (2) 性 | | that of ability to discriminate all the 性 natures of phenomena and transform the living; the 十行 stage; (3) 道 | | (the middle-)way germ-nature, which attains insight into Buddha-laws; the 十廻向; (4) 聖 | | the saint germ-nature which produces holiness by destroying ignorance; the 十地, in which the bodhisattva leaves the ranks of the 賢 and becomes 聖; (5) 等覺 | | the bodhi-rank germ-nature which produces Buddhahood, i.e. 等覺.

五種惡病 Five epidemics in Vaiśālī during the Buddha's lifetime—bleeding from the eyes, pus from the ears, nose-bleeding, lockjaw, and astringent taste of all food.

五種散亂 The five kinds of mental aberration: (1) the five senses themselves not functioning properly; (2) external distraction, or inability to concentrate the attention; (3) internal distraction, or mental confusion; (4) distraction caused by ideas of me and mine, personality, possession, etc.; (5) confusion of thought produced by hīnayāna ideas.

五種比量 The five inferences in (Indian) logic: (1) 相 from appearance, e.g. fire from smoke; (2) 體 from the corporeal, e.g. two or more things from one; (3) 業 from action, e.g. the animal from its footmark; (4) 法 from recognized law, old age from birth; (5) 因果 from cause and effect, that a traveller has a destination.

五種法師 The five kinds of masters of the Law, v. Lotus Sūtra, 法師品—one who receives and keeps; reads; recites; expounds; and copies the sūtra.

五種法界 The Hua-yen school's five forms of dharmadhātu: (1) 有爲法界 or 事 | | the phenomenal realm; (2) 無爲法界 or 理 | | the inactive, quiescent, or noumenal realm; (3) 亦有爲亦無爲 | | or 事理無礙 | | both, i.e. interdependent and interactive; (4) 非有爲非無爲 | | neither active nor inactive, but it is also 事理無礙 | |, e.g. water and wave, wave being water and water wave; (5) 無障礙 | | or 事事無礙 | | the unimpeded realm, the unity of the phenomenal and noumenal, of the collective and individual.

五種法身 The five kinds of a Buddha's dharmakāya. There are four groups. I. (1) 如如智法身 the spiritual body of bhūtatathatā-wisdom; (2) 功德 | | of all virtuous achievement; (3) 自 | | of incarnation in the world; (4) 變化 | | of unlimited powers of transformation; (5) 虛空 | | of unlimited space; the first and second are defined as saṁbhogakāya, the third and fourth as nirmāṇakāya, and the fifth as the dharmakāya, but all are included under dharmakāya as it possesses all the others. II. The esoteric cult uses the first four and adds as fifth 法界身 indicating the universe as pan-Buddha. III. Hua-yen gives (1) 法性生身 the body or person of Buddha born from the dharma-nature; (2) 功德法身 the dharmakāya evolved by Buddha virtue, or achievement; (3) 變化 | | the dharmakāya with unlimited powers of transformation; (4) 實相 | | the real dharmakāya; (5) 虛空 | | the universal dharmakāya. IV. Hīnayāna defines them as 五分 | | q.v.

五種灌頂 The five abhiṣecanī baptisms of the esoteric school—for ordaining ācāryas, teachers, or preachers of the Law; for admitting disciples; for putting an end to calamities or suffering for sins; for advancement, or success; and for controlling (evil spirits) or getting rid of difficulties, cf. 五種修法. Also, baptism of light; of sweet dew (i.e. perfume); of the "germ-word" as seed; of the five baptismal signs of wisdom made on the forehead, shoulders, heart, and throat, indicating the five Dhyāni-Buddhas; and of the "true word" on the breast.

五種藏 The five "stores", or the five differentiations of the one Buddha-nature; (1) 如來 | the Tathāgata-nature, which is the fundamental universal nature possessed by all the living; (2) 正法 | the source or treasury of all right laws and virtues; (3) 法身 | the storehouse of the dharmakāya obtained by all saints; (4) 出世 | the eternal spiritual nature, free from earthly errors; (5) 自性清淨 | the storehouse of the pure Buddha-nature. Another similar group is 如來 |, 法界 |, 法身 |, 出世間上上 |, and 自性清淨 |.

五種般 see | | 不還.

五種行 The acts of the 五種法師 q.v.; also idem | 正行.

五種說人 The five kinds of those who have testified to Buddhism; also 五人說經; 五說; i.e. the Buddha, his disciples, the ṛṣis, devas, and incarnate beings. Also, the Buddha, sages, devas, supernatural beings, and incarnate beings. Also, the Buddha, bodhisattvas, śrāvakas, men, and things. See 五類說法.

五種通 Five kinds of supernatural power: (1) 道通 of bodhisattvas through their insight into truth; (2) 神 | of arhats through their mental concentration; (3) 依 | supernatural or magical powers dependent on drugs, charms, incantations, etc.; (4) 報 | or 業 | reward or karma powers of transformation possessed by devas, nāgas, etc.; (5) 妖 | magical powers of goblins, satyrs, etc.

五種那含 v. 五種不還.

五種鈴 The five kinds of bells used by the Shingon sect in Japan, also called 金剛鈴, i.e. 五鈷 |, 寶 |, 一鈷 |, 三鈷 |, 塔 |; the different names are derived from their handles; the four first named, beginning with the five-pronged one, are placed each at a corner of the altar, the last in the middle.

五種雜行 see 五正行.

五種魔 The five Māras associated with the five skandhas; also 五蘊魔; 五陰魔, 五衆魔.

五箭 The five arrows, i.e. the five desires 五欲.

五納衣 A monk's garment of patches.

五結 The five bonds to mortality: 貪 desire, 恚 hate, 慢 pride, 嫉 envy, 慳 grudging. | | 樂子 One of Indra's musicians who praised Buddha on a crystal lute; v. 中阿含經 33.

五繫 The five suspended corpses, or dead snakes, hanging from the four limbs and neck of Māra as Pāpīyān; v. Nirvāṇa sūtra 6.

五翳 The five films, or intercepters of the light of sun and moon—smoke, cloud, dust, fog, and the hands of asuras.

五聲 idem 五音.

五臺山 Pancaśirsha, Pancaśikha. Wu-t'ai Shan, near the north-eastern border of Shansi, one of the four mountains sacred to Buddhism in China. The principal temple was built A.D. 471–500. There are about 150 monasteries, of which 24 are lamaseries. The chief director is known as Ch'ang-chia Fo (the ever-renewing Buddha). Mañjuśrī is its patron saint. It is also styled 清涼山.

五色 The five primary colours, also called 五正 (or 大) 色 |: 青 blue, 黃 yellow, 赤 red, 白 white, 黑 black. The 五間色 or compound colours are 緋 crimson, 紅 scarlet, 紫 purple, 綠 green, 硫黃 brown. The two sets correspond to the cardinal points as follows: east, blue and green; west, white and crimson; south, red and scarlet; north, black and purple; and centre, yellow and brown. The five are permutated in various ways to represent various ideas. The 五根色 are: faith, white; zeal, red; memory, yellow; meditation, blue; and wisdom, black. These are represented *inter alia* in the 五色線 (or 縷, or 綖, or 繩) the five-coloured emblematic cord; this cord is also a brahman's sign worn on the shoulder and forbidden by the Buddha.

五苦 The five forms of suffering: I. (1) Birth, age, sickness, death; (2) parting with those loved; (3) meeting with the hated or disliked; (4) inability to obtain the desired; (5) the five skandha sufferings, mental and physical. II. Birth, age, sickness, death, and the shackles (for criminals). III. The sufferings of the hells, and as hungry ghosts, animals, asuras, and human beings.

五菩提 The five bodhi, or stages of enlightenment: (1) 發心 | | resolve on supreme bodhi; (2) 伏心 | | mind control, i.e. of the passions and observance of the pāramitās; (3) 明心 | | mental enlightenment, study, and increase in knowledge and in the prajñāpāramitā; (4) 出到 | | mental expansion, freedom from the limitations of reincarnation and attainment of complete knowledge; (5) 無上 | | attainment of a passionless condition and of supreme perfect enlightenment.

五蓋 The five covers, i.e. mental and moral hindrances—desire, anger, drowsiness, excitability, doubt.

五葷 idem | 辛.

五蘊 The five skandhas, Pañcaskandha; also 五陰; 五衆; 五塞犍陀 The five cumulations, substances, or aggregates, i.e. the components of an intelligent being, especially a human being: (1) 色 rūpa, form, matter, the physical form related to the five organs of sense; (2) 受 vedanā, reception, sensation, feeling, the functioning of the mind or senses in connection with affairs and things; (3) 想 sañjñā, conception, or discerning; the functioning of mind in distinguishing; (4) 行 saṁskāra, the functioning of mind in its processes regarding like and dislike, good and evil, etc.; (5) 識 vijñāna, mental faculty in regard to perception and cognition, discriminative of affairs and things. The first is said to be physical, the other four mental qualities; (2), (3), and (4) are associated with mental functioning, and therefore with 心所; (5) is associated with the faculty or nature of the mind 心王 manas. Eitel gives—form, perception, consciousness, action, knowledge. See also Keith's *Buddhist Philosophy*, 85-91. | | (or 陰 or 衆) 世間 The worlds in which the five skandhas exist. | | 宅 The abode of the five skandhas—the human body. | | 論; 大乘 | | | A śāstra by Vasubandhu on the Mahāyāna interpretation of the five skandhas, tr. by Hsüan-tsang; 1 chüan. Other works are the | | 皆空經 tr. by I-ching of the T'ang dynasty. | | 譬喩經 tr. by 安世高 An Shih Kao of the Han dynasty; both are in the 雜阿含經 2 and 10 respectively; also | | 論釋 a commentary by Vinītaprabha. | | 魔 The Māra of the skandhas, v. 五種魔.

五處供養 The five to be constantly served—father, mother, teacher, religious director, the sick. | | 加持 Ceremonial touching of the five places on the body—brow, right and left shoulders, heart, and throat; | | 眞言 has similar reference, v. 五種灌頂.

五衆 idem 五蘊. Also, the five groups, i.e. monks, nuns, nun-candidates, and male and female novices.

五行 The five lines of conduct. I. According to the 起信論 Awakening of Faith they are almsgiving; keeping the commandments; patience under insult; zeal or progress; meditation. II. According to the 涅般經 Nirvāṇa sūtra they are saintly or bodhisattva deeds; arhat, or noble deeds; deva deeds; children's deeds (i.e. normal good deeds of men, devas, and Hinayanists); sickness conditions, e.g. illness, delusion, etc.;—into all these lines of conduct and conditions a Bodhisattva enters. III. The five elements, or tanmātra—wood, fire, earth, metal, and water; or earth, water, fire, air, and ether (or space) as taught by the later Mahāyāna philosophy; idem 五大.

五衍 The five Yānas or Vehicles, idem 五乘.

五衣 The five garments worn by a nun are the three worn by a monk with two others.

五衰 The five signs of decay or approaching death, of which descriptions vary, e.g. uncontrolled discharges, flowers on the head wither, unpleasant odour, sweating armpits, uneasiness (or anxiety); Nirvāṇa sūtra 19.

五見 The five wrong views: (1) 身見 satkāya-dṛṣti, i.e. 我見 and 我所見 the view that there is a real self, an ego, and a mine and thine; (2) 邊見 antargrāha, extreme views, e.g. extinction or permanence; (3) 邪見 mithyā, perverse views, which, denying cause and effect, destroy the foundations of morality; (4) 見取見 dṛṣṭiparāmarśa, stubborn perverted views, viewing inferior things as superior, or counting the worse as the better; (5) 戒禁取見 śīla-vrata-parāmarśa, rigid views in favour of rigorous ascetic prohibitions, e.g. covering oneself with ashes. Cf. | 利使.

五覺 The five bodhi, or states of enlightenment, as described in the 起信論 Awakening of Faith; see also 五菩提 for a different group. (1) 本 | Absolute eternal wisdom, or bodhi; (2) 始 | bodhi in its initial stages, or in action, arising from right observances; (3) 相似 | bodhisattva-attainment of bodhi in action, in the 十信; (4) 隨分 | further bodhisattva-enlightenment according to capacity, i.e. the stages 十住, 十行, and 十廻向; (5) 究竟 | final or complete enlightenment, i.e. the stage of 妙 |, which is one with the first, i.e. 本 |. The 本 | is bodhi in the potential, 始 | is bodhi in the active state, hence (2), (3), (4), and (5) are all the latter, but the fifth has reached the perfect quiescent stage of original bodhi.

五觀 The five meditations referred to in the Lotus 25: (1) 眞 | on the true, idem 空 |, to meditate on the reality of the void, or infinite, in order to be rid of illusion in views and thoughts; (2) 清淨 | on purity, to be rid of any remains of impurity connected with the temporal, idem 假 |; (3) 廣大智慧 | on the wider and greater wisdom, idem 中 |, by study of the "middle" way; (4) 悲 | on pitifulness, or the pitiable condition of the living, and by the above three to meditate on their salvation; (5) 慈 | on mercy and the extension of the first three meditations to the carrying of joy to all the living.

五解脫輪 The five wheels of liberation, or salvation, i.e. the five maṇḍalas in which are the Five Dhyāni-Buddhas, see 五智如來; also called | 大月輪 and | 輪塔婆.

五說 idem 五種說人.

五論 idem 五部大論.

五調子 idem 五音.

五諦 The five axioms: (1) 因 | the cause, which is described as 集 of the Four Noble Truths; (2) 果 | the effect as 苦; (3) 智 | or 能知 | diagnosis as 道; (4) 境 | or 所知 | the end or cure as 滅; to these add (5) 勝 | or 至 | the supreme axiom, i.e. the 眞如; v. 四諦.

五識 The five parijñānas, perceptions or cognitions; ordinarily those arising from the five senses, i.e. of form-and-colour, sound, smell, taste, and touch. The 起信論 Awakening of Faith has a different set of five steps in the history of cognition: (1) 業識 initial functioning of mind under the influence of the original 無明 unenlightenment or state of ignorance; (2) 轉識 the act of turning towards the apparent object for its observation; (3) 現 | observation of the object as it appears; (4) 知 | the deductions derived from its appearance; (5) 相續 | the consequent feelings of like or dislike, pleasure or pain, from which arise the delusions and incarnations.

五趣 The five gati, i.e. destinations, destinies: the hells, hungry ghosts, animals, human beings, devas; cf. 五惡 | and 五道. | | 生死輪 A series of pictures to show the course of life and death, ascribed in the Sarvāstivāda Vinaya 34 to the Buddha.

五身 see 五種法身.

五輪 The five wheels, or things that turn: I. The 五體 or five members, i.e. the knees, the elbows, and the head; when all are placed on the ground it implies the utmost respect. II. The five foundations of the world, first and lowest the wheel or circle of space; above are those of wind; of water; the diamond, or earth; on these rest the nine concentric circles and eight seas. III. The esoteric sect uses the term for the 五大 five elements, earth, water, fire, wind, and space; also for the 五解脫輪 q.v. IV. The five fingers (of a Buddha). | | 六大 The five are the 五大 five elements, to which the sixth 大 is added, i.e. the six elements, earth, water, fire, air and space, and 識 intelligence or mind. | | (率) 塔婆 A stūpa with five wheels at the top; chiefly used by the Shingon sect on graves as indicating the indwelling Vairocana. | | 觀; | | 三摩地 A meditation of the esoteric school on the five elements, earth, water, fire, air, and space, with their germ-words, their forms (i.e. square, round, triangular, half-moon, and spherical), and their colours (i.e. yellow, white, red, black, and blue). The five wheels also represent the Five Dhyāni-Buddhas, v. 五智. The object is that 五輪成身 the individual may be united with the five Buddhas, or Vairocana. | | 際 The fifth wheel limit, or world-foundation, i.e. that of space.

五轉 The five evolutions, or developments: (1) resolve on Buddhahood; (2) observance of the rules; (3) attainment of enlightenment; (4) of nirvāṇa; (5) of power to aid others according to need. | | 成身 idem 五相成身. | | 色 The above five developments are given the colours respectively of yellow, red, white, black, and blue (or green), each colour being symbolic, e.g. yellow of Vairocana, red of Mañjuśrī, etc.

五辛 The five forbidden pungent roots, 五葷 garlic, three kinds of onions, and leeks; if eaten raw they are said to cause irritability of temper, and if eaten cooked, to act as an aphrodisiac; moreover, the breath of the eater, if reading the sūtras, will drive away the good spirits.

五逆 Pañcānantarya; 五無間業. I. The five rebellious acts or deadly sins, parricide, matricide, killing an arhat, shedding the blood of a Buddha, destroying the harmony of the saṅgha, or fraternity. The above definition is common both to Hīnayāna and Mahāyāna. The lightest of these sins is the first; the heaviest the last. II. Another group is: (1) sacrilege, such as destroying temples, burning sūtras, stealing a Buddha's or a monk's things, inducing others to do so, or taking pleasure therein; (2) slander, or abuse of the teaching of śrāvakas, pratyeka-buddhas, or bodhisattvas; (3) ill-treatment or killing of a monk; (4) any one of the five deadly sins given above; (5) denial of the karma consequences of ill deeds, acting or teaching others accordingly, and unceasing evil life. III. There are also five deadly sins, each of which is equal to each of the first set of five: (1) violation of a mother, or a fully ordained nun; (2) killing a bodhisattva in dhyāna; (3) killing anyone in training to be an arhat; (4) preventing the restoration of harmony in a saṅgha; (5) destroying a Buddha's stūpa. IV. The five unpardonable sins of Devadatta who (1) destroyed the harmony of the community; (2) injured Śākyamuni with a stone, shedding his blood; (3) induced the king to let loose a rutting elephant to trample down Śākyamuni; (4) killed a nun; (5) put poison on his finger-nails and saluted Śākyamuni intending to destroy him thereby.

五通 v. 五神通. 丨丨仙 One who by non-Buddhistic methods has attained to the five supernatural powers. 丨丨神 Spirits possessed of the five supernatural powers. They are also identified with five spirits known as the 五聖 or 五顯, of whom there are varying accounts. 丨丨菩薩 The five bodhisattvas of the 鷄頭摩 monastery in India, who, possessed of supernatural powers, went to the Western Paradise and begged the image of Maitreya, whence it is said to have been spread over India.

五道 idem 五趣. 丨丨六道 There is difference of statement whether there are five or six gati, i.e. ways or destinies; if six, then there is added the asura, a being having functions both good and evil, both deva and demon. 丨丨冥官 An officer in the retinue of the ten kings of Hades. 丨丨將軍 A general in the retinue of the ten kings of Hades, who keeps the book of life. 丨丨轉輪王 One of the ten kings of Hades who retries the sufferers on their third year of imprisonment.

五邊 The five alternatives, i.e. (things) exist; do not exist; both exist and non-exist; neither exist nor non-exist; neither non-exist nor are without non-existence.

五遍行 The five universal mental activities associated with every thought—the idea, mental contact, reception, conception, perception, 作意, 觸, 受, 想, 思; cf. 五蘊.

五那含天 idem 五淨居天.

五邪(命) The five improper ways of gain or livelihood for a monk, i.e. (1) changing his appearance, e.g. theatrically; (2) advertising his own powers and virtue; (3) fortune-telling by physiognomy, etc.; (4) hectoring and bullying; (5) praising the generosity of another to induce the hearer to bestow presents.

五部 The five classes, or groups: I. The 四諦 four truths, which four are classified as 見道 or theory, and 修道 practice, e.g. the eightfold path. II. The five early Hīnayāna sects, see 一切有部 or Sarvāstivādāḥ. III. The five groups of the Vajradhātu maṇḍala. 丨丨合斷 To cut off the five classes of misleading things, i.e. four 見 and one 修, i.e. false theory in regard to the 四諦 four truths, and erroneous practice. Each of the two classes is extended into each of the three divisions of past, three of present, and three of future, making eighteen mental conditions. 丨丨大乘經 The five chief Mahāyāna sūtras according to T'ien-t'ai are: 華嚴; 大集; 大品般若; 法華, and 涅槃經, i.e. Avataṁsaka, Mahāsanghāta, Mahāprajñā, Lotus, and Nirvāṇa sūtras. 丨丨大論 Asaṅga, founder of the Yogācāra school, is said, by command of Maitreya, to have edited the five great śāstras, 瑜伽師地丨, 分別瑜伽丨, 大乘莊嚴經丨, 辨中邊丨頌, and 金剛般若丨. 丨丨尊法; 五種壇法 (or 護摩 or 悉地). Ceremonials of the esoteric cult for ridding from calamity; for prosperity; subduing evil (spirits); seeking the love of Buddhas; calling the good to aid; cf. 五種修法. 丨丨座 The five Dhyāni-Buddhas, v. 五智如來. 丨丨律 The first five Hīnayāna sects—Dharmagupta, Sarvāstivāda, Mahīśāsaka, Kāśyapīya, and Vātsīputrīya; see 五師. 丨丨敎主 The five Dhyāni-

Buddhas, v. 五智如來. ||法 idem ||尊法. ||淨(居炎摩羅) Yama as protector in the retinue of the thousand-hand Kuan-yin. ||秘藏 idem ||尊法.

五重世界 The five graduated series of universes: (1) 三千大千世界 Tri-sahasra-mahā-sahasra-loka-dhātu; a universe, or chiliocosm; (2) such chiliocosms, numerous as the sands of Ganges, form one Buddha-universe; (3) an aggregation of these forms a Buddha-universe ocean; (4) an aggregation of these latter forms a Buddha-realm seed; (5) an infinite aggregation of these seeds forms a great Buddha-universe. 智度論 50. Another division is (1) a world, or universe; (2) a Buddha-nature universe, with a different interpretation; and the remaining three are as above, the sea, the seed, and the whole Buddha-universe. ||滯 The five heavy blockages, or serious hindrances; see 五鈍使 infra. ||雲 The five banks of clouds or obstructions for a woman, see 五障.

五鈍使 Pañca-kleśa. 五重滯; 五惑 The five dull, unintelligent, or stupid vices or temptations: 貪 desire, 嗔 anger or resentment, 癡 stupidity or foolishness, 慢 arrogance, 疑 doubt. Overcoming these constitutes the pañca-śīla, five virtues, v. 尸羅. Of the ten 使 or agents the other five are styled 利 keen, acute, intelligent, as they deal with higher qualities.

五鈷(or 胋 or 股)金剛(杵) The five-armed vajra, 五智金剛杵; 五峯||, 五峯光明; emblem of the powers of the 五智如來 q.v.

五門禪 idem 五停心觀; there is also a fivefold meditation on impermanence, suffering, the void, the non-ego, and nirvāṇa.

五間色 The five compound colours, v. 五色.

五闡提羅 The five ṣaṇḍhilas, i.e. five bad monks who died, went to the hells, and were reborn as ṣaṇḍhilas or imperfect males; also |扇||.

五阿含 The five Āgamas, 五阿笈摩, i.e. (1) 長阿含經 Dīrghāgama; (2) 中阿含 Madhyamāgama; (3) 僧育多阿含 Samyuktāgama; (4) 鴦掘多羅阿含 Ekottarikāgama, and (5) 屈陀伽阿含 Kṣudrakāgama.

五陰; 五衆 see 五蘊. 陰 is the older term. ||世間 idem 五蘊世間. ||(盛)苦 idem 五盛陰苦. ||魔 idem 五蘊魔.

五障 The five hindrances, or obstacles; also 五礙; 五雲. I. Of women, i.e. inability to become Brahma-kings, Indras, Māra-kings, Cakravarti-kings, or Buddhas. II. The hindrances to the five 力 powers, i.e. (self-)deception a bar to faith, as sloth is to zeal, anger to remembrance, hatred to meditation, and discontent to wisdom. III. The hindrances of (1) the passion-nature, e.g. original sin; (2) of karma caused in previous lives; (3) the affairs of life; (4) no friendly or competent preceptor; (5) partial knowledge. ||三從 The five hindrances to woman, see above, and her three subordinations, i.e. to father, husband, and son.

五雲 v. |障.

五音 The five musical tones, or pentatonic scale—do, re, mi, sol, la; also 五聲; 五調子.

五頂 Pañcaśikha, the five locks on a boy's head; also used for 五佛頂尊 q.v. ||輪王 idem 五佛頂尊. ||山 idem Wu-t'ai Shan |臺.

五類天 The five kinds of devas: (1) 上界天 in the upper realms of form and non-form; (2) 虛空天 in the sky, i.e. four of the six devas of the desire-realm; (3) 地居天 on the earth, i.e. the other two of the six devas, on Sumeru; (4) 遊虛空天 wandering devas of the sky, e.g. sun, moon, stars; (5) 地下天 under-world devas, e.g. nāgas, asuras, māras, etc. Cf. 五大明王. ||聲 The five groups of five each of the consonants in the syllabary called 悉曇 Siddha. ||說法 The five preachers in the Hua-yen sūtra: the Buddha; bodhisattvas; śrāvakas; the devas in their praise-songs; and material things, e.g. the bodhi-tree; v. 五種說人.

五食 The five kinds of spiritual food by which roots of goodness are nourished: correct thoughts; delight in the Law; pleasure in meditation; firm resolve, or vows of self-control; and deliverance from the karma of illusion.

五香 The incense composed of five ingredients (sandalwood, aloes, cloves, saffron, and camphor) offered by the esoteric sects in building their altars and in performing their rituals. Cf. 五分香.

五體 and ||投地 v. 五輪.

五髻 The five cūḍā, topknots or locks, emblems of the 五智 q.v. 丨丨冠 A five-pointed crown with a similar meaning. 丨丨文殊 Mañjuśrī of the five locks.

今 Now, at present, the present. 丨圓 A T'ien-t'ai term indicating the present "perfect" teaching, i.e. that of the Lotus, as compared with the 昔圓 older "perfect" teaching which preceded it. 丨家 The present school, i.e. my school or sect.

介 Scales, mail; important; resolute, firm; an attendant; petty, small. 丨爾 A transient thought, see kṣaṇa 刹.

仁 Kindness, benevolence, virtue. 丨者 or 丨 Kind sir! 丨尊 Benevolent and honoured, or kindly honoured one, i.e. Buddha. 丨王 The benevolent king, Buddha; the name Śākya is intp. as 能仁 able in generosity. Also an ancient king, probably imaginary, of the "sixteen countries" of India, for whom the Buddha is said to have dictated the 仁王經, a sūtra with two principal translations into Chinese, the first by Kumārajīva styled 丨丨般若經 or 佛說仁王般若波羅蜜經 without magical formulæ, the second by Amogha (不空) styled 丨丨護國般若, etc., into which the magical formulæ were introduced; these were for royal ceremonials to protect the country from all kinds of calamities and induce prosperity. 丨丨供 Service of the 丨丨會 (or 講) the meeting of monks to chant the above incantations. 丨丨咒; 丨丨陀羅尼 The incantations in the above. 丨丨尊 The two Vajrapāṇi 阿 and 吽 who act as door guardians of temples, variously known as 密跡菩薩, 密修力士, 執金剛神, and 那羅延金剛.

什 A file of ten; sundry, what. 丨物 Things (in general), oddments. 丨肇 The 什 is Kumārajīva and the 肇 his disciple 僧肇 Sêng-chao. 丨麽 idem 甚麽 What? What.

允 Sincere, true; to assent. 丨堪 Yün-k'an, a famous monk of the Sung dynasty. 丨若 Yün-jo, a famous monk of the Yüan dynasty.

元 Beginning, first, original, head; dollar; Mongol (dynasty). 丨吉樹 The tree of the origin of felicity, i.e. the bodhi-tree or ficus religiosa, also styled 佛樹; 道樹, and 菩提樹. 丨品無明 Primal ignorance; the original state of avidyā, unenlightenment, or ignorance; original innocence. Also 根本無明; 無始無明. 丨因; 原因 The original or fundamental cause which produces phenomena, e.g. karma, reincarnation, etc.; every cause has its fruit or consequences. The idea of cause and effect is a necessary condition of antecedent and consequence; it includes such relations as interaction, correlation, interdependence, co-ordination based on an intrinsic necessity. 丨妙 The original or fundamental marvel or mystery, i.e. the conception of nirvāṇa. 丨始 Prabhū, 波羅赴; 鉢利部 beginning, in the beginning, primordial. Prabhū is a title of Viṣṇu as a personification of the sun. 丨心 The original or primal mind behind all things, idem the 一心 of the 起信論 Awakening of Faith, the 森羅萬象之元 source of all phenomena, the mind which is in all things. 丨明; 本明 Original brightness or intelligence; the 眞如 or bhūtatathatā as the source of all light or enlightenment. 丨曉 Yüan-hsiao, a famous Korean monk who travelled, and studied and wrote in China during the T'ang dynasty, then returned to Korea; known as 海東師 Hai-tung Shih. 丨照 Name of 湛然 Chan-jan, the seventh head of the T'ien-t'ai School; he died 1116. 丨祖 The original patriarch, or founder of a sect or school; sometimes applied to the Buddha as the founder of virtue. 丨藏 The Yüan Tripitaka, compiled by order of Shih Tsu (Kublai), founder of the Yüan dynasty, and printed from blocks; begun in 1277, the work was finished in 1290, in 1,422 部 works, 6,017 卷 sections, 558 函 cases or covers. It contained 528 Mahāyānist and 242 Hīnayānist sūtras; 25 Mahāyāna and 54 Hīnayāna vinaya; 97 Mahāyāna and 36 Hīnayāna śāstras; 108 biographies; and 332 supplementary or general works. In size, and generally, it was similar to the Sung edition. The 元藏目錄 or Catalogue of the Yüan Tripitaka is also known as 大普寧寺大藏經目錄. 丨辰星; 元神星 A star that controls the attainment of honours, and the riddance of sickness and distresses. The star varies according to the year star of the suppliant which is one of the seven stars in Ursa Major.

內 Within, inner.

內乞 The bhikṣu monk who seeks control from within himself, i.e. by mental processes, as compared with the 外乞 the one who aims at control by physical discipline, e.g. fasting, etc.

內供 (奉) A title for the monk who served at the altar in the imperial palace, instituted in A.D. 756; also called 供奉.

內典 Buddhist scriptures; cf. 外典 non-Buddhist scriptures. There are also divisions of internal and external in Buddhist scriptures.

內凡 The inner or higher ranks of ordinary disciples as contrasted with the 外凡 lower grades; those who are on the road to liberation; Hīnayāna begins the stage at the 四善根位 also styled 丨丨位; Mahāyāna with the 三賢位 from the 十住 upwards. T'ien-t'ai from the 相似卽 of its 六卽 q.v.

內塵 The inner, or sixth 塵 guṇa associated with mind, in contrast with the other five guṇas, qualities or attributes of the visible, audible, etc.

內史 The clerk, or writer of petitions, or prayers, in a monastery; also 內記.

內外 Internal and external; subjective and objective. 丨丨兼明 Inner and outer both "ming"; the first four of the 五明 q.v. are "outer" and the fifth "inner". 丨丨空 Internal organ and external object are both unreal, or not material. 丨丨道 Within and without the religion; Buddhists and non-Buddhists; also, heretics within the religion.

內學 The inner learning, i.e. Buddhism.

內宿食 Food that has been kept overnight in a monastic bedroom and is therefore one of the "unclean" foods; v. 內煮.

內寺 The Buddhist shrines or temples in the palace, v. 內道場.

內心 The mind or heart within; the red lotus is used in the 大日經 as its emblem. 丨丨(or 秘密) 曼荼羅 The "central heart" maṇḍala of the 大日經, or the central throne in the diamond-realm lotus to which it refers.

內我 The antarātman or ego within, one's own soul or self, in contrast with bahirātman 外我 an external soul, or personal, divine ruler.

內教 Buddhism, in contrast with 外教 other cults.

內明 Adhyātma vidyā, a treatise on the inner meaning (of Buddhism), one of the 五明 q.v.

內法 Buddhism, as contrasted with other religions.

內無爲 Inner quiescence, cf. the six 妙門.

內煮 Cooked food in a monastic bedroom, becoming thereby one of the "unclean" foods; v. 丨宿食.

內界 The realm of mind as contrasted with 外界 that of the body; also the realm of cognition as contrasted with externals, e.g. the 五界 five elements.

內秘 The inner mystic mind of the bodhisattva, though externally he may appear to be a śrāvaka.

內種 The seed contained in the eighth 識, i.e. ālaya-vijñāna, the basis of all phenomena.

內空 Empty within, i.e. no soul or self within.

內緣 The condition of perception arising from the five senses; also immediate, conditional, or environmental causes, in contrast with the more remote.

內薰 Inner censing; primal ignorance, or unenlightenment; perfuming, censing, or acting upon original intelligence causes the common uncontrolled mind to resent the miseries of mortality and to seek nirvāṇa; v. 起信論 Awakening of Faith.

內胎 The inner garbhadhātu, i.e. the eight objects in the eight leaves in the central group of the maṇḍala.

內衆 The inner company, i.e. the monks, in contrast with 外俗 the laity.

內衣 Antaravāsaka, one of the three regulation garments of a monk, the inner garment.

內記 The clerk, or writer of petitions, or prayers, in a monastery; also 內史.

內證 The witness or realization within; one's own assurance of the truth.

內識 Internal perception, idem 心識.

內道場 A place for Buddhist worship in the palace, v. 內齋 and 內寺.

內門轉 The psychological elements in the 八識, viz. the seventh and eighth categories.

內陣 The inner ranks, i.e. the part of a temple near the altar, where the monks sit.

內院 The inner court—of the Tuṣita heaven, where Maitreya dwells and preaches; also 善法堂.

內障 Internal, or mental hindrances, or obstacles.

內齋 Buddhist ceremonies in the palace on the emperor's birthday, v. 內道場.

公 Public, general, official; a duke, grandparent, gentleman; just, fair. 丨案 J. Kōan; 因緣 A dossier, or case-record; a cause; public laws, regulations; case-law. Problems set by Zen masters, upon which thought is concentrated as a means to attain inner unity and illumination. 丨界 A public place; in public.

六 Ṣaṭ, ṣaḍ. Six.

六事成就 The six things which enable a bodhisattva to keep perfectly the six pāramitās —worshipful offerings, study of the moral duties, pity, zeal in goodness, isolation, delight in the law; these are described as corresponding to the pāramitās seriatim; v. 莊嚴經 12.

六住 The sixth of the 十住 q.v.

六作 idem 六受.

六位 The six stages of Bodhisattva development, i.e. 十信丨; 十住丨; 十廻向丨; 十地丨; 等覺丨; 佛地丨; these are from the older Hua-yen ching.

六供具 The six articles for worship—flowers, a censer, candles, hot liquid, fruits, tea.

六依 The six senses on which one relies, or from which knowledge is received; v. 丨情.

六入 Ṣaḍāyatana; 六阿耶 (or 也) 怛那 the six entrances, or locations, both the organ and the sensation—eye, ear, nose, tongue, body, and mind; sight, hearing, smell, taste, touch, and perception. The six form one of the twelve nidānas, see 十二因緣. The 六根 are the six organs, the 六境 the six objects, and the 六塵 or guṇas, the six inherent qualities. The later term is 六處 q.v.

六八弘誓 The forty-eight great or surpassing vows of Amitābha, also 六八超世本願.

六決定 v. 六種決定; also 七深信.

六凡 The six stages of rebirth for ordinary people, as contrasted with the saints 聖者: in the hells, and as hungry ghosts, animals, asuras, men, and devas.

六到彼岸 The six things that ferry one to the other shore, i.e. the six pāramitās, v. 六度.

六劍; 六箭 The six swords (or arrows), i.e. the six senses, v. 六塵, which are defined as the qualities of sight, sound, smell, taste, touch, and mind.

六十 Ṣaṣṭi, sixty. 丨丨二見 The sixty-two 見 or views, of which three groups are given: The 大品般若經 in the 佛母品 takes each of the five skandhas under four considerations of 常 time, considered as time past, whether each of the five has had permanence, impermanence, both, neither, $5 \times 4 = 20$; again as to their space, or extension, considered as present time, whether each is finite, infinite, both, neither $= 20$; again as to their destination, i.e. future, as to whether each goes on, or does not, both, neither (e.g. continued personality) $= 20$, or in all 60; add the two ideas whether body and mind 神 are a unity or different $= 62$. The T'ien-t'ai School takes 我見, or personality, as its basis and considers each of the five skandhas under four aspects, e.g (1) rūpa, the organized body, as the ego; (2) the ego as apart from the rūpa; (3) rūpa as the greater, the ego the smaller or inferior, and the ego as dwelling in the rūpa; (4) the ego as the greater, rūpa the inferior, and the rūpa in the ego. Consider these twenty in the past, present, and future $= 60$, and add 斷 and 常 impermanence and permanence as fundamentals $= 62$. There is also a third group. 丨丨卷 The 60 rolls: the T'ien-t'ai 三大部, or three collections of fundamental texts of that school. | | 四書 The sixty-four classes of Indian writing or literature, Brāhmī, Kharoṣṭhī, etc. | | | 梵音 The sixty-four Aryan or noble characteristics of a Buddha's tones or voice, e.g. snigdha 流澤聲 smooth; mṛdukā 柔軟聲 gentle, etc. | | | 眼 Eighteen lictors in the avīci hell each with sixty-four eyes. | | 心 The sixty different mental positions that may occur to the practiser of Yoga, see 大日經住心品; examples of them are desire, non-desire, ire, kindness, foolishness, wisdom, decision, doubt, depression, brightness, contention, dispute, non-contention, the spirit of devas, of asuras, of nagas, of humanity, woman (i.e. lust), mastery, commercial, and so on.

六卽 The six stages of Bodhisattva developments as defined in the T'ien-t'ai 圓敎, i.e. Perfect, or Final Teaching, in contrast with the previous, or ordinary six developments of 十信, 十住, 十行, etc., as found in the 別敎 Differentiated or Separate school. The T'ien-t'ai six are: (1) 理卽 realization that all beings are of Buddha-nature; (2) 名字卽 the apprehension of terms, that those who only hear and believe are in the Buddha-law and potentially Buddha; (3) 觀行卽 advance beyond terminology to meditation, or study and accordant action; it is known as 五品觀行 or 五品弟子位; (4) 相似卽 semblance stage, or approximation to perfection in purity, the 六根清淨位, i.e. the 十信位; (5) 分證卽 discrimination of truth and its progressive experiential proof, i.e. the 十住, 十行, 十廻向, 十地, and 等覺位 of the 別敎, known also as the 聖因 cause or root of holiness. (6) 究竟卽 perfect enlightenment, i.e. the 妙覺位 or 聖果 fruition of holiness. (1) and (2) are known as 外凡 external for, or common to, all. (1) is theoretical; (2) is the first step in practical advance, followed by (3) and (4) styled 內凡 internal for all, and (3), (4), (5), and (6) are known as the 八位 the eight grades. | | 佛 Buddha in six forms: (1) 理佛 as the principle in and through all things, as pan-Buddha—all things being of Buddha-nature; (2) 名字佛 Buddha as a name or person. The other four are the last four forms above.

六受 The six vedanās, i.e. receptions, or sensations from the 六根 six organs. Also 六作.

六合釋 v. 六離合釋.

六和(敬) The six points of reverent harmony or unity in a monastery or convent: 身 bodily unity in form of worship, 口 oral unity in chanting, 意 mental unity in faith, 戒 moral unity in observing the commandments, 見 doctrinal unity in views and explanations, and 利, 行, 學, or 施 economic unity in community of goods, deeds, studies, or charity. | | 合 The six unions of the six sense organs with the six objects of the senses, the eye with the object seen, etc.

六味 The six tastes, or flavours—bitter, sour, sweet, acrid, salt, and insipid.

六喩 The six illustrations of unreality in the Diamond Sūtra: a dream, a phantasm, a bubble, a shadow, dew, and lightning. Also | 如.

六因 The six causations of the 六位 six stages of Bodhisattva development, q.v. Also, the sixfold division of causes of the Vaibhāṣikas (cf. Keith, 177–8); every phenomenon depends upon the union of 因 primary cause and 緣 conditional or environmental cause; and of the 因 there are six kinds: (1) 能作因 Kāraṇahetu, effective causes of two kinds: 與力 | empowering cause, as the earth empowers plant growth, and 不障 | non-resistant cause, as space does not resist, i.e. active and passive causes; (2) 俱有 | Sahabhū-hetu, co-operative causes, as the four elements 四大 in nature, not one of which can be omitted; (3) 同類 | Sabhāgahetu, causes of the same kind as the effect, good producing good, etc.; (4) 相應 | Saṁprayuktahetu, mutual responsive or associated causes, e.g. mind and mental conditions, subject with object; Keith gives "faith and intelligence"; similar to (2); (5) 遍行 | Sarvatragahetu, universal or omnipresent cause, i.e. of illusion, as of false views affecting every act; it resembles (3) but is confined to delusion; (6) 異熟 | Vipākahetu, differential fruition, i.e. the effect different from the cause, as the hells are from evil deeds.

六地藏 Six bodhisattvas in the Ti Tsang group of the garbhadhātu, each controlling one of the 六道 or ways of sentient existence. They deal with rebirth in the hells, as hungry ghosts, animals, asuras, men, and devas.

六垢(法) Six things that defile: 誑 exaggeration, 諂 flattery, 憍 arrogance, 惱 vexation, 恨 hatred, 害 malice.

六城部 Ṣāṇṇagarikāḥ, 山拖那伽梨柯部; or 密林山部. One of the twenty Hīnayāna sects, connected with the Vātsīputtrīyāḥ 犢子部.

六境 The six fields of the senses, i.e. the

objective fields of sight, sound, smell, taste, touch, and idea (or thought); rūpa, form and colour, is the field of vision; sound, of hearing; scent, of smelling; the five flavours, of tasting; physical feeling, of touch; and mental presentation, of discernment; cf. 六入; 六處 and next.

六塵 The six guṇas, qualities produced by the objects and organs of sense, i.e. sight, sound, smell, taste, touch, and idea; the organs are the 六根, 六入, 六處, and the perceptions or discernments the 六識; cf. 六境. Dust 塵 is dirt, and these six qualities are therefore the cause of all impurity. Yet 六塵說法 the Buddha made use of them to preach his law.

六大 The six great or fundamental things, or elements—earth; water; fire; wind (or air); space (or ether); and 識 mind, or perception. These are universal and creative of all things, but the inanimate 非情 are made only of the first five, while the animate 有情 are of all six. The esoteric cult represents the six elements, somewhat differently interpreted in the garbhadhātu and vajradhātu. Also 丨界. 丨丨法性 The unity in variety of the six elements and their products; ordinary eyes see only the differentiated forms or appearances, the sage or philosopher sees the unity. 丨丨無礙 The six elements unimpeded, or interactive; or 六大體大 the six elements in their greater substance, or whole. The doctrine of the esoteric cult of transubstantiation, or the free interchangeability of the six Buddha elements with the human, like with like, whereby yoga becomes possible, i.e. the Buddha elements entering into and possessing the human elements, for both are of the same elemental nature. 丨丨煩惱 The six great kleśa, passions, or distressers: desire, resentment, stupidity, pride, doubt, and false views. 丨丨神 The spirits of the six elements. 丨丨觀 Meditation on the six elements; in the exoteric cult, that they are unreal and unclean; in the esoteric cult, that the Buddha and human elements are of the same substance and interchangeable, see above. 丨丨賊 v. 六賊.

六天 The six devalokas, i.e. the heavens with sense organs above Sumeru, between the brahmalokas and the earth, i.e. 四王天; 忉利丨; 夜摩丨; 兜率天; 樂變化丨; and 他化自在天. The sixth is the heaven of Māra, v. 六欲天.

六夷 The six pārājikas, v. 波羅夷.

六如 The six "likes" or comparisons, like a dream, a phantasm, a bubble, a shadow, dew, and lightning. v. 六喩.

六妄 The six misleaders, i.e. the six senses.

六妙行 idem 六行觀.

六字 The six words or syllables, 南無阿彌陀佛 Namo Amitābha; 丨丨名號 a name for him. The 丨丨文殊 six-word dhāraṇī of Mañjuśrī 闇婆髻䭾(or 計陀)那麽 or 唵縛鷄淡納莫. There are also the esoteric (Shingon) six words connected with the six forms of Kuan-yin and the 丨丨法, 丨丨供, 丨丨河臨法, and 丨丨護摩 ceremonials, some connected with Mañjuśrī, and all with Kuan-yin. There are several 六字 dhāraṇīs, e.g. the Ṣaḍakṣara-vidyāmantra. The six words generally associated with Kuan-yin are 安荼詈(or 隸) 般荼詈 (or 隸). There is also the six-word Lamaistic charm Oṁ maṇi padme hūṁ 唵嚤呢叭彌吽.

六宗 The six schools, i.e. 三論; 法相; 華嚴; 律; 成實, and 俱舍 q.v.; the last two are styled Hīnayāna schools. Mahāyāna in Japan puts in place of them 天台 and 眞言 Tendai and Shingon.

六師 The six tīrthikas or heterodox teachers—Pūraṇa-Kāśyapa, Maskarin, Sañjayin, Ajita-keśakambala, Kakuda-Kātyāyana, and Nirgrantha; see 外道. 丨丨迦王 Name of the king who, thirteen years after the destruction of the Jetavana vihāra, which had been rebuilt "five centuries" after the nirvāṇa, again restored it.

六年苦行 The six years of Śākyamuni's austerities before his enlightenment.

六度 The six things that ferry one beyond the sea of mortality to nirvāṇa, i.e. the six pāramitās 波羅蜜(多): (1) 布施 dāna, charity, or giving, including the bestowing of the truth on others; (2) 持戒 śīla, keeping the commandments; (3) 忍辱 kṣānti, patience under insult; (4) 精進 vīrya, zeal and progress; (5) 闍定 dhyāna, meditation or contemplation; (6) 智慧 prajñā, wisdom, the power to discern reality or truth. It is the last which carries across the saṁsāra (sea of incarnate life) to the shores of nirvāṇa. The opposites of these virtues are meanness, wickedness, anger, sloth, a distracted mind, and ignorance. The 唯識論 adds four other pāramitās: (7) 方便 Upāya, the use of appropriate means; (8) 願 praṇidhāna, pious vows; (9) 力 bala, power of fulfilment; (10) 智 jñana knowledge. ｜｜果報 The rewards stimulated by the six pāramitās are 富 enrichment; 具色 all things, or perfection; 力 power; 壽 long life; 安 peace (or calmness); 辯 discrimination, or powers of exposition of the truth. ｜｜無極 The six infinite means of crossing the sea of mortality, i.e. the six pāramitās 六度.

六德 The six characteristics of a bhagavat, which is one of a Buddha's titles: sovereign, glorious, majestic, famous, propitious, honoured.

六念(法) The six thoughts to dwell upon: Buddha, the Law, the Order, the commands, almsgiving, and heaven with its prospective joys. ｜｜處 The six stages of the above.

六情 The emotions arising from the six organs of sense 六根 for which term 六情 is the older interpretation; v. ｜依.

六慧 The six kinds of wisdom. Each is allotted seriatim to one of the six positions 六位 q.v. (1) 聞慧 the wisdom of hearing and apprehending the truth of the middle way is associated with the 十住; (2) 思｜of thought with the 十行; (3) 修｜of observance with the 十廻向; (4) 無相｜of neither extreme, or the mean, with the 十地; (5) 照寂｜of understanding of nirvāṇa with 等覺｜; (6) 寂照｜of making nirvāṇa illuminate all beings associated with 佛果 Buddha-fruition. They are a 別教 Differentiated School series and all are associated with 中道 the school of the 中 or middle way.

六成就 Six perfections (some say five, some seven) found in the opening phrase of each sūtra: (1) "Thus" implies perfect faith; (2) "have I heard," perfect hearing; (3) "once," the perfect time; (4) "the Buddha," the perfect lord or master; (5) "on Mt. Gṛdhrakūṭa," the perfect place; (6) "with the great assembly of bhikṣus," the perfect assembly.

六方 The six directions—E. W. N. S. above and below. ｜｜禮 The brahman morning act of bathing and paying homage in the six directions; observing the "well-born" do this; the Buddha is said to have given the discourse in the 善生經. ｜｜護念, ｜｜證明 (or 誠) The praises of Amitābha proclaimed by the Buddhas of the six directions.

六時 The six "hours" or periods in a day, three for night and three for day, i.e. morning, noon, evening; night, midnight, and dawn. Also, the six divisions of the year, two each of spring, summer, and winter. ｜｜懺, ｜｜三昧, ｜｜不斷, ｜｜禮讚 all refer respectively to the six daily periods of worship, of meditation, of unintermitting devotions, and of ceremonial.

六染心 The six mental "taints" of the Awakening of Faith 起心論. Though mind-essence is by nature pure and without stain, the condition of 無明 ignorance, or innocence, permits of taint or defilement corresponding to the following six phases: (1) 執相應染 the taint interrelated to attachment, or holding the seeming for the real; it is the state of 執取相 and 名字相 which is cut off in the final pratyeka and śrāvaka stage and the bodhisattva 十住 of faith; (2) 不斷相應染 the taint interrelated to the persisting attraction of the causes of pain and pleasure; it is the 相續相 finally eradicated in the bodhisattva 初地 stage of purity; (3) 分別智相應染 the taint interrelated to the "particularizing intelligence" which discerns things within and without this world; it is the first 智相, cut off in the bodhisattva 七地 stage of spirituality; (4) 現色不相應染 the non-interrelated or primary taint, i.e. of the "ignorant" mind as yet hardly discerning subject from object, of accepting an external world; the third 現相 cut off in the bodhisattva 八地 stage of emancipation from the material; (5) 能見心不相應染 the non-interrelated or primary taint of accepting a perceptive mind, the second 轉相, cut off in the bodhisattva 九地 of intuition, or emancipation from mental effort; (6) 根本業不相應染 the non-interrelated or primary taint of accepting the idea of primal action or activity in the absolute; it is the first 業相, and cut off in the 十地 highest bodhisattva stage, entering on Buddhahood. See Suzuki's translation, 80–1.

六相 The six characteristics found in everything—whole and parts, unity and diversity, entirety and (its) fractions.

六根 The six indriyas or sense-organs: eye, ear, nose, tongue, body, and mind. See also 六入, 六境, 六塵, and 六處. ｜｜五用 Substitution of one organ for another, or use of one organ to do the work of all the others, which is a Buddha's power. ｜｜功德 The powers of the six senses, i.e. the achievement by purification of their interchange of function. ｜｜懺悔 A penitential service over the sins of the six senses. ｜｜(清)淨 The six organs and their purification in order to develop their unlimited power and interchange, as in the case of a Buddha. This full development enables e.g. the eye to see everything in a great chiliocosm from its highest heaven down to its lowest hells and all the beings past, present, and future, with all the karma of each. | | | | 位 The state of the organs thus purified is defined by T'ien-t'ai as the 十信位 of the 別敎, or the 相似卽 of the 圓敎, v. 六卽.

六欲 The six sexual attractions arising from colour; form; carriage; voice (or speech); softness (or smoothness); and features. | | (天) The devalokas, i.e. the heavens of desire, i.e. with sense-organs; the first is described as half-way up Mt. Sumeru, the second at its summit, and the rest between it and the Brahmalokas; for list v. 六天. Descriptions are given in the 智度論 9 and the 俱舍論 8. They are also spoken of as | | | 婬相, i.e. as still in the region of sexual desire. The | | 四禪 are these six heavens where sexual desire continues, and the four dhyāna heavens of purity above them free from such desire.

六法(戒) The six prohibition rules for a female devotee: indelicacy of contact with a male; purloining four cash; killing animals; untruthfulness; food after the midday meal; and wine-drinking. | | is also a term for | 念.

六波 The six pāramitās, v. 波羅蜜.

六無常六譬 v. 六喩.

六煩惱 v. 六大煩惱.

六物 The six things personal to a monk—saṅghāṭī, the patch robe; uttarā saṅghāṭī, the stole of seven pieces; antara-vāsaka, the skirt or inner garment of five pieces; the above are the 三衣 three garments: pātra, begging bowl; niṣīdana, a stool; and a water-strainer: the six are also called the 三衣六物.

六瑞 The six auspicious indications attributed to the Buddha as a preliminary to his delivery of the Lotus Sūtra, see 法華經序品: (1) his opening address on the infinite; (2) his samādhi; (3) the rain of flowers; (4) the earthquake; (5) the delight of the beholders; (6) the Buddha-ray.

六界 The six elements: earth, water, fire, air (or wind), space, and mind; idem | 大. | | 聚 The (human) body, which is composed of these six.

六畜 The six animals likened to the six organs | 根, v. | 衆生.

六神通 The six transcendental, or magical, powers, v. | 通.

六祖 The six patriarchs of the Ch'an (Zen) school 禪宗, who passed down robe and begging bowl in succession, i.e. Bodhidharma, Hui-k'o, Sêng-ts'an, Tao-hsin, Hung-jên, and Hui-nêng 達摩, 慧可, 僧璨, 道信, 弘忍, and 慧能.

六種住 The six Bodhisattva-stages in the Bodhisattvabhūmi sūtra 菩薩地持經 are: (1) 種性 | the attainment of the Buddha-seed nature in the 十住; (2) 解行 | of discernment and practice in the 十行 and 十廻向; (3) 淨心住 of purity by attaining reality in the 初地見道; (4) 行道迹 | of progress in riddance of incorrect thinking, in the 二地 to the 七地; (5) 決定 | of powers of correct decision and judgment in the eighth and ninth 地; (6) 究竟 | of the perfect Bodhisattva-stage in the tenth 地 and the 等覺位, but not including the 妙覺位 which is the Buddha-stage.

六種倶生惑 The six deceivers common to all the living—greed, anger, torpor, ignorance, doubt, and incorrect views.

六種決定 The six kinds of certainty resulting from observance of the six pāramitās: 財成 | | the certainty of wealth; 生勝 | | of rebirth in honourable families; 不退 | | of no retrogression (to lower conditions); 修習 | | of progress in practice; 定業 | | of unfailingly good karma; 無功用 | | of effortless abode in truth and wisdom. 大乘莊嚴論 12.

六種印 The six seals, or proofs, i.e. the six pāramitās, | 度.

六種因 v. 六因.

六種外道 The six kinds of ascetics; also 六種苦行外道; 六術; v. 六行.

六種巧方便 The six able devices of Bodhisattvas: (1) preaching deep truths in simple form to lead on people gladly to believe; (2) promising them every good way of realizing their desires, of wealth, etc.; (3) showing a threatening aspect to the disobedient to induce reform; (4) rebuking and punishing them with a like object; (5) granting wealth to induce grateful offerings and almsgiving; (6) descending from heaven, leaving home, attaining bodhi, and leading all to joy and purity. 菩薩地持經 8.

六種性 For the first five see 五種性; the sixth is the Buddha stage of 妙覺性. The meditation on these is the 丨觀. Cf. 丨位.

六種正行 The fifth of the 五丨丨丨 q.v. is expanded into six kinds of proper practice: reading and intoning, studying, worshipping, invoking, praising, and making offerings.

六種釋 idem 六離合釋.

六種震動 The six earthquakes, or earth-shakings, also 六種動相, of which there are three different categories. I. Those at the Buddha's conception, birth, enlightenment, first preaching, when Māra besought him to live, and at his nirvāṇa; some omit the fifth and after "birth" add "leaving home". II. The six different kinds of shaking of the chiliocosm, or universe, when the Buddha entered into the samādhi of joyful wandering, see 大品般若經 1, i.e. east rose and west sank, and so on with w.e., n.s., s.n., middle and borders, borders and middle. III. Another group is shaking, rising, waving, reverberating, roaring, arousing, the first three referring to motion, the last three to sounds; see the above 般若經; which in later translations gives shaking, rising, reverberating, beating, roaring, crackling.

六窗一猿 Six windows and one monkey (climbing in and out), i.e. the six organs of sense and the active mind.

六箭 The six arrows, i.e. the six senses; v. 丨塵.

六結 A cloth or cord tied in six consecutive double loops and knots. The cloth represents the fundamental unity, the knots the apparent diversity. v. 楞伽經 5.

六罪人 The six kinds of offender, i.e. one who commits any of the 四重 four grave sins, or destroys harmony in the order, or sheds a Buddha's blood.

六羅漢 The six arhats i.e. Śākyamuni and his first five disciples, cf. 五羅漢.

六群比丘 The six common-herd bhikṣus, to whose improper or evil conduct is attributed the laying down of many of the laws by Śākyamuni; also 丨衆; different lists of names are given, the generally accepted list indicating Nanda, Upananda, Aśvaka, Punarvasu, Chanda, and Udāyin. Udāyin is probably Kālodayin, a name given in other lists.

六自在王 The six sovereign rulers, i.e. the six senses, see 六根.

六舟 The six boats, i.e. the six pāramitās 六度 for ferrying to the bank beyond mortality.

六般神足 The six supernatural signs; idem 六瑞.

六苦行 The heretics of the six austerities are referred to as 丨丨丨外道; v. 丨行.

六萬藏 The sixty thousand verses of the Buddha-law which Devadatta could recite, an ability which did not save him from the avīci hell.

六著(心) The six bonds, or the mind of the six bonds: greed, love, hate, doubt, lust, pride.

六蔽 The six sins that smother the six pāramitās: grudging, commandment-breaking, anger, family attachment, confused thoughts, and stupid ignorance.

六處 Ṣaḍāyatana. The six places, or abodes of perception or sensation, one of the nidānas, see 十二因緣; they are the 丨根 or six organs of sense, but the term is also used for the 丨入 and 丨境 q.v.; also 丨塵.

六衆 idem 六羣比丘. 丨丨生 The six senses 丨根 are likened to six wild creatures in confinement always struggling to escape. Only when they are domesticated will they be happy. So is it with the six senses and the taming power of Buddha-truth. The six creatures are a dog, a bird, a snake, a hyena, a crocodile (śiśumāra), and a monkey.

六行 Among Buddhists the term means the practice of the 六度 six pāramitās; it is referred, among outsiders, to the six austerities of the six kinds of heretics: (1) 自餓 starvation; (2) 投淵 naked cave-dwelling (or, throwing oneself down precipices); (3) 赴火 self-immolation, or self-torturing by fire; (4) 自坐 sitting naked in public; (5) 寂默 dwelling in silence among graves; (6) 牛狗 living as animals.

| | 觀 The six meditations, also called 厭欣觀; 六妙行 comparing the 下地 lower realms with the 上地 higher, the six following characters being the subject of meditation: the three lower represent 麤 coarseness, 苦 suffering, and 障 resistance; these in meditation are seen as distasteful; while the higher are the 靜 calm, 妙 mystic, 離 free, which are matters for delight. By this meditation on the distasteful and the delectable the delusions of the lower realms may be overcome.

六術 idem 六種外道; see 六行.

六衰 The six ruiners, i.e. the attractions of the six senses, idem 六塵, 六賊 q.v.

六裁 The six decisions, i.e. the concepts formed through the mental contact of the six senses; later called 六觸.

六親 The six immediate relations—father and mother, wife and child, elder and younger brothers.

六觀(法) Cf. 六種性 and 六位. | | 音 The six kinds of Kuan-yin. There are two groups—I. That of T'ien-t'ai: 大悲 most pitiful; 大慈 most merciful; 師子無畏 of lion-courage; 大光普照 of universal light; 天人丈夫 leader amongst gods and men; 大梵深遠 the great omnipresent Brahmā. Each of this bodhisattva's six qualities of pity, etc., breaks the hindrances 三障 respectively of the hells, pretas, animals, asuras, men, and devas. II. As thousand-handed; the holy one; horse-headed; eleven-faced; Cundī (or Marīci); with the wheel of sovereign power.

六解一亡 "When the six knots are untied the unity disappears." The six knots represent the six organs 六根 causing mortality, the cloth or cord tied in a series of knots represents nirvāṇa. This illustrates the interdependence of nirvāṇa and mortality. Cf. 六結; v. 楞伽經 5.

六觸 idem 六裁.

六論 The six 外道論 vedāṅgas, works which are "regarded as auxiliary to and even in some sense as part of the Veda, their object being to secure the proper pronunciation and correctness of the text and the right employment of the Mantras of sacrifice as taught in the Brāhmaṇas". M. W. They are spoken of together as the 四皮陀六論 four Vedas and six śāstras, and the six are Śikṣā, Chandas, Vyākaraṇa, Nirukta, Jyotiṣa, and Kalpa.

六譬 The six metaphors, v. 六衆生.

六諦 The six logical categories of the Vaiśeṣika philosophy: dravya, substance; guṇa, quality; karman, motion or activity; sāmānya, generality; viśeṣa, particularity; samavāya, inherence: Keith, *Logic*, 179. Eitel has "substance, quality, action, existence, the unum et diversum, and the aggregate".

六賊 The six cauras, or robbers, i.e. the six senses; the 六根 sense organs are the 媒 "match-makers", or medial agents, of the six robbers. The 六賊 are also likened to the six pleasures of the six sense organs. Prevention is by not acting with them, i.e. the eye avoiding beauty, the ear sound, nose scent, tongue flavours, body seductions, and mind uncontrolled thoughts.

六趣 The six directions of reincarnation, also | 道: (1) 地獄趣 naraka-gati, or that of the hells; (2) 餓鬼 | preta-gati, of hungry ghosts; (3) 畜生 | tiryagyoni-gati, of animals; (4) 阿修羅 | asura-gati, of malevolent nature spirits; (5) 人 | manuṣya-gati, of human existence; (6) 天 | deva-gati, of deva existence. The | | 輪迴經 is attributed to Aśvaghoṣa.

六足尊 The six-legged Honoured One, one of the five 明王 fierce guardians of Amitābha, i.e. 大威德, who has six heads, faces, arms, and legs; rides on an ox; and is an incarnation of Mañjuśrī. The | | 阿毗曇摩 Jñāna-prasthāna-ṣaṭpādābhi-dharma is a philosophical work in the Canon.

六輪 The six kinds of cakravartī, or wheel-kings, each allotted to one of the 六位; the iron-wheel king to the 十信位, copper 十住, silver 十行, gold 十廻向, crystal 十地, and pearl 等覺.

六通 Abhijñā, or ṣaḍabhijñā. The six super-natural or universal powers acquired by a Buddha, also by an arhat through the fourth degree of dhyāna. The "southern" Buddhists only have the first five, which are also known in China; v. 五神通; the sixth is 漏盡(智證) | āsravakṣaya-jñāna, super-natural consciousness of the waning of vicious propensities.

六道 The six ways or conditions of sentient existence; v. 丨趣; the three higher are the 上三途, the three lower 下三途. 丨丨佛菩薩 The Buddhas and bodhisattvas of the six gati, i.e. the six Ti-tsang 六地藏 q.v.; also the 六觀音 q.v.; the six Ti-tsang are also styled 丨丨能化菩薩 Bodhisattvas who can change the lot of those in the six gati. 丨丨四生 The four modes of the six rebirths —womb, egg, moisture, or transformation. 丨丨四聖 The six ways of rebirth, see above, and the four holy ways of rebirth, the latter being respectively into the realms of śrāvakas, pratyeka-buddhas, bodhisattvas, and Buddhas; the ten are known as the 十界. 丨丨集經 and 丨丨伽陀經 Two sūtras dealing with the six ways of rebirth.

六部大乘經 The six works chosen by Tz'ŭ-ên 慈恩 as authoritative in the 法相宗 Dharmalakṣaṇa school, i.e. 大方廣佛華嚴丨 of which there are three translations; 解深密丨 4 tr.; 如來出現功德莊嚴丨 untranslated; 阿毘達磨丨 untranslated; 楞伽丨 3 tr.; 厚嚴丨 (also called 大乘密嚴丨).

六離合釋 Ṣaṭ-samāsa; also 丨種 (or 合) 釋 the six interpretations of compound terms, considered in their component parts or together. (1) 持業釋 or 同依丨 karmadhāraya, referring to the equality of dependence of both terms, e.g. 大乘 mahāyāna, "great" and "vehicle", both equally essential to "mahāyāna" with its specific meaning; (2) 依主 (or 士) 丨 tatpuruṣa, containing a principal term, e.g. 眼識 eye-perception, where the eye is the qualifying term; (3) 有 (or 多) 財 丨 bahuvrīhi, the sign of possession, e.g. 覺者 he who has enlightenment; (4) 相違丨 dvandva, a term indicating two separate ideas, e.g. 敎觀 teaching and meditation; (5) 隣近丨 avyayībhava, an adverbial compound, or a term resulting from "neighbouring" association, e.g. 念處 thought or remembering place, i.e. memory; (6) 帶數丨 dvigu, a numerative term, e.g. 五蘊 pañcaskandha, the five skandhas. M. W. gives the order as 4, 3, 1, 2, 6, and 5.

六難 The six difficult things—to be born in a Buddha-age, to hear the true Buddha-law, to beget a good heart, to be born in the central kingdom (India), to be born in human form, and to be perfect; see Nirvāṇa sūtra 23.

六震 idem 六種震.

六面尊 idem 六足尊.

六麤 The six "coarser" stages arising from the 三細 or three finer stages which in turn are produced by original 無明, the unenlightened condition of ignorance; v. Awakening of Faith 起信論. They are the states of (1) 智相 knowledge or consciousness of like and dislike arising from mental conditions; (2) 相續相 consciousness of pain and pleasure resulting from the first, causing continuous responsive memory; (3) 執取相 attachment or clinging, arising from the last; (4) 計名字相 assigning names according to the seeming and unreal (with fixation of ideas); (5) 起業 the consequent activity with all the variety of deeds; (6) 業繫苦相 the suffering resulting from being tied to deeds and their karma consequences.

六齋日 The six monthly poṣadha, or fast days: the 8th, 14th, 15th, 23rd, 29th, and 30th. They are the days on which the Four Mahārājas 四天王 take note of human conduct and when evil demons are busy, so that great care is required and consequently nothing should be eaten after noon, hence the "fast", v. 梵王經 30th command. The 智度論 13 describes them as 惡日 evil or dangerous days, and says they arose from an ancient custom of cutting off the flesh and casting it into the fire.

切 To cut, carve; a whole; urgent; the 反丨 system of spelling, i.e. the combination of the initial sound of one Chinese word with the final sound of another to indicate the sound of a third, a system introduced by translators of Buddhist works; v. 反. 丨勝 A title of Aśvaghoṣa.

分 To divide, separate; a fractional part; a share; a duty.

分位 Avasthā; defined as 時分 time and 地位 position; i.e. a state, e.g. the state of water disturbed into waves, waves being also a state of water; a dependent state.

分別 Vibhajya, or vibhāga; parikalpana; vikalpa; divide, discriminate, discern, reason; to leave. The 三丨丨 three forms are (1) 自性丨丨 natural discrimination, e.g. of present objects; (2) 計度丨丨 calculating discrimination (as to future action); (3) 隨念丨丨 discriminating by remembrance of affairs that are past. 丨丨事識 The third of the three kinds of perception 識, i.e. real (or abstract), manifest, and reasoned (or inferred); it includes all the eight 識 except the ālaya-vijñāna. 丨丨智 Viveka. Differentiating knowledge, discrimination of phenomena, as contrasted with

無 | | | the knowledge of the fundamental identity of all things. | | | 相應染 The taint on mind following upon the action of discriminating, i.e. one of the six 染心; v. Awakening of Faith 起信論. | | 經 There are several sūtras and śāstras with various 分別 titles. | | 說三 The One Vehicle discriminated as "three" for the sake of the ignorant. | | 說部 The Vibhajyavādins. A school the origin of which is obscure. The meaning of the term, not necessarily limited to this school, is the method of particularization in dealing with questions in debate. It is suggested that this school was established to harmonize the differences between the Sthavirās and Mahāsāṅghikās. The Abhidharma Piṭaka "as we have it in the Pali Canon, is the definite work of this school", Keith, 153. | | 識 The discriminating perception, i.e. of 意 mind, the sixth 根 organ. | | 起 Delusions arising from reasoning and teaching, in contrast with 俱生起 errors that arise naturally among people.

分喻 A metaphor only correct in part, e.g. a face like the moon.

分散 Visarj. To dismiss, scatter, separate, as an assembly.

分析 To divide, separate, leave the world, v. 析.

分歲 New Year's eve, the dividing night of the year, also styled 歲夜.

分段 Bhāgya. Lot, dispensation, allotment, fate. | | 生死, | | 死, | | 身, | | 三道 all refer to the mortal lot, or dispensation in regard to the various forms of reincarnation. | | 同居 Those of the same lot, or incarnation, dwelling together, e.g. saints and sinners in this world. | | 輪廻 The wheel of fate, or reincarnation. | | 變易 Includes (1) | | 生死, the condition and station resulting from good or bad karma in the three realms (desire, form, and formlessness) and in the six paths; (2) 變易生死 the condition and station resulting from good karma in the realms beyond transmigration, including arhats and higher saints.

分相門 The doctrine which differentiates the three vehicles from the one vehicle; as 該攝門 is that which maintains the three vehicles to be the one.

分眞卽 idem 分證卽.

分衛 Piṇḍapāta, 賓荼波多; 儐荼夜 food given as alms; piṇḍapātika means one who lives on alms; it is also interpreted as 團墮 lumps (of food) falling (into the begging bowl); the reference is to the Indian method of rolling the cooked food into a bolus for eating, or such a bolus given to the monks.

分證(卽) One of the T'ien-t'ai 六卽 q.v. Also 分眞(卽).

分身 Parturition; in Buddhism it means a Buddha's power to reproduce himself *ad infinitum* and anywhere.

分那柯 Pūrṇaka, i.e. 滿 full; name of a yakṣa, or demon.

分陀利(迦) Puṇḍarīka, 芬陀; 分 (or 奔) 荼利迦 (or 華); 本拏哩迦; the 白蓮花 white lotus (in full bloom). It is also termed 百 (or 八) 葉華 hundred (or eight) leaf flower. For Saddharma-puṇḍarīka, the Lotus Sūtra, v. (妙法) 蓮華經. The eighth and coldest hell is called after this flower, because the cold lays bare the bones of the wicked, so that they resemble the whiteness of this lotus. It is also called 隨色花; when a bud, it is known as 屈摩羅; and when fading, as 迦摩羅.

勿 Not; do not; translit. *m* and *v*. | 伽 Mudga; "phaseolus Mungo (both the plant and its beans)," M. W.; intp. as 胡豆 and 綠豆 kidney beans by the Fan-i-ming-i. | | 羅子 Maudgalyāyana or Maudgalaputra, idem Mahāmaudgalyāyana 目連. | 力伽難提 Mṛgānandi, or 蜜利伽羅 Mṛgala; rejoicing deer; a śramaṇa called 鹿杖 Lu-chang, who was satisfied with the leavings of other monks; also a previous incarnation of Śākyamuni, and of Devadatta, who are both represented as having been deer. | 哩訶娑跛底 Bṛhaspati, Jupiter-lord, 木星 Jupiter.

勾 A hook, to entangle, inveigle, arrest; a tick, mark. | 當 An employee in a monastery, especially of the Shingon sect. In Japan, the second rank of official blind men.

化 To transform, metamorphose: (1) conversion by instruction, salvation into Buddhism; (2) magic powers 通力 of transformation, of which there are said to be fourteen mental and eight formal kinds. It also has the meaning of immediate appearance out of the void, or creation 無而忽起; and of giving alms, spending, digesting, melting, etc.

化主 The lord of transformation, or conversion, i.e. a Buddha; also one who exhorts believers to give alms for worship; also an almsgiver.

化人 A deva or Buddha transformed into human shape; 丨女 is the same in female form.

化他 To save others. 丨丨壽 A Buddha's long or "eternal" life spent in saving others, implying his powers of unlimited salvation.

化佛 Nirmāṇabuddha, an incarnate, or metamorphosed Buddha; Buddhas and bodhisattvas have universal and unlimited powers of appearance, v. 神通力.

化作 To transform (into), create, make.

化俗結緣 For the sake of converting the people.

化儀 The rules or methods laid down by the Buddha for salvation; T'ien-t'ai speaks of 丨丨 as transforming method, and 化法 q.v. as transforming truth; its 丨丨四教 are four modes of conversion or enlightenment: 頓 direct or sudden, 漸 gradual, 秘密 esoteric, and 不定 variable.

化制二教 The twofold division of the Buddha's teaching into converting or enlightening and discipline, as made by the Vinaya School, v. 化行.

化前 In the Amitābha cult the term means before its first sūtra, the 觀無量壽經, just as 爾前 in the Lotus School means "before the Lotus". 丨丨序 the preface to the 觀經疏 by 善導 Shan-tao of the T'ang dynasty. 丨丨方便 All the expedient, or partial, teaching suited to the conditions before the above Wu-liang-shou-ching.

化功歸己 The merit of converting others becomes one's own (in increased insight and liberation); it is the third stage of merit of the T'ien-t'ai five stages of meditation and action 觀行五品位.

化土 One of the 三土 three kinds of lands, or realms; it is any land or realm whose inhabitants are subject to reincarnation; any land which a Buddha is converting, or one in which is the transformed body of a Buddha. These lands are of two kinds, pure like the Tuṣita heaven, and vile or unclean like this world. T'ien-t'ai defines the hua-t'u or the transformation realm of Amitābha as the Pure-land of the West, but other schools speak of hua-t'u as the realm on which depends the nirmāṇakāya, with varying definitions.

化地部 Mahīśāsakah, 磨醯奢娑迦部; 彌喜捨娑阿; 彌娑塞部, 正地部 an offshoot from the 說一切有 丨 or Sarvāstivādah school, supposed to have been founded 300 years after the nirvāṇa. The name Mahīśāsakah is said to be that of a ruler who "converted his land" or people; or 正地 "rectified his land". The doctrines of the school are said to be similar to those of the 大衆 丨 Mahāsāṅghika; and to have maintained, *inter alia*, the reality of the present, but not of the past and future; also the doctrine of the void and the non-ego; the production of taint 染 by the five 識 perceptions; the theory of nine kinds of non-activity, and so on. It was also called 法無去來宗 the school which denied reality to past and future.

化城 The magic, or illusion city, in the Lotus Sūtra; it typifies temporary or incomplete nirvāṇa, i.e. the imperfect nirvāṇa of Hīnayāna.

化境 The region, condition, or environment of Buddha instruction or conversion; similar to 化土.

化壇 The altar of transformation, i.e. a crematorium.

化宮殿 The magical palace, or, palace of joy, held in the fortieth left hand of Kuan-yin of the thousand hands; the hand is styled (丨) 丨丨手 or 寶殿手.

化導 To instruct and guide; the 三輪丨丨 or three sovereign powers for converting others are those of 神變 supernatural transformation (i.e. physical 身); 記心 memory or knowledge of all the thoughts of all beings (i.e. mental 意); and 教誡 teaching and warning (i.e. oral 口). 丨丨力 Power to instruct and guide, one of the 三力.

化尼 The power of a Buddha, or bodhisattva, to be transformed into a nun.

化屬 The converted followers—of a Buddha, or bodhisattva.

化度 To convert and transport, or save.

化心 The mind in the transformation body of a Buddha or bodhisattva, which apprehends things in their reality.

化教 see 化行二教.

化樂天 Nirmāṇarati, 樂變化天 the fifth of the six desire-heavens, 640,000 yojanas above Meru; it is next above the Tuṣita, or fourth deva-loka; a day is equal to 800 human years; life lasts for 8,000 years; its inhabitants are eight yojanas in height, and light-emitting; mutual smiling produces impregnation and children are born on the knees by metamorphosis, at birth equal in development to human children of twelve—hence the "joy-born heaven".

化法 Instruction in the Buddhist principles, as ｜儀 is in practice. T'ien-t'ai in its 化法四教 divides the Buddha's teaching during his lifetime into the four periods of 藏, 通, 別, and 圓 Piṭaka, Interrelated, Differentiated, and Complete, or All-embracing.

化源 The fount of conversion, or salvation, the beginning of the Buddha's teaching.

化現 Metamorphosis and manifestation; the appearance or forms of a Buddha or bodhisattva for saving creatures may take any form required for that end.

化理 The law of phenomenal change—which never rests.

化生 Aupapādaka, or Aupapāduka. Direct metamorphosis, or birth by transformation, one of the 四生, by which existence in any required form is attained in an instant in full maturity. By this birth bodhisattvas residing in Tuṣita appear on earth. Dhyāni Buddhas and Avalokiteśvara are likewise called 化生. It also means unconditional creation at the beginning of a kalpa. Bhūta 部多 is also used with similar meaning. There are various kinds of 化生, e.g. 佛菩薩｜｜the transformation of a Buddha or bodhisattva, in any form at will, without gestation, or intermediary conditions; 極樂｜｜birth in the happy land of Amitābha by transformation through the Lotus; 法身｜｜the dharmakāya, or spiritual body, born or formed on a disciple's conversion.

化疏 A subscription list, or book; an offering burnt for ease of transmission to the spirit-realm.

化相 The transformation form or body (in which the Buddha converts the living). ｜｜三寶 The nirmāṇakāya Buddha in the Triratna forms; in Hīnayāna these are the human 16-foot Buddha, his dharma as revealed in the four axioms and twelve nidānas, and his saṅgha, or disciples, i.e. arhats and pratyeka-buddhas.

化米 Rice obtained by monastic begging and the offering of exhortation or instruction, similarly ｜炭 charcoal and ｜茶 tea; sometimes used with larger connotation.

化緣 The cause of a Buddha's or bodhisattva's coming to the world, i.e. the transformation of the living; also, a contribution to the needs of the community.

化色(身) A Buddha's or bodhisattva's metamorphoses of body, or incarnations at will.

化菩薩 A Buddha or bodhisattva transformed into a (human) bodhisattva; or a bodhisattva in various metamorphoses.

化行(二教) The two lines of teaching: i.e. in the elements, for conversion and admission, and 行教 or 制教 in the practices and moral duties especially for the Order, as represented in the Vinaya; cf. ｜制.

化誘 To convert and entice (into the way of truth).

化身 Nirmāṇakāya, 應(化)身; 變化身 The third characteristic or power of the Trikāya 三身, a Buddha's metamorphosic body, which has power to assume any shape to propagate the Truth. Some interpret the term as connoting pan-Buddha, that all nature in its infinite variety is the phenomenal 佛身 Buddha-body. A narrower interpretation is his appearance in human form expressed by 應身, while 化身 is used for his manifold other forms of appearances. 化生 q.v. means direct "birth" by metamorphosis. It also means the incarnate avatāra of a deity. ｜｜八相 The eight forms of a Buddha from birth to nirvāṇa, v. 八相.

化轉 To transform, convert (from evil to good, delusion to deliverance).

化迹 The traces or evidences of the Buddha's transforming teaching; also 教迹.

化道 The way of conversion, transformation, or development; also 教道.

午 Noon. | 供 The noon offering (of incense).

反 To turn over, turn or send back; contrary; to rebel. | 出生死 One of the seven kinds of mortality, i.e. escape from it into nirvāṇa. | 切 The system of indicating the initial and final sounds of a character by two others, ascribed to Sun Yen 孫炎 in the third century A.D., arising out of the translit. of Sanskrit terms in Buddhist translation. | 叉合掌 One of the twelve forms of folded hands, i.e. with interlocking fingers.

太 Too, very, great. | 子 Kumārarāja. Crown-prince. An epithet of Buddhas, and of Mañjuśrī. | | 和休經; | | 刷護經 There are several 太子, etc. 經. One named the Subāhu-paripṛcchā was translated under the first title between 265–316 A.D., four leaves; under the second title by Dharmarakṣa during the same period. | 孤危生 Life perilous as the (unscaleable) top of the loneliest peak. | 虛空 Space, where nothing exists; also 頑空; 偏空. | 麤生 A ruffian, a rough fellow.

夫 A man; a sage, officer, hero; a husband, mate; a fellow; a particle, i.e. for, so, etc. | 人 A wife; the wife of a king, i.e. a queen, devī. 凡 | The common people, the unenlightened, *hoi polloi*, a common fellow.

天 Heaven; the sky; a day; cf. dyo, dyaus also as 提婆 a deva, or divine being, deity; and as 素羅 sura, shining, bright. 三種天 The three classes of devas: (1) 名天 famous rulers on earth styled 天王, 天子; (2) 生天 the highest incarnations of the six paths; (3) 淨天 the pure, or the saints, from śrāvakas to pratyeka-buddhas. 智度論 7. 四種天 The four classes of devas include (1), (2), (3), above; and (4) 義天 all bodhisattvas above the ten stages 十住. The Buddhas are not included; 智度論 22. 五種天 The above four with the addition of 第一義 | a supreme heaven with bodhisattvas and Buddhas in eternal immutability; 涅槃經 23. Cf. 天宮.

天上 The heavens above, i.e. the six devalokas 六欲天 of the region of desire and the rūpalokas and arūpalokas, i.e. 色 and 無色界.

天上天下唯我獨尊 The first words attributed to Śākyamuni after his first seven steps when born from his mother's right side: "In the heavens above and (earth) beneath I alone am the honoured one." This announcement is ascribed to every Buddha, as are also the same special characteristics attributed to every Buddha, hence he is the 如來 come in the manner of all Buddhas. In Mahāyānism he is the type of countless other Buddhas in countless realms and periods.

天中天 Devātideva; deva of devas. The name given to Siddhārtha (i.e. Śākyamuni) when, on his presentation in the temple of 天王 Maheśvara (Śiva), the statues of all the gods prostrated themselves before him.

天主 Devapati. The Lord of devas, a title of Indra. | | 教法 Devendra-samaya. Doctrinal method of the lord of devas. A work on royalty in the possession of a son of Rājabalendraketu.

天乘 Devayāna. The deva vehicle—one of the 五乘 five vehicles; it transports observers of the ten good qualities 十喜 to one of the six deva realms of desire, and those who observe dhyāna meditation to the higher heavens of form and non-form.

天人 Devas and men; also a name for devas. | | 師 Śāstā Devamanuṣyānām 舍多提婆摩菟舍喃, teacher of devas and men, one of the ten epithets of a Buddha, because he reveals goodness and morality, and is able to save. | | 散花身上 The story of the man who saw a disembodied ghost beating a corpse which he said was his body that had led him into all sin, and further on an angel stroking and scattering flowers on a corpse, which he said was the body he had just left, always his friend. | | 道師 idem 天人師.

天仙 Deva-ṛṣis, or devas and ṛṣis, or immortals. Nāgārjuna gives ten classes of ṛṣis whose lifetime is 100,000 years, then they are reincarnated. Another category is fivefold: 天仙 deva-ṛṣis in the mountains round Sumeru; 神 | spirit-ṛṣis who roam the air; 人 | humans who have attained the powers of immortals; 地 | earth ṛṣis, subterranean; 鬼 | pretas, or malevolent ṛṣis.

天使 Divine messengers, especially those of Yama; also his 三天使 three messengers, or lictors—old age, sickness, death; and his 五天使 or 五大使, i.e. the last three together with rebirth and prisons or punishments on earth.

天(界)力士 idem 那羅延 Nārāyaṇa.

天冠 A deva-crown, surpassing human thought.

天口 The mouth of Brahma, or the gods, a synonym for fire, as that element devours the offerings; to this the 護摩 homa, or fire altar cult is attributed, fire becoming the object of worship for good fortune. Fire is also said to speak for or tell the will of the gods.

天台(山) The T'ien-t'ai or Heavenly Terrace mountain, the location of the T'ien-t'ai sect; its name is attributed to the 三台 six stars at the foot of Ursa Major, under which it is supposed to be, but more likely because of its height and appearance. It gives its name to a hsien in the Chekiang T'aichow prefecture, south-west of Ningpo. The monastery, or group of monasteries, was founded there by 智顗 Chih-i, who is known as 天台大師. 丨丨三教 The three modes of Śākyamuni's teaching as explained by the T'ien-t'ai sect: (1) the sudden, or immediate teaching, by which the learner is taught the whole truth at once 頓教; (2) the gradual teaching 漸教; (3) the undetermined or variable method whereby he is taught what he is capable of receiving 不定. Another category is 漸 gradual, 頓 direct, and 圓 perfect, the last being found in the final or complete doctrine of the 法華經 Lotus Sūtra. Another is: (1) 三藏教 the Tripiṭaka doctrine, i.e. the orthodox Hīnayāna; (2) 通丨intermediate, or interrelated doctrine, i.e. Hīnayāna-cum-Mahāyāna; (3) 別丨differentiated or separated doctrine, i.e. the early Mahāyāna as a cult or development, as distinct from Hīnayāna. 丨丨九祖 The nine patriarchs of the T'ien-t'ai sect: 龍樹 Nāgārjuna; 慧文 Hui-wên of the 北齊 Northern Ch'i dynasty; 慧思 Hui-ssŭ of 南岳 Nan-yo; 智者 (or 顗) Chih-chê, or Chih-i; 灌頂 Kuan-ting of 章安 Chang-an; 法華 Fa-hua; 天宮 T'ien-kung; 左溪 Tso-ch'i; and 湛然 Chan-jan of 荆溪 Ching-ch'i. The ten patriarchs 十祖 are the above nine with 道邃 Tao-sui considered a patriarch in Japan, because he was the teacher of Dengyō Daishi who brought the Tendai system to that country in the ninth century. Some name Hui-wên and Hui-ssŭ as the first and second patriarchs of the school of thought developed by Chih-i at T'ien-t'ai; v. 丨丨宗. 丨丨八教; 八教 The 化法四教 or four periods of teaching, i.e. 藏, 通, 別, and 圓 Hīnayāna, Interrelated, Differentiated, and Complete or Final; the 化儀四教 q.v. are the four modes of teaching, direct, gradual, esoteric, and indefinite. 丨丨四教 The four types each of method and doctrine, as defined by T'ien-t'ai; see last entry. 丨丨大師 The actual founder of the T'ien-t'ai "school" 智顗 Chih-i; his 字 was 德安 Tê-an, and his surname 陳 Ch'ên, A.D. 538–597. Studying under 慧思 Hui-ssŭ of Hunan, he was greatly influenced by his teaching; and found in the Lotus Sūtra the real interpretation of Mahāyānism. In 575 he first came to T'ien-t'ai and established his school, which in turn was the foundation of important Buddhist schools in Korea and Japan. 丨丨宗 The T'ien-t'ai, or Tendai, sect founded by 智顗 Chih-i. It bases its tenets on the Lotus Sūtra 法華經 with the 智度論; 涅槃經, and 大品經; it maintains the identity of the Absolute and the world of phenomena, and attempts to unlock the secrets of all phenomena by means of meditation. It flourished during the T'ang dynasty. Under the Sung, when the school was decadent, arose 四明 Ssŭ-ming, under whom there came the division of 山家 Hill or T'ien-t'ai School and 山外 the School outside, the latter following 悟恩 Wu-ên and in time dying out; the former, a more profound school, adhered to Ssŭ-ming; it was from this school that the T'ien-t'ai doctrine spread to Japan. The three principal works of the T'ien-t'ai founder are called 天台三部, i.e. 玄義 exposition of the deeper meaning of the Lotus; 文句 exposition of its text; and 止觀 meditation; the last was directive and practical; it was in the line of Bodhidharma, stressing the "inner light". 丨丨律 The laws of the T'ien-t'ai sect as given in the Lotus, and the ten primary commandments and forty-eight secondary commandments of 梵網經 the sūtra of Brahma's net (Brahmajāla); they are ascribed as the 大乘圓頓戒 the Mahāyāna perfect and immediate moral precepts, immediate in the sense of the possibility of all instantly becoming Buddha. 丨丨韶國師 T'ien T'ai Shao Kuo Shih, a Chekiang priest who revived the T'ien-t'ai sect by journeying to Korea, where the only copy of Chih I's works existed, copied them, and returned to revive the T'ien-t'ai school. 錢俶 Ch'ien Shu (A.D. 960–997), ruler of 吳越 Wu Yüeh, whose capital was at Hangchow, entitled him Imperial Teacher.

天后 Queen of Heaven, v. 摩利支.

天地鏡 The mirror of heaven and earth, i.e. the Prajñā-pāramitā sūtra, see 般若.

天堂 The mansions of the devas, located between the earth and the Brahmalokas; the heavenly halls; heaven. The Ganges is spoken of as 天堂來者 coming from the heavenly mansions. 丨丨地獄 The heavens and the hells, places of reward or punishment for moral conduct.

天女 Devakanyā; apsaras; goddesses in general; attendants on the regents of the sun and moon; wives of Gandharvas; the division of the sexes is maintained throughout the devalokas 六天.

天子 A son of Heaven. The Emperor-Princes, i.e. those who in previous incarnations have kept the middle and lower grades of the ten good qualities 十善 and, in consequence, are born here as princes. It is the title of one of the four māra, who is 天主 or lord of the sixth heaven of desire; he is also known as 天子(業)魔 and with his following opposes the Buddha-truth.

天宮 Devapura; devaloka; the palace of devas, the abode of the gods, i.e. the six celestial worlds situated above the Meru, between the earth and the Brahmalokas. v. 六天. | | 寶藏 A library of the sūtras. The treasury of all the sūtras in the Tuṣita Heaven in Maitreya's palace. Another collection is said to be in the 龍宮 or Dragon's palace, but is associated with Nāgārjuna.

天尊 The most honoured among devas, a title of a Buddha, i.e. the highest of divine beings; also used for certain mahārāja protectors of Buddhism and others in the sense of honoured devas. Title applied by the Taoists to their divinities as a counterpart to the Buddhist 世尊.

天師 Preceptor of the emperor, a title of the monk 一行 I-hsing, and of the so-called Taoist Pope.

天帝 King, or emperor of Heaven, i.e. 因陀羅 Indra, i.e. 釋(迦); 釋迦婆; 帝(釋); Śakra, king of the devaloka 忉利天, one of the ancient gods of India, the god of the sky who fights the demons with his vajra, or thunderbolt. He is inferior to the trimūrti, Brahma, Viṣṇu, and Śiva, having taken the place of Varuṇa, or sky. Buddhism adopted him as its defender, though, like all the gods, he is considered inferior to a Buddha or any who have attained bodhi. His wife is Indrāṇī. | | 生驢胎 Lord of devas, born in the womb of an ass, a Buddhist fable, that Indra knowing he was to be reborn from the womb of an ass, in sorrow sought to escape his fate, and was told that trust in Buddha was the only way. Before he reached Buddha his life came to an end and he found himself in the ass. His resolve, however, had proved effective, for the master of the ass beat her so hard that she dropped her foal dead. Thus Indra returned to his former existence and began his ascent to Buddha. | | 釋城 The city of Śakra, the Lord of devas, called 善見城 Sudarśana city good to behold, or 喜見城 city a joy to behold.

天弓 The deva-bow, the rainbow.

天德瓶 The vase of deva virtue, i.e. the bodhi heart, because all that one desires comes from it, e.g. the 如意珠 the talismanic pearl. Cf. 天意樹.

天愛 Devānāṁpriya. "Beloved of the gods," i.e. natural fools, simpletons, or the ignorant.

天意樹 The tree in each devaloka which produces whatever the devas desire.

天授 Heaven-bestowed, a name of Devadatta, v. 提.

天有 Existence and joy as a deva, derived from previous devotion, the fourth of the seven forms of existence.

天根 The phallic emblem of Śiva, which Hsüan-tsang found in the temples of India; he says the Hindus "worship it without being ashamed".

天梯山 The ladder-to-heaven hill or monastery, i.e. 天台 T'ien-t'ai mountain in Chekiang.

天樂 Heavenly music, the music of the inhabitants of the heavens. Also one of the three "joys"—that of those in the heavens.

天機 Natural capacity; the nature bestowed by Heaven.

天樹王 The pārijāta tree 波利質多 which grows in front of Indra's palace—the king among the heavenly trees.

天狗 Ulkā, 憂流迦 the "heavenly dog", i.e. a meteor. Also "a star in Argo", Williams.

天獄 The heavens and hells; devalokas and purgatories.

天王 Mahārāja-devas; 四天王 Catur-mahārāja. The four deva kings in the first or lowest devaloka, on its four sides. E. 持國 | | Dhṛtarāṣṭra. S. 增長 | | Virūḍhaka. W. 廣目 | | Virūpākṣa. N. 多聞 | | Dhanada, or Vaiśravaṇa. The four are said to have appeared to 不空 Amogha in a temple in Hsi-an-fu, some time between 742–6, and in consequence he introduced their worship to China as guardians of the monasteries, where their images are seen in the hall at the entrance, which is sometimes called the 天王堂 hall of the deva-kings. | | is also a designation of Śiva the 大自在, i.e. Maheśvara 摩醯首羅, the great sovereign ruler. | | 如來 Devarāja-tathāgata, the name by which Devadatta, v. 提, the enemy of Śākyamuni, will be known on his future appearance as a Buddha in the universe called 天道 Devasopāna; his present residence in hell being temporary for his karmaic expurgation.

天界 idem 天道.

天畫 Deva lines or pictures.

天皇 Deva-king; the T'ang monk 道悟 Tao-wu of the 天皇 T'ien-huang monastery at 荆州 Ching-chou.

天眞 Bhūtatathatā, permanent reality underlying all phenomena, pure and unchanging, e.g. the sea in contrast with the waves; nature, the natural, 天然之眞理, 非人之造作者 natural reality, not of human creation. | | 佛 The real or ultimate Buddha; the bhūtatathatā; another name for the Dharmakāya, the source of all life. | | 獨朗 The fundamental reality, or bhūtatathatā, is the only illumination. It is a dictum of 道邃 Tao-sui of the T'ang to the famous Japanese monk 傳敎 Dengyō. The apprehension of this fundamental reality makes all things clear, including the universality of Buddhahood. It also interprets the phrase 一心三觀 that 空中假 the void, the "mean", the seeming, are all aspects of the one mind.

天眼 Divyacakṣus. The deva-eye; the first abhijñā, v. 六通; one of the five classes of eyes; divine sight, unlimited vision; all things are open to it, large and small, near and distant, the destiny of all beings in future rebirths. It may be obtained among men by their human eyes through the practice of meditation 修得; and as a reward or natural possession by those born in the deva heavens 報得. Cf. 天耳, etc. | | 力 The power of the celestial or deva eye, one of the ten powers of a Buddha. | | 明 One of the three enlightenments 三明, or clear visions of the saint, which enables him to know the future rebirths of himself and all beings. | | 智 The wisdom obtained by the deva eye. | | 智(證)通 The complete universal knowledge and assurance of the deva eye. | | 智通願 The sixth of Amitābha's forty-eight vows, that he would not enter the final stage until all beings had obtained this divine vision. | | 通 idem 天眼; also a term used by those who practise hypnotism.

天督 T'ien-tu, an erroneous form of 天竺, or 印度 Yin-tu, India.

天祠 Devālaya, Devatāgāra, or Devatāgṛha. Brahminical temples.

天神 Deva 提婆 or Devatā 泥縛多. (1) Brahmā and the gods in general, including the inhabitants of the devalokas, all subject to metempsychosis. (2) The fifteenth patriarch, a native of South India, or Ceylon, and disciple of Nāgārjuna; he is also styled Devabodhisattva 提婆菩薩, Āryadeva 聖天, and Nīlanetra 青目 blue-eyed, or 分別明 clear discriminator. He was the author of nine works and a famous antagonist of Brahmanism. | | 地祇 The spirits 天神 are Indra and his retinue; devas in general; the 地祇 are the earth spirits, nāgas, demons, ghosts, etc.

天童 Divine youths, i.e. deva guardians of the Buddha-law who appear as Mercuries, or youthful messengers of the Buddhas and bodhisattvas. | | 山; 天潼山 A famous group of monasteries in the mountains near Ningpo, also called 太白山 Venus-planet mountain; this is one of the five famous mountains of China.

天竺(國) India; 竹 Chu is said to have the same sound as 篤 tu, suggesting a connection with the 度 tu in 印度 Indu; other forms are 身毒 Sindhu, Scinde; 賢豆 Hindu; and 印持伽羅. The term is explained by 月 moon, which is the meaning of Indu, but it is said to be so called because the sages of India illumine the rest of the world; or because of the half-moon shape of the land, which was supposed to be 90,000 li in circumference, and placed among other kingdoms like the moon among the stars. Another name is 因陀羅婆他那 ? Indravadana, or Indrabhavana, the region where Indra dwells. A hill and monastery near Hangchow. | | 三時 (or 際). The three seasons of an Indian year: Grīṣma, the hot season, from first month, sixteenth day, to fifth month, fifteenth; Varṣākāla, the rainy season, fifth month, sixteenth, to ninth month, fifteenth; Hemanta, the cold season, ninth month, sixteenth, to first month, fifteenth. These three are each divided into two, making six seasons, or six periods: Vasanta and grīṣma, varṣākāla and śarad, hemanta and śiśira. The twelve months are Caitra, Vaiśākha, Jyaiṣṭha, Āṣāḍha, Śrāvaṇa, Bhādrapada, Āśvayuja, Kārttika, Mārgaśīrṣa, Pauṣa, Māgha, and Phālguna. | | 九 儀 The nine forms of etiquette of India: speaking softly, bowing the head, raising the hands high, placing hands together, bending knees, kneeling long, hands and knees touching the ground, bowing the head, lowering arms and bending knees, bringing head, arms, and knees to the ground. | | 五 山 The five mountains of India on which the Buddha assembled his disciples: Vaibhāra, Saptaparṇaguhā, Indraśailaguhā, Sarpiṣkuṇḍikā-prāgbhāra, Gṛdhrakūṭa.

天 羅 國 The kingdom of the king with kalmāṣapāda, i.e. spotted, or striped feet 斑 定 王; cf. 仁 王 經.

天 耳 (通) Divyaśrotra, deva-ear, celestial ear. | | 智 (通); | | 智 證 通 The second of the six abhijñās 六 通 by which devas in the form-world, certain arhats through the fourth dhyāna, and others can hear all sounds and understand all languages in the realms of form, with resulting wisdom. For its equivalent interpretation and its 修 得 and 報 得 v. 天 眼. | | 智 通 願 The seventh of the forty-eight vows of Amitābha, not to become Buddha until all obtain the divine ear.

天 臂 城 Devadarśita or Devadiṣṭa, Deva-arm city, but the Sanskrit means deva (or divinely) indicated. The residence of Suprabuddha, 善 覺 長 者 father of Māyā, mother of the Buddha.

天 華 Deva, or divine, flowers, stated in the Lotus sūtra as of four kinds, mandāras, mahāmandāras, mañjūṣakas, and mahāmañjūṣakas, the first two white, the last two red.

天 蓋 A Buddha's canopy, or umbrella; a nimbus of rays of light, a halo.

天 衆 The host of heaven, Brahma, Indra, and all their host. | | 五 相 The five signs of approaching demise among the devas, cf. 五 衰.

天 行 A bodhisattva's natural or spontaneous correspondence with fundamental law; one of the 五 行 of the 涅 槃 經 Nirvāṇa sūtra.

天 衣 Deva garments, of extreme lightness. | | 拂 千 歲 An illustration of the length of a small kalpa: if a great rock, let it be one, two, or even 40 li square, be dusted with a deva-garment once in a hundred years till the rock be worn away, the kalpa would still be unfinished.

天 親 Vasubandhu, 伐 蘇 畔 度; 婆 藪 (or 修) 槃 豆 (or 陀) "akin to the gods", or 世 親 "akin to the world". Vasubandhu is described as a native of Puruṣapura, or Peshawar, by Eitel as of Rājagṛiha, born "900 years after the nirvāṇa", or about A.D. 400; Takakusu suggests 420–500, Péri puts his death not later than 350. In Eitel's day the date of his death was put definitely at A.D. 117. Vasubandhu's great work, the Abhidharmakośa, is only one of his thirty-six works. He is said to be the younger brother of Asaṅga of the Yogācāra school, by whom he was converted from the Sarvāstivāda school of thought to that of Mahāyāna and of Nāgārjuna. On his conversion he would have "cut out his tongue" for its past heresy, but was dissuaded by his brother, who bade him use the same tongue to correct his errors, whereupon he wrote the 唯 識 論 and other Mahāyānist works. He is called the twenty-first patriarch and died in Ayodhyā.

天 語 The deva language, i.e. that of the Brahman, Sanskrit.

天 識 Natural perception, or wisdom; the primal endowment in man; the 眞 如 or Bhūtatathatā.

天 趣 idem 天 道.

天 迦 盧 Devanāgarī, 神 字 the usual form of Sanskrit writing, introduced into Tibet, v. 梵 字.

天 道 Deva-gati, or Devasopāna, 天 趣. (1) The highest of the six paths 六 道, the realm of devas, i.e. the eighteen heavens of form and four of formlessness. A place of enjoyment, where the meritorious enjoy the fruits of good karma, but not a place of progress toward bodhisattva perfection. (2) The Tao of Heaven, natural law, cosmic energy; according to the Taoists, the origin and law of all things.

天 部 The classes of devas; the host of devas; the host of heaven. | | 善 神 Brahmā, Indra, the four devaloka-rājas, and the other spirit guardians of Buddhism.

天 須 菩 提 Deva Subhūti, one of three Subhūtis, disciples of the Buddha; said to have been so called because of his love of fine clothing and purity of life.

天食 Sudhā, food of the gods, sweet dew, ambrosia, nectar; blue, yellow, red, and white in colour, white for the higher ranks, the other colours for the lower.

天香 Deva incense, divine or excellent incense.

天鬼 Gods and demons; gati, or reincarnation, among devas and demons.

天魔 Deva Māra, 魔羅 one of the four Māras, who dwells in the sixth heaven, Paranirmita-vaśa-vartin, at the top of the Kāmadhātu, with his innumerable host, whence he constantly obstructs the Buddha-truth and its followers. He is also styled 殺者 the slayer; also 波旬 explained by 惡愛 sinful love or desire, as he sends his daughters to seduce the saints; also 波卑(夜) Pāpīyān, the evil one. He is the special Māra of the Śākyamuni period; other Buddhas suffer from other Māras; v. 魔. ||外道 Māras and heretics—both enemies of Buddha-truth.

天鼓 The deva drum—in the 善法 Good Law Hall of the Trayas-triṁśas heavens, which sounds of itself, warning the inhabitants of the thirty-three heavens that even their life is impermanent and subject to karma; at the sound of the drum Indra preaches against excess. Hence it is a title of Buddha as the great law-drum, who warns, exhorts, and encourages the good and frightens the evil and the demons. ||雷音佛; 鼓音如來 Divyadundubhimeghanirghoṣa. One of the five Buddhas in the Garbhadhātu maṇḍala, on the north of the central group; said to be one of the dharmakāya of Śākyamuni, his 等流身 or universal emanation body; and is known as 不動尊 corresponding with Akṣobhya, cf. 五智如來 and 大日經疏 4. ||音; 雲自在燈王 Dundubhiṣvara-rāja. Lord of the sound of celestial drums, i.e. the thunder. Name of each of 2,000 koṭis of Buddhas who attained Buddhahood.

天龍 Devas, including Brahmā, Indra, and the devas, together with the nāgas. ||八部 Devas, nāgas, and others of the eight classes: devas, nagas, yakṣas, gandharvas, asuras, garuḍas, kinnaras, mahoragas. 天; 龍; 夜叉; 乾闥婆; 阿修羅; 迦樓羅; 緊那羅; 摩睺羅迦. ||夜叉 Devas, nāgas, yakṣas.

孔 A hole; surname of Confucius; great, very; a peacock. |雀 Mayūra, 摩裕羅 a peacock; the latter form is also given by Eitel for Mauriya as "an ancient city on the north-east frontier of Matipura, the residence of the ancient Maurya (Morya) princes. The present Amrouah near Hurdwar". ||城 Mathurā, or Kṛṣnapura; modern Muttra; 摩度 (or 偷, 突, or 頭) 羅; 秣兔羅 an ancient city and kingdom of Central India, famous for its stūpas, reputed birthplace of Kriṣṇa. ||明王 "Peacock king," a former incarnation of Śākyamuni, when as a peacock he sucked from a rock water of miraculous healing power; now one of the mahārāja bodhisattvas, with four arms, who rides on a peacock; his full title is 佛母大金曜||||. There is another ||王 with two arms.

少 Few; also used as a transliteration of Ṣaṭ, six. |光(天); 廣天 Parīttābhās; the fourth Brahmaloka, i.e. the first region of the second dhyāna heavens, also called 有光壽. |室 Shao-shih, a hill on the 嵩山 Sung shan where Bodhidharma set up his |林寺 *infra.* |室六門集 Six brief treatises attributed to Bodhidharma, but their authenticity is denied. |康 Shao-k'ang, a famous monk of the T'ang dynasty, known as the later 善導 Shan-tao, his master. |林寺 The monastery at |室 in 登封 Têng-fêng hsien, Honanfu, where Bodhidharma sat with his face to a wall for nine years. |林武藝 Wu-i, a cook of the Shao-lin monastery, who is said single-handed to have driven off the Yellow Turban rebels with a three-foot staff, and who was posthumously rewarded with the rank of "general"; a school of adepts of the quarter-staff, etc., was called after him, of whom thirteen were far-famed. |欲知足 Content with few desires. |淨(天) Parīttaśubhas. The first and smallest heaven (brahmaloka) in the third dhyāna region of form. |財鬼 Hungry ghosts who pilfer because they are poor and get but little food.

屯 Collect, mass; to quarter, camp. To sprout; very; stingy. |崙摩 Druma, the king of the kinnara, male and female spirits whose music awakened mystics from their trance; v. 智度論 17.

巴 The open hand, palm; to lay hold of; to flatter. |利 Pali, considered by "Southern" Buddhists to be the language of Magadha, i.e. Māgadhī Prākrit, spoken by Śākyamuni; their Tripiṭaka is written in it. It is closely allied to Sanskrit, but phonetically decayed and grammatically degenerate. |思巴 v. 八思巴. |連弗 Pāṭaliputra, v. 波吒釐. |陵三轉語 The three cryptic sayings of Hao-chien 顥鑑 styled Pa-ling, name of his place in

岳州 Yo-chou. He was the successor of Yün-mên 雲門. "What is the way? The seeing fall into wells. What is the feather-cutting sword (of Truth)? Coral branches (i.e. moonbeams) prop up the moon. What is the divine (or deva) throng? A silver bowl full of snow." | (or 把) 鼻; 巴臂 Something to lay hold of, e.g. a nose or an arm; evidence.

幻 Māyā. Illusion, hallucination, a conjurer's trick, jugglery, i.e. one of the ten illustrations of unreality. | 人 or | 士 An illusionist, a conjurer. | 力 His powers. | 化 Illusion and transformation, or illusory transformation. | 垢 Illusory and defiled, i.e. body and mind are alike illusion and unclean. | 師 An illusionist, a conjurer. | 心 The illusion mind, or mind is unreal. | 惑 Illusory; to delude. | 日王 Bālāditya, 婆羅阿迭多 the morning sun (lit. mock-sun) king, *circa* A.D. 191. 幻 probably should be 幼; a king of Magadha, who fought and captured Mihirakula, the king of 磔迦 Ceka, or the Hūnas, who was an opponent of Buddhism. | 有 Illusory existence. | 法 Conjuring tricks, illusion, methods of Bodhisattva transformation. | 相 Illusion, illusory appearance. | 者 The illusory; anything that is an illusion; all things, for they are illusion. | 身 The illusion-body, i.e. this body is not real but an illusion. | 野 The wilderness of illusion, i.e. mortal life. | 門 The ways or methods of illusion, or of bodhisattva transformation.

引 To stretch, draw, lead, bring in or on. | 入 To introduce, initiate. | 化 Initiate and instruct. | 出佛性 One of the 三佛性 q.v., the Buddha-nature in all the living to be developed by proper processes. | 導 To lead (men into Buddha-truth); also a phrase used at funerals implying the leading of the dead soul to the other world, possibly arising from setting alight the funeral pyre. | 座 A phrase used by one who ushers a preacher into the "pulpit" to expound the Law. | 接; | 攝 To accept, receive, welcome—as a Buddha does all who call on him, as stated in the nineteenth vow of Amitābha. | 果 The stage of fruition, i.e. reward or punishment in the genus, as contrasted with 滿 | the differentiated species or stages, e.g. for each organ, or variety of condition. 唯識論 2. | 業; | 因; 牽 | 業; 總報業 The principal or integral direction of karma, in contrast with 滿 | its more detailed stages; see last entry. | 正太子 Sātavāhana, 沙多婆漢那 a prince of Kosala, whose father the king was the patron of Nāgārjuna; the prince, attributing his father's unduly prolonged life to Nāgārjuna's magic, is said to have compelled the latter to commit suicide, on hearing of which the king died and the prince ascended the throne. 西域記 10. | 發因 One of the 十因 the force or cause that releases other forces or causes. | 磬; 手磬 A hand-bell to direct the attention in services. | 請闍梨 A term for the instructor of beginners. | 飯大師 The great leader who introduces the meal, i.e. the club which beats the call to meals. | 駕大師 One of the 四大師 of the T'ang dynasty; it was his duty to welcome back the emperor on his return to the palace, a duty at times apparently devolving on Buddhist monks.

心 Hrd, hrdaya 汗栗太 (or 馱); 紀哩馱 the heart, mind, soul; citta 質多 the heart as the seat of thought or intelligence. In both senses the heart is likened to a lotus. There are various definitions, of which the following are six instances: (1) 肉團心 hrd, the physical heart of sentient or non-sentient living beings, e.g. men, trees, etc. (2) 集起心 citta, the Ālaya-vijñāna, or totality of mind, and the source of all mental activity. (3) 思量心 manas, the thinking and calculating mind; (4) 緣慮心; 了別心; 慮知心; citta; the discriminating mind; (5) 堅實心 the bhūtatathatā mind, or the permanent mind; (6) 積聚精要心 the mind-essence of the sūtras.

心一境性 One of the seven dhyāna 定, the mind fixed in one condition.

心不相應 (行 or 行法) The functioning of the mind not corresponding with the first three of the 五法 five laws, of which this is the fourth.

心乘 The mind vehicle, i.e. 心觀 meditation, insight.

心亭 The pavilion of the mind, i.e. the body; cf. | 城.

心佛 The Buddha within the heart: from mind is Buddhahood; the Buddha revealed in or to the mind; the mind is Buddha. | | 及衆生, 是三無差別 The mind, Buddha, and all the living—there is no difference between the three, i.e. all are of the same order. This is an important doctrine of the 華嚴經 Hua-yen sūtra, cf. its 夜摩天宮品, by T'ien-t'ai it is called 三法妙 the mystery of the three things.

心作 The karmaic activity of the mind, the 意業 of the three agents, body, mouth, and mind.

心光 The light from (a Buddha's) mind, or merciful heart, especially that of Amitābha.

心印 Mental impression, intuitive certainty; the mind is the Buddha-mind in all, which can seal or assure the truth; the term indicates the intuitive method of the 禪 Ch'an (Zen) school, which was independent of the spoken or written word.

心咒 One of the three classes of spells, idem 一字咒.

心命 Mind life, i.e. the life, longevity, or eternity of the dharmakāya or spiritual body, that of mind; also 慧命. v. 智度論 78.

心器 Mind as the receptacle of all phenomena.

心地 Mind, from which all things spring; the mental ground, or condition; also used for 意 the third of the three agents—body, mouth, mind.

心城 The citadel of the mind, i.e. as guardian over action; others intp. it as the body, cf. 丨亭.

心垢 The impurities of the mind, i.e. 煩惱 passion and delusion; the two phrases are used as synonyms.

心塵 Mind dust or dirt, i.e. 煩惱 the passions, greed, anger, etc.

心宗 The intuitive sect, i.e. the Ch'an (Zen) school; also 佛心宗; 禪宗.

心師 The mind as master, not (like the heretics) mastering (or subduing) the mind 師心.

心心 Every mind; also citta-caitta, mind and mental conditions, i.e 心 and 心所. 丨丨數 The mind and its conditions or emotions; 心數 is an older form of 心所.

心念不空過 Pondering on (Buddha) and not passing (the time) in vain.

心性 Immutable mind-corpus, or mind-nature, the self-existing fundamental pure mind, the all, the tathāgata-garbha, or 如來藏心; 自性清淨心; also described in the 起信論 Awakening of Faith as immortal 不生不滅. Another definition identifies 心 with 性, saying 性即是心心即是佛 the nature is the mind, and mind is Buddha; another, that mind and nature are the same when 悟 awake and understanding, but differ when 迷 in illusion; and further, in reply to the statement that the Buddha-nature is eternal but the mind not eternal, it is said, the nature is like water, the mind like ice, illusion turns nature to mental ice form, awakening melts it back to its proper nature. 丨性三千 The universe in a thought; the mind as a microcosm.

心想 Thought; the thoughts of the mind.

心意識 Mind, thought, and perception (or discernment).

心慧 Wisdom, i.e. mind or heart wisdom, e.g. 身戒心慧 controlled in body and wise in mind.

心懷戀慕 Heart-yearning (for the Buddha).

心所(法) Mental conditions, the attributes of the mind, especially the moral qualities, or emotions, love, hate, etc.; also 心所有法, v. 心心.

心數 An older term for 心所 q.v. the several qualities of the mind. The esoterics make Vairocana the 心王, i.e. Mind or Will, and 心數 the moral qualities, or mental attributes, are personified as his retinue.

心智 Mind and knowledge, or the wisdom of the mind, mind being the organ, knowing the function.

心月 Mind (as the) moon, the natural mind or heart pure and bright as the full moon. 丨丨輪 The mind's or heart's moon-revolutions, i.e. the moon's varying stages, typifying the grades of enlightenment from beginner to saint.

心根 Manas, or the mind-organ, one of the twenty-five tattva 諦 or postulates of a universe.

心極 The pole or extreme of the mind, the mental reach; the Buddha.

心機 The motive power of the mind, the mind the motor.

心水 The mind as a reflecting water-surface; also the mind as water, clear or turbid.

心冰 The heart chaste as ice; the mind congealed as ice, i.e. unable to solve a difficulty.

心法 Mental dharmas, ideas—all "things" are divided into two classes 色 and 心 physical and mental; that which has 質礙 substance and resistance is physical, that which is devoid of these is mental; or the root of all phenomena is mind 緣起諸法之根本者爲心法. The exoteric and esoteric schools differ in their interpretation: the exoterics hold that mental ideas or "things" are 無色無形 unsubstantial and invisible, the esoterics that they 有色有形 have both substance and form. 丨丨身; 心是法身 The mind is dharmakāya, "tathāgata in bonds," 在纏如來.

心波 Mind waves, i.e. mental activity.

心海 Mind as a sea or ocean, external phenomena being the wind, and the 八識 eight forms of cognition being the waves.

心源 The fountain of the mind; the thought-welling fountain; mind as the *fons et origo* of all things.

心無所住 The mind without resting-place, i.e. detached from time and space, e.g. the past being past may be considered as a "non-past" or non-existent, so with present and future, thus realizing their unreality. The result is detachment, or the liberated mind, which is the Buddha-mind, the bodhi-mind, 無生心 the mind free from ideas of creation and extinction, of beginning and end, recognizing that all forms and natures are of the Void, or Absolute.

心燈 The lamp of the mind; inner light, intelligence.

心猿 The mind as a restless monkey.

心王 The mind, the will, the directive or controlling mind, the functioning mind as a whole, distinct from its 心所 or qualities. 丨丨如來 Vairocana as the ultimate mind, the attributes being personified as his retinue. Applied also to the 五佛 and the 九尊. 丨丨心所 The mind and its qualities, or conditions.

心珠 The mind stuff of all the living, being of the pure Buddha-nature, is likened to a translucent gem.

心生滅門 The two gates of mind, creation and destruction, or beginning and end.

心田 The field of the mind, or heart, in which spring up good and evil.

心目 Mind and eye, the chief causes of the emotions.

心相 Heart-shape (of the physical heart); manifestation of mind in action; (the folly of assuming that) mind has shape. 丨丨應行 Actions corresponding with mind, or mind productive of all action.

心眞 Our mind is by nature that of the bhūtatathatā. 丨丨如門 The mind as bhūtatathatā, one of the 二門 of the 起信論 Awakening of Faith.

心眼 The eye of the mind, mental vision.

心神 The spirit of the mind, mental intelligence; mind.

心空 Mind-space, or mind spaciousness, mind holding all things, hence like space; also, the emptied mind, kenosis.

心經 Hṛdaya or "Heart" Sūtra, idem 般若心經; 般若波羅蜜多心經; styled 神分心經 "divinely distributed", when publicly recited to get rid of evil spirits.

心縛 The mind in bondage—taking the seeming for the real.

心緣 Mental cognition of the environment; to lay hold of external things by means of the mind.

心自在者 He whose mind is free, or sovereign, an arhat who has got rid of all hindrances to abstraction.

心華 Heart-flower, the heart in its original innocence resembling a flower.

心蓮 The lotus of the mind or heart; the exoteric school interprets it by original purity; the esoteric by the physical heart, which resembles a closed lotus with eight petals.

心藥 Medicine for the mind, or spirit.

心行 The activities of the mind, or heart; also working on the mind for its control; also mind and action. 丨丨不離 Mind and act not separated, thought and deed in accord, especially in relation to Amitābha.

心要 The very core, or essence.

心觀 Contemplation of the mind and its thoughts, v. 一心三觀.

心證 The inner witness, or assurance, mind and Buddha witnessing together.

心識 The mind and cognition; mind and its contents; the two are considered as identical in the Abhidharma-kośa, but different in Mahāyāna.

心趣 The bent or direction of the mind, or moral nature.

心跡 Footprints, or indications of mind, i.e. the mind revealed by deeds.

心路 The mind-road, i.e. the road to Buddhahood.

心量 Mind-measure; the ordinary man's calculating mind; also, capacity of mind.

心鏡 The heart-mirror, or mirror of the mind, which must be kept clean if it is to reflect the Truth.

心靈 The mind spirit, or genius; intelligence; cf. 丨燈.

心願 The will of the mind, resolve, vow.

心香 The incense of the mind, or heart, i.e. sincere devotion.

心馬 The mind like a horse, that needs breaking in, or stimulating with a whip, cf. 心猿.

心鬼 A perverse mind, whose karma will be that of a wandering ghost.

心魔(賊) The māra-robbers of the mind, i.e. the passions.

戈 A spear. 丨追 idem 俱胝 q.v. Koṭī.

手 Pāṇi; hasta; kara; hand, arm. 丨印 Mudrā, mystic positions of the hand; signet-rings, seals; finger-prints. 丨口意相應 In yoga practices it means correspondence of hand, mouth, and mind, i.e. manual signs, esoteric words or spells, and thought or mental projection. 丨執金剛杵 Vajrapāṇi, or Vajradhara, who holds the thunderbolt. 丨爐 A portable censer (with handle). 丨磬 A hand-chime (or bell) struck with a stick. 丨輪 The lines on the palm and fingers—especially the "thousand" lines on a Buddha's hand.

支 A branch; to branch, put off, pay, advance. 丨伐羅; 至縛羅 Cīvara. A mendicant's garment. 丨佛, 辟支佛 A pratyeka-buddha, who understands the twelve nidānas, or chain of causation, and so attains to complete wisdom. His stage of attainment is the 丨丨地. 丨具; 丨度 The various articles required for worship. 丨提; 丨帝; 丨徵; 丨陀; 脂帝. Newer forms are 制多; 制底(耶); 制地, i.e. 刹, 塔, 廟 Caitya. A tumulus, a mausoleum; a place where the relics of Buddha were collected, hence a place where his sūtras or images are placed. Eight famous Caityas formerly existed: Lumbinī, Buddha-gayā, Vārāṇaśī, Jetavana, Kanyākubja, Rājagṛha, Vaiśālī, and the Sāla grove in Kuśinagara. Considerable difference of opinion exists as to the exact connotation of the terms given, some being referred to graves or stūpas, others to shrines or temples, but in general the meaning is stūpas, shrines, and any collection of objects of worship. 丨提山部; 丨提加部; 制多山部; 只底舸部 ? Caityaśaila; described as one of the twenty sects of the Hīnayāna, and as ascetic dwellers among tombs or in caves. 丨樓迦讖; 丨讖 Chih-lou-chia-ch'an, a śramaṇa who came to China from Yüeh-chih A.D. 147 or A.D. 164 and worked at translations till A.D. 186 at Loyang. 丨用 To divide, distribute for use, i.e. 分用. 丨謙 Chih-ch'ien; name of a Yüeh-chih monk said to have come to Loyang at the end of the Han dynasty and under the Wei; tall, dark, emaciated, with light brown eyes; very learned and wise. 丨那, 指那, 眞丹, 至那, 斯那, 振旦, 震旦, 眞那, 振丹, 脂難, 旃丹; 摩訶至那 Cīna; Mahā-cīna. The name by which China is referred to in the laws of Manu (which assert that the Chinese were degenerate Kṣatriya), in the Mahābhārata, and in Buddhist works. This name may have been derived from families ruling in western China under such titles as 晉 Chin at Fên-chou in Shansi 1106–376 B.C., 陳 Ch'ên in Honan 1122–479 B.C., 秦 Ch'in in Shensi as early as the ninth century B.C., and to this latter dynasty the designation is generally attributed. | 那提婆瞿恒羅; 漢天種 Cīna deva gotra. The "solar deva" of Han descent, first king of Khavandha, born to a princess of the Han dynasty (206 B.C.–A.D. 220) on her way as a bride-elect to Persia, the parentage being attributed to the solar deva. 西域記 12. | 隣陀 Mucilinda, v. 目 or 摩訶 Maha-m. | 郎 Chih-lang, formerly a polite term for a monk, said to have arisen from the fame of the three 支 Chih of the Wei dynasty 支謙 Chih-ch'ien, 支讖 Chih-ch'an, and 支亮 Chih-liang.

文 Letters, literature, writing; refined; culture; civil; a despatch; veined; a cash; to gloss.

文句 Textual explanation or criticism, also termed 章; 疏; 述義; 記, etc.; the term applies to works on canonical texts in general, but has particular reference to the Lotus sūtra, i.e. the 妙法蓮華經文句.

文夾 A portfolio, or satchel for Buddhist books.

文字 The letter; letters; literal; the written word is described as the breath and life of the dharmakāya; cf. 嚕 ruta. | | 人 A literalist, pedant; narrow. | | 法師 A teacher of the letter of the Law, who knows not its spirit.

文尼 Muni, idem 牟尼 and 茂尼, e.g. Śākyamuni.

文殊(師利) Mañjuśrī 滿殊尸利 later 曼殊室利. 文殊 is also used for Mañjunātha, Mañjudeva, Mañjughoṣa, Mañjuṣvara, et al. T., ḫjam-dpal; J., Monju. Origin unknown; presumably, like most Buddhas and bodhisattvas, an idealization of a particular quality, in his case of Wisdom. Mañju is beautiful, Śrī—good fortune, virtue, majesty, lord, an epithet of a god. Six definitions are obtained from various scriptures: 妙首 (or 頭) wonderful (or beautiful) head; 普首 universal head; 濡首 glossy head (probably a transliteration); 敬首 revered head; 妙德 wonderful virtue (or power); 妙吉祥 wonderfully auspicious; the last is a later translation in the 西域記. As guardian of wisdom 智慧 he is often placed on Śākyamuni's left, with 普顯 on the right as guardian of law 理, the latter holding the Law, the former the wisdom or exposition of it; formerly they held the reverse positions. He is often represented with five curls or waves to his hair indicating the 五智 q.v. or the five peaks; his hand holds the sword of wisdom and he sits on a lion emblematic of its stern majesty; but he has other forms. He is represented as a youth, i.e. eternal youth. His present abode is given as east of the universe, known as 清涼山 clear and cool mountain, or a region 寶住 precious abode, or Abode of Treasures, or 寶氏 from which he derives one of his titles, 寶相如來. One of his dhāraṇīs prophesies China as his post-nirvāṇa realm. In past incarnations he is described as being the parent of many Buddhas and as having assisted the Buddha into existence; his title was 龍種上佛 the supreme Buddha of the Nāgas, also 大身佛 or 神仙佛; now his title is 歡喜藏摩尼寶精佛 The spiritual Buddha who joyfully cares for the jewel; and his future title is to be 普現佛 Buddha universally revealed. In the 序品 Introductory Chapter of the Lotus sūtra he is also described as the ninth predecessor or Buddha-ancestor of Śākyamuni. He is looked on as the chief of the Bodhisattvas and represents them, as the chief disciple of the Buddha, or as his son 法王子. Hīnayāna counts Śāriputra as the wisest of the disciples, Mahāyāna gives Mañjuśrī the chief place, hence he is also styled 覺母 mother, or begetter of understanding. He is shown riding on either a lion or a peacock, or sitting on a white lotus; often he holds a book, emblem of wisdom, or a blue lotus; in certain rooms of a monastery he is shown as a monk; and he appears in military array as defender of the faith. His signs, magic words, and so on, are found in various sūtras. His most famous centre in China is Wu-t'ai shan in Shansi, where he is the object of pilgrimages, especially of Mongols. The legends about him are many. He takes the place in Buddhism of Viśvakarman as Vulcan, or architect, of the universe. He is one of the eight Dhyāni-bodhisattvas, and sometimes has the image of Akṣobhya in his crown. He was mentioned in China as early as the fourth century and in the Lotus sūtra he frequently appears, especially as the converter of the daughter of the Dragon-king of the Ocean. He has five messengers 五使者 and eight youths 八童子 attending on him. His hall in the Garbhadhātu maṇḍala is the seventh, in which his group numbers twenty-five. His position is north-east. There are numerous sūtras and other works with his name as title, e.g. 文殊師利問菩提經 Gayāśīrṣa sūtra, tr. by Kumārajīva 384–417; and its 論 or Ṭīkā of Vasubandhu, tr. by Bodhiruci 535, see list in B.N. | | 三昧 The samādhi of Mañjuśrī styled the 無相妙慧 formless wonderful wisdom, or wonderful wisdom in the realm of that which is beyond form. | | 五使者 The five messengers of Mañjuśrī, each bearing one of his 五智 five expressions of wisdom; they are 髻設尼; 優波髻設尼; 質多羅; 地慧, and 請召. | | 八大童子 His eight "pages" are 光網; 地慧; 無垢光; 不思慧; 召請; 髻設尼; 救護慧, and 鄔波髻設尼. | | 悔過 The repentance of Mañjuśrī, i.e. of his former doubting mind, cf. St. Thomas. | | 院 The seventh great court of the thirteen in the Garbhadhātu group; it shows Mañjuśrī in the centre of a group of twenty-five.

文池 The dragon pool by the side of the throne of Vajrapāṇi, called 目眞鄰陀 Mucilinda q.v.

文理 The written word and the truth expressed; written principles, or reasonings; a treatise; literary style.

文證 The evidence of the written word, or scripture.

文陀竭 Mūrdhajāta, Māndhātr, i.e. 頂生王 born from his mother's head, a reputed previous incarnation of the Buddha, who still ambitious, despite his universal earthly sway, his thousand sons, etc., flew to Indra's heaven, saw the 天上玉女 celestial devī, but on the desire arising to rule there on Indra's death, he was hurled to earth; v. | | | 王經.

斗 A bushel, i.e. ten Chinese pints. | 帳 A bushel-shaped curtain, e.g. a state umbrella. | 姥 Dame of the Bushel; queen of heaven 天后 or Marīci, 摩利支. | 父天尊 The husband of 斗姥, a Taoist attribution.

斤 An adze; to chop; a catty, $1\frac{1}{3}$ lb.; penetrating, minute. | 斗; 筋斗; 巾斗 A somersault.

方 Square; place; correct; a means, plan, prescription; then, now, just.

方丈 An abbot, 寺主 head of a monastery; the term is said to arise from the ten-foot cubic dwelling in which 維摩 Vimalakīrti lived, but there seems to be no Sanskrit equivalent.

方便 Upāya. Convenient to the place, or situation, suited to the condition, opportune, appropriate; but 方 is interpreted as 方法 method, mode, plan, and 便 as 便用 convenient for use, i.e. a convenient or expedient method; also 方 as 方正 and 便 as 巧妙, which implies strategically correct. It is also intp. as 權道智 partial, temporary, or relative (teaching of) knowledge of reality, in contrast with 般若智 prajñā, and 眞實 absolute truth, or reality instead of the seeming. The term is a translation of 傴和 upāya, a mode of approach, an expedient, stratagem, device. The meaning is—teaching according to the capacity of the hearer, by any suitable method, including that of device or stratagem, but expedience beneficial to the recipient is understood. Mahāyāna claims that the Buddha used this expedient or partial method in his teaching until near the end of his days, when he enlarged it to the revelation of reality, or the preaching of his final and complete truth. Hīnayāna with reason denies this, and it is evident that the Mahāyāna claim has no foundation, for the whole of its 方等 or 方廣 scriptures are of later invention. T'ien-t'ai speaks of the 三乘 q.v. or Three Vehicles as 方便 expedient or partial revelations, and of its 一乘 or One Vehicle as the complete revelation of universal Buddhahood. This is the teaching of the Lotus sūtra, which itself contains 方便 teaching to lead up to the full revelation; hence the terms 體內 (or 同體) 方便, i.e. expedient or partial truths within the full revelation, meaning the expedient part of the Lotus, and 體外方便 the expedient or partial truths of the teaching which preceded the Lotus; see the 方便品 of that work, also the second chapter of the 維摩經. 方便 is also the seventh of the ten pāramitās. | | 化身土 An intermediate "land" of the Japanese monk 見眞 Kenshin, below the Pure-land, where Amitābha appears in his transformation-body. | | 土 Abbreviation for the last and next but one. | | 智 Upāyajñāna; the wisdom or knowledge of using skilful means (for saving others). | | 有餘土 One of the T'ien-t'ai 四土 Four Lands, which is temporary, as its occupants still have remains to be purged away. | | 殺生 The right of great Bodhisattvas, knowing every one's karma, to kill without sinning, e.g. in order to prevent a person from committing sin involving unintermitted suffering, or to aid him in reaching one of the higher reincarnations. | | 波羅蜜 Upāya, the seventh pāramitā. | | 波羅蜜菩薩 A bodhisattva in the Garbhadhātu group, the second on the right in the hall of Space. | | 現涅槃 Though the Buddha is eternal, he showed himself as temporarily extinct, as necessary to arouse a longing for Buddha, cf. Lotus, 16. | | 門 The gates of upāya, i.e. convenient or expedient gates leading into Truth. | | 假門 Expedient gates or ways of using the seeming for the real.

方典 A term covering the whole of the Mahāyāna sūtras, idem 方等經典.

方口食 Opportunism in obtaining a living, i.e. a monk who makes a living by fawning or by bullying, one of the 四邪命 four illicit ways of livelihood.

方外 Out of the world; the life of a monk.

方廣 Vaipulya, 毘佛略 expansion, enlargement, broad, spacious. 方 is intp. by 方正 correct in doctrine and 廣 by 廣博 broad or wide; some interpret it by elaboration, or fuller explanation of the doctrine; in general it may be taken as the broad school, or wider teaching, in contrast with the narrow school, or Hīnayāna. The term covers the whole of the specifically Mahāyāna sūtras. The sūtras are also known as 無量義經 scriptures of measureless meaning, i.e. universalistic, or the infinite. Cf. 方等. | | 大莊嚴經 A vaipulya sūtra, the Lalita-vistara, in 12 chüan, giving an account of the Buddha in the Tuṣita heaven and his descent to earth as Śākyamuni; tr. by Divākara under the T'ang dynasty; another tr. is the 普曜經. | | 道人 Heretical followers of Mahāyāna, who hold a false doctrine of 空 the Void, teaching it as total non-existence, or nihilism.

方相 Square, four square, one of the five shapes.

方等 Vaipulya; cf. 方廣. 方 is interpreted as referring to the doctrine, 等 as equal, or universal, i.e. everywhere equally. An attempt is made to distinguish between the two above terms, 方廣 being now used for vaipulya, but they are interchangeable. Eitel says the vaipulya sūtras "are distinguished by an expansion of doctrine and style (Sūtras développées, Burnouf). They are apparently of later date, showing the influence of different schools; their style is diffuse and prolix, repeating the same idea over and over again in prose and in verse; they are also frequently interlarded with prophecies and dhāraṇīs"; but the two terms seem to refer rather to the content than the form. The content is that of universalism. Chinese Buddhists assert that all the sūtras from the 華嚴 Hua-yen onwards are of this class and therefore are Mahāyāna. Consequently all 方等 or 方廣 sūtras are claimed by that school. Cf. 方便. | | 三昧 One of T'ien-t'ai's methods of inducing samādhi, partly by walking, partly by sitting, based on the 大方等陀羅尼經; Chih-i delivered the | | | | 行法 to his disciple 灌頂 Kuan-ting who wrote it in one chüan. | | 懺 (悔) One of the subjects of meditation in the above on the hindrances caused by the six organs of sense. | | (戒) 壇 An open altar at which instruction in the commandments was preached to the people, founded on the Mahāyāna-vaipulya sūtras; the system began in 765 in the capital under 代宗 Tai Tsung of the T'ang dynasty and continued, with an interim under 武宗 Wu Tsung, till the 宣宗 Hsüan Tsung period. | | 時 The third of the five periods of T'ien-t'ai 五時教, the eight years from the twelfth to the twentieth years of the Buddha's teaching, i.e. the period of the 維摩, the 金光明, and other vaipulya sūtras. | | 部 The sūtras taught during the | | 時 last-named period.

方服 A monk's robe 袈裟 said to be so called because of its square appearance; also 方袍.

方規 Square-shaped, properly, according to scale.

方詣 Direction.

日 Sūrya; the sun; a day. 蘇利耶. | 光 (菩薩); 蘇利也波羅皮遮那 Sūrya-prabhāsana. Sunlight, and 月光 (| |) Moonlight, name of two Bodhisattva assistants of 藥師 the Master of Healing; Sunlight is the ninth in the Ti-tsang Court of the Garbhadhātu group. | 出論者 The sunrise exponents, a title of the founders of the 經部宗 before the Christian era. | 域 Japan. | 天 (子) Sūrya, 蘇利耶; 修利; 修野 (or 意) 天子; also 寶光天子. The sun-ruler; one of the metamorphoses of Kuan-yin, dwelling in the sun as palace, driving a quadriga. | 天衆 The retinue of Indra in his palace of the sun. | 宮 The sun-palace, the abode of 日天子 *supra*. | 幢華眼鼓 Five characters taken from the names of, and representing five Buddhas in the Vajradhātu 大日, 寶幢, 華開敷, 蓮華眼, and 天鼓雷音. | 想觀 Meditation on, and observing of the setting sun, the first of the sixteen meditations in the 觀無量壽經. | 旋三昧 Sūryāvarta samādhi, one of the sixteen samādhi mentioned in the 法華經妙音品; 日輪三昧 is an older name for it. | 星宿 Nakṣatratārā-rājāditya; a degree of meditation, i.e. the sun, stars and constellations samādhi. | 曜 The sun, one of the nine 曜 luminaries; one of the retinue of | 天 shown in the eastern part of the Garbhadhātu group driving three horses. | 月淨明德 Candra-vimala-sūrya-prabhāsa-śrī. A Buddha whose realm resembles Sukhavatī. | 月燈明佛 Candra-sūrya-pradīpa, or Candrārkadīpa. The title of 20,000 Buddhas who succeeded each other preaching the Lotus sūtra,

v. 法華經序品. | 本 Japan. Buddhism was introduced there from Korea in the sixth century, and in the seventh from China. | 禺中 10 a.m. styled by T'ien-t'ai the hour of 般若 wisdom. | 種 Sūrya-vaṁśa, one of the five surnames of Śākyamuni, sun-seed or lineage, his first ancestors having been produced by the sun from " two stalks of sugar-cane "; v. Ikṣvāku. | 精摩尼 A maṇi, or pearl, crystal-clear as the sun, which gives sight to the blind. | 蓮 Nichiren, the Japanese founder, in A.D. 1252, of the 日蓮宗 Nichiren sect, which is also known as the 法華宗 or Lotus sect. Its chief tenets are the three great mysteries 三大秘法, representing the Trikāya: (1) 本尊 or chief object of worship, being the great maṇḍala of the worlds of the ten directions, or universe, i.e. the body or nirmāṇakāya of Buddha; (2) 題目 the title of the Lotus sūtra 妙法蓮華經 Myō-hō-ren-gwe kyō, preceded by Namo, or, "Adoration to the scripture of the lotus of the wonderful law," for it is Buddha's spiritual body; (3) 戒壇 the altar of the law, which is also the title of the Lotus as above; the believer, wherever he is, dwells in the Pure-land of calm light 寂光淨土, the saṁbhogakāya. | 輪 The sun's disc, which is the exterior of the sun palace of 日天子; it is said to consist of sphaṭika, or fiery crystal.

月 Candra, 旃達(羅); 旃陀羅; 戰達羅; 戰捺羅 the moon, called also 蘇摩 soma, from the fermented juice of *Asclepias acida*, used in worship, and later personified in association with the moon. It has many other epithets, e.g. 印度 Indu, incorrectly intp. as marked like a hare; 創夜神 Niśākara, maker of the night; 星宿王 Nakṣatra-nātha, lord of constellations; 喜懷之頭飾 the crest of Śiva; 蓮華王 Kumuda-pati, lotus lord; 白馬主 Śvetavājin, drawn by (or lord of) white horses; 大白光神 Śītāṁśu, the spirit with white rays; 冷光神 Śītamarīci, the spirit with cool rays; 鹿形神 Mṛgāṅka, the spirit with marks or form like a deer; 野兎形神 Śaśi, ditto like a hare.

月上女經 Candrottarā-dārikā-vyākaraṇa-sūtra of the maid in the moon.

月光 Candraprabha, 戰達羅鉢剌婆 Moonlight. One of the three honoured ones in the Vajradhātu, and in the Mañjuśrī court of the Garbhadhātu, known also as 淸涼金剛. | | 太子 Moonlight prince, name of Śākyamuni in a previous incarnation as a prince, when he split one of his bones to anoint a leper with its marrow and gave him of his blood to drink. 智度論 12. | | 王 The same, called Moonlight king, when he gave his head to a brahman. | | 童子; | | 兒 The son of an elder of the capital of Magadha, who listening to heretics and against his son's pleadings, endeavoured to destroy the Buddha in a pitfall of fire, but, on the Buddha's approach, the fire turned to a pool and the father was converted; the son was then predicted by the Buddha to be king of China in a future incarnation, when all China and the Mongolian and other tribes would be converted, v. | | | | 經. | | 菩薩 The bodhisattva Moonlight who attends on 藥師 the Master of Healing; also in the Mañjuśrī court of the Garbhadhātu; used for | | 王; v. | | | | 經.

月兎 The hare in the moon.

月分 Moon and division, a tr. of Candrabhāgā. 旃達羅婆伽 The two rivers Candra and Bhāga joined. The Chenab river, Punjab, the Acesines of Alexander.

月壇 An external altar in temples in the open, i.e. under the moon.

月天 Candradeva, or Somadeva. 旃達(or 蘇摩)提婆 The ruler of the moon, to whom the terms under 月 *supra* are also applied. | | 子 The male regent of the moon, named 寶吉祥, one of the metamorphoses of the Bodhisattva 勢至 Mahāsthāmaprāpta; the male regent has also his queen 月天妃.

月婆首那 Upaśūnya, 高空 an Indian monk, son of the king of 優禪尼 Udyāna, who tr. 僧伽吒經.

月宮 The moon-palace of the 月天子 made of silver and crystal; it is described as forty-nine yojanas square, but there are other accounts.

月忌 The return of the day in each month when a person died.

月愛三昧 A Buddha's " moon-love samādhi ", in which he rids men of the distresses of love and hate. | | 珠 Candrakānta, the moon-love pearl or moonstone, which bestows abundance of water or rain.

月支(國) The Yüeh-chih, or " Indo-Scythians ", 月氏(國) and a country they at one time occupied, i.e. 都貨羅 Tukhara, Tokharestan, or Badakshan. Driven out from the northern curve of the Yellow River by the Huns, *circa* 165 B.C., they conquered Bactria 大夏, the Punjab, Kashmir, "and the greater part of India." Their expulsion from the north of Shansi was the cause of the famous journey of Chang Ch'ien of the Han dynasty and the beginning of Chinese expansion to the north-west. Kanishka, king of the Yüeh-chih towards the end of the first century A.D., became the great protector and propagator of Buddhism.

月明菩薩 idem 月光菩薩; there is a 月明菩薩經. Also 丨丨童子 (or 男).

月曜 Moon-shining, or Moon-effulgence; a group shown outside the Garbhadhātu group in the Diamond Court.

月燈三昧 Candra-dīpa-samādhi, the samādhi said to have been given to 月光童子 by Buddha, the sūtra of which is in two translations.

月王 Moon-king, 設賞迦 Śaśāṅka, a ruler of Karṇasuvarṇa, who tried to destroy the bodhidruma, Buddha's tree; dethroned by Śīlāditya.

月胄 Candravarma, 旃達羅伐摩 a learned monk of the Nāgavadana monastery.

月眉 New moon eyebrows, i.e. arched like the Buddha's.

月種 Candravaṁśa, descendants of the moon, "the lunar race of kings or the second great line of Kshatriya or royal dynasties in India." M. W.

月精(摩尼) The pearl or jewel in the fortieth hand of the "thousand hand" Kuan-yin, towards which worship is paid in case of fevers; the hand is called 月精手.

月蓋 An elder of Vaiśālī, who at the Buddha's bidding sought the aid of Amitābha, 勢至 (Mahāsthāmaprāpta) and Kuan-yin, especially the last, to rid his people of a pestilence. See Vimalakīrti sūtra.

月輦 The chariot of 月天子.

月輪 The moon's disc, the moon. 丨丨觀 (or 三昧) The moon contemplation (or samādhi) in regard to its sixteen nights of waxing to the full, and the application of this contemplation to the development of bodhi within, especially of the sixteen kinds of bodhisattva mind of the lotus and of the human heart.

月面佛 The "moon-face Buddha", whose life is only a day and a night, in contrast with the sun-face Buddha whose life is 1,800 years.

月黶尊 One of the names of a 明王 Ming Wang, i.e. "moon-black" or "moon-spots", 降三世明王 the mahārāja who subdues all resisters, past, present, and future, represented with black face, three eyes, four protruding teeth, and fierce laugh.

月鼠 The moon rat, one of the two rats, black and white, that gnaw the cord of life, i.e. night and day.

木 Wood; a tree; kāṣṭha, a piece of wood, wood, timber. 丨上座 The elder with the tree, or the wooden elder; the elder's staff. 丨佛 A Buddha of wood, i.e. an image of wood. 丨佉褒折娜 Mukhaproñchana, or face-wiper, towel, handkerchief, one of the thirteen articles of a monk. 丨叉; 丨蛇; 波羅提丨叉 Mokṣa, pratimokṣa; mokṣa is deliverance, emancipation; prati, "towards," implies the getting rid of evils one by one; the 250 rules of the Vinaya for monks for their deliverance from the round of mortality. 丨丨提婆 Mokṣadeva. A title given by the Hīnayānists in India to Mahāyānadeva, i.e. 玄奘 Hsüan-tsang. 丨丨毱多 Mokṣagupta. A monk of Karashahr, protagonist of the Madhyamayāna school, "whose ignorance Hsüan-tsang publicly exposed." Eitel. 丨底 Mukti, 解脫 deliverance, liberation, emancipation; the same meaning is given to 目帝羅 mucira, which has more the sense of being free with (gifts), generosity. 丨律僧 A wooden pettifogging monk; a rigid formalist. 丨得羅 Mudrā, a seal; mystic signs with the hands. 丨星; 勿哩訶娑跛底 Bṛhaspati; "Lord of increase," the planet Jupiter. 丨曜 Jupiter, one of the 九曜 nine luminaries, q.v.; on the south of the diamond hall outside the Garbhadhātu maṇḍala. 丨槵子; 無患子 A tree whose wood can exorcise evil spirits, or whose seeds are used as rosary-beads. It is said to be the ariṣṭa 阿梨瑟迦紫, which means unharmed, secure; it is the name of the soap-berry and other shrubs. 丨欒子 Seeds used for rosary-beads. 丨瓜林; 苦行林 Papaya forest, i.e. Uruvilva, 優樓頻螺 the place near Gayā where Kāśyapa, Śākyamuni, and others practised their austerities before the latter's enlightenment; hence the former is styled Uruvilva Kāśyapa. 丨蘭色 Brownish colour made from bark, probably cinnamon. |頭 Blockhead, a stupid person, one who breaks the commandments. |香; 根香; 薰陸香; 多伽羅 Tagara. An incense-yielding tree, putchuk; *Vangueria spinosa* or *Tabernæ montana coronaria*; Eitel. |食 Living on wild fruits, nuts, etc. |魚 The wooden fish; there are two kinds, one round for use to keep time in chanting, the other long for calling to meals. The origin of the use of a fish is unknown: one version is that as a fish always has its eyes open day and night, so it is an example to monks to be watchful; there is no evidence of connection with the Christian ἰχθύς. |馬 Wooden horse, a symbol of emancipation.

欠 To owe; debt; deficient; to bend, bow, yawn, etc.; the Sanskrit sign ख said to imply 大空不可得 space, great and unattainable or immeasurable.

止 To stop, halt, cease; one of the seven definitions of 禪定 dhyāna described as 奢摩他 śamatha or 三摩地 samādhi; it is defined as 靜息動心 silencing, or putting to rest the active mind, or auto-hypnosis; also 心定止於一處 the mind centred, lit. the mind steadily fixed on one place, or in one position. It differs from 觀 which observes, examines, sifts evidence; 止 has to do with 拂妄 getting rid of distraction for moral ends; it is abstraction, rather than contemplation; see |觀. In practice there are three methods of attaining such abstraction: (*a*) by fixing the mind on the nose, navel, etc.; (*b*) by stopping every thought as it arises; (*c*) by dwelling on the thought that nothing exists of itself, but from a preceding cause. |息 To stop, cease; to stop breathing by self-control; to bring the mind to rest; used for 止觀. |持 Self-control in keeping the commandments or prohibitions relating to deeds and words, which are styled ||戒, ||門, |惡門. |犯; |持作犯 Stopping offences; ceasing to do evil, preventing others from doing wrong. |觀; 奢摩他毗婆 (or 鉢) 舍那 Śamatha-vipaśyanā, which Sanskrit words are intp. by 止觀; 定慧; 寂照; and 明靜; for their respective meanings see 止 and 觀. When the physical organism is at rest it is called 止 Chih, when the mind is seeing clearly it is called 觀 Kuan. The term and form of meditation is specially connected with its chief exponent, the founder of the T'ien-t'ai school, which school is styled 止觀宗 Chih-kuan Tsung, its chief object being concentration of the mind by special methods for the purpose of clear insight into truth, and to be rid of illusion. The T'ien-t'ai work gives ten fields of meditation, or concentration: (1) the five 陰, eighteen 界, and twelve 入; (2) passion and delusion; (3) sickness; (4) karma forms; (5) māra-deeds; (6) dhyāna; (7) (wrong) theories; (8) arrogance; (9) the two Vehicles; (10) bodhisattvahood. ||和尚 A name for the T'ang monk Tao-sui 道邃. ||宗 Another name for the T'ien-t'ai school. ||捨 The upekṣā, indifference to or abandonment of both 止 and 觀, i.e. to rise above both into the universal. ||玄文 Another name for the ||論. ||論; 摩訶止觀論 The foundation work on T'ien-t'ai's modified form of samādhi, rest of body for clearness of vision. It is one of the three foundation works of the T'ien-t'ai School; was delivered by 智顗 Chih-i to his disciple 章安 Chang-an who committed it to writing. The treatises on it are numerous.

比 To compare; than; to assemble, arrive; partisan; each; translit. *pi, bhi, vi*, v. also 毘, 毗. |丘; |呼; 苾芻; 煏芻 Bhikṣu, a religious mendicant, an almsman, one who has left home, been fully ordained, and depends on alms for a living. Some are styled 乞士 mendicant scholars, all are 釋種 Śākya-seed, offspring of Buddha. The Chinese characters are clearly used as a phonetic equivalent, but many attempts have been made to give meanings to the two words, e.g. 比 as 破 and 丘 as 煩惱, hence one who destroys the passions and delusions, also 怖能 able to overawe Māra and his minions; also 除饉 to get rid of dearth, moral and spiritual. Two kinds 內乞 and 外乞; both indicate self-control, the first by internal mental or spiritual methods, the second by externals such as strict diet. 苾芻 is a fragrant plant, emblem of the monastic life. ||尼; 苾芻尼; 尼姑 Bhikṣuṇī. A nun, or almswoman. The first woman to be ordained was the Buddha's aunt Mahāprajāpatī, who had nursed him. In the fourteenth year after his enlightenment the Buddha yielded to persuasion and admitted his aunt and women to his order of religious mendicants, but said that the admission of women would shorten the period of Buddhism by 500 years. The nun, however old, must acknowledge the superiority of every monk; must never scold him or tell his faults; must never accuse him, though he may accuse her; and must in all respects obey the rules as commanded by him. She accepts all the rules for the monks with additional rules for her own order. Such is the theory rather than the practice. The title by which Mahāprajāpatī was addressed was applied to nuns, i.e. āryā, or noble, 阿姨, though some consider the Chinese term entirely native. ||尼戒 The nun's "500 rules" and the eight commanding respect for monks, cf. 五百戒 and 八敬戒; also ||||本 and other works; the |||僧祇律波羅提木叉戒經 Bhikṣuṇī-sāṃghika-vinaya-prātimokṣa sūtra was tr. by

Fa-hsien and also by Buddhabhadra. | | 會 An authoritative assembly of at least four monks; idem 僧伽. | 吒迦俱舍 Piṭaka-kośa, i.e. 藏 a thesaurus, treasury, store. | 摩寺 A monastery five li west of Khotan where Lao Tzŭ is said to have converted the Huns to Buddhism. | 耆陀羨那; 毗戍陀僧訶 Viśuddhasiṁha; the second form is defined by Eitel as 淨師子 pure lion, a Mahāyānist, *circa* A.D. 640; the first is named in the 賢愚經 6, but they may be two different persons. | 智 idem 類智 q.v. | 羅娑落(山) Pīlusāragiri, 象堅山 Hill firm as an elephant, a mountain south-west of the capital of Kapiśā, "the tutelary deity of which was converted by Śākyamuni." Eitel. Aśoka built a stūpa on its summit. 婆 is found in error for 娑 and 洛 for 落. | 那(多); 毗那 Vinata, 不高 A low hill. | 量 Comparison and inference; it is defined as 比 comparison of the known, and 量 inference of the unknown. It is the second form in logic of the three kinds of example, 現, 比 and 聖教量, e.g. the inference of fire from smoke. | | 相違 Viruddha. A contradicting example or analogy in logic, e.g. the vase is permanent (or eternal), because of its nature; one of the nine, in the proposition, of the thirty-three possible fallacies in a syllogism.

毛 Hair; feathers; 毛病 flaw, ailment. | 孔 Hair-hole, pore, the pores. | 繩 A hair rope, i.e. tied up by the passions, as with an unbreakable hair rope. | 道; | 頭 A name for 凡夫 ordinary people, i.e. non-Buddhists, the unenlightened; the 毛 is said to be a translation of vāla, hair or down, which in turn is considered an error for bāla, ignorant, foolish, i.e. simple people who are easily beguiled. It is also said to be a form of Bāla-pṛthag-jana, v. 婆, which is intp. as born in ignorance; the ignorant and untutored in general. | | 生 The ignorant people. | | 凡夫 An ignorant, gullible person. | 頭 idem | 道; also, a barber-monk who shaves the fraternity. | 馱伽羅子 Mudgalaputra, idem Mahāmaudgalyāyana, v. 目連.

水 Water; liquid.

水上泡 A bubble on the water, emblem of all things being transient.

水中月 v. 水月.

水乳 Water and milk—an illustration of the intermingling of things; but their essential separateness is recognized in that the rāja-haṁsa (a kind of goose) is said to be able to drink up the milk leaving behind the water.

水冠 A monk's hat shaped like the character "water" in front.

水器 Water vessel; a filter used by the esoterics in baptismal and other rites.

水圓 Water-globule, a tabu term for the more dangerous term 火珠 fire-pearl or ruby, also altered to 珠圓 pearl ball; it is the ball on top of a pagoda.

水塵 An atom of dust wandering freely in water—one of the smallest of things.

水壇 The water, or round, altar in the Homa, or Fire ceremonial of the esoterics; also an altar in a house, which is cleansed with filtered water in times of peril.

水大 The element water, one of the four elements 四大 q.v.

水天 Varuṇa, 縛嚕拏; 婆樓那 οὐρανός, the heavens, or the sky, where are clouds and dragons; the 水神 water-deva, or dragon-king, who rules the clouds, rains, and water generally. One of the 大神 in the esoteric maṇḍalas; he rules the west; his consort is the | | 妃 represented on his left, and his chief retainer | | 眷屬 is placed on his right. | | 供 or 法 is the method of worshipping him for rain. | | 德佛 The 743rd Buddha of the present universe.

水定 The water dhyāna, in which one becomes identified with water, for during the period of trance one may become water; stories are told of devotees who, having turned to water, on awaking found stones in their bodies which had been thrown into their liquid bodies, and which were only removed during a succeeding similar trance.

水曜 The planet Mercury, one of the nine luminaries; it is shown south of the west door of the diamond court in the Garbhadhātu.

水月 Udakacandra; jalacandra; the moon reflected in the water, i.e. all is illusory and unreal. | | 觀音 Kuan-yin gazing at the moon in the water, i.e. the unreality of all phenomena.

水梭花 Water shuttle flowers, i.e. fish.

水沫泡焰 Spume, bubbles, and flame, e.g. that all is unreal and transient.

水波 Waves of water; the wave and the water are two yet one—an illustration of the identity of differences.

水淨 Cleansed by water; edibles recovered from flowing water are "clean" food to a monk.

水災 The calamity of water, or flood; one of the three final world catastrophes of fire, wind, and water, v. 三災.

水滿 Jalāmbara (third son of 流水 Jalavāhana) reborn as Śākyamuni's son Rāhula.

水燈 The water-lantern festival in the seventh month.

水玉 Sphaṭika, 塞頗胝迦; 娑致迦 water crystal, rock crystal.

水田衣 A monk's robe, because its patches resemble rice-fields; also 稻田衣.

水界 The realm of water, one of the 四大 four elements.

水精 Sphaṭika, crystal, idem 水玉.

水羅 A gauze filter.

水老鶴 A bird, very rarely seen, possibly a snow-goose; also 水白鶴 (or 鷺); 水涸.

水葬 Water-burial, casting a corpse into the water, one of the four forms of burial.

水藏 Water-store, or treasury; second son of Jalavāhana, born as 瞿波 Gopā, see 水滿.

水囊 A water-bag, or filter.

水觀 also 水相觀; 水想 similar to 水定 q.v.

水輪 The third of the four "wheels" on which the earth rests—space, wind (or air), water, and metal. | | 三昧 The samādhi of the above water "wheel", one of the 五輪三昧; water is fertilizing and soft, in like manner the effect of this samādhi is the fertilizing of good roots, and the softening or reduction of ambition and pride.

水陸會 (or 齋) The festival of water and land, attributed to Wu Ti of the Liang dynasty consequent on a dream; it began with placing food in the water for water sprites, and on land for 鬼 ghosts; see 釋門正統 4.

水頭 The waterman in a monastery.

水風火災 The three final catastrophes, see 三災.

火 Fire, flame. Śikhin 尸棄; 式棄, which means fire in the sense of flame, is the name of the 999th Buddha of the kalpa preceding this.

火一切處 Universal conflagration—one of the ten universals, and one of the meditations on the final destruction of all things by fire.

火伴 The fire-tender in a monastic kitchen.

火光 Fire-light, flame. | | 定 The flame dhyāna by which the body is self-immolated. | | 三昧 The flame samādhi, also styled the fourth dhyāna. | | 尊 idem 火天.

火印 The fire sign, for which a triangle pointing upwards is used; a triangular arrangement of fingers of the right hand with the left.

火坑 The fiery pit (of the five desires 五欲); also that of the three ill destinies—the hells, animals, hungry ghosts.

火壇 Fire altar, connected with homa or fire worship; also 爐壇.

火大 The element fire, one of the 四 | four elements.

火天 The fire devas shown as the 12th group in the diamond court of the Garbhadhātu; v. 火神.

火夜 Hāva; to call, invoke; also 訶婆.

火宅 The parable of the burning house; one of the "seven parables" in the Lotus Sūtra 譬喩品, that of the burning house from which the owner tempts his heedless children by the device of the three kinds of carts—goat, deer, and bullock, especially a white-bullock cart, i.e. Mahāyāna. 丨丨僧 Monks in a burning house, i.e. married monks.

火定 The fire dhyāna, v. 火生.

火客 The monk who attends to the fire; also 火伴; 火佃.

火尊 i.e. 火神 q.v.

火帳 The kitchen account of the rice cooked and persons served.

火德星君 The ruler over the fire-star, Mars, whose tablet hangs in the south side of a temple and whose days of worship, to prevent conflagrations, are the fourth and eighteenth of each moon; he is identified with the ancient emperor 炎帝 Yen Ti.

火星 Aṅgāraka, 鴦哦囉迦 the planet Mars.

火曜 Mars, one of the nine luminaries, shown south of the Diamond hall in the Garbhadhātu.

火㮇 Fire-tongs, made of wood, themselves burnt up before all brushwood is used up, a simile of a bodhisattva who so far forgot his vow to save all the living as to enter nirvāṇa before completing his work.

火法 The homa or fire service of the esoterics.

火浣布袈裟 An asbestos cassock; also a non-inflammable robe said to be made of the hair of the 火鼠 fire-rat.

火淨 Purified, food made "clean" by fire, or cooking.

火湯 The hell of liquid fire.

火災 The conflagration catastrophe, for world destruction, v. 三災.

火焚地獄 The scorching hell, where sinners are burnt up.

火燄三昧 A samādhi entered into by the Buddha, in which he emitted flames to overcome a poisonous dragon. Also 火光 (or 火生) 三昧 q.v.

火爐; 火鑪 The homa or fire altar of the esoterics.

火版 The "fire-board", or wooden plaque, hung in the kitchen, the striking of which warns the monks that the meal is ready.

火狗 The fiery dogs—which vomit fire on sinners in hell.

火珠 Fire-pearl, or ruby; the ball on top of a pagoda, see 水圓.

火生三昧 A flame-emitting samādhi, the power to emit flames from the body for auto-holocaust, or other purposes. It is especially associated with 不動尊 q.v. and Shingon practice of the yoga which unites the devotee to him and his powers.

火界 The realm of fire, one of the realms of the four elements 四大, i.e. earth, water, fire, and wind. Cf. 丨院. 丨丨咒 A dhāraṇī of 不動尊 q.v. 丨丨定 Agni-dhātu-samādhi; the meditation on the final destruction of the world by fire.

火神 The gods of fire, stated as numbering forty-four in the Vedic pantheon, with Mahābrahmā as the first; of these the Vairocana sūtra takes twelve, i.e. 大因陀羅; 行滿; 摩嚕多; 盧醯多; 沒㗚拏; 忿怒; 闍吒羅; 吃灑耶; 意生; 羯攞微; (11th unknown); 謨賀那. Cf. 丨尊; 丨天.

火祠法 The directions for the fire sacrifices in the Atharva-veda, the fourth Veda; the esoteric sect has also its 火法 for magical purposes.

火種居士 Brahmans, servers of the sacred fire.

火羅 Horā, hour, hours, time; astrologically a horoscope; said to be the country where 一行 I-hsing studied astronomy.

火聚 Accumulated fires (of hell); accumulating one's own hell-fires; the body as a heap of fire, i.e. to be feared; the fires of angry passions. | | 仙 This genius and his wife are shown above Vaiśramaṇa in the Garbhadhātu. | | 佛頂; 光聚佛頂; 放光 or 放光佛頂 One of the five 佛頂, i.e. one of the incarnations of Śākyamuni, whose Indian name is given as 帝聚羅斫羯羅縛哩底 Tejorāśi-cakravarttī, called by Shingon 神通金剛; this incarnation is placed fourth on Śākyamuni's left in the Garbhadhātu.

火舍 A kind of censer, made in two superimposed circles with a cover.

火葬 Jhāpita, 荼毘; 闍維 cremation, the relics 舍利 being buried.

火蛇 Fire-vomiting serpents in the hells.

火血刀 The hells, animals, and hungry ghosts, i.e. the fiery, bloody, and knife-sharp destinies, the 三惡道.

火車 The fiery chariot (belonging to the hells); there is also the 火車地獄 hell of the fire-chariot, and the fire-pit with its fiery wheels; the sufferer first freezes, then is tempted into the chariot which bursts into flames and he perishes in the fire pit, a process each sufferer repeats daily 90 kotis of times.

火輪 Whirling fire, e.g. fire whirled in a circle, the whole circle seeming to be on fire, emblem of illusion; a fire wheel. | | 印 A sign made by putting the doubled fists together and opening the index fingers to form the fire-sign, a triangle.

火塗 (or 道) The fiery way, i.e. the destiny of the hot hells, one of the three evil destinies.

火辨 Citrabhānu, 質呾羅婆拏 described as one of the ten great writers of the Indian 法相宗 Dharmalakṣaṇa school, a contemporary and colleague of Vasubandhu; but the description is doubtful.

火鈴 Fire-bell—in warning to be careful of fire.

火院 The "fire-court", a kind of contemplation, in which the devotee sees himself encircled by fire after circumambulating three times to the right while making the fire-sign. Also 火界; 金剛炎.

火頂山 A peak near T'ien-t'ai, where the founder of that school overcame Māra.

火頭 A monastery cook. | | 金剛 One of the Ming Wang 明王 v. 烏芻瑟摩.

火食 Burnt offerings, as in the homa worship.

爪 Claws, talons; servants. | (上) 土 The quantity of earth one can put on a toe-nail, i.e. in proportion to the whole earth in the world, such is the rareness of being reborn as a human being; or, according to the Nirvāṇa Sūtra 33, of attaining nirvāṇa. | 塔 A stūpa, or reliquary, for preserving and honouring the nails and hair of the Buddha, said to be the first Buddhist stūpa raised. | 淨 Nail-"cleaned", i.e. fruit, etc., that can be peeled with the nails, one of the five kinds of "clean" food. | 犢 The long-nailed ascetic Brahmacārī (of the) Vātsīputrīyāḥ; it is said that his nails were a treatise and his hair a discourse 爪章髮論.

父 Pitṛ, 比多 Father. 父母 Pitṛ mātṛ, father and mother, parents; 無明 ignorance is referred to as father, and 貪愛 desire, or concupiscence, as mother, the two—ignorance and concupiscence—being the parents of all delusion and karma. Samādhi is also referred to as father, and prajñā (wisdom) as mother, the parents of all knowledge and virtue. In the vast interchanges of rebirth all have been or are my parents, therefore all males are my father and all females my mother: 一切男女我父母 see 心地觀經 2. | 城 The paternal or native city, especially Śākyamuni's, Kapilavastu.

片 A slice, slip, card; brief, few. | 禪 A brief samādhi, or meditation.

牙 Tooth, teeth; toothed; a broker. | 菩薩 The bodhisattva fiercely showing his teeth in defence of the Buddha, also styled 金剛藥叉; he is east of the Buddha in the Vajradhātu.

牛 Go, gaus; ox, bull, bullock, etc. A term applied to the Buddha Gautama as in 牛王 king of bulls, possibly because of the derivation of his name; the phrase 騎牛來 (or 覓) 牛 to ride an ox, to seek an ox, means to use the Buddha to find the Buddha.

牛戒 To live as a cow, eating grass with bent head, etc.—as certain Indian heretics are said to have done, in the belief that a cow's next reincarnation would be in the heavens.

牛毛塵 Go-rajas, the amount of dust that can rest on the top of a cow's hair, i.e. seven times that on a sheep's.

牛狗外道 Go-vratika, or kukkura-vratika. Heretics who lived as oxen or dogs.

牛王 The king of bulls, i.e. a Buddha, or bodhisattva; it is applied to Gautama Buddha, possibly derived from his name. 丨王尊者; 丨呞; 丨相; 丨跡 Gavāṁpati, v. 憍梵波提 and 牛跡比丘.

牛皮 Ox hide—mortal happiness injures the wisdom-life of gods and men, just as ox hide shrinks and crushes a man who is wrapped in it and placed under the hot sun.

牛糞 Gomaya, cow-dung, considered in India as clean and cleansing; used by the esoterics for "cleansing" altars. 丨丨種 The first Gotama ancestor of Śākyamuni, who is reputed to have sprung from cow-dung in the Sugar-cane garden, probably a mere tradition that the family sprang from herdsmen.

牛羊(心)眼 Only the eyes (i.e. vision, or insight) of oxen and sheep.

牛角 Ox-horns, a synonym for things that are even, or on a level. 丨丨一觸 The ox that by merely touching a monk's robe with its horn was transformed into a deva. 丨丨娑羅林 Ox-horns śāla grove, said to be a couple of śāla or teak trees shaped like ox-horns, which grew near Kuśinagara, under which the Buddha preached the Nirvāṇa sūtra. He is reported to have entered nirvāṇa in a grove of eight śāla trees standing in pairs. 丨丨山 v. 牛頭山.

牛貨洲 Godānīya, 瞿伽 (or 耶, or 陀) 尼; 俱助尼; 遇嚩柅; Aparagodāna, 阿鉢唎瞿陀尼, the western of the four continents into which every world is divided, where oxen are the principal product and medium of exchange.

牛跡 Ox-tracks, i.e. the teaching of a Buddha the 牛王 royal bull. 丨丨比丘 the bhikṣu Gavāṁpati, 憍梵波提 q.v., also styled 牛王 (尊者), said to have been a disciple of Śākyamuni; also styled 牛呞 ruminating like a cow, and 牛相 cow-faced; so born because of his previous herdsman's misdeeds.

牛車 Bullock cart, the 白牛車 white-bullock cart as the one universal vehicle of salvation, v. 火宅.

牛頭 The ox-head lictors in the hells. 丨丨(or 角) 山 Gośṛṅga 瞿室餕伽 a mountain 13 li from Khotan. One of the same name exists in Kiang-ning in Kiangsu, which gave its name to a school, the followers of 法融 Fa-jung, called 丨丨山法 Niu-t'ou shan fa, or 丨丨禪 (or 宗); its fundamental teaching was the unreality of all things, that all is dream, or illusion. 丨丨大王 The guardian deity of the Jetavana monastery, and an incarnation of 藥師 q.v. 丨丨栴檀; 牛檀栴檀; 丨丨香 Gośīrsa-candana, ox-head sandal-wood, also styled 赤栴檀 red sandal-wood; said to come from the Ox-head mountains, and if rubbed on the body to make one impervious to fire, also generally protective against fire, curative of wounds and generally medicinal. "The first image of Śākyamuni was made of this wood." Eitel. 西域記 10.

牛驢二乳 The milk of cow and ass, the one turns to "curd", the other to "dung", i.e. alike in appearance, but fundamentally different, as is the case with the Buddha's teaching and that of outsiders.

牛黃(or 王)加持 Cow-bezoar aid, a charm used for childless women to obtain children—the four words should be written with cow bezoar on birch-bark and carried on the person.

王 Rājā, king, prince, royal; to rule. 丨三昧; 三昧王三昧; 三昧王 The king of samādhis, the highest degree of samādhi, the 首楞嚴定 q.v. The first is also applied to invoking Buddha, or sitting in meditation or trance. 丨仙 A royal ṛṣi, i.e. a sovereign who retires from the world and attains to the five transcendent powers. 丨古 Wang Ku, name of a President of the Board of Rites during the Sung dynasty, who was also a devout Buddhist, end of eleventh century. 丨日 idem 八王日. 丨日休 Wang Jih-hsiu, a 進士 doctor who became a devout and learned follower of Amida and Kuan-yin; he was of 龍舒 Lung-shu, was also known as 虛中 Hsü-chung, and compiled the 大阿彌陀經 1160–2. 丨曷邏闍伐彈那 Rājyavardhana, tr. by 王增 Wang Tsêng. A brother of Harshavardhana, king of Kanyākubja. 丨法 Royal law, the law by which a king should rule his country. 丨丨經 A sūtra on royal law, tr. by I-ching; there are other treatises on it. 丨膳 A royal feast referred to in the Lotus sūtra, where the hungry people feared to accept the King's feast till he came himself and called them; i.e. the feast of Buddhahood and the Buddha's call. | 舍 (城) Rājagṛha. King Bimbisāra is said to have removed his capital here from Kuśāgrapura, v. 矩 and 吉, a little further eastward, because of fire and other calamities. Rājagṛha was surrounded by five hills, of which Gṛdhrakūṭa (Vulture Peak) became the most famous. It was the royal city from the time of Bimbisāra "until the time of Aśoka". Its ruins are still extant at the village of Rājgir, some sixteen miles S.S.W. of Bihār; they "form an object of pilgrimages for the Jains". Eitel. The first synod is said to have assembled here.

5. FIVE STROKES

丙 Fire, heat, south; the third of the ten stems, hence | 丁 means a junior, or so-and-so. | | 童子 the boy who attends to the lamps (which are associated with "fire").

且 Moreover, yet, meanwhile. | 喜 So be it, granted, a qualified assent.

丘 A mound, a plot; personal name of Confucius. | 井 A (dry) well on a hill top, symbolical of old age. | 慈; 屈支; 龜茲 q.v. Kuche, Karashahr.

世 Yuga. An age, 1,000th part of a kalpa. Loka, the world. 世 originally meant a human generation, a period of thirty years; it is used in Buddhism both for Yuga, a period of time ever flowing, and Loka, the world, worldly, earthly. The world is that which is to be destroyed; it is sunk in the round of mortality, or transmigration; and conceals, or is a veil over reality.

世世生生 Transmigration after transmigration in the six states of mortal existence.

世主(天) The Lord of the world, Brahmā; Maheśvara; also the four mahārājas 四天王; v. 梵天; 大自在天.

世代 A generation, a lifetime; the world.

世依 He on whom the world relies—Buddha.

世俗 Laukika; common or ordinary things, custom, experiences, common or worldly ways (or views).

世典 Non-Buddhist classical works.

世友 Vasumitra; v. 筏蘇蜜呾羅.

世善 The pleasures of the world, v. | 福.

世尊 Lokajyeṣṭha, world's most venerable, or Lokanātha, lord of worlds. 盧迦委斯諦; 路迦那他 World-honoured, an epithet of every Buddha. Also a tr. of Bhagavat, v. 婆.

世(俗)智 Ordinary or worldly knowledge or wisdom.

世法 Common or ordinary dharmas, i.e. truths, laws, things, etc.

世界 Loka 世間; the finite world, the world, a world, which is of two kinds: (1) 衆生 | | that of the living, who are receiving their 正報 correct recompense or karma; (2) 器 | | that of the material, or that on which karma depends for expression. By the living is meant 有情 the sentient. | | 主 The lord, or ruler over a world or dhyāna heaven, one for each of the four dhyāna heavens. | | 悉檀 One of the four siddhāntas: the Buddha's line of reasoning in earthly or common terms to draw men to the higher truth.

世相 World-state, or condition; appearances, phenomena.

世眼 idem 世間眼.

世福 Earthly happiness, arising from the ordinary good living of those unenlightened by Buddhism, one of the 三福; also, the blessings of this world.

世第一法 The highest of the 四加行位 q.v.

世羅 Śaila 勢羅; 施羅; a crag, a mountain.

世耶那薩喃 Śayanāsana, lying and sitting, couch and seat.

世自在王 Lokeśvararāja, 世饒王 a

Buddha under whom Amitābha, in a previous existence, entered into the ascetic life and made his forty-eight vows.

世英 World hero, i.e. a Buddha; also 世雄.

世親 Vasubandhu, idem 天親 q.v.

世論 Worldly discussions; ordinary unenlightened ways of description or definition; also styled 惡論 evil discussions, especially when applied to the hedonistic Lokāyatika teachings, v. 路迦.

世諦 Ordinary or worldly truth, opposite of 眞諦 truth in reality; also 俗諦; 世俗諦; 覆俗諦. ||不生滅 Ordinary worldly postulates that things are permanent, as contrasted with the doctrine of impermanence advocated by Hīnayāna; both positions are controverted by T'ien-t'ai, which holds that the phenomenal world is neither becoming nor passing, but is an aspect of eternal reality.

世路 The ways, or procedure, of the world; the phenomenal.

世間 The world; in the world; the finite impermanent world, idem 世界. ||乘 The Vehicle, or teaching for the attainment of good fruit in the present life, in contrast with 出世間乘 that for attainment in lives outside this world. ||天 World-devas, i.e. earthly kings. ||天院 The third court in the Garbhadhātu. ||智 Worldly knowledge, i.e. that of ordinary men and those unenlightened by Buddhism. ||檀 Worldly dāna, or giving, i.e. with thoughts of possession, meum, tuum, and the thing given, v. 三礙. ||法 The world-law, or law of this world, especially of birth-and-death; in this respect it is associated with the first two of the four dogmas, i.e. 苦 suffering, and 集 its accumulated consequences in karma. ||相常住 World-forms, systems, or states are eternal (as existing in the Absolute, the 眞如). ||相違 Lokaviruddha; one of the thirty-three logical errors, to set up a premise contrary to human experience. ||眼 The Eye of the world, the eye that sees for all men, i.e. the Buddha, who is also the one that opens the eyes of men. Worldly, or ordinary eyes. Also |眼. ||經 A sūtra discussing causality in regard to the first three of the Four Dogmas 苦集 and 滅 in the 阿含經 34. ||解 Lokavid, 路迦憊 tr. as 知世間 Knower of the world, one of the ten titles of a Buddha. ||難信捷徑 The speedy and straight way to Buddhahood (for all) which the world finds it hard to believe.

世雄兩足尊 The World-hero and two-legged (or human) honoured one, Buddha, or the honoured among human bipeds.

主 Chief, lord, master; to control. |事 Vihāra-svāmin; controller, director, the four heads of affairs in a monastery 監寺, 維那, 典坐, and 直歲. |伴 Chief and attendant, principal and secondary. |宰 Lord, master; to dominate, control; the lord within, the soul; the lord of the universe, God. |方神 The spirits controlling the eight directions. |首 The 監寺 or abbot of a monastery.

乏 Lacking; |道 lacking in the right way, shortcoming, poor,—an expression of humility.

代 Instead of, in place of, acting for, for; e.g. |香 to offer incense in place of another; a generation, v. 世|.

付 To deliver, hand over to, hand down. |屬; 付囑 To deliver, entrust to. |法藏(因緣傳); |法藏傳 or 經. The work explaining the handing down of Śākyamuni's teaching by Mahākāśyapa and the elders, twenty-four in number; tr. in the Yüan dynasty in six chüan; cf. 釋門正統 4.

他 Another, other, the other, his, her, it, etc. |力 Another's strength, especially that of a Buddha, or bodhisattva, obtained through faith in Mahāyāna salvation. ||宗 Those who trust to salvation by faith, contrasted with 自力宗 those who seek salvation by works, or by their own strength. ||念佛 Trusting to and calling on the Buddha, especially Amitābha.

他勝罪 Overcome by specific sin; i.e. any of the four pārājikas, or sins of excommunication. |化(自在)天 Paranirmita-vaśavartin, 婆羅尼蜜婆舍跋提天; 婆那和提; 波舍跋提 the sixth of the six heavens of desire, or passion-heavens, the last of the six devalokas, the abode of Maheśvara (i.e. Śiva), and of Māra. |受用土 That part of a Buddhakṣetra, or reward land of a Buddha, in which all beings receive and obey his truth; cf. 自受用土. |寶 The valuables of another person; other valuables. |己 Another and oneself; both he and I. |心智; |心通; |心智通; 知|心通 Paracittajñāna. Intuitive knowledge of the minds of all other beings. The eighth of the 十智, and the fourth or third of the 六神通. The eighth of Amitābha's forty-eight vows that men and devas in his paradise should all have the joy of this power. |毘梨輿部; |(or 梯)毘利; |鞞羅部; 體

毘履 (or 裏) Sthavirāḥ; 上坐; 老宿 One of the four branches of the Vaibhāṣika School, so called after the Vaibhāṣika śāstra, v. 毘; the school was reputed as later represented by the Mahāvihāra-vāsins, Jetavanīyās, Abhayagirivāsins, in Ceylon; but the history of the Buddhist sects is uncertain, cf. Tāranāth, *Hist. Buddhism*, tr. pp. 270–. |生; |世 Another life, or world, either previous to or after this. |那; 吒那 Sthāna, 處 a place, state, condition.

仙; 僊 Ṛṣi, 哩始 an immortal; 仙人; 人仙 the genii, of whom there is a famous group of eight 八仙; an ascetic, a man of the hills, a hermit; the Buddha. The 楞嚴經 gives ten kinds of immortals, walkers on the earth, fliers, wanderers at will, into space, into the deva heavens, transforming themselves into any form, etc. The names of ten ṛṣis, who preceded Śākyamuni, the first being 闍提首那? Jātisena; there is also a list of sixty-eight 大仙 given in the 大孔雀咒王經下. A classification of five is 天| deva genii, 神| spirit genii, 人| human genii, 地| earth, or cavern genii, and 鬼| ghost genii. |人鹿野苑; |人鹿園, |苑 The Mṛgadāva, a deer park N.E. of Vārāṇaśī, "a favourite resort of Śākyamuni. The modern Sārnath (Sāraṅganātha) near Benares." Eitel. |城 The Ṛṣi's city, i.e. the Buddha's native city, Kapilavastu. |經 Taoist treatises on alchemy and immortality. |音 The voice of Buddha. |鹿王 The royal-stag Genius, i.e. Buddha.

以 By means of, by using, by; whereby, in order to. |心傳心 Direct transmission from mind to mind, as contrasted with the written word; the intuitive principle of the Ch'an (Zen), or intuitive school.

佗 Strong, valiant; suddenly. |那; 繕摩 Jāuman, 生 Jāti, birth, production; rebirth as man, animal, etc.; life, position assigned by birth; race, being; the four methods of birth are egg, womb, water, and transformation.

兄 Elder brother. |弟 Elder and younger brothers; brother, brethren, i.e. members of the fraternity.

囘 Return, turn back, a turn. |忌 The days on which the day of death is remembered. |駕窣塔婆 Nivartana-stūpa, erected on the spot where Śākyamuni sent back his horse after quitting home.

冬 Hima; hemanta; winter. |安居 The winter retreat, 16th of 10th moon to 15th of 1st. |夜 The night before the |至 winter solstice. |朝 The morning of that day. |齋 The observances of that day.

出 To go out, come forth, put forth; exit; beyond.

出世 (1) Appearance in the world, e.g. the Buddha's appearing. (2) To leave the world; a monk or nun. (3) Beyond, or outside this world, not of this world; of nirvāṇa character. ||大事 The great work of the Buddha's appearing, or for which he appeared. ||心 The nirvāṇa, or other-world mind. ||本懷 The aim cherished by the Buddha in appearing in the world. ||果 The fruit of leaving the world; the result in another world; nirvāṇa. ||業 The work or position of one who has quitted the world, that of a monk. ||服 The garment of one who has left the world. ||舍 An abode away from the world, a monastery, hermitage. ||部; ||(間)說 (or 語言) 部; Lokottaravādinaḥ, 盧俱多婆拖部 an offshoot of the Māhāsaṅghikāḥ division of the eighteen Hīnayāna schools; the tenets of the school are unknown, but the name, as implied by the Chinese translation, suggests if not the idea of Ādi-Buddha, yet that of supra-mundane nature. ||間 To go out of the world; the world (or life) beyond this; the supra-mundane; the spiritual world. ||間道, or 法. The way of leaving the world, i.e. of enlightenment, idem 菩提道; the spiritual law.

出佛身血 To shed a Buddha's blood, one of the five grave sins.

出假行 A bodhisattva's entry into time and space, or the phenomenal 假, for the sake of saving others.

出出世間 Surpassing the supra-mundane; the stage of Bodhisattvahood above the eighth 地 or degree.

出塵 To leave the dusty world of passion and delusion.

出定 To come out of the state of dhyāna; to enter into it is 入定.

出家 Pravraj; to leave home and become a monk or nun. || 人 One who has left home and become a monk or nun. Two kinds are named: (1) 身|| one who physically leaves home, and

(2) 心 | | one who does so in spirit and conduct. A further division of four is : (1) one who physically leaves home, but in spirit remains with wife and family ; (2) one who physically remains at home but whose spirit goes forth ; (3) one who leaves home, body and spirit ; and (4) one who, body and mind, refuses to leave home.

出息 To breathe out. | | 不待入 Breathing-out not waiting for breathing-in, breathless.

出慧 The wisdom of leaving mortality, or re-incarnations ; the wisdom of leaving the world.

出曜經 Avadānas, 阿波陀那 stories of memorable deeds. The sixth of the twelve sections of the canon, consisting of 譬喩 parables and comparisons.

出期 The going forth period, i.e. from the sufferings of mortality ; the appointed time of going forth ; the period of setting forth.

出現 To manifest, reveal, be manifested, appear, e.g. as does a Buddha's temporary body, or nirmāṇakāya. Name of Udāyi 優陀夷 a disciple of Buddha to be reborn as Samantaprabhāsa ; also of a son of Ajātaśatru.

出生 To be born ; to produce ; monastic food, superior as bestowed in alms, called | 飯 and 生飯.

出纏眞如 The unfettered, or free bhūtatathatā, as contrasted with the 在纏眞如.

出聖 The surpassing sacred truth, or the sacred immortal truth.

出道 To leave the world and enter the nirvāṇa way.

出陣 To stand out from the class or rank (e.g. to ask a question).

出隊 Outstanding, of outstanding ability, egregious, standing forth. | | 迦提 The public announcement of the distribution of the kaṭhina garment (v. 功德衣) in the last month of the rainy season, i.e. of the coming forth of the monks from their retreat.

出離 To leave, come out from. | | 煩惱 to leave the passions and delusions of life, an intp. of nirvāṇa.

出體 External ; the components of a thing or matter ; to put forth a body.

加 Add, added ; increase ; put on. | 力 Added strength or power (by the Buddhas or bodhisattvas) ; aid. | 尸 ; | 私 ; 迦尸 Kāśa, visibility, splendour ; a species of grass, *Saccharum spontaneum.* M. W. | 持 ; 地瑟娓曩 Adhiṣṭhāna, to depend upon, a base, rule. It is defined as dependence on the Buddha, who 加 confers his strength on all (who seek it), and 持 upholds them ; hence it implies prayer, because of obtaining the Buddha's power and transferring it to others ; in general it is to aid, support. | | 供物 To repeat tantras over offerings, in order to prevent demons from taking them or making them unclean. | | 成佛 By the aid of Buddha to enter Buddhahood. | | 杖 A wand (made of peach wood) laid on in driving out demons, or in healing disease, the painful place being beaten. Tantras are repeated while the wand is used on the patient. | | 身 The body which the Buddha depends upon for his manifestation, i.e. the nirmāṇakāya. | 沙 ; 迦沙 ; 袈裟 Kaṣāya, a colour composed of red and yellow, i.e. brown, described as a mixed colour, but | | 野 is defined as 赤 red. | 蘭伽 Kalaviṅka, v. 迦. | 行 Prayoga. Added progress, intensified effort, earnest endeavour. | | 位 The second of the four stages of the 唯識宗 known also as 四 | |. | | 善 ; 修得善 ; 方便善 Goodness acquired by earnest effort, or "works", as differentiated from 生得善 natural goodness. | 被 ; | 祐 ; | 備 ; | 護 Divine or Buddha aid or power bestowed on the living, for their protection or perfection.

功 Merit, meritorious ; achievement, hence | 力 achieving strength, earnest effort (after the good). | 嘉葛剌思 Kun-dgaḥ-grags, also named 膽巴 Danupa, a famous Tibetan monk of the thirteenth century, who had influence at the Mongol court under Kublai Khan and after, d. 1303. | 巧論 ; 功 (or 巧) 明論 Śilpasthāna-vidyā-śāstra ; "the śāstra of arts and sciences," i.e. of 術 and 數, one of the 五明 five works on knowledge ; it treats of "arts, mechanics, dual philosophy, and calendaric calculations". Eitel. | 德 Virtue achieved ; achievement ; power to do meritorious works ; merit ; meritorious virtue ; the reward of virtue ; a name for 弗若多羅 Puṇyatara, one of the twenty-four 天尊 deva āryas, worshipped in China. | | 叢林 The grove of merit and virtue, i.e. a Buddhist hall, or monastery ; also the scriptures. | | 使 Envoy to the virtuous, or officer supervising virtue, controller of monks and nuns appointed by the T'ang Court. | | 天 (女) idem 吉祥天 (女) Lakṣmī, goddess of fortune. | | 水 (or 池) The water or eight lakes of meritorious deeds, or virtue, in Paradise. | | 田 The field of merit and virtue, i.e. the Triratna 三寶, to be cultivated by the faithful; it is one of the three fields for cultivating welfare 三福田. | | 聚 The assembly of all merit and virtue, i.e. the Buddha; also a stūpa as symbol of him. | | 衣 Kaṭhina, 迦絺那; 羯絺那 the garment of merits, given to monks after their summer retreat of ninety days; it symbolized five merits to which they had attained. | | 遊 Meritorious exercise, i.e. walking about intoning after duty. | 用 Action, functioning, in practice and achievement. | 能 Achieving power; ability, power.

北 Uttara, North. | 山住部; 鬱多世羅部 Uttaraśailāḥ. One of the sects organized in the third century after the Nirvāṇa, whose seat is described as north of 制多山 q.v. | 宗 The northern school of the Ch'an (Zen) sect; from Bodhidharma 達磨 to the fifth patriarch 弘忍 Hung-jên the school was undivided; from 慧能 Hui-nêng began the division of the southern school, 神秀 Shên-hsiu maintaining the northern; it was the southern school which prevailed. | 度 The pupil's position in paying respect to his master, i.e. facing the north where the master sits. | 斗 (七星) Ursa major, the Northern Bushel with its seven stars. | | 堂 The hall for its worship. | 方七曜衆 The seven northern constellations from 胃 wei to 虛 hsü are represented in the Garbhadhātu by their seven devas. Cf. 北辰. | | 佛教 Northern Buddhism, i.e. Mahāyāna, in contrast with Southern Buddhism, Hīnayāna. | 本涅槃經 The northern version of the Nirvāṇa sūtra, in forty chüan. | 枕 The northern pillow, i.e. Śākyamuni, when dying, pillowed his head to the north, pointing the way for the extension of his doctrine. | 洲; | 拘 (or 俱) 盧洲 Uttarakuru, the northern of the four continents surrounding Sumeru; v. 鬱. | 羅 Valabhī. Northern Lāṭa. "An ancient kingdom and city on the Eastern coast of Gujerat." Eitel. | 臺 The northern T'ai, i.e. Wu-t'ai-shan in Shansi, the northernmost of the Four famous Buddhist Mountains. | 藏 The northern collection or edition of 1,621 works first published in Peking by order of Ch'êng Tsu (1403–1424), together with forty-one additional works, published by 密藏 Mi-tsang after thirty years' labour beginning A.D. 1586. Later this edition was published in Japan 1678–1681 by 鐵眼 Tetsugen. | 行 Uttarāyaṇa. The northern ascension of the sun between the winter and summer solstices. | 辰菩薩 The Bodhisattva 妙見 Miao Chien of Ursa Major.

半 Half. Used as translit. for Pan, pun. | 只 (or 支) 迦; 般止柯; 般闍迦; 散支 (迦); 德叉迦 Pāñcika, the third of the eight great yakṣas, husband of Hāritī 鬼子母. | 嗟䇲; | 䇲嗟 Punaca or Pañcasattra or Pañcarāṣṭra, an ancient province and city of Kashmir (now Punch). | 天婆羅門 Half-deva brahmans, a term for hungry ghosts. | 娜 (娑); | 榎娑; 般捺娑; 波那娑 Paṇasa, bread-fruit; 娑 is incorrectly used for 娑. | 字 "Half a character"; a letter of the alphabet. Hīnayāna is likened to a | |, Mahāyāna to a 滿字 complete word; hence 半字教 is Hīnayāna. | 拏囉嚩悉寧; 伴陀羅縛子尼 Pāṇḍara-vāsinī; white-clothed, i.e. the white-clothed Kuan-yin; also tr. as white abode. | 擇迦 Paṇḍaka, intp. as 變 to change from time to time, a general term for eunuchs; see 般荼迦. | 滿教 The half and the complete doctrines, i.e. Hīnayāna and Mahāyāna. | 者珂 (or 佉) 但尼; | 者佉闍尼 Pañcakhādanīya, the five "chewing" foods, not regular foods, i.e. roots, stems, leaves, flowers, fruits; or stems, leaves, flowers, fruits, and their triturations. | 者蒲膳 (or 闍) 尼 Pañcabhojanīya. The five regular articles of food: the 繙譯名義 Fan-i-ming-i gives wheat, rice, parched rice (or cakes), fish, and flesh. Another account is rice, boiled wheat or pulse, parched grain, flesh, cakes. | 託 (or 他) 迦; 槃陀 (迦); 槃特 Panthaka, born on the road; a road; two brothers—one born by a main road, the other by a path—who both became arhats. | 超 A deva who by devotion advances by leaps, escaping from one to thirteen of the sixteen heavens of form. | 跏 (趺) 坐 A bodhisattva's form of sitting, different from the completely cross-legged form of a Buddha. | 遮羅 Pañjara, a basket, or cage. | 齋 Half a day's fast, i.e. fasting all day but eating at night.

占 To divine, prognosticate. | 察 A method of divination in the esoteric school by means of the Sanskrit letter "a". | 戍拏 "Tchañśuṇa" is the highly doubtful form given by Eitel, who describes it as the ancient capital of Vṛji, an "ancient kingdom N. of the Ganges, S.E. of Nepaul".

去 Go, go away; gone, past; depart, leave; to remove, dismiss; the 去 tone. | 來 Go and come. | | 今 Past, future, present. | 來實有宗 The heretical sect which believed in the reality of past and future as well as the present. | (or 式) 叉迦羅尼尸叉罽羅尼; 突吉羅 Śikṣākaraṇī. "A young Brahman studying with his preceptor." M. W. Studies, students. Also interpreted as "evil deeds". Also "a section of the Vinaya called 衆學法 . . . consisting of a series of 100 regulations with reference to the conduct of novices". Eitel.

叫 To call, cry. | 喚 To cry, wail, Raurava, hence the fourth and fifth hot hells. v. 呌.

召 To summon, call. | 請 To invite, especially the Buddhas or bodhisattvas to worship. | | 童子; 阿羯囉灑 The inviter, possibly etymologically connected with achāvāka; he is the youth fifth on the left of Mañjuśrī in his group of the Garbhadhātu, and is supposed to invite all the living to enlightenment.

句 A sentence, phrase, clause; also used for a place. | | Sentence by sentence, every word. | 身 Padakāya, perhaps Prātipadika; an inflected word.

只 Only; a final particle; translit. *j*. | 底舸部; | 底與世羅部; 支提加部; 支提山部; 制多山部; 住支提山部; 逝多林 (or 苑); 祇桓 Jetavanīyāḥ or Jetīyaśailāḥ. School of the dwellers on Mount Jeta, or 勝林部 School of Jetṛvana. A subdivision of the Sthavirāḥ. Cf. 北.

叵 May not, cannot; translit. *ph*. | 囉虞那麼洗; | 勒拏; 頗攞遇捉; 頗勒窶拏 Phālgunamāsa, the twelfth month; M. W. says February–March, the month, māsa, of the Nakṣatra Phālgunī.

可 May, can, able. | 汗 Khan. A Turkish term for "prince". | 漏 (子) A case for books or writings, likened to the shell of an egg (㲉漏). | 賀敦 Khatun. A Turkish term for "queen" or "princess".

古 Ancient, antique, old; of old. | 今 Ancient and modern.

古來實有宗 idem 去來 | | |.

台 A flat place, platform, plateau, terrace; an abbrev. for 臺 and for 天台 T'ien-t'ai, hence | 岳 the T'ien-t'ai mountain; | 宗; | 家 its "school"; | 徒 its disciples; | 教; | 道 its doctrine, or way. | 衡 The school of T'ai-Hêng, or T'ai and Hêng; T'ai is T'ien-t'ai, i.e. Chih-i 智顗 its founder, Hêng is 衡岳 the Hêng-yo monastery, i.e. a term for Hui-ssŭ 慧思 the teacher of Chih-i.

右 Dakṣiṇa. The right hand, on the right, e.g. | 手 right hand, | 旋 right turn, | 繞 pradakṣiṇa, turning or processing with the right shoulder towards an object of reverence.

四 Catur. Four.

四一 The four "ones", or the unity contained (according to T'ien-t'ai) in the 方便品 of the Lotus Sūtra; i.e. 教一 its teaching of one Vehicle; 行一 its sole bodhisattva procedure; 人一 its men all and only as bodhisattvas; 理一 its one ultimate truth of the reality of all existence.

四七品 The twenty-eight chapters of the Lotus Sūtra.

四上 The four times a day of going up to worship—daybreak, noon, evening, and midnight.

四不可得 The four unattainables, perpetual youth, no sickness, perennial life, no death. There is a work, the Catur-lābha-sūtra, tr. into Chinese under this title. | | | 思議 The four things of a Buddha which are beyond human conception: 世界 his world, 衆生 his living beings, 龍 his nāgas, and 佛土境界 the bounds of his Buddha-realm. | | | 輕 The four that may not be treated lightly: a prince though young, a snake though small, a fire though tiny, and above all a "novice" though a beginner, for he may become an arhat. Cf. 阿含經 46.

四不寄附 The four to whom one does not entrust valuables—the old, for death is nigh; the distant, lest one has immediate need of them; the evil; or the 大力 strong; lest the temptation be too strong for the last two.

四不壞淨 (or 信) The four objects of unfailing purity (or faith), i.e. the three precious ones (triratna) and the 戒 moral law.

四不成 Four forms of asiddha or incomplete statement, part of the thirty-three fallacies in logic.

四不生 That a thing is not born or not produced of itself, of another, of both, of neither; cf. 四句推撿.

四不見 The four invisibles—water to fish, wind (or air) to man, the nature (of things) to the deluded, and the 空 "void" to the 悟 enlightened, because he is in his own element, and the Void is beyond conception.

四世 The period of the Buddha's earthly life, styled 聖世 the sacred period (or period of the sage), is added to the three periods of 正法 correct Law; 像法 semblance of the Law; and 末法 decadence of the Law.

四事 The four necessaries of a monk—clothing, victuals, bedding, medicine (or herbs). Another set is a dwelling, clothing, victuals, medicine. | | 供養 The four offerings or provisions for a monk. There is a sūtra, the | | 經, or 阿難 | | |. For | | 不可思議 v. 四不可思議. | | 法門 Four methods of a bodhisattva's preparation for preaching the Law—entry into meditation; into wisdom; into complete moral self-control; and into clear discernment, or reasoning, 辯才門.

四主 The four Lords of the world, whose domains were supposed to stretch E., S., W., and N. of the Himalayas; E. 人 | the lord of men; S. 象 | of elephants; W. 寶 | of jewels (or precious things); N. 馬 | of horses. 西域記 |.

四乘 The goat, deer, and ox carts and the great white-bullock cart of the Lotus sūtra, see 四車.

四人觀世 The world from four points of view: that of men in general—its pleasures, thoughtlessly; of śrāvakas and pratyeka-buddhas—as a burning house, uneasily; of bodhisattvas—as an empty flower; of Buddhas—as mind, all things being for (or of) intelligent mind.

四仙 The three genii, or founders of systems, together with 若提子 Nirgranthajñāti; v. 二天三仙. | | 避死 The four wise men who sought escape from death: one in the mountains, another in the ocean, another in the air, and a fourth in the market place—all in vain.

四住 The four abodes or states in the 智度論 3, i.e. (1) 天 | the devalokas, equivalents of charity, morality, and goodness of heart; (2) 梵 | the brahmalokas, equivalents of benevolence, pity, joy, and indifference; (3) 聖 | the abode of śrāvakas, pratyeka-buddhas, and bodhisattvas, equivalent of the samādhi of the immaterial realm, formless and still; (4) 佛 | the Buddha-abode, the equivalent of the samādhis of the infinite. v. next.

四住(地) The four states or conditions found in mortality; wherein are the delusions of misleading views and desires. They are (1) 見一切住地 the delusions arising from seeing things as they seem, not as they really are. (2) 欲愛 | | the desires in the desire-realm. (3) 色愛 | | the desires in the form-realm. (4) 有愛 | | the desires in the formless realm. When 無明住地 the state of ignorance is added we have the 五住地 five states. These five states condition all error, and are the ground in which spring the roots of the countless passions and delusions of all mortal beings.

四佛 Four of the Five Dhyāni-Buddhas, i.e. the four regional Buddhas; they are variously stated. The 金光明經 gives E. 阿閦; S. 寶相; W. 無量壽; N. 微妙聲. The 大日經 gives E. 寶幢; S. 大勤勇遍覺華開敷; W. 仁勝 (i.e. 無量壽); N. 不動, i.e. 鼓音如來. The 金剛頂經 gives 不動; 寶生; 觀自在, and 不空成就如來. v. 五智如來. | | 土 idem 四土. | | 知見 The four purposes of the Buddha's appearing, that the Buddha-knowledge might be 開示悟入 revealed, proclaimed, understood, and entered; v. Lotus 方便品.

四依 The four necessaries, or things on which the religious rely. (1) 行 | | The four of ascetic practitioners—rag clothing; begging for food; sitting under trees; purgatives and diuretics as moral and spiritual means; these are also termed 四聖種. (2) 法 | | The four of the dharma, i.e. the truth, which is eternal, rather than man, even its propagator; the sūtras of perfect meaning, i.e. of the 中道實相 the truth of the "middle" way; the meaning, or spirit, not the letter; wisdom 智, i.e. Buddha-wisdom rather than mere knowledge 識. There are other groups. Cf. 四事. | | 八正 The first four above, 行 | |, and the 八正道 q.v.

四信 v. | 種信心. | | 五行 The four right objects of faith and the five right modes of procedure; the 眞如 Bhūtatathatā and the 三寶 Three Precious Ones are the four; the five are almsgiving, morality, patience, zeal (or progress), and 止觀 meditation.

四倒 The four viparyaya, i.e. inverted or false beliefs in regard to 常, 樂, 我, 淨. There are two groups: (1) the common belief in the four above, denied by the early Buddhist doctrine that all is impermanent, suffering, impersonal, and impure; (2) the false belief of the Hīnayāna school that nirvāṇa is not a state of permanence, joy, personality, and purity. Hīnayāna refutes the common view in regard to the phenomenal life; bodhisattvism refutes both views.

四優檀那 Yu-t'an-na, ? udāna, the four dogmas: all is impermanent, all is suffering, there is no ego, nirvāṇa.

四八相 The thirty-two marks of a Buddha.

四兵 Catur-aṅgabalakāya; the four divisions of a cakravarti's troops—elephant, hastikāya; horse, aśvakāya; chariot, rathakāya; and foot, pattikāya.

四分 The 法相 Dharmalakṣaṇa school divides the function of 識 cognition into four, i.e. 相分 mental phenomena, 見分 discriminating such phenomena, 自證分 the power that discriminates, and 證自證 the proof or assurance of that power. Another group is: 信 faith, 解 liberty, 行 action, and 證 assurance or realization. | | 僧戒本 Extracts from the 四分律 four-division Vinaya with verses, for use on days when the discipline is recited; there are other works under a similar title. | | 宗 idem 律宗. | | 家 The 法相 school which divides the 識心 cognition-mind into four parts, v. above. | | 律 The four-division Vinaya or discipline of the Dharmagupta school, divided into four sections of 20, 15, 14, and 11 chüan. The | | | 藏 Dharmagupta-vinaya was tr. in A.D. 405 by Buddhayaśas and 竺佛念 Chu Fo-nien; the | | 比丘尼羯磨法 Dharmagupta-bhikṣuṇī-karman was tr. by Guṇavarman in 431; and there are numerous other works of this order.

四劫 The four kalpas, or epochs, of a world, 成 | that of formation and completion; 住 | existing or abiding; 壞 | destruction; and 空 | annihilation, or the succeeding void. 俱舍論 12.

四力 The four powers for attaining enlightenment: independent personal power; power derived from others; power of past good karma; and power arising from environment.

四加行 v. 四善根.

四勝義諦 idem 四諦. | | 身 The four with victorious bodies, who were transformed independently of normal rebirth; also styled 解行身 bodies set free from all physical taint, thus attaining to Buddhahood. The four are the 龍女 dragon-daughter of the Lotus sūtra, who instantly became a male bodhisattva; and three others of the 華嚴 Hua-yen sūtra, i.e. 善財童子; 兜率天子, and 普莊嚴童子.

四化法 The | 無礙辯 q.v. whereby all beings may be saved.

四十 Catvāriṁśat; forty. | | 一位 (or 地) Forty-one of the fifty-two bodhisattva stages (of development), i.e. all except the 十信 and 妙覺. For this and | | 二位 v. 五十二位. | | 九僧 and 燈. The service to 藥師 the Master of Healing, when forty-nine lamps are displayed and forty-nine monks engaged; seven of his images are used, seven of the lamps being placed before each image. | | | 日 The seven times seven days of funeral services; the forty-ninth day. | | | 重摩尼 (or 如意) 殿. The Maṇi, or Pearl palace of forty-nine stories above the Tuṣita heaven. | | 二使者 The forty-two messengers, or angels of 不動尊 q.v. | | | 位 The forty-two stages, i.e. all above the 十信 of the fifty-two stages. | | | 品無明 The forty-two species of ignorance which, according to T'ien-t'ai, are to be cut off seriatim in the above forty-two stages. | | | 字門 The doctrine of the forty-two 悉曇 Siddham letters as given in the 華嚴 76 and 般若經 4. They have special meanings, independent of their use among the fourteen vowels and thirty-five consonants, i.e. forty-nine alphabetic signs. The forty-two are supposed by the 智度論 47 to be the root or basis of all letters; and each letter has its own specific value as a spiritual symbol; T'ien-t'ai associates each of them with one of the forty-two 位. The letters begin with 阿 and end with 荼 or 佗. | | | 章經 The "Sūtra of Forty-two Sections" generally attributed to Kāśyapa Mātaṅga, v. 迦, and Gobharaṇa, v. 竺, the first Indian monks to arrive officially in China. It was, however, probably first produced in China in the 晉 Chin dynasty. There are various editions and commentaries. | | 位 The "forty bodhisattva positions" of the 梵網經. They are classified into four groups: (1) 十發趣 Ten initial stages, i.e. the minds 心 of abandoning things of the world, of keeping the moral law, patience, zealous progress, dhyāna, wisdom, resolve, guarding (the Law), joy, and spiritual baptism by the Buddha. These are associated with the 十住. (2) 十長養 Ten steps in the nourishment of perfection, i.e. minds of kindness, pity, joy, relinquishing, almsgiving, good discourse, benefiting, friendship, dhyāna, wisdom. These are associated with the 十行. (3) 十金剛 Ten "diamond" steps of firmness, i.e. a mind of faith, remembrance, bestowing one's merits on others, understanding, uprightness, no-retreat, mahāyāna, formlessness, wisdom, indestructibility; these are associated with the 十廻向. (4) The 十地 q.v. | | 八使者 The forty-eight demon satellites of Āryācalanātha 不動明王 as subduer of demons, etc. | | | 年 The forty-eight years of service demanded by an old physician of his pupil in order to acquire his skill—likened to the slow and difficult methods of Hīnayāna and of early Mahāyāna. 丨丨丨願 The forty-eight vows of Amitābha that he would not enter into his final nirvāṇa or heaven, unless all beings shared it; the lists vary. 丨丨餘年未顯眞實 For forty and more years (the Buddha) was unable to unfold the full truth (until he first gave it in the Lotus sūtra).

四取 Catuḥ-parāmarśa, the four attachments, i.e. desire, (unenlightened) views, (fakir) morals, and ideas arising from the conception of the self. Also, the possible delusions of the 四住地. Also, seeking fame in the four quarters.

四句 The four terms, phrases, or four-line verses, e.g. 丨丨分別 The four terms of differentiation, e.g. of all things into 有 the existing; 空 non-existing; both; neither; or phenomenal, noumenal, both, neither. Also, double, single, both, neither; and other similar applications. 丨丨執 The four tenets held by various non-Buddhist schools: (1) the permanence of the ego, i.e. that the ego of past lives is the ego of the present; (2) its impermanence, i.e. that the present ego is of independent birth; (3) both permanent and impermanent, that the ego is permanent, the body impermanent; (4) neither permanent nor impermanent; that the body is impermanent but the ego not impermanent. 丨丨成道 The swan-song of an arhat, who has attained to the perfect life:—

All rebirths are ended,
The noble life established,
My work is accomplished.
No further existence is mine.

丨丨推撿 The four-phrase classification that phenomena are 自因 self-caused, 他因 caused by another, 共因 by both, 無因 by neither; cf. 四不生.

四向 The four stages in Hīnayāna sanctity: srota-āpanna, sakṛdāgāmin, anāgāmin, and arhan.

四含 idem 四阿含經.

四味 The four "tastes": the T'ien-t'ai definition of the four periods of the Buddha's teaching preliminary to the fifth, i.e. that of the Lotus sūtra; cf. 五味.

四唱 The four commanders or leaders; see Lotus Sūtra 15.

四善根 Catuṣ-kuśala-mūla, the four good roots, or sources from which spring good fruit or development. In Hīnayāna they form the stage after 總相念住 as represented by the 俱舍 and 成實; in Mahāyāna it is the final stage of the 十廻向 as represented by the 法相宗. There are also four similar stages connected with śrāvaka, pratyeka-buddha, and Buddha, styled 三品丨丨丨. The four of the 俱舍宗 are 煖法, 頂法, 忍法, and 世第一法. The four of the 成實宗 are the same, but are applied differently. The 法相宗 retains the same four terms, but connects them with the four dhyāna stages of the 眞唯識觀 in its four first 加行 developments.

四喩 The four metaphors (of infinity, etc.): 山斤 the weight of all the mountains in pounds; 海 the drops in the ocean; 地塵 the atoms of dust in the earth; 空界 the extent of space.

四園 idem 丨苑.

四土 The four Buddha-kṣetra, or realms, of T'ien-t'ai: (1) 凡聖居同土 Realms where all classes dwell—men, devas, Buddhas, disciples, non-disciples; it has two divisions, the impure, e.g. this world, and the pure, e.g. the "Western" pure-land. (2) 方便有餘土 Temporary realms, where the occupants have got rid of the evils of 見思 unenlightened views and thoughts, but still have to be reborn. (3) 實報無障礙土 Realms of permanent reward and freedom, for those who have attained bodhisattva rank. (4) 常寂光土 Realm of eternal rest and light (i.e. wisdom) and of eternal spirit (dharmakāya), the abode of Buddhas; but in reality all the others are included in this, and are only separated for convenience' sake.

四執 The four erroneous tenets; also 四邪; 四迷; 四術; there are two groups: I. The four of the 外道 outsiders, or non-Buddhists, i.e. of Brahminism, concerning the law of cause and effect: (1) 邪因邪果 heretical theory of causation, e.g. creation by Maheśvara; (2) 無因有果 or 自然, effect independent of cause, e.g. creation without a cause, or spontaneous generation; (3) 有因無果 cause without effect, e.g. no future life as the result of this. (4) 無因無果 neither cause nor effect, e.g. that rewards and punishments are independent of morals. II. The four erroneous tenets of 內外道 insiders and outsiders, Buddhist and Brahman, also styled 四宗 the four schools, as negated in the 中論 Mādhyamika śāstra: (1) outsiders, who do not accept either the 人 jên or 法 fa ideas of 空 k'ung; (2) insiders who hold the Abhidharma or Sarvāstivādāḥ tenet, which recognizes 人空 human impersonality, but not 法空 the unreality of things; (3) also those who hold the 成實 Satyasiddhi tenet which discriminates the two meanings of 空 k'ung but not clearly; and also (4) those in Mahāyāna who hold the tenet of the realists. | | 金剛 The four Vajra-rulers of the four elements —earth, water, fire, wind, and of the S.E., S.W., N.W., and N.E.

四堅信 The four firm or 四不壞信 indestructible beliefs, in the Buddha, the law, the order, and the commandments.

四塔 The four stūpas at the places of Buddha's birth, Kapilavastu; enlightenment, Magadha; preaching, Benares; and parinirvāṇa, Kuśinagara. Four more are located in the heavens of the Trayastriṃśas gods, one each for his hair, nails, begging-bowl, and teeth, E., S., W., N., respectively.

四墮(落法) The four causes of falling from grace and final excommunication of a monk or nun: adultery, stealing, killing, falsity; v. | 波羅夷.

四夜八晝 The four hours of the night 戌亥子丑, i.e. 7 to 3, and the eight hours of the day from 寅 to 酉 3 a.m. to 7 p.m.

四大 Mahābhūta, 四界; 四大界. The four elements of which all things are made; or the four realms; i.e. earth, water, fire, and wind (or air); they represent 堅, 濕, 煖, and 動 solid, liquid, heat, and motion; motion produces and maintains life. As 實 active or formative forces they are styled 四(大)界; as 假 passive or material objects they are 四大; but the 成實論 Satyasiddhi śāstra disputes the 實 and recognizes only the 假. | | 不調 The inharmonious working of the four elements in the body, which causes the 440 ailments; cf. 四蛇. | | 元無主 The verse uttered by 肇法師 Chao Fa-shih when facing death under the 姚秦 Yao Ch'in emperor, fourth century A.D.:—

"No master have the four elements,
Unreal are the five skandhas,
When my head meets the white blade,
'Twill be but slicing the spring wind."

The "four elements" are the physical body. | | 名山 The four famous "hills" or monasteries in China: 普陀 P'u-t'o, for Kuan-yin, element water; 五臺 Wu-t'ai, Wên-shu, wind; 峨眉 O-mei, P'u-hsien, fire; and 九華 Chiu-hua, Ti-tsang, earth. | | 天王 see 四天王. The four deva-kings of the four quarters, guardians in a monastery. | | 明王 v. 大明王. | | 師 The four monastic heads imperially appointed during the T'ang dynasty. | | 弟子 The four great disciples of the Buddha—Śāriputra, Mahāmaudgalyāyana, Subhūti, and Mahākāśyapa. Another group is Mahākāśyapa, Piṇḍola, Rāhula, and ? Kauṇḍinya. | | 海 The four great oceans in a world, around Sumeru, in which are the four great continents; cf. 九山八海. | | (部)洲 The four great continents of a world, v. | 洲. | | 種 idem | 大. | | 聲聞 The four great śrāvakas, idem | 大弟子. | | 菩薩 The four great Bodhisattvas of the Lotus Sūtra, i.e. Maitreya, Mañjuśrī, Avalokiteśvara, and Samantabhadra. Another list of previous Bodhisattvas is 上行 Viśiṣṭacāritra; 無邊行 Anantacāritra; 浄行 Viśuddhacāritra, and 安立行 Supratiṣṭhitacāritra. | | 護 The guardian devas of the four quarters: south 金剛無勝結護; east 無畏結 |; north 壞諸怖結 |; and west 難降伏結 |. The | | 佛護院 is the thirteenth group of the Garbhadhātu. | | 部經 Four great sūtras: 華嚴 Hua-yen; 涅槃 Nirvāṇa; 寶積 Mahāratnakūṭa, and 般若 Prajñā.

四天下 The four quarters or continents of the world. | | 上下 In the upper regions there are the four heavens of the four deva-kings; below are the people of the four continents. | (大) | 王 Catur-mahārājās, or Lokapālas; the four deva-kings. Indra's external "generals" who dwell each on a side of Mount Meru, and who ward off from the world the attacks of malicious spirits, or asuras, hence their name 護世四天王 the four deva-kings, guardians of the world. Their abode is the 四天王天 catur-mahārāja-kāyikas; and their titles are: East 持國天 Deva who keeps (his) kingdom; colour white; name Dhṛtarāṣtra. South 增長天 Deva of increase and growth; blue; name Virūḍhaka. West 廣目天 The broad-eyed (also ugly-eyed) deva (perhaps a form of Śiva); red; name Virūpākṣa. North 多聞 | The deva who hears much and is well-versed; yellow; name Vaiśravaṇa, or Dhanada; he is a form of Kuvera, the god of wealth. These are the four giant temple-guardians introduced as such to China by Amogha; cf. | | | 經. | | 王天 Catur-mahārāja-kāyikas; the four heavens of the four deva-kings.

四夷(戒 or 罪) v. 四波羅夷.

四如實觀 A meditation method on the 四加行位 q.v. | | 意足; 四神足 Ṛddhipāda; the third group of the 三十七科道品 bodhipakṣikadharma; the four steps to ṛddhi, or supernatural powers, making the body independent of ordinary or natural law. The four steps are said to be the 四種禪定 four kinds of dhyāna, but there are several definitions, e.g. 欲神足 chanda-ṛddhi-pāda, desire (or intensive longing, or concentration); 勤神足 vīrya-ṛ.-p., energy (or intensified effort); 心神足 citta-ṛ.-p., memory (or intense holding on to the position reached); 觀神足 mīmāṁsā-ṛ.-p., meditation (or survey, the state of dhyāna).

四姓 The four Indian "clans" or castes—brāhmaṇa, kṣatriya, vaiśya, and śūdra, i.e. (1) priestly, (2) military and ruling, (3) farmers and traders, and (4) serfs; born respectively from the mouth, shoulders, flanks, and feet of Brahmā.

四威儀 Four respect-inspiring forms of demeanour in walking, standing, sitting, lying.

四孟月 The four senior or prime months, i.e. the first of each season, first, fourth, seventh, and tenth.

四安樂(行) The four means of attaining to a happy contentment, by proper direction of the deeds of the body; the words of the mouth; the thoughts of the mind; and the resolve (of the will) to preach to all the Lotus sūtra.

四定 The four dhyāna heavens of form, and the four degrees of dhyāna corresponding to them. For 丨丨記 v. 丨記.

四宗 The four kinds of inference in logic—common, prejudged or opposing, insufficiently founded, arbitrary. Also, the four schools of thought: I. According to 淨影 Ching-ying they are (1) 立性宗 that everything exists, or has its own nature; e.g. Sarvāstivāda, in the "lower" schools of Hīnayāna; (2) 破性宗 that everything has not a nature of its own; e.g. the 成實丨 a "higher" Hīnayāna school, the Satyasiddhi; (3) 破相丨 that form has no reality, because of the doctrine of the void, "lower" Mahāyāna; (4) 顯實丨 revelation of reality, that all comes from the bhūtatathatā, "higher" Mahāyāna. II. According to 曇隱 T'an-yin of the 大衍 monastery they are (1) 因緣丨, i.e. 立性丨 all things are causally produced; (2) 假名丨, i.e. 破性丨 things are but names; (3) 不眞丨, i.e. 破相丨, denying the reality of form, this school fails to define reality; (4) 眞宗, i.e. 顯實丨 the school of the real, in contrast with the seeming.

四家 The schools of 般若, 諦, 捨煩惱, and 苦淸 likened by 章安 Chang-an of the T'ien-t'ai to the 四教, i.e. seriatim: 別, 圓, 通, and 三藏.

四尋思觀 A study or contemplation of the 法相宗 Dharmalakṣaṇa sect, on 名 the terms used, 義 the meanings of the things or phenomena, 自性 the nature of the things, 差別 their differentiation.

四山 Like four closing-in mountains are birth, age, sickness, and death; another group is age, sickness, death, and decay (衰, i.e. of wealth, honours, etc., or 無常 impermanence).

四度加行 Special study of or advancement in the four degrees, a method of the esoterics, formerly extending over 800 or 1,000 days, later contracted to 200. The four "degrees" are 十八道, 胎藏, 金剛, and 護摩, but the order varies.

四弘誓願 The four universal vows of a Buddha or bodhisattva: 衆生無邊誓願度 to save all living beings without limit; 煩惱無數丨丨斷 to put an end to all passions and delusions however numerous; 法門無盡丨丨學 to study and learn all methods and means without end; 佛道無上丨丨成 to become perfect in the supreme Buddha-law. The four vows are considered as arising one by one out of the 四諦 Four Noble Truths.

四律五論 The four vinaya and the five śāstras. The four vinaya, or disciplinary regulations, are the 十誦律 Sarvāstivāda-version tr. in 61 chüan by Puṇyatara; 四分律 Dharmagupta's version, tr. in 60 chüan by Buddhayaśas; 僧祇律 Sāṁghika-version or Māhāsaṁghika-version, tr. in 40 chüan, by Buddhabhadra; and 五部律 Mahīśāsaka-version, tr. in 30 chüan by Buddhajīva and others, also known as Mahīśāsaka-nikāya-pañcavargavinaya. The five śāstras are 毘尼母論; 摩得勒伽丨; 善見丨; 薩婆多丨; and 明了丨. v. 論.

四微 The four minutest forms or atoms perceptible to the four senses of sight, smell, taste, or touch; from these arise the 四大 four elements, from which arise the 五智 five wisdoms, q.v.

四德 The four nirvāṇa virtues, or values, according to the Mahāyāna Nirvāṇa sūtra: (1) 常 permanence or eternity; (2) 樂 joy; (3) 我 personality or the soul; (4) 淨 purity. These four important terms, while denied in the lower realms, are affirmed by the sūtra in the transcendental, or nirvāṇa-realm. | | 樂邦 ; | | 波羅蜜 The joyful realm, or acme of the above four virtues, the nirvāṇa-realm, the abode or dharmakāya of the Tathāgata.

四心 The hearts of kindness, pity, joy, and indifference, idem 四無量心.

四忉利交形 Copulation in the first and in the second devalokas, i.e. 四王 and 忉利 heavens; in the third it is by embrace; in the fourth, by holding hands; in the fifth, by mutual smiling; in the sixth by a mutual look.

四忘 The state of a saint, i.e. beyond, or oblivious of the four conditions of 一異有無 unity, difference, existence, non-existence.

四念住 idem | | 處. | | 珠 The four classes of "prayer-beads", numbering 27, 54, 108, or 1,080, styled 下品, 中品, 最勝, and 上品, lower, middle, superior, and most superior. | | 處(觀); | | 住 Smṛty-upasthāna. The fourfold stage of mindfulness, thought, or meditation that follows the 五停心觀 five-fold procedure for quieting the mind. This fourfold method, or objectivity of thought, is for stimulating the mind in ethical wisdom. It consists of contemplating (1) 身 the body as impure and utterly filthy; (2) 受 sensation, or consciousness, as always resulting in suffering; (3) 心 mind as impermanent, merely one sensation after another; (4) 法 things in general as being dependent and without a nature of their own. The four negate the ideas of permanence, joy, personality, and purity 常, 樂, 我, and 淨, i.e. the four 顚倒, but v. 四德. They are further subdivided into 別 and 總 particular and general, termed 別相念處 and 總相念處, and there are further subdivisions.

四性行 The four kinds of conduct natural to a Bodhisattva, that arising from his native goodness, his vow-nature, his compliant nature, i.e. to the six pāramitās, and his transforming nature, i.e. his powers of conversion or salvation.

四怨 The four enemies—the passions-and-delusion māras, death māra, the five-skandhas māras, and the supreme māra-king.

四恒 As the sands of four Ganges.

四悔 See 五悔 and omit the first.

四悉檀 The four siddhānta, v. 悉. The Buddha taught by (1) mundane or ordinary modes of expression; (2) individual treatment, adapting his teaching to the capacity of his hearers; (3) diagnostic treatment of their moral diseases; and (4) the perfect and highest truth.

四惑 idem 四煩惱.

四意斷 idem 四正勤.

四愛生 (or 起) Four sources of affection: the giving or receiving of clothing, or food, or bedding, or independently of gifts.

四惡 (趣 or 道) The four apāya, or evil destinies: the hells, as hungry ghosts, animals, or asuras. The asuras are sometimes evil, sometimes good, hence the term 三惡道 "three evil destinies" excepts the asuras. | | 比丘 The four wicked bhikṣus who threw over the teaching of their Buddha 大莊嚴 Ta Chuang Yen after his nirvāṇa; these suffered in the deepest hells, came forth purified, but have not been able to attain perfection because of their past unbelief; v. 佛藏經往古品. Also four disobedient bhikṣus who through much purgation ultimately became the Buddhas of the four points of the compass, 阿閦, 寶相, 無量壽, and 微妙聲.

四慧 The four kinds of wisdom received: (1) by birth, or nature; (2) by hearing, or being taught; (3) by thought; (4) by dhyāna meditation.

四戒 Four stages in moral development: that of release, or deliverance from the world on becoming a monk; that arising from the four meditations on the realms of form; that above the stage of 見道 q.v.; that in which all moral evil is ended and delusion ceases.

四持 idem 四種總持.

四捨 The four givings, i.e. of goods of the Truth, of courage (or fearlessness), and the giving up of the passions and delusions; cf. dāna-pāramitā, 捨.

四摩(室) Sīmā. A boundary, a separate dwelling, or dwellings (for monks and/or visitors).

四攝法 (or 事) Catuḥ-saṁgraha-vastu; four all-embracing (bodhisattva) virtues: (1) 布施 dāna, giving what others like, in order to lead them to love and receive the truth; (2) 愛語 priyavacana, affectionate speech, with the same purpose; (3) 利行 arthakṛtya, conduct profitable to others, with the same purpose; (4) 同事 samānārthatā, co-operation with and adaptation of oneself to others, to lead them into the truth. | | 菩薩; | | 衆; | | 金剛 The four bodhisattvas in the Vajradhātu with the hook, the rope, the chain, and the bell, whose office is to 化他 convert the living.

四教 Four teachings, doctrines, or schools; five groups are given, whose titles are abbreviated to 光天曉苑龍: (1) 光宅 | | The four schools of 法雲 Fa-yün of the 光宅 Kuang-chai monastery are the four vehicles referred to in the burning house parable of the Lotus Sūtra, i.e. śrāvaka, pratyeka-buddha, bodhisattva, and the final or one-vehicle teaching. (2) 天台 | | The T'ien-t'ai four are 藏, 通, 別, and 圓, v. 八教. (3) 曉公 | | The group of 元曉 Yüan-hsiao of 海東 Hai-tung are the 三乘別教 represented by the 四諦緣起經; 三乘通教 represented by the 般若深密經; 一乘分教 represented by the 梵網經; and 一乘滿教 represented by the 華嚴經. (4) 苑公 | | The group of 慧苑 Hui-yüan: the schools of unbelievers, who are misled and mislead; of śrāvakas and pratyeka-buddhas who know only the phenomenal bhūtatathatā; of novitiate bodhisattvas who know only the noumenal bhūtatathatā; and of fully developed bodhisattvas, who know both. (5) 龍樹 | | Nāgārjuna's division of the canon into 有 dealing with existence, or reality, cf. the 四阿含; 空 the Void, cf. 般若經; 亦有亦空 both, cf. 深密經; and 非有非空 neither, cf. 中論. | | 三密 Now a 眞言 Shingon term; the 四教 are the T'ien-t'ai four schools of 顯 open or exoteric teaching; the 三密 are the Shingon esoteric teaching in which the three 身口意 body, mouth, and mind have special functions. | | 三觀 The T'ien-t'ai four main doctrinal divisions as above and its three kinds of meditation. | | 五時 T'ien-t'ai's doctrine of the four developments of the Buddha's own teaching, v. above, and the five periods of the same, v. 五時教. | | 儀 A work of 智顗 Chih-i of T'ien-t'ai. | | 地 Four stages, as given in the 大日經具緣品, i.e. 藏, 通, 別, and 圓 q.v.

四方 The four quarters of the compass; a square, square; the E. is ruled by Indra, S. by Yama, W. by Varuṇa, and N. by Vaiśramaṇa; the N.E. is ruled by 伊舍尼 Īśāna, S.E. by 護摩 Homa, S.W. by 涅哩底 Nirṛti, and the N.W. by 嚩瘐 Varuṇa. | | 四佛 The four Buddhas of the four regions—E. the world of 香積 abundant fragrance where reigns 阿閦 Akṣobhya; S. of 歡喜 pleasure, 寶相 Ratnaketu; W. of 安樂 restfulness, or joyful comfort, 無量壽 Amitābha; and N. of 蓮華莊嚴 lotus adornment, 微妙聲 ? Amoghasiddhi, or Śākyamuni. | | 大將 The four "generals" or guardians of the Law, of the four directions: N. 散脂 | |, E. 樂欲 | |, S. 檀帝 | |, W. 善現 | |. Each has 500 followers and twenty-eight companies of demons and spirits. Cf. 四天王.

四施 Four benefactions, i.e. pen, ink, sūtras, preaching.

四日 Catvāraḥ sūryāḥ, the four suns, i.e. Aśvaghoṣa, Devabodhisattva, Nāgārjuna, and Kumāralabdha (or -lāta).

四明 Four Shingon emblems, aids to Yoga-possession by a Buddha or bodhisattva; they are 鉤, 索, 鏁, 鈴, a hook, a cord, a lock, and a bell; the hook for summoning, the cord for leading, the lock for firmly holding, and the bell for the resultant joy. Also, the four Veda śāstras. | | 山 A mountain range in Ningpo prefecture where the 四明 are clearly seen, i.e. sun, moon, stars, and constellations. 知禮 Chih-li of the Sung dynasty is known as the | | 尊者 honoured one of Ssŭ-ming and his school as the | | 家 Ssŭ-ming school in the direct line of T'ien-t'ai. In Japan Mt. Hiyei 比叡山 is known by this title, through Dengyo 傳教 the founder of the Japanese T'ien-t'ai School.

四智 The four forms of wisdom of a Buddha according to the 法相 Dharmalakṣaṇa school: (1) 大圓鏡智 the great mirror wisdom of Akṣobhya; (2) 平等性智 the universal wisdom of Ratnaketu; (3) 妙觀察智 the profound observing wisdom of Amitābha; (4) 成所作智 the perfecting wisdom of Amoghasiddhi. There are various other groups. | | 印 Four wisdom symbols of the Shingon cult: 大智印 or 摩訶岐若勿他羅 mahā-jñāna-mudrā, the forms of the images; 三昧耶印 samaya-jñāna-mudrā, their symbols and manual signs; 法智印 dharma-jñāna-mudrā, the magic formula of each; 羯摩智印 karma-jñāna-mudrā, the emblems of their specific functions. | | 讚 The praise hymns of the four "wisdoms", v. above.

四月 Āṣāḍha, the fourth month. | | 八日 The eighth of the fourth moon, the Buddha's birthday.

四有爲相 The four functioning forms, i.e. 生 birth, 住 stay, 異 change, and 滅 extinction; v. 四相.

四本止觀 The four books of T'ien-t'ai on meditation 止觀, i.e. 摩訶止觀; 禪波羅蜜; 六妙門; and 坐禪法要. ||相 The four fundamental states—birth, stay, change, and extinction (or death), v. 四相.

四果 The four phala, i.e. fruitions, or rewards—srota-āpanna-phala, sakradāgāmi-phala, anāgāmi-phala, arhat-phala, i.e. four grades of saintship; see 須陀洹, 斯陀含, 阿那含, and 阿羅漢. The four titles are also applied to four grades of śramaṇas—yellow and blue flower śramaṇas, lotus śramaṇas, meek śramaṇas, and ultra-meek śramaṇas.

四枯四榮 When the Buddha died, of the eight śāla trees surrounding him four are said to have withered while four continued in full leaf—a sign that the four doctrines of 苦 suffering, 空 the void, 無常 impermanence, and 無我 impersonality were to perish and those of 常 permanence, 樂 joy, 我 personality, and 淨 purity, the transcendent bodhisattva doctrines, were to flourish.

四根本性(or 重)罪 idem 四波羅夷.

四梵住 The noble state of unlimited 慈悲喜捨 love, pity, joy, and indifference. ||堂 Four ways of attaining arhatship, idem ||住, except that the last of the four is 護 protection (of others). ||志 The four Brahmacārins who resolved to escape death each on mountain, sea, in the air, or the market place, and yet failed; v. 山.

四棄 The four pārājika sins resulting in excommunication, v. 波.

四欲 The four desires or passions: 情 sexual love; 色 sexual beauty or attractiveness; 食 food; 婬 lust.

四正勤 Samyakprahāṇa, v. 三十七道品; the four right efforts—to put an end to existing evil; prevent evil arising; bring good into existence; develop existing good; ||斷; 四意斷 are similar but the third point is the conservation of the good.

四比丘 v. 四惡比丘.

四毒蛇 Four poisonous snakes (in a basket), e.g. the four elements, earth, water, fire, and air, of which a man is formed.

四河 The four rivers—Ganges, Sindhu (Indus), Vākṣu (Oxus), and Tārīm, all reputed to arise out of a lake, Anavatapta, in Tibet.

四波 An abbreviation for ||羅蜜(菩薩). The four female attendants on Vairocana in the Vajradhātu, evolved from him, each of them a "mother" of one of the four Buddhas of the four quarters; v. 四佛, etc. ||羅夷; 四重; 四棄, 四極重感墮罪 The four pārājikas, or grievous sins of monks or nuns: (1) abrahmacarya, sexual immorality, or bestiality; (2) adattādāna, stealing; (3) vadha(hiṁsā) killing; (4) uttaramanuṣyadharma-pralāpa, false speaking.

四法 There are several groups of four dharma: (1) 教法 the teaching (of the Buddha); 理 | its principles, or meaning; 行 | its practice; 果 | its fruits or rewards. (2) Another group relates to bodhisattvas, their never losing the bodhi-mind, or the wisdom attained, or perseverance in progress, or the monastic forest life (āraṇyaka). (3) Also 信解行證 faith, discernment, performance, and assurance. (4) The Pure-land "True" sect of Japan has a division: 教法, i.e. the 大無量壽經; 行 | the practice of the seventeenth of Amitābha's vows; 信 | faith in the eighteenth; and 證 | proof of the eleventh. The most important work of Shinran, the founder of the sect, is these four, i.e. 教行信證. (5) A "Lotus" division of 四法 is the answer to a question of P'u-hsien (Samantabhadra) how the Lotus is to be possessed after the Buddha's demise, i.e. by thought (or protection) of the Buddhas; the cultivation of virtue; entry into correct dhyāna; and having a mind to save all creatures. ||三願 idem (4) above; the three vows are the seventeenth, eighteenth, and eleventh of Amitābha. ||不壞 The four imperishables—the correctly receptive heart, the diamond, the relics of a Buddha, and the palace of the devas of light and sound, ābhāsvaras. ||印 The seal or impression of the four dogmas, suffering, impermanence, non-ego, nirvāṇa, see 四法本末. ||成就 idem 四種檀法. ||本末 The alpha and omega in four laws or dogmas—that nothing is permanent, that all things involve suffering, that there is no personality, and that nirvāṇa is 永寂 eternal rest. ||施 The Buddha's gift of the four laws or dogmas, that all things are impermanent, that all (sentient) existence is suffering, that there is no (essential) personality, that all form (or matter) returns to the void. ||界; 四種法界 The four dharma-realms of the Hua-yen School: (1) 事法界 the phenomenal realm, with differentiation; (2) 理 || noumenal, with unity; (3) 理事無礙 ||

both 理 noumenal and 事 phenomenal are interdependent; (4) 事事無礙 | | phenomena are also interdependent.

四洲 Catur-dvīpa; the four inhabited continents of every universe; they are situated S., E., W., and N. of the central mountain Sumeru; S. is Jambūdvīpa 贍部洲; E. Pūrva-videha 東毘提訶; W. Apara-godānīya 牛貨; and N. Uttara-kuru 瞿盧.

四海 The four oceans around Mount Sumeru; cf. 九山八海. | | 論主 Honorific title of the monk 敬脫 Ching-t'o of the Sui dynasty.

四流 The four currents (that carry the unthinking along): i.e. the illusions of 見 seeing things as they seem, not as they really are; 欲 desires; 有 existence, life; 無明 ignorance, or an unenlightened condition.

四淨定 The "pure" dhyāna, i.e. one of the 三定 three dhyānas; this dhyāna is in four parts.

四無(or 非)常偈 Eight stanzas in the 仁王經, two each on 無常 impermanence, 苦 suffering, 空 the void, and 無我 non-personality; the whole four sets embodying the impermanence of all things. | | (所) 畏 The four kinds of fearlessness, or courage, of which there are two groups: Buddha-fearlessness arises from his omniscience; perfection of character; overcoming opposition; and ending of suffering. Bodhisattva-fearlessness arises from powers of memory; of moral diagnosis and application of the remedy; of ratiocination; and of solving doubts. v. 智度論 48 and 5. | | 礙解 (or 智 or 辯). Pratisaṁvid, the four unhindered or unlimited bodhisattva powers of interpretation, or reasoning, i.e. in 法 dharma, the letter of the law; 義 artha, its meaning; 辭 nirukti, in any language, or form of expression; 樂說 pratibhāna, in eloquence, or pleasure in speaking, or argument. | | 色 idem |空處, |空定. | | 量 (心) Catvāri apramāṇāni; the four immeasurables, or infinite Buddha-states of mind, also styled 四等 the four equalities, or universals, and 四梵行 four noble acts or characteristics; i.e. four of the twelve 禪 dhyānas: 慈無量心 boundless kindness, maitrī, or bestowing of joy or happiness; 悲 | | | boundless pity, karuṇā, to save from suffering; 喜 | | | boundless joy, muditā, on seeing others rescued from suffering; 捨 | | | limitless indifference, upekṣā, i.e. rising above these emotions, or giving up all things, e.g. distinctions of friend and enemy, love and hate, etc. The esoteric sect has a special definition of its own, connecting each of the four with 普賢; 虛空藏; 觀自在; or 虛空庫.

四煩惱 The four delusions in reference to the ego: 我癡 ignorance in regard to the ego; 我見 holding to the ego idea; 我慢 self-esteem, egotism, pride; 我愛 self-seeking, or desire, both the latter arising from belief in the ego. Also 四惑.

四爐 The four furnaces, or altars of the esoteric cult, each differing in shape: earth, square; water, round; fire, triangular; wind, half-moon shape.

四王(天) Catur-mahārāja-kāyikās, the four heavens of the four deva-kings, i.e. the lowest of the six heavens of desire; v. 四天王. | | 忉利 The above four and trayastriṁśās, Indra's heaven.

四生 Catur-yoni, the four forms of birth: (1) 胎 or 腹生 jarāyuja, viviparous, as with mammalia; (2) 卵生 aṇḍaja, oviparous, as with birds; (3) 濕生 or 寒熱和合生 saṁsvedaja, moisture, or water-born, as with worms and fishes; (4) 化生 aupapāduka, metamorphic, as with moths from the chrysalis, or with devas, or in the hells, or the first beings in a newly evolved world. | | 百劫 A pratyeka-buddha method of obtaining release, by intensive effort, at the shortest in four rebirths, at the longest in a hundred kalpas.

四田 The four fields for cultivating happiness—animals; the poor; parents, etc.; the religion.

四界 The four realms, idem 四大 earth, water, fire, and air. | | 攝持 The four are the substance and upholders of all things.

四病 The four ailments, or mistaken ways of seeking perfection: 作 | "works" or effort; 任 | *laissez-faire*; 止 | cessation of all mental operation; 滅 | annihilation (of all desire).

四百 Four hundred.

四百四病 The 404 ailments of the body; each of the four elements—earth, water, fire, and wind—is responsible for 101; there are 202 fevers, or hot humours caused by earth and fire; and 202 chills or cold humours caused by water and wind; v. 智

度論 65. 丨丨戒 The 400 disciplinary laws of a bodhisattva, referred to in the 藥師經 but without detail.

四相 The four avasthā, or states of all phenomena, i.e. 生住異滅 birth, being, change (i.e. decay), and death; also 四有爲相. There are several groups, e.g. 果報四相 birth, age, disease, death. Also 藏識四相 of the "Awakening of Faith" referring to the initiation, continuation, change, and cessation of the Ālaya-vijñāna. Also 我人四相 The ideas: (1) that there is an ego; (2) that man is different from other organisms; (3) that all the living are produced by the skandhas; (4) that life is limited to the organism. Also 智境四相 dealing differently with the four last headings 我; 人; 衆生; and 壽相.

四眞(諦) The four noble truths, v. 四(聖)諦, i.e. 苦, 集, 滅, 道 pain, its location, its cessation, the way of cure.

四眼 The four powers of sight of bodhisattvas, a Buddha has a fifth power; v. 五眼.

四知 The four who know the workings of one's mind for good or evil—heaven, earth, one's intimates, and oneself.

四神足 idem 四如意足.

四禪(天) The four dhyāna heavens, 四靜慮(天), i.e. the division of the eighteen brahmalokas into four dhyānas: the disciple attains to one of these heavens according to the dhyāna he observes: (1) 初禪天 The first region, "as large as one whole universe," comprises the three heavens, Brahmapāriṣadya, Brahma-purohita, and Mahābrahma, 梵輔, 梵衆, and 大梵天; the inhabitants are without gustatory or olfactory organs, not needing food, but possess the other four of the six organs. (2) 二禪天 The second region, equal to "a small chiliocosmos" 小千界, comprises the three heavens, according to Eitel, "Parīttābha, Apramāṇābha, and Ābhāsvara," i.e. 少光 minor light, 無量光 infinite light, and 極光淨 utmost light-purity; the inhabitants have ceased to require the five physical organs, possessing only the organ of mind. (3) 三禪天 The third region, equal to "a middling chiliocosmos" 中千界, comprises three heavens; Eitel gives them as Parīttaśubha, Apramāṇaśubha, and Śubhakṛtsna, i.e. 少淨 minor purity, 無量淨 infinite purity, and 徧淨 universal purity; the inhabitants still have the organ of mind and are receptive of great joy. (4) 四禪天 The fourth region, equal to a great chiliocosmos, 大千界, comprises the remaining nine Brahmalokas, namely, Puṇyaprasava, Anabhraka, Bṛhatphala, Asañjñisattva, Avṛha, Atapa, Sudṛśa, Sudarśana, and Akaniṣṭha (Eitel). The Chinese titles are 福生 felicitous birth, 無雲 cloudless, 廣果 large fruitage, 無煩 no vexations, atapa is 無熱 no heat, sudṛśa is 善見 beautiful to see, sudarśana is 善現 beautiful appearing, two others are 色究竟 the end of form, and 無想天 the heaven above thought, but it is difficult to trace avṛha and akaniṣṭha; the inhabitants of this fourth region still have mind. The number of the dhyāna heavens differs; the Sarvāstivādins say 16, the 經 or Sūtra school 17, and the Sthavirāḥ school 18. Eitel points out that the first dhyāna has one world with one moon, one meru, four continents, and six devalokas; the second dhyāna has 1,000 times the worlds of the first; the third has 1,000 times the worlds of the second; the fourth dhyāna has 1,000 times those of the third. Within a kalpa of destruction 壞劫 the first is destroyed fifty-six times by fire, the second seven by water, the third once by wind, the fourth "corresponding to a state of absolute indifference" remains "untouched" by all the other evolutions; when "fate (天命) comes to an end then the fourth Dhyāna may come to an end too, but not sooner". 丨丨八定 The four dhyānas on the form-realms and the eight concentrations, i.e. four on the form-realms and four on the formless-realms. 丨丨定 The four dhyāna-concentrations which lead to the four dhyāna heavenly regions, see above.

四種 Four kinds; where phrases containing the 種 are not found here, they may occur direct, e.g. 四法界. 丨丨三昧(耶) The four samaya, i.e. the four pārājikas—killing, stealing, carnality, lying. 丨丨信心 The four kinds of faith given in the Awakening of Faith, i.e. (1) in the 眞如 q.v. as the teacher of all Buddhas and fount of all action; (2) in Buddha, or the Buddhas; (3) in the Dharma; and (4) in the Saṁgha. 丨丨根本罪 The four deadly sins, i.e. the four pārājikas—killing, stealing, carnality, lying. 丨丨檀法; 丨丨悉地; 丨丨成就法 The four kinds of altar-worship of the esoteric sect for (1) averting calamities from self and others; (2) seeking good fortune; (3) seeking the love and protection of Buddhas; (4) subduing enemies. 丨丨死生 Four kinds of rebirth dependent on present deeds: from obscurity and poverty to be reborn in the same condition; from obscurity and poverty to be reborn in light and honour; from light and honour to be reborn in obscurity and poverty; from light and honour to be reborn in the heavens. 丨丨

法界 v. 四法界. | | 總持 The four kinds of dhāraṇī 陀羅尼 q.v. | | 行人 The four grades of earnest doers, who follow the bodhisattva discipline and attain to the 十住, 十行, 十廻向, and 十地. | | 觀行 The four kinds of examination, a method of repentance as a way to get rid of any sin: study the cause of the sin, which lies in ignorance, or lack of clear understanding, e.g. moth and flame; study its inevitable effect, its karma; study oneself, introspection; and study the Tathāgata in his perfect character, and saving power.

四空(處 or 天) Catur-ārūpya (brahma) lokas; also 四無色界 and see 四空定. The four immaterial or formless heavens, arūpa-dhātu, above the eighteen brahmalokas: (1) 空無邊處 ākāśānantyāyatana, also termed (虛)空處 the state or heaven of boundless space; (2) 識(無邊)處 vijñānanāntyāyatana, of boundless knowledge; (3) 無所有處 ākiñcanyāyatana, of nothing, or non-existence; (4) 非想非非想處 naivasañjnānāsañjñāyatana, also styled 非有想非無想 the state of neither thinking nor not thinking (which may resemble a state of intuition). Existence in the first state lasts 20,000 great kalpas, increasing respectively to 40,000, 60,000 and 80,000 in the other three. | | 定; 四無色定 The last four of the twelve dhyānas; the auto-hypnotic, or ecstatic entry into the four states represented by the four dhyāna heavens, i.e. 四空處 *supra*. In the first, the mind becomes void and vast like space; in the second, the powers of perception and understanding are unlimited; in the third, the discriminative powers of mind are subdued; in the fourth, the realm of consciousness (or knowledge) without thought is reached, e.g. intuitive wisdom. These four are considered both as states of dhyāna, and as heavens into which one who practises these forms of dhyāna may be born.

四第一偈 A verse from the 莊嚴論 Chuang Yen Lun—

> Health is the best wealth,
> Contentment the best riches,
> Friendship the best relationship,
> Nirvāṇa the best joy.

四等 The four virtues which a Buddha out of his infinite heart manifests equally to all; also called 四無量 q.v. They are: 慈悲喜捨 maitrī, karuṇā, muditā, upekṣā, i.e. kindness, pity, joy and indifference, or 護 protection. Another group is 字語法身, i.e. 字 that all Buddhas have the same title or titles; 語 speak the same language; 法 proclaim the same truth; and 身 have each the threefold body, or trikāya. A third group is 諸法 all things are equally included in the bhūtatathatā; 發心 the mind-nature being universal, its field of action is universal; 道等 the way or method is also universal; therefore 慈悲 the mercy (of the Buddhas) is universal for all.

四箇大乘 The four mahāyānas, i.e. the four great schools: (1) 華嚴 Hua-yen or Avataṁsaka; (2) 天台 T'ien-t'ai; (3) 眞言 Chên-yen, Shingon, or esoteric; (4) 禪 Ch'an, Zen, or intuitive school. Another group is the 法相, 三論, 天台, and 華嚴.

四節 The four monastic annual periods—beginning of summer, end of summer, winter solstice, and the new year.

四料簡 A summary of the 臨濟 Ling-chi school, an offshoot of the Ch'an, in reference to subjective, objective, both, neither.

四結 The four knots, or bonds, saṁyojana, which hinder free development; they are likened to the 四翳 q.v. four things that becloud, i.e. rain-clouds, resembling desire; dust-storms, hate; smoke, ignorance; and asuras, gain.

四絶 The four ideas to be got rid of in order to obtain the "mean" or ultimate reality, according to the 中論: they are that things exist, do not exist, both, neither.

四維 The four half points of the compass, N.E., N.W., S.E., S.W.

四縛 The four bandhana, or bonds are (1) desire, resentment, heretical morality, egoism; or (2) desire, possession (or existence), ignorance, and unenlightened views.

四翳 The four films, or things that becloud, i.e. rain-clouds; dust-storms; smoke; and asuras, i.e. eclipses of sun and moon; emblematic of desire, hate, ignorance, and pride; cf. | 結.

四聖 The four kinds of holy men—śrāvakas, pratyeka-buddhas, bodhisattvas, and Buddhas. Also, the four chief disciples of Kumārajīva, i.e. 道生 Tao-shêng, 僧肇 Sêng-chao, 道融 Tao-jung, and 僧叡 Sêng-jui. | | 行 The four holy ways—wearing rags from dust-heaps, begging for food, sitting under trees, and entire withdrawal from the world. The meaning is similar in 四良藥; 行四依; and 四聖種. | | 諦 The four holy or noble truths, idem 四諦.

四股 The four-armed svastika, or thunderbolt.

四自侵 The four self-raidings, or self-injuries —in youth not to study from morn till night; in advancing years not to cease sexual intercourse; wealthy and not being charitable; not accepting the Buddha's teaching. | | 在 The four sovereign powers: 戒 the moral law; 神通 supernatural powers; 智 knowledge; and 慧 wisdom.

四良藥 The four good physicians, or medicines; idem 四聖行.

四花 The four (divine) flowers—mandāra, mahāmandāra, mañjūṣaka, and mahāmañjūṣaka. Also, puṇḍarīka, utpala, padma, and kumuda or white, blue, red, and yellow lotuses.

四苑 The pleasure grounds outside 善見城 Sudarśana, the heavenly city of Indra: E. 衆車 | Caitrarathavana, the park of chariots; S. 麤惡 | Parūṣakavana, the war park; W. 雜林 | Miśrakāvana, intp. as the park where all desires are fulfilled; N. 喜林 | Nandanavana, the park of all delights. Also | 園.

四苦 The four miseries, or sufferings—birth, age, disease, and death.

四菩薩 The four bodhisattvas—Avalokiteśvara, Maitreya, Samantabhadra, and Mañjuśrī. Also, the four chief bodhisattvas in the Garbhadhātu. There are also the 本化 | | | of the Lotus sūtra, named 上行, 無邊行, 淨行, and 安立行.

四處十六會 The sixteen assemblies, or addresses in the four places where the 大般若經 complete Prajñā-pāramitā is said to have been delivered. | | 問訊 To inquire (or worship at) the four places for lighting incense at a monastery.

四蚖蛇 idem next entry.

四蛇 idem 四毒蛇. The Fan-i-ming-i under this heading gives the parable of a man who fled from the two bewildering forms of life and death, and climbed down a rope (of life) 命根, into the well of impermanence 無常, where two mice, night and day, gnawed the rattan rope; on the four sides four snakes 四蛇 sought to poison him, i.e. the 四大 or four elements (of his physical nature); below were three dragons 三毒龍 breathing fire and trying to seize him. On looking up he saw that two 象 elephants (darkness and light) had come to the mouth of the well; he was in despair, when a bee flew by and dropped some honey (the five desires 五欲) into his mouth, which he ate and entirely forgot his peril.

四衆 The four varga (groups, or orders), i.e. bhikṣu, bhikṣuṇī, upāsaka and upāsikā, monks, nuns, male and female devotees. Another group, according to T'ien-t'ai's commentary on the Lotus, is 發起 | the assembly which, through Śāriputra, stirred the Buddha to begin his Lotus Sūtra sermons; 當機 | the pivotal assembly, those who were responsive to him; 影向 | the reflection assembly, those like Mañjuśrī, etc., who reflected on, or drew out the Buddha's teaching; and 結緣 | those who only profited in having seen and heard a Buddha, and therefore whose enlightenment is delayed to a future life.

四行 The four disciplinary processes: enlightenment; good deeds; wisdom; and worship. | | 相 To meditate upon the implications or disciplines of pain, unreality, impermanence, and the non-ego.

四衍 The four yānas or vehicles, idem 四乘.

四術 idem | 執.

四要品 The four most important chapters of the Lotus sūtra, i.e. 方便 |; 安樂行 |; 壽量 |, and 普門 |; this is T'ien-t'ai's selection; the Nichiren sect makes 勸持 | the second and 神力 | the fourth.

四親近 The four bodhisattvas associated with the five dhyāni-buddhas in the Vajradhātu.

四覺 The "four intelligences, or apprehensions" of the Awakening of Faith 起信論, q.v., viz. 本 |, 相似 |, 隨分 |, and 究竟 |.

四記 (or **答**) The Buddha's four methods of dealing with questions: direct answer, discriminating answer, questioning in return, and silence.

四評家 The four great scholars (among the 500 arhats) who made the Vibhāṣā-śāstra, a critical commentary on the Abhidharma. Their names are 世友 Vasumitra, 妙音 Ghoṣa, 法救 Dharmatrāta, and 覺天 Buddhadeva.

四論 Four famous śāstras: (1) 中觀 | Prāṇyamūla-śāstraṭikā by Nāgārjuna, four chüan; (2) 百論 Śata-śāstra by Devabodhisattva, two chüan; (3) 十二門 | Dvādaśanikāya(-mukha)-śāstra by Nāgārjuna, one chüan; (4) 大智度 | Mahāprajñāpāramitā-śāstra by Nāgārjuna, 100 chüan. During the Sui dynasty the followers of these four śāstras formed the 四論宗.

四諦 Catvāri ārya-satyāni; 四聖諦; 四眞諦. The four dogmas, or noble truths, the primary and fundamental doctrines of Śākyamuni, said to approximate to the form of medical diagnosis. They are pain or "suffering, its cause, its ending, the way thereto; that existence is suffering, that human passion (taṇhā, desire) is the cause of continued suffering, that by the destruction of human passion existence may be brought to an end; that by a life of holiness the destruction of human passion may be attained". Childers. The four are 苦, 聚 (or 集), 滅, and 道諦, i.e. duḥkha 豆佉, samudaya 三牟提耶, nirodha 尼樓陀, and mārga 末加. Eitel interprets them (1) "that 'misery' is a necessary attribute of sentient existence"; (2) that "the 'accumulation' of misery is caused by the passions"; (3) that "the 'extinction' of passion is possible; (4) mārga is "the doctrine of the 'path' that leads to the extinction of passion". (1) 苦 suffering is the lot of the 六趣 six states of existence; (2) 集 is the aggregation (or exacerbation) of suffering by reason of the passions; (3) 滅 is nirvāṇa, the extinction of desire and its consequences, and the leaving of the sufferings of mortality as void and extinct; (4) 道 is the way of such extinction, i.e. the 八正道 eightfold correct way. The first two are considered to be related to this life, the last two to 出世間 a life outside or apart from the world. The four are described as the fundamental doctrines first preached to his five former ascetic companions. Those who accepted these truths were in the stage of śrāvaka. There is much dispute as to the meaning of 滅 "extinction" as to whether it means extinction of suffering, of passion, or of existence. The Nirvāṇa sūtra 18 says that whoever accepts the four dogmas will put an end to births and deaths 若能見四諦則得斷生死 which does not of necessity mean the termination of existence but that of continued transmigration. v. 滅. | | 經 The sūtra of the four dogmas, tr. by 安世高 An Shih Kao, one chüan.

四趣 Durgati; the four evil directions or destinations: the hells, hungry ghosts, animals, asuras; v. | 惡.

四身 The four kāya, or "bodies". The Laṅkāvatāra sūtra gives 化佛; 功德佛; 智慧佛, and 如如佛; the first is the nirmāṇakāya, the second and third sambhogakāya, and the fourth dharmakāya. The 唯識論 gives 自性身; 他受用 |; 自受用 |, and 變化 |, the first being 法 |, the second and third 報 |, and the fourth 化 |. The T'ien-t'ai School gives 法 |; 報 |; 應 |, and 化 |. The esoteric sect has four divisions of the 法 |. See 三 |.

四車 The four vehicles 四乘 of the Lotus sūtra 譬喩品, i.e. goat, deer, bullock, and great white-bullock carts. | | 家 The Lotus School, which adds to the Triyāna, or Three Vehicles, a fourth which includes the other three, viz. the 一佛乘 q.v.

四軛 The four yokes, or fetters, i.e. 欲 desire, 有 possessions and existence, 見 (unenlightened or non-Buddhist) views, 無明 ignorance.

四輪 The four wheels or circles: (1) 大地四輪 the four on which the earth rests, wind (or air), water, metal, and space. (2) Four images with wheels, yellow associated with metal or gold, white with water, red with fire, and black with wind. (3) The four dhyāni-buddhas, 金剛輪 Akṣobhya; 寶輪 Ratnasambhava; 法輪 Amitābha; 羯磨輪 Amoghasiddhi. (4) Also the four metals, gold, silver, copper, iron, of the cakravartin kings. | | 王 The four kinds of cakravartin kings.

四輩 The four grades: (1) bhikṣu, bhikṣuṇī, upāsaka, upāsikā, i.e. monks, nuns, male and female disciples, v. | 衆; (2) men, devas, nāgas, and ghosts 鬼.

四迷 idem | 執.

四道 The tao or road means the nirvāṇa-road; the "four" are rather modes of progress, or stages in it: (1) 加行 | discipline or effort, i.e. progress from the 三賢 and 四善根 stages to that of the 三學位, i.e. morality, meditation, and understanding; (2) 無間 | uninterrupted progress to the stage in which all delusion is banished; (3) 解脫 | liberation, or freedom, reaching the state of assurance or proof and knowledge of the truth; and (4) 勝進 | surpassing progress in dhyāni-wisdom. Those four stages are also associated with those of srota-āpanna, sakṛdāgāmin, anāgāmin, and arhat.

四達 Saindhava, 先陀婆 rock-salt, but intp. as salt, water, a utensil, and a horse, the four necessaries, i.e. water for washing, salt for food, a vessel to contain it, and a horse for progress; also called | 實.

四運(心) The four stages of a thought: not yet arisen, its initiation, its realization, its passing away, styled 未念, 欲念, 正念, and 念已.

四邪 idem | 執.

四部 The four classes, e.g. srota-āpanna, sakṛdāgāmin, anāgāmin, and arhat. v. | 道.

四部律 v. 四律五論. | | 經 The four sūtras of the Pure-land sect, according to 慈恩 Tz'ŭ-ên, i.e. the 無量壽經; 觀無量壽經; 阿彌陀經, and 鼓音聲陀羅尼經. | | 衆; | | 弟子; | | 僧; 四衆 The four divisions of disciples—bhikṣu, bhikṣuṇī, upāsaka, and upāsikā, monks, nuns, and male and female devotees.

四重(禁) The four grave prohibitions, or sins, 四重罪 pārājikās: killing, stealing, carnality, lying. Also four of the esoteric sect, i.e. discarding the truth, discarding the bodhi-mind, being mean or selfish in regard to the supreme law, injuring the living. | | 八重 The four pārājikās for monks and eight for nuns. | | 圓壇; | | 曼荼羅 The Garbhadhātu maṇḍala of one central and three surrounding courts. The occupants are described as | | 聖衆 the sacred host of the four courts.

四金剛 The four mahārājas, v. 四天王.

四鉢 The four heavy stone begging-bowls offered to Śākyamuni by the four devas, which he miraculously combined into one and used as if ordinary material.

四鎭 The four guardians, v. 四天王.

四鏡 The four resemblances between a mirror and the bhūtatathatā in the Awakening of Faith 起信論. The bhūtatathatā, like the mirror, is independent of all beings, reveals all objects, is not hindered by objects, and serves all beings.

四門 The four doors, schools of thought, or theories: 有 is the phenomenal world real, or 空 unreal, or both, or neither? According to the T'ien-t'ai school each of the four schools 四教 in discussing these four questions emphasizes one of them, i.e. 三藏教 that it is real, 通教 unreal, 別教 both, 圓教 neither; v. 有 and 空, and each of the four schools. In esoteric symbolism the 四門 are four stages of initiation, development, enlightenment, and nirvāṇa, and are associated with E., S., W., and N.; with the four seasons; with warmth, heat, coolness and cold, etc. | | 遊觀 The four distresses observed during his wanderings by the Buddha when a prince—birth, age, disease, death.

四阿含 The four Āgamas 四阿笈摩, or divisions of the Hīnayāna scriptures: 長阿含 dīrghāgamas, "long" works, cosmological; 中 | | madhyamāgamas, metaphysical; 雜 | | saṁyuktāgamas, general, on dhyāna, trance, etc.; 增一 | | ekottarikāgamas, numerically arranged subjects.

四階成道(or 佛) The four Hīnayāna steps for attaining Buddhahood, i.e. the myriad deeds of the three asaṅkhyeya kalpas; the continually good karma of a hundred great kalpas; in the final body the cutting off of the illusions of the lower eight states; and the taking of one's seat on the bodhi-plot for final enlightenment, and the cutting off of the thirty-four forms of delusive thought.

四隅四行薩埵 The four female attendants on Vairocana in the Vajradhātu 金, 寶, 法, and 業, q.v.; also 四波.

四靜慮(天) v. 四禪(天).

四面毘盧遮那 The four-faced Vairocana, his dharmakāya of Wisdom.

四韋(陀) The four Vedas.

四馬 Four kinds of horses, likened to four classes of monks: those that respond to the shadow of the whip, its lightest touch, its mild application, and those who need the spur to bite the bone.

四須臾 The four short divisions of time—a wink; a snap of the fingers; 羅預 a lava, 20 finger-snaps; and 須臾 kṣaṇa, said to be 20 lava; but a lava is "the sixtieth of a twinkling" (M. W.) and a kṣaṇa an instant.

四食 The four kinds of food, i.e. 段 or 搏 ｜ for the body and its senses; 觸 or 樂 ｜ for the emotions; 思 or 念 ｜ for thought; and 識 ｜ for wisdom, i.e. the 六識 of Hīnayāna and the 八識 of Mahāyāna, of which the eighth, i.e. ālayavijñāna, is the chief.

四食時 The four times for food, i.e. of the devas at dawn, of all Buddhas at noon, of animals in the evening, and of demons and ghosts at night.

四齋日 The four fast days, i.e. at the quarters of the moon—new, full, 8th, and 23rd.

外 Bāhya. Outside, external; opposite to 內 within, inner, e.g. 內證 inner witness, or realization and 外用 external manifestation, function, or use. ｜乞 The mendicant monk who seeks self-control by external means, e.g. abstinence from food, as contrasted with the 內乞 who seeks it by spiritual methods. ｜塵 The external objects of the six internal senses. ｜外道 Outside outsiders, those of other cults. ｜學 Study of outside, or non-Buddhist doctrines. ｜我 An external Ego, e.g. a Creator or ruler of the world, such as Śiva. ｜法; ｜敎; ｜典; ｜執 External doctrines; rules or tenets non-Buddhist, or heretical. ｜海 The sea that surrounds the four world-continents. ｜無爲 Unmoved by externals, none of the senses stirred. ｜相 External appearance or conduct; what is manifested without; externally. The 十二外相 are the hair, teeth, nails, etc. ｜護 External protection, or aid, e.g. food and clothing for monks and nuns, contrasted with the internal aid of the Buddha's teaching. ｜貪欲 Sexual thoughts towards others than one's own wife, or husband. ｜道 Outside doctrines; non-Buddhist; heresy, heretics; the Tīrthyas or Tīrthikas; there are many groups of these: that of the 二天三仙 two devas and three sages, i.e. the Viṣṇuites, the Maheśvarites (or Śivaites), and the followers of Kapila, Ulūka, and Ṛṣabha. Another group of four is given as Kapila, Ulūka, Nirgrantha-putra (Jainas), and Jñātṛ (Jainas). A group of six, known as the ｜｜六師 six heretical masters, is Pūraṇa-Kāśyapa, Maskari-Gośālīputra, Sañjaya-Vairāṭīputra, Ajita-Keśakambala, Kakuda-Kātyāyana, and Nirgrantha-Jñātṛputra; there are also two other groupings of six, one of them indicative of their various forms of asceticism and self-torture. There are also groups of 13, 16, 20, 30, 95, and 96 heretics, or forms of non-Buddhist doctrine, the 95 being divided into 11 classes, beginning with the Sāṅkhya philosophy and ending with that of no-cause, or existence as accidental. ｜金剛部 The external twenty devas in the Vajradhātu group, whose names, many of them doubtful, are given as Nārāyaṇa, Kumāra, Vajragoḍa, Brahmā, Śakra, Āditya, Candra, Vajramāha, ? Musala, Piṅgala, ? Rakṣalevatā, Vāyu, Vajravāsin, Agni, Vaiśravaṇa, Vajrāṅkuśa, Yama, Vajrajaya, Vināyaka, Nāgavajra. ｜｜｜｜院 The last of the thirteen courts in the Garbhadhātu group.

失 To lose, opp. of 得; to err. ｜守 (or 收) 摩羅 Śiśumāra, "child-killing, the Gangetic porpoise, Delphinus Gangeticus," M. W. Tr. by 鱷 a crocodile, which is the kumbhīra 金毘羅. ｜念 To lose the train of thought, or meditation; a wandering mind; loss of memory. ｜羅婆 Śravaṇā, a constellation identified with the Ox, or 9th Chinese constellation, in Aries and Sagittarius.

央 The middle, medial; to solicit; ample, vast. ｜掘(摩羅); ｜仇魔羅; ｜崛鬘; 盎 (or 鴦) 崛 (or 窶) 利摩羅 Aṅgulimālya, Śivaitic fanatics who "made assassination a religious act", and wore finger-bones as a chaplet. One who had assassinated 999, and was about to assassinate his mother for the thousandth, is said to have been then converted by the Buddha.

奴 A slave ｜僕; ｜隸. ｜婢 Male and female slaves.

尼 To stop; a nun; near; translit. *ni*. When used for a nun it is an abbrev. for 比丘尼 bhikṣuṇī. ｜壇 The nun's altar; a convent or nunnery. ｜大師 An abbess. ｜姑 A nun. ｜寺 A nunnery, or convent. ｜戒 The rules for nuns, numbering 341, to which seven more were added making 348, commonly called the 五百戒 500 rules. ｜比丘 A female bhikṣu, i.e. a nun. ｜法師 A nun teacher; effeminate. ｜衆主 The Mistress of the nuns, Gautamī, i.e. Mahāprajāpatī, the foster-mother of Śākyamuni.

尼刺部 (or 浮) 陀 Nirarbuda, ｜羅浮陀 "bursting tumours", the second naraka of the eight cold hells.

尼夜摩 Niyama, restraint, vow; determination, resolve; a degree of Bodhisattva progress, i.e. never turning back.

尼師壇 (or **但那**) Niṣīdana; 𩑦史娜曩 A thing to sit or lie on, a mat.

尼延底 ? Niyati, or Niyantṛ | 近 | tr. as 執取 to restrain, hold, also as 深入 deeply enter, and said to be another term for 貪 to desire, covet.

尼建他迦 Niṣkaṇṭhaka, | 延他柯 a kind of yakṣa, 無咽 throatless.

尼彌留陀 Nirodha, tr. as 滅 extinction, annihilation, cessation, the third of the four noble truths, cf. 尼樓陀.

尼思佛 Sugatacetana, a disciple who slighted Śākyamuni in his former incarnation of 常不輕 Never despise, but who afterwards attained through him to Buddhahood.

尼拘陀 Nyag-rodha, the down-growing tree, Ficus Indica, or banyan; high and wide-spreading, leaves like persimmon-leaves, fruit called 多勒 to-lo used as a cough-medicine; also intp. 楊柳 the willow, probably from its drooping characteristic; the 榕樹 "bastard banyan", Ficus pyrifolia, takes its place as Ficus religiosa in China. Also written | | 律; | | 尼陀; | | 盧 (or 類, 婁, or 屢) 陀; | 瞿陀; | 倶陀 (or 類); 諾瞿陀.

尼抵 Nidhi (Praṇidhāna); also | 低; | 提 The Sanskrit is doubtful. The intp. is 願 vow, or 願志求滿足 seeking the fulfilment of resolves, or aims.

尼提; **尼陀** A scavenger.

尼摩羅 Nirmāṇarati, 須密陀天 devas who "delight in transformations", i.e. 化樂天 or 樂變化天; of the six devalokas of desire they occupy the fifth, where life lasts for 8,000 years.

尼樓陀 Nirodha, restraint, suppression, cessation, annihilation, tr. by 滅 extinction, the third of the four dogmas 四諦; with the breaking of the chain of karma there is left no further bond to reincarnation. Used in Anupūrva-nirodha, or "successive terminations", i.e. nine successive stages of dhyāna. Cf. 尼彌留陀.

尼民陀 (**羅**) Nimindhara, or Nemiṁdhara | | 達羅 maintaining the circle, i.e. the outermost ring of the seven concentric ranges of a world, the 地持山 the mountains that hold the land. Also the name of a sea fish whose head is supposed to resemble this mountain.

尼沙陀 Upaniṣad, v. 鄔.

尼波羅 Nepāla, Nepal, anciently corresponding to that part of Nepal which lies east of the Kāṭhmāṇḍū. Eitel.

尼犍 Nirgrantha, | 健; | 乾 (陀); | 虔, freed from all ties, a naked mendicant, tr. by 離繫不繫, 無結 devotees who are free from all ties, wander naked, and cover themselves with ashes. Mahāvīra, one of this sect, called 若提 Jñāti after his family, and also 尼乾陀若提子 Nirgrantha-jñātiputra, was an opponent of Śākyamuni. His doctrines were determinist, everything being fated, and no religious practices could change one's lot. | | 度 Bhikṣuṇī-khaṇḍa, a division of the Vinaya, containing the rules for nuns. | | 陀弗咀羅 Nirgrantha-putra, idem Jñāti.

尼羅 Nīla, dark blue or green. | | 優曇鉢羅 Nīla-udumbara, v. 優. | | 婆陀羅; 尼藍婆 Nīlavajra, the blue vajra, or thunderbolt. | | 浮陀 idem 尼剌部陀. | | 烏 (or 漚) 鉢羅 Nīlotpala, the blue lotus. | | 蔽荼 Nīlapiṭa, "the blue collection" of annals and royal edicts, mentioned in 西域記.

尼薩曇 Defined as an atom, the smallest possible particle; but its extended form of 優波尼薩曇分 suggests upaniṣad, esoteric doctrine, the secret sense of the sūtras. | | 耆波逸提 Naiḥsargika-prāyaścittika, intp. by 捨 and 墮, the sin in the former case being forgiven on confession and restoration being made, in the latter being not forgiven because of refusal to confess and restore. Cf. 二百五十戒.

尼衛 Nivāsana, an inner garment.

尼近底 v. 尼延底.

尼迦羅 ? Niṣkala, the name of a tree, but niṣkala means *inter alia* seedless, barren.

尼連禪 (**那**) Nairañjanā, | | 河; 希連禪 (or 河) The Nīlajan that flows past Gayā, "an eastern tributary of the Phalgu." Eitel.

尼陀那 Nidāna, a band, bond, link, primary cause. I. The 十二因緣 twelve causes or links in the chain of existence: (1) Jarā-maraṇa 老死 old age and death. (2) Jāti 生 (re)birth. (3) Bhava 有 existence. (4) Upādāna 取 laying hold of, grasping. (5) Tṛṣṇā 愛 love, thirst, desire. (6) Vedanā 受 receiving, perceiving, sensation. (7) Sparśa 觸 touch, contact, feeling. (8) Ṣaḍ-āyatana, 六入 the six senses. (9) Nāma-rūpa 名色 name and form, individuality (of things). (10) Vijñāna 六識 the six forms of perception, awareness or discernment. (11) Saṁskāra 行 action, moral conduct. (12) Avidyā 無明 unenlightenment, "ignorance which mistakes the illusory phenomena of this world for realities." Eitel. These twelve links are stated also in Hīnayāna in reverse order, beginning with Avidyā and ending with Jarā-maraṇa. The Fan-i-ming-i says the whole series arises from 無明 ignorance, and if this can be got rid of the whole process of 生死 births and deaths (or reincarnations) comes to an end. II. Applied to the purpose and occasion of writing sūtras, Nidāna means (1) those written because of a request or query; (2) because certain precepts were violated; (3) because of certain events. | | | 目得迦 Nidāna-mātṛkā, two of the twelve divisions of the sūtras, one dealing with the nidānas, the other with 本事 previous incarnations.

巧 Skilful, clever. | 妙智; | 智慧 is 一切智智 q.v. | 明 v. 功巧論.

巨 Great; translit. *ko*, *kau*, *go*. | 益 Great benefit. | 磨 Gomaya, cow-dung. | 賞彌 Kauśāmbī, (Pali) Kosambi, Vatsa-pattana. Also written 俱睒 (or 賞, or 舍) 彌; 拘睒 (or 剡) 彌; 拘鹽; 拘深; 拘羅瞿; 拘翼; 憍賞 (or 閃) 彌. The country of King Udayana in "Central India", described as 6,000 li in circuit, soil rich, with a famous capital, in which the 西域記 5 says there was a great image of the Buddha. Eitel says: It was "one of the most ancient cities of India, identified by some with Kasia near Kurrah (Lat. 25° 41 N., Long. 81° 27 E.), by others with the village of Kosam on the Jumna 30 miles above Allahabad". It is identified with Kosam.

左 The left hand. | 溪 Tso-ch'i, the eighth T'ien-t'ai patriarch, named Hsüan-lang 玄朗.

市 A market, a fair, an open place for public assembly. | 演得迦 Jetaka, or 娑多婆漢那 Sadvāhana. A king of southern Kosala, patron of Nāgārjuna.

布 Cloth, to spread; translit. *pu*, *po*, *pau*.

布儞阿偈 Pūti-agada, purgatives.

布利迦 Pūrikā, a kind of cake.

布剌拏 Pūraṇa-Kāśyapa, v. 富. Also Pūrṇa of the 釋毘婆少論 v. 毘.

布史 Pauṣa, the 10th month in India.

布咀洛迦 Potala, v. 補 and 普.

布嚕婆毗提訶 Pūrva-Videha, or Videha. 弗婆(毗)提(訶); 弗于毗婆提訶; 逋利婆鼻提賀 One of the four great continents east of Sumeru.

布嚕那跋陀羅 Pūrṇabhadra, one of the eight yakṣa generals.

布如烏伐耶 Puṇyopāya, or 那提 Nadī. A monk of Central India, said to have brought over 1,500 texts of the Mahāyāna and Hīnayāna schools to China A.D. 655. In 656 he was sent to 崑崙山 Pulo Condore Island in the China Sea for some strange medicine. Tr. three works, one lost by A.D. 730.

布字觀 A Shingon meditation on the Sanskrit letter "a" and others, written on the devotee's own body.

布怛那 Pūtanā, | 單 |; 富多 (or 單 or 陀) 那 a female demon poisoning or the cause of wasting in a child; interpreted as a stinking hungry demon, and the most successful of demons.

布教 To publish, or spread abroad the doctrine.

布施 Dāna 檀那; the sixth pāramitā, almsgiving, i.e. of goods, or the doctrine, with resultant benefits now and also hereafter in the forms of reincarnation, as neglect or refusal will produce the opposite consequences. The 二種 | | two kinds of dāna are the pure, or unsullied charity, which looks for no reward here but only hereafter; and the sullied almsgiving whose object is personal benefit. The three kinds of dāna are goods, the doctrine, and courage, or fearlessness. The four kinds are pens to write the sūtras, ink, the sūtras themselves, and preaching. The five kinds are giving to those who have come from a distance, those who are going to a distance, the sick, the hungry, those wise in the doctrine. The seven kinds are giving to visitors, travellers, the sick, their nurses, monasteries, endowments for the sustenance of monks or nuns, and clothing and food according to season. The eight kinds are giving to those who come for aid, giving for fear (of evil), return for kindness received, anticipating gifts in return, continuing the parental example of giving, giving in hope of rebirth in a particular heaven, in hope of an honoured name, for the adornment of the heart and life. 俱舍論 18.

布瑟波 Puṣpa, 補澀波 a flower 華.

布薩 Poṣadha, Upavasatha, Upoṣaṇa; 布沙 (or 灑) 他; 褒沙陀 Pali: Uposatha; fasting, a fast, the nurturing or renewal of vows, intp. by 淨住 or 善宿 or 長養, meaning abiding in retreat for spiritual refreshment. There are other similar terms, e.g. 布薩陀婆; 優補陀婆; also 布薩犍度 which the Vinaya uses for the meeting place; 鉢囉帝提舍耶寐 pratideśanīya, is self-examination and public confession during the fast. It is also an old Indian fast. Buddha's monks should meet at the new and full moons and read the Prātimokṣa sūtra for their moral edification, also disciples at home should observe the six fast days and the eight commands. The | | 日 fast days are the 15th and 29th or 30th of the moon. | | 護 is a term for the lay observance of the first eight commandments on fast days, and it is used as a name for those commands.

布袋和尙 Pu-tai Ho-shang (J.: Hotei Oshō) Cloth-bag monk, an erratic monk 長汀子 Ch'ang-t'ing-tzŭ early in the tenth century, noted, *inter alia*, for his shoulder bag. Often depicted, especially in Japanese art, as a jovial, corpulent monk, scantily clad and surrounded by children.

布路沙 Puruṣa, | 嚕 |; 補盧沙 man, mankind, a man, Man as Nārāyaṇa the soul and origin of the universe, the soul, the Soul, Supreme Being, God, see M. W.; intp. as 人 and 丈夫 man, and an adult man, also by 士夫 master or educated man, "explained by 神我, literally the spiritual self. A metaphysical term; the spirit which together with nature (自性 Svabhāva), through the successive modifications (轉變) of Guṇa (求那 attributes or qualities), or the active principles (作者), produces all forms of existence (作一切物)." Eitel. | | | 布羅; 佛樓沙 Puruṣapura; the ancient capital of Gandhāra, the modern Peshāwar.

布達拉 Potala, 普陀羅 the monastery of the Dalai Lama in Lhasa; v. 普.

平 Even, level, tranquil; ordinary. | 常 Ordinary, usual, common. | 生 Throughout life; all one's life. | 等 Sama; samatā. Level, even, everywhere the same, universal, without partiality; it especially refers to the Buddha in his universal, impartial, and equal attitude towards all beings. | | 力 Universal power, or omnipotence, i.e. to save all beings, a title of a Buddha. | | 大慧 "Universal great wisdom", the declaration by the ancient Buddha in the Lotus sūtra, that all would obtain the Buddha-wisdom. | | 心 An impartial mind, "no respecter of persons," not loving one and hating another. | | 性 The universal nature, i.e. the 眞如 bhūtatathatā q.v. | | 性智 Samatājñāna. The wisdom of rising above such distinctions as I and Thou, meum and tuum, thus being rid of the ego idea, and wisdom in regard to all things equally and universally, cf. 五智. The esoteric school also call it the 灌頂智 and Ratnasambhava wisdom. | | 敎 One of two schools founded by 印法師 Yin Fa-shih early in the T'ang dynasty. | | 智 Samatājñāna, wisdom of universality or sameness, v. *supra*. | | 法 The universal or impartial truth that all become Buddha, 一切衆生平等成佛. | | 法身 Universalized dharmakāya, a stage in Bodhisattva development above the eighth, i.e. above the 八地. | | 王 Yama, the impartial or just judge and awarder. But the name is also applied to one of the Ten Rulers of the Underworld, distinct from Yama. Also, name of the founder of the Kṣatriya caste, to which the Śākyas belonged. | | 義 The meaning of universal, i.e. that the 眞如 q.v. is equally and everywhere in all things. | | 覺 A Buddha's universal and impartial perception, his absolute intuition above the laws of differentiation. | | 觀 One of the three T'ien-t'ai meditations, the 假觀 phenomenal being blended with the noumenal or universal. The term is also used for 空觀 meditation on the universal, or absolute.

平袈裟 A one-coloured robe of seven pieces.

弘 Vast, great; to enlarge, spread abroad; e.g. | 宣; | 敎; | 法; | 通 widely to proclaim the Buddhist truth; | 忍, | 法 Hung-jên and Hung-fa, names of noted monks; | 誓; | (誓) 願 vast or universal vows of a Buddha, or Bodhisattva, especially Amitābha's forty-eight vows.

弗 Not; no; do not. | 于逮; | 于毘婆提訶 idem 布嚕波 Pūrva-Videha. | 伽羅; 福 (or 富) 伽羅; 補特伽羅 Pudgala; Pali, puggala. M. W.

says "handsome", "having form or property", "the soul, personal identity" Keith uses "person", "personality". Eitel, "a general term for all human beings as subject to metempsychosis. A philosophical term denoting personality." It is tr. by 人 man and 衆生 all the living; later by 數取趣 those who go on to repeated reincarnations, but whether this means the individual soul in its rebirths is not clear. | 如檀 Puṇyādarśa, auspicious mirror, interpreted as 法鏡 mirror of the law; name of a man. | 婆勢羅 Pūrvaśaila, "the eastern mountain behind which the sun is supposed to rise." M. W. The eastern mountain, name of a monastery east of Dhānyakaṭaka (Amarāvatī), the 弗 (or 佛) 婆 (or 婆) 勢羅僧伽藍 Pūrvaśaila-saṅghārāma. One of the subdivisions of the Māhāsaṅghika school. | | 呵羅 Puṣpāhara, flower-plucker, 食花 flower-eater, name of a yakṣa. | | 提; | | 鞞陀提 idem 弗毘提訶. | 沙王 Vatsarāja. King Vatsa, idem Udayana, v. 優塡. The | | 迦王經 is another name for the 萍沙王五願經. |沙; 勃 or 富 or 逋 or 補沙; Puṣya; "the sixth (or in later times the eighth) Nakshatra or lunar mansion, also called Tishya." M. W. 底沙. It is the 鬼 group Cancer γδηθ, the 23rd of the Chinese twenty-eight stellar mansions. Name of an ancient Buddha. | | 佛 idem 底沙佛. | | 蜜多 Puṣyamitra, descendant of Aśoka and enemy of Buddhism; possibly a mistake for the next. | | | | 羅 Puṣyamitra, the fourth successor of King Aśoka; asking what he should do to perpetuate his name, he was told that Aśoka had erected 84,000 shrines and he might become famous by destroying them, which he is said to have done, v. 雜阿含經 25. | 栗特 Vṛji, or 三伐特 Saṁvaji. An ancient kingdom north of the Ganges, S.E. of Nepal, the inhabitants, called Saṁvaji, were noted for their heretical proclivities. Eitel. | 毘提訶 Pūrva-Videha, or Videha, the continent east of Sumeru, idem 布嚕波. | 波提; | 把提 Either devapuṣpa, or bhūpadī, the latter being Jasminum Zambæ; both are interpreted by 天華 deva-flowers. | 若多羅; 功德華 Puṇyatara, a śramaṇa of Kubhā 罽賓國 (Kabul), who came to China and in 404 tr. with Kumārajīva the 十誦律 Sarvāstivāda-vinaya. "One of the twenty-four Deva-Ārya (天尊) worshipped in China." Eitel.

必 Certainly, necessary, must. | 定 Certainly, assuredly; tr. of 阿鞞跋致 Avaivartika, intp. as 不退轉 never receding, or turning back, always progressing, and certainly reaching nirvāṇa. | 栗託佐那 Pṛthagjana, interpreted as 獨生, 異生, and 凡夫; pṛthak is separately, individually; with Buddhists the whole term means born an ordinary man; the common people. | 梼家; 比摘迦 Piṭaka, a basket, receptacle, thesaurus, hence the Tripiṭaka 三藏. | 至 Certainly will, certainly arrive at.

忉 Grieved, distressed. | 利天 Trayastriṁśās, 怛唎耶怛唎奢; 多羅夜登陵舍; the heavens of the thirty-three devas, 三十三天, the second of the desire-heavens, the heaven of Indra; it is the Svarga of Hindu mythology, situated on Meru with thirty-two deva-cities, eight on each side; a central city is 善見城 Sudarśana, or Amarāvatī, where Indra, with 1,000 heads and eyes and four arms, lives in his palace called 禪延; 毘闍 (or 禪) 延 ? Vaijayanta, and "revels in numberless sensual pleasures together with his wife" Śacī and with 119,000 concubines. "There he receives the monthly reports of the" four Mahārājas as to the good and evil in the world. "The whole myth may have an astronomical" or meteorological background, e.g. the number thirty-three indicating the "eight Vasus, eleven Rudras, twelve Ādıtyas, and two Aśvins of Vedic mythology." Eitel. Cf. 因陀羅.

戊 Wu, Mou; flourishing; the fifth of the ten "stems". | 地 The Fan-i-ming-i describes this as 西安國, perhaps 安西國 Parthia is meant. | 達羅 A misprint for 戍達羅; 首陁 Śūdra, the caste of farmers and slaves.

打 To beat, strike, make, do; used for many kinds of such action. | 供 To make offerings. | 包 To wrap up or carry a bundle, i.e. a wandering monk. | 坐 To squat, sit down crosslegged. | 成一片 To knock all into one, bring things together, or into order. | 板 To beat the board, or wooden block, e.g. as an announcement, or intimation. | 眠衣 A monk's sleeping garment. | 聽 To make inquiries. | 靜 To beat the silencer, or beat for silence. | 飯 To eat rice, or a meal.

旦 Dawn. | 望 The new moon and full moon, or first and fifteenth of the moon. | 過僧 A wandering monk, who stays for a night. | 過寮 A monastery at which he stays.

未 Not yet; the future; 1–3 p.m. | 了因 The karma of past life not yet fulfilled. | 來; 當來 Anāgata; that which has not come, or will come; the future, e.g. | 來世 a future life, or lives; also the future tense, one of the 三世, i.e. 過, 現, 未 past, present, future. | 受具人 A monk who has not yet formally pledged himself to all the commandments. | 敷蓮華 A half-opened lotus, such as one of the forms of Kuan-yin holds in the hand. |曾有; 希有; 阿浮陀 Adbhuta; never yet been, non-such, rare, marvellous. |||經 Adbhutadharma-paryāya, one of the twelve divisions of the sūtras 十二部經. |||正法經 A Sung translation of the 阿闍世王經 Ajātaśatru-kaukṛīyavinodana. |生怨 Having no enemy, tr. of the name of Ajātaśatru 阿闍世王. There is a sūtra of this name describing his murder of his father Bimbisāra. |至; |到 Not yet arrived, or reached. |陀 ? Arbuda, 100 (or 10) millions. |顯眞實; |開顯 The unrevealed truth, the Truth only revealed by the Buddha in his final Mahāyāna doctrine.

本 Radical, fundamental, original, principal, one's own; the Buddha himself, contrasted with 蹟 chi, traces left by him among men to educate them; also a volume of a book.

本三昧耶印 The first samaya-sign to be made in worship, the forming of the hands after the manner of a lotus.

本不生際 The original status of no rebirth, i.e. every man has a naturally pure heart, which 不生不滅 is independent of the bonds of mortality.

本事經 Itivṛttaka; ityukta; one of the twelve classes of sūtras, in which the Buddha tells of the deeds of his disciples and others in previous lives, cf. 本生經.

本二 His original second (in the house), the wife of a monk, before he retired from the world.

本佛 The Buddha-nature within oneself; the original Buddha.

本來 Coming from the root, originally, fundamentally, 無始以來 from, or before, the very beginning. ||成佛 All things being of Buddha become Buddha. ||法爾 So from the beginning, interpreted as 自始自然. ||無一物 Originally not a thing existing, or before anything existed—a subject of meditation. |(來)空 That all things come from the Void, or Absolute, the 眞如.

本初 In the beginning; originally.

本命星 The life-star of an individual, i.e. the particular star of the seven stars of Ursa Major which is dominant in the year of birth; ||宿 is the constellation, or star-group, under which he is born; ||元辰 is the year of birth, i.e. the year of his birth-star. ||道場 Temple for worship of the emperor's birth-star, for the protection of the imperial family and the state.

本地 Native place, natural position, original body; also the 本身; 本法身; or 本地身 fundamental person or embodiment of a Buddha or bodhisattva, as distinct from his temporal manifestation. ||門 The uncreated dharmakāya of Vairocana is eternal and the source of all things and all virtue.

本尊 ? Satyadevatā, 娑也地提嚩多. The original honoured one; the most honoured of all Buddhas; also the chief object of worship in a group; the specific Buddha, etc., being served.

本山 Native hill; a monk's original or proper monastery; this (or that) monastery; also 本寺.

本師 The original Master or Teacher, Śākyamuni. ||和尙 Upādhyāya 烏波陀耶 an original teacher, or founder; a title of Amitābha.

本形 Original form, or figure; the substantive form.

本心 The original heart, or mind; one's own heart.

本性 The spirit one possesses by nature; hence, the Buddha-nature; the Buddha-nature within; one's own nature.

本惑 The root or origin of delusion; also 根本惑; 根本煩惱.

本拏哩迦 idem Puṇḍarīka, v. 奔.

本據 Mūlagrantha; the original text, or a quotation from it.

本教 The fundamental doctrine, i.e. of the One Vehicle as declared in the Lotus Sūtra, also 根本之敎.

本明 The original light, or potential enlightenment, that is in all beings; also 元明; cf. 本覺.

本時 The original time, the period when Śākyamuni obtained enlightenment; at that time.

本書 The foundation books of any school; a book.

本有 Originally or fundamentally existing; primal existence; the source and substance of all phenomena; also the present life; also the eighth 識, i.e. Ālaya-vijñāna. ｜｜修生. The 本有 means that original dharma is complete in each individual, the 眞如法性之德 the virtue of the bhūtatathatā dharma-nature, being 具足無缺 complete without lack; the 修生 means the development of this original mind in the individual, whether saint or common man, to the realization of Buddha-virtue; 由觀行之力, 開發其本有之德, 漸漸修習而次第開顯佛德也. ｜｜家 A division of the Dharmalakṣaṇa school 法相宗.

本末 Root and twigs, root and branch, first and last, beginning and end, etc.

本母 Upadeśa; mātṛkā; the original "mother" or matrix; the original sūtra, or work.

本淨(無漏) Primal purity.

本生經 Jātaka sūtras 闍陀伽; stories of the Buddha's previous incarnations, one of the twelve classes of sūtras. ｜｜說 The stories thus told. v. 本事經.

本緣 The origin or cause of any phenomenon.

本行 The root of action; the method or motive of attainment; (his) own deeds, e.g. the doings of a Buddha or bodhisattva. ｜｜(集)經 A sūtra of this title.

本囊伽吒 Pūrṇaghaṭa, full pitcher, "one of the sixty-five mystic figures said to be traceable on every footprint (śrīpada) of Buddha." Eitel.

本覺 Original bodhi, i.e. "enlightenment", awareness, knowledge, or wisdom, as contrasted with 始覺 initial knowledge, that is "enlightenment *a priori* is contrasted with enlightenment *a posteriori*". Suzuki, *Awakening of Faith*, p. 62. The reference is to universal mind 衆生之心體, which is conceived as pure and intelligent, with 始覺 as active intelligence. It is considered as the Buddha-dharmakāya, or as it might perhaps be termed, the fundamental mind. Nevertheless in action from the first it was influenced by its antithesis 無明 ignorance, the opposite of awareness, or true knowledge. See 起信論 and 仁王經中. There are two kinds of 本覺, one which is unconditioned, and never sullied by ignorance and delusion, the other which is conditioned and subject to ignorance. In original enlightenment is implied potential enlightenment in each being. ｜｜眞如 The 眞如, i.e. bhūtatathatā, is the 體 corpus, or embodiment; the 本覺 is the 相 or form of primal intelligence; the former is the 理 or fundamental truth, the latter is the 智, i.e. the knowledge or wisdom of it; together they form the whole embodiment of the Buddha-dharmakāya.

本質 Original substance, the substance itself; any real object of the senses.

本誓 Samaya; the original covenant or vow made by every Buddha and Bodhisattva.

本識 The fundamental vijñāna, one of the eighteen names of the Ālaya-vijñāna, the root of all things.

本身 Oneself; it also means 本心 the inner self.

本迹 The original 本 Buddha or Bodhisattva and his 迹 varied manifestations for saving all beings, e.g. Kuan-yin with thirty-three forms. Also ｜地垂迹. ｜｜二門 A division of the Lotus Sūtra into two parts, the 迹門 being the first fourteen chapters, the 本門 the following fourteen chapters; the first half is related to the Buddha's earthly life and previous teaching; the second half to the final revelation of the Buddha as eternal and the Bodhisattva doctrines.

本門 v. 本迹. ｜｜本尊 The especial honoured one of the Nichiren sect, Svādi-devatā, the Supreme Being, whose maṇḍala is considered as the symbol of the Buddha as infinite, eternal, universal. The Nichiren sect has a meditation ｜｜事觀 on the universality of the Buddha and the unity in the diversity of all his phenomena, the whole truth being embodied in the Lotus Sūtra, and in its title of five words, 妙法蓮華經 Wonderful-Law Lotus-Flower Sūtra, which are considered to be the embodiment of the eternal, universal Buddha. Their repetition preceded by 南無 Namah! is equivalent to the 歸命 of other Buddhists.

本願 Pūrvapraṇidhāna. The original vow, or vows, of a Buddha or bodhisattva, e.g. the forty-eight of Amitābha, the twelve of 藥師, etc. ｜｜—

實大道 The great way of the one reality of Amitābha's vows, i.e. that of calling on his name and trusting to his strength and not one's own.

本高迹下 The higher (Buddha) manifesting himself in lower form, e.g. as a bodhisattva.

末 Branch, twig; end; dust; not; translit. *ma*, *va*, *ba*; cf. 摩.

末上 On the last, at last, finally.

末世 The third and last period of a Buddha-kalpa; the first is the first 500 years of correct doctrine, the second is the 1,000 years of semblance law, or approximation to the doctrine, and the third a myriad years of its decline and end. Also 末代.

末伽 Mārga; track, path, way, the way; the fourth of the four dogmas 四諦, i.e. 道, known as the 八聖道, 八正道 (or 門), the eight holy or correct ways, or gates out of suffering into nirvāṇa. Mārga is described as the 因 cause of liberation, bodhi as its 果 result. ||始羅 Mārgaśiras, M. W. says November–December; the Chinese say from the 16th of the 9th moon to the 15th of the 10th. ||梨; ||梨 (or 黎) 拘賒梨 (or 黎); 末佉梨劬奢離 Maskari Gośālīputra, one of the six Tīrthikas 外道六師. He denied that present lot was due to deeds done in previous lives, and the Laṅkāvatāra sūtra says he taught total annihilation at the end of this life.

末利 Mallikā, 摩利; 末羅 (1) Jasminum Zambac, M. W., which suggests the 茉莉花, i.e. the Chinese jasmine; according to Eitel it is the narrow-leaved nyctanthes (with globular berries 柰); the flower, now called kastūrī (musk) because of its odour. By the Fan-i-ming-i it is styled the 鬘花 chaplet flower, as its flowers may be formed into a chaplet. (2) A concoction of various fruits mixed with water offered in worship. ||夫人 The wife of Prasenajit, king of Kośala, so called because she wove or wore jasmine chaplets, or came from a jasmine garden, etc. ||室羅 Mālyaśrī, said to be a daughter of the last and queen in Ayodhyā, capital of Kośala.

末剌諵 Maraṇa, 死 dying, mortal, death.

末化 Buddha transformed into (palm-)branches or leaves; the transformation of the Buddha in the shape of the sūtras.

末嗟羅 Matsara, 慳 grudging, stingy, greedy.

末多利 One of the divisions of the Sarvāstivādāḥ school, said to be the 北山部 q.v.

末奴是若颯縛羅 Manojñasvara 如意音, 樂音 lovely sounds, music; a king of the Gandharvas, Indra's musicians.

末奴沙 Mānuṣa, Manuṣya; 摩奴 (or 努) 娑; 摩奴闍 (or 曬); 摩努史; 摩㝹沙 (or 賒, or 奢, or 舍喃); 摩㝹; 摩拏赦 man, human, intp. by 人 and 意 man and mind or intelligence.

末寺 Subsidiary buildings of a monastery.

末尼 Maṇi 摩尼; a jewel, a crystal, a pearl, symbol of purity, therefore of Buddha and of his doctrine. It is used in Oṁ-maṇi-padmi-hūṁ. ||敎 The Manichean religion, first mentioned in Chinese literature by Hsüan-tsang in his Memoirs, between A.D. 630 and 640. The first Manichean missionary from 大秦 Ta-ch'in reached China in 694. In 732, an imperial edict declared the religion of Mani a perverse doctrine, falsely taking the name of Buddhism. It continued, however, to flourish in parts of China, especially Fukien, even to the end of the Ming dynasty. Chinese writers have often confused it with Mazdeism 火祆敎.

末底 Mati 摩提; devotion, discernment, understanding, tr. by 慧 wisdom. ||僧訶 Matisiṁha, the lion of intelligence, an honorific title.

末度迦 Madhūka 末杜迦; 摩頭; M. W. Bassia latifolia, tr. as 美果 a fine or pleasant fruit.

末捺南 Vandana, 禮 worship, reverence.

末摩 Marman; a vital part, or mortal spot.

末梨 Bali, an asura king.

末法 The last of the three periods 正, 像, and 末; that of degeneration and extinction of the Buddha-law.

末田 Madhyāntika, ||地 (那); ||底加 ||提; ||鐸迦; |彈地; |闡地 or 提 摩 is also used for 末. It is tr. by 中; 日中, 水中

河中, and 金地. One of the two chief disciples of Ānanda, to whom he handed down the Buddha's doctrine. He is reputed to have been sent to convert 罽賓 Kashmir, the other, 商那和修 Śāṇakavāsa, to convert 中國 which is probably Central India, though it is understood as China. Another account makes the latter a disciple of the former. Eitel says that by his magic power he transported a sculptor to the Tuṣita heavens to obtain a correct image of Maitreya.

末睇提舍 Madhyadeśa, 中國 the central kingdom, i.e. Central India.

末笯曷剌他 Manorhita, or Manoratha, tr. by 如意, an Indian prince who became the disciple and successor of Vasubandhu, reputed author of the 毘婆沙論 Vibhāṣā śāstra and the twenty-second patriarch.

末羅 Malla 魔羅; a term for inhabitants of Kuśinagara and Pāvā. 丨丨王經 The sūtra of the king of this name, whose road was blocked by a rock, which his people were unable to remove, but which the Buddha removed easily by his miraculous powers. 丨丨羯多 Marakata, 摩羅迦陀 the emerald. 丨丨遊 Malaya, "the western Ghats in the Deccan (these mountains abound in sandal trees); the country that lies to the east of the Malaya range, Malabar." M. W. Eitel gives 秣羅矩吒 Malakūṭa, i.e. Malaya, as "an ancient kingdom of Southern India, the coast of Malabar, about A.D. 600 a noted haunt of the Nirgrantha sect". It is also identified with 尸利佛逝 Śrībhoja, which is given as 馬來半島 the Malay peninsula; but v. 摩羅耶 Malaya.

末栗者 Marica, pepper.

末迦吒賀邏馱 Markaṭa-hrada; the Apes' Pool, near Vaiśālī.

末達那 Madana; 摩陀 (or 達) 那; 摩陀羅 a fruit called the intoxicating fruit 醉果.

末那 Manaḥ; manas; intp. by 意 mind, the (active) mind. Eitel says: "The sixth of the Chaḍâyatana, the mental faculty which constitutes man as an intelligent and moral being." The 丨丨識 is defined by the 唯識論 4 as the seventh of the 八識, namely 意, which means 思量 thinking and measuring, or calculating. It is the active mind, or activity of mind, but is also used for the mind itself.

末陀 Madya, intoxicating liquor, intoxicating. The two characters are also given as a translation of ? Madhya, and mean 100,000. 丨丨摩 This is intp. as not in the mean or middle way.

末麗曩 Balin 麼攞; strong, strengthening.

正 Right, correct; just, exact; chief, principal; the first month.

正中 Exactly middle; midday.

正依經 The sūtras on which any sect specially relies.

正像末 The three periods of correct law, semblance law, and decadence, or finality; cf. 丨法.

正命 Samyagājīva, the fifth of the 八正道, right livelihood, right life; "abstaining from any of the forbidden modes of living."

正因 The true or direct cause, as compared with 緣因 a contributory cause.

正地部 v. 磨 Mahīśāsakāḥ.

正報 The direct retribution of the individual's previous existence, such as being born as a man, etc. Also 丨果.

正士 Correct scholar, bodhisattva.

正定 Samyaksamādhi, right abstraction or concentration, so that the mind becomes vacant and receptive, the eighth of the 八正道; "right concentration, in the shape of the Four Meditations." Keith. 丨丨業 Concentration upon the eighteenth vow of Amitābha and the Western Paradise, in repeating the name of Amitābha.

正徧智 Samyaksaṁbuddha 三藐三佛陀; omniscience, completely enlightened, the universal knowledge of a Buddha, hence he is the 丨丨丨海 ocean of omniscience. Also 丨丨覺; 丨等正覺.

正忌 The day of decease.

正念 Samyaksmṛti, right remembrance, the seventh of the 八正道; "right mindfulness, the looking on the body and the spirit in such a way as to remain ardent, self-possessed and mindful, having overcome both hankering and dejection." Keith.

正思惟 Samyaksaṁkalpa, right thought and intent, the second of the 八正道; "right aspiration towards renunciation, benevolence and kindness." Keith.

正日 Correct day, the day of a funeral.

正智 Samyagjñāna; correct knowledge; 聖智 sage-like, or saint-like knowledge.

正業 Samyakkarmānta, right action, purity of body, avoiding all wrong, the fourth of the 八正道; "right action, abstaining from taking life, or what is not given, or from carnal indulgence." Keith.

正法 The correct doctrine of the Buddha, whose period was to last 500, some say 1,000 years, be followed by the 像法時 semblance period of 1,000 years, and then by the 末法時 period of decay and termination, lasting 10,000 years. The ||時 is also known as ||壽. ||依 He on whom the Truth depends, a term for a Buddha. ||明如來 The Tathāgata who clearly understands the true law, i.e. Kuan-yin, who attained Buddhahood in the past. ||炬 The torch of truth, i.e. Buddhism. ||華經 The earliest translation of the Lotus sūtra in 10 chüan by Dharmarakṣa, A.D. 286, still in existence.

正當恁麼時 Just at such and such an hour.

正盡覺 idem 正等覺.

正直 Correct and straight; it is also referred to the One Vehicle teaching of T'ien-t'ai. ||捨方便 The straight way which has cast aside expediency.

正精進 Samyagvyāyāma, right effort, zeal, or progress, unintermitting perseverance, the sixth of the 八正道; "right effort, to suppress the rising of evil states, to eradicate those which have arisen, to stimulate good states, and to perfect those which have come into being." Keith.

正等正覺 idem 正徧智.

正等覺 Samyagbuddhi, or -bodhi; the perfect universal wisdom of a Buddha.

正行 Right deeds, or action, opposite of 邪行. The ||經 is an abbreviation of 佛說阿含正行經.

正覺 Saṁbodhi, the wisdom or omniscience of a Buddha.

正見 Samyagdṛṣti, right views, understanding the four noble truths; the first of the 八正道; "knowledge of the four noble truths." Keith.

正語 Samyagvāk, right speech; the third of the 八正道; "abstaining from lying, slander, abuse, and idle talk." Keith.

正量部 Saṁmatīya, Saṁmitīya (三)彌底; the school of correct measures, or correct evaluation. Three hundred years after the Nirvāṇa it is said that from the Vātsīputrīyāḥ school four divisions were formed, of which this was the third.

母 Mātṛ, a mother. |主 The "mother-lord", or mother, as contrasted with 主 and 母, lord and mother, king and queen, in the maṇḍala of Vajradhātu and Garbhadhātu; Vairocana, being the source of all things, has no "mother" as progenitor, and is the 部主 or lord of the maṇḍala; the other four dhyāni-buddhas have "mothers" called 部母, who are supposed to arise from the pāramitās; thus, Akṣobhya has 金剛波羅蜜 for mother; Ratnasambhava has 寶||| for mother; Amitābha has 法||| for mother; Amoghasiddhi has 羯磨||| for mother. |經; 摩怛理迦 Mātṛkā; a text, as distinguished from its commentary; an original text; the Abhidharma. |邑; 摩呾理伽羅摩 Mātṛgrāma, the community of mothers, womankind. |陀 (or 那)摩奴沙 Mṛta-manuṣya; a human corpse. |陀羅; |(or 慕)捺羅; 目陀羅; 末得羅 Mudrā, 印 a seal, stamp, sign, manual sign. |||手 A manual sign of assurance, hence felicitous. |馱; 毋馱 idem 佛陀, i.e. 佛 Buddha.

氷 Ice; chaste. |揭 (or 伽)羅; 畢哩孕迦 Piṅgala, name of the son of Hāritī, 阿利底 the mother of demons. She is now represented as a saint holding a child, Piṅgala, as a beloved son, in her left arm. The sūtra of his name | | | 天童子經 was tr. by 不空金剛 Amoghavajra, middle of the eighth century.

永 Perpetual, eternal, everlasting (like the unceasing flow of water). | 劫 Eternity; the everlasting æon. | 生 Eternal life; immortality; nirvāṇa is defined as 不生 not being born, i.e. not reborn, and therefore 不滅 not dying; | 生 is also perpetual life; the Amitābha cult says in the Pure Land.

犯 To offend against, break (as a law). | 戒 To offend against or break the moral or ceremonial laws (of Buddhism). | 重 To break the weightier laws.

玄 Dark, sombre, black; abstruse, obscure, deep, profound; hence it is used to indicate Taoism, and was afterwards adopted by the Buddhists.

玄一 Hsüan-i, a commentator of the 法相 Dharmalakṣaṇa school during the T'ang dynasty.

玄奘 Hsüan-tsang, whose name is written variously e.g. Hsüan Chuang, Hiüen-tsang, Hiouen Tsang, Yüan Tsang, Yüan Chwang; the famous pilgrim to India, whose surname was 陳 Ch'ên and personal name 禕 Wei; a native of Honan, A.D. 600–664 (Giles). It is said that he entered a monastery at 13 years of age and in 618 with his elder brother, who had preceded him in becoming a monk, went to Ch'ang-an 長安, the capital, where in 622 he was fully ordained. Finding that China possessed only half of the Buddhist classics, he took his staff, bound his feet, and on foot braved the perils of the deserts and mountains of Central Asia. The date of his setting out is uncertain (629 or 627), but the year of his arrival in India is given as 633; after visiting and studying in many parts of India, he returned home, reaching the capital in 645, was received with honour and presented his collection of 657 works, " besides many images and pictures, and one hundred and fifty relics, " to the Court. T'ai Tsung, the emperor, gave him the 弘福寺 Hung Fu monastery in which to work. He presented the manuscript of his famous 大唐西域記 *Record of Western Countries* in 646 and completed it as it now stands by 648. The emperor Kao Tsung called him to Court in 653 and gave him the 慈恩寺 T'zŭ En monastery in which to work, a monastery which ever after was associated with him; in 657 he removed him to the 玉華宮 Yü Hua Kung and made that palace a monastery. He translated seventy-five works in 1335 chüan. In India he received the titles of 摩訶耶那提婆 Mahāyānadeva and 木叉提婆 Mokṣadeva; he was also known as 三藏法師 Tripiṭaka teacher of Dharma. He died in 664, in his 65th year.

玄宗 The profound principles, or propositions, i.e. Buddhism.

玄應 Deep, or abstruse response; also Hsüan-ying, the author in the T'ang dynasty of the | | 音義, i.e. 一切經音義 a Buddhist dictionary in 25 chüan, not considered very reliable.

玄景 Hsüan-ching, a monk, d. 606, noted for his preaching, and for his many changes of garments, as 衡岳 Hêng Yo was noted for wearing one garment all his days.

玄暢 Hsüan-ch'ang, a famous Shensi monk, who was invited to be tutor of the heir-apparent, A.D. 445, but refused, died 484.

玄朗 Hsüan-lang, a Chekiang monk of the T'ang dynasty, died 854, at 83 years of age, noted for his influence on his disciples and for having remained in one room for over thirty years; also called 慧明 Hui-ming and 左溪 Tso-ch'i.

玄疏 The 玄義, a T'ien-t'ai commentary on the contents and meaning of the Lotus Sūtra, and 疏 the critical commentary on the text.

玄沙 Hsüan-sha, a famous Fukien monk who had over 800 disciples, died A.D. 908; his chief subjects were the fundamental ailments of men—blindness, deafness, and dumbness.

玄流 The black-robed sect of monks.

玄琬 Hsüan-yüan, an influential Shensi monk who lived through the persecution of Buddhism in the 北周 Northern Chou dynasty into the Sui and T'ang dynasties.

玄範 Hsüan-fan, a T'ang monk and editor, said to be a contemporary of Hsüan-tsang, some say his disciple.

玄義 The deep meaning; the meaning of the profound; it refers chiefly to the T'ien-t'ai method of teaching which was to proceed from a general explanation of the content and meaning of the various great sūtras to a discussion of the deeper meaning;

the method was : (1) 釋名 explanation of the terms ; (2) 辨體 definition of the substance ; (3) 明宗 making clear the principles ; (4) 論用 discussing their application ; (5) 判教 discriminating the doctrine. v. also | 疏.

玄覺 Hsüan-chio, a Wenchow monk, also named 明道 Ming-tao, who had a large following ; he is said to have attained to enlightenment in one night, hence is known as 一宿覺.

玄贊 An abbreviation of 法華經 | |.

玄道 The profound doctrine, Buddhism.

玄鏡 An abbreviation of 華嚴法界 | |.

玄鑑居士 An Indian, the patron of an Indian monk Dharmapāla, author of the 唯識釋論. After his death the patron gave the MS. to Hsüan-tsang.

玄門 The profound school, i.e. Buddhism. Also that of the 華嚴 Hua-yen (Kegon) which has a division of 十玄門 or 十玄緣起, indicating the ten metaphysical propositions, or lines of thought ; of these there are two or more versions.

玄高 Hsüan-kao, a famous Shensi monk, influential politically, later killed by order of the emperor Wu Ti, *circa* 400.

玉 Jade, a gem ; jade-like, precious ; you, your. | 佛 A famous jade Buddha recovered while digging a well in Khotan, 3 to 4 feet high. | 柔 Pliable jade, i.e. 牛肉 beef. | 泉玉花兩宗 The two schools of the Jade-fountain and Jade-flower, i.e. 天台 T'ien-t'ai and 法相 Dharmalakṣaṇa, the latter with Hsüan-tsang as founder in China. 玉泉 Yü-ch'üan was the name of the monastery in Tang-yang 當陽 Hsien, An-lu Fu, Hupeh, where Chih-i, the founder of the T'ien-t'ai School, lived ; 玉花 Yü-hua, where Hsüan-tsang lived. | 環 The Jade ring in one of the right hands of the " thousand-hand " Kuan-yin. | 耶 The name of the woman to whom the sūtra | | (女) 經 is addressed. | 花 The palace | | 宮 " Yü-hua kung ", transformed into a temple for Hsüan-tsang to work in, where he tr. the 大般若經 Mahāprajñāpāramitā sūtra, 600 chüan, etc. Cf. | 泉. | 豪 ; | 毫 The ūrṇā or white curl between the Buddha's eyebrows, from which he sent forth his ray of light illuminating all worlds.

瓜 Gourd, melon, etc. | 皮 Melon rind.

瓦 Tiles, pottery. | 器金器 An earthen vessel, i.e. the śrāvaka method, and a golden vessel, the bodhisattva method. | 師 The Buddha in a previous incarnation as a potter. | 鉢 An earthenware begging bowl.

甘 Sweet, agreeable, willing ; Kansu. | 丹 Dgaḥ-ldan, the monastery of the yellow sect 30 miles north-east of Lhasa 拉薩, built by Tsoṅ-kha-pa. | 珠爾 Kanjur, one of the two divisions of the Tibetan canon, consisting of 180 chüan, each chüan of 1,000 leaves ; a load for ten yaks. | 菩 (遮) ; 紺蒲 ; 劍蒲 Kamboja, one of the " sixteen great countries of India ", noted for its beautiful women. | 蔗 Sugar-cane, symbol of many things. A tr. of Ikṣvāku, one of the surnames of Śākyamuni, from a legend that one of his ancestors was born from a sugar-cane. | | 王 ; 懿師摩 ; 一叉鳩王 King of the sugar-cane ; Ikṣvāku Virūḍhaka, said to be one of the ancestors of Śākyamuni, but the name is claimed by others.

甘露 ; 阿 (or 啞) 密哩多 (or 達) Amṛta, sweet dew, ambrosia, the nectar of immortality ; tr. by 天酒 deva-wine, the nectar of the gods. Four kinds of ambrosia are mentioned—green, yellow, red, and white, all coming from " edible trees " and known as 蘇陀 sudhā, or 蘇摩 soma. | | 法, or 雨 The ambrosial truth, or rain, i.e. the Buddha truth. | | 法門 The method of the ambrosial truth. | | 滅 The nectar of nirvāṇa, the entrance is the | | 門, and nirvāṇa is the | | 城 or 界 nectar city, or region. | | 王 Amṛta, intp. in its implication of immortality is a name of Amitābha, and connected with him are the | | 咒, | | 陀羅尼咒, 十 | | 咒 (or 明), | | 經, etc. | | 軍荼利明王 ; | | (王) 尊 Amṛtakuṇḍalin, one of the five 明王 Ming Wang, who has three forms, vajra, lotus, and nectar. | | 飯 ; 阿彌都檀那 Amṛtodana. The king whose name was " ambrosia-rice ", a prince of Magadha, father of Anuruddha and Bhadrika, and paternal uncle of Śākyamuni. | | 鼓 The ambrosial drum, the Buddha-truth.

生 Jāti 惹多 ; life ; Utpāda means coming forth, birth, production ; 生 means beget, bear, birth, rebirth, born, begin, produce, life, the living. One of the twelve nidānas, 十二因緣 ; birth takes place in four forms, catur yoni, v. 四生, in each case causing a sentient being to enter one of the 六道 six gati, or paths of transmigration.

生住異滅 Birth, stay, change (or decay), death.

生佛 Buddha alive; a living Buddha; also 生, i.e. 衆生 all the living, and 佛, i.e. Buddha. 丨丨一如; 丨丨一體; 丨丨不二; 凡聖一如 The living and the Buddha are one, i.e. all are the one undivided whole, or absolute; they are all of the same substance; all are Buddha, and of the same 法身 dharmakāya, or spiritual nature; all are of the same 空 infinity. 丨丨不增不減 The indestructibility of the living and the Buddha; they neither increase nor decrease, being the absolute. 丨丨假名 The living and the Buddha are but temporary names, borrowed or derived for temporal indication.

生像; 生似 Natural and similar, i.e. gold and silver, gold being the natural and perfect metal and colour; silver being next, though it will tarnish; the two are also called 生色 and 可染, i.e. the proper natural (unchanging) colour, and the tarnishable.

生化; 化生 Aupapāduka; one of the four forms of birth, i.e. by transformation, without parentage, and in full maturity; thus do bodhisattvas come from the Tuṣita heaven; the dhyāni-buddhas and bodhisattvas are also of such miraculous origin. 丨丨二身 The physical body of Buddha and his transformation body capable of any form; the Nirmāṇakāya in its two forms of 應 and 化.

生即無生, 無生即生 To be born is not to be born, not to be born is to be born—an instance of the identity of contraries. It is an accepted doctrine of the 般若 prajñā teaching and the ultimate doctrine of the 三論 Mādhyamika school. Birth, creation, life, each is but a 假 temporary term, in common statement 俗諦 it is called birth, in truth 眞諦 it is not birth; in the relative it is birth, in the absolute non-birth.

生報 Life's retribution, i.e. the deeds done in this life produce their results in the next reincarnation.

生天 The heavens where those living in this world can be reborn, i.e. from that of the 四天王 to the 非想天; v. 福生天.

生忍 Common or ordinary patience, i.e. of 衆生 the masses.

生念處菩薩 The second Bodhisattva on the right of the Bodhisattva of Space 虛空藏 in the Garbhadhātu.

生支 Liṅga; aṅga-jāta; the male organ, penis.

生有 One of the four forms of existence, cf. 有.

生死 Saṁsāra; birth and death; rebirth and redeath; life and death; 生死, 死生; 生生死死 ever-recurring saṁsāra or transmigrations; the round of mortality. There are two, three, four, seven, and twelve kinds of 生死; the two are 分斷生死 the various karmaic transmigrations, and 不思義變易生死 the inconceivable transformation life in the Pure Land. Among the twelve are final separation from mortality of the arhat, with 無餘 no remains of it causing return; one final death and no rebirth of the anāgāmin; the seven advancing rebirths of the srota-āpanna; down to the births-cum-deaths of hungry ghosts. 丨丨即涅槃 Mortality is nirvāṇa, but there are varying definitions of 即 q.v. 丨丨園 The garden of life-and-death, this mortal world in which the unenlightened find their satisfaction. 丨丨(大)海 The ocean of mortality, mortal life, 輪迴 saṁsāra, or transmigrations. 丨丨岸 The shore of mortal life; as 丨丨流 is its flow; 丨丨泥 its quagmire; 丨丨淵 its abyss; 丨丨野 its wilderness; 丨丨雲 its envelopment in cloud. 丨丨解脫 Release from the bonds of births-and-deaths, nirvāṇa. 丨丨輪 The wheel of births-and-deaths, the round of mortality. 丨丨長夜 The long night of births-and-deaths. 丨丨際 The region of births-and-deaths, as compared with that of nirvāṇa.

生法 The living and things, i.e. 人法, 我法 men and things, the self and things; the 有情 sentient, or those with emotions, i.e. the living; and 非情 those without, i.e. insentient things. 丨丨二身 The physical body and the spiritual body of the Buddha: the Nirmāṇakāya and Dharmakāya.

生津 The ford of life, or mortality.

生滅 Utpādanirodha. Birth and death, production and annihilation; all life, all phenomena, have birth and death, beginning and end; the 三論 Mādhyamika school deny this in the 實 absolute, but recognize it in the 假 relative. 丨丨去來 Coming into existence and ceasing to exist, past and future, are merely relative terms and not true in reality; they are the first two antitheses in the 中論 Mādhyamika-śāstra, the other two antitheses being 一異斷常 unity and difference, impermanence and permanence.

生生 Birth and rebirth (without end).

生田 The three regions 三界 of the constant round of rebirth.

生盲 Born blind.

生空 Empty at birth, i.e. 我空, 人空 void of a permanent ego.

生經 Stories of the previous incarnations of the Buddha and his disciples, tr. by Dharmapāla, 5 chüan, third century A.D.

生老病死 Birth, age, sickness, death, the 四苦 four afflictions that are the lot of every man. The five are the above four and 苦 misery, or suffering.

生肇融叡 Four great disciples of Kumārajīva, the Indian Buddhajīva or 道生 Tao-shêng and the three Chinese 僧肇 Sêng-chao, 道融 Tao-jung, and 僧叡 Sêng-jui.

生色 Jāta-rūpa; gold, v. 生像.

生起 Birth and what arises from it; cause of an act; the beginning and rise.

生趣 The 四生 four forms of birth and the 六趣 six forms of transmigration.

生身 The physical body; also that of a Buddha in contrast with his 法身 dharmakāya; also a bodhisattva's body when born into any mortal form. 丨丨供 The worship paid to Buddha-relics, 丨丨舍利.

生途 The way or lot of those born, i.e. of mortality.

生靈 The mind or intelligence of the living; a living intelligent being; a living soul.

生飯; 出飯 Offerings made before a meal of a small portion of food to ghosts and all the living; cf. Nirvāṇa sūtra 16, and Vinaya 雜事 31. 丨臺 A board on which the offerings are placed. 丨盤 The bowl in which they are contained.

用 To use, to employ; use, function. 丨大 Great in function, the universal activity of the 眞如 bhūtatathatā; v. 起信論; and cf. 性相用 inner nature, form and function. 丨滅 Function or activity ceasing; i.e. matter (or the body 體) does not cease to exist, but only its varying functions or activities.

田 A field, fields; a place, or state, for the cultivation of meritorious or other deeds; cf. 福丨. 丨(相)衣 A patch-robe, its patches resembling the rectangular divisions of fields.

由 From; by; a cause, motive; to allow, let; translit. *yo*, *yu*; e.g. 丨乾; 丨乾陀 (or 陁) 羅, Yugaṁdhara, idem 踰健達羅. 丨旬; 丨延; 兪 (or 揄) 旬; 踰繕 (or 闍 or 延) 那 Yojana; described as anciently a royal day's march for the army; also 40, 30, or 16 li; 8 krośas 拘羅舍, one being the distance at which a bull's bellow can be heard; M. W. says 4 krośas or about 9 English miles, or nearly 30 Chinese li.

甲 Scale, mail; the first of the ten "celestial stems". 丨胄印 A digital or manual sign, indicating mail and helmet. 丨馬 A picture, formerly shaped like a horse, of a god or a Buddha, now a picture of a horse.

申 To draw out, stretch, extend, expand; notify, report; quote. 丨日 Candra, the moon; also the name of an elder. 丨毒; 身毒; 賢頭 Sindhu, Indus, Sindh, v. 印度. 丨河 The river Hiranyavatī, v. 尸賴; otherwise said to be the Nairañjanā 尼連禪河. 丨瑟知林; 丨怒(波)林; 杖林 Yaṣṭi-vana, grove of staves, said to have grown from the staff with which a heretic measured the Buddha and which he threw away because the more he measured the higher the Buddha grew. 丨頭羅 ? Sindūra, the trick of the illusionist who disappears in the air and reappears.

白 White, pure, clear; make clear, inform.

白一 (or 二) 羯磨 Jñaptidvitīyā karmavācanā; to discuss with and explain to the body of monks the proposals or work to be undertaken; 白四羯磨 is to consult with them on matters of grave moment and obtain their complete assent.

白佛 To tell the Buddha.

白傘(or 蓋)佛頂 The white umbrella or canopy over the head of Buddha, indicating him as a cakravartī, or wheel-king.

白報 Pure reward, or the reward of a good life.

白心 A clear heart or conscience.

白拈(賊) Robbing with bare hands and without leaving a trace, as 白戰 is fighting without weapons, and 白折 is killing with bare hands.

白月 Śuklapakṣa 白分; the bright, i.e. first half of the month, as contrasted with the 黑分 kṛṣṇapakṣa, dark or latter half.

白槌; 白椎 The informing baton or hammer, calling attention to a plaint, or for silence to give information.

白檀 White candana, or white sandal-wood.

白毫 The curl between Śākyamuni's eyebrows; from it, in the Mahāyāna sūtras, he sends out a ray of light which reveals all worlds; it is used as a synonym of the Buddha, e.g. 丨丨之賜 (all that a monk has is) a gift from the White-curled One.

白水城 White-river town, Isfijab, "in Turkestan, situated on a small tributary of the Jaxartes in Lat. 38° 30′ N., Long 65° E." Eitel.

白牛 A white ox; 丨丨無角 a hornless white ox: a horse.

白眞 To lay a true information.

白蓮教 The White Lily Society, set up near the end of the Yüan dynasty, announcing the coming of Maitreya, the opening of his white lily, and the day of salvation at hand. It developed into a revolution which influenced the expulsion of the Mongols and establishment of the Ming dynasty. Under the Ch'ing dynasty it was resurrected under a variety of names, and caused various uprisings. 丨丨菜 The Sung vegetarian school of 茅子元 Mao Tzŭ-yüan. 丨丨(華); 分陀利 Puṇḍarīka, the white lotus. 丨丨華座 The lotus throne in the first court of the Garbhadhātu. 丨丨(丨)社; 丨丨之交; 蓮社 A society formed early in the fourth century A.D. by 慧遠 Hui-yüan, who with 123 notable literati, swore to a life of purity before the image of Amitābha, and planted white lotuses in symbol. An account of seven of its succeeding patriarchs is given in the 佛祖統紀 26; as also of eighteen of its worthies.

白衣 White clothing, said to be that of Brahmans and other people, hence it and 白俗 are terms for the common people. It is a name also for Kuan-yin. 丨丨(or 處)觀音; 丨丨大士; 半拏囉嚩悉寧 Pāṇḍaravāsinī, the white-robed form of Kuan-yin on a white lotus.

白象 The six-tusked white elephant which bore the Buddha on his descent from the Tuṣita heaven into Māyā's womb, through her side. Every Buddha descends in similar fashion. The immaculate path, i.e. the immaculate conception (of Buddha).

白贊 To speak praises to the Buddha.

白足(和尚); 丨丨阿練 The white-foot monk, a disciple of Kumārajīva.

白雲(宗) A Buddhist school formed in the White Cloud monastery during the Sung dynasty; its followers were known as the 丨丨菜 White Cloud vegetarians.

白飯王 Śuklodana-rāja, a prince of Kapilavastu, second son of Siṁhahanu, father of Tiṣya 帝沙, Devadatta 調達, and Nandika 難提迦. Eitel.

白馬寺 The White Horse Temple recorded as given to the Indian monks, Mātaṅga and Gobharaṇa, who are reputed to have been fetched from India to China in A.D. 64. The temple was in Honan, in Lo-yang the capital; it was west of the ancient city, east of the later city. According to tradition, originating at the end of the second century A.D., the White Horse Temple was so called because of the white horse which carried the sūtras they brought.

白鷺池 The White Heron Lake in Rājagṛha, the scene of Śākyamuni's reputed delivery of part of the Mahāprajñāpāramitā-sūtra 大般若經 chüan 593–600, the last of the "16 assemblies" of this sūtra, which is also called the 丨丨丨經.

白黑 White and dark, e.g. | | 業 good and evil deeds, or karma; | | 布 薩 light and dark uposatha, the observances of the waxing and waning moon, cf. 白 月.

皮；皮 革 Leather, skin, hide. | 殼 (or 可) 漏 子 The body, lit. "skin and shell leaking". | 衣 Clothing of hides or skins; a name for a monk's garments, implying their roughness and simplicity. | 袋 Skin bag, i.e. the body.

目 Cakṣuḥ, the eye; the organ of vision; the head or chief; translit. *ma*, *mu*. | 佉 Mukha, mouth, opening. | 多 Mukta, release, free, released; muktā, a pearl, jewels in general. | | 伽 Abbrev. for 伊 提 | | | Itivṛttaka, biographical stories. | 帝 羅；木 得 羅 Intp. as mukti, release, emancipation 解 脫, or as the knowledge or experience of liberation. | 支 (or 脂, or 眞) 隣 陀; | (or 支) 隣; 牟 眞 隣 陀; 母 眞 (or 止) 隣 那; 文 眞 隣 陀; 摩 訶 | | | |. Mucilinda, or Mahāmucilinda. A nāga or dragon king who dwelt in a lake near a hill and cave of this name, near Gayā, where Śākyamuni sat absorbed for seven days after his enlightenment, protected by this nāga-king. | 機 銖 兩 The power of the eye to discern trifling differences; quick discernment. | 犍 連; | 連; 摩 訶 | 犍 連 (or 羅 夜 那); 大 | 犍 (or 乾) 連; 沒 特 (or 力) 伽 羅 子; 目 伽 略 (Maha-) Maudgalyāyana, or Maudgalaputra; explained by Mudga 胡 豆 lentil, kidney-bean. One of the ten chief disciples of Śākyamuni, specially noted for miraculous powers; formerly an ascetic, he agreed with Śāriputra that whichever first found the truth would reveal it to the other. Śāriputra found the Buddha and brought Maudgalyāyana to him; the former is placed on the Buddha's right, the latter on his left. He is also known as 拘 栗 Kolita, and when reborn as Buddha his title is to be Tamāla-patra-candana-gandha. In China Mahāsthāmaprapta is accounted a canonization of Maudgalyāyana. Several centuries afterwards there were two other great leaders of the Buddhist church bearing the same name, v. Eitel. | 竭 嵐 Mudgara; a hammer, mallet, mace. | 足 Eye and foot, knowledge and practice; eyes in the feet. | | 仙 Akṣapāda, founder of the Nyāya, or logical school of philosophers. M. W.

矢 An arrow; to take an oath; a marshal; ordure. | 石 Arrow and rock are two incompatibles, for an arrow cannot pierce a rock.

石 Stone, rock. 畫 石 A painting of a rock: though the water of the water-colour rapidly disappears, the painting remains. 難 石 石 裂 Even a rock meeting hard treatment will split. | 壁 經 Sūtras cut in stone in A.D. 829 in the 重 玄 寺 Ch'ung-hsüan temple, Soochow, where Po Chü-i put up a tablet. They consist of 69,550 words of the 法 華, 27,092 of the 維 摩, 5,287 of the 金 剛, 3,020 of the 尊 勝 陀 羅 尼, 1,800 of the 阿 彌 陀, 6,990 of the 普 賢 行 法, 3,150 of the 實 相 法 密, and 258 of the 般 若 心 經. | 女 A barren woman; a woman incompetent for sexual intercourse. | 女 兒 Son of a barren woman, an impossibility. | 榴 The pomegranate, symbol of many children because of its seeds; a symbol held in the hand of 鬼 子 母 神 Hāritī, the deva-mother of demons, converted by the Buddha. | 火 Tinder; lighted tinder, i.e. of but momentary existence. | 經 山 The hill with the stone sūtras, which are said to have been carved in the Sui dynasty in grottoes on 白 帶 山 Pai Tai Shan, west of 涿 州 Cho-chou in Shun-t'ien-fu, Chihli. | 蜜 Stone honey; a toffee, made of sugar, or sugar and cream (or butter). | 鉢 The four heavy stone begging-bowls handed by the four devas to the Buddha on his enlightenment, which he miraculously received one piled on the other.

示 To indicate, notify, proclaim. | 教 To point out and instruct, e.g. | 寂 to indicate the way of nirvāṇa. 告 示 A proclamation; to notify.

禾 Growing grain. | 山 Ho-shan, a monastery in 吉 州 Chi-chou, and its abbot who died A.D. 960.

立 Set up, establish, stand, stand up. | 僧 首 座 The learned monk who occupies the chief seat to edify the body of monks. | 播 Repa, or repha, a "low" garment, a loin-cloth. | 教 To establish a "school", sect, or church. | | 開 宗 To set up a school and start a sect. | 法 To set up, or state a proposition; to make a law, or rule. | 破 To state—and confute—a proposition. | 量 To state a syllogism with its 宗 proposition, 因 reason, and 喩 example.

6. SIX STROKES

亦 Also; moreover. | 有 | 空 門 Both reality and unreality (or, relative and absolute, phenomenal and non-phenomenal), a term for the middle school; Mādhyamika.

交 Interlock, intersect; crossed; mutual; friendship; to hand over, pay. | 代; | 付 To hand over, entrust to. | 堂 To hand over charge of a hall, or monastery. | 蘆; 束 蘆 A tripod of three rushes or canes—an illustration of the mutuality of cause and effect, each cane depending on the other at the point of intersection. 丨露 A curtain festooned with jewels, resembling hanging dewdrops. 丨點 To hand over and check (as in the case of an inventory).

伎 Skill; 丨巧; 丨藝. 丨兒 An actor. 丨藝天女 The metamorphic devī on the head of Śiva, perhaps the moon which is the usual figure on Śiva's head.

伍 A rank of five. 丨官王 Wu-kuan Wang, the fourth of the ten rulers of Hades.

任 Bear, endure, let; office; it is used to connote laisser-faire; one of the 四病, as 丨運 implies laisser-aller; it is intp. by let things follow their own course, or by 自然 naturally, without intervention.

仰 Look up, respectful; lying with the face upward, opposite of 俯; translit. *ṅ* as in aṅga, cf. 我, 俄, 哦. 丨山 To look up to the hills; Yang-shan, name of a noted monk. 丨月點 A half-moon on its back, i.e. ︶, a sign in the esoteric sect.

休 Desist, give up; resign; divorce; blessing, favour. 丨屠 Lit. "Desist from butchering," said to be the earliest Han term for 浮屠, 佛圖, etc., Buddha. The 漢武故事 says that the King of Vaiśālī 毘邪 killed King 休屠 (or the non-butchering kings), took his golden gods, over 10 feet in height, and put them in the 甘泉宮 Sweet-spring palace; they required no sacrifices of bulls or rams, but only worship of incense, so the king ordered that they should be served after their national method.

伏 Prostrate; humble; suffer, bear; ambush; dog-days; hatch; it is used for control, under control, e.g. as delusion; 斷 is contrasted with it as complete extirpation, so that no delusive thought arises. 丨忍 The first of the 五忍 five forms of submission, self-control, or patience. 丨藏 To bury, hide away. 丨陀 The Vedas, v. 韋. 丨馱蜜多 Buddhamitra, of northern India, the ninth patriarch, a Vaiśya by birth (third caste), author of the 五門禪經要用法 Pañcadvāra-dhyāna-sūtra-mahārtha-dharma; he was styled Mahādhyānaguru.

伐 To cut down, chastise; a go-between; to make a display; translit. *va*. 丨伽; 跋渠 Varga, tr. by 部 a class, division, group. 丨剌拏 Varana, "a mountainous province of Kapiśa with city of the same name, probably the country south-east of Wauneh in Lat. 32° 30 N., Long. 69° 25 E." Eitel. Perhaps Bannu, v. Lévi, *J. Asiatique*, XI, v, p. 73. Also v. 障. 丨地 Vadi or Vati. "An ancient little kingdom and city on the Oxus, the modern Betik, Lat. 39° 7 N., Long. 63° 10 E." Eitel. 丨折羅 Vajra. 丨闍羅; 縛 (or 嚩 or 跋) 曰羅 (or 囉); 嚩馹囉; 跋折 (or 闍) 羅; 跋折多; 波 (or 髮) 闍羅, tr. by 金剛 (杵) Diamond club; the thunderbolt, svastika; recently defined by Western scholars as a sun symbol. It is one of the saptaratna, seven precious things; the sceptre of Indra as god of thunder and lightning, with which he slays the enemies of Buddhism; the sceptre of the exorcist; the symbol of the all-conquering power of Buddha. 丨丨丨陀羅; 持 (or 執) 金剛 Vajradhara, the bearer of the vajra. 丨丨丨嚩羅 Vajrajvāla, i.e. flame, tr. as 金剛光 the scintillation of the diamond, the lightning. 丨浪伽 Varāṅga, name of a spirit, or god; a name of Viṣṇu as beautiful. 丨臘毗 Valabhī. Modern Wālā. "An ancient kingdom and city on the eastern coast of Gujerat." Eitel. Known also as 北羅 northern Lāṭa. 丨蘇蜜呾羅 Vasumitra, v. 筏. 丨丨槃 (or 畔) 度; 婆藪槃豆 Vasubandhu, v. 天親. 丨那婆斯 Vanavāsin, one of the sixteen arhats. 丨里沙 Varṣa, rain; name of a noted Sāṁkhya leader, Vārṣagaṇya. 丨闍羅弗多羅 Vajraputra, one of the sixteen arhats.

伊 He, she, it; that; translit. *i*, *ai*, *ṛ*; cf. 壹, 彝 and 意; for the long *ī* the double characters 翳 咿 and 伊伊 are sometimes used. 丨字三點 refers to the Sanskrit sign ∴ as neither across nor upright, being of triangular shape, and indicating neither unity nor difference, before nor after. The Nirvāṇa Sūtra applies the three parts to 法身 dharmakāya, 般若 prajñā, and 解脫 vimokṣa, all three being necessary to complete nirvāṇa. It is also associated with the three eyes of Śiva. When considered across they represent fire, when upright, water. At a later period the three were joined [Siddham sign] in writing.

伊刹尼 Īkṣaṇi, or Īkṣaṇa, defined as a magic mode of reading another's thoughts.

伊吾 (盧) I-wu(-lu), the modern Hami, so called during the Han dynasty. Later it was known as I-wu Chün and I-chou. v. *Serindia*, p. 1147.

伊尼延 Aiṇeya(s); also 伊泥 (or 梨) 延 (陀); 因 (or 黳 or 㖶) 尼延; 翳 (or 瑿) 泥耶 the black antelope; intp. as 鹿 (王) a deer, or royal stag. 甘伊泥延腨 (or 蹲) 相 Aiṇeyajaṅgha. The eighth of the thirty-two characteristic signs of a Buddha, knees like those of a royal stag.

伊師迦 Iṣīkā, an arrow, dart, elephant's eye-ball; Ṛṣigiri, a high hill at Rājagṛha, v. | 私; a type of 我見, 我曼 egoism, etc.

伊帝目 (or 日 or 越) 多伽 Ityuktas, so said, or reported; Itivṛttakam, so occurring; the Buddha's discourses arising out of events; intp. as 本事 q.v. personal events, or Jātaka stories, one of the twelve classes of Buddhist literature, i.e. 十二部經 biographical narratives.

伊梨 (or 利) 沙般荼迦 Īrṣyāpaṇḍaka, also | | | 掌拏 eunuchs, or impotent save when stirred by jealousy, cf. 般.

伊沙 Īśa, master, lord. | | is used for | 舍那 q.v., but | | 那 Īśāna, possessing, is intp. as 聚落 a settled place, locality, and may be Īśānapura, v. *infra* | 賞. | | 陁羅; | | 馱羅 Īṣādhara. A chain of mountains, being the second of the seven concentric circles surrounding Sumeru; defined as 持軸 holding the axis, or axle, also as 車軸 the axle-tree, or 自在持 sovereign control. It is made of the seven precious things, and its sea, 42,000 yojanas wide, is filled with fragrant flowers.

伊爛拏 (鉢伐多) Īriṇa-parvata, or Hiraṇya-parvata. An ancient kingdom noted for a volcano near its capital, the present Monghir, Lat. 25° 16 N., Long. 86° 26 E. Eitel.

伊私耆梨 Ṛṣigiri, 仙山, name of a mountain in Magadha; M. W.

伊羅婆那 Airāvaṇa; | | | 拏; | | (or 那) 鉢那; 伊蘭; 堙羅 (那) q.v.; 噎羅 (or 那) 婆那; 黳 (or 毉) 羅葉, etc. Airāvaṇa, come from the water; Indra's elephant; a tree, the elāpattra; name of a park (i.e. Lumbinī, where the Buddha is said to have been born). | | 跋提河 Erāvatī, Airāvatī, Irāvatī, the river Ravi, also abbrev. to 跋提 Vati. | | 鉢 (多羅) 龍王; | | 多 (or 跋) 羅; | | 婆那; 伊那槃婆龍 and many other forms, v. *supra*. Elāpattra, Erāpattra, Eḍavarṇa, Erāvarṇa. A nāga, or elephant, which is also a meaning of Airāvaṇa and Airāvata. A nāga-guardian of a sea or lake, who had plucked a herb wrongfully in a previous incarnation, been made into a nāga and now begged the Buddha that he might be reborn in a higher sphere. Another version is that he pulled up a tree which stuck to his head and grew there, hence his name. One form is | | 婆那龍象王, which may have an association with Indra's elephant.

伊舍那 (天) Īśāna; 伊邪 (or 賒) 那; v. | 沙 "one of the older names of Śiva-Rudra; one of the Rudras; the sun as a form of Śiva," M. W. Maheśvara; the deva of the sixth desire-heaven; head of the external Vajra-hall of the Vajradhātu group; Śiva with his three fierce eyes and tusks. | | | 后 Īśānī, wife of Śiva, Durgā.

伊葉波羅 Īśvara 伊溼伐羅 (1) King, sovereign; Śiva and others; intp. by 自在 self-existing, independent; applied to Kuan-yin and other popular deities. (2) A śramaṇa of the West, learned in the Tripiṭaka, who *inter alia* translated A.D. 426 Saṃyuktābhidharma-hṛdaya-śāstra, lost since A.D. 730. (3) A bhikṣu of India, commentator on 菩提資糧論 attributed to Nāgārjuna, tr. by Dharmagupta, A.D. 590–616.

伊蒲塞 Upāsaka, a lay member of the Buddhist Church, v. | 優.

伊蘭 Airāvaṇa, Erāvaṇa, 伊羅 and other forms, v. *supra*; name of a tree with beautiful flowers of nauseous scent which spreads its odour for 40 li; typifying 煩惱 the passions and delusions.

伊賞那補羅 Īśānapura. An ancient kingdom in Burma. Eitel. Cf. 伊沙那.

伊迦波提羅那 A title of a Tathāgata, intp. as 最上天王 the supreme deva-king.

兆 An omen; a million. | 載永劫 The perpetual æon of millions of years, the kalpa beyond numbers.

先 Fore, before, former, first; precede. | 世 A previous life, or world. | 哲; | 達 One who has preceded (me) in understanding, or achievement. | 尼; 西儞迦; 霰尼 Sainika, Senika, martial, a commander; a class of non-Buddhists, perhaps the Jains; it may be connected with Śraiṇya, Śreṇika. | 業 Karma from a previous life. | 照高山 The rising sun first shines on the highest mountains. | 生 Senior, sir, teacher, master, Mr.; a previous life. | 進; | 輩 Of earlier, or senior rank or achievement. | 陀 (婆) Saindhava, interpreted as salt, a cup, water, and a horse; born or produced in Sindh, or near the Indus; also a minister of state in personal attendance on the king. | | 客 A man of renown, wealth, and wisdom.

光；光明 Prabhā, light, brightness, splendour, to illuminate.

光世音 idem 觀世音.

光宅 Kuang-chai, name of the temple where 法雲 Fa-yün early in the sixth century wrote his commentary on the Lotus sūtra, which is known as the ｜｜疏；｜｜became his epithet. He made a division of four yāna from the Burning House parable, the goat cart representing the śrāvaka, the deer cart the pratyeka-buddha, the ox-cart the Hīnayāna bodhisattva, and the great white ox-cart the Mahāyāna bodhisattva; a division adopted by T'ien-t'ai.

光寶 Two noted monks of 大慈恩 T'zŭ-en monastery under the T'ang dynasty, 普光 P'u-kuang and 法寶 Fa-pao, the first the author of 俱舍論記, the second of a commentary 疏 on the same śāstra, each in 30 chüan.

光座 Prabhā-maṇḍala; the halo and throne (of a Buddha); also 光趺.

光德國 Avabhāsa, the kingdom of light and virtue, or glorious virtue, in which Mahākāśyapa is to be reborn as a Buddha, under the name of 光明 Raśmiprabhāsa.

光明 v. last entry. ｜｜土 The glory land, or Paradise of Amitābha. ｜｜壇 The fire altar. ｜｜大梵 Jyotiṣprabha, the great illustrious Brahman, whose Buddha-realm "is to contribute some Bodhisattvas for that of Amitābha". Eitel. ｜｜寺；｜｜大師 (or 和尙). Kuang-ming ssŭ, temple and title of 善導 Shan-tao, a noted monk of the T'ang dynasty under Kao Tsung. ｜｜山 The shining hill, or monastery, a name for the abode of Kuan-yin, said to be in India, and called Potala. ｜｜心殿 The temple of the bright or shining heart; the seat of Vairocana, the sun Buddha, in the Vajradhātu maṇḍala. ｜｜王 One of the twenty-five bodhisattvas who, with Amitābha, welcomes to Paradise the dying who call on Buddha. ｜｜眞言 A dhāraṇī by whose repetition the brightness or glory of Buddha may be obtained, and all retribution of sin be averted.

光毫 The ūrṇā, or curl between the Buddha's eyebrows whence streams light that reveals all worlds, one of the thirty-two characteristics of a Buddha.

光照如來相 Vairocana-raśmi-pratimaṇḍita-dhvaja; "a Bodhisattva, disciple of Śākyamuni, who was in a former life Vimaladattā." Eitel.

光燄王佛 The royal Buddha of shining flames, or flaming brightness, Amitābha, with reference to his virtues.

光瑞 The auspicious ray sent from between the Buddha's eyebrows before a revelation.

光目女 The bright-eyed (or wide-eyed) daughter, a former incarnation of 地藏 Kṣitigarbha.

光統 Kuang the general supervisor, i.e. the monk 慧光 Hui-kuang, sixth century, who resigned the high office of 統 and tr. the 十地經論.

光網童子 Jālinīprabhakumāra, 惹哩寧鉢囉婆俱摩羅; one of the eight attendants on Mañjuśrī; he is the youth with the shining net.

光聚佛頂 One of the five 佛頂 q.v.

光記 The above-mentioned 俱舍論記 in 30 chüan by 普光 P'u-kuang, v. ｜寶.

光降 The honoured one descends, i.e. the Buddha or bodhisattva who is worshipped descends.

光音天 Ābhāsvara, light and sound, or light-sound heavens, also styled 極光淨天, the heavens of utmost light and purity, i.e. the third of the second dhyāna heavens, in which the inhabitants converse by light instead of words; they recreate the universe from the hells up to and including the first dhyāna heavens after it has been destroyed by fire during the final series of cataclysms; but they gradually diminish in power and are reborn in lower states. The three heavens of the second dhyāna are 少光, 無量光, and 光音. ｜｜宮 Ābhāsvara-vimāna, the Ābhāsvara palace, idem.

全 All, whole, complete. ｜分戒 or 受 Fully ordained by receiving all the commandments. ｜跏趺坐 The legs completely crossed as in a completely seated image.

共 All, altogether, both, same, in common. ｜不定 Sādhāraṇa; both indeterminate, i.e. one of the six indeterminates in Logic, "when a thesis and its contradiction are both supported by equally valid reasons," e.g. "that sound is not eternal, because it is a product," "that it is eternal, because it is audible." Keith. |十地 The ten stages which śrāvakas, pratyeka-buddhas, and bodhisattvas have in common. |命鳥; 命命鳥; 生生鳥 Jīvajīva, or jīvañjīva, a bird said to have two heads on one body, i.e. mind and perception differing, but the karma one. |報 Collective retribution; reward or punishment of the community, or in common, for the |業 deeds of the community, or even of the individual in their effects on the community. |宗 That which all Buddhist schools have in common. |法; |功德 The totality of truth, or virtue, common to all sages, is found in the Buddha. |相 Sāmānya. Totality, generality, the whole; in common, as contrasted with 自相 individuality, or component parts. |(相)惑 Delusion arising from observing things as a whole, or apart from their relationships. |般若 The interpretation of the Prajñāpāramitā that advanced and ordinary students have in common, as contrasted with its deeper meaning, or 不||| only understood by Bodhisattvas. |許 What is commonly admitted, a term in logic.

再 Again, a second time, also |往.

冰 Ice, chaste. |伽羅 Piṅgala, tawny; tr. as 蒼色 azure, grey.

决 To divide, decide; decidedly; cut off, execute. |了 Decided, defined, and made clear. |定 Fixed and settled, determined. |擇 Deciding and choosing; that which decides and gives reason, i.e. the truth of the saints, or Buddhism. |疑 To resolve doubts, doubts solved; definite.

劣 Inferior, vicious. |智 Inferior wisdom, harmful wisdom.

卍 Sauvastika, 塞縛悉底迦; also styled 室利靺瑳 śrīvatsa, lucky sign, Viṣṇu's breast-curl or mark, tr. by 海雲 sea-cloud, or cirrhus. Used as a fancy form of 萬 or 万; and is also written in a form said to resemble a curl. It is the 4th of the auspicious signs in the footprint of Buddha, and is a mystic diagram of great antiquity. To be distinguished from 卐 svastika, the crampons of which turn to the right.

危 Perilous. |城 A perilous citadel, i.e. the body.

印 Mudrā; seal, sign, symbol, emblem, proof, assurance, approve; also 印契; 契印; 印相. Manual signs indicative of various ideas, e.g. each finger represents one of the five primary elements, earth, water, fire, air, and space, beginning with the little finger; the left hand represents 定 stillness, or meditation, the right hand 慧 discernment or wisdom; they have also many other indications. Also, the various symbols of the Buddhas and Bodhisattvas, e.g. the thunderbolt; cf. 因. |佛 A Buddha made of incense and burnt, a symbolical Buddha. ||作法 An esoteric method of seeking spirit-aid by printing a Buddha on paper, or forming his image on sand, or in the air, and performing specified rites. |光 Illumination from the symbol on a Buddha's or Bodhisattva's breast. |可 Assuredly can, i.e. recognition of ability, or suitability. |土 idem |度 India. |域 The territory of India. |度; |特伽; 身毒; 賢豆; 天竺 Indu (meaning "moon" in Sanskrit), Hindu, Sindhu; see also 信度 and 閻浮 India in general. In the T'ang dynasty its territory is described as extending over 90,000 li in circuit, being bounded on three sides by the sea; north it rested on the Snow mountains 雪山, i.e. Himālayas; wide at the north, narrowing to the south, shaped like a half-moon; it contained over seventy kingdoms, was extremely hot, well watered and damp; from the centre eastwards to 震旦 China was 58,000 li; and the same distance southwards to 金地國, westwards to 阿拘遮國, and northwards to 小香山阿耨達. ||佛教 Indian Buddhism, which began in Magadha, now Bihār, under Śākyamuni, the date of whose nirvāṇa was *circa* 486 B.C. v. 佛 and 佛教. |母 Añjali; the two hands with palms and fingers together—the "mother" of all manual signs. |治 Approval of a course of action. |紙同時 At one and the same time, like printing (which is synchronous, not like writing which is word by word). |達羅 Indra; a thousand quinquillions. 大||| Mahendra; ten times that amount.

各 Each, every. |種 Each kind, every sort.

吐 To spit, excrete, put forth. |淚 Female and male seminal fluids which blend for conception.

吒 To entrust; translit. *t* or *ṭ*. |婆 Something rigid, an obstruction.

吃 To eat; to stutter. |栗多 ? Kṛtya; a 賤人 low or common fellow.

吚剌拏伐底 v. 阿恃多伐底 Hiraṇyavatī, Hiraṇya, Ajitavatī, the river near which Śākyamuni entered into Nirvāṇa; the Gunduck (Gandak), flowing south of Kuśinagara city.

向 Towards, to go towards, facing, heretofore. 丨上 To trace backwards, as from the later to the earlier, primary, the earliest or first; upwards. 丨下 Downwards; to trace downwards, i.e. forwards, "from root to branches." 丨彼悔 pratideśanīya 波羅提提舍尼 sin to be confessed before the assembly.

合 Bring together, unite, unison, in accord. 丨十; 丨爪; 丨掌 To bring the ten fingers or two palms together; a monk's salutation; 丨掌叉手 to put the hands together and fold the fingers. 丨壇 United, or common altar, or altars, as distinguished from 離壇 separate altars. 丨昏(樹); 丨歡; 尸利沙 or 灑 Śirīṣa, the acacia sirisa. 丨殺 The closing note of a chant or song; bring to an end. 丨用 In accordance with need; suitable. 丨蓮華 A closed lotus-flower.

同 Together, with; mutual; same. 丨事 Samānārthatā, working together (with and for others); one of the 四攝法. 丨分; 丨品; 丨類 Of the same class, or order. 丨學 Fellow-students, those who learn or study together. 丨生天; 丨生神; 丨名天 The first two of these terms are intp. as the guardian deva, or spirit, who is sahaja, i.e. born or produced simultaneously with the person he protects; the last is the deva who has the same name as the one he protects. 丨聽異聞 To hear the same (words) but understand differently. 丨行 Those who are practising religion together. 丨體 Of the same body, or nature, as water and wave, but 丨體慈悲 means fellow-feeling and compassion, looking on all sympathetically as of the same nature as oneself. 丨體三寶 idem 一體三寶.

名 Nāman 娜麼 (or 摩); a name, a term; noted, famous. 丨假 Name unreal; one of the 三假; names are not in themselves realities. 丨利 Fame and gain. 丨別義通 Different in name but of the same meaning. 丨字 Name and description, name. 丨丨比丘 A monk in name but not in reality. 丨丨菩薩 A nominal bodhisattva. 丨丨沙彌 One of an age to be a monk, i.e. 20 years of age and over. 丨德 Of notable virtue. 丨目 A name, or descriptive title. 丨相 Name and appearance; everything has a name, e.g. sound, or has appearance, i.e. the visible, v. 丨色; both are unreal and give rise to delusion. The name under which Subhūti will be reborn as Buddha. 丨籍 A register of names. 丨義 Name and meaning; the meaning of a name, or term. 丨丨不離 Connotation; name and meaning not apart, or differing, they are inseparable or identical, the name having equality with the meaning, e.g. a Buddha, or the terms of a dhāraṇī. 丨丨 or 丨丨集 is an abbreviation for the 翻譯名義 Fan-i-ming-i dictionary. 丨聞; 丨聲 Yaśas, renown, fame. 丨臈 A monk of renown and of years. 丨色 Nāmarūpa, name-form, or name and form, one of the twelve nidānas. In Brahminical tradition it served "to denote spirit and matter", "the concrete individual", Keith; in Buddhism it is intp. as the 五蘊 five skandhas or aggregates, i.e. a "body", 受, 想, 行, and 識 vedanā, saṁjñā, karman, and vijñāna being the "name" and 色 rūpa the "form"; the first-named four are mental and the last material. 色 Rūpa is described as the minutest particle of matter, that which has resistance; the embryonic body or fœtus is a nāmarūpa, something that can be named. 丨號 A name, or title, especially that of Amitābha. 丨衲 A name and robe, i.e. a monk. 丨身 A word-group, a term of more than one word. 丨體 Name and embodiment; the identity of name and substance, as in the dhāraṇī of the esoteric sects; somewhat similar to 丨義不離 q.v.

吉 Śrī; auspicious, lucky, fortunate; translit. *k, ke, ku, g.* 丨利; 姞栗陀 Gṛdhra, a vulture. 丨利羅; 髻離吉羅 One of the honourable ones in the Vajradhātu group. 丨庶 (or 遮 or 蔗); 訖利多; 訖栗著 Kṛtyā; a demon, or class of demons, yakṣa and human; explained by 起尸鬼 a corpse-raising demon; 丨利多 is explained by 買得 bought as (a serf or slave). 丨慶 Auspicious, lucky, fortunate. 丨日良辰 A lucky day and propitious star. 丨槃荼 Kumbhāṇḍas, demons of monstrous form, idem 鳩槃荼. 丨河 The auspicious river, the Ganges, because in it the heretics say they can wash away their sins. 丨由羅; 枳由邏; 犄由羅 Keyūra, a bracelet (worn on the upper arm). 丨祥 Auspicious, fortunate, tr. of the name of Lakṣmī, the goddess of fortune. See next, also 室利 and 尸里. 丨丨天女; 功德天; 摩訶室利 Mahāśrī, identified with Lakṣmī, name "of the goddess of fortune and beauty frequently in the later mythology identified with Śrī and regarded as the wife of Vishṇu or Nārāyaṇa", she sprang from the ocean with a lotus in her hand, whence she is also called Padmā, and is connected in other ways with the lotus. M. W. There is some confusion between this goddess and Kuan-yin, possibly through the attribution of Hindu ideas of Lakṣmī to Kuan-yin. 丨丨果 The auspicious fruit, a pomegranate, held by Hāritī 鬼子母 as the bestower of children. 丨丨海雲 The auspicious sea-cloud; tr. as Śrī-vatsa, the breast mark of Viṣṇu, but defined as the svastika, which is the 佛心印 symbol on a Buddha's breast. 丨丨草 (or 茅); 矩奢. Kuśa, auspicious grass used at religious ceremonials, Poa cynosuroides. 丨丨茅國; 矩奢揭羅補羅 Kuśāgrapura, "ancient residence of the kings of Magadha, surrounded by mountains,

14 miles south of Behar. It was deserted under Bimbisāra, who built 'New Rādjagriha' 6 miles farther to the west." Eitel. The distance given is somewhat incorrect, but v. 王舍城. | 羅 Kṛta idem 突 | | Duṣkṛta; one of the grave sins. | 迦夜 Kekaya, a noted monk of the Liu-Sung dynasty.

回; 囘 To turn, revolve, return. | 互 Interchange, intermutation. | 光返照 To turn the light inwards on oneself, concern oneself with one's own duty. | 向; 迴向 Pariṇāmanā. To turn towards; to turn something from one person or thing to another; transference (of merit); the term is intp. by 轉趣 turn towards; it is used for works of supererogation, or rather, it means the bestowing on another, or others, of merits acquired by oneself, especially the merits acquired by a bodhisattva or Buddha for the salvation of all, e.g. the bestowing of his merits by Amitābha on all the living. There are other kinds, such as the turning of acquired merit to attain further progress in bodhi, or nirvāṇa. One definition is | 事向理 to turn (from) practice to theory; | 自向他 from oneself to another; | 因向果 from cause to effect. Other definitions include | 世而向出世 to turn from this world to what is beyond this world, from the worldly to the unworldly. | 小向大 To turn from Hīnayāna to Mahāyāna. | 心; | | 懺悔 To turn the mind from evil to good, to repent. | | 戒 Commandments bestowed on the converted, or repentant. | 悟 To turn and apprehend; be converted. | 禮 To return, or acknowledge a courtesy or gift. | 財; | 祭 Payment by a donor of sums already expended at his request by a monastery. | 趣 To turn from other things to Buddhism.

因 Hetu; a cause; because; a reason; to follow, it follows, that which produces a 果 result or effect. 因 is a primary cause in comparison with 緣 pratyaya, which is an environmental or secondary cause. In the 十因十果 ten causes and ten effects, adultery results in the iron bed, the copper pillar, and the eight hot hells; covetousness in the cold hells; and so on, as shown in the 楞嚴經. Translit. *in*, *yin*. Cf. 印.

因人 Followers of Buddha who have not yet attained Buddhahood, but are still producers of karma and reincarnation.

因位 The causative position, i.e. that of a Buddhist, for he has accepted a cause, or enlightenment, that produces a changed outlook.

因修 The practice of Buddhism as the "cause" of Buddhahood.

因內(二明) Reason and authority; i.e. two of the five 明, v. 因明 and 內明, the latter referring to the statements, therefore authoritative, of the Scriptures.

因分 Cause, as contrasted with effect 果分. | | 可說果分不可說 The causes (that give rise to a Buddha's Buddhahood) may, in a measure, be stated, that is, such part as is humanly manifested; but the full result is beyond description.

因力 The causal force, or cause, contrasted with 緣力 environmental, or secondary forces.

因十四過 The fourteen possible errors or fallacies in the reason in a syllogism.

因同品 (The example in logic must be) of the same order as the reason.

因圓果滿 The cause perfect and the effect complete, i.e. the practice of Buddhism.

因地 The causal ground, fundamental cause; the state of practising the Buddha-religion which leads to the 果地 or resulting Buddhahood.

因尼延 Aiṇeya, black antelope, v. 伊.

因明 Hetuvidyā, 醯都費陀, the science of cause, logical reasoning, logic, with its syllogistic method of the proposition, the reason, the example. The creation of this school of logic is attributed to Akṣapāda, probably a name for the philosopher Gautama (not Śākyamuni). The | | 論 or Hetuvidyā-śāstra is one of the 五明論 pañcavidyā-śāstras, a treatise explaining causality, or the nature of truth and error. | | 入正理論 Nyāyapraveśa; a treatise on logic by 商羯羅主 Śaṅkarasvāmin, follower of Dignāga, tr. by Hsüan-tsang in 1 chüan, on which there are numerous commentaries and works. | | 正理門論 Nyāyadvāratarka-śāstra, a treatise by 陳那 Dignāga, tr. by I-ching, 1 chüan.

因曼陀羅 The Garbhadhātu 胎藏 maṇḍala, which is also east and 因, or cause, as contrasted with the Vajradhātu, which is west and 果, or effect.

因果 Cause and effect; every cause has its effect, as every effect arises from a cause. ||應報 Cause and effect in the moral realm have their corresponding relations, the denial of which destroys all moral responsibility. ||皆空宗 A sect of "heretics" who denied cause and effect both in regard to creation and morals.

因業 The work, or operation, of cause, or causes, i.e. the co-operation of direct and indirect causes, of primary and environmental causes.

因源 Cause; cause and origin.

因異品 Hetu-viruddha; in a syllogism the example not accordant with the reason.

因相 Causation; one of the three forms or characteristics of the Ālayavijñāna, the character of the origin of all things.

因緣 Hetupratyaya. Cause; causes; 因 hetu, is primary cause, 緣 pratyaya, secondary cause, or causes, e.g. a seed is 因, rain, dew, farmer, etc., are 緣. The 十二|| twelve nidānas or links are "the concatenation of cause and effect in the whole range of existence". ||依 Dependent on cause, or the cause or causes on which anything depends. ||生 Causally-produced. ||觀 A meditation on the nidānas.

因能變 The power in a cause to transform itself into an effect; a cause that is also an effect, e.g. a seed.

因行果 Cause, action, effect; e.g. seed, germination, fruit.

因論 idem 因明論.

因道 The way, or principle, of causation.

因達(or 陀)羅大將 Indra as General (guarding the shrine of 藥師 Bhaiṣajya).

因陀囉誓多 Indraceṭa, Indra's attendants, or slaves. |||達婆門佛 Indradhvaja, a Buddha-incarnation of the seventh son of the Buddha Mahābhijñābhibhū 大通智勝.

因陀羅 Indra, 因坻; 因提; 因提梨; 因達羅; 天帝; 天主帝; 帝釋天; originally a god of the atmosphere, i.e. of thunder and rain; idem Śakra; his symbol is the vajra, or thunderbolt, hence he is the 金剛手; he became "lord of the gods of the sky", "regent of the east quarter", "popularly chief after Brahmā, Viṣṇu, and Śiva" (M. W.); in Buddhism he represents the secular power, and is inferior to a Buddhist saint. Cf. 忉利 and 印. |||勢羅窶訶; |||世羅求訶; |||窟; 因沙舊 Indraśailaguhā; explained by 帝釋石窟 Indra's cave; also by 蛇神山 the mountain of the snake god, also by 小孤石山 the mountain of small isolated peaks located near Nālandā, where on the south crag of the west peak is a rock cave, broad but not high, which Śākyamuni frequently visited. Indra is said to have written forty-two questions on stone, to which the Buddha replied. |||呵悉多; |||喝悉哆; |||訶塞多. Probably Indra-hasta, Indra's hand, "a kind of medicament." M. W. Is it the 佛手 "Buddha's hand", a kind of citron? |||婆他那 ? Indravadana, or ? Indrabhavana. A "name for India proper"; Eitel. ||(|)尼羅(目多) Indranīla-(muktā). Indra's blue (or green) stone, which suggests an emerald, Indranīlaka (M.W.); but according to M. W. Indranīla is a sapphire; muktā is a pearl. |||跋帝 Tr. as Indra's city, or Indra's banner, but the latter is Indraketu; ? Indravatī.

在 At, in, on, present. |世 In the world, while alive here. |俗 In and of the world, unenlightened; in a lay condition. |在處處 In every place. |家 At home, a layman or woman, not 出家, i.e. not leaving home as a monk or nun. ||二戒 The two grades of commandments observed by the lay, one the five, the other the eight, v. 五 and 八戒; these are the Hīnayāna rules; the ||戒 of Mahāyāna are the 十善戒 ten good rules. ||出家 One who while remaining at home observes the whole of a monk's or nun's rules. |理教 The Tsai-li secret society, an offshoot of the White Lily Society, was founded in Shantung at the beginning of the Ch'ing dynasty; the title "in the li" indicating that the society associated itself with all three religions, Confucianism, Taoism, and Buddhism; its followers set up no images, burnt no incense, neither smoked nor drank, and were vegetarian. |纏 In bonds, i.e. the ||眞如 the Bhūtatathatā in limitations, e.g. relative, v. 起信論 Awakening of Faith.

地 Pṛthivī, 鉢里體尾 the earth, ground; Bhūmi, 步弭 the earth, place, situation; Talima, 託史 (or 吏) 麼 ground, site; explained by 土地 earth, ground; 能生 capable of producing; 所依

that on which things rely. It is also the spiritual rank, position, or character attained by a Bodhisattva as a result of 住 remaining and developing in a given state in order to attain this 地 rank; v. 十住; 住位 and 十地.

地上 On the ground; above the ground; used for 初地以上 the stages above the initial stage of a Bodhisattva's development.

地中; 地內 Annexes, or subsidiary buildings in the grounds of a monastery.

地(行)仙 Earth-immortals, or genii, one of the classes of ṛṣis; i.e. bhūdeva = Brahman.

地位 Position, place, state.

地前 The stages of a Bodhisattva before the 初地.

地動 Earthquake; the earth shaken, one of the signs of Buddha-power.

地塵 Earth-dust; as dust of earth (in number); atoms of the earth element.

地壇 A square altar used by the esoteric cult.

地大 Earth as one of the 四大 four elements, | earth, 水 water, 火 fire, and 風 air (i.e. air in motion, wind); to these 空 space (Skt. ākāśa) is added to make the 五大 five elements; 識 vijñāna, perception to make the six elements; and 見 darśana, views, concepts, or reasonings to make the seven elements. The esoteric sect use the five fingers, beginning with the little finger, to symbolize the five elements.

地天 The earth-devī, Pṛthivī, one of the four with thunderbolts in the Vajradhātu group; also | | 后 the earth-devī in the Garbhadhātu group. Cf. | 神.

地婆訶羅 Divākara, tr. as 日照 Jih-chao, a śramaṇa from Central India, A.D. 676–688, tr. of eighteen or nineteen works, introduced an alphabet of forty-two letters or characters. | | 達多 (or 兜) Devadatta, v. 提.

地居天 Indra's heaven on the top of Sumeru, below the 空居天 heavens in space.

地底迦 Dhītika, originally Dhṛtaka, an ancient monk, whose name is tr. by 有愧 Yu-k'uei, ashamed, shy.

地 (or 持 or 財) 慧童子 The youth who controls earthly possessions, the fourth on the left of the messengers of Mañjuśrī in the Garbhadhātu group.

地涌 To spring forth, or burst from the earth, a chapter in the Lotus sūtra.

地獄 Naraka, 捺 (or 那) 落迦; Niraya 泥犂; explained by 不樂 joyless; 可厭 disgusting, hateful; 苦具, 苦器 means of suffering; 地獄 earth-prison; 冥府 the shades, or departments of darkness. Earth-prison is generally intp. as hell or the hells; it may also be termed purgatory; one of the six gati or ways of transmigration. The hells are divided into three classes: I. Central, or radical, 根本地獄 consisting of (1) The eight hot hells. These were the original hells of primitive Buddhism, and are supposed to be located under the southern continent Jambudvīpa 瞻部州, 500 yojanas below the surface. (*a*) 等活 or 更活 Saṁjīva, rebirth, where after many kinds of suffering a cold wind blows over the soul and returns it to this life as it was before, hence the name 等活. (*b*) 黑繩 Kālasūtra, where the sufferer is bound with black chains and chopped or sawn asunder. (*c*) 線合; 衆合; 堆壓 Saṁghāta, where are multitudes of implements of torture, or the falling of mountains upon the sufferer. (*d*) 號叫; 呼呼; 叫喚 Raurava, hell of wailing. (*e*) 大叫; 大號叫; 大呼 Mahāraurava, hell of great wailing. (*f*) 炎熱; 燒炙 Tapana, hell of flames and burning. (*g*) 大熱; 大燒炙; 大炎熱 Pratāpana, hell of molten lead. (*h*) 無間; 河鼻旨; 阿惟越致; 阿毗至; 阿鼻; 阿毗 Avīci, unintermitted suffering, where sinners die and are reborn to suffer without interval. (2) The eight cold hells 八寒地獄. (*a*) 頞浮陀 | | Arbuda, where the cold causes blisters. (*b*) 尼剌部陀 Nirarbuda, colder still, causing the blisters to burst. (*c*) 頞哳吒; 阿吒吒 Aṭaṭa, where this is the only possible sound from frozen lips. (*d*) 臛臛婆; 阿波波 Hahava or Apapa, where it is so cold that only this sound can be uttered. (*e*) 虎虎婆 Hāhādhara or Huhuva, where only this sound can be uttered. (*f*) 嗢鉢羅; 鬱 (or 優) 鉢羅 Utpala, or 尼羅烏 (or 漚) 鉢羅 Nīlotpala, where the skin is frozen like blue lotus buds. (*g*) 鉢特摩 Padma, where the skin is frozen and bursts open like red lotus buds. (*h*) 摩訶鉢特摩 Mahāpadma, ditto like great red lotus buds. Somewhat different names are also given. Cf. 俱舍論 8; 智度論 16; 涅槃經 11. II. The secondary hells are called 近邊地獄 adjacent hells or 十六遊增地獄 the sixteen progressive, or 十六小地獄 sixteen inferior hells. Each hot hell has a door on each of its four sides, opening from each such door are four adjacent hells, in all sixteen; thus with the original eight there are 136. A list of eighteen hells is given in the 十八泥梨經. III. A third class is called the 孤 (獨) 地獄 Lokāntarika, or isolated hells in mountains, deserts, below the earth and above it. Eitel says in regard to the eight hot hells that they range "one beneath the other in tiers which begin at a depth of 11,900 yôdjanas and reach to a depth of 40,000 yôdjanas". The cold hells are under "the two Tchakravālas and range shaft-like one below the other, but so that this shaft is gradually widening to the fourth hell and then narrowing itself again so that the first and last hell have the shortest, those in the centre the longest diameter". "Every universe has the same number of hells," but "the northern continent has no hell whatever, the two continents east and west of Meru have only small Lokāntarika hells . . . whilst all the other hells are required for the inhabitants of the southern continent". It may be noted that the purpose of these hells is definitely punitive, as well as purgatorial. Yama is the judge and ruler, assisted by eighteen officers and a host of demons, who order or administer the various degrees of torture. "His sister performs the same duties with regard to female criminals," and it may be mentioned that the Chinese have added the 血盆池 Lake of the bloody bath, or "placenta tank", for women who die in childbirth. Release from the hells is in the power of the monks by tantric means. | | 天子 The immediate transformation of one in hell into a deva because he had in a previous life known of the merit and power of the 華嚴 Hua-yen sūtra. | | 道 or 趣 The hell-gati, or destiny of reincarnation in the hells.

地珂 Dīrgha, long; also 地嘌伽.

地界 The realm of earth, one of the four elements, v. 地大.

地神 The earth devī, Pṛthivī, also styled 堅牢 firm and secure; cf. 地天.

地種 Earth-seed, or atoms of the element earth.

地膩脾 Dravya, substance, thing, object.

地致婆 Tiṭibha, Tiṭilambha, "a particular high mountain," M. W. 1,000 quadrillions; a 大 | | | is said to be 10,000 quadrillions.

地藏 Ti-tsang, J. Jizō, Kṣitigarbha, 乞叉底蘖沙; Earth-store, Earth-treasury, or Earth-womb. One of the group of eight Dhyāni-Bodhisattvas. With hints of a feminine origin, he is now the guardian of the earth. Though associated with Yama as overlord, and with the dead and the hells, his role is that of saviour. Depicted with the alarum staff with its six rings, he is accredited with power over the hells and is devoted to the saving of all creatures between the nirvāṇa of Śākyamuni and the advent of Maitreya. From the fifth century he has been especially considered as the deliverer from the hells. His central place in China is at Chiu-hua-shan, forty li south-west of Ch'ing-yang in Anhui. In Japan he is also the protector of travellers by land and his image accordingly appears on the roads; bereaved parents put stones by his images to seek his aid in relieving the labours of their dead in the task of piling stones on the banks of the Buddhist Styx; he also helps women in labour. He is described as holding a place between the gods and men on the one hand and the hells on the other for saving all in distress; some say he is an incarnation of Yama. At dawn he sits immobile on the earth 地 and meditates on the myriads of its beings 藏. When represented as a monk, it may be through the influence of a Korean monk who is considered to be his incarnation, and who came to China in 653 and died in 728 at the age of 99 after residing at Chiu-hua-shan for seventy-five years; his body, not decaying, is said to have been gilded over and became an object of worship. Many have confused 新羅 part of Korea with 暹羅 Siam. There are other developments of Ti-tsang, such as the 六 | | Six Ti-tsang, i.e. severally converting or transforming those in the hells, pretas, animals, asuras, men, and the devas; these six Ti-tsang have different images and symbols. Ti-tsang has also six messengers 六使者: Yama for transforming those in hell; the pearl-holder for pretas; the strong one for animals; the devī of mercy for asuras; the devī of the treasure for human beings; one who has charge of the heavens for the devas. There is also the 延命 | | Yen-ming Ti-tsang, who controls length of days and who is approached, as also may be P'u-hsien, for that purpose; his two assistants are the Supervisors of good and evil 掌善 and 掌惡. Under another form, as 勝軍 | | Ti-tsang of the conquering host, he is chiefly associated with the esoteric cult. The benefits derived from his worship are many, some say ten, others say twenty-eight. His vows are contained in the | | (菩薩) 本願經. There is also the (大乘大集) | | 十輪經 tr. by Hsüan-tsang in 10 chüan in the seventh century, which probably influenced the spread of the Ti-tsang cult.

地論 idem 十地經論.

地輪 The earth-wheel, one of the 五輪 five circles, i.e. space, wind, water, earth, and above them fire; the five "wheels" or umbrellas shown on the top of certain stūpas or pagodas. ||壇 The earth-altar is four-cornered and used by the esoteric sect.

地迦婆縛那僧伽藍 ? Dīrgha-bhavana-saṁghārāma. A monastery near Khotan 豁旦, with a statue dressed in silk which had "transported itself" thither from Karashahr 庫車. Eitel.

多 Bahu; bhūri. Many; all; translit. *ta*.

多他; 多咃 Tathā; in such a manner, like, so, true; it is tr. by 如 which has the same meanings. It is also said to mean 滅 extinction, or nirvāṇa. v. |陀.

多寶(如來) Prabhūtaratna, abundant treasures, or many jewels. The Ancient Buddha, long in nirvāṇa, who appears in his stūpa to hear the Buddha preach the Lotus doctrine, by his presence revealing, *inter alia*, that nirvāṇa is not annihilation, and that the Lotus doctrine is the Buddha-gospel; v. Lotus Sūtra 寶塔品.

多揭羅 Tagaraka, 木香; 根香 putchuck, Aplotaxis auriculata, or Tabernæmontana coronaria, the shrub and its fragrant powder; also |伽羅 (or 留, or 婁).

多摩梨帝 Tāmralipti, or tī; the modern Tumluk in the estuary of the Hugli; also 呾 (or 躭) 摩栗底. ||羅跋旃檀香 Tamālapattra-candana-gandha; a Buddha-incarnation of the 11th son of Mahābhijña, residing N.W. of our universe; also the name of the Buddha-incarnation of Mahāmaudgalyāyana.

多生 Many births, or productions; many re-incarnations.

多羅 Tārā, in the sense of starry, or scintillation; Tāla, for the fan-palm; Tara, from "to pass over", a ferry, etc. Tārā, starry, piercing, the eye, the pupil; the last two are both Sanskrit and Chinese definitions; it is a term applied to certain female deities and has been adopted especially by Tibetan Buddhism for certain devīs of the Tantric school. The origin of the term is also ascribed to *tar* meaning "to cross", i.e. she who aids to cross the sea of mortality. Getty, 19–27. The Chinese derivation is the eye; the tārā devīs, either as śakti or independent, are little known outside Lamaism. Tāla is the palmyra, or fan-palm, whose leaves are used for writing and known as 貝多 pei-to, pattra. The tree is described as 70 or 80 feet high, with fruit like yellow rice-seeds; the Borassus flabelliformis; a measure of 70 feet. Taras, from to cross over, also means a ferry, and a bank, or the other shore. Also 呾囉. ||夜登陸舍 Trayastriṁśās, v. 三十三天. ||樹; ||果; ||葉; |(|)掌 Tāla, the Tāla tree, its edible fruit resembling the pomegranate, its leaves being used for writing, their palm-shaped parts being made into fans. ||菩薩 Tārā Bodhisattva, as a form of Kuan-yin, is said to have been produced from the eye of Kuan-yin.

多聞 Bahu-śruta; learned, one who has heard much. ||第一 The chief among the Buddha's hearers: Ānanda.

多財鬼 Wealthy ghosts.

多貪 Many desires.

多足 Many-footed, e.g. centipedes.

多陀阿伽陀 Tathāgata, 多他阿伽陀(耶); 多他阿伽駄 (or 度); 多 (or 怛闥 or 怛薩)阿竭; 怛他蘗多; intp. by 如來 Ju-lai, q.v. "thus come", or "so come"; it has distant resemblance to the Messiah, but means one who has arrived according to the norm, one who has attained the goal (of enlightenment). It is also intp. as 如去 Ju-ch'ü, he who so goes, his coming and going being both according to the Buddha-norm. It is the highest of a Buddha's titles. |阿摩羅跋陀羅 Tamālapattra, cassia, "the leaf of the Xanthochymus pictorius, the leaf of the Laurus Cassia," M. W. The Malobathrum of Pliny. Also called 藿葉香 betony, bishopwort, or thyme; also 赤銅葉 copper-leaf.

多體 Many bodies, or forms; many-bodied.

多髮 Kēśini, having long hair, intp. as many locks (of hair), name of a rākṣasī, v. 髻.

多齡(路迦也吠闍也); 帝隸, etc. Trailokyavijaya, one of the 明王 Ming Wang, the term being tr. literally as 三世降(明王) the Ming-Wang defeater (of evil) in the three spheres.

妃 An imperial concubine; as implying production, or giving birth, it is used by the esoteric cult for samaya and dhāraṇī.

好 Good, well; to like, be fond of, love. 丨照 Good at shining, a mirror. 丨生 Love of life; love of the living. 丨相 A good appearance, omen, or sign. 丨聲 (or 音) 鳥 A bird with a beautiful note, the Kokila, or Kalaviṅka, some say Karaṇḍa(ka).

妄 Mithyā; false, untrue, erroneous, wild. 丨執 False tenets, holding on to false views. 丨境界 False environment; the unreal world. 丨塵 The unreal and unclean world. 丨心 A wrong, false, or misleading mind. 丨念 False or misleading thoughts. 丨想 Erroneous thinking. 丨染; 丨風 The spread of lies, or false ideas. 丨法 Bhrānti, going astray, error. 丨緣 The unreality of one's environment; also, the causes of erroneous ideas. 丨見 False views (of reality), taking the seeming as real. 丨言; 丨說 False words, or talk; lies. 丨語 The commandment against lying, either as slander, or false boasting, or deception; for this the 智度論 gives ten evil results on reincarnation: (1) stinking breath; (2) good spirits avoid him, as also do men; (3) none believes him even when telling the truth; (4) wise men never admit him to their deliberations; etc. 丨雲 Clouds of falsity, i.e. delusion.

如 Tathā, 多陀; 但 (or 怛) 他, so, thus, in such manner, like, as. It is used in the sense of the absolute, the 空 śūnya, which is 諸佛之實相 the reality of all Buddhas; hence 如 ju is 實相 the undifferentiated whole of things, the ultimate reality; it is 諸法之性 the nature of all things, hence it connotes 法性 fa-hsing which is 眞實之際極 the ultimate of reality, or the absolute, and therefore connotes 實際 ultimate reality. The ultimate nature of all things being 如 ju, the one undivided same, it also connotes 理 li, the principle or theory behind all things, and this 理 li universal law, being the 眞實 truth or ultimate reality; 如 ju is termed 眞如 bhūtatathatā, the real so, or suchness, or reality, the ultimate or the all, i.e. the 一如 i-ju. In regard to 如 ju as 理 li the Prajñā-pāramitā makes it the 空 śūnya, while the Saddharma-puṇḍarīka makes it the 中 chung, neither matter nor nothingness. It is also used in the ordinary sense of so, like, as (cf. yathā), e.g. 丨幻 as an illusion, or illusory; 丨化 as if transformed; 丨焰 like smoke; 丨雲 like a cloud; 丨電 like lightning; 丨夢 like a dream; 丨泡 like a bubble; 丨影 like a shadow; 丨響 like an echo.

如來 Tathāgata, 多陀阿伽陀 q.v.; 怛他揭多 defined as he who comes as do all other Buddhas; or as he who took the 眞如 chên-ju or absolute way of cause and effect, and attained to perfect wisdom; or as the absolute come; one of the highest titles of a Buddha. It is the Buddha in his nirmāṇakāya, i.e. his "transformation" or corporeal manifestation descended on earth. The two kinds of Tathāgata are (1) 在纏 the Tathāgata in bonds, i.e. limited and subject to the delusions and sufferings of life, and (2) 出纏 unlimited and free from them. There are numerous sūtras and śāstras bearing this title of 如來 Ju-lai. 丨丨乘 Tathāgata-yāna, the Tathāgata vehicle, or means of salvation. 丨丨使 Tathāgata-dūta, or -preṣya; a Tathāgata apostle sent to do his work. 丨丨光明出已還入 According to the Nirvāṇa sūtra, at the Tathāgata's nirvāṇa he sent forth his glory in a wonderful light which finally returned into his mouth. 丨丨地 The state or condition of a Tathāgata. 丨丨室 The abode of the Tathāgata, i.e. 慈悲 mercy, or pity. 丨丨常住 The Tathāgata is eternal, always abiding. 丨丨愍菩薩; 怛他蘖多母隸底多 The seventh Bodhisattva to the right of Śākyamuni in the Garbhadhātu group, in charge of the pity or sympathy of the Tathāgata. There are other bodhisattvas in charge of other Tathāgata forms or qualities in the same group. 丨丨應供正徧智 Tathāgata, Worshipful, Omniscient—three titles of a Buddha. 丨丨日; 實相日 The Tathāgata day, which is without beginning or end and has no limit of past, present, or future. 丨丨神力品; 丨丨壽量品 Chapters in the Lotus sūtra on Tathāgata powers and eternity. 丨丨舞 The play of the Tathāgata, i.e. the exercise of his manifold powers. 丨丨藏 Tathāgatagarbha, the Tathāgata womb or store, defined as (1) the 眞如 chên-ju, q.v. in the midst of 煩惱 the delusion of passions and desires; (2) sūtras of the Buddha's uttering. The first especially refers to the chên-ju as the source of all things: whether compatibles or incompatibles, whether forces of purity or impurity, good or bad, all created things are in the Tathāgatagarbha, which is the womb that gives birth to them all. The second is the storehouse of the Buddha's teaching. 丨丨藏心 idem 眞如心. 丨丨藏性 The natures of all the living are the nature of the Tathāgata; for which v. the 丨丨丨經, 丨丨丨論, etc. 丨丨身 Tathāgatakāya, Buddha-body. 丨丨部 The court of Vairocana-Tathāgata in the Garbhadhātu group.

如去 Tathāgata means both "so-come" and "so-gone", i.e. into Nirvāṇa; v. 如來 and 多陀.

如如 The 眞如 chên-ju or absolute; also the absolute in differentiation, or in the relative.

The | | 境 and | | 智 are the realm or "substance", and the wisdom or law of the absolute.

如實 Real, reality, according to reality (yathābhūtam); true; the 眞如 chên-ju, or bhūtatathatā, for which it is also used; the universal undifferentiated, i.e. 平等不二, or the primary essence out of which the phenomenal arises; | | 空 is this essence in its purity; | | 不空 is this essence in its differentiation. | | 智 Knowledge of reality, i.e. of all things whether whole or divided, universal or particular, as distinguished from their seeming; Buddha-omniscience. | | 知者 The knower of reality, a Buddha. | | 知見 To know and see the reality of all things as does the Buddha. | | 知自心 To know one's heart in reality.

如意 At will; according to desire; a ceremonial emblem, originally a short sword; tr. of Manoratha 末笯曷剌他 successor of Vasubandhu as 22nd patriarch and of Mahāṛddhiprāpta, a king of garuḍas. | | 珠 Cintāmaṇi, a fabulous gem, the philosopher's stone, the talisman-pearl capable of responding to every wish, said to be obtained from the dragon-king of the sea, or the head of the great fish, Makara, or the relics of a Buddha. It is also called | | 寶(珠); | | 摩尼. There is also the | | 瓶 or talismanic vase; the | | 輪 talismanic wheel, as in the case of | | | 觀音 Kuan-yin with the wheel, holding the pearl in her hand symbolizing a response to every prayer, also styled 持寶金剛 the Vajra-bodhisattva with six hands, one holding the pearl, or gem, another the wheel, etc. There are several sūtras, etc., under these titles, associated with Kuan-yin. | | 足 Ṛddhipāda, magical psychic powers of ubiquity, idem 神足. | | 身 Ṛddhi, magic power exempting the body from physical limitations, v. 大教 and 神足.

如是 Evam; thus, so; so it is; so let it be; such and such; (as) . . . so. Most of the sūtras open with the phrase | | 我聞 or 聞如是 Thus have I heard, i.e. from the Buddha.

如法 According to the Law, according to rule. | | 治 punished according to law, i.e. 突吉羅 duṣkṛita, the punishments due to law-breaking monks or nuns.

如理師 A title of the Buddha, the Master who taught according to the truth, or fundamental law.

如語 True words, right discourse.

存 To keep, maintain, preserve; | 生 (命); | 命 to preserve one's life, to preserve alive; | 見 to keep to (wrong) views.

字 Akṣara, 阿乞史囉; 阿刹羅; a letter, character; akṣara is also used for a vowel, especially the vowel "a" as distinguished from the other vowels; a word, words. | 相 | 義 Word-form and word-meaning, differentiated by the esoteric sect for its own ends, 阿 being considered the alpha and root of all sounds and words; the 字 among esoteric Buddhists is the 種子 bīja, or seed-word possessing power through the object with which it is associated; there is also the 字輪, the wheel, rotation, or interchange of words for esoteric purposes, especially the five Sanskrit signs adopted for the five elements, earth, water, fire, air, space. | 母 The Sanskrit alphabet of 42, 47, or 50 letters, the "Siddham" 悉曇 consisting of 35 體文 consonants and 12 摩多 vowels. The | | 表 deals with the alphabet in 1 chüan. The | | 品 is an abbreviation of 文殊問經 | | | |. | 緣; 母音 The 12 or 14 Sanskrit vowels, as contrasted with the 35 or 36 consonants, which are 根本 radical or 字界 limited or fixed letters.

宅 Residential part of a palace, or mansion; a residence.

守 Keep, guard, observe. | 寺 The guardian, or caretaker, of a monastery. | 法 To keep the law. | 護 To guard, protect. | 門天 or 尊 The deva gate-guardian of a temple.

安 Peace, tranquil, quiet, pacify; to put, place; where? how? | 下 To put down. | | 處 A place for putting things down, e.g. baggage; a resting place, a place to stay at. | 名 To give a religious name to a beginner. | 咀羅縛 Andarab, a country through which Hsüan-tsang passed, north of Kapiśā, v. 迦. | 土地 To tranquillize the land, or a plot of land, by freeing it from harmful influences. | 居 Tranquil dwelling. Varṣa, Varṣās, or Varṣāvasāna. A retreat during the three months of the Indian rainy season, and also, say some, in the depth of winter. During the rains it was "difficult to move without injuring insect life". But the object was for study and meditation. In Tokhara the retreat is said to have been in winter, from the middle of the 12th to the middle of the 3rd moon; in India from the middle of the 5th to the 8th, or the 6th to the 9th moons; usually from Śrāvaṇa, Chinese 5th moon, to Aśvayuja, Chinese 8th moon; but the 16th of the 4th to the 15th of the 7th moon has been the common period in China and Japan. The two annual periods are sometimes called 坐夏 and 坐臘 sitting or resting for the summer and for the end of the year. The period is divided into three sections, former, middle, and latter, each of a month. | 底羅 Aṇḍīra, one of the twelve attendants on 藥師 Bhaiṣajya. | 廩 Anlin, a noted monk *circa* A.D. 500. | 心 To quiet the heart, or mind; be at rest. | 息 To rest. | | (國) Parthia, 波斯 modern Persia, from which several monks came to China in the later Han dynasty, such as 安世高 An Shih-kao, 安玄 An-hsüan, 曇無諦 T'an Wu-ti, 安法欽 An Fa-ch'in, 安淸 An-ch'ing. | | 香 Persian incense, or benzoin. | 慧 Settled or firm resolve on wisdom; established wisdom; tr. of 悉耻羅末底 Sthiramati, or Sthitamati, one of the ten great exponents of the 唯識論 Vijñaptimātratāsiddhi śāstra, a native of southern India. | 明 (由) 山 Sumeru, v. 須. | 樂 Happy; ease (of body) and joy (of heart) 身安心樂. The | | 國 or | | 淨土 is Amitābha's Happy Land in the western region, which is his domain; it is also called 安養淨土 or 淨刹, Pure Land of Tranquil Nourishment. | 禪 To enter into dhyāna meditation. | 穩; | 隱 Body and mind at rest. | 立 To set up, establish, stand firm. | | 行 Supratiṣṭhita-cāritra; a Bodhisattva in the Lotus sūtra who rose up out of the earth to greet Śākyamuni. | 膳 (or 繕 or 禪 or 闍) 那 An Indian eye medicine, said to be Añjana. | 遠 Two noted monks of the 晉 Chin dynasty, i.e. 道安 Tao-an and 慧遠 Hui-yüan. | 那般那; | 般; 阿那 (阿) 波那 Ānāpāna, expiration and inspiration, a method of breathing and counting the breaths for purposes of concentration; the 大安般守意經 is a treatise on the subject. | 陁會; | 怛 (or 多) 婆沙 (or 參); | 多 (or 陀) 跋薩 Antarvāsaka, Antarvāsas; a monk's inner garment described as a sort of waistcoat. It is also explained by 裙 ch'ün which means a skirt. This inner garment is said to be worn against desire, the middle one against hate, and the outer one against ignorance and delusion. It is described as the present-day 給子 a jacket or vest.

寺 Vihāra, 毘 or 鼻訶羅; Saṅghārāma 僧伽藍; an official hall, a temple, adopted by Buddhists for a monastery, many other names are given to it, e.g. 淨住; 法同舍; 出世舍; 精舍; 淸淨園; 金剛刹; 寂滅道場; 遠離處; 親近處 "A model vihāra ought to be built of red sandalwood, with 32 chambers, 8 Tāla trees in height, with a garden, park and bathing tank attached; it ought to have promenades for peripatetic meditation and to be richly furnished with stores of clothes, food, bedsteads, mattresses, medicines and all creature comforts." Eitel. | 院 Monastery grounds and buildings, a monastery.

年 A year, years. | 忌 Anniversary of a death, and the ceremonies associated with it. | 戒 The (number of) years since receiving the commandments. | 星 The year-star of an individual. | 滿受具 To receive the full commandments, i.e. be fully ordained at the regulation age of 20. | 臘 The end of a year, also a year. | 少淨行 A young Brahman.

式 Style, shape, fashion, kind. | 棄; | 葉, v. 尸. | 叉 Śikṣā; learning, study. | | (摩那) 尼 Śikṣamāṇā, a female neophyte who from 18 to 20 years of age studies the six rules, in regard to adultery, stealing, killing, lying, alcoholic liquor, not eating at unregulated hours. | | 迦羅尼 Śikṣākāraṇī, intp. as study, or should study or be studied, also as duṣkṛtam, bad deed, breach of the law. The form meaning is suggestive of a female preceptor.

忙 Busy, bustling. | 忙六道 Bustling about and absorbed in the six paths of transmigration. | | 鷄; | 莽鷄 (or 計) 金剛; 麽麽鷄; 麽莫枳 Māmakī, or Māmukhī, tr. as 金剛母 the mother of all the vajra group, whose wisdom is derived from her; she is represented in the Garbhadhātu maṇḍala.

成 See under seven strokes.

戍 The hour from 7–9 p.m.; translit. *śū*, *śu*. | 陀; | 達; | 陀 (or 捺 or 怛) 羅 Śūdra, the fourth or servile caste, whose duty is to serve the three higher castes. | | 戰達羅 Śuddhacandra, 淨月 pure moon, name of one of the ten authorities on 唯識 q.v. | 婆揭羅僧訶 Śubhakarasiṁha. Propitious lion, i.e. auspicious and heroic; fearless. | 縷多 v. 沭. | 羯羅 Śukra; 金星 the planet Venus. | 輪聿提 Śudhyantī; clean or pure. It may be an epithet of *vāk* "voice" in the musical sense of "natural diatonic melody". | 迦 Śuka, a parrot; an epithet of the Buddha. | 迦羅博乞史 Śuklapakṣa, the waxing period of the moon, 1st to 15th.

托 To carry on the palm, entrust to. | 塔天王 The deva-king who bears a pagoda on his palm, one of the four mahārājas, i.e. 毘沙門 Vaiśravaṇa. | 生 That to which birth is entrusted, as a womb, or a lotus in Paradise. | 胎 A womb; conception. | 鉢 An almsbowl; to carry it.

收 To receive; collect, gather; withdraw. | 鈔 To collect paper money, i.e. receive contributions. | 骨 To collect the bones, or relics, after cremation.

早 Early; morning. | 參 The early morning assembly. | 帝梨 Name of a 鬼 demon.

旬 A decade, a period of ten days. | 單 The ten days' account in a monastery.

旨 Purport, will; good. | 歸 The purport, aim, or objective.

曳 To trail, drag. | 瑟知林 Yaṣṭivana, v. 杖林.

曲 Bent, crooked, humpbacked; to oppress; ballads. | 女城 The city of hunchback women, said to be Kanyākubja, an ancient kingdom and capital of Central India, "Canouge Lat. 27° 3 N., Long. 79° 50 E." Eitel. The legend in the 西域記 Record of Western Lands is that ninety-nine of King Brahmadatta's daughters were thus deformed by the ṛṣi Mahāvṛkṣa whom they refused to marry. | 彔; | 錄; | 祿; | 䫞 A bent chair used in monasteries. | 齒; 矩吒檀底 Kūṭadantī, or Mālākūṭadantī, name of a rākṣasī.

有 Bhava; that which exists, the existing, existence; to have, possess, be. It is defined as (1) the opposite of 無 wu and 空 k'ung the non-existent; (2) one of the twelve nidānas, existence; the condition which, considered as cause, produces effect; (3) effect, the consequence of cause; (4) anything that can be relied upon in the visible or invisible realm. It means any state which lies between birth and death, or beginning and end. There are numerous categories—3, 4, 7, 9, 18, 25, and 29. The 三有 are the 三界 trailokya, i.e. 欲, 色 and 無色界 the realms of desire, of form, and of non-form, all of them realms of mortality; another three are 本有 the present body and mind, or existence, 當有 the future ditto, 中有 the intermediate ditto. Other definitions give the different forms or modes of existence.

有上士 A bodhisattva who has reached the stage of 等覺 and is above the state of being, or the existing, i.e. as conceivable by human minds.

有主物 Things that have an owner.

有事 To have affairs, functioning, phenomenal, idem 有爲法.

有作; 有爲 Functioning, effective; phenomenal, the processes resulting from the law of karma; later 安立 came into use.

有分別 The sixth sense of mental discrimination, manas, as contrasted with the other five senses, sight, hearing, etc., each of which deals only with its own perceptions, and is 無分別. | | 識 Discrimination, another name for the ālaya-vijñāna.

有善多 Ujjayanta, a mountain and monastery in Surāṣṭra on the peninsula of Gujerat. Eitel.

有執受 The perceived, perceptive, perception.

有學 Śaikṣa; in Hīnayāna those in the first three stages of training as arhats, the fourth and last stage being 無學 those beyond the need of further teaching or study. There are eighteen grades of śaikṣa.

有對 Pratigha, sapratigha; resistance, opposition, whatever is capable of offering resistance, an object; material; opposing, opposite.

有待 That which is dependent on material things, i.e. the body.

有德女 A woman of Brahman family in Benares, who became a convert and is the questioner of the Buddha in the Śrīmatī-brāhmaṇī-paripṛcchā | | | 所問大乘經.

有性 "To have the nature," i.e. to be a Buddhist, have the bodhi-mind, in contrast with the 無性 absence of this mind, i.e. the 闡提 icchanti, or unconverted.

有情 Sattva, 薩埵 in the sense of any sentient being; the term was formerly tr. 衆生 all the living, which includes the vegetable kingdom, while | | limits the meaning to those endowed with consciousness. | | 居 The nine abodes, or states of conscious beings, v. 九 | | |. | | 數 Among the number, or in the category, of conscious beings. | | 緣慈 Sentience gives rise to pity, or to have feeling causes pity.

有想 To have thoughts, or desires, opp. 無想.

有意 Mati; matimant; possessing mind, intelligent; a tr. of manuṣya, man, a rational being. The name of the eldest son of Candra-sūrya-pradīpa.

有波第耶夜 Upādhyāya, 烏波陀耶

in India a teacher especially of the Vedāṅgas, a term adopted by the Buddhists and gradually applied to all monks. The Chinese form is 和尙, q.v.

有手 To have a hand, or hands. Hastin, possessing a hand, i.e. a trunk; an elephant.

有支 To have a branch; also the category of bhava, one of the twelve nidānas, v. 有.

有教 The realistic school as opposed to the 空教 teaching of unreality; especially (1) the Hīnayāna teaching of the 俱舍宗 Abhidharmakośa school of Vasubandhu, opposed to the 成實宗 Satya-siddhi school of Harivarman; (2) the Mahāyāna 法相宗 Dharma-lakṣaṇa school, also called the 唯識宗, founded in China by Hsüan-tsang, opposed to the 三論宗 Mādhyamika school of Nāgārjuna.

有所緣 Mental activity, the mind being able to climb, or reach anywhere, in contrast with the non-mental activities, which are 無所緣.

有智慧 Manuṣya, an intelligent being, possessing wisdom, cf. 有意.

有根身 The body with its five senses.

有法 A thing that exists, not like "the horns of a hare", which are 無法 non-existent things. Also in logic the subject in contrast with the predicate, e.g. "sound" is the 有法 or thing, "is eternal" the 法 or law stated.

有海 The sea of existence, i.e. of mortality, or births-and-deaths.

有流 The mortal stream of existence with its karma and delusion. Cf. 見流.

有漏 Āsrava, means "outflow, discharge"; "distress, pain, affliction"; it is intp. by 煩惱 kleśa, the passions, distress, trouble, which in turn is intp. as 惑 delusion. Whatever has kleśa, i.e. distress or trouble, is 有漏; all things are of this nature, hence it means whatever is in the stream of births-and-deaths, and also means mortal life or births-and-deaths, i.e. mortality as contrasted with 無漏, which is nirvāṇa. | | 世 (or 三) 界 The world, or worlds, of distress and illusion. | | 善 (or 惡) 法 Good (or evil) done in a mortal body is rewarded accordingly in the character of another mortal body. | | 淨土 A purifying stage which, for certain types, precedes entry into the Pure Land. | | 道 (or 路) The way of mortal saṁsāra, in contrast with 無漏道 that of nirvāṇa.

有無二見 Bhāvābhāva. Existence or non-existence, being or non-being; these two opposite views, opinions, or theories are the basis of all erroneous views, etc. | | | 邊 The two extremes of being or non-being. | | 邪見 Both views are erroneous in the opinion of upholders of the 中道, the Mādhyamika school.

有爲 Active, creative, productive, functioning, causative, phenomenal, the processes resulting from the laws of karma, v. 有作; opposite of 無 | passive, inert, inactive, non-causative, laisser-faire. It is defined by 造作 to make, and associated with saṁskṛta. The three active things 三 | | 法 are 色 material, or things which have form, 心 mental and 非色非心 neither the one nor the other. The four forms of activity 四 | | 相 are 生住異滅 coming into existence, abiding, change, and extinction; they are also spoken of as three, the two middle terms being treated as having like meaning. | | 果 The result or effect of action. | | 無常 Activity implies impermanency. | | 生死 The mortal saṁsāra life of births and deaths, contrasted with 無爲生死 effortless mortality, e.g. transformation such as that of the Bodhisattva. | | 空 The unreality of the phenomenal. | | 轉變 The permutations of activity, or phenomena, in arising, abiding, change, and extinction.

有界 The realm of existence.

有相 To have form, whatever has form, whether ideal or real. | | 業 Action through faith in the idea, e.g. of the Pure Land; the acts which produce such results. | | 敎 The first twelve years of the Buddha's teaching, when he treated the phenomenal as real; v. 有空中. | | 宗 v. 法相宗 and 有部 Sarvāstivāda.

有空 Phenomenal and noumenal; the manifold forms of things exist, but things, being constructed of elements, have no *per se* reality. | | 不二 The phenomenal and the noumenal are identical, the phenomenal expresses the noumenal and the noumenon contains the phenomenon. | | 中 The three terms, phenomenal, noumenal, and the link or mean, v. 中 and 空. | | 中三時 The 法相宗 Dharma-lakṣaṇa school divides the Buddha's teaching into three periods, in which he taught (1) the unreality of the ego, as shown in the 阿含 Āgamas, etc.; (2) the unreality of the dharmas, as in the 般若 Prajñāpāramitā, etc.; and (3) the middle or uniting way, as in the 解深密經 Sandhinirmocana-sūtra, etc., the last being the foundation text of this school.

有結 The bond of existence, or mortal life.

有緣 Those who have the cause, link, or connection, i.e. are influenced by and responsive to the Buddha.

有耶無耶 Existence? non-existence? Material? immaterial? i.e. uncertainty, a wavering mind.

有表業 (or **色**) The manifested activities of the 身口意 body, mouth, and mind (or will) in contrast with their 無表業 unmanifested activities.

有見 The visible, but it is used also in the sense of the erroneous view that things really exist. Another meaning is the 色界 realm of form, as contrasted with the 無見 invisible, or with the formless realms.

有解 The intp. of things as real, or material, opposite of 無 | the intp. of them as unreal, or immaterial.

有識 Perceptive beings, similar to 有情 sentient beings.

有貪 Bhavarāga, the desire for existence, which is the cause of existence; 倶舍論 19.

有輪 The wheel of existence, the round of mortality, of births-and-deaths.

有邊 The one extreme of "existence", the opposite extreme being 無 | "non-existence".

有部; 一切有部; 薩婆多 Sarvāstivāda; the school of the reality of all phenomena, one of the early Hīnayāna sects, said to have been formed, about 300 years after the Nirvāṇa, out of the Sthavira; later it subdivided into five, Dharmaguptāḥ, Mūlasarvāstivādāḥ, Kāśyapīyāḥ, Mahīśāsakāḥ, and the influential Vātsīputrīyāḥ. v. 一切有部. Its scriptures are known as the | | 律; 律書; 十誦律; 根本說一切有部毘那耶; (根本說一切) 有部尼陀那; (根 | | | |) | | 目得迦; 根本薩婆多部律攝 or 有部律攝, etc.

有量 Limited, finite; opposite of 無 | measureless, boundless, infinite. 有相 | | That which has form and measurement is called 麤 coarse, i.e. palpable, that which is without form and measurement 無相無量 is called 細 fine, i.e. impalpable.

有間 Interrupted, not continuous, not intermingled, opposite of 無 |.

有靈 Having souls, sentient beings, similar to | 情; possessing magical or spiritual powers.

有頂(天) Akaniṣṭha, 色究竟天 the highest heaven of form, the ninth and last of the fourth dhyāna heavens. | | 惑 In that region there still exist the possibilities of delusion both in theory (or views) and practice, arising from the taking of the seeming for the real.

有餘 Something more; those who have remainder to fulfil, e.g. of karma; incomplete; extra, additional. | | 土 One of the four lands, or realms, the 方便 | | | to which, according to Mahāyāna, arhats go at their decease; cf. next. | | 涅槃; 有餘依 (涅槃) Incomplete nirvāṇa. Hīnayāna holds that the arhat after his last term of mortal existence enters into nirvāṇa, while alive here he is in the state of sopādhiśeṣa-nirvāṇa, limited, or modified, nirvāṇa, as contrasted with 無餘 | | nirupadhiśeṣa-nirvāṇa. Mahāyāna holds that when the cause 因 of reincarnation is ended the state is that of 有 | | | incomplete nirvāṇa; when the effect 果 is ended, and 得佛之常身 the eternal Buddha-body has been obtained, then there is 無餘 | | complete nirvāṇa. Mahāyāna writers say that in the Hīnayāna 無餘 | | "remainderless" nirvāṇa for the arhat there are still remains of illusion, karma, and suffering, and it is therefore 有餘 | |; in Mahāyāna 無餘 | | these remains of illusion, etc., are ended. | | 說 Something further to say, incomplete explanation. | | 師 Masters, or exponents, in addition to the chief or recognized authorities; also spoken of as 有餘; 餘師; 有諸師; 有人; hence 有餘師說 refers to other than the recognized, or orthodox, explanations.

有體 A thing, form, dharma, anything of ideal or real form; embodied things, bodies; varying list of 75, 84, and 100 are given.

朱 Red, vermilion. | 利 Caura, a thief, robber. | 利草 Caurī, robber-grass or herb, name of a plant. | 羅波梨迦羅 Defined as 雜碎衣, i.e. cīvara, or ragged clothes.

次 Second, secondary; a turn, next. | 第 In turn, one after another. | | 緣; 無間緣 Connected or consequent causes; continuous conditional or accessory cause.

此 This, here. | 世; | 生 This world, or life. | 土著述 Narratives in regard to the present life, part of the 雜藏 miscellaneous piṭaka. | | 耳根利 Clearness of hearing in this world, i.e. the organ of sound fitted to hear the Buddha-gospel and the transcendental. | 岸 This shore, the present life.

死 Maraṇa; 末剌諵; mṛta 母陀; to die, death; dead; also cyuti. 死亡 Dead and gone (or lost). 死刀 The (sharp) sword of death. 死山 The hill of death. | 屍 "Dead corpse," e.g. a wicked monk. | 海 The sea of mortality. | 王 Yama, 焰魔 as lord of death and hell. | 生 Death and life, mortality, transmigration; v. 生. | 相 The appearance of death; signs at death indicating the person's good or evil karma. | 禪和子 Die! monk; dead monk! a term of abuse to, or in regard to, a monk. | 苦 The misery, or pain, of death, one of the Four Sufferings. | 賊 The robber death. | 門; | 關 The gate, or border of death, leading from one incarnation to another. | 靈 The spirit of one who is dead, a ghost. | 風 The destroying wind in the final destruction of the world.

求 v. Seven Strokes.

汙 Stagnant water, impure; but it is explained as a torrent, impermanent; translit. *o* and *u*, and *h*. | 栗馱 Hṛd, Hṛdaya, the 心 heart, core, mind, soul.

汗 Sweat; vast. | (or 干 or 乾) 栗馱; 紇哩陀耶 Hṛd, Hṛdaya, the heart, core, mind, soul; probably an error for 汙.

汚 Impure; to defile. | 家 To defile a household, i.e. by deeming it ungrateful or being dissatisfied with its gifts. | 染 To taint; taint. | 道沙門 A shameless monk who defiles his religion.

江 A river; the River, the Yangtsze. | 天寺 The River and Sky monastery on Golden Island, Chinkiang, Kiangsu. | 湖 Kiangsi and Hunan, where and whence the 禪 Ch'an (Zen) or Intuitive movement had its early spread, the title being applied to followers of this cult. | 西 A title of 馬祖 Ma Tsu, who was a noted monk in Kiangsi, died 788. | 迦葉 River- or Nadī-kāśyapa, one of the three Kāśyapa brothers: v. 三迦葉.

灰 Ash; lime; hot or fiery as ashes. | 人 An image of ashes or lime made and worshipped seven times a day by a woman whose marriage is hindered by unpropitious circumstances. | 山住部 Sect of the Limestone hill dwellers, one of the twenty Hīnayāna schools; ? the Gokulikas, v. 雞. | 沙 Ascetics who cover themselves with ashes, or burn their flesh. | 河 A river of lava or fire, reducing all to ashes. | 身滅智 Destruction of the body and annihilation of the mind—for the attainment of nirvāṇa. | 頭土面 To put ashes on the head and dust on the face.

牟 To low (as an ox); overpass; barley; a grain vessel; weevil; eye-pupil; translit. *mu, ma*. | 呼栗多 Muhūrta, the thirtieth part of an ahorātra, a day-and-night, i.e. forty-eight minutes; a brief space of time, moment; also (wrongly) a firm mind. | | 洛 Mahoraga, boa-demons, v. 摩睺. | (or 摩 or 目) 娑 (羅); | 娑洛 (揭婆); 摩沙羅; 謨 or 牟薩羅 Musāragalva, a kind of coral, white coral, M. W.; defined as 瑪瑙 cornelian, agate; and 硨磲 mother of pearl; it is one of the 七寶 sapta ratna q.v. | 尼 (仙), 文尼; 茂泥; (馬曷) 摩尼 Muni; Mahāmuni; 月摩尼 Vimuni. A sage, saint, ascetic, monk, especially Śākyamuni; interpreted as 寂 retired, secluded, silent, solitary, i.e. withdrawn from the world. See also 百八摩尼. | | 室利 Muniśrī, name of a monk from northern India in the Liu Sung period (5th cent.). | | 王 The monk-king, a title of the Buddha. | 眞鄰陀 Mucilinda, v. 摩 and 目. | 陀羅 Mardala, or Mṛdaṅga, a kind of drum described as having three faces.

百 Śata; a hundred, all. | 一 One out of a hundred; or every one of a hundred, i.e. all.

百不知 (or 會) To know or perceive nothing, insensible (to surroundings).

百丈 A hundred fathoms of 10 feet each, 1,000 feet; the name of a noted T'ang abbot of | | 山 Pai Chang Shan, the monastery of this name in 洪州 Hung-chou.

百二十八根本煩惱 The 128 delusions of 見 views and 思 thoughts; also called 百二十八使 v. 使.

百俱胝 100 koṭīs.

百光遍照王 The king of all light universally shining, i.e. Vairocana.

百八 108. 丨丨丸; 丨丨數珠; 丨丨牟尼 108 beads on a rosary. 丨丨尊 The 108 honourable ones in the Vajradhātu. 丨丨煩惱 The 108 passions and delusions, also called 丨丨結業 the 108 karmaic bonds. 丨丨鐘 The 108 tolls of the monastery bell at dawn and dusk.

百即百生 Of 100 who call on the Buddha 100 will be saved, all will live.

百味 All the (good) tastes, or flavours.

百喩經 The sūtra of the 100 parables, tr. by Guṇavṛddhi, late fifth century; also 百譬經.

百四十不共法 The 140 special, or uncommon, characteristics of a Buddha, i.e. 三十二相; 八十種好; 四淨; 十力; 四無畏; 三念處; 三不護; 大悲; 常不忘失; 斷煩惱習; 一切智.

百會 Where all things meet, i.e. the head, the place of centralization; it is applied also to the Buddha as the centre of all wisdom.

百本疏主 Lord of the hundred commentaries, title of K'uei-chi 窺基 of the 慈恩寺 T'zŭ-ên monastery, because of his work as a commentator; also 丨丨論師.

百法 The hundred divisions of all mental qualities and their agents, of the 唯識 School; also known as the 五位丨丨 five groups of the 100 modes or "things": (1) 心法 the eight 識 perceptions, or forms of consciousness; (2) 心所有法 the fifty-one mental ideas; (3) 色法 the five physical organs and their six modes of sense, e.g. ear and sound; (4) 不相應行 twenty-four indefinites, or unconditioned elements; (5) 無爲 six inactive or metaphysical concepts. 丨丨明門 The door to the knowledge of universal phenomena, one of the first stages of Bodhisattva progress. The 丨丨(丨丨)論 was tr. by Hsüan-tsang in 1 chüan.
丨丨界 The realm of the hundred qualities, i.e. the phenomenal realm; the ten stages from Hades to Buddha, each has ten 如是 or qualities which make up the hundred; cf. 百界.

百界 The ten realms each of ten divisions, so called by the T'ien-t'ai school, i.e. of hells, ghosts, animals, asuras, men, devas, śrāvakas, pratyekabuddhas, bodhisattvas, and Buddhas. Each of the hundred has ten qualities, making in all 丨丨千如 the thousand qualities of the hundred realms; this 1,000 being multiplied by the three of past, present, future, there are 3,000; to behold these 3,000 in an instant is called 一念三千 (之觀法) and the sphere envisaged is the 丨丨千如.

百目 An earthenware lantern, i.e. with many eyes or holes.

百衲衣 A monk's robe made of patches.

百福 The hundred blessings, every kind of happiness.

百萬遍 To repeat Amitābha's name a million times (ensures rebirth in his Paradise; for a seven days' unbroken repetition Paradise may be gained).

百衆學 Śikṣākaraṇīya, what all monks and nuns learn, the offence against which is duṣkṛta, v. 突.

百論 Śataśāstra. One of the 三論 "three śāstras" of the Mādhyamika school, so called because of its 100 verses, each of 32 words; attributed to Deva Bodhisattva, it was written in Sanskrit by Vasubandhu and tr. by Kumārajīva, but the versions differ. There is also the 廣百論本 Catuḥśataka-[śāstrakārikā], an expansion of the above.

竹 Veṇu, bamboo. 丨林(精舍 or 寺); 丨園; 丨苑 Veṇuvana, "bamboo-grove," a park called Karaṇḍaveṇuvana, near Rājagṛha, made by Bimbisāra for a group of ascetics, later given by him to Śākyamuni (Eitel), but another version says by the elder Karaṇḍa, who built there a vihāra for him.

米 Śāli, rice, i.e. hulled rice. The word śāli has been wrongly used for śarīra, relics, and for both words 舍利 has been used. 丨頭 Keeper of the stores. 丨麗耶 Maireya, "a kind of intoxicating drink (extracted from the blossoms of *Lythrum fructicosum* with sugar, etc.)." M. W.

羊 Avi, a sheep, goat, ram. | 毛 塵 The minute speck of dust that can rest on the tip of a sheep's hair. | 石 An abbreviation for 羯 磨 karma, from the radicals of the two words. | 角 A ram's horn is used for 煩 惱 the passions and delusions of life. | 車; | 乘 The inferior, or śrāvaka, form of Buddhism, v. Lotus sūtra, in the parable of the burning house.

老 Jarā; old, old age. | 死 Jarāmaraṇa, decrepitude and death; one of the twelve nidānas, a primary dogma of Buddhism that decrepitude and death are the natural products of the maturity of the five skandhas. | 古 錐 An old awl, an experienced and incisive teacher. | 婆 An old woman; my "old woman", i.e. my wife. | 子 Lao Tzŭ, or Laocius, the accepted founder of the Taoists. The theory that his soul went to India and was reborn as the Buddha is found in the 齊 書 History of the Ch'i dynasty 顧 歡 傳. | 宿 Sthavira, an old man, virtuous elder. | 榴 槌 An old pestle, or drumstick, a baldheaded old man, or monk. | 苦 One of the four sufferings, that of old age.

耳 Śrotra, the ear, one of the 六 根 six organs of sense, hence | 入 is one of the twelve 入, as | 處 is one of the twelve 處. | 根 Śrotrendriya, the organ of hearing. | 語 戒 Secret rules whispered in the ear, an esoteric practice. | 識 Śrotravijñāna. Ear-perception, ear-discernment. | 輪 An ear-ring.

肉 Māṁsa. Flesh. | 心; | 團 心; 紇 利 陀 耶 Hṛdaya; the physical heart. | 燈; | 香 To cremate oneself alive as a lamp or as incense for Buddha. | 眼 Māṁsacakṣus. Eye of flesh, the physical eye. | 色 Flesh-coloured, red. | 身 The physical body. | | 菩 薩 One who becomes a bodhisattva in the physical body, in the present life. | 食 Māṁsa-bhakṣaṇa, meat-eating. | 髻; 烏 (or 鬱) 失 (or 瑟) 尼 沙; 烏 瑟 膩 沙 Uṣṇīṣa. One of the thirty-two marks (lakṣaṇa) of a Buddha; originally a conical or flame-shaped tuft of hair on the crown of a Buddha, in later ages represented as a fleshly excrescence on the skull itself; interpreted as coiffure of flesh. In China it is low and large at the base, sometimes with a tonsure on top of the protuberance.

自 Sva, svayam; the self, one's own, personal; of itself, naturally, of course; also, from (i.e. from the self as central). 自 is used as the opposite of 他 another, other's, etc., e.g. 自 力 (in) one's own strength as contrasted with 他 力 the strength of another, especially in the power to save of a Buddha or Bodhisattva. It is also used in the sense of Ātman 阿 怛 摩 the self, or the soul.

自 作 自 受 As one does one receives, every man receives the reward of his deeds, creating his own karma, 自 業 自 得.

自 內 證 Inner witness.

自 利 Ātmahitam, self-profit; beneficial to oneself. | | 利 他 "Self-profit profit others", i.e. the essential nature and work of a bodhisattva, to benefit himself and benefit others, or himself press forward in the Buddhist life in order to carry others forward. Hīnayāna is considered to be self-advancement, self-salvation by works or discipline; Bodhisattva Buddhism as saving oneself in order to save others, or making progress and helping others to progress, bodhisattvism being essentially altruistic.

自 受 用 土 The third of the four Buddha-kṣetra or Buddha-domains, that in which there is complete response to his teaching and powers; v. 佛 土. | | | 身 One of the two kinds of saṁbhogakāya, for his own enjoyment; cf. 四 身. | | 法 樂 The dharma-delights a Buddha enjoys in the above state.

自 在 Īśvara, 伊 濕 伐 邏; can, king, master, sovereign, independent, royal; intp. as free from resistance; also, the mind free from delusion; in the Avataṁsaka sūtra it translates vaśitā. There are several groups of this independence, or sovereignty—2, 4, 5, 8, and 10, e.g. the 2 are that a bodhisattva has sovereign knowledge and sovereign power; the others are categories of a bodhisattva's sovereign powers. For the eight powers v. 八 大 自 在 我. | | 天 (or 王) Īśvaradeva, a title of Śiva, king of the devas, also known as 大 | | | Maheśvara, q.v. It is a title also applied to Kuan-yin and others. | | | 外 道 Śivaites, who ascribed creation and destruction to Śiva, and that all things form his body, space his head, sun and moon his eyes, earth his body, rivers and seas his urine, mountains his fæces, wind his life, fire his heat, and all living things the vermin on his body. This sect is also known as the | | 等 因 宗. Śiva is represented with eight arms, three eyes, sitting on a bull. | | 王 is also a title of Vairocana; and, as Sureśvara, is the name of a mythical king, contemporary of the mythical Śikhin Buddha.

自 心 Svacitta, self-mind, one's own mind.

自 性 Own nature; of (its) own nature. As an intp. of Pradhāna (and resembling 冥 性) in the Sāṅkhya philosophy it is "Prakṛti, the Originant, primary or original matter or rather the primary germ out of which all material appearances are evolved, the first evolver or source of the material world (hence in a general acceptation 'nature' or rather 'matter' as opposed to *purusha*, or 'spirit')". M. W. As 莎發斡 svabhāva, it is "own state, essential or inherent property, innate or peculiar disposition, natural state or constitution, nature". M. W. The self-substance, self-nature, or unchanging character of anything. 丨丨三寶 The Triratna, each with its own characteristic, Buddha being wisdom 覺; the Law correctness 正; and the Order purity 淨.

自性戒 The ten natural moral laws, i.e. which are natural to man, apart from the Buddha's commands; also 自性善.

自恣 Pravāraṇa, to follow one's own bent, the modern term being 隨意; it means the end of restraint, i.e. following the period of retreat. 丨丨日 The last day of the annual retreat.

自愛 Self-love, cause of all pursuit or seeking, which in turn causes all suffering. All Buddhas put away self-love and all pursuit, or seeking, such elimination being nirvāṇa.

自損損他 To harm oneself and harm others, to harm oneself is to harm others, etc.; opposite of 自利利他.

自殺 To commit suicide; for a monk to commit suicide is said to be against the rules.

自然 Svayambhū, also 自爾; 法爾 self-existing, the self-existent; Brahmā, Viṣṇu, and others; in Chinese it is "self-so", so of itself, natural, of course, spontaneous. It also means uncaused existence, certain sects of heretics 丨丨外道 denying Buddhist cause and effect and holding that things happen spontaneously. 丨丨慈 Intuitive mercy possessed by a bodhisattva, untaught and without causal nexus. 丨丨悟道 Enlightenment by the inner light, independent of external teaching; to become Buddha by one's own power, e.g. Śākyamuni who is called 自然釋迦. 丨丨成佛道 Svayaṁbhuvaḥ. Similar to the last, independent attainment of Buddhahood. 丨丨智 The intuitive or inborn wisdom of a Buddha, untaught to him and outside the causal nexus. 丨丨虛無身 A Buddha's spiritual or absolute body, his dharmakāya; also, those who are born in Paradise, i.e. who are spontaneously and independently produced there.

自生 Self-produced, or naturally existing; also an intp. of bhūta 部多 produced, existing, real; also demons born by transformation 化生 in contrast to the 夜叉 yakṣa who are born from parents.

自相 Svalakṣaṇa; individuality, particular, personal, as contrasted with 共相 general or common.

自行化他 To discipline, or perform, oneself and (or in order to) convert or transform others, v. 自利利他.

自覺悟心 A mind independent of externals, pure thought, capable of enlightenment from within. 丨丨聖智 The uncaused omniscience of Vairocana; it is also called 法界(體性)智 and 金剛智.

自誓受戒 To make the vows and undertake the commandments oneself (before the image of a Buddha), i.e. self-ordination when unable to obtain ordination from the ordained.

自語相違 A manifest contradiction, one of the nine fallacies of a proposition, svārtha-viruddha, e.g. "my mother is barren."

自調自淨自度 The śrāvaka method of salvation by personal discipline, or "works"; 自調 self-progress by keeping the commandments; 自淨 self-purification by emptying the mind; 自度 self-release by the attainment of gnosis, or wisdom.

自證 The witness within, inner assurance. 丨丨壇 or 會 The 成身會 assembly of all the Buddha and bodhisattva embodiments in the Vajradhātu maṇḍala. 丨丨聖智 Pratyātmāryajñāna, personal apprehension of Buddha-truth. 丨丨身 A title of Vairocana, his dharmakāya of self-assurance, or realization, from which issues his retinue of proclaimers of the truth.

自身自佛 One's own body is Buddha.

自類因果 Cause and effect of the same order.

至 Reach, arrive at; utmost, perfect. 丨人 The perfect man, i.e. Śākyamuni. 丨心 With the utmost mind, or a perfect mind. 丨教 Complete or perfect teaching. 丨理 The utmost principle, the fundamental law. | 眞 Perfect truth. | 相 尊 者 The second patriarch of the Hua-yen (Kegon) school 智 儼 Chih-yen. | 言 Perfect words, words of complete explanation. | 那 Cīna, China, hence | | 儞 Cīnānī, the peach-tree, said to have been imported into India from China. | | 僕 底 Cīnapati, Lord (from) China, said in the Record of Western Lands 西 域 記 to have been appointed by the Han rulers; a country so-called because the son of 蕃 維 質 Fan Wei Chih of 河 西 Ho-hsi dwelt (and reigned) there. Eitel says, "A small kingdom in the north-west of India (near Lahore) the inhabitants of which asserted (A.D. 640) that their first kings had come from China." | | 羅 闍 弗 呾 羅 Cīnarājaputra, "son of the China king," intp. by 漢 王 子 Prince of Han, which was also an Indian name for a pear-tree, said to have been imported from China in the Han dynasty; v. 西 域 記 4. | 沙; 帝 沙 Tiṣya, an ancient Buddha. The father of Śāriputra. A son of Śuklodana.

舌 Jihvā, 時 乞 縛; the tongue; | 根 the organ of taste; | 識 tongue-perception; v. 六 根; 六 識. | 相 The broad, long tongue of a Buddha, one of the thirty-two physical signs. | 不 爛 Tongue-unconsumed, a term for Kumārajīva; on his cremation his tongue is said to have remained unconsumed.

色 Rūpa, outward appearance, form, colour, matter, thing; the desirable, especially feminine attraction. It is defined as that which has resistance; or which changes and disappears, i.e. the phenomenal; also as 顯, 形 and 表 色 colour and quality, form or the measurable, and mode or action. There are divisions of two, i.e. inner and outer, as the organs and objects of sense; also colour and form; of three, i.e. the visible object, e.g. colour, the invisible object, e.g. sound, the invisible and immaterial; of eleven, i.e. the five organs and five objects of sense and the immaterial object; of fourteen, the five organs and five objects of sense and the four elements, earth, water, fire, air. Rūpa is one of the six Bāhya-āyatana, the 六 塵; also one of the five Skandhas, 五 蘊, i.e. the 色 身. Keith refers to Rūpa as "material form or matter which is underived (no-utpādā) and which is derived (utpādā)", the underived or independent being the tangible; the derived or dependent being the senses, e.g. of hearing; most of their objects, e.g. sound; the qualities or faculties of feminity, masculinity, vitality; intimation by act and speech; space; qualities of matter, e.g. buoyancy; and physical nutriment.

色 入; 色 處 The entrances, or places, where the organs and objects of physical sense meet, ten in all; cf. 五 入. Also, one of the twelve nidānas.

色 光 Physical light, as contrasted with 心 光 light of the mind; every Buddha has both, e.g. his halo.

色 具 Material objects.

色 味 The flavour of sexual attraction, love of women.

色 塵 The quality of form, colour, or sexual attraction, one of the 六 塵.

色 微 Atoms of things, of form, or colour.

色 心 Matter and mind, the material and immaterial.

色 有 Material existence.

色 欲 Sexual desire, or passion.

色 泡; 色 焰 The material as a bubble, or a flame; impermanent.

色 界 Rūpadhātu, or rūpāvacara, or rūpaloka, any material world, or world of form; it especially refers to the second of the Trailokya 三 界, the Brahmalokas above the Devalokas, comprising sixteen or seventeen or eighteen "Heavens of Form", divided into four Dhyānas, in which life lasts from one-fourth of a mahākalpa to 16,000 mahākalpas, and the average stature is from one-half a yojana to 16,000 yojanas. The inhabitants are above the desire for sex or food. The Rūpadhātu, with variants, are given as— 初 禪 天 The first dhyāna heavens: 梵 衆 天 Brahmapāriṣadya, 梵 輔 天 Brahmapurohita or Brahmakāyika, 大 梵 天 Mahābrahmā. 二 禪 天 The second dhyāna heavens: 少 光 天 Parīttābha, 無 量 光 天 Apramāṇābha, 光 音 天 Ābhāsvara. 三 禪 天 The third dhyāna heavens: 少 淨 天 Parīttaśubha, 無 量 淨 天 Apramāṇaśubha, 徧 淨 天 Śubhakṛtsna. 四 禪 天 The fourth dhyāna heavens: 無 雲 天 Anabhraka, 福 生 天 Puṇyaprasava, 廣 果 天 Bṛhatphala, 無 想 天 Asañjñisattva, 無 煩 天 Avṛha, 無 熱 天 Atapa, 善 現 天 Sudṛśa, 善 見 天 Sudarśana, 色 究 竟 天 Akaniṣṭha, 和 音 天 ? Aghaniṣṭha, 大 自 在 天 Mahāmaheśvara.

色 相 The material, material appearance, or external manifestation, the visible. | | 土 A Buddha's material or visible world.

色究竟天; 色頂 Akaniṣṭha, the highest of the material heavens.

色空外道 Heretics who denied material existence (and consequently sought self-control, or nirvāṇa).

色境 Visible objects, the realm of vision, or form.

色聲 The visible and audible.

色蓋 The concealing, or misleading, character of the visible or material, the seeming concealing reality.

色蘊 The skandha of rūpa, or that which has form, v. 五蘊.

色處 idem 色入.

色衆 idem 色蘊, 色陰.

色諦 idem 假諦.

色身 Rūpa-kāya. The physical body, as contrasted with the 法身 dharma-kāya, the immaterial, spiritual, or immortal body.

虫 Insect, reptile; any creeping thing; animal, man as of the animal kingdom.

血 Blood. 以血洗血 To wash out blood with blood, from one sin to fall into another. 丨書 Written with (one's own) blood. 丨汚池 The pool, or lake, of blood in one of the hells. 丨海 The sea of blood, i.e. the hells and lower incarnations. 丨盆經 The sūtra describing the blood bath for women in Hades; it is a Chinese invention and is called by Eitel "the placenta tank, which consists of an immense pool of blood, and from this hell, it is said, no release is possible"; but there are ceremonies for release from it. 丨脈 The arteries and veins, linked, closely connected. 丨途 The gati or destiny of rebirth as an animal.

行 Go; act; do; perform; action; conduct; functioning; the deed; whatever is done by mind, mouth, or body, i.e. in thought, word, or deed. It is used for ayana, going, road, course; a march, a division of time equal to six months; also for saṁskāra, form, operation, perfecting, as one of the twelve nidānas, similar to karma, action, work, deed, especially moral action, cf. 業.

行乞 To go begging, or asking for alms; also 行鉢; 托鉢.

行人 A traveller, wayfarer; a follower of Buddha; a disciple.

行住坐臥 Walking, standing, sitting, lying—in every state.

行供養 The making of offerings, to go to make offerings.

行信 Act and faith, doing and believing, acting out one's belief.

行儀 To perform the proper duties, especially of monks and nuns.

行化 To go and convert; also 丨敎丨.

行厠 To go to the privy; the privy to which one goes, metaphor of the human body as filthy.

行善 To do good; deeds that are good; to offer up deeds of goodness.

行履 The common acts of daily life—sitting, eating, thinking, etc.

行德 The virtue of performance, or discipline; to perform virtuous deeds.

行教 To carry out the vinaya discipline; the vinaya.

行果 Deed and result; the inevitable sequence of act and its effect.

行業 That which is done, the activities of thought, word, or deed; moral action; karma.

行樹 Trees in rows, avenues of trees.

行母 Mātṛkā, 摩德理迦; the "mother of karma", i.e. the Abhidharma-piṭaka, which shows that karma produces karma, one act producing another.

行滿 Hsing-man, a monk of the 佛龍寺 Fo-lung monastery, about whom little is known, but who is accredited with supplying Dengyō of Japan with T'ien-t'ai scriptures in the latter part of the eighth century.

行犍度 The saṁskāra skandha, the fourth of the five skandhas. v. 丨蘊.

行相 Activity; performance; mental activity.

行籌 To cast lots, divine (length of life).

行者 An abbot's attendant; also ācārin, performing the duties of a disciple.

行脚(僧) A wandering monk.

行苦 The suffering inevitably consequent on action.

行華 To offer flowers.

行蘊 The fourth of the five skandhas, saṁskāra, action which inevitably passes on its effects.

行要 The requirements for action; to do that which is most important.

行證 Action and proof; knowledge or assurance derived from doing; practice of religious discipline and the resulting enlightenment.

行像 To take an image (of Buddha) in procession; it was a custom observed on Buddha's birthday according to the 佛國記.

行足 As works are the feet (so wisdom is the eye).

行道 To walk in the way, follow the Buddha-truth; to make procession round an image, especially of the Buddha, with the right shoulder towards it.

行雨 To rain, or produce rain; Varṣākāra, name of a minister of king Bimbisāra.

行願 Action and vow; act and vow, resolve or intention; to act out one's vows; to vow.

行香 To offer incense.

衣 Clothes, especially a monk's robes which are of two kinds, the compulsory three garments of five, seven, or nine pieces; and the permissive clothing for the manual work of the monastery, etc. The 三衣 or three garments are (1) 安陀會衣 Antarvāsas, an inner garment; the five-piece 袈裟 cassock; (2) 鬱多羅僧衣 Uttarāsaṅga, outer garment, the seven-piece cassock; (3) 僧伽梨衣 Saṁghāṭī, assembly cassock of from nine to twenty-five pieces. The permissive clothing is of ten kinds. 丨座室 The robe, throne, and abode of the Tathāgata, see Lotus sūtra 法師品. 丨法 The robe and the Buddha-truth. 丨珠; 丨寶 The pearl in the garment, i.e. a man starving yet possessed of a priceless pearl in his garment, of which he was unaware; v. Lotus sūtra 五百授記品. 丨服天 The Vajradeva in the Vajradhātu group who guards the placenta and the unborn child; his colour is black and he holds a bow and arrow. 丨丨隨念願 The vow of Amitābha that all the devas and men in his realm shall instantly have whatever beautiful clothing they wish. 丨裓 A towel, cloth, wrapper, or mantle. 丨鉢 Cassock and almsbowl. 丨那 The umbilical cord.

西 Paścima, 跛室制麼; west; it is largely used in the limited sense of Kashmir in such terms as 西方 the west, or western regions; but it is also much used for the western heavens of Amitābha; 西天 is India, the western 天竺國. 丨主 The Lord of the West, Amitābha, who is also the 丨天教主 lord of the cult, or sovereign teacher, of the western paradise. 丨乾 A name for India, cf. 丨天. 丨儞迦; 先尼 Sainika, military. 丨光 The light of the western paradise. 丨刹 Kṣetra, land, region, country.

西域求法高僧傳 Biographies of famous pilgrims, fifty-six in number, with four added; it is by I-ching 義淨. 丨丨記; 大唐西域記; 西域傳 Records of Western countries, by the T'ang dynasty pilgrim 玄奘 Hsüan-tsang, in 12 chüan A.D. 646–8. There was a previous 丨丨傳 by 彥琮 Yen-ts'ung of the Sui dynasty. 丨山住部 Avaraśailā 阿伐羅塾羅 the second subdivision of the Mahāsaṅghika school. A monastery of this name was in Dhana-kaṭaka, said to have been built 600 B.C., deserted A.D. 600. 丨序; 丨班 The western group, i.e. teaching monks stood on the west of the abbot, while those engaged in practical affairs stood on the east; this was in imitation of the Court practice in regard to civil and military officials.

| 方 The west, especially Amitābha's Western Pure Land | | 淨土, Sukhāvatī or Paradise | | 極樂世界, to which Amitābha is the guide and welcomer | | 接引. | 明 Hsi-ming, name of 道宣 Tao-hsüan of the T'ang who founded the Southern Hill school, and also of 圓測 Yüan-ts'ê, both of whom were from the | 明寺 monastery of Western Enlightenment established by Kao Tsung (650–684) at Ch'ang-an, the capital. | 曼陀羅 The "western" maṇḍala is that of the Vajradhātu, as the "eastern" is of the Garbhadhātu. | 河 Hsi-ho, a name for 道綽 Tao-ch'o of the T'ang dynasty. | 淨 The western cleanser, the privy, situated on the west of a monastery. | 牛貨洲; | 瞿陀 (or 耶) 尼 The western continent of a world, Godānīya, v. 瞿, or Aparagodānīya, or Aparagodāna, "western-cattle-giving," where cattle are the medium of exchange, possibly referring to the "pecuniary" barter of the north-west. | 藏 Tibet; | | 佛敎 Tibetan Buddhism, | | 喇嘛敎 Tibetan Lamaism. | 行 Going west; practices of the Amitābha cult, leading to salvation in the Western Paradise.

7. SEVEN STROKES

估 Guess, estimate. | 衣 To estimate the value of a deceased monk's personal possessions, and | 唱 to auction them to the other monks.

伴 Companion, associate; translit. *pan*, *ban*, *van*; cf. 畔. | 僧 Associate or accompanying monks. | 夜; | 靈 To watch with the spirit of a departed monk the night before the cremation. | 談 v. 和南 Vandana. | 陀羅縛子 (or 字) 尼 v. 半 Pāṇḍaravāsinī.

伺 Vicāra, 毘遮羅 Investigation, consideration, search for truth; to spy; wait on.

低 To let down, lower. | 羅擇 (or 釋) 迦 Tiladhāka, Tiladaka, or Tilaśākya. "A monastery, three yôdjanas west of Nālanda, perhaps the modern village of Thelari near Gayā." Eitel.

佗 He, she, it; other; i.e. 他; translit. *thā*, e.g. in sthāna, sthāman.

位 Position, seat, throne. | 不退 One of the 三不退 q.v. three kinds of never receding. | 牌 The board, or record of official position.

何 Translit. *ha*, *hai*, *a*, *ra*, *he*; cf. 賀 and 曷. What? How? | 似生 How does it thus happen? | 夷摩柯 Haimaka, a king at the beginning of a kalpa, 金 by name. | 履那 Hariṇa, a deer. | 羅怙羅 Rāhula, name of Śākyamuni's son, also of an asura. | 耶 Haya, the horse-head form of Kuan-yin. | 耶揭唎婆 Hayagrīva, Horse-neck, a form of Viṣṇu, name of a 明王 Ming-wang.

但 Only. | 空 Only non-existence, or immateriality, a term used by T'ien-t'ai to denote the orthodox Hīnayāna system. 不但空 denotes the 通敎 intermediate system between the Hīnayana and the Mahāyāna; v. 空. | 荼; 單拏 Daṇḍa, a staff, club.

似 Appearance of, seeming as, like, as; than. | 現量 A syllogism assuming e.g. that a vase or garment is real, and not made up of certain elements. | 立宗 A fallacious proposition; containing any one of the nine fallacies connected with the thesis, or pratijñā, of the syllogism. | 能破 A fallacious counter-proposition; containing one of the thirty-three fallacies connected with the thesis (pratijñā 宗), reason (hetu 因), or example (udāharaṇa 喩).

佉 Translit. kha; also khya, ga, gha, khu, khi; cf. 呿, 喀, 吃, 呵, 珂, 佫, 軀; it is used to represent 虛空 space, empty. Skt. kha *inter alia* means "sky", "ether". | 加; 渴伽 Khaḍga, a rhinoceros. | 勒迦 Khārī, a measure (or hamper) of grain; khārīka, equal to a khārī. | 吒迦 Khaṭaka; a manual sign, wrists together, fingers half-closed; M. W. says "the half-closed hand; the doubled fist of wrestlers or boxers". | 啁羅 Khaṭvā, a bed, couch, cot; a long, narrow bed. | 提羅 (迦); | 得羅柯; | 陀羅; 朅地 (or 達) 洛 (迦); 朅那里酤; 羯地羅; 可梨羅; 軻梨羅; Khadiraka, or Karavīka. One of the seven concentric ranges of a world; tr. by Jambu timber, or wood; also by 空破 bare, unwooded. Its sea is covered with scented flowers, and in it are four islands. It is also a tree of the Acacia order. | 梨 Khāri, or khārī. A 斛, i.e. bushel, or measure of about ten 斗; v. | 盧; | 勒. | 樓; | 盧 (風吒); | 路瑟吒 Kharoṣṭhī, tr. by "Ass's lips"; name of an ancient ṛṣi, perhaps Jyotīrasa. Also, "the writing of all the northerners," said to have been introduced by him, consisting of seventy-two characters. | 沙 Kashgar, a country in E. Turkestan, east of the Pamirs, S. of T'ien-shan; the older name, after the name of its capital, is sometimes given as 疏勒 or 室利訖栗多底 Śrīkrītati. | 盧 Khara; said to be a

斗, the tenth of a | 梨; also Khara, the name of a ṛsi. For Kharoṣṭhī, v. above. | 羅陀, or 帝, etc.; v. 伽. | 羅騫馱 Kharakaṇṭha; kings of demons, kings of asuras present when Buddha preached the Lotus Sūtra; also described as rumbling like thunder, or stirring up the waves of the ocean. | 訶囉嚩阿 Kha, ha, ra, va, a, the five 種子 roots, or seed-tones of the five elements, space, wind, fire, water, earth respectively. | 陀 (or 闍) 尼; 珂但尼 Khādanīya, to be chewed; edible; a food; defined as edibles not included in regulation meals.

住 Sthiti. To abide, dwell, stay, stop, settle. 生 | 滅 birth, existence, death. | 位 Abiding place, one of the ten stages, resting and developing places or abodes of the Bodhisattva, which is entered after the stage of belief has been passed; v. 十住; 十地; 地. | 劫 Vivarta siddha kalpa; the abiding or existing kalpa; the kalpa of human existence; v. 劫. | 地 Dwelling-place; abiding place in the Truth, i.e. the acquirement by faith of a self believing in the dharma and producing its fruits. | 定 Fixed, certain, firmly settled. | 定菩薩 A Bodhisattva firmly fixed, or abiding in certainty. After a Bodhisattva has completed three great asaṁkhyeya kalpas he has still one hundred great kalpas to complete. This period is called abiding in fixity or firmness, divided into six kinds: certainty of being born in a good gati, in a noble family, with a good body, a man, knowing the abiding places of his transmigrations, knowing the abiding character of his good works. | 持 To dwell and control; the abbot of a monastery; resident superintendent; to maintain, or firmly hold to (faith in the Buddha, etc.). For | | 身 v. 佛具十身. | 果 Abiding in the fruit; e.g. śrāvakas and pratyeka-buddhas who rest satisfied in their attainments and do not strive for Buddhahood; they are known as | | 緣覺 or | | 羅漢. | 相 Sthiti; abiding, being, the state of existence, one of the four characteristics of all beings and things, i.e. birth, existence, change (or decay), death (or cessation).

作 To make, do, act, be; arise. | 佛 To become or be a Buddha; to cut off illusion, attain complete enlightenment, and end the stage of Bodhisattva discipline. | 佛事 To do the works of Buddha; perform Buddhist ceremonies. | 善 To do good, e.g. worship, bestow alms, etc. | 家 Leader, founder, head of sect, a term used by the 禪 Ch'an (Zen) or Intuitive school. | 惡 To do evil. | 意 Cittotpāda; to have the thought arise, be aroused, beget the resolve, etc. | 戒 Obedience to the commandments, external fulfilment of them; also called 表色, in contrast with 無作戒, 無表色 the inner grace; moral action in contrast with inner moral character. | 持戒 Active keeping of the commandments, active law in contrast with 止持戒 passive, such as not killing, not stealing, etc. v. 持犯. | 梵 (唄) The call to order in the assembly. | 業 Karma produced, i.e. by the action of body, words, and thought, which educe the kernel of the next rebirth. | 法 Karma, which results from action, i.e. the "deeds" of body or mouth; to perform ceremonies. | | 得 To receive ceremonial ordination as a monk. | | 懺 (悔) One of the three kinds of monastic confession and repentance. | | 界 The place of assembly for ceremonial purposes. | 犯 Transgression, sin by action, active sin. | 用 Function, activity, act. | 禮 To pay one's respect by worship; to make an obeisance. | 者 Kartṛ; a doer, he who does things, hence the ātman, ego, or person within; the active element, or principle; one of the sixteen non-Buddhist definitions of the soul. Also kāraṇa, a cause, maker, creator, deity. | 舉 The accusation of sin made against particular monks by the virtuous monk who presides at the pravāraṇa gathering on the last day of the summer's rest. | 願門 To make a vow to benefit self and others, and to fulfil the vow so as to be born in the Pure Land of Amitābha. The third of the five doors or ways of entering the Pure Land. | 麼 (生) How? What? What are you doing?

伽 Interchanged with 迦 q.v.; translit. *ga*, *gha*, *ka*, *khya*, *g*, and in one case for *ha*. | 彌尼 Gamini, a king whom the Buddha is said to have addressed, v. sūtra of this name. | 憊路 idem | | Lokavit. | 梨 Abbrev. for 僧 | | saṅghāṭī, robe. | 梵; | 婆 Abbrev. for Bhagavan, see 婆 | |. A Western Indian monk who tr. a work on 觀自在 was | | 達摩 Bhagavaddharma. | 梵波提; | 傍簸帝 Gavāṁpati. 牛主 Lord of cattle, name of an arhat; v. 憍. | 毗黎 Kapilavastu, v. 劫. | 羅 Abbrev. for 多 | | Tāgara, putchuk, incense. | 羅夜叉 Kālaka, a yakṣa who smote Śāriputra on the head while in meditation, without his perceiving it. | 羅尼; 羯羅拏 Ghrāṇa, smell; scent. | 羅陀 (1) Kharādīya, the mountain where Buddha is supposed to have uttered the 地藏十論經, the abode of Ti-tsang; other names for it are 佉 | |, 佉羅帝 (or 提耶). (2) A Bodhisattva stage attained after many kalpas. | 耶; | 邪; | 闍 Gayā. (1) A city of Magadha, Buddhagayā (north-west of present Gaya), near which Śākyamuni became Buddha. (2) Gaja, an elephant. (3) | | 山 Gajaśīrṣa, Elephant's Head Mountain; two are mentioned, one near "Vulture Peak", one near the Bo-tree. (4) Kāya, the body. | | (or 邪) 舍多 Gayaśāta (? Jayata), the eighteenth Indian patriarch, who laboured among the Tokhari. | | 迦葉 Gayākāśyapa, a brother of Mahākāśyapa, originally a fire-worshipper, one of the eleven foremost disciples of Buddha, to become Samantaprabhāsa Buddha. | 胝 Abbrev. for Saṅghāṭī, robe; v. 僧 | |. | 藍; 僧伽藍摩; 僧藍 Saṅghārāma or Saṅghāgāra. (1) The park of a monastery. (2) A monastery, convent. There are eighteen | | 神 guardian spirits of a monastery. | 蘭他 Grantha, a treatise, section, verse; the scriptures of the Sikhs. | 車提 Gacchati, goes, progresses. | 那 Gana, Ghana; close, solid, thick. 伽伽那卑麗叉那 (or 必利綺那) Gaganaprekṣaṇa, beholding the sky, or looking into space. | | 提婆 Kāṇadeva, i.e. Āryadeva, fifteenth patriarch, disciple of Nāgārjuna, v. 迦. | | 馥力刃 A name of Nāgārjuna. | 陀; | 他 (1) Gātha = song; gāthā, a metrical narrative or hymn, with moral purport, described as generally composed of thirty-two characters, and called 孤起頌 a detached stanza, distinguished from geya, 重頌 which repeats the ideas of preceding prose passages. (2) Agada as adjective = healthy; as noun = antidote. (3) Gata, arrived at, fallen into, or "in a state".

佛 Buddha, from Budh, to "be aware of", "conceive", "observe", "wake"; also 佛陀; 浮圖; 浮陀; 浮頭; 浮塔; 勃陀; 勃馱; 沒馱; 母馱; 母陀; 部陀; 休屠. Buddha means "completely conscious, enlightened", and came to mean the enlightener. The Chinese translation is 覺 to perceive, aware, awake; and 智 gnosis, knowledge. There is an Eternal Buddha, see e.g. the Lotus Sūtra, cap. 16, and multitudes of Buddhas, but the personality of a Supreme Buddha, an Ādi-Buddha, is not defined. Buddha is in and through all things, and some schools are definitely Pan-Buddhist in the pantheistic sense. In the Triratna 三寶 commonly known as 三寶佛, while Śākyamuni Buddha is the first "person" of the Trinity, his Law the second, and the Order the third, all three by some are accounted as manifestations of the All-Buddha. As Śākyamuni, the title indicates him as the last of the line of Buddhas who have appeared in this world, Maitreya is to be the next. As such he is the one who has achieved enlightenment, having discovered the essential evil of existence (some say mundane existence, others all existence), and the way of deliverance from the constant round of reincarnations; this way is through the moral life into nirvāṇa, by means of self-abnegation, the monastic life, and meditation. By this method a Buddha, or enlightened one, himself obtains Supreme Enlightenment, or Omniscience, and according to Mahāyānism leads all beings into the same enlightenment. He sees things not as they seem in their phenomenal but in their noumenal aspects, as they really are. The term is also applied to those who understand the chain of causality (twelve nidānas) and have attained enlightenment surpassing that of the arhat. Four types of the Buddha are referred to: (1) 三藏 | the Buddha of the Tripiṭaka who attained enlightenment on the bare ground under the bodhi-tree; (2) 通 | the Buddha on the deva robe under the bodhi-tree of the seven precious things; (3) 別 | the Buddha on the great precious Lotus throne under the Lotus realm bodhi-tree; and (4) 圓 | the Buddha on the throne of Space in the realm of eternal rest and glory, where he is Vairocana. The Hīnayāna only admits the existence of one Buddha at a time; Mahāyāna claims the existence of many Buddhas at one and the same time, as many Buddhas as there are Buddha-universes, which are infinite in number.

佛世 Buddha-age; especially the age when Buddha was on earth. | | 尊 Buddha, the World-honoured, or honoured of the worlds, a tr. of Bhagavat, revered. | | 界 A Buddha-realm, divided into two categories, the pure and the impure, i.e. the passionless and passion worlds.

佛乘 The Buddha conveyance or vehicle, Buddhism as the vehicle of salvation for all beings; the doctrine of the 華嚴 Hua Yen (Kegon) School that all may become Buddha, which is called 一乘 the One Vehicle, the followers of this school calling it the 圓教 complete or perfect doctrine; this doctrine is also styled in The Lotus 一佛乘 the One Buddha-Vehicle. | | 戒 The rules and commandments conveying beings to salvation.

佛事 Buddha's affairs, the work of transforming all beings; or of doing Buddha-work, e.g. prayers and worship.

佛于逮 Pūrvavideha, v. 佛婆, etc.

佛五姓 The five surnames of Buddha before he became enlightened: 瞿曇 Gautama, a branch of the Śākya clan; 甘蔗 Ikṣvāku, one of Buddha's ancestors; 日種 Sūryavaṁśa, of the sun race; 舍夷 ? Śāka; 釋迦 Śākya, the name of Buddha's clan. This last is generally used in China.

佛位 The state of Buddhahood.

佛使 A messenger of the Tathāgata.

佛供 An offering to Buddha.

佛像 Buddha's image, or pratimā. There is a statement that in the fifth century A.D. the images in China were of Indian features, thick lips, high nose, long eyes, full jaws, etc., but that after the T'ang the form became "more effeminate".

佛光 The light of Buddha, spiritual enlightenment; halo, glory.

佛具 Articles used on an altar in worship of Buddha.

佛具十身 The ten perfect bodies or characteristics of Buddha: (1) 菩提身 Bodhi-body in possession of complete enlightenment. (2) 願身 Vow-body, i.e. the vow to be born in and from the Tuṣita heaven. (3) 化身 Nirmāṇakāya, Buddha incarnate as a man. (4) 住持身 Buddha who still occupies his relics or what he has left behind on earth and thus upholds the dharma. (5) 相好莊嚴身 Saṁbhogakāya, endowed with an idealized body with all Buddha marks and merits. (6) 勢力身 or 心佛 Power-body, embracing all with his heart of mercy. (7) 如意身 or 意生身 At will body, appearing according to wish or need. (8) 福德身 or 三昧身 Samādhi body, or body of blessed virtue. (9) 智身 or 性佛 Wisdom-body, whose nature embraces all wisdom. (10) 法身 Dharmakāya, the absolute Buddha, or essence of all life.

佛凡一體 Buddha and the common people are one, i.e. all are of Buddha-nature.

佛刹 Buddhakṣetra. 丨紇差怛羅 Buddha realm, land or country; see also 佛土, 佛國. The term is absent from Hīnayāna. In Mahāyāna it is the spiritual realm acquired by one who reaches perfect enlightenment, where he instructs all beings born there, preparing them for enlightenment. In the schools where Mahāyāna adopted an Ādi-Buddha, these realms or Buddha-fields interpenetrated each other, since they were coexistent with the universe. There are two classes of Buddha-kṣetra: (1) in the Vairocana Schools, regarded as the regions of progress for the righteous after death; (2) in the Amitābha Schools, regarded as the Pure Land; v. McGovern, *A Manual of Buddhist Philosophy*, pp. 70–2.

佛印 Buddha-seal, the sign of assurance, see 丨心丨.

佛吼 Buddha's nāda, or roar, Buddha's preaching compared to a lion's roar, i.e. authoritative.

佛鳴 Buddhaghoṣa, the famous commentator and writer of the Hīnayāna School and of the Pali canon. He was "born near the Bo Tree, at Buddha Gayā, and came to Ceylon about A.D. 430". "Almost all the commentaries now existing (in Pali) are ascribed to him." Rhys Davids.

佛因 Buddha-cause, that which leads to Buddhahood, i.e. the merit of planting roots of goodness.

佛國 Buddhakṣetra. The country of the Buddha's birth. A country being transformed by a Buddha, also one already transformed; v. 丨土 and 丨刹. 丨丨記 Fa-hsien's Record of Buddhist countries.

佛圍陀 Buddhaveda, i.e. the Tripiṭaka, the Veda of Buddhism.

佛圖澄 or **磴** or **橙** Fo-t'u-ch'êng, an Indian monk who came to Loyang about A.D. 310, also known as 竺丨丨丨, noted for his magic; his name Buddhacinga, or (Eitel) Buddhochinga, is doubtful; he is also called 丨陀僧訶 Buddhasiṁha.

佛土 Buddhakṣetra. 佛國; 紇差怛羅; 差多羅; 刹怛利耶; 佛刹 The land or realm of a Buddha. The land of the Buddha's birth, India. A Buddha-realm in process of transformation, or transformed. A spiritual Buddha-realm. The T'ien-t'ai Sect evolved the idea of four spheres: (1) 同居之國土 Where common beings and saints dwell together, divided into (*a*) a realm where all beings are subject to transmigration and (*b*) the Pure Land. (2) 方便有餘土 or 變易土 The sphere where beings are still subject to higher forms of transmigration, the abode of Hīnayāna saints, i.e. Srota-āpanna 須陀洹; Sakṛdāgāmin 斯陀含; Anāgāmin 阿那含; Arhat 阿羅漢. (3) 實報無障礙 Final unlimited reward, the Bodhisattva realm. (4) 常寂光土 Where permanent tranquillity and enlightenment reign, Buddha-parinirvāṇa.

佛地 Buddha-bhūmi. The Buddha stage, being the tenth stage of the 通 or intermediate school, when the Bodhisattva has arrived at the point of highest enlightenment and is just about to become a Buddha. 丨丨羅 Bodhila, a native of Kashmir and follower of the Māhāsaṅghika school, author of the 集眞論.

佛境 The (spiritual) region of Buddhas.

佛壽 Buddha's life, or age. While he only lived to eighty as a man, in his Saṁbhogakāya he is without end, eternal; cf. Lotus sūtra, 壽量品, where Buddha is declared to be eternal.

佛天 Buddha as Heaven; Buddha and the devas.

佛婆提(訶) Pūrvavideha; 佛提婆; (|)毗提訶; 布嚕婆毗提訶; 逋利婆鼻提賀; 佛于逮 The continent of conquering spirits 勝神洲; one of the four great continents, east of Meru, semi-lunar in shape, its people having faces of similar shape. | | 羅部 idem 犢子部 Vātsīputrīyāḥ.

佛子 Son of Buddha; a bodhisattva; a believer in Buddhism, for every believer is becoming Buddha; a term also applied to all beings, because all are of Buddha-nature. There is a division of three kinds: 外子 external sons, who have not yet believed; 庶子 secondary sons, Hīnayānists; 眞子 true sons, Mahāyānists.

佛宗 Buddhism; principles of the Buddha Law, or dharma.

佛家 The school or family of Buddhism; the Pure Land, where is the family of Buddha. Also all Buddhists from the Srota-āpanna stage upwards.

佛寶, 法寶 僧寶 Buddha, Dharma, Saṅgha, i.e. Buddha, the Law, the Order; these are the three Jewels, or precious ones, the Buddhist Trinity; v. 三寶.

佛弟子 Disciples of Buddha, whether monks or laymen.

佛影 Buddhachāyā; the shadow of Buddha, formerly exhibited in various places in India, visible only to those "of pure mind".

佛後普賢 After having attained Buddhahood still to continue the work of blessing and saving other beings; also P'u-hsien, or Samantabhadra, as continuing the Buddha's work.

佛德 Buddha-virtue, his perfect life, perfect fruit, and perfect mercy in releasing all beings from misery.

佛心 The mind of Buddha, the spiritually enlightened heart. A heart of mercy; a heart abiding in the real, not the seeming; detached from good and evil and other such contrasts. | | 印 The seal of the Buddha heart or mind, the stamp of the universal Buddha-heart in every one; the seal on a Buddha's heart, or breast; the svastika. | | 天子 The Son of Heaven of the Buddha-heart, a name given to Wu Ti of the Liang dynasty, A.D. 502–549. | | 宗 The sect of the Buddha-heart, i.e. the Ch'an (Zen) or Intuitive sect of Bodhidharma, holding that each individual has direct access to Buddha through meditation.

佛性 Buddhatā. The Buddha-nature, i.e. gnosis, enlightenment; potential bodhi remains in every gati, i.e. all have the capacity for enlightenment; for the Buddha-nature remains in all as wheat-nature remains in all wheat. This nature takes two forms: 理 noumenal, in the absolute sense, unproduced and immortal, and 行 phenomenal, in action. While every one possesses the Buddha-nature, it requires to be cultivated in order to produce its ripe fruit. | | 不受羅 The Buddha-nature does not receive punishment in the hells, because it is 空 void of form, or spiritual and above the formal or material, only things with form can enter the hells. | | 常住 The eternity of the Buddha-nature, also of Buddha as immortal and immutable. | | 戒 The moral law which arises out of the Buddha-nature in all beings; also which reveals or evolves the Buddha-nature. | | 眞如 The Buddha-nature, the absolute, as eternally existent, i.e. the Bhūtatathatā.

佛慧 Buddha-wisdom.

佛所行讚經 Buddhacarita-kāvya-sūtra; a poetic narrative of the life of Śākyamuni by Aśvaghoṣa 馬鳴, tr. by Dharmarakṣa A.D. 414–421.

佛戒 The moral commandments of the Buddha; also, the laws of reality observed by all Buddhas.

佛支提 Buddha's Caitya, or Stūpa, v. 支提. A Buddhist reliquary, or pagoda, where relics of the Buddha, 舍利 śarīra, were kept; a stūpa 塔婆 was a tower for relics; such towers are of varying shape; originally sepulchres, then mere cenotaphs, they have become symbols of Buddhism.

佛教 Buddha's teaching; Buddhism. v. 釋敎.

佛敕 Buddha's śāsana or orders, i.e. his teaching.

佛日 The Buddha-sun which drives away the darkness of ignorance; the day of Buddha.

佛智 Anuttara-samyak-sambodhi, Buddha-wisdom, i.e. supreme, universal gnosis, awareness or intelligence; sarvajñatā, omniscience.

佛月 The Buddha-moon, Buddha being mirrored in the human heart like the moon in pure water. Also a meaning similar to 佛日.

佛本行集經 Buddhacarita; a life of Śākyamuni, tr. by Jñānagupta, A.D. 587.

佛果 Buddhaphala; the Buddha fruit, the state of Buddhahood; the fruition of arhatship, arahattvaphala.

佛栗持薩儻那 Urddhasthāna, ? Ūrdvasthāna, Vardhasthāna, or Vṛjisthāna, "an ancient kingdom, the country of the Vardaks, the Ortospana of Ptolemy, the region about Cabool (Lat. 34° 32 N., Long. 68° 55 E.)." Eitel.

佛樓沙 Purushapura, v. 布.

佛桀勢羅 Pūrvaśailāḥ, or Eastern Hill; one of the five divisions of the Māhāsaṅghika school. A monastery east of Dhanakaṭaka, i.e. Amarāvatī, on the R. Godavery.

佛樹 Bodhidruma; 道樹 the Bodhi-tree under which Śākyamuni obtained enlightenment or became Buddha, *Ficus religiosa*.

佛檀 Buddha-dāna, Buddha-giving contrasted with Māra-giving; Buddha-charity as the motive of giving, or preaching, and of self-sacrifice, or self-immolation.

佛歡喜日 The Buddhist joy-day, the 15th of the 7th month, the last day of the summer retreat.

佛母 (1) The mother of the Buddha, Mahāmāyā, 摩耶 Māyā, or Mātṛkā. (2) His aunt who was his foster-mother. (3) The Dharma or Law which produced him. (4) The Prajñā-pāramitā, mother or begetter of all Buddhas. (5) Other "Buddha-mothers", e.g. 准提｜｜; 孔雀｜｜, etc. Cf. ｜眼. ｜｜眞三昧 The samādhi, meditation, or trance by means of which the Buddhas, past, present, and future, become incarnate.

佛法 Buddhadharma; the Dharma or Law preached by the Buddha, the principles underlying these teachings, the truth attained by him, its embodiment in his being. Buddhism. ｜｜僧 Buddha, Dharma, Saṅgha, i.e. the Buddhist Trinity. ｜｜壽命 The life or extent of a period of Buddhism, i.e. as long as his commandments prevail. ｜｜藏 The storehouse of Buddha-law, the Bhūtatathatā as the source of all things.

佛海 Buddha's ocean, the realm of Buddha boundless as the sea.

佛滅(度) Buddha's nirvāṇa; it is interpreted as the extinction of suffering, or delusion, and as transport across the 苦海 bitter sea of mortality, v. 滅.

佛無礙慧 Unhindered, infinite Buddha-wisdom.

佛無差別 The identity of all Buddhas, and of their methods and purposes of enlightenment. One of the three identities, of all Buddhas, of all minds, and of all beings.

佛生日 Buddha's birthday, the 4th month, 8th day, or 2nd month, 8th day, the former having preference for celebration of his birthday in China.

佛田 Buddha field, in which the planting and cultivation of the Buddhist virtues ensure a rich harvest, especially the Buddha as an object of worship and the Order for almsgiving.

佛界 The Buddha realm, the state of Buddhahood, one of the ten realms, which consist of the six gati together with the realms of Buddhas, bodhisattvas, pratyeka-buddhas, and śrāvakas; also a Buddha-land; also the Buddha's country; cf. ｜土.

佛眼 The eye of Buddha, the enlightened one who sees all and is omniscient. ｜｜尊 A term of the esoteric cult for the source or mother of all wisdom, also called ｜｜部母; ｜｜佛母; ｜母身; ｜母尊; 虛空佛.

佛知見 The penetrative power of Buddha's wisdom, or vision.

佛祖 The Buddha and other founders of cults; Buddhist patriarchs; two of the records concerning them are the | | 統紀 and the | | (歷代) 通載.

佛種 The seed of Buddhahood; bodhisattva seeds which, sown in the heart of man, produce the Buddha fruit, enlightenment.

佛種姓 Those of the Buddha-clan, Buddhists.

佛立三昧 A degree of samādhi in which the Buddhas appear to the meditator.

佛經 Buddhist canonical literature; also Buddha's image and sūtras, with special reference to those purporting to have been introduced under Han Ming Ti; sūtras probably existed in China before that reign, but evidence is lacking. The first work, generally attributed to Ming Ti's reign, is known as The Sūtra of Forty-two Sections 四十二章經 but Maspero in *B.E.F.E.O.* ascribes it to the second century A.D.

佛臘日 The Buddhist last day of the old year, i.e. of the summer retreat.

佛舍 A Buddhist temple. | | 利 Buddha's śarīra. Relics or ashes left after Buddha's cremation, literally Buddha's body.

佛般泥洹經; 佛臨涅槃記法住經 The Nirvāṇa or Mahāparinirvāṇa Sūtra.

佛藏 Buddha thesaurus, the sūtras of the Buddha's preaching, etc., also all the teaching of Buddha.

佛見 The correct views, or doctrines, of the Buddha; Buddha doctrines.

佛記 Buddha's prediction, his foretelling of the future of his disciples.

佛說 Buddha's preaching; the Buddha said. Buddha's utterance of the sūtras. There are over 150 sūtras of which the titles begin with these two words, e.g. | | 無量壽經 Aparimitāyus Sūtra, tr. by Saṅghavarman A.D. 252.

佛語 The words, or sayings, of Buddha. | | 心 The Bhūtatathatā, as the mind or storehouse of Buddha's words.

佛跡; 佛迹 Buddha's relic; any trace of Buddha, e.g. the imprint of his foot in stone before he entered nirvāṇa.

佛身 Buddhakāya, a general term for the Trikāya, or threefold embodiment of Buddha. There are numerous categories or forms of the Buddhakāya.

佛道 The way of Buddha, leading to Buddhahood; intp. as bodhi, enlightenment, gnosis.

佛部 The groups in which Buddha appears in the Garbhadhātu and Vajradhātu respectively.

佛陀 v. 佛. There are numerous monks from India and Central Asia bearing this as part of their names, e.g. | | 什 Buddhajīva, who arrived in China from Kashmir or Kabul, A.D. 423; | | 僧訶 Buddhasiṁha, a disciple of Asaṅga, probably fifth century A.D., about whose esoteric practices, lofty talents, and final disappearance a lengthy account is given in the Fan-i-ming-i 翻譯名義; it is also a title of 佛圖澄 q.v. | | 多羅 (多) Buddhatrāta of Kashmir or Kabul, was a translator about 650; | | 扇多 Buddhaśānta, of Central India, translator of some ten works from 525–539; | | 提婆 Buddhadeva; | | 槃遮 Buddhvaca; | | 鞠多 Buddhagupta, "a Buddhistic king of Magadha, son and successor of Śakrāditya," Eitel; | | 波利 Buddhapāla, came from Kabul to China 676; also Buddhapālita, a disciple of Nāgārjuna and founder of the 中論性教; | | 蜜多羅 Buddhamitra, the ninth patriarch; | | 跋陀羅 Buddhabhadra, of Kapilavastu, came to China *circa* 408, introduced an alphabet of forty-two characters and composed numerous works; also name of a disciple of Dharmakoṣa, whom Hsüan-tsang met in India, 630–640; | | 耶舍 Buddhayaśas, of Kashmir or Kabul, tr. four works, 408–412; | | 難提 Buddhanandi, of Kāmarūpa, descendant of the Gautama family and eighth patriarch; | | 馱沙 Buddhadāsa, of Hayamukha 阿耶穆佉, author of the 大毗婆沙論. | | 伐那山 Buddhavanagiri, "a mountain near Rājagṛha famous for its rock caverns, in one of which Śākyamuni lived for a time." Eitel.

佛隴 Name of a peak at the south-west corner of T'ien-t'ai; also a name for Chih-i 智顗 q.v.

佛頂 Śākyamuni in the third court of the Garbhadhātu is represented as the | | 尊 in meditation as Universal Wise Sovereign. The 五 | | q.v. Five Buddhas are on his left representing his Wisdom. The three 佛頂 on his right are called 廣大 | |, 極 | | | |, and 無邊音聲 | |; in all they are the eight 佛頂. | | 印 The characteristic sign on a Buddha's head, short curls, topknot, or uṣṇīṣa. | | 咒; 楞嚴咒 Sitātapatroṣṇīṣa-dhāraṇī; the white-umbrella dhāraṇī in the 首楞嚴經. | | 骨 Buddhoṣṇīṣa; the skull or cranial protuberance on the Buddha's head; one of his characteristic marks.

佛願 The vow of Buddha to save all beings.

佛馱; | 馱 Used in certain names for 佛陀 Buddha, e.g. | | 什 Buddhajīva; | | 斯那 Buddhasena; | | 笈多 Buddhagupta; | | 耶 ? Buddhāya; | | 耶舍 Buddhayaśas, known as the "red-beard Vibhāṣā"; | | 跋陀羅 Buddhabhadra.

佛骨 A bone of the Buddha, especially the bone against whose reception by the emperor Hsien Tsung the famous protest of Han Yü was made in 819.

免 Avoid; remit. | 僧 A monk whose attendance at the daily assembly is excused for other duties.

兎 Śaśa; a rabbit; also a hare. The hare in the moon, hence 懷 | 者 is the moon or śaśin. | 毛塵 The speck of dust that can rest on the point of a hare's down, one-seventh of that on a sheep's hair. | 角 Śaśa-viṣāṇa; Śaśa-śṛṅga; a rabbit's horns, i.e. the non-existent; all phenomena are as unreal as a rabbit's horns.

冷 Cold. | 暖 Cold and warm. | 淘 Cold swill, a name for | 麪 cold dough-strings. | 河 The cold river Sītā, v. 私多.

冶 Smelt, melt; fascinating; translit. for *ya* in Akṣaya; also in Yajurveda, | 受皮陀 one of the four Vedas.

删 Cut, excise; translit. *s*, *ś*. | 地涅暮折那 Sandhinirmocana, name of the 解深密 sūtra. | 提嵐 Described as a fabulous world of the past whose name is given as Śāṇḍilya, but this is doubtful. | 闍夜 (or 耶毘羅胝子); | 逝移毘剌知子 Sañjaya-Vairāṭīputra, or Saṁjayin Vairaḍīputra, one of the six founders of heretical or non-Buddhist schools, whose doctrine was that pain and suffering would end in due course, like unwinding a ball of silk, hence there was no need of seeking the "Way".

判 Divide, judge, decide. | 教 Division of the Buddha's teaching, e.g. that of T'ien-t'ai, into the five periods and eight teachings, that of Hua-yen into five teachings, etc. | 釋 To divide and explain sūtras; to arrange in order, analyse the Buddha's teaching.

利 Paṭu, tīkṣṇa; sharp, keen, clever; profitable, beneficial; gain, advantage; interest. | 人 To benefit or profit men, idem | 他 parahita; the bodhisattva-mind is 自利利他 to improve oneself for the purpose of improving or benefiting others; the Buddha-mind is | 他一心 with single mind to help others, pure altruism; | 生 is the extension of this idea to 衆生 all the living, which of course is not limited to men or this earthly life; | 物 is also used with the same meaning, 物 being the living. | 使 The sharp or clever envoy, i.e. the chief illusion of regarding the ego and its experiences and ideas as real, one of the five chief illusions. | 劍 A sharp sword, used figuratively for Amitābha, and Mañjuśrī, indicating wisdom, discrimination, or power over evil. | 智 Keen intelligence, wisdom, discrimination; pāṭava. | 根 Sharpness, cleverness, intelligence, natural powers, endowment; possessed of powers of the pañca-indryāni (faith, etc.) or the five sense-organs, v. 五根. | 樂 Blessing and joy; the blessing being for the future life, the joy for the present; or aid (for salvation) and the joy of it. | 樂有情 To bless and give joy to the living, or sentient, the work of a bodhisattva. | 波波; 離波多; 黎婆多; 頡隸伐多 Revata; Raivata. (1) A Brahman hermit; one of the disciples of Śākyamuni, to be reborn as Samanta-prabhāsa. (2) President of the second synod, a native of Sāṅkāśya. (3) A contemporary of Aśoka, mentioned in connection with the third synod. Cf. Eitel. | 益 Benefit, aid, to bless; hence | | 妙 the wonder of Buddha's blessing, in opening the minds of all to enter the Buddha-enlightenment. | 行攝 Saṅgraha-vastu, the drawing of all beings to Buddhism through blessing them by deed, word, and will; one of the 四攝法 q.v. | 辯 Sharp and keen discrimination, or ratiocination, one of the seven characteristics 七種辯 of the Bodhisattva. | 養 To nourish oneself by gain; gain; avarice. | 養縛 The bond of selfish greed, one of the two bonds, gain and fame.

別 Separate, divide, part from, other, different, differentiate, special.

別他那 Veṣṭana, 吠率怒天, name of a deva; the second term suggests Viṣṇu, and Veṣṭu might be a conception of Viṣṇu; the intp. 圍 suits both, for Veṣṭana means surrounding, enclosing, and Viṣṇu, pervade, encompass.

別依 Secondary texts or authorities, in contrast with 總依 the principal texts of a school.

別傳 Separately handed down; oral tradition; to pass on the teaching from mind to mind without writing, as in the Ch'an (Zen) or Intuitional school. Also 單傳.

別劫 Antarā-kalpas, small or intermediate kalpas, v. 劫.

別向圓修 The 向 of the 別, i.e. the Separatist or Differentiating School, is the 修 of the 圓 or Perfect School; i.e. when the 別教 Bodhisattva reaches the stage of the 十回向, he has reached the 修 stage of the perfect nature and observance according to the 圓教 or Perfect School.

別圓 The 別 and 圓 schools, q.v. and 四教.

別境 Different realms, regions, states, or conditions. ||心所 Vibhāvanā; the ideas, or mental states, which arise according to the various objects or conditions toward which the mind is directed, e.g. if toward a pleasing object, then desire arises.

別報 Differentiated rewards according to previous deeds, i.e. the differing conditions of people in this life resulting from their previous lives.

別念佛 To intone the name of a special Buddha.

別惑; 別見 Delusions arising from differentiation, mistaking the seeming for the real; these delusions according to the 別教 are gradually eradicated by the Bodhisattva during his first stage.

別教 The "different" teaching of the 華嚴宗. Both the Hua-yen school and the Lotus school are founded on the 一乘 or One Vehicle idea; the Lotus school asserts that the Three Vehicles are really the One Vehicle; the Hua-yen school that the One Vehicle differs from the Three Vehicles; hence the Lotus school is called the 同教一乘 unitary, while the Hua-yen school is the 別教一乘 Differentiating school.

別時念佛 To call upon Buddha at special times. When the ordinary religious practices are ineffective the Pure Land sect call upon Buddha for a period of one to seven days, or ten to ninety days. Also 如法念佛.

別業 Differentiated karma (the cause of different resultant conditions); cf. 總業.

別理隨緣 The 理 li is the 眞如 Bhūtatathatā, which one school says is different in operation, while another asserts that it is the same, for all things are the chên-ju.

別相 Viśeṣa; differentiation; difference, one of the 六相 of the Hua-yen school. ||三觀 The three views of the 別教 in regard to the absolute, the phenomenal, the medial 空假中 as separate ideas.

別衆 For a monk schismatically or perversely to separate himself in religious duties from his fellow-monks is called duṣkṛta, an offence or wickedness, v. 突.

別見 Unenlightened, or heterodox, views.

別解脫戒 Another name for the commandments, which liberate by the avoidance of evil; also |||律儀.

別請 Special deference paid by singling out or inviting one member of the community; which procedure is against monastic rules.

別願 Special vows, as the forty-eight of Amitābha, or the twelve of 藥師佛 Yao Shih Fo (Bhaiṣajya), as contrasted with general vows taken by all Bodhisattvas.

劬 Toil; translit. *k*, *gh*. |嬪(陀) Kapphiṇa, v. 劫. |師羅 Ghoṣira, v. 具. |毗耶; 瞿波 Gopā, i.e. Yaśodharā, wife of Śākyamuni, v. 耶.

助 Help, aid, assist; auxiliary. |音 To assist in singing, or intoning. |業 Auxiliary karma, i.e. deeds or works, e.g. reciting the sūtras about the Pure Land, worship, praise, and offering, as additional to direct karma 正業, i.e. faith in Amitābha, expressed by constant thought of him and calling on his name. |道 Auxiliary means, e.g. of meditation; auxiliary discipline; any aid to faith or virtue.

劫; 刧 A kalpa, æon, age; also translit. *ka*; "a fabulous period of time, a day of Brahmā or 1,000 Yugas, a period of four hundred and thirty-two million years of mortals, measuring the duration of the world; (a month of Brahmā is supposed to contain thirty such kalpas; according to the Mahābhārata twelve months of Brahmā constitute his year, and one hundred such years his lifetime; fifty years of Brahmā are supposed to have elapsed . . .)." M. W. An æon of incalculable time, therefore called a 大時節 great time-node. v. |波.

劫初 The beginning of the kalpa of formation; the kalpa of creation; also 成劫.

劫地羅 Khadira, v. 竭.

劫婆吒; 劫縛拏 Kaparda, a shell, cowrie, small coin.

劫婆羅樹 v. 劫波樹 and 劫沙波娑 or 劫具, for both of which it is used.

劫布怛 (or 呾 or 咀 or 俎) 那 Kapotana, or Kebudhana; an ancient kingdom, the modern Kebud or Keshbūd, north of Samarkand.

劫布羅 Karpūra, camphor, described as 龍腦香 dragon-brain scent.

劫比他 Kapittha. (1) An ancient kingdom of Central India, also called 僧佉尸 Sāṁkāśya. (2) A Brahman of Vṛji who ill-treated the Buddhists of his time, was reborn as a fish, and was finally converted by Śākyamuni. Eitel.

劫比拏 idem |賓那.

劫比(羅) Kapila; also |畢羅; 迦比 (or 毗) 羅 The meaning is "brown", but it is chiefly used for "the sage Kapila, founder of the classical Sāṁkhya" philosophy and the school of that name. |||天; 金比羅天; 倶鞞羅天 A deva, or demon, called Kapila, or Kumbhīra, or Kubera.

劫比羅伐窣堵 (or 都) Kapilavastu, |||國; 迦毘羅衛; 迦 (or 伽) 毗羅蘇 (or 皤窣) 都; 迦羅 (or 夷 or 維); 伽毗黎, etc. Capital of the principality occupied by the Śākya clan; destroyed during Śākyamuni's life, according to legend; about 100 miles due north of Benares, north-west of present Gorakhpur; referred to in 西域記.

劫比舍也 Said to be 罽賓 Kashmir.

劫水 The flood in the kalpa of destruction, v. 三災.

劫波 Kalpa; also |簸; |跛; v. 劫. Æon, age. The period of time between the creation and recreation of a world or universe; also the kalpas of formation, existence, destruction, and non-existence, which four as a complete period are called mahākalpa 大劫. Each great kalpa is subdivided into four asaṅkhyeya-kalpas (阿僧企耶 i.e. numberless, incalculable): (1) kalpa of destruction 壞劫 saṁvarta; (2) kalpa of utter annihilation, or empty kalpa 增減劫; 空劫 saṁvartasiddha; (3) kalpa of formation 成劫 vivarta; (4) kalpa of existence 住劫 vivartasiddha; or they may be taken in the order 成住壞空. Each of the four kalpas is subdivided into twenty antarakalpas, 小劫 or small kalpas, so that a mahākalpa consists of eighty small kalpas. Each small kalpa is divided into a period of 增 increase and 減 decrease; the increase period is ruled over by the four cakravartīs in succession, i.e. the four ages of iron, copper, silver, gold, during which the length of human life increases by one year every century to 84,000 years, and the length of the human body to 8,400 feet. Then comes the kalpa of decrease divided into periods of the three woes, pestilence, war, famine, during which the length of human life is gradually reduced to ten years and the human body to 1 foot in height. There are other distinctions of the kalpas. A small kalpa is represented as 16,800,000 years, a kalpa as 336,000,000 years, and a mahākalpa as 1,334,000,000 years. There are many ways of illustrating the length of a kalpa, e.g. pass a soft cloth over a solid rock 40 li in size once in a hundred years, when finally the rock has been thus worn away a kalpa will not yet have passed; or a city of 40 li, filled with mustard seeds, one being removed every century till all have gone, a kalpa will not yet have passed. Cf. 成劫. ||娑 (or 育 or 羅 or 薩); |婆羅; |具(娑) Kārpāsa is cotton, Gossypium Herbaceum; but this refers especially to Kārpāsī, the cotton tree. ||杯 Kapāla, a bowl, skull; the drinking bowl of Śiva, a skull filled with blood. ||樹 Kalpataru.

A tree in Indra's garden bearing fruit according to the seasons. 丨丨羅 Kapāla, a skull; also Kārpāsa, see 丨丨婆. 丨丨丨天 Yama, as ruler of time, 時分天.

劫海 The ocean of kalpas, i.e. their great number.

劫濁 The impure or turbid kalpa, when the age of life is decreasing and all kinds of diseases afflict men.

劫火 The fire in the kalpa of destruction; also 劫盡火; 劫焰; 劫燒 v. 三災.

劫灰 Kalpa-ash, the ashes after the fire kalpa of destruction.

劫災 The calamity of fire, wind, and water, during the 壞劫 kalpa of destruction.

劫焰 Kalpa-flames, idem 丨火.

劫燒 idem 劫火.

劫簸 idem 劫波.

劫具 v. 劫波娑.

劫賓那 Kapphiṇa; also 劫比拏王; 劫庀 (or 比, or 譬) 那; or Kampilla, 金毗羅; whose monastic name was Mahā-kapphiṇa; intp. as 房宿 (born) under the constellation Scorpio; he is said to have understood astronomy and been king of Southern Kośala; he became a disciple of Śākyamuni and is to be reborn as Samantaprabhāsa Buddha.

劫跛劫跛夜帝 ? Kalpa-kalpāyati, perhaps connected with klṛp, intp. as 離 (or 無) 分別 indiscriminate, undifferentiate.

卵生 Aṇḍaja. Egg-born, one of the four ways of coming into existence, v. 四生.

却 Decline, reject; but, yet. 丨入生死 To leave his perfect life to enter into the round of births and deaths, as a Bodhisattva does.

告 To inform; plead; accuse. 丨香 To inform by offering incense.

吸 To suck up, inhale; 呼丨 exhale and inhale.

吟 Chant, hum, mutter. 丨詠; 丨諷 To intone, repeat.

吹 To blow; puff, praise. 丨光 To blow out a light, a blown-out light. 丨毛 Name of a sharp sword, or Excalibur, that would sever a falling feather; to blow hair or fur. 丨法螺 To blow the conch of the Law, the Buddha's preaching.

吽; 件 Translit. for Hūṁ, which is interpreted as the bodhi, or omniscience, of all Buddhas. 丨丨 The lowing of oxen. 丨迦囉身 Hūṁkāra, P'u-hsien 普賢 Samantabhadra in his minatory aspect against demons.

叫喚 Raurava; also 號叫; 呼呼. The wailing hells, the fourth of the eight hot hells, where the inmates cry aloud on account of pain.

君 Prince, noble, ideal man or woman; translit. *kun*. 丨持; 丨遲; 軍持; 捃稚 (or 稚) 迦 Kuṇḍa, Kuṇḍikā, a pitcher, waterpot; washbowl. 丨(or 軍) 荼 Kuṇḍa, a hole in the ground for the fire at the fire altar; the homa or fire altar.

吠 To bark (as a dog); translit. *ve, vi, vai*; cf. 毘; 鞞; 衛; 別. 丨世師; 丨丨史迦 Vaiśeṣika, v. 衛. 丨努璃耶 Vaiḍūrya, lapis lazuli. 丨嚧遮那; 丨路者那 Vairocana; v. 毘. 丨室囉末拏 Vaiśravaṇa, v. 鞞. 丨嵐 Vairambha, v. 毘. 丨摩質怛利 Vimalacitra, v. 毘. 丨率怒 Veṣṭana, v. 別. 丨瑠璃 (耶) Vaiḍūrya, lapis lazuli. 丨舍; 鞞 (or 毘) 丨; 丨奢 Vaiśya; the third of the four Indian castes, that of agriculture and trade. 丨 (or 薜) 舍佉; 鼻奢迦 Vaiśākha; the second Indian month, from 15th of 2nd to 16th of 3rd Chinese months. 丨舍釐 (or 離) Vaiśālī, v. 毘. 丨陀 Veda, v. 韋.

含 To hold in the mouth; cherish; restrain. 丨中教 A T'ien-t'ai term for the 通教 which was midway between or interrelated with Hīnayāna and Mahāyāna. 丨情 All beings possessing feeling, sentience. 丨生; 丨靈 Living beings, all beings possessing life, especially sentient life. 丨華 In the closed lotus flower, i.e. those who await the opening of the flower for rebirth in Paradise. 丨識; 丨類 All sentient beings.

坊 A place, locality; a temple, place of assembly, etc.

均 Equal, in balance, all; used for Kun in 丨提 Kunti, (*a*) said to be a devoted disciple of Śāriputra; (*b*) one of the attendants on Mañjuśrī.

坐 Niṣad; niṣaṇṇa; sit; rest; situated. 丨具 given as Niṣīdana, an article for sitting on, said to be a cloth, or mat. 丨久成勞 To accomplish one's labour by prolonged sitting, as did Bodhidharma. 丨參 The evening meditation at a monastery (preceding instruction by the abbot). 丨堂 A sitting-room, the assembly room of the monks. 丨夏; 丨臘 Varṣā; the retreat or rest during the summer rains. 丨丨由 A certificate of "retreat" given to a wandering monk. 丨禪 To sit in dhyāna, i.e. abstract meditation, fixed abstraction, contemplation; its introduction to China is attributed to Bodhidharma (though it came earlier), and its extension to T'ien-t'ai. 丨丨堂 The monks' assembly room. 丨證 Another term for dhyāna contemplation.

夾 Squeeze, clip, nip; lined. 丨山 Name of a monastery and monk in 澧州 Li-chou under the T'ang dynasty.

妓 A singing-girl, courtesan. 丨樂 Female musicians and performers.

妖 An imp; to bewitch; magical. 丨通 The power to change miraculously into trees and animals; v. 五種通.

妙 Su, sat, mañju, sūkṣma. Wonderful, beautiful, mystic, supernatural, profound, subtle, mysterious. Su means good, excellent, surpassing, beautiful, fine, easy. Sat means existing, real, good. Mañju means beautiful, lovely, charming. Intp. in Chinese as 不可思議 beyond thought or discussion; 絕待 special, outstanding; 無比 incomparable; 精微深遠 subtle and profound.

妙中 The profound medium (madhya); the universal life essence, the absolute, the bhūtatathatā which expresses the unity of all things, i.e. the doctrine held by T'ien-t'ai as distinguished from the 別敎 which holds the madhya doctrine but emphasizes the dichotomy of the 空 transcendental and 假 phenomenal.

妙假 The profound meaning of phenomena of T'ien-t'ai, that they are the bhūtatathatā (e.g. water and wave) as distinguished from the 別敎 view; cf. 丨中.

妙光 Varaprabha, Wonderful Light, an ancient incarnation of Mañjuśrī. 丨丨佛 Sūryaraśmi, the 930th Buddha of the present kalpa.

妙典 The classics of the wonderful dharma, i.e. Mahāyāna.

妙吉祥 Wonderful and auspicious, the meaning of Mañjuśrī, 妙 for Mañju and 吉祥 for śrī; v. 文殊.

妙喜世界 The realm of profound joy, the country of Vimalakīrti 維摩居士, who is stated to have been a contemporary of Śākyamuni; v. 維摩詰經 12. 丨丨足天 The heaven full of wonderful joy, idem Tuṣita, v. 兜.

妙善公主 The princess of wonderful goodness, name of Kuan-yin as third daughter of King 莊嚴 Chuang Yen.

妙因 The profound cause, the discipline of the bodhisattva, i.e. chastity, and the six pāramitās, etc., as producing the Buddha-fruit.

妙土 The wonderful land; a Buddha's reward-land; especially the Western Paradise of Amitābha.

妙宗 Profound principles; the Lotus School.

妙幢 Ruciraketu. Name of a Bodhisattva. The 丨丨相三昧 Dhvajāgrakeyūra, "the ring on the top of a standard," a degree of ecstatic meditation mentioned in the Lotus sūtra.

妙德 Wonderful virtue, title of Mañjuśrī; also an intp. of the meaning of Kapilavastu, v. 劫比, etc.

妙心 The mind or heart wonderful and profound beyond human thought. According to T'ien-t'ai the 別敎 limited this to the mind 眞心 of the Buddha, while the 圓敎 universalized it to include the unenlightened heart 妄心 of all men.

妙意菩薩 Mānavaka, i.e. Śākyamuni in a previous incarnation as disciple of Dīpaṅkara 然燈佛.

妙應 The miraculous response, or self-manifestation of Buddhas and bodhisattvas.

妙教 Admirable, profound teaching; i.e. that of the Lotus Sūtra.

妙明 Profoundly enlightened heart or mind, i.e. the knowledge of the finality of the stream of reincarnation.

妙智 The wonderful Buddha-wisdom.

妙有 The absolute reality, the incomprehensible entity, as contrasted with the superficial reality of phenomena; supernatural existence.

妙果 Wonderful fruit, i.e. bodhi or enlightenment and nirvāṇa.

妙樂 Wonderful music (in the Pure Land). Miao-yo, the sixth T'ien-t'ai patriarch.

妙法 Saddharma, 薩達(刺)摩 The wonderful law or truth (of the Lotus Sūtra). ||一乘 The One Vehicle of the wonderful dharma, or perfect Mahāyāna. ||堂; 善法堂 The hall of wonderful dharma, situated in the south-west corner of the Trayastriṁśas heaven, v. 忉, where the thirty-three devas discuss whether affairs are according to law or truth or the contrary. ||宮 The palace of the wonderful law, in which the Buddha ever dwells. ||燈 The lamp of the wonderful Law shining into the darkness of ignorance. ||船 The bark or boat of wonderful dharma, capable of transporting men over the sea of life into nirvāṇa. ||華 idem ||蓮華. ||藏 The treasury of the wonderful dharma. ||輪 The wheel of the wonderful Law, Buddha's doctrine regarded as a great cakra or wheel. ||蓮華; 法華 The wonderful truth as found in the Lotus Sūtra, the One Vehicle sūtra; which is said to contain 實法 Buddha's complete truth as compared with his previous 權法 or 方便法, i.e. partial, or expedient teaching, but both are included in this perfect truth. The sūtra is the Saddharmapuṇḍarīka 正法華經 or (添品) 妙法蓮華經, also known as 薩曇芬陀利經, of which several translations in whole or part were made from Sanskrit into Chinese, the most popular being by Kumārajīva. It was the special classic of the T'ien-t'ai school, which is sometimes known as the 蓮宗 Lotus School, and it profoundly influenced Buddhist doctrine in China, Japan, and Tibet. The commentaries and treatises on it are very numerous; two by Chih-i 智顗 of the T'ien-t'ai school being the ||||經文句 and the 玄義.

妙無 Asat, the mystery of non-existence.

妙玄 Wonderful and profound; an abbreviation for |法蓮華經玄義 the T'ien-t'ai commentary on the Lotus Sūtra.

妙眞如性 The profound nature of the Bhūtatathatā, the totality, or fundamental nature, of all things.

妙臂菩薩 Subāhu-kumāra, the bodhisattva of the wonderful arm; there is a sūtra of this name.

妙色 Surūpa, 蘇樓波. The wonderful form or body, i.e. of a Buddha's saṁbhogakāya and his Buddha-land. ||身如來 Surūpakāya Tathāgata (Akṣobhya, the Buddha of the East), who is thus addressed when offerings are made to the hungry spirits.

妙莊(嚴)王 Śubhavyūha, the king who is the subject and title of the twenty-seventh chapter of the Lotus sūtra. He is also reputed to be the father of Kuan-yin.

妙蓮華 The wonderful lotus, symbol of the pure wisdom of Buddha, unsullied in the midst of the impurity of the world.

妙行 The profound act by which a good karma is produced, e.g. faith; v. 一行一切行.

妙見 The beautiful sight, i.e. Ursa Major, or the Bodhisattva who rules there, styled ||大士 (or 菩薩), though some say Śākyamuni, others Kuan-yin, others 藥師 Bhaiṣajya, others the seven Buddhas. His image is that of a youth in golden armour.

妙覺 The wonderful enlightenment of Mahāyāna, or self-enlightenment to enlighten others. ||地 The stage of wonderful enlightenment, Buddhahood. ||性 The profound, enlightened nature, that of Buddha, one of the 六性.

妙觀 The wonderful system of the three T'ien-t'ai meditations; v. 三諦, 三觀.

妙語藏 The storehouse of miraculous words, mantras, dhāraṇī, or magic spells of Shingon.

妙賢 Subhadra, 善賢 A monk referred to in the 西域記 Records of Western Lands.

妙趣 The wonderful destiny or metempsychosis, i.e. that of Mahāyāna.

妙車 The wonderful vehicles (mentioned in the Lotus sūtra).

妙門 The wonderful door of dharma; nirvāṇa; the six T'ien-t'ai methods leading through meditation to enlightenment and the state of nirvāṇa.

妙音 Wonderful sound. (1) Gadgadasvara, | | 菩薩 (or 大士) a Bodhisattva, master of seventeen degrees of samādhi, residing in Vairocanaraśmi-pratimaṇḍita, whose name heads cap. 24 of the Lotus sūtra. (2) Sughoṣa, a sister of Kuan-yin; also a Buddha like Varuṇa controlling the waters 水天德佛, the 743rd Buddha of the present kalpa. (3) Ghoṣa, 瞿沙 an arhat, famous for exegesis, who "restored the eyesight of Dharmavivardhana by washing his eyes with the tears of people who were moved by his eloquence". Eitel. | | 徧滿 Universal wonderful sound, Manojña-śabdābhigarjita, the kalpa of Ānanda as Buddha. | | (樂) 天 Sarasvatī, the wife or female energy of Brahmā. Also called 辨才天 (女) Jap. Benzaiten, or Benten; goddess of eloquence, learning, and music, bestower of the Sanskrit language and letters, and the bestower of 財 riches; also the river goddess. Sometimes considered as masculine. Honoured among the seven gods of luck, and often represented as mounted on a dragon or a serpent. | | 鳥 The wonderful-voice bird, the Kalaviṅka.

妙顯山 The mountain of marvellous appearance, i.e. Sumeru.

妙高山 (王) The wonderful high mountain, Sumeru; the king of mountains.

孝 Filial, obedient. | 子 A filial son. | 服 Mourning clothes for parents. | 順 Obedient.

孛 Po; plants shooting; a comet. | 伽夷 Bhagai. A city south of Khotan, formerly famous for a statue exhibiting all the thirty-two lakṣaṇas or marks on the body of Buddha.

宏 Vast, spacious. | 智 Hung-chih, posthumous name of a monk of 天童 T'ien-t'ung monastery, Ningpo, early in the twelfth century.

宋 The Sung dynasty, A.D. 960–1280. | 元入藏諸大小乘經 Sūtras of the Hīnayāna and Mahāyāna admitted into the canon during the Northern and Southern Sung (A.D. 960–1127 and 1127–1280) and Yüan (A.D. 1280–1368) dynasties. B.N., 782–1081. | 帝王 The third of the ten rulers of Hades, who presides over the Kālasūtra, the hell of black ropes.

尾 Tail; end. | 儞也 Vibhā, to shine, illuminate, tr. by 明, a name for the Shingon sect 眞言 because of its power to dispel the darkness of delusion. | 嚕博乞叉 Virūpākṣa, epithet for the three-eyed deva, Śiva. See also 毘流波叉. | | 荼迦 Virūḍhaka idem 毘瑠璃, one of the four mahārāja-devas.

尿 Urine, urinate. | 牀鬼子 A urinating ghost; a term of abuse. | 閭 A urinal.

希 Rare, seldom, few; to hope for. | 奇 Rare and extraordinary. | 天施; | 求施 Giving in hope of heaven, or bliss; one of the 八種布施. | 有 Rare, extraordinary, uncommon, few. | | 人 There are few, a sad exclamation, indicating that those who accept Buddha's teaching are few, or that those who do evil and repent, or give favours and remember favours, etc., are few. | 法 Adbhuta-dharma; supernatural things, prodigies, miracles, a section of the twelve classical books. | 祀鬼 Ghosts that hope for sacrificial offerings (from their descendants). | 連河; | | 禪 The river Nairañjanā, v. 尼. | 麟音義 The dictionary compiled by Hsi-lin of the T'ang dynasty, supplementing the 慧琳音義 Hui-lin-yin-i. Sound and meaning accord with Hui-lin, and terms used in translations made subsequent to that work are added.

序 Seriatim; preface, introduction; the opening phrase of a sūtra, "Thus have I heard"; an opening phrase leading up to a subject. | 王 The introduction by Chih-i to the Lotus sūtra. Introductions are divided into 序, 正, and 流通, the first relating to the reason for the book; the second to its method; and the third to its subsequent history.

弟 Younger brother. | 子 Disciple, disciples.

形 Form, figure, appearance, the body. | 像 Pratimā, an image or likeness (of Buddha). | 山 The body, comparable to a mountain. | 貌 Form, appearance. | 貌欲 The desire awakened on seeing a beautiful form, one of the 六欲 six desires. | 色

Saṁsthānarūpa, the characteristics of form—long, short, square, round, high, low, straight, crooked. It is also associated with Rūpāvacara as personal appearance, and as a class of gods in the realm of form.

志 Will, resolve, 丨意; 心丨; also data, records.

快 Glad, joyful; quick, sharp. 丨樂 Joyful. 丨目王 The quick-eyed king, Sudhīra, or highly intelligent, who could see through a wall 40 li away, yet who took out his eyes to give as alms; v. 賢愚經 6.

忻 Delight, joy.

忌 Avoid, tabu, dread; hate, jealous. 丨日; 諱日 The tabu day, i.e. the anniversary of the death of a parent or prince, when all thoughts are directed to him, and other things avoided.

忍 Kṣānti, 羼提 (or 底); patience, endurance, (*a*) in adverse circumstances, (*b*) in the religious state. There are groups of two, three, four, five, six, ten, and fourteen, indicating various forms of patience, equanimity, repression, forbearance, endurance, constancy, or "perseverance of the saints", both in mundane and spiritual things. 丨不墮惡趣 The stage of patience ensures that there will be no falling into the lower paths of transmigration. 丨仙 The patient ṛṣi, or immortal of patience, i.e. the Buddha. 丨位 The stage of patience. 丨加行 The discipline of patience, in the 四加行 four Hīnayāna disciplines; also in the Mahāyāna. 丨善 The patient and good; or patient in doing good. 丨土 The place of patience or endurance, this world. 丨地 The stage of patience, i.e. of enlightenment separating from the chain of transmigration. 丨智 Patience and wisdom. In the Hīnayāna, patience is cause, wisdom effect; in Mahāyāna, the two are merged, though patience precedes wisdom. 丨水 Patience in its depth and expanse compared to water. 丨法 (位) The method or stage of patience, the sixth of the seven stages of the Hīnayāna in the attainment of arhatship, or sainthood; also the third of the four roots of goodness. 丨波羅蜜 The patience pāramitā, v. 丨辱. 丨界 Sahā, or Sahāloka, or Sahālokadhātu. The universe of persons subject to transmigration, the universe of endurance. 丨調 Patiently to harmonize, i.e. the patient heart tempers and subdues anger and hatred. 丨辱; 羼提 (or 底) 波羅蜜多 Kṣānti pāramitā; patience, especially bearing insult and distress without resentment, the third of the six pāramitās 六度. Its guardian bodhisattva is the third on the left in the hall of space in the Garbhadhātu. 丨辱仙 Kṣāntyṛṣi; the ṛṣi who patiently suffered insult, i.e. Śākyamuni, in a former life, suffering mutilation to convert Kalirāja. 丨辱地 The stage of patience. Two kinds are distinguished, patience which endures (1) insults originating in men, such as hatred, or abuse, (2) distresses arising from natural causes such as heat, cold, age, sickness, etc. 丨辱太子 The patient prince, of Vārāṇaśī (Benares), who gave a piece of his flesh to heal his sick parents, which was efficacious because he had never given way to anger. 丨辱衣 The robe of patience, a patient heart which, like a garment, wards off all outward sin. A general name for the kaṣāya, monk's robe. 丨(辱) 鎧 Patience as armour, protecting against evils; also the kaṣāya, monk's robe.

成 Complete, finish, perfect, become.

成佛 To become Buddha, as a Bodhisattva does on reaching supreme perfect bodhi. 丨丨得脫 To become Buddha and obtain deliverance (from the round of mortality).

成劫 Vivarta kalpa, one of the four kalpas, consisting of twenty small kalpas during which worlds and the beings on them are formed. The others are: 住丨 Vivarta-siddha kalpa, kalpa of abiding, or existence, sun and moon rise, sexes are differentiated, heroes arise, four castes are formed, social life evolves. 壞丨 Saṁvarta kalpa, that of destruction, consisting of sixty-four small kalpas when fire, water, and wind destroy everything except the fourth Dhyāna. 空丨 Saṁvarta-siddha kalpa, i.e. of annihilation. v. 劫波. 丨唯識論 Vidyā-mātra-siddhi śāstra, in 10 chüan, being Vasubandhu's 唯識 in 30 chüan reduced by Hsüan-tsang, also by others, to 10. There are works on it by various authors.

成實 Completely true, or reliable, perfect truth, an abbreviation for 丨丨宗, 丨丨論, 丨丨師.

成實宗 Satyasiddhi sect (Jap. Jōjitsu-shū), based upon the Satyasiddhi śāstra of Harivarman, v. 訶, tr. by Kumārajīva. In China it was a branch of the 三論 San Lun Sect. It was a Hīnayāna variation of the Śūnya 空 doctrine. The term is defined as perfectly establishing the real meaning of the sūtras. The 丨丨論 tr. as above is in 16 chüan; there are other works on it. 丨就 Siddhi; accomplishment, fulfilment, completion, to bring to perfection. 丨丨衆生 To transform all beings by developing their Buddha-nature and causing them to obtain enlightenment. 丨熟者 The ripe; those who attain; those in whom the good nature, immanent in all the living, completes their salvation. | 等正覺 To attain to perfect enlightenment, become Buddha. | 自然覺 To attain to natural enlightenment as all may do by beholding eternal truth 實相 within their own hearts. | 身會; 根本會; 羯磨會 The first group in the nine Vajradhātu groups. | 道 To attain the Way, or become enlightened, e.g. the Buddha under the bodhi tree. | 道會; 臘八 The annual commemoration of the Buddha's enlightenment on the 8th day of the 12th month.

我 I, my, mine; the ego, the master of the body, compared to the ruler of a country. Composed of the five skandhas and hence not a permanent entity. It is used for ātman, the self, personality. Buddhism takes as a fundamental dogma 無我, i.e. no 常我, no permanent ego, only recognizing a temporal or functional ego. The erroneous idea of a permanent self continued in reincarnation is the source of all illusion. But the Nirvāṇa sūtra definitely asserts a permanent ego in the transcendental world, above the range of reincarnation; and the trend of Mahāyāna supports such permanence; v. 常我樂淨.

我事 My body; myself; my affair.

我人四相 The four ejects of the ego in the Diamond Sūtra: (1) 我相 the illusion that in the five skandhas there is a real ego; (2) 人相 that this ego is a man, and different from beings of the other paths; (3) 衆生相 that all beings have an ego born of the five skandhas; (4) 壽相 that the ego has age, i.e. a determined or fated period of existence.

我倒 The illusion of an ego, one of the four inverted or upside-down ideas.

我劣慢 Ūnamāna; the pride of thinking myself not much inferior to those who far surpass me. One of the 九慢 q.v.

我勝慢 Adhimāna; the pride of thinking oneself superior to equals. One of the 九慢.

我執 Ātma-grāha; holding to the concept of the ego; also 人執.

我室 The ego as the abode (of all suffering).

我德 Power or virtue of the ego, the ego being defined as 自在 sovereign, master, free; v. | 波羅蜜.

我愚 Ego ignorance, holding to the illusion of the reality of the ego.

我想 The thought that the ego has reality.

我愛 Self-love; the love of or attachment to the ego, arising with the eighth vijñāna.

我慢 Abhimāna, ātma-mada. Egotism; exalting self and depreciating others; self-intoxication, pride.

我我所 I and mine; the self and its possessions.

我所; 我所有; 我所事 Mine, personal, subjective; personal conditions, possessions, or anything related to the self. | | 心 The mind that thinks it is owner of things. | | 見 The incorrect view that anything is really mine, for all things are but temporal combinations.

我有 The illusion that the ego has real existence.

我法 Self (or the ego), and things. | | 俱有宗 The school that regards the ego and things as real; the 犢子部 Vātsīputrīyā school.

我波羅蜜 The ego pāramitā in the four based on the Nirvāṇa sūtra in which the transcendental ego is 自在, i.e. has a real and permanent nature; the four are 常 permanency, 樂 joy, 我 personality, 淨 purity.

我痴 Ego-infatuation, confused by the belief in the reality of the ego.

我相 Egoism, the concept of the ego as real. Anyone who believes in | |, 人 |, 衆生 |, 壽 | is not a true bodhisattva, v. | 人四相.

我空; (衆)生空; 人空 Illusion of the concept of the reality of the ego, man being composed of elements and disintegrated when these are dissolved. | | 眞如 The Hīnayāna doctrine of impersonality in the absolute, that in truth there is no ego; this position abrogates moral responsibility, cf. 原人論.

我等慢 Mānātimāna; the pride of thinking oneself equal to those who surpass us. One of the 九慢.

我見; 身見 The erroneous doctrine that the ego, or self, composed of the temporary five skandhas, is a reality and permanent.

我語取 The attachment to doctrines or statements about the ego. One of the 四取.

我顛倒 The illusion that the ego is real; also the incorrect view that the Nirvāṇa-ego is non-ego. One of the 四顛倒.

戒 Śīla, 尸羅. Precept, command, prohibition, discipline, rule; morality. It is applied to the five, eight, ten, 250, and other commandments. The five are: (1) not to kill; (2) not to steal; (3) not to commit adultery; (4) not to speak falsely; (5) not to drink wine. These are the commands for lay disciples; those who observe them will be reborn in the human realm. The Sarvāstivādins did not sanction the observance of a limited selection from them as did the 成實宗 Satyasiddhi school. Each of the five precepts has five guardian spirits, in all twenty-five, 五戒二十五神. The eight for lay disciples are the above five together with Nos. 7, 8, and 9 of the following; the ten commands for the ordained, monks and nuns, are the above five with the following: (6) not to use adornments of flowers, nor perfumes; (7) not to perform as an actor, juggler, acrobat, or go to watch and hear them; (8) not to sit on elevated, broad, and large divans (or beds); (9) not to eat except in regulation hours; (10) not to possess money, gold or silver, or precious things. The 具足 | full commands for a monk number 250, those for a nun are 348, commonly called 500. Śīla is also the first of the 五分法身, i.e. a condition above all moral error. The Sūtra of Brahma's Net has the following after the first five: (6) not to speak of the sins of those in orders; (7) not to vaunt self and depreciate others; (8) not to be avaricious; (9) not to be angry; (10) not to slander the Triratna.

戒力 The power derived from observing the commandments, enabling one who observes the five commandments to be reborn among men, and one who observes the ten positive commands 十善 to be born among devas, or as a king.

戒取 Clinging to the commandments of heterodox teachers, e.g. those of ultra-asceticism, one of the four attachments, 四取 catuḥ-parāmarśa. | | 使 The delusion resulting from clinging to heterodox commandments. | | 見; | 禁取見 Clinging to heterodox ascetic views; one of the five darśana 五見.

戒品 The different groupings or subjects of the commandments, or discipline; i.e. the 5, 10, 250, etc.

戒善 The good root of keeping the commandments, from which springs the power for one who keeps the five to be reborn as a man; or for one who keeps the ten to be reborn in the heavens, or as a king.

戒器 A utensil fit to receive the rules, i.e. one who is not debarred from entering the Order, as is a eunuch, slave, minor, etc.

戒垢 The source of defiling the commandments, i.e. woman.

戒場 The place where monks are given the commandments.

戒壇 The altar at which the commandments are received by the novice; the 方等 | | is the Mahāyāna altar.

戒學 The study of the rules or discipline; one of the three departments 三學, the other two being meditation and philosophy.

戒定慧 Discipline, meditation, wisdom; discipline wards off bodily evil, meditation calms mental disturbance, wisdom gets rid of delusion and proves truth.

戒師 The teacher of the discipline, or of the commandments (to the novice); also 戒和尙.

戒師五德 The five virtues of the teacher of the discipline: obedience to the rules, twenty years as monk, ability to explain the vinaya, meditation, ability to explain the abhidharma.

戒律 Śīla and Vinaya. The rules. | | 藏 The Vinaya Piṭaka, the second main division of the Buddhist Canon.

戒德 The power of the discipline.

戒忍 Patience acquired by the observance of the discipline; the first of the ten kṣānti.

戒急乘緩 Zealous for the discipline rather than for knowledge, e.g. Hīnayāna; 乘急戒緩 one who is zealous for knowledge rather than the discipline, e.g. Vimalakirtti 維摩; 乘戒俱急 one who emphasizes both, the bodhisattva; 乘戒俱緩 one who is indifferent to both.

戒本 The Prātimokṣa 波羅提木叉 q.v. The | | 經 is the latter half of the 梵網經.

戒波羅蜜 Moral precepts, the second of the six pāramitās.

戒波離 Upāli, a śūdra, disciple of Śākyamuni, famous for his knowledge of the Vinaya; v. 優波離.

戒海 The rules are pure and purify like the waters of the ocean.

戒牒; 戒驗; 度牒 Certificate of ordination of a monk.

戒珠 The commandments, or rules, are like pure white pearls, adorning the wearer.

戒相 The commandments or rules in their various forms; also the commandments as expressions for restraining evil, etc.

戒禁 Prohibitions arising out of the fundamental rules; by-laws. | | 取見 v. 戒取.

戒膝 The "commandments' knee", i.e. the right knee bent as when receiving the commandments.

戒臘 The number of years a monk has been ordained. 臘 is the name of an offering made at the end of the year in ancient times. Also | 蠟; | 臈; 僧臘.

戒藏 The Vinaya Piṭaka; the collection of rules.

戒賢 Śīlabhadra, see 尸.

戒躅 The rut or way of the commandments; the rules.

戒門 The way or method of the commandments or rules; obedience to the commandments as a way of salvation.

戒香 The perfume of the commandments, or rules, i.e. their pervading influence.

戒體 The embodiment of the commandments in the heart of the recipient. v. 無表; also the basis, or body, of the commandments.

技人 A magician, trickster, conjurer.

批 An order of a court, rescript; a contract, lease; to comment, criticize. | 那 Vīṇā; the Indian lute.

抖 To shake. | 擻; 斗藪 Dhūta; stirring up to duty; discipline. v. 頭陀.

折 To snap, break; decide; compound; fold. | 伏攝受 To subdue the evil and receive the good; cf. 抑. | 利怛 (or 但) 羅 Caritra, 發行城 "A port on the south-east frontier of Uḍa (Orissa) whence a considerable trade was carried on with Ceylon." Eitel. | 句迦; 斫 (or 所) | | Cakoka, i.e. Karghalik in Turkestan. | 石 A broken stone, i.e. irreparable. | 蘆 The snapped-off reed on which Bodhidharma is said to have crossed the Yangtsze from Nanking.

投 To cast, throw into, surrender, tender. | 子 T'ou-tzŭ, name of a hill and monastery at 舒州 Shu-chou and of 義青 I-ch'ing its noted monk. | 機 To avail oneself of an opportunity; to surrender oneself to the principles of the Buddha in the search for perfect enlightenment. | 淵 To cast oneself into an abyss (hoping for eternal life). | 華 To cast, or offer flowers in worship. | 身 To cast away, or surrender, one's body, or oneself.

抑 Curb, repress; or. | 揚教 The third of the five periods of Buddha's teaching, as held by the Nirvāṇa sect of China 涅槃宗, during which the 維摩思益 is attributed to him. | 止 To suppress, e.g. | | 惡事 suppress evil deeds. | | 攝取 The suppression or universal reception of evil beings; pity demands the latter course.

扶 Aid, support, uphold. | 塵根 The external organs, i.e. of sight, etc., which aid the senses; 扶 is also written 浮 meaning fleeting, vacuous, these external things having an illusory existence; the real organs, or indriya, are the 正根 or 勝義根 which evolve the ideas. |律談常(敎) The teaching which supports the rules and speaks of the eternal, i.e. the 涅槃經 Nirvāṇa Sūtra. |疏 "Supporting commentary", another name for the same sūtra, because according to T'ien-t'ai it is an amplification of the Lotus Sūtra. |薩 Bodhisattva, idem 菩薩.

改 To change, correct. |宗 To change one's cult, school of thought, or religion. |悔 To repent and reform.

更 To change; a night watch; again; the more. |藥 Medicines that should be taken between dawn and the first watch, of which eight are named, v. 百一羯磨 5.

李 Plum. |園 Āmravana, the wild-plum (or mango) grove, see 菴.

束蘆 To tie reeds together in order to make them stand up, illustration of the interdependence of things and principles.

杖林 Yaṣṭivana, 洩瑟知林; the forest in which a Brahman tried to measure Buddha's height with a 16 ft. bamboo pole, but the more he measured the higher the body became; another part of the legend is that the forest grew from the bamboo which he left behind in chagrin.

杜 Stop, prevent; azalea. |口 To shut the mouth, render speechless. |嚕 Turuṣka olibanum, Indian incense, resin, gum used for incense. It is said to resemble peach resin and to grow in Aṭali. Its leaves resemble the pear's and produce pepper; it is said to flourish in the sands of Central Asia and its gum to flow out on to the sands. |多; |荼; 頭陀 q.v. Dhūta, discipline (to shake off sin, etc.). |底 Dūta, a messenger; dūtī, a female messenger. |魯婆跋吒 Dhruvapaṭu, a king of Valabhī, son-in-law of Śilāditya.

步 Pada; step, pace. |他 v. 佛 Buddha. |擲金剛 or 明王; 播般曩結使波 A form of 普賢 Samantabhadra as a vajra-king.

每 Each, every. |怛里 v. 彌勒 Maitreya. | | |末那 Maitrīmanas, of kindly mind, tr. by 慈悲 merciful.

汲 Draw water; emulate, eager; the round of reincarnations is like the |井輪 waterwheel at the well ever revolving up and down.

沐 To bathe; translit. *mu, mo*; |魄太子 is 慕魄 one of the former incarnations of Śākyamuni.

沈; 沉 To sink; heavy. |冥 Sunk in the gloom of reincarnations and ignorance. |檀 Agaru, or aguru, sandal incense. |(水)香 Aguru, the tree and incense of that name. |空 To sink into emptiness, or uselessness.

沃 Wet, wash, enrich. |焦石 (or 山) The rock, or mountain, Pātāla, on the bottom of the ocean, just above the hot purgatory, which absorbs the water and thus keeps the sea from increasing and overflowing. | |海 is the ocean which contains this rock, or mountain.

汚 Filthy, impure. Kleśa; contamination of attachment to the pleasures of sense, to heretical views, to moral and ascetic practices regarded as adequate to salvation, to the belief in the self, all which cause misery.

沒 Sunk, gone; not; translit. *m, mu, mo, mau, ma, bu, v*, etc. |交涉 No inter-relation. |劫 Moha, delusion, bewilderment, infatuation, tr. by 愚 foolishness; cf. 謨. |哩底野吠 Derived from mṛtyu, death; one of Yama's 明王 or rājas. |巴鼻 No nose to lay hold of; no lead, no bases. |度 Buddha, v. 佛. |栗度 Mṛdu, soft, pliant, weak. |栗多 Vrata, temporary chastity, or observance. |曳達利瑟致 Māyādṛṣṭi, illusion-views, intp. by 我見 egoism, the false doctrine that there is a real ego. |滋味 Tasteless, valueless, useless, e.g. the discussion of the colour of milk by blind people. |特 (or 刀) 伽羅子 v. 目(犍)連 Maudgalaputra, or Maudgalyāyana. |馱 Buddha, v. 佛.

求 To seek, beseech, pray. |不得苦 The pain which results from not receiving what one seeks, from disappointed hope, or unrewarded effort. One of the eight sorrows. |名菩薩 The Ch'iu-ming (fame-seeking) bodhisattva, v. Lotus sūtra, a name of Maitreya in a previous life. Also, Yaśaskāma, "A disciple of Varaprabhā noted for his boundless ambition and utter want of memory." Eitel. |寂 Seeking nirvāṇa, i.e. the disciple who accepts the ten commandments. |那 Guṇa, a quality, characteristic, or virtue, e.g. sound, taste, etc. |那毘地

Guṇavṛddhi, 德進, an Indian monk who came to China 492–5, tr. three works, d. 502. |那跋摩 Guṇavarman, tr. 功德鎧, a prince of Kubhā (Cashmere), who refused the throne, wandered alone, reached China, tr. ten works, two of which were lost by A.D. 730. Born in 367, he died in Nanking in A.D. 431. He taught that truth is within, not without, and that the truth (dharma) is of oneself, not of another. The centre of his work is placed in 揚州 Yang-chou. It is said that he started the order of nuns in China, v. 翻譯名義 Fan-i-ming-i. |那跋陀羅 Guṇabhadra, tr. 德賢. (1) A follower of the Mahīśāsakā in Kapiśā. (2) A Brāhmaṇa of Central India, tr. into Chinese some seventy-eight works A.D. 435–443; b. 394, d. 468.

沙 Bālukā. Sand; sands, e.g. of Ganges 恒河, implying countless; translit. ṣ, ś, ṣ. Cf. 莎.

沙劫 Kalpas countless as the sands of Ganges.

沙婆婆瑟 Ṣaḍ-varṣa; the sexennial assembly.

沙彌 Śrāmaṇera, 室羅摩拏洛迦; 室末那伊洛迦; 室羅摩尼羅 The male religious novice, who has taken vows to obey the ten commandments. The term is explained by 息惡行慈 one who ceases from evil and does works of mercy, or lives altruistically; 勤策男 a zealous man; 求寂 one who seeks rest; 求涅槃寂 one who seeks the peace of nirvāṇa. Three kinds are recognized according to age, i.e. 7 to 13 years old, old enough to 驅烏 "drive away crows"; 14 to 19, called 應法 able to respond to or follow the doctrine; 20 to 70. |(|)尼 Śrāmaṇerikā 室羅摩拏理迦. A female religious novice who has taken a vow to obey the ten commandments, i.e. 勤策女 a zealous woman, devoted. ||尼戒 The ten commandments taken by the śrāmaṇerikā: not to kill living beings, not to steal, not to lie or speak evil, not to have sexual intercourse, not to use perfumes or decorate oneself with flowers, not to occupy high beds, not to sing or dance, not to possess wealth, not to eat out of regulation hours, not to drink wine. ||戒 The ten commandments of the śrāmaṇēra; v. 十戒.

沙心 Mind like sand in its countless functionings.

沙摩帝 Saṁmatīya, 正量部 one of the eighteen Hīnayāna sects.

沙波訶 Svāha, hail! 娑訶 v. 蘇.

沙界 Worlds as numerous as the sands of Ganges.

沙羅 Sāla, or Śāla, 娑羅 the Sāl or Śal tree; the teak tree; the Shorea (or Valeria) Robusta; a tree in general. ||王 Sālarāja, a title of the Buddha. ||那 (or 拏); 娑刺拏王 ? Śāraṇa (said to be a son of King Udayana) who became a monk. ||雙樹 The twin trees in the grove 娑羅林 in which Śākyamuni entered nirvāṇa.

沙落迦 "Charaka, a monastery in Kapiśa." Eitel.

沙訶 Sahā, 娑訶; 索訶 the world around us, the present world. Also Svāha, see above.

沙那利迦 Ṣāṇnagarika, one of the eighteen Hīnayāna sects.

沙門 Śramaṇa. 桑門; 娑門; 喪門; 沙門那; 舍羅磨拏; 沙迦懣曩; 室摩那拏 (1) Ascetics of all kinds; "the Sarmanai, or Samanaioi, or Germanai of the Greeks, perhaps identical also with the Tungusian Saman or Shaman." Eitel. (2) Buddhist monks "who 'have left their families and quitted the passions', the Semnoi of the Greeks". Eitel. Explained by 功勞 toilful achievement, 勤息 diligent quieting (of the mind and the passions), 淨志 purity of mind, 貧道 poverty. "He must keep well the Truth, guard well every uprising (of desire), be uncontaminated by outward attractions, be merciful to all and impure to none, be not elated to joy nor harrowed by distress, and able to bear whatever may come." The Sanskrit root is śram, to make effort; exert oneself, do austerities. ||果 The fruit, or rebirth, resulting from the practices of the śramaṇa. ||統 The national superintendent or archbishop over the Order appointed under the Wei dynasty.

牢 A gaol, fold, pen; secure, firm. |關 A firm barrier, a place shut tight, type of the deluded mind. |籠 Pen, pit, or fold (for animals) and cage (for birds).

狂 Deranged, mad, wild. |亂往生 Saved out of terror into the next life; however distressed by thoughts of hell as the result of past evil life, ten repetitions, or even one, of the name of Amitābha ensures entry into his Paradise. |慧 Foolish wisdom; clever but without calm meditation. |狗

A mad dog. | 華 Muscæ volitantes, dancing flowers before the eyes; | 象 a mad elephant, such is the deluded mind.

男 Male. | 女 Male and female. | 根 The male organ.

矣 A particle of finality, pronounced *i*, used in | 栗馱 Hṛd, the heart; the essence of a thing.

禿 Bald. | 人; | 居士; | 奴 A monk; a nun, sometimes used as a term of abuse.

秀能 The two patriarchs 神秀 Shên-hsiu and 慧能 Hui-nêng, q.v.

私 Private, secret, selfish, illicit. | 印 A monk's private seal, which should resemble a skull as reminder of the brevity of life. | 婆吒 Vasiṣṭha, v. 婆. | 婆婆 Svabhāva, "own state, essential or inherent property, innate or peculiar disposition, natural state or constitution nature" (M. W.), intp. as 自體體 or 自性性. | 多; | 陀; 悉陀; 徙多; 枲多 Sītā. Described as the "cold" river; one of the four great rivers flowing from the Anavatapta or Anavadata Lake 阿耨達池 in Tibet. One account makes it "an eastern outflux" which subsequently becomes the Yellow River. It is also said to issue from the west. Again, "the Ganges flows eastward, the Indus south, Vatsch (Oxus) west, Sītā north." Vatsch = Vākṣu. "According to Hiuentsang, however, it is the northern outflux of the Sirikol [Sarikkol] Lake (Lat. 38° 20′ N., Long. 74° E.) now called Yarkand daria, which flows into Lake Lop, thence underneath the desert of Gobi, and reappears as the source of the Hoangho." Eitel. According to Richard, the Hwangho "rises a little above two neighbouring lakes of Khchara (Charing-nor) and Khnora (Oring-nor). Both are connected by a channel and are situated at an elevation of 14,000 feet. It may perhaps be at first confounded with Djaghing-gol, a river 110 miles long, which flows from the south and empties into the channel joining the two lakes".

究 To go to the bottom of; inquire into; end, fundamental, supreme. v. 鳩 for | 槃荼 Kumbhāṇḍa and | 磨羅 Kumāra; v. 拘尸那 for | 施 Kuśināgra. | 究吒 Kukkuṭa, a cock, or fowl. | 竟 Examine exhaustively; utmost, final, at the end, a tr. of *uttara*, upper, superior, hence 至極 ultimate, supreme. | 竟佛 The fundamental, ultimate, or supreme Buddha, who has complete comprehension of truth; Buddha in his supreme reality. | 竟位 The supreme class or stage, i.e. that of Buddhahood. The Mahāyāna groups the various stages in the attainment of Buddhahood into five, of which this is the highest. | 竟即 The stage of complete comprehension of truth, being the sixth stage of the T'ien-t'ai School, v. 六即. | 竟樂 The supreme joy, i.e. nirvāṇa. | 竟法身 The supreme Dharmakāya, the highest conception of Buddha as the absolute. | 竟覺 Supreme enlightenment, that of Buddha; one of the four kinds of enlightenment in the 起信論 Awakening of Faith.

肘 Hasta, forearm, the 16,000th part of a yōjana; it varies from 1 ft. 4 in. to 1 ft. 8 in. in length.

良 Good, virtuous, beneficial. | 日; 吉日 A good, or auspicious, day. | 忍 Ryōnin, founder of the Japanese 融通念佛 school. | 賁 Liang-pên, the T'ang monk who assisted Amogha in the translation of the 仁王經 Jên Wang Ching. | 福田 The field of blessedness, cultivated by offerings to Buddha, the Law, and the Order.

虬宮 The dragon palace in which Nāgārjuna recited the 華嚴經 Hua-yen ching.

見 Darśana, 捺喇捨曩; also Dṛṣṭi; seeing, discerning, judgment, views, opinions; it is thinking, reasoning, discriminating, selecting truth, including the whole process of deducing conclusions from premises. It is commonly used in the sense of wrong or heterodox views or theories, i.e. 邪見 or 有見, especially such as viewing the seeming as real and the ego as real. There are groups of two, four, five, seven, ten, and sixty-two kinds of 見.

見佛 Beholding Buddha; to see Buddha. Hīnayāna sees only the nirmāṇakāya or body of incarnation, Mahāyāna sees the spiritual body, or body in bliss, the saṁbhogakāya.

見修 Views and practice; heterodoxy; cf. | 思.

見地 The stage of insight, or discernment of reality, the fourth of the ten stages of progress toward Buddhahood, agreeing with the 預流果 of Hīnayāna.

見大 Visibility (or perceptibility) as one of the seven elements of the universe.

見性 To behold the Buddha-nature within oneself, a common saying of the Ch'an (Zen) or Intuitive School.

見思 Views and thoughts, in general 見惑思惑 illusory or misleading views and thoughts; 見 refers partly to the visible world, but also to views derived therefrom, e.g. the ego, with the consequent illusion; 思 to the mental and moral world also with its illusion. The 三惑 three delusions which hinder the 三諦 three axioms are | |, 塵沙, and 無明 q.v. Hīnayāna numbers 88 kinds and the Mahāyāna 112 of 見惑, of 思惑 10 and 16 respectively.

見愛 Views and desires, e.g. the illusion that the ego is a reality and the consequent desires and passions; the two are the root of all suffering.

見慧 The wisdom of right views, arising from dhyāna meditation.

見正 Seeing correctly; said to be the name of a disciple of the Buddha who doubted a future life, to whom the Buddha is said to have delivered the contents of the | | 經.

見毒 The poison of wrong views.

見漏 The illusion of viewing the seeming as real, v. 四漏.

見濁 Dṛṣṭi-kaṣāya. Corruption of doctrinal views, one of the five final corruptions.

見王齋 The service on the third day when the deceased goes to see King Yama.

見相 The state or condition of visibility, which according to the 起信論 Awakening of Faith arises from motion, hence is also called 轉相.

見眞 To behold truth, or ultimate reality.

見結 The bond of heterodox views, which fastens the individual to the chain of transmigration, one of the nine attachments; v. | 縛.

見網 The net of heterodox views, or doctrines.

見縛 The bond of the illusion of heterodox opinions, i.e. of mistaking the seeming for the real, which binds men and robs them of freedom; v. | 結.

見取 Clinging to heterodox views, one of the four 取; or as | | 見, one of the 五見 q.v. | | 使 The trials of delusion and suffering from holding to heterodox doctrines; one of the ten sufferings or messengers. | | 見 Dṛṣṭiparāmarśa; to hold heterodox doctrines and be obsessed with the sense of the self, v. 五見.

見聞 Seeing and hearing, i.e. beholding Buddha with the eyes and hearing his truth with the ears.

見處 The state of wrong views, i.e. the state of transmigration, because wrong views give rise to it, or maintain it.

見諦 The realization of correct views, i.e. the Hīnayāna stage of one who has entered the stream of holy living; the Mahāyāna stage after the first Bodhisattva stage.

見諍 Wrangling on behalf of heterodox views; striving to prove them.

見道 The way or stage of beholding the truth (of no reincarnation), i.e. that of the śrāvaka and the first stage of the Bodhisattva. The second stage is 修道 cultivating the truth; the third 無學道 completely comprehending the truth without further study.

見障 The obstruction of heterodox views to enlightenment.

見非見 The visible and invisible; phenomenal and noumenal.

見顚倒 To see things upside down; to regard illusion as reality.

角 Viṣāṇa; a horn, a trumpet; also a corner, an angle; to contend. | 馱 Perverted doctrines and wrong thoughts, which weigh down a monk as a pack on an animal.

言 Words, speech; to speak. | 依 Word-dependence, i.e. that which can be expressed in words, the phenomenal, or describable. | 句 Sentences. | 詮 Words as explaining meaning; explanation; 離 | | is beyond explanation. | 敎 The teaching of Buddha as embodied in words. | 行 Words and deeds. | 語; | 說 Words, speech, verbal expression. | 陳 Set out in words, i.e. a syllogism.

谷 A gully. | 呱呱 Ku-wa-wa, the cry of a ghost, made in proof of its existence to one who had written a treatise on the non-existence of 鬼 ghosts.

豆 Māṣa, 摩沙; 磨灑 Legumes, beans, peas, lentils, etc. 豆伽藍 Masūra Saṅghārāma, Lentil Monastery, "an ancient vihāra about 200 li south-east of Moṅgali." Eitel. | 佉 Duḥkha, trouble, suffering, pain, defined by 逼惱 harassed, distressed. The first of the four dogmas, or "Noble Truths" 四諦 is that all life is involved, through impermanence, in distress. There are many kinds of 苦 q.v.

貝 Śaṅkha; a shell, cowry, conch; valuables, riches; a large trumpet sounded to call the assembly together; | 鐘 conch and bell. | 多; | 多羅 (葉); | 葉 Pattra; palm leaves from the *Borassus flabelliformis*, used for writing material. | 文 The scriptures written on such leaves. | 支迦 Pratyeka, v. 辟 | |. | 牒 Pattra tablets, sūtras written on them.

赤 Kaṣāya 袈沙野, red, hot; south; naked. | 梅檀 A tree used for incense. | 白二渧 The "drops" of red and white, i.e. female and male sperm which unite in conception. | 眼 The red-eye, i.e. a turtle. | 肉 (團) The red flesh (lump), the heart. | 鄂衍那 Chagayana. "An ancient province and city of Tukhāra, the present Chaganian in Lat. 38° 21 N., Long. 69° 21 E." Eitel. | 髭毘婆沙 The red-moustached (or bearded) Vibhāṣā, a name for 佛陀耶舍 Buddhayaśas.

赤鬼 The red demons of purgatory, one with the head of a bull, another with that of a horse, etc.

走 To walk, go. | 海 To travel by sea.

足 Foot, leg; enough, full. | 目 "Eyes in his feet," name of Akṣapāda Gotama, to whom is ascribed the beginning of logic; his work is seen "in five books of aphorisms on the Nyāya." Keith.

身 Kāya; tanu; deha. The body; the self. | 入 The sense of touch, one of the 六入 six senses.

身三口四意三 The three commandments dealing with the body, prohibiting taking of life, theft, unchastity; the four dealing with the mouth, against lying, exaggeration, abuse, and ambiguous talk; the three belonging to the mind, covetousness, malice, and unbelief.

身光 The glory shining from the person of a Buddha, or Bodhisattva; a halo.

身命 Body and life; bodily life.

身器 The body as a utensil, i.e. containing all the twelve parts, skin, flesh, blood, hair, etc.

身土 Body and environment. The body is the direct fruit of the previous life; the environment is the indirect fruit of the previous life.

身城 The body as the citadel of the mind.

身如意通 Ṛddhividhi-jñāna. Also 身通, 身足通; the power to transfer oneself to various regions at will, also to change the body at will.

身座 The body as the throne of Buddha.

身心 Body and mind, the direct fruit of the previous life. The body is rūpa, the first skandha; mind embraces the other four, consciousness, perception, action, and knowledge; v. 五蘊.

身根 Kāyendriya; the organ of touch, one of the six senses.

身業 The karma operating in the body; the body as representing the fruit of action in previous existence. One of the three karmas, the other two referring to speech and thought.

身毒 Sindhu, Scinde, v. 印度.

身毛上靡相 The hairs on Buddha's body curled upwards, one of the thirty-two marks.

身燈 The body as a lamp, burnt in offering to a Buddha, e.g. the Medicine King in the Lotus sūtra.

身田 The body regarded as a field which produces good and evil fruit in future existence.

身相 Bodily form; the body.

身蓮 The lotus in the body, i.e. the heart, or eight-leaved lotus in all beings; it represents also the Garbhadhātu, which is the matrix of the material world out of which all beings come.

身見 Satkāyadṛṣṭi; the illusion that the body, or self, is real and not simply a compound of the five skandhas; one of the five wrong views 五見.

身識 Kāya-vijñāna. Cognition of the objects of touch, one of the five forms of cognition; v. 五根.

身車 The body as the vehicle which, according with previous karma, carries one into the paths of transmigration.

身通 The power to transfer the body through space at will, one of the marks of the Buddha.

身雲 The numberless bodies of Buddhas, hovering like clouds over men; the numberless forms which the Buddhas take to protect and save men, resembling clouds; the numberless saints compared to clouds.

車 A cart, wheeled conveyance. | 也 Chāyā, 陰 shade, shadow. | 匿; 闡鐸迦 Chandaka, the driver of Śākyamuni when he left his home. | 帝 The name of a cave, said to be Śataparṇa, or Saptaparṇaguhā. | 軸 The hub of a cart; applied to large drops (of rain). | 鉢羅婆 Name of a spirit.

辛頭 The Indus; Sindh; idem 信度. | | 波羅香 Sindhupāra (? Sindhuvāra), incense or perfume, from a fragrant plant said to grow on the banks (pāra) of the Indus (Sindhu).

辰 Hour; time; the celestial bodies. | 那 Jina, victorious, applied to a Buddha, a saint, etc.; forms part of the names of | | 呾邏多 Jinatrāta; | | 弗多羅 Jinaputra; | | 飯荼 Jinabandhu; three Indian monks in China, the first and last during the seventh century.

巡 Wander about, patrol, inspect. | 堂 To patrol, or circumambulate the hall. | 寮 To inspect all the buildings of a monastery. | 案 To patrol and receive any complaints. | 更 To patrol as night-watchman, or | 火 as guarding against fire. | 錫 To walk about with a metal staff, i.e. to teach.

邠 The ancient state of Pin, south-west Shensi; translit. *p*, e.g. in Pūrṇamaitrāyaṇīputra | 祁文陀弗, Anāthapiṇḍada 阿那 | 抵, etc.

邪 Deflected, erroneous, heterodox, depraved; the opposite of 正; also erroneously used for 耶.

邪倒見 Heterodoxy; perverted views or opinions.

邪命(食) Heterodox or improper ways of obtaining a living on the part of a monk, e.g. by doing work with his hands, by astrology, his wits, flattery, magic, etc. Begging, or seeking alms, was the orthodox way of obtaining a living. | | 說法 The heterodox way of preaching or teaching, for the purpose of making a living.

邪執 Heterodox tenets and attachment to them.

邪婬 Adultery.

邪山 A mountain of error or heterodox ideas; such ideas as great as a mountain.

邪思惟 Heterodox reflection, or thought.

邪性定(聚) The accumulation (of suffering) to be endured in purgatory by one of heterodox nature; one of the three accumulations 三聚.

邪慢 Mithyāmāna; perverse or evil pride, doing evil for self-advancement; to hold to heterodox views and not to reverence the Triratna.

邪扇 Heterodox fanning, i.e. to influence people by false doctrines.

邪旬 Jhāpita, 旬 being erroneously used to represent the syllable *pi*, v. 荼.

邪法 Heterodoxy, false doctrines or methods.

邪私 Depraved and selfish desires, lust.

邪網 The net of heterodoxy, or falsity.

邪聚 The accumulation of misery produced by false views, one of the 三聚.

邪行 Erroneous ways, the ninety-six heretical ways; the disciplines of non-Buddhist sects. | | 眞如 The phenomenal bhūtatathatā, from which arises the accumulation of misery.

邪見 Heterodox views, not recognizing the doctrine of moral karma, one of the five heterodox opinions and ten evils 五見十惡. | | 乘 The Hīnayāna, the Vehicle of perverted views. | | 稠林 The thickets of heterodoxy.

邪道 Heterodox ways, or doctrines.

邪雲 Clouds of falsity or heterodoxy, which cover over the Buddha-nature in the heart.

邪魔 Evil demons and spirits, māras. | | 外道 Māras and heretics.

那 Where? How? What? That. Translit. *na, ne, no, nya*; cf. 娜, 拏, 曩.

那他 Nada, a river.

那伽 Nāga. Snake, dragon, elephant. It is tr. by 龍 dragon and by 象 elephant. (1) As dragon it represents the chief of the scaly reptiles; it can disappear or be manifest, increase or decrease, lengthen or shrink; in spring it mounts in the sky and in winter enters the earth. The dragon is of many kinds. Dragons are regarded as beneficent, bringing the rains and guarding the heavens (again Draco); they control rivers and lakes, and hibernate in the deep. Nāga and Mahānāga are titles of a Buddha, (also of those freed from reincarnation) because of his powers, or because like the dragon he soars above earthly desires and ties. One of his former reincarnations was a powerful poisonous dragon which, out of pity, permitted itself to be skinned alive and its flesh eaten by worms. (2) A race of serpent-worshippers. | | 閼剌 (or 曷) 樹那 Nāgārjuna, 龍樹 the dragon-arjuna tree, or Nāgakrośana, intp. probably wrongly as 龍猛 dragon-fierce. One of the "four suns" and reputed founder of Mahāyāna (but see 阿 for Aśvaghoṣa), native of South India, the fourteenth patriarch; he is said to have cut off his head as an offering. "He probably flourished in the latter half of the second century A.D." Eliot. v. 龍樹. He founded the Mādhyamika or 中 School, generally considered as advocating doctrines of negation or nihilism, but his aim seems to have been a reality beyond the limitations of positive and negative, the identification of contraries in a higher synthesis, e.g. birth and death, existence and non-existence, eternal and non-eternal; v. 中論.

那先 Nāgasena 那伽犀那. The instructor of the king in the Milindapañha, v. | | (比丘) 經.

那利(薊)羅 Nārikela, Nārikera, 捺唎羅吉唎 The coco-nut. Nārikeladvīpa is described as "an island several thousand li south of Ceylon, inhabited by dwarfs 3 feet high, who have human bodies with beaks like birds, and live upon coco-nuts". Eitel.

那吒 Naṭa, said to be the eldest son of Vaiśravaṇa, and represented with three faces, eight arms, a powerful demon-king.

那含; 那金含 Anāgāmin, v. 阿.

那婆(摩利) Nava; Navamālikā. Variegated or mixed flowers.

那律 Aniruddha, v. 阿.

那提 Nadī, river, torrent; name of Puṇyopāya, 布如 | |, 布焉伐耶 a noted monk of Central India. | | 迦葉; 捺地迦葉波 Nadīkāśyapa, brother of Mahākāśyapa, to become Samantaprabhāsa Buddha.

那揭(羅喝羅) Nagara; Nagarahāra. 曩哦囉賀囉 "An ancient kingdom and city on the southern bank of the Cabool River about 30 miles west of Jellalabad (Lat. 34° 28 N., Long. 70° 30 E.). The Nagara of Ptolemy." Eitel.

那摩 Nāman 娜 (or 曇) 麽. A name 名.

那爛陁 Nālandā, a famous monastery 7 miles north of Rājagṛha, built by the king Śakrāditya. Nālandā is intp. as 施無厭 "Unwearying benefactor", a title attributed to the Nāga which dwelt in the lake Āmra there. The village is identified in Eitel as Baragong, i.e. Vihāragrāma. For Nālandā excavations see Archæological Survey Reports, and cf. Hsüan-tsang's account.

那由他 Nayuta, 那庾 (or 由) 多; 那術 (or 述) a numeral, 100,000, or one million, or ten million.

那羅 Naṭa; cf. ｜吒; a dancer or actor 伎戲; or perhaps Narya, manly, strong, one definition being 力. ｜｜延(那); ｜｜野拏 Nārāyaṇa, "son of Nara or the original man, patronymic of the personified Purusha or first living being, author of the Purusha hymn," M. W. He is also identified with Brahmā, Viṣṇu, or Kṛṣṇa; intp. by 人生本 the originator of human life; 堅固 firm and stable; 力士 or 天界力士 hero of divine power; and 金剛 vajra; the term is used adjectivally with the meaning of manly and strong. Nārāyaṇa is represented with three faces, of greenish-yellow colour, right hand with a wheel, riding a garuḍa-bird. ｜｜延天 Nārāyaṇa-deva, idem Nārāyaṇa. His ｜｜｜｜后 śakti or female energy is shown in the Garbhadhātu group. ｜｜摩那 (or 納) Naramānava, a young Brahman, a descendant of Manu. ｜｜那里 Nara-nārī, union of the male and female natures. ｜｜陀? Narādhāra, a flower, tr. 人持花 carried about for its scent.

那耶 Naya; leading, conduct, politic, prudent, method; intp. by 正理 right principle; 乘 conveyance, i.e. mode of progress; and 道 way, or method. ｜｜修摩 Nāya is a name of Jñātṛ, v. 尼 Nirgrantha.

那落迦 Naraka, "hell, the place of torment, . . . the lower regions" (M. W.), intp. by 地獄 q.v.

那謨 Namaḥ, Namo, idem 南無 q.v.

那辣遮 Nāraca, an arrow, intp. 錐 a pointed implement.

那連(提黎)耶舍 Narendrayaśas, a monk of Udyāna, north-west India; sixth century A.D.; tr. the Candra-garbha, Sūrya-garbha, and other sūtras.

那阿賴耶曼荼羅 Nālaya-maṇḍala, the non-ālaya maṇḍala, or the 道場 bodhi-site or seat, which is 無依處 without fixed place, independent of place, and entirely pure.

那鞞 Nābhi; navel, nave of a wheel.

那麻 Namaḥ, Namo, idem 南無.

里 A village, neighbourhood, third of an English mile; translit. *r* and *ṛ*; perhaps also for *l* and *lṛ*.

防 Ward off, protect, beware; to counter. ｜難 To counter, or solve difficulties, especially difficult questions. ｜羅 (idem 邏) Warders or patrols in Hades. ｜那 Vāna, weaving, sewing; tr. as a tailoress.

8. EIGHT STROKES

乳 Milk, which in its five forms illustrates the T'ien-t'ai 五時教 five periods of the Buddha's teaching. ｜味 The flavour of fresh milk, to which the Buddha's teaching in the 華嚴經 Hua-yen ching is compared. ｜木 Resinous wood (for homa, or fire sacrifice). ｜水眼 The eye able to distinguish milk from water; as the goose drinks the milk and rejects the water, so the student should distinguish orthodox from heterodox teaching. ｜經 T'ien-t'ai compares the Avataṁsaka-sūtra 華嚴經 to milk, from which come all its other products. ｜香 Kunduruka, *Boswellia thurifera*, both the plant and its resin.

事 Artha 曰迦他 (迦 being an error for 遏); affair, concern, matter; action, practice; phenomena; to serve. It is "practice" or the thing, affair, matter, in contrast with 理 theory, or the underlying principle. ｜度 Salvation by observing the five commandments, the ten good deeds, etc.

事教 Teaching dealing with phenomena. The characterization by T'ien-t'ai of the Tripiṭaka or Hīnayāna teaching as 界內｜｜ within the three realms of desire, form, and formlessness; and the 別教 "different teaching" as 界外｜｜ outside or superior to those realms; the one dealt with the activities of time and sense, the other transcended these but was still involved in the transient; the 別教 was initial Mahāyāna incompletely developed.

事法界 The phenomenal world, phenomenal existence. v. 四法界. ｜｜｜身 The Buddha-nature in practice, cf. 理法身, which is the Buddha-nature in principle, or essence, or the truth itself.

事火 Phenomenal fire, v. 性火 fire as an element; also, fire-worship.

事理 Practice and theory; phenomenon and noumenon, activity and principle, or the absolute; phenomena ever change, the underlying principle, being absolute, neither changes nor acts, it is the 眞如 q.v. also v. 理. For | | (無礙) 法界 v. 四法界. | | 三千 The three thousand phenomenal activities and three thousand principles, a term of the T'ien-t'ai School. | | 五法 v. 五法.

事相 Phenomenon, affair, practice. The practices of the esoterics are called | | 部 as contrasted with their open teaching called 敎相部. | | 禪師 A mystic, or monk in meditation, yet busy with affairs: an epithet of reproach.

事論 Discussion of phenomena in contrast with 理論.

事造 Phenomenal activities. According to T'ien-t'ai there are 3,000 underlying factors or principles 理具 giving rise to the 3,000 phenomenal activities.

事迹 Traces of the deeds or life of an individual; biography.

事障 Phenomenal hindrances to entry into nirvāṇa, such as desire, etc.; 理 | are noumenal hindrances, such as false doctrine, etc.

亟 Haste, urgency. | 縛屣 Leather sandals.

亞 Second, inferior; used in translit. as 阿 "a", e.g. | 畧 Ārya.

享 Offer up; enjoy. | 堂 The hall of offerings, an ancestral hall.

侍 Attend; wait on; attendant. | 者 An attendant, e.g. as Ānanda was to the Buddha; assistants in general, e.g. the incense-assistant in a temple.

使 To send; cause; a messenger; a pursuer, molester, lictor, disturber, troubler, intp. as 煩惱 kleśa, affliction, distress, worldly cares, vexations, and as consequent reincarnation. There are categories of 10, 16, 98, 112, and 128 such troublers, e.g. desire, hate, stupor, pride, doubt, erroneous views, etc., leading to painful results in future rebirths, for they are karma-messengers executing its purpose. Also 金剛童子 q.v.

供 Pūjā; to offer (in worship), to honour; also to supply; evidence. | 佛 To offer to Buddha. | 具; | 物 Offerings, i.e. flowers, unguents; water, incense, food, light. | 天; 天 | The devas who serve Indra. | 奉 To offer; the monk who serves at the great altar. | 帳 The T'ang dynasty register, or census of monks and nuns, supplied to the government every three years. | | 雲 The cloud of Bodhisattvas who serve the Tathāgata. | 養 To make offerings of whatever nourishes, e.g. food, goods, incense, lamps, scriptures, the doctrine, etc., any offering for body or mind.

來 Āgama; āgam-; āgata. Come, the coming, future. | 世 Future world, or rebirth. | 應 To come in response to an invitation; to answer prayer (by a miracle). | 果 The fruit or condition of the next rebirth, regarded as the result of the present. | 生 Future rebirth; the future life. | 迎 The coming of Buddhas to meet the dying believer and bid welcome to the Pure Land; the three special welcomers are Amitābha, Avalokiteśvara, and Mahāsthāmaprāpta.

依 To depend, rely on; dependent, conditioned; accord with. | 他 Dependent on or trusting to someone or something else; trusting on another, not on self or "works". | | (起) 性 Not having an independent nature, not a nature of its own, but constituted of elements. | | 自性 One of the 三性 dependent on constructive elements and without a nature of its own. | | 心 The mind in a dependent state, that of the Buddha in incarnation. | | 十喩 The unreality of dependent or conditioned things, e.g. the body, or self, illustrated in ten comparisons: foam, bubble, flame, plantain, illusion, dream, shadow, echo, cloud, lightning; v. 維摩詰經 2. | 圓 Dependent and perfect, i.e. the dependent or conditioned nature, and the perfect nature of the unconditioned bhūtatathatā. | 地 The ground on which one relies; the body, on which sight, hearing, etc., depend; the degree of samādhi attained; cf. | 身. | 報 v. | 正. | 怙 To rely on, depend on. | 果 idem | 報 v. | 正. | 止 To depend and rest upon. | 止甚深 The profundity on which all things depend, i.e. the bhūtatathatā; also the Buddha. | 止師, | 止阿闍梨 The ācārya, or master of a junior monk. | 正 The two forms of karma resulting from one's past; 正報 being the resultant person, 依報 being the dependent condition or environment, e.g. country, family, possessions, etc. | 法不依人 To rely upon the dharma, or truth itself, and not upon (the false interpretations of) men. | 版; 禪版 A board to lean against when in meditation. | 言眞如 The bhūtatathatā in its expressible form, as distinguished from it as 離言 inexpressible. | 身 The body on which one depends, or on which its parts depend, cf. | 他. | 通 The magical powers which depend upon drugs, spells, etc., v. 五 通.

兩 Two, a couple, both; an ounce, or tael. | 卷 經 The two-chüan sūtra, i.e. the 佛 說 無 量 壽 經. | 垢 (如 如) The contaminated and uncontaminated Bhūtatathatā, or Buddha-nature, v. 止 觀 2 and 起 信 論 Awakening of Faith. | 權 The two temporary vehicles, Śrāvaka and Pratyeka-buddha, as contrasted with the 實 complete Bodhisattva doctrine of Mahāyāna. | 河 The "two rivers", Nairañjanā, v. 尼, where Buddha attained enlightenment, and Hiraṇyavatī, see 尸, where he entered Nirvāṇa. | 翅 The two wings of 定 and 慧 meditation and wisdom. | 肩 神 The two recording spirits, one at each shoulder, v. 同 名 and 同 坐 神. | 界 v. | 部. | 舌 Double tongue. One of the ten forms of evil conduct 十 惡 業. | 財 The two talents, or rewards from previous incarnations, 內 inner, i.e. bodily or personal conditions, and 外 external, i.e. wealth or poverty, etc. | 足 尊 The most honoured among men and devas (lit. among two-footed beings), a title of the Buddha. The two feet are compared to the commandments and meditation, blessing and wisdom, relative and absolute teaching (i.e. Hīnayāna and Mahāyāna), meditation and action. | 部; | 界 Two sections, or classes. | | 曼 荼 羅 Maṇḍala of the two sections, i.e. dual powers of the two Japanese groups symbolizing the Vajradhātu and Garbhadhātu, v. 金 剛 界 and 胎 藏 界. | 鼠 The two rats (or black and white mice), night and day.

典 Canon, rule; allusion; to take charge of; mortgage. | 客 (or 賓); 知 客 The one who takes charge of visitors in a monastery. | 座 The verger who indicates the order of sitting, etc. | 攬 Summary of the essentials of a sūtra, or canonical book. 辭 | A dictionary, phrase-book.

具 All; complete; to present; implements; translit. *gh*. | (or 瞿) 史 羅 or 劬 師 羅 Ghoṣira, a wealthy householder of Kauśāmbī, who gave Śākyamuni the Ghoṣiravana park and vihāra. | 壽 ? Āyuṣmant. Having long life, a term by which a monk, a pupil, or a youth may be addressed. | 戒 idem | 足 戒. | 戒 方 便 The "expedient" method of giving the whole rules by stages. | 戒 地 The second of the bodhisattva ten stages in which all the rules are kept. | 支 灌 頂 One of the three abhiṣeka or baptisms of the 大 日 經. A ceremonial sprinkling of the head of a monarch at his investiture with water from the seas and rivers (in his domain). It is a mode also employed in the investiture of certain high officials of Buddhism. | 縛 Completely bound, all men are in bondage to illusion. | 說 To discuss completely, state fully. | 譚 Gautama, v. 瞿. | 足 All, complete. | | 戒 The complete rules or commandments—250 for the monk, 500 (actually 348) for the nun. | | 德 本 願 The forty-fourth of Amitābha's forty-eight vows, that all universally should acquire his virtue.

函 A box, receptacle; to enfold; a letter. | 蓋 相 應 Agreeing like a box and lid.

刻 Cut, carve, engrave; oppress; a quarter of an hour, instant. | 藏 To engrave the canon.

到 Arrive, reach, to. | 彼 岸 Pāramitā, cf. 波; to reach the other shore, i.e. nirvāṇa. | 頭 At the end, when the end is reached.

制 Restrain, govern; regulations; mourning. | 多; | (or 質) 底; | 體 Caitya, a tumulus, mausoleum, monastery, temple, spire, flagstaff on a pagoda, sacred place or thing, idem 支 提 (or 帝), cf. 剎. | 多 山 部 Jetavanīyāḥ, a Hīnayāna sect. | 底 畔 睇 (or 畔 彈 那) Caitya-vandana, to pay reverence to, or worship a stūpa, image, etc. | 怛 羅 Caitra, the spring month in which the full moon is in this constellation, i.e. Virgo or 角; M. W. gives it as March–April, in China it is the first month of spring from the 16th of the first moon to the 15th of the second. Also idem | 多 Caitya. | 戒, | 教 The restraints, or rules, i.e. of the Vinaya. | 門 The way or method of discipline, contrasted with the 化 門, i.e. of teaching, both methods used by the Buddha, hence called 化 制 二 門.

剎 Ch'a; translit. *kṣ*, | 土; 乞 叉; 乞 灑 kṣetra, land, fields, country, place; also a universe consisting of three thousand large chiliocosms; also, a spire, or flagstaff on a pagoda, a monastery, but this interprets caitya, cf. 制. Other forms are | (or 制 or 差) 多 羅; 紇 差 怛 羅. | 塵 Lands, countless as the dust. | (帝) 利; | 怛 利 耶 Kṣatriya. The second, or warrior and ruling caste; Chinese render it as 田 主 landowners and 王 種 royal caste; the caste from which the Buddha came forth and therefore from which all Buddhas (如 來) spring. | 摩 Kṣema, a residence, dwelling, abcde, land, property; idem 剎 and | 竿. | 海 Land and sea. | 竿 Yaṣṭi. The flagpole of a monastery, surmounted by a gilt ball or pearl, symbolical of Buddhism; inferentially a monastery with its land. Also | 柱, 金 (or 表) 剎. | 那 Kṣaṇa. An indefinite space of time, a moment, an instant; the shortest measure of time, as kalpa is the longest; it is defined as 一 念 a thought; but according to another definition 60 kṣaṇa equal one finger-snap, 90 a thought 念, 4,500 a minute; there are other definitions. In each kṣaṇa 900 persons are born and die. | | 三 世 The moments past, present, future. | | 無 常 Not a moment is permanent, but passes through the stages of birth, stay, change, death. | | 生 滅 All things are in continuous flow, born and destroyed every instant.

初 To cut cloth for clothes; beginning, first. | 夜 The first of the three divisions of the night. | 位 The initial stage on the road to enlightenment. | 住 The first of the ten stages, or resting-places, of the bodhisattva. 住 is the resting-place or stage for a particular course of development; 地 is the position or rank attained by the spiritual characteristics achieved in this place. | 僧 祇 The first of the three asaṁkhyeya or incalculable kalpas. | 刹 那 識 The initial kṣaṇa, initial consciousness, i.e. the eighth or ālaya-vijñāna, from which arises consciousness. | 地 The first of the 十 地 ten bodhisattva stages to perfect enlightenment and nirvāṇa. | 心 The initial resolve or mind of the novice. | 日 分 The first of the three divisions of the day, beginning, middle, end | 中 後. | 更 The first watch of the night. | 時 敎 A term of the 法 相 宗 Dharmalakṣaṇa school, the first of the three periods of the Buddha's teaching, in which he overcame the ideas of heterodox teachers that the ego is real, and preached the four noble truths and the five skandhas, etc. | 果 The initial fruit, or achievement, the stage of Srota-āpanna, illusion being discarded and the stream of enlightenment entered. | | 向 is the aiming at this. The other stages of Hīnayāna are Sakṛdāgāmin, Anāgāmin, and Arhat. | 歡 喜 地 The first of the ten stages toward Buddhahood, that of joy. | 發 心 The initial determination to seek enlightenment; about which the 晉 Chin dynasty Hua-yen Ching says: | | | 時 便 成 正 覺 at this very moment the novice enters into the status of perfect enlightenment; but other schools dispute the point. | 禪 天 The first of the four dhyāna heavens, corresponding to the first stage of dhyāna meditation. | 禪 梵 天 Devas in the realms of form, who have purged themselves from all sexuality. | 禪 定 The first dhyāna, the first degree of dhyāna-meditation, which produces rebirth in the first dhyāna heaven. | 能 變 The initiator of change, or mutation, i.e. the ālaya-vijñāna, so called because the other vijñānas are derived from it.

卓 Lofty, tall, erect. | 錫 Tall, or erect staves, i.e. their place, a monastery.

卑 Low, inferior; translit. *p, pi, v, vy, m.* | (下) 慢 The pride of regarding self as little inferior to those who far surpass one; one of the 七 慢. | 先 匿 Prasenajit, v. 波. | 帝 利 Pitṛ, a kind of hungry demon. | 鉢 羅 Pippala, the bodhidruma, v. 菩. | 摩 羅 叉 Vimalākṣa, the pure-eyed, described as of Kabul, expositor of the 十 誦 律, teacher of Kumārajīva at Karashahr; came to China A.D. 406, tr. two works. | 栗 蹉; 蔑 戾 車 Mlecchas, border people, hence outside the borders of Buddhism, non-Buddhist.

叔 A father's younger brother; translit. *śi, śu.* | | (摩) 羅 Śiśumāra, a crocodile. | (or 叺叔) 迦 (婆) Śuka, a parrot. | 離 Śukla, or Śukra, white, silvery; the waxing half of the moon, or month; one of the asterisms, "the twenty-fourth of the astronomical Yogas," M. W.; associated with Venus.

取 Upādāna. To grasp, hold on to, held by, be attached to, love; used as indicating both 愛 love or desire and 煩 惱 the vexing passions and illusions. It is one of the twelve nidānas 十 二 因 緣 or 十 二 支 the grasping at or holding on to self-existence and things. | 次 語 Easy, facile, loose talk or explanations. | 相 The state of holding to the illusions of life as realities. | 相 懺 To hold repentance before the mind until the sign of Buddha's presence annihilates the sin. | 與 The producing seed is called | 果, that which it gives, or produces, is called 與 果. | 著 To grasp, hold on to, or be held by any thing or idea. | 蘊 The skandhas which give rise to grasping or desire, which in turn produces the skandhas. 見 | v. 見.

受 To receive, be, bear; intp. of Vedanā, "perception," "knowledge obtained by the senses, feeling, sensation." M. W. It is defined as mental reaction to the object, but in general it means receptivity, or sensation; the two forms of sensation of physical and mental objects are indicated. It is one of the five skandhas; as one of the twelve nidānas it indicates the incipient stage of sensation in the embryo. | 具 To receive the entire commandments, as does a fully ordained monk or nun. | 想 行 識 The four immaterial skandhas—vedanā, saṁjñā, saṁskāra, vijñāna, i.e. feeling, ideation, reaction, consciousness. | 戒 To receive, or accept, the commandments, or rules; a disciple; the beginner receives the first five, the monk, nun, and the earnest laity proceed to the reception of eight, the fully ordained accepts the ten. The term is also applied by the esoteric sects to the reception of their rules on admission. | 持 To receive and retain, or hold on to, or keep (the Buddha's teaching). | 業 Duties of the receiver of the rules; also to receive the results or karma of one's deeds. | 歲 To receive, or add, a year to his monastic age, on the conclusion of the summer's retreat.

| 用 Received for use. | 用身 The Saṁbhogakāya 報身 v. 三身 Trikāya, i.e. the functioning glorious body, 自受用 for a Buddha's own use, or bliss; 他受用 for the spiritual benefit of others. | 用土 The realm of the Saṁbhogakāya. | 者 A recipient (e.g. of the rules). The illusory view that the ego will receive reward or punishment in a future life, one of the sixteen false views. | 蘊 Vedanā, sensation, one of the five skandhas. | 記; | 決; | 別 To receive from a Buddha predestination (to become a Buddha); the prophecy of a bodhisattva's future Buddhahood. | 隨 To receive the rules and follow them out | 體隨行.

呿 To gape; translit. *kha*.

咃 Translit. *ṭha*.

咄嚕瑟劍 Turuṣka, olibanum, incense; also the name of an Indo-Scythian or Turkish race.

呼 Call; breathe out. | | The raurava or fourth hot hell. | 圖 (or 胡土) 克圖 Hutuktu, a chief Lama of Mongolian Buddhism, who is repeatedly reincarnated. | 摩; 護摩 Homa, an oblation by fire.

呬摩怛羅 Himatala 雪山下. "An ancient kingdom ruled in A.D. 43 by a descendant of the Śākya family. Probably the region south of Kundoot and Issar north of Hindukush near the principal source of the Oxus." Eitel. 西域記 3.

呵 Ho, k'o. Breathe out, yawn, scold; ha, laughter; used for 訶 and 阿. | 也怛那 Āyatana, an organ of sense, v. 六入. | (or 阿) 利 (or 梨) 陀 Hāritī, the demon-mother; also Harita, Haridrā, tawny, yellow, turmeric. | (or 訶) 吒迦 Hāṭaka; gold, thorn-apple. | 婆婆 Hahava, or Ababa, the fourth and | 羅羅 Aṭaṭa the third of the eight cold hells, in which the sufferers can only utter these sounds. | 責犍度 The eleventh of the twenty rules for monks, dealing with rebuke and punishment of a wrongdoer.

呾 Ta. Call; stutter; translit. *ta.*. | 你 (or 儞) 也他 Tadyathā, i.e. 所謂, as or what is said or meant, it means, i.e., etc. | 刹那 Tatkṣaṇa, "the 2250th part of an hour." Eitel. | 喇健 Talekān, "an ancient kingdom on the frontiers of Persia," its modern town is Talikhan. | 叉始羅; 竺刹尸羅 Takṣaśilā, "ancient kingdom and city, the Taxila of the Greeks, the region near Hoosum Abdaul in Lat. 35° 48 N., Long. 72° 44 E." Eitel. | (or 躭) 摩栗底; 多摩梨帝 Tāmralipti (or tī), the modern Tamluk near the mouth of the Hooghly, formerly "the principal emporium for the trade with Ceylon and China". Eitel. | 羅斯 Talas, or Taras; "(1) an ancient city in Turkestan 150 li west of Ming bulak (according to Hiuentsang). (2) A river which rises on the mountains west of Lake Issikoul and flows into a large lake to the north-west." Eitel. | 蜜 Termed, or Tirmez, or Tirmidh. "An ancient kingdom and city on the Oxus in Lat. 37° 5 N., Long. 67° 6 E." Eitel.

味 Rasa. Taste, flavour; the sense of taste. One of the six sensations. | 塵 Taste-dust, one of the six "particles" which form the material or medium of sensation. | 欲; | 著 The taste-desire, hankering after the pleasures of food, etc.; the bond of such desire. | 道 Taste, flavour; the taste of Buddha-truth, or tasting the doctrine.

咒 Dhāraṇī 陀羅尼; mantra; an incantation, spell, oath, curse; also a vow with penalties for failure. Mystical, or magical, formulæ employed in Yoga. In Lamaism they consist of sets of Tibetan words connected with Sanskrit syllables. In a wider sense dhāraṇī is a treatise with mystical meaning, or explaining it. | 咀; | 殺; | 起死 (or 屍) 鬼 An incantation for raising the vetāla 畏陀羅 or corpse-demons to cause the death of another person. | 心 The heart of a spell, or vow. | 藏 One of the four piṭakas, the thesaurus of dhāraṇīs. | 術 Sorcery, the sorcerer's arts. | 願 Vows, prayers, or formulas uttered in behalf of donors, or of the dead; especially at the All Souls Day's offerings to the seven generations of ancestors. Every word and deed of a bodhisattva should be a dhāraṇī.

命 Jīvita. Life, vital, length of life, fate, decree. | 光 The light of a life, i.e. soon gone. | | 鳥; 耆婆耆婆迦 Jīvajīvaka; Jīvaṁjīva, a bird with two heads, a sweet songster; 生生鳥 or 共命鳥 is the same bird. | 寳 The precious possession of life. | 根 A root, or basis for life, or reincarnation, the nexus of Hīnayāna between two life-periods, accepted by Mahāyāna as nominal but not real. | 梵 Life and honour, i.e. perils to life and perils to noble character. | 濁 One of the 五濁, turbidity or decay of the vital principle, reducing the length of life. | 終 Life's end; nearing the end. | 者 The living being; the one possessing life; life. | 藤 The rope of life (gnawed by the two rats, i.e. night and day). | 道沙門 A śramaṇa who makes the commandments, meditation, and knowledge his very life, as Ānanda did. | 難 Life's hardships; the distress of living.

周 Around, on every side, complete. | 利 (or 梨) 槃陀加 Kṣudrapanthaka; little (or mean) path. Twin brothers were born on the road, one called Śuddhipanthaka, Purity-path, the other born soon after and called as above, intp. 小路 small road, and 繼道 successor by the road. The elder was clever, the younger stupid, not even remembering his name, but became one of the earliest disciples of Buddha, and finally an arhat. The records are uncertain and confusing. Also, | | 般兎; | 稚般他迦, | | 槃特 (迦); 朱荼半託迦; | 陀· | 忌; | 闕 The first anniversary of a death, when | | 齋 anniversary masses are said. | 祥 The anniversary of Buddha's birthday. | 羅 (髮); 首羅 Cūḍā; a topknot left on the head of an ordinand when he receives the commandments; the locks are later taken off by his teacher as a sign of his complete devotion. | 遍 Universal, everywhere, on every side. | | 法界 The universal dharmadhātu; the universe as an expression of the dharmakāya; the universe; cf. 法界. | 那 Cundā, said to be the same as 純陀. | 陀 ? Kṣudra, said to be the same as | 利 *supra.*

和 Harmony, peace; to blend, mix; with, unite with; respond, rhyme, e.g. | 順 harmonious and compliant; | 會 to blend, unite. | 伽羅 (那); | 伽那; | 羅那 Vyākaraṇa, grammar, analysis, change of form; intp. as 授記 prediction, i.e. by the Buddha of the future felicity and realm of a disciple, hence Kauṇḍinya is known as Vyākaraṇa-Kauṇḍinya. | 南; 婆南; 伴談 (or 題); 畔睇; 畔彈南; 槃淡; 槃那寐; 盤荼味; 煩淡 Vandana. Obeisance, prostration, bowing the head, reverencing, worshipping. | 合 To blend, unite, be of one mind, harmonize. | (合) 僧; | (合) 衆 A saṁgha 僧伽, a monastery. | | 海 A monastery where all are of one mind as the sea is of one taste. | 尙 A general term for a monk. It is said to be derived from Khotan in the form of | 闍 or | (or 烏) 社 which might be a translit. of Vandya (Tibetan and Khotanī *ban-de*), "reverend." Later it took the form of | 尙 or | 上. The 律宗 use | 上, others generally | 尙. The Sanskrit term used in its interpretation is 烏波陀耶 Upādhyāya, a "sub-teacher" of the Vedas, inferior to an ācārya; this is intp. as 力生 strong in producing (knowledge), or in begetting strength in his disciples; also by 知有罪知無罪 a discerner of sin from not-sin, or the sinful from the not-sinful. It has been used as a synonym for 法師 a teacher of doctrine, in distinction from 律師 a teacher of the vinaya, also from 禪師 a teacher of the Intuitive school. | 夷羅 Vajra, | | | 洹閱叉; 跋闍羅波膩 Vajrapāṇi, the 金剛手 Bodhisattva holding the sceptre or thunderbolt, or 金剛神 one of the names of Indra, as a demon king and protector of Buddhism. | 闐 Khotan, Kustana, cf. 于. | 須吉 Vāsuki, lord of nāgas, name of a "dragon-king", with nine heads, hydra-headed; also | 修 |. | 須蜜 (多) Vasumitra. A distinction is made (probably in error) between Vasumitra, noted as a libertine and for his beauty, and Vasumitra 筏蘇蜜呾羅 q.v., a converted profligate who became president of the synod under Kaniṣka. | 香丸 A pill compounded of many kinds of incense typifying that in the one Buddha-truth lies all truth.

垂 Drop, droop, let down, pass down; regard. | 示; | 語 To make an announcement. | 迹 Traces, vestiges; manifestations or incarnations of Buddhas and bodhisattvas in their work of saving the living.

夜 Night; translit. *ya.* | 他跋 Yathāvat, suitably, exactly, solid, really. | 叉; | 乞叉; 藥叉; 閱叉 Yakṣa, (1) demons in the earth, or in the air, or in the lower heavens; they are malignant, and violent, and devourers (of human flesh). (2) The 八大將, the eight attendants on Kuvera, or Vaiśravaṇa, the god of wealth; those on earth bestow wealth, those in the empyrean houses and carriages, those in the lower heavens guard the moat and gates of the heavenly city. There is another set of sixteen. The names of all are given in 陀羅尼集經 3. See also 羅 for rakṣa and 吉 for kṛtya. Yakṣa-kṛtya are credited with the powers of both yakṣa and kṛtya. | 摩 Yama, "originally the Aryan god of the dead, living in a heaven above the world, the regent of the South; but Brahminism transferred his abode to hell. Both views have been retained by Buddhism." Eitel. Yama in Indian mythology is ruler over the dead and judge in the hells, is "grim in aspect, green in colour, clothed in red, riding on a buffalo, and holding a club in one hand and noose in the other": he has two four-eyed watch-dogs. M. W. The usual form is 閻摩 q.v. | 摩天 Yama deva; the third devaloka, which is also called 須 | 摩 or 蘇 | 摩, intp. as 時分 or 善時分 the place where the times, or seasons, are always good. | 摩盧迦 Yamaloka, the realm of Yama, the third devaloka. | 殊 Yajurveda, "the sacrificial Veda" of the Brahmans; the liturgy associated with Brahminical sacrificial services.

奉 To receive respectfully; honoured by, have the honour to, be favoured by, serve, offer. | 事 To carry out orders. | 加, | 納 To make offerings. | 行 To obey and do (the Buddha's teaching).

奈 Remedy, alternative, how? what? a yellow plum. | 利 idem 泥犂 Niraya, hell. | 河 The inevitable river in purgatory to be crossed by all souls. |河橋 The bridge in one of the hells, from which certain sinners always fall. |耻羅訶羅 Rudhirāhāra, name of a yakṣa.

奇 Āścarya, adbhuta; wonderful, rare, extraordinary; odd. |妙 Beautiful, or wonderful beyond compare. |特 Wonderful, rare, special, the three incomparable kinds of 神通 | | power to convert all beings, 慧心 | | Buddha-wisdom, and 攝受 | | Buddha-power to attract and save all beings. |異 Extraordinary, uncommon, rare.

奔 To run; translit. *pun* and *p*. |攘舍羅 Puṇyaśālā, almshouse or asylum for sick and poor. |荼(利迦) Puṇḍarīka, the white lotus, v. 分 or 芬; also the last of the eight great cold hells, v. 地獄. |那伐戰那 Puṇḍra-vardhana, an ancient kingdom and city in Bengal. |那伽 Puṣpanāga, the flowering dragon-tree under which Maitreya is said to have attained enlightenment.

委 To throw down, depute; really; crooked; the end. |順 To die, said of a monk.

妬 Jealous, envious. |不男 Īrṣyāpaṇḍaka. Impotent except when aroused by jealousy, one of the five classes of "eunuchs".

姑 Paternal aunt, husband's sister, a nun; to tolerate; however; leave. |尸草, 矩奢 Kuśa grass, grass of good omen for divination. |臧 Ku-tsang, formerly a city in Liangchow, Kansu, and an important centre for communication with Tibet.

始 Beginning, first, initial; thereupon. |士 An initiator; a Bodhisattva who stimulates beings to enlightenment. |教 According to T'ien-t'ai, the preliminary teaching of the Mahāyāna, made by the Avataṁsaka (Kegon) School; also called 相始教; it discussed the nature of all phenomena as in the 唯識論, 空始教; and held to the immateriality of all things, but did not teach that all beings have the Buddha-nature. |終 Beginning and end, first and last. |行人 A beginner. |覺 The initial functioning of mind or intelligence as a process of "becoming", arising from 本覺 which is Mind or Intelligence, self-contained, unsullied, and considered as universal, the source of all enlightenment. The "initial intelligence" or enlightenment arises from the inner influence 熏 of the Mind and from external teaching. In the "original intelligence" are the four values adopted and made transcendent by the Nirvāṇa-sūtra, viz. 常, 樂, 我, 淨 perpetuity, joy, personality, and purity; these are acquired through the 始覺 process of enlightenment. Cf. 起信論 Awakening of Faith.

孟 Eldest, first; Mencius; rude. |八郎 The eight violent fellows, a general term for plotters, ruffians, and those who write books opposed to the truth. |婆神 The Mêng family dame, said to have been born under the Han dynasty, and to have become a Buddhist; later deified as the bestower of |婆湯 the drug of forgetfulness, or oblivion of the past, on the spirits of the dead.

孤 Orphan, solitary. |山 An isolated hill; a monastery in Kiangsu and name of one of its monks. |(獨)地獄 Lokāntarika, solitary hells situated in space, or the wilds, etc. |(獨)園; 給園; 祇洹; 逝多林 Jetavana, the seven-storey abode and park presented to Śākyamuni by Anāthapiṇḍaka, who bought it from the prince Jeta. It was a favourite resort of the Buddha, and "most of the sūtras (authentic and suppositious) date from this spot". Eitel. |獨園 is also a term for an orphanage, asylum, etc. |落迦 A fruit syrup. |調 Self-arranging, the Hīnayāna method of salvation by individual effort.

官 Official, public. |難 In danger from the law; official oppression.

定 To fix, settle. Samādhi. "Composing the mind"; "intent contemplation"; "perfect absorption of thought into the one object of meditation." M. W. Abstract meditation, the mind fixed in one direction, or field. (1) 散定 scattered or general meditation (in the world of desire). (2) 禪定 abstract meditation (in the realms of form and beyond form). It is also one of the five attributes of the Dharmakāya 法身, i.e. an internal state of imperturbability or tranquillity, exempt from all external sensations, 超受陰; cf. 三摩提.

定侶 Fellow-meditators; fellow-monks.

定光 (1) Dīpaṁkara 提洹羯; 然燈佛, to whom Śākyamuni offered five lotuses when the latter was 儒童 Ju-t'ung Bodhisattva, and was thereupon designated as a coming Buddha. He is called the twenty-fourth predecessor of Śākyamuni. He appears whenever a Buddha preaches the Lotus sūtra. (2) Crystal, or some other bright stone.

定判 To determine, adjudge, settle.

定力 Samādhibala. The power of abstract or ecstatic meditation, ability to overcome all disturbing thoughts, the fourth of the five bala 五力; described also as 攝心 powers of mind-control.

定聚 One of the 三聚 q.v.

定命 Determined period of life; fate.

定妃 The female figures representing meditation in the maṇḍalas; male is wisdom, female is meditation.

定學 Learning through meditation, one of the three forms of learning 三學.

定心; 定意 A mind fixed in meditation. |心三昧 A fixed mind samādhi, i.e. fixed on the Pure Land and its glories.

定忍 Patience and perseverance in meditation.

定性 Fixed nature; settled mind. A classification of "five kinds of nature" 五種性 is made by the 法相宗, the first two being the ||二乘, i.e. śrāvakas and pratyeka-buddhas, whose mind is fixed on arhatship, and not on Buddhahood. The ||喜樂地 is the second dhyāna heaven of form, in which the occupants abide in surpassing meditation or trance, which produces mental joy.

定慧 Meditation and wisdom, two of the six pāramitās; likened to the two hands, the left meditation, the right wisdom.

定散 A settled, or a wandering mind; the mind organized by meditation, or disorganized by distraction. The first is characteristic of the saint and sage, the second of the common untutored man. The fixed heart may or may not belong to the realm of transmigration; the distracted heart has the distinctions of good, bad, or indifferent. ||二善 Both a definite subject for meditation and an undefined field are considered as valuable.

定智 Meditation and wisdom.

定根 Samādhīndriya. Meditation as the root of all virtue, being the fourth of the five indriya 五根.

定業 Fixed karma, rebirth determined by the good or bad actions of the past. Also, the work of meditation with its result. ||亦能轉 Even the determined fate can be changed (by the power of Buddhas and bodhisattvas).

定水 Calm waters; quieting the waters of the heart (and so beholding the Buddha, as the moon is reflected in still water).

定相 Fixity, determined, determination, settled, unchanging, nirvāṇa. The appearance of meditation.

定覺支 The enlightenment of meditation, the sixth of the Sapta bodhyaṅga 七菩提分 q.v.

定身 The Dharmakāya of meditation, one of the 五分法身 five forms of the Buddha-dharmakāya.

宗 Ancestors, ancestral; clan; class, category, kind; school, sect; siddhānta, summary, main doctrine, syllogism, proposition, conclusion, realization. Sects are of two kinds: (1) those founded on principles having historic continuity, as the twenty sects of the Hīnayāna, the thirteen sects of China, and the fourteen sects of Japan; (2) those arising from an individual interpretation of the general teaching of Buddhism, as the sub-sects founded by Yung-ming 永明 (d. 975), 法相|, 法性|, 破相|, or those based on a peculiar interpretation of one of the recognized sects, as the Jōdo-shinshū 淨土眞宗 founed by Shinran-shōnin. There are also divisions of five, six, and ten, which have reference to specific doctrinal differences. Cf. |派.

宗乘 The vehicle of a sect, i.e. its essential tenets.

宗元 The basic principles of a sect; its origin or cause of existence.

宗儀 The rules or ritual of a sect.

宗依 That on which a sect depends, v. 宗法.

宗匠 The master workman of a sect who founded its doctrines.

宗因喻 Proposition, reason, example, the three parts of a syllogism.

宗學 The study or teaching of a sect.

宗客巴 Sumatikīrti (Tib. Tsoṅ-kha-pa), the reformer of the Tibetan church, founder of the Yellow Sect (黃帽教); according to the 西藏新志 b. A.D. 1417 at Hsining, Kansu. His sect was founded on strict discipline, as opposed to the lax practices of the Red sect, which permitted marriage of monks, sorcery, etc. He is considered to be an incarnation of Mañjuśrī; others say of Amitābha.

宗密 Tsung-mi, one of the five patriarchs of the Hua-yen (Avataṁsaka) sect, d. 841.

宗旨 The main thesis, or ideas, e.g. of a text.

宗極 Ultimate or fundamental principles.

宗法, 宗體 The thesis of a syllogism consisting of two terms, each of which has five different names: 自性 subject; 差別 its differentiation; 有法 that which acts; 法 the action; 所別 that which is differentiated; 能別 that which differentiates; 前陳 first statement; 後陳 following statement; 宗依 that on which the syllogism depends, both for subject and predicate.

宗派 Sects (of Buddhism). In India, according to Chinese accounts, the two schools of Hīnayāna became divided into twenty sects. Mahāyāna had two main schools, the Mādhyamika, ascribed to Nāgārjuna and Āryadeva about the second century A.D., and the Yogācārya, ascribed to Asaṅga and Vasubandhu in the fourth century A.D. In China thirteen sects were founded: (1) 俱舍宗 Abhidharma or Kośa sect, representing Hīnayāna, based upon the Abhidharma-kośa-śāstra or 俱舍論. (2) 成實宗 Satyasiddhi sect, based on the 成實論 Satyasiddhi-śāstra, tr. by Kumārajīva; no sect corresponds to it in India; in China and Japan it became incorporated in the 三論宗. (3) 律宗 Vinaya or Discipline sect, based on 十誦律, 四分律, 僧祇律, etc. (4) 三論宗 The three-śāstra sect, based on the Mādhyamika-śāstra 中觀論 of Nāgārjuna, the Śata-śāstra 百論 of Āryadeva, and the Dvādaśa-nikāya-śāstra 十二門論 of Nāgārjuna; this school dates back to the translation of the three śāstras by Kumārajīva in A.D. 409. (5) 涅槃宗 Nirvāṇa sect, based upon the Mahāparinirvāṇa-sūtra 涅槃經 tr. by Dharmarakṣa in 423; later incorporated in T'ien-t'ai, with which it had much in common. (6) 地論宗 Daśabhūmikā sect, based on Vasubandhu's work on the ten stages of the bodhisattva's path to Buddhahood, tr. by Bodhiruci 508, absorbed by the Avataṁsaka school, *infra.* (7) 淨土宗 Pure-land or Sukhāvatī sect, founded in China by Bodhiruci; its doctrine was salvation through faith in Amitābha into the Western Paradise. (8) 禪宗 Dhyāna, meditative or intuitional sect, attributed to Bodhidharma about A.D. 527, but it existed before he came to China. (9) 攝論宗, based upon the 攝大乘論 Mahāyāna-samparigraha-śāstra by Asaṅga, tr. by Paramartha in 563, subsequently absorbed by the Avataṁsaka sect. (10) 天台宗 T'ien-t'ai, based on the 法華經 Saddharma-puṇḍarīka Sūtra, or the Lotus of the Good Law; it is a consummation of the Mādhyamika tradition. (11) 華嚴宗 Avataṁsaka sect, based on the Buddhāvataṁsaka-sūtra, or Gandha-vyūha 華嚴經 tr. in 418. (12) 法相宗 Dharmalakṣaṇa sect, established after the return of Hsüan-tsang from India and his trans. of the important Yogācārya works. (13) 眞言宗 Mantra sect, A.D. 716. In Japan twelve sects are named: Sanron, Hossō, Kegon, Kusha, Jōjitsu, Ritsu, Tendai, Shingon; these are known as the ancient sects, the two last being styled mediaeval; there follow the Zen and Jōdo; the remaining two are Shin and Nichiren; at present there are the Hossō, Kegon, Tendai, Shingon, Zen, Jōdo, Shin, and Nichiren sects.

宗用 Principles and their practice, or application.

宗祖 The founder of a sect or school. | 家 A name for Shan-tao 善導 (d. 681), a writer of commentaries on the sūtras of the Pure Land sect, and one of its principal literary men; cf. 念佛宗.

宗義 The tenets of a sect.

宗致 The ultimate or fundamental tenets of a sect.

宗要 The fundamental tenets of a sect; the important elements, or main principle.

宗說俱通 In doctrine and expression both thorough, a term applied to a great teacher.

宗門 Originally the general name for sects. Later appropriated to itself by the 禪 Ch'an (Zen) or Intuitional school, which refers to the other schools as 敎門 teaching sects, i.e. those who rely on the written word rather than on the "inner light".

宗風 The customs or traditions of a sect. In the Ch'an sect it means the regulations of the founder.

宗骨 The "bones" or essential tenets of a sect.

宗體 The body of doctrine of a sect. The thesis of a syllogism, v. 丨法.

居 Dwell, reside; be. 丨士; 倶攞鉢底; 迦羅越 Kulapati. A chief, head of a family, squire, landlord. A householder who practises Buddhism at home without becoming a monk. The female counterpart is 女丨士. The 丨士傳 is a compilation giving the biography of many devout Buddhists. 丨倫; 丨(or 倶)隣; 拘輪 idem Ājñāta-kauṇḍinya, v. 憍.

屈 To bend; oppression, wrong. 丨丨吒播 (or 波) 陀 Kukkuṭapādagiri; Cock's foot, a mountain said to be 100 li east of the bodhi tree, and, by Eitel, 7 miles south-east of Gayā, where Kāśyapa entered into nirvāṇa; also known as 窶盧播陀山 tr. by 尊足 "honoured foot". The legend is that these three sharply rising peaks, on Kāśyapa entering, closed together over him. Later, when Mañjuśrī ascended, he snapped his fingers, the peaks opened, Kāśyapa gave him his robe and entered nirvāṇa by fire. 丨吒阿濫摩 Kukkuṭa-ārāma, a monastery built on the above mountain by Aśoka, cf. 西域記 8. 丨支; 丨茨; 庫車; 龜兹; 丘兹 Kutche (Kucha). An ancient kingdom and city in Turkestan, north-east of Kashgar. 丨浪那 (or 拏) Kūrān, anciently a kingdom in Tokhara, "the modern Garana, with mines of lapis lazuli (Lat. 36° 28 N., Long. 71° 2 E.)." Eitel. 丨摩羅; 丨滿囉 A lotus bud. 丨眴 A cottony material of fine texture. 丨陀迦阿含 The Pali Khuddakāgama, the fifth of the Āgamas, containing fifteen (or fourteen) works, including such as the Dharmapada, Itivṛttaka, Jātaka, Buddhavaṁsa, etc. 丨霜儞迦 Kashanian, a region near Kermina, Lat. 39° 50 N., Long. 65° 25 E. Eitel. 丨露多 Kulūta. An ancient kingdom in north India famous for its rock temples; Kulu, north of Kangra.

岸 Kūla. Shore, bank. 丨樹 A tree on a river's brink, life's uncertainty. 丨頭 The shore of the ocean of suffering. 彼丨 The other shore; nirvāṇa.

帕 Kerchief, veil. 丨克斯巴 Bashpa, v. 八 and 巴.

庚 Age; change; west; to reward; the seventh of the ten celestial stems. 丨申會 An assembly for offerings on the night of Kêng-shên to an image in the form of a monkey, which is the shên symbolical animal; a Taoist rite adopted by Buddhism.

底 Bottom, basis; translit. *t*, *d*, *dh*. 丨下 At the bottom, below, the lowest class (of men). 丨哩 Tri, three, in Trisamaya, etc. 丨彥多; 丁岸哆 Tiṅanta, Tryanta, described as the singular, dual, and plural endings in verbs. 丨栗車 Tiryagyoni, the animal species, animals, especially the six domestic animals. 丨沙 Tiṣya. (1) The twenty-third of the twenty-eight constellations 鬼宿 $\gamma\,\delta\,\eta\,\theta$ in Cancer; it has connection with Śiva. (2) Name of a Buddha who taught Śākyamuni and Maitreya in a former incarnation. 丨理 The fundamental principle or law.

廻 v. 回 6.

延 Prolong, prolonged, delay; invite. 丨年; 丨壽; 丨命 Prolonged life. 丨年轉壽 Prolonged years and returning anniversaries. 丨命法 Methods of worship of the 丨命菩薩 life-prolonging bodhisattvas to increase length of life; these bodhisattvas are 普賢; 金剛薩埵; 地藏; 觀音, and others. 丨促劫智 Buddha-wisdom, which surmounts all extending or shrinking kalpas, v. 劫波. 丨壽 Prolonged life, the name of Yen-shou, a noted Hangchow monk of the Sung dynasty. 丨壽堂 The hall or room into which a dying person is taken to enter upon his "long life". 丨慶寺 Yen-ch'ing ssŭ, the monastery in which is the ancient lecture hall of T'ien-t'ai at 四明山 Ssŭ-ming Shan in Chekiang.

弩 Crossbow, bow. 丨達囉灑 Durdharṣa, hard to hold, or hard to overcome, or hard to behold, guardian of the inner gate in Vairocana's maṇḍala. 丨櫱帝 Anvāgati, approaching, arriving.

彼 That, the other, in contrast with 此 this. 丨岸; 波羅 Pāra, yonder shore, i.e. nirvāṇa. The saṁsāra life of reincarnation is 此岸 this shore; the stream of karma is 中流 the stream between the one shore and the other. Metaphor for an end to any affair. Pāramitā (an incorrect etymology, no doubt old) is the way to reach the other shore. 丨茶 Peṭa, or Piṭaka, a basket.

往 To go; gone, past; to be going to, future. 丨生 The future life, the life to which anyone is going; to go to be born in the Pure Land of Amitābha. (1) 往相回向 To transfer one's merits to all beings that they may attain the Pure Land of Amitābha. (2) 還相回向 Having been born in the Pure Land to return to mortality and by one's merits to bring mortals to the Pure Land.

忠 Loyal. | 心 Loyal, faithful, honest.

忽 Suddenly; hastily; a millionth. | 懍 Khulm, an ancient kingdom and city between Balkh and Kunduz. | 露摩 Shadumān, "a district of ancient Tukhāra, north of the Wakhan." Eitel.

怖 Uttras-; santras-; fear, afraid. | 捍; 霍 罕 Ferghana, in Russian Turkestan. | 畏施 Almsgiving to remove one's fears. | 魔 Scare-demon, a supposed tr. of the term Bhikṣu.

怛 Distressed; pity. Translit. for *t*, *ta*, *tan*, etc. | 他 Tadyathā, 所謂 whereas, as here follows. || 揭 (or 蘖) 多; | 陀竭多; | 佗議多; | 薩 (or 闥) 阿竭 Tathāgata, v. 多. | 利耶怛喇舍 (or 奢) Trayastriṁśa, the thirty-three heavens of Indra, cf. 多. | 刹那 ? Tṛṇa, a length of time consisting of 120 kṣaṇa, or moments; or "a wink", the time for twenty thoughts. | 哩支伐離迦 Tricīvaraka, the three garments of a monk. | 囉麼洗 Caitra-māsa, tr. as the 正月 or first month; M. W. gives March–April. | 索迦 Takṣaka, name of a dragon-king. | 縛 Tvam, thou, you. | 羅夜耶 Traya, three, with special reference to the Triratna. | 荼 Daṇḍa, cf. 檀拏 a staff. | 那 idem 檀那 Dāna, alms, giving, charity. | 鉢那 Tapana, burning, scorched; parched grain. | 麼 Ātman, an ego, or self, personal, permanent existence, both 人我 and 法我 q.v.

忿 Anger. | 怒 Anger, angry, fierce, over-awing; a term for the | 王 or | 怒 (明) 王 the fierce mahārājas as opponents of evil and guardians of Buddhism; one of the two bodhisattva forms, resisting evil, in contrast with the other form, manifesting goodness. There are three forms of this fierceness in the Garbhadhātu group and five in the Diamond group. | 怒鉤 A form of Kuan-yin with a hook. | 結 The bond of anger.

念 Smṛti. Recollection, memory; to think on, reflect; repeat, intone; a thought; a moment. | 力 Smṛtibala, one of the five bala or powers, that of memory. Also one of the seven bodhyaṅga 七菩提分. | 佛 To repeat the name of a Buddha, audibly or inaudibly. | 佛者 One who repeats the name of a Buddha, especially of Amitābha, with the hope of entering the Pure Land. | 佛宗 or 門. The sect which repeats only the name of Amitābha, founded in the T'ang dynasty by 道綽 Tao-ch'o, 善道 Shan-tao, and others. | 佛三昧 The samādhi in which the individual whole-heartedly thinks of the appearance of the Buddha, or of the Dharmakāya, or repeats the Buddha's name. The one who enters into this samādhi, or merely repeats the name of Amitābha, however evil his life may have been, will acquire the merits of Amitābha and be received into Paradise, hence the term | 佛往生. This is the basis or primary cause of such salvation | 佛爲本 or 先. Amitābha's merits by this means revert to the one who repeats his name | 佛廻向, the | 佛往生願 being the eighteenth of Amitābha's forty-eight vows. | 天 One of the six devalokas, that of recollection and desire. | 定 Correct memory and correct samādhi. | 念 Kṣaṇa of a kṣaṇa, a kṣaṇa is the ninetieth part of the duration of a thought; an instant; thought after thought. || 無常 Instant after instant, no permanence, i.e. the impermanence of all phenomena; unceasing change. || 相續 Unbroken continuity; continuing instant in unbroken thought or meditation on a subject; also unceasing invocation of a Buddha's name. | 持 To apprehend and hold in memory. | 根 Smṛtīndriya. The root or organ of memory, one of the five indriya 五根. | 漏 The leakages, or stream of delusive memory. | 珠 To tell beads. | 經 To repeat the sūtras, or other books; to intone them. | 著 Through perverted memory to cling to illusion. | 處 Smṛtyupasthāna. The presence in the mind of all memories, or the region which is contemplated by memory. 四 | 處 Four objects on which memory or the thought should dwell—the impurity of the body, that all sensations lead to suffering, that mind is impermanent, and that there is no such thing as an ego. There are other categories for thought or meditation. | 覺支 Holding in memory continually, one of the Sapta bodhyaṅga 七覺支. | 言 (As) the mind remembers, (so) the mouth speaks; also the words of memory. | 誦 To recite, repeat, intone, e.g. the name of a Buddha; to recite a dhāraṇī, or spell.

性 Svabhāva, prakṛti, pradhāna. The nature, intp. as embodied, causative, unchanging; also as independent or self-dependent; fundamental nature behind the manifestation or expression. Also, the Buddha-nature immanent in all beings, the Buddha heart or mind.

性佛 The Dharmakāya 法性佛, v. 法身.

性具 The T'ien-t'ai doctrine that the Buddha-nature includes both good and evil; v. 觀音玄義記 2. Cf. 體具; 理具 of similar meaning.

性分 The nature of anything; the various natures of various things.

性命 The life of conscious beings; nature and life.

性善 Good by nature (rather than by effort); naturally good; in contrast with | 惡 evil by nature. Cf. | 具.

性土 The sphere of the dharma-nature, i.e. the bhūtatathatā, idem 法性土.

性地 Spiritual nature, the second of the ten stages as defined by the 通教 Intermediate School, in which the illusion produced by 見思 seeing and thinking is subdued and the mind obtains a glimmer of the immateriality of things. Cf. 十地.

性宗 v. 法性宗.

性得 Natural attainment, i.e. not acquired by effort; also 生得.

性德 Natural capacity for good (or evil), in contrast with 修 | powers (of goodness) attained by practice.

性心 The perfectly clear and unsullied mind, i.e. the Buddha mind or heart. The Ch'an (Zen) school use 性心 or 心性 indifferently.

性念處 Citta-smṛtyupasthāna, one of the four objects of thought, i.e. that the original nature is the same as the Buddha-nature, v. 四念處.

性戒 The natural moral law, e.g. not to kill, steal, etc., not requiring the law of Buddha.

性我 The Buddha-nature ego, which is apperceived when the illusory ego is banished.

性橫修縱 A division of the Triratna in its three aspects into the categories of 橫 and 縱, i.e. cause and effect, or effect and cause; a 別教 division, not that of the 圓教.

性欲 Desires that have become second nature; desires of the nature.

性海 The ocean of the bhūtatathatā, the all-containing, immaterial nature of the Dharmakāya.

性火 Fire as one of the five elements, contrasted with 事火 phenomenal fire.

性相 The nature (of anything) and its phenomenal expression; hsing being 無爲 non-functional, or noumenal, and hsiang 有爲 functional, or phenomenal. | 相學 The philosophy of the above, i.e. of the noumenal and phenomenal. There are ten points of difference between the | 相二宗, i.e. between the 性 and 相 schools, v. 二宗.

性種性 Nature-seed nature, i.e. original or primary nature, in contrast with 習 | 性 active or functioning nature; it is also the bodhisattva 十行 stage. | 種戒 idem 性戒.

性空 The nature void, i.e. the immateriality of the nature of all things. | 空教 One of the three 南山 Nan-shan sects which regarded the nature of things as unreal or immaterial, but held that the things were temporally entities. | 空觀 The meditation of this sect on the unreality, or immateriality, of the nature of things.

性罪 Sins that are such according to natural law, apart from Buddha's teaching, e.g. murder, etc.

性色 Transcendent rūpa or form within or of the Tathāgata-garbha; also 眞色.

性覺 Inherent intelligence, or knowledge, i.e. that of the bhūtatathatā.

性識 Natural powers of perception, or the knowledge acquired through the sense organs; mental knowledge.

性起 Arising from the primal nature, or bhūtatathatā, in contrast with 緣起 arising from secondary causes.

性遮 Natural and conventional sins, i.e. sins against natural law, e.g. murder, and sins against conventional or religious law, e.g. for a monk to drink wine, cut down trees, etc.

房 House, room. The rooms for monks and nuns in a monastery or nunnery. | 宿 Scorpio, idem 㤀賓那.

所 A place; where, what, that which, he (etc.) who. | 作 That which is done, or to be done, or made, or set up, etc. 丨依 Āśraya, that on which anything depends, the basis of the vijñānas. 丨別 The subject of the thesis of a syllogism in contrast with 能別 the predicate; that which is differentiated. 丨化 The one who is transformed or instructed. 丨引 That which is brought forward or out; a quotation. 丨有 What one has, what there is, whatever exists. 丨知依 That on which all knowledge depends, i.e. the ālayavijñāna, the other vijñānas being derived from it; cf. 八識. 丨知障 The barrier of the known, arising from regarding the seeming as real. 丨立 A thesis; that which is set up. 丨緣 Ālambana; that upon which something rests or depends, hence object of perception; that which is the environmental or contributory cause; attendant circumstances. 丨緣緣 Adhipati-pratyaya. The influence of one factor in causing others; one of the 四緣. 丨詮 That which is expounded, explained, or commented on. 丨遍計 That by which the mind is circumscribed, i.e. impregnated with the false view that the ego and things possess reality. 丨量 That which is estimated; the content of reasoning, or judgment.

拄 A prop, a post. 丨杖(子) A crutch, staff.

抹 Rub out or on, efface. 丨香 Powdered incense to scatter over images.

拓 Carry (on the palm), entrust to, pretext, extend. 丨林羅 One of the twelve generals in the Yao-shih (Bhaiṣajya) sūtra.

拍掌; 丨手 Clapping of hands at the beginning and end of worship, a Shingon custom.

抱 Embrace, enfold, cherish. 丨佛脚 (Only when old or in trouble) to embrace the Buddha's feet.

承 Receive, succeed to, undertake, serve. 丨事 Entrusted with duties, serve, obey, and minister. 丨露盤 or 槃 The "dew-receivers", or metal circles at the top of a pagoda.

拙 Stupid, clumsy. 丨(or 窶)具羅; 求求羅 Kukura, Kukkura; a plant and its perfume. 丨度 A stupid, powerless salvation, that of Hīnayāna.

抵 Knock; arrive; resist, bear; substitute. 丨彌 Timi, Timiṅgila, a huge fish, perhaps a whale.

折 Tear open, break down. 丨摩馱那 Calmadana or 涅末 Nimat, "An ancient kingdom and city at the south-east borders of the desert of Gobi." Eitel.

抽 Draw, withdraw, pull out. 丨籤 To draw lots, seek divine indications, etc. 丨脫 To go to the latrine.

拖 Tow, tug; delay; implicate. 丨泥帶水; 和泥合水 Mud and water hauler, or made of mud and water, a Ch'an (Zen) school censure of facile remarks.

拂 To rub, wipe, dust. 丨子 A duster, fly brush. 丨石; 槃石劫 A kalpa as measured by the time it would take to wear away an immense rock by rubbing it with a deva-garment; cf. 芥 and 劫波. 丨迹入玄 To rub out the traces of past impurity and enter into the profundity of Buddha.

招 Call, beckon, notify, cause; confess. 丨魂 To call back the spirit (of the dead). 丨提; 拓鬪提舍 Caturdiśah, the four directions of space; cāturdiśa, belonging to the four quarters, i.e. the Saṃgha or Church; name for a monastery.

披 To spread open, unroll, thrown on (as a cloak). 丨 is to wear the garment over both shoulders; 袒 is to throw it over one shoulder. 丨剃 The first donning of the robe and shaving of the head (by a novice).

拈 To take in the fingers, pluck, pinch. 丨古; 丨提 To refer to ancient examples. 丨花微笑 "Buddha held up a flower and Kāśyapa smiled". This incident does not appear till about A.D. 800, but is regarded as the beginning of the tradition on which the Ch'an (Zen) or Intuitional sect based its existence. 丨衣 To gather up the garment. 丨香 To take and offer incense. 丨語 To take up and pass on a verbal tradition, a Ch'an (Zen) term.

拔 Pull up, or out; raise. 丨婆; 丨波 Vatsa, calf, young child. 丨底耶 Upādhyāya, a spiritual teacher, or monk 和尙 v. 烏. 丨提 -vatī, a terminal of names of certain rivers, e.g. Hiraṇyavatī. 丨褐達多 Bhadradatta, name of a king. 丨濟 To rescue, save from trouble. 丨舌地獄 The hell where the tongue is pulled out, as punishment for oral sins. 丨苦與樂 To save from suffering and give joy. 丨羅魔囉 Bhramara, a kind of black bee. 丨思發; 丨合思巴; 八思巴 Baschpa (Phags-pa), Tibetan Buddhist and adviser of Kublai Khan, v. 八發(思).

拘 Seize, take, arrest; translit. *k* sounds, cf. 巨, 矩, 俱, 憍.

拘利; 拘胝 Koṭi. A million. Also explained by 億 100,000; or 100 lakṣa, i.e. ten millions. Also 俱利 or 胝.

拘利太子 Kolita, the eldest son of Droṇodana, uncle of Śākyamuni; said to be Mahānāma, but others say Mahāmaudgalyāyana. Also 拘栗; 拘肄多.

拘吒賒摩利 Kūṭaśālmali. Also 居|奢|| (or 離) A fabulous tree on which garuḍas find nāgas to eat; M. W. describes it as "a fabulous cotton-tree with sharp thorns with which the wicked are tortured in the world of Yama". |吒迦 Kuṭaṅgaka, thatched; a hut.

拘尸那 Kuśinagara; |||竭 or 揭羅; 拘 (or 俱) 夷那竭; 俱尸那; 究施 a city identified by Professor Vogel with Kasiah, 180 miles north-west of Patna, "capital city of the Mallas" (M. W.); the place where Śākyamuni died; "so called after the sacred Kuśa grass." Eitel. Not the same as Kuśāgārapura, v. 矩.

拘摩羅 Kumāra; also 矩 (or 鳩) 摩羅; a child, youth, prince, tr. by 童子 a youth. |||天; 鳩摩羅伽天 Kumārakadeva, Indra of the first dhyāna heaven whose face is like that of a youth, sitting on a peacock, holding a cock, a bell, and a flag. |||肏 Kumārata, v. 鳩.

拘沙 A branch of the Yüeh-chih people, v. 月.

拘流沙 Kuru, the country where Buddha is said to have delivered the sūtra 長阿含大緣方便經.

拘物頭 Kumuda; also ||陀; ||度; |勿頭 (or 投); |牟 (or 貿 or 某 or 那) 頭; |母陀; 句文羅; 俱勿頭; 屈摩羅; 究牟陀 a lotus; an opening lotus; but kumuda refers especially to the esculent white lotus. M. W.

拘理迦 Kulika. "A city 9 li south-west of Nālanda in Magadha." Eitel.

拘瑟耻羅 Kauṣṭhila, also 俱|祉|; an arhat, maternal uncle of Śāriputra, who became an eminent disciple of Śākyamuni.

拘留孫佛 Krakucchanda; also ||秦佛; |樓秦; 俱留孫; 鳩樓孫; 迦羅鳩餐陀 (or 村馱); 羯洛迦孫馱; 羯羅迦寸地; 羯句忖那, etc. The first of the Buddhas of the present Bhadrakalpa, the fourth of the seven ancient Buddhas.

拘盧(舍) Krośa; also |樓賒; |屢; 俱盧舍; the distance a bull's bellow can be heard, the eighth part of a yojana, or 5 li; another less probable definition is 2 li. For || Uttarakuru, see 俱.

拘睒彌 Kauśāmbī, or Vatsapattana |暹; 憍賞彌; a country in Central India; also called |羅瞿 v. 巨.

拘羯羅 Cakra, v. 斫.

拘耆(那羅) Kokila, also |翅羅, the cuckoo. M. W.

拘蘇摩 Kusuma, "the white China aster." Eitel. |||補羅 Kusumapura, city of flower-palaces; two are named, Pāṭaliputra, ancient capital of Magadha, the modern Patna; and Kanyākubja, Kanauj (classical Canogyza), a noted city in northern Hindustan; v. 羯.

拘謎陀 Kumidha. "An ancient kingdom on the Beloortagh to the north of Badakhshan. The *vallis Comedorum* of Ptolemy." Eitel.

拘那(含)牟尼 Kanakamuni, |那含; 迦諾迦牟尼 q.v., lit. 金寂 the golden recluse, or 金仙 golden ṛṣi; a Brahman of the Kāśyapa family, native of Śobhanavatī, second of the five Buddhas of the present Bhadra-kalpa, fifth of the seven ancient Buddhas; possibly a sage who preceded Śākyamuni in India.

拘那羅 Kuṇāla; also |拏羅; |浪拏; 鳩那羅 a bird with beautiful eyes; name of Dharmavivardhana (son of Aśoka), whose son Sampadi "became the successor of Aśoka". Eitel. Kuṇāla is also tr. as an evil man, possibly of the evil eye. |||陀 (or 他); |蘭難陀 ? Guṇarata, name of Paramārtha, who was known as 眞諦三藏, also as Kulanātha, came to China A.D. 546 from Ujjain in Western India, tr. many books, especially the treatises of Vasubandhu.

拘隣 Kauṇḍinya; also | (or 俱) 輪; 俱隣: 居隣 (or 倫). v. 憍.

拘粺陀羅 Kovidāra, *Bauhinia variegata*, fragrant trees in the great pleasure ground (of the child Śākyamuni).

放 To let go, release, send out; put, place. 丨下 To put down, let down, lay down. 丨光 Light-emitting; to send out an illuminating ray. 丨丨三昧 A samādhi in which all kinds and colours of light are emitted. 丨丨瑞 The auspicious ray emitted from between the eyebrows of the Buddha before pronouncing the Lotus sūtra. 丨燈 Lighting strings of lanterns, on the fifteenth of the first month, a custom wrongly attributed to Han Ming Ti, to celebrate the victory of Buddhism in the debate with Taoists; later extended to the seventh and fifteenth full moons. 丨生 To release living creatures as a work of merit. 丨逸 Loose, unrestrained.

於 At, in, on, to, from, by, than. 丨諦 All Buddha's teaching is "based upon the dogmas" that all things are unreal, and that the world is illusion; a 三論 phrase. 丨麾 A name for Ladakh. "The upper Indus valley under Cashmerian rule but inhabited by Tibetans." Eitel.

易 Change; easy. 丨行 Easy progress, easy to do. 變丨 To change.

昔 Of old, formerly. 丨哩 Śrī, fortunate, idem 室 (or 尸) 利.

昆勒 Piṭaka, also 蜫勒 defined as the śāstras; a misprint for 毘.

昏 Dusk, dull, confused. 丨城 The dim city, the abode of the common, unenlightened man. 丨識 Dull, or confused, knowledge. 丨醉 Matta, drunk, intoxicated. 丨鐘; 丨鼓 The bell, or drum, at dusk. 丨默多 Kandat, the capital of Tamasthiti, perhaps the modern Kunduz, but Eitel says "Kundoot about 40 miles above Jshtrakh, Lat. 36° 42 N., Long. 71° 39 E."

明 Vidyā, knowledge. Ming means bright, clear, enlightenment, intp. by 智慧 or 聰明 wisdom, wise; to understand. It represents Buddha-wisdom and its revelation; also the manifestation of a Buddha's light or effulgence; it is a term for 眞言 because the "true word" can destroy the obscurity of illusion; the "manifestation" of the power of the object of worship; it means also dhāraṇīs or mantras of mystic wisdom. Also, the Ming dynasty A.D. 1368–1644. 丨了 To understand thoroughly; complete enlightenment. 無明 Commonly tr. "ignorance", means an unenlightened condition, non-perception, before the stirrings of intelligence, belief that the phenomenal is real, etc.

明信佛智 To believe clearly in Buddha's wisdom (as leading to rebirth in the Pure Land).

明冥 The (powers of) light and darkness, the devas and Yama, gods and demons, also the visible and invisible.

明利 Clear and keen (to penetrate all mystery).

明地 The stage of illumination, or 發光地 the third of the ten stages, v. 十地.

明妃 Another name for dhāraṇī as the queen of mystic knowledge and able to overcome all evil. Also the female consorts shown in the maṇḍalas.

明度無極 An old intp. of Prajñā 明 pāramitā 度, the wisdom that ferries to the other shore without limit; for which 明炬 a shining torch is also used.

明得(定) A samādhi in the Bodhisattva's 四加行 in which there are the bright beginnings of release from illusion. 丨丨菩薩 The Bodhisattva who has reached that stage, i.e. the 煖位.

明心 The enlightened heart.

明慧 The three enlightenments 三明, and the three wisdoms 三慧.

明敏 Śīghrabodhi. "A famous priest of the Nālanda monastery." Eitel.

明星 Venus 太白 and the 天子 or deva-prince who dwells in that planet; but it is also said to be Aruṇa, which indicates the Dawn.

明月 The bright moon. 丨丨珠; 明珠; 摩尼 The bright-moon maṇi or pearl, emblem of Buddha, Buddhism, the Buddhist Scriptures, purity, etc. 丨丨天子 The moon-deva, in Indra's retinue.

明法 The law or method of mantras, or magic formulæ.

明熏 The inner light, enlightenment censing and overcoming ignorance, like incense perfuming and interpenetrating.

明王 The rājas, ming-wang, or fierce spirits who are the messengers and manifestation of Vairocana's wrath against evil spirits.

明相 Early dawn, the proper time for the monk's breakfast; brightness.

明神 The bright spirits, i.e. devas, gods, demons.

明脫 Enlightenment (from ignorance) and release (from desire).

明藏 The Buddhist canon of the Ming dynasty; there were two editions, one the Southern at Nanking made by T'ai Tsu, the Northern at Peking by Tai Tsung. A later edition was produced in the reign of Shên Tsung (Wan Li), which became the standard in Japan.

明處 The regions or realms of study which produce wisdom, five in number, v. 五明(處).

明行足 Vidyā-caraṇa-saṁpanna; knowledge-conduct-perfect 婢侈遮羅那三般那. (1) The unexcelled universal enlightenment of the Buddha based upon the discipline, meditation, and wisdom regarded as feet; one of the ten epithets of Buddha. Nirvāṇa sūtra 18. (2) The 智度論 2 interprets 明 by the 三明 q.v., the 行 by the 三業 q.v., and the 足 by complete, or perfect.

明道 The bright or clear way; the way of the mantras and dhāraṇīs.

明達 Enlightenment 明 in the case of the saint includes knowledge of future incarnations of self and others, of the past incarnations of self and others, and that the present incarnation will end illusion. In the case of the Buddha such knowledge is called 達 thorough or perfect enlightenment.

服 Submit, serve; clothing, to wear; mourning; to swallow; a dose. |水論師 The sect of non-Buddhist philosophers who considered water the beginning and end of all things.

板 A board; a board struck for calling, e.g. to meals.

杯 A cup. |度 Pei-tu, a fifth-century Buddhist monk said to be able to cross a river in a cup or bowl, hence his name.

枉 Oppression, wrong; crooked; in vain. |死 Wrongly done to death.

析 To divide, separate, differentiate, explain. 分| To divide; leave the world; separation. |小 To traverse or expose the fallacy of Hīnayāna arguments. |微塵 To subdivide molecules till nothing is reached. |水 To rinse (the alms-bowl). |智 Analytical wisdom, which analyses Hīnayāna dharmas and attains to the truth that neither the ego nor things have a basis in reality.

枝 A branch. |香 Incense made of branches of trees, one of the three kinds of incense, the other two being from roots and flowers. |末惑 or |末無明 Branch and twig illusion, or ignorance in detail, contrasted with 根本無明 root, or radical ignorance, i.e. original ignorance out of which arises karma, false views, and realms of illusion which are the "branch and twig" condition or unenlightenment in detail or result. Also, the first four of the 五住地 five causal relationships, the fifth being 根本無明.

林 A grove, or wood; a band. |微(or 毘)尼; 嵐毘尼; 龍(or 流)彌你; 臘伐尼; 論民; |毘, etc. Lumbinī, the park in which Śākyamuni was born, "15 miles east of Kapilavastu." Eitel. |葬 Forest burial, to cast the corpse into a forest to be eaten by animals. |藤 Vegetable food, used by men at the beginning of a kalpa. |變 The trees of the wood turned white when the Buddha died.

東 Pūrva, East. |勝身洲; (佛婆)毘提訶; 佛婆提; 佛于逮; 逋利婆; 鼻提賀; 布嚕婆, etc. Pūrvavideha. The eastern of the four great continents of a world, east of Mt. Meru, semicircular in shape. |司; |淨; |厠 The privy in a monastery. |土 The eastern land, i.e. China. |密 The eastern esoteric or Shingon sect of Japan, in contrast with the T'ien-t'ai esoteric sect. |山 An eastern hill, or monastery, general and specific, especially the 黃梅|| Huang-mei eastern monastery of the fourth and fifth patriarchs of the Ch'an (Zen) school. |山部; 佛婆勢羅部 Pūrvaśailāḥ; one of the five divisions of the Māhāsaṁghikāḥ school. |山寺 Pūrvaśailā-saṁghārāma, a monastery east of Dhanakaṭaka. |嶽 The Eastern Peak,

T'ai Shan in Shantung, one of the five sacred peaks; the god or spirit of this peak, whose protection is claimed all over China. | 庵 The eastern hall of a monastery. | 方 The east, or eastern region. | 曼陀羅 The eastern maṇḍala, that of the Garbhadhātu.

果 Phala, 頗羅 fruit; offspring; result, consequence, effect; reward, retribution; it contrasts with cause, i.e. 因 | cause and effect. The effect by causing a further effect becomes also a cause.

果上 In the stage when the individual receives the consequences of deeds done.

果人 Those who have obtained the fruit, i.e. escaped the chain of transmigration, e.g. Buddha, Pratyeka-buddha, Arhat.

果位 The stage of attainment, or reward as contrasted with the cause-stage, i.e. the deed.

果佛性 Fruition of the Buddha-enlightenment, its perfection, one of the five forms of the Buddha-nature.

果分 The reward, e.g. of ineffable nirvāṇa, or dharmakāya.

果名; 果號 Attainment-name, or reward-name or title, i.e. of every Buddha, indicating his enlightenment.

果唯識 The wisdom attained from investigating and thinking about philosophy, or Buddha-truth, i.e. of the sūtras and abhidharmas; this includes the first four under 五種唯識.

果圓 Fruit complete, i.e. perfect enlightenment, one of the eight T'ien-t'ai perfections.

果地 The stage of attainment of the goal of any disciplinary course.

果報; 異熟 Retribution for good or evil deeds, implying that different conditions in this (or any) life are the variant ripenings, or fruit, of seed sown in previous life or lives. | | 土 The realm of reward, where bodhisattvas attain the full reward of their deeds, also called 實報無障礙土, one of the 四土 of T'ien-t'ai. | | 四相 The four forms of retribution—birth, age, sickness, death.

果德 The merits of nirvāṇa, i.e. 常樂我淨 q.v., eternal, blissful, personal (or autonomous), and pure, all transcendental.

果斷 To cut off the fruit, or results, of former karma. The arhat who has a "remnant of karma", though he has cut off the seed of misery, has not yet cut off its fruits.

果果 The fruit of fruit, i.e. nirvāṇa, the fruition of bodhi. | | 佛性 The fruit of the fruit of Buddhahood, i.e. parinirvāṇa, one of the 五佛性.

果極 Fruition perfect, the perfect virtue or merit of Buddha-enlightenment. | | 法身 The dharmakāya of complete enlightenment.

果海 The ocean of bodhi or enlightenment.

果滿 The full or complete fruition of merit; perfect reward.

果熟識 The Ālaya-vijñāna, i.e. storehouse or source of consciousness, from which both subject and object are derived.

果界圓現 In the Buddha-realm, i.e. of complete bodhi-enlightenment, all things are perfectly manifest.

果相 Reward, retribution, or effect; especially as one of the three forms of the ālaya-vijñāna.

果縛 Retribution-bond; the bitter fruit of transmigration binds the individual so that he cannot attain release. This fruit produces 子縛 or further seeds of bondage. | | 斷 Cutting off the ties of retribution, i.e. entering nirvāṇa, e.g. entering salvation.

果脣 Fruit lips, Buddha's were "red like the fruit of the Bimba tree".

果遂 The fruit follows. | | 願 The assurance of universal salvation, the twentieth of Amitābha's forty-eight vows.

果頭 The condition of retribution, especially the reward of bodhi or enlightenment, idem | 上, hence | | 佛 is he who has attained the Buddha-condition, a T'ien-t'ai term.

欣 Joyful, elated, elevated. | 求 To seek gladly. | 界 The joyful realm (of saints and sages).

毒 Poison. | 器 The poison vessel, the body. | 天二鼓 The two kinds of drum: poison-drum, harsh or stern words for repressing evil, and deva-drum, gentle words for producing good; also, misleading contrasted with correct teaching. The | 鼓 is likened also to the Buddha-nature which can slay all evil. | 樹 Poison tree, an evil monk. | 氣 Poison vapour, emitted by the three poisons, 貪瞋痴, desire, hate (or anger), stupor (or ignorance). | 箭 Poison arrow, i.e. illusion. | 藥 Poison, cf. the sons who drank their father's poisons in the 普門 chapter of The Lotus Sūtra. | 蛇 Poisonous snakes, the four elements of the body—earth, water, fire, wind (or air)—which harm a man by their variation, i.e. increase and decrease. Also, gold. | 龍 The poisonous dragon, who accepted the commandments and thus escaped from his dragon form, i.e. Śākyamuni in a former incarnation. 智度論 14.

注 Fix, record; flow. | 荼半托迦 Cūḍapanthaka, the sixteenth of the sixteen arhats.

油 Oil. | 鉢 A bowl of oil. 持 | | As careful as carrying a bowl of oil.

泡 A bubble, a blister; to infuse. | 影 Bubble and shadow, such is everything.

河 River (in north), canal (in south), especially the Yellow River in China and the Ganges 恒 | in India. | 沙 The sands of Ganges, vast in number. | 鼻旨 Avīci, the hell of uninterrupted suffering, where the sufferers die and are reborn to torture without intermission.

沓 Ripple, babble; join. Translit. *t*, *d*, etc., e.g. | 婆; | | 摩羅 Dravya Mallaputra, an arhat who was converted to the Mahāyāna faith.

治 Rule, govern; prepare; treat, cure; repress, punish. | (or 持) 國天 One of the four devas or mahārājas, guarding the eastern quarter. | 地住 One of the 十住 q.v. | 生 A living, that by which one maintains life.

泯 Vast; to flow off; ruin, confusion. | 權歸實 To depart from the temporary and find a home in the real, i.e. forget Hīnayāna, partial salvation, and turn to Mahāyāna for full and complete salvation.

泥 Mud; paste; clogged; bigoted; translit. *n*; v. 尼; | 人 A sufferer in niraya, or hell, or doomed to it. | 哩底 Nirṛti, one of the rakṣa-kings. | 塔 Paste pagoda; a mediaeval Indian custom was to make a small dagoba five or six inches high of incense, place scriptures in and make offerings to it. The esoterics adopted the custom, and worshipped for the purpose of prolonging life and ridding themselves of sins, or sufferings. | 洹 Nirvāṇa; also | 丸; | 曰; | 桓; | 畔, v. 涅. | 犁 Niraya, intp. as joyless, i.e. hell; also | 梨(耶); | 梨迦; | 黎; | 囉耶; | 底 v. 捺落迦 Naraka. | 盧鉢羅 Nīla-utpala; the blue lotus, portrayed in the hand of Mañjuśrī. | | 都 One of the sixteen hells. | 縛些那 Nivāsana, a garment, a skirt. Also | 婆娑; | 伐散娜; 涅槃僧.

波 Taraṅga. A wave, waves; to involve; translit. *p*, *b*, *v*; cf. 婆; 般; 鉢, etc.

波儞 (or 你) 尼 Pāṇini, the great Indian grammarian and writer of the fourth century B.C., also known as Śālāturīya.

波利 Pari, round, round about; complete, all. | (|) 伽羅 Parikara, an auxiliary garment, loin-cloth, towel, etc. | | 婆沙 Parivāsa, sent to a separate abode, isolation for improper conduct. | | 質(多)羅; | 疑質姤; | | 樹 Paricitra, a tree in the Trayastriṁśas heavens which fills the heavens with fragrance; also Pārijāta, a tree in Indra's heaven, one of the five trees of paradise, the coral-tree, Erythina Indica. | | 涅縛南; | | 暱縛㖷 Parinirvāṇa, v. 般.

波卑 idem 波旬.

波叉 Virūpākṣa, 毘留博叉; 鼻溜波阿叉 irregular-eyed, a syn. of Śiva; the guardian king of the West.

波吒羅 Pāṭalī, 鉢怛羅 a tree with scented blossoms, the trumpet-flower, *Bignonia Suaveolens*. A kingdom, i.e. | | 釐(子); | | 利弗; | | 梨耶; | 羅利弗多羅; 巴連弗 Pāṭaliputra, originally Kusumapura, the modern Patna; capital of Aśoka, where the third synod was held.

波哆迦 Patākā, a flag.

波夷羅 Vajra, one of the generals of Yao-shih, Bhaiṣajya, the Buddha of Healing.

波 奴 ? Vidhu, a syn. for the moon.

波 婆 (or 和) 利 Pravarī, or perhaps Pravara, woollen or hairy cloth, name of a monastery, the 丨丨梨 奄 婆. Also 丨丨丨 or 丨丨離 name of a maternal aunt of Maitreya.

波 尼; 波 抳 Pāna, drink, beverage; tr. as water (to drink); 丨丨藍 tr. as "water", but may be Pānila, a drinking vessel.

波 崙 v. 薩 陀.

波 帝 Pati, 鉢 底 master, lord, proprietor, husband.

波 戍 Paśu, any animal.

波 斯 Pārasī, Persian, Persia. 丨嘶; 丨剌 斯 or 私; 丨羅 悉. In its capital of Surasthāna the Buddha's almsbowl was said to be in A.D. 600. Eitel. 丨丨(匿); 鉢 邏 犀 (or 斯) 那 恃 (or 時) 多; 丨剌 斯 Prasenajit, king of Śrāvastī, contemporary of the Buddha, and known *inter alia* as (勝) 光 王; father of Virūḍhaka, who supplanted him.

波 旬 (踰); 波 鞞 Pāpīyān. Pāpīmān. Pāpīmā. Pāpīyān is very wicked. Pāpīyān is a Buddhist term for 惡 者 the Evil One; 殺 者 the Murderer; Māra; because he strives to kill all goodness; v. 魔. Also 丨卑 面 or 椽 or 緣.

波 (栗) 濕 縛; 波 奢 Pārśva, the ribs. The tenth patriarch, previously a Brahman of Gandhāra, who took a vow not to lie down until he had mastered the meaning of the Tripiṭaka, cut off all desire in the realms of sense, form and non-form, and obtained the six supernatural powers and the eight pāramitās. This he accomplished after three years. His death is put at 36 B.C. His name is tr. as 脇 尊 者 his Worship of the Ribs.

波 樓 那 A fierce wind, hurricane, perhaps Vātyā. 丨丨沙 迦 Paruṣaka, a park in the Trayastriṁśas heaven.

波 波 Running hither and thither. Also, Pāvā, a place near Rājagṛha. 丨丨劫 劫 Rushing about for ever. 丨丨羅 Pippala, *Ficus religiosa*.

波 浪 Taraṅga, a wave, waves.

波 演 (or 衍) 那 ? Paryayaṇa, suggesting an ambulatory; intp. as a courtyard.

波 羅 伽 Pāraka, carrying over, saving; the pāramitā boat. 丨丨迦 Pāraga, a title of Buddha who has reached the other shore. 丨丨伽 羅; 鉢 囉 迦 羅 Prākāra, a containing wall, fence.

波 羅 夷 Pārājika. The first section of the Vinaya piṭaka containing rules of expulsion from the order, for unpardonable sin. Also 丨丨闍 巳 迦; 丨丨市 迦. Cf. 四 丨丨丨. There are in Hīnayāna eight sins for expulsion of nuns, and in Mahāyāna ten. The esoteric sects have their own rules. The 丨丨丨四 喩 four metaphors addressed by the Buddha to monks are: he who breaks the vow of chastity is as a needle without an eye, a dead man, a broken stone which cannot be united, a tree cut in two which cannot live.

波 羅 奈 (斯) Vārāṇasī. Ancient kingdom and city on the Ganges, now Benares, where was the Mṛgadāva park. Also 丨丨捺 (寫); 丨丨痆 斯; 丨剌 那 斯.

波 羅 奢 華 Palāśa; a leaf, petal, foliage; the blossom of the *Butea frondosa*, a tree with red flowers, whose sap is used for dye; said to be black before sunrise, red during the day, and yellow after sunset.

波 羅 尼 密 婆 舍 跋 提 天 Paranirmita-vaśavartin, "obedient to the will of those who are transformed by others," M. W.; v. 他 化 自 在 天.

波 羅 提 (提) 舍 尼 Pratideśanīya. A section of the Vinaya concerning public confession of sins. Explained by 向 彼 悔 罪 confession of sins before another or others. Also 丨丨舍 尼; 提 舍 尼; 丨胝 丨丨丨; 鉢 剌 底 丨丨丨.

波 羅 提 木 叉 Pratimokṣa; emancipation, deliverance, absolution. Prātimokṣa; the 250 commandments for monks in the Vinaya, v. 木 叉, also 婆; the rules in the Vinaya from the four major to the seventy-five minor offences; they should be read in assembly twice a month and each monk invited to confess his sins for absolution.

波 羅 提 (or 梯) 毘 Pṛthivī, the earth. Also 鉢 里 體 尾. See 地.

波羅末陀 Paramārtha, the highest truth, ultimate truth, reality, fundamental meaning, 眞諦. Name of a famous monk from Western India, Guṇarata, v. 拘, whose title was 眞諦三藏; reached China 547 or 548, but the country was so disturbed that he set off to return by sea; his ship was driven back to Canton, where he translated some fifty works.

波羅蜜多 Pāramitā, 播囉弭多, derived from parama, highest, acme, is intp. as to cross over from this shore of births and deaths to the other shore, or nirvāṇa. The six pāramitās or means of so doing are: (1) dāna, charity; (2) śīla, moral conduct; (3) kṣānti, patience; (4) vīrya, energy, or devotion; (5) dhyāna, contemplation, or abstraction; (6) prajñā, knowledge. The 十度 ten are the above with (7) upāya, use of expedient or proper means; (8) praṇidhana, vows, for bodhi and helpfulness; (9) bala, strength, purpose; (10) wisdom. Childers gives the list of ten as the perfect exercise of almsgiving, morality, abnegation of the world and of self, wisdom, energy, patience, truth, resolution, kindness, and resignation. Each of the ten is divisible into ordinary, superior, and unlimited perfection, or thirty in all. Pāramitā is tr. by 度; 度無極; 到彼岸; 究竟.

波羅赴 Prabhu, 鉢喇部 surpassing, powerful; a title of Viṣṇu "as personification of the sun", of Brahmā, Śiva, Indra, etc. Prabhū, come into being, originate, original.

波羅越 Pārāvata, a dove; the fifth row of a rock-cut temple in the Deccan, said to resemble a dove, described by Fa-hsien.

波羅門 Brahmin, v. 婆.

波羅頗婆底 Prabhāvatī, younger sister of Aśoka. |||迦羅蜜多羅 Prabhākaramitra, enlightener, v. |頗.

波耶 Payas, water; in Sanskrit it also means milk, juice, vital force.

波謎羅 Pamira, the Pamirs, "the centre of the Tsung-ling mountains with the Sirikol lake (v. Anavatapta) in Lat. 38° 20 N., Long. 74° E." Eitel.

波輸鉢多 Pāśupata; a particular sect of Sivaites who smeared their bodies with ashes.

波逸提; 波藥致 Pātaka. A sin causing one to fall into purgatory. Also ||底迦; |夜|; |羅逸尼柯; |(羅夜)質胝迦; but there seems to be a connection with prāyaścitta, meaning expiation, atonement, restitution.

波那娑 Panasa, 半那娑 the bread-fruit tree, jaka or jack-fruit.

波里衣多羅 Pāriyātra, "an ancient kingdom 800 li south-west of Śatadru, a centre of heretical sects. The present city of Birat, west of Mathurā." Eitel.

波闍波提 Prajāpatī, |(邏)|鉢| aunt and nurse of the Buddha, v. 摩訶. ||羅 Vajra, the diamond sceptre, v. 金剛杵.

波陀 Pada; a step, footprint, position; a complete word; u.f. 阿||那 avadāna. ||劫; 跋達羅劫 Bhadra-kalpa, v. 賢劫 and 颰.

波離 Upāli, v. 優.

波鞞 v. |旬.

波頗 Prabhā(kara)mitra, an Indian monk, who came to China in A.D. 626.

波頭摩 Padma, |曇|; |暮; etc., the red lotus; v. 鉢; tr. 華 or 蓮. |||巴尼 Padmapāṇi, one of the forms of Kuan-yin, holding a lotus.

法 Dharma, 達磨; 曇無 (or 摩); 達摩 (or 謨) Law, truth, religion, thing, anything Buddhist. Dharma is "that which is held fast or kept, ordinance, statute, law, usage, practice, custom"; "duty"; "right"; "proper"; "morality"; "character". M. W. It is used in the sense of 一切 all things, or anything small or great, visible or invisible, real or unreal, affairs, truth, principle, method, concrete things, abstract ideas, etc. Dharma is described as that which has entity and bears its own attributes. It connotes Buddhism as the perfect religion; it also has the second place in the Triratna 佛法僧, and in the sense of |身 Dharmakāya it approaches the Western idea of "spiritual". It is also one of the six media of sensation, i.e. the thing or object in relation to mind, v. 六塵.

法主 Dharma-lord, Buddha.

法乳 The milk of the dharma which nourishes the spiritual nature.

法事; 佛事 Religious affairs, e.g. assemblies and services; discipline and ritual.

法位 (1) Dharma-state, the bhūtatathatā. (2) The grade or position of a monk.

法住 Dharma abode, i.e. the omnipresent bhūtatathatā in all things. Dharmasthititā, continuity of dharma.

法佛 idem 丨身丨, or 丨性丨.

法侶 A companion of the Dharma, a disciple.

法供養 Dharmapūjā. Serving the Dharma, i.e. believing, explaining, keeping, obeying it, cultivating the spiritual nature, protecting and assisting Buddhism. Also, offerings of or to the Dharma.

法光定 Samādhi of the light of Truth, that of the bodhisattva in the first stage.

法入; 法處 The sense-data of direct mental perception, one of the 十二入 or 處.

法公 Signior of the Law, a courtesy title of any monk.

法典 The scriptures of Buddhism.

法利 The blessing, or benefits, of Buddhism.

法劍 The sword of Buddha-truth, able to cut off the functioning of illusion.

法力 The power of Buddha-truth to do away with calamity and subdue evil.

法化 Transformation by Buddha-truth; teaching in or by it. 丨丨生身 The nirmāṇakāya, or corporeal manifestation of the spiritual Buddha.

法匠 Dharma workman, a teacher able to mould his pupils.

法印 The seal of Buddha-truth, expressing its reality and immutability, also its universality and its authentic transmission from one Buddha or patriarch to another.

法句經 Dharmapāda, 曇鉢經 a work by Dharmatrāta, of which there are four Chinese translations, A.D. 224, 290–306, 399, 980–1001.

法名 A monk's name, given to him on ordination, a term chiefly used by the 眞 Shin sect, 戒名 being the usual term.

法同舍 A communal religious abode, i.e. a monastery or convent where religion and food are provided for spiritual and temporal needs.

法味 The taste or flavour of the dharma.

法命 The wisdom-life of the Dharmakāya, intp. as 法身慧命. The age or lifetime of a monk.

法喜 Joy in the Law, the joy of hearing or tasting dharma. Name of Dharmanandi, v. 曇. 丨丨食 The food of joy in the Law.

法號 The name received by a monk on ordination, i.e. his 戒名; also his posthumous title.

法器 Implements used in worship; one who obeys the Buddha; a vessel of the Law.

法四依 The four trusts of dharma: trust in the Law, not in men; trust in sūtras containing ultimate truth; trust in truth, not in words; trust in wisdom growing out of eternal truth and not in illusory knowledge.

法城 Dharma as a citadel against the false; the secure nirvāṇa abode; the sūtras as the guardians of truth.

法域 The realm of dharma, nirvāṇa; also 法性土.

法堂 The chief temple, so called by the Ch'an (Zen) sect; amongst others it is 講堂 preaching hall.

法堅那羅王 Druma, king of the Kinnaras.

法場 Any place set aside for religious practices, or purposes; also 道場.

法執 Holding to things as realities, i.e the false tenet that things are real.

法報化三身 The Trikāya: 法 Dharmakāya, the absolute or spiritual body; 報 Saṁbhogakāya, the body of bliss; 化 Nirmāṇakāya, the body of incarnation. In Hīnayāna 法身 is described as the commandments, meditations, wisdom, nirvāṇa, and nirvāṇa-enlightenment; 報身 is the reward-body of bliss; 化 or 應 (化) is the body in its various incarnations. In Mahāyāna, the three bodies are regarded as distinct, but also as aspects of one body which pervades all beings. Cf. 三身.

法塵 A mental object, any direct mental perception, not dependent on the sense organs. Cf. 六塵.

法夏 Dharma summers, the years or age of a monk; v. 法臘.

法天 Dharmadeva, a monk from the Nālandāsaṁghārāma who tr. under this name forty-six works, 973–981, and under the name of Dharmabhadra seventy-two works, 982–1001.

法子 Child of the Dharma, one who makes his living by following Buddhism.

法宇 Dharma roof, or canopy, a monastery.

法定 One of the twelve names for the Dharma-nature, implying that it is the basis of all phenomena.

法家 Buddhism; cf. 法門.

法密 Dharmagupta, founder of the school of this name in Ceylon, one of the seven divisions of the Sarvāstivādāḥ.

法寶 Dharmaratna. (1) Dharma-treasure, i.e. the Law or Buddha-truth, the second personification in the Triratna 三寶. (2) The personal articles of a monk or nun—robe, almsbowl, etc. | | 藏 The storehouse of all law and truth, i.e. the sūtras.

法尼 A nun.

法山 Buddha-truth mountain, i.e. the exalted dharma.

法帝 Dharma emperor, i.e. the Buddha.

法師 A Buddhist teacher, master of the Law; five kinds are given—a custodian (of the sūtras), reader, intoner, expounder, and copier.

法幢 The standard of Buddha-truth as an emblem of power over the hosts of Māra.

法平等 Dharmasamatā; the sameness of truth as taught by all Buddhas.

法度 Rules, or disciplines and methods.

法弟 A Buddhist disciple.

法律 Laws or rules (of the Order).

法忍 Patience attained through dharma, to the overcoming of illusion; also ability to bear patiently external hardships.

法念處 The position of insight into the truth that nothing has reality in itself; v. 四念處.

法性 Dharmatā. Dharma-nature, the nature underlying all things, the bhūtatathatā, a Mahāyāna philosophical concept unknown in Hīnayāna, v. 眞如 and its various definitions in the 法相, 三論 (or 法性), 華嚴, and 天台 Schools. It is discussed both in its absolute and relative senses, or static and dynamic. In the Mahāparinirvāṇa sūtra and various śāstras the term has numerous alternative forms, which may be taken as definitions, i.e. 法定 inherent dharma, or Buddha-nature; | 住 abiding dharma-nature; | 界 dharmakṣetra, realm of dharma; | 身 dharmakāya, embodiment of dharma; 實際 region of reality; 實相 reality; 空性 nature of the Void, i.e. immaterial nature; 佛性 Buddha-nature; 無相 appearance of nothingness, or immateriality; 眞如 bhūtatathatā; 如來藏 Tathāgatagarbha; 平等性 universal nature; 離生性 immortal nature; 無我性 impersonal nature; 虛定界 realm of abstraction; 不虛妄性 nature of no illusion; 不變異性 immutable nature; 不思議界 realm beyond thought; 自性清淨心 mind of absolute purity, or unsulliedness, etc. Of these the terms 眞如, 法性, and 實際 are most used by the Prajñāpāramitā sūtras. | | 土 The kṣetra, or region of the dharma-nature, i.e. the bhūtatathatā, or 眞如, in its dynamic relations. | | 宗 The sects, e.g. 華嚴, 天台, 眞言 Hua-yen, T'ien-t'ai, Shingon, which hold that all things proceed from the bhūtatathatā, i.e. the Dharmakāya, and that all phenomena are of the same essence as the noumenon. | | 山 The dharma-nature as a mountain, i.e. fixed, immovable. | | 常樂 The eternity and bliss of the dharma-nature, v. 常樂我淨. | | 水 The water of the dharma-nature, i.e. pure. | | 海 The ocean of the dharma-nature, vast, unfathomable, v. | 水. | | 眞如 Dharma-nature and bhūtatathatā, different terms but of the same meaning. | | 身 idem 法身. | | 隨妄 The dharma-nature in the sphere of delusion; i.e. | | | 緣; 眞如隨緣 the dharma-nature, or bhūtatathatā, in its phenomenal character; the dharma-nature may be static or dynamic; when dynamic it may by environment either become sullied, producing the world of illusion, or remain unsullied, resulting in nirvāṇa. Static, it is likened to a smooth sea; dynamic, to its waves.

法恩 Dharma-grace, i.e. the grace of the Triratna.

法悅 Joy from hearing and meditating on the Law.

法慳 Meanness in offering Buddha-truth, avariciously holding on to it for oneself.

法愛 Religious love in contrast with 欲愛 ordinary love; Dharma-love may be Hīnayāna desire for nirvāṇa; or bodhisattva attachment to illusory things, both of which are to be eradicated; or Tathāgata-love, which goes out to all beings for salvation.

法成就 Siddhi 悉地 ceremony successful, a term of the esoteric sect when prayer is answered.

法我 A thing *per se*, i.e. the false notion of anything being a thing in itself, individual, independent, and not merely composed of elements to be disintegrated. | | 見 The false view as above, cf. 我見.

法教 Buddhism.

法數 The categories of Buddhism such as the three realms, five skandhas, five regions, four dogmas, six paths, twelve nidānas, etc.

法文 The literature of Buddhism.

法施 The almsgiving of the Buddha-truth, i.e. its preaching or explanation; also 法布施.

法明 Dharmaprabhāsa, brightness of the law, a Buddha who will appear in our universe in the Ratnāvabhāsa-kalpa in a realm called Suviśuddha 善淨, when there will be no sexual difference, birth taking place by transformation. | | 道 The wisdom of the pure heart which illumines the Way of all Buddhas. | | 門 The teaching which sheds light on everything, differentiating and explaining them.

法智 Dharma-wisdom, which enables one to understand the four dogmas 四諦; also, the understanding of the law, or of things.

法會 An assembly for worship or preaching. | | 社 A monastery.

法有 The false view of Hīnayāna that things, or the elements of which they are made, are real. | | 我無宗 The Sarvāstivādins who while disclaiming the reality of personality claimed the reality of things.

法服; 法衣 Dharma garment, the robe.

法本 The root or essence of all things, the bhūtatathatā.

法樂 Religious joy, in contrast with the joy of common desire; that of hearing the dharma, worshipping Buddha, laying up merit, making offerings, repeating sūtras, etc.

法樹 The dharma-tree which bears nirvāṇa-fruit.

法橋 The bridge of Buddha-truth, which is able to carry all across to nirvāṇa.

法殿 The temple, or hall, of the Law, the main hall of a monastery; also the Kuan-yin hall.

法比量 Inferring one thing from another, as from birth deducing death, etc.

法水 Buddha-truth likened to water able to wash away the stains of illusion; | 河 to a deep river; | 海 to a vast deep ocean.

法沙 Kashgar, "or (after the name of the capital) 疏勒. An ancient Buddhistic kingdom in Central Asia. The *Casia regis* of the ancients." Eitel.

法波羅蜜 One of the four Pāramitā Bodhisattvas in the Diamond realm.

法滅 The extinction of the Law, or Buddhism, after the third of the three stages 正像末.

法炬 The torch of Buddhism.

法照 Dharma-shining; name of the fourth patriarch of the 蓮宗 Lotus sect.

法然 According to rule, naturally; also 法爾; 自然.

法燈 The lamp of dharma, which dispels the darkness of ignorance.

法無我 Dharmanairātmya. Things are without independent individuality, i.e. the tenet that things have no independent reality, no reality in themselves. | | | 智 The knowledge or wisdom of the above. | | 礙 (解 or 智) Wisdom or power of explanation in unembarrassed accord with the Law, or Buddha-truth.

法爾 idem 法然.

法將 Dharma-generals, i.e. monks of high character and leadership.

法王 Dharmarāja, King of the Law, Buddha. | | 子 Son of the Dharma-king, a Bodhisattva.

法界 Dharmadhātu, 法性; 實相; 達磨馱都 Dharma-element, -factor, or -realm. (1) A name for "things" in general, noumenal or phenomenal; for the physical universe, or any portion or phase of it. (2) The unifying underlying spiritual reality regarded as the ground or cause of all things, the absolute from which all proceeds. It is one of the eighteen dhātus. There are categories of three, four, five, and ten dharmadhātus; the first three are combinations of 事 and 理 or active and passive, dynamic and static; the ten are: Buddha-realm, Bodhisattva-realm, Pratyekabuddha-realm, Śrāvaka, Deva, Human, Asura, Demon, Animal, and Hades realms—a Hua-yen category. T'ien-t'ai has ten for meditation, i.e. the realms of the eighteen media of perception (the six organs, six objects, and six sense-data or sensations), of illusion, sickness, karma, māra, samādhi, (false) views, pride, the two lower Vehicles, and the Bodhisattva Vehicle. | | 一相 The essential unity of the phenomenal realm.

法界佛 The Dharmadhātu Buddha, i.e. the Dharmakāya; the universal Buddha; the Buddha of a Buddha-realm. | | 加持 Mutual dependence and aid of all beings in a universe. | | 唯心 The universe is mind only; cf. Hua-yen sūtra, Laṅkāvatāra sūtra, etc. | | 圓融 The perfect intercommunion or blending of all things in the Dharmadhātu; the 無礙 of Hua-yen and the 性具 of T'ien-t'ai. | | 定 In dharmadhātu meditation, a term for Vairocana in both maṇḍalas. | | 宮 The dharmadhātu-palace, i.e. the shrine of Vairocana in the Garbhadhātu. | | 實相 Dharmadhātu-reality, or Dharmadhātu is Reality, different names but one idea, i.e. 實相 is used for 理 or noumenon by the 別教 and 法界 by the 圓教. | | 性 idem | 界 and | 性. | | 無礙智; | | | 邊智 The unimpeded or unlimited knowledge or omniscience of a Buddha in regard to all beings and things in his realm. | | 等流 The universal outflow of the spiritual body of the Buddha, i.e. his teaching. | | 緣起 The Dharmadhātu as the environmental cause of all phenomena, everything being dependent on everything else, therefore one is in all and all in one. | | 藏 The treasury or storehouse or source of all phenomena, or truth. | | 身 The Dharmakāya (manifesting itself in all beings); the Dharmadhātu as the Buddhakāya, all things being Buddha. | | 體性智 Intelligence as the fundamental nature of the universe; Vairocana as cosmic energy and wisdom interpenetrating all elements of the universe, a term used by the esoteric sects.

法相 The aspects or characteristics of things—all things are of monad nature but differ in form. A name of the 法相宗 Fa-hsiang or Dharmalakṣaṇa sect (Jap. Hossō), called also 慈恩宗 Tz'ŭ-ên sect from the T'ang temple, in which lived 窺基 K'uei-chi, known also as 慈恩. It "aims at discovering the ultimate entity of cosmic existence in contemplation, through investigation into the specific characteristics (the marks or criteria) of all existence, and through the realization of the fundamental nature of the soul in mystic illumination". "An inexhaustible number" of "seeds" are "stored up in the Ālaya-soul; they manifest themselves in innumerable varieties of existence, both physical and mental". "Though there are infinite varieties . . they all participate in the prime nature of the Ālaya." Anesaki. The Fa-hsiang School is one of the "eight schools", and was established in China on the return of Hsüan-tsang, consequent on his translation of the Yogācārya works. Its aim is to understand the principle underlying the 萬法性相 or nature and characteristics of all things. Its foundation works are the 解深密經, the 唯識論, and the 瑜伽論. It is one of the Mahāyāna realistic schools, opposed by the idealistic schools, e.g. the 三論 school; yet it was a "combination of realism and idealism, and its religion a profoundly mystic one". Anesaki. (大乘)||敎 The third of the five periods of doctrinal development as distinguished by 圭峯 Kuei-fêng.

法眼 The (bodhisattva) dharma-eye able to penetrate all things. Name of the founder of the ||宗 Fa-yen sect, one of the five Ch'an (Zen) schools. ||淨 To see clearly or purely the truth: in Hīnayāna, to see the truth of the four dogmas; in Mahāyāna, to see the truth which releases from reincarnation.

法空 The emptiness or unreality of things, everything being dependent on something else and having no individual existence apart from other things; hence the illusory nature of all things as being composed of elements and not possessing reality. ||眞如 The Bhūtatathatā as understood when this non-individuality or unreality of "things" is perceived. ||觀 Meditative insight into the unreality of all things.

法緣 Dharma-caused, i.e. the sense of universal altruism giving rise to pity and mercy.

法縛 idem 法執.

法臘 The end of the monk's year after the summer retreat; a Buddhist year; the number of 夏 or 戒臘 summer or discipline years indicating the years since a monk's ordination.

法臣 Ministers of the Law, i.e. Bodhisattvas; the Buddha is King of the Law, these are his ministers.

法自在 A bodhisattva's complete dialectical freedom and power, so that he can expound all things unimpeded.

法自相相違因 One of the four fallacies connected with the reason (因), in which the reason is contrary to the truth of the premiss.

法舟; 法船 The barque of Buddha-truth which ferries men out from the sea of mortality and reincarnation to nirvāṇa.

法芽 The sprout or bud of Buddhism.

法苑 The garden of Dharma, Buddhism.

法華 The Dharma-flower, i.e. the Lotus Sūtra, the ||經 or 妙法蓮華經 q.v., Saddharma-puṇḍarīka-sūtra; also the ||宗 Lotus sect, i.e. that of T'ien-t'ai, which had this sūtra for its basis. There are many treatises with this as part of the title. ||法, ||會, ||講 ceremonials, meetings, or explications connected with this sūtra. ||一實 The one perfect Vehicle of the Lotus gospel. ||八年 The last eight years of the Buddha's life, when, according to T'ien-t'ai, from 72 to 80 years of age he preached the Lotus gospel. ||三昧 The samādhi which sees into the three 諦 dogmas of 空假中 unreality, dependent reality, and transcendence, or the noumenal, phenomenal, and the absolute which unites them; it is derived from the "sixteen" samādhis in chapter 24 of The Lotus. There is a |||| 經 independent of this samādhi.

法藏 Dharma-store; also 佛法藏; 如來藏 (1) The absolute, unitary storehouse of the universe, the primal source of all things. (2) The Treasury of Buddha's teaching, the sūtras, etc. (3) Any Buddhist library. (4) Dharmākara, mine of the Law; one of the incarnations of Amitābha. (5) Title of the founder of the Hua-yen School 賢首|| Hsien-shou Fa-tsang.

法藥 The medicine of the Law, capable of healing all misery.

法蘊 The Buddha's detailed teaching, and in this respect similar to |藏.

法蘭 Gobharana, 竺||, companion of Mātaṅga, these two being the first Indian monks said to have come to China, in the middle of the first century A.D.

法螺 Conch of the Law, a symbol of the universality, power, or command of the Buddha's teaching. Cf. 商佉 Śaṅkha.

法衆 The Buddhist monkhood; an assembly of monks or nuns.

法衣 The religious dress, general name of monastic garments.

法要 The essentials of the Truth; v. | 會.

法見 Maintaining one tenet and considering others wrong; narrow-minded. bigoted.

法語 Dharma-words, religious discourses.

法誓 A religious vow.

法譬 Similes or illustrations of the dharma.

法財 The riches of the Law, or the Law as wealth.

法身 Dharmakāya, embodiment of Truth and Law, the "spiritual" or true body; essential Buddhahood; the essence of being; the absolute, the norm of the universe; the first of the Trikāya, v. 三身. The Dharmakāya is divided into 總 unity and 別 diversity; as in the noumenal absolute and phenomenal activities, or potential and dynamic; but there are differences of interpretation, e.g. as between the 法相 and 法性 schools. Cf. | | 體性. There are many categories of the Dharmakāya. In the 2 group 二法身 are five kinds: (1) 理 "substance" and 智 wisdom or expression; (2) 法性 | | essential nature and 應化 | | manifestation; the other three couples are similar. In the 3 group 三法身 are (1) the manifested Buddha, i.e. Śākyamuni; (2) the power of his teaching, etc.; (3) the absolute or ultimate reality. There are other categories. | | 佛 The Dharmakāya Buddha. | | 如來 The Dharmakāya Tathāgata, the Buddha who reveals the spiritual body. | | 塔 The Pagoda where abides a spiritual relic of Buddha; the esoteric sect uses the letter वं as such an abode of the dharmakāya. | | 流轉 Dharmakāya in its phenomenal character, conceived as becoming, as expressing itself in the stream of being. | (|) 舍利; | | 偈 The śarīra, or spiritual relics of the Buddha, his sūtras, or verses, his doctrine and immutable law. | | 菩薩; | | 大士 Dharmakāya Mahāsattva, one who has freed himself from illusion and attained the six spiritual powers 六神通; he is above the 初地, or, according to T'ien-t'ai, above the 初住. | | 藏 The storehouse of the Dharmakāya, the essence of Buddhahood, by contemplating which the holy man attains to it. | | 觀 Meditation on, or insight into, the Dharmakāya, varying in definition in the various schools. | | 體性 The embodiment, totality, or nature of the Dharmakāya. In Hīnayāna the Buddha-nature in its 理 or absolute side is described as not discussed, being synonymous with the 五分 five divisions of the commandments, meditation, wisdom, release, and doctrine, 戒, 定, 慧, 解脫, and 知見. In the Mahāyāna the 三論宗 defines the absolute or ultimate reality as the formless which contains all forms, the essence of being, the noumenon of the other two manifestations of the Triratna. The 法相宗 defines it as (*a*) the nature or essence of the whole Triratna; (*b*) the particular form of the Dharma in that trinity. The One-Vehicle schools represented by the 華嚴宗, 天台, etc., consider it to be the Bhūtatathatā, 理 and 智 being one and undivided. The Shingon sect takes the six elements—earth, water, fire, air, space, mind—as the 理 or fundamental Dharmakāya and the sixth, mind, intelligence, or knowledge, as the 智 Wisdom Dharmakāya.

法輪 Dharma-cakra, the Wheel of the Law, Buddha-truth which is able to crush all evil and all opposition, like Indra's wheel, and which rolls on from man to man, place to place, age to age. 轉 | | To turn, or roll along the Law-wheel, i.e. to preach Buddha-truth.

法鈴 The dharma-bell; the pleasing sound of intoning the sūtras.

法鏡 The Dharma mirror, reflecting the Buddha-wisdom.

法門 Dharmaparyāya. The doctrines, or wisdom of Buddha regarded as the door to enlightenment. A method. Any sect. As the living have 84,000 delusions, so the Buddha provides 84,000 methods | | of dealing with them. Hence the | | 海 ocean of Buddha's methods. | | 身 A T'ien-t'ai definition of the Dharmakāya of the Trinity, i.e. the qualities, powers, and methods of the Buddha. The various representations of the respective characteristics of Buddhas and bodhisattvas in the maṇḍalas.

法陀羅尼 One of the four kinds of dhāraṇī: holding firmly to the truth one has heard, also called 聞 | | |.

法阿育 Dharmāśoka; name given to Aśoka on his conversion; cf. 阿育.

法集 idem 佛會.

法雨 The rain of Buddha-truth which fertilizes all beings.

法雲 Dharmamegha. Buddhism as a fertilizing cloud. | | 地 The tenth bodhisattva-stage, when the dharma-clouds everywhere drop their sweet dew. | | 等覺 The stage after the last, that of universal knowledge, or enlightenment.

法雷 The thunder of dharma, awakening man from stupor and stimulating the growth of virtue, the awful voice of Buddha-truth. | 電 The lightning of the Truth.

法非法 Dharmādharma; real and unreal; thing and nothing; being and non-being, etc.

法音 The sound of the Truth, or of preaching.

法顯 Fa-hsien, the famous pilgrim who with fellow-monks left Ch'ang-an A.D. 399 overland for India, finally reached it, remained alone for six years, and spent three years on the return journey, arriving by sea in 414. His 佛國記 *Records of the Buddhistic Kingdoms* were made, on his information, by Buddhabhadra, an Indian monk in China. His own chief translation is the 僧祇律, a work on monastic discipline.

法食 Dharmāhāra. Diet in harmony with the rules of Buddhism; truth as food. | | 時 The regulation time for meals, at or before noon, and not after.

法體 Embodiment of the Law, or of things. (1) Elements into which the Buddhists divided the universe; the Abhidharma-kośa has 75, the 成實論 Satyasiddhi-śāstra 84, the Yogācārya 100. (2) A monk.

法魔 Bemused by things; the illusion that things are real and not merely seeming.

法鼓 The drum of the Law, stirring all to advance in virtue.

法齋日 The day of abstinence observed at the end of each half month, also the six abstinence days, in all making the eight days for keeping the eight commandments.

炙 Broil, burn, roast, dry; intimate. | 茄會 A Ch'an (Zen) School winter festival at which roasted lily roots were eaten.

炎 Blazing, burning. | 熱地獄 Tapana, the hell of burning or roasting, the sixth of the eight hot hells, where 24 hours equal 2,600 years on earth, life lasting 16,000 years. | 經 A name for the Nirvāṇa sūtra, referring to the Buddha's cremation; also to its glorious teaching. | 點 Nirvāṇa, which burns up metempsychosis.

牧 To herd, pastor. | 牛 Cowherd.

物 Thing, things in general, beings, living beings, matters; "substance," cf. 陀羅驃 Dravya. | 施 One of the three kinds of almsgiving, that of things. | 機 That on which anything depends, or turns; the motive or vital principle.

狐 A fox; seems to be used also for a jackal.

狗 A dog. | 心 A dog's heart, satisfied with trifles, unreceptive of Buddha's teaching. | 戒 Dog-rule, dog-morals, i.e. heretics who sought salvation by living like dogs, eating garbage, etc. | 法 Dog-law, fighting and hating, characteristics of the monks in the last days of the world. | 臨井吠 Like the dog barking at its own reflection in the well. | 著獅子皮 The dog in the lion's skin—all the dogs fear him till he barks.

盂蘭(盆); 烏藍婆(拏) Ullambana 盂蘭 may be another form of Lambana, or Avalamba, "hanging down," "depending," "support"; it is intp. "to hang upside down", or "to be in suspense", referring to extreme suffering in purgatory; but there is a suggestion of the dependence of the dead on the living. By some 盆 is regarded as a Chinese word, not part of the transliteration, meaning a vessel filled with offerings of food. The term is applied to the festival of All Souls, held about the 15th of the 7th moon, when masses are read by Buddhist and Taoist priests and elaborate offerings made to the Buddhist Trinity for the purpose of releasing from purgatory the souls of those who have died on land or sea. The Ullambanapātra-sūtra is attributed to Śākyamuni, of course incorrectly; it was first tr. into Chinese by Dharmaraksha, A.D. 266–313 or 317; the first masses are not reported until the time of Liang Wu-ti, A.D. 538; and were popularized by Amogha (A.D. 732) under the influence of the Yogācārya School. They are generally observed in China, but are unknown to Southern

Buddhism. The "idea of intercession on the part of the priesthood for the benefit of" souls in hell "is utterly antagonistic to the explicit teaching of primitive Buddhism". The origin of the custom is unknown, but it is foisted on to Śākyamuni, whose disciple Maudgalyāyana is represented as having been to purgatory to relieve his mother's sufferings. Śākyamuni told him that only the united efforts of the whole priesthood 十方衆會 could alleviate the pains of the suffering. The mere suggestion of an All Souls Day with a great national day for the monks is sufficient to account for the spread of the festival. Eitel says: "Engrafted upon the native ancestral worship, this ceremonial for feeding the ghosts of deceased ancestors of seven generations obtained immense popularity and is now practised by everybody in China, by Taoists even and by Confucianists." All kinds of food offerings are made and paper garments, etc., burnt. The occasion, 7th moon, 15th day, is known as the | | (|) 會 (or 齋) and the sūtra as | | (|) 經.

盲 Blind. | 冥 Blind and in darkness, ignorant of the truth. | 跛 Blind and lame, an ignorant teacher. | 龍 The blind dragon who appealed to the Buddha and was told that his blindness was due to his having been formerly a sinning monk. | 龜 It is as easy for a blind turtle to find a floating log as it is for a man to be reborn as a man, or to meet with a Buddha and his teaching.

直 Straight, upright, direct; to arrange. | 傳 Direct information or transmission (by word of mouth). | 堂 The servant who attends in the hall; an announcer. | 心 Straightforward, sincere, blunt. | 裰; | 裰 A monk's garment, upper and lower in one. | 歲 A straight year, a year's (plans, or duties). | 說 Straight, or direct, speech; the sūtras. | 道 The direct way (to nirvāṇa and Buddha-land).

知 To know. Sanskrit root Vid, hence vidyā, knowledge; the vedas, etc. 知 vijñā is to know, 智 is vijñāna, wisdom arising from perception or knowing.

知一切法智 The Buddha-wisdom of knowing every thing or method (of salvation). | | | 衆生智 The Buddha-wisdom which knows (the karma of) all beings.

知世間 Lokavid. He who knows the world, one of the ten characteristics of a Buddha.

知事 To know affairs. The karmadāna, or director of affairs in a monastery, next below the abbot.

知客 The director of guests, i.e. the host.

知寮 Warden of the monasterial abodes.

知庫 The bursar (of a monastery).

知根 The organs of perception. To know the roots, or capacities (of all beings, as does a Bodhisattva; hence he has no fears).

知殿 The warden of a temple.

知法 To know the Buddha-law, or the rules; to know things; in the exoteric sects, to know the deep meaning of the sūtras; in the esoteric sects, to know the mysteries.

知無邊諸佛智 To have the infinite Buddha-wisdom (of knowing all the Buddha-worlds and how to save the beings in them).

知禮 Knowing the right modes of respect, or ceremonial; courteous, reverential; Chih-li, name of the famous tenth-century monk of the Sung dynasty, Ssŭ-ming 四明, so called after the name of his monastery, a follower of the T'ien-t'ai school, sought out by a Japanese deputation in 1017.

知者 The knower, the cognizer, the person within who perceives.

知苦斷集 To know (the dogma of) suffering and be able to cut off its accumulation; cf. 四諦.

知見 To know, to know by seeing, becoming aware, intellection; the function of knowing; views, doctrines. | | 波羅蜜 The Prajñāpāramitā, v. 般若.

知論 A name for the Prajñāpāramitā, v. 般若.

知識 (1) To know and perceive, perception, knowledge. (2) A friend, an intimate. (3) The false ideas produced in the mind by common, or unenlightened knowledge; one of the 五識 in 起信論. | | 衆 A body of friends, all you friends.

知足 Complete knowledge; satisfaction. | | (天) Tuṣita, the fourth Devaloka, Maitreya's heaven of full knowledge, where all bodhisattvas are reborn before rebirth as Buddhas; the inner court is | | 院.

知道者 The one who knows the path to salvation, an epithet of the Buddha.

社 Gods of the land; a village, clan, society. | 伽 Jagat, all the living. | 得迦 Jātaka, previous births or incarnations (especially of Buddhas or bodhisattvas). | | | 摩羅 Jātakamālā, a garland of incarnation stories in verse.

秉 To lay hold of, grasp. | 拂 To hold the fly-brush, or whisk, the head of an assembly, the five heads of a monastery have this privilege. | 持 To hold firmly (to the discipline, or rules). | 炬 To carry the torch (for cremation).

空 Śūnya, empty, void, hollow, vacant, non-existent. Śūnyatā, 舜若多, vacuity, voidness, emptiness, non-existence, immateriality, perhaps spirituality, unreality, the false or illusory nature of all existence, the seeming 假 being unreal. The doctrine that all phenomena and the ego have no reality, but are composed of a certain number of skandhas or elements, which disintegrate. The void, the sky, space. The universal, the absolute, complete abstraction without relativity. There are classifications into 2, 3, 4, 6, 7, 11, 13, 16, and 18 categories. The doctrine is that all things are compounds, or unstable organisms, possessing no self-essence, i.e. are dependent, or caused, come into existence only to perish. The underlying reality, the principle of eternal relativity, or non-infinity, i.e. śūnya, permeates all phenomena making possible their evolution. From this doctrine the Yogācārya school developed the idea of the permanent reality, which is Essence of Mind, the unknowable noumenon behind all phenomena, the entity void of ideas and phenomena, neither matter nor mind, but the root of both.

空一切處 Universal emptiness, or space; the samādhi which removes all limitations of space; also 空徧處.

空三昧 The samādhi which regards the ego and things as unreal; one of the 三三昧.

空假中 Unreality, reality, and the middle or mean doctrine; noumenon, phenomenon, and the principle or absolute which unifies both. 空 Unreality, that things do not exist in reality; 假 reality, that things exist though in "derived" or "borrowed" form, consisting of elements which are permanent; 中 the "middle" doctrine of the Madhyamaka School, which denies both positions in the interests of the transcendental, or absolute. 空以破一切法, 假以立一切法, 中以妙一切法 Śūnya (universality) annihilates all relativities, particularity establishes all relativities, the middle path transcends and unites all relativities. T'ien-t'ai asserts that there is no contradiction in them and calls them a unity, the one including the other 即空即假即中.

空劫 The empty kalpa, v. 劫.

空即是色 The immaterial is the material, śūnya is rūpa, and vice versa, 色不異空.

空執 v. 空有二執.

空塵 Śūnya as sub-material, ghostly, or spiritual, as having diaphanous form, a non-Buddhist view of the immaterial as an entity, hence the false view of a soul or ego that is real.

空大 Space, one of the five elements (earth, water, fire, wind, space); v. 五大.

空如來藏 The Bhūtatathatā in its purity, or absoluteness.

空始教 The initial teaching of the undeveloped Mahāyāna doctrines is the second of the five periods of Śākyamuni's teaching as defined by the Hua-yen School. This consists of two parts: 空始教 the initial doctrine of śūnya, the texts for which are the 般若, 三論, etc.; and 相始教, the initial doctrine of the essential nature as held by the esoterics; intp. in the 深密 and 瑜伽 texts.

空定 The meditation which dwells on the Void or the Immaterial; it is divided into 內道, i.e. the 三三昧, and 外道, the latter limited to the four dhyānas 四空定 q.v., except the illusion that things have a reality in themselves, as individuals 法我 q.v.

空宗 The Śūnya sects, i.e. those which make the unreality of the ego and things their fundamental tenet.

空寂 Immaterial; a condition beyond disturbance, the condition of nirvāṇa.

空居天 Devas dwelling in space, or the heavenly regions, i.e. the devalokas and rūpalokas.

空徧處 idem | 一切 |.

空心 An empty mind, or heart; a mind meditating on the void, or infinite; a mind not entangled in cause and effect, i.e. detached from the phenomenal.

空忍 Patience attained by regarding suffering as unreal; one of the 十忍.

空性 Śūnyatā, v. 空, the nature of the Void, or immaterial, the Bhūtatathatā, the universal substance, which is not 我法 ego and things, but while not Void is of the Void-nature.

空想 Thinking of immateriality. Also, vainly thinking, or desiring.

空慧 The wisdom which beholds spiritual truth.

空拳 Riktamuṣṭi; empty fist, i.e. deceiving a child by pretending to have something for it in the closed hand; not the Buddha's method.

空教 The teaching that all is unreal. The 法相宗 Dharmalakṣaṇa School divided Buddha's teaching into three periods: (1) the Hīnayāna period, teaching that 法有 things are real; (2) the 般若 Prajñā period, that 法空 things are unreal; (3) the Hua-yen and Lotus period of the middle or transcendental doctrine 中道教.

空有 Unreal and real, non-existent and existent, abstract and concrete, negative and positive. | | 二執 (or 見). The two (false) tenets, or views, that karma and nirvāṇa are not real, and that the ego and phenomena are real; these wrong views are overcome by the | | 二觀 meditating on the unreality of the ego and phenomena, and the reality of karma and nirvāṇa. | | 二宗 The two schools 空 and 有 in Hīnayāna are given as 俱舍 Kośa for 有 and 成實 Satyasiddhi for 空, in Mahāyāna 法相 for 有 and 三論 for 空.

空果 Empty fruit; also fruit of freedom from the illusion that things and the ego are real.

空法 (1) To regard everything as unreal, i.e. the ego, things, the dynamic, the static. (2) The nirvāṇa of Hīnayāna.

空海 Like sky and sea; like space and the ocean for magnitude.

空無 Unreality, or immateriality, of things, which is defined as nothing existing of independent or self-contained nature. | | 我 Unreal and without ego. | | 邊處 v. 空處.

空王 The king of immateriality, or spirituality, Buddha, who is lord of all things. | | 佛 Dharmagahanābhyudgata-rāja. A Buddha who is said to have taught absolute intelligence, or knowledge of the absolute, cf. Lotus sūtra 9.

空理 The śūnya principle, or law, i.e. the unreality of the ego and phenomena.

空生 The one who expounded vacuity or immateriality, i.e. Subhūti, one of the ten great pupils of the Buddha.

空界 The realm of space, one of the six realms, earth, water, fire, wind, space, knowledge. The | | 色 is the visible realm of space, the sky, beyond which is real space.

空相 Voidness, emptiness, space, the immaterial, that which cannot be expressed in terms of the material. The characteristic of all things is unreality, i.e. they are composed of elements which disintegrate. v. 空.

空空 Unreality of unreality. When all has been regarded as illusion, or unreal, the abstract idea of unreality itself must be destroyed. | | 寂寂 Void and silent, i.e. everything in the universe, with form or without form, is unreal and not to be considered as real.

空經 The sūtras of unreality or immateriality, e.g. the Prajñāpāramitā.

空聖 A saint who bears the name without possessing the character.

空聚 (1) An empty abode or place. (2) The body as composed of the six skandhas, which is a temporary assemblage without underlying reality.

空色 Formless and with form; noumena and phenomena.

空華; 空花 Khapuṣpa, flowers in the sky, spots before the eyes, *Muscœ volitantes*; illusion. The Indian Hīnayānists style Mahāyānists | | 外道 Śūnyapuṣpa, sky-flower heretics, or followers of illusion.

空處; 空無邊處 Ākāśānantyāyatana; the abode of infinite space, the formless, or immaterial world 無色界 the first of the Arūpaloka heavens, one of the four Brahmalokas. | (| |) | 定 The dhyāna, or meditation connected with the above, in which all thought of form is suppressed.

空行 The discipline or practice of the immaterial, or infinite, thus overcoming the illusion that the ego and all phenomena are realities.

空見 The heterodox view that karma and nirvāṇa are not real, v. | 有.

空觀 v. 空有二觀.

空解 The interpretation (or doctrine) of ultimate reality. | | 脫門 The gate of salvation or deliverance by the realization of the immaterial, i.e. that the ego and things are formed of elements and have no reality in themselves; one of the three deliverances.

空諦 The doctrine of immateriality, one of the three dogmas of T'ien-t'ai, that all things animate and inanimate, seeing that they result from previous causes and are without reality in themselves, are therefore 空 or not material, but "spiritual".

空輪 The wheel of space below the water and wind wheels of a world. The element space is called the wheel of space.

空門 (1) The teaching which regards everything as unreal, or immaterial. (2) The school of unreality, one of the four divisions made by T'ien-t'ai. (3) The teaching of immateriality, the door to nirvāṇa, a general name for Buddhism; hence | | 子 are Buddhist monks.

空閑處 A tr. of 阿蘭若 araṇya, i.e. "forest". A retired place, 300 to 600 steps away from human habitation, suitable for the religious practices of monks.

空際 The region of immateriality, or nirvāṇa. Also called 實際, the region of reality.

空魔 The demons who arouse in the heart the false belief that karma is not real.

空鳥 The bird that cries 空空, the cuckoo, i.e. one who, while not knowing the wonderful law of true immateriality (or spirituality), yet prates about it.

空點 The dot over the ṁ or ṅ in Sanskrit, symbolizing that all things are empty or unreal; used by the Shingon sect with various meanings.

竺 Indian. | 土; 天 |; | India. | 經 Indian, i.e. Buddhist, sūtras. Several Indians are known by this term, e.g. | 曇摩羅察; | 法護 Dharmarakṣa, or Indu-dharmarakṣa, a native of Tukhāra, who knew thirty-six languages and tr. (A.D. 266–317) some 175 works. | 法蘭 Dharmarakṣa, or Indu-dharmāraṇya, to whom with Kāśyapa Mātaṅga the translation of the sūtra of 42 sections is wrongly attributed; he tr. five works in A.D. 68–70. | 法力 Dharmabala, translator A.D. 419 of the larger Sukhāvatī-vyūha, now lost. | 葉摩騰 Kāśyapa Mātaṅga, v. 迦. | 刹尸羅 Takṣaśilā, v. 呾.

肥 Fat. | 者耶 ? Vajradhātrī, the wife or female energy of Vairocana. | 膩 A grass or herb said to enrich the milk of cattle.

肩 Shoulder; | 次; | 下; 下 | shoulder by shoulder, one next to another.

育 To rear, nurture. | 坻; | 抵 Yukti, yoking, joining, combination, plan. | | 華 Yuktā, a kind of celestial flower. | 多婆提 ? Yukta-bodhi, steps in Yoga wisdom.

卧 Śayana, lying down, sleeping. | 具 A couch, bed, mat, bedding, sleeping garments, etc. | 佛寺 A shrine of the "sleeping Buddha", i.e. of the dying Buddha.

舍 A shelter, cottage; used as a term of humility for "my"; to lodge; let go, relinquish.

舍利 (1) Śārī, Śārikā; a bird able to talk, intp. variously, but M. W. says the maina. Śārikā was the name of Śāriputra's mother, because her eyes were bright and clever like those of a maina; there are other interpretations. (2) Śarīra(m). 設 (or 室) 利羅; 實利; 攝𠼝悉藍 Relics or ashes left after the cremation of a Buddha or saint; placed in stūpas and worshipped. The white represent bones; the black, hair; and the red, flesh. Also called dhātu- or dharma-śarīra. The body, a dead body. The body looked upon as dead by reason of obedience to the discipline, meditation, and wisdom. The Lotus and other sūtras are counted as relics. Śākyamuni's relics are said to have amounted to 八斛四斗 84 pecks, for which Aśoka is reputed to have built in one day 84,000 stūpas; but other figures are also given. Śarīra is also intp. by grains of rice, etc., and by rice as food. ||塔 Śarīra-stūpa, a reliquary, or pagoda for a relic (of Buddha). ||娑婆 Sarṣapa, a mustard seed, 芥子 q.v., the 10,816,000th part of a yojana 由旬 q.v. ||弗; 奢利弗 (or 富)(多) 羅; 奢利補担羅; ||子 Śāriputra. One of the principal disciples of Śākyamuni, born at Nālandāgrāma, the son of Śārikā and Tiṣya, hence known as Upatiṣya; noted for his wisdom and learning; he is the "right-hand attendant on Śākyamuni". The followers of the Abhidharma count him as their founder and other works are attributed, without evidence, to him. He figures prominently in certain sūtras. He is said to have died before his master; he is represented as standing with Maudgalyāyana by the Buddha when entering nirvāṇa. He is to reappear as Padmaprabha Buddha 華光佛.

舍囉摩拏 Śramaṇa. 室拏; 沙迦滿囊; 沙門; 桑門; v. 沙門.

舍多提婆魔㝹舍諵 Śāstādeva-manuṣyāṇām, intp. as 天人師 teacher of gods and men, one of the ten titles of a Buddha.

舍多毘沙 Śatabhiṣā, a constellation identified with 危 in Aquarius.

舍夷 ? Śākya, one of the five surnames of the Buddha.

舍婆提 v. |衛.

舍摩 Śama, calm, quiet, a name for the bodhi tree. For ||陀 v. 奢.

舍支 Śaśa, 設施 a hare; Śaśī, or Śaśin, the moon; Śakti, energy. (1) The hare (which threw itself into the fire to save starving people), transferred by Indra to the centre of the moon. (2) Śakti is the wife or female energy of a deity, cf. |脂. (3) The female organ.

舍樓伽 Śāluka, esculent lotus roots; intp. as a kind of cooked liquid food.

舍磨奢那 Śmaśāna, a cemetery or crematorium; a low mound of stone under which the remains of monks are buried in countries west of China. Also 奢|||.

舍羅 Śārikā, Śārī, v. |利. Śalākā, bamboo or wooden tallies used in numbering monks. ||婆迦 Śrāvaka; a hearer, disciple, 聲聞 q.v. (1) He who has heard (the voice of Buddha). All the personal disciples of Śākyamuni, the chief disciples being called Mahāśrāvaka. (2) The lowest degree of saintship, the others being Pratyeka-buddha, Bodhisattva, Buddha.

舍脂 Śācī, 舍支; 設施 power of speech and action. Name of Indra's chief consort. Indra is known as ||鉢低 Śacīpati.

舍舍迦 Śaśaka, a hare, rabbit, v. |支.

舍衛 Śrāvastī, 舍婆提; 室羅伐 (悉底); 尸羅跋提; 捨羅婆悉帝耶; intp as 聞物 the city of famous things, or men, or the famous city; it was a city and ancient kingdom 500 li north-west of Kapilavastu, now Rapetmapet south of Rapti River (M. W. says Sāhet-Māhet). It is said to have been in 北憍薩羅 northern Kośala, distinct from the southern kingdom of that name. It was a favourite resort of Śākyamuni, the 祇園 Jetavana being there.

舍那身 The body or person of Vairocana; ||尊特 is defined as Locana; the || in both cases seems to be "cana", an abbreviation of Vairocana, or Locana.

舍勒 Śāṭaka, 舍吒迦; 舍 (or 奢) 那 An inner garment, a skirt.

舍頭諫 Śārdūla-karṇa. The original name of Ānanda, intp. 虎耳 tiger's ears.

芝 A felicitous plant; sesamum. |苑 Name for 元照 Yüan-chao of 靈芝 Ling-chih monastery, Hangchow.

芬 Fragrant; confused; translit. *pun* in 丨陀 (or 陁) 利 Puṇḍarīka. the white lotus, v. 分.

花; 華 Puṣpa, a flower, flowers; especially the lotus, and celestial flowers. 丨座 The lotus throne on which Buddhas and Bodhisattvas sit. 丨筥; 丨籠; 丨皿 Flower baskets for scattering lotus flowers, or leaves and flowers in general.

芥子 Sarṣapa, 薩利刹跛; 舍利沙婆 Mustard seed. (1) A measure of length, 10,816,000th part of a yojana, v. 由旬. (2) A weight, the 32nd part of a 賴提 or 草子 raktikā, $2\frac{3}{16}$ grains. (3) A trifle. (4) On account of its hardness and bitter taste it is used as a symbol for overcoming illusions and demons by the esoteric sects. (5) The appearance of a Buddha is as rare as the hitting of a needle's point with a mustard-seed thrown from afar. 丨丨劫 A mustard-seed kalpa, i.e. as long as the time it would take to empty a city 100 yojanas square, by extracting a seed once every century. 丨石 Mustard-seed kalpa and rock kalpa, the former as above, the latter the time required to rub away a rock 40 li square by passing a soft cloth over it once every century.

虎 Vyāghra, 弭也竭羅 a tiger. 丨丘山 Hu-ch'iu Shan, a monastery at Soochow, which gave rise to a branch of the Ch'an (Zen) school, founded by 紹隆 Shao-lung. 丨丨婆 Hahava, the fifth hell. For 丨耳 v. 舍頭.

表 Indicate, manifest, express, expose; external. 丨刹 The flagpole on a pagoda. 丨德 To manifest virtue, in contrast with 遮情 to repress the passions; the positive in deed and thought, as expounded by the 華嚴宗 Hua-yen school. 丨無表戒 The expressed and unexpressed moral law, the letter and the spirit. 丨白 To explain, expound, clear up. 丨示 To indicate, explain. 丨色 Active expression, as walking, sitting, taking, refusing, bending, stretching, etc.; one of the three 色 forms, the other two being 顯 the colours, red, blue, etc., and 形 shape, long, short, etc. 丨銓 Positive or open exposition, contrasted with 遮銓 negative or hidden exposition; a term of the 法相宗 Dharmalakṣaṇa school.

迎 Go to meet, receive, welcome. 丨接 To receive, or be received, e.g. by Amitābha into Paradise.

近 Near, near to, approach, intimate, close. 丨事 Those who attend on and serve the Triratna, the 丨丨男 upāsaka, male servant or disciple, and 丨丨女 upāsikā, female servant or disciple, i.e. laymen or women who undertake to obey the five commandments. 丨住 Laymen or women who remain at home and observe the eight commandments, i.e. the 丨丨律儀. 丨圓 Nearing perfection, i.e. the ten commands, which are "near to" nirvāṇa. 丨童 A devotee, or disciple, idem upāsaka.

邲輸跋陀 Viśvabhadra, name of 普賢 P'u-hsien, Samantabhadra.

金 Hiraṇya, 伊爛拏 which means gold, any precious metal, semen, etc.; or 蘇伐剌 Suvarṇa, which means "of a good or beautiful colour", "golden", "yellow", "gold", "a gold coin", etc. The Chinese means metal, gold, money.

金人 Buddha; an image of Buddha of metal or gold, also 丨佛.

金仙 Golden ṛsi, or immortal, i.e. Buddha; also Taoist genii.

金光(明) Golden light, an intp. of suvarṇa, prabhāsa, or uttama. It is variously applied, e.g. 丨丨丨女 Wife of 丨天童子; 丨丨丨鼓 Golden-light drum. 丨丨丨經 Golden-light sūtra, tr. in the sixth century and twice later, used by the founder of T'ien-t'ai; it is given in its fullest form in the 丨丨丨最勝王經 Suvarṇa-prabhāsa-uttamarāja sūtra. 丨丨佛刹 The lowest of the Buddha-kṣetra, or lands.

金刹 A "golden" pagoda; the nine "golden" circles on top of a pagoda.

金剛 Vajra, 伐闍羅; 跋折(or 闍)羅; 縛日(or 日)羅 The thunderbolt of Indra, often called the diamond club; but recent research considers it a sun symbol. The diamond, synonym of hardness, indestructibility, power, the least frangible of minerals. It is one of the Saptaratna 七寶. 丨丨杵 The Vajra, or thunderbolt; it is generally shaped as such, but has various other forms. Any one of the beings represented with the vajra is a 金剛. The vajra is also intp. as a weapon of Indian soldiers. It is employed by the esoteric sects, and others, as a symbol of wisdom and power over illusion and evil spirits. When straight as a sceptre it is 獨股 one limbed, when three-pronged it is 三股, and so on with five and nine limbs.

金剛不壞(身) The diamond indestructible (body), the Buddha.

金剛乘 Vajrayāna. The diamond vehicle, another name of the 眞言 Shingon.

金剛夜 (or 藥) 叉 Vajrayakṣa. One of the five 大明王, fierce guardian of the north in the region of Amoghasiddhi, or Śākyamuni, also styled the Bodhisattva with the fangs.

金剛佛 Vajra-buddha. Vairocana, or 大日 the Sun-buddha; sometimes applied to Śākyamuni as embodiment of the Truth, of Wisdom, and of Purity. 丨丨丨子 A son of the Vajra-buddha, i.e. of Vairocana, a term applied to those newly baptized into the esoteric sect.

金剛刹 Vajrakṣetra, a vajra or Buddhist monastery or building.

金剛力 Vajra-power, irresistible strength; 丨丨丨(士) is the 丨丨神 q.v.

金剛口 Diamond mouth, that of a Buddha.

金剛天 The vajra-devas twenty in number in the Vajradhātu group.

金剛子 Rudrākṣa, a seed similar to a peach-stone used for beads, especially in invoking one of the 丨丨. Also a vajra son.

金剛定 Vajrasamādhi, 丨丨喩定; 丨丨三昧; 丨丨滅定 diamond meditation, that of the last stage of the Bodhisattva, characterized by firm, indestructible knowledge, penetrating all reality: attained after all remains of illusion have been cu off.

金剛密迹 The deva-guardians of the secrets of Vairocana, his inner or personal group of guardians in contrast with the outer or major group of P'u-hsien, Mañjuśrī, etc. Similarly, Śāriputra, the śrāvakas, etc., are the "inner" guardians of Śākyamuni, the Bodhisattvas being the major group. Idem 丨丨手; 丨丨力士; 密迹力士, etc.

金剛寶戒 The Mahāyāna rules according to the 梵網 sūtra. 丨丨丨藏 The "Diamond" treasury, i.e. nirvāṇa and the pure bodhi-mind, as the source of the mind of all sentient beings, v. Nirvāṇa sūtra.

金剛 (圍 or 輪) 山 The concentric iron mountains about the world; also Sumeru; also the name of a fabulous mountain. Cf. 金山.

金剛幡 Vajraketu. A flag, hung to a pole with a dragon's head. 丨丨丨菩薩 Vajraketu Bodhisattva, the flag-bearer, one of the sixteen in the Vajradhātu group.

金剛座 (or 床) Vajrāsana, or Bodhimaṇḍa, Buddha's seat on attaining enlightenment, the "diamond" throne. Also a posture or manner of sitting. M. W.

金剛心 Diamond heart, that of the Bodhisattva, i.e. infrangible, unmoved by "illusion". 丨丨丨殿 The Vajradhātu (maṇḍala), in which Vairocana dwells, also called 不壞丨丨光明心殿 the shrine of the indestructible diamond-brilliant heart.

金剛念誦 Silent repetition; also 丨丨語言.

金剛慧 Diamond wisdom, which by its reality overcomes all illusory knowledge.

金剛手 Vajrapāṇi, a holder of the vajra, a protector, any image with this symbol; 丨丨部 Groups of the same in the 金 and 胎 maṇḍalas. 丨丨丨菩薩 (or 薩埵) Vajrapāṇi Bodhisattva, especially P'u-hsien 普賢 Samantabhadra.

金剛拳 Vajra-fist, the hands doubled together on the breast. 丨丨丨菩薩 One of the Bodhisattvas in the Diamond group.

金剛智 Vajramati. The indestructible and enriching diamond wisdom of the Buddha. Also the ame of an Indian who came to China A.D. 619; ne is said to have introduced the Yogācāra system and founded the esoteric school, but this is attributed to Amoghavajra, v. 大教. 丨丨丨三藏 Vajrabodhi may be the same person, but there is doubt about the matter, cf. 大教.

金剛曼荼羅 v. 丨丨界.

金剛杵 (or 杖) v. 金剛.

金剛水 Diamond or vajra water, drunk by a prince on investiture, or by a person who receives the esoteric baptismal rite; also 誓水.

金剛法界宮 The palace or shrine of Vairocana in the Garbhadhātu.

金剛炎 Diamond-blaze, a circle of fire to forbid the entry of evil spirits, also called 丨炎; 火院 (界印 or 密縫印).

金剛王 The vajra-king, i.e. the strongest, or finest, e.g. a powerful bull. 丨丨丨寶覺 The diamond royal-gem enlightenment, i.e. that of the Buddha. 丨丨丨菩薩 One of the sixteen bodhisattvas in the Diamond-realm, one of Akṣobhya's retinue; also known as 丨丨鉤王 the vajra hook king.

金剛界 Vajradhātu, 金界 The "diamond", or vajra, element of the universe; it is the 智 wisdom of Vairocana in its indestructibility and activity; it arises from the Garbhadhātu 胎藏界 q.v., the womb or store of the Vairocana 理 reason or principles of such wisdom, v. 理智. The two, Garbhadhātu and Vajradhātu, are shown by the esoteric school, especially in the Japanese Shingon, in two maṇḍalas, i.e. groups or circles, representing in various portrayals the ideas arising from the two fundamental concepts. Vajradhātu is intp. as the 智 realm of intellection, and Garbhadhātu as the 理 substance underlying it, or the matrix; the latter is the womb or fundamental reason of all things, and occupies the eastern position as "cause" of the Vajradhātu, which is on the west as the resultant intellectual or spiritual expression. But both are one as are Reason and Wisdom, and Vairocana (the illuminator, the 大日 great sun) presides over both, as source and supply. The Vajradhātu represents the spiritual world of complete enlightenment, the esoteric Dharmakāya doctrine as contrasted with the exoteric Nirmāṇakāya doctrine. It is the sixth element 識 mind, and is symbolized by a triangle with the point downwards and by the full moon, which represents 智 wisdom or understanding; it corresponds to 果 fruit, or effect, garbhadhātu being 因 or cause. The 丨丨丨五部 or five divisions of the Vajradhātu are represented by the Five Dhyāni-Buddhas, thus: centre 大日 Vairocana; east 阿閦 Akṣobhya; south 寶生 Ratnasambhava; west 阿彌陀 Amitābha; north 不空成就 Amoghasiddhi, or Śākyamuni. They are seated respectively on a lion, an elephant, a horse, a peacock, and a garuda. v. 五佛; also 胎.

金剛神 The guardian spirits of the Buddhist order; the large idols at the entrance of Buddhist monasteries; also 丨丨手; 丨丨力士.

金剛童子 Vajrakumāra, 丨丨使者 a vajra-messenger of the Buddhas or bodhisattvas; also an incarnation of Amitābha in the form of a youth with fierce looks holding a vajra.

金剛索 Vajrapāśa, the diamond lasso, or noose, in the hand of 不動明王 and others. 丨丨丨菩薩 Vajrapāśa-bodhisattva in the Vajradhātu maṇḍala, who carries the snare of compassion to bind the souls of the living.

金剛經 The "Diamond" Sūtra; Vajracchedikā-prajñāpāramitā-sūtra 金剛能斷般若波羅蜜經 A condensation of the Prājñāpāramitā; first tr. by Kumārajīva, later by others under slightly varying titles.

金剛菩薩 There are many of these Vajrabodhisattvas, e.g.: 丨丨因丨丨Vajrahetu, 丨丨手丨丨 Vajrapāṇi, 丨丨寶丨丨 Vajraratna, 丨丨藏丨丨 Vajragarbha, 丨丨針丨丨 Vajrasūci, 丨丨將丨丨 Vajrasena, 丨丨索丨丨 Vajrapāśa, 丨丨鉤丨丨 Vajrāṅkuśa, 丨丨香丨丨 Vajradhūpa, 丨丨光丨丨 Vajratejaḥ, 丨丨法丨丨 Vajradharma, 丨丨利丨丨 Vajratīkṣṇa, and others.

金剛藏 Vajragarbha, the Bodhisattva in the Laṅkāvatāra sūtra. 丨丨丨王 A form of the next entry; also Śākyamuni.

金剛薩埵 Vajrasattva(-mahāsattva). 金薩 A form of P'u-hsien (Samantabhadra), reckoned as the second of the eight patriarchs of the 眞言宗 Shingon sect, also known as 丨丨手 (秘密王 or 菩薩) and other similar titles. The term is also applied to all vajra-beings, or vajra-bodhisattvas; especially those in the moon-circle in the east of the Diamond maṇḍala. Śākyamuni also takes the vajrasattva form. (1) All beings are vajrasattva, because of their Buddha-nature. (2) So are all beginners in the faith and practice. (3) So are the retinue of Akṣobhya. (4) So is Great P'u-hsien.

金剛衆 The retinue of the 丨丨神 Vajradevas.

金剛觀 The diamond insight or vision which penetrates into reality.

金剛語言 idem 丨丨念誦.

金剛身 The diamond body, the indestructible body of Buddha.

金剛輪 The diamond or vajra wheel, symbolical of the esoteric sects. The lowest of the circles beneath the earth.

金剛部 The various groups in the two maṇḍalas, each having a 主 or head; in the Diamond maṇḍala Akṣobhya, or Vajrasattva, is spoken of as such. |||母; 忙莽鷄 Māmakī is "mother" in this group.

金(剛)針 The straight vajra, or sceptre; also v. ||菩薩.

金剛鈴 The diamond or vajra bell for attracting the attention of the objects of worship, and stimulating all who hear it. |||菩薩 Vajra-ghaṇṭā, a Bodhisattva holding a bell in the Vajra-dhātu maṇḍala.

金剛鏁 Vajra-śṛṅkhalā. The vajra chain, or fetter. |||菩薩 The chain-bearer in the Diamond group.

金剛門 The diamond door of the Garbha-dhātu maṇḍala.

金剛頂 The diamond apex or crown, a general name of the esoteric doctrines and sūtras of Vairocana. The sūtra |||經 is the authority for the |||宗 sect.

金剛體 The diamond body, that of Buddha, and his merits.

金口 The golden mouth of the Buddha, a reference *inter alia* to 金剛口 the diamond-like firmness of his doctrine. ||相承; ||祖承 The doctrines of the golden mouth transmitted in "apostolic succession" through generations (of patriarchs).

金地 A Buddhist monastery; v. also 逝 Jetavana. ||國 Suvarṇabhūmi, said to be a country south of Śrāvastī, to which Aśoka sent missionaries. Also |出; |田.

金大王 Protector of travellers, shown in the train of the 1,000-hand Kuan-yin.

金山 Metal or golden mountain, i.e. Buddha, or the Buddha's body. ||王 Buddha, especially Amitābha. The 七|| are the seven concentric ranges around Sumeru, v. 須; viz. Yugaṁdhara, Īśādhara, Khadiraka, Sudarśana, Aśvakarṇa, Vinataka, Nemiṁdhara, v. respectively 踰, 伊, 竭, 蘇, 頞, 毘, and 尼.

金星 Śukra, the planet Venus.

金杖 The golden staff broken into eighteen pieces and the skirt similarly torn, seen in a dream by king Bimbisāra, prophetic of the eighteen divisions of Hīnayāna.

金毘羅 Kumbhīra, ||囉; 金波羅; 禁(or 宮)毘羅; a crocodile, alligator, described as 蛟龍 a "boa-dragon"; cf. 失. A yakṣa-king who was converted and became a guardian of Buddhism, also known as |||陀(迦毘羅); |||神; |||大將. For |||比丘 Kampilla, v. 劫.

金毛獅子 The lion with golden hair on which Mañjuśrī (Wên-shu) rides; also a previous incarnation of the Buddha.

金水 Golden water, i.e. wisdom.

金沙 Golden-sand (river), an imaginary river in the Nirvāṇa sūtra 10. Also the Hiraṇyavatī, v. 尸.

金河 Hiraṇyavatī, v. 尸.

金粟如來 The golden grain Tathāgata, a title of Vimalakīrti 維摩 in a previous incarnation.

金翅鳥(王) Garuḍa, 妙翅; 迦樓羅 the king of birds, with golden wings, companion of Viṣṇu; a syn. of the Buddha.

金胎 idem 金剛界 and 胎藏界.

金色 Golden coloured. ||世界 The golden-hued heaven of Mañjuśrī (Wên-shu). ||女 The princess of Vārāṇaśī, who is said to have been offered in marriage to Śākyamuni because he was of the same colour as herself. ||孔雀王 The golden-hued peacock king, protector of travellers, in the retinue of the 1,000-hands Kuan-yin. ||王 A previous incarnation of the Buddha. ||迦葉; ||尊者; ||頭陀 Names for Mahākāśyapa, as he is said to have 飲光 swallowed light, hence his golden hue.

金藏 Golden treasury, i.e. the Buddha-nature in all the living. | | 雲 The first golden-treasury cloud when a new world is completed, arising in the 光音天 ābhāsvara heaven and bringing the first rain.

金襴衣 A kāṣāya or robe embroidered with gold; a golden robe; also 金襴袈裟; 金色衣.

金言 Golden words, i.e. those of Buddha.

金蹄 Kaṇṭhaka aśvarāja, 金泥; 犍涉駒 name of the steed on which Śākyamuni left his home.

金身; 金軀 The golden body or person, that of Buddha.

金輪 The metal circle on which the earth rests, above the water circle which is above the wind (or air) circle which rests on space. Also the cakra, wheel or disc, emblem of sovereignty, one of the seven precious possessions of a king. | | 王 A golden-wheel king, the highest in comparison with silver, copper, and iron cakravartin.

金鷄 The golden cock (or fowl), with a grain of millet in its beak, a name for Bodhidharma.

金骨 Golden bones, i.e. Buddha's relics.

金龜 The golden tortoise on which the world rests, idem | 輪.

長 Ch'ang, long; always; Chang, to grow, rising, senior. | 乞食 Always to ask food as alms, one of the twelve duties of a monk. | 壽 Long life. | 壽天 Devas of long life, in the fourth dhyāna heaven where life is 500 great kalpas, and in the fourth arūpaloka where life extends over 80,000 kalpas. | 夜 The whole night, the long night of mortality or transmigration. | 日 The long day, or succeeding days prolonged. | 生 Long or eternal life (in Paradise), | 生不死, | 生不老 long life without death, or growing old, immortality. | 生符 The charm for immortality, i.e. Buddhism. | 老 Senior, venerable, title for aged and virtuous monks; also an abbot. | 者; 揭利呵跋底; 疑叻賀鉢底 Gṛhapati. A householder; one who is just, straightforward, truthful, honest, advanced in age, and wealthy; an elder. | 衣; | 物; | 鉢 Clothes, things, or almsbowls in excess of the permitted number. | 跪 Kneeling with knees and toes touching the ground and thighs and body erect; tall kneeling. | 阿含經 Dīrghāgama, the long āgamas, cf. 阿含. | 食 Ample supplies of food, i.e. for a long time.

門 A door; gate; a sect, school, teaching, especially one leading to salvation or nirvāṇa. | 侶 Disciple, fellow-student. | 師 Preceptor, the monk who is recognized as teacher by any family. | 徒 Disciple. | 派; | 流; | 葉; | 跡 The followers, or development of any sect. | 狀; 參狀 or 榜 A name paper, card, visiting-card. | 神; | 丞 The gate-gods or guardians. | 經 The funeral service read at the house-door. | 答辣 Maṇḍala, see 曼. | 首; | 主 The controller of a gate, or sect.

附 Adjoin, attached to, append, near. | 佛法外道 Heretics within Buddhism.

陀 Steep bank, declivity; translit. *t*, *th*, *d*, *dh*, *ty*, *dy*, *dhy*; cf. 荼, 多, 檀. | 呵 Dāha, burning. | 多竭多 Tathāgata, v. 多. | 摩 Dama, tamed, domiciled, obedient, good. | 歷 Darada, "the country of the ancient Dardae mentioned by Strabo and Pliny. The region near Dardu Lat. 35° 11 N., Long. 73° 54 E." Eitel. | 毘羅 (or 荼); 達羅毘 (or 弭) 荼 Damila, Dravila, probably Drāviḍa, or Drāvira, anciently a kingdom in Southern India, "bounded in the South by the Cauveri and reaching northward as far as Arcot or Madras." Eitel.

陀羅 Tārā, star, shining, radiating, a female deity, v. 多. | 羅尼 (or 那); 陀隣尼 Dhāraṇī. Able to lay hold of the good so that it cannot be lost, and likewise of the evil so that it cannot arise. Magical formulas, or mystic forms of prayer, or spells of Tantric order, often in Sanskrit, found in China as early as the third century A.D.; they form a portion of the Dhāraṇīpiṭaka; made popular chiefly through the Yogācārya 瑜伽 or 密教 esoteric school. Four divisions are given, i.e. 法, 義, 咒, and 忍 | | |; the 咒, i.e. mantra or spell, is emphasized by the 眞言 Shingon sect. There are numerous treatises, e.g. | | | 集經; 瑜伽師地論, attributed to Asaṅga, founder of the Buddhist Yoga school. | | | 菩薩 Dhāraṇī-bodhisattva, one who has great power to protect and save. | | 那 Name of a yakṣa. | | 羅 Name of a ṛṣi. | | 驃 Dravya, the nine "substances" in the Nyāya philosophy, earth, water, fire, air, ether 空, time, space 方, soul 神, and mind 意. | 那 Dāna, bestow, alms; the marks on a scale; ādāna, another name for the ālaya-vijñāna. | 那婆 Dānavat, name of a god. 丨那伽他 Dānagāthā, or Dakṣiṇāgāthā, the verse or utterance of the almsgiver. 丨那鉢底 or 施主 Dānapati, almsgiver.

陁 idem 陀.

阿 A or Ā; अ, आ. It is the first letter of the Sanskrit Siddham alphabet, and is also translit. by 曷, 遏, 安, 頞, 韻, 噁, etc. From it are supposed to be born all the other letters, and it is the first sound uttered by the human mouth. It has therefore numerous mystical indications. Being also a negation it symbolizes the unproduced, the impermanent, the immaterial; but it is employed in many ways indicative of the positive. Amongst other uses it indicates Amitābha, from the first syllable in that name. It is much in use for esoteric purposes.

阿世耶 Āśaya, 丨奢也, disposition, mind; pleased to, desire to, pleasure.

阿他婆吠陀 Atharvaveda, also Ātharvaṇa, the fourth Veda, dealing with sorcery or magic; also 丨達婆鞞陀; 丨闥波陀.

阿伐羅勢羅 Avaraśāilāḥ, the school of the dwellers in the Western mountains 西山寺 in Dhanakaṭaka; it was a subdivision of the Mahāsaṅghikāḥ.

阿伽 Arghya, argha, 閼伽; 遏伽; 遏迦 tr. by water, but it specially indicates ceremonial water, e.g. offerings of scented water, or water containing fragrant flowers. 丨丨坏 The vase or bowl so used. 丨丨嚧; 丨丨樓; 惡揭嚕 Agaru, Aguru, fragrant aloe-wood, intp. 沉香 the incense that sinks in water, the Agallochum; "the Ahalim or Ahaloth of the Hebrews." Eitel. 丨丨摩 v. 阿含 Āgama. 丨丨羅伽 Aṅgāraka, the planet Mars; a star of ill omen; a representation in the Garbhadhātu. 丨丨陀; 丨竭陀; 丨揭(陀) Agada, free from disease, an antidote, intp. as 普去 a medicine that entirely rids (cf disease), elixir of life, universal remedy. 丨丨曇 Aghana, not solid, not dense.

阿修羅 Asura, 修羅 originally meaning a spirit, spirits, or even the gods, it generally indicates titanic demons, enemies of the gods, with whom, especially Indra, they wage constant war. They are defined as "not devas", and "ugly", and "without wine". Other forms are 丨須(or 蘇, or 素)羅; 丨丨(or 須)倫 or 輪; 丨素洛; 丨差. Four classes are named according to their manner of rebirth—egg-born, womb-born, transformation-born, and spawn- or water-born. Their abode is in the ocean, north of Sumeru, but certain of the weaker dwell in a western mountain cave. They have realms, rulers, and palaces, as have the devas. The 丨丨丨道 is one of the six gatis, or ways of reincarnation. The 修羅場 or 巷 is the battlefield of the asuras against Indra. The 丨丨丨琴 are their harps.

阿傍; 阿防 The ox-head torturers in Hades. Also 丨丨羅刹.

阿儞囉迦 Ārdraka, raw ginger.

阿僧(伽) Asaṅga, Āryāsaṅga, intp. as 無著 unattached, free; lived "a thousand years after the Nirvāṇa", probably the fourth century A.D., said to be the eldest brother of 天親 Vasubandhu, whom he converted to Mahāyāna. He was first a follower of the Mahīśāsaka school, but founded the Yogācārya or Tantric school with his Yogācārabhūmi-śāstra 瑜伽師地論, which in the 三藏傳 is said to have been dictated to him by Maitreya in the Tuṣita heaven, along with the 莊嚴大乘論 and the 中邊分別論. He was a native of Gandhāra, but lived mostly in Ayodhyā (Oudh).

阿僧祇 Asaṅkhya, Asaṅkhyeya, 阿僧企耶; 僧祇 intp. 無數 innumerable, countless, said to be 一千萬萬萬萬萬萬萬萬兆 kalpas. There are four asaṅkhya kalpas in the rise, duration, and end of every universe, cf. 刦.

阿㝹樓馱 v. 阿那律 Aniruddha. 丨丨羅陀補羅 Anurādhapura, a northern city of Ceylon, at which tradition says Buddhism was introduced into the island; cf. Abhayagiri, 丨跋.

阿利尼 Alni or Arni; "a kingdom which formed part of ancient Tukhāra, situated near to the sources of the Oxus." Eitel.

阿利(or 黎)沙 Ārṣa, connected with the ṛṣis, or holy men; especially their religious utterances in verse 丨丨丨偈; also a title of a Buddha; and 丨丨丨住處 is the highest position of achievement, perfection.

阿利羅跋提 Ajitavatī, 丨恃多伐底, see 尸 Hiraṇyavatī.

阿利耶 idem 丨賴丨Ālaya, and 丨梨丨

阿制多 Ajita, v. 阿逸多.

阿剡底訶羅 Name of a demon burnt up by the fire it eats.

阿卑羅吽欠 A (or Āḥ)-vi-ra-hūm-kham, the Shingon "true word" or spell of Vairocana, for subduing all māras, each sound representing one of the five elements, earth, water, fire, wind (or air), and space (or ether). Also, 丨毘 (or 尾) 丨丨丨 (or 劍); 丨味囉𠵇欠.

阿叉摩羅 Akṣamālā, a rosary, especially of the seeds of the Eleocarpus. M. W. Also a symbol of the ten perfections.

阿吒利 Aṭāli, 丨丨釐 a province of the ancient kingdom of Malwa, or Malava; its people rejected Buddhism. 丨丨吒 Aṭaṭa; the third of the four cold hells. 丨丨婆拘; 丨丨嚩迦; 丨(or 遏) 丨薄倶 Āṭavika, name of a demon-general. 丨丨筏底 Alakavatī, the city of Vaiśravaṇa.

阿含 Āgama, 丨丨暮; 丨鋡; 丨伽 (or 笈) 摩, the Āgamas, a collection of doctrines, general name for the Hīnayāna scriptures: tr. 法歸 the home or collecting-place of the Law or Truth; 無比法 peerless Law; or 趣無 *ne plus ultra*, ultimate, absolute truth. The 四丨丨經 or Four Āgamas are (1) 長阿含 Dīrghāgama, "Long" treatises on cosmogony. (2) Madhyamāgama, 中丨丨, "middle" treatises on metaphysics. (3) Saṁyuktāgama, 雜丨丨 "miscellaneous" treatises on abstract contemplation. (4) Ekottarāgama 增一丨丨 "numerical" treatises, subjects treated numerically. There is also a division of Five Āgamas. 丨丨時 The period when the Buddha taught Hīnayāna doctrine in the Lumbinī garden during the first twelve years of his ministry. 丨丨部 Hīnayāna.

阿吽 Ahūṁ, the supposed foundation of all sounds and writing, "A" being the open and "hūṁ" the closed sound. "A" is the seed of Vairocana, "hūṁ" that of Vajrasattva, and both have other indications. "A" represents the absolute, "hūṁ" the particular, or phenomenal.

阿呼 Ahu! Aho! an interjection, e.g. 奇哉 Wonderful! Also Arka, a flash, ray, the sun; praise; name of a mountain; cf. 丨羅歌. 丨丨地獄 The hell of groaning.

阿呵呵 Ahaha, sound of laughter.

阿周陀 The name of 目連 Mahāmaudgalyāyana as a ṛṣi. 丨丨丨那 Arjuna, v. 丨順那.

阿唎(耶)多羅 Ārya-tārā; one of the titles of Kuan-yin, Āryāvalokiteśvara 丨丨丨婆盧羯帝爍鉢囉耶.

阿地目得迦 Ati-muktata, v. 丨提.

阿夜健多 Ayaḥkāṇḍa, an iron arrow; also 丨丨塞健那.

阿失麗沙 Aśleṣā, the 柳 or 24th constellation, stars in Hydra; M. W. says the 9th Nakṣatra containing five stars.

阿夷 Arhan, a worthy, noble, or saintly man; especially 丨私陀 Asita, q.v. 丨丨恬 ? Ādikarmika, a beginner, neophyte. 丨丨頭 idem 丨耆多 Ajita. 丨丨羅和 (or 婆) 帝 or 底 or 跋提, v. 丨恃 the river Ajiravatī. v. 阿羅漢.

阿奢也 v. 阿世耶. 丨丨理貳 or 兒 Āścarya, rare, extraordinary. Part of the name of an ancient monastery in Karashahr.

阿奴謨柁 Anumoda, concurrence, a term of thanks from a monk to a donor on parting. 丨丨邏陀 Anurādhā, the seventeenth of the twenty-eight Nakṣatras, or lunar mansions. M. W. The 房 constellation in Scorpio.

阿娑嚩 A-sa-va, a formula covering the three sections of the Garbhadhātu—"a" the Tathāgata section, "sa" the Lotus section, and "va" the Diamond section. 丨丨摩補多 Asamāpta, incomplete, unended. 丨丨磨 (or 摩) 娑摩 Asamasama, one of the titles of a Buddha; it is defined as 無等等 which has various interpretations, but generally means of unequalled rank. 丨丨弭 has similar meaning. 丨丨羅 Asaru, a medicine; a plant, *Blumea lacera*; or perhaps Asāra, the castor-oil plant, or the aloe. 丨丨頗那伽 Āśvāsa-apānaka, contemplation by counting the breathings; cf. 阿那波那.

阿婆 Apa, abha, ava, etc. 丨丨(娑)摩羅 Apasmāra, epileptic demons, demons of epilepsy. 丨丨孕迦羅 Abhayaṁkara, giving security from fear, name of a Tathāgata. 丨丨盧吉低舍婆羅 Avalokiteśvara, name of Kuan-yin. 丨丨磨 Anupama, applied to a Buddha as 無等等 of unequalled rank, cf. 丨娑磨.

阿密哩多 Amṛta, ||嘌帝; |沒嘌都 nectar, ambrosia. ||||軍荼利 One of the five 明王 q.v.

阿尸羅婆那 Śravaṇā, which M. W. gives as " one of the lunar asterisms . . . α, β, γ, Aquilae ". Śrāvaṇa is the month which falls in July–August.

阿尾捨 Āveśa, spiritualistic possession, a youthful medium. Also ||舍, ||奢, ||賒, |毘舍.

阿底 (or **跌**) **哩** Atri, a devourer; one of the stars in Ursa Major; one of the assistants of Agni shown in the Garbhadhātu; an ancient ṛṣi.

阿庾多 idem 阿由多.

阿差末 Akṣayamati, unceasing devotion, with an unfailing mind; name of a bodhisattva.

阿彌(陀) Amita, boundless, infinite; tr. by 無量 immeasurable. The Buddha of infinite qualities, known as |||婆 (or 佛) Amitābha, tr. 無量光 boundless light; |||庾斯 Amitāyus, tr. 無量壽 boundless age, or life; and among the esoteric sects Amṛta 甘露(王) sweet-dew (king). An imaginary being unknown to ancient Buddhism, possibly of Persian or Iranian origin, who has eclipsed the historical Buddha in becoming the most popular divinity in the Mahāyāna pantheon. His name indicates an idealization rather than an historic personality, the idea of eternal light and life. The origin and date of the concept are unknown, but he has always been associated with the west, where in his Paradise, Sukhāvatī, the Western Pure Land, he receives to unbounded happiness all who call upon his name (cf. the Pure Lands 淨土 of Maitreya and Akṣobhya). This is consequent on his forty-eight vows, especially the eighteenth, in which he vows to refuse Buddhahood until he has saved all living beings to his Paradise, except those who had committed the five unpardonable sins, or were guilty of blasphemy against the Faith. While his Paradise is theoretically only a stage on the way to rebirth in the final joys of Nirvāṇa, it is popularly considered as the final resting-place of those who cry Na-mo A-mi-to-Fo, or Blessed be, or Adoration to, Amita Buddha. The 淨土 Pure-land (Jap. Jōdo) sect is especially devoted to this cult, which arises chiefly out of the Sukhāvatīvyūha, but Amita is referred to in many other texts and recognized, with differing interpretations and emphasis, by the other sects. Eitel attributes the first preaching of the dogma to " a priest from Tokhara " in A.D. 147, and says that Fa-hsien and Hsüan-tsang make no mention of the cult. But the Chinese pilgrim 慧日 Hui-jih says he found it prevalent in India 702–719. The first translation of the Amitāyus sūtra, *circa* A.D. 223–253, had disappeared when the K'ai-yuan catalogue was compiled A.D. 730. The eighteenth vow occurs in the tr. by Dharmarakṣa A.D. 308. With Amita is closely associated Avalokiteśvara, who is also considered as his incarnation, and appears crowned with, or bearing the image of Amita. In the trinity of Amita, Avalokiteśvara appears on his left and Mahāsthāmaprāpta on his right. Another group, of five, includes Kṣitigarbha and Nāgārjuna, the latter counted as the second patriarch of the Pure-land sect. One who calls on the name of Amitābha is styled |||聖 a saint of Amitābha. Amitābha is one of the Five " Dhyāni Buddhas " 五佛, q.v. He has many titles, amongst which are the following twelve relating to him as Buddha of light, also his title of eternal life: 無量光佛 B. of boundless light; 無邊光佛 B. of unlimited light; 無礙光佛 B. of irresistible light; 無對光佛 B. of incomparable light; 燄王光佛 B. of yama or flame-king light; 清淨光佛 B. of pure light; 歡喜光佛 B. of joyous light; 智慧光佛 B. of wisdom light; 不斷光佛 B. of unending light; 難思光佛 B. of inconceivable light; 無稱光佛 B. of indescribable light; 超日月光佛 B. of light surpassing that of sun and moon; 無量壽 B. of boundless age. As Buddha he has, of course, all the attributes of a Buddha, including the Trikāya, or 法報化身, about which in *re* Amita there are differences of opinion in the various schools. His esoteric germ-letter is Hrīḥ, and he has specific manual-signs. Cf. |||經, of which with commentaries there are numerous editions.

阿彌陀檀那 Amṛtodana 甘露王. A king of Magadha, father of Anuruddha and Bhadrika, uncle of Śākyamuni.

阿恃多伐底 Ajiravatī; v. 尸. The river Hiraṇyavatī, also |利 (or 夷) 羅跋 (or 拔) 提; |夷 (or 脂 or 寅) 羅婆底; |爾多嚩底. It is probable that 阿恃多, intp. 無勝 unconquered, is Ajita and an error. Cf. 阿嗜.

阿折羅 Ācāra, an arhat of the kingdom of Andhra, founder of a monastery.

阿拘盧奢 Ākrośa; 罵 scolding, abusing.

阿拏 Aṇu, 阿菟; 阿耨 Minute, infinitesimal, the smallest aggregation of matter, a molecule consisting of 七微 seven atoms.

阿提佛陀 Ādi-buddha, the primal Buddha of ancient Lamaism (Tib. chos-kyi-daṅ-poḥi-saṅs-rgyas); by the older school he is associated with P'u-hsien born of Vairocana, i.e. Kuntu-bzan-po, or Dharmakāya-Samantabhadra; by the later school with Vajradhara, or Vajrasattva, who are considered as identical, and spoken of as omniscient, omnipotent, omnipresent, eternal, infinite, uncaused, and causing all things. | | (or 地) 目 多 (伽) Adhimukti or Atimukti, entire freedom of mind, confidence, intp. by 善 思 惟 "pious thoughtfulness", good propensity. Atimuktaka, a plant like the "dragon-lick", suggestive of hemp, with red flowers and bluish-green leaves; its seeds produce fragrant oil, sesame. Also, a kind of tree. | | 阿 耨 波 陀 Ādyanutpāda, or -panna; 本 初 不 生 the original uncreated letter *ā* or *a*.

阿摩 Ambā, or mother, a title of respect. | | 爹 爹 Mother and father. | | (or 麽) 提; | | 隷 The 21st of the thirty-three forms of Kuan-yin, three eyes, four arms, two playing a lute with a phœnix-head, one foot on a lion, the other pendent. | | 羅 Amala; spotless, unstained, pure; the permanent and unchanging in contrast with the changing; the pure and unsullied, e.g. saintliness; the true nirvāṇa. Also 菴 | |; | 末 | q.v.

阿擅 Anātman, 阿 檀; 阿 捺 摩, i.e. 無 我 without an ego, impersonality, different from soul or spirit.

阿施 Artha, 義 reason, sense, purpose. 施 is probably a misprint for 陁; the Hua-yen uses 曷 攞 多; also 他 is used for 施.

阿末羅 Āmra, Āmalaka, Āmrāta. | 摩 洛 迦; 菴 摩 洛 (or 羅 or 勒) 迦 Āmra, mango, *Mangifera indica*; Āmalaka, *Emblic myrobalan*, or *Phyllanthus emblica*, whose nuts are valued medicinally; Āmrāta, hog-plum, *Spondias mangifera*. Also used for discernment of mental ideas, the ninth of the nine kinds of 心 識. 菴 沒 (or 摩 or 婆) 羅 should apply to Āmra the mango, but the forms are used indiscriminately. Cf. | 摩 |.

阿梨宜 Āliṅg-; to embrace; āliṅgī, a small drum; a kind of ecstatic meditation. | | (or 棃) 樹 Arjaka, ? *Ocymum pilosum*, a tree with white scented flowers, said to fall in seven parts, like an epidendrum, styled also 頞 杜 (? 社) 迦 曼 折 利. | | (瑟) 吒 Ariṣṭa(ka), the soap-berry tree, *Sapindus detergens*, 木 槵 子, whose berries are used for rosaries. Name of a bhikṣu. | | 耶 Ārya, | 利 |; | 棃 |; | 黎 |; | 犁 |; | 離 |; | 哩 夜; | 略 or 夷; 梨 耶 loyal, honourable, noble, Āryan, "a man who has thought on the four chief principles of Buddhism and lives according to them," intp. by 尊 honourable, and 聖 sage, wise, saintly, sacred. Also, ulūka, an owl. | | 呵 Arhan, | 羅 漢 q.v. | | 耶 伐 摩 Āryavarman, of the Śarvāstivādin school, author of a work on the Vaibhāṣika philosophy. | | (|) 斯 那 Āryasena, a monk of the Mahāsaṅghikāḥ. | | | 馱 娑 Āryadāsa, ditto.

阿槃陀羅 Avāntara, intermediate, within limits, included.

阿歐 Au! An exclamation, e.g. Ho! Oh! Ah! Also | 傴; | 嘔; | 漚 or | 優. The two letters *a* and *u* fell from the corners of Brahmā's mouth when he gave the seventy-two letters of Kharoṣṭhī, and they are said to be placed at the beginning of the Brahminical sacred books as divine letters, the Buddhists adopting 如 是 "Thus" (*Evam*) instead.

阿毗 Avīci, 毘 (至) cf. | 鼻. | | 三 佛 (陀); | 惟 | | Abhisaṁbuddha, Abhisaṁbodha; realizing or manifesting universal enlightenment; fully awake, complete realization. | | 目 底 Abhimukti, probably in error for Adhimukti, implicit faith, conviction. | | (or 比) | 佉 Abhimukham, towards, approaching, in presence of, tr. 現 前. Abhimukhī, the sixth of the ten stages 十 住. | | 私 度 Abhijit, 女 宿 the tenth Chinese stellar mansion, stars in Aquarius. | | 跋 致; | 鞞 | |; | 惟 越 致 Avivartin, 不 退 No retrogression. | | 達 磨; | | 曇; | 鼻 達 磨 Abhidharma. The śāstras, which discuss Buddhist philosophy or metaphysics; defined by Buddhaghōsa as the law or truth (dharma) which (abhi) goes beyond or behind the law; explained by 傳 tradition, 勝 法 surpassing law, 無 比 法 incomparable law, 對 法 comparing the law, 向 法 directional law, showing cause and effect. The | | | | 藏 or 論 藏 is the Abhidharma-piṭaka, the third part of the Tripiṭaka. In the Chinese canon it consists of 大 乘 論 Mahāyāna treatises, 小 乘 論 Hīnayāna treatises, and 藏 諸 論 those brought in during the Sung and Yüan dynasties. The | | | | 俱 舍 論 Abhidharma-kośa-śāstra, tr. by Hsüan-tsang, is a philosophical work by Vasubandhu refuting doctrines of the Vibhāṣā school. There are many works of which Abhidharma forms part of the title. | | 遮 羅 Abhicāra. A hungry ghost. | | | 嚕 迦; | | 拓 (or 左) 嚕 迦; | | 左 囉 Abhicāraka, exorcism; an exorciser, or controller (of demons).

阿沙陀 Āṣāḍha, | | 荼; 頞 沙 荼 the fourth

month, part of June and July. Name of a monk. Aṣāḍhā, an Indian constellation comprising 箕 and 斗, stars in Sagittarius. Cf. 阿薩多.

阿泥底耶 Āditya, the sons of Aditi, the gods; Varuṇa; the sun; the sky; son of the sun-deva.

阿波摩羅 Apasmāra, malevolent demons, epilepsy, and the demons who cause it; also 丨婆丨丨; 丨跋丨丨; 丨跛娑丨囉. 丨丨會; 丨丨會; 丨婆譮; 丨丨羅 Ābhāsvara(-vimāna), the sixth of the Brahmalokas 光音天 of light and sound (ābhāsvara) and its devas, but it is better intp. as ābhās, shining and vara, ground, or splendid, the splendid devas or heaven; shown in the Garbhadhātu. Like other devas they are subject to rebirth. Also 丨會亘修 (or 差); 丨丨嘬羅 (庶); 丨衛貨羅. 丨丨(or 婆) 末加; 丨丨麼羅誐 Apāmārga, 牛膝草 *Achryanthes aspera.* 丨丨波 Ababa, Hahava, the only sound possible to those in the fourth of the eight cold hells. 丨丨羅囉; 丨丨邏丨; 丨丨丨利; 丨丨波; 丨鉢丨; and ? 丨羅婆樓 Apalāla, "not fond of flesh" (M. W.), a destroyer by flood of the crops; the nāga of the source of the river Śubhavăstu (Swat) of Udyāna, about which there are various legends; he, his wife 比壽尼, and his children were all converted to Buddhism. 丨丨(羅) 摩那 (阿) 婆; 丨(or 盧) 婆 (or 鉢) 摩那婆; 丨丨丨那; 波摩那 Apramāṇābha, intp. as 無量光 immeasurable light, the fifth of the Brahmalokas. 丨丨那伽低 Aparagati, the three evil paths, i.e. animal, hungry ghost, hell, but some say only the path to the hells. 丨丨陀那; 丨丨陁丨; 丨丨他丨 Avadāna, parables, metaphors, stories, illustrations; one of the twelve classes of sūtras; the stories, etc., are divided into eight categories.

阿浮呵 (or 訶) 那 Āvāhana, or Āpattivyutthāna, the calling of a monk or nun into the assembly for penance, or to rid the delinquent of sin. 丨丨(陀) 達摩 Adbhuta-dharma, miraculous or supernatural things, a section of the canon recounting miracles and prodigies.

阿潘 A-p'an, name of the "first" Chinese Buddhist nun, of Lo-yang in Honan.

阿濕喝咃波力叉 Aśvattha-vṛkṣa; v. 菩提樹 the *Ficus religiosa.* 丨丨婆 Aśva, a horse. 丨丨丨迷陀 Aśvamedha, the ancient royal horse-sacrifice. 丨丨摩 (or 麼 or 魔) Aśman, a stone, rock. 丨丨丨揭婆 Aśmagarbha; emerald, tr. by 石藏, but also by 馬腦 agate, the idea apparently being derived from another form 丨丨嚩揭波 aśvagarbha, horse matrix. Other forms are 丨丨(or 輸 or 舍) 丨碣 (or 揭 or 竭) 丨or 波; 遏丨丨丨丨. 丨丨毘儞 Aśvinī. M. W. says it is the first of the twenty-eight Nakshatras; the eleventh of the Chinese twenty-eight constellations, Hsü, β Aquarii, α Equulei. 丨丨波 Aśvin, the twins of the Zodiac, Castor and Pollux, sons of the Sun and Aśvinī; they appear in the sky before dawn riding in a golden carriage drawn by horses or birds. 丨丨縛伐多; 丨丨婆恃; 丨丨婆 (氏多); 丨丨波持; 丨說示 (or 旨); 丨輸實; 頞鞞 Aśvajit 馬勝 "Gaining horses by conquest." M. W. Name of one of the first five disciples and a relative of Śākyamuni; teacher of Śāriputra. 丨丨縛庾闍; 丨丨嚩喩若 Aśvayuja. The month in which the moon is in conjunction with Aśvinī, 16th of the 8th moon to 15th of the 9th; it is the middle month of autumn. 丨丨(or 溼) 縛窶沙; 馬鳴 q.v. Aśvaghoṣa. 丨丨縛羯拏; 丨輸割那 Aśvakarṇa, 馬耳 the horse-ear mountains, fifth of the seven concentric mountains around Sumeru.

阿點婆翅羅國 Atyambakela, an ancient kingdom near Karachi.

阿牟伽 v. 丨目佉 Amogha. 丨丨丨皤賒 Amoghapāśa, Kuan-yin with the noose.

阿犍 (or 揵) 多 Āgantuka, any visitant, or incident; a visiting monk; accidental.

阿由 Āyurvēda, one of the Vedas, the science of life or longevity. 丨丨(or 庾) 多 Ayuta, variously stated as a million or a thousand millions; and a 大丨丨丨 as ten thousand millions.

阿盧那 Aruṇa, 阿留 (or 樓) 那 ruddy, dawn-colour, dawn, south, fire, Mars, etc. 丨丨丨花 Aruṇakamala, the red lotus. 丨丨丨跋底 A red-coloured incense.

阿目佉 (跋折羅) Amogha, or Amoghavajra, 阿牟 (or 謨 or 穆) 伽 intp. 不空 (金剛) a monk from northern India, a follower of the mystic teachings of Samantabhadra. Vajramati 金剛智 is reputed to have founded the Yogācārya or Tantric school in China about A.D. 719–720. Amogha succeeded him in its leadership in 732. From a journey through India and Ceylon, 741–6, he brought to China more than 500 sūtras and śāstras; introduced a new form for transliterating Sanskrit and published 108 works. He is credited with the introduction of the Ullambana festival of All Souls, 15th of 7th moon, v. 盂. He is the chief representative of Buddhist mysticism in China, spreading it widely through the patronage of three successive emperors, Hsüan Tsung, Su Tsung, who gave him the title of 大廣智三藏 q.v., and Tai Tsung, who gave him the posthumous rank and title of a Minister of State. He died 774.

阿祇儞 or **尼** Agni, 阿耆 (or 擬) 尼 Fire, the fire-deva.

阿私仙 Asita-ṛṣi. | | (or 斯) 陀; | 氏多; | 夷. (1) A ṛṣi who spoke the Saddharma-puṇḍarīka-sūtra to Śākyamuni in a former incarnation. (2) The aged saint who pointed out the Buddha-signs on Buddha's body at his birth.

阿竭 (or **揭**) **多** Agastya, the star Canopus, also intp. as lightning. | | | 仙 One of the genii in the Nirvāṇa sūtra, who stopped the flow of the Ganges for twelve years by allowing it to run into one of his ears.

阿維 (or **比**) **羅提** Abhirati, the eastern Pure Land of Akṣobhya.

阿縛羅訶佉 A-va-ra-ha-kha, a spell uniting the powers respectively of earth, water, fire, air, and space. | | 盧枳低濕伐邏 Avalokiteśvara, | | | | 帝 (or 多伊) | | |; | 婆 | 吉帝舍婆羅; 阿那婆婁吉低輸; 阿梨耶婆樓吉弖稅; also Āryāvalokiteśvara. Intp. as 觀世音 or 光世音 "Regarder (or Observer) of the world's sounds, or cries"; or ? "Sounds that enlighten the world". Also 觀自在 The Sovereign beholder, a tr. of īśvara, lord, sovereign. There is much debate as to whether the latter part of the word is svara, sound, or īśvara, lord; Chinese interpretations vary. Cf. 觀音.

阿羅伽 Rāga, desire, emotion, feeling, greed, anger, wrath; and many other meanings; derived from to dye, colour, etc. | | 歌; 阿迦 or 伽 Arka, or white flower, *Asclepias* (M. W. says *Calotropis*) *gigantea*. Cf. 阿呼. | | 波 (or 婆) 遮那 Arapacana, a mystical formula, v. Lévi's article on arapacana, Batavian Society Feestbundel, 1929, II, pp. 100 seq. | | 漢 Arhan, arhat, lohan; worthy, venerable; an enlightened, saintly man; the highest type or ideal saint in Hīnayāna in contrast with the bodhisattva as the saint in Mahāyāna; intp. as 應供 worthy of worship, or respect; intp. as 殺賊 arihat, arihan, slayer of the enemy, i.e. of mortality; for the arhat enters nirvāṇa 不生 not to be reborn, having destroyed the karma of reincarnation; he is also in the stage of 不學 no longer learning, having attained. Also 羅漢; | 盧 |; | | 訶 or 呵; | 梨 (or 黎) 呵; 羅呵, etc.; cf. | 夷; | 畧. | | | 向 The direction leading to arhatship, by cutting off all illusion in the realms of form and beyond form. | | | 果 The fruit of arhat discipline. | | | 訶 One of the titles of Buddha, the Arhan who has overcome mortality. | | 磨 Ārāma, garden, grove, pleasaunce; hence saṅghārāma, a monastery with its gardens. Also, | |; | | 彌; | 藍麼 or 摩; 藍. | | 邏 Ārāḍa Kālāma, v. next. Also the Atata or Hahava cold hells. | | 邏迦藍 Ālāra- or Ārāḍa-Kālāma, the ṛṣi to whom Śākyamuni went on leaving home; another was Udraka Rāmaputra; they had attained to the concept of nothingness, including the non-existence of ideas. Other forms are | | | | 羅摩; | | 荼迦邏摩; | 藍迦; | 藍 (伽藍); | 蘭迦蘭; 羅勒迦藍. | | 闍 Rāja, a king. | | | 界 Rāja-dhātu, a dominion; kingdom.

阿羯羅 Āgāra, a house, dwelling, receptacle; tr. 境 and used in the sense of an organ, e.g. the ear for sound, etc.

阿耆多 Ajita, v. | 逸 |. | | | 翅 (or 頸) 舍欽 (or 甘) 婆羅; 阿末多 Ajita Keśa Kambalin, the unyielding one whose cloak is his hair. One of the six Tīrthyas, or Brahminical heretics, given to extravagant austerities; his doctrine was that the happiness of the next life is correlative to the sufferings of this life. | | 尼 Agni, fire, v. | 祇儞. Also "Agni or Akni, name of a kingdom . . . north of lake Lop". Eitel. | | (|) 達 or 陀 Agnidatta, name of a king. | | 毘伽 Ājīvika, or Ājīvaka, 邪命 One who lives on others, i.e. by improper means; an improper livelihood (for one in orders).

阿耨 v. 阿拏 Aṇu; and used for Anavatapta, *infra*. | | (多羅三藐三) 菩提 Anuttara-samyak-saṁbodhi; or Anubodhi. Unexcelled complete enlightenment, an attribute of every Buddha; tr. by 無上正徧知; 無上正等正覺, the highest correct and complete, or universal knowledge or awareness, the perfect wisdom of a Buddha, omniscience. | | 樓陀 Anuruddha, son of Amṛtodana, and "cousin german" to Śākyamuni (Eitel); not Aniruddha; cf. 阿那. | | 窣都婆 Anuṣṭubh; v. 阿菟. | | 觀音 Anu Kuanyin, the twentieth of the thirty-three forms of the "Goddess of Mercy", seated on a rock scanning the sea to protect or save voyagers. | | 達; 阿那婆答 (or 波達) 多 Anavatapta, a lake in Jambudvīpa, north of the Himālayas, south of 香山 Gandha-mādana, described as about 800 li in circumference, bordered by gold, silver, precious stones, etc. It is said to be the source of the four great rivers: east, the Ganges out of a silver ox mouth; south, the Indus out of that of an elephant; west, the Oxus; and north, the Śītā, said to be the Yellow River. Eitel has the Brahmaputra, Ganges, Śatadru (or Sutlej), and the Oxus; but there is confusion in the records. The Dragon-king of this lake became a bodhisattva and is exempt from the distresses of the other seven dragon-kings. The | | | 山 are the mountains north of the lake.

阿耶 Āya, approach, drawing near; | | 羅 Āyāna has the same meaning, but is intp. by 觀 to contemplate, look into. | | (or 也) 怛那 Āyatana, seat, abode, intp. by 入 or 處 entrance, or place, i.e. the ṣaḍāyatanas, six entrances or places of sense-data, or sensation; v. 六入. | | 揭哩 (or 唎) 婆 Hayagrīva, the horse-head Kuan-yin. | | 穆佉 Ayamukha, Hayamukha, an ancient kingdom in Central India.

阿育 Aśoka, | 恕伽; | 輸 or 舒, or 叔) 迦 Grandson of Candragupta (Sandrokottos), who united India and reached the summit of his career about 315 B.C. Aśoka reigned from about 274 to 237 B.C. His name Aśoka, "free from care," may have been adopted on his conversion. He is accused of the assassination of his brother and relatives to gain the throne, and of a fierce temperament in his earlier days. Converted, he became the first famous patron of Buddhism, encouraging its development and propaganda at home and abroad, to which existing pillars, etc., bear witness; his propaganda is said to have spread from the borders of China to Macedonia, Epirus, Egypt, and Cyrene. His title is Dharmāśoka; he should be distinguished from Kālāśoka, grandson of Ajātaśatru. Cf. | | 伽經, | | 伽傳, etc. | | 伽樹 The name of a tree under which the mother of the Buddha was painlessly delivered of her son, for which Chinese texts give eight different dates; the Jonesia aśoka; it is also called 畢利叉 Vṛkṣa.

阿若(多) Ājñāta-kāuṇḍinya, 阿若憍陳如 one of the first five disciples of Śākyamuni, said to be the first to realize the Buddha-truth. Ājñāta, his designation (i.e. recognized or confessed), is intp. as 已知 Having known and 無知 Not knowing, or knowledge of non-existence. Or perhaps for Ājñātṛ, confessor. Kauṇḍinya, his surname, is said to mean a "fire holder" from "the early fire-worship of the Brahmins".

阿菟 Aṇu, v. 阿拏. | | 吒闡提 Anuṣṭubh-chandas, a metre of two lines each in 8 + 8 syllables; also 阿耨窣都婆.

阿落刹娑 Rākṣasa, | | 迦娑 demons, evil spirits; rākṣasī are female demons, but are also said to be protectresses, cf. 羅叉娑.

阿薄健 Avakan, Vakhan, Khavakan; Wakhan, an ancient kingdom on the borders of the present Afghanistan, described by Hsüan-tsang as 200 li south-east of Badakshan. Also 濕 | |; 劫 | |.

阿薩多 Asāḍhā is a double nakṣatra (two lunar mansions) associated with 箕, stars in Sagittarius; this form is said to be Pūrvāṣāḍhā and is intp. as 軫, i.e. stars in Corvus, but these stars are in the Indian constellation Hastā, the Hand, which may be the more correct trans-literation; cf. | 沙陀. | | 闍 Asādhya, incurable.

阿蘭若 Āraṇya; from araṇya, "forest"; | | | 迦 āraṇyaka, one who lives there. Intp. by 無諍聲 no sound of discord; 閑靜 shut in and quiet; 遠離 far removed; 空寂 uninhabited and still; a lonely abode 500 bow-lengths from any village. A hermitage, or place of retirement for meditation. Three kinds of occupants are given: 達磨 | | | | Dharma-ā., meditators on the principle of inactivity, or letting Nature have its course; 摩祭 | | | | Mātaṅga-ā., those who dwell among the dead, away from human voices; 檀陀 | | | | Daṇḍaka-ā., those who dwell in sandy deserts and among rocks (as in the ancient Deccan). Other forms are: | | 那 or 攘; | | 陀 or 拖; | 練若 or 茹; 曷刺覣.

阿術達 Āśu-cittā, daughter of Ajātaśatru, king of Magadha, noted for her wisdom at 12 years of age.

阿詣羅 Aṅgiras, one of the seven deva-ṛṣis born from Brahma's mouth, shown in the Diamond Court of the Garbhadhātu, red coloured, holding a lotus on which is a vase; in Sanskrit the planet Jupiter. A title of the Buddha. Also 鴦耆伽羅和.

阿誓(or 恃)單闍那 Ajitaṁjaya, invincible, a charm for entering the meditation on invincibility. Cf. 阿恃.

阿說他 Aśvattha, a tree, the *Ficus religiosa*, or bodhi-tree, called also the 無罪樹 no-sin tree,

because whoever goes around it three times is rid of sin. Also 丨濕波他；丨舍波陀；丨輸他.
丨丨羅部 Aiśvarikas, a theistic school of Nepāl, which set up Ādi-Buddha as a supreme divinity.

阿賀羅 Āhāra, v. 食 9.

阿賒迦 A kind of hungry ghost; ? connected with Aśanāyuka.

阿賴耶 Ālaya, an abode, resting-place (hence Himālaya, the storehouse of snow), intp. as 無沒 non-disappearing, perhaps non-melting, also as 藏 store. Other forms are 丨利 (or 梨, 黎, or 羅) 耶; also 賴 or 梨 耶. Any of these terms is used in abbreviation for Ālaya-vijñāna. 丨丨丨外道 The ālaya heresy, one of the thirty heretical sects named in the 大日經, 住心, chapter 1, that the ālaya is a sort of eternal substance or matter, creative and containing all forms; when considered as a whole, it is non-existent, or contains nothing; when considered "unrolled", or phenomenal, it fills the universe. It seems to be of the nature of materialism as opposed to the idealistic conception of the Ālaya-vijñāna. 丨丨丨識 Ālaya-vijñāna. "The receptacle intellect or consciousness"; "the originating or receptacle intelligence"; "basic consciousness" (Keith). It is the store or totality of consciousness, both absolute and relative, impersonal in the whole, temporally personal or individual in its separated parts, always reproductive. It is described as 有情根本之心識 the fundamental mind-consciousness of conscious beings, which lays hold of all the experiences of the individual life; and which as storehouse holds the germs 種子 of all affairs; it is at the root of all experience, of the skandhas, and of all things on which sentient beings depend for existence. Mind is another term for it, as it both stores and gives rise to all seeds of phenomena and knowledge. It is called 本識 original mind, because it is the root of all things; 無沒識 inexhaustible mind, because none of its seeds (or products) is lost; 現識 manifested mind, because all things are revealed in or by it; 種子識 seeds mind, because from it spring all individualities, or particulars; 所知依識 because it is the basis of all knowledge; 異熟識 because it produces the rounds of mortality, good and evil karma, etc.; 執持識 or 阿陀那 q.v., that which holds together, or is the seed of another rebirth, or phenomena, the causal nexus; 第一識 the prime or supreme mind or consciousness; 宅識 abode (of) consciousness; 無垢識 unsullied consciousness when considered in the absolute, i.e. the Tathāgata; and 第八識, as the last of the eight vijñānas. There has been much discussion as to the meaning and implications of the Ālaya-vijñāna. It may also be termed the unconscious, or unconscious absolute, out of whose ignorance or unconsciousness arises all consciousness.

阿跋多羅 Avatāra, descent or epiphany, especially of a deity; but intp. as 無上 peerless and 入 to enter, the former at least in mistake for anuttara. 丨丨耶祇釐 Abhayagiri, Mount Fearless, in Ceylon at Anurādhapura; in its monastery a broad school of the Sthavirāḥ arose.

阿路巴 Rūpya, silver. 丨丨猱 Aruṇa, a mountain in the Punjab said formerly to fluctuate in height.

阿踰闍 Ayodhyā, 丨丨陀; 阿輸闍 capital of Kośala, headquarters of ancient Buddhism, the present Oudh, Lat. 26° N., Long. 82° 4 E.

阿軫䩉 Acintya, beyond conception, v. 不思議.

阿輸柯 Younger brother of Aśoka; he is said to have reigned for seven days and then resigned to Aśoka, but cf. Mahendra under 摩.

阿轆轆地 The land where all goes smoothly along (a-lu-lu) at will; idem 轉丨丨丨.

阿迦 Translit. *aka*, *agha*, etc. 丨丨奢 Ākāśa, the sky space, the air, ether, atmosphere. 丨丨色 Agha, but may be Ākāśa; it has two opposite interpretations, substantial and unsubstantial, the latter having special reference to the empyrean. 丨丨囊; 丨丨; 丨揭多 A flash in the east, the lightning god; the term is defined as 無厚 not solid, liquid, Sanskrit aghana(m). 丨丨雲 A physician, a healer, probably should be 丨丨曇 Agadaṁ; especially Bhaiṣajyarāja, the King of Medicine, or Healing. 丨丨尼(瑟)吒 Akaniṣṭha, not the least, i.e. the highest, or eighteenth of the heavens of form, or Brahmalokas; also 丨丨丨沙(or 師)吒 or 託; 丨丨貳吒; 丨丨尼(瑟)搋; 尼(師)吒; 二吒.

阿逸(多) Ajita, 無能勝 invincible, title of Maitreya; and of others. Also 丨氏 (or 底, 哳, or 嗜) 丨; 丨私陀; 丨夷頭.

阿遮利耶 Ācārya, (阿) 闍黎 or 梨; 丨舍梨; 丨祇利 or 梨 spiritual teacher, master, preceptor; one of 正行 correct conduct, and able to teach others. There are various categories, e.g.

出家｜｜｜ one who has charge of novices; 教授｜｜｜ a teacher of the discipline; 羯磨｜｜｜ of duties; 授經｜｜｜ of the scriptures; 依止｜｜｜ the master of the community. ｜｜(羅 or 攞); ｜奢羅 Acala, Immovable, the name of Āryācalanātha 不動明王, the one who executes the orders of Vairocana. Also, a stage in Bodhisattva development, the eighth in the ten stages towards Buddhahood. ｜｜樓 Name of a mountain.

阿避陀羯剌拏 Aviddhakarṇa, unpierced ears, name of an ancient monastery near Benares; "near Yodhapatipura" (Eitel).

阿那 Āna, 安那 inhalation, v. ｜｜波那. ｜｜他 Anātha, protector-less. ｜｜｜賓低 Anāthapiṇḍada, a wealthy elder of Śrāvastī, famous for liberality to the needy, and his gift of the Jetavana with its gardens and buildings to the Buddha, cf. 祇. His original name was 須達多 Sudatta and his wife's 毘舍佉 Viśākhā. ｜｜含 (or 鋡); ｜｜伽迷 (or 彌) Anāgāmin, the 不來 non-coming, or 不還 non-returning arhat or saint, who will not be reborn in this world, but in the rūpa and arūpa heavens, where he will attain to nirvāṇa. ｜｜｜向 One who is aiming at the above stage. ｜｜｜果 The third of the 四果 four fruits, i.e. the reward of the seeker after the above stage. ｜｜婆婁吉低輸 Āryāvalokiteśvara, a title of Kuan-yin, v. ｜縛. ｜｜律; ｜｜律徒 (or 陀); ｜兔 (or 寃) 樓馱; ｜尼 (or 菟) 盧豆 (or 律陀) Aniruddha, "unrestrained," tr. by 無滅 unceasing, i.e. the benefits resulting from his charity; or 如意無貪 able to gratify every wish and without desire. One of the ten chief disciples of Buddha; to reappear as the Buddha Samantaprabhāsa; he was considered supreme in 天眼 deva insight. Cf. 阿耨. ｜｜(阿) 波那; 安般; 安 (or 阿) 那般那 Ānāpāna, breathing, especially controlled breathing; āna is intp. as exhaling and apāna as inhaling, which is the opposite of the correct meaning; the process is for calming body and mind for contemplation by counting the breathing. ｜｜耆智羅 A spell for healing sickness, or charm for preventing it; others of similar title are for other saving purposes. ｜｜藪囉 (or 羅攞) 嚩 Anāsrava, free from mortality and its delusions.

阿部曇 The Arbuda hell, cf. 頞.

阿鉢唎瞿陀尼 Aparagodāna; apara, west; godāna, ox-exchange, where oxen are used as money; the western of the four continents of every world, circular in shape and with circular-faced people. Also 啞陌囉孤答尼耶. Cf. 瞿. ｜｜底鉢喇底提舍那 Āpatti-pratideśanā, confession, 懺悔. ｜｜羅嘁訶譎 Apratihata, irresistible, unaffected by. ｜｜｜市多 Aparājita, name of a yakṣa; also ｜跋｜爾多; ｜波羅實多; as a symbol of invincibility it is written ｜波羅質多.

阿鑁 Avaṁ. "A" is the Vairocana germ-word in the Garbhadhātu, "Vaṁ" the same in the Vajradhātu, hence Avaṁ includes both. ｜｜覽唅欠 A-vaṁ-raṁ-haṁ-khaṁ, is the highest formula of the 眞言 Shingon sect; it represents all the five elements, or composite parts of Vairocana in his corporeal nature, but also represents him in his 法身 or spiritual nature; cf. 阿卑, etc., and 阿羅 Arapacana.

阿閦 Akṣobhya, 阿閦鞞; 阿閦婆; 阿芻鞞耶 unmoved, imperturbable; tr. 不動; 無動 also 無怒; 無瞋恚 free from anger, according to his Buddha-vow. One of the Five Buddhas, his realm Abhirata, Delightful, now being in the east, as Amitābha's is in the west. He is represented in the Lotus as the eldest son of Mahābhijñābhibhū 大通智勝, and was the Bodhisattva ? Jñānākara 智積 before he became Buddha; he has other appearances. Akṣobhya is also said to mean 100 vivaras, or 1 followed by 17 ciphers, and a 大｜｜｜ is ten times that figure.

阿闍世 Ajātaśatru, ｜｜貰; ｜｜多設咄路; 未生怨 "Enemy before birth"; a king of Magadha whose father, Bimbisāra, is said to have sought to kill him as ill-omened. When grown up he killed his father and ascended the throne. At first inimical to Śākyamuni, later he was converted and became noted for his liberality; died *circa* 519 B.C. Also called "Broken fingers" and Kṣemadarśin. His son and successor was Udāyi; and a daughter was ? Aśu-dharā. According to a Tibetan legend an infant son of Ajātaśatru was kidnapped, or exposed, and finally became king of Tibet named Ña-khri-btsan-po. ｜｜梨 Ācārya, ācārin, v. 阿遮.

阿闡底(迦) Anicchantika, without desire, averse from, i.e. undesirous of nirvāṇa.

阿闥(or 達)婆那(or 波陀) Ātharvaṇa, v. 阿他 the Atharva Veda.

阿陀 Agada, v. ｜伽陀. ｜｜那 Ādāna, intp. by 執持 holding on to, maintaining; holding together the karma, good or evil, maintaining the sentient organism, or the germ in the seed or plant. It is another name for the ālaya-vijñāna, and is known as the ｜｜｜識 ādānavijñāna.

阿難 Ānanda, 丨難陀; intp. by 歡喜 Joy; son of Droṇodana-rāja, and younger brother of Devadatta; he was noted as the most learned disciple of Buddha, and famed for hearing and remembering his teaching, hence is styled 多聞; after the Buddha's death he is said to have compiled the sūtras in the Vaibhāra cave, v. 畢, where the disciples were assembled in Magadha. He is reckoned as the second patriarch. Ānandabhadra and Ānandasāgara are generally given as two other Ānandas, but this is uncertain. 丨丨丨夜叉 A yakṣa, called White Teeth. 丨丨丨補羅 Ānandapura, a place given by Eitel as north-east of Gujerat; "the present Bārnagar, near Kurree," which was "one of the strongholds of the Jain sect".

阿鞞跋致 Avaivartika, Avivartin, Aparivartya, 不退轉 One who never recedes; a bodhisattva who, in his progress towards Buddhahood, never retrogrades to a lower state than that to which he has attained. Also 丨毘丨丨; 丨惟越丨.

阿順那 Arjuna, white, silvery; the tree *Terminalia arjuna*; part of the name of 那伽閼刺樹那, Nāgārjuna q.v. Also 丨闍丨; 丨周陀丨; 頞丨丨; 夷離淳那.

阿顛底迦 Ātyantika, final, endless, tr. by 畢竟 to or at the end, e.g. no mind for attaining Buddhahood; cf. 阿闡.

阿馱囉 Ādara 丨陀丨 to salute with folded hands, palms together.

阿鳩羅加羅 Ākulakara, disturbing, upsetting; name of a wind.

阿鼻 Avīci, 丨丨旨; 丨丨脂; 丨丨至; the last and deepest of the eight hot hells, where the culprits suffer, die, and are instantly reborn to suffering, without interruption 無間. It is the 丨丨(丨)地獄 or the 丨丨焦熱地獄 hell of unintermitted scorching; or the 丨丨喚地獄 hell of unintermitted wailing; its wall, out of which there is no escape, is the 丨丨大城.

雨 Varṣa. Rain; to rain. 丨乞 To pray for rain. 丨安居; 丨時; 丨期 Varṣās; varṣavasāna; the rains, the rainy season, when was the summer retreat, v. 安居. 丨花, 丨華 To rain down (celestial) flowers. 丨衆 The disciples of 伐里沙 Vārṣya, i.e. Vārṣagaṇya, a leader of the Sāṅkhya school.

青 Nīla, blue, dark-coloured; also green, black, or grey; clear. 丨心 An unperturbed mind. 丨提女 The mother of Maudgalyāyana in a former incarnation, noted for her meanness. 丨河; 清河 The blue, or clear river, Vaṅksu, Vākṣu, the Oxus. 丨目 Blue-eyed. 丨蓮 Utpala, v. 優 Blue lotus. 丨面金剛 The blue-faced rāja, protector of Buddhism, king of the yakṣas, with open mouth, dog's fangs, three eyes, four arms, wearing skulls on his head, serpents on his legs, etc. 丨頭; 丨頸觀音 The blue-head, or blue-neck Kuan-yin, the former seated on a cliff, the latter with three faces, the front one of pity, the side ones of a tiger and a pig. 丨鬼 Blue (or green) demons who abuse the sufferers in Hades. 丨龍 Blue or Green dragon.

非 Not; un-; without, apart from; wrong.

非三非一 Neither three nor one; a T'ien-t'ai phrase, that the 空假中 or noumenon, phenomenon, and madhya or mean, are three aspects of absolute truth, but are not merely three nor merely one; idem the 三德 three powers, i.e. dharmakāya, wisdom, and nirvāṇa.

非二聚 Apart from the two categories of matter and mind; v. 非色非心.

非人 Not-men, not of the human race, i.e. devas, kinnaras, nāgas, māras, rakṣas, and all beings of darkness; sometimes applied to monks who have secluded themselves from the world and to beggars, i.e. not like ordinary men.

非六生 Not arising directly from the mind, which is the sixth sense, but from the other senses.

非喩 An imaginary and not factual metaphor, one of the eight forms of comparison 八喩.

非器 A vessel unfit for Buddha or Buddhism, e.g. a woman's body, which is unclean, v. Lotus Sūtra 提婆 chapter 12.

非天 Not devas, i.e. asuras, v. 阿修羅.

非學者 Those who do not learn Buddha-truth, hence 丨丨世者 is a world of such.

非安立 The unestablished, or undetermined; that which is beyond terminology. 丨丨丨諦 The doctrine of 丨丨丨眞如 the bhūtatathatā, the absolute as it exists in itself, i.e. indefinable, contrasted with the absolute as expressible in words and thought, a distinction made by the 唯識論.

非常 Anitya, 無常 impermanent, transient, illusory, as evidenced by old age, disease, and death. 丨丨苦空非我 Impermanent, suffering, empty, non-ego—such is life.

非心 Apart from mind, without mind, beyond mentation.

非心非佛 Apart from mind there is no Buddha; the positive statement is 是心是佛 this mind is Buddha.

非思量底 According to the orthodox or teaching sects, not to discriminate, or reason out; according to the Ch'an sect, to get rid of wrong thoughts (by freeing the mind from active operation).

非情 Non-sentient objects such as grass, wood, earth, stone. 丨丨成佛 The insentient become (or are) Buddha, a tenet of the 圓教, i.e. the doctrine of pan-Buddha.

非想 Beyond the condition of thinking or not-thinking, of active consciousness or unconsciousness; an abbrev. for 丨丨非非想天 or 處, v. 非有想. The 定 or degree of meditation of this name leads to rebirth in the arūpa heaven; which is not entirely free from distress, of which it has 八苦 eight forms.

非所斷 Not to be cut off, i.e. active or passive nirvāṇa (discipline); one of the 三所斷.

非時 Untimely; not the proper, or regulation time (for meals), which is from dawn to noon; hence 丨丨食 to eat out of hours, i.e. after noon.

非有 Abhāva. Non-existent, not real. 丨丨想非無想天 (or 處) Nāivasaṁjñānāsaṁjñāyatana. 非想非非想天 The heaven or place where there is neither thinking nor not-thinking; it is beyond thinking; the fourth of the 四空天 four immaterial heavens, known also as the 有頂天.

非有非空 Neither existing nor empty; neither material nor immaterial; the characterization of the bhūtatathatā (in the 唯識論), i.e. the ontological reality underlying all phenomena. In the light of this, though the phenomenal has no reality in itself 非有, the noumenal is not void 非空.

非業 Death by accident said not to be determined by previous karma; a sudden, unnatural, accidental death.

非滅 The Buddha's "extinction" or death not considered as real, v. next.

非生非滅 The doctrine that the Buddha was not really born and did not really die, for he is eternal; resembling Docetism.

非色 Arūpa, formless, i.e. without rūpa, form, or shape, not composed of the four elements. Also the four skandhas, 丨丨四蘊, excluding rūpa or form. 丨丨非心 Neither matter nor mind, neither phenomenal nor noumenal; the triple division of all things is into 色, 心, and 非色非心 phenomenal, noumenal, and neither.

非菩薩 Not bodhisattvas, those who have not yet inclined their hearts to Mahāyāna.

非道 Wrong ways, heterodox views, or doctrines.

非非想天 or **處** v. 非有.

非食 Not to eat out of regulation hours, v. 丨時丨.

非黑非白業 Neither black nor white karma, karma which does not affect metempsychosis either for evil or good; negative or indifferent karma.

9. NINE STROKES

係 Connect, bind, involve; is, are. 丨念 To think of, be drawn to.

俄 Suddenly, on the point of. 丨那鉢底 Gaṇapati, v. 誐.

�伽定 The nāga meditation, which enables one to become a dragon, hibernate in the deep, prolong one's life and meet Maitreya, the Messiah.

保 Protect, ward, guard; guarantee. 丨境將軍 The guardian general of the region.

便 Convenient, convenience; then, so; easy;

cheap. | 利 Convenient and beneficial; to urinate or evacuate the bowels; a latrine. | 旋 A mere turn, i.e. immediate and easy. | 膳 (or 善 or 社) 那; 䩭 膳 | Vyañjana, "making clear, marking, distinguishing," M. W. a "relish"; intp. by 文 a mark, sign, or script which manifests the meaning; also 味 a taste or flavour, that which distinguishes one taste from another.

俗 Common, ordinary, usual, vulgar. | 人 Gṛhastha, an ordinary householder; an ordinary man; the laity. | 塵 Common dust, earthly pollution. | 形 Of ordinary appearance, e.g. the laity. | 戒 The common commandments for the laity. | 我 The popular idea of the ego or soul, i.e. the empirical or false ego 假 我, composed of the five skandhas. This is to be distinguished from the true ego 眞 我 or 實 我, the metaphysical substratum from which all empirical elements have been eliminated; v. 八 大 自 在 我. | 智 Common or worldly wisdom, which by its illusion blurs or colours the mind, blinding it to reality. | 流 The common run or flow. | 諦; 世 諦 Common principles, or axioms; normal unenlightened ideas, in contrast with reality.

信 Śraddhā. Faith; to believe; belief; faith regarded as the faculty of the mind which sees, appropriates, and trusts the things of religion; it joyfully trusts in the Buddha, in the pure virtue of the Triratna and earthly and transcendental goodness; it is the cause of the pure life, and the solvent of doubt. Two forms are mentioned: (1) Adhimukti, intuition, tr. by self-assured enlightenment. (2) Śraddhā, faith through hearing or being taught. For the Awakening of Faith, Śraddhotpāda, v. 起 信 論.

信 伏 To believe in and submit oneself to.

信 仰 To believe in and look up to.

信 力 Śraddhābala. The power of faith; one of the five bala or powers.

信 受 The receptivity and obedience of faith; to believe and receive (the doctrine). | | 奉 行 In faith receive and obey, a sentence found at the end of sūtras.

信 向 To believe in and entrust oneself to the Triratna 三 寳.

信 士 Upāsaka, 信 事 男 a male devotee, who remains in the world as a lay disciple. A bestower of alms. Cf. 優.

信 女 Upāsikā. A female devotee, who remains at home. Cf. 優.

信 度 Sindhu, Sindh, Scinde, 辛 頭 the country of | | 河 the Indus, one of the "four great rivers". Sindhu is a general name for India, but refers especially to the kingdom along the banks of the river Indus, whose capital was Vichavapura.

信 德 The merit of the believing heart; the power of faith.

信 心 A believing mind, which receives without doubting.

信 忍 Faith-patience, faith-endurance: (1) To abide patiently in the faith and repeat the name of Amitābha. (2) To believe in the Truth and attain the nature of patient faith. (3) According to T'ien-t'ai the 別 敎 meaning is the unperturbed faith of the Bodhisattva (that all dharma is unreal).

信 慧 Faith and wisdom, two of the 五 根.

信 戒 Faith and morals, i.e. the moral law, or commandments; to put faith in the commandments.

信 手 Faith, regarded as a hand grasping the precious truth of Buddha.

信 施 Almsgiving because of faith; the gifts of the faithful.

信 根 Śraddhendriya. Faith, one of the five roots or organs producing a sound moral life.

信 樂 To believe and rejoice in the dharma; the joy of believing.

信 水 Faith pure and purifying like water.

信 海 The ocean of faith; the true virtue of the believing heart is vast and boundless as the ocean.

信 珠 The pearl of faith; as faith purifies the heart it is likened to a pearl of the purest water.

信現觀 Firm faith in the Triratna as revealing true knowledge; one of the 六現觀.

信種 The seed of faith.

信藏 The treasury of faith (which contains all merits).

信行 Believing action; faith and practice. Action resulting from faith in another's teaching, in contrast with 法行 action resulting from direct apprehension of the doctrine; the former is found among the 鈍根, i.e. those of inferior ability, the latter among the 利根, i.e. the mentally acute.

信解 Faith and interpretation, i.e. to believe and understand or explain the doctrine; the dull or unintellectual believe, the intelligent interpret; also, faith rids of heresy, interpretation of ignorance. ｜｜行證 Faith, interpretation, performance, and evidence or realization of the fruit of Buddha's doctrine.

信順 To believe and obey.

信首 Faith as the first and leading step.

信鼓 The drum or stimulant of faith.

冒 To risk; rash; counterfeit; introduce. ｜地 Bodhi. ｜｜質多 Bodhicitta, the enlightened mind, idem 菩提心. ｜｜薩怛𠴨縛 Bodhisattva. Cf. 菩提.

則 Pattern, rule; then, therefore. ｜劇 To play; a form of play.

剃 To shave. ｜刀 A razor. ｜頭 To shave the head. ｜髮 To shave the hair, following Śākyamuni, who cut off his locks with a sharp sword or knife to signify his cutting himself off from the world.

前 Pūrva. Before; former, previous; in front. ｜世; ｜生 Former life or lives. ｜中後 Former, intermediate, after. ｜佛 A preceding Buddha; former Buddhas who have entered into nirvāṇa. ｜堂 The front hall, or its front part. ｜塵 Previous impure conditions (influencing the succeeding stage or stages). ｜正覺山 Prāgbodhi, v. 鉢 A mountain in Magadha, reported to have been ascended by Śākyamuni before his enlightenment, hence its name. ｜身 The previous body, or incarnation. ｜後際斷 Discontinuous function, though seemingly continuous, e.g. a "Catherine-wheel", or torch whirled around.

剌 To cut, slash; translit. *la, ra, ya.* ｜瑟胝 Yaṣṭi, pole, staff, stick, intp. flagpole. ｜ (or 欏) 竭節 Laguḍa, a staff, stick. ｜那 cf. 囉, 羅 Ratna, precious thing, jewel, etc. ｜｜尸棄 Ratnaśikhin, cf. 尸, "the 999th Buddha of the preceding kalpa, the second of the Sapta Buddha." Eitel. ｜｜伽羅 Ratnākara, a "jewel-mine, the ocean" (M. W.), intp. jewel-heap; name of a Buddha and bodhisattva; the 112th Buddha of the present kalpa; also of "a native of Vaiśālī, contemporary of Śākyamuni". ｜闍; 囉惹 Rajas, atmosphere, vapour, gloom, dust, dirt, etc.; intp. dust, minute; also hatred, suffering.

勅 Imperial commands. ｜命 The sovereign commands of the Buddha.

勇 Brave, bold, courageous, fearless. ｜猛精進 Bold advance, or progress. ｜施菩薩 Pradhānaśūra, a bodhisattva now in Śākyamuni's retinue.

勃 Shooting plants; a comet. ｜沙; 弗沙 Puṣya; foam; a lunar mansion, i.e. the three arrow stars in the 鬼 constellation of which δ Cancri is one. ｜陀; ｜馱; ｜塔耶; 脖陀; 佛陀 Buddha; intp. by 覺 and 佛 q.v. ｜伽夷 Bhagai, "a city south of Khotan with a Buddha-statue which exhibits all the" lakṣaṇāni, or thirty-two signs, "brought there from Cashmere." Eitel.

南 Dakṣiṇa, south; translit. *nām*, and as a suffix intp. as meaning plural, several, i.e. more than three.

南中三教 The three modes of Śākyamuni's teaching as expounded by the teachers south of the Yangtze after the Ch'i dynasty A.D. 479–501. (1) The 漸教 gradual method, leading the disciples step by step to nirvāṇa. (2) The 頓｜ immediate method, by which he instructed the bodhisattvas, revealing the whole truth. (3) The 不定教 undetermined method, by which the teaching is adapted to each individual or group.

南天(竺) Southern India.

南宗 The Southern sect, or Bodhidharma School, divided into northern and southern, the northern under 神秀 Shên-hsiu, the southern under 慧能 Hui-nêng, *circa* A.D. 700, hence ｜能北秀; the southern came to be considered the orthodox Intuitional school. The phrase 丨頓北漸 or "Southern immediate, northern gradual" refers to the method of enlightenment which separated the two schools.

南山 Southern hill, name of a monastery which gave its name to 道宣 Tao-hsüan of the T'ang dynasty, founder of the 四分律 school.

南方 The southern quarter; south. 丨丨佛教 Southern Buddhism in contrast with 北方 northern Buddhism. 丨(丨)無垢(世界) The Southern Pure Land to which the dragon-maid went on attaining Buddhahood, cf. Lotus Sūtra.

南泉 Nan-ch'üan, a monk of the T'ang dynasty *circa* 800, noted for his cryptic sayings, inheritor of the principles of his master, Ma Tsu 馬祖.

南海摩羅耶山 Malayagiri, "the Malaya mountains in Malabar answering to the western Ghāts; a district in the south of India." M. W. A mountain in Ceylon, also called Laṅkā.

南無 Namaḥ; Pali: Namo; to submit oneself to, from to bend, bow to, make obeisance, pay homage to; an expression of submission to command, complete commitment, reverence, devotion, trust for salvation, etc. Also written 丨牟; 丨謨; 丨忙; 那謨 (or 模 or 麻); 納莫 (or 慕); 娜母; 曩莫 (or 謨); 捺麻 (or 謨), etc. It is used constantly in liturgy, incantations, etc., especially as in Namaḥ Amitābha, which is the formula of faith of the Pure-land sect, representing the believing heart of all beings and Amitābha's power and will to save; repeated in the hour of death it opens the entrance to the Pure Land. 丨丨佛; 丨丨三寶 I devote myself entirely to the Buddha, or Triratna, or Amitābha, etc. 丨丨師 Masters of Namaḥ, i.e. Buddhist or Taoist priests and sorcerers.

南羅 Southern Lāra; Mālava, an ancient kingdom in Central India; headquarters of heretical sects, in the present Malwa. 北丨 was Valabhī, in Gujarat.

南能北秀 v. 南宗.

南藏 The Southern Collection, or Edition, of the Chinese Buddhist Canon, published at Nanking under the reign of T'ai Tsu, the first emperor of the Ming dynasty, who reigned A.D. 1368–1398.

南行 Dakṣiṇāyana. The course or declination of the sun to the south; the half-year in which it moves from north to south; a period of six months.

南贍部洲; 南閻浮提 Jambūdvīpa. One of the four continents, that situated south of Mt. Meru, comprising the world known to the early Indians. Also 丨洲; 丨浮; 丨部.

南陽 Nan-yang, a noted monk who had influence with the T'ang emperors Su Tsung and Tai Tsung, *circa* 761–775.

南頓北漸 v. 南宗.

即 To draw up to, or near; approach; forthwith; to be; i.e. *alias*; if, even if; 就是. It is intp. as 和融 united together; 不二 not two, i.e. identical; 不離 not separate, inseparable. It resembles implication, e.g. the afflictions or passions imply, or are, bodhi; births-and-deaths imply, or are, nirvāṇa; the indication being that the one is contained in or leads to the other. T'ien-t'ai has three definitions: (1) The union, or unity, of two things, e.g. 煩惱 and 菩提, i.e. the passions and enlightenment, the former being taken as the 相 form, the latter 性 spirit, which two are inseparable; in other words, apart from the subjugation of the passions there is no enlightenment. (2) Back and front are inseparables; also (3) substance and quality, e.g. water and wave.

即中 The *via media* is that which lies between or embraces both the 空 and the 假, i.e. the void, or noumenal, and the phenomenal.

即事即理 The identity of phenomena with their underlying principle, e.g. body and spirit are a unity; 丨丨而眞 approximates to the same meaning that phenomena are identical with reality, e.g. water and wave.

即得 Immediately to obtain, e.g. rebirth in the Pure Land, or the new birth here and now.

即心 Of the mind, mental, i.e. all things are mental, and are not apart from mind. 丨丨即佛, 丨丨是 (or 成) 佛 The identity of mind and Buddha, mind is Buddha, the highest doctrine of Mahāyāna;

the negative form is 非心非佛 no mind no Buddha, or apart from mind there is no Buddha; and all the living are of the one mind. | | 念佛 To remember, or call upon, Amitābha Buddha within the heart, which is his Pure Land.

即時 Immediately, forthwith.

即有即空 All things, or phenomena, are identical with the void, or the noumenon.

即相即心 Both form and mind are identical, e.g. the Pure Land as a place is identical with the Pure Land in the mind or heart—a doctrine of the Pure-land or Jōdo sect.

即空即假即中 All things are void, or noumenal, are phenomenal, are medial, the three meditations 三觀 of T'ien-t'ai.

即身 The doctrine of the Shingon 眞言 sect that the body is also Buddha; in other words Buddha is not only 即心 mind, but body; hence | | 成佛; | | 菩提 the body is to become (consciously) Buddha by Yoga practices.

即離 Identity and difference, agreement and disagreement.

即非 Identity and difference.

哀 Alas! mourn, wail. | 愍; | 憐 Pity for one in misery. | 雅 Ai ya! an exclamation of pain, or surprise.

咥 To laugh; to bite. Translit. *t*. | 哩若底 Trijāti, the three stages of birth, past, present, future. (摩) | 哩迦 Mātṛkā, a name for the Abhidharma-piṭaka.

咥吒 Kheṭa, name of a preta, or hungry ghost.

哈密 Hami, "an ancient city and kingdom in Central Asia north-east of lake Lop in Lat. 43° 3 N., Long. 93° 10 E." Eitel. From Han to T'ang times known as I-wu 伊吾, now called Kumul by Turki Mohammadans. For more than 1500 years, owing to its location and supply of water, Hami was a bridge-head for the expansion and control of the outposts of the Chinese empire in Central Asia.

咸 All, entirely. | 同 All together.

品 Varga, 跋渠 class, series, rank, character; a chapter of a sūtra. 上中下 | Superior, middle, and lower class, grade, or rank.

垢 Mala. Dust, impurity, dregs; moral impurity; mental impurity. Whatever misleads or deludes the mind; illusion; defilement; the six forms are vexation, malevolence, hatred, flattery, wild talk, pride; the seven are desire, false views, doubt, presumption, arrogance, inertia, and meanness. | 有 v. 二眞如. | 染 Taint of earthly things, or illusion. | 汙 Defilement (of the physical as type of mental illusion). | 結 The bond of the defiling, i.e. the material, and of reincarnation; illusion. | 習 Habituation to defilement; the influence of its practice. | 識 Defiling knowledge, the common worldly knowledge that does not discriminate the seeming from the real.

城 See under Ten Strokes.

契 A tally, covenant, bond; to agree with; devoted to; adopted (by). | 吒 Kakṣa; Kacha; Kach; ancient kingdom of Mālava, now the peninsula Cutch. | 會 To meet, rally to, or unite in the right or middle path, and not in either extreme. | 範 The covenants and rules, or standard contracts, i.e. the sūtras. | 線; | 經 The sūtras, because they tally with the mind of man and the laws of nature.

姞 Chi, name of the concubine of Huang Ti; translit. *g*. | 栗陀(羅矩吒) Gṛdhra, a vulture; Gṛdhrakūṭa, the Vulture Peak, v. 耆.

姟 Ten millions, tr. of Ayuta 阿由他, Nayuta 那由他; but another account says 100 millions.

姥 Matron, dame. | 達羅 Mudrā(-bala), 100,000 sexillions; 大 | | | a septillion; v. 洛.

威 Prabhāva. Awe-inspiring majesty; also | 力 and | 神力. | 儀 Respect-inspiring deportment; dignity, i.e. in walking, standing, sitting, lying. There are said to be 3,000 and also 80,000 forms of such deportment. | | (法)師; | | 僧 A master of ceremonies. | 德 Of respect-inspiring virtue; dignified. | 怒 Awe-inspiring; wrathful majesty. | | 王 The wrathful Mahārāja guardians of Buddhism. | 神 The awe-inspiring gods, or spirits. | 音王 Bhīṣma-garjita-ghoṣa-svara-rāja, the king with the awe-inspiring voice, the name of countless

Buddhas successively appearing during the 離衰 kalpa; cf. Lotus Sūtra.

宣 Proclaim; spread abroad; widespread. 丨流; 丨說.

客 A guest, visitor, traveller, outsider, merchant. 丨司 Guest room; reception of guests. 丨山 The guest hill, or branch monastery, in contrast with the 主山 chief one. 丨塵 Āgantu-kleśa, the foreign atom, or intruding element, which enters the mind and causes distress and delusion; the mind is naturally pure or innocent till the evil element enters; v. 煩惱.

室 House, household, abode; translit. *ś*, *s*, *śr*, *śl*. Cf. 尸; 舍; 首; for 丨摩 v. 沙門.

室利 Śrī, fortunate, lucky, prosperous; wealth; beauty; name applied to Lakṣmī and Sarasvatī, also used as a prefix to names of various deities and men; an abbrev. for Mañjuśrī. 丨丨靺塞迦 Śrīvāsas, turpentine. 丨丨蜜多羅 Śrīmitra, a prince of India, who became a monk and tr. three works in Nanking A.D. 317–322. 丨丨揭婆 Śrīgarbha, Fortune's womb, epithet of Viṣṇu. M. W. also tr. it "a sword", but it is intp. as a precious stone. 丨丨提婆 Śrīdeva, name of 道希 Tao-hsi, a noted monk. 丨丨毱 Śrīgupta, an enemy of Śākyamuni, whom he tried to destroy with a pitfall of fire and a poisoned drink. 丨丨羅 Śarīra, relics, v. 舍. 丨丨羅 (or 邏) 多 Śrīlabdha, a celebrated commentator, to whom is attributed, *inter alia*, the chief commentary on the 起信論 Awakening of Faith; he was called the enlightener of northern India. 丨丨差呾羅 Śrīkṣetra, "an ancient kingdom near the mouth of the Brahmaputtra"; capital probably "modern Silhet (Śrīhatta)". Eitel. 丨丨訖栗多底 Śrīkrītati, ancient name of Kashgar; Eitel. 丨丨靺蹉 Śrīvatsa, the mark of Viṣṇu and Kṛṣṇa, a curl of hair on their breasts, resembling a cruciform flower (M. W.), intp. as resembling the svastika.

室星 The Revatī constellation in India, that of the "house" or the thirteenth constellation in China.

室灑 Śiṣya, a pupil, disciple.

室獸摩羅 Śiśumāra, a crocodile; see 失收丨丨.

室羅末尼羅 Śrāmaṇera, v. 沙彌; also for 丨丨摩拏洛 (or 理) 迦.

室羅筏 (or 縛) 拏 (磨洗) Śrāvaṇa(-māsa). The hottest month of summer, July–August (from 16th of 5th moon to 15th of 6th moon).

室羅筏悉底 Śrāvastī or Śarāvatī, also 丨丨伐, v. 舍衛國.

封 To seal, close (a letter); classifier, or numerative of letters, etc.; to appoint (imperially). 丨體 To seal up a god or Buddha in a body by secret methods.

屋 A house, a room. 丨裏人 The master of the house; the mind within; also a wife.

屍 Corpse (of a murdered person). v. 尸 and 毘陀羅. 丨鬼 A corpse-ghost (called up to kill an enemy). 丨陀林 Śītavana, a cemetery. 丨黎密 Śrīmitra, cf. 室.

屎 Excrement. 丨擔子 A load of night-soil, i.e. the human body that has to be carried about. 丨糞地獄 The excrement hell.

帝 Ruler, sovereign; translit. *t*. 丨利耶瞿榆泥伽; 傍行 Tiryagyoni-gati; the animal path of reincarnation. 丨失羅叉 Tiṣya-rakṣitā; "a concubine of Aśoka, the rejected lover and enemy of Kuṇāla" (Eitel). M. W. says Aśoka's second wife. 丨居 The abode of Indra. 丨心 Title given to 杜順 Tu Shun, founder of the Hua-yen school, by T'ang T'ai Tsung. 丨沙 Tiṣya; an ancient Buddha; also the father of Śāriputra. 丨相 Indra-dhvaja, a Buddha "said to have been a contemporary of Śākyamuni, living south-west of our universe, an incarnation of the seventh son of Mahābhijña-jñānābhibhū". Eitel. 丨釋 Sovereign Śakra; Indra; 能天帝 mighty lord of devas; Lord of the Trayastriṁśas, i.e. the thirty-three heavens 三十三天 q.v.; he is also styled 釋迦提桓 (or 婆) 因陀 (or 達) 羅; 釋帝桓因 Śakra-devānām Indra. 丨(丨) 弓; 天弓 Indradhanus, the rainbow. 丨丨巖; 丨丨窟 Indraśilāguhā, Indra's cave at Nālandā in Magadha, where Indra is supposed to have sought relief for his doubts from the Buddha. 丨丨瓶 The vase of Indra, from which came all things he needed; called also 德 (or 賢 or 吉) 祥瓶 vase of virtue, or of worth, or of good fortune. 丨(丨) 網 ? Indra-jāla. The net of Indra, hanging in Indra's 宮 hall, out of which all things can be produced; also the name of an incantation considered all-powerful. 丨隸路迦也

跃闍耶 Trailokya-vijaya, victor or lord over the 三世 three realms. | 青 Indranīla, an emerald.

幽 Hidden, dark, mysterious. | 儀 The mysterious form, the spirit of the dead. | 冥 Mysterious, beyond comprehension; the shades. | 途 The dark paths, i.e. of rebirth in purgatory or as hungry ghosts or animals. | 靈 Invisible spirits, the spirits in the shades, the souls of the departed.

度 Pāramitā, 波羅蜜; intp. by 渡 to ferry over; to save. The mortal life of reincarnations is the sea; nirvāṇa is the other shore; v. Pāramitā, 波. Also, to leave the world as a monk or nun, such is a |僧 or |者. |一切世間苦惱 Sarvalōkadhātūpadravodvega - pratyuttīrṇa. "One who redeems men from the misery of all worlds. A fictitious Buddha who dwelled west of our universe, an incarnation of the tenth son of Mahābhijñājñānābhibhū." Eitel. | 世 To get through life; to pass safely through this life. Also, to save the world. | 沃焦 An epithet of Buddha who rescues all the living from being consumed by their desires, which resemble the burning rock in the ocean above purgatory. |洛叉 Daśalakṣa, 10 lakhs, a million. |無極 To ferry across, or save, without limit. | 生 To save, rescue all beings; also idem | 世. | 科 The portion of the sūtras supposed to be learned by religious novices as preparation for leaving the world as monks. | 脫 To give release from the wheel of transmigration; enlightenment.

建 To found, set up, establish, build. | 佗歌 Kaṇṭhaka, the horse on which Śākyamuni rode when he left home. |志補羅; |志城 Kāñcīpura, capital of Drāviḍa, the modern Conjevaram, about 48 miles south-west of Madras. | 立 To found (a school of thought or practice); to set up; e.g. samāropa, assertion, postulation, theory, opp. of 誹謗 apavāda, refutation.

廻 Return, turn back, turn to, give back; a turn. |大入一 To turn to and enter the One Vehicle of Mahāyāna. | 心 To turn the mind or heart towards (Mahāyāna). | 向 The goal or direction of any discipline such as that of bodhisattva, Buddha, etc.; to devote one's merits to the salvation of others; works of supererogation; | 施 is similar; cf. 回向; 十|向; 五悔; 三心; 九方便.

弭 Stop, put down. |曼差 The Mīmāṁsā system of Indian philosophy founded by Jaimini, especially the Pūrva-mīmāṁsā. It was "one of the three great divisions of orthodox Hindu philosophy". M. W. Cf. the Nyāya and Sāṅkhya. | 秣賀 Mimaha, "an ancient kingdom about seventy miles east of Samarkand, the present Moughian or Maghīn in Turkestan." Eitel.

彥 Accomplished, refined. | 琮 Yen-ts'ung, a famous monk, translator and writer, A.D. 557–610. | 悰 Yen-ts'ung, T'ang monk, translator and writer, date unknown. | 達縛 Gandharva, v. 乾.

待 To wait, treat, behave to. | 對 Relationship, in relation with, one thing associated with another.

後 After, behind, later, posterior. | 世 The life after this; later generations or ages. | 五(百年 or 歲) The pratirūpaka 象 (or 像) 法 symbol, formal, or image period, to begin 500 years after the Nirvāṇa; also the last of the periods of 500 years when strife would prevail. | 光 The halo behind an image. | 唄 The third of the three chants in praise of Buddha. | 報 The retribution received in further incarnation (for the deeds done in this life). | 夜 The third division of the night. | 得智; 分別智 Detailed, or specific, knowledge or wisdom succeeding upon or arising from 根本智 fundamental knowledge. | 有 Future karma; the person in the subsequent incarnation; also, the final incarnation of the arhat, or bodhisattva. | 法; 像法 The latter, or symbol, age of Buddhism; see above. | 生 The after condition of rebirth; later born; youth. | 說 Spoken later, or after; the predicate of the major premiss of a syllogism. | 身 The body or person in the next stage of transmigration.

律 Vinaya, from Vi-nī, to lead, train; discipline; v. 毘奈耶; other names are pratimokṣa, śīla, and upalakṣa. The discipline, or monastic rules; one of the three divisions of the Canon, or Tripiṭaka, and said to have been compiled by Upāli. | 乘 The Vinaya-vehicle, the teaching which emphasizes the discipline. | 儀 Rules and ceremonies, an intuitive apprehension of which, both written and unwritten, enables the individual to act properly under all circumstances. | 儀戒 The first of the three 聚戒, i.e. to avoid evil by keeping to the discipline. | 宗 The Vinaya school, emphasizing the monastic discipline, founded in China by 道宣 Tao-hsüan of the T'ang dynasty. | 派 The discipline branch, or school. | 師 Master and teacher of the rules of the discipline. | 懺 Repentance and penance according to the rules. | 法 The laws or methods of the discipline; rules and laws. | 相 The discipline, or its characteristics. | 禪 The two schools of Discipline and Intuition. | 藏 The Vinaya-piṭaka. | 行 The discipline in practice, to act according to the rules.

怎 How? What? Why? Anything. | 生 How born? How did it arise?

急 Haste, urgency; promptly. | 施 Alms made under stress of urgency. | | 如 律 令 "Swiftly as Lü-ling runs," used by sorcerers in their incantations.

恨 Hate, annoyed, vexed. | 心; 怨 |; | 怒.

恒 Constant; perseverance, persistence; translit. *ga, ha*. | 常 Constant, regular. | 伽 河 The Ganges, v. | 河. | 伽 提 婆 Gaṅgādevī, name of a female disciple of the Buddha. | | 達 Gaṅgādatta, son of a wealthy landowner and disciple of the Buddha. | (or 亘) 娑 Haṁsa, a goose. | 河; | 水; | (競, 殑, or 強) 伽 Gaṅgā, the river Ganges, "said to drop from the centre of Śiva's ear into the Anavatapta lake" (Eitel), passing through an orifice called variously ox's mouth, lion's mouth, golden elephant's mouth, then round the lake and out to the ocean on the south-east. | 伽 沙 more commonly | 沙 Gaṅgā-nadī-vālukā; as the sands of Ganges, numberless.

思 Cint- 指 底. Think, thought; turn the attention to; intp. by 心 所 法 mental action or contents, mentality, intellection. | 假 Thought or its content as illusion. | 惟 To consider or reflect on an object with discrimination; thought, reflection. | 惑 The illusion of thought. | 慧 The wisdom attained by meditating (on the principles and doctrines of Buddhism). | 擇 力 Power in thought and selection (of correct principles). | 量 Thinking and measuring, or comparing; reasoning. | 量 (能 變) 識 The seventh vijñāna, intellection, reasoning. | 食 Thought-food, mental food; to desire food.

怨 Resentment, grievance, hatred. | 家; | 敵 An enemy. | 憎 會 苦 One of the eight sufferings, to have to meet the hateful. | 結 The knot of hatred. | 親 Hate and affection. | 賊 The robber hatred, hurtful to life and goods. | 靈 An avenging spirit or ghost.

按 To place, lay down, lay the hand on; examine; accord with. | 指 To make a finger-mark, or sign.

拏 Take, lay hold of; translit. for *ḍ, ṇ*; e.g. ḍāmara, to affright (demons); v. 荼.

拜 Pay respect (with the hands), worship; the forms of bowing and kneeling are meticulously regulated. | 佛 To worship the Buddhas, etc.

拾 To gather, pick up, arrange; ten. | 得 To gather; gathered up, picked up, a foundling.

指 Finger, toe; to point, indicate. | 兎 idem | 月 To indicate the hare (in the moon). | 印 To sign by a thumb-mark; a sign. | 多; 質 多 Citta, the mind. | 方 立 相 To point to the west, the location of the Pure Land, and to set up in the mind the presence of Amitābha; to hold this idea, and to trust in Amitābha, and thus attain salvation. The mystics regard this as a mental experience, while the ordinary believer regards it as an objective reality. | 月 To point a finger at the moon: the finger represents the sūtras, the moon represents their doctrines. | 環; 草 |; | (or 草) 釧 Finger-ring; sometimes of grass, used by the esoteric sect. | 節 Aṅgulī-parvan; finger-joint; a measure, the 24th part of a forearm (hasta). | 腹 親 Related by the betrothal of son and daughter still in the womb. | 難 idem 支 那 China. | 鬘 Aṅgulīmālya, name of a convert of Śākyamuni, who had belonged to a Śivaitic sect which wore chaplets of finger-bones, and "made assassination a religious act".

持 Dhṛ; Dhara. Lay hold of, grasp, hold, maintain, keep; control. | 句 One who holds to or retains the words (of the dhāraṇī). | 名 to hold to, i.e. rely on the name (of Amitābha). | 國 者 A sovereign, ruler of a kingdom. | (or 治) 國 天 Dhṛtarāṣṭra, one of the four deva-guardians or mahārājas, controlling the east, of white colour. | 地 Dharaṇimdhara, holder, or ruler of the earth, or land; name of a Bodhisattva, who predicted the future of Avalokiteśvara. | 律 A keeper or observer of the discipline. | 念 To hold in memory. | 息 念 The contemplation in which the breathing is controlled, v. Ānāpāna 阿 那. | 戒 To keep the commandments, or rules. | 戒 波 羅 蜜 One of the six pāramitās, morality, keeping the moral law. | 本 Holding to the root, or fundamental; ruler of the earth, which is the root and source of all things. | 明 The dhāraṇī illuminant, i.e. the effective "true word" or magical term. | 明 仙 The magician who possesses this term. | 明 藏 The canon of the dhāraṇīs; vidyādhara-piṭaka. | 水 Jātiṁdhara, a physician who adjusted prescriptions and diet to the seasons; reborn as Śuddhodana. | 法 者 A keeper or protector of the Buddha-law. | 犯 "maintaining and transgressing", i.e. keeping the commandments by 止 持 ceasing to do wrong and 作 持 doing what is right, e.g. worship, the monastic life, etc.; transgression is also of two kinds, i.e. 作 犯 positive in doing evil and 止 犯 negative in not doing good. | 牛 戒 Keepers of the law of oxen, an ascetic sect who ate and acted like oxen. | 瓔 珞 Mālādharī, wearing a chaplet, name of a rākṣasī, or demoness. | 素 To keep to vegetarian diet; vegetarian. | 軸 山 Īṣādhara, the second of the seven concentric mountains round Mt. Meru, rounded like a hub. | 邊 山 Nemiṁdhara, the outermost of the seven mountain circles around Mt. Meru. | 雙 山 Yugaṁdhara; the first of the seven concentric mountains. | 金 剛; 執 金 剛 Vajradhara, or Vajrapāṇi, a Bodhisattva who holds a vajra or thunderbolt, of these there are several; a name for Indra. | 齋 To keep the fast, i.e. not eat after noon.

政 Government, administration, policy, politics. | 教 Political teaching, governmental education; politics and the church (or religion).

故 Old, of old; from of old; cause; purposely; to die; tr. pūrva. | 二 Pūrva-dvitīya, the former mate or wife of a monk. | 思 (or 作) 業 The karma produced by former intention. | 意 Intentionally. | 意 方 行 位 The third to the seventh of the 十 地 ten bodhisattva stages of development. | 紙 Old or waste paper. | 苦 Old suffering; also the suffering resulting from prolongation, e.g. too much lying, standing, walking, at first a joy, becomes wearying. | 骨 Old bones, bones of a former incarnation or generation.

斫 To chop; translit. *ca*, *cha*. | (or 拆 or 所) 句 迦 Chakoka, or Cugopa. "An ancient kingdom and city in Little Bukharia, probably the modern Yerkiang (葉 爾 羌) in Lat. 38° 13 N., Long. 78° 49 E." Eitel. Or perhaps Karghalik in the Khotan region. | (乞) 芻 Cakṣu(s), the eye, one of the six organs of sense. Cakṣurdhātu is the 眼 界 eye-realm, or sight-faculty. There are definitions such as the eye of body, mind, wisdom, Buddha-truth, Buddha; or human, deva, bodhisattva, dharma, and Buddha vision. | 訖 羅 idem | (or 柘) 迦 羅; 遮 伽 (or 迦) 羅; 賒 羯 羅 Cakra, a wheel, disc, cycle; the wheel of the sun's chariot, of time, etc.; like the vajra it is a symbol of sovereignty, of advancing or doing at will; to revolve the wheel is to manifest power or wisdom. It is a symbol of a | | | 伐 辣 底; 遮 迦 越 羅; 轉 輪 (王) Cakravartī(-rāja), sovereign ruler, whose chariot wheels roll everywhere without hindrance; the extent of his realm and power are indicated by the quality of the metal, iron, copper, silver, or, for universality, gold. The highest cakravartī uses the wheel or thunderbolt as a weapon and "hurls his Tchakra into the midst of his enemies", but the Buddha "meekly turns the wheel of doctrine and conquers every universe by his teaching". Eitel. The cakra is one of the thirty-two signs on a Buddha's soles. | | | 婆 (迦) Cakravāka, Cakrāhva, "the ruddy goose", "the Brāhmany duck". M. W. The mandarin duck. | | | 山 Cakravāla, Cakravāḍa, the circle of iron mountains "forming the periphery of a universe".

施 Dāna 檀 那 Alms; charity. To give, bestow. See also 實. | 主 Dānapati; an almsgiver, a patron of Buddhism. | 僧 To give alms to monks. | 化 To bestow the transforming truth. | 林 To give to the forest, i.e. burial by casting the corpse into the forest. | 無 厭 (寺), i.e. 那 爛 陀 Nālandā-saṅghārāma, a monastery seven miles north of Rājagṛha, where Hsüan-tsang studied; built by Śakrāditya; now "Baragong (i.e. vihāragrāma)". Eitel. | 無 畏 Abhayandada; abhayadāna; the bestower of fearlessness, a title of Kuan-yin; a bodhisattva in the Garbhadhātu. | 行 The practice of charity. | 設 To set up, establish, start. | 設 論 部 Kārmikāḥ, the school of Kārma, which taught the superiority of morality over knowledge. | 護 Dānapāla, a native of Udyāna who translated into Chinese some 111 works and in A.D. 982 received the title of Great Master and brilliant expositor of the faith. | 開 廢 A T'ien-t'ai term indicating the three periods of the Buddha's teaching: (1) bestowing the truth in Hīnayāna and other partial forms; (2) opening of the perfect truth like the lotus, as in the Lotus sūtra; (3) abrogating the earlier imperfect forms. | 食 To bestow food (on monks), and on hungry ghosts.

昭 Bright, illustrious. | 玄 寺 The bureau for nuns in the fifth century A.D.

是 The verb to be, is, are, etc.; right; this, these. | 心 | 佛 This mind is Buddha; the mind is Buddha, cf. 即. | 處 非 處 力 The power to distinguish right from wrong, one of the ten Buddha-powers.

星 Tārā, a star; the 25th constellation consisting of stars in Hydra; a spark. | 宿 The twenty-eight Chinese constellations 二 十 八 宿; also the twenty-eight nakṣatras; the 十 二 宮 twelve rāśi, or zodiacal mansions; and the 七 曜 seven mobile stars: sun, moon, and five graha or planets; all which are used as auguries in | 占 法 astrology. A list giving Sanskrit and Chinese names, etc., is given in 佛 學 大 辭 典, pp. 1579–1580. | 宿 劫 A future kalpa of the constellations in which a thousand Buddhas will appear. | 曆 Jyotiṣa, relating to astronomy, or the calendar; Jyotiṣka 殊底色迦 was a native of Rājagṛha, who gave all his goods to the poor. | 祭; | 供 To sacrifice, or pay homage to a star, especially one's natal star.

曷 How? What? Why? Translit. *a*, *ha*, *ra*, *ro*. | 利拏 Hariṇa, deer of several kinds. | 利沙伐彈那 Harṣavardhana, king of Kanyākubja, protector of Buddhism about A.D. 625. | 剌怛那揭婆 Ratnagarbha, jewel treasury, or throne. | 剌䄍 Āraṇya, v. 阿. | 羅怙羅 Rāhula, v. 羅. | 羅胡 Rohu, "an ancient city and province of Tukhāra, south of the Oxus." Eitel. | 羅闍姞利呬; 羅閱城 Rājagṛha, v. 王舍城. | | | 補羅 Rājapura, a province and city, now Rajaori in south-west Kashmir. | 部多 Adbhuta, remarkable, miraculous, supernatural.

栅 Palisades, rails. | 門那, idem 訕若 Sañjaya.

枳 Thorn, thorns; translit. *ke*, *ki*. | 哩 | 哩 Kelikila, one of the rājas who subdues demons. | 吒; | 怛(那) An island which rises out of the sea. | 羅蘇 (or 娑) Kilāsa, white leprosy, tr. as "white" and a "hill".

柴 See under Ten Strokes.

柱 Pillar, post, support. | 塔 A pagoda.

枸 A spinous shrub; translit. *k*. | 蘇摩 Kusuma, a flower; especially the white China-aster. | | | 補羅 Kusumapura, the city of flowers, Pāṭaliputra, i.e. Patna. | 盧舍 Krośa, cf. 拘, 俱; the distance the lowing of an ox can be heard, the eighth part of a yojana.

柔 Pliant, yielding, soft. | 和 Gentle, forbearing, tolerant. | 輭 (A heart) mild and pliable (responsive to the truth). | 輭語 Gentle, persuasive words. | 順忍 The patience of meekness, i.e. in meekness to accord with the truth.

柯 Axe-handle; agent; translit. *k*, v. 呵, 迦, 哥, etc. | 尸悲與 The Kāśyapīya school.

枯 Wither, decay. | 木 Withered timber, decayed, dried-up trees; applied to a class of ascetic Buddhists, who sat in meditation, never lying down, like 石霜 | 木 petrified rocks and withered stumps.

| 木堂 The hall in which they sat. | 筏羅闍 1,000 sextillions, cf. 洛.

柰 Berries of the *Nyctanthes* or musk. Āmra, a mango. | 女 (or 氏) Āmradārikā, Āmrapālī, a woman who is said to have been born on a mango-tree, and to have given the Plum-garden | 苑 (or 園) to the Buddha, cf. 菴羅.

柳 A willow. | 枝 Willow branches put in clean water to keep away evil spirits.

柏 Cypress, cedar, *Arbor vitæ*.

柄 A handle; authority, power. | 語 Authoritative or pivotal words.

染 To dye, infect, contaminate, pollute; lust. | 垢; | 汚 Soiled, contaminated, impure, especially by holding on to the illusory ideas and things of life; deluded. The kleśas or contaminations of attachment to the pleasures of the senses, to false views, to moral and ascetic practices regarded as adequate for salvation, to the belief in a self which causes suffering, etc. | 心 A mind contaminated (with desire, or sexual passion). | 恚痴 Lust, anger, stupidity (or ignorance); also 婬怒痴; 貪瞋痴. | 愛 Polluting desire. | 法 Polluted thing, i.e. all phenomena; mode of contamination. | 汚 idem 染垢. | | 意 A name for the seventh vijñāna, the mind of contamination, i.e. in egoism, or wrong notions of the self. | 淨 Impurity and purity; the thoughts and things of desire are impure, the thoughts and methods of salvation are pure. | | 不二門 Impurity and purity as aspects of the total reality and not fundamentally ideas apart, one of the 十不二門 q.v. | | 眞如 The bhūtatathatā as contaminated in phenomena and as pure being. | 界 The sphere of pollution, i.e. the inhabited part of every universe, as subject to reincarnation. | 緣 The nidāna or link of pollution, which connects illusion with the karmaic miseries of reincarnation. From the "water" of the bhūtatathatā, affected by the "waves" of this nidāna-pollution, arise the waves of reincarnation.

染習 Contaminated by bad customs, or habit. | 著 Pollution-bond; a heart polluted by the things to which it cleaves. | (色) 衣 Dyed garments, i.e. the kaṣāya of the early Indian monks, dyed to distinguish them from the white garments of the laity.

段 A piece; a section, paragraph. Piṇḍa, a ball, lump, especially of palatable food, sustenance.

毘 Contiguous; surrounded; hemmed in; liberal; to aid; manifest; translit. *v, vi, vai, vya, ve, pi, bh, bhi*. Cf. 鞞, 鼻, 吠.

毘佛略 Vaipulya, large, spacious, intp. 方廣 q.v., expanded, enlarged. The term is applied to sūtras of an expanded nature, especially expansion of the doctrine; in Hīnayāna the Āgamas, in Mahāyāna the sūtras of Hua-yen and Lotus type; they are found in the tenth of the 十二部經 twelve sections of the classics. Other forms are 鞞 or 裴佛略; 毘富羅.

毘伽羅 Vyākaraṇa, grammatical analysis, grammar; "formal prophecy," Keith; tr. 聲明記論 which may be intp. as a record and discussion to make clear the sounds; in other words, a grammar, or sūtras to reveal right forms of speech; said to have been first given by Brahmā in a million stanzas, abridged by Indra to 100,000, by Pāṇini to 8,000, and later reduced by him to 300. Also |耶羯剌諵; |何羯喇拏; in the form of 和伽羅 Vyākaraṇas q.v. it is prediction.

毘佉 (or 低) 羅 Vikāra, an old housekeeper with many keys round her waist who had charge of the Śākya household, and who loved her things so much that she did not wish to be enlightened.

毘俱胝 (or 知) Bhrūkuṭi, knitted brow; one of the forms of Kuan-yin.

毘利差 Vṛkṣa means a tree, but as the intp. is "a hungry ghost," vṛka, wolf, seems more correct.

毘勒 Piṭaka 蜫勒. A T'ien-t'ai term for the 藏教 or Hīnayāna.

毘吠伽 Viveka, "discrimination," intp. 淸辯 clear distinction or discrimination. (婆) | | | Bhāvaviveka, a disciple of Nāgārjuna, who "retired to a rock cavern to await the coming of Maitreya". Eitel.

毘囉拏羯車婆 Vīraṇakacchapa, a tortoise, turtle.

毘多輸 Vītaśoka, younger brother of Aśoka, v. 阿.

毘奢蜜多羅 Viśvāmitra, name of Śākyamuni's school-teacher.

毘婆尸 Vipaśyin, 弗沙; 底沙 the first of the seven Buddhas of antiquity, Śākyamuni being the seventh. Also | |沙; |頗沙; |(or 微) 鉢沙; 鞞 (or 鼻) 婆沙; 維衛. | |沙 Vibhāṣā, option, alternative, tr. 廣解 wider interpretation, or 異說 different explanation. (1) The Vibhāṣā-śāstra, a philosophical treatise by Kātyāyanīputra, tr. by Saṅghabhūti A.D. 383. The Vaibhāṣikas | | |論師 were the followers of this realistic school, "in Chinese texts mostly quoted under the name of Sarvāstivādāḥ." Eitel. (2) A figure stated at several tens of thousands of millions. (3) Vipaśyin, v. above. | | (or 鉢) 舍那 Vipaśyanā, discernment, intp. as 觀 insight, 正見 correct perception, or views, etc. Vipaśyanā-vipaśyanā, thorough insight and perception. | |闍婆提 Vibhajyavādins, answerers in detail, intp. as 分別說, discriminating explanation, or particularizing; a school of logicians. "It is reasonable to accept the view that the *Abhidhamma Piṭaka*, as we have it in the Pali Canon, is the definite work of this school." Keith.

毘富羅 Vipula, 毘布羅 broad, large, spacious. A mountain near Kuśāgārapura, in Magadha; v. 毘佛略.

毘尸沙 Viśeṣa, the doctrine of "particularity or individual essence", i.e. the *sui generis* nature of the nine fundamental substances; it is the doctrine of the Vaiśeṣika school of philosophy founded by Kaṇāda.

毘尼 Vinaya, v. 律 and 毘奈耶.

毘嵐風 Vairambha. The great wind which finally scatters the universe; the circle of wind under the circle of water on which the world rests. Also | (or 鞞 or 吠) 藍 (婆); 鞞嵐; 吠嵐婆 (or 僧伽); |樓那; and |藍婆 which is also Pralambā, one of the rāksasīs.

毘怛迦 Vitarka, "initial attention," "cognition in initial application," "judgment," Keith; intp. as 尋 search or inquiry, and contrasted with 伺 spying out, careful examination; also as 計度 conjecture, supposition. Cf. |遮羅 vicāra.

毘指多婆多 Vijitavat, one who has conquered, conqueror, intp. as the sun.

毘提訶 Videha, 佛提媻; 弗於逮. (1) Abbrev. for Pūrvavideha, 佛婆 | | | the continent east of Meru. (2) "Another name for Vaiśālī and the region near Māthava." Eitel.

毘摩 Bhīmǎ. (1) Śiva, also a form of Durgā, his wife (the terrible). (2) A city west of Khotan, possessing a statue of Buddha said to have transported itself thither from Udyāna. Eitel. Also used for ｜｜羅 Vimalā, unsullied, pure; name of a river, and especially of Śiva's wife. ｜｜羅詰; 鼻磨羅鷄利帝; 維磨詰; Vimalakīrti, name of a disciple at Vaiśālī, whom Śākyamuni is said to have instructed, see the sūtra of this name. ｜｜質多; 吠摩質呾利 Vimalacitra, a king of asuras, residing at the bottom of the ocean, father of Indra's wife.

毘播奢 Vipāśā, a river in the Punjab, "the Hyphasis of the Greeks," now called the Beas. ｜播迦 Vipāka, ripeness, maturity, change of state; another name for the eighth 識.

毘曇 v. 阿毘達磨 Abhidharma.

毘木叉 v. 毘目叉.

毘奈耶 Vinaya, ｜那耶; ｜(or 鞞)尼(or 泥迦); 鼻那夜 Moral training; the disciplinary rules; the precepts and commands of moral asceticism and monastic discipline (said to have been given by Buddha); explained by 律 q.v ordinances; 滅 destroying sin; 調伏 subjugation of deed, word, and thought; 離行 separation from action, e.g. evil. ｜｜｜藏 The Vinayapiṭaka, the second portion of the Tripiṭaka, said to have been compiled by Upāli; cf. 律.

毘梨耶 Vīrya, virility, strength, energy; "well-doing," Keith; intp. 精進 zeal, pure progress, the fourth of the ten pāramitās; it is also intp. as enduring shame. Also ｜利 (or 黎 or 離) ｜; 尾唎也.

毘沙拏 Viṣāṇa, a horn. It is used for the single horn of the rhinoceros, as an epithet for a pratyeka-buddha, v. 緣覺, whose aim is his own salvation. ｜｜門(天王) Vaiśravaṇa. Cf. 財 and 俱. One of the four Mahārājas, guardian of the North, king of the Yakṣas. Has the title 多聞; 普聞; universal or much hearing or learning, said to be so called because he heard the Buddha's preaching; but Vaiśravaṇa was son of Viśravas, which is from viśru, to be heard of far and wide, celebrated, and should be understood in this sense. Vaiśravaṇa is Kuvera, or Kubera, the Indian Pluto; originally a chief of evil spirits, afterwards the god of riches, and ruler of the northern quarter. Hsüan Tsung built a temple to him in A.D. 753, since which he has been the god of wealth in China and guardian at the entrance of Buddhist temples. In his right hand he often holds a banner or a lance, in his left a pearl or shrine, or a mongoose out of whose mouth jewels are pouring; under his feet are two demons. Colour, yellow. ｜｜｜五童子 The five messengers of Vaiśravaṇa. Other forms are 毗捨明; 鞞舍羅婆拏; 鞞室羅懣囊.

毘流波叉 Virūpākṣa, "irregular-eyed," "three-eyed like Śiva," translated wide-eyed, or evil-eyed; one of the four mahārājas, guardian of the West, lord of nāgas, colour red. Also 毘流(or 樓)博叉; 鼻溜波阿叉; 鞞路波阿迄.

毘濕婆 (or **波**). A wind, said to be a transliteration of Viśva, universal, cf. ｜嵐.

毘灑迦 ? Viśākhā, one of the retinue of Vaiśravaṇa.

毘瑠璃 Virūḍhaka. Known as Crystal king, and as 惡生王 Ill-born king. (1) A king of Kośala (son of Prasenajit), destroyer of Kapilavastu. (2) Ikṣvāku, father of the four founders of Kapilavastu. (3) One of the four mahārājas, guardian of the south, king of kumbhāṇḍas, worshipped in China as one of the twenty-four deva āryas; colour blue. Also, ｜｜王; 流離王; (毘)婁勒王; (維)樓黎王; ｜盧釋(or 宅)迦王; 鼻溜茶迦, etc.

毘盧舍耶 Vairocana, "belonging to or coming from the sun" (M. W.), i.e. light. The 眞身 q.v. true or real Buddha-body, e.g. godhead. There are different definitions. T'ien-t'ai says Vairocana represents the 法身 dharmakāya, Rocana or Locana the 報身 saṁbhogakāya, Śākyamuni the 應身 nirmāṇakāya. Vairocana is generally recognized as the spiritual or essential body of Buddha-truth, and like light 徧一切處 pervading everywhere. The esoteric school intp. it by the sun, or its light, and take the sun as symbol. It has also been intp. by 淨滿 purity and fullness, or fullness of purity. Vairocana is the chief of the Five Dhyāni Buddhas, occupying the central position; and is the 大日如來 Great Sun Tathāgata. There are numerous treatises on the subject. Other forms are ｜｜; ｜｜遮(or 折)｜; 吠嚧遮那; 鞞嚧杜那.

毘目叉 Vimokṣa, Vimukti, 毘木叉 or 底 liberation, emancipation, deliverance, salvation, tr. 解脫 q.v. ｜｜瞿沙 Vimuktaghoṣa, the Buddha's voice of liberation (from all fear); also ｜｜多羅.

毘睇 Vidyā, 尾底牙 knowledge, learning, philosophy, science; incantation; intp. 明呪 an incantation to get rid of all delusion. The Vidyādharapiṭaka is a section of incantations, etc., added to the Tripiṭaka.

毘羅刪拏 Vīrasana. "An ancient kingdom and city in the Doab between the Ganges and the Yamuna. The modern Karsanah." Eitel.

毘耶娑 Vyāsa, arranger, compiler; to distribute, diffuse, arrange; a sage reputed to be the compiler of the Vedas and founder of the Vedānta philosophy.

毘舍 Veśa, entrance, house, adornment, prostitute; but it is probably Vaiśya, the third caste of farmers and traders, explained by 居士 burghers, or 商賈 merchants; cf. 吠. | | 佉 Vaiśākha, viśākhā 吠 | |; 鼻奢佉; one of the constellations similar to Ti 底, the third of the Chinese constellations, in Libra; M. W. says the first month in the year, the Chinese interpret it as from the middle of their second to the middle of their third month. | | | 母; 鹿母 A wealthy matron who with her husband gave a vihāra to Śākyamuni, wife of Anāthapiṇḍika; v. 阿那. | | 支 (or 遮) ? Piśācī, female sprites, or demons, said to inhabit privies. | | 浮 Viśvabhū, the second Buddha of the 31st kalpa. Eitel says: "The last (1,000th) Buddha of the preceding kalpa, the third of the Sapta Buddha 七佛 q.v., who converted on two occasions 130,000 persons." Also | | 婆 (or 符); | 濕婆部; | 恕沙付; | 攝羅; 鞞恕婆附; 鞞舍; 隨葉; 浮舍. | | 羅 Viśāla, a deity who is said to have protected the image of Buddha brought to Ming Ti of the Han dynasty. | | 闍 Piśācāḥ. Imps, goblins, demons in the retinue of 持國天 Dhṛtarāṣṭra. Also | (or 畢) 舍遮 (or 支); 辟 (or 臂) 舍柘. | | 離; 吠舍離 (or 釐). Vaiśālī, an ancient kingdom and city of the Licchavis, where the second synod was held, near Basarh, or "Bassahar, north of Patna". Eitel. Also | 耶 (|); | 城; 鞞 | |; 鞞隸夜; 維耶 (離).

毘若底 Vijñapti, information, report, representation; intp. as 識 knowledge, understanding, hence the | | | 摩呾剌多 Vijñaptimātratā, or 唯識. Reality is nothing but representations or ideas. For | | 南 v. | 闍那.

毘苫婆補羅 Vichavapura. "The ancient capital of Sindh." Eitel.

毘荼 Bhiḍa, or Pañca-nada, an ancient kingdom called after its capital of Bhiḍa; the present Punjab. Eitel.

毘訖羅摩阿迭多 Vikramāditya, Valour-sun, intp. as surpassing the sun, a celebrated king who drove out the Sakas, or Scythians, and ruled over northern India from 57 B.C., patron of literature and famous benefactor of Buddhism. Also 超柯 | | | | |.

毘訶羅 Vihāra, a pleasure garden, monastery, temple, intp. as 遊行處 place for walking about, and 寺 monastery, or temple. Also 鼻 | |; 鞞 | |; 尾賀 |. | | | 波羅 Vihārapāla, the guardian of a monastery. | | | 莎弭 Vihārasvāmin, the patron or bestower of the monastery.

毘跋耶斯 The smṛti-upasthāna 四念處, or four departments of memory; possibly connected with Vipaśyanā, v. | 婆.

毘遮羅 Vicāra, "applied attention," Keith, cf. | 怛迦 intp. as pondering, investigating; the state of the mind in the early stage of dhyāna meditation.

毘那夜加 Vināyaka, a hinderer, the elephant god, Gaṇeśa; a demon with a man's body and elephant's head, which places obstacles in the way. | | 怛迦; | 泥吒迦 Vinataka, bowed, stooping, is used with the same meaning, and also for the sixth of the seven concentric circles around Mt. Meru; any mountain resembling an elephant. Also | | 耶加; 頻 | 也 |; | | 耶怛 |; 吠 | 野怛 |. For | | 耶 v. | 柰 |.

毘闍那 Vijñāna, 毘若南 "consciousness or intellect", knowledge, perception, understanding, v. 識.

毘陀 The Vedas; also 皮 |; 圍 |; 韋 |. | | 羅 Vetāla, an incantation for raising a corpse to kill another person.

毘離耶犀那 Vīryasena, an instructor of Hsüan-tsang at the Bhadravihāra, v. 跋.

毘頭利 Vaiḍūrya, lapis lazuli, one of the seven precious things. A mountain near Vārāṇaśī. Also | or 吠瑠璃; 鞞稠利夜.

毘首(羯磨) Viśvakarman, all-doer, or maker,

the Indian Vulcan, architect of the universe and patron of artisans; intp. as minister of Indra, and his director of works. Also | 守 | |; | 濕縛 | |.

津 Ford, ferry, place of crossing a stream. | 梁 A bridge or ferry across a stream; i.e. religion. | 送 To escort to the ferry, either the living to deliverance or more generally the dead; to bid goodbye (to a guest).

洲 An islet; a continent. | 渚 An island, i.e. cut off, separated, a synonym for nirvāṇa.

洗 To wash, cleanse. | 淨 Cleansing, especially after stool.

洩 To leak, diminish. | 瑟知林 Yaṣṭivana, forest of the bamboo staff which took root when thrown away by the Brahman who did not believe the Buddha was 16 feet in height; but the more he measured the taller grew the Buddha, hence his chagrin. Name of a forest near Rājagṛha.

活 Jīva, jīvaka; alive, living, lively, revive, movable. | 國 ? Ghūr, or Ghori, name of an ancient country in Turkestan, which Eitel gives as Lat. 35° 41 N., Long. 68° 59 E., mentioned in Hsüan-tsang's *Records of Western Countries*, 12. | 佛 A living Buddha, i.e. a reincarnation Buddha, e.g. Hutuktu, Dalai Lama, etc. | 兒子 A name for the bodhi-tree. | 命 Life, living; to revive.

洴舍 Bimbisāra, v. 頻.

洞 A hole, cave; to see through, know. | 山 Cave hill or monastery in Yün-chou, modern Jui-chou, Kiangsi, noted for its T'ang teacher 悟本 Wu-pên. | 家; | 上; | 下 refer to the 曹洞 school of 慧能 Hui-nêng.

洛 Lo-yang | 陽, the ancient capital of China. | 叉 or 沙 Lakṣa, a lakh, 100,000. The series of higher numbers is as follows:

度 | 叉 a million
兆 俱胝 10 millions 京
末陀 100 millions 秭
阿庾多 1,000 millions 垓
大 ditto 10,000 millions 壤
那庾多 100,000 mill. 溝
大 ditto 1 billion 澗
鉢羅庾多 10 billions 正
大 ditto 100 billions 載
矜羯羅; 甄迦羅 1,000 billions
大 ditto 10,000 billions
頻婆 (or 跋) 羅 100,000 billions
大 ditto 1 trillion
阿閦 (or 芻) 婆 10 tr.
大 ditto 100 tr.
毘婆訶 1,000 tr.
大 ditto 10,000 tr.
嗢蹭伽 100,000 tr.
大 ditto 1 quadrillion
婆喝那 10 quadr.
大 ditto 100 quadr.
地致婆 1,000 quadr.
大 ditto 10,000 quadr.
醯都 100,000 quadr.
大 ditto 1 quintillion
羯臘縛 10 quint.
大 ditto 100 quint.
印達羅 1,000 quint.
大 ditto 10,000 quint.
三磨鉢躭 100,000 quint.
大 ditto 1 sextillion
揭底 10 sext.
大 ditto 100 sext.
枯筏羅闍 1,000 sext.
大 ditto 10,000 sext.
姥達羅 100,000 sext.
大 ditto 1 septillion
跋藍 10 sept.
大 ditto 100 sept.
珊若 1,000 sept.
大 ditto 10,000 sept.
毘步多 100,000 sept.
大 ditto 1 octillion
跋羅攙 10 octillions
大 ditto 100 octillions
阿僧企耶 asaṁkhyeya, innumerable.

炭 Charcoal, coal. | 頭 The fire-tender in a monastery.

珍 Precious; rare. | 域 The precious region, or Pure Lanu of a Buddha. | 寶 A pearl; jewel; precious thing. | 重 To esteem and treat as precious.

珂 White jade shell; translit. *k*, *khr*. | 但尼; 佉陀 (or 闍尼) Khādanīya, food that can be masticated, or eaten. | 咄羅 Kotlan, "an ancient kingdom west of the Tsung-ling, south of the Karakal lake, in Lat. 39° N., Long. 72° E." Eitel. | 月 The jade-like or pearly moon. | 貝 Jade (or white quartz) and shells (cowries), used as money in ancient times. | 雪 Snow-white as jade (or white quartz).

玻璃 Sphaṭika. Rock crystal, one of the seven precious things. Also 頗梨 or 黎; 塞頗致迦, etc.

珊 Coral; translit. for *san*, *saṁ*. | 尼羅闍 Sanirājā, a river of Udyāna. | 瑚 Pravāḍa, or prabāla, coral, one of the seven treasures. | 若 Sañjñā, "a particularly high number," M. W. 1,000 septillions, a 大 | 若 is 10,000 septillions. | 若婆 A wasting disease. | 闍邪 (or 夜) 毘羅胝 Sañjaya-vairāṭi, a king of yakṣas; also the teacher of Maudgalyāyana and Śāriputra before their conversion.

甚 What? any; very, extreme. | 深 The profundity (of Buddha-truth).

界 Dhātu. 馱都 Whatever is differentiated; a boundary, limit, region, that which is contained, or limited, e.g. the nature of a thing; provenance;

a species, class, variety; the underlying principle; the root or underlying principles of a discourse.

界內 Within the region, limited, within the confines of the 三界, i.e. the three regions of desire, form, and formlessness, and not reaching out to the infinite. |內事教 T'ien-t'ai's term for the Tripiṭaka school, i.e. Hīnayāna, which deals rather with immediate practice, confining itself to the five skandhas, twelve stages, and eighteen regions, and having but imperfect ideas of 空 the illimitable. |內理教 T'ien-t'ai's 通教, which is considered to be an advance in doctrine on the last, partially dealing with the 空 and advancing beyond the merely relative. Cf. |外. |內教 The above two schools. |內惑 Illusion of these two schools; illusion of, or in, the above three realms which gives rise to rebirths. |分 Any region or division, especially the regions of desire, form, and formlessness. |外 The pure realms, or illimitable "spiritual" regions of the Buddhas outside the three limitations of desire, form, and formlessness. |外事教 T'ien-t'ai's term for the 別教, which concerned itself with the practice of the bodhisattva life, a life not limited to three regions of reincarnation, but which had not attained to its fundamental principles. ||理教 T'ien-t'ai's 圓教 the school of the complete Buddha-teaching, i.e. that of T'ien-t'ai, which concerns itself with the Śūnya doctrines of the infinite, beyond the realms of reincarnation, and the development of the bodhisattva in those realms. |外教 The above two schools. |如 The 十界 and 十如 q.v. |繫 The karma which binds to the finite, i.e. to any one of the three regions. |趣 The three regions (desire, form, and formlessness) and the six paths (gati), i.e. the spheres of transmigration.

疥 Itch, the itch, scabby. |癩野干 A scabby dog, or jackal.

皆 All. |空 All is empty and void.

皈 idem 歸. |依 To turn to and rely on the Triratna.

盆 Bowl, basin, tub. |會 The All-Souls anniversary, v. 盂.

省 Look into minutely, inspect, examine; arouse; spare, save; an inspectorate, hence a province. |行堂 another name for 延壽堂.

看 Look, see; watch over. |方便 To fix the mind or attention, a Ch'an (Zen) term. |病 To nurse the sick; also to attend a patient medically.

眉 Eyebrow, the eyebrows. |間白毫相 Ūrṇā. The curl of white hairs, between the eyebrows of the Buddha, one of the thirty-two signs of Buddhahood. ||光 The ray of light which issued therefrom lighting up all worlds, v. Lotus sūtra.

相 Lakṣaṇa 攞乞尖拏. Also, nimitta. A "distinctive mark, sign", "indication, characteristic", "designation". M. W. External appearance; the appearance of things; form; a phenomenon 有爲法 in the sense of appearance; mutual; to regard. The four forms taken by every phenomenon are 生住異滅 rise, stay, change, cease, i.e. birth, life, old age, death. The Hua-yen school has a six-fold division of form, namely, whole and parts, together and separate, integrate and disintegrate. A Buddha or Cakravartī is recognized by his thirty-two lakṣaṇa, i.e. his thirty-two characteristic physiological marks. |性 Form and nature; phenomenon and noumenon.

相似 Alike, like, similar, identical. 相似佛 Approximation or identity of the individual and Buddha, a doctrine of T'ien-t'ai; the stage of 十信. ||即(佛) One of the six of such identities, similarity in form. ||覺 The approximate enlightenment which in the stages of 十住, 十行 and 十廻向 approximates to perfect enlightenment by the subjection of all illusion; the second of the four degrees of bodhi in the Awakening of Faith 起信論.

相入 Mutual entry; the blending of things, e.g. the common light from many lamps.

相分 An idea, a mental eject; a form.

相即 Phenomenal identity, e.g. the wave is water and water the wave.

相名五法 v. 五法.

相違因 Mutually opposing causes; one of the 十因.

相大 The greatness of the potentialities, or attributes of the Tathāgata; v. the Awakening of Faith 起信論.

相好 Lakṣaṇa-vyañjana; the thirty-two 相

or marks and the eighty 好 or signs on the physical body of Buddha. The marks on a Buddha's saṁbhogakāya number 84,000. 相 is intp. as larger signs, 好 as smaller; but as they are also intp. as marks that please, 好 may be a euphemism for 號.

相宗 idem 法相宗.

相對 Opposite, opposed; in comparison.

相待 The doctrine of mutual dependence or relativity of all things for their existence, e.g. the triangle depends on its three lines, the eye on things having colour and form, long on short.

相想俱絶宗 One of the ten schools, as classified by Hsien-shou of Hua-yen, which sought to eliminate phenomena and thought about them, in favour of intuition.

相應 Response, correspond, tally, agreement, yukta, or yoga, interpreted by 契合 union of the tallies, one agreeing or uniting with the other. 丨丨因 Corresponding, or mutual causation, e.g. mind, or mental conditions causing mentation, and vice versa. 丨丨宗 Yoga, the sect of mutual response between the man and his object of worship, resulting in correspondence in body, mouth, and mind, i.e. deed, word, and thought; it is a term for the Shingon or 眞言 school. 丨丨法 The correspondence of mind with mental data dependent on five correspondences common to both, i.e. the senses, reasoning, process, time, and object. 丨丨阿笈摩 The Saṁyuktāgamas, or "miscellaneous" āgamas; v. 阿. 丨丨縛 The bond (of illusion) which hinders the response of mind to the higher data.

相智 Knowledge derived from phenomena.

相承 Mutually receiving, handing on and receiving, mutually connected.

相無性 Unreal in phenomena, e.g. turtle-hair or rabbit's horns; the unreality of phenomena, one of the 三無性.

相空 The unreality of form; the doctrine that phenomena have no reality in themselves, in contrast with that of Hīnayāna which only held that the ego had no reality.

相縛 To be bound by externals, by the six guṇas, or objects of sensation. Cf. 丨應丨.

相續 Santati. Continuity, especially of cause and effect. 丨丨假 Illusory ideas continuously succeed one another producing other illusory ideas, one of the three hypotheses of the 成實論 Satyasiddhi-śāstra. 丨丨常 Nodal or successive continuity in contrast with 不斷常 uninterrupted continuity. 丨丨心 A continuous mind, unceasing thought. 丨丨相 Continuity of memory, or sensation, in regard to agreeables or disagreeables, remaining through other succeeding sensations, cf. 起信論 Awakening of Faith. 丨丨識 Continuity-consciousness which never loses any past karma or fails to mature it.

相輪 The sign or form of wheels, also 輪相, i.e. the nine wheels or circles at the top of a pagoda.

矜 To pity; boast; attend to; vigorous. 丨哀 To pity. 丨羯羅; 金伽羅 Kiṁkara, a servant, slave; the seventh of the eight messengers of 不重明王.

砂 Gravel, sand. 以丨施佛 The legend of Aśoka when a child giving a handful of gravel as alms to the Buddha in a previous incarnation, hence his rebirth as a king.

祆 Hsien, commonly but incorrectly written 祅 a Western Asian name for Heaven, or the 天神 God of Heaven, adopted by the Zoroastrians and borrowed later by the Manicheans; also intp. as Maheśvara. 丨寺 A Manichean monastery. 丨(or 末尼) 教 The Manichean religion.

祈 Yācñā. Pray; prayer is spoken of as absent from Hīnayāna, and only known in Mahāyāna, especially in the esoteric sect. 丨禱; 丨念; 丨請 To pray, beg, implore, invite. 丨雨 To pray for rain. 丨願 To vow.

祇 The Earth-Spirit; repose; vast; translit. *j, g*. 丨哆槃那 (or 林); 丨園 (精舍); 丨樹園; 丨樹給孤獨園; 丨樹花林窟; 丨桓 (or 洹) 林; 丨陀林 (or 園); also 逝 or 誓多, etc. Jetavana, a park near Śrāvastī, said to have been obtained from Prince Jeta by the elder Anāthapiṇḍika, in which monasterial buildings were erected, the favourite resort of Śākyamuni. Two hundred years later it is said to have been destroyed by fire, rebuilt smaller 500 years after, and again a century later burnt down; thirteen years afterwards it was rebuilt on the earlier scale, but a century later entirely destroyed. This is the account given in 法苑珠林 39. 丨多蜜 Gītamitra, tr. 謌友 "friend of song", who in the fourth century tr. some twenty-five works into Chinese. | 夜 Geya, singing; Geyam, a song; preceding prose repeated in verse; odes in honour of the saints; cf. 伽陀 gāthā. | 支 v. 僧 | |. | 陀 Jetṛ; Jetā; victor, a prince of Śrāvastī, son of king Prasenajit, and previous owner of the Jetavana.

禺 A monkey; begin; the 巳 hour, 9–11 a.m.; | 中 the middle of that hour, 10 a.m. T'ien-t'ai called the fourth period of Buddha's teaching the | 中.

科 A class, lesson, examination. | 文 A set portion of a book, a lesson. | 儀 The rule of the lesson.

穿 To bore, pierce; to thread; to don, put on. To bore a well, and gradually discover water, likened to the gradual discovery of the Buddha-nature. | 耳僧 Pierced-ear monks, many of the Indian monks wore ear-rings; Bodhidharma was called | | 客 the ear-pierced guest.

突 Rush out; protrude; rude; suddenly. | 婆 Dhūpa, incense, frankincense, fragrant gum; intp. as 茅香 lemon-grass, perhaps *Andropogen nardus*. | 吉羅; | 膝 (or 悉) 吉栗多; | 瑟儿理多 Duṣkṛta (Pali Dukkaṭa), wrong-doing, evil action, misdeed, sin; external sins of body and mouth, i.e. deed and word. Cf. 吉羅. | 迦 Durgā, Bhīmā, or Marīci, "the wife of Maheśvara, to whom human flesh was offered once a year in autumn." Eitel. | 路拏 Droṇa, a Brahman who is said to have divided the cremation remains of the Buddha to prevent strife for them among contending princes.

紀 To record; regulate; a year, a period (of twelve years). | 綱寮 The office of the director of duties.

紇 Tassels; the Uigur tribe; a knot. | 利陀耶; | | 俱; | 哩陀 (or 乃 or 娜) 耶; 訖利馱耶; 釳利陀; 汗栗馱; 肝栗大 Hṛdaya, the heart, the mind; some forms are applied to the physical heart, others somewhat indiscriminately to the tathāgata-heart, or the true, natural, innocent heart; | 哩 or 利 (俱); 纈利 Hrīḥ is a germ-word of Amitābha and Kuan-yin. | 差怛羅 Kṣetra, a land, country, especially a Buddha-realm, cf. 刹. | 露悉泥 Hrosminkan or Semenghān, an ancient kingdom near Khulm and Kunduz. "Lat. 35° 40 N., Long. 68° 22 E." Eitel.

紅 Aruṇa, rakta; red. | 教; | 衣派 The red sect, i.e. the Zva-dmar, or Shamar, the older Lamaistic sect of Tibet, who wear red clothes and hats. | 蓮花 Padma, the red lotus, after which the | | 地獄 red lotus hell is called, the seventh of the eight cold hells, where the flesh of the sufferers bursts open like red lotuses.

約 Bind, restrain; agree, covenant; about. | 機 To avail oneself of opportunity, or suitable conditions. | 教; | 部 According to their doctrine or according to their school. | 法 According to the doctrine, or method.

美 Fine, handsome, beautiful, admirable. Madhura, sweet, pleasant. | 音 Beautiful sound, a king of the Gandharvas (乾闥婆), Indra's musicians. Also, the name of a son of Sudhīra and Sumitra converted by Ānanda. | | (天女); 妙音天 Sarasvatī, 薩囉薩伐底, the Muse of India, goddess of speech and learning, hence called 大辯才天女, goddess of rhetoric; she is the female energy or wife of Brahmā, and also goddess of the river Sarasvatī.

耐 To endure, bear. | 怨害忍 The patience which endures enmity and injury. | 秣陀 Narmadā, the modern Nerbudda river.

耶 An interrogative particle; translit. for *jha*, *ya*; | 旬; | 維 cf 荼毘 Jhāpita, cremation. | 婆 Yava, barley; a barleycorn, the 2,688,000th part of a yojana; also a measure in general of varying weight and length. | 婆提 Yavana, Yavadvīpa, i.e. Java. | 婆盧吉帝 cf. 觀音 Avalokiteśvara. | 舍 Yaśas, or | 舍陀 Yaśojā. There were two persons of this name: (1) a disciple of Ānanda; (2) another who is said to have "played an important part in connection with the second synod". | 輸陀 (羅); | 輸多羅; | 戍達羅 Yaśodharā; the wife of Śākyamuni, mother of Rāhula, who became a nun five years after her husband's enlightenment. She is to become the Buddha Raśmi-śata-sahasra-paripūrṇa-dhvaja; v. Lotus sūtra. Her name was also Gōpā, 瞿波; 劬毘耶 is perhaps Gopī.

胐 v. 僧.

背 Back, behind; turn the back on, go contrary to; carry on the back. | 念 To turn one's back on the transmigration life and abide quietly in the nirvāṇa-mind. | 捨 To turn the back on and leave (the world). | 正 To turn the back on Buddha-truth.

| 鱠 經 屏 To mince fish on the back of an image, and paste up the scriptures as a screen from the wind—a man without conscience.

胡 How? Why? Hun; Turk; random; hemp; long-lived; pepper, etc.; translit. *go*, *hu*. | 亂 Disorderly, without order. | 嚧 遮 那 Gorocanā, "a bright yellow pigment prepared from the urine or bile of a cow." M. W. | 子 Hun, or Turk, a term applied to the people west and north of China; a nickname for Bodhidharma. | 種 族 Of West Asian race, a term applied to the Buddha, as the sūtras were also styled | 經 Hun classics and 老 | Old Hun was also a nickname for the Buddha. | 蘇 多 A charm, or incantation against evil vapours, etc. | 跪 The Hun way of kneeling, right knee on the ground, left knee up. | 道 人 Monks from Central Asia or India. | 實 健 Hujikan, "an ancient kingdom south-west of Balkh . . . in Lat. 35° 20′ N., Long. 65° E." Eitel.

胞 Placenta, womb; bladder. | 胎 Womb, uterine, v. 胎 生.

胎 Garbha, the womb, uterus.

胎內五位 The five periods of the child in the uterus. | 外 | | Ditto after birth, i.e. infancy, childhood, youth, middle age, old age.

胎卵濕化 The four yoni or modes of birth—womb-born, egg-born, spawn-born, and born by transformation (e.g. moths, certain deities, etc.).

胎大日 Vairocana in the Garbhadhātu.

胎獄; 胎宮 The womb prison, the womb regarded as a prison; see next.

胎生 Uterine birth, womb-born. Before the differentiation of the sexes birth is supposed to have been by transformation. The term is also applied to beings enclosed in unopened lotuses in paradise, who have not had faith in Amitābha but trusted to their own strength to attain salvation; there they remain for proportionate periods, happy, but without the presence of the Buddha, or Bodhisattvas, or the sacred host, and do not hear their teaching. The condition is also known as | 宮, the womb-palace.

胎藏界 Garbhadhātu, or Garbhakośa-(dhātu), the womb treasury, the universal source from which all things are produced; the matrix; the embryo; likened to a womb in which all of a child is conceived —its body, mind, etc. It is container and content; it covers and nourishes; and is the source of all supply. It represents the 理 性 fundamental nature, both material elements and pure bodhi, or wisdom in essence or purity; 理 being the garbhadhātu as fundamental wisdom, and 智 acquired wisdom or knowledge, the vajradhātu. It also represents the human heart in its innocence or pristine purity, which is considered as the source of all Buddha-pity and moral knowledge. And it indicates that from the central being in the maṇḍala, viz. the Sun as symbol of Vairocana, there issue all the other manifestations of wisdom and power, Buddhas, bodhisattvas, demons, etc. It is 本 覺 original intellect, or the static intellectuality, in contrast with 始 覺 intellection, the initial or dynamic intellectuality represented in the vajradhātu; hence it is the 因 cause and vajradhātu the 果 effect; though as both are a unity, the reverse may be the rule, the effect being also the cause; it is also likened to 利 他 enriching others, as vajradhātu is to 自 利 enriching self. Kōbō Daishi, founder of the Yoga or Shingon 眞 言 School in Japan, adopted the representation of the ideas in maṇḍalas, or diagrams, as the best way of revealing the mystic doctrine to the ignorant. The garbhadhātu is the womb or treasury of all things, the universe; the 理 fundamental principle, the source; its symbols are a triangle on its base, and an open lotus as representing the sun and Vairocana. In Japan this maṇḍala is placed on the east, typifying the rising sun as source, or 理. The vajradhātu is placed west and represents 智 wisdom or knowledge as derived from 理 the underlying principle, but the two are essential one to the other, neither existing apart. The material and spiritual; wisdom-source and intelligence; essence and substance; and similar complementary ideas are thus portrayed; the garbhadhātu may be generally considered as the static and the vajradhātu as the dynamic categories, which are nevertheless a unity. The garbhadhātu is divided into 三 部 three sections representing samādhi or quiescence, wisdom-store, and pity-store, or thought, knowledge, pity; one is called the Buddha-section, the others the Vajra and Lotus sections respectively; the three also typify vimokṣa, prajñā, and dharmakāya, or freedom, understanding, and spirituality. There are three heads of these sections, i.e. Vairocana, Vajrapāṇi, and Avalokiteśvara; each has a mother or source, e.g. Vairocana from Buddha's-eye; and each has a 明 王 or emanation of protection against evil; also a śakti or female energy; a germ-letter, etc. The diagram of five Buddhas contains also four bodhisattvas, making nine in all, and there are altogether thirteen 大院 or great courts of various types of ideas, of varying numbers, generally spoken of as 414. Cf. 金剛界; 大日; 兩部.

胎金 The Garbhadhātu and the Vajradhātu.

苫 Thatch; mat; mourning. | 婆羅; 擔步羅 Jambhala, Jambhīra, the citron tree, *Blyxa octandra*. | 末羅 Cāmara, name of several plants, āmra, betel-nut, etc.; the resort of "golden-winged birds".

茅 Thatch. | 蓋頭 A handful of thatch to cover one's head, a hut, or simple monastery.

若 If; as, like; the said; translit. *j* or *jñ* sounds. | 那 (or 南); 惹那 Jñāna, tr. by 智 knowledge, understanding, intellectual judgments, as compared with 慧 wisdom, moral judgments; prajñā is supposed to cover both meanings. | 提子 Jñātīputra, v. 尼 Nirgranthajñāti.

茂 Flourishing | 泥; 文尼; 牟尼 Muni, a solitary, a recluse, e.g. Śākyamuni, the recluse of the Śākya family; genii; intp. as one who seeks solitude, and one who is able to be kind. | 羅三部盧 Mūlasthānapura, the modern Multan. | 遮 Moca, the plantain tree, *Musa sapientum*, associated with the idea of liberation from the passions.

苾 Fragrant. | 芻; 煏芻; 比丘 q.v. Bhikṣu, a beggar, religious mendicant; a Buddhist monk. | 芻尼 Bhikṣuṇī, a nun. | 芻律儀 The 250 rules for monks.

苑 A park, imperial park, a collection; v. Jetavana 祇. | 公四敎 v. 四敎.

苦 Duḥkha, 豆佉 bitterness; unhappiness, suffering, pain, distress, misery; difficulty. There are lists of two, three, four, five, eight, and ten categories; the two are internal, i.e. physical and mental, and external, i.e. attacks from without. The four are birth, growing old, illness, and death. The eight are these four along with the pain of parting from the loved, of meeting with the hated, of failure in one's aims, and that caused by the five skandhas; cf. 四諦.

苦厄 The obstruction caused by pain, or suffering.

苦因 The cause of pain.

苦域 The region of misery, i.e. every realm of reincarnation.

苦性 The nature of misery; a sorrowful spirit.

苦惱 Misery and trouble; distress.

苦智 The knowledge or understanding of the axiom of suffering.

苦本 The root of misery, i.e. desire.

苦果 The physical and mental suffering resulting from evil conduct (chiefly in previous existences).

苦業 The karma of suffering.

苦河 Misery deep as a river.

苦津 The deep ford or flood of misery which must be crossed in order to reach enlightenment.

苦海 The ocean of misery, its limitlessness.

苦法智 The knowledge of the law of suffering and the way of release, one of the 八智. | | | 忍 One of the 八忍 q.v.

苦空 Misery and unreality, pain and emptiness.

苦網 The net of suffering.

苦縛 The bond of suffering.

苦苦 Duḥkha-duḥkhatā. The pain or painfulness of pain; pain produced by misery or pain; suffering arising from external circumstances, e.g. famine, storm, sickness, torture, etc.

苦蘊 The bundle of suffering, i.e. the body as composed of the five skandhas.

苦行 Duṣkara-caryā, undergoing difficulties, hardships, or sufferings; also Tapas, burning, torment; hence asceticism, religious austerity, mortification. | | 林; 木瓜林 Uruvilvā-kāśyapa, the forest near Gayā where Śākyamuni underwent rigorous ascetic discipline; v. 優.

苦言 Bitter words, words of rebuke.

苦(聖)諦 Duḥkha-ārya-satyam. The first of the four dogmas, that of suffering; v. | 集.

苦輪 The wheel of suffering, i.e. reincarnation.

苦道 The path of suffering; from illusion arises karma, from karma suffering, from suffering illusion, in a vicious circle.

苦際 The limit of suffering, i.e. entrance to nirv ṇa.

苦陰 The body with its five skandhas 五 | enmeshed in suffering.

苦集 Samudaya, arising, coming together, collection, multitude. The second of the four axioms, that of "accumulation", that misery is intensified by craving or desire and the passions, which are the cause of reincarnation. | | 滅道 The four axioms or truths: i.e. duḥkha, pain; samudaya, as above; nirodha, the extinguishing of pain and reincarnation; mārga, the way to such extinction; cf. 四諦.

苦類智 The wisdom which releases from suffering in all worlds. | | (|) 忍 One of the eight forms of endurance arising out of the above, v. 八忍.

苦餘 Remains of suffering awaiting the Hīnayāna disciple who escapes suffering in this world, but still meets it in succeeding worlds.

衍 Overflow, inundate; abundant; ample; superfluous; fertile; used in 摩訶 | Mahāyāna. | 門 The ample door, school, or way, the Mahāyāna.

要 Important, essential, necessary, strategic; want, need; about to; intercept; coerce; agree, etc. | 妙 The essential and mystic nature (of Buddha-truth). | 文 The important text or texts. | 旨 The important meaning or aim. | 津 The essential ford, or road. | 行 The essential mode of action, or conduct. | 言 Important, or essential words. | 門 Essential door, or opening. | 路; | 道 The essential or strategic way.

計 To reckon, count (on); scheme; add to, annex; translit. *ke*; cf. 罽, 鷄. | 名字相 The stage of giving names (to seeming things, etc.), v. 六麤. Cf. Awakening of Faith 起信論. | 度 Tarka; vitarka, conjecture, reckon, calculate, differentiate. | 我實有宗 The sect that reckons on, or advocates, the reality of personality. | 捨羅; | (or 鷄) 薩羅 Kesara, hair, filament, intp. as stamens and pistils. | 着 To maintain determinedly, bigotedly, on the basis of illusory thinking. | 都; | 部; 鷄都 or 兜 Ketu, any bright appearance, comet, ensign, eminent, discernment, etc.; the name of two constellations to the left and right of Aquila.

貞 Chaste, lucky. | 實 Pure and true.

負 To bear on the back; turn the back on; lose. | 門 Positions that have been withdrawn from in argument; defeated.

赴 To go to, or into. | 火外道 Ascetics who burn themselves alive. | 請 To go in response to an invitation; go to invite. | 機 To go or to preach according to the need or opportunity.

軍 An army; military; martial; translit. *kuṇ*, cf. 君. | 持 Kuṇḍī, Kuan-yin with the vase, also | (or 鍕) 鉼 ; 運 握; 君 持; 君 遲; also 君 (or 捃) 稚 迦 for Kuṇḍikā, idem. | 持 and 君 遲 are also used for Kuḍikā, an ascetic's water-bottle. | 茶 Kuṇḍa, firepot, brazier, or fire-hole used by the esoterics in fire-worship. | 荼利; | 遲 Kuṇḍalin, ring-shaped, intp. as a vase, bottle. | 荼利明王 Amṛta, v. 阿, one of the five ming wang, the ambrosia king, also known as a 夜叉 yakṣa in his fierce form of queller of demons. | 那 Kunda, a flower, perhaps jasmine, oleander, or *Boswellia thurifera*.

軌 A rut, rule; axle. | 持 A rule and its observance, intp. as to know the rule or doctrine and hold it without confusion with other rules or doctrines. | 範 Rule, mode. | 範師 A teacher of rules, discipline, morals; an ācārya. | 儀 Rule, form.

迴 v. 廻.

述 Narrate, publish; narration. | 嚕怛羅; 戍 縷 多 Śrotra, the ear.

迦 Translit. *ka, kā*; cf. 伽; 各; 嘎; 揭; 柯; 箇; 紺; 羯.

迦利 Kali, strife, striver; ill-born; also |梨; |棃; |藍浮; |羅富; |陵伽王;

哥 (or 歌) 利; 羯利 Kalirāja, Kaliṅgarāja, a king of Magadha noted for his violence; it is said that in a former incarnation he cut off the ears, nose, and hands of the Buddha, who bore it all unmoved; cf. Nirvāṇa sūtra, 31. 丨丨沙 (那) Karṣa, Karṣaṇa; dragging, pulling, ploughing; a weight, intp. as half a Chinese ounce. 丨丨丨波拏 Kārṣāpaṇa, tr. as 400 candareens, but the weights vary; also 丨丨丨般 (or 婆 or 鉢) 拏; 羯丨丨鉢那 (or 拏); 罽利沙盤.

迦吒富單那 Kaṭapūtana, 羯吒布怛那 Pretas, or demons, of remarkably evil odour.

迦奢 Kāśa, a species of grass, used for mats, thatch, etc.; personified as one of Yama's attendants. M. W. Eitel says a broom made of it and used by Śākyamuni " is still an object of worship ". 丨丨布羅 Kāśapura, a city which Eitel locates between Lucknow and Oudh.

迦尸 Kāśī 丨私, a place said to be so called because its bamboos were good for arrows, north of Kosala; but it is also given by M. W. as Benares.

迦尼迦 Kanaka, or Kanika; a tree or plant, probably a kind of sandal-wood.

迦布德迦 Kapotaka, 迦逋唐 a dove, pigeon. 丨丨丨丨伽藍; 鴿園 Kapotaka-saṁghārāma, a monastery of the Sarvāstivādaḥ school, so called because the Buddha in a previous incarnation is said to have changed himself into a pigeon and to have thrown himself into the fire in order to provide food for a hunter who was prevented from catching game because of Buddha's preaching. When the hunter learned of Buddha's power, he repented and attained enlightenment.

迦師 ? Kṛsara, " rice and peas boiled together "; " grain and sesamum." M. W. It is intp. as a wheat porridge.

迦摩 Kāma, desire, love, wish. A hungry spirit. 丨丨浪迦 Kāmalaṅkā, an ancient country " probably part of the present Chittagong opposite the mouth of the Ganges ". Eitel. 丨丨(or 末) 羅 Kāmalā, jaundice. 丨丨縷波 Kāmarūpa, now Kamrup; " an ancient kingdom formed by the western portion of Assam." Eitel. 丨丨馱都 Kāmadhātu; the realm of desire, of sensuous gratification; this world and the six devalokas; any world in which the elements of desire have not been suppressed.

迦旃 (延子) Kātyāyana; Mahākātyāyana; Mahākātyāyanīputra; one of the ten noted disciples of Śākyamuni. The foundation work of the Abhidharma philosophy, viz. the Abhidharma-jñāna-prasthāna-śāstra, has been attributed to him, but it is by an author of the same name 300 to 500 years later. Other forms are 丨多衍那; 丨多衍 (or 演) 尼子; 丨底耶夜那; 丨氈延 (尼子). There are others of the same name; e.g. the seventh of the ten non-Buddhist philosophers, perhaps Kakuda Kātyāyana, associated with mathematics, but spoken of as " a violent adversary of Śākyamuni." M. W.

迦曇波 (or 婆) Kadamba, a tree or plant with fragrant flowers; the *Nauclea cadamba*; the mustard plant.

迦柘 Kāca, glass, crystal; tr. as a precious stone.

迦梨沙舍尼 Karṣaṇīya; to be drawn, attracted, conciliated; intp. as forgiveness. 丨丨(or 羅) 迦 Kālīyaka, a nāga inhabiting the Yamunā (Jumna), slain by Kṛṣna; intp. as a black dragon. Also Kālikā, a garment of diverse colours.

迦樓羅 Garuḍa; " a mythical bird, the chief of the feathered race, the enemy of the serpent race, the vehicle of Vishṇu." M. W. Tr. as golden-winged, with an expanse of 3,360,000 li, carrying the ju-i pearl or talisman on its neck; among other accounts one says it dwells in great trees and feeds on snakes or dragons. Also 丨婁丨; 丨留丨; 丨嘍荼; 伽樓羅; 揭路荼; 誐 or (蘗) 嚕拏. The association of the garuḍa, like the phœnix, with fire makes it also a symbol of flame 丨丨丨炎. 丨丨那; 丨盧拏 Karuṇā, pitying, pity.

迦比 (or **毘**) **羅** Kapila, author of the Sāṅkhya philosophy, v. 劫; also Kapilavastu, v. 劫.

迦毘摩羅 Kapimala, of Patna, second century A.D., converted by Aśvaghoṣa 馬鳴; he himself is said to have converted Nāgārjuna; he was the thirteenth Patriarch.

迦毘羅 Kapila; tawny, brown, red; intp. as red head, or yellow head; name of the founder of the Sāṅkhya philosophy; also 丨丨梨; 丨比丨; 劫丨丨; cf. 僧劫 and 數. Kapilavastu, v. 劫; also written in a dozen varieties, e.g. 丨丨(or 比) 丨(婆); 丨丨丨皤窣都; 丨維 (羅閱 or 越).

迦波釐 Kāpālikas, followers of Śiva who wore skulls.

迦濕彌羅 Kāśmīra, Kashmir, formerly known in Chinese as 罽賓 Chi-pin ("the Kophen of the Greeks, the modern Kabul", Kubhā); under Kaniṣka the seat of the final synod for determining the Canon. Other forms are | 葉彌羅; 羯濕弭羅.

迦留陀夷 Kālodāyin, also called 烏陀夷 Udayin or Black Udayin, but there are other interpretations; said to have been schoolmaster to Śākyamuni when young and one of the early disciples; also to have been murdered.

迦畢試 Kapiśā, an ancient kingdom, south of the Hindukush, said to be 4,000 li around, with a capital of the same name 10 li in circumference; formerly a summer resort of Kaniṣka.

迦絺那 Kaṭhina, | 提; 羯 | | hard, inflexible, unyielding; a robe of merit. | | | 月 Kārttika-māsa, the month in October–November, intp. as the month after the summer retreat, when monks received the "kaṭhina" robe of merit; the date of the month is variously given, but it follows the summer retreat; also | 提月; | (or 羯) 栗底迦月; | 利邸迦月; | 哩 (or 剌) 底迦麽洗.

迦羅 Kalā, 哥 |; 歌 |; a minute part, an atom; the hundredth part lengthwise of a human hair; also a sixteenth part of anything. Also Kāla (and | 攞), a definite time, a division of time; the time of work, study, etc., as opposed to leisure time. Kāla, among other meanings, also means black, for which | | 迦 Kālaka is sometimes used, e.g. the black nāga. | | 毘囉 Karavīra, a fragrant oleander; tr. as 羊躑躅 a plant whose leaves on pressure exude juice. | | 毘迦 Probably an incorrect form of Kapilavastu, v. | 毘. | (|) 沙曳 (or 野 or 異) Kaṣāya, a monk's dyed robe, in contrast with white lay garb. | | 臂拏迦 Kālapināka, a "city of Magadha, 20 li south-east of Kulika, south of the present city of Behar". Eitel. | | 越 Kulapati, the head of a clan, or family. | | 迦吒 The crab in the zodiac. | | 邏 Karāla, "having projecting teeth, formidable," "epithet of the Rākshasas, of Śiva, of Kāla, of Vishṇu," etc. M. W. | | 鎮頭 Kālaka and tinduka, the first a poisonous fruit, the second non-poisonous, similar in appearance; a simile for bad and good monks. | | 鳩馱 Krakucchanda, v. 拘留孫; also Kakuda-Kātyāyana, v. 迦旃.

迦耶 Kāya, the body; an assemblage; cf. Trikāya.

迦膩(色)伽 Kaniṣka, king of 月支 the Yüeh-chih, i.e. of Tukhāra and the Indo-Scythians, ruler of Gandhāra in northern Punjab, who conquered northern India and as far as Bactria. He became a patron of Buddhism, the greatest after Aśoka. His date is variously given; Keith says "probably at the close of the first century A.D." It is also put at A.D. 125–165. He convoked "the third (or fourth) synod" in Kashmir, of 500 leading monks, under the presidency of 世友 Vasumitra, when the canon was revised and settled; this he is said to have had engraved on brass and placed in a stūpa.

迦葉(波) Kāśyapa, 迦攝(波) *inter alia* "a class of divine beings similar to or equal to Prajāpati"; the father "of gods, demons, men, fish, reptiles, and all animals"; also "a constellation". M. W. It is intp. as "drinking light", i.e. swallowing sun and moon, but without apparent justification. (1) One of the seven or ten ancient Indian sages. (2) Name of a tribe or race. (3) Kāśyapa Buddha, the third of the five Buddhas of the present kalpa, the sixth of the seven ancient Buddhas. (4) Mahākāśyapa, a brahman of Magadha, who became one of the principal disciples of Śākyamuni, and after his death became leader of the disciples, "convoked and directed the first synod, whence his title Ārya Sthavira (上坐, lit. chairman) is derived." Eitel. He is accounted the chief of the ascetics before the enlightenment; the first compiler of the canon and the first patriarch. (5) There were five Kāśyapas, disciples of the Buddha, Mahā-Kāśyapa, Uruvilvā-Kāśyapa, Gayā-Kāśyapa, Nadī-Kāśyapa, and Daśabala-Kāśyapa; the second, third, and fourth are said to have been brothers. (6) A bodhisattva, whose name heads a chapter in the Nirvāṇa sūtra. (7) | | 摩騰 Kāśyapa-Mātaṅga, the monk who with Gobharana, or Dharmarakṣa, i.e. Chu Fa-lan 竺法蘭, according to Buddhist statements, brought images and scriptures to China with the commissioners sent by Ming Ti, arriving in Lo-yang A.D. 67. | | 遺 Kāśyapīya, a school formed on the division of the Mahāsaṅghikāḥ into five schools a century after the Nirvāṇa. Keith gives the southern order, in the second century after the Nirvāṇa, as Theravāda (Sthavira), Mahīśāsaka, Sarvāstivādin, Kāśyapīya. Other forms: | | 毘; | | 維; | | 波; | | 臂耶; 柯尸悲與.

迦蘭陀 ? Karaṇḍa, ? Karaṇḍaka. A bird which flies in flocks and has a pleasant note; also, a squirrel which awakened Bimbisāra to warn him against a snake. (2) The Karaṇḍa-venuvana, a garden belonging to an elder called Karaṇḍa, used by a Nirgrantha sect, then presented by King Bimbisāra to Śākyamuni. Other forms: | | | 夷; | | 馱; | | 多 迦; | 藍 |; 伽 隣; 羯 | 鐸 (or 馱) 迦.

迦 迦 Kāka, Kākāla; a crow, also | | |; | | 羅. | | 羅 蟲 is said to be Kākala, a black insect or worm. | | 婁 多 Kākaruta. A crow's caw. | | 婆 迦 頻 闍 邏 Perhaps kapiñjala, a francolin, partridge, or pheasant. | | 那 Gagana, the firmament, space.

迦 遮 (or 柘) 末 尼 Kācamaṇi, crystal, quartz. | | 鄰 地 ? Kācalindikāka, or Kācilindi, also | | (or 眞) 粦 底 迦; | 旃 粦 提 (or 陀); | 止 栗 那; | 鄰 提 (or 陀) A sea bird, from whose feathers robes are made.

迦 邏 迦 Kāra(ka), one who does, or causes; an agent.

迦 逋 唐 v. | 布.

迦 那 伽 牟 尼 Kanakamuni, v. 拘. | | 提 婆 Kāṇadeva, a disciple of Nāgārjuna and fifteenth patriarch, a native of South India, of the Vaiśya caste; said to have only one eye, hence Kāṇa his name; known also as Deva Bodhisattva.

迦 陵 (頻) 伽 Kalaviṅka. A bird described as having a melodious voice, found in the valleys of the Himalayas. M. W. says "a sparrow". It may be the Kalandaka, or Kokila, the cuckoo. It "sings in the shell" before hatching out. Other forms are | 蘭 (頻) or 毘 |; | 毘 伽 (羅); | 尾 羅; 羯 羅 | |; 羯 毘 (or 鶡 鵯) 伽 羅, etc. | 頻 (or 賓) 闍 羅; 鵤 鴒 Kapiñjala, a francolin, partridge, or pheasant. | | | | 王 Kapiṅjalarāja, a previous incarnation of Śākyamuni as a pheasant.

郁 Elegant, refined, translit. *y* and *u*. | 伽 Yoga, cf. 瑜. | 伽 支 羅 Ukkacela, is a place unknown. | 多 (羅 僧 伽) Uttarāsaṅga, the cassock, the seven-patch robe; for this and Uttarakuru cf. 鬱. | 迦 Ugra, an elder of Śrāvastī, whose name is given to a sūtra.

重 Heavy, weighty, grave, serious; to lay stress upon, regard respectfully; again, double, repeated. | 如 v. 如 如 the double ju. | 山 The heavy mountain (of delusion). | 火 To pay respect to the god of fire. | 空 The double space, i.e. the space beyond space, the void beyond the void. | 重 Repeated, again and again, manifold, e.g. | | 帝 網 The multi-meshed net of Indra. | 關 The grave barriers (to meditation and enlightenment). | 閣 講 堂 The double-storeyed hall at Vaiśālī where the Buddha stayed. | 障 Serious hindrances (to enlightenment), e.g. delusion, sin, retribution (or the results of one's previous lives). | 頌; 祇 夜 Geya, repetition in verse of a prose section.

限 Limit, boundary, to fix. | 分 limited, e.g. limited culpability by reason of accident, unintentional error.

降 Descend, send down; degrade; subdue; submit. | 世 To descend to earth from above, as recorded of the Buddha. | 三 世 To subdue the three worlds, as conqueror of them, e.g. | | | 明 王 Trailokya-vijaya-rāja, Rāja subduing the three realms above, here, below, one of the five great 明 王 q.v.; the one controlling the east; subduer of the three realms of desire, resentment, and stupidity; also of these three passions in past, present, future. There are other similar rājas. | 伏 Abhicāraka, exorciser; magic; subjugator (of demons). | 焰 魔 尊 Yamāntaka, cf. 焰 the fierce mahārāja with six legs who controls the demons of the West. | 生 To descend into the world, as the Buddha is said to have done from the Tuṣita heaven. | 神 The descent of Buddha's spirit into Māyā's womb; also to bring down spirits as does a spiritualistic medium. | 胎 The descent into Māyā's womb. | 臨 To descend, draw near from above, condescend, e.g. the Buddha, the spirits, etc. | 誕 The anniversary of the descent, i.e. the Buddha's birthday, not the conception. | 魔 To overcome demons, e.g. as the Buddha did at his enlightenment. | 龍 To subdue nāgas, e.g. | | 鉢 to compel a nāga to enter an almsbowl as did the Buddha; | | 伏 虎 to subdue nāgas and subjugate tigers.

面 Face. | 目 Face and eyes, face, looks. | 門 Forehead, or mouth, or the line across the upper lip. | 授 Personal or face-to-face instruction. | 壁 To sit in meditation with the face to a wall, as did Bodhidharma for nine years, without uttering a word.

革 Skins, hides, pelts; strip, cut off. | 葱; 茖 葱 Latārka, "green onions" (M. W.), tr. as 蒜 garlic.

韋 A thong; translit. for *vi*, *ve*, *vai* sounds. | (天) 將 軍 One of the generals under the southern Mahārāja guardian in a temple. | 提 (希); 毘 (or 吠) 提 希; 吠 題 呬 弗 多 羅 Vaidehī, wife of Bimbisāra, and mother of Ajātaśatru; also called

Śrībhadra. 丨紐天；丨糅；違紐；毘紐；毘瑟紐；丨搜紐；丨廋紐；毘瑟怒 (or 笯) Viṣṇu, all-pervading, encompassing; "the preserver" in the Trimūrti, Brahmā, Viṣṇu, Śiva, creator, preserver, destroyer; the Vaiṣṇavas (Vishnuites) are devoted to him as the Śaivas are to Śiva. His wife is Lakṣmī, or Śrī. The Chinese describe him as born out of water at the beginning of a world-kalpa with 1,000 heads and 2,000 hands; from his navel springs a lotus, from which is evolved Brahmā. 丨陀；圍丨；毘丨；皮丨；吠丨(or 馱)；薜丨；鞞丨 Veda; knowledge, tr. 明智, or 明分 clear knowledge or discernment. The four Vedas are the Ṛgveda, Yajurveda, Sāmaveda, and Atharvaveda; they were never translated into Chinese, being accounted heretical. 丨陀 (or 馱) 輸 Vītāśoka, Vigatāśoka, younger brother of king Āśoka. 丨陀羅 Vetāla, v. 毘. 丨馱(天) Wei-to, the guardian facing the main hall of a temple; the origin of Wei-to is uncertain.

音 Sound, note, that which is heard. 丨教 Vocal teaching, Buddha's preaching. 丨木 Sounding block, or board for keeping time or rhythm. 丨樂 Music, a musical accompaniment to a service. 丨義 Sound and meaning, i.e. a pronouncing dictionary. 丨聲 Sound, note, preaching. 丨聲佛事 Buddha's work in saving by his preaching. 丨響忍 Sound and echo perseverance, the patience which realizes that all is as unreal as sound and echo.

風 Vāyu. Wind, air; rumour, repute; custom; temper, lust. 丨三昧；丨奮丨丨 A samādhi in which the whole body is conceived of as scattered. 丨(中 or 前) 燈 or 燭 "As a lamp (or candle) in the wind", such is the evanescence of the world and man. 丨刀 The wind knife, i.e. the approach of death and its agonies. 丨大 Wind or air as one of the four elements. 丨天 The wind deva. 丨界 The realm of wind, or air, with motion as its principle, one of the 四大 q.v. 丨災 The calamity of destruction by wind at the end of the third period of destruction of a world. 丨色 Wind colour, i.e. non-existent, like a rabbit's horns, tortoise-hair, or scent of salt. 丨輪 The wheel, or circle, of wind below the circle of water and metal on which the earth rests; the circle of wind rests on space. 丨(輪) 際 The region of the wind-circle.

飛 To fly. 丨(行) 仙 Flying genii. 丨化 Flying and changing. 丨行 Flying anywhere (at will). 丨行夜叉 Flying yakṣas, or demons. 丨(行皇) 帝 Flying ruler, synonym for a sovereign. 丨錫 Flying staff, synonym for a travelling monk.

食 Āhāra, 阿賀羅 food; to eat, feed. The rules are numerous, and seem to have changed; originally flesh food was not improper and vegetarianism was a later development; the early three rules in regard to "clean" foods are that "I shall not have seen the creature killed, nor heard it killed for me, nor have any doubt that it was killed for me". The five "unclean" foods are the above three, with creatures that have died a natural death; and creatures that have been killed by other creatures. The nine classes add to the five, creatures not killed for me; raw flesh, or creatures mauled by other creatures; things not seasonable or at the right time; things previously killed. The Laṅkāvatāra and certain other sūtras forbid all killed food. 丨前 Before food, i.e. before the principal meal at noon; but 丨後 after food, especially after breakfast till noon. 丨(or 齋) 堂 The dining-hall of a monastery. 丨時 The time of eating the principal meal, i.e. noon; nothing might be eaten by members of the Order after noon. 丨欲 The lust for food, one of the four cravings. 丨物五果 The five kinds of edible fruits and grains: those with stones (or pips), rinds, shells, seeds (e.g. grains), pods. 丨蘭碣 To eat some kind of poisonous herb. 丨蜜 To eat honey, i.e. to absorb the Buddha's teaching. 丨頃 The time of a meal, i.e. but a short time.

首 Head. 丨圖馱那；輸 (or 閱) 頭檀 Śuddhodana, intp. "pure food", king of Kapilavastu, husband of Mahāmāyā, and father of Śākyamuni. 丨座 The chief seat, president, chief. 丨悔 Voluntary confession and repentance. 丨楞嚴；丨丨伽摩 Śūraṁgama, intp. 健相 heroic, resolute; the virtue or power which enables a Buddha to overcome every obstacle, obtained in the 丨楞嚴定 or 三昧 Śūraṁgama dhyāna or samādhi; 丨楞嚴經 is the sūtra on the subject, whose full title commences 大佛頂, etc. 丨盧 (迦 or 柯)；輸 (or 室) 盧迦 (波)；室路迦 Śloka, a stanza of thirty-two syllables, either in four lines of eight each, or two of sixteen. 丨(or 周) 羅 (髮) Cūlaka, Cūḍa; one of the eight yakṣas, or demons. 丨訶 (or 阿) 旣那 Śubhakṛtsna, the ninth brahmaloka, i.e. the third region of the third dhyāna of form. 丨陀 (羅)；戍陀 (or 達 or 捺) 羅 Śūdra, the fourth of the four castes, peasants. 丨(or 私) 陀 (娑) 婆 Śuddhāvāsa, the five pure abodes, or heavens. 丨題 Heading or title (of a sūtra).

香 Gandha. Fragrance; incense; the sense of smell, i.e. one of the ṣaḍayātana, six senses. Incense is one of the 使 Buddha's messengers to stimulate faith and devotion.

香丸 Incense balls.

香(光莊)嚴 The one whose mind meditates on Buddha becomes interpenetrated and glorified by Buddha-fragrance (and light). There are several deva-sons and others called Hsiang-yen.

香入 The sense of smell and its organ, the nose.

香刹 An incense kṣetra, i.e. a monastery.

香厨 The fragrant kitchen, i.e. a monastery kitchen.

香塵 The atom or element of smell, one of the six guṇas.

香室 Gandhakuṭī; house of incense, i.e. where Buddha dwells, a temple.

香山 Gandhamādana. Incense mountain, one of the ten fabulous mountains known to Chinese Buddhism, located in the region of the Anavatapta lake in Tibet; also placed in the Kunlun range. Among its great trees dwell the Kinnaras, Indra's musicians.

香染 Incense-coloured, yellowish-grey, the colour of a monk's robe; also | 色; | (複) 衣.

香樓 The fragrant pyre on which the body of Buddha was consumed.

香欲 The desire for fragrance, the lust of the nasal organ, one of the five desires.

香殿 The incense hall, especially the large hall of the Triratna.

香水 Liquid scent, or perfume. | | 錢 Money given to monks. | (|) 海 The scented ocean surrounding Sumeru.

香湯 A fragrant liquid made of thirty-two ingredients, used by the secret sects in washing the body at the time of initiation.

香火 Incense and candles (or lamps).

香炷 Thread incense (in coils); a lamp or candle giving a fragrant odour; incense and candles.

香爐 A censer.

香王 Gandharāja, a bodhisattva in whose image the finger tips are shown as dripping ambrosia. There is also a | | Kuanyin.

香界 Incense region, a temple.

香神; 香音神 The gods of fragrance (and music), i.e. the Gandharvas who live on Gandhamādana; the musicians of Indra, with Dhṛtarāṣṭra as their ruler.

香積 Hsiang-chi, the Buddha of Fragrance-land | 國, described in the 維摩經. The inhabitants live on the odour of incense, which surpasses that of all other lands; cf. | 象; also the kitchen and food of a monastery.

香篆 Incense made in coils and burnt to measure the time; also | 盤; | 印.

香華 Incense and flowers, offerings to Buddha.

香象 Gandhahastī. Fragrant elephant; one of the sixteen honoured ones of the Bhadra-kalpa; also a bodhisattva in the north who lives on the | 聚山 or | 醉 | with Buddha | 積; cf. | 集. | | 之文 A narrative in the Abhidharma-kośa; also a title for the Buddhist canon. | | 大師 The third patriarch of the Hua-yen school, Fa-tsang 法藏.

香集 The name of the western Buddha-land in which Ākāśa Bodhisattva lives, described in the 虛空藏菩薩經 Ākāśagarbha sūtra; cf. | 象.

香風山 The abode of the Bodhisattva of fragrance and light.

香食 Fragrance for food; fragrant food.

香龍腦 Scented dragon's brains, camphor; v. 羯布羅.

10. TEN STROKES

乘 Yāna 衍; 野那 a vehicle, wain, any means of conveyance; a term applied to Buddhism as carrying men to salvation. The two chief divisions are the 小 | Hīnayāna and 大 | Mahāyāna; but there are categories of one, two, three, four, and five shêng q.v., and they have further subdivisions. | 津 The vehicle and ford to nirvāṇa, i.e. Buddha-truth. | 種 The vehicle-seed, or seed issuing from the Buddha-vehicle.

借 To borrow, lend. | 花獻佛 To borrow a flower to offer to Buddha, i.e. to serve him with another's gift.

値 To meet; happen on; attend to; worth, valued at. | 遇 To meet, happen on unexpectedly.

俾 To cause, enable. | 沙闍羅所 Bhaiṣajya-rāja, the Buddha of medicine, or king of healing, v. 藥師 19. | 禮多 Preta, a hungry ghost, v. 鬼 10.

倍 Double, double-fold, a fold; to turn from or against, to revolt. | 離 To turn from and depart from.

條 A length (of anything); a law, order. | 支 The Tajiks anciently settled "near the Sirikol lake". Eitel. | 衣 The monk's patch-robe.

倒 To fall, lie down; to pour; upside down, inverted, perverted; on the contrary. | 凡 Perverted folk, the unenlightened who see things upside down. | 合 A fallacious comparison in a syllogism. | 懸 Hanging upside down; the condition of certain condemned souls, especially for whom the Ullambana (or Lambana, cf. 盂) festival is held in the seventh month; the phrase is used as a tr. of Ullambana, and as such seems meant for Lambana. | 我 The conventional ego, the reverse of reality. | 見 Cf. 顚 19. Upside-down or inverted views, seeing things as they seem, not as they are, e.g. the impermanent as permanent, misery as joy, non-ego as ego, and impurity as purity. | 離 The fallacy of using a comparison in a syllogism which does not apply.

修 To put in order, mend, cultivate, observe. Translit. *su*, *sū*. Cf. 須; 蘇.

修伽陀 Sugata, one who has gone the right way, one of a Buddha's titles; sometimes intp. as well-come (Svāgata). Also | | 多; | | 度; | (or 蘇) 揭多; 沙婆揭多; 莎伽(陀).

修利 Sūrya, 蘇利耶 the sun; also name of a yakṣa, the ruler of the sun.

修善 To cultivate goodness; the goodness that is cultivated, in contrast with natural goodness.

修堅 Firmness in observing or maintaining; established conviction, e.g. of the 別敎 bodhisattva that all phenomena in essence are identical.

修多羅 Sūtra; from *siv*, to sew, to thread, to string together, intp. as 綖, i.e. 線 thread, string; strung together as a garland of flowers. Sūtras or addresses attributed to the Buddha, usually introduced by 如是我聞 thus have I heard, Evam mayā śrutam. It is intp. by 經 a warp, i.e. the threads on which a piece is woven; it is the Sūtra-piṭaka, or first portion of the Tripiṭaka; but is sometimes applied to the whole canon. It is also intp. 契 or 契經 scriptures. Also 修單羅; | 妬路; | 多闌; | 單蘭多; 素呾(or 怛)纜; 蘇多(or 呾)羅. A clasp on the seven-piece robe of the 眞宗 Shin sect.

修性 To cultivate the nature; the natural proclivities. | | 不二門 The identity of cultivation and the cultivated.

修惡 To cultivate evil; cultivated evil in contrast with evil by nature.

修懺 To undergo the discipline of penitence.

修所斷 To cut off illusion in practice, or performance.

修惑 Illusion, such as desire, hate, etc., in practice or performance, i.e. in the process of attaining enlightenment; cf. 思惑.

修生 That which is produced by cultivation, or observance.

修禪六妙門 The six mysterious gates or ways of practising meditation, consisting mostly of breathing exercises.

修羅 Asura, demons who war with Indra; v. 阿｜｜; it is also Sura, which means a god, or deity. ｜｜軍 The army of asuras, fighting on the ｜｜場 asura battlefield against Indra. ｜｜酒 Surā, wine, spirits; but it is also intp. as asura wine, i.e. the non-existent. ｜｜道 or 趣 Asura way, or destiny.

修習力 The power acquired by the practice of all (good) conduct; the power of habit.

修行 Caryā, conduct; to observe and do; to mend one's ways; to cultivate oneself in right practice; be religious, or pious. ｜｜住 A bodhisattva's stage of conduct, the third of his ten stages.

修跋拏 Suvarṇa; ｜越｜; 蘇伐剌 gold.

修道 To cultivate the way of religion; be religious; the way of self-cultivation. In the Hīnayāna the stage from anāgāmin to arhat; in Mahāyāna one of the bodhisattva stages.

修造局 A workshop (in a monastery).

修陀里舍那 Sudarśana, intp. 善見 beautiful, given as the name of a yakṣa; cf. also 蘇.

俱 All, every; translit. *ku*, *ko*; cf. 拘; 鳩; 究; 居; 窟; 瞿.

俱不(極)成 All incomplete; a fallacy in the comparison, or example, which leaves the syllogism incomplete.

俱不遣 A fallacy in a syllogism caused by introducing an irrelevant example, one of the thirty-three fallacies.

俱俱羅 Kukkuṭa is a cock, or fowl; this is intp. as the clucking of fowls; cf. 究 and 拘. The ｜｜｜部 Kaukkuṭikāḥ is described as one of the eighteen schools of Hīnayāna; cf. 拘; 鳩; 窟; 居.

俱利伽羅 A kind of black dragon; also ｜力迦(羅); ｜哩迦(or 劍); 古力迦; 加梨加; 迦羅迦; 律迦, etc. It is one of the symbols of 不動明王, connected with his sword.

俱吠羅 Kuvera; kubera; the god of riches, Vaiśravaṇa, regent of the north; having three legs and eight teeth; in Japan Bishamon. Also ｜乞羅 and numerous other names; cf. 毘.

俱夜羅 Things that go with the almsbowl, e.g. spoon, chopsticks, etc.

俱摩羅 Kumāra, a boy, youth; cf. 拘. ｜｜｜天 A youthful deva.

俱攞 Kūla, a slope, a shore; a mound; a small dagoba in which the ashes of a layman are kept. Kula, a herd, family, household. ｜｜鉢底 Kulapati, the head of a family, a householder.

俱有 Existing together; all being, existing, or having. ｜｜依; ｜｜根 Things or conditions on which one relies, or from which things spring, e.g. knowledge. ｜｜因 Sahabhūhetu, mutual causation, the simultaneous causal interaction of a number of things, e.g. earth, water, fire, and air. ｜｜法 Co-existent, co-operative things or conditions.

俱毘留波叉 Defined variously, but indicative of Virūpākṣa, the three-eyed Śiva; the guardian ruler of the West, v. 毘.

俱毘羅 (1) Kumbhīra, crocodile; also 鳩鞞羅; 俱尾羅. (2) Kuvera, Kubera, the guardian king of the north, v. 毘沙門 Vaiśravaṇa, the god of wealth.

俱毘陀羅 Kovidāra, 拘鞞｜｜ *Bauhinia variegata*; also one of the trees of paradise. M. W. Said to be the tree of the great playground (where the child Śākyamuni played).

俱生 Natural, spontaneous, inborn as opposed to acquired. ｜｜惑 Natural doubt, inborn illusion, in contrast to doubt or illusion acquired, e.g. by being taught. ｜｜(法) Spontaneous ideas or things. ｜｜神 The spirit, born at the same time as the individual, which records his deeds and reports to Yama. Another version is the two spirits who record one's good and evil. Another says it is the Ālaya-vijñāna. ｜｜起 Arising and born with one; spontaneous.

俱留孫 Krakkucchanda, fourth of the seven ancient Buddhas, first of the Buddhas of the present age. Cf. 拘.

俱盧洲 Kurudvīpa; Uttarakuru. The

northern of the four continents of a world; cf. 大洲 and 鬱.

俱盧舍 Krośa, the distance the lowing of an ox or the sound of a drum can be heard, *circa* 5 li. Cf. 拘.

俱睒彌 Kauśāmbī; 丨賞 (or 舍) 彌 Vatsapattana, an ancient city of central India, identified with the village of Kosam on the Jumna, 30 miles above Allahabad. These are old forms, as are 拘深; 拘翼; 拘鹽惟, and forms with 巨 and 鳩; the newer forms being 憍賞 (or 閃) 彌.

俱空 Both or all empty, or unreal, i.e. both ego and things have no reality.

俱緣果 Bījapūra, or Bījapūraka; described as a citron. M. W. A fruit held in one of the hands of Kunti Kuan-yin.

俱胝 Koṭī, 丨致; 拘致; a crore, 10 millions; intp. as 100,000; 1,000,000; or 10,000,000.

俱舍 Kośa, 句捨 cask, box, treasury; translated 藏 store, also 鞘 sheath, scabbard; especially the 丨丨論 Abhidharma-kośa-śāstra, v. 阿, composed by Vasubandhu, tr. by Paramārtha and Hsüan-tsang. 丨丨宗 The Abhidharma or Piṭaka School.

俱蘇摩 Kusuma, a flower, flowers; v. 拘. 丨丨丨跋低 Kusumavatī; name of a Buddha-realm. 丨丨丨摩羅 Kusumamālā, a wreath, garland. 丨丨洛 (迦) Kuśūla; a "bin" skirt, worn by nuns; also 厥蘇丨丨; 祇 (or 瞿 or 厥) 修羅.

俱蘭吒 Kuraṇṭa; yellow amaranth; intp. as a red flower, among men with 10 leaves, among devas 100, among Buddhas 1,000; also as a material thing, i.e. something with resistance. Cf. 拘.

俱解脫 Complete release, i.e. the freedom of the arhat from moral and meditative hindrances.

俱遜婆 Kusumbha; safflower, saffron.

兼 Both; also; to unite, join, comprehend. 丨利 Mutual benefit; to benefit self and others. 丨但對帶 The first four of the five periods of Buddha's teaching are also defined by T'ien-t'ai as: (1) 兼 Combined teaching; including 圓 and 別教 doctrine, the period of the Avataṁsaka-sūtra. (2) 但 Sole; i.e. 藏 or Hīnayāna only, that of the Āgamas. (3) 對 Comparative; all four forms of doctrines being compared. 帶 Inclusive, that of the 般若 Prajñā, when the perfect teaching was revealed as the fulfilment of the rest.

冥 Darkness, obscurity; deep, Hades; used chiefly in the sense of 無知 ignorance, profound, secret, invisible, e.g. as opposed to 顯 open, manifest. 丨一 Entire obscurity, pristine darkness. 丨使 Lictors, or messengers of Hades. 丨利; 丨益 Invisible benefit, or merit, i.e. within, spiritual. 丨初 The primitive darkness (at the beginning of existence). 丨加 The invisible aid of the spiritual powers. 丨官 The rulers in Hades. 丨府 The palace of darkness, Hades. 丨往 Going into the shades, death. 丨思; 丨慮 The unfathomable thought or care of the Buddhas and bodhisattvas, beyond the realization of men. 丨應 Response from the invisible. 丨(or 內) 熏 Fumigation within, inner influence. 丨界 Hades, or the three lower forms of incarnation, i.e. hell, preta, animal. 丨福 The happiness of the dead. 丨衆 The invisible powers—Brahmā, Śakra, Yama; the spirits in general. 丨諦; 丨性; 自性 The Sāṅkhya doctrine of primordial profundity, beyond estimation, the original nature out of which all things arose. 丨資 Possessions of or for the dead; their happiness. 丨道; 丨途; 丨土 The dark way, or land of darkness, the shades, Hades, pretas, etc. 丨通 Mysterious, supernatural, omnipresent power. 丨陽會 The assembly (for offerings) of the spirits below and above, pretas, etc. 丨顯兩界 The two regions of the dead and of the living

准 To permit, grant, acknowledge; used for 準 in 丨提 q.v.

剝 To peel, flay; kill. 丨皮 To flay, or peel. In one of the previous incarnations of Śākyamuni he is said to have written a certain gāthā containing the Holy Law on a piece of his own flayed skin with one of his bones split into the shape of a pen, and his blood instead of ink. 智度論 27.

剜 To scoop out. 丨燈 To scoop out (one's body) and turn (it) into a lamp, attributed to Śākyamuni in a former incarnation.

剡 Pointed, sharp. 丨浮 Jambūdvīpa, and Yama, v. 閻.

原 Origin, original. (華嚴) 丨人論 A treatise on the original or fundamental nature of man, by

宗密 Tsung-mi, the fifth patriarch of the Hua-yen school, explaining its doctrine, in one chüan.

哥 Elder brother. │大 Skandha, v. 塞. │(利)王 cf. 迦. │羅羅 Kalala. The womb, uterus; an embryo shortly after conception.

哭 To weep. │泣 To weep. │啼 To weep and wail.

哦 Translit. *ga*; cf. 我, 誐, 伽, 哧, 疙. │哆也 Gatayaḥ, nom. pl. of gati, intp. as going, coming.

唄 Pāṭha; pāṭhaka; read, recite, intone, chant, hymns in praise of Buddha; 唄匿 is erroneously said to transliterate the Sanskrit root vi-ne and to be the same as 婆陟 (or 婆師), but these are bhāṣa. │器 Instruments for keeping time during chanting. │士; │師 Leader of the chanting. │比丘; 鈴聲比丘 A famous Buddhist singer of old, ugly but with bell-like voice. │讚 To sing hymns of praise.

唐 Rude, wild; the T'ang dynasty A.D. 618–907. │三藏 The T'ang Tripiṭaka, a name for Hsüan-tsang. │僧 T'ang monks, especially Hsüan-tsang as the T'ang monk. │捐 To cast away as valueless.

城 A city (or defensive) wall; a city, a walled town. │隍神 The city god, protector of the wall and moat and all they contain.

夏 Summer. │中 During the summer, the middle of the summer; the rainy reason spent by the monks of India in retirement. │坐; 坐│; │安居 The period of the summer retreat for meditation, known as varṣās, the rains. │末; │滿; │竟; │解 The end of the summer (retreat), the 15th of the 7th month. │臘; 法臘 The age of a monk as monk, the years of his ordination. │衆 The assembly of monks at the summer retreat. │首 The first day, or beginning, of the retreat.

娘 Lady, wife, mother, aunt. 師│ A nun.

娜 Translit. *da* and *na*, e.g. │多 Danta, tooth, tusk, fang. │伽 Naga, mountain, hill. │耶 Naya, conduct, course, leading.

娑 To play, careless, idle, easy going; translit. *s*, *ś*, chiefly *sa*, *sā*. 娑也地提嚩多 ? Satyadevatā, intp. as 本尊 the fundamental, or original, or principal honoured one. │伽羅 Sāgara. │竭│ The Ocean. The Nāga king of the ocean palace north of Mt. Meru, possessed of priceless pearls; the dragon king of rain; his eight-year-old daughter instantly attained Buddhahood, v. the Lotus sūtra. │呵 Sahā, a herb in the Himālayas imparting immortality to the finder, v. │婆. │多吉哩 ? Śatakri, name of one of the yakṣa generals. ││婆(漢)那 Sadvāhana, Śātavāhana, name of a royal patron of Nāgārjuna. │婆 Sahā; that which bears, the earth, v. 地; intp. as bearing, enduring; the place of good and evil; a universe, or great chiliocosm, where all are subject to transmigration and which a Buddha transforms; it is divided into three regions 三界 and Mahābrahmā Sahāmpati is its lord. Other forms: ││世界; │界; │婆; │訶; 沙訶; 索訶. │訶樓陀 Sahā-lokadhātu, the world. │婆訶; │縛賀 Svāhā, an oblation by fire, also Hail! a brahminical salutation at the end of a sacrifice. │底也 Satya, true; satyatā, truth, a truth. │度 Sādhu, good, virtuous, perfect, a sage, saint, tr. 善 good. │毘迦羅; 劫毘羅 Kapila, possibly Sāṅkhya Kapila, the founder of the Sāṅkhya philosophy. │磨 Sāmaveda, the third of the Vedas, containing the hymns. │羅; 沙羅 Śāla, Sāla; the Sāl tree, ││樹 *Shorea robusta*, the teak tree. │羅林 Śālavana, the grove of Sāl trees near Kuśinagara, the reputed place of the Buddha's death. │羅(樹)王 Śālendra-rāja, a title of a Buddha; also of Śubhavyūha, father of Kuan-yin. │羅娑 Sārasa, the Indian crane. │羅梨弗 ? "Salaribhu, an ancient kingdom or province in India. Exact position unknown." Eitel. │路多羅; 戍縷多 Śrotra, the ear. │麼囉 Smara, recollection, remembrance.

孫 Grandchild; grandson; translit. *sun*. │陀利 Sundarī, wife of Sundarananda; Sundari, name of an arhat; also a courtesan who defamed the Buddha. │陀羅難陀 Sundarananda, or Sunanda, said to be younger brother of Śākyamuni, his wife being the above Sundarī; thus called to distinguish him from Ānanda.

家 Family; home; school, sect; genus. │世國 v. 呾 Takṣaśilā, Taxila. │主 Kulapati, the head of a family. │狗 A domestic dog, i.e. trouble, which ever dogs one steps.

害 Hiṁsā; vihiṁsā; hurt, harm, injure. │想; │覺 The wish, or thought, to injure another.

容 Contain; bear; allow; bearing, face, looks; easy. │有釋 (or 說) An admissible though indirect interpretation; containing that meaning.

宮 A palace, mansion; a eunuch. 丨毘羅 Kumbhīra, v. 金丨丨 a crocodile. 丨胎 The palace-womb, where those who call on Amitābha but are in doubt of him are confined for 500 years, devoid of the riches of Buddha-truth, till born into the Pure Land; idem 疑城胎宮.

宴 A banquet; to repose; at ease. 丨坐 To sit in meditation. 丨寂 To enter into rest, to die. 丨默 Peaceful and silent.

尅 To overcome; successfully attain to. 丨實 To discover the truth. 丨果 To obtain the fruit of endeavour; the fruit of effort, i.e. salvation. 丨終 Successful end, certainty of obtaining the fruit of one's action. 丨聖 The certainty of attaining arhatship. 丨證 The assurance of success in attaining enlightenment. 丨識 The certainty of the knowledge (by the spirits, of men's good and evil).

展 To extend, expand, stretch. 丨轉力 Powers of extension or expansion.

峨 High, commanding. 丨(or 峩)眉山 O-mei Shan or Mt. Omi in Szechwan. Two of its peaks are said to be like 蛾眉 a moth's eyebrows, also pronounced O-mei; the monastery at the top is the 光相寺 where P'u-hsien (Samantabhadra) is supreme.

差 To send; to differ, err; translit. *kṣ*. 丨別 Pariccheda. Difference, different, discrimination; opposite of 平等 on a level, equal, identical. 丨利尼迦 Kṣīriṇikā, sap-bearing, a tree of that kind. 丨多羅 Kṣetra, land, region, country. 丨羅波尼 Kṣārapānīya, alkaline water, caustic liquid; also said to be a kind of garment.

師 A host, army; a leader, preceptor, teacher, model; tr. of upādhyāya, an "under-teacher", generally intp. as a Buddhist monk.

師子 Siṁha, a lion; also 枲伽; idem 獅子 Buddha, likened to the lion, the king of animals, in respect of his fearlessness.

師子乳 Lion's milk, like bodhi-enlightenment, which is able to annihilate countless ages of the karma of affliction, just as one drop of lion's milk can disintegrate an ocean of ordinary milk.

師子光 Siṁharaśmi. "A learned opponent of the Yogācāra school who lived about A.D. 630." Eitel.

師子吼 Siṁhanāda. The lion's roar, a term designating authoritative or powerful preaching. As the lion's roar makes all animals tremble, subdues elephants, arrests birds in their flight and fishes in the water, so Buddha's preaching overthrows all other religions, subdues devils, conquers heretics, and arrests the misery of life.

師子國 Siṁhala, Ceylon, the kingdom reputed to be founded by Siṁha, first an Indian merchant, later king of the country, who overcame the "demons" of Ceylon and conquered the island.

師子座 (or 牀) Siṁhāsana. A lion throne, or couch. A Buddha throne, or seat; wherever the Buddha sits, even the bare ground; a royal throne.

師子奮迅 The lion aroused to anger, i.e. the Buddha's power of arousing awe.

師子尊者; 師子比丘 Āryasiṁha, or Siṁha-bhikṣu. The 23rd or 24th patriarch, Brahman by birth; a native of Central India; laboured in Kashmir, where he died a martyr A.D. 259.

師子王 The lion king, Buddha.

師子相 Siṁdhadhvaja; "lion-flag," a Buddha south-east of our universe, fourth son of Mahābhijña.

師子胄 or 鎧 Harivarman, to whom the 成實論 Satyasiddhi-śāstra is ascribed.

師子身中蟲 Just as no animal eats a dead lion, but it is destroyed by worms produced within itself, so no outside force can destroy Buddhism, only evil monks within it can destroy it.

師子遊戲三昧 The joyous samādhi which is likened to the play of the lion with his prey. When a Buddha enters this degree of samādhi he causes the earth to tremble, and the purgatories to give up their inmates.

師子音 Siṁhaghoṣa; "lion's voice," a Buddha south-east of our universe, third son of Mahābhijña.

師子頰玉 Siṁhahanu. The paternal grandfather of Śākyamuni, a king of Kapilavastu, father of Śuddhodana, Śuklodana, Droṇodana, and Amṛtodana.

師孫 Disciple of a disciple.

師姑 A nun; also 尼姑.

師檀 Teacher and donor, or monk and patron.

師祖 The teacher of one's teacher.

師絃 or **筋** A tiger's tendons as lute-strings, i.e. bodhi music silences all minor strings.

庫 Treasury; storehouse. | 倫 K'urun, Urga, the Lamaistic centre in Mongolia, the sacred city. | 車 K'u-ch'ê, or Karashahr, v. 屈.

庭 Court, hall, family; forehead. | 儀 The ceremony on entering the hall for service.

座 Āsana. A seat; throne; classifier of buildings, etc. | 主; 上 |; 首 |; | 元 A chairman, president; the head of the monks; an abbot. | 光; 光 | The halo behind the throne of an image; a halo throne. | 臘 The end of the summer retreat; the monastic end of the year.

徑 A short cut, a diameter. | 山 A monastery at Ling-an Hsien, Chekiang.

徒 On foot; a follower, disciple; in vain; banishment. | 弟 A disciple, neophyte, apprentice. | 衆 The company of disciples.

悔 Regret, repent. | 懺 法 The rules for repentance and confession. | 過 To repent of error.

恚 Hate, anger, rage. | 怒 Hate and anger. | 結 The fetter of hatred binding to transmigration.

息 To breathe; breath; rest, stop, settle, cease; produce, interest. | 化 To cease the transforming work (and enter nirvāṇa as did the Buddha). | 心 To set the heart at rest; a disciple. | 忌 伽 彌; | 忌 陀 伽 迷 Sakṛdāgāmin, he who is to be reborn only once before entering nirvāṇa. | 慈 At rest and kind, an old translation of śramaṇa, one who has entered into the life of rest and shows loving-kindness to all. | 災 To cause calamities to cease, for which the esoteric sect uses magical formulæ, especially for illness, or personal misfortune. | 苦 To put an end to suffering.

恭 Respect, reverence. | 御 陀 Konyodha, a kingdom mentioned by Hsüan-tsang as a stronghold of unbelievers; it is said to be in south-east Orissa, possibly Ganjam as suggested in Eitel; there is a Konnāda further south. | 敬 Reverence, worship. | 敬 施 Worship as an offering, one of the three forms of giving. | 畔 荼 Kumbhāṇḍa, a demon, v. 鳩. | 建 那 補 羅 Koṅkaṇapura, "An ancient kingdom on the West Coast of India," including Konkan, Goa, and "North Canara, between Lat. 14° 37 N. and Lat. 18° N." Eitel.

恩 Grace, favour. | 度 One who graciously saves—a term for a monk. | 愛 Grace and love; human affection, which is one of the causes of rebirth. | 愛 獄 The prison of affection, which holds men in bondage. | 憐 Loving-kindness and pity. | 河 The river of grace. | 海 The sea of grace. | 田 The field of grace, i.e. parents, teachers, elders, monks, in return for the benefits they have conferred; one of the 三 福 田

悅 To please, pleased. | 衆 Please all, name for the manager of affairs in a monastery, also called 知 事 karmadāna.

悟 Awaken to, apprehend, perceive, become aware; similar to 覺, hence 覺 |. | 入 To apprehend or perceive and enter into (the idea of reality). Name of a Kashmir monk, Sugandhara. | 刹 The kṣetra or land of perception or enlightenment. | 忍 The patience of enlightenment, obtained by Vaidehī, wife of Bimbisāra, "on her vision of Amitābha," also known as Joy-perseverance, or Faith-perseverance; one of the ten stages of faith. | 道 To awaken to the truth.

扇 Fan; door-leaf; translit. *ś*, *ṣ*. | 底 迦 Śāntika, propitiatory, producing ease or quiet; a ceremony for causing calamities to cease. | 搋; | | 半 擇 (or 般 荼) 迦 Ṣaṇḍhaka, a eunuch, sexually impotent; v. 般; 半.

振 To shake, rouse, restore. | 地 To shake the earth. | 鈴 To shake or ring a bell.

挾 To clasp under the arm; to cherish; to presume on. |侍; 脇士 The two assistants of a Buddha, etc., right and left.

捃 v. 君.

捕 Arrest, catch. |喝; |喃; |揭 Bukhara. The present Bokhara, 39° 47 N., 64° 25 E.

料 To measure (grain), calculate; control, direct; materials; glassware. |簡 To expound, explain, comment upon; T'ien-t'ai uses the term for question and answer, catechism.

旁 A side, beside, adjoining, near. |生: 傍生 Rebirth as an animal. In some parts of China |生 means the next life.

旃 A flag on a bent pole; to warn; translit. generally *can*, rarely *śan, ṣan, cin, kim*. |丹 v. 震 China. |延 v. 迦 abbrev. for Kātyāyana. |提羅 Śaṇḍha or Ṣaṇḍhaka, a eunuch. |檀 (娜) Candana, from cand, to brighten, gladden; sandal-wood, either the tree, wood, or incense-powder, from southern India; there are various kinds, e.g. 牛頭 | | q.v. |檀耳 A fungus or fruit of the sandal tree, a broth or decoction of which is said to have been given to the Buddha at his last meal, by Cunda 純陀 q.v.; v. 長阿含經 3. |簓迦 Campaka, also 瞻蔔 (or 博 or 波). A tree with yellow fragrant flowers, *Michelia champaka*; a kind of perfume; a kind of bread-fruit tree; a district in the upper Punjab. |荼羅 Caṇḍāla, v. below. |達羅婆伽; 月分 Candrabhāgā. "The largest Pundjab stream, the Acesines of Alexander, now called Chenab." Eitel. |達羅; |達提婆 Candradeva, the moon, the moon-deva, the male ruler of the moon. |遮 Ciñca-Māṇavikā, or Sundarī, also |闍, 戰遮 name of a brahmin woman who falsely accused the Buddha of adultery with her, 興起行經下 q.v. |陀羅 Caṇḍāla, derived from violent, and intp. as a butcher, bad man. |陀利 Caṇḍāla, "an outcast," "a man of the lowest and most despised of the mixed tribes, born from a Śūdra father and Brāhman mother." M. W. He bore a flag and sounded a bell to warn of his presence. Converts from this class were admitted to ordination in Buddhism. |陀阿輸柯 Cāṇḍāśoka, Cruel Aśoka, a name given to Aśoka before his conversion.

時 Time, hour, period; constantly; as kāla, time in general, e.g. year, month, season, period; as samaya, it means kṣaṇa, momentary, passing; translit. *ji*. |乞縛 Jihvā, the tongue. |分 Time-division of the day, variously made in Buddhist works: (1) Three periods each of day and night. (2) Eight periods of day and night, each divided into four parts. (3) Twelve periods, each under its animal, as in China. (4) Thirty hours, sixty hours, of varying definition. |(散) 外道 The non-Buddhist sect which regarded Time, or Chronos, as creator of all things. |婆時婆迦 Jīvajīvaka, v. 耆. |(or 精) 媚鬼 One of the three classes of demons; capable of changing at the 子 tzŭ hour (midnight) into the form of a rat, boy, girl, or old, sick person. |宗; 六|往生宗 A Japanese sect, whose members by dividing day and night into six periods of worship seek immortality. |成就 The third of the six initial statements in a sūtra, i.e. 一時 "at one time" or "once", cf. 六成就. |毘多迦羅 Jīvitākāra, name of a spirit described as a devourer of life or length of days. |縛迦 Jīvaka, one of the eight principal drugs; living, making or seeking a living, causing to live, etc.; an "illegitimate son of king Bimbisāra by Āmradārikā", who resigned his claim to the throne to Ajātaśātru and practised medicine; a physician. |處諸緣 The conditions or causes of time and place into which one is born. |衆 The present company, i.e. of monks and laity; the community in general. |衣 Garments suited to the time or occasion. |食 Seasonable or timely food, especially roots used as food in sickness, part of the 五藥, i.e. turnip, onion, arrowroot, radish (or carrot), and a root curing poison.

書 Likh; to write; pustaka, a writing, book; lekha, a letter, document. |寫 To write, record; a recorder. |記 A record.

案 A judge's desk; a case at law. |達羅 Andhra, a kingdom in southern India, between the Krishnā and Godāvarī rivers, whose capital was Veṅgī; the country south-east of this was known as 大|||.

柴 Fuel, firewood, brushwood. |頭 The one who looks after it in a monastery.

校 Compare, collate, compared with, similar to 較. |量 To compare, or collate, and measure; comparative. |飾 To adorn, ornament.

桓 A tree whose hard, black seeds are used for beads; a pillar, post, tablet. |因 Indra, abbrev. for 釋提||.

格 A rule, line, pattern; reach, research, science. |外 Extraordinary.

栗 Chestnut; translit. *l, hṛ*. 丨咕(婆)毘 Licchavi, v. 梨. 丨馱 Hṛd, hṛdaya, the heart, v. 汙.

桑 Mulberry. 丨渴耶 v. 僧 Saṅgha. 丨門 v. 沙 Śramaṇa.

根 Mūla, a root, basis, origin; but when meaning an organ of sense, Indriyam, a "power", "faculty of sense, sense, organ of sense". M. W. A root, or source; that which is capable of producing or growing, as the eye is able to produce knowledge, as faith is able to bring forth good works, as human nature is able to produce good or evil karma. v. 五丨and 二十二丨. 丨上下智力 One of a Buddha's ten powers, to know the capacities of all beings, their nature and karma. 丨利 Of penetrative powers, intelligent, in contrast with 丨鈍 dull powers. 丨力 Organs and their powers, the five organs of sense and their five powers. 丨器 Natural capacity, capacity of any organ, or being. 丨境 The field of any organ, its field of operation. 丨塵 The object or sensation of any organ of sense. 丨性 Nature and character; the nature of the powers of any sense. 丨本 Fundamental, basal, radical, original, elemental; when referring to a fundamental text, 丨丨經 mūlagrantha, it indicates a sūtra supposed to contain the original words of the Buddha. 丨丨定; 丨丨禪; 丨丨等至 The stages of dhyāna in the formless or immaterial realm. 丨丨心 Root or fundamental mind. 丨丨惑; 丨丨煩惱 The fundamental illusions, passions, or afflictions—desire, hate, delusion (moha), pride, doubt, bad views (or false opinions); the first five are the 五鈍使; the last represents 五利使 q.v. 丨丨智 Fundamental, original, or primal wisdom, source of all truth and virtue; knowledge of fundamental principles; intuitive knowledge or wisdom, in contrast with acquired wisdom. 丨丨無明; 無始 (or 元始) 無明 Primal ignorance, the condition before discernment and differentiation. 丨丨說一切有部 The Sarvāstivādins, v. 一切有. 丨丨識 Original or fundamental mind or intelligence, a name for the ālayavijñāna. 丨敗 Decay of the powers, or senses. 丨機 Motive power, fundamental ability, opportunity. 丨淨 The purity of the six organs of sense. 丨緣 Nature and environment; natural powers and conditioning environment. 丨門 The senses as doors (through which illusion enters). 丨闕; 丨缺 Defective in any organ of sense, e.g. blind or deaf. 丨香 Putchuk, idem 木香.

殊 To kill, exterminate; different; very. 丨勝 Rare, extraordinary, surpassing, as the 丨勝殿 and 池 surpassing palace and lake of Indra. 丨妙身 Surpassingly wonderful body, i.e. Padmottara, the 729th Buddha of the present kalpa. 丨底(色)迦 Jyotiṣka, 丨丨穡丨; 聚底色迦; 樹提迦 "a luminary, a heavenly body." M. W. Name of a wealthy elder of Rājagṛha, who gave all his goods to the poor. 丨徵伽 One of the four kinds of ascetics who dressed in rags and ate garbage. 丨致阿羅婆 Jyotīrasa, tr. as 光味 flavour of light, said to be the proper name of Kharoṣṭha, v. 佉.

殺 To kill, cut down, cut off. 丨三摩娑 Shaṭsamāsa, cf. 三. 丨業 The karma resulting from killing. 丨生 To take life, kill the living, or any conscious being; the taking of human life offends against the major commands, of animal life against the less stringent commands. Suicide also leads to severe penalties. 丨者 The murderer, a name for Māra. 丨賊 Kṣīṇāsrava, thief-destroyer, i.e. conqueror of the passions, an arhat. 丨鬼 To slay demons; a ghost of the slain; a murderous demon; a metaphor for impermanence.

浮 Floating, drifting, unsettled. 丨孔 A hole in a floating log, through which a one-eyed turtle accidentally obtains a glimpse of the moon, the rarest of chances, e.g. the rareness of meeting a Buddha. 丨囊 A floating bag, a swimming float, a lifebuoy. 丨圖; 丨陀; 丨頭; 丨屠 Buddha; also a stūpa, v. 佛 and 塔. 丨塵 Floating dust or atoms, unstable matter, i.e. phenomena, which hide reality. 丨想 Passing thoughts, unreal fancies. 丨木 A floating log, v. 丨孔. 丨(塵)根; 扶(塵)根 Indriya, the organs of sensation, eye, ear, etc., in contrast with 勝義根 the function or faculty of sensation. 丨雲 A drifting cloud, e.g. this life, the body, etc.

海 Sāgara, the ocean, the sea. 丨印 The ocean symbol, indicating the vastness of the meditation of the Buddha, the vision of all things. 丨德 The eight virtues, or powers of the ocean, i.e. vastness, tidal regularity, throwing out of the dead, containing the seven kinds of pearls, absorption of all rivers, of all rain without increase, holding the most mighty fish, universal unvarying saltness. 丨會 The assembly of the saints; also a cemetery. 丨潮音 The ocean-tide voice, i.e. of the Buddha. 丨珠 Ocean pearls, things hard to obtain. 丨衆 Ocean assembly, i.e. a great assembly of monks, the whole body of monks. 丨龍王 The Ocean-nāga, or Dragon King of the Ocean; hence the 丨丨丨經 sūtra of this name.

浩 Vast, great. 丨妙 Vast and mysterious.

消 Melt, disperse, expend, digest, dispose of.

| 滅 To put an end to, cause to cease. | 災 To disperse, or put an end to calamity. | 瘦 服 The monk's robe as putting an end to illusion. | 釋 To solve and explain. | 除 To eradicate.

流 Flow; float; spread; wander. | 來 Flowed or floated down; that which has come down from the past. | 來 生 死 Transmigration which has come down from the state of primal ignorance. | 支 An abbreviation for Bodhiruci, v. 菩. | 毘 尼; | 彌 尼 Lumbinī, cf. 嵐. | 水 Flowing water, name of a former incarnation of Śākyamuni. | 沙 Floating or shifting sands. | 注 Continuous flow, ceaseless. | 漿 Liquid broth of molten copper, or grains of red-hot iron, in one of the hells. | 舍 那 Locana. Cf. 毘. Often regarded as the body of bliss of Vairocana. | 轉 Saṁsāra, transmigration, flowing and returning, flowing back again. | 轉 門 The way of transmigration, as contrasted with 滅 門 that of nirvāṇa. | 轉 眞 如 The bhūtatathatā, or absolute, in transmigratory forms. | 通 Spread abroad; permeate; flowing through, or everywhere, without effective hindrance.

泰 Prosperous, exalted; many. | 山 T'ai Shan in Shantung, the eastern sacred mountain of China.

浴 To bathe, wash. | 主; 知 |; | 頭 Bath-controller. | 佛; | 像 To wash the image of the Buddha; this is a ceremony on his birthday, 8th of the 4th month. | 室 A bath-house. | 鼓 The bathing-drum, announcing the time for washing in the Ch'an monasteries.

涌 To well up, spring up. | 出 To spring forth. | 泉 The springing fountain, i.e. the sūtras.

涅; 湼 Black mud at the bottom of a pool; muddy; to blacken, defile; the first form is more correct, but the second is more common.

涅哩底 Nirṛti, destruction, the goddess of death and corruption, regent of the south-west. | | | 方 The south-west quarter.

涅槃 Nirvāṇa, "blown out, gone out, put out, extinguished"; "liberated from existence"; "dead, deceased, defunct." "Liberation, eternal bliss"; "(with Buddhists and Jainas) absolute extinction or annihilation, complete extinction of individual existence." M. W. Other forms are | | 那; 泥 日; 泥 洹; 泥 畔 Originally translated 滅 to extinguish, extinction, put out (as a lamp or fire), it was also described as 解 脫 release, 寂 滅 tranquil extinction; 無 爲 inaction, without effort, passiveness; 不 生 no (re)birth; 安 樂 calm joy; 滅 度 transmigration to "extinction". The meaning given to "extinction" varies, e.g. individual extinction; cessation of rebirth; annihilation of passion; extinction of all misery and entry into bliss. While the meaning of individual extinction is not without advocates, the general acceptation is the extinction or end of all return to reincarnation with its concomitant suffering, and the entry into bliss. Nirvāṇa may be enjoyed in the present life as an attainable state, with entry into parinirvāṇa, or perfect bliss to follow. It may be (*a*) with a "remainder", i.e. the cause, but not all the effect (karma), of reincarnation having been destroyed; (*b*) without "remainder", both cause and effect having been extinguished. The answer of the Buddha as to the continued personal existence of the Tathāgata in Nirvāṇa is, in the Hīnayāna canon, relegated "to the sphere of the indeterminates" (Keith), as one of the questions which are not essential to salvation. One argument is that flame when blown out does not perish but returns to the totality of Fire. The Nirvāṇa Sūtra claims for nirvāṇa the ancient ideas of 常 樂 我 淨 permanence, bliss, personality, purity in the transcendental realm. Mahāyāna declares that Hīnayāna by denying personality in the transcendental realm denies the existence of the Buddha. In Mahāyāna final nirvāṇa is transcendental, and is also used as a term for the absolute. The place where the Buddha entered his earthly nirvāṇa is given as Kuśinagara, cf. 拘. | | 佛 The nirvāṇa-form of Buddha; also | | 像 the "sleeping Buddha", i.e. the Buddha entering nirvāṇa. | | 僧 Nivāsana, an inner garment, cf. 泥. | | 八 味 The eight rasa, i.e. flavours, or characteristics of nirvāṇa—permanence, peace, no growing old, no death, purity, transcendence, unperturbedness, joy. | | 分 The part, or lot, of nirvāṇa. | | (寂 靜) 印 The seal or teaching of nirvāṇa, one of the three proofs that a sūtra was uttered by the Buddha, i.e. its teaching of impermanence, non-ego, nirvāṇa; also the witness within to the attainment of nirvāṇa. | | 城 The nirvāṇa city, the abode of the saints. | | 堂 The nirvāṇa hall, or dying place of a monk in a monastery. | | 宗 The School based on the 大 般 | | 經 Mahāparinirvāṇa Sūtra, first tr. by Dharmarakṣa A.D. 423. Under the 陳 Ch'ên dynasty this Nirvāṇa school became merged in the T'ien-t'ai sect. | | 宮 The nirvāṇa palace of the saints. | | 山 The steadfast mountain of nirvāṇa in contrast with the changing stream of mortality. | | 忌; | | 會 The Nirvāṇa assembly, 2nd moon 15th day, on the anniversary of the Buddha's death. | | 月 日 The date of the Buddha's death, variously stated as 2nd moon 15th or 8th day; 8th moon 8th; 3rd moon 15th; and 9th moon 8th. | | 樂 Nirvāṇa-joy or bliss. | | 洲 Nirvāṇa-island, i.e. in the stream of mortality, from which stream the Buddha saves men with his eight-oar boat of truth, v. 八聖道. | | 界 Nirvāṇa-dhātu; the realm of nirvāṇa, or bliss, where all virtues are stored and whence all good comes; one of the 三無爲法. | | 疊那 ? Nidhāpana, Nirdahana, cremation. | | 相 The 8th sign of the Buddha, his entry into nirvāṇa, i.e. his death, after delivering "in one day and night" the 大般 | | 經 Mahāparinirvāṇa sūtra. | | 經 Nirvāṇa sūtra. There are two versions, one the Hīnayāna, the other the Mahāyāna, both of which are translated into Chinese, in several versions, and there are numerous treatises on them. Hīnayāna: 佛般泥洹經 Mahāparinirvāṇa-sūtra, tr. by Po Fa-tsu A.D. 290–306 of the Western Chin dynasty, B.N. 552. 大般涅槃經 tr. by Fa-hsien, B.N. 118. 般泥洹經 translator unknown. These are different translations of the same work. In the Āgamas 阿含 there is also a Hīnayāna Nirvāṇa sūtra. Mahāyāna: 佛說方等般泥洹經 Caturdāraka-samādhi-sūtra, tr. by Dharmarakṣa of the Western Chin A.D. 265–316, B.N. 116. 大般泥洹經 Mahāparinirvāṇa-sūtra, tr. by Fa-hsien, together with Buddhabhadra of the Eastern Chin, A.D. 317–420, B.N. 120, being a similar and incomplete translation of B.N. 113, 114. 四童子三昧經 Caturdāraka-samādhi-sūtra, tr. by Jñānagupta of the Sui dynasty, A.D. 589–618, B.N. 121. The above three differ, though they are the first part of the Nirvāṇa sūtra of the Mahāyāna. The complete translation is 大般涅槃經 tr. by Dharmarakṣa A.D. 423, B.N. 113; v. a partial translation of fasc. 12 and 39 by Beal, in his *Catena of Buddhist Scriptures*, pp. 160–188. It is sometimes called 北本 or Northern Book, when compared with its revision, the Southern Book, i.e. 南本大般涅槃經 Mahāparinirvāṇa-sūtra, produced in Chien-yeh, the modern Nanking, by two Chinese monks, Hui-yen and Hui-kuan, and a literary man, Hsieh Ling-yün. B.N. 114. 大般涅槃經後分 The latter part of the Mahāparinirvāṇa-sūtra tr. by Jñānabhadra together with Hui-ning and others of the T'ang dynasty, B.N. 115, a continuation of the last chapter of B.N. 113 and 114. | | 縛 The fetter of nirvāṇa, i.e. the desire for it, which hinders entry upon the Bodhisattva life of saving others; it is the fetter of Hīnayāna, resulting in imperfect nirvāṇa. | | 聖 Nickname of 道生 Tao-shêng, pupil of Kumārajīva, tr. part of the Nirvāṇa sūtra, asserted the eternity of Buddha, for which he was much abused, hence the nickname. | | 色 Nirvāṇa-colour, i.e. black, representing the north. | | 門 The gate or door into nirvāṇa; also the northern gate of a cemetery. | | 際 The region of nirvāṇa in contrast with that of mortality. | | 風 The nirvāṇa-wind which wafts the believer into bodhi. | | 食 Nirvāṇa food; the passions are faggots, wisdom is fire, the two prepare nirvāṇa as food.

涅迦羅 Niṣkala, without parts; seedless; indivisible; or perhaps niṣkāla, but a short time to live, intp. as 暫時 a short time, temporary.

烝 To steam; advance; all. | 砂作飯 Like cooking sand for food.

烈 Burning, fierce; virtuous, heroic. | 士池 Tyāgihrada, Jīvakahrada, the lake of the renouncer, or of the hero, near to the Mrgadāva.

烟 Smoke; also tobacco, opium. | 蓋 Smoke (of incense) like a canopy.

烏 The crow; black, not; ah! alas! translit. chiefly *u*; cf. 優; 盂; 鬱; 鄔; 塢.

烏仗那 Udyāna, a park or garden; the park (of Aśoka); an "ancient kingdom in the north-west of India, the country along the Śubhavastu; the Suastene of the Greeks, noted for its forests, flowers, and fruits". Eitel. Also | 杖那; | 場; | 萇; | 孫; | 儞也曩; | 耆延那 said to be the present Yūsufzai.

烏倶婆誐 Ugra-bhaga, formidable or fierce lord, one of the eight servants of 不動明王 q.v.

烏剌尸 Uraśī, or Uraśā; anciently in Kashmir, "the region south-west of Serinagur, Lat. 33° 23 N., Long. 74° 47 E." Eitel. The Hazāra district.

烏地多 "The king of an unknown country in Northern India who patronized Hsüan-tsang (A.D. 640)." Eitel.

烏摩 Unmada, 優摩陀 a demon or god of craziness or intoxication. | | 妃 Umā, "flax," "wife of Rudra and Śiva" (M. W.), intp. as wife of Śiva, and as a symbol of 貪 covetousness, desire, Umā being described as trampling Śiva under her left foot.

烏枕南 Udāna, breathing upwards a solemn utterance, or song of joy, intp. as unsolicited or voluntary statements, i.e. by the Buddha, in contrast with replies to questions; it is a section of Buddhist literature.

烏沙斯 Uṣas. The dawn, but intp. as the planet Venus.

烏波 Upādāna, laying hold of, grasp; hence material, things; it transliterates Bhāva, and is intp. as 有 to have, be, exist, things, the resultant or karma of all previous and the cause of all future lives. v. 取 and 優. 丨丨斯迦; 優丨夷 (or 賜迦) Upāsikā, female disciples who remain at home. 丨丨提 Upādhi; a condition; peculiar, limited, special; the upādhi-nirvāṇa is the 苦 or wretched condition of heretics. 丨丨级多 Upagupta, also 鄔 and 優, a Śūdra by birth, who became the fourth patriarch. 丨丨第鑠; 鄔丨提丨; 優丨提舍 Upadeśa, a section of Buddhist literature, general treatises; a synonym for the Abhidharmapiṭaka, and for the Tantras of the Yogācāra school. 丨丨索 (or 娑) 迦; 優婆塞; 優波娑迦 Upāsaka, lay male disciples who remain at home and observe the moral commandments. 丨丨陀耶; 有波弟耶夜; 和尙 (or 闍 or 闍) Upādhyāya, originally a subsidiary teacher of the Vedāṅgas; later, through Central Asia, it became a term for a teacher of Buddhism, in distinction from 律師 disciplinists and 禪師 intuitionalists, but as Ho-shang it attained universal application to all masters. 丨(or 塢)丨難陀 Upananda, a disciple of Śākyamuni; also one of the eight Nāga-kings in the Garbhadhātu. 丨丨髻使者; 丨婆計設尼 Upakeśinī, one of the messengers of Mañjuśrī.

烏洛迦旃檀 Uraga(sāra)-candana, serpent-sandal, a kind of sandal wood, used as a febrifuge. 丨丨丨; 丨羅伽 Uraga, going on the belly, a serpent.

烏瑟(膩沙) Uṣṇīṣa, a turban, diadem, distinguishing mark; intp. as 佛頂 the crown of the Buddha's head; and 肉髻 fleshy tuft or coif, one of the thirty-two lakṣaṇāni of a Buddha, generally represented as a protuberance on the frontal crown. Also 塢丨丨丨; 丨失尼丨; 鬱 (or 嗢) 丨丨丨.

烏耆 Agni, or Akni, an ancient kingdom north of Lop Nor, identified with Karashahr. Also 阿耆尼; 偽夷.

烏芻瑟摩 ? Ucchuṣma. One of the 明王 ming wang; he presides over the cesspool and is described both as "unclean" and as "fire-head"; he is credited with purifying the unclean. Also 丨丨沙丨; 丨丨澁丨; 丨樞丨丨(or 沙 丨); 丨素沙丨.

烏茶 Uḍa, Uḍradeśa, Oḍra, Oḍivisa; an ancient country of eastern India with a busy port called 折利呾羅 Charitrapura (Hsüan-tsang), probably the province of Orissa.

烏落 Ulak; Ulag; a Uigur term meaning horse, indicating relays of post-horses.

烏菴 Om or Aum; cf. 唵.

烏逋沙他 Upavasatha (Pali, Uposatha). A fast-day, originally in preparation for the brahminical soma sacrifice; in Buddhism there are six fast-days in the month.

烏鐸迦漢茶 ? Uṭabhāṇḍa, or Uḍakhāṇḍa, an ancient city of Gandhāra, on the northern bank of the Indus, identified with Ohind; Eitel gives it as "the modern Attok".

烏闍衍那 Ujjayinī, Ujjain, Oujein, 優禪那 the Greek Ozēnē, in Avanti (Mālava), one of the seven sacred cities of the Hindus, and the first meridian of their geographers, from which they calculate longitude; the modern Ujjain is about a mile south of the ancient city. M. W.

烏陀衍那 Udayana, a king of Vatsa, or Kauśāmbī, "contemporary of Śākyamuni," of whom he is said to have had the first statue made.

特 A bull, stallion; outstanding, special, alone. 丨勝 Special, extraordinary. 丨尊 The outstanding honoured one. 丨欹拏伽陀 Dakṣiṇāgāthā, a song offering, or expression of gratitude by a monk for food or gifts.

狼 A wolf; fierce. 丨跡山 Wolf track hill, another name for 鷄足山 q.v.

珠 Maṇi. A pearl; a bead; synonym for Buddha-truth. 丨利耶 Culya, Caula, Cola. "An ancient kingdom in the north-east corner of the present Madras presidency, described A.D. 640 as a scarcely cultivated country with semi-savage and anti-Buddhistic inhabitants." Eitel.

班 A class, rank, band; translit. *pan*. 丨禪喇嘛; 丨禪額爾德尼 The Tibetan Panchen-lama.

留 Keep, detain; hand down. 丨拏 Ruṇṇapaṇḍakas, castrated males. 丨難 The difficulty of one's good deeds being hindered by evil spirits.

畔 A path between fields, or boundary; to trespass; translit. *ban*, *van*, *par*, *pra*. v. 船, 班, etc.

｜喋婆 ? Vātyā. A great calamitous wind. ｜彈南 ; ｜睇 Vandana, v. 和.

畜 To rear, feed, domesticate ; restrain ; cattle. ｜生 Tiryagyoni, 底栗車 ; 傍生 "Born of or as an animal," rebirth as an animal ; animals in general ; especially domestic animals. ｜｜因 The cause, or karma, of rebirth as an animal. ｜｜界 The animal kingdom. ｜｜道 ; ｜｜趣 The way, destiny, or gati of rebirth as animals, cf. 六道 ; 六趣.

疾 Sickness, an attack of illness ; haste, speedy ; angry. ｜書 Hasty writing ; a hurried note ; write speedily, or at once.

病 Illness, disease ; to hurt. ｜子 Just as a mother loves the sick child most, so Buddha loves the most wicked sinner. Nirvāṇa Sūtra 30.

盎 A bowl ; abundant ; translit. *ang*. ｜哦囉迦 Aṅgāraka, the planet Mars. ｜窶利魔羅 Aṅgulimālīya ; 指鬘 A wreath, or chaplet, of finger-bones ; a Śivaitic sect which practised assassination as a religious act.

眠 To close the eyes, to sleep. ｜藏 A monastic sleeping-room.

眞 True, real ; verisimilitude, e.g. a portrait. 眞丹 ; 震旦 ; 神丹 An ancient Indian term for China ; v. 支那.

眞乘 The true vehicle, i.e. the true teaching or doctrine.

眞人 One who embodies the Truth, an arhat ; a Buddha.

眞俗 Truth and convention ; the true view and the ordinary ; reality and appearance. 眞 is 空, and 俗 is 假.

眞佛 The real Buddha, i.e. the saṁbhogakāya, or reward body, in contrast to the nirmāṇakāya, or manifested body. Also the Dharmakāya 法身 q.v. ｜｜子 A true Buddha son, i.e. one who has attained the first stage of bodhisattvahood according to the 別教 definition, i.e. the unreality of the ego and phenomena.

眞化 The teaching of the 眞宗 True (or Shin) sect. ｜化二身 The 眞 is the dharmakāya and saṁbhogakāya, and the 化 the nirmāṇakāya ; v. 三身.

眞因 The true cause ; reality as cause.

眞境 The region of truth or reality.

眞妄 True and false, real and unreal. (1) That which has its rise in Buddha-truth, meditation, and wisdom is true ; that which arises from the influences of unenlightenment is untrue. (2) The essential bhūtatathatā as the real, phenomena as the unreal. ｜妄二心 The true and false minds, i.e. (1) The true bhūtatathatā mind, defined as the ninth or Amalavijñāna. (2) The false or illusion mind as represented by the eight vijñānas, 八識.

眞如 Bhūtatathatā, 部多多他多. The 眞 is intp. as ｜實 the real, 如 as 如常 thus always, or eternally so ; i.e. reality as contrasted with 虛妄 unreality, or appearance, and 不變不改 unchanging or immutable as contrasted with form and phenomena. It resembles the ocean in contrast with the waves. It is the eternal, impersonal, unchangeable reality behind all phenomena. Bhūta is substance, that which exists ; tathatā is suchness, thusness, i.e. such is its nature. The word is fundamental to Mahāyana philosophy, implying the absolute, the ultimate source and character of all phenomena, it is the All. It is also called 自性清淨心 self-existent pure Mind ; 佛性 Buddha-nature ; 法身 Dharmakāya ; 如來藏 Tathāgata-garbha, or Buddha-treasury ; 實相 reality ; 法界 Dharma-realm ; 法性 Dharma-nature ; 圓成實性 The complete and perfect real nature, or reality. There are categories of 1, 2, 3, 7, 10, and 12 in number : (1) The undifferentiated whole. (2) There are several antithetical classes, e.g. the unconditioned and the conditioned ; the 空 void, static, abstract, noumenal, and the 不空 not-void, dynamic, phenomenal ; pure, and affected (or infected) ; undefiled (or innocent), i.e. that of Buddhas, defiled, that of all beings ; in bonds and free ; inexpressible, and expressible in words. (3) 無相 Formless ; 無生 uncreated ; 無性 without nature, i.e. without characteristics or qualities, absolute in itself. Also, as relative, i.e. good, bad, and indeterminate. (7, 10, 12) The 7 are given in the 唯識論 8 ; the 10 are in two classes, one of the 別教, cf. 唯識論 8 ; the other of the 圓教, cf. 菩提心義 4 ; the 12 are given in the Nirvāṇa sūtra.

眞如一實 Bhūtatathatā the only reality, the one bhūtatathatā reality.

眞如三昧 The meditation in which all phenomena are eliminated and the bhūtatathatā or absolute is realized.

眞如內熏 The internal perfuming or influence of the bhūtatathatā, or Buddha-spirituality.

眞如實相 The essential characteristic or mark (lakṣaṇa) of the bhūtatathatā, i.e. reality. 眞如 is bhūtatathatā from the point of view of the void, attributeless absolute; 實相 is bhūtatathatā from the point of view of phenomena.

眞如海 The ocean of the bhūtatathatā, limitless.

眞如法身 The absolute as dharmakāya, or spiritual body, all embracing.

眞如緣起 The absolute in its causative or relative condition; the bhūtatathatā influenced by environment, or pure and impure conditions, produces all things, v. 緣起.

眞如隨緣 The conditioned bhūtatathatā, i.e. as becoming; it accords with the 無明染緣 unconscious and tainting environment to produce all phenomena.

眞妙 The mysterious reality; reality in its profundity.

眞子 A son of the True One, i.e. the Tathāgata; a Buddha-son, one who embodies Buddha's teaching.

眞宗 The true sect or teaching, a term applied by each sect to its own teaching; the teaching which makes clear the truth of the bhūtatathatā. The True Sect, or Shin Sect of Japan, founded by Shinran in A.D. 1224, known also as the Hongwanji sect; celibacy of priests is not required; Amida is the especial object of trust, and his Pure Land of hope.

眞實 Tattva. Truth, reality; true, real. | | 明 The Truth-wisdom, or Buddha-illumination, i.e. prajñā. | | 智 Tattvajñāna, knowledge of absolute truth. | | 際 The region of reality, the bhūtatathatā.

眞寂 The true Buddha-nirvāṇa as contrasted with that of the Hīnayāna.

眞常 True and eternal; the eternal reality of Buddha-truth.

眞影 A reflection of the true, i.e. a portrait, photograph, image, etc.

眞性 The true nature; the fundamental nature of each individual, i.e. the Buddha-nature.

眞應二身 The Dharmakāya and Nirmāṇakāya; v. 三身.

眞我 (1) The real or nirvāṇa ego, the transcendental ego, as contrasted with the illusory or temporal ego. (2) The ego as considered real by non-Buddhists.

眞文 The writings of Truth, those giving the words of the Buddha or bodhisattvas.

眞明 True knowledge or enlightenment (in regard to reality in contrast with appearance).

眞智 Wisdom or knowledge of ultimate truth, or the absolute, also called 無智 knowledge of the no-thing, i.e. of the immaterial or absolute; also 聖智 sage wisdom, or wisdom of the sage.

眞普賢 A true P'u-hsien or Samantabhadra, a living incarnation of him.

眞法 The real or absolute dharma without attributes, in contrast to phenomena which are regarded as momentary constructs. | | 界 The region of reality apart from the temporal and unreal.

眞淨 The true and pure teaching of the Mahāyāna, in contrast to the Hīnayāna.

眞無漏智 The true knowledge of the Mahāyāna in its concept of mental reality, in contrast with Hīnayāna concepts of material reality.

眞理 Truth, the true principle, the principle of truth; the absolute apart from phenomena.

眞發明性 The spirit of true enlightenment, i.e. the discipline of the mind for the development of the fundamental spiritual or Buddha-nature.

眞空 (1) The absolute void, complete vacuity, said to be the nirvāṇa of the Hīnayāna. (2) The essence of the bhūtatathatā, as the 空眞如 of the 起信論, 唯識, and 華嚴. (3) The void or immaterial as reality, as essential or substantial, the 非空之空 not-void void, the ultimate reality, the highest Mahāyāna concept of true voidness, or of ultimate reality. | | 妙有 The true void is the mysteriously existing; truly void, or immaterial, yet transcendentally existing.

眞色 The mystic or subtle form of the bhūtatathatā, or absolute, the form of the void, or immaterial, Dharmakāya.

眞解脫 Release from all the hindrances of passion and attainment of the Buddha's nirvāṇa, which is not a permanent state of absence from the needs of the living, but is spiritual, omniscient, and liberating.

眞見道 The realization of reality in the absolute as whole and undivided, one of the 見道位.

眞覺 The true and complete enlightenment, i.e. the perfect nirvāṇa of the Buddha; the perception of ultimate truth.

眞言 True words, words of Truth, the words of the Tathāgata, Buddha-truth. The term is used for mantra and dhāraṇī, indicating magical formulæ, spells, charms, esoteric words. Buddhas and Bodhisattvas have each an esoteric sound represented by a Sanskrit letter, the primary Vairocana letter, the alpha of all sounds being "a" 阿, which is also styled | | 救世者 the True Word that saves the world. | | 乘 The True Word, or Mantra-Vehicle, called also the supernatural vehicle, because of immediate attainment of the Buddha-land through tantric methods. | | 宗 The True-word or Shingon sect, founded on the mystical teaching "of all Buddhas", the "very words" of the Buddhas; the especial authority being Vairocana; cf. the 大日 sūtra, 金剛頂經; 蘇悉地經, etc. The founding of the esoteric sect is attributed to Vairocana, through the imaginary Bodhisattva Vajrasattva, then through Nāgārjuna to Vajramati and to Amoghavajra, *circa* A.D. 733; the latter became the effective propagator of the Yogācāra school in China; he is counted as the sixth patriarch of the school and the second in China. The three esoteric duties of body, mouth, and mind are to hold the symbol in the hand, recite the dhāraṇīs, and ponder over the word "a" 阿 as the principle of the ungenerated, i.e. the eternal. | | 智 The mantra wisdom, which surpasses all other wisdom. | | 秘密 The mystic nature of the mantras and dhāraṇīs; the esoteric things of Shingon.

眞說 True speech or teaching; the words of the Buddha.

眞詮 Commentaries or treatises on reality.

眞語 True words, especially as expressing the truth of the bhūtatathatā; the words of the Tathāgata as true and consistent.

眞諦 The asseverations or categories of reality, in contrast with 俗 | ordinary categories; they are those of the sage, or man of insight, in contrast with those of the common man, who knows only appearance and not reality. | | 三藏 Paramārtha 波羅末陀, also called ? Guṇarata 拘那羅陀 or Kulanātha, from Ujjain in western India, who came to China A.D. 546, and is famous as translator or editor, e.g. of the 起信論.

眞證 Real evidence, proof, or assurance, or realization of truth. The knowledge, concept, or idea which corresponds to reality.

眞識 Buddha-wisdom; the original unadulterated, or innocent mind in all, which is independent of birth and death; cf. 楞伽經 and 起信論. Real knowledge free from illusion, the sixth vijñāna.

眞身 The true body, corpus of truth, dharmakāya, Buddha as absolute.

眞道 The Truth; the true way; reality.

眞金 Pure gold. | | 像 An image of pure gold; the body of the Buddha. | | 山 A mountain of pure gold, i.e. Buddha's body.

眞門 The gateway of truth, or reality; the Truth; the school of perfect truth, in contrast with partial truth adapted to the condition of the disciple.

眞際 The region of reality, ultimate truth, idem | 實 |.

矩 A carpenter's square, a rule; translit. *ku*,

cf. 姑, 拘, 鳩. 丨奢揭羅補羅 Kuśāgrapura, v. 吉祥 and cf. 拘尸那. 丨拉婆 Kurava or Uttarakuru, v. 鬱 the northern of the four great continents. 丨矩吒 Kukkuṭa, a cock, fowl. 丨丨丨瑿說羅 Kukkuṭeśvara, Korea.

破 To break, disrupt, destroy, cause schism; solve, disprove, refute, negate. 丨僧 To disrupt a monk's meditation or preaching, also 丨和合僧 Saṅghabheda, disrupt the harmony of the community of monks, to cause schism, e.g. by heretical opinions. 丨地獄 To break open the gates of hell, by chants and incantations, for the release of a departed spirit. 丨執 To refute (false) tenets, e.g. the belief in the reality of the ego and things. 丨壞 To destroy. 丨壞善 Destroyer of good, a name for Māra. 丨夏 To neglect the summer retreat. 丨戒 To break the commandments. 丨有 To refute the belief in the reality of things; to break the power of transmigration as does the Buddha. 丨正 That which denies the truth, e.g. heresy. 丨正命 An incorrect or wrong form of livelihood. 丨法 To break the (Buddha-)law, e.g. by the adoption of heresy. 丨相宗 The sects established by Yung-ming 永明, Ching-ying 淨影, and Hui-yüan 慧遠, which held the unreality of all things. 丨立 also called 遮照 Refuting and establishing; by refuting to prove, or to establish, i.e. in refuting the particular to prove the universal, and vice versa. 丨薩提 Upaśānti, tranquillity, calm. 丨(邪)顯(正) To break, or disprove the false and make manifest the right. 丨門 To break a door, leave a sect. 丨闇滿願 To destroy darkness or ignorance and fulfil the Buddha-vow, i.e. that of Amitābha. 丨顏微笑 To break into a smile, the mark of Kāśyapa's enlightenment when Buddha announced on Vulture Peak that he had a teaching which was propagated from mind to mind, a speech taken as authoritative by the Intuitional School. 丨魔 To overcome the māras, exorcise demons. 丨齋 To break the monastic rule of the regulation food, or time for meals, for which the punishment is hell, or to become a hungry ghost like the kind with throats small as needles and distended bellies, or to become an animal.

祝 To invoke, either to bless or curse. 丨聖 To invoke blessings on the emperor's birthday.

祖 Grandfather; ancestor; patriarch; founder; origin. See 二十八丨. 丨師 A first teacher, or leader, founder of a school or sect; it has particular reference to Bodhidharma.

祠 The spring ancestral sacrifice; the spring; ancestral temple, tablet, etc. 丨堂 An ancestral temple or hall. 丨堂銀 An endowment for masses to be said for the departed, also 長生銀; 無盡財.

祇 To revere, venerate; only; translit. *j* in 丨園精舍; 丨樹給孤獨園 The vihāra and garden Jetavana, bought by Anāthapiṇḍaka from prince Jeta and given to Śākyamuni.

神 Inscrutable spiritual powers, or power; a spirit; a deva, god, or divinity; the human spirit; divine, spiritual, supernatural.

神人 Gods, or spirits, and men.

神仙; 丨僊 The genii, immortals, ṛṣi, of whom the five kinds are 天, 神, 人, 地, and 鬼仙, i.e. deva, spirit, human, earth (or cave), and preta immortals.

神供 Offerings placed before the gods or spirits.

神光 Deva-light, the light of the gods.

神力 v. 丨通.

神咒 Ṛddhi-mantra, or dhāraṇī; divine or magic incantations.

神坐 Deva or spirit thrones.

神域 The realm of spirit, of reality, surpassing thought, supra-natural.

神女 A devī, a female spirit; a sorceress.

神妙 Mysterious, mystic, occult, recondite, marvellous.

神我 Puruṣa, or Ātman. The soul, the spiritual ego, or permanent person, which by non-Buddhists was said to migrate on the death of the body. Puruṣa is also the Supreme Soul, or Spirit, which produces all forms of existence.

神明 The spirits of heaven and earth, the gods; also the intelligent or spiritual nature.

神智 Spiritual wisdom, divine wisdom which comprehends all things, material and immaterial.

神根 The vital spirit as the basis of bodily life.

神識 The intelligent spirit, also called 靈魂 the soul; incomprehensible or divine wisdom.

神變 Supernatural influences causing the changes in natural events; miracles; miraculous transformations, e.g. the transforming powers of a Buddha, both in regard to himself and others; also his miraculous acts, e.g. unharmed by poisonous snakes, unburnt by dragon fire, etc. Tantra, or Yogācāra.

神足(通) Deva-foot ubiquity. Ṛddhipāda; ṛddhi-sākṣātkriyā. Also 神境智通; 如意通 Supernatural power to appear at will in any place, to fly or go without hindrance, to have absolute freedom; cf. 大敎. 丨丨月 The first, fifth, and ninth months, when the devas go on circuit throughout the earth.

神通(力) Ubiquitous supernatural power, especially of a Buddha, his ten powers including power to shake the earth, to issue light from his pores, extend his tongue to the Brahma-heavens effulgent with light, cause divine flowers, etc., to rain from the sky, be omnipresent, and other powers. Supernatural powers of eye, ear, body, mind, etc. 丨丨月 idem 丨足月. 丨丨乘 The supernatural or magic vehicle, i.e. the esoteric sect of 眞言 Shingon.

神道 The spirit world of devas, asuras, and pretas. Psychology, or the doctrines concerning the soul. The teaching of Buddha. Shintō, the Way of the Gods, a Japanese national religion.

神闇 The darkened mind without faith.

秦 The Ch'in state and dynasty, 255–205 B.C. 大丨 Syria, the Eastern Roman Empire. 丨廣王 Ch'in-kuang, the first of the ten kings of Hades.

秣 To feed a horse; translit. *ma*. 丨兎羅 Mathurā, v. 摩. 丨奴若瞿沙 Manojñaghoṣa, an ancient bhikṣu. 丨底補羅 Matipura, an "ancient kingdom (and city) the kings of which in A.D. 600 belonged to the Śūdra caste, the home of many famous priests. The present Rohilcund (Rohilkhand) between the Ganges and Rāmagaṅgā". 丨羅娑 Malasa. "A mountain valley in the upper Pundjab." 丨羅矩吒 Malakūṭa. "An ancient kingdom of Southern India, the coast of Malabar, about A.D. 600 a noted haunt of the Nirgrantha sect." Eitel.

秘 Secret, occult, esoteric; opposite of 顯. 丨印 Esoteric signs, or seals. 丨奥 Secret, mysterious. 丨宗; 密敎 The esoteric Mantra or Yogācāra sect, developed especially in 眞言 Shingon, with Vairocana 大日如來 as the chief object of worship, and the maṇḍalas of the Garbhadhātu and Vajradhātu. 丨密 Secret, occult, esoteric, mysterious, profound. 丨丨(上)乘 The esoteric (superior) vehicle, i.e. the above sect. 丨丨主 Vajrasattva, cf. 金剛薩埵, who is king of Yakṣas and guardian of the secrets of Buddhas. 丨丨咒 The mantras, or incantations of the above sect. 丨丨號 Its dhāraṇīs. 丨丨壇 Its altars. 丨丨宗 The (above) esoteric sect. 丨丨戒 Its commandments. 丨(丨)敎 Its teaching; the sect itself; one of the four modes of teaching defined by the T'ien-t'ai; a name for the 圓敎. 丨丨瑜伽 The yoga rules of the esoteric sect; also a name for the sect. 丨(丨)經 Its sūtras. 丨丨結集 The collection of mantras, dhāraṇīs, etc., and of the Vajradhātu and Garbhadhātu literature, attributed to Ānanda, or Vajrasattva, or both. 丨(丨)藏 The treasury of the profound wisdom, or mysteries, variously interpreted. 丨決 or 訣 Secret, magical incantations. 丨法 The mysteries of the esoteric sect. 丨要 The essence, the profoundly important.

竝 Together, idem 並. 丨起 To arise together.

笈 A satchel, book-box; translit. *g*. 丨多 Upagupta, v. 優. 丨房鉢底; 憍梵波提 Gavāṁpati, a monk with the feet and cud-chewing characteristic of an ox, because he had spilled some grains from an ear of corn he plucked in a former life.

粉 Flour, meal, powder. 丨骨碎身 Bones ground to powder and body in fragments.

紙 Paper. 丨葉 Palm-leaves. 丨衣, 丨冠, 丨錢 Paper clothing, hats, money, etc., burnt as offerings to the dead.

純 One-coloured, unadulterated, pure, sincere. 丨一 Pure, unmixed, solely, simply, entirely. 丨眞 Sincere, true; name of a man who asked the Buddha questions which are replied to in a sūtra. 丨陀 Cunda, who is believed to have supplied Śākyamuni with his last meal; it is said to have been of 旃檀耳 q.v., but there are other accounts including a stew of flesh food; also 准丨, 淳丨, 周那.

索 Cord; to extort, express; the cord or noose of Kuan-yin by which she binds the good; the cord of the vajra-king by which he binds the evil; translit. *sa.* 丨哆 v. 薩 Sattva. 丨訶; 丨阿 v. 娑 Sahā, the world. 丨語; 丨話 Express, expression (in words); forced statements, a demand or request (e.g. for information).

素 Original colour or state; plain, white; heretofore, usual; translit. *su.* 丨具 Already prepared. 丨嚩哩拏; 蘇伐羅; 修跋拏 Suvarṇa; v. 金 gold. 丨意; 丨懷 Ordinary thoughts, or hopes; the common purposes of the mind. 丨怛纜 v. 修 Sūtra. 丨法身 Possessing the fundamental dharmakāya nature though still in sin, i.e. the beings in the three lowest orders of transmigration. 丨絹 Plain silk lustring, thin silk. 丨豪 The ūrṇā, or white curl between the Buddha's eyebrows. 丨食; 丨饌 Vegetarian food.

納 Offer; pay, give; receive, take; translit. *na*; cf. 衲. 丨具 To accept all the commandments, or rules. 丨加梨 v. 衲. 丨受; 丨得 To receive, accept. 丨帽 A cap made of bits of given material. 丨慕; 丨莫; 丨謨 v. 南無 Namaḥ. 丨戒 To receive or accept the commandments. 丨播 A stole worn during teaching. 丨縛僧伽藍 Navasaṅghārāma. "An ancient monastery near Baktra, famous for three relics of Śākyamuni (a tooth, basin, and staff)." Eitel. 丨縛提婆矩羅 Navadevakula. "An ancient city, a few miles south-east of Kanyākūbdja, on the eastern bank of the Ganges. The present Nobatgang." Eitel. 丨縛波 Na-fu-po, Hsüan-tsang's name for a city on the ancient site of I-hsün 伊循, capital of Shan-shan 鄯善 in the Former Han dynasty, afterwards known as Nob or Lop (in Marco Polo). It corresponds to the modern Charkhlik. 丨蛇於筒 To put a snake into a tube, i.e. meditation able to confine unruly thoughts. 丨衣 Garments made of castaway rags, the patch-robe of a monk. 丨骨 To bury bones, or a skeleton.

缺 Broken; deficient, lacking; a vacancy, a post. 丨漏 A breach and leakage, a breach of the discipline.

罣 See under Eleven Strokes.

翅 A wing, fin; translit. *ke.* 丨夷羅 Feather robes. 丨内邏; 枳丨羅; 吉丨攞 Keyūra, an armlet, necklace. 丨舍欽婆羅 Keśakambala, a hair garment or covering; name of one of the ten heretical Indian schools.

耆 Old, 60 years of age, experienced; translit. *ji, g.* 丨婆; 丨域; 時縛迦 Jīva, Jīvaka. Son of Bimbisāra by the concubine Āmrapālī. On his birth he is said to have seized the acupuncture needle and bag. He became famed for his medical skill. 丨婆天 Jīva, the deva of long life. 丨婆鳥 idem 命命鳥, also 丨婆丨婆(迦); 闍婆者婆(丨) A bird of the partridge family; there is a fable about such a bird having two heads, called 迦嘍嗏 garuḍa, and 憂波丨丨丨 upagaruḍa; one ate a delicious flower while the other was asleep; when the latter awoke, it was so annoyed at not sharing it that it ate a poisonous flower and the bird died; thus there is a Jekyll and Hyde in every one. 丨那 Jina, victor, he who overcomes, a title of every Buddha; also the name of various persons; the Jaina religion, the Jains. 丨闍 Gṛdhra, a vulture, also an abbrev. for 丨丨崛; 伊沙堀; 揭梨馱羅鳩胝; 姞栗陀羅矩吒 Gṛdhrakūṭa; a mountain near Rājagṛha said to be shaped like a vulture's head, or to be famous for its vultures and its caverns inhabited by ascetics, where Piśuna (Māra), in the shape of a vulture, hindered the meditations of Ānanda. It has numerous other names.

耻; 恥 Shame; ashamed. 丨小慕大 Ashamed of the small (Hīnayāna) and in love with the great (Mahāyāna).

脂 Fat, lard; gum; soapstone; wealth; translit. *ci, cai*; see 支. 丨那 China; intp. as the country of culture, with a people clothed and capped; also as a frontier (of India), a place of banishment. 丨帝浮圖 Caitya, a stūpa, a mausoleum, a place or object of worship.

脇 The ribs, flanks, sides; forceful, to coerce. 丨侍; 挾侍; 丨士 Bodhisattvas, or other images on either side of a Buddha. 丨尊 v. 波 Pārśva.

胸 The breast. 丨字 The svastika on Buddha's breast, one of the thirty-two marks. 丨行 Creatures that crawl on their bellies, like snakes.

能 Śak. Able to, can; capability, power. 丨人 An able man, i.e. Buddha as the all-powerful man able to transform the world. 丨仁 Mighty in loving-kindness, an incorrect interpretation of Śākyamuni, but probably indicating his character. 丨依 Dependent on, that which relies on something else, e.g. vegetation on land; 所依 is that on which it relies. 丨信 Can believe, or can be believed, contrasted with 所信 that which is believed. 丨大師; 丨行者 The sixth patriarch 慧丨 Hui-nêng of the

Ch'an (Zen) School. | 所 These two terms indicate active and passive ideas, e.g. ability to transform, or transformable and the object that is transformed. | 持 Ability to maintain, e.g. to keep the commandments. | 斷金剛經 Vajracchedikā-sūtra, the "Diamond Sūtra", translated by Hsüan-tsang, an extract from the Prajñāpāramitā-sūtra. | 施太子 Prince "Giver", a former incarnation of Śākyamuni, when he obtained the magic dragon-pearl and by its power relieved the needs of all the poor. | 立 A proposition in logic that can be established, or postulated. | 緣 The conditioning power in contrast with the conditioned, e.g. the power of seeing and hearing in contrast with that which is seen and heard.

臭 Stink, stinking; smell. | 口 (or 毛) 鬼 Demons with stinking breath, or hair.

般 A sort, a kind; translit. *par*, *pra*, *pan*, *pa*, etc.

般利伐羅句迦 Parivrājaka, or Wanderer. "A Śivaitic sect, worshippers of Mahēśvara, who wear clothes of the colour of red soil and leave a little hair about the crown of the head, shaving off the rest." Eitel. Also 波利呾羅拘迦; 簸利婆闍迦.

般剌蜜帝 Pramiti, Paramiti, a monk from Central India, tr. the Śūraṅgama sūtra 首楞嚴經 A.D. 705.

般泥洹 Parinirvāṇa; v. next entry.

般涅槃(那) Parinirvāṇa; "quite extinguished, quite brought to an end; the final extinction of the individual." M. W. The death of the Buddha. Nirvāṇa may be attained in this life, parinirvāṇa after it; for the meaning of "extinction" v. 涅槃. It may also correspond to the suppression of all mental activity. It is also the second of the three grades of nirvāṇa, parinirvāṇa, and mahānirvāṇa, which are later developments and have association with the ideas of Hīnayāna, Madhyamayāna, and Mahāyāna, or the small, middle, and great vehicles; also with the three grades of bodhi which these three vehicles represent; and the three classes of śrāvakas, pratyeka-buddhas, and bodhisattvas. Other forms are: | 利 | | |; 波利 | | |; | 尼洹.

般羅颯迷 Parasmaipada. "The transitive or active verb and its terminations." M. W

般舟 Pratyutpanna, present; multiplied. | | (三昧) Pratyutpannasamādhi, the samādhi in which the Buddhas of the ten directions are seen as clearly as the stars at night. Also called 常行道 or 常行三昧 the prolonged samādhi, because of the length of time required, either seven or ninety days. Its sūtra is the | | | | 經.

般荼迦 Paṇḍaka. The general name for eunuchs. The five classes with various degrees of sexual impotence: (1) 扇搋 Ṣaṇḍha(paṇḍaka); by birth impotent. (2) 留拏 Rugṇa or Ruṇḍa paṇḍaka; "maimed," i.e. emasculated males. (3) 伊梨沙掌拏 Īrṣyā(paṇḍaka); those whose sexual desires are only aroused by jealousy. (4) 半擇迦 Paṇḍaka are eunuchs in general, but in this category are described as hermaphrodites. (5) 博叉 Pakṣa-(pāṇḍaka); impotent during one-half of the month. A newer classification distinguishes those with incomplete from those with complete organs; the incomplete being (1) Ṣaṇḍha, or Jātipaṇḍaka as above; and (2) emasculated males; the complete are the others; the fifth being stimulated when bathing or evacuating. Other forms: | 吒; 半托; 半擇迦 tr. 黃門. | | 盧伽法 The Pāṇḍaka and Lohitaka rule is that derived from the conduct of these two disciples in the Vinaya, and is against quarrelling and fighting.

般若 Prajñā, "to know, understand"; "Wisdom." M. W. Intp. 慧 wisdom; 智慧 understanding, or wisdom; 明 clear, intelligent, the sixth pāramitā. The Prajñā-pāramitā-sūtra describes it as supreme, highest, incomparable, unequalled, unsurpassed. It is spoken of as the principal means, by its enlightenment, of attaining to nirvāṇa, through its revelation of the unreality of all things. Other forms are | 羅 |; | 賴 |; 鉢 |; 鉢剌 |; 鉢羅枳孃; 鉢腎禳; 波(賴) |; 波羅孃; 班 |. | (賴) | Prajñā is also the name of a monk from Kabul, A.D. 810, styled 三藏法師; tr. four works and author of an alphabet.

般若佛母 Wisdom, or salvation through wisdom (Prajñā-pāramitā), is the mother or source of all Buddhas. 智度論 34.

般若多羅 Prajñātāra. The 27th patriarch, native of eastern India, who laboured in southern India and consumed himself "by the fire of transformation", A.D. 457, teacher of Bodhidharma.

般若心經 The sūtra of the heart of prajñā; there have been several translations, under various titles, the generally accepted version being by Kumārajīva, which gives the essence of the Wisdom Sūtras. There are many treatises on the 心 經.

般若時 The prajñā period, the fourth of the (T'ien-t'ai) five periods of the Buddha's teaching.

般若毱多 Prajñāgupta. A Hīnayāna monk of southern India, who wrote against the Mahāyāna.

般若波羅蜜(多) Prajñāpāramitā. The acme of wisdom, enabling one to reach the other shore, i.e. wisdom for salvation; the highest of the six pāramitās, the virtue of wisdom as the principal means of attaining to Nirvāṇa. It connotes a knowledge of the illusory character of everything earthly, and destroys error, ignorance, prejudice, and heresy. For the sūtra of this name see below.

般若湯 The soup of wisdom, a name for wine.

般若經 The wisdom sūtras, especially the 大般若波羅密多經 tr. by Hsüan-tsang in 600 chüan. A compendium of five wisdom sūtras is 摩訶 | |; 金剛 | |; 天王問 | |; 光讚 | | and 仁王 | |; cf. the last. Another compendium contains eight books.

般若船 The boat of wisdom, the means of attaining nirvāṇa.

般若菩薩 Prajñā-bodhisattva; wisdom as a female bodhisattva in the Garbhadhātu group; also known as 智慧金剛.

般若鋒 The spear of wisdom (which is able to cut off illusion and evil).

般若頭 The monk in charge of the Prajñā sūtras.

般遮 Pañca, five; also 半者. | | 子旬 Pāñcika. Described as the gods of music, i.e. the gandharvas, also as | | 旬 Pañcābhijñāna, the five supernatural powers. | | 于瑟 Pañca-vārṣika; Pañca-pariṣad; Mokṣa-mahāpariṣad, the great quinquennial assembly instituted by Aśoka for the confession of sins, the inculcation of morality and discipline, and the distribution of charity; also | | 婆瑟; | | 跋瑟迦; | | 越師; | | 婆栗迦史; | | 跋利沙; | 闍于瑟.

般那 Prāṇa, exhalation, breathing out, cf. 阿那. | | 摩 Padma, lotus, cf. 鉢.

茶 Tea; tea-leaves; translit. *ja, jha*. | 湯 Tea and hot water, used as offerings to the spirits. | 毘 v. 荼. | 矩磨 Fragrant flowers, i.e. 鬱金 from Western or Central Asia for scenting wine, and for calling down the spirits. | 闍他 Jaḍatā, coldness, apathy, stupidity.

荆 Thorns. | 溪 Ching-ch'i, thorn-stream, name of the ninth T'ien-t'ai patriarch 湛然 Chan-jan.

芻 Hay, straw; translit. *kṣ*. | 摩; 芻 |; 須 | (迦) Kṣaumā, kṣaumaka, flax, linen, linen garment.

荒 Wild, waste; wilds; empty; famine; reckless; to nullify; an angry appearance. | 野 | 郊 A wilderness, uncultivated. | 空 Empty, deserted.

荅 To undertake; translit. *ta, da*. Tathāgata, v. 多. | 攝蒲密卜羅牒瑟吒諦 Daśabhūmi-pratiṣṭhite, "Thou who art established in the ten stages"—said to the Tathāgatas in invocations. | 秣蘇伐那 Tāmasavana, 闇林 the dark forest. "A monastery situated at the junction of the Vipāśā and Śatadru, 50 li south-east of Tchīnapati. It is probably identical with the so-called Djālandhara monastery in which the IV Synod under Kanichka held its sessions." Eitel.

草 Grass, herbs, plants; rough; female (of animals, birds, etc.). | 創 Newly or roughly built, unfinished. | 堂 The building in the | | 寺 monastery at Ch'ang-an where Kumārajīva translated. | 座 Mats or cushions to sit on. | 庵 A thatched hut as a monastery or retreat. | 木 Herbs and trees—equally recipients of rain, as all humanity is of the Buddha's truth. | 木成佛 Even inanimate things, e.g. grass and trees, are Buddha, all being of the 一如 q.v., a T'ien-t'ai and Chên-yen (Shingon) doctrine. | (or 茅) 環 A grass finger-ring used by the esoteric sect. | 鞋 Straw shoes. | 飯 A coarse or rough meal.

衰 Decay, fade, decline; frayed, i.e. mourning clothes. | 相 The (five) indications of approaching death, v. 五 |. | 患 The calamities of decadence, famine, epidemics, etc.

衲 To patch, line, pad; a monk's garment, supposed to be made of rags. 丨伽梨 The saṅghāṭī, or coat of patches varying from 9 to 25. 丨子 A monk, especially a peripatetic monk. 丨(or 納)衣 A monk's robe. 丨袈裟 A monk's robe of seven pieces and upwards. 丨衆 Monks who wear these robes.

記 To remember, to record; to record as foretelling, prophesy. 丨別; 丨莂; 授丨 To record and differentiate, the Buddha's foretelling of the future of his disciples to Buddhahood, and to their respective Buddha-kalpas, Buddha-realms, titles, etc.; see the 丨別經 and 和伽羅那 Vyākaraṇa, predictions, one of the twelve divisions of the Canon. 丨室; 書丨 Secretary's office, secretary, writer. 丨心 Memory. 丨論 Vyākaraṇa, a treatise on Sanskrit grammar, cf. 毘伽羅論.

訖 To finish, end, stop, to reach (an end); until; entirely; translit. *k*. 丨利多 Kṛta, Kṛtya, v. 吉; a slave, serf, bought or hired worker. 丨丨丨王 King Kṛta of Kashmir, whose descendants were opposed to Buddhism; they were dethroned by Kaniṣka, who restored Buddhism; but later the royal line regained the throne and drove out the Buddhist monks. 丨里瑟拏 Kṛṣṇa, black, dark, dark blue; Krishna, the hero-god of India, "with Buddhists he is chief of the black demons, who are enemies of Buddha and the white demons." M. W.

訓 To teach. 教丨; 丨誨 To teach, instruct.

訕 Abuse, slander; translit. *san*, *śan*. 丨底 v. 扇 Śāntika. 丨若 Sañjaya, "entirely vanquishing," name of the founder of one of the ten heretical sects. Also, one of the six Tīrthyas, former teacher of Maudgalyāyana and Śāriputra; also, a king of yakṣas; cf. 珊.

豺狼 A wolf. 丨丨地獄 One of the sixteen hells, where sinners are devoured by wolves.

貢 Tribute; best. 丨高 Elevated, proud.

財 Vasu; Artha. Wealth, riches. 丨主 A wealthy man, rich. 丨供養; 丨施 Offerings or gifts of material goods. 丨慳 Meanness, stinginess. 丨欲 The desire for wealth, one of the five wrong desires. 丨神 Kuvera, v. 俱 Vaiśravaṇa, v. 毘 the god of wealth. 丨色 Wealth and beauty (i.e. woman).

起 To rise, raise, start, begin; uprising; tr. utpāda. 丨信 The uprise or awakening of faith. 丨丨論 Śraddhotpāda Śāstra; it is one of the earliest remaining Mahāyāna texts and is attributed to Aśvaghoṣa; cf. 馬鳴; two tr. have been made, one by Paramārtha in A.D. 554, another by Śikṣānanda, *circa* 700; the first text is more generally accepted, as Chih-i, the founder of T'ien-t'ai, was Paramārtha's amanuensis, and 法藏 Fa-tsang (643–712) made the standard commentary on it, the 丨丨丨義記, though he had assisted Śikṣānanda in his translation. It gives the fundamental principles of Mahāyāna, and was tr. into English by Teitaro Suzuki (1900), also by T. Richard. There are several commentaries and treatises on it. 丨丨二門 Two characteristics of mind in the śāstra, as eternal and phenomenal. 丨尸鬼 To resurrect a corpse by demoniacal influence and cause it to kill another person; v. 毘 vetāla; 丨死人 is similar, i.e. to raise the newly dead to slay an enemy. 丨止處 A latrine, cesspool. 丨滅 Rise and extinction, birth and death, beginning and end. 丨盡 Beginning and end, similar to the last. 丨者 One who begins, or starts; one who thinks he creates his own welfare or otherwise. 丨行 To start out (for the life to come). 丨請 To call on the gods or the Buddhas (as witness to the truth of one's statements).

迹 Traces, footsteps; external evidences or indications. 丨化 Teaching or lessons derived from external events, i.e. of the Buddha's life and work, shown in the first fourteen sections of the Lotus Sūtra; the second fourteen sections of that work are called 本化 his direct teaching. The lessons from the external indications are called 丨化十妙 the ten marvellous indications, cf. 十妙.

追 To pursue, follow after; to follow the dead with thoughts and services. 丨修 To follow the departed with observances. 丨福 To pursue the departed with rites for their happiness. 丨薦 and 丨善 have similar meaning; also 丨嚴 for a sovereign.

迷 Māyā; delude, deceive, confuse, mislead; delusion, illusion, etc. 丨事 Delusive phenomena, or affairs, deluded in regard to phenomena, cf. 丨理 *infra*. 丨人咒 Incantations to delude or confuse others. 丨倒 Deluded, confused, to delude and upset. 丨妄 Deluded and misled; deluding and false. 丨子 The deluded son who held a gold coin in his hand while starving in poverty; such is the man with Buddha-nature who fails to use it. v. 金剛三昧經. 丨岸 The shore of delusion. 丨底履 v. 彌 Maitreya. 丨心 A deluded mind. 丨惑 Deluded and confused, deceived in regard to reality. 丨悟 Illusion and enlightenment; 丨悟一如 the two are aspects of the one reality, as water and ice are the same substance, | 悟不二 and fundamentally are the same. | 悟因果 In the four axioms, that of "accumulation" is caused by illusion, with suffering as effect; that of "the way" is caused by enlightenment, with extinction (of suffering) as effect. | 沒 Deluded and sunk (in the passions). | 津 The ford of delusion, i.e. mortality. | 理 Deluded in regard to the fundamental principle, i.e. ignorant of reality; cf. | 事. | 生 All deluded beings. | 界 Any world of illusion. | 盧 v. 蘇 | | Sumeru. | 隸 (or 麗) 耶 Maireya, a kind of intoxicating drink. | 黎麻羅 (and other forms) Confused sight; blurred.

逆 Vāma. To go against, contrary, adverse, reverse, rebellious, oppose, resist. | 修; 豫修 To observe in contrary order; to observe before death the Buddhist rites in preparation for it. | 化 (The ability of the Buddhas and bodhisattvas) to convert the heterodox or opponents. | 喩 Argument by illustration from effect to cause, e.g. the source of the ocean is the river, of the river the streams, of these the ponds. | 流 To go against the current, i.e. the stream of transmigration, and enter the path of Nirvāṇa, also called 預流, the Śrota-āpanna, or śrāvaka first stage. | 緣 Resisting accessory-cause; as goodness is the 順 or accordant cause so evil is the resisting cause of the Buddha way. | 觀 The inverse method in meditation. | 謗 To resist and abuse. | 路伽耶陀 Vāma-lokāyata; the Lokāyata were materialistic and "worldly" followers of the Cārvāka school; the Vāma-lokāyata were opposed to the conventions of the world. An earlier intp. of Lokāyata is, Ill response to questions, the sophistical method of Chuang Tzŭ being mentioned as comparison. Vāma-lokāyata is also described as Evil questioning, which is the above method reversed. | 順 The adversatives, resisting and complying, opposing and according with, reverse or direct, backward or forward.

送 To escort, send, give as a present. | 亡 To escort or take the departed to the grave. | 葬 To escort for burial.

逃 To flee, escape. | 禪 To escape in or from meditation or thought.

退 Retire, withdraw, backslide, recede, yield. | 大 To backslide from Mahāyāna (and revert to Hīnayāna). | 屈 To yield or recede, as is possible to a Bodhisattva facing the hardships of further progress. | 座 To withdraw from one's seat. | 沒 To be reborn in a lower stage of existence. | 轉 To withdraw and turn back, i.e. from any position attained.

酒 Surā; Maireya; Madya. Wine, alcoholic liquor; forbidden to monks and nuns by the fifth commandment.

針 Sūci; a needle. | 孔 A needle's eye; it is as difficult to be reborn as a man as it is to thread a needle on earth by throwing the thread at it from the sky. | 口鬼 Needle-mouth ghosts, with mouths so small that they cannot satisfy their hunger or thirst. | 毛鬼 Ghosts with needle hair, distressing to themselves and others. | 芥 Needle and mustard seed; the appearance of Buddha is as rare as hitting the point of a needle on earth by a mustard seed thrown from the sky. | 鋒 A needle's point, similar to the last.

閃 Flash; get out of the way. | 多 A demon; one of Yama's names. | 電光 Lightning-flashing, therefore awe-inspiring.

陞 To ascend; rise, raise. | 座 To ascend the platform to expound the sūtras.

院 Ārāma, pleasaunce, garden, grove; a monastery, hall, court. | 主 The abbot of a monastery.

除 Get rid of. | 一切惡 To get rid of all evil. | 散 Get rid of and scatter away. | 斷 Get rid of completely, cut off. | 災 Get rid of calamity. | 疑 Eliminate doubt. | 蓋障 To dispose of hindrances. | 覺支 To get rid of mental effort and produce mental and physical buoyancy. | 饉 He (or she) who puts away want (by receiving alms), an intp. of bhikṣu and bhikṣuṇī.

馬 Aśva, a horse; a stallion; one of the seven treasures of a sovereign. | 勝; | 師 Aśvajit. Horse-breaker or Horse-master. The name of several persons, including one of the first five disciples. | 鳴; 阿濕縛窶沙 Aśvaghoṣa, the famous writer, whose patron was the Indo-Scythian king Kaniṣka q.v., was a Brahmin converted to Buddhism; he finally settled at Benares, and became the twelfth patriarch. His name is attached to ten works (v. Hōbōgirin 192, 201, 726, 727, 846, 1643, 1666, 1667, 1669, 1687). The two which have exerted great influence on Buddhism are 佛所行讚經 Buddha-carita-kāvya-sūtra, tr. by Dharmarakṣa A.D. 414–421, tr. into English by Beal, S.B.E.; and 大乘起信論 Mahāyāna śraddhotpāda-śāstra, tr. by Paramārtha,

A.D. 554, and by Śikṣānanda, A.D. 695–700, tr. into English by Teitaro Suzuki 1900, and also by T. Richard, v. 起. He gave to Buddhism the philosophical basis for its Mahāyāna development. There are at least six others who bear this name. Other forms: | | 比丘; | | 大士; | | 菩薩, etc. | 曷麻諦 Mahāmati, 大慧, the bodhisattva addressed in the Laṅkāvatāra Sūtra; v. 摩訶摩底. | 祀 Aśvamedha, the horse sacrifice, either as an annual oblation to Heaven, or for specific purposes. | 祖 Ma Tsu, founder of the Southern Peak school of the Ch'an or Intuitional sect in Kiangsi, known as 江西道一. | 耳山 Aśvakarṇa, v. 頞, one of the seven concentric rings around Meru. | 苑 The horse park, i.e. 白馬寺 the White Horse Monastery at Loyang in the Later Han dynasty, where, according to tradition, the first missionaries dwelt. | 陰藏 A retractable penis, e.g. that of the horse, one of the thirty-two signs of a Buddha. | 頭 Horse-head. | | 羅刹 The horse-head rākṣasa in Hades. | | 觀音; | | 大士; | | 明王 Hayagrīva, the horse-neck or horse-head Kuan-yin, in awe-inspiring attitude towards evil spirits. | 麥 Horse-grain, Buddha's food when he spent three months with the Brahmin ruler Agnidatta with 500 monks, one of his ten sufferings.

骨 Bone; bones, relics. | 人 Skeleton. | 佛 A bone-buddha, a corpse. | 塔 A dagoba for the ashes of the dead. | 目 The bones and eyes, the essentials. | 身 The bones of the body, the śarīra or remains after cremation. | 鏁天 The bone-chain deva 商羯羅 Śaṅkara, i.e. Śiva.

高 High, lofty, eminent. | 士 Eminent scholar; old tr. for Bodhisattva. | 世耶; 憍奢耶; 憍尸; Kauśeya, thin silk, lustring; wild silk-worms. | 僧 Eminent monks. | 昌; | 車 Karakhojo, the ancient town of Kao-ch'ang, which lay 30 li east of Turfān in Turkestan, formerly an important Buddhist centre, whence came scriptures and monks to China. | 祖 A founder of a sect or school. | 薩羅 v. 憍 Kośala. | 足 Superior pupils or disciples. | 麗 Korea. | | 藏 The Korean canon of Buddhism, one of the three collections which still exists in the 海印寺 in 639 cases, 1521 部 and 6589 卷.

鬼 Preta 薜荔多, departed, dead; a disembodied spirit, dead person, ghost; a demon, evil being; especially a 餓 | hungry ghost. They are of many kinds. The Fan-i ming i classifies them as poor, medium, and rich; each again thrice subdivided: (1) (*a*) with mouths like burning torches; (*b*) throats no bigger than needles; (*c*) vile breath, disgusting to themselves; (2) (*a*) needle-haired, self-piercing; (*b*) hair sharp and stinking; (*c*) having great wens on whose pus they must feed. (3) (*a*) living on the remains of sacrifices; (*b*) on leavings in general; (*c*) powerful ones, yakṣas, rākṣasas, piśācas, etc. All belong to the realm of Yama, whence they are sent everywhere, consequently are ubiquitous in every house, lane, market, mound, stream, tree, etc. | 子母 Hāritī, 訶梨帝 intp. as pleased, or pleasing. A "woman who having vowed to devour all the babies at Rādjagriha was reborn as a Rākshasī, and gave birth to 500 children, one of which she was to devour every day. Converted by Śākyamuni she entered a convent. Her image is to be seen in all nunneries". Eitel. Another account is that she is the mother of 500 demons, and that from being an evil goddess or spirit she was converted to become a protectress of Buddhism. | | | 神 A rākṣasī who devours men. | 城 The demon-city, that of the Gandharvas. | (法) 界 The region or realm of demons; one of the ten regions. | 火 Spirit lights, *ignis fatuus*. | 病 Sickness caused by demons, or ghosts. | 神 Ghosts and spirits, a general term which includes the spirits of the dead, together with demons and the eight classes of spirits, such as devas, etc. 鬼 is intp. as 威 causing fear, 神 as 能 potent, powerful. | | 食時 The time when they feed, i.e. night. | 見 Demon views, i.e. heterodox teaching. | 道; | 趣 The way or destiny of yakṣas, rākṣasas, and hungry ghosts; | 道 also means in league with demons, or following devilish ways. | 錄 The iron record, containing the sins of men, in Yama's office in Hades. | 門 The north-east corner of a house, or of a city-gate enceinte, through which the spirits can come and go. | 魅 Imps or demons who cause sickness, especially malaria in certain regions.

11. ELEVEN STROKES

乾 Dry, dried up, clean; heaven, male, masculine, enduring, continual. Translit. *gan* and *h*. | 屎橛 A stick used in India as "toilet paper", in China paper, straw, or bamboo. | 慧地 The dry or unfertilized stage of wisdom, the first of the ten stages. | 栗陀耶; | | 馱 Hṛdaya, heart, soul, mind, core. | (達) 城 Gandharva city, *infra*. | 闥婆; | 沓婆 or 和; 健達 (or 闥) 婆; 犍達縛; 犍陀羅; 彥達縛 Gandharva or Gandharva Kāyikās, spirits on Gandha-mādana

香山 the fragrant or incense mountains, so called because the Gandharvas do not drink wine or eat meat, but feed on incense or fragrance and give off fragrant odours. As musicians of Indra, or in the retinue of Dhṛtarāṣtra, they are said to be the same as, or similar to, the Kinnaras. They are, or according to M. W., Dhṛtarāṣtra is associated with soma, the moon, and with medicine. They cause ecstasy, are erotic, and the patrons of marriageable girls; the Apsaras are their wives, and both are patrons of dicers. ||| 城 A Gandharva city, i.e. a mirage city. ||| 王 The king of the Gandharvas, named Citraratha (M. W.), but tr. as Druma, a tree. | 陀 Yugaṁdhara, cf. 踰, the first of the concentric mountains of a world; also name of a tree. | 陀羅 (or 越 or 衛 or 婆那) Gandhāra, an ancient kingdom in the north of the Punjab, "Lat. 35° 5 N., Long. 71° 16 E." (Eitel); famous as a centre of Buddhism. Śākyamuni, in a former life, is said to have lived there and torn out his eyes to benefit others, "probably a distortion of the story of Dharmavivardhana, who as governor of Gandhāra was blinded by order of a concubine of his father, Aśoka." Eitel. M. W. associates Gandhāra with Kandahar. Also, name of a fragrant tree, and of a yellow colour. || 訶提 Gandhahastin, "fragrant elephant," name of a Bodhisattva.

停 To stop, rest, settle, delay. | 心 To fix or settle the mind in meditation, cf. 五 | 心觀.

偶 An image; a mate; unexpectedly. | 像 An image, an idol.

偷 Remiss; to steal; stealthy. | 婆 Stūpa, cf. 塔. | 盜 Steal, rob; one of the ten sins. | 蘭 (遮耶), 薩 | 羅; 因蘭 Sthūlātyaya, a great transgression, one of the major transgressions of a monk or nun.

偈 Gāthā, metrical hymn or chant, often occurring in sūtras, and usually of 4, 5, or 7 words to the line. Also | 他 cf. 伽陀. | 讚 To sing in verse the praises of the object adored. | 頌, | 陀 Hymn, chant; to hymn.

健 Sturdy, strong, hard, bold; unwearied; translit. *ga, gha*. | 勇坐 The heroic posture of the Buddha with his feet on his thighs soles upward. | 南 Ghana, a mass, also | 男; 鍵 (or 蹇 or 羯) 南; it is intp. as a hard, solid lump, the human embryo formed from the fourth to the seventh day. | 拏驃訶 Gandha-vyūha, tr. by 華嚴 q.v. | 陀; | 杜; | 達 Gandha, smell, scent; a tree producing incense; the first and last also mean (as do 乾陀 and 乾馱) kaṣāya, a colour composed of red and yellow, the monk's robe, but the sounds agree better with kanthā, the patch-robe. Also used for skandha, v. 塞, the five constituents; also for gandharvas, v. 乾. | 陀俱知 Gandhakuṭī, the house of scent, or incense, a temple. | 陀摩陀摩羅 Gandhamādanamāla, the hill of intoxicating perfume. | 達縛 Gandharva, v. 乾. | 馱梨 ? Gandhārī, a spell that gives power to fly. | 馱羅 Gāndhāra, v. 乾.

假 To borrow, pretend, assume, suppose; unreal, false, fallacious. In Buddhism it means empirical; nothing is real and permanent, all is temporal and merely phenomenal, fallacious, and unreal; hence the term is used in the sense of empirical, phenomenal, temporal, relative, unreal, seeming, fallacious, etc. The three fundamental propositions or 三諦 are 空 | 中 the void, or noumenon; the empirical, or phenomenal; and the mean. | 合; | 和合 Phenomena, empirical combinations without permanent reality. | 合之身 The empirical body. | 名 Unreal names, i.e. nothing has a name of itself, for all names are mere human appellations. | 名世間 The world of unreal names, i.e. the phenomenal world of sentient beings. | 名有 Things which exist only in name, i.e. all things are combinations of other things and are empirically named. | 名菩薩 One who may be called a bodhisattva because he has attained the 十信 q.v. | 實 False and true, unreal and real, empirical and real, etc. | 我 The empirical ego of the five skandhas. | 有 The phenomenal, which in reality no more exists than turtle's hair or rabbit's horns. | 色 Invisible, or internal form, i.e. spiritual form. | 觀 The meditation on relative truth, or phenomenal and therefore illusory existence, in comparison with 空 and 中 q.v. | 設 Prajñapti; ordinary teaching, doctrines derived from the phenomenal. | 門 The sects which rely on externals, i.e. on "works" for salvation, in contrast with faith in Amitābha.

偏 To or on one side, deflected, one-sided, biased, partial, prejudiced. | 圓 Partial and all-embracing, relative and complete, e.g. Hīnayāna and Mahāyāna, also the intermediate schools (between Hīnayāna and Mahāyāna) and the perfect school of T'ien-t'ai. | 執 To hold firmly to a one-sided interpretation; bigoted. | 小 The partial and minor teaching of the Buddha during the first twelve years of his ministry. | 小情 The partial or narrower Hīnayāna idea that though the ego is unreal, things are real. | 教; 權教 Partial or relative teaching; T'ien-t'ai regarded its own teaching as the complete, or final and all-embracing teaching of the Buddha, while that of the 法相, 三論, etc., was partial and imperfect; in like manner, the three schools, 藏, 通, and 別, piṭaka, intermediate, and separate, were partial and imperfect. | 眞, | 空, 單空 The Hīnayāna doctrine of unreality, a one-sided dogma in contrast with the transcendental reality of Mahāyāna. | 衫 The monk's toga, or robe, thrown over one shoulder, some say the right, others the left. | 袒 Bare on one side, i.e. to wear the toga, or robe, over the right shoulder, baring the other as a mark of respect. | 門 A side door, one through which offenders are expelled.

兜 Helmet, hood; pocket, bag; translit. *tu*. | 夜 The Tuṣita and the Yama heavens. | 婆 A stūpa. | 沙 Tuṣāra, frost. | 牟盧 Tumburu, probably gandharvas. | 樓婆; 妬路婆? Turuṣka; olibanum; Indian incense. | 率 (陀 or 哆); | 術; 珊都 (or 覩) 史多; 鬭瑟多 Tuṣita, from Tuṣ, contented, satisfied, gratified; name of the Tuṣita heaven, the fourth devaloka in the 欲界 passion-realm, or desire realm, between the Yama and Nirmāṇarati heavens. Its inner department is the Pure Land of Maitreya who, like Śākyamuni and all Buddhas, is reborn there before descending to earth as the next Buddha; his life there is 4,000 Tuṣita years, or (each day there being equal to 400 earth-years) 584 million such years. | 率天子 The Tuṣita prince, i.e. Śākyamuni, whose light while he was in Tuṣita shone into hell and saved all its occupants to that heaven; hence he is also called 地獄天子 Prince of Hades. | 羅; 妬 (or 堵 or 蠹) 羅 Tūla, floss, e.g. willow-floss, wild silk; cotton, also called | 羅綿 (or 毦); also a tree producing such floss.

減; 减 Diminish, decrease, abate, reduce, abbreviate; opp. 增. | 劫 The decreasing kalpas in which the period of life is gradually reduced, as the 增 | are the kalpas of increase; together they form twenty kalpas, ten diminishing and ten increasing; but there are other definitions. | 費 To cut down one's personal expenditure (for the sake of charity).

副 To aid, assist, second; a deputy. | 寮 Deputy in a monastery.

勘 To investigate, examine, collate. | 辨 To examine and define.

勒 Rein; extort, force; a left stroke; to draw in. | 沙 Lākṣā, lac; a reddish colour, probably cochineal. | 沙婆 Ṛṣabha, described as one of three famous ṛṣi, before the days of Śākyamuni, of the Nirgrantha type of naked ascetics. | 那摩 (or 婆) 提? Ratnamati, a monk from Central India, *circa* A.D. 500, who translated three works of which two remain.

動 Move, stir, motion, mutable; movement arises from the nature of wind which is the cause of motion. | 不動法 The mutable and the immutable, the changing and the unchanging, the Kāmadhātu, or realms of metempsychosis and the two higher realms, Rūpadhātu and Arūpadhātu. Cf. 不動.

厠 A privy, cesspool; also called 西淨; 東淨; 東司; 雪隱; 後架; 起止處, etc. Ucchuṣma, v. 烏, is the guardian spirit of the cesspool.

參 Reflect on, counsel, visit superior. An assembly, a gathering for the purpose of meditation, preaching, worship. Read *shên*, the twenty-first constellation, α, β, γ, δ, ϵ, ζ, η, and k in Orion. 早 | Morning assembly; 晚 | evening assembly; 小 | a special meeting; a discussion following an address. | 前 Before the evening assembly; | 後; | 退 after the evening assembly. | 問 To seek instruction—generally as a class. | 堂 The initiation to the services of one newly ordained. | 禪 To inquire, discuss, seek religious instruction. | 詣 To approach the gods or Buddhas in worship. | 請 To request instruction, or discussion. | 頭 One versed in the ceremonies and capable of leading others.

啓 To open, begin, inform. | 白 idem 表白 To inform, make clear, especially to inform the Buddhas.

唱 To cry out, sing. | 名 To cry out names; to call (on) the name (of Buddha). | 寂 To cry out nirvāṇa, as the Buddha is said to have done at his death. | 導 To preach to people and lead them to conversion. | 禮 To announce the ceremonial duty. | 衣 To cry for sale the robes of a deceased monk, or person. | 道師 A preacher; the president of a monastic assembly. | 食 To give the "blessing" at meals.

唵 Om; aum; "a word of solemn affirmation and respectful assent (sometimes translated by yes, verily, so be it, and in this sense compared with Amen)." M. W. It is "the mystic name for the Hindū triad", and has other significations. It was adopted by Buddhists, especially by the Tantric school, as a mystic spell, and as an object of meditation. It forms the first syllable of certain mystical combinations, e.g. | 㗚呢叭𡁠吽 Om maṇi padme hūṃ, which is a formula of the Lamaistic branch, said to be a prayer to Padmapāṇi; each of the six syllables having its own mystic power of salvation from the lower paths of transmigration, etc.; the formula is used in sorcery, auguries, etc.; other forms of it are | | | 鉢頭迷吽; | 麽抳鉢訥銘吽.

啞 Eḍa, dumb; eḍamūka, deaf and dumb, unable to express oneself; translit. *a*, v. 阿. | 呧囉孤答尼耶 Aparagodāna, the Western continent, see 阿. | 子得夢 A dumb man who has had a dream—but cannot tell it. | 密哩達 Amṛta, ambrosia v. 阿. | 撳釋該而 Abhiṣeka, "consecrate me by sprinkling," said in prayer. | 曷囉啞曷囉馬麻藹由而傘塔囉尼 Āhāra āharaṇam āyuḥ, saṁtāraṇe "Give me, give me, old age, oh protector". | 法 The doctrine of a deaf and dumb person, which he cannot p oclaim. | 羊 (僧) A dumb sheep (monk), stupid, one who does not know good from bad, nor enough to repent of sin.

問 To ask, inquire, question; to adjudicate, sentence. | 法印 The manual sign indicating the putting of a question. | 訊 To make inquiry; ask about another's welfare, orally or by folding the hands; interrogate; try a case.

商 To consult, arrange; trade, a merchant; translit. *śaṅ*, *śām*, *śa*, *śā*. | 佉; | 迦 Śaṅkha, 餉 (or 傷, 勝, 儴, 曠, 霜) 佉; 勝伽; | 企羅; 償起羅 A conch, shell. | 羯羅 Śaṅkara, "auspicious" (M. W.), a name for "Śiva", and intp. as 骨鏁 bone-chains; name of | | | 阿闍梨 Śaṅkarācārya, the celebrated Indian philosopher of the eighth century A.D. who is known as a great opponent of Buddhism. | 諾 (迦) 縛娑; | 那和修; 舍那和修 (or 波私) Śaṇakavāsa; Śaṇavāsa; a younger brother of Ānanda. Also an arhat, whom Eitel gives as the third patriarch, a native of Mathurā, and says: "A Tibetan tradition identifies him with Yaśas, the leader of the II Synod." Because of his name he is associated with a hemp or linen garment, or a covering with which he was born. | 賈 A trader, one of the vaiśya caste. | 量 To consult, discuss together, e.g. as master and pupil.

唯 Eva. Affirmative, yes; to answer, respond; said to interpret Mātratā, and is defined as discrimination, decision, approval. It is also used for only, alone, but. | 名 Nāmamātra; name only. | 境無識 Realism as opposed to | 識無境 Idealism; implying that the four elements are real and permanent. | 心 Idealism, mind only, the theory that the only reality is mental, that of the mind. Similar to | 識 q.v. and v. Lankāvatāra sūtra. | | 偈 The eight-line verse of the older 華嚴 sūtra, which summarizes the idealistic idea. | 色 All things are matter, because mind and matter are identical, for matter is mind. | 識 Vijñānamātra-(vāda); cittamātra. Idealism, the doctrine that nothing exists apart from mind, 識外無法. | 識中道 The madhya, or medial doctrine of idealism as held by the 法相 Dharmalakṣaṇa school, that all things are of mind-evolution, and are neither in themselves real nor unreal. | 識修道五位 The five stages of attaining enlightenment in the idealistic sect: stage of reason and speculation; of asceticism; of apprehension of truth; of practice of contemplation from the first to the tenth stage; of complete comprehension of truth. | 識圓教 The third of the three divisions of the Buddha's teaching as defined by Tao-hsüan of Nan-shan, the perfect doctrine of idealism. | 識宗 The Dharmalakṣaṇa sect 法相宗, which holds that all is mind in its ultimate nature. Also | | 家. | 識觀 The three subjects of idealistic reflection: that the ego and things are realities; that things are produced by cause and circumstance; that the bhūtatathatā is the only reality. Also called | | 心定; | | 三性觀, cf. 三性. | 識論 Vijñaptimātrasiddhi-śāstra, also called the 成 | | |; 唯識二十 | Vidyāmātrasiddhi-viṃśakakārikā-śāstra; another is the | | 三十 | Vidyāmātrasiddhi-tridaśakārikā-śāstra. There are numerous commentaries and treatises on the subject. See de la Vallée Poussin's version.

國 A country, a nation; national. | 僧正 National superintendent of the clergy, an office which at one time existed. | 土 A country, land, native land, abode of a race, or races. | 土世間 The world of countries on which people depend for existence. | 土身 The Buddha as Buddhakṣetra, or abode of the living; the world as the body of Vairocana. | 師 Imperial preceptor, a title conferred on certain Buddhist monks, especially on 慧能 Hui-nêng, q.v. | 王 A king, prince, i.e. one who has attained to his present high estate consequent on keeping all the ten commandments in a previous incarnation; and being protected by devas 天, he is called 天子 deva son, or Son of Heaven.

域 Frontier, limit; region; tomb. | 心; | 懷 The limits of the mind, natural endowment. | 龍 Dignāga, Diṅnāga, a celebrated Buddhist philosopher 陳那, author of a famous treatise on logic.

堆 A heap, a pile. | 壓地獄 The hell of crushing, also 衆合地獄, the third great hell in which sinners are crushed to death.

堂 Prāsāda. A hall, temple, court. | 上; | 頭 The head of the hall, the abbot of a monastery. | 主 The head of a hall on specific occasion. | 司 The controller of the business in a monastery. | 塔 Temples and monasteries in general. | 達 The distributor of the liturgies, etc.

堅 Dṛḍha, Sthira; firm, firmly fixed, reliable. | 固 Firm and sure. | 固意 Firm-willed, name of a bodhisattva in the Garbhadhātu. | 固慧 Strong in wisdom, ditto. | (固) 林 The grove of Śāla trees, in which Śākyamuni died. | 牢 Firm and stable; that which is stable, the earth. | 牢地神 (or 天, or 祇) The earth-goddess, or deity, or spirits. | 實 Firm and solid. | 實心 With firm heart. | 意; | 慧 Sthiramati, of firm mind, or wisdom. An early Indian monk of the Mahāyāna; perhaps two monks. | 智 Firm knowledge, or wisdom, a name of Vajrapāṇi. | 法 The three things assured to the faithful (in reincarnation)—a good body, long life, and boundless wealth. | 滿菩薩 Dhṛtiparipūrṇa, the firm and complete Bodhisattva, who is to be Buddha Padma-vṛṣabha-vikrāmin, attending on Padmaprabha. | 誓師子 The firmly vowing lion, i.e. Śākyamuni in a previous incarnation.

執 Grah, grabh; graha. To seize, grasp, hold on to, maintain; obstinate. | 事 To manage, control; a manager. | 受 Impressions, ideas grasped and held. | 取相 Retention of memories of past joys and sorrows as if they were realities and not illusions, one of the 六麤 in the Awakening of Faith. | 師子國 Siṁhala, Ceylon. | 心 The mind which clings to (things as real). | 情 The foolish passion of clinging to the unreal. | 持 To hold firmly. | 持識 Ādāna-vijñāna, a name for the ālaya-vijñāna. | 曜 Graha, the planets, nine or seven. | 著 To cling to things as real; used for abhiniveśa. | 見 Views obstinately held, with consequent delusion; bigoted. | 金剛神 Vajrapāṇi, vajradhara. Any deva-holder of the vajra. (1) Indra, who in a former incarnation took an oath to defend Buddhism, was reborn as king of the Yakṣas, hence he and his yakṣas carry vajras. (2) Mañjuśrī as the spiritual reflex of the Dhyāni Buddha Akṣobhya. (3) A popular deity, the terror of all enemies of Buddhist believers, specially worshipped in exorcisms and sorcery by the Yoga school. | 障 The holding on to the reality of self and things and the consequent hindrance to entrance into nirvāṇa.

婦 A woman; a wife. | 人. "Nothing is so dangerous to monastic chastity as woman"; she is the root of all misery, hindrance, destruction, bondage, sorrow, hatred, blindness, etc.

婬 Licentious, lewd; adultery, fornication; similar to 淫 q.v. | 怒癡 The three poisons of sexual desire, anger, and ignorance (or heedlessness). | 戒 The commandment against adultery. | 欲 Sexual desire. | 火 The fire of sexual passion. | 羅網 Its net.

婆 A dame, mother, wife, granny, crone; translit. *pa*, *ba*, *va*, *pha*, *bha*, and similar labial sounds.

婆利 Vaḍiśa, Valiśa, or Vakrī, a hook, bent. | | 師 Varṣās, v. 雨, the rainy season of retreat. | | 師 (迦); | | 史迦羅 v. | 師迦. | | 耶 Bhāryā, a wife. | | 質 (多) 羅 ? Pārijāta, v. 波, a tree in Indra's heaven. | | 闍多迦 Pārijātaka, a deva flower.

婆叉 Vākṣu; Vaṅkṣu; the Oxus; Vaṅkṣu is also a small branch of the Ganges, idem 縛芻.

婆伽 Bhāga, a portion, division, fraction. | | 婆 (帝) Bhagavat, or | | 梵; | | 伴; | 誐鑁; 薄伽 (or 阿) 梵 Bhagavān, "fortunate," "excellent," "revered, sacred," "the holy one" (M. W.); generally intp. by 世尊 world-honoured, but there are other intps.; an epithet of a Buddha.

婆哩野 Bhāryā, a dependent, a wife; also | 利 (or 梨) 耶; | 庚.

婆喝那 Vāhana, 10 quadrillions. 大 | | | 100 quadrillions.

婆嚩誐帝 Bhagavat, v. | 伽.

婆城 A gandharva city, a mirage, an illusion city, v. 乾.

婆婆伽利 Pāpakārin; evil-doer, name of a prince.

婆差優婆差 Upāsaka-upāsikā, male and female disciples dwelling at home; lay disciples.

婆師波 Vāṣpa, Bāṣpa; one of the first five disciples, Daśabala-Kāśyapa, identified with Mahā-Kāśyapa; also | | (or 濕) 婆; | 沙波.

婆師(迦) Vārṣika, the flower that blooms in the rains, the aloe, Agallochum; also 丨利師(迦) q.v.; 丨利史迦羅; 丨使迦; 丨師波利 Varṣākāla, Varṣipālī.

婆捺囉婆捺麼洗 Bhādrapadamāsa, the sixth month, middle of August to middle of September; the third and fourth Nakṣatras or lunar mansions, Pūrva and Uttara; also 跋丨丨丨娜; 跋陀娜婆娜; 丨達羅鉢陀.

婆提 Bhadrika, one of the first disciples; cf. 跋. Also Vana, a grove; or Vanī.

婆斯仙 One of the fire devas and his 后 wife in the Garbhadhātu group; perhaps Vasu.

婆梨 Vāri; water; fluid, fluidity; also 丨利; 波利.

婆樓那 Varuṇa, v. 水天.

婆檀陀 Bhadanta, 大德, laudable, praiseworthy, blessed, of great virtue—a term of respect for a Buddha, or for monks, especially of the Hīnayāna school.

婆毘吠伽 Bhāvaviveka, a learned monk who retired from the world to await the coming of Maitreya, v. 西域記 10.

婆沙 v. 毘 Vibhāṣā. 丨丨波; 丨敷 Bāṣpa, v. 丨師波.

婆珊婆演底 Vasanta-vayantī, spring-weaving, but the description is of a guardian of the night or of sleep.

婆瘦 Vāyu, wind, god of the wind. Also 丨牖; 縛臾.

婆盧枳底濕伐羅 Avalokiteśvara, see 觀音.

婆私(吒) Vasiṣṭha, a Brahman who is said to have denied the eternity of nirvāṇa, and maintained that plants had lives and intelligence; Nirvāṇa Sūtra 39. One of the seven ancient ṛṣis of Brahmanic mythology, one of the champions in the Ṛgveda of the priesthood. Name of a Brahman whose mother lost her six sons, she became mad, wandered naked, met the Buddha, was restored and became a disciple. Also 丨吒; 私丨吒; 丨私瑟搋 or 侘.

婆稚 Bandhi, or Bali, the origin and meaning are obscure, defined as "bound" and also as round, full-orbed, complete. Bandhiasura, an asura-king. Also, 丨梨; 跋稚; 跋墀; 跋移; 末利.

婆羅 Pāla; keeper, guardian, warden; vihārapāla, warden of a monastery. Bala; power, strength, especially the 五力 five powers, pañca balāni, i.e. 五根; also the 十力 daśabala, ten powers. Name of the sister of Ānanda who offered milk to Śākyamuni. Bāla; "young," "immature," "simpleton, fool," "hair" (M. W.); ignorant, unenlightened, see Bālapṛthagjana, *infra*. 丨丨吸摩補羅 Brahmapura. "An ancient kingdom of Northern India, the dynastic title of which was entailed upon the female line exclusively"; hence styled 女國. Said to be Garhwal. 丨丨奢 Phalasa, the bread-fruit tree; intp. as a tree with red flowers. 丨丨必栗託仡那; 丨丨丨哩他丨丨; 丨丨丨利他伽闍那 Bālapṛthagjana, low, foolish people; natural-minded, as children, of common intelligence and ideas, a man in his natural state, unilluminated, unenlightened. 丨丨捨佉; 鉢羅奢佉 Praśākha, a fœtus of five to seven days. 丨丨提木叉 Pratimokṣa, v. 波. 丨丨痆斯; 丨丨捺寫 Vārāṇasī, an ancient kingdom and city, noted (A.D. 640) as the headquarters of Śivaism; Benares; cf. 波. 丨丨(訶) Balāhaka, a king of horses, or possessing horses. 丨丨賀磨 or 摩 Brahmā; 丨丨丨丨拏; 丨丨欱末拏 Brāhmaṇa; v. *infra*. 丨丨那馱 Varanāda, a bellowing yakṣa. 丨丨門; 跋濫摩; 沒囉憾摩 Brāhmaṇa; Brāhmanical; Brāhman; 淨行; 丨志 of pure life or mind; the highest of the four castes, those who serve Brahma, his offspring, the keepers of the Vedas. 丨丨丨國 Brāhmaṇarāṣṭra, the realm of the Brahmans, India. 丨丨丨城 A city of Brahmans, from which the Buddha returned with his begging bowl empty. 丨丨丨書 Brahman writing; the alphabet. 丨丨丨邑 Brāhmaṇapura, "a city north-east of the capital of Mālava." Eitel.

婆耶 Payas; liquid, fluid, juice, water.

婆致迦 Sphātika, v. 水玉.

婆舍斯多 Basiasita (Sk. Vāsi-Asita) or Naśaśata, the twenty-fifth Patriarch who laboured in Central India; the date of his death is given as A.D. 325.

婆舍跋提 Vaśavartin, the sixth desire-heaven, the abode of Māra, the god of lust, sin, and death; its occupants avail themselves of the merits of others for their own pleasure; it is also called the abode of Śikhin (Brahma) as lord of fire; also 他化自在天 and | 羅尼蜜 | | | | Paranirmita-vaśavartin.

婆藪 Vasu | 萸; good; rich; sweet; dry; according to Monier-Williams, eight personifications of natural phenomena; eight; the sun, etc.; father of Kṛṣṇa; intp. as the first to offer slain sacrifices to Heaven, to have been cast into hell, but after countless kalpas to have become a disciple of Buddha. Also called Vasudeva. Also name of certain devas, e.g. Viṣṇu; and other beings whom men serve, e.g. a father. | | 槃豆; | | | 陀; | | 盤豆; | 修盤頭; 伐蘇畔徒; 筏蘇畔徒 or 盤豆 Vasubandhu, known as 天親 q.v., and 世親 kinsman of devas, or of the world.

婆訶 Vāha; it means bearing, carrying, a beast of burden, but is used in the sense of a large grain-container of twenty bushels 斛; supernatural life, or adbhuta, is compared to a vāha full of hemp seed, from which one seed is withdrawn every century. Also | | 摩.

婆誐 Bhaṅga, breaking, fracture, fragment, broken. Also | 伽; 薄伽.

婆蹉 Vatsa, a calf, offspring, a term of endearment for a child. The founder of the Vātsīputrīyāḥ school. | | 婆 A term for Śakra. | | 富(多)羅 The above school, a branch of the Sarvāstivādins, v. 犢. | | 那婆 Vatsanābha, a strong poison, "from the root of a kind of aconite." M. W.

婆那 Vana, a wood, grove; also 飯 |; 嚩泥.

婆里旱 Balin, intp. 力士 a strong man, hero.

婆闍羅波尼婆里旱 Vajrapāṇibalin, the powerful one with the thunderbolt, one of the two gate-guardians.

婆陀 Baddha, bound, tied, fettered, fixed; also 縛馱; also an abbrev. for 阿波陀那 Avadāna.

婆雌子部 Vātsīputra, also | 麤富羅, v. | 蹉 and 犢子.

婆須蜜(多) Vasumitra, v. 筏蘇蜜呾羅.

婆頗娑 Prabhāsa, light, bright.

冤 To oppress, wrong; a grievance; enmity. | 親 Enmity and friendship. | | 平等心 A mind that knows neither enmity nor friendship, no discrimination of persons.

寄 To go or put under cover, lodge, confide to, deliver, convey, transfer; to enter, put in a list. | 庫 To convey to the treasury, i.e. as paper money or goods are transferred to credit in the next world not only of the dead, but also by the living in store for themselves.

密 Closed in; close together; intimate; quiet, still; secret, occult, esoteric; fine, small; contrasted with 顯 open, exoteric. Cf. 秘. | 付 To pass down esoterically, or by word of mouth. | 印 The esoteric digital sign of a Buddha or bodhisattva indicative of his vow. | 咒 A dhāraṇī, or esoteric incantation. | 號 The esoteric name of Vairocana; also any "true word" (Shingon) or esoteric spell. | 嚴國; | | 淨土 The Pure Land of Vairocana; also in the Hua-yen sūtra called the 華藏 world; the doctrine is found in this sūtra. | 因 The esoteric, occult, recondite cause. | 字 The esoteric letter of Vairocana, or of a Buddha or bodhisattva. | 宗 The esoteric, mantra, Shingon, or "True word" sect, especially prevalent in Japan, where its two chief texts are 毘盧遮那成佛經 and 金剛頂經; founded by Kōbō Daishi, it developed the two maṇḍalas of the Garbhadhātu and Vajradhātu, q.v. | 家 idem the last. | 教 idem, also esoteric teaching in general; the two classes are divided into the | 教 esoteric or Yoga school, and 顯教 the open schools or teaching, comprising all the sects of Buddhism, except the esoteric sect. The | 教三藏 Tripiṭaka of the esoteric sect are, as its sūtra, the 大毘盧舍那金剛頂經; as its vinaya, the 蘇婆呼經根本部; as its śāstras, the 莊嚴菩提心經, etc., q.v. | 機 The motive power, or fundamental element, in the esoteric; the opportunity of learning a mantra. | 法 Esoteric methods. | 灌 The baptism of the esoteric sect. | 經 The foundation texts of the esoteric school, i.e. the 大日經 and 金剛頂經 and various sūtras, especially but not exclusively those with mantras; another group is the first two and the 蘇悉地經. | 義 Esoteric meaning, or doctrine. | 藏 The esoteric canon. | 衆 The followers of the esoteric school. | 行 Esoteric practice, or discipline, the origin of which is attributed to Rāhula. | 語 Occult, or esoteric expressions. | 迹 ; | 跡 Secret or invisible tracks. | 迹金剛力士 Vajrapāṇi, guardian of Buddhas, driving away all yakṣa disturbers, a form of Indra ; his dhāraṇīs have been twice translated into Chinese, v. B.N. The | 奢兜 esoteric "Cintya" is a mantra said to have been used by all the seven Buddhas down to and including Śākyamuni.

宿 A halting-place ; to pass the night, sojourn, stay ; early, former ; left over ; nakṣatra, the constellations. | 世 A former existence. | 作 The deeds of a former life. | 作外道 One of the ascetic sects who sought release from penalties for the deeds of a former life by severe austerities now. | 住 Pūrva-nivāsa, former abidings, or habitations, hence | | (隨念智證) 通, i.e. Buddha-knowledge of the former incarnations of himself and others. | 債 The unrepaid debts from, or sins of, former incarnations. | 哈 idem 娑訶 Svāhā. | 命 Previous life, or lives ; v. | 住. | 命力 Buddha-power to know all previous transmigrations. | 命明 The knowledge of the arhat of his own and other previous transmigrations. | 命 (智) 通 Pūrvanivāsānusmṛti-(jñāna) ; Buddha-knowledge of all forms of previous existence of self and others ; one of the 六 (神) 通. | 善 Good deeds done in previous existence. | 因 Good or evil cause in previous existence. | 執 The character acquired in a previous existence and maintained. | 執開發 The present fruition of the meritorious character developed in previous existence. | 報 The consequence of deeds done in former existence. | 夜 To stay the night ; the previous night, e.g. the night before any special service. | 忌 The night before a fast-day. | 意 A former intention, or vow. | 曜 The twenty-eight constellations and seven luminaries. | 根 ; | 植 The root of one's present lot planted in previous existence. | 業 Former karma, the karma of previous existence. | 王戲 Nakṣatra-rāja-vikrīḍita, the play of the star-king, or king of the constellations, one of the samādhi in the Lotus Sūtra. | 王華 Nakṣatra-rāja-saṅkusumitābhijña, king of the star-flowers, a bodhisattva in the Lotus. | 福 Happy karma from previous existence. | 緣 Causation or inheritance from previous existence. | 習 The practices, habits, or deeds of or inherited from former existence. | 願 The vow made in a former existence. | 願力 The power of an ancient vow.

寂 Praśama ; vivikta ; śānti. Still, silent, quiet, solitary, calm, tranquil, nirvāṇa. | 光 Calm and illuminating as are Truth and Knowledge ; the hidden truth illuminating. | 光 (土) The land (of Buddhas) where is calm illumination. | 命智 Buddha-knowledge of the transmigratory forms of all beings. | 定 Tranquil concentration ; contemplation in which disturbing illusion is eliminated. | 岸 The shore of peace, nirvāṇa. | 常 Peace eternal, eternal nirvāṇa. | 忍 Calmness and endurance, quiet patience. | 念 Calm thoughts ; to calm the mind ; contemplation. | 業師子 The lion of nirvāṇa, Śākyamuni. | 滅 Calmness and extinction, nirvāṇa. | 滅忍 Nirvāṇa-patience ; the patience of the nirvāṇa (the suppression of all passion). | 滅法 The nirvāṇa-method. | 滅無二 Nirvāṇa as absolute without disunity or phenomena. | 滅相 Nirvāṇa considered independently of the phenomenal. | (滅道) 場 The place where a Buddha attains the truth of nirvāṇa, especially where Śākyamuni attained it. | 災 To quell calamities (by spells, or ceremonies). | 然 In calmness, quietude, silence ; undisturbed. | 然界 The Hīnayāna nirvāṇa-realm or border. | 照 Nirvāṇa-illumination ; ultimate reality shining forth. | 照慧 Buddha-wisdom which comprehends nirvāṇa reality and its functioning. | 用湛然 Character (nirvāṇa-like) and function concomitant in the absolute and relative, in being and becoming, etc. | 種 The nirvāṇa class, i.e. the Hinayanists who are said to seek only their own salvation. | 靜 Calm and quiet ; free from temptation and distress ; nirvāṇa. | 靜法 Ceremonies for restoring peace from calamity. | 靜行 Hīnayāna discipline to ensure nirvāṇa. | 靜門 Nirvāṇa, or the absolute — 切諸法, as the door of release from trouble and suffering. | 默外道 Ascetics vowed to silence who dwell among tombs or in solitude.

專 Single ; special ; solely. | 心 With single mind ; whole-heartedly. | 念 To fix the mind, or attention, upon ; solely to invoke (a certain Buddha). | 想 To think wholly, or only, of or upon. | 精 Solely and purely (to advance in the Way).

屏 Screen ; to exclude, expel, turn away. | 莎 Bimbisāra, v. 苹.

崛 Lofty, distinguished. | 山 Vulture peak, abbrev. for 耆闍 | 山. | 多 Abbrev. for Upagupta, cf. 優.

崇 Lofty, eminent, honourable ; to reverence, adore. | 信 Reverence and faith, to revere and trust. | 敬 To reverence and respect.

崑崙 K'un-lun, or Pulo Condore Island, or islands generally in the southern seas, hence | | 子 or | | 奴 is a native of those islands of black colour, and | | 國 is described as Java, Sumatra, etc. | | The K'un-lun range north of Tibet, th 香山 lhamādana.

帶 A girdle, belt, bandage, tape, appendage; connect; implicate; take along. 丨刀臥; 丨丨睡 To take one's sword to bed, which being worn on the left side compels the wearer to sleep on the right, or proper side. 丨塔尊; 丨丨德菩薩 Maitreya, bearer of the pagoda.

常 Nitya; śāśvata. Prolonged, constant, always, unceasing, permanent, perpetual, ever, eternal; normal, ordinary, regular. 丨不輕 Sadāparibhūta, the monk who never slighted others, but assured all of Buddhahood, a former incarnation of Śākyamuni; Lotus Sūtra 20. 丨住 Permanent, always abiding, eternal. 丨住一相 The eternal unity or reality behind all things. 丨光 The unceasing radiance of the Buddha's body, represented as a halo. 丨力 Unfailing powers. 丨啼菩薩 v. 薩陀. 丨境 The eternal realm. 丨寂 Eternal peace, nirvāṇa. 丨寂光土 The realm (of spirit) where all are in perpetual peace and glory; T'ien-t'ai's fourth Buddhakṣetra. 丨恒 Constantly. 丨念 Always remembering; always repeating. 丨智 Knowledge *sub specie æternitatis*, not conditioned by phenomena, abstract. 丨樂我淨 The four pāramitās of knowledge: eternity, bliss, personality, purity, the four transcendental realities in nirvāṇa, v. Nirvāṇa Sūtra. 丨沒 Ever drowning in the sea of mortality. 丨波羅蜜 The first of the four pāramitās, eternity. 丨眼 The ordinary physical eye. 丨立勝幡 An-avanāmita-vaijayanta. With ever erect victorious banner; name of Ānanda's future Buddha-realm. 丨行 Constantly doing, or practising; ordinary procedure. 丨見 The view that (personality) is permanent. 丨身 The eternal Buddha-body, the Dharmakāya. 丨途 Regular ways, or methods. 丨道 Eternal Tao; the way of eternity; regular ways, the regulation path.

庵 A thatched hut, shelter, place of retirement from the world; a small temple; especially a nunnery, hence 丨室; 丨寺 generally applies to such, and 丨主 is the abbess.

庶 A multitude; all; the; a concubine; so that; nearly so. 丨類 The common people. 丨迦(羅) Cakra, a wheel, hence Cakravartī or wheel-king.

康 At ease, in repose; undisturbed; well, hale. 丨居 Samarkand, or Soghdiana, cf. 西域記 1. 丨僧鎧 (or 會) Saṅghavarman, also said to be Saṅghapāla; an Indian monk supposed to be of Tibetan descent; but Saṅghapāla is described as the eldest son of the prime minister of Soghdiana, and is probably a different person. Saṅghavarman tr. at the White Horse Temple, Loyang, in A.D. 252; *inter alia* the 無量壽經 is accredited to him, but a more reliable tradition of the Canon ascribes the tr. to Dharmarakṣa A.D. 308.

徙 Remove, flit. 丨多 v. 私 Śītā.

從 To follow, agree with, obey; from; followers, secondary. 丨地踊出 Springing out of the earth, chapter 15 in the Lotus Sūtra. 丨容 Of calm demeanour, easy and natural, unperturbed. 丨僧 A "half-monk", a neophyte.

得 Prāp; Prāpta. To get, obtain, attain to; got, obtained, etc. 丨入 To attain entry, e.g. to Buddha-truth. 丨勝 To obtain the victory. 丨大勢; (大)勢至 Mahāsthāmaprāpta, he who has obtained great power, or stability, who sits on the right of Amitābha, controlling all wisdom. 丨度 To obtain transport across the river of transmigration, to obtain salvation; to enter the monastic life. 丨意 To obtain one's desires, or aims; to obtain the meaning (of a sūtra). 丨戒 To obtain the commandments; to attain to the understanding and performance of the moral law. 丨戒沙彌 A monk who is restored, or not unfrocked, on confession of his sin. 丨果 To obtain the fruit of deeds or life. 丨眼林 Āptanetravana, the forest of recovered eyes. 丨繩 The cord, or bond, of attaining; the bondage of possessing. 丨羅盧迦 Trailokya, 三界 q.v. 丨藏 Śrīgarbha, idem 淨眼 Vimalanetra. 丨脫 To attain to deliverance (from the miseries of reincarnation). 丨道 To obtain the way, or the religion; by obedience to the commandments, practice of meditation, and knowledge, to attain enlightenment. 丨髓 To obtain the marrow, the secret, the essence.

惛 Confused, stupefied. 丨沈 Sunk in stupor.

惜 To care for, regard, compassionate, pity; spare. 丨囊 To be as careful of (the monastic law as of) the skin-floats when swimming a river.

惟 To reflect on; but, only; verbal particle; cf. 唯. 丨予 (or 于) 頗羅 Bṛhatphala 廣果, "great fruit," or abundant merits; the twelfth Brahmaloka, or second region of the fourth dhyāna.

情 The feelings, passions, desires, affections, sensations; sentient; affinities; affairs, facts. Particular affections, duties, or affairs. 丨塵 The six guṇas or objects of sensation of the six organs of sense; sensation and its data; sensation-data;

passion-defilement. | 有 The realm of feeling, i.e. any world of sentience or feeling, especially this world as empirically considered; 有 | is to have consciousness, the conscious, or sentient. | 有理無 Empirically or sentiently existing, in essence or reality non-existent. | 欲 The passions, desires. | 猿 The passions like an ape, never still. | 見 The perverted views produced by passion or affection.

悉 Investigate thoroughly; fully, minutely; all; translit. *si, sa, s, śr*. | 伽羅 Śṛgāla, 野干 a jackal. | 他薜攞; | 替耶 Sthavira, an elder, a term applied to a monk of 20–50 years of age and of ten years' standing; the Sthaviranikāya | 他陛攞尼迦耶, or 上坐部 q.v., was one of the four branches of the Vaibhāṣika school. | 利 idem 室利 q.v. | 地 Siddhi, accomplishment, complete attainment, perfection, proof, truth, final emancipation, supreme felicity, magical or supernatural powers; cf. M. W. As supernatural power it is used to end calamities, subdue demons, etc. | 多頞他 Siddhārtha, *infra*. | 底 Siddhi, *supra*. | 怛多般怛羅 Sitātapatra, a white umbrella, or canopy. | 曇; | 檀; | 談 Siddha(m), accomplished, finished, v. Siddhi above; and next. | | 章 Siddhavastu, the first of twelve chapters of a syllabary attributed to Brahmā, originating the thirty-six letters of the alphabet, later said to be expanded to as many as fifty-two. | 檀; | 談 Siddhānta, an established conclusion, proved fact, axiom, dogma, a text or authoritative work, cf. M. W.; intp. as 成就 complete, and incorrectly as the Buddha's unstinted gift of the 四法 q.v. | 耻羅末底 Sthiramati, one of the 唯識 writers. | 達(多) Siddhārtha, Sarvārthasiddha, also | 多(頞他); | 陀 the realization of all aims, prosperous; personal name of Śākyamuni. | 陁 idem 私多.

掘 To dig. | 倫 ? Kulun, i.e. Pulo Condore, also called 崑崙. | 具羅 A kind of western incense.

捫打勒 Maṇḍala, v. 曼.

捺 To press down; a pen-stroke to the right; translit. *na*. | 地迦葉波 Nadī-Kāśyapa, also 那提 a brother of Mahā-Kāśyapa, to be reborn as Buddha Samanta-prabhāsa. | (or 那) 落迦 Naraka, hell, the hells, v. 地獄; | 落迦 sometimes refers to the place of torment, and 那 | | nāraka to the sufferer there. | 讟; | 麻 Namaḥ, v. 南.

捧 To hold in both hands, offer, receive; a double handful. | 物 To bear or offer gifts in both hands.

掃 To sweep. | 地 To sweep the floor, or ground, an act to which the Buddha is said to have attributed five kinds of merit; v. 毘奈耶雜事.

探 To feel for, explore, investigate, search; to spy, inquire into. | 水 To sound the depth of water, the lower part of a staff, i.e. for sounding depth.

掉 To shake, change, arrange; to fall. | 悔 Discontent and regret, ambition and repining. | 散 Unsteady in act, word, and thought; unreliable | (舉) Ambitious, unsettled.

推 To push away, recede from, decline, resign, push, put, put off; investigate. | 功歸本 To put off minor merit for the sake of fundamentals. | 究 To search out, investigate. | 却 To decline.

採 To pick, gather, choose. | 花; | 華 To pick flowers. | 菽氏 Bean-picker, a tr. of the name of Maudgalyāyana, from mudga, kidney-beans.

掩 To cover (with the hand), screen, shut up. | 土 To bury, inter. | 室 To shut (oneself) in a room, as did the Buddha for meditation. | 色 To cover the form, or face, i.e. the death of the Buddha, or a noted monk, referring to the covering of the face.

掛 To hang, suspend. | 子 A peg for a garment. | 搭; | 褡; | 單 One who hangs up all his possessions, i.e. a wandering monk who stays for the night in a monastery. | 眞 To hang up a picture (of a Buddha, etc.). | 絡; | 落; | 羅 A short garment, or cover; a waistcoat. | 錫 To hang up one's staff, similar to | 搭; to dwell in a place.

接 To receive, take; join on; graft. | 引 To receive and lead, to welcome. | 待 To receive and treat, or wait upon. | 生 To receive the living; also to receive at birth as a midwife does. | 足作禮 To embrace the (Buddha's) feet in reverence or pleading, or to extend the arms in that posture.

授 To give, confer, deliver, communicate to, hand down. | 事 Karmadāna, the director of duties, the one who gives out the work. | 手 To proffer the hand, to come in person to welcome the dying, as e.g. does Kuan-yin in certain cases. | 決 To give decisions, idem | 記. | 衣 To give out winter garments in the ninth month. | 記; 和伽羅

Vyākaraṇa, Vyākāra; the giving of a record, prediction; foretelling; the prophetic books of the Canon predicting the future glory of individuals and groups of disciples, both final and temporary, and the various stages of progress. There are several classifications, v. 二 and 八 記. Cf. 憍.

捨 Upekṣā, neglect, indifference, abandoning, M. W. To relinquish, renounce, abandon, reject, give. One of the chief Buddhist virtues, that of renunciation, leading to a state of "indifference without pleasure or pain" (Keith), or independence of both. v. 舍. It is defined as the mind 平等 in equilibrium, i.e. above the distinction of things or persons, of self or others; indifferent, having abandoned the world and all things, and having no affections or desires. One of the seven bodhyaṅgas. Translit. *sa*, *śa*, *s(r)*. | 囉梵 Śarāva, a shard, an earthenware vessel. | 心 The mind of renunciation. | 念清淨地 The pure land or heaven free from thinking, the fifth of the nine Brahmalokaṣ in the fourth dhyāna region. | 攞馱 Śraddhā, faith, confidence, trust, belief. | 受 The state of renunciation, or indifference to sensation. | 家棄欲 To leave home and cast off desire, i.e. to become a monk. | 無量心 Upekṣā, one of the four forms of the unsparing or unlimited mind, complete abandonment, absolute indifference, renunciation of the mental faculties. | 身 Bodily sacrifice, e.g. by burning, or cutting off a limb, etc.

救 To save, rescue, prevent from ill. | 世 To save the world; a saviour of the world, i.e. | | 者 or 尊; | | 菩薩 Buddhas and bodhisattvas as world-saviours, especially | | 觀世音 Kuan-yin, also called | | 圓滿 complete saviour of the world. | | 輪 The wheel of salvation. | | 闡提 The world-saving Icchanti, q.v., the Bodhisattva who defers entry into Buddhahood to fulfil his vow of saving all beings. | 拔 To save and drag out of suffering, e.g. hell. | 脫 To save and set free; to be saved and freed. | 苦 To save from suffering, to save the suffering. | 護 To save and protect.

敏 Clever, active, ingenious, witty. | 倶理 ? Hingulā, an Indian name doubtfully intp. as Korea. 聰 | Wise, clever.

敗 Subvert, defeat, ruin, spoil, destroy. | 壞菩薩 Bodhisattvas who defeat their proper end of becoming Buddha, and who are reborn in lower positions, e.g. as kings or princes, or as dragon-kings, etc. | 根; | 種 Spoiled roots, or seed, i.e. Hīnayānists who do not seek Buddhahood, but are content with the rewards of asceticism.

教 Pravacana, to teach, instruct, inculcate; śāśana, teaching, precept, doctrine; āgama, sect, school, church.

教主 The founder of a religion, e.g. the Buddha.

教令 To instruct, command; the commands of a sect or school.

教內 Within instruction; in the sect or church; especially those who receive normal instruction from the written canon, opposite of 敎外.

教典 The sacred books of a religion, or sect.

教判 The various divisions of teaching or doctrine, such as the T'ien-t'ai theory of the five periods of Śākyamuni's life, the four classes of doctrine, the four styles of teaching, etc.

教勅 The commands of a master or father.

教化 To transform by instruction; teach and convert; to cause another to give alms.

教外 Outside the sect, or school, or church; also not undergoing normal instruction, i.e. the intuitive school which does not rely on texts or writings, but on personal communication of its tenets, either oral or otherwise, including direct contact with the Buddha or object of worship, e.g. "guidance".

教導 To instruct and lead.

教授 To instruct, give instruction. | | 師; | | 阿闍梨 An ācārya, or instructor, preceptor.

教會 An assembly for instruction; a congregation; a church.

教理 The fundamental principles of a religion; its doctrines, or dogmas, e.g. the four truths, the twelve nidānas, the eightfold noble path. | | 行果 The fruit or results arising from the practice of a religion.

教相 The particular teaching of a sect.

教網 The teaching (of Buddha) viewed as a net to catch and save mortals.

教義 The meaning of a teaching, or doctrine.

教行 Instruction and conduct; teaching and practice; also the progress of the teaching, or doctrine. 丨丨證 Teaching, practice and its realization, its evidential results.

教觀 Teaching and meditation; the Buddha's doctrine and meditation on it; also 丨丨二門.

教語 The words of Buddhism; words of instruction.

教證 Teaching and evidence, doctrine and its evidential results, or realization.

教迹 The vestiges, or evidences of a religion; e.g. the doctrines, institutions, and example of the teachings of Buddha and the saints.

教道 To teach a way, or religion; a taught way contrasted with an intuitional way; the way of teaching.

教門 A religion, a sect, different religious teachings.

教體 The body, or corpus of doctrine; the whole teaching.

斛 Droṇa, a tub, or wooden vessel; a measure of capacity. A square wooden vessel, a bushel, a picul. 丨飯 Droṇodana, cf. 途.

旋 Revolve, turn round, whirl. 丨嵐 A whirlwind, cyclone. 丨火輪 A whirling wheel of fire, a circle yet not a circle, a simile of the seeming but unreal, i.e. the unreality of phenomena. 丨陀羅尼 A spell which endows with extensive powers of evolution; also varied involutions of magical terms.

晝 Day, daytime, daylight. 丨暗林 The grove of daylight darkness, a cemetery.

晨 Dawn, morning. 丨朝 The morning period, the first of the three divisions of the day.

晦 The last day of the moon; night; dark, obscure; unlucky. 昏 丨 Obscure, dark.

晚 Sunset, evening, twilight; late. 丨參 The evening service. 丨粥 The evening gruel, which being against the rule of not eating after midday is styled medicine.

晤 Clear; to meet; to explain. 丨恩 Wu-ssŭ, founder of the 山外 external school of the T'ien-t'ai, died A.D. 986.

曹 Company, class; used as the plural of pronouns, etc. 丨山 Ts'ao-shan in Kiangsu, where the Ts'ao-tung sect 丨洞宗, a branch of the Ch'an school, was founded by Tung-shan 洞山; Ts'ao-shan was the name of the second patriarch of this sect. 丨溪 Ts'ao-ch'i, a stream, south-east of Shao-chou, Kwangtung, which gave its name to 慧能 Hui-nêng.

曼 Long, prolonged, extended, widespread. 丨供 Offerings of mandārava flowers, cf. *infra*. 丨勝尊 A title of a Buddha. 丨怛 (or 特) 羅 v. *infra* and 滿怛羅 are also used for mantra, an incantation, spell, magical formula, or muttered sound. 丨殊室 (or 尸) 利 Mañjuśrī, v. 文殊, and the 丨丨丨丨經. 丨丨沙; 丨丨顏 Mañjūṣaka, the "*Rubia cordifolia*, the roots of which yield the madder of Bengal called Munjeeth". Eitel. 丨荼羅; 丨怛丨; 丨特丨; 丨陀丨; 丨拏丨; 蔓陀囉; 滿荼邏 Maṇḍala, a circle, globe, wheel, ring; "any circular figure or diagram" (M. W.); a magic circle; a plot or place of enlightenment; a round or square altar on which Buddhas and bodhisattvas are placed; a group of such, especially the Garbhadhātu and Vajradhātu groups of the Shingon sect; these were arranged by Kōbō Daishi to express the mystic doctrine of the two dhātu by way of illustration, the Garbhadhātu representing the 理 and the 因 principle and cause, the Vajradhātu the 智 and the 果 intelligence (or reason) and the effect, i.e. the fundamental realm of being, and mind as inherent in it; v. 胎 and 金剛. The two realms are fundamentally one, as are the absolute and phenomenal, e.g. water and wave. There are many kinds of maṇḍalas, e.g. the group of the Lotus Sūtra; of the 觀經; of the nine luminaries; of the Buddha's entering into nirvāṇa, etc. The real purpose of a maṇḍala is to gather the spiritual powers together, in order to promote the operation of the dharma or law. The term is commonly applied to a magic circle, subdivided into circles or squares in which are painted Buddhist divinities and symbols. Maṇḍalas also reveal the direct retribution of each of the ten worlds of beings (purgatory, pretas, animals, asuras, men, devas, the heavens of form, formless heavens, bodhisattvas, and Buddhas). Each world has its maṇḍala which represents the originating principle that brings it to completion. The maṇḍala of the tenth world indicates the fulfilment and completion of the nine worlds. ｜｜｜敎 Maṇḍala doctrine, mantra teaching, magic, yoga, the True word or Shingon sect. ｜陀 (or 陁) 羅; 漫陀羅 Mandāra(va), the coral-tree; the *Erythrina indica*, or this tree regarded as one of the five trees of Paradise, i.e. Indra's heaven; a white variety of *Calotropis gigantea*. Name of a noted monk, and of one called Mandra. ｜首 idem 文殊.

望 To look at, or for; expect, hope; towards; the full moon. 失｜To lose hope. 盼｜To hope for.

梅 The plum. ｜呾利(耶); ｜｜｜曳那; ｜｜囉曳尼; ｜呾黎; ｜呾麗藥; 昧怛履曳 v. 彌勒 Maitreya, friendly, benevolent; the expected Buddhist Messiah.

梖 Pattra; ｜多葉 the palm-leaves used for writing; the ｜｜樹 is erroneously said to be the *Borassus flabelliformis*, described as 60 or 70 feet high, not deciduous, the bark used for writing.

梯 A ladder, stairs. ｜隥 Ladder rungs, or steps, used for the 漸敎 school of gradual revelation in contrast with the 頓敎 full and immediate revelation.

桶 A tub, bucket, barrel. ｜頭 The monk who looks after these things in a large establishment.

梨 The pear. ｜耶 v. 阿 Ārya. ｜車; 黎車; 離車; 栗呫婆 Licchavi, the ancient republic of Vaiśālī, whose people were among the earliest followers of Śākyamuni.

梁皇懺 The litany of Liang Wu Ti for his wife, who became a large snake, or dragon, after her death, and troubled the emperor's dreams. After the litany was performed, she became a devī, thanked the emperor, and departed.

梵 Brahman (from roots *bṛh*, *vṛh*, connected with *bṛṁh*), "religious devotion," "prayer," "a sacred text," or mantra, "the mystic syllable *Om*"; "sacred learning," "the religious life," "the Supreme Being regarded as impersonal," "the Absolute," "the priestly or sacerdotal class," etc. M. W. Translit. ｜摩; ｜覽摩 or 磨; 勃嚂摩; 婆羅賀摩; 沒羅憾摩; intp. as Brahmā, see ｜天; and brahman, or priest; it is used both in a noble and ignoble sense, ignoble when disparaging brahman opposition; it is intp. by 淨 pure, also by 離欲清淨 celibate and pure.

梵世界 The Brahmaloka of the realm of form; also ｜｜天.

梵乘 The brahmayāna, i.e. the noblest of the vehicles, that of the bodhisattva.

梵僧 A monk from India. Also a monk who maintains his purity.

梵典 Buddhist sūtras, or books.

梵剎 Brahmakṣetra, Buddha-land; a name for a Buddhist monastery, i.e. a place of purity.

梵唄 Buddhist hymns, cf. 唄. They are sung to repress externals and calm the mind within for religious service; also in praise of Buddha.

梵土 Brahman-land, India.

梵壇 (or 怛) Brahmadaṇḍa, Brahma-staff ｜杖, the Brahma (i.e. religious) punishment (stick), but the derivation is uncertain; the explanation is "to send to Coventry" a recalcitrant monk, the forbidding of any conversation with him, called also 默擯 exclusion to silence.

梵天 Brahmadeva. Brahmā, the ruler of this world. India. Brahmaloka, the eighteen heavens of the realm of form, divided into four dhyāna regions (sixteen heavens in Southern Buddhism). The first three contain the ｜衆天 assembly of brahmadevas, i.e. the Brahmakāyika; the ｜輔天 Brahmapurohitas, retinue of Brahmā; and 大｜天 Mahābrahman, Brahman himself. ｜｜外道 Brahmadeva heretics; the Brahmans consider Brahmā to be the Creator of all things and the Supreme Being, which is heresy with Buddhism. ｜｜后 The queen, or wife of Brahmā. ｜｜女 A devī in the Garbhadhātu group. ｜｜王 Brahmā, v. above, and cf. ｜王. ｜｜界 His realm.

梵夾 Palm-leaf scriptures; also ｜筴; ｜篋; ｜挾; 經夾.

梵女 A noble woman, a woman of high character.

梵學 The study of Buddhism; the study of Brahmanism.

梵宇 A sacred house, i.e. a Buddhist monastery, or temple.

梵字 Brahma letters; Saṁskṛtam; Sanskrit; also 丨書 The classical Aryan language of India, systematized by scholars, in contradistinction to Prākrit, representing the languages as ordinarily spoken. With the exception of a few ancient translations probably from Pāli versions, most of the original texts used in China were Sanskrit. Various alphabets have been introduced into China for transliterating Indian texts, the Devanāgarī alphabet, which was introduced via Tibet, is still used on charms and in sorcery. Pāli is considered by some Chinese writers to be more ancient than Sanskrit both as a written and spoken language.

梵室 A dwelling where celibate discipline is practised, a monastery, temple.

梵宮 Brahmā's palace; a Buddhist temple.

梵富樓 Brahmapurohita, the ministers, or assistants of Brahmā; the second Brahmaloka; the second region of the first dhyāna heaven of form. Also 丨輔.

梵延 Brahmā and Nārāyaṇa.

梵德 The power, or bliss, of Brahmā.

梵心 The noble or pure mind (which practises the discipline that ensures rebirth in the realm without form).

梵志 Brahmacārin. "Studying sacred learning; practising continence or chastity." M. W. A Brahmacārī is a "young Brahman in the first āśrama or period of his life" (M. W.); there are four such periods. A Buddhist ascetic with his will set on 梵 purity, also intp. as nirvāṇa.

梵摩 Brahmā; brahman, etc., v. 梵; 丨天, etc. 丨丨三鉢 Brahmā-sahāmpati, or Mahābrahmā-sahāmpati; Brahmā, lord of the world. 丨丨尼 Brahma-maṇi, pure pearl, or the magic pearl of Brahmā. 丨丨羅 Brahman, i.e. Brahmā; or Brahmā and Māra; or both as one. 丨丨達 Brahmadatta, a king of Kanyākubja. A king of Vārāṇaśī, father of Kāśyapa.

梵服 The kaṣāya or monk's robe; the garment of celibacy.

梵本 Sūtras in the Indian language.

梵王 Brahmā, cf. 丨天. The father of all living beings; the first person of the Brahminical Trimūrti, Brahmā, Viṣṇu, and Śiva, recognized by Buddhism as devas but as inferior to a Buddha, or enlightened man. 丨丨宮 The palace of Brahmā.

梵宮 The realm of Brahmā; the first dhyāna heaven of the realm of form.

梵皇 The Indian Emperor, Buddha.

梵相 Brahmadhvaja, one of the sons of Mahābhijña; his Buddha domain is south-west of our universe.

梵章 Brahmavastu, a Sanskrit syllabary in twelve parts.

梵網 Brahmajāla; Brahma-net. 丨丨宗 The sect of Ritsu 律宗, brought into Japan by the Chinese monk 鑑眞 Chien-chên in A.D. 754. 丨丨經 Brahmajāla-sūtra, tr. by Kumārajīva A.D. 406, the infinitude of worlds being as the eyes or holes in Indra's net, which is all-embracing, like the Buddha's teaching. There are many treatises on it. 丨丨戒品 A name for the above, or the next. 丨丨戒本; 菩薩戒經 The latter part of the above sūtra.

梵聲 The voice of Buddha.

梵苑 A monastery or any place where celibate discipline is practised.

梵衆 Monks, so called because of their religious practices. 丨丨天 Brahmapāriṣadya (or pārṣadya), belonging to the retinue of Brahmā; the first Brahmaloka; the first region of the first dhyāna heaven of form.

梵行 Pure living; noble action; the discipline of celibacy which ensures rebirth in the Brahmaloka, or in the realms beyond form.

梵衍那 Bayana, "an ancient kingdom and city in Bokhara famous for a colossal statue of Buddha (entering Nirvāṇa) believed to be 1,000 feet long." Eitel. The modern Bamian.

梵語 Brahma language, Sanskrit, the Sanskrit alphabet; "the language of India"; supposed to come from Brahmā.

梵身 The pure spiritual body, or dharmakāya, of the Buddha, v. 法 |. | | 天 The Brahmakāyika, or retinue of Brahmā..

梵輪 The brahma-wheel, the wheel of the law, or pure preaching of the Buddha; his four | 行 v. 四無量心; the first sermon at the request of Brahmā; the doctrine or preaching of the Brahmans.

梵迦夷 Brahma-kāyikas; the Brahma-devas; v. | 天.

梵道 The way of purity, or celibacy; the brahman way.

梵釋 Brahmā, the lord of the form-realm, and Śakra of the desire-realm. | | 四天 Brahmā, Śakra, and the four Mahārājas.

梵鐘 A temple or monastery bell.

梵難 The difficulty of maintaining celibacy, or purity.

梵面佛 A Buddha with Brahma's face, said to be 23,000 years old.

梵音 (1) Brahma voice, clear, melodious, pure, deep, far-reaching, one of the thirty-two marks of a Buddha. (2) Singing in praise of Buddha.

梵響 The sound of Buddha's voice; his preaching.

梵魔 Brahmā and Māra, the former lord of the realm of form, the latter of desire or passion.

欲 Rajas, passion. Also Kāma, desire, love. The Chinese word means to breathe after, aspire to, desire, and is also used as 慾 for lust, passion; it is *inter alia* intp. as 染愛塵 tainted with the dust (or dirt) of love, or lust. The three desires are for beauty, demeanour, and softness; the five are those of the five physical senses.

欲刺 The sharp point of desire.

欲塵 The dust, or dirt, or infection of the passions; the guṇas, or qualities, or material factors of desire regarded as forces. Also the six desires and the five guṇas 六欲五塵.

欲天 The six heavens of desire or passion, the kāmadhātu. | | 五婬 The five methods of sexual intercourse in the heavens of desire; in the heaven of the Four Great Kings and in Trayastriṁśās the method is the same as on earth; in the Yama-devaloka a mere embrace is sufficient; in the Tuṣita-heaven, holding hands; in the Nirmāṇarati heaven, mutual smiles; in the other heavens of Transformation, regarding each other.

欲心 A desirous, covetous, passionate, or lustful heart.

欲性 Desire-nature, the lusts.

欲愛 Passion-love; love inspired by desire, through any of the five senses; love in the passion-realm as contrasted to 法愛 the love inspired by the dharma. | | 住地 One of the five fundamental conditions of the passions, v. 五住(地).

欲有 The realm of desire, one of the 三有. | | 見無明 The unenlightened condition of desire; kāma-bhava-dṛṣṭi-avidyā are the four constituents which produce 漏 q.v.

欲染 The tainting, or contaminating influence of desire.

欲樂 The joys of the five desires.

欲氣 Desire-breath, passion-influence, the spirit or influence of desire, lust.

欲泥 The mire of desire, or lust.

欲河 The river of desire, or lust (which drowns).

欲海 The ocean of desire, so called because of its extent and depth.

欲流 The stream of the passions, i.e. the illusions of cupidity, anger, etc., which keep the individual in the realm of desire; the stream of transmigration, which results from desire.

欲漏 The stream or flow of existence, evoked by desire interpenetrated by unenlightened views and thoughts; these stimulating desires produce karma which in turn produces reincarnation; v. 三漏.

欲火 The fire of desire.

欲界 Kāmadhātu. The realm, or realms, of desire for food, sleep, and sex, consisting of souls in purgatory, hungry spirits, animals, asuras, men, and the six heavens of desire, so called because the beings in these states are dominated by desire. The Kāmadhātu realms are given as: 地居 Bhauma. 虛空天 Antarikṣa. 四天王天 Caturmahārājakāyika [i.e. the realms of 持國天 Dhṛtarāṣṭra, east; 增長天 Virūḍhaka, south; 廣目天 Virūpakṣa, west; 多聞天 Vaiśramaṇa (Dhanada), north]. 忉利天 Trayastriṁśa. 兜率天 Tuṣita. 化樂天 Nirmāṇarati. 他化自在天 Paranirmitavaśavartin.

欲箭 The arrows of desire, or lust. Also the darts of the Bodhisattva 欲金剛, who hooks and draws all beings to Buddha.

欲色 The two realms of desire and form, or the passions and the sensuous.

欲苦 The sufferings of desire, or in desire-realms.

欲覺 Passion-consciousness; the consciousness of desire.

欲貪 Desire and coveting, or coveting as the result of passion; craving.

欲邪行 Adulterous conduct, prohibited in the five commandments.

欲鉤 The hook of desire; the bodhisattva attracts men through desire, and then draws them to the enlightenment of Buddha.

欲魔 The evil demon of lust.

殑伽 Gaṅgā, the Ganges; also 丨河 v. 恒. 丨者 Gaṅgā, the goddess of the Ganges.

毫 Down, soft hair; minute, trifling, tiny. 丨眉 The white hair between Buddha's eyebrows, the 丨相, i.e. one of the thirty-two signs of a Buddha.

混 Turbid, intermingled, confused, chaotic. 丨沌 Mixed, confused, in disorder.

淋 To drip, sprinkle, soak. 丨汗 Dripping sweat; to sprinkle or pour water on the body to cleanse it.

淚 Tears. 丨墮 Falling tears.

淘 To scour, swill, wash, cleanse; tricky, playful. 丨汰 The fourth of the five periods of Buddha's teaching, according to T'ien-t'ai, i.e. the sweeping away of false ideas, produced by appearance, with the doctrine of the Void, or the reality behind the seeming.

添 Add, additional, increase. 丨品 Additional chapter, or chapters.

淫 Excess, excessive; licentious, lewd; adultery, fornication. 丨欲 Sexual passion. 丨丨火 Its fire, or burning. 丨丨病 The (spiritual) disease it causes. 丨湯 A kind of rice soup, or gruel. 丨羅 The net of passion. Also 婬.

淺 Shallow; superficial; light in colour; simple, easy. 丨略 Superficial, simple, not profound. 丨臘 Of few years, i.e. youthful in monastic years.

深 Deep, profound, abstruse. 丨入 Deep entering, or the deep sense, i.e. 貪 desire, covetousness, cupidity. 丨奧; 丨妙; 丨密; 丨秘 Deep, profound, abstruse. 丨坑 A deep or fathomless pit. 丨信 Deep faith. 丨心 A mind profoundly engrossed (in Buddha-truth, or thought, or illusion, etc.). 丨摩舍那 Śmaśāna, v. 尸, place for disposing of the dead. 丨智 Profound knowledge or wisdom. 丨法(門) Profound truth, or method. 丨法忍 Patience, or perseverance, in faith and practice. 丨淨 Profoundly pure. 丨玄 Deep, abstruse, dark, deep black. 丨理 Profound principle, law, or truth. 丨經; 丨藏 The profound sūtras, or texts, those of Mahāyāna. 丨行 Deep or deepening progress, that above the initial bodhisattva stage.

清 Amala. Pure, clear. 丨信士 or 丨信男 and 丨信女 Upāsaka and Upāsikā, male and female lay devotees. 丨揚 Clear and resonant. 丨明 Clear and bright; the Chinese spring festival on the

19th of the 2nd moon, when honour is paid to departed spirits. | 梵 Pure Sanskrit; Buddha's resonant voice, or pure enunciation. | 涼; | 涼 Clear and cool; clear, pure. | 涼國師 Pure-minded preceptor of the State, title of the fourth patriarch of the Hua-yen school. | 涼寺 A monastery at Wu-t'ai shan. | 涼山 A name for Wu-t'ai in north Shansi; also the abode of Mañjuśrī, north-east of our universe. | 涼月 The pure moon, i.e. the Buddha. | 涼池 The pure lake, or pool, i.e. nirvāṇa. | 淨 Pariśuddhi; viśuddhi. Pure and clean, free from evil and defilement, perfectly clean. | 淨人 The pure and clean man, especially the Buddha. | 淨光明身 The pure, shining body or appearance (of the Buddha). | 淨園 Pure garden, or garden of purity, i.e. a monastery or convent. | 淨心 A pure mind free from doubt or defilement. | | 智 Undefiled knowledge. | | 本然 Purely and naturally so, spontaneous. | | 業處 The state which one who has a pure karma reaches. | | 法 Dharmaviraja, pure truth. | | 法界 The pure Buddha-truth (realm). | | 法眼 The pure dharma-eye, with which the Hīnayāna disciple first discerns the four noble truths, and the Mahāyāna disciple discerns the unreality of self and things. | | 眞如 One of the seven Chên-ju, q.v. | | 覺海 The pure ocean of enlightenment, which underlies the disturbed life of all. | | 解脫三昧 A samādhi free from all impurity and in which complete freedom is obtained. | | 識 Amalavijñāna, pure, uncontaminated knowledge; earlier regarded as the ninth, later as the eighth or ālaya-vijñāna. | 白 Pure and white, pure white, as Buddha-truth, or as pure goodness. | 辯 Bhāvaviveka, a noted Buddhist philosopher *circa* A.D. 600, a follower of Nāgārjuna. | 齋 Pure observance of monastic rules for food; to eat purely, i.e. vegetarian food; fasting.

淨 Vimala. Clean, pure; to cleanse, purify; chastity. In Buddhism it also has reference to the place of cleansing, the latrine, etc. Also 凈.

淨主 The donor of chastity, i.e. of an abode for monks or nuns.

淨住 A pure rest, or abode of purity, a term for a Buddhist monastery.

淨佛 Pure Buddha, perfect Buddhahood, of the dharmakāya nature.

淨侶 The company of pure ones, i.e. monks or nuns.

淨信 Pure faith.

淨刹 The pure kṣetra, i.e. Buddha-land.

淨命 Pure livelihood, 正命, i.e. that of the monk. Also the life of a pure or unperturbed mind.

淨國 The pure land, i.e. Buddha-land.

淨圓覺心 Pure and perfect enlightened mind: the complete enlightenment of the Buddha.

淨土 Sukhāvatī. The Pure Land, or Paradise of the West, presided over by Amitābha. Other Buddhas have their Pure Lands; seventeen other kinds of pure land are also described, all of them of moral or spiritual conditions of development, e.g. the pure land of patience, zeal, wisdom, etc. | | 宗 The Pure-land sect, whose chief tenet is salvation by faith in Amitābha; it is the popular cult in China, also in Japan, where it is the Jōdo sect; it is also called 蓮(花)宗 the Lotus sect. Established by Hui-yüan 慧遠 of the Chin dynasty (317–419), it claims P'u-hsien 普賢 Samantabhadra as founder. Its seven chief textbooks are 無量清淨平等覺經; 大阿彌陀經; 無量壽經; 觀無量壽經; 阿彌陀經; 稱讚淨土佛攝受經; and 鼓音聲三陀羅尼經. The | | 眞宗 is the Jōdo-Shin, or Shin sect of Japan.

淨地 Pure locality, i.e. where a chaste monk dwells.

淨域 The Pure Lands of all Buddhas.

淨天 Pure heaven, or pure devas; śrota-āpannas to pratyeka-buddhas are so called. | | 眼 The pure deva eye, which can see all things small and great, near and far, and the forms of all beings before their transmigration.

淨宗 idem | 土 |.

淨家 The Pure-land sect.

淨居天 The five heavens of purity, in the fourth dhyāna heaven, where the saints dwell who will not return to another rebirth. Also Śuddhāvāsa-deva, "a deva who served as guardian angel to Śākyamuni and brought about his conversion." Eitel.

淨屋 House of chastity, i.e. a monastery or convent.

淨心 The pure heart or mind, which is the original Buddha-nature in every man. ||住 The pure heart stage, the third of the six resting-places of a bodhisattva, in which all illusory views are abandoned.

淨戒 The pure commandments, or to keep them in purity.

淨方 The Pure Land of Amitābha, v. |土.

淨施 Pure charity, which does not seek fame or blessing in this world, but only desires to sow nirvāṇa-seed.

淨梵王 Brahmā, as the pure divine ruler. Also |飯王 q.v.

淨業 Good karma; also the deeds which lead to birth in the Pure Land.

淨法界 The realm of pure dharma, the unsullied realm, i.e. the bhūtatathatā.

淨波羅蜜 The fourth pāramitā of the Nirvāṇa sūtra, 常樂我淨 v. 常.

淨潔五欲 The five pure desires, or senses, i.e. of the higher worlds in contrast with the coarse senses of the lower worlds.

淨瑠璃世界 The pure crystal realm in the eastern region, the paradise of Yao Shih 藥師 Buddha; it is the Bhaiṣajyaguruvaiḍūrya-prabhāsa.

淨眼 The clear or pure eyes that behold, with enlightened vision, things not only as they seem but in their reality. Also Vimalanetra, second son of Śubhavyūha in the Lotus Sūtra.

淨聖 Pure saint, the superior class of saints.

淨肉 Pure flesh, the kind which may be eaten by a monk without sin, three, five, and nine classes being given.

淨菩提心 Pure bodhi mind, or mind of pure enlightenment, the first stage of the practitioner in the esoteric sect.

淨華衆 The pure flower multitude, i.e. those who are born into the Pure Land by means of a lotus flower.

淨藏 Vimalagarbha, eldest son of Śubhavyūha in the Lotus Sūtra.

淨衆 Pure assembly, the company of the chaste, the body of monks.

淨行者 One who observes ascetic practices; one of pure or celibate conduct; a Brahman; also 梵志.

淨裔 Of pure descent, or line; a young Brahman; an ascetic in general.

淨覺 Pure enlightenment.

淨觀 Pure contemplation, such as the sixteen mentioned in the 無量壽經.

淨語 Pure words; words that express reality.

淨諸根 Undefiled senses; i.e. undefiled eye, ear, mouth, nose, body.

淨道 The pure enlightenment of Buddha.

淨邦 idem |土.

淨門 Gate of purity to nirvāṇa, one of the 六妙.

淨頭 The monk who controls the latrines.

淨飯王 Pure rice king, Śuddhodana, the father of Śākyamuni; v. 首.

淨髮 To cleanse the hair, i.e. shave the head as do the monks.

牽 To haul, drag, influence, implicate. |引因 Sarvatraga-hetu, "omnipresent causes, like false views which affect every act." Keith. |道八道

行城 To advance on the city from all sides as in chess 波羅塞 prāsaka, i.e. to employ the omnipresent dharmas (sarvatraga) for salvation.

猊 A fabulous beast like a lion, of extraordinary powers. | 下 A kind of lion-throne for Buddhas, etc.; a term of respect like 足下. | 座 A lion-throne.

猛 Fierce, violent; determined; sudden | 利 Fierce, sudden. | 火 Fierce fire, conflagration.

率 A net with handle; to pursue, follow after; lead on; suddenly; generally. | 都婆 Stūpa, a mound, v. 塔. | 祿勤那 Srughna. "An ancient kingdom and city near the upper course of the Yamunā, probably the region between" Saharanpur and Srinagar. Eitel.

現 Appear, apparent; manifest, visible; now; present; ready.

現世 The present world.

現前 Now present, manifest before one. | | 地 The sixth of the ten stages of the bodhisattva, in which the bhūtatathatā is manifested to him.

現喩 A comparison consisting of immediate facts, or circumstances.

現圖曼陀羅 The two revealed or revealing maṇḍalas, the Garbhadhātu and Vajradhātu.

現在 Now, at present, the present. | | 世 The present world. | | 賢劫 The present bhadrakalpa. | |, 過去, 未來 Present, past, and future.

現報 Present-life recompense for good or evil done in the present life.

現成 Manifest, existing, evident, ready-made, self-evident or self-existing.

現生 The present life. | | 利益 Benefits in the present life (from serving Buddha).

現相 Manifest forms, i.e. the external or phenomenal world, the 境界相, one of the 三細 q.v. of the 起信論 Awakening of Faith.

現當 Present and future (i.e. 當來).

現益 Benefit in the present life.

現行 Now going, or proceeding; present or manifest activities. | | 法 Things in present or manifested action, phenomena in general.

現觀 Insight into, or meditation on, immediate presentations; present insight into the deep truth of Buddhism.

現證 The immediate realization of enlightenment, or nirvāṇa; abhisamaya, inner realization; pratyakṣa, immediate perception, evidence of the eye or other organ.

現識 Direct knowledge, manifesting wisdom, another name of the ālayavijñāna, on which all things depend for realization, for it completes the knowledge of the other vijñānas. Also the "representation-consciousness" or perception of an external world, one of the 五識 q.v. of the 起信論.

現過未 (or 當) Present, past, and future.

現起光 The phenomenal radiance of Buddha which shines out when circumstances require it, as contrasted to his noumenal radiance which is constant.

現身 The present body. Also the various bodies or manifestations in which the Buddhas and bodhisattvas reveal themselves.

現量 Reasoning from the manifest, pratyakṣa. (1) Immediate, or direct reasoning, whereby the eye apprehends and distinguishes colour and form, the ear sound, etc. (2) Immediate insight into, or direct inference in a trance (定) of all the conditions of the ālayavijñāna. | | 相違 A fallacy of the major premiss in which the premiss contradicts experience, e.g. sound is something not heard, this being one of the nine fallacies of the major premiss.

理 Siddhānta; hetu. Ruling principle, fundamental law, intrinsicality, universal basis, essential element; nidāna, reason; pramāṇa, to arrange, regulate, rule, rectify.

理事 Noumena and phenomena, principle and practice, absolute and relative, real and empirical, cause and effect, fundamental essence and external activity, potential and actual; e.g. store and distribution, ocean and wave, static and kinetic. | | 無礙 Unimpeded interaction of noumenon and phenomenon, principle and practice, etc.; no barrier in either of the two. Cf. 十門.

理佛 The fundamental or intrinsic Buddha, i.e. the Dharmakāya; also the T'ien-t'ai doctrine of Buddha as immanent in all beings, even those of the three lowest orders; which doctrine is also called 素法身 the plain, or undeveloped Dharmakāya. | | 性 The fundamental Buddha-nature in contrast with 行佛性 the Buddha-nature in action or development.

理入 Entry by the truth, or by means of the doctrine, or reason, as 行入 is entry by conduct or practice, the two depending one on the other, cf. 二入.

理具 Wholly noumenal, or all things as aspects of the absolute, a doctrine of the T'ien-t'ai "profounder" school, in contrast with the 事造 of the "shallower" school, which considered all things to be phenomenally produced. | | 三千 The things of a 三千大千世界 great chiliocosm considered as noumenal throughout, or all dharmakāya.

理即(佛) The underlying truth of all things is Buddha; immanent reason; Buddhahood; the T'ien-t'ai doctrine of essential universal Buddhahood, or the undeveloped Buddha in all beings.

理在絶言 Truth is in eliminating words; it is independent of words; it does not require words to express it.

理性 Absolute nature, immutable reality, fundamental principle or character.

理惑 Illusion in regard to fundamental truth, e.g. the reality of the ego and things; as 事惑 is illusion in regard to things themselves. Also, fundamental illusion; reality and illusion.

理智 Principle and gnosis (or reason); the noumenal in essence and in knowledge; the truth in itself and in knowledge; *li* is also the fundamental principle of the phenomenon under observation, *chih* the observing wisdom; one is reality, the other the knower or knowing; one is the known object, the other the knower, the knowing, or what is known; each is dependent on the other, *chih* depends on *li*, *li* is revealed by *chih*. Also knowledge or enlightenment in its essence or purity, free from incarnational influences. | | 五法 v. 五法.

理曼陀羅 The noumenal maṇḍala, i.e. the Garbhadhātu in contrast with the 智 or Vajradhātu maṇḍala.

理法身 The Dharmakāya as absolute being, in contrast with 智法身 the Dharmakāya as wisdom, both according to the older school being 無爲 noumenal; later writers treat 理 | | as noumenal and 智 | | as kinetic or active. | 法界 One of the 四界, that of the common essence or dharmakāya of all beings.

理界 The realm of *li* in contrast with 智界; cf. | 智.

理禪 The dhyāna of or concentration on absolute truth free from phenomenal contamination.

理觀 The concept of absolute truth; the concentration of the mind upon reality.

理論 Reasoning on, or discussion of, principles, or fundamental truth.

理身理土 The dharmakāya in the dharmakṣetra, e.g. the spiritual Vairocana in the eternal light.

理障 The hindrance caused by incorrect views of truth.

理體 The fundamental substance or body of all things.

瓶 A bottle, vase, jar, pitcher, etc. 天德 | The vase of divine virtue, i.e. bodhi; also a sort of cornucopia. | 沙王 Bimbisāra, v. 頻. | 窣都波 Droṇastūpa, a stūpa said to contain a jar of relics of Śākyamuni's body, surreptitiously collected after his cremation by a Brahman. | 耆羅 Eitel gives this as Viṅgila, Viṅkila, Varaṅgala; the ancient capital of Andhra, cf. 案; but it is doubtful.

略 To mark off, define; abridge, outline, sketch; summarize in general; rather, somewhat.

要 | An outline of the important points. | 戒 The first period of general moral law, before the detailed commandments became necessary; i.e. the first twelve years of the Buddha's ministry.

畢 To end, final, complete, all; translit. *p*, *v*; |利叉; |洛叉; |剌叉 Vṛkṣa is a tree; here it is described as *the* tree, i.e. the *Jonesia aśoka*, a tree under which the Buddha is said to have been born. |利多 Preta, hungry ghost. |力 (or 栗) 迦 Pṛkkā, Spṛkkā, a fragrant plant, said to be the *Trigonella corniculata*. |勒支底迦(佛); |支佛; 辟支佛; 鉢攞底迦佛 Pratyeka(-buddha). Cf. 辟. Singly, individually, one "who lives in seclusion and obtains emancipation for himself only". M. W. It is intp. as 獨覺 lonely (or alone) enlightenment, i.e. for self alone; also 緣覺 enlightened in the 十二因緣 twelve nidānas; or 圓覺 completely enlightened, i.e. for self. |境 Atyanta. At bottom, finally, at last, fundamental, final, ultimate. |境依 A final trust, ultimate reliance, i.e. Buddha. |境智 Ultimate, or final wisdom, or knowledge of the ultimate. |境無 Never, fundamentally not, or none. |境空 Fundamentally unreal, immaterial, or void, see 空. |境覺 The ultimate enlightenment, or bodhi, that of a Buddha. |舍遮; 毘||; 毘|闍; 臂奢柘 Piśāca, demons that eat flesh, malignant sprites or demons. |鉢(羅) Pippala, one of the names of the *Ficus religiosa*; also the name of Mahā-Kāśyapa. |陵(伽婆蹉) Pilindavatsa, who for 500 generations had been a Brahman, cursed the god of the Ganges, became a disciple, but still has to do penance for his ill-temper.

異 Pṛthak. Different, separate, unlike, not the same; diverse, diversity; strange; heterodox; extraordinary. |人 Different person, another. |口同音 Different or many mouths, but the same response, unanimous. |品 Of different order, or class. |因 A different cause, or origin. |執 A different tenet; to hold to heterodoxy. |學 Different studies; heterodoxy. |心 Different mind; heterodox mind; amazed. |慧 Heterodox wisdom. |方便 Extraordinary, or unusual adaptations, devices, or means. |熟 Vipāka, different when cooked, or matured, i.e. the effect differing from the cause, e.g. pleasure differing from goodness its cause, and pain from evil. Also, maturing or producing its effects in another life. |熟因 Vipāka-hetu, heterogeneous cause, i.e. a cause producing a different effect, known as 無記 neutral, or not ethical, e.g. goodness resulting in pleasure, evil in pain. |熟果 Fruit ripening differently, i.e. in another incarnation, or life, e.g. the condition of the eye and other organs now resulting from specific sins or otherwise in previous existence. The |熟等五果 are the five fruits of karma; pañcaphalāni, or effects produced by one or more of the six hetus or causes. They are as follows: (1) 異熟果 Vipāka-phala, heterogeneous effect produced by heterogeneous cause. (2) 等流果 Niṣyanda-phala, uniformly continuous effect. (3) 士用果 Puruṣakāra-phala, simultaneous effect produced by the sahabhū-hetu and the saṁprayukta-hetu; v. 六因. (4) 增上果 Adhipati-phala, aggregate effect produced by the karma-hetu. (5) 離繫果 Visaṁyoga-phala, emancipated effect produced by all the six causes. |熟生 A difference is made in Mahāyāna between |熟(識) which is considered as Ālaya-vijñāna, and |熟生 the six senses, which are produced from the Ālaya-vijñāna. |生 Pṛthag-jana; bālapṛthagjana, v. 婆; an ordinary person unenlightened by Buddhism; an unbeliever, sinner; childish, ignorant, foolish; the lower orders. |生羝羊心 Common "butting goat", or animal, propensities for food and lust. |相 Difference, differentiation. |端 Heterodoxy. |緣 Ālambana-pratyaya, things distracting the attention, distracting thoughts; the action of external objects conditioning consciousness. |見 A different view, heterodoxy. |解 A different, or heterodox, interpretation. |說 A ditto explanation. |部 Of a different class, or sect; heterodox schools, etc.

眷 Regard, love; wife; family; relatives; retainers. |屬 Retinue, retainers, suite, especially the retinue of a god, Buddha, etc.

眼 Cakṣuḥ, the eye. |入 The eye entrance, one of the twelve entrances, i.e. the basis of sight consciousness. |智 Knowledge obtained from seeing. |根 The organ of sight. |界 The element or realm of sight. |目 The eye, eyes. |識 Sight-perception, the first vijñāna. |識界 Cakṣur-vijñāna-dhātu, the element or realm of sight-perception.

祭 Sacrifice, sacrificial. |文; 齋文. The prayer or statement read and burnt at a funeral. |祠論 The Yajurveda, v. 韋.

祥 Felicitous. |月 Felicitous month, an anniversary. |瑞 Auspicious. |草 The felicitous herb, or grass, that on which the Buddha sat when he attained enlightenment.

移 To transplant, transpose, transmit, convey, remove. |山 To remove mountains. |龕 To remove the coffin to the hall for the masses for the dead on the third day after the encoffinment.

章 A section, chapter; finished, elegant; essay, document; rule, according to pattern. 丨服 Regulation dress.

笯赤建 Nujkend, or Nujketh in Turkestan, between Taras and Khojend.

第 Number, degree, sign of the ordinals; only. 丨一 The first, chief, prime, supreme. 丨丨乘 The supreme vehicle, Mahāyāna. 丨丨句 The first and supreme letter, *a*, the alpha of all wisdom. 丨丨寂滅 The supreme reality, nirvāṇa. 丨丨義 The supreme, or fundamental meaning, the supreme reality, i.e. enlightenment. 丨丨丨悉檀 The highest Siddhānta, or Truth, the highest universal gift of Buddha, his teaching which awakens the highest capacity in all beings to attain salvation. 丨丨丨智 The highest knowledge, or wisdom. 丨丨丨樂 The highest bliss, i.e. nirvāṇa. 丨丨丨空 The highest Void, or reality, the Mahāyāna nirvāṇa, though it is also applied to Hīnayāna nirvāṇa. 丨丨丨觀 The highest meditation of T'ien-t'ai, that on 中 the Mean. 丨丨丨諦 The supreme truth, or reality in contrast with the seeming; also called Veritable truth, sage-truth, surpassing truth, nirvāṇa, bhūtatathatā, madhya, śūnyatā, etc. 丨三禪 The third dhyāna, a degree of contemplation in which ecstasy gives way to serenity; also a state, or heaven, corresponding to this degree of contemplation, including the third three of the rūpa heavens. 丨丨能變 The third power of change, i.e. the six senses, or vijñānas, 能變 means 識. 丨七仙 The seventh "immortal", the last of the seven Buddhas, Śākyamuni. 丨丨情 A seventh sense; non-existent, like a 十三入 thirteenth base of perception, or a 十九界 19th dhātu. 丨二月 A double or second moon, which is an optical illusion, unreal. 丨丨禪 The second dhyāna, a degree of contemplation where reasoning gives way to intuition. The second three rūpa heavens. 丨丨能變 The second power of change, the kliṣṭamano-vijñāna, disturbed-mind, consciousness, or self-consciousness which gives form to the universe. The first power of change is the Ālaya-vijñāna. 丨五大 A fifth element, the non-existent. 丨六陰 A sixth skandha: as there are only five skandhas it means the non-existent. 丨八識 The eighth, or ālaya-vijñāna, mind-essence, the root and essence of all things. 丨十八願 The eighteenth of Amitābha's forty-eight vows, the one vowing salvation to all believers. 丨四禪 The fourth dhyāna, a degree of contemplation when the mind becomes indifferent to pleasure and pain; also the last eight rūpa heavens. 丨那那 v. 禪 Dhyāna. 丨黎多曷羅殺吒羅 Dhṛtarāṣṭra, one of the four mahārājas, the white guardian of the east, one of the lokapālas, a king of gandharvas and piśacas; cf. 提.

紹 To continue, hand down. 丨隆 To continue (or perpetuate) and prosper Buddhist truth, or the Triratna.

終 End, termination, final, utmost, death, the whole; opposite of 始. 丨南山 Chung-nan Shan, a mountain in Shensi; a posthumous name for Tu Shun 杜順, founder of the Hua-yen or Avataṁsaka School in China. 丨教 The "final teaching", i.e. the third in the category of the Hua-yen School, cf. 五教; the final metaphysical concepts of Mahāyāna, as presented in the Laṅkāvatāra sūtra, Awakening of Faith, etc. 丨歸於空 All things in the end return to the Void.

累 To tie; accumulate; repeatedly; to implicate, involve. 丨七齋 The sevenfold repetition of masses for the dead. 丨劫 Repeated, or many kalpas. 丨形 The body as involved in the distresses of life. 丨障 The hindrances of many vexations, responsibilities or affairs.

紺 A violet or purplish colour, a blend of blue and red, also called 丨青 and 丨瑠璃, the colour of the roots 丨髮 or 丨頂 of the Buddha's hair. 丨宇; 丨園; 丨坊; 丨殿 Names for a Buddhist monastery. 丨睫 The Buddha's violet or red-blue eyebrows. 丨蒲 Kamboja, described as a round, reddish fruit, the Buddha having something resembling it on his neck, one of his characteristic marks. 丨丨國 The country of Kamboja.

細 Fine, small, minute; in detail; careful. 丨四相 The four states of 生住異滅 birth, abiding, change, extinction, e.g. birth, life, decay, death. 丨心 Carefully, in detail, similar to 丨意識 the vijñāna of detailed, unintermitting attention. 丨滑欲 Sexual attraction through softness and smoothness. 丨色 Refined appearance. Cf. 微.

罣 A snare; impediment; cause of anxiety, anxious. 丨念 To be anxious about. 丨礙 A hindrance, impediment.

習 Repetition, practice, habit, skilled; u.f. 丨氣 intp. vāsanā. 丨因丨果 The continuity of cause and effect, as the cause so the effect. 丨氣 Habit, the force of habit; the uprising or recurrence of thoughts, passions, or delusions after the passion or delusion has itself been overcome, the remainder or remaining influence of illusion. 丨滅 To practise (the good) and destroy (the evil).

脚 Foot, leg. | 布 A bath towel, foot-towel.

脫 To take the flesh from the bones; to strip, undress, doff; to escape, avoid; let go, relinquish. | 珍著弊 To doff jewels and don rags, as did the Buddha, on leaving home, but it is intp. as a kenosis, the putting off of his celestial body for an incarnate, earthly body. 解 | v. 解. | 闍 Dhvaja, a banner, flag. | 體 To strip the body, naked; to get rid of the body.

皐 A marsh, pool, bank; high; the fifth month. | 諦 Kuntī, name of one of the rākṣasī, a female demon.

船 A boat, ship. | 師 Captain, i.e. the Buddha as captain of salvation, ferrying across to the nirvāṇa shore. | 筏 A boat, or raft, i.e. Buddhism.

莽 Jungle; wild; rude; translit. *ma*, cf. 摩; intp. as 無 and 空.

荷 A small-leaved water-lily, a marshmallow; to carry, bear. | 力皮陀 v. 吠 The Ṛigveda. | 擔 To carry, bear on the back or shoulder.

茶 A bitter herb; weeds; to encroach; translit. *ḍa, ḍha, dhya, dhu.* | 吉尼 Ḍākinī, also | 枳尼; 吒吉尼; 拏吉儞 Yakṣas or demons in general, but especially those which eat a man's vitals; they are invoked in witchcraft to obtain power. | 毘; 闍毘 (or 維, or 鼻多); also 耶維; 耶旬 Jhāpita; cremation. | 矩磨 Kuṅkuma, saffron, or turmeric, or the musk-root.

莎 A species of grass, or sedge; cf. 娑. | 揭哆 Svāgata 善來 "well come", a term of salutation; also 善逝 "well departed". It is a title of every Buddha; also | 迦 (or 伽) 陀; 沙伽 (or 竭) 陀; 娑婆羯多; 蘇揭多. | 羅樹 The Sala-tree. | 髻 A crown of grass put on the head of 不動尊 q.v. as a servant of the Buddhas.

莫 Not; none; no; do not; translit. *ma, mu*; cf. 摩. | 伽 Magha, donation, wealth; maghā, seven stars; M. W. says a constellation of five stars α, γ, ζ, η, ν Leonis. | 訶 Mahā, cf. 摩; Mahī, or Mahānada, a small river in Magadha, and one flowing into the gulf of Cambay. | 訶僧祇尼迦耶 Māhāsaṅghika-nikāya, cf. 摩. | 訶婆伽 The musk deer. | 訶衍磧 The great Shamo (Gobi) desert. | 賀延 The same; also called "Makhai". Eitel. | 醯 v. 摩 Maheśvara, i.e. Śiva.

莊 Sedate, serious, proper, stern. | 王 v. 妙 Śubhavyūha, reputed father of Kuan-yin. | 嚴 Alaṁkāraka. Adorn, adornment, glory, honour, ornament, ornate; e.g. the adornments of morality, meditation, wisdom, and the control of good and evil forces. In Amitābha's paradise twenty-nine forms of adornment are described, v. 淨土論. | 嚴劫 The glorious kalpa to which the thousand Buddhas, one succeeding another, bring their contribution of adornment. | 嚴王 Vyūharāja, a bodhisattva in the retinue of Śākyamuni. | | | 經 Vyūharāja sūtra, an exposition of the principal doctrines of the Tantra school. | 嚴門 The gate or school of the adornment of the spirit, in contrast with external practices, ceremonies, asceticism, etc.

處 To dwell, abide; fix, decide, punish; a place, state. Āyatana, 阿耶怛那, also tr. 入, place or entrance of the sense, both the organ and the sensation, or sense datum; hence the 十二 | twelve āyatana, i.e. six organs, and six sense data that enter for discrimination. | 不退 Not to fall away from the status attained. | 中 To abide in the *via media*, which transcends ideas both of existence and non-existence.

蛇 Sarpa, a serpent, snake. 毒 | A poisonous snake. 佛口 | 心 A Buddha's mouth but a serpent's heart. | 繩麻 The seeming snake, which is only a rope, and in reality hemp. | 藥 Snake-medicine, name of the Sarpāuṣadhi monastery in Udyāna, where Śākyamuni in a former incarnation appeared as an immense snake, and by giving his flesh saved the starving people from death. | 行 To crawl, go on the belly. | 足 Snake's legs, i.e. the non-existent.

術 Way or method; art; trick, plan. | 婆迦 Śubhakara, a fisherman who was burnt up by his own sexual love.

被 A quilt, coverlet; to cover; to suffer; sign of the passive. | 位 Covered seats for meditation. | 葉衣觀音 Kuan-yin clad in leaves.

袈裟 Kaṣāya, the monk's robe, or cassock. The word is intp. as decayed, impure (in colour), dyed, not of primary colour, so as to distinguish it from the normal white dress of the people. The patch-robe, v. 二十五條. A dyed robe "of a colour composed of red and yellow" (M. W.); it has a number of poetic names, e.g. robe of patience, or endurance. Also 迦 (邏) 沙曳.

袍 A robe. ｜休羅蘭 Bahularatna, i.e. Prabhūtaratna, abundance of precious things, the 多寳 Buddha of the Lotus sūtra. ｜裳；｜服 Upper and lower garments.

許 Grant, permit, admit, promise; very. ｜可 Grant, permit, admit.

設 To set up, establish, institute; arrange, spread; suppose; translit. *ś*. ｜利（羅）Śarīra, relics, remains, see 舍. ｜｜弗怛羅 Śāriputra, v. 舍. ｜多圖盧 Śatadru, "an ancient kingdom of northern India, noted for its mineral wealth. Exact position unknown." Eitel. Also, the River Sutlej. ｜施 Śacī, Śakti, v. 舍. ｜覩嚕 Śatru, an enemy, a destroyer, the enemy, also ｜咄｜；｜都嚧；捨（or 爍）覩嚧；宰覩喚；娑訥嚕. ｜賞迦 Śaśāṅka. "A king of Karṇasuvarṇa, who tried to destroy the sacred Bodhidruma. He was dethroned by Śīlāditya." Eitel.

貨 Goods, wares. ｜利習彌迦 Khārismiga, an "ancient kingdom on the upper Oxus, which formed part of Tukhāra, the Kharizm of Arabic geographers." Eitel.

貫 To string, thread, pass through. ｜花 A string of flowers, a term for the gāthās in sūtras, i.e. the prose recapitulated in verse. ｜首；｜頂 A superintendent, head.

貧 Poor, in poverty. ｜女 A poor woman. ｜女寳藏 The poor woman in whose dwelling was a treasure of gold of which she was unaware, v. Nirvāṇa sūtra 7. Another incident, of a poor woman's gift, is in the 智度論 8, and there are others. ｜窮 Poor, poverty. ｜道 The way of poverty, that of the monk and nun; also, a poor religion, i.e. without the Buddha-truth.

貪 Rāga; colouring, dyeing, tint, red; affection, passion; vehement longing or desire; cf. M. W. In Chinese: cupidity, desire; intp. as tainted by and in bondage to the five desires; it is the first in order of the 五鈍使 pañca kleśa q.v., and means hankering after, desire for, greed, which causes clinging to earthly life and things, therefore reincarnation. ｜（欲）使 The messenger, or temptation of desire. ｜恚痴 v. *infra*. ｜惜 To begrudge; be unwilling to give. ｜愛 Desire, cupidity. ｜染 The taint of desire, or greed. ｜欲 Desire for and love of (the things of this life). ｜欲即是道 Desire is part of the universal law, and may be used for leading into the truth, a tenet of T'ien-t'ai. ｜欲瞋恚愚痴 Rāga, dveṣa, moha; desire, anger, ignorance (or stupidity), the three poisons. ｜欲蓋 The cover of desire which overlays the mind and prevents the good from appearing. ｜毒 The poison of desire. ｜水 Desire is like water carrying things along. ｜濁 The contamination of desire. ｜煩惱 The kleśa, temptation or passion of desire. ｜狼 Greedy wolf, wolfish desire or cupidity. ｜瞋痴 Rāgadveṣa-moha, the three poisons, v. *supra*. ｜結 The bond of desire, binding in the chain of transmigration. ｜縛 The tie of desire. ｜習 The habit of desire, desire become habitual. ｜習因 Habitual cupidity leading to punishment in the cold hells, one of the 十因. ｜著 The attachment of desire. ｜見 The illusions or false views caused by desire.

赦 To pardon. ｜儞娑 The son of Vaiśravaṇa, see 毘.

趺 To sit cross-legged ｜坐, cf. 跏.

躭摩栗底 Tamluk, v. 多.

軟 Soft, yielding. ｜語 Soft or gentle words adapted to the feelings of men.

這 This; these. ｜裏 This place, here. ｜箇 This.

逍 To roam, saunter. ｜遙自在 To go anywhere at will, to roam where one will.

連 To connect, continue; contiguous; and, even. ｜河 The Nairañjanā river, v. 尼；希.

逐 To drive, urge; expel; exorcise. ｜機頓 Immediate accordance with opportunity; ｜is used as 遂; i.e. to avail oneself of receptivity to expound the whole truth at once instead of gradually.

速 Haste, quick; speedily, urgent. ｜得 Speedily obtain, or ensure. ｜成 Speedily completed. ｜疾鬼 Hurrying demons, rākṣasa. ｜香 Quickly burnt inferior incense.

途 A road, way, method. ｜盧（諾）檀那 Droṇodana, a prince of Magadha, father of Devadatta and Mahānāma, and uncle of Śākyamuni.

逗 Delay, loiter; skulk; beguile. ｜會；｜機 Adaptation of the teaching to the taught.

逝 Pass away, depart, die, evanescent. 丨多 Jeta; jetṛ; v. 祇. 丨宮 The transient mansions of Brahmā and of men. Astronomical "mansions". 丨瑟吒 The month Jyaiṣṭha (May-June), when the full moon is in the constellation Jyeṣṭhā.

逋 Abscond, default, owe; translit. *po, pu, va*. 丨利婆鼻提賀 Pūrvavideha, the eastern of the 四大洲 four continents. 丨多(羅) Potalaka, v. 補. 丨沙 Puruṣa, v. 布. 丨沙他 Upavasatha, a fast day. 丨盧羯底攝伐羅 Avalokiteśvara, v. 觀音.

造 Create, make, build. Hurried, careless. 丨像 To make an image; the first one made of the Buddha is attributed to Udayana, king of Kauśāmbī, a contemporary of Śākyamuni, who is said to have made an image of him, after his death, in sandalwood, 5 feet high. 丨化 To create; to make and transform. 丨書天 The deva-creator of writing, Brahmā. 丨花 To make flowers, especially paper flowers.

通 Permeate, pass through, pervade; perceive, know thoroughly; communicate; current; free, without hindrance, unimpeded, universal; e.g. 神丨 supernatural, ubiquitous powers. There are categories of 五丨, 六丨, and 十丨, all referring to supernatural powers; the five are (1) knowledge of the supernatural world; (2) deva vision; (3) deva hearing; (4) knowledge of the minds of all others; (5) knowledge of all the transmigrations of self and all others. The six are the above together with perfect wisdom for ending moral hindrance and delusion. The ten are knowing all previous transmigrations, having deva hearing, knowing the minds of others, having deva vision, showing deva powers, manifesting many bodies or forms, being anywhere instantly, power of bringing glory to one's domain, manifesting a body of transformation, and power to end evil and transmigration.

通利 Intelligence keen as a blade, able to penetrate truth.

通別二序 The general and specific introductions to a sūtra; 如是我聞 being the 通序 general introduction in every sūtra.

通力 The capacity to employ supernatural powers without hindrance. Buddhas, bodhisattvas, etc., have 神力 spiritual or transcendent power; demons have 業力 power acquired through their karma.

通化 Perspicacious, or influential teaching; universal powers of teaching.

通夜 The whole night, i.e. to recite or intone throughout the night.

通念佛 To call on the Buddhas in general, i.e. not limited to one Buddha.

通惑 The two all-pervading deluders 見 and 思 seeing and thinking wrongly, i.e. taking appearance for reality.

通慧 Supernatural powers and wisdom, the former being based on the latter.

通教 T'ien-t'ai classified Buddhist schools into four periods 藏, 通, 別, and 圓. The 藏 Piṭaka school was that of Hīnayāna. The 通 T'ung, interrelated or intermediate school, was the first stage of Mahāyāna, having in it elements of all the three vehicles, śrāvaka, pratyekabuddha, and bodhisattva. Its developing doctrine linked it with Hīnayāna on the one hand and on the other with the two further developments of the 別 "separate", or "differentiated" Mahāyāna teaching, and the 圓 full-orbed, complete, or perfect Mahāyāna. The 通教 held the doctrine of the Void, but had not arrived at the doctrine of the Mean.

通明慧 The six 通, three 明, and three 慧 q.v.

通會 To harmonize differences of teaching.

通行 The thoroughfare, or path which leads to nirvāṇa.

通途 Thoroughfare, an open way.

通達 To pervade, perceive, unimpeded, universal. 丨丨心; 丨丨菩提心 To attain to the enlightened mind; the stage of one who has passed through the novitiate and understands the truth.

部 A group, tribe, class, division, section; a board, office; school, sect; a work in volumes, a heading or section of a work. 丨引陀 or 陁 The planet Mercury, i.e. Buddha. 丨主 The founder of a sect, or school, or group. 丨執 The tenets of a sect, or school. 丨多 Bhūta, "been, become, produced, formed, being, existing," etc. (M. W.); intp.

as the consciously existing; the four great elements, earth, fire, wind, water, as apprehended by touch; also a kind of demon produced by metamorphosis. Also, the 眞如 bhūtatathatā. | 敎 The sūtras, or canon, and their exposition.

野 The country, wilderness, wild, rustic, uncultivated, rude. | 寐尼 Yamani, Java. | 布施 To scatter offerings at the grave to satisfy hungry ghosts. | 干 Śṛgāla; jackal, or an animal resembling a fox which cries in the night. | 狐 A wild fox, a fox sprite. | 狐禪 Wild-fox meditators, i.e. non-Buddhist ascetics, heterodoxy in general. | 盤僧 A roaming monk without fixed abode. | 葬 Burial by abandoning the corpse in the wilds.

釣 To angle, fish. | 語 Angling words or questions, to fish out what a student knows.

閉 To close, stop, block. | 尸 Peśī v. 八位胎藏 A piece of flesh; a mass; a fœtus. | 爐 To cease lighting the stove (in spring). | 關 To shut in; to isolate oneself for meditation. | 黎多 Preta, hungry ghost, see 薜.

陵 A mound, tomb; cf. 畢 |.

陪 To accompany, associated with; add to, assist. | 食 To keep one company at meals. | 臚; | 囉嚩 Bhairava, the terrible, name of Śiva, also of Viṣṇu and other devas, also of a 金剛神.

陶 Pottery, kiln. | 家輪 A potter's wheel.

陳 Arrange, marshal, spread, state; old, stale. | 棄藥; 腐爛藥 Purgative medicines. | 那 Dignāga, Dinnāga; a native of southern India, the great Buddhist logician, *circa* A.D. 500 or 550, founder of the new logic, cf. 因明; he is known also as 童授 and 域龍. Also used for Jina, victorious, the overcomer, a title of a Buddha.

陰 Shade, dark, the shades, the negative as opposed to the positive principle, female, the moon, back, secret. In Buddhism it is the phenomenal, as obscuring the true nature of things; also the aggregation of phenomenal things resulting in births and deaths, hence it is used as a translation like 蘊 q.v. for skandha, the 五 | being the five skandhas or aggregates. | 入界 The five skandhas, the twelve entrances, or bases through which consciousness enters (āyatana), and the eighteen dhātu or elements, called the 三科. | 境 The present world as the state of the five skandhas. | 妄 The skandha-illusion, or the unreality of the skandhas. | 妄一念 The illusion of the skandhas like a passing thought. | 幻 The five skandhas like a passing illusion. | 界 The five skandhas and the eighteen dhātu. | 藏 A retractable penis—one of the thirty-two marks of a Buddha. | 錢 Paper money for use in services to the dead. | 魔 The five skandhas considered as māras or demons fighting against the Buddha-nature of men.

雪 Snow. | 山; | 嶺 The snow mountains, the Himālayas. | 山大士; | 山童子 The great man, or youth of the Himālayas, the Buddha in a former incarnation. | 山部 Haimavatāḥ, the Himālaya school, one of the five divisions of the Māhāsaṅghikaḥ.

頂 Top of the head, crown, summit, apex, zenith; highest; to rise; oppose; an official's "button". | 光 The halo round the head of an image. | 巢 Contemplation so profound that a bird may build its nest on the individual's head. | 珠 The gem in the head-dress, or coiffure; the protuberance on the Buddha's brow. | 生王 Mūrdhaja-rāja, the king born from the crown of the head, name of the first cakravartī ancestors of the Śākya clan; the name is also applied to a former incarnation of Śākyamuni. | 相 The protuberance on the Buddha's brow, one of the thirty-two marks of a Buddha; also an image, or portrait of the upper half of the body. | 石 Like a heavy stone on the head, to be got rid of with speed, e.g. transmigration. | 禮 To prostrate oneself with the head at the feet of the one reverenced. | 輪 A wheel or disc at the top, or on the head, idem 金輪佛頂 q.v. | 門眼 The middle upstanding eye in Maheśvara's forehead.

魚 Matsya. Fish. | 兎 Like a fish or a hare, when caught the net may be ignored, i.e. the meaning or spirit of a sūtra more valuable than the letter. | 子 Spawn, vast in multitude compared with those that develop. | 板 The wooden fish in monasteries, beaten to announce meals, and to beat time at the services. | 母 The care of a mother-fish for its multitudinous young, e.g. Amitābha's care of all in leading them to his Pure Land. | 鼓 Similar to | 板.

鳥 A bird. | 迹 The tracks left in the air by a flying bird, unreal. | 道 The path of the birds, evasive, mysterious, difficult, as is the mystic life. Also a fabulous island only reached by flight. | 鼠僧 A "bat monk", i.e. one who breaks the commandments, with the elusiveness of a creature that is partly bird and partly mouse ; also who chatters without meaning like the twittering of birds or the squeaking of rats.

鹿 Mṛga ; a deer ; as Śākyamuni first preached the four noble truths in the Deer-garden, the deer is a symbol of his preaching. | 仙 Śākyamuni as royal stag : he and Devadatta had both been deer in a previous incarnation. | 戒 Deer morals i.e. to live, as some ascetics, like deer. | 苑 ; | 野園 Mṛgadāva, known also as 仙人園, etc., the park, abode, or retreat of wise men, whose resort it formed ; " a famous park north-east of Vārāṇaśī, a favourite resort of Śākyamuni. The modern Sārnāth (Śāraṅganātha) near Benares." M. W. Here he is reputed to have preached his first sermon and converted his first five disciples. T'ien-t'ai also counts it as the scene of the second period of his teaching, when during twelve years he delivered the Āgama sūtras. | 車 Deer carts, one of the three kinds of vehicle referred to in the Lotus Sūtra, the medium kind ; v. 三車.

麥 Yava. 耶婆 Corn, wheat, barley, etc. Corn, especially barley ; a grain of barley is the 2,688,000th part of a yojana.

麻 Hemp, flax, linen, translit. *ma*, cf. 牟, 麽, etc. | 蹉 Matsya, a fish. | 豆瞿羅 Madhugola, sweet balls, or biscuits.

12. TWELVE STROKES

傅 To superintend, teach ; a tutor ; to paint ; a function ; annex. | 訓 The instructions of a teacher ; to instruct.

傀 Gigantic, monstrous, part man part devil ; a puppet. | 儡子 A puppet, marionette.

傍 Near, adjoining, side, dependent. | 生 Tiryagyoni, " born of or as an animal " (M. W.) ; born to walk on one side, i.e. belly downwards, because of sin in past existence. | 生趣 The animal path, that of rebirth as an animal, one of the six gati.

傌彝 Uighurs, | 胡 ; 回鶻 ; 高車 ; 高昌. A branch of the Turks first heard of in the seventh century in the Orkhon district where they remained until A.D. 840, when they were defeated and driven out by the Kirghiz ; one group went to Kansu, where they remained until about 1020 ; another group founded a kingdom in the Turfān country which survived until Mongol times. They had an alphabet which was copied from the Soghdian. Chingis Khan adopted it for writing Mongolian. A.D. 1294 the whole Buddhist canon was translated into Uighur.

割 To cut, gash, sever. | 斷 To cut off.

勞 Toil, labour, trouble ; to reward. | 侶 Troublesome companions, e.g. the passions. | 怨 The annoyance or hatred of labour, or trouble, or the passions, or demons. | 結 The troublers, or passions, those which hold one in bondage.

勝 Jina, victorious, from *ji*, to overcome, surpass. | 乘 The victorious vehicle, i.e. Mahāyāna. | 友 Jinamitra, friend of the Jina, or, having the Jina for friend ; also the name of an eloquent monk of Nālandā, *circa* A.D. 630, author of Sarvāstivāda-vinaya-saṅgraha, tr. A.D. 700. | 士 Victor, one who keeps the commandments. | 子樹 v. 祇. The Jeta grove, Jetavana. | 宗 v. | 論宗 *infra.* | 州 Uttarakuru, v. 鬱 the continent north of Meru | 心 The victorious mind, which carries out the Buddhist discipline. | 應身 A T'ien-t'ai term for the superior incarnational Buddha-body, i.e. his compensation-body under the aspect of 他受用身 saving others. | 林 v. 祇 The Jeta grove, Jetavana. | 果 The surpassing fruit, i.e. that of the attainment of Buddhahood, in contrast with Hīnayāna lower aims ; two of these fruits are transcendent nirvāṇa and complete bodhi. | 業 Surpassing karma. | 神州 Pūrvavideha, Videha, the continent east of Meru. | 義 Beyond description, that which surpasses mere earthly ideas ; superlative, inscrutable. | | 根 The surpassing organ, i.e. intellectual perception, behind the ordinary organs of perception, e.g. eyes, ears, etc. | | 法 The superlative dharma, nirvāṇa. | | 空 Nirvāṇa as surpassingly real or transcendental. | | 諦 The superior truth, enlightened truth as contrasted with worldly truth. | | | 論 Paramārtha-satya-śāstra, a philosophical work by Vasubandhu. | 者 Pradhāna, pre-eminent, predominant. | 論 v. 吠 Vaiśeṣika-śāstra, and | 論宗 The Vaiśeṣika school of Indian philosophy, whose foundation is ascribed to Kaṇāda (Ulūka) ; he and his successors are respectfully styled 論師 or slightingly 論外道 ; the school, when combined with the Nyāya, is also known as Nyāya-vaiśeṣika. | 軍 Prasenajit, conquering army, or conqueror of an army; king of Kośala and patron of Śākyamuni; also one of the Mahārājas, v. 明王. | 鬘夫人 Mālyaśrī, daughter of Prasenajit, wife of the king of Kośala (Oudh), after whom the Śrīmālā-devī-siṁhanāda 會 and 經 are named.

博 Wide, universal; widely read, versed in; to cause; gamble; barter. | 叉 Vaṅkṣu; Vakṣu; v. 縛 the Oxus. | | 般荼迦; | | 半擇 | Pakṣa-paṇḍakās; partial eunuchs, cf. 半. | 吃蒭 Pakṣa, half a lunar month; also used for Māra's army.

厥 Third personal pronoun; demonstrative pronoun; also used instead of 俱.

喫 To eat. | 素 To eat ordinary, or vegetarian food. | 棄羅 Khakkhara, a beggar's staff; an abbot's staff.

喝 To shout, bawl, call, scold; to drink. | 捍 Gahan, an ancient kingdom, also called 東安國, i.e. Eastern Parthia, west of Samarkand, now a district of Bukhara.

喚 To call, summon. | 鐘; 半 (or 飯) 鐘 The dinner bell or gong.

啼 To wail; crow. | 哭 To weep and wail; to weep. | | 佛 The ever-wailing Buddha, the final Buddha of the present kalpa; cf. 薩陀.

喬 Lofty. | 答摩 Gautama; | | 彌 Gautamī; v. 瞿.

喪 Mourning. To lose; destroy. | 䞋 Gifts to monks for masses for the dead.

喇嘛 Lama, the Lamaistic form of Buddhism found chiefly in Tibet, and Mongolia, and the smaller Himalayan States. In Tibet it is divided into two schools, the older one wearing red robes, the later, which was founded by Tson-kha-pa in the fifteenth century, wearing yellow; its chiefs are the Dalai Lama and the Panchen Lama, respectively.

單 Single, alone; only; the odd numbers; poor, deficient; a bill, cheque, etc.; cf. 但. | 位 A single seat, or position; also a fixed, or listed position, or seat. | 前 In front of one's listed name, i.e. in one's allotted place. | 麻 The single hempseed a day to which the Buddha reduced his food before his enlightenment.

喻 Illustrate, example; to know 宗因喻 q.v. The example (dṛṣṭānta) in a syllogism. | 依 The subject of the example, e.g. a vase, or bottle; as contrasted with | 體 the predicate, e.g. (the vase) is not eternal.

喜 Prīti; ānanda. Joy; glad; delighted, rejoice; to like. | 受 The sensation, or receptivity, of joy; to receive with pleasure. | 忍 The "patience" of joy, achieved on beholding by faith Amitābha and his Pure Land; one of the 三忍. | 悅; | 歡; | 樂 Pleased, delighted. | 捨 Joyful giving. | 林苑 Joy-grove garden, a name for Indra's garden or paradise. | 見 Priyadarśana. Joyful to see, beautiful, name of a kalpa. | 見城 Sudarśana, the city beautiful, the chief city, or capital, of the thirty-three Indra-heavens; also 善見城. | 見天 The Trayastriṁśās, or thirty-three devas or gods of Indra's heaven, on the summit of Meru. | 見菩薩 The Bodhisattva Beautiful, an incarnation of 藥王. | 覺支 The third bodhyaṅga, the stage of joy on attaining the truth.

善 Su; sādhu; bhadra; kuśala. Good, virtuous, well; good at; skilful.

善人 A good man, especially one who believes in Buddhist ideas of causality and lives a good life.

善來 Svāgata, susvāgata; "welcome"; well come, a title of a Buddha; v. | 逝.

善劫 A good kalpa, bhadrakalpa, especially that in which we now live.

善友 Kalyāṇamitra, "a friend of virtue, a religious counsellor," M. W.; a friend in the good life, or one who stimulates to goodness.

善哉 Sādhu. Good! excellent!

善因 Good causation, i.e. a good cause for a good effect.

善宿 Abiding in goodness, disciples who keep eight commandments, upavasatha, poṣadha.

善巧 Clever, skilful, adroit, apt.

善心 A good heart, or mind.

善性 Good nature, good in nature, or in fundamental quality.

善惡 Good and evil; good, *inter alia*, is defined as 順理, evil as 違理; i.e. to accord with, or to disobey the right. The 十善十惡 are the keeping or breaking of the ten commandments.

善慧地 Sādhumatī, v. 十地.

善月 Good months, i.e. the first, fifth, and ninth; because they are the most important in which to do good works and thus obtain a good report in the spirit realm.

善本 Good stock, or roots, planting good seed or roots; good in the root of enlightenment.

善果 Good fruit from | 因 q.v.; good fortune in life resulting from previous goodness.

善根 Kuśala-mūla. Good roots, good qualities, good seed sown by a good life to be reaped later.

善現 Well appearing, name of Subhūti, v. 蘇. | | 天 (or 色) Sudṛśa, the seventh Brahmaloka; the eighth region of the fourth dhyāna.

善生 Sujāta, "well born, of high birth," M. W. Also tr. of Susaṁbhava, a former incarnation of Śākyamuni.

善男子 Good sons, or sons of good families, one of the Buddha's terms of address to his disciples, somewhat resembling "gentlemen". | 男信女 Good men and believing women.

善知 Vibhāvana, clear perception. | | 識 A good friend or intimate, one well known and intimate.

善神 The good devas, or spirits, who protect Buddhism, 8, 16, or 36 in number; the 8 are also called | 鬼 |.

善見 Sudarśana, good to see, good for seeing, belle vue, etc., similar to 喜見 q.v.

善財童子 Sudhana, a disciple mentioned in the 華嚴經 34 and elsewhere, one of the 四勝身 q.v.; the story is given in Divyāvadāna, ed. Cowell and Neil, pp. 441 seq.

善逝 Sugata, well departed, gone as he should go; a title of a Buddha; cf. | 來.

圍 Surround, enclose, encircle, go round. | 繞 To surround, go round; especially to make three complete turns to the right round an image of Buddha.

堙羅那 Airāvaṇa, a king of the elephants; Indra's white elephant, cf. 伊. It is also confused with Airāvata in the above senses, and for certain trees, herbs, etc.; also with Elāpattra, name of a nāga.

場 Area, arena, field, especially the bodhi-plot, or place of enlightenment, etc.; cf. 道 |; 菩提 |.

堪 To bear, sustain, be adequate to. | 忍 Sahā; to bear, patiently endure. | 忍世界 The sahā world of endurance of suffering; any world of transmigration. | 忍地 The stage of endurance, the first of the ten bodhisattva stages. | 能 Ability to bear, or undertake.

報 Recompense, retribution, reward, punishment, to acknowledge, requite, thank; to report, announce, tell. | 佛 To thank the Buddha; also idem | 身 *infra*. | 命 The life of reward or punishment for former deeds. | 因 The cause of retribution. | 土 The land of reward, the Pure Land. | 恩 To acknowledge, or requite favours. | 恩施 Almsgiving out of gratitude. | 恩田 The field for requiting blessings received, e.g. parents, teachers, etc. | 應 Recompense, reward, punishment; also the | 身 and 應身 q.v. | 果 The reward-fruit, or consequences of past deeds. | 沙 Pauṣa, the first of the three Indian winter months, from the 16th of the 10th Chinese month. | 生三昧 A degree of bodhisattva samādhi, in which transcendental powers are obtained. | 緣 The circumstantial cause of retribution. | 身 Reward body, the saṁbhoga-kāya of a Buddha, in which he enjoys the reward of his labours, v. 三身 Trikāya. | 謝 To acknowledge and thank; also, retribution ended. | 通 The supernatural powers that have been acquired as karma by demons, spirits, nāgas, etc. | 障 The veil of delusion which accompanies retribution.

奠 To settle, offer, condole. | 茶 To make an offering of tea to a Buddha, a spirit, etc.

奢 To spread out; profuse; extravagant. 丨利; 丨利弗 (or 富) 多羅; 丨利補担羅 v. 舍 Śāriputra. 丨彌; 丨弭 Śamī, a leguminous tree associated with Śiva. 丨摩他 (or 陀); 舍 丨 丨. Śamatha, "quiet, tranquillity, calmness of mind, absence of passion." M. W. Rest, peace, power to end (passion, etc.), one of the seven names for dhyāna. 丨羯羅 Śākala, the ancient capital of Ṭakka and (under Mihirakula) of the whole Punjab; the Sagala of Ptolemy; Eitel gives it as the present village of Sanga a few miles south-west of Amritsar, but this is doubtful. 丨薩怛羅; 舍 丨 丨 丨; 設婆 丨 丨 Śāstra, intp. by 論 treatise, q.v. 丨陀 Śāṭhya, knavery, fawning, crooked.

寓 To dwell, lodge; appertain, belong to, resemble. 丨宗 A branch sect; one school appertaining to another. 丨錢 Semblance money, i.e. paper money.

寒 Śīta. Cold; in poverty; plain. 丨暑 Cold and heat. 丨林 The cold forest, where the dead were exposed (to be devoured by vultures, etc.); a cemetery; v 尸 for śītavana and śmaśāna. 丨獄 The cold hells, v. 地獄.

富 Rich, wealthy, affluent, well supplied; translit. *pu* and *ve* sounds; cf. 不, 布, 補, 婆.

富單 (or 陀) 那 Pūtana. A class of pretas in charge of fevers, v. 布.

富婁 (or 留) 沙富羅 Puruṣapura, the ancient capital of Gandhara, the modern Peshawar, stated to be the native country of Vasubandhu.

富樓沙 Puruṣa, v. 布; a man, mankind. Man personified as Nārāyaṇa; the soul and source of the universe; soul. Explained by 神我 the spiritual self; the Ātman whose characteristic is thought, and which produces, through successive modifications, all forms of existence.

富樓那 Pūrṇa; also 丨丨丨彌多羅尼子 and other similar phonetic forms; Pūrṇamaitrāyaṇīputra, or Maitrāyaṇīputra, a disciple of Śākyamuni, son of Bhava by a slave girl, often confounded with Maitreya. The chief preacher among the ten principal disciples of Śākyamuni; ill-treated by his brother, engaged in business, saved his brothers from shipwreck by conquering Indra through samādhi; built a vihāra for Śākyamuni; expected to reappear as 法明如來 Dharmaprabhāsa Buddha.

富沙 Puṣya. An ancient ṛṣi. A constellation, v. 弗.

富 (特) 伽羅 Pudgala, that which has (handsome) form; body; soul; beings subject to metempsychosis. Cf. 弗, 補.

富羅 A translit. for a short-legged, or ornamented boot, as 丨維跋陀羅 is boot or shoe ornamentation. 丨丨 is also intp. as land, country; perhaps pura, a city.

富蘭那 Purāṇas. A class of Brahmanic mythological literature; also 布 (or 補) 剌拏. 丨丨丨迦葉; 布 (晡 or 棓) 剌拏 (or 那); 不蘭; 補剌那, etc. Pūraṇa Kāśyapa; one of the six heretics opposed by Śākyamuni; he taught the non-existence of all things, that all was illusion, and that there was neither birth nor death; ergo, neither prince nor subject, parent nor child, nor their duties. 丨丨陀羅 Purandara; stronghold-breaker, fortress-destroyer, a name for Indra as thunder-god.

富那 Puṇya; Punar; Pūrṇa. 丨丨奇 Name of a preta, or hungry ghost; and of a monk named Pūrṇeccha. 丨丨婆蘇 Punarvasu; an asterism, i.e. the 弗宿; name of a monk. 丨丨耶舍; 丨丨(夜)奢 Puṇyayaśas; the tenth (or eleventh) patriarch; a descendant of the Gautama family; born in Pāṭaliputra, laboured in Vārāṇāśi and converted Aśvaghoṣa. 丨丨跋陀 Pūrṇabhadra, name of a spirit-general.

尋 To seek; investigate; to continue; usually; a fathom, 8 Chinese feet. 丨伺 Vitarka and vicāra, two conditions in dhyāna discovery and analysis of principles; vitarka 毘怛迦 a dharma which tends to increase, and vicāra 毘遮羅 one which tends to diminish, definiteness and clearness in the stream of consciousness; cf. 中間定. 丨常念佛 Normal or ordinary worship of Buddha, in contrast with special occasions.

尊 To honour. Ārya; honoured, honourable. 丨勅 The honourable commands, Buddha's teaching. 丨勝 Honoured and victorious, the honoured victorious one, one of the five 佛頂, also known as 除障佛頂, one of the divinities of the Yoga school. 丨宿 A monk honoured and advanced in years. 丨者 Ārya, honourable one, a sage, a saint, an arhat. 丨記 The prediction of Buddhahood to his disciples by the Honoured One; the honourable prediction. 丨貴; 丨重 Honoured, honourable; to honour.

屠 To butcher, kill; a butcher. | 沽 Butcher and huckster; caṇḍāla is "the generic name for a man of the lowest and most despised of the mixed tribes". M. W.

嵐 Mountain mist; vapour. | 毘尼 Lumbinī, the park in which Māyā gave birth to Śākyamuni, 15 miles east of Kapilavastu; also Limbinī, Lambinī, Lavinī. | 鞞尼; 藍 (or 留, 流, 林, 樓) 毘尼; 流彌尼; 林微尼; 臘伐尼; 龍彌你; 論民尼; 藍毫尼.

強 Strong, forceful, violent; to force; to strengthen. | 伽 The Ganges, v. 恒.

復 Again, return, revert, reply. | 活 To live again, return to life. | 飾 To return to ordinary garments, i.e. to doff the robe for lay life.

循 To follow, accord with, according to. | 環 Pradakṣina; moving round so that the right shoulder is towards the object of reverence. | 身觀 The meditation which observes the body in detail and considers its filthiness.

徧 Sarvatraga. On every side, ambit, everywhere, universal, pervade, all, the whole. | 一切處 Pervading everywhere, omnipresent, an epithet for Vairocana. | 吉 Universally auspicious, a tr. of 普賢 Samantabhadra. | 成 To complete wholly, fulfil in every detail. | 淨 Universal purity. | 照 Universally shining, everywhere illuminating. | 界 The whole universe. | 行因 Sarvatragahetu, "omnipresent causes, like false views which affect every act." Keith. | 覺 The omniscience, absolute enlightenment, or universal awareness of a Buddha. | 計 Parikalpita. Counting everything as real, the way of the unenlightened. | 計所執性 The nature of the unenlightened, holding to the tenet that everything is calculable or reliable, i.e. is what it appears to be.

悶 Depressed, oppressed, sad, melancholy; to cover, shut down, or in. 憂 |; 愁 | Distress, grief, sadness.

惱 Vexation, irritation, annoyance, e.g. 懊 | and especially 煩 | kleśa, q.v.

惠 Kind, gracious, forbearing, accordant. 恩惠 Grace, kindness. 施 | To bestow kindness, or charity. | 利 To show kindness to and benefit others.

惑 Moha. Illusion, delusion, doubt, unbelief; it is also used for kleśa, passion, temptation, distress, care, trouble. | 人 A deluded person, to delude others. | 染 The taint of delusion, the contamination of illusion. | 業苦 Illusion, accordant action, and suffering; the pains arising from a life of illusion. | 著 The bond of illusion, the delusive bondage of desire to its environment. | 趣 The way or direction of illusion, delusive objective, intp. as deluded in fundamental principles. | 障 The hindrance, or obstruction of the delusive passions to entry into truth.

悲 Karuṇā; kṛpā. Sympathy, pity for another in distress and the desire to help him, sad. | 心 A heart of pity, of sympathy, or sadness. | 手 A pitying hand. | 智 Pity and wisdom; the two characteristics of a bodhisattva seeking to attain perfect enlightenment and the salvation of all beings. In the esoteric sects pity is represented by the garbadhātu or the womb treasury, while wisdom is represented by the vajradhātu, the diamond treasury. Pity is typified by Kuan-yin, wisdom by Mahāsthāmaprāpta, the two associates of Amitābha. | 無量心 Infinite pity for all. | 田 The field of pity, cultivated by helping those in trouble, one of the three fields of blessing. | 觀慈觀 The pitying contemplation for saving beings from suffering, and the merciful contemplation for giving joy to all beings. | 願 The great pitying vow of Buddhas and bodhisattvas to save all beings. | | 船 The boat of this vow for ferrying beings to salvation.

惡 Agha. Bad, evil, wicked, hateful; to hate, dislike; translit. *a*, cf. 阿.

惡世界 An evil world.

惡作 Evil doings; also to hate that which one has done, to repent.

惡叉 Akṣa, "a seed of which rosaries are made (in compound words, like Indrāksha, Rudrāksha); a shrub producing that seed (*Eleocarpus ganitrus*)." M. W. It is called the | | 聚 because its seeds are said to be formed in triplets, and illustrate the simultaneous character of 惑行苦 illusion, action, and suffering; another version is that the seeds fall in clusters, and illustrate numbers, or numerous; they are also known as 金剛子.

惡取空 To have evil ideas of the doctrine of voidness, to deny the doctrine of cause and effect.

惡口 Evil mouth, evil speech; a slanderous, evil-speaking person.

惡因 A cause of evil, or of a bad fate; an evil cause.

惡報 Recompense for ill, punishment.

惡察那 (or **羅**) Akṣara; imperishable, unalterable; a syllable; words; intp. as an unchanging word, a root word, or word-root. Also 丨刹羅; 阿乞史羅.

惡師 An evil teacher who teaches harmful doctrines.

惡律儀 Bad, or evil rules and customs.

惡揭嚕 Aguru, Lignum Aloes, v. 沉水香.

惡果 Evil fruit from evil deeds.

惡業 Evil conduct in thought, word, or deed, which leads to evil recompense; evil karma.

惡無過 That it is not wrong to do evil; that there are no consequences attached to an evil life.

惡癩野干心 A scabby pariah, a phrase describing the evil of the mind.

惡知識 A bad intimate, or friend, or teacher.

惡祁尼 Agni; intp. by 火神 the god of fire, cf. 阿.

惡緣 External conditions or circumstances which stir or tempt one to do evil.

惡見 Evil or heterodox views. 丨丨處 The place in Hades whence the sinner beholds the evil done in life, one of the sixteen special hells.

惡覺 Contemplation or thought contrary to Buddhist principles.

惡觸 Evil touch; contaminated as is food by being handled or touched.

惡趣 The evil directions, or incarnations, i.e. those of animals, pretas, and beings in purgatory; to which some add asuras.

惡道 Evil ways; also the three evil paths or destinies—animals, pretas, and purgatory.

惡露 Foul discharges from the body; also evil revealed.

惡鬼神 Evil demons and evil spirits, yakṣas, rākṣasas, etc.

惡魔 Evil māras, demon enemies of Buddhism.

插 To insert, stick in. 丨單 To insert one's slip, or credentials.

掌 A palm, a paw; to grasp, control, administer. 丨果 (As easy to see) as a mango in the hand.

揀 To pick, choose, select. 丨擇 To choose, select. 丨師 One chosen to be a teacher, but not yet fit for a full appointment.

揵達婆 Gandharva, v. 乾.

揣 To estimate, conjecture, guess; said also to mean 摶 to roll into a ball, roll together. 丨食 The Indian way of eating by first rolling the food into a ball in the hand; also 團食.

揄 To draw out, extol. 丨旬 Yojana, v. 由.

揭 To lift up, or off, uncover; make known, stick up, publish; translit. *g*, *ga*, *kha*. 丨利呵跋底 Gṛhapati, an elder, householder, proprietor, landlord. 丨底 Gati, "a particular high number" (M. W.), 10 sexillions; 大丨丨 100 sexillions, v. 洛叉 lakṣa. 丨盤陀 Khavandha, an ancient kingdom and city, "modern Kartchou" south-east of the Sirikol Lake. Eitel. 丨職 Gachi, an ancient kingdom between Balkh and Bamian, about Rui. Eitel. 丨路茶 Garuḍa, the mythical bird on which Viṣṇu rides, v. 迦樓羅.

提 To raise, mention, bring forward, summon, lead.

提和 Deva. 丨丨竭羅 Dīpaṃkara, v. 然燈.

提唱 To mention, to deliver oral instruction, or the gist of a subject, as done in the Intuitional School. Also 丨綱; 丨要.

提多羅吒 Dhṛtarāṣṭra, one of the four mahārājas, the yellow guardian eastward of Sumeru; also 頭賴吒; 第黎多曷羅殺吒羅. 丨丨迦 Dhṛtaka; the fifth patriarch "unknown to Southern Buddhists, born in Magadha, a disciple of Upagupta, he went to Madhyadēśa where he converted the heretic Micchaka and his 8,000 followers". Eitel.

提婆 Deva. Explained by 天 celestial; also by 梵天人 inhabitants of the Brahmalokas, or by 天神 celestial spirits. General designation of the gods of Brahmanism, and of all the inhabitants of Devalokas who are subject to metempsychosis. Also 丨波; 丨和; 丨桓. Used also for Devadatta, *infra*. 丨丨地丨丨 Devātideva, the god of gods, Viṣṇu; also name of the Buddha before he left home. 丨丨宗 The school of Nāgārjuna, so called after Āryadeva, *infra*. 丨丨犀那 Devasena, celestial host, name of an arhat. 丨丨菩薩 Devabodhisattva, or Āryadeva, or Kāṇadeva, the one-eyed deva, disciple of Nāgārjuna, and one of the "four sons" of Buddhism; fourteenth patriarch; a monk of Pāṭaliputra; along with Nāgārjuna he is counted as founder of the 三論宗 q.v. 丨丨設摩 Devakṣema, or Devaśarman, an arhat who wrote the 阿毘達磨識身足論 tr. by Hsüan-tsang, A.D. 649, in which he denied the ego. 丨丨達多; 丨丨; 丨丨達; 丨丨丨兜; 達兜; 地婆達多 (or 兜); 禘丨丨丨; 調丨丨丨 Devadatta, son of Droṇodana rāja 斛飯王, and cousin of Śākyamuni, of whom he was enemy and rival, cultivating magical powers. For his wicked designs on the Buddha he is said to have been swallowed up alive in hell; nevertheless, he is predicted to become a Buddha as Devarāja; he was worshipped as a Buddha by a sect "up to A.D. 400". Eitel. 丨丨魔囉播稗 Deva-māra-pāpīyān, Māra, the evil one, king of demons.

提撕 To arouse or stimulate a student.

提桓 Deva, v. 丨婆.

提樹 The bodhidruma tree, v. 菩.

提波 Deva, v. 丨婆.

提洹竭 Dīpaṁkara, cf. 然燈.

提羅 One with abnormal sexual organs; abbreviation of ṣaṇḍhila, cf. 般, 半.

提舍 Intp. as preaching to and ferrying people over the stream of transmigration; also 底沙. 丨丨尼 Pratideśanīya, v. 波. 丨丨那 Deśanīya, confession.

提訶 Deha; the body. Also v. 八中洲.

提調 To arrange, or manage, as deputy; a deputy manager or director.

提謂波利 Trapuṣa and Bhallika, the two merchants who offered Śākyamuni barley and honey after his enlightenment.

提那婆 "Dinabha," or Dineśvara, the sun-god, worshipped by "heretics in Persia". Eitel.

提雲般若 Devaprajña, a Śramaṇa of Kustana (Khotan) who tr. six works A.D. 689–691; in B.N. eight works are ascribed to him. Also 丨曇陀若那.

提鞞 Devī. Female devas; apsaras. 丨丨沙 Dveṣa, hatred, dislike, enmity, one of the 三毒 three poisons. 丨丨波 Dvīpa, an island, or continent; four dvīpa compose a world, v. 四洲.

敢 To dare, venture. 丨曼 Kambala, a woollen or hair mantle; a loin cloth.

敦 Staunch, honest, substantial; to consolidate; urge, etc. 丨(or 燉) 煌 The city in Kansu near which are the 千佛洞 Cave-temples of the thousand Buddhas; where a monk in A.D. 1900, sweeping away the collected sand, broke through a partition and found a room full of MSS. ranging in date from the beginning of the 5th to the end of the 10th century, together with block prints and paintings, first brought to light by Sir Aurel Stein.

散 Viprakṝ. Scatter, disperse, dismiss; scattered; broken, powder; translit. *saṁ*, *san*. 丨亂 Scattered, dispersed, unsettled, disturbed, restless. 丨供 To scatter paper money, etc., as offerings. 丨善 Goodness cultivated during normal life, not as 定善, i.e. by meditation. 丨地 The stage of distraction, i.e. the world of desire. 丨心 A distracted or unsettled mind; inattentive. 丨拓羅 Saṁsāra, course, passage, transmigration. 丨支; 丨脂 (迦); 半

只 (or 支) 迦 Pañcika, one of the eight generals of Vaiśravaṇa, cf. 毘. | 日 The dispersing day, the last of an assembly. | 業 The good karma acquired in a life of activity. | 業念佛 To repeat the name of Buddha generally and habitually. | 生齋 Almsgiving in petition for restoration from illness. | 疑三昧 A samādhi free from all doubt. | 花; | 華 To scatter flowers in honour of a Buddha, etc. | 錢 To scatter paper money as offerings. | 陀那 Sandānikā, a kind of flower.

斑 Spotted, striped, streaked, variegated. | 足王 The king with the marks on his feet, Kalmāṣapāda, said to be the name of a previous incarnation of the Buddha.

斯 This, these; to rive; forthwith; translit. *s*. | 哩牙 Sūrya, the sun, the sun-deva. | 陀含 Sakṛdāgāmin, once more to arrive, or be born; the second grade of arhatship involving only one rebirth. Cf. 四向 and 四果.

景 Prospect, view, circumstances. | 命日 The day of the king's accession, when services were conducted monthly on that day for his welfare. | 敎 The Luminous Religion, i.e. Nestorian Christianity.

普 Viśva; universal, all; pervasive, ubiquitous; translit. *po, pa, pu*. | 光 Universal light, to shine everywhere. | 化 Universal change, or transformation. | 明 Samantaprabhāsa, pervading-light, name of 500 arhats on their attaining Buddhahood. | 法 Universal dharmas, or things; all things. | 渡 Universally to ferry across; | | 衆生 to deliver, or save all beings. | 王 Universal king, title of Yama when he has expiated all his sins. | 現 Universal manifestation, especially the manifestation of a Buddha or bodhisattva in any shape at will. | 知 Omniscience, hence | | 者 the Omniscient, i.e. Buddha. | 禮 To worship all the Buddhas. | 等 Everywhere alike, universal equality, all equally. | 莎 Puṣya, the asterism Tiṣya, and the month Pauṣa; blossom, foam, scum; but intp. as 吉祥 auspicious. | 賢 Samantabhadra, Viśvabhadra; cf. 三曼 Universal sagacity, or favour; lord of the 理 or fundamental law, the dhyāna, and the practice of all Buddhas. He and Mañjuśrī are the right- and left-hand assistants of Buddha, representing 理 and 智 respectively. He rides on a white elephant, is the patron of the Lotus Sūtra and its devotees, and has close connection with the Hua-yen Sūtra. His region is in the east. The esoteric school has its own special representation of him, with emphasis on the sword indicative of 理 as the basis of 智. He has ten vows. | 通 Universal, reaching everywhere, common to all. | 遍; | 徧 Universal, everywhere, on all sides. | 門 Universal door, the opening into all things, or universality; the universe in anything; the unlimited doors open to a Buddha, or bodhisattva, and the forms in which he can reveal himself. | 陀 Potala, cf. 補, 布; it is also Pattala, an ancient port near the mouth of the Indus; the Potala in Lhasa, etc., but in this form especially the sacred island of Pootoo, off Ningpo; also called | | 洛伽山 Potaraka monastery.

智 Jñāna 若那; 闍那 Knowledge; wisdom; defined as 於事理決斷也 decision or judgment as to phenomena or affairs and their principles, of things and their fundamental laws. There are numerous categories, up to 20, 48, and 77, v. 一智; 二智 and others. It is also used as a tr. of prajñā, cf. | 度.

智儼 Fourth patriarch of the 華嚴 Hua-yen school, also called 雲華 Yün-hua, A.D. 600–668.

智光 Jñānaprabha. Having the light of knowledge; name of a disciple of Śīlabhadra.

智刃 The sword of knowledge; knowledge like a sword.

智力 Knowledge and supernatural power; power of knowledge; the efficient use of mystic knowledge.

智度 Prajñā pāramitā, the sixth of the six pāramitās, wisdom which brings men to nirvāṇa. (大) | | 論 The śāstra, or commentary on the Prajñā-pāramitā sūtra; cf. 般若. It is a famous philosophical Mahāyāna work.

智城 The city of mystic wisdom, Buddhahood.

智境 The objects of wisdom, or its state, or conditions.

智妙 Mystic knowledge (which reveals spiritual realities).

智山 The mountain of knowledge; knowledge exalted as a mountain.

智心 The mind of knowledge; a wise mind.

智悲 All-knowing and all-pitying; these two with 定 "contemplative" make up the 三德 three virtues or qualities of a Buddha.

智惑 Wisdom and delusion.

智慧 Jñāna as 智 knowledge and prajñā as 慧 discernment, i.e. knowledge of things and realization of truth; in general, knowledge and wisdom; but sometimes implying mental and moral wisdom. | | 力 Wisdom, insight. | | 光佛 Wisdom-light Buddha, i.e. Amitābha. | (|) 劍 The sword of wisdom which cuts away passion and severs the link of transmigration. | | 水 The water of wisdom which washes away the filth of passion. | | 海 Buddha-wisdom deep and wide as the ocean. | | 觀 One of the meditations of Kuan-yin, insight into reality. | | 門 The gate of Buddha-wisdom which leads into all truth.

智手 The knowing hand, the right hand.

智斷 Mystic wisdom which attains absolute truth, and cuts off misery.

智智 Wisdom of wisdom; Buddha-omniscience.

智月 Jñānacandra. Knowledge bright as the moon; name of a prince of Karashahr who became a monk A.D. 625.

智杵 The wisdom hammer, the vajra or "diamond club".

智果 The fruit of knowledge, enlightenment.

智楫 Oar of wisdom, that rows across to nirvāṇa.

智母 The mother of knowledge; wisdom-mother; v. Mātṛkā 摩.

智波羅蜜 Prajñā pāramitā, see | 度.

智淨相 Pure-wisdom-aspect; pure wisdom; wisdom and purity.

智火 The fire of knowledge which burns up misery.

智炬 The torch of wisdom.

智界 The realm of knowledge in contrast with 理界 that of fundamental principles or law.

智相 Wise mien or appearance, the wisdom-light shining from the Buddha's face; also human intelligence.

智眼 The eye of wisdom; wisdom as an eye.

智礙 Obstacles to attaining Buddha-wisdom, especially original ignorance.

智積 Jñānākara. Accumulation of knowledge. Eldest son of Mahābhijña; also said to be Akṣobhya. Prajñākūṭa. A Bodhisattva in the retinue of Prabhūtratna, v. Lotus Sūtra.

智者 The knower, or wise man; a name for | 顗 q.v.

智藏 The treasury of Buddha-wisdom; posthumous title of Amogha.

智證 Wisdom assurance, the witness of knowledge, the wisdom which realizes nirvāṇa.

智辯 Wisdom and dialectic power; wise discrimination; argument from knowledge.

智象 Prajñā, or Wisdom, likened to an elephant, a title of Buddha, famous monks, the Nirvāṇa-sūtra, the Prajñā-pāramitā sūtra, etc.

智身 Jñānakāya, wisdom-body, the Tathāgata.

智鏡 The mirror of wisdom.

智門 Wisdom gate; Buddha-wisdom and Buddha-pity are the two gates or ways through which Buddhism expresses itself: the way of enlightenment directed to the self, and the way of pity directed to others.

智顗 Chih-i, founder of the T'ien-t'ai school, also known as | 者 and 天台 (大師); his surname was 陳 Ch'ên; his 字 was 德安 Tê-an; born about A.D. 538, he died in 597 at 60 years of age.

He was a native of 潁川 Ying-ch'uan in Anhui, became a neophyte at 7, was fully ordained at 20. At first a follower of 慧思 Hui-ssŭ, in 575 he went to the T'ien-t'ai mountain in Chekiang, where he founded his famous school on the Lotus Sūtra as containing the complete gospel of the Buddha.

替 Substitute, deputy, on behalf of, for, exchange. 丨僧 A youth who becomes a monk as deputy for a new-born prince.

最 Most, very, superlative. 丨上 Supreme, superlative. 丨上乘 The supreme vehicle, or teaching. 丨上大悉地 The stage of supreme siddhi or wisdom, Buddhahood. 丨勝 Jina; vijaya; conquering, all-conquering, pre-eminent, peerless, supreme. 丨勝乘 The supreme vehicle, Mahāyāna. 丨勝尊 The most honoured one, Buddha. 丨(末)後 The last of all, ultimate; final, finally, at death. 丨後十念 To call on Amitābha ten times when dying. 丨後心; 丨後念 The final mind, or ultimate thought, on entering final nirvāṇa. 丨後身; 丨後生 The final body, or rebirth, that of an arhat, or a bodhisattva in the last stage. 丨正覺 Supreme perfect enlightenment, i.e. Buddhahood.

期 A set time; a limit of time; times, seasons; to expect. 滿丨 The time fulfilled. 過丨 Beyond the time. 丨望 To look for, expect, hope.

朝 Morning. Court, dynasty; towards. 丨夕; 丨暮 Morning and evening. 丨山 To worship (towards) the hills, pay court to a noted monastery, especially to pay court to the Dalai Lama. 丨露 Morning dew, e.g man's life as transient. 丨鮮 Korea, Chosen.

棲 Roost, rest. 丨光 To bring his light to rest, the Buddha's nirvāṇa. 丨身 To take one's rest, retire from the world. 丨神 To rest the spirit, or mind, be unperturbed.

植 To plant, set up. 丨衆德本 To plant all virtuous roots, cultivate all capacities and powers.

椎 A hammer, especially for a gong, etc.; idem 槌.

棺 A coffin 丨材.

棱 A corner, a shaped edge, trimmed timber, corner-like; intractable, uncertain. 丨嚴經 The Laṅkāvatāra Sūtra, v. 楞.

棒 A stick, cudgel. 丨喝 To bang and bawl, in rebuke of a student.

棓 A flail. 丨剌拏 Pūraṇa, v. 富.

森 Dense, forest-like. 丨羅萬象 The myriad forms dense and close, i.e. the universe. 丨丨丨丨即法身 The universe in its vast variety is the Dharmakāya, or Buddha-body; in the esoteric school it is the Vairocana-body.

棄 To cast aside, reject, abandon. 丨世 To leave the world; to die. 自丨 To throw oneself away.

欽 Imperial; to respect, reverence. 丨婆羅 Kambala, a woollen or hair mantle, v. 敢 12.

殘 To spoil, injure; cruel. 丨果 Spoiled fruit, i.e. a corpse.

殼 Husk, shell. 丨(or 可)漏子 A leaking husk or shell, i.e. the body of a man.

毳 Down, feathered. 丨衣 A garment wadded with down.

減 v. 減.

湛 Deep, clear, placid, to soak. 丨然 Chan-jan, the sixth T'ien-t'ai patriarch, also known as 荊溪 Ching-ch'i; died A.D. 784; author of many books.

湖 A lake. 丨南 The province of Hunan.

湯 Hot liquid, hot water, soup, etc. 丨頭 The monk in charge of the kettles, etc.

溫 Warm, mild, bland, gentle; acquainted with; to warm. 丨室 Bath-house; bathroom. 丨宿 Wên-su, a district in Sinkiang, on the river Aksu. 丨陀羅 Uttara, cf. 嗢.

游 Bhrāmyati; to ramble, travel; swim. 丨藍 Ambrosia, nectar.

渴 Tṛṣṇā. Thirst, thirsty; translit. *kha*. 丨仰 To long for as one thirsts for water. 丨伽 Khaḍga, a rhinoceros. 丨地獄 The thirst-hell, where red-hot iron pills are administered. 丨愛 Thirsty desire or longing; the will to live. | 樹羅 Kharjūra, a date, the wild date, the Persian date. | 法 To thirst for the truth, or for the Buddha-way. | 鹿 The thirsty deer which mistakes a mirage for water, i.e. human illusion.

涅 Black mud at the bottom of pools; to defile, black. | 槃 Nirvāṇa, v. 涅 10. | 末 Nimat, or Calmadana, "an ancient kingdom and city at the south-east borders of the desert of Gobi." Eitel. | 疊般那 Niṣṭapana, burning, cremation.

焦 Scorch, harass. | 熱地獄 Tapana, the sixth of the eight hot hells; the | | 大焦熱 is the seventh, i.e. Pratāpana.

焚 To burn, consume by fire. | 香 To burn incense.

然 To burn, simmer; so, yes; but, however. | 燈佛 Dīpaṁkara Buddha, the twenty-fourth predecessor of Śākyamuni, who always appears when a Buddha preaches the gospel found in the Lotus Sūtra, in which sūtra he is an important hearer; also 錠光; 提洹 (or 和) 竭; 大和竭羅.

焔 Flame, blaze; nirvāṇa; translit. *ya*. Cf. 炎; 閻; 夜. | 慧地 The stage of flaming wisdom, the fourth of the ten Bodhisattva-stages. | 摩大火仙 Jamadagni, one of the seven ancient sage-ṛṣis. | 摩天 Yamadevaloka, the third of the desire-heavens, above the Trayastriṁśas; also deva Yama, v. 夜, whose wife is | | | 妃 in the Yama-maṇḍala. | 王光佛 The fifth of the twelve shining Buddhas. | 網 The flaming, or shining net of Buddha, the glory of Buddha, which encloses everything like the net of Indra. | 胎 The flaming womb, the garbhadhātu which surrounds with light.

無 Sanskrit *A*, or before a vowel *An*, similar to English *un-*, *in-*, in a negative sense; not, no, none, non-existent, v. 不, 非, 否; opposite of 有. | 一 Not one. | 二 | 三 Neither two nor three, but only 一乘 one Vehicle.

無上 Anuttara. Unsurpassed, unexcelled, supreme, peerless. | 上上 Above the supreme, the supreme of the supreme, i.e. Buddha. | | (|) 乘 The most supreme Vehicle, the Mahāyāna. | | (兩足) 尊 The peerless (two-legged) honoured one. | | 士 The peerless nobleman, the Buddha. | | 妙覺 The supreme mystic enlightenment. | | 忍 The highest patient equanimity in receiving the truth; also, to believe the truth of impermanence without doubt, v. 十忍. | | 慧 Supreme wisdom, that of Buddha. | | 慚愧衣 The supreme garment of sensitiveness to the shameful, the monk's robe. | | 福田衣 The supreme garment of the field of blessedness, i.e. good works. | | 正徧智, or 道 or 覺, the last being the later tr., Anuttara-samyak-sambodhi, supreme perfect enlightenment, or wisdom. | | 法 The supreme dharma, nirvāṇa. | | 法王 Its lord, Buddha. | | 法輪 Its preaching, or propagation. | | 涅槃 The supreme nirvāṇa, that of Mahāyāna in contrast with the inferior nirvāṇa of Hīnayāna. | | 燈 The supreme lamp, that of nirvāṇa, as dispersing the gloom of passion-illusion. | | 眼 The supreme eye, able to discern the inward significance of all things. | | 菩提 The supreme bodhi or enlightenment, that of Buddha. | | 覺 Ditto. | | 道 The supreme way, or truth, that of Buddha.

無不 A double negative, making a positive; also | 非; | 沒.

無住 Not abiding; impermanence; things having no independent nature of their own, they have no real existence as separate entities. | | 三昧 The samādhi which contemplates all things as temporal and evanescent.

無依 Nothing on which to rely; unreliable. | | 涅槃 Final nirvāṇa, v. | 餘, nothing for reincarnation to lay hold of.

無倒 Not upside-down, seeing things right-side up, or correctly, i.e. correct views of truth and things, e.g. not regarding the seeming as real, the temporal as eternal, etc.

無作 Not creating; uncreated; not doing; inactive, physically or mentally; independent of action, word, or will, i.e. natural, intuitive. | | 戒; | 表戒 The intangible, invisible moral law that influences the ordinand when he receives visible ordination; i.e. the internal spiritual moral law and its influence; the invisible grace of which the visible ordination is a sign; v. | 表 avijñapti.

無光佛 An unilluminating Buddha, a useless Buddha who gives out no light.

無刀大賊 A bandit without a sword, e.g. a virtueless monk robbing others of their virtue.

無分別 Nirvikalpa. Non-discriminating. 丨丨丨心 The mind free from particularization, especially from affection and feelings; passionless; translates avikalpa; (*a*) unconditioned or absolute, as in the 眞如; (*b*) conditioned, as in dhyāna. Particularization includes memory, reason, self-consciousness; the mind free from particularization is free from these. 丨丨丨智 The unconditioned or passionless mind as above. 丨丨丨法 The absolute dharma underlying all particular dharmas, the absolute as contrasted with the relative.

無功用 Without effort. 丨丨德 Without merit, or virtue.

無動 Akṣobha; imperturbable, calm, serene, unagitated. 丨丨佛 Akṣobhya, cf. 阿閦婆 and 不動佛 The unperturbed Buddha, sometimes tr. as motionless, but the reference is to his calmness, serenity, and absence of passion; he is one of the Five Dhyāni-Buddhas, and generally reigns over the east, his kingdom being Abhirati, realm of mystic pleasure. In the Lotus Sūtra he is named as the first of the sixteen sons of Mahābhijñābhibhu. One of his principal characteristics is that of subduing the passions. 丨丨尊 idem 不動明王.

無勝 Ajita; invincible, unsurpassed. 丨丨國 The unexcelled land, the Pure Land located west of this universe.

無厭足 Insatiable, name of a rākṣasī, v. 十羅刹女.

無去無來 Neither going nor coming, eternal like the dharmakāya.

無叉羅 Mokṣala, also 丨羅叉 "A native of Kustana who laboured in China as a translator and introduced there a new alphabet (A.D. 291) for the transliteration of Sanskrit." Eitel.

無問 Unasked; not to ask; volunteered. 丨丨自說 Udāna, that part of the canon spoken voluntarily and not in reply to questions or appeals; but Kern defines udāna as "enthusiastic utterances in prose and verse".

無垢 Vimala; Amala. Undefiled, stainless; similar to 無漏. 丨丨地 The stage of undefilement, the second stage of a bodhisattva; also applied to the final stage before attaining Buddhahood. 丨丨忍 The stage of undefiled endurance, the final stage of a bodhisattva as above. 丨丨衣 The stainless garment, the monastic robe of purity. 丨丨識 Amala, undefiled or pure knowing or knowledge, formerly considered as the ninth, later as the eighth vijñāna.

無塵 Dustless, without an atom of the material or unclean, immaterial, pure. 丨丨法界 The immaterial realm out of which all things come.

無央數劫 Asaṅkhyeya kalpa, a period of numberless kalpas.

無始 Without beginning, as is the chain of transmigration. 丨丨曠劫 Transmigration which has existed without beginning through vast kalpas. 丨丨無明; 元品 (or 根本) 無明 The period of unenlightenment or ignorance without beginning, primal ignorance, also called 丨丨間隔, the period of transmigration which has no beginning; since under the law of causality everything has a cause, therefore no beginning is possible; for if there were a beginning it would be without cause, which is impossible. Also primal ignorance is without beginning; and the 眞如 is without beginning, the two terms connoting the same idea. 生死 Birth and death, or transmigration are 無始無終 also without beginning or end, but about the "end" there is difference of interpretation. 丨丨無邊 The Buddha-truth is without beginning and infinite. 丨丨空 Without beginning and unreal, void without beginning, the abstract idea of 無始, i.e. without beginning.

無學 Aśaikṣa. No longer learning, beyond study, the state of arhatship, the fourth of the śrāvaka stages; the preceding three stages requiring study; there are nine grades of arhats who have completed their course of learning. 丨丨道 The way of the arhat, especially his attainment to complete truth and freedom from all illusion, with nothing more to learn.

無常 Anitya. Impermanent; the first of the 三明 Trividyā; that all things are impermanent, their birth, existence, change, and death never resting for a moment. 丨丨依 The reliance of the impermanent, i.e. Buddha, upon whom mortals can rely. 丨丨堂; 丨丨院; 延壽堂; 涅槃堂 The room where a dying monk was placed, in the direction of the sunset at the north-west corner. 丨丨磬; 丨丨鐘 The passing bell, or gong, for the dying. 丨丨鵰 The bird which cries of impermanence, messenger of the shades, the goat-sucker.

無師智 Self-attained enlightenment, wisdom attained without a teacher, that of Buddha.

無影像 Nirābhāsa, without image or shadow, without semblance or appearance.

無後生死 No more birth-and-death, the bodhisattva who will not again be subject to the wheel of transmigration.

無心 Mindless, without thought, will, or purpose; the real immaterial mind free from illusion; unconsciousness, or effortless action. 丨丨三昧; 丨丨定 The samādhi in which active thought has ceased. 丨丨道人 The hermit or saint in ecstatic contemplation, as with emptied mind he becomes the receptacle of mystic influences.

無性 Without a nature, nothing has an independent nature of its own; cf. 三丨丨. 丨丨有情 Men and devas with passions and devoid of natures for enlightenment, hence destined to remain in the six paths of transmigration; a doctrine of the 法相宗 Dharmalakṣaṇa school.

無念 Without a thought; without recollection; absence of false ideas or thoughts, i.e. correct ideas or thoughts; apart from thought (nothing exists).

無想 Without thought, absence of thinking. 丨丨天; 丨丨界; 丨丨處 Avṛha, the thirteenth Brahmaloka, the fourth in the fourth dhyana, where thinking, or the necessity for thought, ceases. 丨丨定 The concentration in which all thinking ceases, in the desire to enter avṛha, v. above; such entry is into 丨丨果. The 丨丨門 is parinirvāṇa.

無愛 Without love, or craving, or attachment.

無意 Absence of objective thought, of will or intention; absence of idea, the highest stage of dhyāna.

無慚 Ahrīka, without shame, shameless.

無憂 Aśoka, "without sorrow, not feeling or not causing sorrow." M. W. 丨丨王 v. 阿 King Aśoka. 丨丨樹 *Jonesia Aśoka* Roxb., the tree under which Śākyamuni is said to have been born. 丨丨伽藍 Aśokārāma, a vihara in Pāṭaliputra in which the "third synod was held". Eitel.

無我 Anātman; nairātmya; no ego, no soul (of an independent and self-contained character), impersonal, no individual independent existence (of conscious or unconscious beings, anātmaka). The empirical ego is merely an aggregation of various elements, and with their disintegration it ceases to exist; therefore it has no ultimate reality of its own, but the Nirvāṇa Sūtra asserts the reality of the ego in the transcendental realm. The non-Buddhist definition of ego is that it has permanent individuality 常一之體 and is independent or sovereign 有主宰之用. When applied to men it is 人丨, when to things it is 法丨. Cf. 常 11.

無所 Nothing, nowhere. 丨丨不能 Nothing (he) cannot do, omnipotent. 丨丨不至 Nowhere (it) does not reach. 丨丨住 Apratiṣṭhita. No means of staying, non-abiding. 丨丨得 Nowhere, or nothing obtainable, the immaterial universal reality behind all phenomena. 丨丨有 Avidyamāna, non-existing; nothing existing, the immaterial. 丨丨丨處 The third region in the realm of formlessness. 丨丨丨丨定 Akiñcanāyatana. The contemplation of the state of nothingness, or the immaterial, in which ecstasy gives place to serenity. 丨丨著 Not bound by any tie, i.e. free from all influence of the passion-nature, an epithet of Buddha. 丨丨觀 The contemplation of the immaterial reality behind all phenomena.

無擇地獄 idem 丨間丨丨 q.v.

無數 Asaṁkhyeya, numberless.

無方 No place, nowhere; unlimited to place or method, i.e. Buddha's power.

無明 Avidyā, ignorance, and in some senses Māyā, illusion; it is darkness without illumination, the ignorance which mistakes seeming for being, or illusory phenomena for realities; it is also intp. as 痴 ignorant, stupid, fatuous; but it means generally, unenlightened, unillumined. The 起信論 distinguishes two kinds as 根本 the radical, fundamental, original darkness or ignorance considered as a 無始無明 primal condition, and 枝末 "branch and twig" conditions, considered as phenomenal. There is also a list of fifteen distinctions in the Vibhāṣā-śāstra 2. Avidyā is also the first, or last of the twelve nidānas. 丨丨使 One of the ten lictors, messengers or misleaders, i.e. of ignorance, who drives beings into the chain of transmigration. 丨丨住地 The fifth of the five 住地, i.e. the fundamental, unenlightened condition; the source or nucleus of ignorance; also ignorance as to the nature of things, i.e. of their fundamental unreality. | | 惑 The illusion arising from primal ignorance which covers and hinders the truth of the *via media*; one of the 三惑 of T'ien-t'ai; in the 別教 it is overcome by the bodhisattva from the first 地 stage, in the 圓教 in the first 住 resting-place. | | 業愛 Ajñānakarmatṛṣnā. Ignorance, karma, desire—the three forces that cause reincarnation. | | 法性一體 Avidyā and the Bhūtatathatā are of the same nature, as are ice and water; the ice of avidyā is the water of all things, the source out of which all enlightenment has come. | | 流 Unenlightenment, or ignorance, the cause of the stream of transmigration. | | 漏 The stream of unenlightenment which carries one along into reincarnation. | | 熏習 v. 四熏習. | | 父 Ignorance as father and desire as mother produce the ego. | | 結 The bond of ignorance which binds to transmigration. | | 網 The snare of ignorance. | | 藏 The storehouse of ignorance, from which issues all illusion and misery. | | 見 Views produced by ignorance, ignorant perception of phenomena producing all sorts of illusion.

無有 Non-existent and existent; also, non-existent, have not, there is none, etc.

無根 Without root; without organs; without the organs of sex. | | 信 Faith produced not of oneself but by Buddha in the heart.

無極 Limitless, infinite. | | 之體 The limitless bodies of those in the Pure Land; the state of one who has attained nirvāṇa.

無比 Without comparison, no comparing, incomparable. | | 法 Incomparable truth or law, an incorrect tr. of abhidharma. | | 身 The incomparable body (of the Buddha).

無滅 The undiminished powers of a bodhisattva after attaining Buddhahood; i.e. undiminished power and zeal to save all beings, power of memory, wisdom, nirvāṇa, and insight attained through nirvāṇa; cf. 智度論 26; also for a list of twenty-two cf. 唯識論 10.

無漏 Anāsrava. No drip, leak, or flow; outside the passion-stream; passionless; outside the stream (of transmigratory suffering); away from the down-flow into lower forms of rebirth. | | 因 Passionless purity as a cause for attaining nirvāṇa. | | 實相 Reality as passionless or pure. | | (最) 後身 The final pure or passionless body. | | 慧; | | 智 Passionless, or pure, wisdom, knowledge, or enlightenment. | | 根 The three roots which produce pure knowledge, 三 | | | q.v. | | 果 The result of following the way of 戒, 定, and 慧, i.e. purity, meditation, and wisdom, with liberation from the passions and from lower incarnation. | | 法 The way of purity, or escape from the passions and lower transmigration. | | 法性 The pure, passionless dharma-nature. | | 道 The way of purity, or deliverance from the passions, i.e. 戒定慧 *supra*; the fourth of the four dogmas 滅 cessation, or annihilation of suffering. | | 門 Āsravakṣaya-jñāna, entry into spiritual knowledge free from all faults, the last of the 六通 q.v.

無爲 Non-active, passive; *laisser-faire*; spontaneous, natural; uncaused, not subject to cause, condition, or dependence; transcendental, not in time, unchanging, eternal, inactive, and free from the passions or senses; non-phenomenal, noumenal; also intp. as nirvāṇa, dharma-nature, reality, and dharmadhātu. | | 法 Asaṁskṛta dharmas, anything not subject to cause, condition, or dependence; out of time, eternal, inactive, supra-mundane. Sarvāstivādins enumerate three: ākāśa, space or ether; pratisaṁkhyā-nirodha, conscious cessation of the contamination of the passions; apratisaṁkhyā-nirodha, unconscious or effortless cessation. | | 法身 Asaṁskṛta dharmakāya, the eternal body of Buddha not conditioned by cause and effect. | | 涅槃 (界) The realm of the eternal, unconditioned nirvāṇa, the Pure Land. | | 生死 The birth-and-death of saints, i.e. without any action; transformation. | | 空 Asaṁskṛta śūnyatā, the immaterial character of the transcendent. | | 自然 Causeless and spontaneous, a tr. of nivṛtti. | | 舍 The nirvāṇa home.

無熱 Anavatapta, heatless. | | 天 The Anavatapta, or Atapta heaven, without heat or affliction 熱惱; the second of the 五淨天 in the fourth dhyāna heaven. | | 池 The lake without heat, or cold lake, called Mānasarovara, or Mānasa-saro-vara, "excellent mānasa lake," or modern Manasarovar, 31° N., 81° 3 E., "which overflows at certain seasons and forms one lake with" Rakas-tal, which is the source of the Sutlej. It is under the protection of the nāga-king Anavatapta and is also known by his name. It is said to lie south of the Gandha-mādana mountains, and is erroneously reputed as the source of the four rivers Ganges, Indus, Śītā (Tārīm River), and Oxus.

無生 Not born, without being born or produced; uncreated; no rebirth; immortal; nirvāṇa as not subject to birth and death, or reincarnation, and which negates them; the condition of the absolute. | | 之生 A life that is without birth, an immortal life, a nirmāṇakāya, or transformation appearance of a Buddha in the world. | | 寶國 The precious country beyond birth-and-death, the immortal paradise of Amitābha. | | 忍 The patient rest in belief in immortality, or no rebirth. | | 智 The final knowledge attained by the arhat, his release from the chain of transmigration; cf. 十智. Also, the knowledge of the bodhisattva of the assurance of immortality, or no rebirth. | | 法 The law of no-birth, or immortality, as the fundamental law of the 眞如 and the embodiment of nirvāṇa. | | 法忍 idem | | 忍. | | 藏 The scriptures which deal with the absolute, e.g. the 中論 Mādhyamika-śāstra. | | 身 The immortal one, i.e. the Dharmakāya. | | 門 The doctrine of reality as beyond birth, or creation, i.e. that of the bhūtatathatā; the gate or school of immortality. | | 際 The uncreate, or absolute; the region of the eternal.

無畏 Abhaya. Fearless, dauntless, secure, nothing and nobody to fear; also Vīra, courageous, bold. | | 山 Abhayagiri, Mount Fearless in Ceylon, with an ancient monastery where Fa-hsien found 5,000 monks. | | 授; 勤授 Vīradatta, "hero-giver," a prominent layman, contemporary with Śākyamuni. | | 施 Abhayapradāna. The bestowing of confidence by every true Buddhist, i.e. that none may fear him. | | 藏 Storehouse of fearlessness, said of members of the esoteric sect.

無疑 Undoubted, without doubt.

無盡 Inexhaustible, without limit. It is a term applied by the 權教 to the noumenal or absolute; by the 實教 to the phenomenal, both being considered as infinite. The Hua-yen sūtra 十地品 has ten limitless things, the infinitude of living beings, of worlds, of space, of the dharmadhātu, of nirvāṇa, etc. | | 意 Inexhaustible intention, or meaning, name of Akṣayamati, a bodhisattva to whom Śākyamuni is supposed to have addressed the Avalokiteśvara chapter in the Lotus Sūtra. | | 海 The Buddha-truth as inexhaustible as the ocean. | | 燈 The one lamp which is yet limitless in the lighting of other lamps; the influence of one disciple may be limitless and inexhaustible; also limitless mirrored reflections; also an altar light always burning. | | 緣起; 法界緣起 Unlimited causation, or the unlimited influence of everything on all things and all things on everything; one of the Hua-yen 四種緣起. | | 藏 The inexhaustible treasury.

無相 Animitta; nirābhāsa. Without form, or sign; no marks, or characteristics; nothingness; absolute truth as having no differentiated ideas; nirvāṇa. | | 佛 Nirlakṣaṇa-buddha; alakṣaṇa-buddha; the Buddha without the thirty-two or eighty marks, i.e. Nāgārjuna. | | 好佛 Ditto, Upagupta, the fourth patriarch. | | 宗; | | 大乘; | | 教; | | 空教 The San-lun or Mādhyamika school because of its "nihilism". | | 福田衣 The garment of nothingness for cultivating the field of blessing, i.e. the robe, which separates the monk from earthly contamination. | | 菩提 The enlightenment of seclusion, obtained by oneself, or of nirvāṇa, or nothingness, or immateriality. | | 解脫門 The nirvāṇa type of liberation, cf. 三三昧.

無知 Ignorant; ignorance; absence of perception. Also, ultimate wisdom considered as static, and independent of differentiation.

無礙 Apratihata. Unhindered, without obstacle, resistless, without resistance, permeating everywhere, all pervasive, dynamic omnipresence which enters everywhere without hindrance like the light of a candle. | | 人 The unhindered one, the Buddha, who unbarred the way to nirvāṇa, which releases from all limitations; the omnipresent one; the one who realizes nirvāṇa-truth. | | 光 The all-pervasive light or glory, that of Amitābha. | | 大會 cf. | 蓋 | |. | | 智 The omniscience of Buddha.

無種性 The nature without the seed of goodness and so unable to escape from the stream of transmigration. | | 闡提 An icchanti, or evil person without the Buddha-seed of goodness.

無等 Asama; unequal, unequalled; the one without equal, Buddha. | | 等 Asamasama; of rank unequalled, or equal with the unequalled, Buddha and Buddhism. | | | 乘 The unequalled vehicle, Mahāyāna. | | 覺 The unequalled enlightenment possessed by Buddhas.

無緣 Causeless, without immediate causal connection, uncaused, underived, independent. | | 三昧 Anilambha or "unpropped samādhi", in which all mental functions cease to connect with environment and cease to function. | | 乘 The vehicle, or method, of the subjective mind, by which all existence is seen as mental and not external. The | | 乘心 is the sixth of the ten 住 stages. | | 塔; | | 塚 A stūpa, or funeral monument not connected with any one person, a general cemetery.

無聞比丘 A monk who refuses instruction, untutored, self-confident.

無聲漏 The silent clepsydra, incense in the shape of ancient characters used to indicate the time.

無能 Unable, without power. | | 勝 Ajita. Invincible, unsurpassable, unconquerable; especially applied to Maitreya, cf. 阿逸多; also to various others.

無自性 Asvabhāva; without self-nature, without a nature of its own, no individual nature; all things are without 自然性 individual nature or independent existence, being composed of elements which disintegrate.

無色 Arūpa, formless, shapeless, immaterial. | | 有 Existence in the formless or immaterial realm. | | 界 Arūpaloka, or Arūpadhātu, the heavens without form, immaterial, consisting only of mind in contemplation, being four in number, which are defined as the 四空天 Catūrūpabrahmaloka, and given as: 空無邊處 Ākāśānantyāyatana, 識無邊處 Vijñānānantyāyatana, 無所有處 Akiñcanyāyatana, 非想非非想處 Naivasaṁjñānāsaṁjñāyatana. | | 貪 The desire in the world without form of holding on to the illusion of contemplation.

無著 Unattached, not in bondage to anything. Name of Asaṅga, brother of Vasubandhu, and others. | | 天親宗 The school of Asaṅga and Vasubandhu, i.e. the 法相宗 q.v. | | 行 Unfettered action, power to overcome all obstacles.

無蓋 That which cannot be covered or contained, universal; also that which includes all, a characteristic of the pity of Buddha, hence | | 大悲, uncontainable, or superlative, pity.

無表 Avijñapti. Unconscious, latent, not expressed, subjective, e.g. "the taking of a religious vow impresses on a man's character a peculiar bent," Keith. This is internal and not visible to others. It has a "quasi-material" basis styled | | 色 or | 作色 which has power to resist evil. It is the Sarvāstivādin view, though certain other schools repudiated the material basis and defined it as mental. This invisible power may be both for good and evil, and may perhaps be compared to "animal magnetism" or hypnotic powers. It means occult power whether for higher spiritual ends or for base purposes. | | 戒 The inward invisible power received with the commandments during ordination. | | 業 The invisible power conferred at ordination, cf. | 作 | *supra*.

無見頂相 The uṣṇīṣa, or lump, on Buddha's head, called "the invisible mark on the head", because it was supposed to contain an invisible sign; perhaps because it was covered.

無言 Without words, silent, speechless. | | 說道 The way, or teaching, without speech; the school which teaches that speaking of things is speaking of nothing, or the non-existent; the acquisition of truth through contemplation without the aid of words.

無記 ? Avyākṛta, or Avyākhyāta. Unrecordable (either as good or bad); neutral, neither good nor bad; things that are innocent or cannot be classified under moral categories. Cf. 三性.

無諍 Without strife, debate, or contradiction; passionless; abiding in the "empty" or spiritual life without debate, or without striving with others. | | 三昧 The samādhi in which there is absence of debate or disputation, or distinction of self and other.

無遮 Unconcealing, unconfined; illimitable. Buddha-grace, -mercy, or -love; cf. | 蓋. | | (大) 會 Pañca(varṣikā)pariṣad; the 五年大會 quinquennial assembly, for having all things in common, and for confession, penance, and remission.

無邊 Ananta; endless, boundless, limitless, infinite, e.g. like space. | | 世界 The infinite world, i.e. space; also infinite worlds; the numberless worlds in infinite space. | | 法界 The infinite world of things; the realm of things infinite in number; the infinite universe behind all phenomena. | | 身 The immeasurable body of the Buddha: the more the Brahman measured it the higher it grew, so he threw away his measuring rod, which struck root and became a forest.

無量 Apramāṇa; Amita; Ananta; immeasurable, unlimited, e.g. the "four infinite" characteristics of a bodhisattva are 慈悲喜捨 kindness, pity, joy, and self-sacrifice. | | 光 Apramāṇābha. Immeasurable, or infinite light or splendour. | |

光佛 Amitābha, v. 阿. | | 光天 The heaven of boundless light, the fifth of the Brahmalokas. | | 光明 Amitābha. | | 光明土 His land of infinite light. | | 壽 Boundless, infinite life, a name for Amitābha, as in | | 壽佛; | | 壽如來; | | 壽王. | | 壽經 The Sukhāvatīvyūha-sūtra is tr. as the Amitāyus sūtra, and there are other treatises with similar titles, cf. 觀 | | 壽經, etc. | | 尊 The infinite honoured one, Amitābha. | | 慧 Infinite wisdom, a term applied to a Buddha. | | 意 Anantamati, boundless mind, intention, will, or meaning. | | 淨(天) Apramāṇaśubha, boundless purity, the second of the heavens in the third dhyāna heavens of form. | | 淸淨佛 The Buddha of boundless purity, Amitābha. | | 義 Infinite meaning, or the meaning of infinity; the meaning of the all, or of all things. | | 義處三昧 The anantanirdeśapratiṣṭhāna samādhi, into which the Buddha is represented as entering before preaching the doctrine of infinity as given in the Lotus Sūtra. | | 覺 Infinite enlightenment, name of Amitābha.

無門宗 The unsectarian, Ch'an or meditative sect, so called because it claimed to derive its authority directly from the mind of Buddha.

無間 Avīci, uninterrupted, unseparated, without intermission. | | 地獄 The avīci hell, the last of the eight hot hells, in which punishment, pain, form, birth, death continue without intermission. | | 業 The unintermitted karma, or unintermitted punishment for any of the five unpardonable sins; the place of such punishment, the avīci hell; also styled ānantarya.

無際 Unlimited, boundless.

無餘 Aśeṣa. Without remainder, no remnant, final; applied to the section of the Vinaya regarding expulsion for unpardonable sin from the monkhood; also to final nirvāṇa without remainder of reincarnation. | | (依)涅槃 Anupadhiśeṣa, the nirvāṇa state in which exists no remainder of the karma of suffering; it is also the nirvāṇa of arhat extinction of body and mind, described as | | 灰斷. | | 記 Complete or final prediction, e.g. to Buddhahood, as contrasted with partial prediction.

無煩 Free from trouble, the thirteenth Brahmaloka, the fifth region of the fourth dhyāna.

無齒大蟲 A toothless great creature, i.e. a toothless tiger.

爲 To do; to make; to effect; to be; because of; for. 有 | 無 | Action and inaction; active and passive; dynamic and static; things and phenomena in general are 有 |; nirvāṇa, quiescence, the void, etc., are 無 |. 名 | Its name is (so-and-so). | 善 To do good, be good, because of the good, etc. | 利 For gain, or profit. | 己 For self. 以 | To take to be, consider as, etc.

猪 A hog, pig. | 頭和尙 Pig-head monk, because of his meditative or dormant appearance.

猴 The monkey; 3–5 p.m. 獼 | The larger monkey, mischievous, restless, like the passions.

猶 A monkey; doubtful; if, so; like, as; yet, still; to scheme. | 若 As if. | 未定 Still unsettled, uncertain.

琵琶 The p'i-p'a, a Chinese stringed musical instrument somewhat resembling a guitar.

琥珀 Amber; intp. of aśmagarbha, v. 阿, one of the saptaratna; cf. 七寶.

琰魔 Yama, the lord of Hades; v. 夜. | | 界 Yamaloka, the hells under the earth. | | 王廳 Yama's judgment hall. | | 使 His messengers. | | 卒 His lictors. | 母那; 閻牟那 Yamunā, the River Jumna.

番 Barbarian, foreign; a time, a turn. | 僧 Foreign monk, especially from India or the west; also a temple warden or watchman.

畫 Draw, paint, picture, sketch; devise, fix. | 水 Like drawing a line across water, which leaves no trace, unlike | 石 sculpture in stone, which remains. | 餅 Pictured biscuits, a term of the Intuitive School for the scriptures, i.e. useless as food. | 像 Portraits, paintings of images, maṇḍalas.

疏; 踈 Open, wide apart; distant, coarse; estrange; lax, careless; to state, report; commentary; also used for 蔬 vegetarian food. | 勒 Su-lo, a hsien or district in Western Kashgaria and a Han name for Kashgar. | 所緣緣 A distant circumstance, or remote cause, one of the four conditional causes in the 唯識 school. | 頭 Written incantations, spells, or prayers burnt before the spirits.

登 Ascend, advance, start; attain, ripen; to note, fix. | 時 At once. | 住 The advance of the bodhisattva to the 十住 q.v. | 地 idem 十地 q.v. | 座 To ascend the throne, or pulpit, etc.

發 To shoot forth, send, issue; start, initiate; expound; prosper. | 光 To send forth light, radiate. | 心 Mental initiation or initiative, resolve, make up the mind to; to start out for bodhi, or perfect enlightenment; to show kindness of heart, give alms. | | 供養 To make an offering with pious intent. | 思八, v. 八 Bāṣpa. | 意 To resolve on, have a mind to; similar to | 心. | 戒 To issue to, or bestow the commandments on a disciple. | 生 To produce, grow, initiate, prosper. | 眞 To exhibit the truth, tell the truth; to manifest the 眞如 or innate Buddha. | 講 To commence expounding, to expound. | 起 To spring up, begin, develop, stimulate. | 露 To reveal, manifest, confess. | 願 To vow, resolve.

盜 To rob; a robber, bandit, pirate, e.g. | 賊, 強 |, 海 |, etc.

硬 Hard, obstinate. | 軟 Hard and soft.

硨磲 Musāragalva; Musālagarbha. One of the saptaratna 七寶; M. W. says coral; others cornelian, or agate.

童 A youth, boy, girl, virgin. | 子 Kumāra, a boy, youth, son; a prince; a neophyte; a bodhisattva as son of the Tathāgata. | 眞 A term for a monk, who should have the child-nature of simplicity. | 眞住 The stage of youth in Buddhahood, the eighth of the 十住. | 籠磨 Druma, a tree in general; a king of the Kinnaras, or Gandharvas, the celestial musicians.

筌 A bamboo fishing-trap. | 魚 Trap and fish, a difficult passage in a book and its interpretation. 得魚忘 | Having caught the fish, the trap may be forgotten, i.e. it is of secondary importance; also ingratitude.

筆 A pen. | 受 To receive in writing; to record, write down from dictation.

策 A treatise, book, memo, tablet, card; a plan, scheme; question; whip; etc. | 修 To stimulate to cultivation of the good; to keep oneself up to the mark.

答 A bamboo hawser, to draw out, to respond, reply, return thanks. | 香 To stick in incense sticks, as a monk does in acknowledgment of those of worshippers. | 摩 Tamas, darkness, gloom, grief, anger, suffering. | 哩磨 idem 達磨 dharma. | 秣蘇伐那 Tāmasavana, a monastery "Dark forest", possibly that of Jālandhara where the "fourth synod" under Kaniṣka held its sessions; "at the junction of the Vipāśā and Śatadru," i.e. Beas and Sutlej. Eitel.

筏 A raft. | 喩 Raft parable. Buddha's teaching is like a raft, a means of crossing the river, the raft being left when the crossing has been made. | (or 伐 or 婆) 蘇蜜呾 (or 多) 羅; 婆須蜜; 和須蜜多; 世友 Vasumitra, described as a native of northern India, converted from riotous living by Micchaka, "was a follower of the Sarvāstivādaḥ school," became president of the last synod for the revision of the Canon under Kaniṣka, q.v., was seventh patriarch, and "wrote the Abhidharma-prakaraṇa-pāda śāstra" (Eitel). | 蘇盤豆; v. 婆 Vasubandhu. | 蘇枳 Vāsuki, or 和須吉; lord of snakes, or nāgas. | 蹉子 Vātsīputra, founder of the 犢子部 v. 跋.

等 To pair; parallel, equal, of like order; a class, grade, rank; common; to wait; sign of plural. In Buddhist writings it is also used for "equal everywhere", "equally everywhere", "universal".

等一大車 The highest class great cart, i.e. universal salvation; cf. Lotus Sūtra 3.

等一切諸佛 The third of the 十迴向 q.v.

等供 Synchronous offering, also | 得, i.e. the simultaneous beginning of a meal when the master of ceremonies cries that the meal is served.

等侶 Of the same class, or company; fellows, equals.

等味 Of equal flavour, of the same character.

等妙 The two supreme forms of Buddha-enlightenment 等覺 and 妙覺, being the 51st and 52nd stages of the Mahāyāna 階位. A Buddha is known as | | 覺王, king of these two forms of universal and supernatural illumination.

等引 Samāhita, body and mind both fixed or concentrated in samādhi.

等心 Equal mind; of the same mental characteristics; the universal mind common to all.

等慈 Universal or equal mercy toward all beings without distinction.

等持 Holding oneself in equanimity, a tr. of samādhi, as also is 三 | |, i.e. samādhi-equilibrium; also of samāpatti, v. 三摩鉢底 and 等至.

等智 Common knowledge, which only knows phenomena.

等正覺 Samyak-sambodhi; complete perfect knowledge; Buddha-knowledge; omniscience; the bodhi of all Buddhas; cf. | 覺; 三藐.

等活 Saṁjīv. Revive, re-animate; resurrection. | | 地獄 The first of the eight hot hells, in which the denizens are chopped, stabbed, ground, and pounded, but by a cool wind are brought back to life, to undergo renewed torment. Also 更活.

等流 Niṣyanda, outflow, regular flow, equal current; like producing like; the equality of cause and effect; like causes produce like effects; of the same order. | | 果 Like effects arise from like causes, e.g. good from good, evil from evil; present condition in life from conduct in previous existence; hearing from sound, etc. | | 相續 Of the same nature, or character; connected as cause and effect.

等無間緣 Uninterrupted continuity, especially of thought, or time.

等空 Equal with space, universal.

等至 A name for fixation of the mind, or concentration in dhyāna; an equivalent of samāpatti.

等衆生界 The universal realm of living beings.

等覺 Samyak-sambodhi; absolute universal enlightenment, omniscience, a quality of and term for a Buddha; also the 51st stage in the enlightenment of a bodhisattva, the attainment of the Buddha-enlightenment which precedes 妙覺.

等觀 The beholding of all things as equal, e.g. as 空 unreal, or immaterial; or of all beings without distinction, as one beholds one's child, i.e. without respect of persons.

等諦 Ordinary rules of life; common morality.

等身 A life-size image or portrait.

等願 The universal vows common to Buddhas.

粥 Congee, gruel. | 飯僧 A rice-gruel monk, or gruel and rice monk, i.e. useless.

粟 Maize, millet. | 散 Like scattered millet. | 散王 Scattered kings, or rulers who own allegiance to a supreme sovereign, as | 散國 means their territories.

給 Dā. To give. | 孤(獨) To give to orphans and widows; a benefactor; almsgiver; e.g. Anāthapiṇḍika, v. 阿那.

絞 Intertwine, twist, intermingle. | 飾 Adorned or robed in grey, a mixture of black and yellow.

紝 To lay a warp, wind, weave. | 婆; 任婆 Nimba, the Neemb tree, which has a small bitter fruit like the 苦楝; its leaves in India are "chewed at funeral ceremonies". M. W.

絡 Continuous; fibres, veins. 聯 | Connected, linked.

紫 Purple, dark red. | 姑 The goddess of the cesspool. | 磨 Pure gold, hence | | 金; also | | 忍辱 the Buddha's image in attitude of calmness and indifference to pleasure or pain. | 衣; | 袈; | 服 The purple robe, said to have been bestowed on certain monks during the T'ang dynasty.

絶 To cut off, sunder, terminate, end; decidedly, superlatively. | 大 Superlatively great. | 學 To cease study, beyond the need of study, a hint being enough. | 對 Beyond compare, supreme. | 待 Final, supreme, special. | 待眞如 Bhūtatathatā as absolute, apart from all phenomena and limiting terms; or as being, in contrast to the bhūtatathatā as becoming. | 食 To cut off food, cease to eat.

結 Knot, tie, bond; bound; settle, wind up; to form. The bond of transmigration. There are categories of three, five, and nine bonds; e.g. false views, the passions, etc.

結使 The bondage and instigators of the passions.

結印 A binding agreement sealed as a contract, employed by the esoteric sects.

結嘆 A sigh of praise at the close of a passage of a sūtra.

結夏 The end of the summer retreat.

結戒 Bound by the commandments.

結業 The karma resulting from the bondage to passion, or delusion.

結河 The river of bondage, i.e. of suffering or illusion.

結漏 Bondage and reincarnation because of the passions.

結生 The bond of rebirth.

結界 A fixed place, or territory; a definite area; to fix a place for a monastery, or an altar; a determined number, e.g. for an assembly of monks; a limit. It is a term specially used by the esoteric sects for an altar and its area, altars being of five different shapes.

結病 The disease of bondage to the passions and reincarnation.

結經 The end of a sūtra; also its continuation.

結縛 To tie and knot, i.e. in the bondage of the passions, or delusion.

結緣 To form a cause or basis, to form a connection, e.g. for future salvation. 大通 | | The basis or condition laid 84,000 kalpas ago (by Mahābhijña-jñānābhibhū 大通智勝佛 in his teaching of the Lotus scriptures to 16 disciples who became incarnate as 16 Buddhas) for the subsequent teaching of the Lotus scriptures by Śākyamuni, the last of the 16 incarnations, to his disciples. | | 衆 The company or multitude of those who now become Buddhists in the hope of improved karma in the future.

結胄 To make the sign of the vajra armour and helmet, i.e. of Vairocana, in order to control the spirits—a method of the esoteric sects.

結解 Bondage and release; release from bondage.

結講 Concluding an address, or the addresses, i.e. the final day of an assembly.

結賊 Binders and robbers, the passions, or delusion.

結跏 (趺坐) The Buddha's sitting posture with legs crossed and soles upward, left over right being the attitude for subduing demons, right over left for blessing, the hands being placed one above the other in similar order. Also, said to be paryaṅkabandha, or utkuṭukāsana, sitting on the hams like ascetics in meditation.

結集 The collection and fixing of the Buddhist canon; especially the first assembly which gathered to recite the scriptures, Saṅgīti. Six assemblies for creation or revision of the canon are named, the first at the Pippala cave at Rājagṛha under Ajātaśatru, the second at Vaiśālī, the third at Pāṭaliputra under Aśoka, the fourth in Kashmir under Kaniṣka, the fifth at the Vulture Peak for the Mahāyāna, and the sixth for the esoteric canon. The first is sometimes divided into two, that of those within "the cave", and that of those without, i.e. the intimate disciples, and the greater assembly without; the accounts are conflicting and unreliable. The notable three disciples to whom the first reciting is attributed are Kāśyapa, as presiding elder, Ānanda for the Sūtras and the Abhidharma, and Upāli for the Vinaya; others attribute the Abhidharma to Pūrṇa, or Kāśyapa; but, granted the premises, whatever form their work may have taken, it cannot have been that of the existing Tripiṭaka. The fifth and sixth assemblies are certainly imaginary.

結願 Concluding the vows, the last day of an assembly.

羡 To desire; praise; surplus. 丨那 Senā, an army.

著 To cover, put on; cause; place; complete; ought, must. 丨衣 To don clothes. 丨鎧 Put on (the Buddha-)armour.

舜 The legendary Emperor Shun, 2255–2205 B.C. 丨若 Śūnya, empty, unreal, incorporeal, immaterial, 空 q.v. 丨若多 Śūnyatā; emptiness, unreality, i.e. 空性 of the nature of the void.

菊 Chrysanthemum; aster. 丨燈 A chrysanthemum-shaped lamp used in temples.

萍 Duckweed; floating. 丨沙 Bimbisāra, see 頻.

菜 Vegetables. 丨蔬 Vegetarian food. 丨頭 The monk who has charge of this department.

菴 Hut, thatched cottage, small temple, nunnery; translit. *am*, *ām*. 丨乜呢必滅堪 Om-maṇi-padme-hūṁ, cf. 唵. 丨園 The Āmravana garden. 丨婆(羅)女 Āmradārika, Āmrapālī, Ambapālī; the guardian of the āmra tree; a female who presented to Śākyamuni the Āmravana garden; another legend says she was born of an āmra tree; mother of Jīvaka, son of Bimbisāra. 丨婆羅多迦 Āmrātaka, a celestial fruit; similar to 丨羅. 丨婆利沙 Ambarīṣa, name of a king. 丨弭羅 Āmla; Amlikā, the tamarisk indica. 丨摩勒 Amalā, *Emblica officinalis*, like the betel nut, used as a cure for colds. 丨摩(or 沒)羅 Amala, spotless, stainless, pure, white. Āmra, cf. 阿末羅 and *infra*; the term is variously used, sometimes for pure, at others for the amalā, at others for the āmra, or mango. 丨摩羅識 Pure knowledge, 眞如 knowledge, v. 阿末羅識. 丨沒羅 v. *supra*. 丨羅 Āmra, the mango, though its definition in Chinese is uncertain; v. *supra*. 丨羅(樹 or 衛)園 Āmravana, Āmrapālī, Āmrāvatī, v. *supra*. 丨羅女 Ditto. 丨華 The āmra flower.

華 Kusuma; Puṣpa; Padma; a flower, blossom; flowery; especially the lotus; also 花, which also means pleasure, vice; to spend, waste, profligate. 華 also means splendour, glory, ornate; to decorate; China.

華光 Padmaprabha, Lotus-radiance, the name by which Śāriputra is to be known as a Buddha. 丨丨大帝 The Chinese god of fire, Aśvakarṇa, see 阿, "mentioned in a list of 1,000 Buddhas" and who "is reported to have lived here in his first incarnation". Eitel.

華嚴 Avataṁsa, a garland, a ring-shaped ornament, M. W.; the flower-adorned, or a garland; the name of the Hua-yen sūtra, and the Hua-yen (Jap. Kegon) school; cf. 健. 丨丨一乘 The one Hua-yen yāna, or vehicle, for bringing all to Buddhahood. 丨丨三昧 The Buddha-samādhi of an eternal spiritual realm from which all Buddha-activities are evolved. 丨丨三王 The three Hua-yen kings, Vairocana in the centre with Samantabhadra and Mañjuśrī left and right. 丨丨宗 The Hua-yen (Kegon) school, whose foundation work is the Avataṁsaka-sūtra; founded in China by 帝心杜順 Ti-hsin Tu-shun; he died A.D. 640 and was followed by 雲華智嚴 Yün-hua Chih-yen; 賢首法藏 Hsien-shou Fa-tsang; 清涼澄觀 Ch'ing-liang Ch'êng-kuan; 圭峯宗密 Kuei-fêng Tsung-mi, and other noted patriarchs of the sect; its chief patron is Mañjuśrī. The school was imported into Japan early in the T'ang dynasty and flourished there. It held the doctrine of the 法性 Dharma-nature, by which name it was also called. 丨丨時 The first of the "five periods" as defined by T'ien-t'ai, according to which school this sūtra was delivered by Śākyamuni immediately after his enlightenment; but accounts vary as to whether it was on the second or third seventh day; all these claims are, however, devoid of evidence, the sūtra being a Mahāyāna creation. 丨丨經 Avataṁsaka-sūtra, also 大方廣佛丨丨丨. Three tr. have been made: (1) by Buddhabhadra, who arrived in China A.D. 406, in 60 chüan, known also as the 晉經 Chin sūtra and 舊經 the old sūtra; (2) by Śikṣānanda, about A.D. 700, in 80 chüan, known also as the 唐經 T'ang sūtra and 新經 the new sūtra; (3) by Prajña about A.D. 800, in 40 chüan. The treatises on this sūtra are very numerous, and the whole are known as the 丨丨部; they include the 丨丨音義 dictionary of the Classic by 慧苑 Hui-yüan, about A.D. 700.

華天 The Hua-yen and T'ien-t'ai Schools.

華報 Flower recompense, i.e. flowers to him who cultivates them, and fruit corresponding to the seed sown, i.e. retribution for good or evil living.

華山 Mt. Hua in Shensi, one of the Five Sacred Mountains of China; v. also 九華山.

華座 The lotus throne.

華德菩薩 Padmaśrī, Lotus-brilliance Bodhisattva, tr. as Lotus-virtue, name of Śubhavyūha, v. 妙, when incarnated as a member of Śākyamuni's retinue.

華手 The hands folded lotus-fashion.

華方 The flowery region, the south.

華梵 China and India.

華氏城 Kusumapura, Puṣpapura; the city of flowers, or of the palace of flowers, also known as Pāṭaliputra, the modern Patna. It was the residence of Aśoka, to whom the title of | | is applied. He there convoked the third synod.

華王世界 The world of the lotus-king, that of Vairocana.

華目 Eyes like the blue lotus, i.e. pure.

華瞖 Flowery films, motes, specks, *muscæ volitantes.*

華胎 The lotus womb in which doubters and those of little virtue are detained in semi-bliss for 500 years before they can be born into the Pure Land by the opening of the lotus.

華臺 The lotus dais, seat, or throne.

華蓋 A flowery umbrella, a canopy of flowers.

華藏 Lotus-treasury. | |(世)界 The lotus-store, or lotus-world, the Pure Land of Vairocana, also the Pure Land of all Buddhas in their saṁbhogakāya, or enjoyment bodies. Above the wind or air circle is a sea of fragrant water, in which is the thousand-petal lotus with its infinite variety of worlds, hence the meaning is the Lotus which contains a store of myriads of worlds; cf. the T'ang Hua-yen sūtra 8, 9, and 10; the 梵網經 ch. 1, etc. | | 八葉 The maṇḍala of the Garbhadhātu. | | 與極樂 The Lotus-world and that of Perfect Joy (of Amitābha and others); they are the same.

華鬘 Kusuma-mālā, a wreath, or chaplet of flowers.

華齒 Puṣpadantī. Flowery or ornate teeth, name of a rākṣasī.

菩 A kind of fragrant grass.

菩提 Bodhi; from budh; knowledge, understanding; perfect wisdom; the illuminated or enlightened mind; anciently intp. by 道, later by 覺 to be aware, perceive; for Saṁbodhi v. 三.

菩提分 Bodhyaṅga, a general term for the thirty-seven 道品, more strictly applied to the 七覺支 q.v., the seven branches of bodhi-illumination. Also | | | 法.

菩提場 A place, plot, or site of enlightenment, especially Śākyamuni's under the bodhi-tree.

菩提子 Bodhi-seeds, or beads, the hard seeds of a kind of Himalayan grass, also of a tree at T'ien-t'ai, used for rosaries.

菩提寺 Bodhi-vihāra, temple of or for enlightenment, a name used for many monasteries; also | | 所.

菩提心 The mind for or of bodhi; the awakened, or enlightened mind; the mind that perceives the real behind the seeming, believes in moral consequences, and that all have the Buddha-nature, and aims at Buddhahood.

菩提樹 Bodhidruma, Bodhitaru, Bodhivṛkṣa; the wisdom-tree, i.e. that under which Śākyamuni attained his enlightenment, and became Buddha. The *Ficus religiosa* is the pippala, or aśvattha, wrongly identified by Fa-hsien as the palm-tree; it is described as an evergreen, to have been 400 feet high, been cut down several times, but in the T'ang dynasty still to be 40 or 50 feet high. A branch of it is said to have been sent by Aśoka to Ceylon, from which sprang the celebrated Bo-tree still flourishing there. | | | 神 The goddess-guardian of the Bo-tree.

菩提流志 Bodhiruci, intp. as 覺愛, a monk from southern India whose original name 達磨流支 Dharmaruci was changed as above by order of the Empress Wu; he tr. 53 works in A.D. 693–713. | | | 支 Bodhiruci, intp. as 道希, a monk from northern India who arrived at Loyang in

A.D. 508 and tr. some 30 works; also | | 留 |, | | 鶴露支.

菩提薩埵 Bodhisattva, a being of enlightenment; "one whose essence is wisdom"; "one who has Bodhi or perfect wisdom as his essence," M. W. Also | | 索多 v. 菩薩.

菩提達磨 Bodhidharma, commonly known as Ta-mo, v. 達; reputed as the founder of the 禪 Ch'an (Zen) or Intuitional or Mystic School. His original name is given as | | 多羅 Bodhitara.

菩提道場 Bodhimaṇḍa, the bodhi-site, or plot or seat which raised itself where Śākyamuni attained Buddhahood. It is said to be diamond-like, the navel or centre of the earth; every bodhisattva sits down on such a seat before becoming Buddha.

菩提門 The gate of enlightenment; name for a cemetery.

菩薩 Bodhisattva, cf. | 提薩埵. While the idea is not foreign to Hīnayāna, its extension of meaning is one of the chief marks of Mahāyāna. "The Bodhisattva is indeed the characteristic feature of the Mahāyāna." Keith. According to Mahāyāna the Hinayanists, i.e. the śrāvaka and pratyeka-buddha, seek their own salvation, while the bodhisattva's aim is the salvation of others and of all. The earlier intp. of bodhisattva was 大道心衆生 all beings with mind for the truth; later it became 大覺有情 conscious beings of or for the great intelligence, or enlightenment. It is also intp. in terms of leadership, heroism, etc. In general it is a Mahayanist seeking Buddhahood, but seeking it altruistically; whether monk or layman, he seeks enlightenment to enlighten others, and he will sacrifice himself to save others; he is devoid of egoism and devoted to helping others. All conscious beings having the Buddha-nature are natural bodhisattvas, but require to undergo development. The mahāsattva is sufficiently advanced to become a Buddha and enter Nirvāṇa, but according to his vow he remains in the realm of incarnation to save all conscious beings. A monk should enter on the arduous course of discipline which leads to Bodhisattvahood and Buddhahood. | | 乘 One of the "five vehicles", which teaches the observance of the six pāramitās, the perfecting of the two 利, i.e. 自利利他 the perfecting of self for perfecting others, and the attaining of Buddhahood. | | 五智 The five-fold knowledge of the Bodhisattva: that of all things by ntuition, of past events, of establishing men in sound religious life, of the elements in or details of all things, of attaining everything at will. | | 僧 The Bodhisattvasaṅgha, or monks, i.e. Mahāyāna, though there has been dispute whether Hīnayāna monks may be included. | | 十住; | | 十地 Ten stages in a Bodhisattva's progress; v. 十. | | 大士 Bodhisattva-Mahāsattva, a great Bodhisattva, e.g. Mañjuśrī, Kuan-yin, etc. v. *infra*. | | 性 Bodhisattva nature, or character. | | 戒 The rules are found in the sūtra of this name, taken from the 梵網經. | | 摩訶薩 Bodhisattva-Mahāsattva. Mahāsattva is the perfected Bodhisattva, greater than any other being except a Buddha. | | 聖衆 The Bodhisattva saints who have overcome illusion, from the first stage upwards, as contrasted with ordinary bodhisattvas. | | 藏 The Mahāyāna scriptures, i.e. those of the bodhisattva school. | | 行 The way or discipline of the bodhisattva, 自利利他, i.e. to benefit self and benefit others, leading to Buddhahood. | | 道 ditto.

虛 Śūnya. Empty, vacant; unreal, unsubstantial, untrue; space; humble; in vain. | 假 Baseless, false. | 僞 Unreal, deceptive. | 堂 Hsü-t'ang, name of a noted monk of the Sung dynasty. | 妄 Vitatha. Unreal and false, baseless; abhūta, non-existent. | 妄法 Unreal things or sensations, such as those perceived by the senses. | 妄輪 The unreal wheel of life, or transmigration. | 心 With humble mind, or heart. | 無 Empty, non-existent, unreal, incorporeal, immaterial. | 無身 The immaterial Buddha-body, the spirit free from all limitations. | 空 Śūnya; empty, void, space; ākāśa, in the sense of space, or the ether; gagana, the sky, atmosphere, heaven; kha, space, sky, ether. 虛 is defined as that which is without shape or substantiality, 空 as that which has no resistance. The immaterial universe behind all phenomena. | 空住 Ākāśa-pratiṣṭhita, abiding in space, the fifth son of Mahābhijña, a bodhisattva to the south of our universe. | 空天 The four heavens of desire above Meru in space, from the Yama heaven upwards. | 空孕 The womb of space, ākāśagarbha, idem | 空藏 *infra*. | 空法身 The Dharmakāya as being like space which enfolds all things, omniscient and pure. | 空無爲 Ākāśa, one of the asaṁskṛta dharmas, passive void or space; two kinds of space, or the immaterial, are named, the active and passive, or phenomenal and non-phenomenal (i.e. noumenal). The phenomenal is differentiated and limited, and apprehended by sight; the noumenal is without bounds or limitations, and belongs entirely to mental conception. | 空界 The visible vault of space. | 空眼 The eye of space, or of the immaterial; name of the mother of Buddhas in the garbhadhātu group. | 空神 Śūnyatā, the god of space. | 空華 Spots before the eyes, *Muscæ volitantes.* | 空藏 Ākāśagarbha, or Gaganagarbha, the central bodhisattva in the court of space in the garbhadhātu group; guardian of the treasury of all wisdom and achievement; his powers extend to the five directions of space; five forms of him are portrayed under different names; he is also identified with the dawn, Aruṇa, and the 明星 or Venus. | 空身 The body which fills space, Vairocana. | 言 Empty words, baseless talk. | 誑語 Untrue or misleading talk, which is against the fourth commandment.

蛭 A leech. | 數 idem 底沙 Tiṣya.

蛤 Bivalves, clams. | 唎觀音 One of the thirty-three forms of Kuan-yin, seated on a shell.

衆 All, the many; a company of at least three. | 僧 Saṁgha, all the monks, an assembly of at least three monks. | 合 (地獄); | 磕 The third of the eight hot hells, Saṁghāta, where two ranges of mountains meet to crush the sinners. | 園; | 寮 Saṁghārāma, a monastery, a nunnery; originally only the surrounding park. | 徒 The whole body of followers; also the monks, all the monks. | 會 An assembly (of all the monks). | 生 Sattva; all the living, living beings, older tr. 有情 sentient, or conscious beings; also many lives, i.e. many transmigrations. | 生世間 The world of beings from Hades to Buddha-land; also all beings subject to transformation by Buddha. | 生垢 The common defilement of all beings by the false view that the ego has real existence. | 生忍 Patience towards all living beings under all circumstances. | 生想 The false notion that all beings have reality. | 生本性 The original nature of all the living, i.e. the Bhūtatathatā in its phenomenal aspect. | 生根 The nature, or root, of all beings, cf. last entry. | 生濁 The fourth of the five periods of decay, sattvakaṣāya, when all creatures are stupid and unclean. | 生無始無終 As all beings are part of the 法身 dharmakāya they have neither beginning nor end. | 生界 The realm of all the living in contrast with the Buddha-realm. | 生相; | 生見 The concept that all beings have reality. | 祐 Protector or Benefactor of all, an old intp. of Bhagavat. | 聖 All saints, all who have realized the Buddha-truth. | 苦 All the miseries of existence, the sufferings of all. | 道 The way of all; all the three yāna, or vehicles of salvation. | 香國土 The country of all fragrance, i.e. the Pure Land, also the Sūtras.

街 A street (especially with shops), a market. | 方 The busy mart of life.

裂 To rip, split, crack. | 裳 The torn robe (of Buddhism), i.e. split into eighteen pieces, like the Hīnayāna sects.

視 Look, see, behold. | 那 Jina, victor, idem 耆那.

觝突 To butt against, gore, as an angry bull.

詐 Impose on, deceive, feign, pretend. 奸 | Fraudulent, crafty, to cheat.

註 Explain, open up the meaning, define. | 疏 Notes and comments.

評 Criticize, discuss. | 註 Criticize, comment on. | 論 Discuss. 譏 | Censure, criticize.

詞 An expression, phrase, word. | 無礙智 Pratimsaṁvid, v. 四.

訶 To blame, reprove, scold; ridicule; translit. *ha*, *ka*, *kha*, *ga*, and similar sounds. | 佛罵祖 To scold a Buddha and abuse an elder. | 利; | 梨; 呬歌里 Hari, tawny, a lion. | 利底 Hāritī, also | 利 (or 哩) 帝; 呵利底; 呵利帝 (or 陀); 阿利底 Aritī; intp. as captivating, charming; cruel; dark green, yellow, etc.; mother of demons, a rākṣasī who was under a vow to devour the children of Rājagṛha, but was converted by the Buddha, and became the guardian of nunneries, where her image, carrying a child and with children by her, is worshipped for children or in children's ailments. | 利底母 or 南 idem. | 利枳舍; 呬歌里鷄舍 Harikeśa, yellow-haired, lion's mane, name of a yakṣa. | 悉多 Hasta, an arm, a hand. | 梨勒 Harītakī, the yellow Myrobalan tree and fruit, used for medicine; also | 梨怛鷄 (or 得枳), | 子, etc. | 梨跋摩 Harivarman, tawny armour, and 師子鎧 lion armour; a Brahman who, "900 years" after the Nirvāṇa, appeared in Central India and joined the Sarvāstivādin and Satyasiddhi school by the publication of the Satyasiddhi śāstra (tr. as the 成實論 by Kumārajīva, 407–418). | 羅 | 羅 Halāhala, Hālāhala, etc., a deadly poison.

象 Gaja; Hastin; also Nāga; an elephant; v. 像 14. | 主 The southern division of India, v. 四主. | 堅山 Pīlusāragiri, a mountain south-west of Kapiśā, on the top of which Aśoka erected a stūpa, the Pīlusāra-stūpa. | 墮阬 Hastigarta, "elephant's hole," i.e. the hollow formed by the elephant's fall, when Śākyamuni flung aside a dead elephant put in his path by Devadatta. | 尊國 The elephant-honouring country, India. | 教 The teaching by images or symbols, i.e. Buddhism, v. 像教. | 牙 Elephant's tusk, ivory. | 王 Gajapati, Lord of Elephants, a term for Śākyamuni; also the fabulous ruler of the southern division of the Jambudvīpa continent. | 軍 Hastikāya, the elephant corps of an Indian army. | 頭山 Gayāśiras, tr. as elephant-head mountain, name of two mountains, one near Gayā, the other said to be near the river Nairañjanā, 150 li away. | 駕 The elephant chariot, or riding forward, i.e. the eastward progress of Buddhism. | 鼻 Elephant's trunk; a wrong way of wearing a monk's robe.

貳 Two; translit. *ni*, e.g. | 吒 Akaniṣṭha, not the smallest, i.e. the highest of the Brahmalokas, v. 阿迦.

賀 To make offerings in congratulation; congratulate; translit. *h*, cf. 訶. | 捺婆 Haṁsa, a goose. | 羅 (or 邏) 馱 Hrada, a lake, pool, ray of light. | 野紇 (or | 演屹) 哩嚩 Hayagrīva, the horse-necked one, a form of Viṣṇu and of Kuan-yin.

費 To spend, lavish, waste, squander; expense; translit. *vi*, *ve*, in Vidyā, v. 明; Vīṇā, a lute, v. 批; Veda, the Vedas, v. 韋.

貴 Honourable, dear, precious. | 賤 Dear and cheap; noble and base; your and my.

買 To buy, purchase. | 林 Vikrītavana, a "monastery 200 li north-west of the capital of Cashmere". Eitel.

貼 To stick, attach to; make up, add. | 嚫 Dakṣiṇa, right-hand, south, dexterity; donations, offerings, etc.

超 Vikrama. Leap over, surpass; exempt from; to save. | 世 Surpassing the world, superior to anything in the world. | 八 Surpassing the eight other schools, as does the teaching of the Lotus and Nirvāṇa Sūtras, according to T'ien-t'ai. | 日王 Vikramāditya, "a celebrated Hindu king," 57 B.C., who drove out the Śakas or Scythians, ruled all northern India, was one of the wisest of Hindu kings and a great patron of literature. M. W. | 越 Surpassing, supreme; to pass over, be exempt from. | 過 Samatikram, to go beyond, cross over, transgress.

越 To step over, pass over, surpass, exceed; similar to 超, with which it is often connected. | 喜三昧 The samādhi of Yaśodharā, wife of Śākyamuni and mother of Rāhula, which causes all kinds of joy to self and others. | 罪 Exceeding sin, or transgression of the law, particularly of esoteric law or monastic vows. | 闍 Vajra, cf. 金剛.

跏 To sit cross-legged | 趺坐, v. 結.

跋 Trudge, tread on, travel; heel, base; a summary; translit. *pa*, *ba*, *bha*, *va* sounds; cf. 波, 婆, 簸. | 伽仙 (or 婆) Bhārgava, Bhagava, Bhaga, the ascetic under whom Śākyamuni practised the austere life. | 利沙 Varṣās, cf. 雨 the rains. | 折羅 Vajra, v. 金剛 diamond; thunderbolt. | 折羅吒訶沙 Vajrāṭṭahāsa, i.e. Śiva, one of the guardians, the laughing Mahārāja. | 捺羅婆娜 Bhādrapada, the sixth Indian month. | 提 Bhadra, or Bhadrika, v. next; used also for Vatī, the river Hiraṇyavatī, or Gunduck. | 提梨 (or 唎) 迦 Bhadrika, also 婆提 or 帝, one of the first five disciples, said to be a son of king Amṛtodana. | 摩 Harivarman, and his school, v. 訶. | 日羅 Vajra, v. 金剛. | 渠 Varga, a class, group, cf. 伐. | 濫摩; 婆羅門 Brāhmaṇa, Brahman, the caste, or character, i.e. pure. | 盧沙 Varuṣa, now Attock, east of Peshawar. | 祿羯呫婆 Bharukaccha, an ancient state in Gujarat, near Baruch, on the Narbudda. | 祿迦 An ancient state in east Turkestan, the present Aksu. Eitel. | 私弗多羅 Vātsīputra, 犢子 founder of the sect of this name, one of the Vaibhāṣika schools. | 窣堵 Vastu, real, substance; intp. as the Vinaya, or part of it; may be tr. by 事, 物, 本, 有. | 羅娑馱 Prāsāda, a temple, palace, assembly hall. | 羅攙 Tallakṣaṇa (Julien), 10 octillions; a 大 | | | is 100 octillions, v. 洛叉. | 羅縷支 Bhadraruci, a monk of west India, of great subtlety and reasoning power; he opposed an arrogant Brahman, who, defeated, sank alive into hell. | 藍 Bala, or Mudrābala, 10 septillions; 大 | | 100 septillions, v. 洛. | 路婆 (or 娑) 陀 Prāsāda, v. above. | 達羅 Bhadra, good, auspicious, gracious, excellent, virtuous; an epithet for every Buddha; the present 賢劫 Bhadrakalpa. | 邏末羅耆釐 Bhramaragiri (Beal), a monastery built by Sadvaha for Nāgārjuna on this mountain, 300 li south-west of Kośala. | 那 Varaṇa, v. 伐, a province of Kapiśā, v. 障. | 陂 Bhadrapāla, name of 賢護 a bodhisattva. | 陀 Bhadra, v. above. | 陀婆 Bhadrapāla, v. above. | 陀羅 Bhādrapadā, the 壁 constellation in Pegasus and Andromeda. Bhadrā, a female disciple of Śākyamuni. Guṇabhadra, v. 求, a nāga-king; a tree. | 陀羅樓支 Bhadraruci, v. above. | 陀羅耶尼 Bhadrayāniyāḥ,

v. 小乘, one of the eighteen Hīnayāna sects. | 陀羅迦卑梨耶 Bhadrakapilā, also | 陀迦毘羅 a female disciple of Śākyamuni. | 闍 Vṛji, the modern Vraja or Braj, west of Delhi and Agra; also given as Vaiśālī, cf. 毘, where the second assembly met and where the ten unlawful acts permitted by the Vṛjiputra monks were condemned. | 闍羅 Vajra, v. 金剛. | | | 波膩 Vajrapāni, "thunderbolt handed" (M. W.), v. 金剛手. | 難陀 Upananda, a disciple who rejoiced over the Buddha's death because it freed the disciples from restraint. A nāga king.

躭摩栗底 Tāmralipti, Tamlook, v. 多摩.

軻地羅 Khadira, the *Acacia catechu*; the mimosa; also | 梨羅; 珂 | |; 朅 | |; 佉陀 (or 達) 羅; 佉提迦; 朅達羅. | | | 山 The Khadira circle of mountains, the fifth of the seven concentric mountain chains of a world. | 梨; 朅地 (or 達) 洛迦 Khadiraka, idem.

進 Advance, progress, enter. | 具 To reach the age (20) and advance to full ordination. 精 | Vīrya, zeal, unchecked progress.

逸 To get away from; retire, be at ease, indulgence, excess. | 多 Ajita, Maitreya, v. 阿 | 多.

逮 To reach, catch up, until, when, wait for. | 夜 The night previous to a fast day, or to any special occasion.

都 Metropolis, imperial city or domain; a district, ward, territory. All. | 史 (多 or 天) the Tuṣita heaven, v. 兜. | 吒迦 Joyful sound, united voices; (derivation uncertain). | 監寺; | 總 The director or second in command of a monastery. | 市王 The ruler of the eighth hot hell. | 率天 Tuṣita, see above. | 貨羅 Tukhāra, the 月支 Yüeh-chih country; "(1) A topographical term designating a country of ice and frost (tukhāra), and corresponding to the present Badakchan which Arab geographers still call Tokharestan. (2) An ethnographical term used by the Greeks to designate the Tocharoi or Indo-Scythians, and likewise by Chinese writers applied to the Tochari Tartars who driven on by the Huns (180 B.C.) conquered Trans-oxania, destroyed the Bactrian kingdom (大夏) 126 B.C., and finally conquered the Pundjab, Cashmere, and the greater part of India. Their greatest king was Kanichka." Eitel.

酤 To deal in spirits, or alcoholic liquor. | 酒戒 The commandment against it.

酥 Curd, butter; crisp. It is described as produced by churning milk or treating it with herbs. Milk produces 酪, then 生酥, then 熟酥, then 醍醐. | 燈 A lamp burning butter-oil.

量 Pramāṇa. Measure, capacity, length, ability; to measure, deliberate; a syllogism in logic, v. 比 |. A syllogism, consisting of 宗 pratijñā, proposition; 因 hetu, reason; 喩 udāharaṇa, example; but the syllogism varies in the number of its avayava, or members. There are other divisions from 2 to 6, e.g. 現 | and 比 | direct or sense inferences, and comparative or logical inferences; to these are added 聖敎 | arguments based on authority; 譬喩 | analogy; 義准 postulation, or general assent; and 無體 negation, or non-existence. | 果 Conditioned by various external objects, different types of consciousness arise (ālambana-pratyaya). The 法相宗 held that the percipient mind is conditioned by existing things, and when the two are in conjunction the ultimate consequence of any action may be known. | 等身 The immanence of the Tathāgata in all things, phenomenal and noumenal, he being the all in all.

鈔 A voucher, banknote, paper-money, taxes; to pinch up, take up; to seize all, sequestrate; to copy, transcribe, extract.

鈎 Hook, barb; also 鉤. | 召法 Vaśīkaraṇa, the method in esoteric practice of summoning and influencing the beneficent powers. | 鈕 To knot, tie, e.g. a girdle; to button. | 菩薩 The bodhisattva guardian with the trident, one of the four with barb, noose, chain or bell.

鈍 Dull, blunt, stupid. | 使 The five envoys of stupidity, i.e. of the lower passions, in contrast with the higher 五利使; the 使 is intp. as 煩惱 kleśa, the afflicters, or passions; the five are 貪, 瞋, 痴, 慢, 疑 greed, hate, stupidity, arrogance, doubt. | 根; | 機 Of dull capacity, unable to receive Buddha-truth.

間 A crevice, interval, space, room; separate, intermission; between, during, in; to divide, interfere, intervene. | 斷 To interrupt, interfere and stop. | 色 Intermediate colours, i.e. not primary colours. | 隔 Interval, intermission, but it is chiefly used for during, while, the period of an event. Cf. 無 | Avīci.

閑 To bar, a barrier; to shut out; trained. 丨居十德 Ten advantages of a hermitage given in verse, i.e. absence of sex and passion; of temptation to say wrong things; of enemies, and so of strife; of friends to praise or blame; of others' faults, and so of talk about them; of followers or servants, and so no longing for companions; of society, and so no burden of politenesss; of guests, and so no preparations; of social intercourse, and so no trouble about garments; of hindrance from others in mystic practice. 丨文字; 丨塵境 Words, or expressions to be shut out; unnecessary words. 丨處 A shut-in place, a place of peace, a hermitage, a Buddhist monastery. 丨道人 One well-trained in the religion; a practitioner.

開 To open, begin, institute, unfold, disclose; dismiss; write out; unloose; to heat, boil.

開三顯一 To explain the three vehicles, and reveal the reality of the one method of salvation, as found in the Lotus Sūtra.

開元 The K'ai-yüan period of the T'ang emperor Hsüan Tsung, A.D. 713–741; during which the monk 智昇 Chih-shêng in 730 issued his "complete list of all the translations of Buddhist books into the Chinese language from the year A.D. 67 up to the date of publication, embracing the labours of 176 individuals, the whole amounting to 2,278 separate works, many of which, however, were at that time already lost." Wylie. Its title was 丨丨釋教錄. He also issued the 丨丨丨丨丨略出, an abbreviated version.

開光 Introducing the light, the ceremony of "opening the eyes" of an image, i.e. painting or touching in the pupil; also 丨眼.

開具 To make an inventory.

開化 To transform the character by instruction; to teach.

開士 The hero who is enlightened, or who opens the way of enlightenment, an epithet of the bodhisattva; also applied to monks.

開山 To establish a monastery; to found a sect.

開廢 idem 丨遮.

開心 To open the heart; to develop the mind; to initiate into truth.

開悟 To awaken, arouse, open up the intelligence and bring enlightenment.

開本 To commence; the very beginning; at the beginning; to explain the beginning.

開枕 To display the pillows, i.e. retire to bed.

開法 To found a sect or teaching, e.g. as Buddha founded Buddhism; the method of opening, or beginning.

開演 To lecture, explain at length, expound.

開甘露門 To open the ambrosial door, i.e. provide for hungry ghosts.

開發 To start, begin, send forth.

開白 To start from the bare ground; to begin a ceremony.

開示悟入 The four reasons for a Buddha's appearing in the world: to open up the treasury of truth; to indicate its meaning; to cause men to apprehend it; and to lead them into it.

開祖 The founder of a sect, or clan.

開葷; 開素 To abandon vegetarianism, as is permitted in case of sickness.

開覺 To arouse, awaken; to allow the original Buddha-nature to open and enlighten the mind.

開解 To expound, explain.

開道者 The Way-opener, Buddha; anyone who opens the way, or truth.

開遮 The adversatives, permit 開 or prohibit 遮; also 丨廢.

開靜 To break the silence, i.e. rouse from sleep.

開顯 To open up and reveal; to expose the one and make manifest the other. It is a term used by T'ien-t'ai, i.e. 開權顯實, to expose and dispose of the temporary or partial teaching, and reveal the final and real truth as in the Lotus Sūtra.

開齋 To break the fast, breakfast.

陽 The side on which the sun shines, the sun, heat, this life, positive, masculine, dynamic, etc. | 光 The sun's light, also idem | 餤 sun flames, or heat, i.e. the mirage causing the illusion of lakes.

雁 A hawk, also used for Haṁsa, a wild goose. | 塔 The Wild Goose pagoda, name of a famous monastery. | 宇 A term for a monastery. | 行 To pass in V-shaped formation like wild geese.

集 Samudāya. To assemble, collect together, aggregate, accumulate. | 會 To assemble, an assembly. | 會所 A place of assembly. | 衆 To assemble all, or everybody. | 諦 Samudaya, the second of the four dogmas, that the cause of suffering lies in the passions and their resultant karma. The Chinese 集 "accumulation" does not correctly translate Samudaya, which means "origination". | 起 A term for citta, the mind, and for ālayavijñāna, as giving rise to the mass of things.

雲 Megha. Cloud, cloudy, abundant. | 兄水弟; | 衆水衆 Brothers or men of the clouds and waters, fellow-monks. | 宗 idem 白 | |. | 堂 The assembly hall of a monastery, because of the massed congregation. | 心 Clouded heart, depressed. | 水; | 兄水弟; | 衲; | 納 Homeless or roaming monks. | 海 Many as the clouds and the waters of the ocean. | 版 A sort of cloud-shaped gong, struck to indicate the hour. | 雷音王 Megha-dundubhi-svara-rāja, or | | | 宿王華智 Jaladhara-garjita-ghoṣa-susvara-nakṣatra-rāja-saṅkusumitā-bhijña. A Buddha "having a voice musical as the sound of the thunder of the clouds and conversant with the appearance of the regents of the nakshatras". M. W. A Buddha possessing the wisdom of the Thunder-god and of the flowery stars. | 自在王 Meghasvara-rāja, ruler of the cloud drums, a son of Mahābhijñābhibhu. | 門 The Cloud-gate monastery in Kwangtung, from which 文偃 Wên-yen derived his title; his name was 張雪峯 Chang Hsüeh-fêng; he lived early in the tenth century and founded the | 門 (禪) 宗, v. 三句. | 集 Flocking like clouds, a great assembly. | 鼓 A drum ornamented with clouds for calling to midday meals.

順 Accord with, comply, yield, obey, agreeable; v. 逆 to resist. | 世 To accord with the world, its ways and customs; to die. | 上分結 The five ties in the higher realm which hold the individual in the realms of form and formlessness: desire for form, desire for formlessness, restlessness, pride, and ignorance. | 下分結 The five ties in the lower realm which hold the individual in the realms of desire, i.e. desire, resentment, egoism, false tenets, and doubt. | 分 To follow out one's duty; to accord with one's calling; to carry out the line of bodhisattva progress according to plan. | 化 To accord with one's lessons; to follow the custom; to die. | 忍 The third of the five bodhisattva stages of endurance, i.e. from the fourth to sixth stage. | 次 According to order or rank, one after another, the next life in Paradise to follow immediately after this without intervening stages. | 流 Going with the stream, i.e. of transmigration, custom, etc. | 牙 Śūnya, v. 空. | 逆 To go with, or resist, e.g. the stream to reincarnation, or to nirvāṇa.

須 To expect, wait for, wait on; necessary, must; moment, small, translit. for *su*; cf. 蘇. | 夜摩 Suyāma, also | 炎 (or 餤) 摩, intp. as Yama, the ruler of the Yama heaven; and in other similar ways. | 大拏 Sudāna, *infra*. | 彌 Sumeru, also | | 樓; 彌樓; 蘇 | |; 修迷樓; later 蘇迷盧; the central mountain of every world, tr. as 妙高; 妙光, etc., wonderful height, wonderful brilliancy, etc.; at the top is Indra's heaven, or heavens, below them are the four devalokas; around are eight circles of mountains and between them the eight seas, the whole forming nine mountains and eight seas. | 彌座; | 彌壇 A kind of throne for a Buddha. | 彌相 Merudhvaja, or Merukalpa, name of the universe of | 彌燈王佛, in the north-west, twelfth son of Mahābhijñā. | 彌頂 Merukūṭa, second son of Mahābhijñā, whose name is | 蜜羅天 Abhirati. | 扇多 Suśānta, a Buddha of this name, "very placid," M. W.; entirely pure; also | 延頭 ? Suyata. | 摩提 (or 題) Sumati, of wonderful meaning, or wisdom, the abode of Amitābha, his Pure Land. | 摩那 Sumanā, also 修 (or 蘇) | |; | 曼那; a plant 4 or 5 feet high with light yellow flowers, the "great flowered jasmine". M. W. | 梨耶 Sūrya, the sun. | 涅蜜陀 Sunirmita, but suggestive in meaning of nirmāṇarati, heavens or devas of joyful transformation. | 眞 ? Sucinti, or Sucintā, or Sucitti, name of a deva. | 臾 A kṣaṇa, a moment. | 菩提 Subhūti, also | 扶 |; | 浮帝; 蘇補 (or 部) 底; one of the ten chief disciples, said to have been the best exponent of Śūnya, or the void 解空第一; he is the principal interlocutor in the Prajñāpāramitā sūtra. There are two later personages of this name. | 跋 陀 (羅) Subhadra; the last convert of the Buddha, "a Brahman 120 years old." | 達 (多); 蘇 | | Sudatta, well-given, intp. as a good giver, beneficent; known as 給 獨 benefactor of orphans, etc. His name was Anāthapiṇḍaka, who bestowed the Jetavana vihāra on the Buddha. | 達 天 Sudṛśās, the 善 現 天; seventh Brahmaloka, eighth of the Dhyāna heavens. | 達 拏 Sudāna, also | 大 |; | 提 梨 拏; 蘇 | |, a previous incarnation of the Buddha, when he forfeited the throne by almsgiving; it is confused in meaning with 善 牙 Sudanta, good teeth. | 達 梨 舍 那; | 帶 Sudarśana, the heaven of beautiful appearance, the sixteenth Brahmaloka, and seventh of the fourth Dhyāna. | 陀 Śūdra, the fourth caste, cultivators, etc., cf. 首; also sudhā, nectar. | 陀 洹 Srota-āpanna; also | 陀 般 那; 窣 路 多 (or 陀) 阿 半 那 (or 鉢 囊); intp. by 入 流, one who has entered the stream of holy living, also 逆 流, one who goes against the stream of transmigration; the first stage of the arhat, that of a śrāvaka, v. 聲 聞. | 陀 (須) 摩 Sudhāman, a king mentioned in the 智 度 論 4.

黃 Yellow. | 壚 A grave, idem | 沓. | 旛 Yellow paper streamers hung on a grave. | 敎; | 帽 敎 The yellow sect of Lamaism, founded in 1417 by 宗 喀 巴 Tsoṅ-kha-pa, Sumatikīrti, who overthrew the decadent sect, which wears red robes, and established the sect that wears yellow, and which at first was noted for the austere life of the monks; it is found chiefly in Tibet, Mongolia, and Ili. | 昏 Evening. | 楊 木 禪 The yellow poplar meditation. The yellow poplar grows slowly, and in years with intercalary months is supposed to recede in growth; hence the term refers to the backwardness, or decline of stupid disciples. | 檗 Huang-po, *Phallodendron amurense*, a tree which gave its name to a monastery in Fukien, and to a sect founded by 希 運 Hsi-yün, its noted abbot of the T'ang dynasty. | 泉 The yellow springs, the shades. | 葉 Yellow willow leaves, resembling gold, given to children to stop their crying; the evanescent joys of the heavens offered by Buddha to curb evil. | 衣 Yellow robes (of the monks), but as yellow is a prime colour and therefore unlawful, the garments are dyed a mixture, yellowish-grey. | 金 The yellow metal, i.e. gold. | 金 宅 Golden abode, i.e. a monastery, so called after the Jetavana vihāra, for whose purchase the site was "covered with gold". | 門 Eunuchs, paṇḍakas, v. 般 10. | 面 The yellow-faced Lao Tzŭ, i.e. Buddha, because his images are gold-colour. | 龍 寺 Huang-lung, the Yellow Dragon monastery in Kiangsi after which 慧 南 Hui-nan was called.

黑 Kāla; kṛṣṇa; black; dark. | 分; | 月 Kṛṣṇapakṣa, the darkening, or latter half of the month, the period of the waning moon. | 夜 神 Kālarātri, also | | 天; | 闇 天; 闇 夜 天; one of the three queens of Yama, who controls midnight. | 天 Mahākāla, the black deva, a title of Śiva, the fierce Rudra, a black or dark-blue deity with eight arms and three eyes. | 業 Black karma, or evil deeds, which produce like karmaic results. | 漆 桶 Black varnish tub, blank ignorance. | 白 Black and white, evil and good; also the two halves of the month, the waning and waxing moon. | 繩 Kālasūtra, the black-rope or black-bonds hell. | 蚖 The black adder, or venomous snake, i.e. kleśa, passion, or illusion. | 衣; | 袈 Black, or dark monastic garments. | 闇 Black, dark, secluded, shut off; in darkness, ignorant. | 風 Black wind, i.e. a dark storm. | 齒 Maṭutacaṇḍī, black teeth, name of one of the rākṣasī.

13. THIRTEEN STROKES

亂 Disturb, perturb, confusion, disorder, rebellion. | 僧 A disorderly monk. | 善 To disturb the good, confound goodness; the confused goodness of those who worship, etc., with divided mind. | 心 A perturbed or confused mind, to disturb or unsettle the mind. | 想 To think confusedly, or improperly. | 行 Disorderly conduct.

傳 To transmit, pass on, hand down, promulgate, propagate; tradition; summon; interpret; record; the Abhidharma. | 心 To pass from mind to mind, to pass by narration or tradition, to transmit the mind of Buddha as in the Intuitional school, mental transmission. | 戒 To transmit the commandments, to grant them as at ordination. | 持 To maintain what has been transmitted; to transmit and maintain. | 敎 To spread the teaching, or doctrine; to transmit and instruct. | 法 To transmit, or spread abroad the Buddha truth. | 燈 To transmit the light, pass on the lamp of truth. | 衣 To hand down the mantle, or garments. | 通 Universal propagation; unhindered transmission.

傷 To injure, wound, hurt, harm, distress. A tr. of yakṣa. | 和 氣 To disturb the harmony. | 命 Injury to life.

募 To solicit, call upon, invite; enrol, enlist, subscribe. | 緣; | 化 To raise subscriptions.

勢 Bala, sthāman. Power, influence, authority; aspect, circumstances. | 力鬼 A powerful demon. | 羅 Śaila, craggy, mountainous, mountain. | 至 He whose wisdom and power reach everywhere, Mahāsthāmaprāpta, i.e. 大 | | q.v. Great power arrived (at maturity), the bodhisattva on the right of Amitābha, who is the guardian of Buddha-wisdom.

勤 Vīrya, energy, zeal, fortitude, virility; intp. also as 精進 one of the pāramitās. | 息 A tr. of śramaṇa, one who diligently pursues the good, and ceases from evil. | 求 To seek diligently (after the good). | 苦 Devoted and suffering, zealously suffering. | 行 Diligently going forward, zealous conduct, devoted to service, worship, etc.

嗟 To sigh. | 嘆 Alas! translit. *cha*.

嗚 Oh! alas! to wail. | 嚕捺囉叉 Rudrākṣa, the *Elceocarpus ganitrus*, whose berries are used for rosaries; hence, a rosary.

嗜 Fond of, given up to, doting; translit. *sh*, *j* sounds, e.g. | 那耶舍 Jinayaśas, a noted monk.

嗣 To succeed to, continue, adopt, posterity, follow after. | 法 To succeed to the dharma, or methods, of the master, a term used by the meditative school; 傳法 is used by the esoteric sect.

嗢 To clear the throat; translit. *u*, cf. 鬱, 烏, 温, 優. | 呾 (or 怛) 羅 Uttara, tr. by 上 superior, predominant, above all. | | | 矩嚕 Uttarakuru, one of the four continents, that north of Meru. | | | 犀那 Uttarasena, a king of Udyāna who obtained part of Śākyamuni's relics. | | | 頞沙荼 Uttarāṣāḍhā, the nakṣatra presiding over the second half of the 4th month, "the month in which Śākyamuni was conceived." Eitel. | 尸羅 Uśīra, fragrant root of *Andropogon muricatus*. | 屈竹迦; | 倶吒 Utkuṭukāsana, v. 結跏 to squat on the heels. | 瑟尼沙 Uṣṇīṣa, the protuberance on the Buddha's head, v. 烏. | 蹭伽 Utsaṅga, 100,000 trillions, a 大 | | | being a quadrillion, v. 洛叉. | 鉢 (羅) Utpala, the blue lotus; the 6th cold hell.

園 Vihāra; place for walking about, pleasure-ground, garden, park. | 觀 A garden look-out, or terrace. | 頭 A gardener, or head of a monastery-garden, either for pleasure, or for vegetables.

圓 Round, all-round, full-orbed, inclusive, all-embracing, whole, perfect, complete.

圓乘 The all-complete vehicle, the final teaching of Buddha.

圓信 Complete faith; the faith of the "perfect" school. A T'ien-t'ai doctrine that a moment's faith embraces the universe.

圓修 (1) To observe the complete T'ien-t'ai meditation, at one and the same time to comprehend the three ideas of 空假中 q.v. (2) To keep all the commandments perfectly.

圓位 The perfect status, the position of the "perfect" school, perfect unity which embraces all diversity.

圓光 The halo surrounding the head of a Buddha, etc.

圓佛 The Buddha of the "perfect" school, the perfect pan-Buddha embracing all things in every direction; the dharmakāya; Vairocana, identified with Śākyamuni.

圓凝 Complete crystallization, or formation, i.e. perfect nirvāṇa.

圓合 All-embracing, all inclusive.

圓壇 Round altar; a complete group of objects of worship, a maṇḍala.

圓妙 The mystery of the "perfect" school, i.e. the complete harmony of 空假中 noumenon, phenomenon, and the middle way.

圓宗 The sect of the complete or final Buddha-truth, i.e. T'ien-t'ai; cf. | 教.

圓密 The complete teaching of T'ien-t'ai and the esoteric teaching. Also, the harmony of both as one.

圓寂 Perfect rest, i.e. parinirvāṇa; the perfection of all virtue and the elimination of all evil, release from the miseries of transmigration and entrance into the fullest joy.

圓實 Perfect reality; the T'ien-t'ai perfect doctrine which enables one to attain reality or Buddhahood at once.

圓心 The perfect mind, the mind that seeks perfection, i.e. nirvāṇa.

圓悟 Completely to apprehend the truth. In T'ien-t'ai, the complete apprehension at the same time of noumenon, phenomenon, and the middle way.

圓成 Complete perfection. | | 實性 The perfect true nature, absolute reality, the bhūtatathatā.

圓戒 v. 圓頓戒.

圓教 The complete, perfect, or comprehensive doctrine; the school or sect of Mahāyāna which represents it. The term has had three references. The first was by 光統 Kuang-t'ung of the Later Wei, sixth century, who defined three schools, 漸 gradual, 頓 immediate, and 圓 inclusive or complete. The T'ien-t'ai called its fourth section the inclusive, complete, or perfect teaching 圓, the other three being 三藏 Hīnayāna, 通 Mahāyāna-cum-Hīnayāna, 別 Mahāyāna. The Hua-yen so called its fifth section, i.e. 小乘; 大乘始; 大乘終; 頓 and 圓. It is the T'ien-t'ai version that is in general acceptance, defined as a perfect whole and as complete in its parts; for the whole is the absolute and its parts are therefore the absolute; the two may be called noumenon and phenomenon, or 空 and 假 (or 俗), but in reality they are one, i.e. the 中 medial condition. To conceive these three as a whole is the T'ien-t'ai inclusive or "perfect" doctrine. The Hua-yen "perfect" doctrine also taught that unity and differentiation, or absolute and relative, were one, a similar doctrine to that of the identity of contraries. In T'ien-t'ai teaching the harmony is due to its underlying unity; its completeness to the permeation of this unity in all phenomena; these two are united in the medial 中 principle; to comprehend these three principles at one and the same time is the complete, all-containing, or "perfect" doctrine of T'ien-t'ai. There are other definitions of the all-inclusive doctrine, e.g. the eight complete things, complete in teaching, principles, knowledge, etc. | | 四門 v. 四門.

圓斷 The T'ien-t'ai doctrine of the complete cutting off, at one remove, of the three illusions, i.e. 見思 associated with 空; 塵沙 with 假; and 無明 with 中; q.v.

圓果 Perfect fruit, nirvāṇa.

圓極 Inclusive to the uttermost; absolute perfection.

圓機 The potentiality of becoming fully enlightened at once.

圓海 The all-embracing ocean, i.e. the perfection or power of the Tathāgata.

圓滿 Completely full; wholly complete; the fulfilling of the whole, i.e. that the part contains the whole, the absolute in the relative. | | 經 The complete, or all-inclusive sūtra, a term applied to the Hua-yen ching.

圓空 Complete vacuity, i.e. 空空, from which even the idea of vacuity is absent.

圓融 Complete combination; the absolute in the relative and vice versa; the identity of apparent contraries; perfect harmony among all differences, as in water and waves, passion and enlightenment, transmigration and nirvāṇa, or life and death, etc.; all are of the same fundamental nature, all are bhūtatathatā, and bhūtatathatā is all; waves are one with waves, and water is one with water, and water and wave are one. | | 三諦 The three dogmas of 空假中 as combined, as one and the same, as a unity, according to the T'ien-t'ai inclusive or perfect school. The universal 空 apart from the particular 假 is an abstraction. The particular apart from the universal is unreal. The universal realizes its true nature in the particular, and the particular derives its meaning from the universal. The middle path 中 unites these two aspects of one reality.

圓行 The conduct or discipline of the T'ien-t'ai "perfect" school.

圓覺 Complete enlightenment potentially present in each being, for all have 本覺 primal awareness, or 眞心 the true heart (e.g. conscience), which has always remained pure and shining; considered as essence it is the 一心 one mind, considered causally it is the Tathāgata-garbha, considered in its result it is | | perfect enlightenment, cf. | | 經.

圓詮 Exposition of the perfect or all-embracing doctrine, as found in the Hua-yen and Lotus sūtras.

圓具 Whole and complete, i.e. the whole of the commandments, by the observance of which one is near to nirvāṇa.

圓通 Universally penetrating; supernatural powers of omnipresence; universality; by wisdom to penetrate the nature or truth of all things. | | 三昧 The various samādhi of supernatural powers of the twenty-five "great ones" of the 楞嚴經 Śūraṅgama sūtra, especially of | | 大士 the omnipresent hearer of those who call, i.e. Kuan-yin.

圓道 The perfect way (of the three principles of T'ien-t'ai, v. above).

圓頓 Complete and immediate, i.e. to comprehend the three principles 空假中 at one and the same time, cf. | 敎. | | 一乘 The complete immediate vehicle, that of T'ien-t'ai. | | 宗; | | 敎 ditto. | | 戒 The rules of the T'ien-t'ai school, especially for attaining immediate enlightenment as above; also called | | 無作 (or 菩薩) 大戒. | | (止) 觀 as given in the 摩訶止觀 is the concentration, or mental state, in which is perceived, at one and the same time, the unity in the diversity and the diversity in the unity, a method ascribed by T'ien-t'ai to the Lotus sūtra; v. above.

塚 A tomb, mound, cemetery; śmaśāna, v. 舍.

塑 To model in clay. 泥 | 木雕 Modelled clay and carved wood, images. | 像 To model images.

塡 To fill up. | 王 Udayana, v. 優 | king of Kauśāmbī. | 陵 A raised mound, a stūpa.

塢 A bank, wall, entrenchment, dock; translit. *u*, for which many other characters are used, e.g. 烏; 憂; 于, etc.

塗 To smear, rub on. | 割 To anoint the hand, or cut it off, instances of love and hatred. | 毒鼓 A drum smeared with poison to destroy those who hear it. | 灰外道 Pāṁśupatas, perhaps Pāsupatas, followers of Śiva, Śaiva ascetics; a class of heretics who smeared themselves with ashes. | 足油 Oil rubbed on the feet to avoid disease. | 香 To rub the body with incense or scent to worship Buddha.

塔 Stūpa; tope; a tumulus, or mound, for the bones, or remains of the dead, or for other sacred relics, especially of the Buddha, whether relics of the body or the mind, e.g. bones or scriptures. As the body is supposed to consist of 84,000 atoms, Aśoka is said to have buil 84,000 stūpas to preserve relics of Śākyamuni. Pagodas, dagobas, or towers with an odd number of stories are used in China for the purpose of controlling the geomantic influences of a neighbourhood. Also | 婆; 兜婆; 偸婆; 藪斗波; 窣堵波; 率都婆; 素覩波; 私鍮簸, etc. The stūpas erected over relics of the Buddha vary from the four at his birthplace, the scene of his enlightenment, of his first sermon, and of his death, to the 84,000 accredited to Aśoka. | 像 Stūpas and images. | 廟 Pagodas and temples.

塞 To stop up, block, gag; dull; honest; a barrier, frontier; translit. *s*. | 建陀(羅); | 健陀 Skandha, "the shoulder"; "the body"; "the trunk of a tree"; "a section," etc. M. W. "Five psychological constituents." "Five attributes of every human being." Eitel. Commonly known as the five aggregates, constituents, or groups; the pañcaskandha; under the Han dynasty 陰 was used, under the Chin 衆, under the T'ang 蘊. The five are: 色 Rūpa, form, or sensuous quality; 受 Vedanā, reception, feeling, sensation; 想 Sañjñā, thought, consciousness, perception; 行 Karman, or Saṁskāra, action, mental activity; 識 Vijñāna, cognition. The last four are mental constituents of the ego. Skandha is also the name of an arhat, and Skanda, also | | 那, of a deva. | 畢力迦 Sprkkā, clover, lucern. | 縛悉底迦 Svastika, v. 萬. | 頗胝加 Sphāṭika, crystal, quartz, one of the saptaratna, seven treasures.

奥 South-west corner where were the lares; retired, quiet; abstruse, mysterious; blended; warm; translit. *au*. | 箄迦 Aupayika, proper, fit, suitable.

嫉 Īrṣyā; envy of other's possessions, jealousy.

媽 Nurse, mother. | 哈薩督呀 Mahāsattva, a great or noble being; the perfect bodhisattva, greater (mahā) than any other being (sattva) except a Buddha; v. 摩訶薩埵.

媲 To pair. Small. | 摩 Bhīmā, terrible, fearful; name of Śiva's wife. "A city west of Khoten noted for a Buddha-statue, which had transported itself thither from Udjyana." Eitel. Hsüan-tsang's P'i-mo. v. 毗.

𣪍 To and fro, to roll; translit. *bha, va.* | 毗吠伽 Bhāvaviveka, a disciple of Nāgārjuna, who retired to a rock cavern to await the coming of Maitreya. | 羅犀那 Varasena (the Aparasvin of the Zend-Avesta), a pass on the Paropamisus, now called Khawak, south of Indarab. | 藪天 Vasudeva, in Brahmanic mythology the father of Kṛṣṇa. | 達羅鉢陀 Bhādrapada, the last month of summer.

嵯 Irregular, uneven; translit. *jha.*

廅 A cave. | 天 Parīttābha, the fourth Brahmaloka, the first region of the second dhyāna. | 樓亘 An early attempt to translate the name of Kuan-yin. | 波(摩那) Apramāṇābha, the heaven of infinite light, the second region of the second dhyāna.

微 Sūkṣma. Minute, small, slight; abstruse, subtle; disguised; not; used in the sense of a molecule seven times larger than 極微 an atom; translit. *vi, bi.* | 塵 A molecule, v. above. | 塵數 Numerous as molecules, or atoms; numberless. | 妙 Abstruse, recondite, mysterious. | 密 Mysterious, secret, occult. | 戍陀 Viśuddha, purified, pure. | 沙落起多 ? Vibhārakṣita, a form of Tiṣyarakṣita, Aśoka's queen. | 瑟紐 Viṣṇu, also 毘 | | (or 笈 or 怒); 毘紐; 毘搜 (or 瘦) 紐; 韋紐; the second in the Trimūrti, Brahmā, Viṣṇu, Śiva; the "preserver", and all-pervading, or encompassing; identified with Nārāyaṇa-deva. | 若布雷迦 Bījapūraka; a citron, citron medicus. M. W. | 細 Minute, fine, refined, subtle. | 細身 A refined, subtle body. | 聚 A molecule, the smallest aggregation of atoms. | 行 Minute, refined, or subtle action. | 誓耶 Vijayā, also | 惹 |; 毘社耶 the overcomer, Durgā, intp. as the wife, or female manifestation, of Vairocana.

愼 Careful, cautious, attentive, heedful. | 謹; translit. *ji*, e.g. | 那弗怛羅 Jinaputra, author of the Yogācāryabhūmi-śāstra-kārikā, tr. by Hsüan-tsang A.D. 654.

㨔惕鬼 A demon of the nerves who troubles those who sit in meditation. Also 堆 | |; 埠 | |.

愧 Ashamed, intp. as ashamed for the misdeeds of others. v. 慚.

惹 Incite, provoke, irritate; translit. *j, ja, jña*; cf. 社; 闍. | 那 Jñāna, v. 智 knowledge, wisdom.

愍 idem 憫. Grieve for, mourn, sympathize. | 忌 A day of remembrance for a virtuous elder on the anniversary of his birthday.

感 To influence, move. | 應 Response to appeal or need; Buddha moved to respond. | 果 The result that is sought. | 進 To move to zeal, or inspire to progress.

想 To think, meditate, reflect, expect; a function of mind. | 地獄 Sañjīva, idem 等地獄 the resurrecting hell. | 念 To think and reflect. | 愛 Thought of and desire for, thought leading to desire. | 蘊 Sañjñā, one of the five skandhas, perception. | 顚倒 Inverted thoughts or perceptions, i.e. the illusion of regarding the seeming as real.

愚 Monkey-witted, silly, stupid, ignorant. | 僧 Ignorant monk. | 夫 Bāla; ignorant, immature, a simpleton, the unenlightened. | 惑 Deluded by ignorance, the delusion of ignorance. | 法 Ignorant, or immature law, or method, i.e. that of śrāvakas and pratyeka-buddhas, Hīnayāna. | 痴 Muḍha; ignorant and unenlightened, v. 痴. | 鈍 Ignorant and dull-witted.

慈 Affection (as that of a mother), mercy, compassion, tenderness; mother. | 光 Merciful light, that of the Buddhas. | 力王 Maitrībala-rāja, king of merciful virtue, or power, a former incarnation of the Buddha when, as all his people had embraced the vegetarian life, and yakṣas had no animal food and were suffering, the king fed five of them with his own blood. | 嚴 Compassion and strictness, the maternal-cum-paternal spirit. | 子 Sons of compassion, i.e. the disciples of Maitreya. | 尊 The compassionate honoured one, Maitreya. | 心 A compassionate heart. | 忍 Compassion and patience, compassionate tolerance. | 恩 Compassion and grace, merciful favour; name of a temple in Loyang, under the T'ang dynasty, which gave its name to K'uei-chi 窺基 q.v., founder of the 法相 school, known also as the 慈恩 or 唯識 school; he was a disciple of and collaborator with Hsüan-tsang, and died A.D. 682. | 悲 Compassion and pity, merciful, compassionate. | 悲室 The abode of compassion, the dwelling of Buddha, v. Lotus sūtra. | 悲萬行 Tender compassion in all things, or with compassion all things succeed. | 悲衣 Compassionate garment, the monk's robe. | 悲觀 The compassion-contemplation, in which pity destroys resentment. | 意 The mind or spirit of compassion and kindness. | 敬 Loving reverence. | 明 Tz'ŭ-ming, a noted monk of the Sung dynasty. | 氏

The compassionate one, Maitreya. | 水 Mercy as water fertilizing the life. | 眼 The compassionate eye (of Buddha). | 航 The bark of mercy. | 辯 To discuss compassionately. | 門 The gate of mercy, Buddhism. | 雲 The over-spreading, fructifying cloud of compassion, the Buddha-heart; also Tz'ŭ-yün, the name of a noted Sung monk. | 霔 To rain down compassion on men.

意 Manas, the sixth of the ṣaḍāyatanas or six means of perception, i.e. sight, hearing, smell, taste, touch, and mind. Manas means "mind (in its widest sense as applied to all the mental powers), intellect, intelligence, understanding, perception, sense, conscience, will". M. W. It is "the intellectual function of consciousness", Keith. In Chinese it connotes thought, idea, intention, meaning, will; but in Buddhist terminology its distinctive meaning is mind, or the faculty of thought.

意三 The three evils which belong to intellect—lobha, dveṣa, moha, i.e. desire, dislike, delusion.

意力 Mental power or intention; the purpose to attain bodhi or enlightenment.

意地 The stage of intellectual consciousness, being the sixth vijñāna, the source of all concepts.

意學 Mental learning, learning by meditation rather than from books, the special cult of the Ch'an or Intuitional school, which is also called the School of the Buddha-mind.

意安樂行 The calmly joyful life of the mind—one of the four in the Lotus sūtra 14; v. 四 | | |.

意念往生 By thought and remembrance or invocation of Amitābha to enter into his Pure Land.

意憤天 A deva who sinned and was sent down to be born among men.

意成 Mentally evolved, or evolved at will. | | 天 Devas independent of the nourishment of the realms of form and formlessness, who live only in the realm of mind. | | 身 idem | 生 | q.v.

意根 The mind-sense, or indriya, the sixth of the senses; v. 六處.

意業 The function of mind or thought, one of the 三業 thought, word, deed.

意樂 Joy of the mind, the mind satisfied and joyful. Manobhirāma, the realm foretold for Maudgalyāyana as a Buddha.

意水 The mind or will to become calm as still water, on entering samādhi.

意猿 The mind as intractable as a monkey.

意生身 A body mentally produced, or produced at will, a tr. of manomaya. Bodhisattvas from the first stage 地 upwards are able to take any form at will to save the living; also | | 化 |; | 成 |.

意界 Manodhātu, the realm of mind.

意處 The mind-sense, the mind, the sixth of the six senses, v. 六處.

意見 Thoughts, ideas, concepts, views.

意解 Intellectual explanation; liberation of the mind, or thought.

意言 Mental words, words within the intellectual consciousness; thought and words.

意識 Manovijñāna; the faculty of mind, one of the six vijñānas.

意趣 The direction of the mind, or will.

意車 The mind vehicle, the vehicle of intellectual consciousness, the imagination.

意馬 The mind as a horse, ever running from one thing to another. | | 心猿 The mind like a horse and the heart like a monkey—restless and intractable.

愛 Kāma; rāga. Love, affection, desire; also used for tṛṣṇā, thirst, avidity, desire, one of the twelve nidānas. It is intp. as 貪 coveting, and 染著 defiling attachment; also defined as defiling love like that toward wife and children, and undefiling love like that toward one's teachers and elders.

愛假 The falseness or unreality of desire.

愛別離苦 The suffering of being separated from those whom one loves. v. 八苦.

愛刺 The thorn of love; the suffering of attachment which pierces like a thorn.

愛執 The grip of love and desire.

愛心 A loving heart; a mind full of desire; a mind dominated by desire.

愛恚 Love and hate, desire and hate.

愛惜 Love and care for; to be unwilling to give up; sparing.

愛惑 The illusion of love, or desire.

愛憎 Love and hate, desire and dislike.

愛果 The fruit of desire and attachment, i.e. suffering.

愛根 The root of desire, which produces the passions.

愛業 The karma which follows desire.

愛樂 The joy of right love, i.e. the love of the good.

愛欲 Love and desire; love of family. | | 海 The ocean of desire.

愛毒 The poison of desire, or love, which harms devotion to Buddha.

愛水 Semen; also the passion of desire which fertilizes evil fruit.

愛法 Love for Buddha-truth; the method of love.

愛河 The river of desire in which men are drowned.

愛染 The taint of desire. | | 王 Rāga, one of the 明王 with angry appearance, three faces and six arms.

愛涎 The mouth watering with desire.

愛海 The ocean of desire.

愛流 The flood of desire which overwhelms.

愛渇 The thirst of desire, also 渇愛 thirstily to desire.

愛潤 The fertilizing of desire; i.e. when dying the illusion of attachment fertilizes the seed of future karma, producing the fruit of further suffering.

愛火 Love as fire that burns.

愛獄 The prison of desire.

愛界 The realm of desire, or love; those who dwell in it.

愛眼 The eye of love, that of Buddha.

愛種 The seed of desire, with its harvest of pain.

愛結 The tie of love or desire.

愛緣 Love or desire as a contributory cause, or attachment.

愛繫 The bond of love, or desire.

愛羂 The noose, or net, of desire.

愛羅刹女 The rākṣasī, or female demon, of desire.

愛著 The strong attachment of love; the bondage of desire. From this bond of love also arises pity 慈悲, which is fundamental to Buddhism. There is also | | 生死 bondage to rebirth and mortality by love of life, and to be rid of this love is essential to deliverance. | | 迷 The delusion of love for and attachment to the transient and perishing.

愛繭 The cocoon of desire spun about beings as a silkworm spins a cocoon about itself.

愛行 Emotional behaviour, or the emotions of desire, as contrasted with 見行 rational behaviour.

愛見 Attachment or love growing from thinking of others. Also, attachment to things 愛 and attachment to false views 見; also emotional and rational.

愛語 Loving speech; the words of love of a bodhisattva.

愛論 Talk of love or desire, which gives rise to improper conversation.

愛身天 The heaven of lovely form in the desire-realm, but said to be above the devalokas; cf. sudṛśa 善現.

愛輪 The wheel of desire which turns men into the six paths of transmigration.

愛鬼 The demon of desire.

損 To spoil, hurt, damage. | 伏斷 To spoil, subject and destroy (the passions).

敬 Reverence, respect. | 愛 Reverence and love; reverent love. | 田 The field of reverence, i.e. worship and support of the Buddha, Dharma, and Saṁgha as a means to obtain blessing. | 禮 Vandanī, paying reverence, worship.

新 New, newly, just, opposite of 舊 old. | 戒 One who has newly been admitted; a novice. | 歲 The new year of the monks, beginning on the day after the summer retreat. | 發意 One who has newly resolved on becoming a Buddhist, or on any new line of conduct. | 舊兩譯 Old and new methods of or terms in translation, the old before, the new with Hsüan-tsang. | | 醫 Old and new methods of healing, e.g. Hīnayāna and Mahāyāna, v. Nirvāṇa Sūtra 2.

暖 Warm; to warm. | 寮; | 寺; | 洞; | 席 Presents of tea, fruit, etc., brought to a monastery, or offered to a new arrival.

暗 Dark, dim, gloom, dull; secret, hidden. | 蔽 Dark, ignorant. | 證禪師; | 證; | 禪, etc. A charlatan who teaches intuitional meditation differently from the methods of that school; an ignorant preceptor.

會 Meet, assemble, collect, associate, unite; assembly, company; communicate; comprehend, skilled in, can, will; a time, moment. | 三歸一 To unite the three vehicles in one, as in the Lotus sūtra. | 下 The lower, or junior members of an assembly, or company. | 得 To comprehend, understand; to meet with. | 式 The manners, customs, or rules of an assembly, or community. | 釋 To assemble and explain the meaning; to comprehend and explain. | 衆 To assemble the community, or company; to meet all. | 通 To compare and adjust; compound; bring into agreement; solve and unify conflicting ideas.

楚 Brambles, spinous; painful, grievous; to flog; clear up; the Ch'u state. | 江王 King of the grievous river, the second of the ten rulers of Hades.

椽 Rafters.

楊 Willow; aspen, poplar, arbutus; syphilis. | 枝 Willow branches, or twigs, used as dantakāṣṭha, i.e. for cleansing the teeth by chewing or rubbing. | 柳觀音 Kuan-yin with the willow-branch. | 葉 Willow leaves, e.g. yellow willow leaves given to a child as golden leaves to stop its crying, a parallel to the Buddha's opportune methods of teaching.

楞伽 Laṅkā, a mountain in the south-east part of Ceylon, now called Adam's Peak; the island of Ceylon 錫蘭; also 稜伽; 駿伽. | | 經 The Laṅkāvatāra sūtra, a philosophical discourse attributed to Śākyamuni as delivered on the Laṅka mountain in Ceylon. It may have been composed in the fourth or fifth century A.D.; it "represents a mature phase of speculation and not only criticizes the Sāṅkhya, Pāśupata and other Hindu schools, but is conscious of the growing resemblance of Mahāyānism to Brahmanic philosophy and tries to explain it". Eliot. There have been four translations into Chinese, the first by Dharmarakṣa between 412–433, which no longer exists; the second was by Guṇabhadra in 443, called 楞伽阿跋多羅寶經 4 chüan; the third by Bodhiruci in 513, called 入楞伽經 10 chüan; the fourth by Śikṣānanda in 700–704, called 大乘入楞伽經 7 chüan. There are many treatises and commentaries on it, by Fa-hsien and others. See *Studies in the Laṅkāvatāra Sūtra* by Suzuki and his translation of it. This was the sūtra allowed by Bodhidharma, and is the recognized text of the Ch'an (Zen) School. There are numerous treatises on it. 丨嚴經 Śūraṅgama-sūtra, a Tantric work tr. by Pāramiti in 705; v. 首丨丨丨; there are many treatises under both titles.

極 Highest point, apex; utmost, ultimate, extreme, the limit, finality; reaching to. 丨位 The highest stage of enlightenment, that of Buddha. 丨光淨天 Pure heaven of utmost light, the highest of the second dhyāna heavens of the form-world; the first to be re-formed after a universal destruction and in it Brahmā and devas come into existence; also 丨光音天 Ābhāsvara. 丨喜地 The stage of utmost joy, the first of the ten stages 十地 of the bodhisattva. 丨地 Reaching the ground; utmost; fundamental principle; the highest of all, i.e. Buddha. 丨妙 Of utmost beauty, wonder, or mystery. 丨尊 The highest revered one, Buddha. 丨微 An atom, especially as a mental concept, in contrast with 色聚之微, i.e. a material atom which has a centre and the six directions, an actual but imperceptible atom; seven atoms make a 微塵 molecule, the smallest perceptible aggregation, called an aṇu 阿菟 or 阿拏; the perceptibility is ascribed to the deva-eye rather than to the human eye. There is much disputation as to whether the ultimate atom has real existence or not, whether it is eternal and immutable and so on. 丨果 The highest fruit, perfect Buddha-enlightenment. 丨樂 Sukhāvatī, highest joy, name of the Pure Land of Amitābha in the West, also called 丨丨世界 the world of utmost joy. 丨熱地獄 Pratāpana; Mahātāpana; the hottest hell, the seventh of the eight hells. 丨略色 The smallest perceptible particle into which matter can be divided, an atom. 丨聖 The highest saint, Buddha. 丨臈 The oldest monk in orders. 丨致 Utmost, ultimate, final point; reaching to. 丨覺 Profound enlightenment, utmost awareness. 丨靜 Utmost quiescence, or mental repose; meditation, trance. 丨難勝地 The stage in which the bodhisattva has overcome his worst difficulties, the fifth stage.

業 Karman, Karma, "action, work, deed"; "moral duty"; "product, result, effect." M. W. The doctrine of the act; deeds and their effects on the character, especially in their relation to succeeding forms of transmigration. The 三業 are thought, word, and deed, each as good, bad, or indifferent. Karma from former lives is 宿丨, from present conduct 現丨. Karma is moral action which causes future retribution, and either good or evil transmigration. It is also that moral kernel in each being which survives death for further rebirth or metempsychosis. There are categories of 2, 3, 4, 6, and 10; the 六丨 are rebirth in the hells, or as animals, hungry ghosts, men, devas, or asuras: v. 六趣.

業力 The power of karma to produce good and evil fruit.

業厄 The constraints of karma; i.e. restricted conditions now as resulting from previous lives.

業受 That which is received as the result of former karmaic conduct, e.g. long or short life, etc.

業因 The deed as cause; the cause of good or bad karma.

業垢 Karma defilement.

業報 Karma-reward; the retribution of karma, good or evil. 丨丨身 The body of karmaic-retribution, especially that assumed by a bodhisattva to accord with the conditions of those he seeks to save.

業塵 Karma-dirt, the defilement or remains of evil karma.

業天 The karma of heaven, i.e. the natural inevitable law of cause and effect.

業壽 Life, long or short, as determined by previous karma.

業影 Karma-shadow, karma dogging one's steps like a shadow.

業性 The nature of karma, its essential being; idem 丨體.

業惱 Karmaic distress; karma and distress.

業感 The influence of karma; caused by karma.

業有 Reality of karma, idem 行有.

業果 The fruit of karma, conditions of rebirth depending on previous karmaic conduct.

業海 The vast, deep ocean of (evil) karma.

業火 The fires of evil karma; the fires of the hells.

業田 The field of karma; the life in which the seeds of future harvest are sown.

業病 Illness as the result of previous karma.

業相 Action, activity, the karmaic, the condition of karmaic action. The first of the three 相 of the Awakening of Faith, when mental activity is stirred to action by unenlightenment.

業秤 The scales of karma, in which good and evil are weighed by the rulers of Hades.

業種 Karmabīja; karma-seed which springs up in happy or in suffering rebirth.

業簿 The record, or account book, kept by the rulers of Hades, recording the deeds of all sentient beings.

業結 The bond of karma; karma and the bond (of the passions).

業網 The net of karma which entangles beings in the sufferings of rebirth.

業緣 Karma-cause, karma-circumstance, condition resulting from karma.

業縛 Karma-bonds; the binding power of karma.

業繩 Karma-cords, the bonds of karma.

業繫 Karma-bonds; karma-fetters. | | 苦相 The suffering state of karma-bondage.

業羂 The noose of karma which entangles in transmigration.

業苦 Karmaic suffering.

業處 Karmasthāna; a place for working, of business, etc.; the place, or condition, in which the mind is maintained in meditation; by inference, the Pure Land, etc.

業行 Deeds, actions; karma deeds, moral action which influences future rebirth.

業識 "Activity-consciousness in the sense that through the agency of ignorance an unenlightened mind begins to be disturbed (or awakened)." Suzuki's *Awakening of Faith*, 76.

業賊 Robber-karma; evil karma harms as does a robber.

業輪 The wheel of karma which turns men into the six paths of transmigration.

業通 Supernatural powers obtained from former karma; idem 報 |.

業道 The way of karma. | | (神) The gods who watch over men's deeds.

業鏡 Karma-mirror, that kept in Hades reveals all karma.

業障 Karmāvaraṇa; the screen, or hindrance, of past karma, hindering the attainment of bodhi. | | 除 A symbol indicating the cutting away of all karmaic hindrances by the sword of wisdom.

業風 Karma-wind: (1) the fierce wind of evil karma and the wind from the hells, at the end of the age; (2) karma as wind blowing a person into good or evil rebirth.

業食 Karma as nutritive basis for succeeding existence.

業餘 A remnant of karma after the six paths of existence. v. 三 餘.

業體 idem | 性.

業魔 Karma-māras, the demons who or the karma which hinders and harms goodness.

歲 Vatsara, a year; cf. 臘 19 strokes.

毀 To break down, destroy, abolish, defame. | 呰 To defame, vilify. | 釋 To slander the Buddha or Buddhism.

殿 A temple, hall, palace; rearguard. | 主; | 司 The warden of a temple.

準 Correct, exact, a rule. | 提 Candī, or Cundi; also 准胝; 尊提. (1) In Brahmanic mythology a vindictive form of Durgā, or Pārvatī, wife of Śiva. (2) In China identified with Marīci 摩里支 or 天后 Queen of Heaven. She is represented with three eyes and eighteen arms; also as a form of Kuan-yin, or in Kuan-yin's retinue. | 陀; 純陀 Cunda, a native of Kuśinagara from whom Śākyamuni accepted his last meal.

溥 Universal. | 首 A name of Mañjuśrī, v. 文.

溼 The class of beings produced by moisture, such as fish, etc. v. 四生.

源 Spring, source, origin, *fons et origo*. | 底 The very beginning, source, or basis.

滅 Extinguish, exterminate, destroy; a tr. of Nirodha, suppression, annihilation; of Nirvāṇa, blown out, extinguished, dead, perfect rest, highest felicity, etc.; and of Nivṛtti, cessation, disappearance. Nirodha is the third of the four axioms: 苦, 集, 滅, 道 pain, its focussing, its cessation (or cure), the way of such cure. Various ideas are expressed as to the meaning of 滅, i.e. annihilation or extinction of existence; or of rebirth and mortal existence; or of the passions as the cause of pain; and it is the two latter views which generally prevail; cf. 涅 10 strokes.

滅劫 The saṁvarta-kalpa of world-destruction, cf. 壞 |.

滅受想定 A samādhi in which there is complete extinction of sensation and thought; one of the highest forms of kenosis, resulting from concentration.

滅場 The plot or arena where the extinction (of the passions) is attained; the place of perfect repose, or nirvāṇa.

滅定 idem | 盡 |. | | 智通 The freedom or supernatural power of the wisdom attained in nirvāṇa, or perfect passivity.

滅度 Nirvāṇa; extinction of reincarnation and escape from suffering.

滅後 After the Nirvāṇa, after the Buddha's death.

滅擯 Blotting out the name and the expulsion of a monk who has committed a grievous sin without repentance.

滅智 The knowledge, or wisdom, of the third axiom, nirodha or the extinction of suffering.

滅果 Nirvāṇa as the fruit of extinction (of desire).

滅業 The work or karma of nirodha, the karma resulting from the extinction of suffering, i.e. nirvāṇa.

滅法 The unconditioned dharma, the ultimate inertia from which all forms come, the noumenal source of all phenomena. | | 智 The knowledge or wisdom of the dogma of extinction (of passion and reincarnation); one of the 八智 q.v. | | | 忍 One of the 八忍, the endurance and patience associated with the last. | | 界 The realm of the absolute, of perfect quiescence.

滅理 The principle or law of extinction, i.e. nirvāṇa.

滅病 One of the 四病 four sick or faulty ways of seeking perfection, the Hīnayāna method of endeavouring to extinguish all perturbing passions so that nothing of them remains.

滅盡定 idem 滅受想定, also called | 定 and | 盡三昧.

滅相 Extinction, as when the present passes into the past. Also, the absolute, unconditioned aspect of bhūtatathatā.

滅種 To destroy one's seed of Buddhahood.

滅羯磨 The extinguishing karma, or the blotting out of the name of a monk and his expulsion.

滅觀 The contemplation of extinction: the destruction of ignorance is followed by the annihilation of karma, of birth, old age, and death.

滅 諦 Nirodha-āryasatya, the third of the four dogmas, the extinction of suffering, which is rooted in reincarnation, v. 四 諦.

滅 道 Extinction of suffering and the way of extinction, nirodha and mārga ; v. *supra*.

照 To shine, illumine ; to superintend ; a dispatch, pass ; as, according to. | 寂 The shining mystic purity of Buddha, or the bhūtatathatā. | 拂 The manager of affairs in a monastery. | 牌 A notice board, especially allotting seats. | 覽 To shine upon and behold ; to survey ; to enlighten. | 鏡 To look at oneself in a mirror, forbidden to monks except for specified reasons.

煎 To simmer, fry. | 點 To fry cakes.

煮 To boil, cook. | 沙 Like boiling sand for food.

熙 Light, bright, splendid, prosperous. | 連 The river Hiraṇyavatī, see 尸.

煙 Smoke, tobacco, opium. | 蓋 A smoke cover, i.e. a cloud of incense.

煗 Warm, idem 暖. | 法 The first of the 四 加 行 位 ; the stage in which dialectic processes are left behind and the mind dwells only on the four dogmas and the sixteen disciplines.

煠 To heat ; a pot. | 牒 薩 督 呀 Bodhisattva, v. 菩.

煏 To dry by the fire. | 芻 Bhikṣu, v. 比.

煆 To forge metal, work upon, calcine. | 髮 To burn up the hair of a novice, male or female.

煩 Trouble, annoyance, perplexity.

煩 惱 Kleśa, " pain, affliction, distress," " care, trouble " (M. W.). The Chinese tr. is similar, distress, worry, trouble, and whatever causes them. Keith interprets kleśa by " infection ", " contamination ", " defilement ". The Chinese intp. is the delusions, trials, or temptations of the passions and of ignorance which disturb and distress the mind ; also in brief as the three poisons 貪 瞋 痴 desire, detestation, and delusion. There is a division into the six fundamental | |, or afflictions, v. below, and the twenty which result or follow them ; and there are other dual divisions. The six are : 貪 瞋 痴 慢 疑 and 惡 見 desire, detestation, delusion, pride, doubt, and evil views, which last are the false views of a permanent ego, etc. The ten | | are the first five, and the sixth subdivided into five. | |, like kleśa, implies moral affliction or distress, trial, temptation, tempting, sin. Cf. 使.

煩 惱 即 菩 提 The passions, or moral afflictions, are bodhi, i.e. the one is included in the other ; it is a T'ien-t'ai term, and said to be the highest expression of Mahāyāna thought ; cf. 即.

煩 惱 林 The forest of moral affliction.

煩 惱 業 苦 The suffering arising out of the working of the passions, which produce good or evil karma, which in turn results in a happy or suffering lot in one of the three realms, and again from the lot of suffering (or mortality) arises the karma of the passions ; also known as 惑 業 苦, 三 輪, and 三 道.

煩 惱 冰 The ice of moral affliction, i.e. its congealing, chilling influence on bodhi.

煩 惱 泥 The soil or mud of moral affliction, out of which grows the lotus of enlightenment.

煩 惱 河 The river of moral affliction which overwhelms all beings.

煩 惱 海 The ocean of moral affliction which engulfs all beings.

煩 惱 濁 The impurity, or defiling nature of the passions, one of the five 濁.

煩 惱 病 The disease of moral affliction.

煩 惱 礙 The obstruction of temptation, or defilement, to entrance into nirvāṇa peace by perturbing the mind.

煩 惱 習 The habit or influence of the passions after they have been cut off.

煩 惱 薪 The faggots of passion, which are burnt up by the fire of wisdom.

煩惱藏 The store of moral affliction, or defilement, contained in the five 住地, q.v.

煩惱賊 Temptation, or passion, as a thief injuring the spiritual nature.

煩惱道 The way of temptation, or passion, in producing bad karma.

煩惱陣 The army of temptations, tempters, or allurements.

煩惱障 The barrier of temptation, passion, or defilement, which obstructs the attainment of the nirvāṇa-mind.

煩惱餘 The remnants of illusion after it has been cut off in the realms of desire, form, and formlessness—a Hīnayāna term.

煩惱魔 The māra of the passions who troubles mind and body; the tempter; cf. 使.

煩籠 The basket of the troublers, i.e. the passions.

煩談 Vandana, obeisance, worship, v. 和.

牒 Tablets, records. 戒 | A monk's certificate, useful to a wandering or travelling monk.

犍 A gelded bull, an ox; a creature half man, half leopard. | 不男 A eunuch by castration, cf. paṇḍaka. | 地 v. | 稚 *infra.* | 度 Khaṇḍa, a piece, fragment, portion, section, chapter; a collection; the rules, monastic rules; also used for skandha, v. 塞. There are categories of eight, and twenty subjective divisions for the eight, v. the Abhidharma 八 | | 論 B.N. 1273. | 德; | 陟 (馬) Kaṇṭhaka, name of the steed on which Śākyamuni rode away from home. | 沓 Gandharva, v. 乾. | 稚 Ghaṇṭā, also | 地; | 椎; | 槌; | 遲; a bell, gong, or any similar resonant article. | 陀 Skandha, v. 塞; | | 羅; | | 衙; | | 訶; | 馱邏 Gandhāra; v. 乾. | 黄門 Palace eunuchs.

獅 A lion; cf. 師子.

瑚 Coral. | 璉 A sacrificial grain-vessel; described as a precious stone.

瑞 Auspicious; a jade token. | 像 Auspicious image, especially the first image of Śākyamuni made of sandalwood and attributed to Udayana, king of Kauśāmbī, a contemporary of Śākyamuni. Cf. 西域記 5. | 應 Auspicious response, the name of the Udumbara flower, v. 優. | 相 Auspicious, auspicious sign, or aspect.

瑟 A lute; massive. | |; | 石 The stone of which the throne of 不動明王 q.v. consists.

瑜 Lustre of gems; a beautiful stone; excellences, virtues; translit. *yu, yo.* | 乾馱羅 Yugaṁdhara, v. 踰, the first of the seven concentric circles around Meru. | 伽 Yoga; also | 誐; 遊迦; a yoke, yoking, union, especially an ecstatic union of the individual soul with a divine being, or spirit, also of the individual soul with the universal soul. The method requires the mutual response or relation of 境, 行, 理, 果 and 機; i.e. (1) state, or environment, referred to mind; (2) action, or mode of practice; (3) right principle; (4) results in enlightenment; (5) motivity, i.e. practical application in saving others. Also the mutual relation of hand, mouth, and mind referring to manifestation, incantation, and mental operation; these are known as | 伽三密, the three esoteric (means) of Yoga. The older practice of meditation as a means of obtaining spiritual or magical power was distorted in Tantrism to exorcism, sorcery, and juggling in general. | 伽宗 The Yogācāra, Vijñānavāda, Tantric, or esoteric sect. The principles of Yoga are accredited to Patañjali in the second century B.C., later founded as a school in Buddhism by Asaṅga, fourth century A.D. Cf. 大教. Hsüan-tsang became a disciple and advocate of this school. | 伽師; | 伽阿闍梨 Yogācāra, a teacher, or master of magic, or of this school. | 伽師地論 Yogācāryabhūmi-śāstra, the work of Asaṅga, said to have been dictated to him in or from the Tuṣita heaven by Maitreya, tr. by Hsüan-tsang, is the foundation text of this school, on which there are numerous treatises, the | | | | | 釋 being a commentary on it by Jinaputra, tr. by Hsüan-tsang. | | 祇; | 岐; | 祁 Yogin, one who practises yoga.

當 Suitable, adequate, equal to; to bear, undertake; ought; proper; to regard as, as; to pawn, put in place of; at, in the future. | 位即妙 According to its place, or application, wonderful or effective; e.g. poison as poison, medicine as medicine. | 來 That which is to come, the future, the future life, etc. | 分 According to condition, position, duty, etc. | 機 To suit the capacity or ability, i.e. of hearers, as did the Buddha; to avail oneself of an opportunity. | 機 衆 Those hearers of the Lotus who were adaptable to its teaching, and received it; one of the 四 衆 q.v. | 陽 In the sun, in the light. | 體 The present body, or person; the body before you, or in question; in body, or person. | 體 即 空 idem 體 空 Corporeal entities are unreal, for they disintegrate.

痾 Sickness, pain; diarrhœa. | 略 祇 Ārogya, freedom from sickness, healthy; a greeting from a superior monk, Are you well? or Be you well!

痺 Numb. | 鉢 羅 Pippala, the peepul tree, *Ficus religiosa*, v. 畢.

痴 Moha, "unconsciousness," "delusion," "perplexity," "ignorance, folly," "infatuation," etc. M. W. Also, Mūḍha. In Chinese it is silly, foolish, daft, stupid. It is intp. by 無 明 unenlightened, i.e. misled by appearances, taking the seeming for real; from this unenlightened condition arises every kind of kleśa, i.e. affliction or defilement by the passions, etc. It is one of the three poisons, desire, dislike, delusion. | 使 The messenger, lictor, or affliction of unenlightenment. | 凡; | 子 The common, unenlightened people. | 取 The kleśa of moha, held in unenlightenment. | 定 The samādhi of ignorance, i.e. without mystic insight. | 心 An unenlightened mind, ignorance darkening the mind. | 惑 Unenlightened and deluded, ignorant of the right way of seeing life and phenomena. | 愛 Ignorance and desire, or unenlightened desire, ignorance being father, desire mother, which produce all affliction and evil karma. | 慢 Ignorance and pride, or ignorant pride. | 毒 The poison of ignorance, or delusion, one of the three poisons. | 水 The turbid waters of ignorance; also to drink the water of delusion. | 燈 The lamp of delusion, attracting the unenlightened as a lamp does the moth. | 狗 Deluded dogs, i.e. the Hīnayāna śrāvakas and pratyeka-buddhas. | 猴 The deluded monkey seizing the reflection of the moon in the water, e.g. unenlightened men who take the seeming for the real. | 迷 Unenlightened and led astray. | 網 The net of delusion, or ignorance. | 縛 The bond of unenlightenment. | 闇 The darkness of the unenlightened condition.

睦 Amicable, friendly. 和 | Concord, harmony.

睡 Śaya, asleep; sleep; śay, to sleep. | 眠 idem; also Middha, drowsiness, torpor, sloth. | 眠 欲 The lust for sleep, physical and spiritual, hence | 眠 蓋 sleep, drowsiness, or sloth as a hindrance to progress.

睒 Glance; lustrous; translit. *śa*. | 彌 Śamī, a kind of acacia. | 摩 Śāmaka, a bodhisattva born to a blind couple, clad in deerskin, slain by the king in hunting, restored to life and to his blind parents by the gods.

碑 A stone tablet, or monument.

碎 Broken, fragments. | 身 舍 利 Relics of a cremated body.

禁 Prohibitions, to forbid, prohibit. | 戒 Prohibitions, commandments, especially the Vinaya as containing the laws and regulations of Buddhism. | 呪 藏 The Vidyādharapiṭaka, or Dhāraṇīpiṭaka, the canon of dhāraṇīs, a later addition to the Tripiṭaka.

稟 To petition, report, request, beg; to receive (from above); endowment. | 具 To be fully ordained, i.e. receive all the commandments. | 教 To receive the Buddha's teaching.

稠 Thick-set as growing grain, dense. | 林 A dense forest, e.g. the passions, etc.

稗 Tares, weeds. | 沙 門 Lazy monks, cumberers of the ground. | 稊 tares, weeds, only fit to be ploughed up.

窟 Guhā. A cave. | 內 "Within the cave," the assembly of the elder disciples, after Śākyamuni's death, in the cave near Magadha, when, according to tradition, Kāśyapa presided over the compiling of the Tripiṭaka; while at the same time the | 外 disciples "without the cave" compiled another canon known as the 五 藏 Pañcapiṭaka. To this separation is ascribed, without evidence, the formation of the two schools of the 上 座 部 Mahāsthavirāḥ and 大 衆 部 Mahāsaṅghikāḥ.

窣 Rustle, move, rush; translit. *s*. | 兔 黎 濕 伐 羅 ? Sūnurīśvara, ancient capital of Laṅgala, in the Punjab. | 利 ? Suri, "an ancient kingdom to the west of Kachgar, peopled by Turks (A.D. 600)." Eitel. | 唎; | 羅 Surī, or Surā, distilled liquor. | 堵 波 Stūpa, a tumulus, or building over relics, v. 率. | 莎 揭 哆 Susvāgata, most welcome (a greeting). | 路 多 阿 半 那 Srota-āpanna, one who has entered the stream of the holy life, cf. 須 and 入 流. | 都 利 慧 那 Sutriṣna, Satruṣna, Osrushna, Ura-tepe, "an ancient city in Turkestan between Kojend and Samarcand." Eitel.

豎 To stand, erect, upright. | 底沙論 The Jyotiṣa śāstra. | 敵 Protagonist and antagonist in debate. | 義; 立義 To propound a thesis and defend it. | 者 One who supplies answers to difficulties.

縱 The threads of beads or gems which hang, front and back, from the ceremonial square cap. | 經 or 線經 A sūtra, or sūtras.

經 A warp, that which runs lengthwise; to pass through or by, past; to manage, regulate; laws, canons, classics. Skt. Sūtras; threads, threaded together, classical works. Also called 契 | and | 本. The sūtras in the Tripiṭaka are the sermons attributed to the Buddha; the other two divisions are 律 the Vinaya, and 論 the śāstras, or Abhidharma; cf. 三藏. Every sūtra begins with the words 如是我聞 "Thus did I hear", indicating that it contains the words of Śākyamuni.

經典 The discourses of Buddha, the sūtra-piṭaka.

經唄 Intoning the sūtras.

經塔 A pagoda containing the scriptures as relics of the Buddha, or having verses on or in the building material.

經宗 The sūtra school, any school which bases its doctrines on the sūtras, e.g. the T'ien-t'ai, or Hua-yen, in contrast to schools based on the śāstras, or philosophical discourses.

經家 One who collected or collects the sūtras, especially Ānanda, who according to tradition recorded the first Buddhist sūtras.

經師 A teacher of the sūtras, or canon in general.

經律論 Sūtras, Vinaya, Abhidharma śāstras, the three divisions of the Buddhist canon.

經戒 Sūtras and commandments; the sūtras and morality, or discipline. The commandments found in the sūtras. The commandments regarded as permanent and fundamental.

經手 A copier of classical works; also called | 生.

經教 The teaching of the sūtras, cf. | 量部.

經法 The doctrines of the sūtras as spoken by the Buddha.

經生 To pass through life; also a copier of classical works.

經笥 A case for the scriptures, bookcase or box, also | 箱 *et al.* 有脚 | | A walking bookcase, a learned monk.

經者 One who expounds the sūtras and śāstras; one who keeps the teaching of the Lotus sūtra.

經藏 The sūtra-piṭaka.

經行 To walk about when meditating to prevent sleepiness; also as exercise to keep in health; the caṅkramaṇa was a place for such exercise, e.g. a cloister, a corridor.

經衣 The garment with sūtras in which the dead were dressed, so called because it had quotations from the sūtras written on it; also | 帷子.

經論 The sūtras and śāstras.

經軌 Sūtras and regulations (of the esoteric sects).

經道 The doctrines of the sūtras.

經(量)部 Sautrāntika, an important Hīnayāna school, which based its doctrine on the sūtras alone, cf. Keith, 151, *et al.*

置 To set up, place, arrange; set aside, buy. | 答 To reply by ignoring a question.

罪 That which is blameworthy and brings about bad karma; entangled in the net of wrong-doing; sin, crime. | 垢 The filth of sin, moral defilement. | 報 The retribution of sin, its punishment in suffering. | 性 A sinful nature; the nature of sin. | 惡 Sin and evil. | 根 The root of sin, i.e. unenlightenment or ignorance. | 業 That which sin does, its karma, producing subsequent suffering. | 福 Sinfulness and blessedness. | 福無主 Sinfulness and blessedness have no lord, or governor, i.e. we induce them ourselves. | 行 Sinful acts, or conduct. | 障 The veil, or barrier of sin, which hinders the obtaining of good karma, and the obedient hearing of the truth.

羣 A flock of sheep, herd, multitude, the flock, crowd, all. | 有 All that exists. | 生 All the living, especially all living, conscious beings. | 萌 All the shoots, sprouts, or immature things, i.e. all the living as ignorant and undeveloped. | 迷 All the deluded; all delusions. | 類 All classes of living beings, especially the sentient.

義 The right; proper, righteous; loyal; public-spirited, public; meaning, significance. It is used for the Skt. Artha, object, purpose, meaning, etc.; also for abhidheya. | 例 Meaning and rules, or method, abbrev. for 止觀 | 例 q.v. | 意 Meaning and aim. | 淨 I-ching, A.D. 635–713, the famous monk who in 671 set out by the sea-route for India, where he remained for over twenty years, spending half this period in the Nālandā monastery. He returned to China in 695, was received with much honour, brought back some four hundred works, tr. with Śikṣānanda the Avataṁsaka-sūtra, later tr. many other works and left a valuable account of his travels and life in India, died aged 79. | 無礙 Unobstructed knowledge of the meaning, or the truth; complete knowledge. | 疏 Meaning and comments on or explanations. | 相 Truth, meaning; meaning and form, truth and its aspect. | 辯 One of the seven powers of reasoning, or discourse of a bodhisattva, that on the things that are profitable to the attainment of nirvāṇa. | 趣 The path of truth, the right direction, or objective. | 門 The gate of righteousness; the schools, or sects of the meaning or truth of Buddhism. | 陀羅尼 Truth dhāraṇī, the power of the bodhisattva to retain all truth he hears.

聖 Ārya; sādhu; a sage; wise and good; upright, or correct in all his character; sacred, holy, saintly. The | 人 is the opposite of the 凡人 common, or unenlightened man.

聖主天中天 The holy lord, deva of devas, i.e. Buddha; also | 主師子 the holy lion-lord.

聖仙 The holy ṛṣi, Buddha.

聖位 The holy position, the holy life of Buddhism.

聖供 Holy offerings, or those made to the saints, especially to the Triratna.

聖僧 The holy monk, the image in the monks' assembly room; in Mahāyāna that of Mañjuśrī, in Hīnayāna that of Kāśyapa, or Subhūti, etc.

聖儀 The saintly appearance, i.e. an image of Buddha.

聖典 The sacred canon, or holy classics, the Tripiṭaka.

聖寶藏神 The deva, or devas, of the sacred treasury of precious things (who bestows them on the living).

聖尊 The holy honoured one, Buddha.

聖師子 The holy lion, Buddha.

聖心 The holy mind, that of Buddha.

聖性 The holy nature, according to the Abhidharma-kośa 俱舍論, of the passionless life; according to the Vijñānamātrasiddhi 唯識論, of enlightenment and wisdom. | 性離生 The life of holiness apart or distinguished from the life of common unenlightened people.

聖應 The influence of Buddha; the response of the Buddhas, or saints.

聖提婆 Āryadeva, or Devabodhisattva, a native of Ceylon and disciple of Nāgārjuna, famous for his writings and discussions.

聖教 The teaching of the sage, or holy one; holy teaching. | 教量 The argument or evidence of authority in logic, i.e. that of the sacred books.

聖方 Āryadeśa, the holy land, India; the land of the sage, Buddha.

聖明 Holy enlightenment; or the enlightenment of saints.

聖智 Ārya-jñāna; the wisdom of Buddha, or the saints, or sages; the wisdom which is above all particularization, i.e. that of transcendental truth.

聖果 The holy fruit, or fruit of the saintly life, i.e. bodhi, nirvāṇa.

聖法 The holy law of Buddha; the law or teaching of the saints, or sages.

聖淨 The schools of Buddhism and the Pure-land School, cf. | 道.

聖福 Holy happiness, that of Buddhism, in contrast with 梵福 that of Brahma and Brahmanism.

聖種 (1) The holy seed, i.e. the community of monks; (2) that which produces the discipline of the saints, or monastic community.

聖網 The holy jāla, or net, of Buddha's teaching which gathers all into the truth.

聖緣 Holy conditions of, or aids to the holy life.

聖者 Ārya, holy or saintly one; one who has started on the path to nirvāṇa; holiness.

聖胎 The womb of holiness which enfolds and develops the bodhisattva, i.e. the 三賢位 three excellent positions attained in the 十住, 十行 and 十廻向.

聖衆 The holy multitude, all the saints. | 衆來迎 Amitābha's saintly host come to welcome at death those who call upon him.

聖行 The holy bodhisattva life of 戒定慧 the (monastic) commandments, meditation and wisdom.

聖言 Holy words; the words of a saint, or sage; the correct words of Buddhism.

聖語 Āryabhāṣā. Sacred speech, language, words, or sayings; Sanskrit.

聖諦 The sacred principles or dogmas, or those of the saints, or sages; especially the four noble truths, cf. 四 | |

聖道 The holy way, Buddhism; the way of the saints, or sages; also the noble eightfold path. | 道門 The ordinary schools of the way of holiness by the processes of devotion, in contrast with immediate salvation by faith in Amitābha.

聖靈 The saintly spirits (of the dead).

腹 The belly. | 中 Within the belly, the heart, womb, unborn child, etc.

腰 The waist, middle. | 衣 A skirt, "shorts," etc. | 白 A white, or undyed, sash worn in mourning.

葷 Strongly smelling vegetables, e.g. onions, garlic, leeks, etc., forbidden to Buddhist vegetarians; any non-vegetarian food. | 辛 Strong or peppery vegetables, or foods. | 酒 Non-vegetarian foods and wine.

葛 The rambling, or creeping bean. | 藤 Creepers, trailers, clinging vines, etc., i.e. the afflicting passions; troublesome people; talk, words (so used by the Intuitional School). | 哩麻 Karma, v. 業. | 耶 Kāya, body, v. 身.

落 Falling leaves; to fall, drop, descend, settle; translit. *la*, *na*. | 叉 A lakh, 100,000, v. 洛. | 吃澁弭 Lakṣmī, the goddess of fortune, of good auspices, etc. | 賺 A humbug, trickster, impostor, deceiver. | 迦 Naraka, hell, v. 那. | 髮 To cut off the hair of the head, shave, become a monk. | 髮染衣; | 染 To shave the head and dye the clothing, i.e. to dye grey the normal white Indian garment; to become a monk.

葬 Inter, bury. | 送; 送 | To escort the deceased to the grave.

葉 Pattra; Parṇa; leaf, leaves. | 蓋 A leaf-hat, or cover made of leaves. | 衣觀音 A form of Kuan-yin clad in leaves to represent the 84,000 merits.

著 To manifest, display, publish, fix; interchanged with 着. In a Buddhist sense it is used for attachment to anything, e.g. the attachment of love, desire, greed, etc. | 心 The mind of attachment, or attached. | 想 The attachment of thought, or desire. | 我 Attachment to the ego, or idea of a permanent self. | 樂 Attachment to bliss, or pleasure regarded as real and permanent. | 法 Attachment to things; attachment and its object. | 衣喫飯 To wear clothes and eat food, i.e. the common things of life.

萬 Myriad, 10,000; all. | 八千世界 The 18,000 easterly worlds lighted by the ray from the Buddha's brows, v. Lotus sūtra. | 善 All goodness, all good works. | 境 All realms, all regions. | 字 The sauvastika 卍, also styled śrīvatsa-lakṣaṇa, the mark on the breast of Viṣṇu, "a particular curl of hair on the breast"; the lightning; a sun symbol; a sign of all power over evil and all favour to the good; a sign shown on the Buddha's breast. One of the marks on a Buddha's feet. | 法 All things, everything that has noumenal or phenomenal existence. | 法一如 The absolute in everything; the ultimate reality behind everything. | 法一心 Myriad things but one mind; all things as noumenal. | 物 All things. | 行 All procedures, all actions, all disciplines, or modes of salvation.

號 To roar, call, cry, scream; sign, mark, designation. | 叫地獄 Raurava; the hell of wailing.

蜃 Mirage; sea-serpent; frog. | 樓臺 A mirage palace, cf. 乾.

蛾 A moth. 如 | 趣燈火 Like a moth flying into the lamp—is man after his pleasures.

裙 A skirt. Nivāsana, cf. 泥, a kind of garment, especially an under garment.

裝 To dress, make up, pretend, pack, load, store; a fashion. | 像 To dress an image. | 香 To put incense into a censer.

補 To patch, repair, restore; tonic; translit. *pu*, *po*, cf. 富, 弗, 佛, 布. | 伽羅 Pudgala, *infra*. | 剌拏 v. 富; intp. by 滿 Pūrṇa. | 囉嚩 Pūrva, in Pūrva-videha, the eastern continent. | 怛洛迦 Potaraka, Potala, *infra*. | 沙 Puṣya, the 鬼 asterism, v. 富. | 澁波 Puṣpa, a flower, a bloom, v. 布. | 特伽羅 Pudgala, "the body, matter; the soul, personal identity" (M. W.); intp. by man, men, human being, and 衆生 all the living; also by 趣向 direction, or transmigration; and 有情 the sentient, v. 弗. | 瑟置 (or 迦) Pauṣṭika, promoting advancement, invigorating, protective. | 盧沙 Puruṣa, "man collectively or individually"; "Man personified"; "the Soul of the universe" (M. W.); intp. by 丈夫 and 人; v. 布; also the first form of the masculine gender; (2) puruṣam | | 衫; (3) puruṣeṇa | | 沙拏; (4) puruṣāya | | 沙耶; (5) puruṣāt | | 沙多頞; (6) puruṣasya | | 殺沙; (7) puruṣe | | 鎩. | 羯娑 Paulkasa, an aboriginal, or the son "of a śūdra father and of a kshatriyā mother" (M. W.); intp. as low caste, scavenger, also an unbeliever (in the Buddhist doctrine of 因果 or retribution). | 處 One who repairs, or occupies a vacated place, a Buddha who succeeds a Buddha, as Maitreya is to succeed Śākyamuni. | 陀; | 陁; | | 落(迦) Potala; Potalaka. (1) A sea-port on the Indus, the πατάλα of the ancients, identified by some with Ṭhaṭtha, said to be the ancient home of Śākyamuni's ancestors. (2) A mountain south-east of Malakūṭa, reputed as the home of Avalokiteśvara. (3) The island of Pootoo, east of Ningpo, the Kuan-yin centre. (4) The Lhasa Potala in Tibet; the seat of the Dalai Lama, an incarnation of Avalokiteśvara; cf. 普; also written | 怛 (or 但) 落迦; 逋多(羅); 布咀洛加.

解 To unloose, let go, release, untie, disentangle, explain, expound; intp. by mokṣa, mukti, vimokṣa, vimukti, cf. | 脫.

解一切衆生言語 Sarva-ruta-kauśalya, supernatural power of interpreting all the language of all beings.

解境十佛 All existence discriminated as ten forms of Buddha. The Hua-yen school sees all things as pan-Buddha, but discriminates them into ten forms: all the living, countries (or places), karma, śrāvakas, pratyeka-buddhas, bodhisattvas, tathāgatas, 智 jñānakāya, dharmakāya, and space; i.e. each is a 身 corpus of the Buddha.

解夏 The dismissing of the summer retreat; also | 制.

解悟 Release and awareness; the attaining of liberation through enlightenment.

解深蜜經 Sandhi-nirmocana-sūtra, tr. by Hsüan-tsang, the chief text of the Dharmalakṣaṇa school, 法相宗. Four tr. have been made, three preceding that of Hsüan-tsang, the first in the fifth century A.D.

解界 To release or liberate the powers by magic words, in esoteric practice.

解知見 A Buddha's understanding, or intp. of release, or nirvāṇa, the fifth of the 五分法身.

解空 To apprehend, or interpret the immateriality of all things.

解脫 Mukti, "loosing, release, deliverance, liberation, setting free, . . . emancipation." M. W.

Mokṣa, "emancipation, deliverance, freedom, liberation, escape, release." M. W. Escape from bonds and the obtaining of freedom, freedom from transmigration, from karma, from illusion, from suffering; it denotes nirvāṇa and also the freedom obtained in dhyāna-meditation; it is one of the five characteristics of Buddha; v. 五分法身. It is also vimukti and vimokṣa, especially in the sense of final emancipation. There are several categories of two kinds of emancipation, also categories of three and eight. Cf. 毘; and 八 | |.

解脫冠 The crown of release.

解脫味 The flavour of release, i.e. nirvāṇa.

解脫天 Mokṣadeva, a name given to Hsüan-tsang in India.

解脫戒 The commandments accepted on leaving the world and becoming a disciple or a monk.

解脫海 The ocean of liberation.

解脫清淨法殿 The pure dharma-court of nirvāṇa, the sphere of nirvāṇa, the abode of the dharmakāya.

解脫相 Liberation; the mark, or condition, of liberation, release from the idea of transmigration.

解脫知見 The knowledge and experience of nirvāṇa, v. | 知見.

解脫耳 The ear of deliverance, the ear freed, hearing the truth is the entrance to nirvāṇa.

解脫處 v. 八 | |.

解脫衣 The garment of liberation, the robe; also | | 幢相衣; | | 服.

解脫身 The body of liberation, the body of Buddha released from kleśa, i.e. passion-affliction.

解脫道 The way or doctrine of liberation, Buddhism.

解脫門 The door of release, the stage of meditation characterized by vacuity and absence of perception or wishes.

解脫風 The wind of liberation from the fires of worldly suffering.

解行 Interpretation and conduct; to understand and do. | | 地 The stage of apprehending and following the teaching.

誠 See under Fourteen Strokes.

詮 Explain, expound, discourse upon. | 旨 To explain the meaning, or import. | 辯 To explain, comment on.

詵 Talking, inquiring, buzzing, swarming. | 遮 Abhiṣecana, to baptize, or sprinkle upon; also 毘 | |.

話 Words, language, talk. | 則 Word-norm, the spoken words of the Buddha the norm of conduct.

該 To connect, belong to; proper; ought, owe; the said; the whole. | 羅; | 攝 Containing, inclusive, undivided, whole; the one vehicle containing the three.

試 To try, test, attempt; tempt. | 經 To test or prove the scriptures; to examine them. | 羅 Śilā, a stone, flat stone, intp. as "probably a coral" (Eitel), also as "mother"-of-pearl.

賊 A thief, robber, spoiler; to rob, steal, etc. | 住 An unordained person who passes himself off as a monk.

資 Funds, basis, property, supplies; fees; to depend on; disposition; expenditure. | 生 Necessaries of life. | 糧 Saṁbhāra; supplies for body or soul, e.g. food, almsgiving, wisdom, etc. | 緣 The material necessaries of a monk, clothing, food, and shelter. | 財帳 Schedule of property (of a monastery).

跨 To straddle, bestride, pass over. | 節 To interpret one sūtra by another, a T'ien-t'ai term, e.g. interpreting all other sūtras in the light of the Lotus sūtra.

跪 To kneel. | 拜 To kneel and worship, or pay respect. | 爐 To kneel and offer incense.

路 A road, way. 丨伽 idem 丨迦. 丨伽多 Lohita, red, copper-coloured. 丨伽祇夜 Lokageya, intp. as repetition in verse, but also as singing after common fashion. 丨賀 Loha, copper, also gold, iron, etc. 丨迦 Loka, intp. by 世間, the world, a region or realm, a division of the universe. 丨丨(or 伽) 憊 Lokavit, Lokavid, he who knows, or interprets the world, a title of a Buddha. 丨丨耶底迦; 丨伽丨(陀); 丨柯耶胝柯 Lokāyatika. "A materialist, follower of the Cārvāka system, atheist, unbeliever" (M. W.); intp. as 順世 worldly, epicurean, the soul perishes with the body, and the pleasures of the senses are the highest good. 丨丨那他 intp. 世尊 Lokajyeṣṭha; Lokanātha, most excellent of the world, lord of the world, epithet of Brahmā and of a Buddha.

辟 A prince, sovereign, lord; split; punish, repress; perverse; toady; quiet. 丨支(迦) Pratyeka, each one, individual, oneself only. 丨丨(丨)佛(陀) Pratyeka-buddha, one who seeks enlightenment for himself, defined in the Lotus sūtra as a believer who is diligent and zealous in seeking wisdom, loves loneliness and seclusion, and understands deeply the nidānas. Also called 緣覺; 獨覺; 倶存. It is a stage above the śrāvaka 聲聞 and is known as the 中乘 middle vehicle. T'ien-t'ai distinguishes 獨覺 as an ascetic in a period without a Buddha, 緣覺 as a pratyeka-buddha. He attains his enlightenment alone, independently of a teacher, and with the object of attaining nirvāṇa and his own salvation rather than that of others, as is the object of a bodhisattva. Cf. 畢. 丨支佛乘 The middle vehicle, that of the pratyeka-buddha, one of the three vehicles. 丨除 To suppress, get rid of. 丨雷 To rend as thunder, to thunder. 丨鬼 To suppress demons.

農 Farm, farming, agriculture; an intp. of the śūdra caste.

遁 To retire, vanish. 丨世 To retire from the world and become a monk; also to withdraw from the community and become a hermit.

遏 Check, stop. 丨部多 Adbhuta, the marvellous; name of a stūpa in Udyāna, north-west India.

逼 To press, constrain, urge, harass. 丨廹 To constrain, compel, bring strong pressure to bear.

違 To oppose, disregard, disobey; leave, avoid. 丨他順自 To disregard or oppose others and follow one's own way; the opposite of 丨自順他. 丨境 To oppose or disregard conditions; opposing or unfavourable circumstances. 丨緣 Opposing or hostile conditions. 丨陀 Veda, knowledge, the Vedas, cf. 韋, 毘. 丨順 To oppose, or accord with; hostile or favourable.

運 Revolve; turn of the wheel, luck; carry, transport. 丨心 Revolve in the mind; indecision; to have in mind; to carry the mind, or thought, towards.

逾 To pass over, exceed. 丨越 To pass over. 丨時 To exceed the time. 丨健達羅 Yugaṁdhara, v. 踰.

遊 Bhrāmyati. Ramble, wander, travel, go from place to place. 丨化 To go about preaching and converting men. 丨山 To go from monastery to monastery; ramble about the hills. 丨増地獄 The sixteen subsidiary hells of each of the eight hot hells. 丨心法界 A mind free to wander in the realm of all things; that realm as the realm of the liberated mind. 丨戲 Vikrīḍita. To roam for pleasure; play, sport. 丨戲神通 The supernatural powers in which Buddhas and bodhisattvas indulge, or take their pleasure. 丨方 To wander from place to place. 丨虛空天 To roam in space, as do the devas of the sun, moon, stars, etc.; also the four upper devalokas. 丨行 To roam, wander, travel, etc.

過 To pass; past; gone; transgression, error. 丨去 Passed, past. 丨去世 The past, past time, past world or age. 丨去七佛 The seven past Buddhas: Vipaśyin, Śikhin, Viśvabhū (of the previous 莊嚴 kalpa), and Krakucchanda, Kanakamuni, Kāśyapa, and Śākyamuni (of the 賢 or present kalpa). 丨去聖靈 The spirit of the departed. 丨夏 To pass the summer, or the summer retreat. 丨度 To pass from mortal life. 丨慢 The pride which among equals regards self as superior and among superiors as equal; one of the seven arrogances. 丨木橋 To cross over the single log bridge, i.e. only one string to the bow. 丨現未 Past, present, future. 丨惡 Dauṣṭhulya. Surpassing evil; extremely evil.

遍 Sarvatraga. Everywhere, universe, whole; a time. 丨依圓 The three points of view: 丨計 which regards the seeming as real; 依他 which sees things as derived; 圓成 which sees them in their true nature; cf. 三性. 丨出外道 Ascetics who entirely separate themselves from their fellow-men. 丨周 Universal, everywhere. 丨智 Universal knowledge, omniscience. 丨淨天 The heaven of universal purity, the third of the third dhyāna heavens. | 法界身 The universal dharmakāya, i.e. the universal body of Buddha, pan-Buddha. | 照如來 The universally shining Tathāgata, i.e. Vairocana. | 至 Universally reaching, universal. | 行 Universally operative; omnipresent. | 計所執性 The nature that maintains the seeming to be real. | 處 Everywhere, universal.

達 Permeate, penetrate, reach to, transfer, inform, promote, successful, reaching everywhere; translit. *ta*, *da*, *dha*, etc.

達利瑟致 Dṛṣṭi, 見 seeing, viewing, views, ideas, opinions; especially seeing the seeming as if real, therefore incorrect views, false opinions, e.g. 我見 the false idea of a permanent self; cf. Darśana, *infra*.

達嚫(拏) Dakṣiṇā, a gift or fee; acknowledgment of a gift; the right hand (which receives the gift); the south. Eitel says it is an ancient name for Deccan, "situated south of Behar," and that it is "often confounded with 大秦國 the eastern Roman empire". Also 達賧 (or 親 or 櫬); 噠嚫; 大嚫; 檀嚫.

達多 Devadatta, v. 提.

達婆 Gandharva, v. 乾.

達梨舍那 Darśana, seeing, a view, views, viewing, showing; 見 v. above, Dṛṣṭi.

達水 Also | 池, Anavatapta, v. 阿.

達磨 Dharma; also | 摩; | 麼; | 而麻耶; 曇摩; 馱摩 tr. by 法. Dharma is from dhara, holding, bearing, possessing, etc.; and means "that which is to be held fast or kept, ordinance, statute, law, usage, practice"; "anything right." M. W. It may be variously intp. as (1) characteristic, attribute, predicate; (2) the bearer, the transcendent substratum of single elements of conscious life; (3) element, i.e. a part of conscious life; (4) nirvāṇa, i.e. the Dharma *par excellence*, the object of Buddhist teaching; (5) the absolute, the real; (6) the teaching or religion of Buddha; (7) thing, object, appearance. Also, Tamo, or Bodhidharma, the twenty-eighth Indian and first Chinese patriarch, who arrived in China A.D. 520, the reputed founder of the Ch'an or Intuitional School in China. He is described as son of a king in southern India; originally called Bodhitara. He arrived at Canton, bringing it is said the sacred begging-bowl, and settled in Loyang, where he engaged in silent meditation for nine years, whence he received the title of wall-gazing Brahman 壁觀婆羅門, though he was a kṣattriya. His doctrine and practice were those of the "inner light", independent of the written word, but to 慧可 Hui-k'o, his successor, he commended the Laṅkāvatāra-sūtra as nearest to his views. There are many names with Dharma as initial: Dharmapāla, Dharmagupta, Dharmayaśas, Dharmaruci, Dharmarakṣa, Dharmatrāta, Dharmavardhana, etc. | | 宗 The Tamo, or Dharma sect, i.e. the 禪宗 Meditation, or Intuitional School. | | 忌 The anniversary of Bodhidharma's death, fifth of the tenth month. | | 馱都 Dharmadhātu, tr. 法界 "the element of law or of existence" (M. W.); all psychic and non-psychic processes (64 dharmas), with the exception of rūpa-skandha and mano-ayatana (11), grouped as one dharma element; the storehouse or matrix of phenomena, all-embracing totality of things; in the Tantric school, Vairocana divided into Garbhadhātu (material) and Vajradhātu (indestructible); a relic of the Buddha.

達羅毘荼 Draviḍa, a district on the east coast of the Deccan.

達賴喇嘛 Dalai Lama, the head of the Yellow-robe sect of Tibetan Buddhism, and chief of the nation.

達須 Dasyu, barbarians; demons; also | 首; | 架. Used for Sudarśana, v. 須.

道 Mārga. A way, road; the right path; principle, Truth, Reason, Logos, Cosmic energy; to lead; to say. The way of transmigration by which one arrives at a good or bad existence; any of the six gati, or paths of destiny. The way of bodhi, or enlightenment leading to nirvāṇa through spiritual stages. Essential nirvāṇa, in which absolute freedom reigns. For the eightfold noble path v. 八聖道.

道交 Mutual interaction between the individual seeking the truth and the Buddha who responds to his aspirations; mutual intercourse through religion.

道人 One who has entered the way, one who seeks enlightenment, a general name for early Buddhists and also for Taoists.

道位 The stages in the attainment of Buddha-truth.

道俗 Monks and laymen.

道元 The beginning of right doctrine, i.e. faith.

道光 The light of Buddha-truth.

道具 The implements of the faith, such as garments, begging-bowl, and other accessories which aid one in the Way.

道力 The power which comes from enlightenment, or the right doctrine.

道化 To transform others through the truth of Buddhism; converted by the Truth.

道品 Religious or monastic grade, or grades.

道器 A vessel of religion, the capacity for Buddhism.

道士 A Taoist (hermit), also applied to Buddhists, and to Śākyamuni.

道場 Truth-plot. Bodhimaṇḍala, circle, or place of enlightenment. The place where Buddha attained enlightenment. A place, or method, for attaining to Buddha-truth. An object of or place for religious offerings. A place for teaching, learning, or practising religion. | | 樹 The bodhidruma, or tree under which the Buddha attained enlightenment. | | 神 Tutelary deities of Buddhist religious places, etc.

道宣 A celebrated T'ang monk, Tao-hsüan, who assisted Hsüan-tsang in his translations.

道德 Religion and virtue; the power of religion.

道心 The mind which is bent on the right way, which seeks enlightenment. A mind not free from the five gati, i.e. transmigration. Also | 意.

道教 Taoism. The teaching of the right way, i.e. of Buddhism.

道智 Religious wisdom; the wisdom which understands the principles of mārga, the eightfold path.

道果 The result of the Buddha-way, i.e. nirvāṇa.

道業 The karma of religion which leads to Buddhahood.

道樂 The joy of religion.

道樹 The bodhi-tree, under which Buddha attained enlightenment; also as a synonym of Buddhism with its powers of growth and fruitfulness.

道檢 The restraints, or control, of religion.

道次 The stages of enlightenment, or attainment.

道氣 The breath, or vital energy, of the Way, i.e. of Buddhist religion.

道水 The water of Truth which washes away defilement.

道法 The way or methods to obtain nirvāṇa. | | 智 The wisdom attained by them; the wisdom which rids one of false views in regard to mārga, or the eightfold noble path.

道流 The stream of Truth; the flow, or progress, of Buddha-truth; the spread of a particular movement, e.g. the Ch'an school.

道理 Truth, doctrine, principle; the principles of Buddhism, Taoism, etc.

道眼 The eye attained through the cultivation of Buddha-truth; the eye which sees that truth.

道禁 Whatever is prohibited by the religion, or the religious life; śīla, the second pāramitā, moral purity.

道種性 The nature possessing the seed of Buddhahood. The stage in which the "middle" way is realized. | | 智 The wisdom which adopts all means to save all the living; one of the 三智.

道者 One who practises Buddhism; the Truth, the religion.

道舊 An old monastic, or religious, friend.

道芽 The sprouts, or seedlings, of Buddha-truth.

道衆 Those who practise religion, the body of monks.

道號 The hao, or literary name of a monk.

道行 Conduct according to Buddha-truth; the discipline of religion.

道術 The methods, or arts, of the Buddhist religion.

道要 The fundamentals of Buddhism.

道觀 Religious practice (or external influence) and internal vision.

道諦 Mārga, the dogma of the path leading to the extinction of passion, the fourth of the four axioms, i.e. the eightfold noble path, v. 八聖道.

道識 The knowledge of religion; the wisdom, or insight, attained through Buddhism.

道門 The gate of the Way, or of truth, religion, etc.; the various schools of Buddhism.

道類智 The wisdom obtained through insight into the way of release in the upper realms of form and formlessness; one of the 八智.

道風 The wind of Buddha-truth, as a transforming power; also as a prognosis of future events.

道體 The embodiment of truth, the fundament of religion, i.e. the natural heart or mind, the pure nature, the universal mind, the bhūtatathatā.

鄉 The country, rural, village. | 人 Country people, people of one's village.

鄔 Translit. *u*, *ū*, cf. 烏, 塢, 優, e.g. | 波尼殺曇 Upaniṣad, cf. 優; variously intp. but in general refers to drawing near (to a teacher to hear instruction); the Upanishads. | 闍衍那 Ujjayinī, Oujein; cf. 烏 | 陀延; | | 衍那 Udayana, king of Kauśāmbī, cf. 烏.

酬 Pledge, toast, requite. | 還 To pay a vow, repay.

酪 Dadhi, a thick, sour milk which is highly esteemed as a food and as a remedy or preventive. | 味 Sour, one of the five tastes. T'ien-t'ai compared the second period of the Hīnayāna with this. | 經 T'ien-t'ai term for the Hīnayāna sūtras.

鉦 A small gong struck during the worship, or service. | 鼓 Cymbals, or small gongs and drums.

鈴 A hand-bell with a tongue.

鈸 Cymbals.

鉢 Pātra, a bowl, vessel, receptacle, an almsbowl; translit. *p*, *pa*, *ba*.

鉢伐多 Parvata, crags, mountain range. An ancient city and province of Ṭakka, 700 li north-east of Mûlasthānapura, perhaps the modern Futtihpoor between Multan and Lahore. Also | 羅 | |.

鉢位 Bowl seat, the place each monk occupies at table.

鉢健提 Pākhaṇḍa, i.e. Pāṣaṇḍa, Pāṣaṇḍin, heresy, a heretic, intp. 堅固 firm, stubborn; name of a deva.

鉢刺底羯爛多 Pratikrānta, following in order, or by degrees. | | 翳迦佛陀 v. 辟, Pratyeka-buddha. | | 迦羅 Prakaraṇa, intp. as 章 a section, chapter, etc.

鉢吒 Paṭa, woven cloth or silk. | | 補怛囉 Pāṭaliputra, the present Patna.

鉢吉帝 Prakṛti, natural; woman; etc. Name of the woman at the well who supplied water to Ānanda, seduced him, but became a nun.

鉢和羅 Pravāraṇa. A freewill offering made, or the rejoicings on the last day of the summer retreat. Also described as the day of mutual confession; also 鉢和蘭; | 剌婆剌拏; 盋和羅.

鉢哩體吠 Pṛthivī, the earth, world, ground, soil, etc.

鉢喇部 Prabhu, mighty, intp. by 自在 sovereign, a title of Viṣṇu, Brahmā, and others.

鉢喇底木叉 Pratimokṣa, idem mokṣa, v. 木, 波, 解. Prātimokṣa, a portion of the Vinaya, called the sūtra of emancipation. | | | 提舍尼 (or 那) Pratideśanā, public confession; prātideśanīya, offences to be confessed; a section of the Vinaya, v. 波. | | 特崎拏 Pradakṣiṇa, circumambulation with the right shoulder towards the object of homage.

鉢囉惹(鉢多曳) Prajāpati, "lord of creatures," "bestower of progeny," "creator"; tr. as 生主 lord of life, or production, and intp. as Brahmā. Also, v. Mahāprajāpatī, name of the Buddha's aunt and nurse.

鉢塞莫 Pāśakamālā, dice-chain, i.e. a rosary.

鉢多(羅) Pātra, a bowl, vessel, receptacle, an almsbowl; also | 咀 |; | 和 | (or 蘭); 波 (or 播) 怛囉; in brief 鉢. The almsbowl of the Buddha is said to have been brought by Bodhidharma to China in A.D. 520.

鉢摩羅伽 Padmarāga, lotus-hued, a ruby; also | 曇 | | |.

鉢曇 Pada, v. | 陀.

鉢特(摩) Padma, or Raktapadma, the red lotus; one of the signs on the foot of a Buddha; the seventh hell; also | | 忙; | 頭 (or 弩 or 曇) 摩; | 納摩; | 頭 (or 曇) 㦄.

鉢羅 Pala, a particular measure or weight, intp. as 4 ounces; also 波 |; 波賴他; but pala also means flesh, meat, and palāda, a flesh-eater, a rākṣasa; translit. *pra, para.* | | 吠奢 Praveśa, entrance, 入 q.v. | | 奢 (or 賒) 佉 Praśākha; praśaka; the fifth stage of the fœtus, the limbs being formed. | | 底也 Pratyaya, a concurrent or environmental cause. | | 弭 Parama; highest, supreme, first. | | 摩菩提 Parama-bodhi, supreme enlightenment. | | 斯 (or 犀) 那特多; 波斯匿 Prasenajit, a king of Kośala, patron of Śākyamuni, who is reputed as the first to make an image of the Buddha. | | 枳孃; | | 賢禳 v. 般 Prajñā. | | 步 (or 部) 多囉怛曩野, i.e. 多寶 q.v. Prabhūtaratna. | | 由 (or 庾) 他; also 波 | | |; ? Prayuta; ten billions; 大 | | | | 100 billions, v. 洛. | | 笈菩提 Prāgbodhi. A mountain in Magadha, which Śākyamuni ascended "before entering upon Bodhi"; wrongly explained by 前正覺 anterior to supreme enlightenment. | | 耶伽 Prayāga, now Allahabad. | | 若 v. 般 Prajñā. | | 薩他 Prastha, a weight tr. as a 斤 Chinese pound; a measure.

鉢里薩囉伐拏 Parisrāvaṇa, a filtering bag, or cloth, for straining water (to save the lives of insects), part of the equipment of a monk.

鉢鐸創那 Badakshan, "a mountainous district of Tukhāra" (M. W.); also 巴達克山.

鉢陀 Pada, footstep, pace, stride, position; also | 曇; 波 |; 播 |; also tr. as foot; and stop.

鉢露兒 Bolor, a kingdom north of the Indus, south-east of the Pamir, rich in minerals, i.e. Hunza-Nagar; it is to be distinguished from Bolor in Tukhāra. | | 羅 Polulo, perhaps Baltistan.

鉢頭摩 Padma, v. | 特.

隙 A crack, crevice, rift; translit. *kha.* | 遊塵 Motes in a sunbeam; a minute particle. | 棄羅 Khakkhara, a mendicant's staff; a monk's staff.

隔 To divide off, separate, part. | 宿 Separated by a night, i.e. the previous day. | 生 Divided by birth; on rebirth to be parted from all knowledge of a previous life. | 歷 Separate, distinct. | 歷三諦 To differentiate and apprehend the three distinctive principles 空假中 noumenon, phenomenon, and the mean.

雉 A pheasant; a parapet. | 救林火 The pheasant which busied itself in putting out the forest on fire and was pitied and saved by the fire-god.

雷 Garjita, thunder, thundering.

電 Lightning, symbolizes the impermanent and transient. | 光石火 Lightning and flint-fire, transient. | 影 Impermanence of all things like lightning and shadow.

頌 Extol, praise. Gāthā, hymns, songs, verses, stanzas, the metrical part of a sūtra; cf. 伽陀.

頑 Stupid, obstinate. | 石點頭 (Moved by the reciting of the Mahāparinirvāṇa Sūtra,) even the stupid stones nodded their heads.

預 At ease, contented, pleased; arranged, provided for; beforehand; an autumn trip. | 流 According with the stream of holy living, the srota-āpanna disciple of the śrāvaka stage, who has overcome the illusion of the seeming, the first stage in Hīnayāna. | 彌國 Yāmī, the land or state of Yama, where is no Buddha.

頓 To fall headlong, prostrate; at one time, at once; suddenly; immediate; a pause; to stamp; make ready; used chiefly in contrast with 漸 gradually. | 圓 The immediate and complete way of enlightenment of the T'ien-t'ai Lotus school. | 頓圓 Instantaneous perfect enlightenment of the Hua-yen, a term used by 澄觀 Ch'êng-kuan, who left the Lotus for the Hua-yen. | 大 The immediate school and sūtra of the Mahāyāna, i.e. the Hua-yen. | 寫; | 經; 一日經 To copy the Lotus sūtra at one sitting. | 悟 Instantly to apprehend, or attain to Buddha-enlightenment, in contrast with Hīnayāna and other methods of gradual attainment. | 悟菩薩 A bodhisattva who attains immediately without passing through the various stages. | 成諸行 The immediate fulfilment of all acts, processes, or disciplines (by the fulfilment of one). | 教 The doctrine that enlightenment or Buddhahood may be attained at once; also immediate teaching of the higher truth without preliminary stages. | 斷 To cut off at one stroke all the passions, etc. | 機 The capacity, or opportunity, for immediate enlightenment. | 漸 Immediate, or sudden, attainment in contrast with gradualness. | 旨 The will, or aim, of immediate attainment. | 法 The method of immediacy. | 覺 Immediate apprehension or enlightenment as opposed to gradual development.

飯 Rice (cooked); food; to eat. 磬 The dinner-gong. | 袋子 A rice-bag fellow, a monk only devoted to his food, useless. | 那 Vana, a grove, a wood. | 頭 A cook.

飲 To drink, swallow; to water cattle | 光 Drinking light, a tr. of the name of Kāśyapa, v. 迦, or his patronymic, possibly because it is a title of Aruṇa, the charioteer of the sun, but said to be because of Kāśyapa's radiant body. | 光部 Māhākāśyapīyāḥ, or school of the Māhāsaṅghikāḥ. | 血地獄 The hell where they have to drink blood. | 酒 To drink wine, or alcoholic liquor, forbidden by the fifth of the five commandments; 10, 35, and 36 reasons for abstinence from it are given. | 食 Drink and food, two things on which sentient beings depend; desire for them is one of the three passions; offerings of them are one of the five forms of offerings.

鳩 A dove; to collect; translit. *ku*, *gu*, *ko*, *ki*; cf. 瞿, 拘, 倶, 矩. | 垣 Kupana, | 洹; 仇桓; an asura who swells with anger. | 夷羅 Kokila, the cuckoo; or | 那羅 Kuṇāla, cf. 拘. There are other forms beginning with 拘, 倶, 瞿. | 摩(羅) Kumāra, a child, youth, prince. | | |; | | | 什(婆); | | | 時 (or 耆) |; 羅什 Kumārajīva, one of the "four suns" of Mahāyāna Buddhism, of which he was the early and most effective propagator in China. He died in Ch'ang-an about A.D. 412. His father was an Indian, his mother a princess of Karashahr. He is noted for the number of his translations and commentaries, which he is said to have dictated to some 800 monastic scribes. After cremation his tongue remained "unconsumed". | | | 伽 Kumāraka, idem Kumāra. | | | | 地 Kumāraka-stage, or | | | 浮多 Kumāra-bhūta, youthful state, i.e. a bodhisattva state or condition, e.g. the position of a prince to the throne. | | | 炎 Kumārāyaṇa, father of Kumārajīva. | | 邏多 (or 陀) Kumāralabdha, also 矩 and 拘; two noted monks, one during the period of Aśoka, of the Sautrāntika sect; the other Kumāralabdha, or "Kumarata" (Eitel), the nineteenth patriarch. | 槃茶 Kumbhāṇḍa, a demon shaped like a gourd, or pot; or with a scrotum like one; it devours the vitality of men; also written with initials 弓, 恭, 究, 拘, 倶, and 吉; also | 滿拏. | 鳩吒 Kukkuṭa, a fowl.

鼓 A drum. | 樂絃歌 Drum-music and singing with stringed instruments. | 音 The rolling of drums. | 天 The drum-deva, thunder.

鼠 Mūṣa; ākhu; a mouse, rat. 白黑二 | The two mice in the parable, one white, the other black, gnawing at the rope of life, i.e. day and night, or sun and moon. | 唧鳥空 Vain discussions, like rat-squeakings and cuckoo-callings.

14. FOURTEEN STROKES

僕 A servant. 丨呼繕那 Bahujanya, intp. 衆生 all the living, all who are born. 丨拏 Intp. as a digital sign; the fourth of the twelve ways of placing the hands together.

僞 False, counterfeit, forged. False or forged sūtras which were produced after the Wei dynasty; catalogues of these forged sūtras are given in various books.

像 Pratirūpa; pratirūpaka. Like, similar, resemblance; semblance; image; portrait; form, formal. 丨化 The religion of the image or symbol, Buddhism. Also the second or formal period of the teaching of Buddhism by symbol, v. 丨法. 丨始 The beginning of the formal period. 丨季 The end of that period. 丨敎 idem 丨化. 丨末 The two final stages of Buddhism. 丨法 Saddharma-pratirūpaka, the formal or image period of Buddhism; the three periods are 正像末, those of the real, the formal, and the final; or correct, semblance, and termination. The first period is of 500 years; the second of 1,000 years; the third 3,000 years, when Maitreya is to appear and restore all things. There are varied statements about periods and dates, e.g. there is a division of four periods, that while the Buddha was alive, the early stage after his death, then the formal and the final periods. 丨經 Images and sūtras. 丨運 The period of formality, or symbolism.

僧; 僧伽 Saṅgha, an assembly, collection, company, society. The corporate assembly of at least three (formerly four) monks under a chairman, empowered to hear confession, grant absolution, and ordain. The church or monastic order, the third member of the Triratna. The term 僧 used alone has come to mean a monk, or monks in general. Also 丨佉, 丨加, 丨企耶. 丨伽吒; 丨丨多; 丨丨陀 Saṅghāta, an assemblage; also the final hurricane in the kalpa of destruction. 丨丨婆尸沙 v. 丨殘. 丨丨婆羅 Saṅghapāla; a monk of 扶南國? Siam, who tr. ten or eleven works A.D. 506–520. 丨丨梨 or 黎 v. 丨丨胝 Saṅghāṭī. 丨丨羅 Siṁhala, Ceylon; also name of the Buddha in a previous incarnation when, as a travelling merchant, he, along with 500 others, was driven on to the island; there the rākṣasīs bewitched them; later the Buddha and his companions (like the Argonauts) escaped, and ultimately he destroyed the witches and founded his kingdom there. 丨丨胝 Saṅghāṭī. The patch-robe, one of the three garments of a monk reaching from shoulders to the knees and fastened around the waist, made up of nine to twenty-five pieces and so called 重雜衣; also 大衣 great robe; also 重 in layers and 合 composite; v. 九品. 丨丨藍 (摩) Saṅghārāma, a monastery with its garden or grove; also 伽藍. 十丨補羅 Siṁhapura. Eitel says "an ancient province and city of Cashmere, probably the modern Simla". 丨丨跋摩 Saṅghavarman, an Indian monk who arrived in Nanking A.D. 433, tr. five works in 434, went westward in 442. 丨丨跋陀羅 Saṅghabhadra. "A learned priest of Cashmere, a follower of the Sarvāstivādāḥ school, the author of many philosophical works." Eitel. 丨丨難提 Saṅghanandi, a prince of Śrāvastī, lived in a cave, was discovered by Rāhulata, became the sixteenth patriarch.

僧佉 Saṅkhyā, 丨企耶; intp. 數 number, reckon, calculate; sāṅkhya, "one of the great divisions of Hindu philosophy ascribed to the sage Kapila, and so called as 'reckoning up' or 'enumerating' twenty-five Tattvas or true principles, its object being to effect the final liberation of the twenty-fifth (Purusha, the Soul) from the fetters of the phenomenal creation by conveying the correct knowledge of the twenty-four other Tattvas, and rightly discriminating the soul from them." M. W. Cf. 迦 and 數.

僧儀 The monastic custom, i.e. shaving head and beard, wearing the robe, etc.

僧侶 Monastic companions, or company.

僧俗 Monks and the laity.

僧伍 The monastic ranks.

僧可 Name of 慧可 Hui-k'o, second patriarch of the Intuitive School.

僧吉隷鑠 Saṅkleśa, whatever defiles, e.g. the passions.

僧坊; 僧房 A vihāra, or saṅghārāma, a monastery; also a nunnery.

僧塞迦羅 Saṁskāra, impressions resulting from action, the fourth skandha.

僧官 Director of monks, an official first appointed by the government in the fourth century A.D.; then and later the office was called 丨正; 丨統; 丨錄(司).

僧寶 Saṅgha, the idealized church, the third member of the Triratna. 丨丨果 The perfect arhat who has not to be reborn.

僧尼 Monks and nuns.

僧戒 The ten prohibitions; the complete commands for monks.

僧柯者 idem 丨迦舍. Sāṅkāśya. 丨丨慄多弭 Saṁskṛtam, which means composite, compounded, perfected, but intp. as active, phenomenal, causally produced, characterized by birth, existence, change, and death.

僧次 In order of monastic age, according to years of ordination. 丨自恣日 The 15th of the 7th month; the last day of the summer retreat, on which the monks confessed their sins.

僧殘 Saṅghāvaśeṣa; Pali, Saṅghādiśeṣa. A sin of an ordained person, requiring open confession before the assembly for absolution, or riddance 殘; failing confession, dismissal from the order. Thirteen of these sins are of sexual thoughts, or their verbal expression, also greed, even for the sake of the order, etc.

僧祇 Sāṅghika, relating to a saṅgha; a complete set of land and buildings for a monastery. 丨丨支 Saṅkakṣikā, or Uttarasaṅghāṭī, described as a kind of toga passed over the left shoulder and under the right armpit; also 丨迦; 丨竭支; 丨却崎; 丨脚欹迦; 祇支; 竭支. 丨丨物 Monastic possessions, or things. 丨丨律 Sāṅghika-vinaya, the rules for monks and nuns. 丨丨部 Sāṅghikāḥ, the Māhāsaṅghikāḥ school, v. 大衆部.

僧若 Sañjñā; saṁjñā, the third of the five skandhas, i.e. 想 thought, ideation, consciousness.

僧衆 The body or assembly of monks.

僧訶 Siṁha, a lion, also 丨伽.

僧迦舍 Sāṅkāśya, an ancient kingdom and city in Northern India (v. Kapitha 劫). The modern Samkassam, now a village 45 miles north-west of Kanauj. Also 丨伽施.

僧那(僧涅) Sannāha (-sannaddha), girding on armour, intp. as a Buddha's or bodhisattva's great vow.

厮 Attendant, an attendant, servant; to serve.

厭 Satiated; weary of; disgusted with. 丨世 Weary of the world; to renounce the world. 丨欣 Disgusted with, or rejoicing in. 丨求 Weary of the miseries of earth and seeking deliverance. 丨離 To weary of the world and abandon it. 丨魅; 丨禱鬼 Vetāla, a demon appealed to in order to raise a corpse and with it to cause the death of an enemy.

嘔 To vomit, spit, disgorge. 丨侯侯 Ahaha, or Hahava, the fifth of the cold hells, where the condemned neither stir nor speak, but the cold air passing through their throats produces this sound —a hell unknown to Southern Buddhism.

嘉 Good, excellent, praiseworthy, to commend. 丨會; 丨集 Delightful assembly, an excellent meeting.

嘆 To praise, extol; to sigh. 丨佛 To praise Buddha. 丨德 To praise the virtue of others. 丨靈 To praise the spirit of the departed.

嗽 Cough. 丨卑 Upāsikā, an old form, see 烏 a female disciple.

圖 A plan, map; seal; to plan, scheme, calculate.

團 Round; a ball, mass, lump; a group, company, train-band. 丨拜 To kneel, or worship altogether as a company. 丨食 To roll rice, etc., into a ball in eating, Hindu fashion.

境 Viṣaya; artha; gocara. A region, territory, environment, surroundings, area, field, sphere, e.g. the sphere of mind, the sphere of form for the eye, of sound for the ear, etc.; any objective mental projection regarded as reality. 丨智 The objective world and the subjective mind, or knowledge of the objective sphere. 丨界 Sphere, region, realm, as above. 丨界相 The external, or phenomenal world, the third aspect referred to in the Awakening of Faith; the three are blind or unintelligent action, the subjective mind, and the objective illusory world. | 界般若 External world prajñā, or wisdom of all things; prajñā is subjective, all things are its objective.

塵 Guṇa, in Sanskrit *inter alia* means "a secondary element", "a quality", "an attribute of the five elements", e.g. "ether has śabda or sound for its guṇa and the ear for its organ". In Chinese it means "dust, small particles; molecules, atoms, exhalations". It may be intp. as an atom, or matter, which is considered as defilement; or as an active, conditioned principle in nature, minute, subtle, and generally speaking defiling to pure mind; worldly, earthly, the world. The six guṇas or sensation-data are those of sight, sound, smell, taste, touch, and thought. | 刹 Guṇakṣetra, "field of qualities," certain sins. | 勞 The trouble of the world, the passions. | 境 The environment of the six guṇas or qualities of sight, sound, smell, taste, touch, and thought. | 塵三昧 The samādhi in which, in a moment of time, entry is made into all samādhis. | | 刹土 Numberless lands; also in every grain, or atom, there is a whole realm. | 妄 Impure and false, as are all temporal things. | 垢 Material, or phenomenal defilement; the defilement of the passions. | 欲 The desires connected with the six guṇas. | 沙 Dust and sand, i.e. numberless as the atoms. T'ien-t'ai uses the term as one of the three illusions, i.e. the trial of the bodhisattva in facing the vast amount of detail in knowledge and operation required for his task of saving the world. | 洲 Worlds as numerous as atoms. | (點) 劫 A period of time as impossible of calculation as the atoms of a ground-up world, an attempt to define the infinite, v. Lotus sūtra 7 and 16. | 累 The passion-karma which entangles the mind. | 網 The net of the six guṇas, i.e. those connected with the six senses. | 緣 The circumstances or conditions environing the mind created by the six guṇas. | 表 Outside of the secular, i.e. the doctrine of Buddha. | 道 The dusty path, the phenomenal world, or worlds. | 那羅 Dīnāra, a coin, a gold coin, from δηνάριον. | 鄉 The native place or home of the six guṇas, i.e. that of transmigration.

壽 Long life, longevity, age, v. 耆婆 jīva. | 像 A portrait, or statue of a man of years while still alive. | 命 Jīvita, life, length of days, age. | 命無有量; | 命無數劫 The infinite life of Buddha. | 論; 阿由 The Āyurveda, the medical Vedas, v. 韋. | 量品 The chapter in the Lotus sūtra where Buddha declares his eternity; v. also the 無量 | 經.

夢 A dream, a simile of the things of the world. | 幻 Dream and illusion, the characteristics of all phenomena. | 揭釐 Moṅgali, or Maṅgala, ancient capital of Udyāna, the present Manglavor on the left bank of the Swat, a trans-Indus State west of Kashmir. | 想 To "dream" a thing, to think of in a dream, to imagine. | 見 To see in a dream, to imagine one sees, or has seen.

奪 Snatch, carry off, take by force; decide. | 魂鬼 A demon that carries off the soul. | 精鬼 One that carries off the vital breath of the dying.

寢 To sleep, rest; stop; a retiring room, resting-place. | 堂 A dormitory.

寧 Repose; settle; better than; rather; how? | 安 Reposeful, at ease.

實 Real, true, honest, sincere; solid; fixed; full; to fill; fruit, kernel, effects; verily, in fact; it is used for 眞, as in — | the supreme fact, or ultimate reality; also for bhūta.

實化 The real or noumenal Buddha as contrasted with 權化 the temporal or phenomenal Buddha; the | | 二身 are his 報身 saṁbhogakāya and his 化身 nirmāṇakāya.

實利 Śarīra, relics, see 舍.

實叉難陀 Śikṣānanda. A śramaṇa of Kustana (Khotan) who in A.D. 695 introduced a new alphabet into China and translated nineteen works; the Empress Wu invited him to bring a complete copy of the Hua-yen sūtra to Lo-yang; sixteen works in the present collection are assigned to him. Also 施乞义難陀.

實唱 Reality-proclamation, i.e. to preach the Tathāgata's law of Reality.

實報土 The land of Buddha-reward in Reality free from all barriers, that of the bodhisattva, the third of the four "lands" of T'ien-t'ai. A Buddha-kṣetra.

實大乘教 The real Mahāyāna, freed from temporal, relative, or expedient ideas; the T'ien-t'ai, Hua-yen, Intuitional, and Shingon schools claim to be such.

實性 Real nature, or essence, i.e. the 眞如 bhūtatathatā.

實我 The true ego, in contrast with the 假 | phenomenal ego.

實教 The teaching of Reality; also, the real or reliable teaching.

實智 The knowledge or wisdom of Reality, in contrast with knowledge of the 權 relative.

實本 Fundamental reality, applied to the teaching of the Lotus sūtra, as opposed to the previous Buddhist teaching.

實眼 An eye able to discern reality, i.e. the Buddha-eye.

實相 Reality, in contrast with 虛妄; absolute fundamental reality, the ultimate, the absolute; the 法身, i.e. Dharmakāya, or 眞如 Bhūtatathatā. Other terms are 一實; 一如; 一相; 無相; 法證; 法位; 涅槃; 無爲; 眞諦; 眞性; 眞空; 實性; 實諦; 實際, q.v. | | 三昧 The samādhi of reality, in which the unreality of the phenomenal is realized. | | 印 The seal or witness of reality, which is passed on from Buddha to Buddha. | | 慧 Wisdom in regard to reality. | | 智身 The body of absolute knowledge, or of complete knowledge of Reality, i.e. that of Vairocana. | | 法界 The first half is a Lotus sūtra term for Reality, the latter half a Hua-yen term for the same. | | 爲物二身 The Dharmakāya or spiritual Buddha, and the Nirmāṇakāya, i.e. manifested or phenomenal Buddha. | | 無相 Reality is Nullity, i.e. is devoid of phenomenal characteristics, unconditioned. | | 花; | | 風 The flower, or breeze, of Reality, i.e. the truth, or glory, of Buddhist teaching. | | 觀 Insight into, or meditation on Reality.

實空 Absolute śūnya, or vacuity; all things being produced by cause and environment are unreal.

實經 The true sūtras as contrasted to the relative or temporary sūtras, a term of the Lotus school.

實色身 The real Buddha-body, or his saṁbhogakāya in contrast with his nirmāṇakāya.

實語 True, or reliable words; words corresponding to reality; discussions of Reality.

實諦 A truth; the true statement of a fundamental principle.

實道 The true way, the true religion, absolute Buddha-truth.

實際 The region of Reality. | | 理地 The noumenal universe, the bhūtatathatā.

對 To respond, reply, face, opposite, pair, compare; the opposite of; agreeing with. | 告衆 The intermediary for the Buddha's address to the assembly, especially Ānanda. | 揚 One who drew out remarks or sermons from the Buddha. | 機 To respond to the opportunity, or the capacity of hearers. | 法 The corresponding law, the philosophy in the Buddha's teaching, the Abhidharma; comparison of cause and effect. | 法宗 The Abhidharma sect. | 法藏 The third section of the Tripiṭaka, the śāstras, or Abhidharma. | 治 To respond or face up to and control. | 觸禮 To worship, or pay respects, face to face. | 首 Face to face (confession).

幖 A streamer, pennant | 幟.

廓 Wide, spacious, open, vacant. | 然大悟 Widely to have a great apprehension of the truth.

彰 Variegated, adorned; to display, show, make manifest.

慚 Shame, ashamed; i.e. for one's own faults, cf. 愧.

慳 Matsara; lobha; grudging, sparing, stingy, avaricious. | 心; | 惜 A grudging, mean heart. | 法 Mean and grudging of the Truth to others, unwillingness to part with it. | 貪 Grudging and greed.

慢 Māna. Pride, arrogance, self-conceit, looking down on others, supercilious, etc.; there are categories of seven and nine kinds of pride. | 使 The messenger, or lictor, of pride, cf. 五使. | 坑 The pit, or pitfall of pride. | 山 Pride as high as a mountain. | 幢 Pride as a banner rearing itself aloft. | 惑 One of the ten great delusions, that of pride. | 想 Proud, arrogant thoughts. | 結 The bondage of pride. | 舉 To hold oneself arrogantly. | 見 Pride, regarding oneself as superior, one of the ten wrong views. | 過 | Regarding oneself as superior to superiors.

慇 Anxious; | 懃 zealous, careful.

截 To cut off, intercept. | 雨呪 Incantations for the cessation of rain.

摸 To feel, grope, e.g. as a blind man. | 象 The blind man who tried to describe an elephant by feeling it, v. Nirvāṇa Sūtra 32.

敲 To knock, beat, pound, e.g. a drum, gong, or gate.

斡 A handle for turning a wheel, a wheel, to revolve, circulate. | 資羅 Vajra, v. 跋 and 金剛.

朅 To and fro; translit. *kha*; cf. 竭; 軻. | 伽; | 誐 Khaḍga, a sword, rhinoceros' horn, rhinoceros. | | 毘沙拏; | | 婆沙 Khaḍga-viṣāṇa, a rhinoceros' horn. | 地洛迦 Khadiraka, the Acacia, or Acacia mountain, i.e. | 達羅 one of the seven concentric mountains around Sumeru.

槌 Hammer, mallet. | 砧; | 墩 Hammer and block, or anvil.

槃 Vitasti, a span; the 32,000th part of a yojana.

榮 Glory, splendour. | 華 Glory, the glory of life, viewed as transient.

槃 A tray; a hut; to turn; translit. *pan, van, va*. | 淡 cf. 和 Vandana, obeisance, worship. | 特; | 陀 cf. 半 Paṇḍaka, eunuch. | 遮 Vac, speech, talk. | 頭 Pāṇḍu, father of Vipaśyin, the 998th Buddha of the last kalpa.

榜 A placard, list; model, example.

歌 To sing; a song; translit. *ka*; cf. 迦, 羯. | 偈 Verses for singing; to sing verses. | 利 Kali, the present evil age. | | 王 v. 羯 Kalirāja. | 唄; | 嘆; | 咏; | 頌 To sing, chant. | 栗底迦 Kārttika, the month October–November. | 舞 To sing and dance. | 羅 (分) v. 迦 Kalā, a fraction. | 羅邏 Kalala, an embryo, the womb. | 羅頻迦 v. 迦, Kalaviṅka. | 聲 The sound of singing, the singing of Kinnaras, cf. 緊.

殞 To perish, die; fall; become extinct.

漆 Varnish, lacquer. | 桶 Varnish tub, a stupid, unseeing fellow.

漢 The River Han; the Han dynasty; a fine fellow; China.

漉 To strain, filter. | 水袋 or 囊 A monk's filtering-bag to strain off living creatures.

漫 Overflowing, boundless; translit. *man, van*; cf. 曼, 滿. | 提 Vande, "I worship." | 荼 (or 怛 or 陀) 羅 v. 曼 Maṇḍala. | 荼迦 Maṇḍaka, a cake, pastry.

漚 To steep, macerate, rot; bubble; translit. *u, o*, etc. | (or 傴) 和俱 (or 拘) 舍羅 Upāyakauśalya, intp. by 方便善巧 expediency and skill, adaptable, suited to conditions, opportunist, the adaptation of teaching to the capacity of the hearer. | 多羅僧 v. 鬱 Uttarāsaṅga, a toga worn over the left shoulder. | 波耶波羅蜜 Upāya-pāramitā, saving by the method of expedient teaching, v. above. | 鉢羅 Utpala, also 嗢 | |; 優 | |; 烏 | | the blue lotus; also a lord of Nāgas and his blue lotus lake.

漕 A channel, canal; transport, especially by the | 河 Grand Canal. | 矩吒 Tsaukūṭa, an "ancient (Arachotos) kingdom in N.W. India (near Ghuznee)". Eitel.

演 To extend, expound, practise, perform. | 暢 To expound and make clear. | 若(達多) Yajña-datta, "obtained from sacrifice," a crazy man who saw his eyebrows and eyes in a mirror but not seeing them in his own head thought himself bedevilled; the eyes and head are a symbol of 正性 reality, those in the mirror of 妄相 unreality. | 說 To expound, dilate upon, discourse.

漸 Gradual, by degrees, to flow little by little, | 次 step by step, by degrees, gradually. | 教 The gradual method of teaching by beginning with the Hīnayāna and proceeding to the Mahāyāna, in contrast with 頓教 q.v. the immediate teaching of the Mahāyāna doctrine, or of any truth directly; e.g. the Hua-yen school considers the Hua-yen sūtra as the immediate or direct teaching, and the Lotus sūtra as both gradual and direct; T'ien-t'ai considers the Lotus direct and complete; but there are other definitions. | 斷 Gradually to cut off, as contrasted with 頓 | sudden or instantaneous excision. | 熱 Increasing heat; grīṣma, the two months from middle of May to middle of July.

滿 Pūrṇa. Full, whole, complete. | 分戒 The whole of the commandments, i.e. of the monk. | 字 The complete word, i.e. Mahāyāna, as compared with the 半字 half word, or incomplete word of Hīnayāna. | 座 A complete, or full assembly; also the last day of a general assembly. | 怛羅; | 荼邏 v. 曼 Maṇḍala. | 慈子; | 祝子; | 見子; | 願子 see 富 Pūrṇa. | 成 Fully complete, perfect. | 月尊 The full-moon honoured one, Buddha. | 果; | 業 The fruit, or karma, which fills out the details of any incarnation, as distinguished from 引業 which determines the type, e.g. man, animal, etc., of that incarnation. | 殊尸利 v. 文 Mañjuśrī. | 泥; 漫提 Vande, "I worship." | 濡; 曼殊 or 乳 Mañju, beautiful, lovely. | 荼 Maṇḍa, solid, the diamond throne. | 足 Full, complete.

漏 Āsrava, "flowing, running, discharge; distress, pain, affliction." M. W. It is defined as another term for 煩惱 q.v.; also as the discharge, or outflow, from the organs of sense, wherever those exist, hence it is applied to the passions and their filth; impure efflux from the mind, v. 欲有; also to the leakage or loss thereby of the 正道 truth; also to the stream of transmigration. | 永盡無所畏 Absolute confidence (of Buddha) that transmigration would cease for ever. | 戒 To make a leak in the commandments, i.e. break them. | 業 The deeds of the sinner in the stream of transmigration, which produce his karma. | 無漏 Transmigration and nirvāṇa. | 盡 Āsravakṣaya. The end of the passions, or the exhaustion of the stream of transmigration. | 盡明 The realization that the stream of transmigration is ended. | 盡意解 The passions ended and the mind freed, the state of the arhat. | 盡智 The wisdom of the arhat. | 盡比丘 The monk who has ended the stream of transmigration, the arhat. | 盡證明 The assurance or realization that the stream of transmigration is ended and nirvāṇa attained. | 盡通 The supernatural insight into the ending of the stream of transmigration; one of the six abhijñās.

熏 To smoke, fumigate, cense, perfume, exhale; fog, becloud. | 習 To fumigate, perfume, i.e. the influence of unenlightenment, ignorance, or blind fate, on the unconditioned producing the conditioned, v. 薰 18.

熊 A bear. | 耳山 Bear's ear mount, the place where Bodhidharma was buried.

熒 Glitter, twinkle. | 惑心 (or 天) Aṅgāraka, the planet Mars; also 火曜日; it is also described as a nakṣatra, or asterism, and as such is represented in feminine form in the Vajradhātu group.

爾 You, thou; so, thus; used adverbially. | 前 Before this, formerly, used by T'ien-t'ai to denote the time preceding the Lotus sūtra. | 燄; | 炎 Jñeya, cognizable, the region or basis of knowledge.

獄 Litigation, law-case; a prison; 地 | q.v. Earth-prison, the hells.

瑠璃 Vaiḍūrya, described as a green indestructible gem, one of the seven precious things. A mountain near Vārāṇaśī. Also 吠 | | (耶); 毘頭梨. | | 王 Virūḍhaka, cf. 毘.

瑪 Agate | 瑙.

瑤 Jasper (green), green crystal. | 花宮 cf. 玉.

甄 Mould, influence, discern; translit. *kim*, *kin*. | 叔迦 Kiṁśuka, the tree *Butea frondosa*, with beautiful red blossoms; a red stone, perhaps a ruby. | 迦羅 Kiṁkara, 10,000,000,000. | 陀 Kinnara, v. 緊.

疑 Vicikitsā; doubt, suspect; hesitate, be uncertain, fear, surmise. | 使 The messenger, tempter, or lictor, of doubt. | 刺 The thorn of doubt. | 城胎宮 The palace for doubters outside Amitābha's heaven, where all doubters of him are confined for 500 years until fit to enjoy his paradise. | 執 The holding to doubt. | 心 A doubting heart, dubious, suspicious. | 惑 Doubt and delusion, doubt, uncertainty. | 悔 To repent of doubt. | 結 The bondage of doubt. | 蓋 The overhanging cover of doubt. | 見 Doubtfully to view, doubtful views, doubt.

監 To survey, examine; a palace-eunuch; the Academy; to superintend, oversee; warden of a jail, warder, jail. | 寺; | 院; | 收 The warden, or superintendent of a monastery, especially the one who controls its material affairs.

盡 An emptied vessel, all used up; end, finish, complete, nothing left; all, utmost, entirely. | 七日 At the end of seven days, seven days being completed. | 十方 The entire ten directions, the universe, everywhere. | 未來際 To the end of all time, eternal. | 淨虛融 The identity of the absolute and the empirical, a doctrine of the Prajñāpāramitā.

碧 Jade-green, or blue. | 眼胡 The blue-eyed barbarian, Bodhidharma.

禍 Woe, calamity, misfortune.

福 Blessing, happiness, felicity, good fortune. | 地 A place of blessedness, a monastery. | 報 A blessed reward, e.g. to be reborn as a man or a deva. | 因 That which causes or gives rise to blessing, i.e. all good deeds. | 庭 A court, or hall, of blessedness, a monastery. | 德 Puṇya. Blessed virtues, all good deeds; the blessing arising from good deeds. | 德莊嚴 The adornment of blessedness and virtue, i.e. of good deeds. | 德資糧 The nutriment of blessedness, i.e. deeds of charity. | 德身 The Buddhakāya, or body of Buddha, in the enjoyment of the highest samādhi bliss. | 德門 The gates of blessedness and virtue, the first five of the six pāramitās. | 慧 Blessedness and wisdom; or virtue and wisdom. | 慶 Blessedness and felicity, blessed felicity; to congratulate on good fortune. | 智 Blessedness and wisdom, the two virtues which adorn. | 果 The reward of blessedness. | 業 The karma of blessedness, a happy karma. | 生 Born of or to happiness. | 生天 Puṇyaprasavās, the tenth brahmaloka, the first region of the fourth dhyāna. | 田 The field of blessedness, i.e. any sphere of kindness, charity, or virtue; there are categories of 2, 3, 4, and 8, e.g. that of study and that of charity; parents, teachers, etc.; the field of poverty as a monk, etc. | 田衣 The garment of the field of blessing, the monk's robe. | 相法身 The Buddha-dharmakāya as blessedness, in contrast with it as wisdom. | 祿 Happiness and emolument, good fortune here or hereafter. | 蓋 The cover, or canopy, of blessing. | 行 The life or conduct which results in blessing, e.g. being reborn as a man or a deva. | 觀 Blessedness and insight, similar to | 慧; | 智. | 足 The feet of blessedness, one consisting of the first five pāramitās, the other being the sixth pāramitā, i.e. wisdom; happiness replete.

稱 To call, style, invoke; to weigh; a steelyard, scale; to suit, tally with. | 佛 To invoke a Buddha. | 名 To invoke the (Buddha's) name, especially that of Amitābha. | 名雜行 To worship a variety of Buddhas, etc., instead of cleaving to Amitābha alone. | 意華 The soma plant, suggested by Sir Aurel Stein as possibly wild rhubarb. | 讚 To praise.

種 Vīja; bīja. Seed, germ; sort, species; also to sow, plant. | 子 Seed, germ; the content of the ālayavijñāna as the seed of all phenomena; the esoterics also have certain Sanskrit letters, especially the first letter *a*, as a seed or germ containing supernatural powers. | 子識 Ālayavijñāna, the abode or seed-store of consciousness from which all phenomena spring, producing and reproducing momentarily. | 性 Seed nature, germ nature; derivative or inherited nature. | 智 Omniscience, knowledge of the seed or cause of all phenomena. | 根器 The three categories of the Ālayavijñāna: (1) the seed, or cause, of all phenomena; (2) the five organs of sensation; (3) the material environment on which they depend. | 熟脫 The seed of Buddha-truth implanted, its ripening, and its liberation or harvest. | 種色世界 A world of every kind of thing. | 覺 The insight into all seeds or causes, Buddha-knowledge, omniscience. | 識 The ālayavijñāna.

端 Beginning, coming forth, elementary principles; a point either beginning or end; straight, proper. | 嚴 In strict propriety. | 坐 To sit straight and proper. | 心正意 With a proper mind and regulated will, doing no evil. | 正 Proper, properly ordered, rectitude, integrity.

竭 Exhaust, used up, finished; utmost. | 叉 A place said to be in the Karakoram mountains, where according to Fa-hsien formerly great assemblies were held under royal patronage and with royal treatment. Eitel gives it as Khaśa, and says "an ancient tribe on the Paropamisus, the Kasioi of Ptolemy"; others give different places, e.g. Kashmir, Iskardu, Kartchou. | 支 v. 僧祇支. | 誐 Khaḍga (sometimes in error Khaṅga), a sword, a rhinoceros' horn, a rhinoceros. | 陀羅 Khadira, the *Acacia catechu*; khadīra, the *Mimosa pudica*. M. W. A hard wood, also Karavīra.

箋 A tablet, slip. | 書 Sūtras.

箇 Each, every. | | 圓常道 Every single thing is the complete eternal Tao.

管 A pipe, tube; to rule, control. | 絃講 Pipes, strings, and preaching, an "accompanied" service—in India.

算 Reckon, count, calculate. | 數 To count numbers, to count, number.

精 Cleaned rice, freed from the husk, pure; essential, essence, germinating principle, spirit; fine, best, finest. | 室; | 廬; | 舍 A place for pure, or spiritual, cultivation, a pure abode, the abode of the celibate, a monastery or nunnery. | 氣 Vitality, virility. | 眞 Pure truth, apprehension of ultimate reality. | 神 Vitality; also the pure and spiritual, the subtle, or recondite. | 進 Vīrya, one of the seven Bodhyaṅga; "vigour," "valour, fortitude," "virility" (M. W.); "well-doing" (Keith). The Chinese interpretation may be defined as pure or unadulterated progress, i.e. 勤 zeal, zealous, courageously progressing in the good and eliminating the evil. | 進力 Vīryabala. The power of unfailing progress, one of the five moral powers. | 進弓智慧箭 Zeal as the bow, wisdom the arrow. | 進波羅蜜 Zeal, energy, or progress as the fourth of the six pāramitās. | 靈棚 The booth, or canopy, where the feast of all souls is provided.

綺 A kind of open-work variegated silk. 綺語 Sexual talk; improper remarks.

緊 Tight; to bind tight; press tight; pressing, urgent; translit. *kin*. | 祝迦 Kiṁśuka, v. 甄 ruby-colour. | 要 Important. | 那羅; | 捺 (or 陀) 羅; 甄 (or 眞) 陀羅 Kinnara; the musicians of Kuvera, with men's bodies and horses' heads; they are described as 人非人 men yet not men, and 疑神 mythical beings; one of the eight classes of heavenly musicians; they are also described as horned, as having crystal lutes, the females singing and dancing, and as ranking below gandharvas.

綫 Thread; a clue, continuation. An intp. of sūtra.

綱 A net rope, bond, social nexus, constant obligation, the restraints of society. | 維 The controller of a monastery.

網 Jāla. A net, a web. | 目 The "eyes", or meshes of a net. For the Brahmajāla sūtra v. 梵 | 經.

緇 Black garments; at one time black was used for monastic robes. | 徒; | 流 Monks. | 林 A monastery. | 衣 Black robes, monks. | 門 The black-robe order, monks.

維 A carriage-curtain; a net; a corner, cardinal point; to tie or hold together, connect; a copula, also, but, whereas, now. | 口食 Improper means of existence by spells, fortune-telling, etc., one of the four cardinal improper ways of earning a livelihood. | 摩 Vimalakīrti, | | (羅) 詰; 毘摩羅詰 undefiled or spotless reputation, "a native of Vaiśālī, said to have been a contemporary of Śākyamuni, and to have visited China." Eitel. The Vimalakīrti-nirdeśa sūtra | | 詰所說經 is an apocryphal account of "conversations between Śākyamuni and some residents of Vaiśālī", tr. by Kumārājīva; an earlier tr. was the | | 詰經, a later was by Hsüan-tsang, and there are numerous treatises. | 耶離 cf. 毘 Vaiśālī. | 衛 (佛) cf. 毘 Vipaśyin, one of the seven ancient Buddhas. | 越 Avaivartika, cf. 阿, one who never reverts to a lower condition. | 那; 羯磨陀那 Karmadāna, the duty-distributor, deacon, arranger of duties, second in command of a monastery.

聚 Samāsa; assemble, collect; an assemblage. | 沫 The phenomenal world likened to assembled scum, or bubbles. | 諦 Samudaya, the second of the four dogmas, that of "accumulation", i.e. that suffering is caused by the passions. | 集 To assemble, flock together.

聞 To hear; to make known to; to smell. | 光力 To hear of the power of the light of Amitābha. | 名 To hear the name of; fame, famous; to hear the name of Buddha, or a Buddha. | 慧 Hearing the word and becoming wise in it; wisdom obtained from hearing. | 持 To hear and keep; hearing and keeping in mind; hearing and obeying. | 法 To hear the doctrine. | (持) 陀羅尼 To hear and keep, hear and remember the teaching, dhāraṇī 陀 | | meaning to hold to, maintain.

肇 To begin, initiate. | 法師 or 僧肇 Sêng-chao, name of a monk in the fourth century whose treatise is called by this name.

腐 Rotten, corrupt, putrid, sloughing. | 爛藥 Purgatives, diuretics.

膏 Fat, oil, unguent. | 明 Oil and light, oil being right conduct, with the resultant shining before men.

臺 A terrace, platform, stage, look-out; also written 台. | 座 A platform, or stage, for an image.

與 Give, grant; with, associate; present at, share in; mark of interrogation or exclamation. | 力 To give strength. | 願 To be willing (or vow) to grant.

舞 To posture, brandish, play; urge. | 戲 To play, perform plays.

蒸 Twigs; to steam, vapour. | 沙 Steaming or cooking sand for food: an impossibility, like Ānanda trying to meditate without cutting off evil conduct.

蒺 Thorny bushes, furze. | 蔾 The calthrop, *Tribulus terrestris*.

蒭 Hay, straw, fodder. | 摩 Kṣumā, kṣauma, linen, flax, linen garments; also 芻 | 迦; 菆 |; 須 |; 蘇 |; 讖 |.

蓱沙王 Bimbisāra, v. 頻.

蒲 Rushes, flags, grass. | 團 A rush cushion, or hassock. | 塞 Upāsaka, 伊 | | cf. 優. | 闍尼; | 膳 | Bhojanīya, to be eaten, edible; what is suitable as the fare of monks and nuns, proper food; one list gives wheat, rice (boiled), parched rice, fish, and flesh; another gives cakes (or loaves), porridge, parched grain, flesh, and boiled rice.

蓋 A cover, anything that screens, hides, or hinders; to build; then, for. The passions which delude the real mind so that it does not develop. A hat, or umbrella, or any cover. The canopy over a Buddha. | 纏 Cover and bonds, i.e. the passions which stunt growth and hold in bondage.

蒙 To cover; stupid, ignorant; receive (from above); Mongol. | 古 Mongolia, Mongol. | 惑 Stupid and deluded.

蒼 Azure; the heavens; grey, old. | 龍窟 The cave of the azure or green dragon, where it lies curled over the talismanic pearl, which only a hero can obtain.

蜫 Insects, creeping things. | 蟲作佛 Even insects may attain Buddhahood; v. 智度論 93.

蜜 Honey; translit. *m*. | 利伽羅 Mṛga; a deer; mṛga-rāja, royal stag, Buddha. | 利車 Mleccha, cf. 彌 heathen, non-Buddhist nations, the barbarians. | 栗伽悉他鉢娜 Mṛga-sthāpana, Mṛgadāva, a famous park north-east of Varāṇaśī, a favourite resort of Śākyamuni. The modern Sārnath, near Benares. Eitel.

裴 Beautifully robed. | 弗略 Vaipulya, enlarged, v. 方.

裸 Naked. | 形外道 Nirgranthas, naked ascetics.

誠 Truthful, true, truth; real; sincere, sincerity. | 信 True and trustworthy, true, reliable. | 諦 Truth, a truth, the true teaching of Buddhism.

誡 Commandment, precept, prohibition, warning, rule. | 罰 To warn and punish; to punish for breach of the commandments or rules. | 勸 Prohibitions from evil and exhortations to good. See 戒.

誌 To remember, record.

誐 To intone, hum; translit. *ga*. | 囉娜 Gardabha, defined as an ass. | 嚕 Garuḍa, v. 迦. | 那鉢氐 Gaṇapati, a leader, Gaṇeśa, the "elephant god"; it is, however, defined as 歡喜 pleased, joyful.

認 To recognize | 識; to acknowledge, e.g. sin | 罪.

誑 Imposition, deception, lying.

誦 To murmur, recite, intone, memorize by repeating in a murmur, cf. 念. | 經 To intone sūtras.

誕 A birthday; to bear, produce; wide, boastful. | 生會 An assembly to celebrate a birthday, e.g. the Buddha's on the 8th of the 4th month.

誓 To swear, vow, engage to, enter into a contract. | 約 To swear and engage to. | 願 To swear and vow, e.g. the forty-eight vows of Amitābha to save all beings.

語 Words, discourse, conversation, speech, language; to say, speak with; cf. 嚕 ruta. | 業 The karma produced by speech. | 義 Rutārtha word-meaning; word and meaning. | 言 Abhidhāna. Words, talk, speech; naming.

說 To speak, say, talk, discourse, expound; speech, etc. Used for 悅 pleased. | 一切有部 v. — and 有; the Sarvāstivādāḥ realistic school. | 假部 The Prajñāptivādinaḥ school, a branch of the Māhāsaṅghikāḥ, which took the view of phenomenality and reality, ? founded on the Prajñapti-śāstra. | 出世部 The Lokottaravādinaḥ school, a branch of the Māhāsaṅghikāḥ, which held the view that all in the world is merely phenomenal and that reality exists outside it. | 因部 Hetu-vādinaḥ, idem Sarvāstivādāḥ. | 戒 The bi-monthly reading of the prohibitions for the order and of mutual confession. | 法 To tell or expound the law, or doctrine; to preach. | 示 To tell and indicate. | 經 To expound the sūtras. | 罪 To confess sin, or wrong-doing. | 轉部 idem 經(量)部 Sautrāntika school. | 通 To expound thoroughly, penetrating exposition. | 默 Speech and silence.

賒 To buy or sell on credit; to borrow; slow, remiss, shirk. | 乃以室折羅 Śanaiścara 土星, Saturn, or its regent. | 多 Śānta, pacified, at ease, ceased, dead, liberated; also 奢多.

賓 A guest; to entertain; to submit. | 伽羅 Piṅgala, an Indian sage to whom is attributed "the Chandas" (M. W.), i.e. a treatise on metre. | 吒羅 ? Piṇḍāra, ? Piṇḍala, one of the painless purgatories. | 坻 Piṇḍada, abbrev. for Anathapiṇḍada, v. 阿. | 撥利力叉 Pippala, pippala-vṛkṣa, the bodhi-druma, or tree under which Śākyamuni obtained insight. | 波羅窟 Vaibhāra, the Vaibhāra cavern; "a rock-cut temple on a mountain near Rādjagṛha, now called Baibhargiri. Śākyamuni used to resort thither for meditation." Eitel. | 鉢羅 Pippala, v. above. | 頭 One of the purgatories, v. above. | | 盧頗羅墮 Piṇḍola-bhāradvāja, name of the first of the sixteen arhats, who became the old man of the mountains, white hair and beard, bushy eyebrows, one of the genii.

趙 To hasten to, return; a long time. | 州 A prefecture in south-west Chihli, with a monastery, from which the T'ang monk Chao-chou got his pseudonym.

輕 Light; frivolous; to slight. | 安 Not oppressed, at ease. | 慢 To despise; the pride of thinking lightly of others. | 毛 As light as a hair, as unstable as a feather. | 重 Light and heavy.

遣 To send; to drive away. | 喚 To send, and to call.

遜 To yield, accord; modest.

遠 Far, distant, far removed. | 塵離垢 To be far removed from the dust and defilement of the world. | 師 idem 慧遠 q.v. | 行地 The seventh stage of the bodhisattva, in which he leaves the world of phenomena and enjoys mystic contemplation. | 離 Vivṛj; vivarjana; leave afar off, be far removed; absolute separation of unconditioned reality from the realm of phenomena. | 離樂 The joy of the first dhyāna heaven, in which the defilement of desire is left far behind in mystic contemplation.

銘 To engrave, on metal, stone, or the tablets of the heart.

銖 A weight equal to the twenty-fourth part of a tael; a small ancient coin; a scruple; trifles. | 衣 The gossamer clothing of the devas, or angels.

銅 Tāmra. Copper, brass. | 錢 Copper money, cash. | 鑼 A gong.

銀 Rūpya. Silver; money. | 色 Silver-colour.

閣 A pavilion, temple building; chamber, council, cabinet.

際 A border, region, juncture, limit; between; to join on; then, since, now. 生死之 | Between life and death. 無 | Unlimited. | 史吒 Jyaiṣṭha, the month in May–June.

障 Varaṇa; āvaraṇa; a screen, barricade, partition, a term for the passions or any delusion which hinders enlightenment. | 礙 Screen and obstruction, i.e. anything that hinders. | 盡解脫 Salvation through the complete removal of the obstruction of illusion.

韎 Red socks. | 嘌沙迦; | 師迦 Vārṣika; a flower that blooms during the rainy season, described as of a white colour and very fragrant; the aloe.

領 Neck, collar; lead, direct; receive. | 納 To receive, accept. | 解 To receive and interpret.

頗 Somewhat, quite, very; partial; translit. *pha*, *bha*. Cf. 叵. | 勒具那 (or 窶拏) Phālguna, the twelfth month in India (February–March). | 尼多 Phāṇita, the inspissated juice of the sugar cane, raw sugar. | 羅 Phala, fruit, produce, progeny, profit, etc. | 羅墮 (or 吒) Bhāradvāja, descendant of the ancient sage Bharadvāja, intp. as one of the six (or eighteen) Brahmin surnames, and as meaning 利根 of keen mind, clever. | 胝迦; | 置 |; | 黎; | 梨 Sphāṭika, rock crystal.

颯 In gusts, suddenly. | 秣建 Samakan, the modern Samarkand. Eitel. | 破檖迦 Sphaṭika, see 頗.

飽 Replete, full. | 學 Replete with learning; fed full with study.

飾 To adorn; gloss over; pretend. 裝 |.

馝柯 Vikramāditya, a king of Śrāvastī and famous benefactor of Buddhism, v. 毘.

馺 v. 蘇 Svāhā.

駄; 馱 Translit. *dha, dhya.* | 南 Dhyāna, also | (那) 演那; | 衍那 tr. by 定 and 禪 q.v. | 器尼 v. 達 The Deccan. | 麼 v. 達 Dharma. | 索迦 Dāsaka, a slave, or dāsikā, a female slave. | 縛若 Dhvaja, a flag. | 那羯磔迦 Dhanakaṭaka, or Amarāvatī, an ancient kingdom in the north-east of the modern Madras presidency. | 都 Dhātu, intp. by 界 field, area, sphere; 體 embodiment, body, corpus; 性 nature, characteristic. It means that which is placed or laid; a deposit, foundation, constituent, ingredient, element; also a śarīra, or relic of Buddha. The two dhātus are the conditioned and unconditioned, phenomenal and noumenal; the three are the realms of desire, of form, and of the formless; the four are earth, water, fire, and air; the six add space and intelligence; the eighteen are the twelve āyatanas, with six sensations added.

魂 The mind, the soul, conscious mind, vijñāna; also | 神. | 魄 Animus and anima; the spiritual nature or mind, and the animal soul; the two are defined as mind and body or mental and physical, the invisible soul inhabiting the visible body, the former being celestial, the latter terrestrial.

鳳 The "phœnix", the auspicious bird. | 刹 "Phœnix"-kṣetra, a term for a Buddhist temple.

鳴 Cry, sound, note of a bird, etc. | 魚 To sound the wooden fish to announce a meal time. | 錫 A rattling staff shaken to warn the spirits.

麽 Interrogative particle; translit. *ma, ba*; cf. 摩. | 也 Māyā, illusion, hallucination; also intp. as 體 body. | 度羅 Mathurā, the modern Muttra. | 攞; | 羅 Mālā, a head-dress, wreath. | 洗 Māsa, a month. | 羅庾 Malaya, a kind of incense from the Malaya mountains in Malabar. | 麽 Mama, my, mine, genitive case of the first personal pronoun. | 麽鷄 Māmakī; 忙忙 |; 忙莽 | (or 計); 摩莫枳; the Vajra mother, mother of the 金剛部 or of wisdom in all the vajra group.

鼻 Ghrāṇa. The nose; one of the five 根 indriyas; the organ of smell; one of the six vijñānas (六識) or perceptions, the sense of smell; translit. *vai, vi.* | 入 Organ and sense of smell. | 奢佉 Vaiśākha, the second month of spring. | 婆沙 see 毘, Vibhāṣā. | 根 The organ of smell. | 息 The breath of the nostrils; also the perception of smell. | 溜荼迦 v. 毘 Virūḍhaka. | 訶羅 v. 毘 Vihāra. | 識 The sensation, or perception of smell. | 路波阿叉 Virūpākṣa. One of the Lokapāla, or guardians of the four cardinal points of Mount Sumeru. In China known as 廣目 wide-eyed, red in colour, with a small pagoda in his right hand, and a serpent in his left; in China worshipped as one of the twenty-four Deva Ārya 天尊. Also, a name for Maheśvara or Rudra (Śiva). Cf. 毘 and 髀. | 那夜 cf. 毘 Vinaya. | 隔禪師 Dhyāna master with nose (and other organs) shut off from sensation, i.e. a stupid mystic. | 鼓 (or 致) 迦 Bījaka, a seed, v. 種.

齊 Even, level, equal, uniform; complete, perfect; equalize; tranquillize; alike; all; at the same time, altogether. | 業身 The final body which brings to an end all former karma. | 說 | 聞 Speaking and hearing together, or at the same time.

15. FIFTEEN STROKES

僵 Stiff, rigid; prostrate. | 娑洛 Saṁsāra, course, transmigration, v. 散 and 生死.

億 A number varying from the Chinese 100,000 to a Buddhist 1,000,000, 10,000,000, and 100,000,000.

儀 Manner, mode, style; ceremony, etiquette. | 式; | 軌 Mode, style, manner.

僻 Perverse, base, depraved; partial, prejudiced; rustic, secluded. | 見 Perverse, incorrect, or depraved views.

劍 A sword, two-edged sword. | 山; | 樹地獄 Asipattra. The hill of swords, or sword-leaf trees hell, one of the sixteen hells; also called 刀刃路.

劈 To split, rend, tear. | 箭急 Rapid as an arrow cleaving (the air).

厨 A kitchen; also a cabinet for an image.

噜喹 Bhūrom, an exclamation frequently occurring at the beginning of mantras, probably in imitation of Brahmanic mantras, which begin by invoking bhūr earth, bhuvaḥ air, and svar heaven; or it may be a combination of bhūr, earth, and om, the mystic interjection.

嘶 To neigh; a crashing noise. | 夜那 Śyena, a hawk, falcon.

嗷 Bite, eat, feed on; a bite, morsel; to lure. | 月 To gnaw the moon.

墳 A grave | 墓.

墨 Ink; black; dyed black, e.g. | 衣 black clothes, at one time said to have been the garb of the monk to distinguish him from the ordinary people who wore white. | 竭提 Magadha, v. 摩.

墜 To fall, sink, settle, slide. | 芥 To drop a mustard seed from the Tuṣita heaven on to the point of a needle on the earth, most difficult, rare.

墮 To fall; dilapidated; to fall from a higher to a lower place or condition; a tr. of Prāyaś-citta, expiation, a section in the Vinaya of ninety offences for which atonement is required. | 羅鉢底 Dvārapati or -vatī, "an ancient kingdom on the upper Irawaddy." Eitel.

增 To increase, add, augment, more. | 一阿含經 Ekottara-āgama. The āgama in which the sections each increase by one, e.g. the Aṅguttara Nikāya of the Hīnayāna; a branch of literature classifying subjects numerically, cf. 阿 āgama. | 上 Additional, increase, superior, strengthened. | 上心 Advancing or improving mind, superior mind. | 上心學 The study of increased powers of mind (through meditation). | 上慢 Arrogance, pride (of superior knowledge); e.g. the 5,000 disciples who, in their Hīnayāna superiority, thought they had gained all wisdom and refused to hear the Lotus gospel. | 上果 Adhipatiphala, v. 異熟果, dominant effect; increased or superior effect, e.g. eye-sight as an advance on the eye-organ. | 上緣 The cause, condition, or organ of advance to a higher stage, e.g. the eye as able to produce sight. | 劫 The kalpa of increment, during which human life increases by one year every century, from an initial life of ten years, till it reaches 84,000 (and the body from 1 foot to 8,400 feet in height), in the 減劫 similarly diminishing. | 息 Increasing (power of prayer for) cessation of calamity. | 悲 Augmented pity of a bodhisattva, who remains to save, though his | 智 advanced knowledge would justify his withdrawal to nirvāṇa. | 戒學 Advanced or increasing study of the moral law; the study of the higher moral law. | 益 Increasing, improving. | 進 Advance, progress. | 道損生 A bodhisattva's progress in the doctrine with concurrent reduction in reincarnation. | 長 Increasing both broad and long, | referring to breadth and 長 to height, or length. | 長天 Virūḍhaka, the Mahārāja of the southern quarter. | 長廣目 Virūḍhaka and Śiva.

嬉 Play, pleasure. | 戲 To play, perform.

寫 To write. | 經 To copy the scriptures.

寮 A hut, study, monastery; fellow-student. | 主; | 元; | 長 The head, or manager of a monastery.

審 To try, judge, examine. | 慮思 Discriminating thought.

幢 Dhvaja; Ketu. A pennant, streamer, flag, sign. | 幡 A flag, banner. | 相 A sign, symbol, i.e. the monk's robe.

幡 Patākā, a flag, banner.

廢 To fall in ruins; come to nought; cast aside, do away with, discard; spoil, waste. | 前敎 The discarding of previous rules in the Nirvāṇa sūtra, e.g. previously monks were allowed the three kinds of clean meat; in this sūtra all are forbidden. | 惡修善 To cast aside evil and perform the good. | 權立實 To set aside the temporary and establish the real and permanent. | 迹顯本 To set aside the temporal life (of the Buddha) and reveal the fundamental eternal life.

廟 A fane, temple, palace; an intp. of caitya, cf. 支.

廣 Vipula. Broad, wide, extensive, spacious; extended, enlarged, expanded; for vaipulya v. 方 |, for which | is also used alone to indicate vaipulya sūtras, etc. | 博 Wide and spacious, extensively read, very learned. | 博身 The one whose body fills space, Vairocana. | 嚴城 Vaiśālī, broad ornate city, cf. 毘. | 大 Broad and great. | 大智 The vast wisdom of Buddha beyond measure. | 大會 The centre where vast virtues meet, a term for Amitābha. | 慧 Vipulaprajña, or Vipulamati, vast wisdom, an epithet of a Buddha, one able to transform all beings. | 敎 Full or detailed teaching by the Buddha about the duties of the order, in contrast with 略敎 general or summarized teaching; the detailed teaching resulting from errors which had crept in among his disciples. | 果天 Bṛhatphala, the twelfth Brahmaloka, the third of the eight heavens of the fourth dhyāna realm of form. | 狹 Broad and narrow. | 目天 The wide-eyed deva, Virūpākṣa, diversely-eyed, having deformed eyes, an epithet of Śiva, as represented with three eyes; name of one of the four Mahārājas, he who guards the west. | 長舌 A broad and long tongue, one of the thirty-two marks of a Buddha, big enough to cover his face; it is also one of the "marvels" in the Lotus sūtra.

弊 Worn out, reduced to extremities, corrupt, deceptive; my, mine. | 欲 Corrupt, or base desires.

彈 A bullet, shot; to strum, snap; repress, impeach; translit. *dan*. | 多 Danta, a tooth. | 多抳瑟搋 Dantakāṣṭha, a tooth stick, v. 憚. | 多落迦 Dantalokagiri, a mountain (the montes Daedali of Justinian) near Varuṣa with its cavern (now called Kashmiri-Ghār), where Sudāna lived. | 宅迦 Daṇḍaka, name of a king. | 宅迦林 The forest of Daṇḍaka, destroyed by a ṛsi because the king had carried off the ṛsi's wife, saying a ṛsi had no need for one. | 指 To snap the fingers—in assent, in joy, in warning; a measure of time equal to twenty winks.

影 Shadow, picture, image, reflection, hint; one of the twelve "colours". | 事 Shadow things, i.e. all things are mere shadows. | 供 Image worship. | 像 Pratibimba. Shadows, reflections, with no real existence or nature of their own. | 向 The coming of a deity, responding, responsive. | 堂 A hall where are the images, or pictures, of objects of worship. | 現 The epiphany of the shadow, i.e. the temporal Buddha. | 護 Like a shadow-guardian, always following like a shadow the substance. | 響衆; | 向 | The responsive group in the Lotus sūtra, who came in response to a call, e.g. Mañjuśrī, Kuan-yin, etc.

徹 Penetrate, pervious, perspicacious; throughout; communal. | 心 To penetrate or reach the heart or mind.

德 Virtue, moral excellence, moral power, power; also translates guṇa; translit. *ta*. | (叉)尸羅 Takṣaśilā, an ancient kingdom and city, the Taxila of the Greeks. Lat. 35° 8′ N., Long. 72° 44′ E. | 叉迦 Takṣaka, one of the four dragon-kings. | 士 Virtuous scholar, a term for a monk in the T'ang dynasty. | 字 The svastika. | 本 The root of the moral life, or of religious power; also a name for Amitābha as the root of all virtue. | 母 The mother of virtue, i.e. faith which is the root of the religious life. | 海 The ocean-like character and influence of virtue. | 瓶 The vase or talisman of power, cf. 賢 |. | 田 Field of virtue, or of religious power, i.e. the cult of arhats and Buddhas. | 行 Moral conduct and religious exercises, or discipline; moral conduct. | 風 The wind of virtue, or of religious power. | 香 The fragrance of virtue.

慶 Felicity, felicitous, felicitate. | 懺; | 讚 A service of felicitation, e.g. on the dedication of an image, temple, etc.

憐 Commiserate, pity, sympathize, charitable. | 念 Sympathetic thoughts. | 愛 To pity, love, care for. | 愍 To pity, commiserate.

慕 To long for, hanker after, love; translit. *mo*, *mu*. | 何 Moha, v. 謨 Unenlightened, stupid. | 捺囉 Mudrā, a seal, sign, token, hand or finger signs. | 攞; | 羅 Mūla, root, fundamental, hence mūlagrantha, fundamental works, original texts; Mūla-sarvāstivādāḥ, the Hīnayāna school of that name.

憚 Dread; dislike; translit. *dan*. | 哆 Danta, tooth, teeth; cf. 彈 and 娜. | 哆家瑟多 Dantakāṣṭha, tooth stick, said to be chewed as a dentifrice; also, to be the name of a tree grown from a toothpick of the Buddha.

憎 Hate, dislike. | 愛 Hate and love.

慾 Passion, inordinate desire, lust, v. 欲. | 愛 To hanker after, desire.

憍 Boastful, bragging; self-indulgent; indulgent; translit. *ko*, *kau*, *go*, *gau*; cf. 瞿, 倶, 拘, 巨. | 坑 The pit of pride and arrogance. | 奢耶 Kauśeya, also | 舍 |; 高世耶 cloth made of wild silk. | 尸 Idem. | 尸 (or 支) 迦 Kauśika, of the family of Kuśika, family name of Indra; one account says Amitābha was of the same family name. | 慢 Arrogance and pride. | 曇彌; | 答 |; 倶 | | Gautamī, feminine of the patronymic Gautama, the family name of Śākyamuni. Gautamī is a name for Mahāprajāpatī, his aunt and nurse, who in the Lotus sūtra is predicted to become Buddha. | 梵 (波提) Gavāṁpati, also | 梵鉢 |; 迦 | 波提; 笈房鉢底 intp. as chewing the cud; lord of cattle, etc. A man who became a monk, born with a mouth always ruminating like a cow because of former oral sin. | 薩羅 Kosala, Kośala; also 居 (or 拘) | |; 拘娑 |, i.e. Northern Kosala, or Uttarakosala, an ancient kingdom, the modern Oude; also Southern Kosala, or Dakṣiṇakosala, an ancient kingdom, part of the present Central Provinces. | 賞彌 Kauśāmbī, also | 閃 (or 睒) |; 倶睒 |; "an ancient city on the Ganges in the lower part of the Doab." M. W. It has been identified by some with Kusia near Kurrah; but is the village of Kosam on the Jumna, 30 miles above Allahabad. Cf. 巨. | 陳如 (or 那) Kauṇḍinya; also 阿若拘隣; 阿若憍陳那 Ājñātakauṇḍinya. (1) A prince of Magadha, uncle and first disciple of Śākyamuni. (2) A grammarian mentioned in the Prātiśākhya sūtras. (3) Vyākaraṇa-Kauṇḍinya, who was told by the Buddha that a Buddha is too spiritual to leave any relics behind. Eitel.

憂 Sorrow, grief, melancholy, anxiety; to mourn, grieve; translit. *u*, *yu*; cf. 優, 烏. | 世 The world of trouble and sorrow. | 受 Sorrow, one of the five emotions. | 婆提舍 Upatiṣya, perhaps a name of Śāriputra. | 火 The fires of sorrow or distress. | 畢叉 Upekṣā, cf. 優 indifference attained in abstraction, i.e. "indifference to pain or pleasure, equanimity, resignation, stoicism". Childers. "Looking on, hedonic neutrality or indifference, zero point between joy and sorrow, disinterestedness, neutral feeling, equanimity." *Pali Text Society's Dictionary*. | 陀伽 Udaka, water. | 陀那 Udāna, cf. 優, 烏, etc. Breathing upwards from the throat into the head; guttural sounds; the navel, umbilical; the middle; volunteered remarks or addresses by the Buddha, sermons that came from within him without external request; voluntarily to testify.

慧 Prajñā; sometimes Jñāna. Wisdom, discernment, understanding; the power to discern things and their underlying principles and to decide the doubtful. It is often interchanged with 智, though not correctly, for *chih* means knowledge, the science of the phenomenal, while *hui* refers more generally to principles or morals. It is part of the name of many monks, e.g. | 可 Hui-k'o; | 思 Hui-ssŭ.

慧劍 The sword of wisdom which cuts away illusion.

慧力 Prajñābala, one of the five powers, that of wisdom.

慧印 Wisdom-sign, or seal; also 智印.

慧可 Hui-k'o, the successor of Bodhidharma, v. 達; he previously cut off his arm in appeal to be received as disciple, and finally inherited his mantle and alms-bowl.

慧命 Wisdom-life, or wisdom as life, wisdom being the basis of spiritual character. A term of address to a monk, also | 壽, and to a monk by a superior.

慧學 The study of wisdom, e.g. the Abhidharma.

慧幻 Wisdom-illusion, wisdom-conjuring; the kaleidoscope of wisdom.

慧忍 Wisdom-patience, one of the 十忍.

慧思 Hui-ssŭ, the second patriarch of the T'ien-t'ai school 南嶽大師.

慧愷 Hui-k'ai, a monk and author, also known as 智愷 Chih-k'ai of the sixth century A.D.

慧數 Mental conditions in contrast to mind itself.

慧日 Wisdom-sun, Buddha-wisdom. Hui-jih, a celebrated T'ang monk and author (disciple of I-ching) who also went on pilgrimage to India and spent thirteen years there, died A.D. 748; entitled 慈愍三藏.

慧月 Jñānacandra, author of the non-Buddhist 勝宗十句義論, Vaiśeṣika-nikāya-daśapadārtha-śāstra, tr. by Hsüan-tsang; perhaps the same as 智月.

慧根 The root, i.e. the organ, of wisdom.

慧業 Undertaking and doing; practical goodness resulting from wisdom.

慧流 The living stream of wisdom able to cleanse all impurity.

慧淨 Hui-ching, a noted T'ang monk, translator and author, who was commanded to assist Hsüan-tsang in his translations but was unable through failing health.

慧炬 The torch of wisdom.

慧燈 The lamp of wisdom. | | 王 A king who gave his flesh and blood to save the lives of others.

慧琳 Hui-lin, a disciple of the Indian monk Amogha 不空; he made the | | 音義 dictionary of sounds and meanings of Buddhist words and phrases, based upon the works of 玄應 Hsüan-ying, 慧苑 Hui-yüan, 窺基 K'uei-chi, and 雲公 Yün-kung, in 100 chüan, beginning the work in A.D. 788 and ending it in 810. He is also called 大藏音義; died 820.

慧目 The eye of wisdom. | 眼 The wisdom-eye that sees all things as unreal.

慧縛 The bond of ignorance and stupidity which fetters wisdom.

慧義 The apprehension of the meaning of reality through wisdom.

慧能 The power of wisdom. Hui-nêng, name of a noted monk, sixth patriarch of the Intuitional or Meditation sect; died 713.

慧苑 Hui-yüan, a noted T'ang monk and lexicographer, author of the | | 音義 dictionary of sounds and meanings, cf. | 琳.

慧藏 Wisdom-store, the Abhidharma Piṭaka, which embodies the science of ascertaining the meaning of the sūtras. Also, the whole of the Tripiṭaka.

慧見 Wise views, or insight into wisdom, the views of wisdom.

慧觀 Hui-kuan, one of Kumārajīva's chief assistants in translation, died 424.

慧解 The function of wisdom—to explain all things. | | 脫 The escape by, or into wisdom, i.e. of the arhat who overcomes the hindrances to wisdom, or insight, but not the practical side of abstraction, etc.; better able to understand than to do.

慧超 Hui-ch'ao, a monk who travelled in India.

慧足 The leg of wisdom, the other being 福足 q.v.

慧身 Wisdom body, one of the five divisions of the Dharmakāya, which is the embodiment *inter alia* of inherent wisdom.

慧鏡 The mirror of wisdom.

慧雲 The clouds of wisdom with which the Tathāgata covers all beings.

撰 To compose, compile. | 號 Compiler's name, author's title.

播 To sow, publish; reject; to winnow; to stir up, cheat; translit. *pa*, *pā*. | 尼 Pāṇi, the palm of the hand. | 捨 Pāśa, a noose, snare. | 磨 Upamā, a resemblance, simile. | 輸鉢多 Pāśupata, followers of the lord of cattle, Śiva, who smeared themselves with ashes, also 波 | | |.

撥 To spread, open out, scatter, disseminate, detach, uproot. | 無因果 To dispense with, or deny the law of karma, one of the five heresies | 草瞻風 (or 參玄) To uproot the weeds (of ignorance) and look for the mystic Buddha-breeze.

撒 To scatter, set loose, sow. | 馬兒罕 Samakan, Samarkand, v. 颯.

摩 To feel, handle, rub; translit. *m*, *ma*, *mu*, *ba*; cf. 末, 磨.

摩休勒 Mahoraga, cf. | 睺羅.

摩伽 Maghā, an asterism "containing five stars figured like a house, apparently $\alpha, \gamma, \zeta, \eta, \nu$ Leonis"

(M. W.); intp. as governing the eleventh month; for which 丨佉; 丨袪 are also used. 丨丨羅 Makara, cf. 丨竭 a sea monster. 丨丨陀 Magadha, cf. 丨竭陀 also used for Māgha, the month January–February.

摩偷 Madhu, sweet, an intoxicating liquor. 丨丨羅 Mathurā; Madhurā. Ancient kingdom and city, the modern Muttra on the bank of the Jumna; the reputed birthplace of Kṛṣṇa, one of the seven sacred cities, called Peacock City 孔雀城 Kṛṣṇapura, famous for its stūpas. The ancient name Madhu is given in 摩度. Other forms are 丨突 (or 度, or 頭) 羅; 秣菟羅.

摩利 Mallikā, a fragrant flower variously described as jasmine, aloes, musk, etc. Name of the wife of king Prasenajit, also called 丨丨室羅 Mālyaśrī. 丨丨伽羅耶 Malaya in Malabar, cf. 丨羅. 丨丨(or 梨, or 里) 支; 末丨支 Marīci. Rays of light, the sun's rays, said to go before the sun; mirage; also intp. as a wreath. A goddess, independent and sovereign, protectress against all violence and peril. "In Brahmanic mythology, the personification of light, offspring of Brahmā, parent of Sūrya." "Among Chinese Buddhists Maritchi is represented as a female with eight arms, two of which are holding aloft emblems of sun and moon, and worshipped as goddess of light and as the guardian of all nations, whom she protects from the fury of war. She is addressed as 天后 queen of heaven, or as 斗姥 lit. mother of the Southern measure ($\mu\ \lambda\ \rho\ \sigma\ \tau\ \zeta$ Sagittarii), and identified with Tchundi" and "with Mahēśvarī, the wife of Mahēśvara, and has therefore the attribute Mātrikā", mother of Buddhas. Eitel. Taoists address her as Queen of Heaven.

摩哂陀 Mahendra, younger brother of Aśoka, reputed as founder of Buddhism in Ceylon.

摩呼洛迦 Mahoraga, described as large-bellied; a class of demons shaped like the boa; a spirit in the retinue of Śākyamuni; a form taken by Vairocana; also 莫丨丨丨(摩); 丨睺羅伽; 丨護囉誐.

摩多 Mātṛ, a measurer, maker, former, mother. 丨丨羅迦 Mātṛkā, cf. 丨怛.

摩夷 Mātṛkā, cf. 丨怛.

摩娑 Māṁsa, flesh. 丨丨羅 Musāra-galva, agate, cf. 牟.

摩奴沙 (or 闍), v. 末奴沙 Manuṣya, Mānuṣa, man, any rational being. 丨丨是若 Manojña, agreeable to the mind, attractive, at will. 丨丨(or 菟) 末耶 Manomaya, "consisting of spirit or mind, spiritual, mental." M. W. Intp. as mind-produced body, or form, any appearance produced at will.

摩菟沙 Manuṣya, 丨丨奢; 丨丨賒 man, any rational being, v. 末丨丨, 摩奴沙.

摩尼 Maṇi; "a jewel, gem, precious stone (especially a pearl, bead, or other globular ornament)." M. W. A bright luminous pearl, symbol of Buddha and his doctrines. Tr. "as wished", or at wish, whoever possesses the pearl receives whatever he desires. One of the seven treasures. With Shivaites a symbol of the Liṅga. Also 末尼. 丨丨跋陀 (羅) Maṇibhadra, one of the eight generals; "a king of the Yakshas (the tutelary deity of travellers and merchants, probably another name for Kuvera)." M. W. 丨丨犍大龍王 Maṇiskandhanāga. The nāga-king in whose hand is the talismanic pearl.

摩度羅 Mathurā, modern Mutra, v. 丨偷.

摩怛里 Mātṛ, a mother. 丨丨丨迦 Mātṛkā, also 丨咀里迦; 丨丨履迦; 丨得 (or 德) 勒. 伽; 丨多羅迦; 丨侄梨迦; 丨室里迦; 丨夷; the Abhidharma-piṭaka, as the mother of Buddhist philosophy.

摩愉羅伽藍 Masūra Saṅghārāma. An ancient vihāra about 200 li south-east of Mongali. Eitel. Cf. 豆.

摩揭 v. 丨竭.

摩提 Mati, understanding; v. 末底.

摩拏 v. 丨奴沙. 丨拏羅 Manorhita, or Manorhata, an Indian prince who became disciple and successor to Vasubandhu as 22nd Patriarch. Author of the Vibhāṣā śāstra. "He laboured in Western India and in Ferghana where he died in A.D. 165." Eitel. Also 丨奴丨; 末笯曷利他.

摩賴耶 v. 丨羅丨.

摩沙羅 Musara-galva, v. 牟.

摩沓婆 Māthava; Mādhava; Madhu. "The Mathai of Megasthenes, a tribe of Indian aborigines who lived north of Kośala in Rohilcund and along the southern frontier of Nepaul. They gave the name to Mathurā and Matipura." Eitel. The last statement at least is doubtful.

摩由羅 Mayūra, 孔雀 a peacock; also 丨裕丨; 丨庾囉.

摩登伽阿蘭若 Mātaṅga-āraṇyakāḥ. The second class of hermits (probably called after the lowest caste), living in cemeteries, at a distance of 500 bow-lengths (*circa* 3,000 feet) from a village. 丨丨丨經 A sūtra on Mātaṅgī, and on the stars. Cf. 丨鄧.

摩睺羅 Muhūrta, a moment. Mahoraga, also 丨丨勒 v. 丨呼.

摩祇 A medicine that can eradicate poison, and so overpowering that serpents avoid it; also 丨蛇; 丨蚳; 丨醯; 莫耆.

摩竭(羅) Makara. A sea monster, either in the form of a great fish, e.g. a whale, or a great turtle. Also 丨伽 (or 迦) 丨. 丨丨陀 Magadha, also 丨丨提; 丨揭陀; 丨伽陀; 丨訶陀 "A kingdom in Central India, the headquarters of ancient Buddhism up to A.D. 400; the holy land of all Buddhists, covered with vihāras and therefore called Bahar, the southern portion of which corresponds to ancient Magadha." Eitel. A ṛṣi after whom the country of Southern Behar is said to be called. Name of a previous incarnation of Indra; and of the asterism Maghā 丨伽.

摩納(婆迦) Māṇavaka, a Brahman youth, a youth, a man; also 丨丨縛 (迦); 丨那槃; 那羅摩那 (naramana). 丨丨仙 Śākyamuni in a previous incarnation.

摩羅 Mālā, a wreath, garland, chaplet, head-dress; also tr. as Māra, a huge fish, cf. 丨竭羅 Makara. 丨丨伽 (or 迦) 陀 Marakata, the emerald. 丨丨提; 丨丨耶提 (or 底) 數; 丨離 Malaya-deśa, Malaya country. 丨丨耶 Malaya, the Malabar hills, noted for their sandalwood, cf. 末; also 丨丨延; 丨梨; 丨利伽羅耶; 丨賴耶.

摩耶 Māyā, v. Mahāmāya, *infra*.

摩臘婆 Mālava, or Lāra (Lāṭa). An ancient state in Central India, in the present Gujarat.

摩裕羅 v. 丨由丨.

摩訶 Mahā, great, large, very; also 丨醯; 莫訶.

摩訶僧祇部 Māhāsāṅghikāḥ, or Mahāsaṅghanikāya; 大衆部 one of the four branches of the Vāibhāṣika, said to have been formed after the second synod in opposition to the Sthavirās, marking the first division in the Buddhist church. Followers of Mahākāśyapa. After the third synod this school split into five sects: Pūrvaśāila, Avaraśāila, Haimavatā, Lokottaravādinas, Prajñaptivādinas. 丨丨丨丨律 The great canon of monastic rules, tr. by Buddhabhadra and Fa-hsien in 40 chüan.

摩訶剌佗 Mahārāṣtra. "The Mahratta country, an ancient kingdom in the north-west corner of the Deccan, near the upper course of the Godavery." Eitel.

摩訶因陀羅 Mahendra, v. 丨哂.

摩訶娑(or 娑)羅 Mahāsāra. "An ancient city in Central India, the present Masar, about 30 miles west of Patna." Eitel.

摩訶尼(or 泥)羅 Mahānīla, dark-blue, a sapphire; described as the large blue pearl of Indra, perhaps the Indranīla.

摩訶憍曇彌 Mahāgautamī, aunt and nurse of Śākyamuni. Cf. 憍.

摩訶曼殊沙華 Mahāmañjūṣaka, a red flower yielding the madder (munjeeth of Bengal). 丨丨丨陀羅華 Mahāmandārava, a large white lotus; cf. 曼.

摩訶拘絺羅 Mahākauṣṭhila, a disciple of the Buddha; also 丨丨俱瑟耻羅; v. 拘.

摩訶摩耶 Mahāmāyā, intp. by M. W. as "great deceit or illusion, worldly illusion, the divine power of illusion (which makes the material universe appear as if really existing and renders it cognizable by the senses), the Great Illusion (the illusory nature of worldly objects personified and identified with

Durgā)". Mahāmāyā was the wife of Śuddhodana, and mother of Śākyamuni. He, Siddhārtha, was born "from her right side", and she died seven days later, her sister Mahāprajāpati becoming his foster-mother. Also called | | 第 脾 Mahādevī; | | 夫人 Lady Māyā, etc.

摩訶毘盧遮那 v. 毘. Mahāvairocana. | | | 訶羅 Mahāvihāra. A monastery near Anurādhāpura, Ceylon, where Fa-hsien (A.D. 400) found 3,000 inmates. | | | | | 住部 Mahāvihāravāsināḥ. "A subdivision of the Mahāsthavirah school, which combated the Mahāyāna system." Eitel.

摩訶提婆 Mahādeva, the great deva, Maheśvara, i.e. Śiva; also a former incarnation of Śākyamuni; and name of an arhat.

摩訶波闍波提 Mahāprajāpatī, title of aunt and nurse of Śākyamuni; reputed as the first abbess; according to the Lotus she is to become a Buddha, under the title of Sarvasattva-priya-darśana. Also | | 鉢剌闍鉢底; cf. 憍 Gautamī.

摩訶盧瑟拏 Mahāroṣaṇa, the angry deva.

摩訶目犍連 Mahāmaudgalyāyana, v. 目, one of the chief disciples of Śākyamuni, at whose left his image is placed, Śāriputra being on the right. Mahāsthāmaprāpta is said to be a form of Maudgalyāyana. | | 目脂 (or 眞) 隣陀 Mahāmucilinda, name of a Nāga-king, etc., v. 目.

摩訶怛特 Mahātantra(dhāraṇī), great spell power for overcoming the evil and cleaving to the good.

摩訶羅 Mahallakas, old, stupid, ignorant; also | 迦 |; 莫訶 (or 喝) 洛迦. | | | 闍 Mahārāja, a great or superior king; a king.

摩訶耶那提婆 Mahāyānadeva, a title given to Hsüan-tsang in India; cf. 玄.

摩訶般涅槃那 Mahāparinirvāṇa, v. 涅, the great complete nirvāṇa, final release, perfect rest. | | | 若 Mahāprajñā, v. 般, great wisdom, great insight into all truth. | | | | 波羅蜜 Mahāprajñāpāramitā, v. 般, the great wisdom method of crossing the stream to nirvāṇa, i.e. Buddha-truth.

摩訶菩提寺 Mahābodhi-saṅghārāma. The monastery of the great enlightenment, a vihāra near the Bodhidruma at Gayā; cf. 西域記 8 and Fa-hsien.

摩訶薩 (埵) Mahāsattva, "great being," one with great compassion and energy, who brings salvation to all living beings; a Bodhisattva; also | | 刹頭. | | | | 王子 Mahāsattva-kumāra-rāja, the noble and royal prince, Śākyamuni.

摩訶衍 (那) Mahāyāna, 大乘 q.v. the Great Vehicle, in contrast with Hīnayāna 小乘. Also | | 夜那 (or 泥).

摩訶諾伽那 Mahānagna, "quite naked" (M. W.); great naked powerful spirits, cf. 諾.

摩訶質帝薩埵 Mahācittasattva. A great-mind being, a Bodhisattva. Also | | 菩提質帝 | |.

摩訶迦葉(波) Mahākāśyapa, or Kāśyapa-dhātu 迦葉 (頭陀), a Brahman of Magadha, disciple of Śākyamuni; accredited with presiding over the first synod, hence known as 上座; also with supervising the first compilation of the Buddha's sermons; is reckoned as the first Patriarch, v. 二十八祖 and 迦. | | | 旃延 Mahākātyāyana, one of the principal disciples of Śākyamuni; v. 大 and 迦. | | | 羅 Mahākāla, the great black deva, v. 大黑.

摩訶那伽 Mahānāga, the great Nāga, "one of the elephants that support the world." M. W. A title of a Buddha, or of an arhat. | | | 摩; | | 男 Mahānāman, one of the first five of Śākyamuni's converts. | | | 鉢 Mahāsthāmaprāpta, the Bodhisattva 大勢至 q.v.

摩訶鉢特摩 Mahāpadma, defined by M. W. as a great "white" lotus; but intp. in China as the great red lotus, after which the eighth cold hell is named. As the great white lotus it is a Buddha-throne, of purity and fragrance.

摩迦吒 Markaṭa, a monkey; also | 斯 |.

摩那埵 Mānatta, joy to the penitent and his fellow monks caused by confession and absolution; also a term for penance, or punishment; and for offences involving reprimand (Pali). | | 婆 v.

| 納 Māṇava. | | 斯; | | 蘇婆帝 Mānasa; Manasvatī. A lake in the Himālayas, one of the four lakes formed when the ocean fell from heaven upon Mount Meru. The dragon who is the tutelary deity of this lake.

摩鄧伽 Mātaṅga, also | 登 (or 燈) 伽 Elephant, greatest, utmost, lowest caste, outcast, barbarian. | | 祇 Mātaṅgī. Both words bear a low meaning in Chinese, e.g. low caste. Mātaṅgī is the name of the low-caste woman who inveigled Ānanda. The | | | 咒 spell is performed with blood, etc.

摩醯(or 訶)因陀羅 Mahendra, younger brother of Aśoka, who, on repenting of his dissolute life, became an arhat and is said to have founded Buddhism in Ceylon. | | 奢娑迦 Mahīśāsakāḥ, cf. 彌, one of the subdivisions of the Sarvāstivādāḥ school. | | 徑伐羅; 魔醯首羅; 魔醯 Mahēśvara. Explained by 大自在天 great sovereign deva, 天王 king of devas. Śiva, lord of one great chiliocosm, a deity with eight arms, three eyes, riding on a white bull. Hsüan-tsang says specially worshipped in the Panjab. It is a term also for certain bodhisattvas and certain heavens.

摩頂 To lay the hand on the top of the head, a custom of Buddha in teaching his disciples, from which the burning of the spots on the head of a monk is said to have originated.

摩騰 Kāśyapa Mātaṅga who, according to tradition, accompanied the first envoys back to China. A.D. 64; cf. 迦.

敷 Diffuse, spread, promulgate, announce. | 具 The displayed, or promulgating article, i.e. the monk's robe. | 曼荼羅 To spread a magic cloth, or maṇḍala, on the ground.

敵 To oppose, compete; an enemy. | 證 Opposition and affirmation, negative and positive.

數 To number, count, enumerate, figure out, calculate, reason, reprimand; numbers, an account, fate, destiny; flurried. It is also used for 智 knowledge, and for mental content or conditions as in 心 |. | 人; | 法人 Those of the Sarvāstivādāḥ school, cf. 薩, who held that all things are real. | 取趣 A definition of Pudgala, i.e. all beings subject to transmigration. | 息 To count the breathings in order to calm mind and body for meditation, e.g. | | 觀; | (|) 門; cf. 阿 Ānāpāna. | 珠 A rosary; to tell beads, which consist of various numbers, generally 108. | 緣盡; | 滅無爲 idem 擇滅. | 行煩惱 The common passions and their consequences. | 論 The śāstras of the Sarvāstivādins; also Kapila, called | | 外道; | | 師 founder of the Sāṅkhya philosophy; v. 僧伽, 劫, and 迦. It is an attempt to place all concepts in twenty-five categories, with Puruṣa at the head and the others in ordered progress. *Inter alia* it also teaches "the eternity and multiplicity of souls" (Eitel). Vasubandhu wrote in criticism of the system.

暫 Temporarily, briefly, meanwhile, suddenly. | 暇 A brief relief, or leave of absence.

樞 A pivot, axis. | 要 The pivot; principles.

樊 A cage, fence. | 籠 A cage, the cage of karma, or the world with its suffering, etc.

槵 A species of Sapindus, or soap-berry tree, whose seeds | 子 are used for rosaries.

樓 An upper storey, storied building, tower; one of the eighteen hells. | 夷亘羅 Lokeśvararāja, an ancient Buddha, successor to 定光 Buddha. | 炭 A tower or pile of charcoal, e.g. the world for conflagration, | 毘 cf. 嵐 Lumbinī. | 由; | 至 Rucika, also 盧至 (or 遮), the last of the 1,000 Buddhas of the present kalpa. | 陀 (羅) Rudra, the howler, or god of tempests. | 黎 Vaiḍūrya, lapis lazuli, cf. 琉.

標 Signal, flag, banner; the troops under a particular banner; a notice, list, signboard, ticket; to publish. | 幟 Signals, symbols, especially those used by the Yoga sect. | 月 To indicate the moon. | 領 The leader, chief.

槽 A trough, manger, channel. | 廠 A stable.

樂 Music, that which causes joy, hence joy, joyful, glad, rejoice; also to find joy in, enjoy. | 乾闥婆 The Gandharvas, Indra's musicians. | 受 The sensation, or perception of pleasure. | 土 A happy land. | 天 Deva musicians, see above. | 施 Joyful giver, tr. of Sudatta, i.e. Anāthapiṇḍika, v. 阿. | 果 Joyful fruit, i.e. nirvāṇa. | 根 The organs of pleasure—eyes, ears, nose, tongue, and body. | 欲 Desire for the pleasant, or pleasure. | 法 Delight in Buddha-truth, or the religion. | 波羅蜜 The pāramitā of joy, one of the 四德 | | | four transcendent pāramitās q.v., i.e. 常, |, 我, and 淨. | 神 Deva musicians, v. above. | 著 The bond of pleasure binding to the phenomenal life. | 說 Joy in preaching, or telling the way of salvation; joy in that which is preached. It is also called pratibhāna, bold and illuminating discourse, or freedom in expounding the truth with correct meaning and appropriate words, one of the 無礙智 four pratisaṁvids. | 說辯才 similar to the last. | 變化天 Sunirmita, the fifth of the six desire-heavens, where every form of joy is attainable at will; also 化(自)|天; 妙|化天. | 邦 The joyful country, the paradise of the West. | 音 The sound of music. | 音樹 The trees in Amitābha's paradise which give forth music to the breeze.

歎 To praise; to sigh. | 波那 Broken rice, v. 麨.

潮 The tide; tidal; damp. 乘 | To take advantage of the tide.

澄 Clear, limpid. | 觀 Ch'êng-kuan, a famous monk and author, a follower of 賢首 Hsien-shou and supporter of the Hua-yen school, died A.D. 806.

潔 Clean, pure. | 齋 To purify a monastery, cleanse away all immorality and impropriety; a pure establishment.

澆 To sprinkle, to water; perfidious, infamous. | 季 The evil period of the world's existence leading to its end.

澁 Acrid, astringent, rough; | 觸 one of the eight sensations of touch.

潭 A deep, a pool. | 恩 Profound grace, or favour.

潙 Name of several streams, etc. | 山 Kuei-shan, a noted mountain, monastery, and T'ang monk in Fukien, by whom the | 仰 Kuei-yang branch of the Ch'an school was founded.

潤 Moisten, soak, enrich, fertilize, sleek, smooth, profit. | 業 Fertilized karma, the original karma fertilized by the passions and distresses of life. | 生 The fertilization of the natural conditions which produce rebirth, especially those of the three kinds of attachment in the hour of death, love of body, of home, and of life.

熟 Ripe. | 酥經 The sūtras of ripe curds or cheese, the Prajñā group.

熱 Tap, tapana, tapas. Hot; to heat. | 惱 Perturbed, feverish, troubled, distressed. | 時炎 Mirage, idem 陽炎. | 病 Fever. | 鐵地獄 The hell of red-hot iron (pills).

犛 A yak | 牛.

瘡 A sore, ulcer. | 門 Ulcerating orifices, i.e. the nine orifices in the body which discharge.

瘞 To bury, offer in sacrifice. | 錢 Offerings of paper money at the grave.

瘧 Fever, ague. | 加持; | 病法 Treatment of feverish ailments by tantric measures. | 鬼 Apasmāra, a demon supposed to cause the above.

盤 A dish, plate; round, to coil, wind up; to go about, travel, convey; to inquire about, interrogate. Translit. *pa*, *ba*, *bha*, *va*; cf. 般, 半, etc. | 坐 To sit with folded legs. | 茶味 Vandanī, praise, adore, v. 和.

瞎 Blind. | 屢生 A blind, stupid man. | 驢 A blind or blind-folded donkey, stupid.

瞋 Krodha; pratigha; dveṣa; one of the six fundamental kleśas, anger, ire, wrath, resentment, one of the three poisons; also called | 恚. | 恚使 The messenger, or lictor of anger. | 心; | 恚心 A heart of anger. | 火 The fire of anger. | 煩惱 The passion or defilement of anger.

磋 To polish; translit. *cha*; cf. 車, etc.

磐 A rock. | 石劫 The rock kalpa. Let a rock 40 li in extent be brushed once in a hundred years by a deva garment; when brushed away the kalpa is ended.

磁 Porcelain crockery, chinaware. | 石 A lodestone, magnet.

稽 Investigate; delay; to prostrate oneself. | 首 Vandana; vandi. To make obeisance by prostration. | 薑那 Kikaṇa. "A people in Afghanistan (east of Kandahar, south of Ghazna) ruled A.D. 630

by independent chieftains, perhaps identical with the Kykānān of Arabic chroniclers." Eitel.

穀 Grain; rice unhulled. | 頭 The monk in charge of the grain.

稻 Growing rice. | 稈 Rice straw.

窮 Poor, impoverished, exhausted; to exhaust, investigate thoroughly. | 子 The poor son, or prodigal son, of the Lotus sūtra. | 生死蘊 To exhaust the concomitants of reincarnation, be free from transmigration.

篅 A round grain bin. | 衣 A nun's skirt.

箭 An arrow, dart. | 道 An arrow-shot, or bow-shot, in distance.

範 Pattern, rule, method. | 衛 Rule and restraint; to guard by proper means.

篇 A slip of bamboo, a slip, leaf, page, books. | 目 A subject or text exposed on a slip; the publication, e.g., of the name of a wrong-doer. | 聚 Two divisions of wrong-doing, one called the 五 | five p'ien, the other the six and seven chü. The five p'ien are: (1) pārājika, v. 波, sins demanding expulsion from the order; (2) saṅghāvaśeṣa, v. 僧, sins verging on expulsion, which demand confession before and absolution by the assembly; (3) ? prāyaścitta, v. 波逸, sins deserving hell which may be forgiven; (4) pratideśanīya, v. 波羅 and 提舍, sins which must be confessed; (5) duṣkṛta, v. 突, light sins, errors, or faults. The six chü are the five above with sthūlātyaya, v. 偸, associated with the third, implying thought not developed in action. The seven chü are the above with the division of the fifth into two, action and speech. There are further divisions of eight and nine.

線 A thread, wire, clue, spy, lead, connection. | 香 Thread or string incense, slow-burning and prolonged.

練 To train, practise, drill, exercise. | 磨 To drill and grind, three bodhisattva conditions for maintaining progress: the fixing of attention on those who have attained enlightenment; the examination of one's purpose; and the realization of the power at work in others; v. 三退屈. | 若 Araṇya, hermitage, etc., cf. 阿. | 行 Religious training or discipline.

編 To plait; enroll; compile. | 髮 To plait the hair, or roll it into conch-shape.

緣 Pratyaya means conviction, reliance, but with Buddhists especially it means "a co-operating cause, the concurrent occasion of an event as distinguished from its proximate cause". M. W. It is the circumstantial, conditioning, or secondary cause, in contrast with 因 hetu, the direct or fundamental cause. Hetu is as the seed, pratyaya the soil, rain, sunshine, etc. To reason, conclude. To climb, lay hold of. The mind 能 | can reason, the objective is 所 |, the two in contact constitute the reasoning process. The four kinds of causes are 因 |; 次第 |; | |, and 增上 | q.v.

緣中 The place or idea on which the mind is centralized.

緣事 To lay hold of, or study things or phenomena, in contrast to principles or noumena, cf. | 理; meditation on the Buddha's nirmāṇakāya and saṁbhogakāya, in contrast with the dharmakāya.

緣佛 A deceased relative or friend, i.e. a Buddha connected with me.

緣力 Pratyaya-bala; the power of the conditioning cause, circumstance, or contributing environment, in contrast with the 因力 direct cause.

緣化 To convert or instruct those under influence.

緣因 Developing cause, i.e. development of the fundamental Buddha-nature, cf. | 正.

緣塵 The guṇas, qualities, or sense-data which cause the six sensations of form, sound, odour, taste, touch, and thought.

緣心 The conditioned mind, the mind held by the phenomenal.

緣念; 緣想 Thoughts arising from environment, similar to the last entry.

緣成 The phenomenal, whatever is produced by causal conditions.

緣日 The day of the month on which a particular Buddha or bodhisattva is worshipped, he being in special charge of mundane affairs on that day, e.g. the 5th is Maitreya, 15th Amitābha, 25th Mañjuśrī, 30th Śākyamuni.

緣機 Conditions opportune; favourable circumstances; cause and conditions co-operating for achieving Buddhahood.

緣正 Conditioned and fundamental; 正 refers to the Buddha-nature, the bhūtatathatā 正因佛性; 緣 to the Buddha-nature in all undergoing development 緣因佛性.

緣理 To study, or reason on fundamental principles; to contemplate ultimate reality, cf. | 事. | | 斷九 By the consideration of the tenth realm only, i.e. the Buddha-realm, to cut off the illusion of the nine other realms of time and sense.

緣生 Produced by causal conditions. The twelve nidānas are also called 十二 | |. Cf. | 起.

緣慮心 The rational cogitating mind; also 慮知心 the cogitating perceiving mind.

緣相 Reasoning, mentality, the mind.

緣緣 The reasoning mind, or the mind reasoning, intelligence in contact with its object; later termed 所 | |, i.e. 所 | being the object and | the mind; the relationship being like that of form or colour to the eye.

緣覺 Pratyeka-buddha 辟支佛; 辟支迦佛; 鉢剌翳伽(佛)陀. In the early translations it was rendered 緣覺, i.e. enlightened through reasoning on the riddle of life, especially as defined in the twelve nidānas. Later it was rendered 獨覺 or individual enlightenment, i.e. one who lives apart from others and attains enlightenment alone, or for himself, in contrast with the altruism of the bodhisattva principle. The term pratyeka-buddha is not limited to Buddhists, but is also general for recluses pondering alone over the meaning of life, an illustration being the rhinoceros, which lives in isolation. The non-Buddhist enlightenment is illusion, e.g. from observing the "flying flowers and falling leaves"; the Buddhist enlightenment arises from pondering over the twelve nidānas. As a degree of saintship it is undefined by early Buddhism, receiving its definition at a later period. | | 乘 The "middle conveyance" period, characterized as that of the pratyeka-buddha, who is enlightened by the twelve nidānas; it is considered as an advance on the Hīnayāna, cf. śrāvaka, but not yet the standard of the altruistic bodhisattva-vehicle, the Mahāyāna. | | 法界 The pratyeka-buddha realm, one of the ten T'ien-t'ai categories of intelligent beings. | | 菩提 The pratyeka-buddha form of enlightenment, for self. | | 身 The pratyeka-buddha or personal appearing of the Buddha.

緣觀 The phenomenal and noumenal, i.e. the observed and the observing, the object and subject.

緣起 Arising from conditional causation; everything arises from conditions, and not being spontaneous and self-contained has no separate and independent nature; cf. | 生. It is a fundamental doctrine of the Hua-yen school, which defines four principal uses of the term: (1) 業感 | | that of the Hīnayāna, i.e. under the influence of karma the conditions of reincarnation arise; (2) 賴耶 | | that of the primitive Mahāyāna school, i.e. that all things arise from the Ālaya, or 藏 fundamental store; (3) 如來藏 | | that of the advancing Mahāyāna, that all things arise from the Tathāgatagarbha, or bhūtatathatā; (4) 法界 | | that of complete Mahāyāna, in which one is all and all are one, each being a universal cause. | | 法 Pratītya-samutpāda; idem 十二 | |, i.e. the twelve nidānas, cf. 十二因 |. | | 偈; | | (法) 頌 The gāthā of three of the four fundamental dogmas of Buddhism; that all is suffering, that suffering is intensified by desire, and that extinction of desire is practicable. This is found in the 智度論. It is also called 緣起法頌. It is placed in the foundations of pagodas and inside of images of Buddha and so is called 法身偈 dharmakāya gāthā.

罵 To curse, scold. 呪 | To curse.

罷 Cease, stop; mark of finality. | 參 To dismiss the assembly.

羯 To castrate; deer-skin; translit. *ka*, *gha*. Cf. 迦, 拘, 軻, 朅, 竭, etc.

羯利王 Kalirāja, a former incarnation of Kauṇḍinya, when as king he cut off the hands and feet of Kṣānti-ṛṣi because his concubines had strayed to the hermit's hut. Converted by the hermit's indifference, it was predicted that he would become a disciple of Buddha. | | 沙鉢 Kārṣāpaṇa, a coin weighing *ca.* 176 grains.

羯吒布怛那 Kaṭapūtana, a kind of ill-smelling demon, a preta in the lower regions. M. W.

羯地洛迦 Khadiraka, the third of the seven circles around Meru. Cf. 佉.

羯尼(迦) Kanaka, gold; name of several yellow plants, e.g. thorn apple; *Butea frondosa*; a species of sandalwood, etc.

羯布羅 Karpūra, dragon-brain scent, camphor.

羯拏僕 Kaṇabhuj; Kaṇāda 蹇尼陀, founder of the Vaiśeṣika school of Indian philosophy.

羯摩 Karma, v. 業 and cf. | 磨.

羯毘(迦羅) Kalaviṅka, v. 迦.

羯洛迦孫馱 Krakucchanda, v. 迦.

羯磨 Karma; action, work, deed, performance, service, "duty"; religious action, moral duty; especially a meeting of the monks for the purpose of ordination, or for the confession of sins and absolution, or for expulsion of the unrepentant. There are numerous kinds of karma, or assemblies for such business, ordinarily requiring the presence of four monks, but others five, ten, or twenty. Cf. 業 for definition of Karma, deeds or character as the cause of future conditions; also 五蘊 for karma as the fourth skandha. | | 僧 A monastic assembly; also a monk on duty, e.g. in meditation. | | 印 An image showing the symbol of a bodhisattva's activity. | | 會 An assembly for monastic duty; also the central group of the Vajradhātu maṇḍala. | | 身 An image, a term used by the esoterics. | | 陀那 Karmadāna, i.e. the 維那 or director of duties.

羯羅拏蘇伐刺那 Karṇasuvarṇa. "An ancient kingdom in Gundwana, the region about Gangpoor, Lat. 21° 54 N., Long. 84° 30 E." Eitel. | | 舍 Kalaśa, a water-pot, pitcher, jar, dish, also 迦 | |; | 攞賒. | | 頻迦 cf. | 陵. For Krakucchanda, v. 迦.

羯耻那 Khaṭṭika. Lictors in hades; possibly from the root khād, to devour; also | | 羅; 伽絺那; it is also defined as "dog-cookers", butchers, hunters, those who live by killing and selling animals, persons of very low caste.

羯臘婆 or **縛** Karaphu, or Kalahu, "a particularly high number" (M. W.), 10 quintillions; 大 | | | 100 quintillions; cf. 洛叉.

羯若鞠闍 Kanyākubja, "hump-backed maidens." An ancient city and kingdom of Central India. In antiquity this city ranks next to Ayodhyā in Oudh. It is known to classical geography as Canogyza. The etymology refers to the legend of the hundred daughters of Kuśanābha its king, who refused the licentious desires of Vāyu (Mahāvṛkṣa 大樹仙) and were turned by him into hunchbacks. M. W. Eitel says "the modern Canouge".

羯蘭鐸迦 Kalandaka, "a species of bird" (M. W.); cf. 迦.

羯蠅揭羅 Kajiṅghara, Kajangala, or Kajūghira, a kingdom whose ruling family was extinct in A.D. 400. "The ruins of the capital are situated at the village of Kadjéri near Farakhabad (Lat. 27° 24 N., Long. 79° 27 E.) in the province of Agra." Eitel. Also | 殊嗢祇羅.

羯達羅 Khadira | 陀 |; v. 竭.

羯邏藍 Kalala, the human embryo during the first seven days; the womb; also | 羅 |, 歌羅邏, etc.

羯陵伽 Kaliṅga, also | 餕 |. An ancient kingdom south-east of Kośala, a nursery of heretical sects, the present Kalingapatnam. Eitel. Also with | 羅頻迦 used for Kalaviṅka, v. 迦.

羯霜那 Kaśanna. "An ancient kingdom 300 li south-west of Kharismiga on the Oxus, the present Koorshee," Karshi. Eitel.

膠 Glue, gum. | 盆子 A glue-pot, referring to running handwriting. | 香 Incense of the liquidambar tree.

膜 A membrane. | 拜 To raise the hands to the head in making obeisance.

蔡 Chāyā, a shadow, reflection; gnomon, dial. | 華 A lotus.

蔑 Without, not; minute, small. | 戾車 Mleccha, barbarians, non-Aryan, heathen, frontier tribes. Also 篾, 彌, 畢.

蓮 Puṇḍarīka, the lotus, especially the white lotus, *Nymphœa alba*; Padma, especially the *Nelumbium speciosum*; Utpala, the *Nymphœa cærulea*, the blue lotus; Kumuda, *Nymphœa esculenta*, white lotus, or *N. rubra*, red lotus; Nīlotpala, *N. cyanea*, a blue lotus. The first four are called white, red, blue, and yellow lotuses; but the white lotus is generally meant unless otherwise specified. | 刹 Lotus-kṣetra, or Lotus-land, the paradise of Amitābha. | 子 Lotus seeds. | 宗 The Lotus sect founded by 慧遠 Hui-yuan *circa* A.D. 390 at his monastery, in which was a 白蓮池 white lotus pond. It has no connection with the White Lily Secret Society which arose during the Mongol or Yüan dynasty. The Lotus sect is traced to the awakening of Hui-yüan by the reading of the Prajñāpāramitā sūtra. He then turned his attention to calling on the name of Buddha to obtain salvation direct to his Pure Land. The school became that of the Amitābha or Pure-land sect, which in later years developed into the principal Buddhist cult in the Far East. | 宮 Padmavimāna. Lotus-palace, the Pure Land of the Saṁbhogakāya; also the eight-leaved lotus of the heart. | 座 The lotus throne on which are seated the images; Buddha-throne. | 理 The mystic doctrine of the Lotus faith. | 眼 The eye of the blue lotus, i.e. the wonderful eye of Buddha. | 社 The White Lotus sect, idem | 宗. | 祐 Mutual protectors, or helpers of the Lotus sect, i.e. members. | 經 The Lotus sūtra; v. 法華. | 胎 The Lotus-womb in which the believers of Amitābha are born into his paradise; it is also described as the believer's heart in embryo. | 華 or 花 The lotus flower. | | 國 The pure land of every Buddha, the land of his enjoyment. | | 坐 Padmāsana; to sit with crossed legs; also a lotus throne. | | 子 Disciples, or followers, shown in the | | 部 of the maṇḍalas. | | 手菩薩 Padmapāṇi, Kuan-yin holding a lotus flower. | | 智 The lotus or mystic wisdom of Amitābha, one of the five 智. | | 眼 The blue-lotus eyes of Kuan-yin. | | 臺 Lotus throne for images of Buddhas and bodhisattvas. | | 藏世界 The lotus world or universe of each Buddha for his saṁbhogakāya. | | 衣 or 服 The lotus-garment, or robe of purity, the robe of the monk or nun. | 邦 The Lotus land, the Pure Land, of Amitābha. | 門 The Lotus sect, idem | 宗.

蝦 A shrimp, prawn; a frog. | 蟆禪 Frog samādhi, which causes one to leap with joy at half-truths.

蝙 The bat. | 蝠僧 A bat monk, v. 鳥.

衛 Guard, defend, restrain, an outpost, garrison; to escort. | 世師 Vaiśeṣika; derived from viśeṣa, characteristic, individuality, particularity or individual essence. M. W. Also 鞞 | | (or 思迦); 吠世史迦; 勝論宗 An atomistic school founded by Kaṇāda. Like the Saṅkhya philosophy it taught a dualism and an endless number of souls, also by its doctrine of particularity or individual essence maintained "the eternally distinct or *sui generis* nature of the nine substances" (see below), "of which the first five including mind are held to be atomic." M. W. The interaction of these with the six mentioned below produces cosmic evolution. It chiefly occupied itself, like the orthodox Nyāya philosophy, with the theory of knowledge, but it differed by distinguishing only six categories of cognition 六諦, viz. substance, quality, activity, species, distinction, and correlation, also a seventh of non-existence, and nine substances possessed of qualities, these 九陰 being: the five elements, air, fire, water, earth, ether, together with time, space, spirit (manas), and soul (ātman). Cf. Keith, *Indian Logic and Atomism*, and Dasgupta, *History of Indian Philosophy*.

複 Double garments, wadded, lined; double; repeated.

褒 To praise; salutation. Poṣadha, v. 布.

褐 Coarse serge, hence poverty. | 刺 (or 賴) 縭 (or 褵) Harali, cloth woven of fine hair. | 麗 (筏多) Revata, name of several persons, v. 利, 離.

諂 To flatter, fawn, cajole, sycophancy. | 曲 Flattery and fawning.

諍 Remonstrate with; debate, dispute. | 論 Debate, dispute, disputation.

請 Request, ask, invite; please; engage; acknowledge, announce. | 佛 To invite a Buddha. | 假; 暫假 To ask for leave of absence, or permission to go out. | 折 To ask for, or reject. | 益 To ask for an increase, for more, for advancement, etc. | 雨 To pray for rain.

諄那 Cūrṇa, powder, flour, dust, sand, etc.

誹 Slander. | 謗 Apavāda. Slander, refute, deny. | | 正 法 To slander, or deny, the truth, i.e. Buddhism.

談 To talk, chat, discuss. | 林 A monastic schoolroom. | 空 說 有 To discuss non-existence and talk of existence; i.e. to discuss the meaning of reality; in discussing non-existence to talk of the existing; it is a phrase expressing confusion of ideas or argument. | 義 To discuss the meaning. | 議 To discuss and consult, or deliberate.

論 To discourse upon, discuss, reason over; tr. for śāstra, abhidharma, and upadeśa, i.e. discourses, discussions, or treatises on dogma, philosophy, discipline, etc. | 宗 The Madhyamaka school of the 三 論 San-lun (Sanron); also the Abhidharma, or Śāstra school; also the same as | 家; | 師 śāstra-writers, or interpreters, or philosophers. | 民 v. 嵐 Lumbinī. | 疏 Śāstras with commentary. | 藏 Thesaurus of discussions or discourses, the Abhidharma Piṭaka, one of the three divisions of the Tripiṭaka. It comprises the philosophical works. The first compilation is accredited to Mahā-Kāśyapa, disciple of Buddha, but the work is of a later period. The Chinese version is in three sections: 大 乘 論 the Mahāyāna philosophy; 小 乘 論 the Hīnayāna philosophy; 宋 元 續 入 藏 諸 論 The Sung and Yüan Addenda, A.D. 960–1368. | 議 Upadeśa, dogmatic treatises, the twelfth and last section of the Canon.

調 To harmonize, blend; regulate, control; to change about, exchange; a song, tune. | 伏 To discipline, bring under control, e.g. bring into submission the body, mouth, and will; control, or subjugate evil spirits, etc.; it is one of the intp. of vinaya. | (婆) 達 (多) v. 提 Devadatta. | 度 To arrange, calculate, manage, especially relating to provision for material needs. | 御 To tame and control as a master does a wild elephant or horse, or as the Buddha brings the passions of men under control, hence he is termed | | 丈 夫 and | | 師 Puruṣa-damya-sārathi. | 意 To control the will, to subdue its evil. | 直 定 To harmonize the discords of the mind, to straighten its irregularities, and quiet its distractions, an explanation of samādhi given by T'ien-t'ai. | 頌 Hymns and chants, an intp. of gāthā.

賣 To sell. | 弄 To show off, boast.

質 Substance, matter; to substantiate, to confront; substantial, honest, sound; translit. *ci*, *ce*. | 多 (耶); | 帝 Citta(m), the heart considered as the seat of intellect; the thinking, reflecting mind. | 多 羅 Citra, variegated, of mixed colours, not of a primary colour. Citrā, the name of a star, Spica in Virgo. | 底 Ci, to assemble, pile up; caitya, a funeral pile, or mound. | 直 Substantial and straight; honestly, firmly, straight without dissemblance. Cf. 火 辨.

賢 Bhadra. Wise and virtuous, sage, second in rank to a 聖 saint; good, excellent in character, virtuous. | 人 A wise and virtuous man. | 劫 Bhadrakalpa, the present period; the last was 莊 嚴 劫, the next is to be 星 宿 劫. A Bhadrakalpa has 1,000 Buddhas, hence its name "the good kalpa", also called 善 劫. There are varied statements in regard to the thousand Buddhas, and variety as to their names. Śākyamuni is the fourth of the present kalpa, Maitreya is to follow and 995 to succeed him. "It is to last 236 million years, but over 151 millions have already elapsed." Eitel. Cf. | 劫 經; 現 在 | 劫 千 佛 經 and 颰 陂 for Bhadra. | 瓶 Bhadra-kumbha; auspicious jar, magic bottle, from which all good things may be wished. | 者 A good and wise man, not yet free from illusion or fully comprehending reality; also anyone occupying a superior position, or a good man in general. | 聖 Those who are noted for goodness, and those who are also noted for wisdom, or insight; the hsien are still of ordinary human standard, the shêng transcend them in wisdom and character; the attainments from 見 道 upwards are those of the shêng; the hsien is on the moral plane, and has not eliminated illusion; the shêng has cut off illusion and has insight into absolute reality. The Mahāyāna has three stages for the hsien and ten for the shêng; the Hīnayāna has seven for each. | 護 Bhadrapāla, a disciple who kept the faith at home at the time of the Buddha. Also, a bodhisattva who with 500 others slighted Śākyamuni in a previous existence, was converted and became a Buddha. An image of Bhadrapāla is kept in the monastic bathroom; cf. 楞 嚴 經 5. | 豆 Hindu, India, cf. 印. | 首 Sage head or leader, a term of address to a monk. A bodhisattva in the Hua-yen sūtra. A queen mentioned in the same sūtra, and in the | 首 經. The third patriarch 法 藏 Fa-tsang, of the Hua-yen sect, which is also known by his title | 首 宗 Hsien Shou Tsung.

趣 Destination, destiny (especially on rebirth); v. 五 |, i.e. the hells, pretas, animals, man, devas. | 寂 The destiny of nirvāṇa, as understood by the Hīnayāna.

踞 To squat. | 地 獅 子 A crouching lion.

踏 Tread, trample. | 床 A footstool.

踢 To kick. | 倒 To kick over.

輪 Cakra; wheel, disc, rotation, to revolve; v. 斫. The three wheels are 惑 業 苦 illusion, karma, suffering, in constant revolution. The five are earth, water, fire, wind, and space; the earth rests on revolving spheres of water, fire, wind, and space. The nine are seen on the tops of pagodas, cf. 九 |. | 圍 山 Cakravāla, the double concentric circles of mountains forming the periphery of a world. | 圓 (具 足) A complete maṇḍala showing the Buddhas and others, symbolizing their works; a magic circle. | 埵 Ears round and full, a mark of a Buddha. | (多 梨) 華 A precious pearl that purifies; also a specially fragrant flower. | 寶 A cakravartin's wheel, i.e. either gold, silver, copper, or iron, manifesting his rank and power. | 差; | 番 To take turns, used to indicate a rota or rotation of duties. | 座 The throne of a cakravartin, or Buddha. | 廻; | 轉 Saṁsāra, the turning of the wheel, to revolve, i.e. transmigration in the six ways, the wheel of transmigration; the round of existence. 火 | Alātacakra, a wheel of fire, produced by rapidly whirling a fire-brand, a symbol of the unreality of the visible, since such a wheel does not exist. | 王 A cakravartin, "a ruler the wheels of whose chariot roll everywhere without obstruction; an emperor, a sovereign of the world, a supreme ruler." M. W. A Buddha, whose truth and realm are universal. There are four kinds of cakravartin, symbolized by wheels of gold, silver, copper, and iron; each possesses the seven precious things, 七 寶 q.v. | 相 The wheel sign, on the top of a pagoda, or on the feet of a cakravartin, or Buddha. | 臍 The navel, or hub of a wheel. | 藏 Revolving scriptures, a revolving stand with eight faces, representing the eight directions, each containing a portion of the sacred canon; a praying-wheel, the revolving of which brings as much merit to the operator as if he had read the the whole. | 輻 Wheel-spokes. | 輞; | 緣 A felly, or tire.

適 To go to, reach; happen; follow, accord with; suddenly, now, then. | 化 To adapt teaching to circumstances. | 莫 Pro and con, according or contrary (to wishes).

遮 To cover, screen, veil, hide, hinder; translit. *ca*, *cha*, *tya*. | 制; | 戒 A secondary commandment, deriving from the mandate of Buddha, e.g. against drinking wine, as opposed to 性 戒 a commandment based on the primary laws of human nature, e.g. against murder, etc.; cf 二 戒. | 吒 迦 Cāṭaka, a sparrow; the bird *Cuculus melanoleucus*, which is supposed only to drink falling rain. | 性 The two kinds of commandment mentioned above. | 惡; | 罪 The second kind of sin as above, e.g. drinking. | 文 荼 ? Cāmuṇḍā, a jealous woman; angry spirit; evil demon, one used to call up the dead to slay an ememy. | 斷 To prevent, suppress, cut off. | 末 邏; | 摩 羅 Cāmara, name of one of the central parts of the southern continent, Jambudvīpa. | 梨 夜; | 唎 耶 Caryā, actions, doings, proceedings, course. | 照 To suppress or to reveal (or illuminate); destructive or constructive; to negate or to affirm. | 遣 To negate, disprove, dispose of. | 那; 毘 盧 | | Vairocana, v. 毘. | 難 Tests for applicants for full orders; there are sixteen (or ten) 遮 and thirteen 難, the former relating to general character and fitness, the latter referring to moral conduct.

醉 Drunk, intoxicated. | 象 A mad elephant, like evil hard to subdue.

鋒 The point of a sword, or weapon; points, bristling; a knife edge.

銷 To melt metal, dissolve, dispel, dissipate, spend, cancel, end. | 釋 To solve, explain.

鋪 多 Bhūtāḥ, a sect of ascetics who smeared themselves with ashes.

閱 Examine, inspect, look over. | 藏 To examine (and dust) the scriptures, or library. | 叉 Yakṣa, v. 夜. | 頭 檀 Śuddhodana, v. 首.

隣 Neighbouring, adjacent, near. | 單 One's neighbouring monks, i.e. in the right and left seats. | 圓 Near to perfect enlightenment, the stage before it. | 智 Similar to the last entry. | 珍 A neighbour's pearls—no aid to me. | 虛 Next to nothing, the minutest particle, an atom. | 近 Near to, approaching, adjoining, approximate.

震 To shake, thunder, tremble, awe, quicken; translit. *cin*, *ci*. | 動 To shake, agitate. | 多 末 尼 Cintāmaṇi, the philosopher's stone, granting all one's wishes. | 旦 Cīna, name of China in ancient India; also 振 |; 眞 |; 神 | intp. as the place where the sun rises, but a translit. of Cīnasthāna. | 嶺 China. | 越 Cīvara, a garment; an article for sleeping on, or in.

頞 The root of the nose, the brow; a saddle; translit. *a*, *an*, *ar*, cf. 阿. | 哳吒 Aṭaṭa, one of the cold hells. | 悉多 Asta, the western hill behind which the sun sets, sunset, death, home. | 杜迦 Andūka, v. 阿梨. | 沙荼 Āṣādha, the first month of summer, 16th of 4th Chinese moon to 15th of 5th. | 浮陀; | 部陀 (or 曇) Arbuda, cf. 阿, the first of the eight cold hells, where the cold raises tumours on the skin; also a fœtus of twenty-seven days. | 濕縛羯拏 Aśvakarṇa, the fifth of the seven circles round Meru. | 濕縛 (or 婆) 庾闍 Aśvayuja, the first month of autumn (September–October). | 瑟吒 Aṣṭan, eight, the eight divisions of the 24-hour day. | 那 Anna, food, but intp. as the name of a mountain. | 鞞 Upasena, v. 阿濕 one of the first five converts, idem Aśvajit. | 順那 v. 阿 Arjuna. | 飯底 v. 阿 Avantī.

颰 A gale; translit. *pha*, *bha*; cf. 跋 and 婆. | 陀; | | 和 (羅); | | 波羅 Bhadra, | | 羅波梨 Bhadrapāla, v. 跋. | | 劫 Bhadrakalpa, v. 跋.

養 Poṣa. Nourish, rear, support.

餉 Rations, food; revenue. | 供 Offerings of food.

髮 Hair (of the head), locks. | 塔 A pagoda over a hair of Buddha's head. | 論 The śāstra of the non-Buddhist Kapila, the 勝論 q.v.

魅 An ogre, evil spirit. | 女 A young woman used as a medium for such a spirit to injure others.

魯 Stupid, vulgar, honest. | 達羅 Rudra, roaring, awful, terrible, intp. terribly evil, a name for Śiva; also 澇 | |; 嚕捺 |.

鴈 A wild goose. | 王 King or leader of the flight, or flock; Buddha, hence | 門 Buddhism.

麨 Broken dry rice, grits, crumbled grain.

黎 Black, black-haired; cf. 離, 利, 梨, etc. | 耶 Ālaya, v. 阿.

齒 The teeth, especially the front and upper teeth; toothed, serrated; age, class. | 印 A serrated seal, or serrations as evidence. | 木 Dantakāṣṭha. A stick for cleaning the teeth.

16. SIXTEEN STROKES.

儒 A scholar; learned. Confucian. | 童菩薩 Learned-youth Bodhisattva, i.e. Confucius, he having been sent from India by the Buddha to instruct China! Also a name of Śākyamuni in a previous existence.

凝 To congeal, consolidate, form. | 然常 Solid, unchanging, immutable.

劍 A sword, a two-edged sword. | 摩舍帝 A spirit or demon, ? Aniruddha, the unobstructed, the ungovernable, son of Kāma (Love, Lust). | 林 (or 樹) 地獄 Asipattra, the hell of the forest of swords, or sword-leaf trees. | 波 Kampa, Bhūkampa; deva of earthquakes. | 輪法 A system of revolving swords for subduing demons.

噱叉 Vakṣu, the Oxus, v. 縛.

器 A vessel, utensil, tool. | 世間; | 世界; | 界 The world as a vessel containing countries and peoples; the material world, a realm of things. | 界說 The supernatural power of the Buddha to make the material realm (trees and the like) proclaim his truth. | 量 Capacity.

壁 A wall, partition-wall, screen. | 定 Wall-meditation, i.e. steady, not restless, meditation. | 觀 The wall-gazer, applied to Bodhidharma, who is said to have gazed at a wall for nine years. Also a name for the meditation of the Ch'an school.

壇 An altar; an open altar. In the esoteric cult it also means a maṇḍala, objects of worship grouped together.

奮 To rouse, excite, exert; impetuous, energetic. | 迅 Speedy, immediate (sāmadhi), cf. 師.

學 Śikṣ; to study, learn, the process of acquiring knowledge; learning. | 侶 Fellow-students, the company of monks who are studying. | 悔 Studying to repent, as when a monk having committed sin seeks to repent. | 敎成迷 To study the Buddha's teaching yet interpret it misleadingly, or falsely. | 法女 v. 式 Śikṣamāṇa. | 無 | One who is still learning, and one who has attained; 學 is to study religion in order to get rid of illusion; 無學 begins when illusion is cast off. In Hīnayāna the first three stages, v. 四果, belong to the period of 學; the arhat to the 無學. In the Mahāyāna, the ten stages of the bodhisattva belong to 學; the stage of Buddha to 無學. | 生; | 人; | 匠; | 徒 A student, a neophyte. | 者 Śaikṣa; one still under instruction, who has not yet reached the arhat position; a student.

導 To lead, indicate, educe, induce. | 化 To lead and convert, or transform. | 引 To lead. | 師 Nāyaka; a leader, guide, one who guides men to Buddha's teaching; applied also to Buddhas and bodhisattvas, and to the leaders of the ritual in Buddhist services; v. 天人道師.

廨 An official building; a monastic granary; | 院主 the head of it.

彊 Strong, violent; to force; idem 強.

懊 Vexed, distressed; regret. | 惱 Harassed, uneasy, distressed.

懈 Idle, lazy, negligent. | 怠 Kausīdya, indolent, lazy or remiss (in discipline). | 怠賊 The robber indolence, robber of religious progress. | 慢國; | 慢界 A country that lies between this world and the Western Paradise, in which those who are reborn become slothful and proud, and have no desire to be reborn in Paradise.

憶 To recall, reflect on. | 念 To keep in mind. | 持 To keep in mind, to remember and maintain.

憺 Tranquil, content. | 怕 Tranquil and inactive, retired.

戰 War, hostilities, battle; alarm, anxiety, terrified; translit. *can*. | 勝林 The grove of victory, v. 逝 Jetavana, Jetṛvana. | 達 (or 捺) 羅 Candra, shining; the moon, especially as the moon-deity. | | | 鉢喇婆 Candraprabha, moonlight, name of Śākyamuni when a king in a former incarnation, who cut off his head as a gift to others.

撿 To check, revise, gather. | 挍 To check, tally.

據 To lay hold of, tangible, evidential, according to. | 事 According to fact.

擁 To crowd, press; embrace, hug. | 護 To hug in the bosom and guard.

擔 To carry, undertake; a load; also 担. | 步羅; 耽餔羅 Tāmbūla, betel, Piper Betel. Eitel says Djambalā, *Citrus acida.*

擇 To select, pick, choose; used for pravicāra, the second of the seven bodhyaṅga, cf. 覺分; dharmapravicaya, discrimination, the faculty of discerning the true from the false. | 乳眼 The power to choose and drink the milk out of watered milk, leaving the water, as Haṇsarāja, the "king of geese", is said to do. | 力 The power of discrimination. | 地 To select a site. | 法眼; | 法覺支 The bodhyaṅga of discrimination, v. above. | 滅 Pratisaṁkhyānirodha, Nirvāṇa as a result of the above discrimination, the elimination of desire by means of mind and will.

曉 Dawn, shining, clear; to know, to make known. | 了 To make clear. | 公, i.e. 元 | Yüan-hsiao, the author-monk. | 鼓 The reveillé drum at dawn.

曇 Clouds covering the sun, spreading clouds; translit. *dh* in dharma | 摩, | 磨, | 無; v. 達 and 法. Dharma is also the initial character for a number of names of noted Indian monks, e.g. | 磨鞠多; 達摩瞿諦; | 無德 Dharmagupta, founder of a school, the | 無德部 which flourished in Ceylon A.D. 400. Also Dharmajātayaśas, Dharmakāla, Dharmākara, Dharmamitra, Dharmanandi, Dharmapriya, Dharmarakṣa, Dharmaruci, Dharmasatya, Dharmayaśas, etc. | 花 The udumbara tree, v. 優.

橋 A bridge; cross-beam; curved; lofty. | 梁 A bridge, trampled on by all but patiently bearing them, a synonym for patience, endurance.

橫 A crossbar, crosswise, athwart, across, perverse, arrogant; unexpected, i.e. lucky or unlucky. | 出 By discipline to attain to temporary nirvāṇa in contrast with | 超 happy salvation to Amitābha's paradise through trust in him. | 截 To thwart, intercept, cut off, e.g. to end reincarnation and enter

Paradise. | 竪 Crosswise and upright, to lay across or to stand upright. | 縱 Across and direct, crosswise and lengthwise.

樹 Vṛkṣa, a tree; to stand, erect, establish. | 提 (伽); 殊底色迦 Jyotiṣka, "a luminary, a heavenly body" (M. W.); tr. asterisms, shining, fire, or fate. A wealthy man of Rājagṛha, who gave all his goods to the poor; there is a sūtra called after him. | 林 A grove, a forest. | 經 Scriptures written on tree-leaves or bark, chiefly on palm-leaves.

機 The spring, or motive principle, machine, contrivance, artifice, occasion, opportunity; basis, root or germ; natural bent, fundamental quality. | 宜 Opportune and suitable; natural qualification (for receiving the truth). | 性; | 根 Natural or fundamental quality, original endowment and nature, suitability, capacity. | 感 Potentiality and response, the potentiality of all to respond to the Buddha; the response of the Buddha to the good in all the living. | 應 Potentiality and response, similar to last entry. | 教 Potentiality and teaching, opportune teaching, suited to the occasion. | 緣 Potentiality and conditions; favourable circumstances; opportunity. | 要 Opportunity, strategical possibility, or point. | 見 Vision according to natural capacity, seeing the Buddha according to natural endowment. | 語 Opportune words; fundamental words. | 關 Spring, motive force, cause, opportunity, etc.

歷 To pass through, over or to; successive; separated; calendar, astronomical calculations. | 劫 To pass through a kalpa; in the course of a kalpa. | 然 Separate(ly). | 緣對境 Passing circumstances and the objects of the senses.

澳 The south-west corner of a hall where the lares were kept; secluded, deep, profound, mysterious. | 那 Kustana, Khotan, v. 于.

澡 To bathe, wash, cleanse. | 瓶; | 罐 Kuṇḍikā, a water-pot. | 瓶天子; 作 | | | Śuddhāvāsadeva, who appeared to Śākyamuni when a prince, leading him to leave home.

濁 Turbid, muddy, impure, opposite of 清. An intp. of kaṣāya, especially in reference to the 五 | five stages of a world's existence. | 亂 Impure and lawless, the reign of evil. | 世 An impure world in its five stages, v. 五 |. | 劫 An impure kalpa, the kalpa of impurity, degenerate, corrupt; an age of disease, famine, and war. | 惡世 A world of impurity or degeneration, i.e. of the 五 | and 十惡. | 惡處 The present contaminated evil world. | 業 Contaminated karma, that produced by 貪 desire.

熾 Blaze, flame, burn, effulgent. | 盛光佛 Name of a Buddha, noted for effulgence, light streaming from every pore.

燃 To set fire to, light, burn; idem 然 12 q.v.

燒 To burn. | 炙地獄 The burning, blistering hell. | 香 To burn incense.

燈 Dīpa, a lamp, lantern; cf. 然 | 12. | 光 The light of a lamp; lantern light. | 明 The lamp hung before a Buddha, etc., as symbol of his wisdom. | 明佛; 日月 | | | A Buddha mentioned in the Lotus Sūtra. | 滅 The extinction of a lamp. | 火 Dīpapradīpa, lamp-light. | 籠; | 爐 A lantern.

燄 Flame, blaze; idem 焰; 爓 q.v. | 口 Ulkā-mukha. Flaming mouth, a hungry ghost or preta, that is represented as appearing to Ānanda in the 救拔 | 口餓鬼陀羅尼經 (B.N. 984).

獨 Only, alone, solitary. | 一法界 The one and only universal dharma-realm, or reality, behind all phenomena. | 園 v. 給 and 阿 Anāthapiṇḍika. | 孤洛加 Dukūla is a fine cloth, and may be the origin of this Chinese term, which is intp. as 紵 a kind of linen. | 尊 The alone honoured one, Buddha. | 居 Dwelling alone, e.g. as a hermit. | 影境 Imaginary or illusory conditions, ideal and unsubstantial. | 柯多 v. 突 Duṣkṛta, offence. | 生 | 死 | 去 | 來 Alone we are born and die, go and come. | 空 The one immaterial reality behind all phenomena. | 股杵; | 鈷 (杵) The single-arm vajra. | 覺 Pratyeka-buddha, v. 緣 one who seeks his own enlightenment. | 角仙人 Ekaśṛṅga, or Unicorn ṛṣi, cf. 一角, the ascetic who fell through the wiles of a woman. | 頭無明 idem 不共無明 q.v.

盧 A rice-vessel; a fire-pan; dram-shop; black; translit. *lo*, *ro*, *ru*; cf. 樓; 路; 流. | 俱多婆拖部 Lokottaravādinaḥ, superior to the world, an important sect of the Māhāsaṅghikāḥ. | 呬胝訶目多 Lohita- or Rohita(ka)-muktā, rubies or red pearls, one of the seven treasures. | 脂那 Rocana, illuminating, bright; name of a flower; perhaps also spots before the eyes; identified with | 遮那

v. 毘 Vairocana. | 至佛; | 遮佛 v. 樓 Rucika. | 舍 v. 俱 Krośa. | 舍那 Rocana, illuminating, also v. 毘 Vairocana. | 行者 Surname and title of 慧能 Hui-nêng. | 迦委斯謌 Lokeśvara-rāja, lord of the world, an epithet of Kuan-yin and others. | 醯咀 (or 多) 迦 Rohita(ka); Lohita(ka); red. | 陀羅耶 Rudra, roaring, terrible, a name of Siva, the Rudras or Maruts, storm-gods, etc.

瞖 Timira, an affection of the eye, eye-film, cataract, dim sight, blindness.

磬 A piece of flat stone or metal, used as a gong, or for musical percussion.

磨 To grind, rub, polish; a mill for grinding; translit. *ma*; cf. 摩. | 多 Mātā, mātṛ, a mother. | 下; | 司; | 院 The place in a monastery for grinding corn. | 灑; 摩沙 Māṣa, a bean, also a weight of gold valued at 80 Chinese cash; the stealing of goods to the value of 5 māṣa involved expulsion from the monkhood, as also in India it is said to have involved exile. | 牛 The ox turning the millstone, a formalist, i.e. a disciple who performs the bodily motions, but without heart in his religion. | 磚 To grind a brick to make a mirror, useless labour. | 磨迦羅 Mamakāra, feeling of "mine", of interest to oneself. | 衲 A monk's robe, a Korean term. | 訶 Mahā, 磨醯 Mahi; v. 摩. | 頭 The monk who looks after the mill.

積 Accumulate, pile up; many, long. | 功累德; | 累 To accumulate or lay up merit. | 石山 Aśmakūṭa, stone-heap mountains, the eastern border of the Gobi desert.

窶 Rustic, poor; translit. *ku, gu*; v. 求, 瞿, 屈.

窺 To peep, spy; furtive.

篤 Sincere; serious; consolidate. | 進 Toksun, "a city in Mongolia." Eitel.

緣 v. Fifteen Strokes.

縛 Bandha. Tie, attachment, bind, bond, another name for kleśa-afflictions, the passions, etc., which bind men; the "three bonds" are 貪瞋痴 desire, resentment, stupidity; translit. *pa, ba, va*; cf. 跋, 婆, 飯. | 伽浪 Baghelān, "the country west of the Bunghee river between Koondooz and Ghoree (about Lat. 36° N., Long. 78° E.)." Eitel. | 利沙鍵拏 v. 伐里 Vārṣagaṇya. | 喝 (羅) Baktra, the present Balkh, once a nursery of Buddhism and in A.D. 600 still famous for relics and monuments. Eitel. | 尼 Vana, v. 飯 a grove. | 底 Patnī, a mistress, wife, female. | 摩 Vāma, the left, contrary, crooked. | 斯仙 Vasiṣṭha, "a very celebrated Vedic Ṛishi or inspired sage," owner of the cow of plenty and able therefore to grant all desires. M. W. One of the six fire-devas in the maṇḍala. | 日羅 Vajra, 嚩日 (or 馹) 囉; 跋日 (or 折, or 闍) |; 跋折 |; 波闍羅; 伐折 (or 闍) 羅; intp. as 金剛 (杵), a diamond (club). Adamantine, hard. The sceptre of Indra as god of thunder and lightning with which he slays the enemies of Buddhism. Used by monks to indicate spiritual authority, and the all-subduing power of Buddha. | 脫 Bonds and freedom, escape from entanglement. | 臾 Vāyu, air, wind, the god of the wind; he controls the | 臾方 or north-west. | 芻 Vakṣu; Vaṅkṣu; 婆 | (or 槎 or 輸); 薄叉; 博叉; the Oxus 青河 or Blue River, one of the "four great rivers of Jambudvipa", rising in the west of the Anavatapta lake (Tibet) and flowing into the north-west sea, the Caspian; cf. 西域記 1. | 薩怛羅 Vastra, cloth, clothes. | 迦 Vākya, speech, saying, sentence, word. | 野吠 Vāyavī, the deva of the north-west, v. Vāyu above. | 馬答 An argument or reply in a "vicious circle", like a horse tethered to a peg.

興 Abhyudaya. Rise, begin; prosper; elated. | 世 The raising, or beginning of the salvation, of the world, i.e. the birth of Buddha. | 渠; | 舊; | 宜; 刑具 Hiṅgu. Asafœtida, 阿魏; there are other interpretations. | 盛 Prosper, successful. | 行 Prospering and progressing.

蕭寺 A name for monasteries in the Liang dynasty, A.D. 502–557, because Liang Wu Ti built so many that they were called after his surname 蕭 Hsiao.

蔽尸 Peśī, the embryo in the third of its five stages, a thirty-seven days' fœtus, lit. a lump of flesh. 閉尸; 箄尸; 蜱羅尸.

融 Blending, combining; melting, thawing; clear, intelligent. | 通 To blend, combine, mix, unite, assemble. | 識 Perspicacity, insight into both the phenomenal and noumenal.

衡 A cross-bar, crosswise; a balance; to weigh, balance, compare, adjust, adjudge, judgment. | 山 The Hêng mountains in Hunan, where was the 南岳 Southern Peak monastery, from which came 慧思

Hui-ssŭ, second patriarch of T'ien-t'ai. | 量 Balancing and measuring, judging.

覩 To look at, see. | 史多天 The Tuṣita heaven, v. 兜. | 貨羅 Tukhāra, "the present Badakchan which Arab geographers still call Tokharestan"; the country of the Indo-Scythians, the Tocharoi of the Greeks, idem 月支.

親 Personally related, own, intimate; family; a wife, marriage. 父 |; 母 | Father; mother. | 友 An intimate friend. | 戚; | 眷 Relatives. | 愛 To love, beloved. | 教 (師) One's own teacher, a tr. of upādhyāya, v. 鄔.

諫 To admonish. | 王 To admonish a king.

諷 To intone; to satirize. | 經 To intone a scripture, especially one suited to the occasion. | 誦 To intone, sing. | 頌 A gāthā, or hymn, v. 伽.

諾 To answer; promise; yes; translit. *na, nya*. | 健那; 荼 | |; 諾伽 | Nagna; naked, a naked mendicant; a name of Śiva; a vajra-king. | 詎羅; | 矩 | Nakula, one of the sixteen arhats. | 瞿陀 Nyagrodha. The Indian figtree, *Ficus indica*, cf. 尼.

諦 To judge, examine into, investigate, used in Buddhism for satya, a truth, a dogma, an axiom; applied to the Āryasatyāni, the four dogmas, or noble truths, of 苦, 集, 滅, and 道 suffering, (the cause of its) assembly, (the possibility of its cure, or) extinction, and the way (to extinction), i.e. the eightfold noble path, v. 四 | and 八聖道. There are other categories of 諦, e.g. (2) 眞 and 俗 Reality in contrast with ordinary ideas of things; (3) 空, 假 and 中 q.v.; (6) by the 勝論宗; and (8) by the 法相宗. | 婆達兜 v. 提 Devadatta. | 殊羅施 Tejorāśi, the flame-god, one of the five 佛頂 crowned Buddhas.

諸 The diverse kinds, many, the many, all, every; on, at, in regard to; a final interrogative particle, also a rhythmic ending; used for sarva.

諸仙 All the hermits, mystics, ṛṣi; a term also applied to the Brahmans.

諸佛家 The home of all Buddhas, i.e. the Pure Land. | | 母菩薩 v. 虚空眼 The mother of all Buddhas.

諸冥 All darkness, i.e. all ignorance.

諸塵 All the atoms, or active principles of form, sound, smell, taste, touch.

諸天 All the devas.

諸尊 All the honoured ones.

諸惡無作 "To do no evil, to do only good, to purify the will, is the doctrine of all Buddhas," i.e. | | | |, | 善奉行, 自淨其意, 是諸佛教. These four sentences are said to include all the Buddha-teaching: cf. 阿含經 1.

諸數 All the variety of things, all phenomena.

諸有 All that exists; all beings.

諸根 All roots, powers, or organs, e.g. (1) faith, energy, memory, meditation, wisdom; (2) eyes, ears, nose, tongue, and body.

諸法 Sarvadharma; sarvabhāva; all things; every dharma, law, thing, method, etc. | | 五位 v. 五位 The five orders of things. | | 寂滅相 All things in their nirvāṇa aspect, inscrutable. | | 實相 All things in their real aspect, i.e. the reality beneath all things, the Bhūtatathatā, or Dharmakāya, or Ultimate; the term also connotes 空 śūnya, nirvāṇa, Amitābha, the eight negations of the Mādhyamika school, etc. | | 無我 Nothing has an ego, or is independent of the law of causation. | | 皆空 All things being produced by causes and accessory conditions have no reality, a doctrine differently interpreted in different schools of Buddhism.

諸相 All the differentiating characteristics of things.

諸緣 All the accessory conditions, or environmental causes which influence life.

諸著 All attachments: the ordinary man is attached to life, the arhat to nirvāṇa, the bodhisattva to his saving work.

諸蘊 All the skandhas.

諸色 All kinds of things.

諸行 All phenomenal changes; all conduct or action. | | 無常 Whatever is phenomenal is impermanent.

諸見 All the diverse views; all heterodox opinions, sixty-two in number.

諸趣 All paths or destinies of sentient existence, i.e. devas, men, asuras, beings in purgatory, pretas, and animals.

諸通 All spiritual or magical powers.

諸釋法王 The dharma-king of all the Śākyas, a title of Buddha.

諸閑不閑 All in happy and unhappy conditions of metempsychosis.

豫 At ease; beforehand; prepared, v. 預 13.

賴 To rely upon, depend on; throw the burden on, repudiate. | 吒 (啝 羅) Rāṣṭrapāla, protector of a kingdom, king. | 耶 Ālaya, v. 阿.

赭 Ochre, brown; translit. *cha*. | 時 "Tchadj or Tchāsch"; Kingdom of stone or stones. An ancient place "in Turkestan on the Sir; the modern Tashkend". Eitel. | 羯 "Tchakas. A race of people near Samarkand who furnished excellent soldiers." Eitel.

踰 To pass over, or by; exceed; beyond; translit. *yo, yu*. | 健達羅; | 乾陀羅; v. 瑜 Yugandhara. | 繕那; | 闍那 v. 由 Yojana. | 闍 v. 阿 Ayodhyā.

輭 Soft, yielding, pliant, supple. | 賊 Treacherous thieves, i.e. fame and gain, which injure the aspiration of the religious man.

輸 To pay one's dues, to lose, be beaten, ruined; translit. *su, śu*; cf. 首; 室; 蘇. | 拘盧那 Śuklodana, a prince of Kapilavastu, younger brother of Śuddhodana, and father of Tiṣya, Devadatta, and Nandika. | 波 (or 婆) 迦羅 Śubhakarasiṁha, name of 善無畏三藏 a famous Indian monk. | 羅; | 那 Śūla, a lance, dart, etc.; also Śūra, hero, heroic. | 盧迦 (波) v. 首 Śloka. | 達羅 Śūdra, the fourth caste, i.e. of slaves, servants, labourers, farmers, etc.

辦 To transact, carry out; prepare; punish. | 事 To transact affairs, attend to, arrange. | 道 To carry out religious duty or discipline.

辨 Discriminate, distinguish; v. 辯 21. | 才天 One of the devas, of the gandharva order.

遷 To move, remove, improve, promote, dismiss. | 化 To be taken away, i.e. die.

遵 To comply with, accord with, obey; accordingly. | 守 To obey and keep, e.g. the rules.

選 To choose; a myriad. | 友 Śākyamuni's schoolmaster, usually named Viśvāmitra, or Kauśika. | 擇 To choose, select.

遺 To leave behind, bequeath, bestow, residue. | 弟 The disciples left behind by a deceased master. | 形 Relics of the Buddha. | 教; | 化; | 法; | 訓 Doctrine, or transforming teaching, handed down or bequeathed (by a Buddha). | 跡 Traces, tracks, evidences, examples left behind.

遶 To go round, revolve around, encompass; to pay respect by walking around the object of regard. | 佛; | 塔 To circumambulate an image of the Buddha, or a pagoda.

醍 Oil of butter; | 醐 a rich liquor skimmed from boiled butter; clarified butter; ghee; used for the perfect Buddha-truth as found, according to T'ien-t'ai, in the Nirvāṇa and Lotus sūtras. | 鞞沙 Dveṣa, hatred, dislike.

錫 Pewter, tin; to bestow; a monk's staff. | 丈 Khakkara, a monk's staff partly of metal, especially with metal rings for shaking to make announcement of one's presence, and also used for demon expulsion, etc. | 崙 Ceylon.

閼 To obstruct, stop; hoodwink. | 伽 Arghya, v. 阿伽 scented water, or flowers in water as an offering, the word arghya meaning primarily something valuable, or presentable; hence | | 杯, a golden or metal vessel to hold such water; | | 花 the flowers which float on its surface, etc.

閻 A gate, border-gate, hamlet, lane; translit. *ya, ja*; cf. 夜; 炎; 焔; 餤; 剡; 琰. | 婆度 A bird in purgatory as large as an elephant, who picks up the wicked, flies with and drops them, when they are broken to pieces. 丨 摩 Yama; v. *infra*. 丨 摩那洲國 Yavana, Yamana, the island nation of Java, visited by Fa-hsien and Hsüan-tsang. 丨 曼德迦 Yamāntaka, the destroyer; Śiva, Yama's destroyer; one of the 明王 represented with six legs, guardian of the West. 丨 浮; 瞻部 Jambu (at present the rose-apple, the *Eugenia jambolana*), described as a lofty tree giving its name to 丨 丨 提 Jambudvīpa, "one of the seven continents or rather large islands surrounding the mountain Meru; it is so named either from the Jambu trees abounding in it, or from an enormous Jambu tree on Mount Meru visible like a standard to the whole continent"; "the central division of the world." M. W. With Buddhists it is the southern of the four continents, shaped like a triangle resembling the triangular leaves of the Jambu tree, and called after a forest of such trees on Meru. 丨 浮檀金; 丨 浮那提金 Jambūnada-suvarṇa, Jambu-river gold, the golden sand of the Jambu. 丨 牟那 Yamunā, the modern river Jamna. 丨 王; 丨 羅; 丨 魔(王); 丨 摩羅; 丨 老 Yama, also v. 夜; 丨 羅王 Yama. (1) In the Vedas the god of the dead, with whom the spirits of the departed dwell. He was son of the Sun and had a twin sister Yamī or Yamuna. By some they were looked upon as the first human pair. (2) In later Brahmanic mythology, one of the eight Lokapālas, guardian of the South and ruler of the Yamadevaloka and judge of the dead. (3) In Buddhist mythology, the regent of the Nārakas, residing south of Jambudvīpa, outside of the Cakravālas, in a palace of copper and iron. Originally he is described as a king of Vaiśālī, who, when engaged in a bloody war, wished he were master of hell, and was accordingly reborn as Yama in hell, together with his eighteen generals and his army of 80,000 men, who now serve him in purgatory. His sister Yamī deals with female culprits. Three times in every twenty-four hours a demon pours into Yama's mouth boiling copper (by way of punishment), his subordinates receiving the same dose at the same time, until their sins are expiated, when he will be reborn as Samantarāja 普王. In China he rules the fifth court of purgatory. In some sources he is spoken of as ruling the eighteen judges of purgatory.

隨 Follow, comply with; sequent, consequent, after, according to, as; often used for the prefix *anu*.

隨信行 The religious life which is evolved from faith in the teaching of others; it is that of the 鈍根 unintellectual type.

隨分 According to the part assigned or expected; according to lot, or duty. 丨 丨 覺 Partial enlightenment, the third of the 四覺 in the Awakening of Faith 起信論.

隨喜 To rejoice in the welfare of others. To do that which one enjoys, to follow one's inclination.

隨宜 As suitable, proper, or needed.

隨形好 Excellent in every detail; the individual excellences of others united in the Buddha.

隨心 According to mind, or wish.

隨情 Compliant, yielding to other people's wishes.

隨意 At will, following one's own wishes.

隨方 According to place; suitable to the place; in whatever place; wherever. 丨 丨 毘尼 Vinaya, or rules, suitable to local conditions; or to conditions everywhere.

隨機 According to capacity, capability, or opportunity, e.g. the teaching of the Buddha according with the capacity of everyone.

隨求 According to prayer. Name of a deva who was formerly a wicked monk who died and went to hell, but when dying repented, prayed, and was reborn the deva 丨 丨 天子 or 丨 丨 即得天子. Also, a bodhisattva in the Kuan-yin group of the Garbhadhātu, a metamorphosis of Kuan-yin, who sees that all prayers are answered, 丨 丨 菩薩.

隨法行 Those who follow the truth by reason of intellectual ability, in contrast with the non-intellectual, who put their trust in others. v. 丨 信行.

隨煩惱 Sequent, or associated kleśa-trials, or evils, either all of them as always dogging the footsteps; or, especially those which follow the six 丨 眠 q.v. Also called 丨 惑.

隨相 The secondary states, i.e. of birth, stay, change, and death, in all phenomena. 丨 丨 戒 To follow the forms and discipline of the Buddha, i.e. become a monk.

隨眠 Yielding to sleep, sleepiness, drowsiness, comatose, one of the kleśa, or temptations; also used by the Sarvāstivādins as an equivalent for kleśa, the passions and delusions; by the 唯識 school as the seed of kleśa; there are categories of 6, 7, 10, 12, and 98 kinds of | |.

隨經律 According to the discipline as described in the sūtras, i.e. the various regulations for conduct in the Sūtra-piṭaka; the phrase 隨律經 means according to the wisdom and insight as described in the Vinaya-piṭaka.

隨緣 According with, or resulting from conditioning causes, or circumstances, as waves result from wind; also, sequent conditions; also, according to circumstances, e.g. | | 化物 to convert or transform people according to their conditions, or to circumstances in general. | | 不變 Ever changing in conditions yet immutable in essence; i.e. the 眞如, in its two aspects of | | 眞如 the absolute in its phenomenal relativity; and considered as immutable, the 不變眞如, which is likened to the water as opposed to the waves.

隨義 According to intention, to meaning, or to the right.

隨自 At one's own will; voluntary. | | 意語 Voluntary addresses, or remarks volunteered by the Buddha.

隨舍利 ? Vaiśālī; the Licchavis were the people of "the ancient republic of Vaiśāli who were among the earliest followers of Śākyamuni". Also | 邪利 and v. 梨.

隨色摩尼 A precious stone that takes on the colour of its surroundings.

隨轉(理門) The sects or teaching of adaptable philosophies not revealed by the Buddhas and bodhisattvas, in contrast with 眞實 (| |) the truth as revealed by them.

隨逐 To attach oneself to and follow, e.g. Buddha.

隨順 To follow, accord with, obey; to believe and follow the teaching of another.

隨類 According to class, or type. | | 應同 Buddhas and bodhisattvas reveal themselves in varying forms according to the need or nature of the beings whom they desire to save. | | 生 They are also born into the conditions of those they seek to save.

霍 Quickly, suddenly. | 罕; 怖捍 Ferghana, "a mountainous province and city in Turkestan on the upper Jaxartes." Eitel.

靜 Cessation of strife, peace, calm, quietness, stillness. | 主 The elder presiding over a company of monks in meditation. | 力 The power of abstract meditation. | 室 Abode of peace, the quiet heart. | 思 Calm thought; meditation, a meditator, i.e. a monk. | 息 A tr. of Yama, he who restrains, curbs, controls, keeps in check. | 慧 Calm wisdom, insight into the void, or immaterial, removed from the transient. | 慮 A tr. of dhyāna, calm thought, unperturbed abstraction. | 智 Calm wisdom, the wisdom derived from quietness, or mystic trance.

頰 Cheeks, jaws. | 車 The cheeks rounded—one of the characteristics of a Buddha.

頻 Urgent, pressing; repeated; translit. *bim, vi, vim, vin.* | 伽 Kalaviṅka, v. 迦. | 伽餅 The kalaviṅka pitcher, an illustration in the 楞嚴 sūtra of emptiness or non-existence. | 伽陀; 毘笈摩 Vigata; vigama; gone away, disappearance, a medicine which causes diseases to disappear. | 來果 Once more to be reborn, v. 斯 Sakṛdāgāmin. | 婆 Vimba; Bimba; a bright red gourd, *Momordica monadelphia*; a tree with red fruit; fruit of the Bimba-tree. | 婆(羅) Vimbara, differently stated as ten millions, and 100,000 billions, a 大 | | | as a trillion; it is also intp. as a king of fragrance, or incense. | 婆娑羅 Bimbisāra, or Bimbasāra | 毘 | |; 洴 (or 瓶 or 萍) 沙. A king of Magadha, residing at Rājagṛha, converted by Śākyamuni, to whom he gave the Vēṇuvana park; imprisoned by his son Ajātaśatru, and died. | 那夜迦 Vināyaka (Gaṇeśa), name of a demon or spirit, cf. 毘.

頭 The head; chief, first. | 光 A halo or nimbus round the head (of an image). | 北面西 Head north face west, the proper attitude in which to sleep, the position of the dying Buddha. | 袖 Head-sleeve, name for a cap. | 陀 Dhūta, also 杜多; 杜荼 shaken, shaken off, cleansed. To get rid of the trials of life; discipline to remove them and attain nirvāṇa. There are twelve relating to release from ties to clothing, food, and dwelling: (1) garments of cast-off rags; (2) only the three garments; (3) eat only food begged; (4) only breakfast and the noon meal; (5) no food between them; (6) limited amount; (7) dwelling as a hermit; (8) among tombs; (9) under a tree; (10) under the open sky; (11) anywhere; (12) sitting and not lying down. There are other groups. | 面作禮 To bow the head and face in worship or reverence, to fall prostrate in reverence. | 首 The chief monks in a monastery, known as the western band, in contrast with the eastern band of subordinates. | 鳩羅 Dukūla, a species of plant, fine cloth made of the inner bark of this plant, silken cloth.

餓 Hungry, famished, starving. | 鬼 Pretas, hungry spirits, one of the three lower destinies. They are of varied classes, numbering nine or thirty-six, and are in differing degrees and kinds of suffering, some wealthy and of light torment, others possessing nothing and in perpetual torment; some are jailers and executioners of Yama in the hells, others wander to and fro amongst men, especially at night. Their city or region is called | | 城; | | 界. Their destination or path is the | | 趣 or | | 道. | | 愛 Desire as eager as that of a hungry ghost.

餘 Remains, remainder, the rest, the other; surplus. | 宗; | 乘 Other schools; other vehicles, i.e. other than one's own. | 念 Divided thoughts, inattentive. | 甘子 Āmraphala, v. 菴. | 習 The remnants of habit which persist after passion has been subdued; also called | 氣; 習氣; 殘習.

髻 Topknot, tuft, the hair coiled on top. | 珠; | 寶 The precious stone worn in it; a king's most prized possession in the Lotus sūtra parable. | 利吉羅; 計利 (or 里) 枳 (or 計) 攞 (or 羅) Kelikila, the attendant of a deva; one of the Vajrapāṇis.

鴛 Drake of mandarin duck; v. next. | 班 Paired bands, i.e. to stand facing each other when reciting sūtras.

鴦 Hen of mandarin duck, symbolizing conjugal fidelity; translit. *aṅg*. | 伽; | 掘多羅 ? Aṅga, described as a country north of Magadha. | | 社哆 Aṅgajāta, "produced from or on the body," a son, but intp. as the membrum virile. | 俱舍 Aṅgūṣa, an arrow, a barbed weapon. | 哦囉迦 Aṅgāraka, charcoal; intp. fire star, the planet Mars. | 崛 (利) 摩羅 Aṅgulimālya, chaplet of finger-bones; the Śivaitic sect that wore such chaplets; also | 堀 | |; | 掘 | |; | 窶 | | | v. 央. One converted by the Buddha is known by this name. | 輸伐摩 Aṃśu-varman, a king of ancient Nepal, descendant of the Licchavis, author of the 聲明論.

麈 A great deer, whose tail is used as a fly-whip; the use of which is forbidden to monks.

默 Dark, secret, silent, profound. | 傳 Silent teaching or propagation, i.e. from mind to mind, without words or writing. | 擯; 梵壇 Brahma-naṇḍa; to "send to Coventry" an obnoxious monk, all intercourse with him being forbidden. | 然 Silent, without words. | 理 The principle of silence, that the absolute is indefinable, the doctrine of Vimalakīrti. | 置記 Answering a foolish or improper question by silence.

龍 A dragon, dragon-like, imperial; tr. for nāga, which means snake, serpent; also elephant, elephantine, serpent-like, etc., cf. 那.

龍天 Dragon kings and devas; also Nāgārjuna and Vasubandhu. | | 八部 Nāgas, devas, rakṣasas, gandharvas, asuras, garuḍas, kinnaras, and mahoragas.

龍奮迅三昧 A samādhi powerful like the dragon; abstract meditation which results in great spiritual power.

龍女 Nāgakanyā, a nāga maiden. Daughter of Sāgara-nāgarāja, the dragon king at the bottom of the ocean; she is presented in the Lotus sūtra, though a female and only eight years old, as instantly becoming a Buddha, under the tuition of Mañjuśrī.

龍宮 Dragon palace; palaces of the dragon kings; also | 戶.

龍彌你 Lumbinī, v. 嵐.

龍方 The dragon-quarter, i.e. the north.

龍樹 Nāgārjuna, v. 那.

龍河 Another name for the river Nairañjanā, cf. 尼.

龍湯 Dragon soup, a purgative concocted of human and animal urine and excrement; also called 黃 | |.

龍猛 Nāgārjuna, v. 那.

龍王 Nāgarāja, dragon king, a title for the tutelary deity of a lake, river, sea, and other places; there are lists of 5, 7, 8, 81, and 185 dragon kings.

龍珠 Dragon-pearl; pearl below the dragon's jaws; the sun or moon associated with the dragon and spring.

龍神 A dragon-god, or spirit.

龍種(上)尊(王佛) The Buddha of the race of honourable dragon kings, a title of Mañjuśrī.

龍章 Dragon books, i.e. the sūtras, so called because the Sanskrit writing seemed to the Chinese to resemble the forms of snakes and dragons.

龍華樹 Nāga-puṣpa; 奔那伽 puṣpanāga, the dragon-flower tree, which will be the bodhi-tree of Maitreya, the Buddhist Messiah, when he comes to earth. | | 會 His assembly under it for preaching the Buddha-truth. The eighth of the fourth moon has been so called, an occasion when the images are washed with fragrant water, in connection with the expected Messiah.

龍藏 The Dragon Treasury or library, formerly in the | 興 Lung Hsing monastery at Ch'ang-an.

龍象 Dragon elephant, or dragon and elephant, i.e. great saints, Buddhas, bodhisattvas. A large elephant is called a dragon elephant. The term is also one of respect applied to a monk.

龍軍 A tr. of Nāgasena, v. 那先; 那伽犀那; and the 那先比丘經 Milindapañha sūtra.

龍鉢 A begging-bowl formerly used by a certain monk for obtaining rain, the dragon descending into his bowl.

龍龕 Dragon coffins, i.e. those for monks.

龜 Tortoise, turtle. The rareness of meeting a Buddha is compared with the difficulty of a blind sea-turtle finding a log to float on, or a one-eyed tortoise finding a log with a spy-hole through it. | 毛 The hair on a tortoise, i.e. the non-existent. | 玆 Kuchā, also 庫車; 屈支 (or 茨); 丘玆; 俱支 An ancient kingdom and city in Eastern Turkestan, 41° 45′ N., 83° E. It is recorded as the native place of Kumārajīva. | 藏六 The parable of the tortoise and the jackal, the tortoise hiding its six vulnerable parts, symbolizing the six senses, the jackal wailing and starving to death.

17. SEVENTEEN STROKES

償 To repay, compensate; cf. 商.

優 Abundant, excessive; exceptional, extra; at ease; an actor; chiefly translit. *u* sounds, cf. 鬱, 憂, 烏, etc.

優塡 Udayana, king of Kauśāmbī and contemporary of Śākyamuni, who is reputed to have made the first image of the Buddha; also | 陀延; 于闐; 鄔陀衍那; 嗢陀演那伐蹉 Udayana Vatsa. Cf. 巨, 俱, 拘, and 弗沙王.

優多羅 Uttara. Upper, superior, higher, further.

優婆 cf. | 波. | | 塞 Upāsaka, | | 娑柯; | 波娑迦; 鄔波塞(加); 鄔波索 (or 素) 迦; 伊蒲塞. Originally meaning a servant, one of low caste, it became the name for a Buddhist layman who engages to observe the first five commandments, a follower, disciple, devotee. | | 夷 Upāsikā. | 波 |; | | 斯; | | 私柯; | 波賜迦; 鄔 | (or 波) 斯迦 Female lay disciples who engage to observe the first five commandments. | | 尼沙陀 (or 曇) Upaniṣad, v. | 波. | | 掘多 v. Upagupta, *infra*. | | 提舍 Upadeśa; | | 題 |; | 波 | (or 替) |; 鄔波題 (or 弟) 鑠. Discourses and discussions by question and answer; one of the twelve divisions of the Canon; a synonym for the Abhidharma, also for the Tantras. | | 毱多 Upagupta, | | 鞠 (or 掘) 多; | 波笈 (or 毱) 多; 鄔波毱 (or 級 or 屈) 多; 烏波 | |. A "Śūdra by birth, who entered upon monastic life when 17 years old". Eitel. He was renowned as almost a Buddha, lived under King Aśoka, and is reputed as the fifth patriarch, 200 years after the Nirvāṇa. | | 至 (or 室) 沙 Upatiṣya, i.e. Śāriputra, v. 舍. | | 離 Upāli | | 利; | 波利 (or 離); 鄔波離. A barber of śūdra caste, who became a disciple of Śākyamuni, was one of the three sthaviras of the first Synod, and reputed as the principal compiler of the Vinaya, hence his title 持戒 Keeper of the laws. There was another Upāli, a Nirgrantha ascetic. 丨丨馱耶 Upādhyāya, "a sub-teacher"; "a spiritual teacher." M. W. A general term for monk. There are various names, etc., beginning with 優; 憂; 鄔; 塢; 郁, etc.

優曇(鉢) The udumbara tree; supposed to produce fruit without flowers; once in 3,000 years it is said to flower, hence is a symbol of the rare appearance of a Buddha. The *Ficus glomerata*. Also 丨丨婆羅; 烏丨跋羅; 鄔丨丨羅.

優樓(迦) Ulūka, the owl; a ṛṣi "800 years" before Śākyamuni, reputed as founder of the Vaiśeṣika philosophy. Also 丨婁佉; 憂流迦; 嘔盧伽; 漚樓; 嗢露迦.

優樓頻螺 Uruvilvā, papaya tree; name of the forest near Gayā where Śākyamuni practised austere asceticism before his enlightenment. Also 丨丨丨(or 毘)蠡; 烏盧丨丨(or 羅); 漚丨丨丨. 丨丨丨丨迦葉 and other forms; Uruvilvā Kāśyapa; "one of the principal disciples of Śākyamuni, so called because he practised asceticism in the Uruvilvā forest," or "because he had on his breast a mark resembling the fruit of the" papaya. He "is to reappear as Buddha Samantaprabhāsa". Eitel.

優檀那 ? Uddāna, fasten, bind, seal.

優波 v. 丨婆. 丨丨娑迦 v. 丨婆塞 Upāsaka. 丨丨婆娑 Upavāsa, to dwell in, or by; fasting, abstinence; to keep eight of the ten prohibitions. 丨丨尼沙土(or 陀) Upaniṣad, also 丨婆丨丨曇; certain philosophical or mystical writings by various authors at various periods "attached to the Brāhmaṇas, the aim of which is the ascertainment of the secret sense of the Veda (they are more than a hundred in number, and are said to have been the source of the six darśanas, or systems of philosophy)". M. W. The best known is the Bṛhad-āraṇyaka. 丨丨憍舍羅 Upāyakauśalya, the seventh pāramitā, cf. 波. 丨丨替(舍) v. 舍 Upatiṣya (son of Tiṣya), i.e. Śāriputra. 丨丨羅懺; 丨婆丨叉 Upalakṣaṇa, a mark or property, tr. as 律 the law, or the monastic rules. 丨丨陀 v. 丨鉢羅 Utpala. 丨丨那訶 v. 丨婆馱耶 Upādhyāya. 丨丨難陀 Upananda, a disciple of Śākyamuni; also a nāga king. 丨丨離 Upāli, v. 丨婆.

優流漫陀 Urumuṇḍa, name of a mountain in the Aśoka sūtra.

優畢捨(or 叉) Upekṣā. The state of mental equilibrium in which the mind has no bent or attachment, and neither meditates nor acts, a state of indifference. Explained by 捨 abandonment.

優禪尼 Ujjayanī, Oujein, v. 烏闍.

優鉢羅 Utpala, the blue lotus, to the shape of whose leaves the Buddha's eyes are likened; also applied to other water lilies. Name of a dragon king; also of one of the cold hells, and one of the hot hells. Also 丨丨剌; 鄔丨丨; 漚丨丨.

優陀夷 Udāyin, to rise, shine forth; a disciple of Śākyamuni, to appear as Buddha Samantaprabhāsa. 丨丨延 v. *supra* and 鄔 Udayana. 丨丨那 Udāna(ya), voluntary discourses, a section of the canon.

壓 To press, squeeze, crush; repress. 丨沙油 To press oil out of sand, impossible. 丨油 To crush seed for oil. 丨丨輪罪 The sin of the oil-presser, i.e. the killing of insects among the seeds crushed.

嬰 Infant, baby. 丨童 A child.

彌 To shoot, reach everywhere, pervade; complete, universal; prevent, stop; more; long.

彌伽 Megha, a cloud; name of one of the bodhisattvas renowned as a healer, or as a cloud-controller for producing rain.

彌勒 Maitreya, friendly, benevolent. The Buddhist Messiah, or next Buddha, now in the Tuṣita heaven, who is to come 5,000 years after the nirvāṇa of Śākyamuni, or according to other reckoning after 4,000 heavenly years, i.e. 5,670,000,000 human years. According to tradition he was born in Southern India of a Brahman family. His two epithets are 慈氏 Benevolent, and Ajita 阿逸多 "Invincible". He presides over the spread of the church, protects its members and will usher in ultimate victory for Buddhism. His image is usually in the hall of the four guardians facing outward, where he is represented as the fat laughing Buddha, but in some places his image is tall, e.g. in Peking in the Yung Ho Kung. Other forms are 丨帝隸; 迷諦隸; 梅低梨; 梅怛麗(藥 or 邪); 每怛哩; 昧怛喱曳; 丨羅. There are numerous Maitreya sūtras.

彌底 Miti, measure, accurate knowledge, evidential. 三 | |; 三蜜 The Sammatīya school.

彌戾車 Mleccha, barbarian, foreigner, wicked; defined as "ill-looking", a term for a non-Buddhist tribe or people. Also | 離 |; cf. 蜜.

彌樓 Meru, "the Olympus of Hindu mythology." M. W. Sumeru, cf. 須; but there is dispute as to the identity of the two. Meru also refers to the mountains represented by the Himalayas, in this not differing from Sumeru. It also has the general meaning of "lofty".

彌沙塞(部) Mahāśāsakāḥ. One of the divisions of the Sarvāstivādāḥ school; cf. 磨. Also name of the 五分律 tr. by Buddhajīva A.D. 423–4. Also | 喜捨娑阿.

彌蘭 King Milinda, v. 那先.

彌迦 Mekā, said to be the name of the girl who gave milk congee to Śākyamuni immediately after his enlightenment; seemingly the same as Sujātā, Senā, or Nandā. | | (or 呵) 羅 Mekhalā, a girdle, name of an elder.

彌遮迦 Miccaka or Mikkaka. "A native of Central India, the sixth patriarch, who having laboured in Northern India transported himself to Ferghana where he chose Vasumitra as his successor. He died 'by the fire of samādhi'." Eitel.

彌陀 Amitābha, v. 阿. | | 三尊 (or 聖) The three Amitābha honoured ones; Amitābha, whose mercy and wisdom are perfect; Kuan-yin, Avalokiteśvara, on his left, who is the embodiment of mercy; Ta Shih Chih, Mahāsthāmaprāpta, on his right, the embodiment of wisdom. | | 山 Mitraśānta, a monk from Tukhara.

應 Respond, correspond, answer, reply; ought, should, proper, deserving, worthy of.

應人 Arhat, arhan; deserving (worship), an old tr. of arhat.

應佛 idem | 身 q.v.

應作 Responsive appearance, revelation, idem | 現.

應伽 Aṅga, a limb, member, body.

應供 Worthy of worship, a tr. of the term arhat; one of the ten titles of a Tathāgata.

應儀 Deserving of respect, or corresponding to the correct, an old tr. of arhat.

應化 Nirmāṇa means formation, with Buddhists transformation, or incarnation. Responsive incarnation, or manifestation, in accordance with the nature or needs of different beings. | | 利生 Revelation or incarnation for the benefit of the living. | | 法身 Responsive manifestation of the Dharmakāya, or Absolute Buddha, in infinite forms. | | 聲聞 Buddhas or bodhisattvas incarnate as śrāvakas, or disciples. | | 身; 應身; 化身 Nirmāṇakāya, the Buddha incarnate, the transformation body, capable of assuming any form (for the propagation of Buddha-truth).

應器 The pātra, or begging-bowl, the utensil corresponding to the dharma; the utensil which responds to the respectful gifts of others; the vessel which corresponds with one's needs; also | 量 |.

應土 Any land or realm suited to the needs of its occupants; also called 化土.

應報 Corresponding retribution; rewards and punishments in accordance with previous moral action.

應形 The form of manifestation, the nirmāṇakāya, idem | 身.

應感 The response of Buddhas and spirits (to the needs of men).

應應 Nirmāṇakāya response, its response to the needs of all; that of the Dharmakāya is called 法應.

應文 Ying Wên; the grandson of the founder of the Ming dynasty, T'ai Tsu, to whom he succeeded, but was dethroned by Yung Lo and escaped disguised as a monk; he remained hidden as a monk till his 64th year, afterwards he was provided for by the reigning ruler. His name is also given as | 能 Ying Nêng; | 賢 Ying Hsien; and posthumously as 允炆 Yün Wên.

應果 Arhat-fruit, the reward of arhatship.

應正遍知 The arhat of perfect knowledge, a title of a Buddha.

應法 In harmony with dharma or law. | | 妙服 The mystic (or beautiful) garment of accordance with Buddha-truth, i.e. the monk's robe. | | 沙彌 A novice, preparing for the monkhood, between 14 and 19 years of age.

應現 Responsive manifestation, revelation through a suitable medium.

應理(圓實)宗 A name of the Dharmalakṣaṇa school, 法相宗 q.v.

應用無邊 Omnipresent response to need; universal ability to aid.

應病與藥 To give medicine suited to the disease, the Buddha's mode of teaching.

應眞 A worthy true one, an old tr. of the term arhat. Also, one who is in harmony with truth.

應護 The response and protection of Buddhas and bodhisattvas according to the desires of all beings.

應身 Nirmāṇakāya, one of the 三身 q.v. Any incarnation of Buddha. The Buddha-incarnation of the 眞如 q.v. Also occasionally used for the saṁbhogakāya. There are various interpretations: (*a*) The 同性經 says the Buddha as revealed supernaturally in glory to bodhisattvas is | |, in contrast with 化身, which latter is the revelation on earth to his disciples. (*b*) The 起信論 makes no difference between the two, the | | being the Buddha of the thirty-two marks who revealed himself to the earthly disciples. The 金光明經 makes all revelations of Buddha as Buddha to be | |; while all incarnations not as Buddha, but in the form of any of the five paths of existence, are Buddha's 化身. T'ien-t'ai has the distinction of 勝應身 and 劣應身, i.e. superior and inferior nirmāṇakāya, or supernatural and natural. | | 土 Any realm in which a Buddha is incarnate.

應迹 Evidential nirmāṇakāya, manifestations or indications of incarnation.

應頌 Geya, corresponding verses, i.e. a prose address repeated in verse, idem 重頌; the verse section of the canon.

戲 Khelā, krīḍā. Play, sport, take one's pleasure; theatricals, which are forbidden to a monk or nun. | 忘(念)天 One of the six devalokas of the desire-heavens, where amusement and laughter cause forgetfulness of the true and right. | 論 Prapañca. Sophistry; meaningless argument; frivolous or unreal discourse.

擦 To rub, wipe. | 汗 To wipe off sweat.

擬 To compare, estimate, guess, adjudge, decide, intend. | 罪 To judge a case.

擯 To expel. | 治 The punishment of expulsion, which is of three orders: (1) | 出 expulsion from a particular monastery or nunnery, to which there may be a return on repentance; (2) 默擯 prohibition of any intercourse; (3) 滅擯 entire expulsion and deletion from the order.

檢 A case; rule; to collate; compose; pick up. | 校 To check, compare.

檐 Eaves, v. 𧶘 20.

檀 A hard wood, translit. *da, dan*. Dāna, a giver; donation, charity, almsgiving, bestowing. | 主 Dānapati, lord of charity, a patron. | 中 Among the patrons. | 信 The faith of an almsgiver; almsgiving and faith. | 嚫 Dakṣiṇā, cf. 達, the Deccan. | 家 A patron, patrons. | 度 cf. 六度. The pāramitā of charity, or almsgiving. | 捨; | 施 Almsgiving, bestowing, charity. | 拏; | 陀 Daṇḍa, also 但荼 a staff, club. | 林; 旃 | 之林 Forest of sandal-wood, or incense, a monastery. | 波羅蜜 v. 六度 Dānapāramitā. | 特; | 陀; 彈多落迦 Dantaloka, a mountain "near Varucha", with a cavern (now called Kashmiri-Ghār) where Sudāna (cf. 須) lived, or as some say the place where Śākyamuni, when Siddhārtha, underwent his ascetic sufferings. | 耳 v. 旃 | | Candana. | 越 Dānapati, an almsgiver, patron; various definitions are given, e.g. one who escapes the karma of poverty by giving. | 那; 陀那 Dāna, to give, donate, bestow, charity, alms. | | 鉢底 Dānapati, v. *supra*. | 陁迦阿蘭若 ? Daṇḍaka-āraṇyaka, Daṇḍaka forest hermits, one of the three classes of hermits, intp. as those who live on rocks by the seashore.

濟 To cross a stream; aid; cause, bring about. 丨家; 丨下 The school, or disciples of 臨丨 Lin-chi. 丨度 To ferry the living across the sea of reincarnation to the shore of nirvāṇa.

濡 To dip, wet, soak; damp; glossy; forbearing. 丨佛 An image of Vairocana in the open. 丨首 A faulty tr. of Mañjuśrī, cf. 文.

濫 Overflowing, excess. 丨波 Lampā(ka); the district of Lamghan.

濕 Wet, humid, moist. 丨生 Moisture-born; born in damp or wet places; spawn, etc., one of the four forms of birth, v. 四生.

獲 To catch, seize, obtain, recover, 丨得.

療 To heal, cure, 丨病.

皤 Grey, white. 丨利 Bali, the offering of a portion of a meal to all creatures; also royal revenue, a sacrifice, etc. 丨雌子部 v. 犢.

瞥 A glance. 丨地 Instant, quickly.

禪 To level a place for an altar, to sacrifice to the hills and fountains; to abdicate. Adopted by Buddhists for dhyāna, 丨 or 丨那, i.e. meditation, abstraction, trance. Dhyāna is "meditation, thought, reflection, especially profound and abstract religious contemplation". M. W. It was intp. as "getting rid of evil", etc., later as 靜慮 quiet meditation. It is a form of 定, but that word is more closely allied with samādhi, cf. 丨定. The term also connotes Buddhism and Buddhist things in general, but has special application to the 丨宗 q.v. It is one of the six pāramitās, cf. 波. There are numerous methods and subjects of meditation. The eighteen Brahmalokas are divided into four dhyāna regions "corresponding to certain frames of mind where individuals might be reborn in strict accordance with their spiritual state". The first three are the first dhyāna, the second three the second dhyāna, the third three the third dhyāna, and the remaining nine the fourth dhyāna. See Eitel. According to Childers' *Pali Dictionary*, "The four Jhānas are four stages of mystic meditation, whereby the believer's mind is purged from all earthly emotions, and detached as it were from his body, which remains plunged in a profound trance." Seated cross-legged, the practiser "concentrates his mind upon a single thought. Gradually his soul becomes filled with a supernatural ecstasy and serenity", his mind still reasoning: this is the first jhána. Concentrating his mind on the same subject, he frees it from reasoning, the ecstasy and serenity remaining, which is the second jhána. Then he divests himself of ecstasy, reaching the third stage of serenity. Lastly, in the fourth stage the mind becomes indifferent to all emotions, being exalted above them and purified. There are differences in the Mahāyāna methods, but similarity of aim.

禪三昧 Dhyāna and samādhi, dhyāna considered as 思惟 meditating, samādhi as 定 abstraction; or meditation in the realms of 色 the visible, or known, and concentration on 無色 the invisible, or supramundane; v. 丨定.

禪人 A member of the Ch'an (Jap. Zen), i.e. the Intuitional or Meditative sect.

禪侶 Fellow-meditators; fellow-monks.

禪僧 A monk of the Ch'an sect; a monk in meditation.

禪化 The transforming character of Ch'an.

禪卷 The meditation fist (muṣṭi), the sign of meditation shown by the left fist, the right indicating wisdom.

禪味 Meditation-flavour, the mysterious taste or sensation experienced by one who enters abstract meditat on.

禪和 Meditation-associates, fellow-monks; also 丨丨子; 丨丨者.

禪坐 To sit cross-legged in meditation.

禪堂 Meditation-hall of the Ch'an sect. A common name for the monastic hall.

禪天 Dhyāna heavens, four in number, where those who practise meditation may be reborn, v. 禪.

禪定 Ch'an is dhyāna, probably a transliteration; ting is an interpretation of samādhi. Ch'an is an element in ting, or samādhi, which covers the whole ground of meditation, concentration, abstraction, reaching to the ultimate beyond emotion or thinking; cf. 禪, for which the two words ch'an-ting are loosely used.

禪宗 The Ch'an, meditative or intuitional, sect usually said to have been established in China by Bodhidharma, v. 達, the twenty-eighth patriarch, who brought the tradition of the Buddha-mind from India. Cf. 楞 13 Laṅkāvatāra sūtra. This sect, believing in direct enlightenment, disregarded ritual and sūtras and depended upon the inner light and personal influence for the propagation of its tenets, founding itself on the esoteric tradition supposed to have been imparted to Kāśyapa by the Buddha, who indicated his meaning by plucking a flower without further explanation. Kāśyapa smiled in apprehension and is supposed to have passed on this mystic method to the patriarchs. The successor of Bodhidharma was 慧可 Hui-k'o, and he was succeeded by 僧璨 Sêng-ts'an; 道信 Tao-hsin; 弘忍 Hung-jên; 慧能 Hui-nêng, and 神秀 Shên-hsiu, the sect dividing under the two latter into the southern and northern schools; the southern school became prominent, producing 南嶽 Nan-yo and 靑原 Ch'ing-yüan, the former succeeded by 馬祖 Ma-tsu, the latter by 石頭 Shih-t'ou. From Ma-tsu's school arose the five later schools, v. | 門.

禪室 Meditation hall or room; other similar terms are | 屋; | 房; | 院; | 堂; | 居.

禪家 The Ch'an sect, v. | 宗; | 門.

禪尼 A nun.

禪居 A meditation abode; to dwell in meditation; a hermitage; a hermit monk.

禪師 A master, or teacher, of meditation, or of the Ch'an school.

禪律 The Ch'an and Lü (Vinaya) sects; i.e. the Meditative and Disciplinary schools.

禪思 Meditation thoughts; the mystic trance.

禪悅 Joy of the mystic trance. | | 食 Its nourishing powers.

禪慧 The mystic trance and wisdom.

禪房 Meditation abode, a room for meditation, a cell, a hermitage, general name for a monastery.

禪敎 The teaching of the Ch'an sect. Also, | the esoteric tradition and 敎 the teaching of the scriptures.

禪智 Meditation and wisdom, cf. | 卷.

禪杖 A staff or pole for touching those who fall asleep while assembled in meditation.

禪林 Grove of meditation, i.e. a monastery. Monasteries as numerous as trees in a forest. Also | 苑.

禪梵天 The three Brahmaloka heavens of the first Dhyāna; cf. |.

禪樂 The joy of abstract meditation.

禪毬 A ball of hair used to throw at and awaken those who fell asleep during meditation.

禪波 Disturbing waves, or thoughts, during meditation. | | 羅密 The sixth or dhyāna pāramitā, the attainment of perfection in the mystic trance.

禪法 Methods of mysticism as found in (1) the dhyānas recorded in the sūtras, called 如來禪 Tathagata-dhyānas; (2) traditional dhyāna, or the intuitional method brought to China by Bodhidharma, called 祖師禪, which also includes dhyāna ideas represented by some external act having an occult indication.

禪河 The dhyāna river, i.e. the mystic trance like a river extinguishes the fires of the mind. The 尼連禪 river Nairañjanā (Niladyan), which flows past Gayā.

禪病 The ills of meditation, i.e. wandering thoughts, illusions. The illusions and nervous troubles of the mystic.

禪窟 A cell, or cave, for meditation, or retirement from the world.

禪習 The practice of religion through the mystic trance.

禪行 The methods employed in meditation; the practices, or discipline, of the Ch'an school.

禪觀 Dhyāna-contemplation.

禪那 Dhyāna, abstract contemplation. There are four degrees through which the mind frees itself from all subjective and objective hindrances and reaches a state of absolute indifference and annihilation of thought, perception, and will; v. 禪. The River Jumna.

禪錄 The records of the Ch'an sect.

禪鎭 The meditation-warden, a piece of wood so hung as to strike the monk's head when he nodded in sleep.

禪門 The meditative method in general. The dhyāna pāramitā, v. 六度. The intuitional school established in China according to tradition by Bodhidharma, personally propagated from mind to mind as an esoteric school. | | 五宗 Five Ch'an schools, viz. 臨濟宗; 潙仰 |; 雲門 |; 法眼 |, and 曹洞 |; the fourth was removed to Korea; the second disappeared; the other three remained, the first being most successful; in the Sung it divided into the two sects of 楊岐 and 黃龍. Cf. 楞 13 Laṅkāvatāra sūtra.

禪靜 Dhyāna and its Chinese translation, quieting of thought, or its control, or suppression, silent meditation.

禪髓 The marrow of meditation—a term for the Laṅkāvatāra sūtra.

禪齋 idem | 室.

篾 Bamboo splints, or strips. | 隸車 Mlecchas, v. 蔑 15.

糞 Ordure, sweepings, garbage. | 掃 Sweepings, garbage. | 掃衣; 衲衣 The monk's garment of cast-off rags. | 果 The āmraka fruit in the midden, or a pearl in the mud, cf. Nirvāṇa sūtra 12. | 除 To get rid of garbage, scavenge; cf. Lotus sūtra 4.

糟糠 Dregs and chaff, said of a proud monk, or of inferior teaching.

總 Sādhāraṇa. Altogether, all, whole, general; certainly. | 供 A general offering to all spirits in contrast with specific worship. | 別 General and particular. | 報業 General karma determining the species, race, and country into which one is born; 別報 is the particular karma relating to one's condition in that species, e.g. rich, poor, well, ill, etc. | 持 Dhāraṇī, cf. 陀, entire control, a tr. of the Sanskrit word, and associated with the Yogācārya school; absolute control over good and evil passions and influences. | 持門 The esoteric or Tantric sects and methods. | 明論 A name for the Abhidharma-kośa. | 相 Universal characteristics of all phenomena, in contrast with 別相 specific characteristics. | 相戒 The general commandments for all disciples, in contrast with the 別 | |, e.g. the 250 monastic rules. | 願 Universal vows common to all Buddhas, in contrast with 別 | specific vows, e.g. the forty-eight of Amitābha.

罽 A fishing net (of hair); translit. *k, c, r*. | 利沙盤 cf. 迦 Kārṣāpaṇa. | 羅多 Kirāta. A tribe north-west of the Himalayas, which invaded Kashmir during the Han dynasty. | 膩吒王 Caṇḍa-Kaniṣka, 吒王; the Scythian king, conqueror of northern India and Central Asia, noted for violence, the seizure of Aśvaghoṣa, and, later, patronage of Buddhism. | 賓 Kubhā, Kubhāna; the Kōphēn of the Greeks; also a Han name for Kashmir; modern Kabul; cf. Hupian 護苾那. | 那尸棄佛 v. 尸棄 Ratnaśikhin. | 饒夷 Kanyākubja, Kanauj, in Central India, cf. 羯.

翳 A film; screen; fan; hide, invisible; translit. *e, a*. | 迦 Eka, one, once, single, unique. | 羅鉢咀羅 Elāpattra, a nāga who is said to have consulted Śākyamuni about rebirth in a higher sphere; also, a palm-tree formerly destroyed by that nāga. | 身藥 A drug for making the body invisible.

聰 Quick at hearing, sharp, clever, astute, wise, | 明.

聲 Śabda. Sound, tone, voice, repute; one of the five physical senses or sensations, i.e. sound, the | 入, | 根, or | 塵, cf. 六 and 十二入. | 念誦 Vocal intonation. | 敎 Vocal teaching. | 杖 The sounding or rattling staff, said to have been ordained by the Buddha to drive away crawling poisonous insects. | 明 Śabdavidyā, one of the 五明 five sciences, the | | 論 Śabdavidyā śāstra being a treatise on words and their meanings. | 獨; | 緣 Śrāvakas and pratyeka-buddhas, cf. next entry and 緣 覺. | 聞 Śrāvaka, a hearer, a term applied to the personal disciples of the Buddha, distinguished as mahā-śrāvaka; it is also applied to hearers, or disciples in general; but its general connotation relates it to Hīnayāna disciples who understand the four dogmas, rid themselves of the unreality of the phenomenal, and enter nirvāṇa; it is the initial stage; cf. 舍. | 聞 乘 Śrāvakayāna; the śrāvaka vehicle or sect, the initial stage, Hīnayāna, the second stage being that of pratyeka-buddha, v. above. | 聞 僧 A Hīnayāna monk. | 聞 藏 The Hīnayāna canon. | 論 cf. | 明, also vyākaraṇam, a treatise on sounds and the structure of Sanskrit.

臘 The end of a Buddhist year; a Buddhist year; v. 臘.

膿 Pus. | 血 地 獄 The hell of pus and blood.

臂 The arm; forearm; translit. *pi*, cf. 畢, 毘. | 卑 履 也 Pipīla(ka), an ant. | 多 勢 羅 Pitāśilā, "an ancient kingdom and city in the province of Sindh, 700 li north of Adhyavakīla, 300 li south-west of Avaṇḍa. Exact position unknown." Eitel. | 奢 柘 Piśāca, a class of demons.

臊 Rancid, rank; shame; translit. *su*, in | 陀 intp. as Śuka, parrot; more correctly 叔 迦.

臨 To regard with kindness; approach, on the brink of, about to; whilst. | 終 Approach the end, dying. | 濟 A monastery during the T'ang dynasty in 眞 定 府 Chên-ting fu, Chihli, from which the founder of the | | school derived his title; his name was 義 玄 I-hsüan; cf. 禪 門. | 齋 Approaching the midday meal; near noon.

薑 Ginger. | 羯 羅 Kaṅkara, "a high number, 100 niyutas." M. W.

薪 Fuel, firewood; wages. | 盡 (火 滅) Fuel consumed fire extinguished, a term for nirvāṇa, especially the Buddha's death or nirvāṇa.

薜 Wild hemp; translit. *p, ve, vai*; cf. 毘, 吠, 閉, etc. | 室 羅 末 拏 v. 毘 Vaiśravaṇa. | 攞 斫 羯 羅 Velācakra, a kind of clock. | 服 Hemp garments, the coarse monastic dress. | 舍 (離) v. 毘 Vaiśālī. | 荔 (多) cf. 閉 Preta, intp. as an ancestral spirit, but chiefly as a hungry ghost who is also harmful. | 陀 Veda, cf. 吠.

薄 Thin, poor, shabby; to slight, despise; to reach to; the herb mint. | 佉 羅 Bactria (or Bukhāra), the country of the Yüeh-chih, described as north-west of the Himalayas. | 健 v. 濕 Wakhan. | 地 Poor land, i.e. the world, as full of trouble. | 拘 羅 also | 矩 |; | 俱 |; | 羅 婆 拘 |; 縛 矩 |; 波 鳩 蠡 Vakula, a disciple who, during his eighty years of life, never had a moment's illness or pain. | 福 Unfortunate; poor condition due to poor karma; ill luck. | 證 Shallow insight, weak in mystic experience. | 迦 (梵); | 伽 (梵) Bhagavan, Bhagavat, 世 尊 World-honoured, cf. 婆.

薊 A thistle. | 利 耶 Sūrya, the sun, the sun-god, v. 蘇.

螺 A conch, snail, spiral, screw. | 髻 Tuft of hair on Brahmā's head resembling a conch, hence a name for Brahmā. | | 仙 人 A former incarnation of the Buddha, when a bird built its nest in his hair during his prolonged meditation. | | 梵 (志) A name for Brahmā, and for the Buddha. | 髮 The curly hair of the Buddha.

蟒 A boa, python; a class of demons resembling such, a mahoraga.

謳 To sing; song. | 舞 To sing and dance.

謝 To thank; return (with thanks), decline; fall; apologize; accept with thanks. | 戒 To give thanks for being given the commandments, i.e. being ordained.

謗 To slander. 誹 | To slander, vilify, defame. | 三 寶 戒 One of the commandments against speaking falsely of the Three Precious Ones. | 法 To slander the Truth.

講 To talk, explain, preach, discourse. | 下 Descend the pulpit, end the discourse. | 堂 The preaching hall, lecture hall. | 宗 The preaching sects, i.e. all except the Ch'an, or intuitional, and the Vinaya, or ritual sects. | 師 An expounder, or teacher. | 演; | 說 To expound, discourse, preach. | 經 To expound the sūtras.

豁 Open, clear; intelligent. | 旦 Kustana; Khoten; v. 于, 瞿.

賻 Pecuniary aid (for funerals), | 儀.

賽 Money offerings | 錢 (to the Buddhas or gods); to compete.

蹇 Halt, lame; unfortunate; proud; translit. *ka, kha, ska.* | 尼陀 Kaṇāda, | 拏僕 Kaṇabhuj, atom-eater, Kaṇāda's nickname, the reputed founder of the Vaiśeṣika school. | 荼 Khaṇḍa, candy, broken bits.

蹈 To trample, tread on. | 七寶華 Saptaratnapadmavikrāmin, the name of Rāhula as Buddha, he whose steps are on flowers of the seven precious things.

避 Avoid, escape, flee. | 死 To avoid death. | 羅 Vimbara, idem 頻婆羅.

還 To return; repay; still, yet. | 年藥 A drug to return the years and restore one's youth. | 俗 To return to lay life, leave the monastic order. | 相 To return to the world, from the Pure Land, to save its people; i.e. one of the forms of 迴向 q.v. | 滅 To return to nirvāṇa and escape from the backward flow to transmigration. | 源 To return to the source, i.e. abandon illusion and turn to enlightenment. | 生 To return to life; to be reborn in this world; to be reborn from the Hīnayāna nirvāṇa in order to be able to attain to Mahāyāna Buddhahood; also, restoration to the order, after repentance for sin. | 禮; | 拜; | 香 Return of courtesy, of a salute, of incense offered, etc. | 門 One of the six 妙門, i.e. to realize by introspection that the thinker, or introspecting agent, is unreal.

醜 Ugly, shameful, shame, disgraceful. | 目; | 眼 Virūpākṣa; ugly-eyed, i.e. Śiva with his three eyes; also the name of the mahārāja-protector of the West, v. 毘. | 陋 Ugly, vile.

鍋 A pan. | 頭 The one who attends to the cooking-stoves, etc., in a monastery.

鍵 The bolt of a lock; to lock; translit. *gha.* | 南 Ghana, also 伽訶那, solid, compact, firm, viscid, mass; a fœtus of forty-seven days. | 鎔 A bowl, small almsbowl; also | 鎡; 犍 茨; 健支; 建鎡.

鍱 A thin metal plate. | 腹 The Indian philosopher who is said to have worn a rice-pan over his belly, the seat of wisdom, lest it should be injured and his wisdom be lost.

闊 Broad, wide, spacious; well-off, liberal. | 悉多 Khusta, "a district of ancient Tukhara, probably the region south of Talikhan, Lat. 36° 42 N., Long. 69° 25 E." Eitel. But it may be Khost in Afghanistan, south-west of Peshawar.

闇 To shut; dark; retired; translit. *am,* cf. 暗, 菴. | 室 A dark room, a place for meditation. | 密里帝軍荼利 Amṛtakuṇḍalī, the vase of ambrosia. | 心 A dark, ignorant, or doubting mind. | 林 Tāmasavana, see 答 10. | 鈍 Ignorant and dull. | 障 The hindrance of ignorance.

闍 Translit. *c, j, k, g* sounds. | 世 cf. 阿 Ajātaśatru. | 伊那 Jaina, the Jains, founded by Jñātṛputra, cf. 若, contemporary of Śākyamuni. | 利 Jala, water. | 嚩囉 Jvala, shining; light. | 多伽 Jātaka, stories of previous incarnations of Buddhas and bodhisattvas. | 夜 Jaya, conquering, a manual sign of overcoming. | 夜多 Jayata, twentieth Indian patriarch, teacher of Vasubandhu. | 婆隸 Jvālā, flame(-mouth), a class of hungry demons. | 崛山 Gṛdhrakūṭa, cf. 耆 Vulture peak. | 提 Jāti, 生 birth, production; genus; name of several plants, e.g. marigold. | 提闍羅 Jātijarā, birth and decrepitude. | 提首那 Jātisena, an ancient sage mentioned in the Nirvāṇa sūtra. | 梨; | 黎 Ācārya, cf. 阿, a teacher, instructor, exemplar. | 樓 Jarāyu, a placenta, an after-birth. | 毘 idem 荼毘 Jhapita. | 演帝 (or 底) Jayanta, conqueror, name of Śiva and others. | 爛達羅 Jālandhara, an ancient kingdom and city in the Punjab, the present Jalandar. | 王 v. 阿 Ajātaśatru. | 維 A monk's funeral pyre, perhaps jhāpita. | 耶因陀羅 Jayendra, a monastery of Pravarasenapura, now Srinagar, Kashmir. | 耶毱多 Jayagupta, a teacher of Hsüan-tsang in Srughna. | 耶犀 (or 宰) 那 Jayasena, a noted Buddhist scholar of the Vedas. | 耶補羅 Jayapura, "an anc'ent city in the Punjab, probably the present Hasaurah, 30 miles north-west of Lahore." Eitel. | 那崛多 Jñānagupta, a native of Gandhāra, tr. forty-three works into Chinese A.D. 561–592. | 那耶舍 Jñānayaśas, a native of Magadha, teacher of Yaśogupta and Jñānagupta, co-translator of six works, A.D. 564–572. | 陀伽 idem | 多 | Jātaka. | 鼻多 Jhāpita, idem 荼毘.

隱 To hide, conceal; obscure, esoteric; retired. | 密 Esoteric meaning in contrast with 顯了 exoteric, or plain meaning. | 形; | 身 To vanish, become invisible. | 所 A privy. | 覆 To hide, conceal; secret.

隸 To control; retainers. | 車 v. 離.

鞠 To nourish, exhaust, address; a ball; translit. *ku, gu.* 丨利衔那 Kuryana; Kuvayana; also 鞠和丨丨. "An ancient kingdom south-east of Ferghana, north of the upper Oxus, the present Kurrategeen." Eitel. 丨多 Upagupta, v. 優.

鞞 A scabbard; translit. *vi, ve, vai, vya, bhi, bhya, be*; cf. 毘, 吠, 韋. 丨世師; 丨崽迦 The Vaiśesika school of philosophy, cf. 衛. 丨(or 毘) 侈 (or 多) 遮羅那 (三般那) Vidyā-caraṇa-saṁpanna, perfect in knowledge and conduct 明行足, one of the ten epithets of a Buddha. 丨嚧杜那 v. 毘 Vairocana. 丨奢隸夜 v. 毘 Vaiśālī. 丨婆尸 (or 沙) v. 毘 Vibhāṣā. 丨婆訶羅 (Eka)vyavahārika, tr. 一說部, a branch of the Māhāsaṅghika. 丨室羅懣囊 v. 毘 Vaiśravaṇa. 丨尼 v. 毘 Vinaya. 丨恕婆附 v. 毘 Viśvabhū. 丨殺社 v. 藥 Bhaiṣajya, healing, medical, remedial. 丨沙門 v. 毘 Vaiśravaṇa. 丨稠利夜; 丨頭梨 v. 毘, 吠 Vaiḍūrya. 丨索迦 Vaiśākha, the second month of spring, i.e. Chinese second month 16th to the 3rd month 15th day; name of a wealthy patroness of Śākyamuni and his disciples. 丨紐婆那 Veṇuvana, 竹林, a park near Rājagṛha, the Karaṇḍaveṇuvana, a favourite resort of Śākyamuni. 丨舍 (隸夜 or 離) v. 毘 Vaiśālī. 丨舍羅婆拏 v. 毘 Vaiśravaṇa. 丨跋致 Vaivartika; intp. by 退 to recede, fall back, backslide. 丨陀 v. 韋 The Vedas. 丨丨路婆 v. 毘 Vetāla.

鵂 Ulūka, an owl. 丨鶹 Ulūka, i.e. Kaṇāda, a celebrated philosopher, said to have lived "800 years" before Śākyamuni.

鴿 Pārāvata; kapotaka; a dove, pigeon. 丨園 A famous monastery said to be in Kashmir, the Kapotakasaṁghārāma, v. 迦布德迦.

點 To dot, touch, punctuate, light, nod; the stroke of a clock; to check off; a speck, dot, drop, etc. 丨化 Touched into activity, or conversion. 丨心 A snack, slight repast, not a proper meal. 丨燈 To light a lamp. 丨石 The stones nodded in approval (when 道生 Tao-shêng read the Nirvāṇa sūtra).

齋 To reverence; abstinence; to purify as by fasting, or abstaining, e.g. from flesh food; religious or abstinential duties, or times; upavasatha (uposatha), a fast; the ritual period for food, i.e. before noon; a room for meditation, a study, a building, etc., devoted to abstinence, chastity, or the Buddhist religion; mourning (for parents). 丨七 The seven periods of masses for the dead, during the seven sevens or forty-nine days after death. 丨主 The donor of monastic food. 丨僧 To provide a meal for monks. 丨堂 Abstinence hall, i.e. monastic dining-hall. 丨場 Similarly a dining-place. 丨席 A table of food for monks, or nuns. 丨戒 Purification, or abstinential rules, e.g. the eight prohibitions. 丨持 To observe the law of abstinence, i.e. food at the regulation times. 丨日 Days of offerings to the dead, ceremonial days. 丨時 The regulation hours for monastic meals, especially the midday meal, after which no food should be eaten. 丨月 The three special months of abstinence and care, the first, fifth, and ninth months. 丨會 An assembly of monks for chanting, with food provided. 丨法 The rule of not eating after noon; also the discipline of the order, or the establishment. 丨筵 Offerings of food to the Triratna. 丨粥 The midday and morning meals, breakfast of rice or millet congee, dinner of vegetarian foods. 丨罷; 丨退 Afternoon, i.e. after the midday meal. 丨鐘; 丨鼓 The bell, or drum, calling to the midday meal. 丨食 The midday meal; not eating after noon; abstinential food, i.e. vegetarian food, excluding vegetables of strong odour, as garlic, or onions.

18. EIGHTEEN STROKES

叢 A copse, grove, wood; crowded. 丨林 A thickly populated monastery; a monastery. 丨規 The rules of the establishment.

嚕 Translit. *ru, rau.* 丨多 Ruta, a loud sound, or voice. 丨羅婆 The Raurava hell of crying and wailing.

戴 To wear (on the head); to bear, sustain. 丨塔 To have a pagoda represented on the head, as in certain images; a form of Maitreya, āryastūpamahāśrī, 丨塔吉祥; also applied to Kuan-yin, etc.

擲 To throw, throw away, reject. 丨惡人 To cast away, or reject, wicked men. 丨枳多 Chikdha, the modern Chitor, or Chittore, in Central India. Eitel.

斷 Uccheda; to cut off, end, get rid of, cause to cease; decide, decidedly. 丨七 The final seventh, i.e. the forty-ninth day of obsequies for the dead. 丨伏 To cut off and overcome. 丨和 To decide a dispute and cause harmony. 丨善根 To cut off, or destroy, roots of goodness. 丨善闡提 The icchanti, or outcast, who cannot attain Buddhahood, i.e. a man of great wickedness; or, a bodhisattva who separates himself from Buddhahood to save all beings. | 屠 To prohibit the butchering of animals —on special occasions. | 常 End or continuance, annihilation or permanence, death or immortality. | 德 The power or virtue of bringing to an end all passion and illusion—one of the three powers of a Buddha. | 惑 To bring delusion to an end. | 惡 To cut off evil, or wickedness. | 末摩 Marmacchid, to cut through, wound, or reach vital parts; cause to die. | 滅 The heterodox teaching which denies the law of cause and effect, i.e. of karma. | 結 To snap the bonds, i.e. of passion, etc. | 肉 To forbid flesh; meat was permitted by the Buddha under the Hīnayāna cult, but forbidden in Mahāyāna under the bodhisattva cult, and also by Hīnayāna. | 見 Ucchedadarśana; the view that death ends life, in contrast with 常見 that body and soul are eternal—both views being heterodox; also world-extinction and the end of causation. | 道 The stage in development when illusion is cut off. | 頭罪 The "lop off the head" sins, i.e. adultery, stealing, killing, lying, sins which entail immediate exclusion from the order. | 食 To fast; voluntarily to starve oneself.

旛 Patākā, a flag, streamer. 旗 | Banners and flags, flags.

曜 Brilliant, shining. 七 | The sun, moon, and five planets. | 宿 These seven and the constellations, the celestial orbs.

櫈 A stool, bench, footstool, etc.

櫃 A counter, cupboard, bureau. | 頭 Bursar, storekeeper.

檳 The areca or betel-nut, i.e. | 榔 Pūga, the areca catechu, or betel-nut tree.

歸 Return to, give oneself up to; commit oneself to, surrender; cf. 三歸 Śaraṇa-gamana. | 仰 To turn to in expectancy or adoration, put trust in. | 依 To turn to and rely on. | 依佛; | 依法; | 依僧 To commit oneself to the Triratna, i.e. Buddha, Dharma, Saṅgha; Buddha, his Truth and his Church. | 俗 To return to lay life. | 元 To return to one's origin, enter nirvāṇa, i.e. to die; also | 化; | 寂; | 本; | 眞, etc. | 入 To turn to and enter, e.g. a religion, church, society, etc. | 命; 南無 Namas, namaḥ, namo; to devote one's life (to the Buddha, etc.); to entrust one's life; to obey Buddha's teaching. | 性 To turn from the world of phenomena to that of eternal reality, to devote oneself to the spiritual rather than the material. | 敬 To turn to in reverence, put one's trust in and worship.

瀉 To purge, drain. | 藥 Purgatives.

濾 To strain, filter. | 水囊; | 羅 A filtering bag, or cloth; cf. 漉.

瀑 A torrent, cataract, cascade. | 流 A torrent, the stream of passion, or illusion.

獵 To hunt. | 師 A hunter, e.g. a disguised person, a monk who wears the robe but breaks the commandments.

甕 Kumbha, a pitcher, jar, pot. | 形 Jar-shaped, pot-shaped; kumbhāṇḍaka, v. 鳩.

瞻 To look up to, or for; revere, adore, expect, i.e. | 仰; translit. *ca, ja*. | 蔔 (迦) Campa, Campaka, a yellow fragrant flower, *Michelia champaka*; also | 波; | 婆; | 博 (迦); 睒婆; 占婆; 旃波迦, etc. | 波國; | 婆城 The country and city of Campā, given by M. W. as "the modern Bhāgalpur or a place in its vicinity, founded by Campa"; by Eitel as "a district in the upper Pundjab". | 病 To examine a sick person medically. | 部 v. 閻 Jambudvīpa. | 風 To hope for the wind (of Buddha truth or aid).

瞿 The wary look of a bird, anxious; translit. *ga, kau, gau, ko, go, gho, ku, gu*; cf. 鳩, 俱, 仇, 拘, etc.

瞿伽尼 Godāna; Godāniya; Godhanya, also | 陀 |; | 耶 |; 劬 | |; v. 牛 The continent west of Sumeru; also Aparagodāna. | | 離 Gokālī; Kokālī; Kokāliya; Kokālika; | 迦 |; 仇 | |; 俱 | |; 俱迦利, etc. The 智度論 1 says a follower of Devadatta who was sent to hell for accusing Śariputra and Maudgalyāyana of fornication. Eitel says "the parent of Devadatta".

瞿修羅 Kuśūla is a place for grain, but is intp. as a nuṅ's skirt, cf. 俱.

瞿夷 Gopā; Gopikā, a name of Yaśodharā, wife of Gautama and mother of Rāhula, cf. 憍 Gautamī; also | 毘耶; | 比迦; | 波; | 婆.

瞿室餕伽 Gośṛṅga, cow's horn, a mountain near Khotan.

瞿師羅 Ghoṣira; 丨私丨; 具史丨; 劬史丨 name of the donor of the park of this name to Śākyamuni, "identified by Beal as Gopsahasa, a village near Kosam." Eitel.

瞿折羅 Gurjara, an ancient tribe and kingdom in Rajputana, which moved south and gave its name to Gujerat. Eitel.

瞿拏鉢刺婆 Guṇaprabha, of Parvata, who deserted the Mahāyāna for the Hīnayāna; author of many treatises. A fanciful account is given of his seeking Maitreya in his heavenly palace to solve his doubts, but Maitreya declined because of the inquirer's self-sufficiency.

瞿摸怛羅 Gomūtra, cow's urine.

瞿摩(夷) Gomaya, cow-dung. 丨丨帝 Gomatī; abounding in herds of cattle. The river Gumti which "flows into the Ganges below Benares". Eitel. A monastery A.D. 400 in Khotan.

瞿曇 Gautama, the surname of Buddha's family; hence a name of Śākyamuni. Also 俱 (or 具) 譚 later 喬答摩 q.v. 丨丨仙 An ancient ṛsi, said to be one of the founders of the clan. 丨丨僧伽提婆 Gautama-saṅghadeva, a native of Kabul, tr. of some seven works, A.D. 383–398. 丨丨彌 Gautamī, the feminine of Gautama, especially applied to the aunt and nurse of Śākyamuni, who is also known as Mahāprajāpatī, v. 摩. 丨丨(般若) 留 (or 流) 支 Gautama-prajñāruci, from Benares, tr. some eighteen works, A.D. 538–543. 丨丨達磨闍那; 丨丨法智 Gautama-dharmajñāna, son of the last; tr. 582 a work on karma.

瞿枳羅 The Kokila, or Kalaviṅka bird, cf. 鳩.

瞿沙 Ghoṣa, murmur; sound of voices, etc., noise, roar; tr. sound of speaking, and 妙音; 美音 beautiful voice or speech; name of a famous dialectician and preacher who is accredited with restoration of sight to Dharmavivardhana, i.e. Kuṇāla, son of Aśoka, "by washing his eyes with the tears of people who were moved by his eloquence." Eitel. Also author of the Abhidharmāmṛta śāstra, which is called 丨丨經.

瞿波 idem 丨夷. 丨丨羅 Gopāla, name of a nāga-king, of a yakṣa, and an arhat.

瞿盧折那 Gorocanā, 丨嚧者丨, a bright yellow pigment prepared from the urine or bile of a cow. 丨丨薩謗 said to be Grosapam, or Karsana, or Bhagārāma, the ārāma (garden or grove) of the god Bhaga, i.e. the capital of Kapiśā, cf. 迦.

瞿薩怛那 Kustana, i.e. Khotan, v. 于.

瞿那末底 Guṇamati, a native of Parvata, who lived at Valabhī, a noted antagonist of Brahmanism; his 隨相論 was tr. by Paramārtha A.D. 557–569

瞿陀尼 v. 丨伽丨.

禮 Worship, offerings, rites; ritual, ceremonial, decorum, courtesy, etiquette. 丨懺 Worship and repentance, penitential offering. 丨拜 Vandana; or, when invoking the name of the object of worship, namas-kāra; to worship, pay reverence. 丨敬 To worship, reverence, pay respect.

穢 Foul, filthy, unclean, impure. 丨佉阿悉底迦 v. 塞 Svastika. 丨土; 丨刹; 丨國 This impure world, in contrast with the Pure Land. 丨業 Impure karma, one of the 三業 q.v. 丨身 The impure or sinful body. 丨迹金剛 The vajra-ruler who controls unclean places. 丨食 Unclean, or contaminated food, e.g. left over, or used by the sick.

簡 A tablet, memorandum; to abridge; appoint; examine; abrupt, concise, direct. 丨別 To select, or differentiate.

繡 To embroider, embellish. 丨佛 Embroidered pictures of the Buddha, etc. 丨利蜜多 ? Sūrya-mitra, the sun-god.

繕 To repair, put in order, write out, copy. 丨摩末剌諵 Janma-maraṇa, 生死 birth and death. 丨都 Jantu, 衆生 all living beings; also 禪豆; 丨頭; 丨兜.

繒 Silk pongee; an arrow, dart. 丨蓋 A large embroidered canopy of silk.

繞 To wind round, go round. 丨佛 To go three times around the Buddha to his right in worship.

羂 Pāśa. A noose, bird-net; to hang, or bind. 丨索 A noose, or net for catching birds; a symbol of Buddha-love in catching and saving the living.

翻; 繙 To translate, interpret. | 梵 To translate from Sanskrit. | 經 To translate the scriptures. | 譯 To translate, interpret. | | 名 義 集 *Fan i ming i chi*, a dictionary of Buddhist technical terms compiled by 法 雲 Fa-yün *circa* A.D. 1150.

職 To record, oversee, direct; office, official duty. | 分 Duty, responsibility.

舉 To raise (a thing, matter, subject, etc.); conduct; the whole, all. | 一 蔽 諸 To raise, or refer to, one point and include all others. | 人 One who has taken his second degree, an M.A. | 動 Conduct, movements. | 家 The whole family.

舊 Old, ancient. | 住 Formerly lived there, dwelt of old. | 經 Old writings, or versions. | 言 The vernacular language of Magadha, the country of South Behar, called Māgadhī Prākrit, cf. 巴 利 Pālī, which is the language of the Ceylon canon. The Ceylon Buddhists speak of it as Māgadhī, but that was quite a different dialect from Pālī. | 譯 The older translations, i.e. before the T'ang dynasty; those of Hsüan-tsang and afterwards are called the new.

藉 To rely on, avail oneself of. | 通 開 導 (The two other schools 別 and 圓) depended on the T'ung or Intermediate school for their evolution.

薰 A fragrant plant which expels noxious influences; vāsanā, perfume, fumigate, becloud. | 習 Fumigation, influence, "perfuming"; defiling, the inter-perfuming of bhūtatathatā, v. 眞 如, of ignorance (avidyā), of the empirical mind, and of the empirical world. | 陸 香 Kunduruka, "the resin of the plant *Boswellia thurifera*." M. W.

藁 Straw. | 幹 The farmer farms for grain, not for straw, but also gets the latter, a parable.

藍 Blue, indigo; translit. *ram, lam*. | 勃 羅 Lambura; Lambhara, a mountain north of Kabul. | 婆 Lambā, name of a rākṣasī. | 宇 A saṅghārāma, monastery, monastery-buildings. | 摩; | 莫 Rāma; Rāmagrāma, an ancient kingdom and city of Northern India between Kapilavastu and Kuśinagara. | 風 Vairambhavāta, a hostile or fierce storm, v. 毘 嵐.

藏 Treasury, thesaurus, store, to hide; the Canon. An intp. of piṭaka, a basket, box, granary, collection of writings. The 二 | twofold canon may be the sūtras and the vinaya; or the Hīnayāna and Mahāyāna scriptures. The 三 | or Tripiṭaka consists of the sūtras, vinaya, and śāstras (Abhidharma). The 四 | fourfold canon adds a miscellaneous collection. The 五 | fivefold collection is sūtras, vinaya, abhidharma, miscellaneous, and spells, or, instead of the spells, a bodhisattva collection. There is also an esoteric fivefold canon, the first three being the above, the last two being the Prājñāpāramitā and the Dhāraṇīs. | 主 Librarian. | 司 Library; librarian. | 塵 The store of dust, i.e. the earthly body of Buddha, his nirmāṇakāya. | 敎 The Piṭaka, i.e. Tripiṭaka school, one of the four divisions | 通 別 圓 as classified by T'ien-t'ai; it is the Hīnayāna school of the śrāvaka and pratyekabuddha type, based on the Tripiṭaka and its four dogmas, with the bodhisattva doctrine as an unimportant side issue. It is also subdivided into four others, 有 the reality of things, 空 their unreality, both and neither. The bodhisattva of the Piṭaka school is defined as undergoing seven stages, beginning with the four dogmas and ending with complete enlightenment under the bodhi-tree. | 殿 A library of the scriptures. | 理 The Tathāgatagarbha, or universal storehouse whence all truth comes. | 經 The Canon, of which there are catalogues varying in number of contents, the first by Liang Wu Ti of 5,400 chüan; the K'ai Yüan Catalogue contained 5,048 chüan. The oldest existing canon is believed to be the Korean with 6,467 chüan; the Sung canon has 5,714; the Yüan, 5,397; the Japanese, 665 covers; the Ming, 6,771 chüan, reprinted in the Ts'ing dynasty with supplement; and a new and much enlarged edition has recently been published in Shanghai, and one in Tokyo; cf. 三 藏 and 一 切 經. | 識 The Ālayavijñāna, the storehouse of all knowledge, the eighth of the vijñānas, cf. 阿 and 八. | 通 The Tsang and T'ung schools as classified by T'ien-t'ai, v. *supra*.

薩 A character introduced by the Buddhists, used as a translit. of *sa* sounds.

薩不荅 Sapta, seven; | | | 羅 的 捺 Saptaratna, the seven precious things, 七 寶.

薩他泥濕伐羅 Sthāṇvīśvara, "a kingdom and city in Central India. The scene of the battle between the Pandus and Kurus." The modern Thanesar.

薩利殺跛 Sarṣapa, mustard-seed.

薩埵 Sattva, being, existence, essence, nature, life, sense, consciousness, substance, any living or sentient being, etc. M. W. Tr. by 情 sentient, 有情 possessing sentience, feeling, or consciousness; and by 衆生 all the living. Abbrev. for Bodhisattva. Also 丨多婆; 丨怛嚩; 索埵, etc.

薩多琦梨 Name of a demon king, intp. as a deva of great strength or power.

薩婆 Sarva, "all, every; whole, entire, universal, complete." M. W. 丨丨吃隸奢 Sarvakleśa, all the passions or afflictions. 丨丨多(部) Sarvāstivāda, the doctrine that all things are real, the school of this name, v. 有 and 一切有. 丨丨悉多; 丨丨悉達多; 丨丨曷剌他悉陀 Sarvārthasiddha, Sarvasiddhārtha, every object (or desire) attained, personal birthname of Śākyamuni; also 丨丨頞他悉陀; 丨縛頞他悉地; abbrev. to 悉達. 丨丨愼若提婆 Sarvajñadeva, the omniscient deva, a title of a Buddha. 丨丨若 Sarvajña, having complete knowledge, omniscience, the perfect knowledge attained by Śākyamuni on attaining Buddhahood; also 丨丨若囊 (or 那 or 多); 丨云若 (or 然); 丨芸然; 丨雲若; 丨伐 (or 柀) 若, etc. 丨丨迦摩 Sarvakāma, all kinds of desires; fulfilling all wishes. M. W. 丨丨阿私底婆拖 Sarvāstivāda, v. *supra*.

薩怛多般怛羅 A dhāraṇī, intp. as a large white canopy indicating the purity of the Tathāgata-garbha.

薩縛達 Sarvada, the all-giving, or all-abandoning, a name for the Buddha in a former incarnation.

薩羅 Sālva, Śālva, a country, a tribe "inhabiting Bhāratavarsha". M. W. 丨丨薩伐底; 丨丨娑縛底; 丨丨酸底 Sarasvatī, "the goddess of speech and learning," interpretation of music and of rhetoric.

薩裒煞地 Sarpauṣadhi, serpent-medicine, said to have been provided by (the Buddha when he was) Indra, as a python, in giving his flesh to feed the starving. A monastery in Udyāna built on the reputed spot. Also 丨丨施殺.

薩跢也 Satya, true, genuine, virtuous, etc., tr. 諦 a proved, or accepted, truth. Also 丨底丨.

薩迦耶見 Satkāya-darśana, the view of the reality of personality.

薩達喇摩 Saddharma, the good, true, beautiful, or excellent law, tr. by 正法, the right, or correct law, or method; or by 妙法 the wonderful law, or method, i.e. the 丨丨磨芬陀利(迦); 丨丨磨奔荼利迦; 丨曇分陀利 Saddharmapuṇḍarīka, the Lotus Sūtra, v. 法華經 and 妙.

薩遮尼乾(連陀) ? Jñāti Nirgrantha, v. 尼.

薩闍羅娑 Sarjarasa; 丨折丨丨; resin of the Sal-tree, resin used as scent or incense.

薩陀波崙 Sadāpralāpa; ever chattering, or bewailing, name of a Bodhisattva, some say who wept while searching for truth. Also the 常啼佛 ever-wailing Buddha, name of the final Buddha of the present kalpa.

蟣 Likṣā, a nit; young louse, the egg of a louse; a minute measure of weight.

蟲 The animal kingdom including man, but generally applied to worms, snails, insects, etc.; also 虫 6 q.v. 丨食 To eat as do grubs, moth-eat, etc.

覆 To throw over, overthrow; prostrate; to and fro; repeated; to report; to cover. 丨(俗)諦 The unenlightened inversion of reality, common views of things. 丨器 Things for turning off, e.g. water, as tiles do; impermeable, resistant to teaching. 丨墓 To return to or visit a grave on the third day after interment. 丨帛 To throw a coverlet (over an image). 丨肩 To throw a robe over the shoulder. 丨講 To repeat a lesson to a teacher. 丨鉢 The inverted bowl at the top of a pagoda below the nine circles. 丨面 A veil for the face; to cover the face.

謦 To speak softly; to clear the throat. It is in contrast with 咳 to speak loudly, etc.; the two together indicate laughter.

謨 Plans, schemes; counterfeit, forge; translit. *mo, mu*. 丨薩羅 Musalagarbha, v. 牟. 丨賀 Moha, intp. as 痴 unconsciousness, delusion, ignorance, foolishness, infatuation. M. W. It is used in the sense of unenlightenment, and is one of the three poisons 貪瞋痴, i.e. the ignorant, unenlightened state which is deceived by appearances, taking the seeming for real. Also 慕何.

豐 Abundant. 丨財 Wealthy.

轉 Vartana; pravartana; vṛtti. Turn, transform, revolve, evolve, change, the process of birth and rebirth; again, re-.

轉世 To return to this life.

轉大般若經 To turn over the leaves of and scan (for acquiring merit) the 600 chüan of the complete Prajñā-pāramitā; cf. 丨經.

轉女成男 To be transformed from, or transform, a female into a male.

轉廻 To return, revolve, be reborn; idem 輪廻.

轉教 To teach or preach through a deputy; to pass on the doctrine from one to another.

轉格欄 The circuit of the central Lhasa temple, made by prostrations every third step, to get rid of evils or obtain blessings.

轉梵輪 To turn the noble or pure wheel, idem 丨法.

轉法輪 To turn the dharma-cakra, or wheel of dharma, to preach, to teach, to explain the religion of Buddha. 丨丨丨日 The day when the Buddha first preached, in the Deer Park, i.e. the eighth day of the eighth month. 丨丨丨相 The sign of preaching, one of the eight signs that Śākyamuni was a Buddha. 丨丨丨菩薩 The preaching Bodhisattva, especially the Pāramitā (i.e. Prajñā) Bodhisattva.

轉物 To transform things, especially by supernatural power.

轉經 To recite a scripture; to scan a scripture by reading the beginning, middle, and end of each chapter; cf. 丨大. To roll or unroll a scripture-roll. To copy a scripture. 丨藏; 丨讀 are similar in meaning.

轉識 (1) Pravṛtti-vijñāna; knowledge or mind being stirred, the external world enters into consciousness, the second of the five processes of mental evolution in the 起信論. (2) The seven stages of knowledge (vijñāna), other than the ālaya-vijñāna, of the 唯識論. (3) Knowledge which transmutes the common knowledge of this transmigration-world into Buddha-knowledge.

轉變 Pariṇāma; change, transform, evolve. 丨丨無常 Change and impermanence.

轉輪 Cakravartī, "a ruler the wheels of whose chariot roll everywhere without hindrance." M. W. Revolving wheels; to turn a wheel; also 丨丨(聖)王; 輪王; 丨丨聖帝, cf. 斫. The symbol is the cakra or disc, which is of four kinds indicating the rank, i.e. gold, silver, copper, or iron, the iron cakravartī ruling over one continent, the south; the copper, over two, east and south; the silver, over three, east, west, and south; the golden being supreme over all the four continents. The term is also applied to the gods over a universe, and to a Buddha as universal spiritual king, and as preacher of the supreme doctrine. Only a cakravartī possesses the 七寳 Saptaratna and 1,000 sons. The cakra, or discus, is also a missile used by a cakravartī for overthrowing his enemies. Its origin is probably the sun with its myriad rays.

轉迷開悟 To reject the illusion of the transmigrational worlds and enter into nirvāṇa-enlightenment.

醫 To heal. 丨子 The parable of the healing of his poisoned sons by the doctor in the Lotus Sūtra. 丨方 A prescription. 丨王 The Buddha as healer of sufferings; also the Medicine King, v. 藥 19. 丨羅鉢呾邏 Elāpattra, the nāga- or dragon-king of this name; also a place in Taxila.

醞 A potation, or drinking; a secret or private drinking; private. 丨忘臺 The terrace of the potation of forgetfulness, e.g. the waters of Lethe. Also the birds, animals, fish, and creeping things about to be reincarnated as human beings are taken to this terrace and given the drink which produces oblivion of the past.

鎭 To guard, protect, repress; a town with a guard, a market town. 丨守 To protect, watch over. 丨頭迦 Tinduka, the *Diospyros embryopteros*, or *glutinosa*; tr. 柿 the persimmon; the 丨丨丨羅 are two fruits, i.e. 鎭頭 and 迦羅, the former good, the latter poisonous.

鎧 Armour, mail. 丨甲.

鎌 A sickle. 丨子.

鎖 Lock, chain. 丨匙; 丨鑰 Lock and key; key.

闕 A city gate; a blank, deficiency, wanting, waning; imperial reserve. | 文 A hiatus in a text.

雞 Kukkuṭa, a cock, fowl, chicken, hen; translit. *ku, ke, go.* | 園 Kukkuṭārāma, a monastery on the | 足 山 built by Aśoka; also called | 頭 摩 (or 末) 寺; | 雀 寺. | 毒 India, Hindu, idem 身毒. | 狗 戒 Cock or dog discipline, e.g. standing on one leg all day, or eating ordure, like certain ascetics. | 胤 部 The Gokulikas; Kukkulikas; Kukkuṭikas; Kaukkuṭikas; a branch of the Mahāsaṅghikas which early disappeared; also 窟 居; 高 拘 梨 訶; 憍 矩 胝. | 薩 羅 Keśara, hair, mane (of a lion, etc.), curly, name of a gem. | 貴 Honouring, or reverencing the cock, said to be tr. of Kukkuteśvara, a name for Korea. 雞 足 山 Kukkuṭapāda, cock's foot mountain, in Magadha, on which Kāśyapa entered into nirvāṇa, but where he is still supposed to be living; also | 峯; | 嶺. 狼 跡 山 Wolf-track, or 尊 足 山 Buddha's foot mountain, Gurupada.

雛 A fledgling. | 僧 A fledgling priest, neophyte.

雙 A pair, couple, twin; mates, matched. | 木; | 林; | 樹 Twin trees, the śāla-trees under which the Buddha entered nirvāṇa. | 持 The Yugaṁdhara, v. 踰. | 流 The twin streams of teaching and mystic contemplation. | 王 A term for Yama, v. 夜. | 身 Twin-bodied, especially the two bodies of Vaiśramaṇa, v. 毘.

雜 Mixed, variegated, heterogeneous, hybrid, confused, disordered. | 住 界 The world of mixed dwellers, i.e. the five species 五 趣, v. *infra*; this or any similar world. | 含 The Saṁyuktāgama, tr. by Guṇabhadra. | 業 A world of varied karma. | 染 All kinds of moral infection, the various causes of transmigration. | 生 世 界 A world of various beings, i.e. that of the five destinies, hells, demons, animals, men, and devas. | 華 (經) A name for the Hua-yen sūtra. | 藏 Saṁyuktapiṭaka, the miscellaneous canon, at first said to relate to bodhisattvas, but it contains miscellaneous works of Indian and Chinese authors, collections made under the Ming dynasty and supplements of the northern Chinese canon with their case marks from the southern canon.

額 The forehead; a fixed (number); suddenly; translit. *a*; v. 阿, 安, etc. | 上 珠 The pearl on the forehead, e.g. the Buddha-nature in every one.

題 Heading, theme, thesis, subject, text; to state, mention, refer to. | 目 A heading, theme, etc. 立 | To set a subject, state a proposition.

騎 To ride, sit astride. | 驢 覓 驢 To search for your ass while riding it, i.e. not to recognize the mind of Buddha in one's self.

駿 Laṅkā. | 迦 Ceylon, v. 楞.

髀 The pelvic bones, the rump. | 路 波 阿 迄 Virūpākṣa, the western of the four Mahārājas, v. 毘.

鵝 王 Rāja-haṃsa, the king-goose, leader of the flight, i.e. Buddha, one of whose thirty-two marks is webbed hands and feet; also the walk of a Buddha is dignified like that of the goose. | | 別 乳 A king-goose is reputed to be able to absorb the milk from a mixture of milk and water, leaving the water behind, so with the bodhisattva and truth. | (|) 眼 The eye of the king-goose, distinguishing milk from water, used for the eye of the truth-discerner.

黠 Smart, clever, intelligent. | 慧 Worldly wisdom, cleverness, intelligence.

19. NINETEEN STROKES

嚫 Translit. *kṣi* in dakṣiṇā, which means a donation, gift, e.g. | 施; | 物; | 財; | 資; | 金; | 錢 cf. 噠.

嚩 Translit. *va, ba*; cf. 縛; e.g. | 日 羅 Vajra. | 泥 v. 婆 那 Vana. | 盧 枳 諦 Avalokita, cf. 觀 to behold, see. | 嚕 拏 Varuṇa, the deva of the sky, and of the waters, of the ocean, etc.

嚧 Translit. *ru, ro, lṛ, lo,* v. 盧.

壞 To go to ruin, decay, perish, destroy, spoil, worn out, rotten, bad. | 劫 Saṁvarta, v. 劫 7, the periodical gradual destruction of a universe, one of its four kalpas, i.e. 成 Vivarta, formation; 住 Vivarta-siddha; abiding, or existence; 壞 Saṁvarta, decay, or destruction; 滅 Saṁvarta-siddha, final annihilation. | 山 As the hills wear down, so is it with man. | 法 Any process of destruction, or decay; to burn the bones of a deceased person so that they may not draw him to rebirth. | 相

The aspect, or state of destruction or decay. | 色 Kaṣāya, cf. 袈 a brown colour; but it is described as a neutral colour through the dyeing out of the other colours, i.e. for the monk's | 色 衣 or | 衲 rag-robe. | 苦 The suffering of decay, or destruction, e.g. of the body, reaction from joy, etc. | 見 Corrupt, or bad views; the advocacy of total annihilation. | 道 To destroy the truth, or the religion, e.g. by evil conduct. | 驢 車 A worn-out donkey cart—i.e. Hīnayāna.

寳 v. 寶 20.

廬 A hut, shelter, hovel. | 舍 那 Locana; illuminating; one of the forms of the Trikāya, similar to the saṁbhogakāya. Also used for Vairocana, v. 毘.

懷 To carry in the bosom, mind, or heart; to embrace, cherish; the bosom. | 兎 Śaśa-dhara, the i.e. the hare-bearer, or in Chinese the hare-embracer, moon. | 靈 Spirit-enfolders, i.e. all conscious beings.

懶 Lazy, negligent, disinclined. | 惰.

攀 To grasp, drag, pull, detain; climb, clamber. | 緣 Something to lay hold of, a reality, cause, basis; used for 緣 q.v. | 覺 Seizing and perceiving, like a monkey jumping from branch to branch, i.e. attracted by externals, unstable.

曠 Spacious, extensive; waste; wilderness; far, long, wide. | 劫 A past kalpa; the part of a kalpa that is past. | 野 A wilderness, wild, prairie.

爍 Bright, glistening, flashing, shining; translit. *c*, *ś*. | 羯 囉 Śakra, cf. 賒; 釋 name of Indra. | 覩 嚧 cf. 設 Śatru, enemy, a demon. | 迦 羅 Cakra, a wheel, cf. 斫.

犢 Vatsa; a calf, young animal, offspring, child. | 子 Vatsa, the founder of the | | 部, Vātsīputrīyas (Pali Vajjiputtakas), one of the main divisions of the Sarvāstivāda (Vaibhāṣika) school; they were considered schismatics through their insistence on the reality of the ego; "their failure in points of discipline," etc.; the Vinaya as taught by this school "has never reached China". Eitel. For other forms of Vātsīputrīya, v. 跋 私; also 婆 and 佛.

獸 An animal, a brute. | 主 Paśupati, lord of the animals, or herds; Śiva; also name of a non-Buddhist sect. Cf. 畜 生 10.

瓣 A section, or division (of a melon). | 香 Incense with sections resembling a melon.

甕 Kumbha, a pitcher, jar, pot. | 形 Jar-shaped, kumbhāṇḍaka, v. 鳩.

癡 v. 痴 13.

礙 A stumbling-block; hindrance; cf. 障.

簸 A winnowing fan; to winnow. | 臈 復 多 Prabhūta, abundant, numerous; a yakṣa. | 利 婆 羅 闍 迦 Parivrājaka, a Śivaitic sect; v. 般.

簿 Notebook, register, etc. | 句 (or 拘) 羅 Vakula, an intelligent disciple of Śākyamuni. A demon.

繩 String, cord. | 床 A string-bed.

繫 To fasten, attach to, connect; think of, be attached to, fix the thoughts on. | 念 To fix the mind, attention, or thought on. | 珠 A pearl fastened in a man's garment, yet he, in ignorance of it, is a beggar. | 縛 To fasten, tie; tied to, e.g. things, or the passions; | 緣 and | 著 are similar.

羆 A bear. | 菩 薩 The bodhisattva who appeared as a bear and saved a dying man by providing him with food; he told hunters of its lair; they killed it, gave him of its flesh, and he died.

羅 A net (for catching birds), gauze, openwork; sieve; to arrange in order; translit. *la* and *ra* sounds, e.g. 南 | S. Lāra; Lāḍa; Lāṭa, in Gujarāt; 北 | N. Lāra, Valabhī, on the western coast of Gujarāt.

羅 剎 (娑) Rākṣasa, also | 叉 娑; from rakṣas, harm, injuring. Malignant spirits, demons; sometimes considered inferior to yakṣas, sometimes similar. Their place of abode was Laṅkā in Ceylon, where they are described as the original inhabitants, anthropophagi, once the terror of shipwrecked mariners; also described as the barbarian races of ancient India. As demons they are described as terrifying, with black bodies, red hair, green eyes, devourers of men. | | 私 Rākṣasī, also | 叉 私; | | 斯; | | 女 Female demons, of whom the names of eight, ten, and twelve are given, and 500 are also mentioned. | | 天 The deva controlling these demons, who has his abode in the south-west corner of the heavens. | | 國 An island in the Indian Ocean, supposed to be Ceylon. | | 羅 Akṣara, a syllable, word, letter.

羅十 Kumārajīva, also | 什; v. 鳩.

羅婆 Lava, also | 預 A division of time, an instant. | | 那 Rāvaṇa, king of Ceylon and ruler of the Rākṣasas, overcome by Rāmacandra, v. the Rāmāyaṇa.

羅惹 Rājan, Rāja; king, sovereign, ruler.

羅摩 Rāma, delightful, joyful; also the name of a grove, perhaps ārāma, a pleasaunce, garden. | | 伽 is tr. as 入法界 entering the realm of the law. | | 印度 Helmend, a river rising in Afghanistan.

羅縠 A gauze-like ethereal garment.

羅漢 Arhan, arhat; worthy, worshipful, an arhat, the saint, or perfect man of Hīnayāna; the sixteen, eighteen, or 500 famous disciples appointed to witness to Buddha-truth and save the world; v. 阿.

羅睺 Rāhu, also | 護; | 虎; "the demon who is supposed to seize the sun and moon and thus cause eclipses." M. W. | | 羅 Rāhula, the eldest son of Śākyamuni and Yaśodharā; also | 睺; | 吼 |; | 云; | 雲; 曷 (or 何 or 羅) 怙羅. He is supposed to have been in the womb for six years and born when his father attained Buddhahood; also said to have been born during an eclipse, and thus acquired his name, though it is defined in other ways; his father did not see him till he was six years old. He became a disciple of the Hīnayāna, but is said to have become a Mahāyānist when his father preached this final perfect doctrine, a statement gainsaid by his being recognized as founder of the Vaibhāṣika school. He is to be reborn as the eldest son of every Buddha, hence is sometimes called the son of Ānanda. | | | 多 Rāhulata, of Kapila, the sixteenth Patriarch, "who miraculously transported himself to the kingdom of Śrāvastī, where he saw on the Hiraṇyavatī the shadow of five Buddhas"; a sage, Saṅghanandi, was there in meditation, and him he appointed as his successor. | | 阿修羅 Rāhu-asura, the asura who in fighting with Indra can seize sun and moon, i.e. cause eclipses.

羅被那 Ravaṇa, clamorous, demanding.

羅誐 Rāga, desire, covetousness.

羅越 Rājagṛha, v. | 閱.

羅門 Brāhmaṇa, v. 婆 | |.

羅閱 Rājagṛha, also | | 祇 (迦 羅); | | 耆; | | 揭黎醯; | 越; 囉惹訖哩呬 The capital of Magadha, at the foot of the Gṛdhrakūṭa mountain, first metropolis of Buddhism and seat of the first synod; v. 王舍.

羅陀(那) Ratna, anything precious, a gem, etc.; also | 怛那 or 曩 or 囊. Cf. 寶 and 七寶.

羅齋 To collect contributions of food; an almsbowl.

臘 Dried flesh; to sacrifice to the gods three days after the winter solstice; the end of the year; a year; a monastic year, i.e. the end of the annual summer retreat, also called 戒 |; 夏 |; 法 |. | 八 The 8th day of the last month of the year, the 8th of the 12th month, the day of the Buddha's enlightenment. | 次 In order of years, i.e. of ordination. | 伐尼 v. 嵐 Lumbinī. | 佛 The offerings to Buddha after the summer retreat, maintained on the 15th day of the 7th month; also All Souls' Day, v. 盂 8; the | 餅 annual cakes are then offered and eaten. | 縛 Lava, a brief time; the 900th part of a day and night, or 1 minute 36 seconds.

藕 The water-lily root, arrowroot. | 絲 Lily-root fibres.

藪 A marsh, reserve, retreat, refuge, lair; translit. *s, su.* | 斗婆 v. 塔 13 Stūpa. | 達梨舍苑 Sudarśana, the fourth circle round Meru, cf. 蘇 20.

藤 Creepers, canes. | 蛇 Seeing a cane and thinking it a snake.

藥 Medicine, chemicals. | 上菩薩 Bhaiṣajya-samudgata, bodhisattva of healing, he whose office, together with his brother, is to heal the sick. He is described as the younger of two brothers, the elder of whom is the | 王 *infra.* | 叉 Yakṣa; also | 乞叉 v. 夜. | 師 Bhaiṣajya-guru-vaiḍūrya-prabhāṣa; | 師瑠璃光如來; 大醫王佛;

醫王善逝, etc. The Buddha of Medicine, who heals all diseases, including the disease of ignorance. His image is often at the left of Śākyamuni Buddha's, and he is associated with the east. The history of this personification is not yet known, but cf. the chapter on the | 王 in the Lotus Sūtra. There are several sūtras relating to him, the | | 瑠璃光, etc., tr. by Hsüan-tsang *circa* A.D. 650, and others. There are shrines of the | | 三尊 the three honoured doctors, with Yao-shih in the middle and as assistants 日光邊照 the Bodhisattva Sunlight everywhere shining on his right and 月光邊照 the Bodhisattva Moonlight, etc., on his left. The | | 七佛 seven healing Buddhas are also all in the east. There are also the | | 十二神將 twelve spiritual generals or protectors of Yao-shih, for guarding his worshippers. | | 十二誓願 The twelve vows of the Buddha of Medicine are: (1) To shine upon all beings with his light; (2) to reveal his great power to all beings; (3) to fulfil the desires of all beings; (4) to cause all beings to enter the Great Vehicle; (5) to enable all beings to observe all the moral laws; (6) to heal all those whose senses are imperfect; (7) to remove all diseases and give perfect health of body and mind and bring all to perfect enlightenment; (8) to transform women into men (in the next rebirth); (9) to enable all beings to escape false doctrines and bonds and attain to truth; (10) to enable all beings to escape evil kalpas, etc.; (11) to give superior food to the hungry; (12) and wonderful garments to the naked. | 王菩薩 Bhaiṣajya-rāja Bodhisattva, the elder of the two brothers, who was the first to decide on his career as Bodhisattva of healing, and led his younger brother to adopt the same course; *supra.* They are also styled Pure-eyed and Pure-treasury, which may indicate diagnosis and treatment. He is referred to in the Lotus sūtra as offering his arms as a burnt sacrifice to his Buddha. | 王樹; | 樹王 The king of healing herbs and trees. | 樹王身 The body or form which is taken by this bodhisattva at any time for healing the sick. | 草 Medicine, herbs.

蟻 Ant. | 術 The duty and mode of saving the lives of ants.

譏 Ridicule, jeer at; inspect. | 嫌 To hold in contempt; to satirize.

譚 Gossip, talk; to boast. | 婆 Translit. of a term defined as eaters of dog's flesh.

證 To prove, witness to, testify, substantiate, attain to; evidence; experience; realize; assurance, conviction; v. 阿 Abhisaṁbuddha. | 入 Experiential entry into Buddha-truth, (1) partial, as in Hīnayāna and the earlier Mahāyāna; (2) complete, as in the perfect school of Mahāyāna. | 得 To realize, to attain truth by personal experience. | 大菩提 To experience, attain to, realize, or prove, perfect enlightenment. | 德 Attainment of virtue, or spiritual power, through the four dogmas, twelve nidānas and six pāramitās, in the Hīnayāna and Madhyamayāna. | 悟 Mystic insight; conviction by thinking, realization, to prove and ponder. | 明 To prove clearly, have the clear witness within. | 智 Adhigamāvabodha. Experiential knowledge; realization; the attainment of truth by the bodhisattva in the first stage. | 果 The fruits or rewards of the various stages of attainment. | 覺 To prove and perceive, to know by experience. | 道 The way of (mystic) experience; to witness to the truth. 教 | The two ways of learning, by teaching or experience.

識 Vijñāna, "the art of distinguishing, or perceiving, or recognizing, discerning, understanding, comprehending, distinction, intelligence, knowledge, science, learning . . . wisdom." M. W. Parijñāna, "perception, thorough knowledge," etc. M. W. It is intp. by 心 the mind, mental discernment, perception, in contrast with the object discerned; also by 了別 understanding and discrimination. There are classifications of 一 | that all things are the one mind, or are metaphysical; 二 | q.v. discriminating the ālaya-vijñāna or primal undivided condition from the mano-vijñāna or that of discrimination; 三 | in the Laṅkāvatāra sūtra, fundamental, manifested and discriminate; 五 | q.v. in the 起信論, i.e. 業, 轉, 現, 知, and 相續 |; 六 | the perceptions and discernings of the six organs of sense; also of 8, 9, 10, and 11 識. The most important is the eight of the 起信論, i.e. the perceptions of the six organs of sense, eye, ear, nose, tongue, body (or touch), and mind, together with manas, intp. as 意 | the consciousness of the previous moment, on which the other six depend; the eighth is the ālaya-vijñāna, v. 阿賴耶 |, in which is contained the seed or stock of all phenomena and which 無沒 loses none, or nothing, is indestructible; a substitute for the seventh is ādāna "receiving" of the 唯 |, which is intp. as 無解 undiscriminated, or indefinite perception; there is a difference of view between the 相 and the 性 schools in regard to the seventh and eighth 識; and the latter school add a ninth called the amala, or pure vijñāna, i.e. the non-phenomenal 眞如 |. The esoterics add that all phenomena are mental and all things are the one mind, hence the one mind is 無量 | unlimited mind or knowledge, every kind of knowledge, or omniscience. Vijñāna is one of the twelve nidānas.

識主 The lord of the intellect, the mind, the ālaya-vijñāna as discriminator.

識住 That on which perception, or mind, is dependent; the four | | are phenomenon, receptivity, cognition, and reaction; a further category of seven | | is divided into phenomenal and supra-phenomenal.

識宿命通 Pūrva - nivāsānusmṛti - jñāna; knowledge of all forms of previous existence of oneself and others.

識幻 The illusion of perception, or mind.

識心 The perceptive mind.

識浪 The waves or nodes of particularized discernment, produced on the bhūtatathatā considered as the sea of mind.

識海 The ocean of mind, i.e. the bhūtatathatā as the store of all mind.

識無邊處 The Brahmaloka of limitless knowledge or perception, v. 四空天 or 處 and |處天. | | | |定 The dhyāna corresponding to it. | | | |解脫 The vimokṣa, or liberation from it to a higher stage.

識牛 Intellect the motive power of the body, as the ox is of the cart.

識界 Vijñāna dhātu, the elements of consciousness, the realm of mind, the sphere of mind, mind as a distinct realm.

識精 Pure or correct discernment or knowledge; the essence of mind.

識藏 The storehouse of mind, or discernment, the ālaya-vijñāna whence all intelligence or discrimination comes.

識蘊 Vijñāna-skandha, one of the five aggregates or attributes.

識處天 The heaven of (limitless) knowledge, the second of the catur ārūpya brahmalokas, or four formless heavens, also v. *supra*. | |定 The dhyāna, or abstract state, which corresponds to the above.

識變 Mental changes, i.e. all transformations, or phenomenal changes, are mental, a term of the 法相 school.

識食 Spiritual food, mental food, by which are kept alive the devas of the formless realms and the dwellers in the hells.

贊 To assist. |寧 Tsan-ning, a learned Sung monk of the tenth century, author of many works, e.g. 宋高僧傳 the biographies of noted monks. |那曩 Candana, sandal-wood incense.

贈 A present (at parting), a souvenir; posthumous honours; a title patent. |五重 A service of the Pure-land sect, consisting of five esoteric rituals, for admitting the deceased into the lineage of the Buddha to ensure his welfare in the next life. |別夜 The night (of ceremony) before a funeral.

辭 A phrase, words, language; to decline, resign. |無礙智 Unhindered knowledge of all languages or terms.

邊 A side, edge, margin, border. |地 The countries bordering on Jambudvīpa. The border land to Amitābha's Pure Land, where the lax and haughty, cf. 懈慢, are detained for 500 years, also called 胎宮 womb-palace, and |界 border-realm. |州 The countries bordering on, or outside of India. |獄 The side hells, or lokāntarika hells. |罪 Sins of expulsion from the order, i.e. sexual intercourse, killing, stealing, lying. |見; |執見 The two extreme views of annihilation and personal immortality. |際 Utmost limit, ultimate, final. |際智 The perfect wisdom of a bodhisattva who has attained complete enlightenment.

醮 Libations or offerings, especially to ancestors; the offerings of All Souls' Day, v. 盂 8; emptied, finished.

醯 Pickle. Translit. *hi*; *he*, *hai*. |兜婆拖部 Hetuvādapūrva Sthavirāḥ, the first school of the Sthavirās treating of causality, or hetuvāda, the 因論 school; it was a subdivision of the Sarvāstivādāḥ. |摩嚩多; | |跋陀 A ruler of the

Himālayas, in the retinue of Vaiśravaṇa, v. 毘. | | | 多部 Haimavatāḥ, school of the snow mountains, "a schismatic philosophical school, one of the five subdivisions" of the Māhāsaṅghikāḥ. Eitel. | 羅 Hiḍḍa, five miles south of Jellālabad. Eitel. | 都 Hetu, a cause, logical reason. | | 費陀 Hetuvidyā, 因明, logic. | | 鉢羅底也 Hetu-pratyaya, primary and secondary cause.

鏡 Ādarśa. A mirror. | 像 The image in a mirror, i.e. the transient. | 谷 Mirror and gully, reflection and echo, i.e. the response of the Buddhas to prayers.

鏧 A metal chime.

關 To shut, a closed place, barrier, frontier; to include, concern, involve. | 帝 Kuan Ti, the god of War, a deified hero of the Three Kingdoms, a protector of Buddhism.

難 Difficult, hard; distress, adversity; opposite of 易 easy; translit. *nan*, *nam*. | 伏 Hard to subdue, or submit; unconquerable. | 入 Hard to enter, or attain. | 勝 Hard to overcome, or be overcome; unconquerable; the fifth of the ten bodhisattva 地 stages when all passion and illusion is overcome and understanding of all things attained. | 化 Difficult of conversion, or transformation. | 度 Hard to cross over, to save or be saved. | 度海 The ocean hard to cross, the sea of life and death, or mortality. | 思 Hard to think of, hard to realize, incredible. | 拏 Daṇḍa, 檀 |; a club, mace, Yama's symbol. | 提 Nandi, "the happy one," name of Viṣṇu, Śiva, and of a Buddhist monk; also said to be a term for stūpa. | 提迦 Nandika, brother of 調達 Devadatta. | 提迦物多 Nandikāvarta; nandyāvarta; joyous, or auspicious turning; defined as turning to the right, i.e. curling as a Buddha's hair. | 有 Hard to have, similar to 希有, rare. | 陀; | 陁 Nanda, "happiness, pleasure, joy, felicity." M. W. Name of disciples not easy to discriminate; one is called Cowherd Nanda, an arhat; another Sundarananda, to distinguish him from Ānanda, and the above; also, of a milkman who gave Śākyamuni milk; of a poor woman who could only offer a cash to buy oil for a lamp to Buddha; of a Nāga king; etc. | 陀跋難陀 Nanda Upananda, two nāga brothers, who protected Magadha.

離 To leave, part from, apart from, abandon; translit. *li*, *le*, *r*, *re*, *rai*. | 佉 Likh, to write; lekha, writings, documents. | 垢 To leave the impure, abandon the defiling influence of the passions, or illusion. | 垢世界 The world free from impurity, the name of Śāriputra's Buddha-realm. | 垢地 The second of the ten bodhisattva stages in which he overcomes all passion and impurity. | 垢眼 To abandon the eye of impurity, or contamination, and attain the eye which beholds truth and reality. | 塵服 The monk's robe, or kaṣāya, freed from the dusty world, i.e. free from the contamination of the senses. | 婆多; | 波 |; | 越; | 曰; 梨婆多 Revata; one of the twenty-eight Indian constellations, corresponding with 室 the "house", (*a*) Markab, (*b*) Scheat, Pegasus; name of a disciple of Śākyamuni; of the leader of the second synod; of a member of the third synod; cf. 頡. | 微 Apart from all the phenomenal; *li* is intp. as spirit, *wei* as its subtle, mysterious functioning; *li* is also intp. as nirvāṇa in character, *wei* as prajñā, or intelligence, knowledge, discrimination. | 性無別佛 Apart from mind, or the soul, there is no other Buddha, i.e. the 性 is Buddha. | 染服 The monk's robe which separates him from contamination; also the nun's. | 欲 To leave, or be free from desire, or the passions. | 生 To leave the chain of rebirth. | 生性 The true nature of the holy man which leaves the round of mortality. | 生喜樂地 The first dhyāna heaven, where is experienced the joy of leaving the evils of life. | 相 One of the 三相 q.v. | 相戒; 無相戒 The inner commands, or observance in the heart, in contrast with external observance or ritual. | 繫子 The Nirgrantha sect of naked devotees who abandoned all ties and forms. | 蓋 To abandon the 五蓋 q.v. five obscurers, or hindrances to truth. | 言 That which cannot be described in words, e.g. the bhūtatathatā, which is beyond definition. | 車(毘); | 奢; 利車; 梨車毘; 隷車; 黎昌; 栗唱; 栗呫婆 or 毘. Licchavi, the kṣatriyas who formed the republic of Vaiśālī, and were "among the earliest followers of Śākyamuni". Eitel. The term is intp. as 皮薄 thin-skinned, or 豪 heroic, etc. | 間語 Talk which causes estrangement between friends; alienating words; one of the ten wicked things.

類 Class, species; to classify. | 智 Knowledge which is of the same order, e.g. the four fundamental dogmas (四諦 or 法智) applicable on earth which are also extended to the higher realms of form and non-form and are called | 智.

顚 Overturn, upset, upside down; the forehead, top. | 倒 Viparyaya; error. Upside down, inverted; contrary to reality; to believe things to be as they seem to be, e.g. the impermanent to be permanent, the apparent ego to be real; cf. 七 and 八 | |. | | 忘想 Upside-down and delusive ideas.

願 Praṇihita; praṇidhāna; resolve, will, desire, cf. 誓. | 主 The original resolve in a previous existence which incites a man to build a pagoda, copy a sūtra, etc., leading him to become Buddha or reach the Pure Land. | 佛 A Buddha of the vow, who passes through the eight forms of an incarnate Buddha, v. 八 相. | 作 Resolve to be or become, e.g. | 作 佛 resolve to become Buddha. | 力 The power of the vow. | 土 The land of the vow, the Pure Land of Amitābha. | 度 Salvation through trust in the vow, e.g. of Amitābha. | 心 The heart of resolve (of Buddha to save all beings). | 智 Wisdom resulting from the vow. | 波 羅 蜜 The vow pāramitā, the eighth of the ten pāramitās, a bodhisattva's vow to attain bodhi, and save all beings to the other shore. | 海 The Bodhisattva vow is deep and wide like the ocean. | 船 The Amitābha's vow likened to a boat which ferries all beings to his Pure Land. | 行 To vow and perform the discipline the vow involves. | 身 The resolve of a Buddha to be born in the Tuṣita heaven for the work of saving all beings, also idem | 佛 *supra.* | 輪 The vow-wheel, which overcomes all opposition; also the revolving of the bodhisattva's life around his vow. | 食 Vow-food; to nourish the life by the vow, and thus have strength to fulfil its duties.

鯨 A whale. | 魚 Makara, sea-monster, whale. | 音 A reverberating sound,–like that of a bell, or gong.

鵲 A magpie; jay, daw. | 巢 A magpie's nest, sometimes applied to a place of meditation. | 園 Magpie garden, applied to the Veṇuvana, v. 竹 林.

麗 Elegant, beautiful; to display. | 塔 An elegant pagoda. | 掣 毘 Licchavi, v. 離, 梨. | 藏 The Korean Tripiṭaka. 高 | Korea.

20. TWENTY STROKES

勸 To exhort, persuade, admonish. | 化 To exhort to conversion, to convert. | 發 To exhort to start (in the Buddhist way). | 誡 Exhortation and prohibition; to exhort and admonish; exhort to be good and forbid the doing of evil. | 轉 The second, or exhortation turn of the Buddha's wheel, v. 三 轉 法 輪, men must know the meaning and cause of suffering, cut off its accumulation, realize that it may be extinguished, and follow the eightfold path to attainment. | 門 The method of exhortation or persuasion, in contrast with prohibition or command.

嚴 Commanding, strict, awe-inspiring, glorious. For 華 | v. Twelve Strokes. | 淨 Glorious and pure, gloriously pure. | 王, i.e. 妙 莊 王 in the Lotus sūtra. | 飾 Gloriously adorned.

孽 Retribution; an illicit son; son of a concubine. 罪 | Sins, crimes.

寶 Ratna, precious, a treasure, gem, pearl, anything valuable; for saptaratna, v. 七 |. Also maṇi, a pearl, gem.

寶 乘 The precious vehicle of the Lotus sūtra; the Mahāyāna.

寶 光 天 子 Precious light deva, Sūrya-deva, the sun-prince, a manifestation of Kuan-yin. | | 明 池 A lake in Magadha, where the Buddha is said to have preached.

寶 典 The precious records, or scriptures.

寶 剎 The precious kṣetra, or Buddha-realm; a monastery.

寶 勝 Ratnaketu, one of the seven Tathāgatas; also said to be a name for | 生 q.v.

寶 印 Precious seal, or symbol. (1) The second of the Triratna, i.e. 法 寶. (2) The three evidences of the genuineness of a sūtra, v. 三 法 印. (3) The symbols of Buddhas, or bodhisattvas. (4) Their magical 種 子, i.e. germ-letters, or sounds. | | 三 昧 The ratnamudrā samādhi, in which are realized the unreality of the ego, the impermanence of all things, and nirvāṇa.

寶 吉 祥 天 Deva of the precious omen, i.e. Candradeva, deva of the moon, a manifestation of Mahāsthāmaprāpta.

寶 國 Precious country, the Pure Land.

寶 坊 Precious place, or the abode of the Triratna, a monastery. 大 寶 坊 is the place between the desire-world and the form-world where Buddha expounded the 大集經.

寶城 The city full of precious things, in the Nirvāṇa sūtra, i.e. the teaching of the Buddha.

寶塔 A stūpa, or fane for precious things, or relics; a pagoda adorned with gems; the shrine of 多寶 Prabhūtaratna in the Lotus sūtra.

寶女 Kanyā-ratna; precious maidens, one of the seven treasures of the Cakravartin; also 玉女.

寶幢 Ratnadhvaja; a banner decorated with gems. A deva in the Tuṣita heaven who presides over music.

寶性 The precious nature, or Tathāgatagarbha, underlying all phenomena, always pure despite phenomenal conditions.

寶悉底迦 The precious svastika, or sign on Buddha's breast.

寶手 Precious hand, the hand which gives alms and precious things.

寶所 The place of precious things, i.e. the perfect Nirvāṇa.

寶林 The groves, or avenues of precious trees (in the Pure Land). The monastery of Hui-nêng, sixth patriarch of the Ch'an sect, in 韶州典江縣 Tien-chiang Hsien, Shao Chou, Kwangtung, cf. 慧 15. The | | 傳 and supplement contain the teachings of this school.

寶樹 The jewel-trees (of the Pure Land).

寶池 The precious lake of the eight virtuous characteristics in the Pure Land.

寶沙麼洗 Pauṣamāsa, the tenth Indian month, "beginning on the 16th day of the 12th Chinese month." Eitel.

寶洲 The precious continent, or wonderful land of a Buddha.

寶渚 Ratnadvīpa; precious islet, island of pearls or gems; synonym for perfect nirvāṇa; also an old name for Ceylon. (Eitel.)

寶王 The Precious King, or King of Treasures, a title of Buddha; the ruler of the continent west of Sumeru, also called 寶主 Jewel-lord, or Lord of jewels. | 王三昧 The King of Treasures samādhi, achieved by fixing the mind on Buddha.

寶珠 Maṇi, a precious pearl, or gem; a talisman; a symbol of Śāriputra.

寶瓶 Kuṇḍikā, a precious vase, vessels used in worship; a baptismal vase used by the esoteric sects for pouring water on the head.

寶生 Ratnasaṁbhava, one of the five Dhyāni-Buddhas, the central figure in the southern "diamond" maṇḍala. The realm of Subhūti on his becoming Buddha.

寶界 The saptaratna realm of every Buddha, his Pure Land.

寶相 The precious likeness, or image (of Buddha). Ratnaketu, one of the seven Tathāgatas; a name of Ānanda as a future Buddha; the name under which 2,000 of Śākyamuni's disciples are to be reborn as Buddhas.

寶積 Ratna-rāśi, or ratna-kūṭa. Gem-heap; collection of gems; accumulated treasures. | | 三昧 The samādhi by which the origin and end of all things are seen. | | 佛 Buddha adorned with heaps of treasures, i.e. powers, truths, etc. | | 經 v. 大 | | |. | | 長者子 The sons of the elders of Vaiśālī, who are said to have offered canopies of the seven precious things to Śākyamuni in praise of his teaching.

寶筏 The precious raft of Buddha-truth, which ferries over the sea of mortality to nirvāṇa.

寶篋 Ratna-piṭaka, or Ratna-karaṇḍaka; a precious box, or box of precious things.

寶網 Indra's net of gems; also 帝網; 因陀羅網.

寶聚 Jewel-collection; a collection of precious things, e.g. the Buddhist religion.

寶華 Precious flowers, deva-flowers.

寶蓋 A canopy above an image or dais, decorated with gems.

寶藏 The treasury of precious things, the wonderful religion of Buddha. | | 如來 Ratnagarbha; a Buddha to whom Śākyamuni and Amitābha are said to have owed their awakening.

寶處三昧 The samādhi of the precious place, the ecstatic trance of Śākyamuni by which he dispensed powers and riches to all beings.

寶號 Precious name or title, especially that of Buddhas and bodhisattvas.

寶車 The precious cart (in the Lotus sūtra), i.e. the one vehicle, the Mahāyāna.

寶鐸 Bells hung on pagodas, etc.; also 風 |; 簷 |.

寶陀巖 Potalaka, the abode of Kuan-yin, v. 補.

寶雲 Pao-yün, a monk of 涼州 Liang-chou, who travelled to India, *circa* A.D. 397, returned to Ch'ang-an, and died 449 aged 74.

懸 Suspend, hang. | 曠 Hanging and wide-spread, e.g. sun and sky, the mystery and extensiveness (or all-embracing character of Buddha-truth). | 記 Prophecy; to prophesy. | 談 A foreword, or introduction, to a discourse on a scripture, outlining the main ideas; also 玄 |.

懺 Kṣamayati, "to ask pardon"; to seek forgiveness, patience or indulgence, kṣamā meaning patience, forbearance, tr. as 悔過 repentance, or regret for error; also as confession. It especially refers to the regular confessional service for monks and for nuns. | 儀 The rules for confession and pardon. | 悔 Ch'an is the translit. of Kṣamā, 悔 its translation, i.e. repentance; but also the first is intp. as confession, cf. 提 deśanā, the second as repentance and reform. | 摩; 叉磨 Kṣama, kṣamayati, v. *supra*; to forbear, have patience with; ask for consideration, or pardon. | 摩衣 Clothing made of kṣauma, i.e. wild flax. | 法 The mode of action, or ritual, at the confessional; also the various types of confessional, e.g. that of Kuan-yin, Amitābha, etc. | 除 Confession and forgiveness.

爐 A stove, fireplace, censer. | 壇 A fire-altar.

獻 To offer up, present. | 身 To offer up one's body as a sacrifice.

獼 Markaṭa, | 猴 a monkey, typical of the mind of illusion, pictured as trying to pluck the moon out of the water; also of the five desires; of foolishness; of restlessness. | | 地; | | 江 The place in Vaiśālī where Buddha preached.

癢 To itch. | 和子 A back-scratcher; a term for 如意, a ceremonial sceptre, a talisman.

競 To wrangle, emulate. | 伽 v. 恒河. Gaṅgā, the Ganges, | | 河門 Gaṅgādvāra, the gate of the Ganges. "A famous devālaya, the object of pilgrimages, the present Hurdwar," or Haridwar. Eitel.

籌 To calculate, devise, plan; a tally. | 量 Reckoning, to reckon and measure.

繼 To continue, inherit, adopt, 相 |; | 嗣.

辮 To plait, a plait, queue. | 髮 To plait the hair.

臛臛婆 The third of the cold hells, where the sinner's tongue is so cold that he can only utter the word Ho-ho-p'o or Apapa. Also 嚯嚯婆, 阿波波.

藹 Luxuriant, graceful; translit. *ai*. | 吉 (支) v. 毘; idem vetāla. | 羅筏拏 Airāvaṇa, a king of the nāgas; Indra's elephant; also elāpattra, v. 伊.

藿 Greens, bean-stalks, etc.; bishopwort, a kind of mint; the Tamāla, 多摩羅 (跋) *Xanthochymus pictorius*, *Laurus cassia*, and other odoriferous shrubs. | 香 A scent from the above.

蘆 Reeds, rushes. | 葉達磨 Bodhidharma and his rush-leaf boat in which he is said to have crossed the Yangtse.

蘊 Skandha, v. 塞; older tr. 陰, intp. as that which covers or conceals, implying that physical and mental forms obstruct realization of the truth; while the tr. 蘊, implying an accumulation or heap, is a nearer connotation to Skandha, which, originally meaning the shoulder, becomes stem, branch, combination, the objects of sense, the elements of being or mundane consciousness. The term is intp. as the five physical and mental constituents, which combine to form the intelligent 性 or nature; rūpa, the first of the five, is considered as physical, the remaining four as mental; v. 五 |. The skandhas refer only to the phenomenal, not to the 無為 non-phenomenal. | 落 Any unit, or body, consisting of skandhas. | 處界 The five skandhas, twelve 處 āyatana or bases, and eighteen 界 dhātu or elements. | 識 The skandha of intelligence, or intellectuation; also intp. as 有情 consciousness, or emotion. | 馱南 Udāna, v. 優, an expression of joy, or praise; voluntary addresses (by the Buddha). | 魔 The evil spirit (or spirits) that works (or work) through the five skandhas.

蘇 Refreshing thyme; revive, cheer; Soochow; translit. *su, so, sa, s*. Most frequently it translit. the Sanskrit *su*, which means good, well, excellent, very. Cf. 須, 修.

蘇伐刺 Suvarṇa, gold, v. 金; also | | 羅; | 嚩囉 and v. 素. | | | 拏瞿怛繼 Suvarṇa-gotra, a matriarchal kingdom, somewhere in the Himālayas, described as the Golden Clan.

蘇偷婆 Stūpa, v. 率.

蘇利耶 Sūrya, the sun, also | 哩 |; 須梨耶.

蘇囉多 Surata, enjoyment, amorous pleasures.

蘇怛羅 Sūtra; thread; a classical work 經, especially the sermons or sayings of the Buddha, v. 素 and 修.

蘇悉地 Susiddhi, a mystic word of the Tantra School, meaning "may it be excellently accomplished", v. the | | | 經 Susiddhi and | | | 羯羅經 Susiddhikāra sūtras.

蘇揭多 Sugata; Svāgata; well come, or well departed, title of a Buddha; also | 伽 | or 陁; v. 修, 沙, 莎, 索.

蘇摩 Soma, to distil, extract, generate; the moon-plant, hence the moon; probably wild rhubarb (Stein). The alcoholic drink made from the plant and formerly offered to the Brahminical gods; tr. 神酒, wine of the gods. Also rendered 香油 a sweet-smelling oil. | | 提婆 Soma-deva, i.e. Candra-deva, the moon-deva. | | 蛇 ? Sūma-sarpa, a former incarnation of Śākyamuni when he gave his body as a great snake to feed the starving people.

蘇末那 Sumanā. A yellow sweet-smelling flower growing on a bush 3 or 4 feet high, perhaps the "great-flowered jasmine"; associated by some with the soma plant, saumanā, a blossom; also | 摩 |; | 蔓 |; 須摩 |.

蘇槃多 Subanta, also | 漫多, the case of a noun. | | 伐窣多; | 婆薩都 Śubhavastu, the river Swat.

蘇樓波 Surūpa, of beautiful form, handsome.

蘇油 Ghṛta, ghee, or clarified butter; scented oil extracted from the sumanā plant.

蘇波訶 Svāhā, Hail! A kind of Amen; a mystic word indicating completion, good luck, nirvāṇa, may evil disappear and good be increased; in India it also indicates an oblation, especially a burnt offering; the oblation as a female deity. Also | 和 |; | 婆 |; | 呵, also with 沙, 娑, 莎, 薩, 率, 馺 as initial syllable.

蘇燈 A lamp using butter and fragrant oil; also 酥燈.

蘇盧多波那 Srota-āpanna 入流 v. 須 and 窣.

蘇跋陀羅 Subhadra, a learned Brahmin, 120 years old, the last convert made by Śākyamuni.

蘇迷(盧) Sumeru, "the Olympus of Hindu mythology," M. W. It is the central mountain of every world. Also | 彌樓 v. 須.

蘇達多 Sudatta, v. 須 name of Anāthapiṇḍaka. | | 拏 Sudāna, name of Śākyamuni as a great almsgiver in a previous incarnation. | | 梨舍那 Sudarśana, the fourth of the seven concentric circles around Sumeru; also | 跌里 | |; v. 修 and 須.

蘇部底 Subhūti, also | 補 |; v. 須 and the 般若 sūtra.

蠕 Wrigglers, crawlers, e.g. worms. | 動 To wriggle, etc.

襪 Stockings, socks; also 韈.

覺 Bodhi, from bodha, "knowing, understanding", means enlightenment, illumination; 覺 is to awake, apprehend, perceive, realize; awake, aware; (also, to sleep). It is illumination, enlightenment, or awakening in regard to the real in contrast to the seeming; also, enlightenment in regard to moral evil. Cf. 菩提 and 佛.

覺了 Completely and clearly enlightened; clearly to apprehend.

覺人 An enlightened man who has apprehended Buddha-truth.

覺他 To awaken others; to enlighten others.

覺位 The stage of perfect enlightenment, that of Buddha.

覺分 Bodhyaṅga, the seven 菩提分 q.v.; also applied to the thirty-seven Bodhipakṣika, 三十七道品, q.v.

覺城 The walled city of enlightenment, into which illusion cannot enter. Gayā, where the Buddha attained enlightenment.

覺堅 Firm, or secure, enlightenment.

覺如 idem 覺眞如 v. 眞如.

覺山 The mountain of enlightenment, i.e. Buddha-truth.

覺岸 The shore of enlightenment, which Buddha has reached after crossing the sea of illusion.

覺心 The mind of enlightenment, the illuminated mind, the original nature of man.

覺性 The enlightened mind free from all illusion. The mind as the agent of knowledge, or enlightenment. Also used for Dharmakāya, v. 三身; 三寶, etc.

覺悟 To awake, become enlightened, comprehend spiritual reality. | | 智 Enlightened wisdom; wisdom that extends beyond the limitations of time and sense; omniscience.

覺支 The various branches or modes of enlightenment; for the seven | | v. 七菩提分.

覺日 Timelessness, eternity, changelessness, the bodhi-day which has no change. Also | 時.

覺樹 The tree of knowledge, or enlightenment, the pippala under which the Buddha attained enlightenment, also called Bodhidruma and *Ficus religiosa*. To plant virtue in order to attain enlightenment.

覺母 Mother of enlightenment, a title of Mañjuśrī as the eternal guardian of mystic wisdom, all Buddhas, past, present, and future, deriving their enlightenment from him as its guardian; also 佛母.

覺海 The fathomless ocean of enlightenment, or Buddha-wisdom.

覺王 The king of enlightenment, the enlightened king, Buddha; also | 帝.

覺用 Nirmāṇakāya, v. 三身; 三寶, etc.

覺相 Saṁbhogakāya, ditto.

覺策 To awaken and stimulate the mind against illusion and evil.

覺者 An enlightened one, especially a Buddha, enlightening self and others, 自覺覺他.

覺苑 Garden of enlightenment, a Pure Land, or Paradise; also the mind.

覺華 The flower of enlightenment, which opens like a flower.

覺行 The procedure, or discipline, of the attainment of enlightenment for self and others.

覺觀 Awareness and pondering, acts of intellectuation, later called 尋伺, both of them hindrances to abstraction, or dhyāna. They are described as 麤 and 細, general and particular, respectively.

覺道 The way of enlightenment, also | 路. | | (支) The 七覺 and 八正道 q.v.

覺雄 The lord, or hero, of enlightenment, Buddha; also 世雄.

觸 To butt, strike against; contact. Sparśa, touch, contact, collision, the quality of tangibility, feeling, sensation. M. W. Eleven kinds of sensation are given—hot, cold, hard, soft, etc. Sparśa is one of the twelve nidānas, cf. 十二因緣, and of the ṣaḍāyatana, cf. 六入. It is also used with the meaning of 濁 unclean. | 因 Touch, or sensation cause, v. 二十五圓通. | 塵 The medium or quality of touch. | 指 The fourth and fifth fingers of the left hand which in India are used at stool, the unclean fingers. | 桶; | 瓶 A commode, ordure tub, etc. | 樂 The pleasure produced by touch. | 欲 Desire awakened by touch. | 毒 The poison of touch, a term applied to woman. | 禮 To prostrate one's head to a stool, or footstool, in reverence. | 穢 To touch anything unclean and become unclean. | 鐘 To strike a bell. | 食 Food made unclean by being touched, or handled; any food soiled, or unclean; the food of sensation, or imagination, mentally conceived.

警 To warn. | 覺 To warn, arouse, stimulate. | 策 A switch to awaken sleepers during an assembly for meditation.

譯 To translate, 繙 |; 翻 |. An oral interpreter, 傳 |; | 官.

譬 To compare, allegorize; like, resembling; parable, metaphor, simile. | 喩 A parable, metaphor; the avadāna section of the canon, v. 阿波; there are numerous categories, e.g. the seven parables of the Lotus sūtra, the ten of the Prajña and Vimalakīrti sūtras, etc. | 喩(論)師 Reputed founder of the 經量部 Sautrāntika school, also known as 日出論者. | 喩量 The example in Logic.

譫 Incoherent talk. | 浮洲 Jambudvīpa, v. 贍.

贍 To supply; supplied, enough; translit. *jam*. | 部 Jambū, "a fruit tree, the rose apple, *Eugenia jambolana*, or another species of Eugenia." M. W. Also | | 提; 閻浮; 剡浮; 譫浮; also applied to the next. | | 洲 Jambudvīpa. Name of the southern of the four great continents, said to be of triangular shape, and to be called after the shape of the leaf of an immense Jambutree on Mount Meru; or after fine gold that is found below the tree. It is divided into four parts: south of the Himalayas by the lord of elephants, because of their number; north by the lord of horses; west by the lord of jewels; east by the lord of men. This seems to imply a region larger than India, and Eitel includes in Jambudvīpa the following countries around the Anavatapta lake and the Himalayas. North: Huns, Uigurs, Turks. East: China, Corea, Japan, and some islands. South: Northern India with twenty-seven kingdoms, Eastern India ten kingdoms, Southern India fifteen kingdoms, Central India thirty kingdoms. West: Thirty-four kingdoms. | | (金) Jāmbūnada, the produce of the river Jambūnadī, i.e. gold, hence | | 光像 is an image of golden glory, especially the image of Śākyamuni attributed to Anathapiṇḍaka. | | 捺陀金 Jambūnadasuvarṇa, the gold from the Jambūnadī river.

釋 To separate out, set free, unloose, explain; Buddhism, Buddhist; translit. *śa*, *śi*; also *ḍ*, *ḍh*.

釋侶 Any follower or disciple of the Buddha; any Buddhist comrade; Buddhists.

釋典 The scriptures of Buddhism.

釋女 The women of the Śākya clan.

釋子 Śākyaputrīya, sons of Śākyamuni, i.e. his disciples in general.

釋宮 The Śākya palace, from which prince Siddhārtha went forth to become Buddha.

釋家 The Śākya family, i.e. the expounders of Buddhist sūtras and scriptures.

釋帝 Śakra, Indra, lord of the thirty-three heavens; also 帝釋; | 迦(婆) q.v.

釋師 The Śākya teacher, Buddha. | | 子 The lion of the Śākyas, Buddha.

釋提桓因 Śakro-devānāmindra, 釋 Śakra 提桓 devānām 因 Indra; Śakra the Indra of the devas, the sky-god, the god of the nature-gods, ruler of the thirty-three heavens, considered by Buddhists as inferior to the Buddhist saint, but as a deva-protector of Buddhism. Also | 羅; 賒羯羅因陀羅; 帝釋; 釋帝; v. | 迦. He has numerous other appellations.

釋摩男 Śākya Mahānāma Kulika, one of the first five of the Buddha's disciples, i.e. prince Kulika.

釋教 Buddhism; the teaching or school of Śākyamuni.

釋梵 Indra and Brahma, both protectors of Buddhism.

釋氏 The Śākya clan, or family name; Śākyamuni.

釋疑 Explanation of doubtful points, solution of doubts.

釋種 Śākya-seed; the Śākya clan; the disciples of Śākyamuni, especially monks and nuns.

釋翅(搜) ? Śākyeṣu, defined as a name for Kapilavastu city; also | 氏廋.

釋藏 The Śākya thesaurus, i.e. the Tripiṭaka, the Buddhist scriptures, cf. 藏.

釋論 The Prajñā-pāramitā-sūtra; also explanatory discussions, or notes on foundation treatises.

釋輪 Śakra's wheel, the discus of Indra, symbol of the earth.

釋迦 Śākya, the clan or family of the Buddha, said to be derived from śāka, vegetables, but intp. in Chinese as powerful, strong, and explained by 能 powerful, also erroneously by 仁 charitable, which belongs rather to association with Śākyamuni. The clan, which is said to have wandered hither from the delta of the Indus, occupied a district of a few thousand square miles lying on the slopes of the Nepalese hills and on the plains to the south. Its capital was Kapilavastu. At the time of Buddha the clan was under the suzerainty of Kosala, an adjoining kingdom. Later Buddhists, in order to surpass Brahmans, invented a fabulous line of five kings of the Vivartakalpa headed by Mahāsammata 大三末多; these were followed by five cakravartī, the first being Mūrdhaja 頂生王; after these came nineteen kings, the first being Cetiya 捨帝, the last Mahādeva 大天; these were succeeded by dynasties of 5,000, 7,000, 8,000, 9,000, 10,000, 15,000 kings; after which king Gautama opens a line of 1,100 kings, the last, Ikṣvāku, reigning at Potala. With Ikṣvāku the Śākyas are said to have begun. His four sons reigned at Kapilavastu. "Śākyamuni was one of his descendants in the seventh generation." Later, after the destruction of Kapilavastu by Virūḍhaka, four survivors of the family founded the kingdoms of Udyana, Bamyam, Himatala, and Śāmbī. Eitel. | | (婆) Śakra. | | 提婆 (or 桓) 因 (陀羅) Śakra-devendra; Śakro-devānāmindra; v. | 帝, i.e. Indra. | | 尊 The honoured one of the Śākyas, i.e. Śākyamuni. | | 牟尼; | | 文 (尼); | 伽文 Śākyamuni, the saint of the Śākya tribe. Muni is saint, holy man, sage, ascetic, monk; it is intp. as 仁 benevolent, charitable, kind, also as 寂默 one who dwells in seclusion. After "500 or 550" previous incarnations, Śākyamuni finally attained to the state of Bodhisattva, was born in the Tuṣita heaven, and descended as a white elephant, through her right side, into the womb of the immaculate Māyā, the purest woman on earth; this was on the 8th day of the 4th month; next year on the 8th day of the 2nd month he was born from her right side painlessly as she stood under a tree in the Lumbinī garden. For the subsequent miraculous events v. Eitel, also the 神通遊戲經 (Lalitavistara), the 釋迦如來成道記, etc. Simpler statements say that he was born the son of Śuddhodana, of the kṣatriya caste, ruler of Kapilavastu, and Māyā his wife; that Māyā died seven days later, leaving him to be brought up by her sister Prajāpatī; that in due course he was married to Yaśodharā who bore him a son, Rāhula; that in search of truth he left home, became an ascetic, severely disciplined himself, and finally at 35 years of age, under a tree, realized that the way of release from the chain of rebirth and death lay not in asceticism but in moral purity; this he explained first in his four dogmas, v. 四諦 and eightfold noble way 八正道, later amplified and developed in many sermons. He founded his community on the basis of poverty, chastity, and insight or meditation, and it became known as Buddhism, as he became known as Buddha, the enlightened. His death was probably in or near 487 B.C., a few years before that of Confucius in 479. The sacerdotal name of his family is Gautama, said to be the original name of the whole clan, Śākya being that of his branch, v. 瞿, 喬; his personal name was Siddhārtha, or Sarvārthasiddha, v. 悉. | | 獅子 Śākyasiṁha, the lion of the Śākyas, i.e. the Buddha. | | 菩薩 Śākya-bodhisattva, one of the previous incarnations of the Buddha.

釋門 The school of Śākyamuni, Buddhism.

釋雄 The hero of the Śākyas, Buddha; also 世雄.

釋風 The custom of Buddhism; also its "breeze" or progress.

鐘 Ghaṇṭā, 犍稚 a bell, a chime. 百八｜ The 108 strokes of the temple bell struck at dawn and dusk. ｜樓 Bell-tower.

鐼子 Hsün-tzŭ, a bowl (or bowls) within an almsbowl. Buddha's bowl consisted of four heavy deva-bowls which he received miraculously one on the other; they are to be recovered with the advent of Maitreya; v. 鍵鎔.

鐃 A hand-bell, cymbals.

闡 To open, spread, enlarge, expand, expound; translit. *chan*. ｜提 v. 一｜｜ Icchantika, intp. as unable to become Buddha (*a*) because of unbelief, or abandoned character; (*b*) because of a bodhisattva vow. ｜陀 Chandaka, name of the Buddha's driver when he left home; he became a monk; also ｜那; ｜擇迦;｜釋迦; ｜鐸迦; 車匿; also a form of metre; poetry; hymns; a style of poetic recitation.

騷 Trouble, sad; poetic, learned; translit. *su*, *s*. ｜伽陁; ｜揭多 Sugata, v. 修. ｜毗羅 ? Parisrāvaṇa, a filtering cloth or bag, v. 鉢里.

騰 To mount, rise; translit. *tang*. ｜蘭 Tang and Ran, i.e. Mātaṅga (Kāśyapa Mātaṅga) and Gobharaṇa, the two monks brought to China, according to tradition, by Ming Ti's emissaries, v. 摩, 迦, and 竺.

鰐 A crocodile. ｜魚 v. 金 Kumbhīra.

鶖 A stork. ｜(鶩)子 Śāriputra, also 秋露子 meaning son of Śārī, his mother; Śārī is a kind of bird "commonly called the Maina". M. W. It is tr. as a stork. Cf. 舍.

鹹 Salty, salted. ｜水 Salt water.

21. TWENTY-ONE STROKES

嚼 To chew. ｜蠟 Chewing wax, tasteless.

嚩 Translit. *vā*. ｜羅呬 Vārāhī, tr. as the gods below the earth.

懼 Fear, dread; translit. *gu*. ｜曩 Guṇa, a power, quality, v. 求.

攝 To collect, gather together, combine, include; lay hold of; assist, act for or with; control, direct, attend to; translit. *ś*, *śa*. ｜取, ｜受 To gather, gather up, receive. ｜哩藍 Śarīra, v. 舍 relics. ｜嚩縛 Śava, a corpse (not yet decayed). ｜大乘論 Mahāyāna-saṁparigraha-śāstra, a collection of Mahāyāna śāstras, ascribed to Asaṅga, of which three tr. were made into Chinese. ｜心 To collect the mind, concentrate the attention. ｜念山林 The hill-grove for concentrating the thoughts, a monastery. ｜意音樂 Music that calms the mind, or helps to concentration. ｜拖苾馱 Śabda-vidyā, (a śāstra on) grammar, logic. ｜摩騰 Kāśyapa-Mātaṅga, v. 迦, according to tradition the first official Indian monk (along with Gobharaṇa) to arrive in China, *circa* A.D. 67; tr. the Sūtra of the Forty-two Sections. ｜衆生戒; 接生戒 The commands which include or confer blessing on all the living. ｜論 The collected śāstras, v. *supra*. ｜論宗 The school of the collected śāstras.

曩 Of old, ancient; translit. *na*. ｜莫 Namaḥ, v. 南.

欄 A rail, handrail; pen, fold. ｜楯 Barrier, railing.

灌 To water, sprinkle, pour; to flow together, or into, accumulate. ｜佛; 浴佛 To wash a Buddha's image with scented water, which is a work of great merit and done with much ceremony. ｜室 The building in which the esoterics practise the rite of baptism. ｜洗 To wash a Buddha's image. ｜臘 The washing of a Buddha's image at the end of the monastic year, the end of summer. ｜頂 Abhiṣecana; Mūrdhābhiṣikta; inauguration or consecration by sprinkling, or pouring water on the head; an Indian custom on the investiture of a king, whose head was baptized with water from the four seas and from the rivers in his domain; in China it is administered as a Buddhist rite chiefly to high personages, and for ordination purposes. Amongst the esoterics it is a rite especially administered to their disciples; and they have several categories of baptism, e.g. that of ordinary disciples, of teacher, or preacher, of leader, of office-bearer; also for special causes such as relief from calamity, preparation for the next life, etc. | 頂住 The tenth stage of a bodhisattva when he is anointed by the Buddhas as a Buddha.

爛 Glittering, as iridescent fish, | 魚; rotten, soft; pulp.

瓔 A gem, a necklace. | 珞 A necklace of precious stones; things strung together.

竈 A kitchen-stove. | 神 The kitchen-stove god, or kitchen-god who at the end of each year is supposed to report above on the conduct of members of the family.

纏 To bind with cords; bonds; another name for 煩惱 the passions and delusions, etc. | 報 The retribution of transmigrational-bondage. | 無明 The bondage of unenlightenment. | 縛 Bondage; to bind; also the 十 | and 四縛 q.v.

續 To join on, continue, add, supplementary, a supplement. | 命 (Prayers for) continued life, for which the | | 神幡 flag of five colours is displayed.

羼 Crowding sheep, confusion; translit. *kṣan*, *ṣan*. | 底 (or 提) Kṣānti, patience, forbearance, enduring shame, one of the six pāramitās. | 提仙人 Kṣāntirṣi, name of Śākyamuni in a previous incarnation, the patient or enduring ṛṣi. | | 羅 Ṣaṇḍila, a sterile woman, cf. 扇.

蘭 The epidendrum, orchid; scented, refined; pledged, sworn; translit. *ra*, *ram*, *ran*; abbrev. for 偸 | 遮 q.v. | 室; | 若 Araṇya, lit. forest, hence hermitage, v. 阿; a monastery. | 盆 (會) Ullambana, Lambana, Avalamba, v. 盂. The festival of masses for destitute ghosts on the 15th of the 7th month. | 菊 Orchid and chrysanthemum, spring and autumn, emblems of beauty. | 闍; | 奢 (待) A Mongol or Turkish word implying praise. | 香 Orchid fragrance, spring.

蘗 A shrub, tree stump, etc., translit. *g*, *ga*, *gan*. | 哩訶; | 羅訶 Gṛha; Grāha; the seizer, name of a demon. | 喇婆 Garbha, tr. 中心; the womb, interior part. | 嚕拏 v. 迦 Garuḍa. | 馱矩吒 Gandhakuṭī, a temple for offering incense (in the Jetavana monastery and elsewhere).

蠟 Wax. | 印 To seal with wax, a wax seal.

覽 To look at, view; translit. *raṁ*-; associated with fire.

護 To protect, guard, succour. | 世者 The four Lokapālas, each protecting one of the four quarters of space, the guardians of the world and of the Buddhist faith. | 命 Protection of life. | 國 The four Lokapālas, or Rāṣṭrapālas, who protect a country. | 寺 Vihārapāla, guardian deity of a monastery. | 念 To guard and care for, protect and keep in mind. | 戒神 The five guardian-spirits of each of the five commandments, cf. 二十五神. | 摩 Homa, also | 磨; 呼麼; described as originally a burnt offering to Heaven; the esoterics adopted the idea of worshipping with fire, symbolizing wisdom as fire burning up the faggots of passion and illusion, and therewith preparing nirvāṇa as food, etc.; cf. 大日經; four kinds of braziers are used, round, semi-circular, square, and octagonal; four, five, or six purposes are recorded, i.e. Śāntika, to end calamities; Pauṣṭika (or puṣṭikarman) for prosperity; Vaśīkaraṇa, "dominating," intp. as calling down the good by means of enchantments; Abhicāraka, exorcising the evil; a fifth is to obtain the loving protection of the Buddhas and bodhisattvas; a sixth divides Puṣṭikarman into two parts, the second part being length of life; each of these six has its controlling Buddha and bodhisattvas, and different forms and accessories of worship. | 明大士 Prabhāpāla; guardian of light, or illumination, name of Śākyamuni when in the Tuṣita heaven before earthly incarnation. | 法 To protect or maintain the Buddha-truth; also name of Dharmapāla q.v. | 法神 The four lokapālas, seen at the entrance to Buddhist temples, v. *supra*. | 童子法 Method of protecting the young against the fifteen evil spirits which seek to harm them. | 符 A charm used by the esoterics. | 苾那 Hupian, "the capital of Vridjisthāna, probably in the neighbourhood of the present Charekoor . . . to the north of Cabool." Eitel. | 身 Protection of the body, for which the charm last named is used, and also other methods.

辯 To discuss, argue, discourse. | 才 Ability to discuss, debate, discourse; rhetoric. | 才天 Sarasvatī, goddess of speech and learning, v. 大 | 才天. | 無礙 Power of unhindered discourse, perfect freedom of speech or debate, a bodhisattva power.

鑁 Translit. *vaṁ*, associated with water and the ocean; also, the embodiment of wisdom.

鐶 A metal ring; a ring. | 釧 Finger-rings and armlets.

鐵 Iron. | 圍山 Cakravāla, Cakravāḍa. The iron enclosing mountains supposed to encircle the earth, forming the periphery of a world. Mount Meru is the centre and between it and the Iron mountains are the seven 金山 metal-mountains and the eight seas. | 城 The iron city, hell. | 札 Iron tablets in Hades, on which are recorded each person's crimes and merits. | 輪 The iron wheel; also cakravāla, *supra.* | 輪王 Iron-wheel king, ruler of the south and of Jambudvīpa, one of the 四輪王. | 鉢 Cf. 四鉢. Iron pātra, or almsbowl. | 際 The boundary of the cakravāla, v. *supra.*

鐸 A bell with a clapper; translit. *da.* | 曷攞 Dahara, small, young; a monk ordained less than ten years.

闢 To open; translit. *pi*, v. 毘. | 妄 To explain, or set free from, illusion. | 展 Pidjan, or Pi-chang, near Turfān.

闥 An inner door (especially of the women's rooms); a recess, corner; translit. *da, dha*, etc. | 婆 Gandharvas, v. 乾.

露 Dew; symbol of transience; to expose, disclose. | 命 Dew-like life; transient. | 地 Bare ground; like dew on the ground, dewy ground. | 形; | 身 Exposed form, naked, e.g. the Nirgrantha ascetics. | 牛 The great white ox and ox-cart revealed in the open, i.e. the Mahāyāna, v. Lotus sūtra.

霹 Crash, rumble. | 靂 A thunder-crash.

饑 Hunger, famine. | 餓地獄 The hell of hunger. | 饉災 The calamity of famine.

饒 Spare; abundance, surplus; to pardon. | 王 (佛) Lokeśvara, "the lord or ruler of the world; N. of a Buddha" (M. W.); probably a development of the idea of Brahmā, Viṣṇu, or Śiva as lokanātha, "lord of worlds." In Indo-China especially it refers to Avalokiteśvara, whose image or face, in masculine form, is frequently seen, e.g. at Angkor. Also 世 | | |. It is to Lokeśvara that Amitābha announces his forty-eight vows. | 益 To enrich. | 舌 A fluent tongue; loquacious.

驅 To drive out or away, expel, urge. | 烏 Scarecrow, term for an acolyte of from seven to thirteen years of age, he being old enough to drive away crows. | 龍 Dragon-expeller, a term for an arhat of high character and powers, who can drive away evil nāgas.

髏 Kapāla; a skull. | 鬘 A chaplet or wreath of skulls, worn by the Kāpālikas, a Śivaitic sect; kapālī is an epithet of Śiva as the skull-wearer.

鬘 A head-dress, coiffure; a chaplet, wreath, etc.; idem 末利.

魑 A mountain demon resembling a tiger; 魅 is a demon of marshes having the head of a pig and body of a man. The two words are used together indicating evil spirits.

魔; 魔羅 Māra, killing, destroying; "the Destroyer, Evil One, Devil" (M. W.); explained by murderer, hinderer, disturber, destroyer; he is a deva "often represented with a hundred arms and riding on an elephant". Eitel. He sends his daughters, or assumes monstrous forms, or inspires wicked men, to seduce or frighten the saints. He "resides with legions of subordinates in the heaven Paranirmita Vaśavartin situated on the top of the Kāmadhātu". Eitel. Earlier form 磨; also v. 波 Pāpīyān. He is also called 他化自在天. There are various categories of māras, e.g. the skandha-māra, passion-māra, etc.

魔事 Māra-deeds, especially in hindering Buddha-truth.

魔天 Māra-deva, the god of lust, sin, and death, cf. Māra.

魔女 The daughters of Māra, who tempt men to their ruin.

魔忍 Māra-servitude, the condition of those who obey Māra.

魔怨 Māra enmity; Māra, the enemy of Buddha.

魔戒 Māra-laws, Māra-rules, i.e. those of monks who seek fame and luxury.

魔梵 Māra and Brahmā; i.e. Māra, lord of the sixth desire-heaven, and Brahmā, lord of the heavens of form.

魔檀 Māra-gifts, in contrast with those of Buddha.

魔民 Mārakāyikas, also 丨子丨女 Māra's people, or subjects.

魔(波)旬 Māra-pāpīyān, cf. 波.

魔王 The king of māras, the lord of the sixth heaven of the desire-realm.

魔界 The realm of the māras; also 丨境; 丨道.

魔禪 Māra-dhyāna, evil thoughts, wrong and harmful meditation.

魔縛 Māra-cords; Māra-bonds; also 丨繫.

魔緣 Māra-circumstance, or environment, or conditioning cause, i.e. hindering the good.

魔網 The net of Māra.

魔羅 Māra, v. 魔; also 麼丨; for 丨丨耶 v. 摩.

魔軍 The army of Māra.

魔道 The māra path, or way, i.e. one of the six destinies.

魔鄉 Māra-country, i.e. the world.

魔醯首羅 Maheśvara, Śiva. 丨丨因陀羅 Mahendra, a younger brother of Aśoka. 丨丨溼羅補羅 Maheśvarapura, the present Machery in Rajputana. 丨丨邏矩羅 Mihirakula, king of the Punjab, later of Kashmir, about A.D. 400, a persecutor of Buddhism, v. 摩.

魔障 Māra-hindrances; also 障 is an interpretation of 魔.

鷄 v. 雞 Eighteen Strokes.

鶴 The crane; the egret; translit. *ha, ho*. 丨林; 丨樹 Crane grove, a name for the place where Śākyamuni died, when the trees burst into white blossom resembling a flock of white cranes. 丨勒那夜奢 Haklenayaśas, or Padmaratna, the twenty-third patriarch, born in the palace of the king of Tokhara. 丨悉那 Hosna, or Ghazna, "the capital of Tsaukūṭa, the present Ghuznee" (Ghazni) in Afghanistan. Eitel. 丨秣 Homa, "a city on the eastern frontier of Persia, perhaps the modern Humoon." Eitel. 丨苑 Crane-garden, a term for a monastery. 丨薩羅 Hasara, "the second capital of Tsaukūṭa, perhaps the modern Assaia Hazaréh between Ghuznee and Kandahar in Afghanistan." Eitel.

22. TWENTY-TWO STROKES

囉 To chatter, translit. *ra* sounds; cf. 羅, 邏, 嚕, e.g. 丨逝 Rājñī, a queen, a princess. 丨惹 Rāja, a king.

囊 A bag, sack, purse; translit. *na*. 丨莫; 丨謨; v. 南 Namaḥ. 丨哦羅賀羅 Nagarahāra, Nagara, a city on the Kabul river, v. 那.

攞 To split; wipe; choose; translit. *la*. 丨乞尖拏 v. 相 Lakṣaṇa. 丨都迦 Laḍḍuka, a cake, or sweetmeat, identified with the 歡喜丸 joy-buns, q.v.

權 The weight (on a steelyard), weight, authority, power; to balance, adjudge; bias, expediency, partial, provisional, temporary, positional; in Buddhist scriptures it is used like 方便 expediency, or temporary; it is the adversative of 實 q.v. 丨化 The power of Buddhas and bodhisattvas to transform themselves into any kind of temporal body. 丨大乘 The temporary, or partial, schools of Mahāyāna, the 通 and 別, in contrast with the 實大乘 schools which taught universal Buddhahood, e.g. the Hua-yen and T'ien-t'ai schools. 丨實 Temporal and real; 權 referring to the conditional, functional, differential, or temporary, 實 to the fundamental, absolute, or real. 丨實不二門 The two divisions, the provisional and the perfect, are not two but complementary, v. 丨敎 and 十不二門. 丨悲 Pity in regard to beings in time and sense, arising from the Buddhas 丨智 *infra*. 丨敎 Temporary, expedient, or functional teaching, preparatory to the perfect teaching, a distinguishing term of the T'ien-t'ai and Hua-yen sects, i.e. the teachings of the three previous periods 藏, 通 and 別 which were regarded as preparatory to their own, cf. 圓 敎. | 方 便 Expedients of Buddhas and bodhisattvas for saving all beings. | 智 Buddha-wisdom of the phenomenal, in contrast with 實 智 knowledge of the fundamental or absolute. | 現 Temporary, or *ad hoc* manifestations, similar to | 化. | 理 Partial, or incomplete truth. | 者 A Buddha or bodhisattva who has assumed a temporary form in order to aid beings; also 化 者; | 化; 大 權, etc. | 謀 Temporary plans, methods suited to immediate needs, similar to 方 便. | 迹 Temporal traces, evidences of the incarnation of a Buddha in human form. | 門 The sects which emphasize 方 便, i.e. expediency, or expedients; the undeveloped school, *supra*.

歡 Nanda. Pleased, glad. | 喜 Pleased, glad; pleasure, gladness. | | 丸 (or 團) Joy-buns, a name for a kind of honey-cake. | | 光 佛 Buddha of joyful light, Amitābha. | | 國; 妙 喜 國 Abhirati, the happy land, or paradise of Akṣobhya, east of our universe. | | 苑; | 樂 園; 喜 林 苑 Nandana-vana. Garden of joy; one of the four gardens of Indra's paradise, north of his central city. | | 地 Pramuditā. The bodhisattva's stage of joy, the first of his ten stages (bhūmi). | | 天; 大 聖 | | 天; (大) 聖 天 The joyful devas, or devas of pleasure, represented as two figures embracing each other, with elephants' heads and human bodies; the two embracing figures are interpreted as Gaṇeśa (the eldest son of Śiva) and an incarnation of Kuan-yin; the elephant-head represents Gaṇeśa; the origin is older than the Kuan-yin idea and seems to be a derivation from the Śivaitic linga-worship. | | 日 The happy day of the Buddha, and of the order, i.e. that ending the "retreat", 15th day of the 7th (or 8th) moon; also every 15th day of the month. | | 會 The festival of All Souls, v. 盂.

灑 To sprinkle, translit. *sa*. | 水 To sprinkle water. | 淨 To purify by sprinkling.

禳 To pray to avert; e.g. | 日 蝕; | 月 | to avert the calamity threatened by an eclipse of sun or moon. | 災 Ceremonies to avert calamity, indicating also the Atharva-veda, and other incantations.

籠 A cage, crate; to ensnare. | 頭 Blinkers for a horse's head.

聽 To hear, listen, hearken; listen to, obey. | 敎 Those who hear the Buddha's doctrine; those who obey. | 聞 To hear; to hear and obey.

讀 To read; a comma, full stop. | 師 A reader to an assembly. | 經 Ditto; also to read the scriptures. | 誦 Reading and reciting.

贖 To redeem, ransom. | 命 To redeem life; a redeemer of life, said of the Nirvāṇa sūtra.

鑑 A mirror 明 |; to note, survey, | 察.

鑊 Caldron, rice pan. | 沙; 烏 鎩 Ōsh, or Ūsh, "an ancient kingdom north of the Śītā, probably the present Ingachar"; possibly Uch-Turfān or Yangishahr, 依 耐 or 英 吉 沙 爾. | 湯 地 獄 The purgatory of caldrons of molten iron.

響 Pratiśrut. Echo, resonance. 影 | Shadow and echo.

顩 Translit. *kam* ir | 鉢 羅 Kambala, a woollen garment, or blanket.

鷓 A partridge | 鴣. | | 斑 Spotted like a partridge, a kind of incense.

龕 A shrine; a cabinet, box; a coffin (for a monk); to contain. | 塔 A pagoda with shrines.

23. TWENTY-THREE STROKES

巖 A crag, cliff. | 谷 Cliffs and gullies.

戀 To be fond of, hanker after, cleave to; | 慕.

曬 To dry in the sun. | 厨 Sukha, delight, joy.

癰 A tumour, abscess. | 瘡 A tumour of pus, a running sore.

蘿 Creeping or climbing plants. | 衣 Coarse garments worn by ascetics.

變 To change, alter, transmute, transform. | 化 To transform, change, change into, become, especially the mutations of Buddhas and bodhisattvas, e.g. | 化人 becoming men; also | 化土 the land where they dwell, whether the Pure Land or any impure world where they live for its enlightenment. | 化法身 The dharmakāya in its power of transmutation, or incarnation. | 化生 Birth by transformation, not by gestation. | 化身 The nirmāṇakāya, i.e. transformation-body, or incarnation-body, one of the 三身 Trikāya, q.v. | 壞 Destroyed, spoilt, turned bad. | 成 To become, turn into, be transformed into. | 成王 Pien-ch'êng Wang, one of the kings, or judges of Hades. | 成男子 To be transformed from a female to a male. Every Buddha is supposed to vow to change all women into men. | 易 Change, to change, similar to | 化. | 易生死 Mortal changes, or a body that is being transformed from mortality, e.g. | 易身 bodies that are being transformed in a Pure Land, or transformed bodies.

邏 Patrol; translit. *la*, *ra*. | 吃灑; | 乞洒 Lakṣaṇa, v. 相, a distinguishing mark, sign, or characteristic. | 求 Laghu, light, nimble. | 闍 Rāja, v. 羅.

鑠 To melt; bright; translit. *śa*. | 枳底; | 訖底 Śakti, a halberd or lance; a tally or sign. | 迦羅阿逸多 Śakrāditya, also 帝日, a king of Magadha, some time after Śākyamuni's death, to whom he built a temple. | 雞謨儞 Śākyamuni, v. 釋.

顯 Manifest, reveal, open, clear, plain, known, illustrious; exoteric. | 典; | 經 The exoteric or general scriptures, as distinguished from the 蜜 esoteric, occult, or tantric scriptures. | 冥 Open or hidden, external or internal (illumination, or powers). | 宗; | 家 The exoteric sects, in contrast with the 蜜 esoteric. | 教 The open, or general teaching; the exoteric schools. | 明 Open, manifest; pure; to reveal. | 本 The revelation of his fundamental or eternal life by the Buddha in the Lotus Sūtra. | 正 To show the truth, reveal that which is correct. | 示 To reveal, indicate. | 色 The visible or light colours. | 蜜 Exoteric and esoteric; the 眞言 Shingon, or True-word sect, is the esoteric sect, which exercises occult rites of Yoga character, and considers all the other sects as exoteric. | 識 Manifest, revealing, or open knowledge, the store of knowledge where all is revealed both good and bad, a name for the ālaya-vijñāna. | 露 To reveal, disclose.

驚 Uttras-; santras-; alarm, startle, arouse. | 覺 Arouse, stimulate.

驗 To examine into, hold an inquest; to come true, verify. | 生人中 An inquiry into the mode of a person's death, to judge whether he will be reborn as a man, and so on with the other possible destinies, e.g. | | 地獄 whether he will be reborn in the hells.

髑 A skull | 髏.

體 Body, limbs; corpus, corporeal; the substance, the essentials; to show respect to, accord with. | 內方便; | 外 | | A term of the T'ien-t'ai school indicating that the "expedient" methods of the 方便 chapter of the Lotus sūtra are within the ultimate reality of that sūtra, while those of other schools are without it. | 大 Great in substance, the "greatness of quintessence" or the fundamental immutable substance of all things; cf. Awakening of Faith 起信論. | 性 Ātmakatva; dharmatā; the essential, or substantial nature of anything, self-substance. | 智 Fundamental wisdom which penetrates all reality. | 毘履 v. 他 Sthavira, elder, president. | 法 The universality of substance and the unreality of dharmas or phenomena, the view of the 通教 as contrasted with that of the 藏教. | 用 Substance, or body, and function; the fundamental and phenomenal; the function of any body. | 相 Substance and phenomena or characteristics, substance being unity and phenomena diversity. | 相用 The three great fundamentals in the Awakening of Faith—substance, characteristics, function. | 空 The emptiness, unreality, or immateriality of substance, the "mind-only" theory, that all is mind or mental, a Mahāyāna doctrine. | 達 The universal fundamental principle all pervasive. | 露 Complete exposure or manifestation.

鷲 A vulture. | 山 Gṛdhrakūṭa, Vulture Peak near Rājagṛha, "the modern Giddore, so called because Piśuna (Māra) once assumed there the guise of a vulture to interrupt the meditation of Ānanda" (Eitel); more probably because of its shape, or because of the vultures who fed there on the dead; a place frequented by the Buddha; the imaginary scene of the preaching of the Lotus sūtra, and called 靈 | 山 Spiritual Vulture Peak, as the Lotus sūtra is also known as the | 峯偈 Vulture Peak gāthā. The peak is also called | 峯; | 頭(山); | 臺; | 嶽; | 巖; 靈山; cf. 耆闍崛山.

麟 The lin, or female unicorn. 麒 | Male and female unicorns; the ch'i-lin in general. | 角 The unicorn with its single horn is a simile for 獨覺 q.v. pratyeka-buddha.

24. TWENTY-FOUR STROKES

囑 To bid, order, tell, enjoin on. | 累 To entrust to, lay responsibility upon.

攬 To seize, hold in the arms, embrace; monopolize.

蠶 The silkworm. | 繭 A silkworm's cocoon, simile of the self-binding effects of the passions, etc.

衢 A thoroughfare, a way, cf. 瞿 18.

讖 To prognosticate, prophesy; supplicate, fulfil, a password; translit. *kṣa*. | 羅半尼 Kṣārapāṇīya, ash-water, also intp. as an ash-coloured garment, v. 差 10.

靈 Spirit, spiritual, energy, effective, clever. | 供 Offerings to the spirits who are about the dead during the forty-nine days of masses. | 像 Spirit-image, that of a Buddha or a god. | 妙 Abstruse, mysterious; clever. | 山; | 嶽; | 鷲山 The Spirit Vulture Peak, Gṛdhrakūṭa, v. 耆 10 and 鷲 23. | 感; | 應 Spirit-response, efficacious as in response to prayer. | 瑞華 The udumbara flower, which appears but once in 3,000 years, a symbol of Buddha; v. 優曇 17. | 界 The realm of departed spirits; the world of spirits. | 神 The spirit, soul; an efficacious spirit. | 祠 Spirit-temple, a monastery. | 芝 The auspicious plant, emblem of good luck, or long life; name of 元照 Yüan-chao, q.v. | 骨 Spirit-bones, Buddha-relics. | 魂 A spirit, soul. | 龕 A coffin.

鬭 To contest, fight. | 勝 To overcome in a contest of any kind. | 諍 Argument, debate, contention. | 諍王 The fractious king, Kalirāja, v. 羯 15.

鹽 Salt; translit. *ya*. | 天 Yama, v. 焰 12. | 牟(尼)那; 搖尤那 The river Yamunā, or Jamna, a tributary of the Ganges. | 香 Salt-smell, i.e. non-existent.

鼇 A turtle, tortoise. | 不愼口 The tortoise, clinging to a stick with its mouth, being carried in flight, warned not to open its mouth to speak, yet did, fell and perished; moral, guard your lips.

25. TWENTY-FIVE STROKES

觀 Vipaśyanā; vidarśanā. To look into, study, examine, contemplate; contemplation, insight; a study, a Taoist monastery; to consider illusion and discern illusion, or discern the seeming from the real; to contemplate and mentally enter into truth. 覺 is defined as awakening, or awareness, 觀 as examination or study. It is also an old tr. of the word Yoga; and cf. 禪 17. Kuan is especially a doctrine of the T'ien-t'ai school as shown in the 止 | q.v.

觀世音 Regarder of the world's sounds, or cries, the so-called Goddess of Mercy; also known as | 音; | 世音菩薩; |(世)自在; | 尹; 光世音 (the last being the older form). Avalokiteśvara, v. 阿 8. Originally represented as a male, the images are now generally those of a female figure. The meaning of the term is in doubt; it is intp. as above, but the term |(世)自在 accords with the idea of Sovereign Regarder and is not associated with sounds or cries. Kuan-yin is one of the triad of Amida, is represented on his left, and is also represented as crowned with Amida; but there are as many as thirty-three different forms of Kuan-yin, sometimes with a bird, a vase, a willow wand, a pearl, a "thousand" eyes and hands, etc., and, when as bestower of children, carrying a child. The island of P'u-t'o (Potala) is the chief centre of Kuan-yin worship, where she is the protector of all in distress, especially of those who go to sea. There are many sūtras, etc., devoted to the cult, but its provenance and the date of its introduction to China are still in doubt. Chapter 25 of the Lotus sūtra is devoted to Kuan-yin, and is the principal scripture of the cult; its date is uncertain. Kuan-yin is sometimes confounded with Amitābha and Maitreya. She is said to be the daughter of king Śubhavyūha 妙莊王, who had her killed by "stifling because the sword of the executioner broke without hurting her. Her spirit went to hell; but hell changed into paradise. Yama sent her back to life to save his hell, when she was miraculously transported on a Lotus flower to the island of Poo-too". Eitel. | | | 母 Tārā, the śakti, or female energy of the masculine Avalokiteśvara.

觀佛 To contemplate, or meditate upon, Buddha. | | 三昧 A samādhi on the characteristic marks of a Buddha.

觀像念佛 To contemplate the image of (Amitābha) Buddha and repeat his name.

觀在薩埵 Idem Kuan-yin Bodhisattva, v. 丨世音.

觀察 Pravicaya; investigation; meditation on and inquiry into; vibhāvana, clear perception. 丨丨門 Contemplation of the joys of Amitābha's Pure Land, one of the 五念門.

觀心 Contemplation of the mind, mental contemplation, contemplation of all things as mind.

觀念 To look into and think over, contemplate and ponder.

觀想 To meditate and think. 丨丨念佛 To contemplate Buddha (especially Amitābha) in the mind and repeat his name.

觀慧 The wisdom which penetrates to ultimate reality.

觀智 Wisdom obtained from contemplation.

觀樹 Contemplating the tree (of knowledge, as Śākyamuni is said to have done after his enlightenment).

觀法 Methods of contemplation, or obtaining of insight into truth, cf. 六丨丨 and 止觀.

觀無量壽經 An important sūtra relating to Amitāyus, or Amitābha, and his Pure Land, known also as 佛說丨丨丨丨佛經. There are numerous commentaries on it. The title is commonly abbreviated to 丨經.

觀照 To be enlightened (or enlighten) as the result of insight, or intelligent contemplation. 丨丨般若 The prajñā or wisdom of meditative enlightenment on reality.

觀禪 Contemplation and meditation, to sit in abstract trance.

觀空 To regard all things as unreal, or as having no fundamental reality.

觀行 Contemplation and (accordant) action; method of contemplating. 丨丨佛; 丨丨卽 The third of the 六卽, the bodhisattva or disciple who has attained to the 五品 stage of Buddhahood.

觀解 To contemplate ultimate reality and unravel or expound it.

觀象 Describing an elephant from sight rather than 摸丨, as would a blind man, from feeling it; i.e. immediate and correct knowledge.

觀道 Contemplation, meditation, insight.

觀達 To penetrate to reality through contemplation.

觀門 Contemplation or meditation as one of the two methods of entry into truth, i.e. instruction and meditation; also one of the 六妙門. 丨丨十法界 cf. 十 and 法.

觀頂三昧 The samādhi of the summit of contemplation, i.e. the peak whence all the samādhis may be surveyed.

觀音 v. 丨世丨.

26. TWENTY-SIX STROKES

讚 Stotra, hymn, praise. 丨佛 To praise Buddha. 丨唄 A hymn in praise (of Buddha). 丨嘆; 丨歎 To praise (Buddha). 丨禮 To praise and worship. 丨衆 The assembly of praise-singers, led by the 丨頭 precentor. 丨誦 To praise and intone; to sing praises; a tr. of Rigveda.

驢 Khara, an ass, donkey. 丨年 Donkey-year, i.e. without date or period, because the ass does not appear in the list of cyclic animals. 丨脣 Kharoṣṭha, "donkey lips," name of a sage celebrated for his astronomical knowledge.

27. TWENTY-SEVEN STROKES

鬮 A lot, tally, ballot, ticket, made of wood, bamboo, or paper; also 鬮. To cast lots for good or ill fortune.

鑽 To bore, pierce; an awl. | 水求酥 To churn water to get curd.

28. TWENTY-EIGHT STROKES

鸚 Śuka; a parrot | 鵡. | 鵡賓 v. 甄 14 Kiṁśuka, "a tree with red flowers, said to be the *Butea frondosa.*" Eitel.

29. TWENTY-NINE STROKES

鬱 Dense, oppressive, anxious; translit. *u* sounds; cf. 郁, 優, 嗢, 殟, 烏. | 多摩 Uttama, highest, chief, greatest. | 多羅 Uttara, upper, higher, superior; subsequent; result; excess; the north; also | 怛羅, etc. | 多羅僧 (伽) Uttarāsaṅga, an upper or outer garment; the seven-patch robe of a monk; also used for the robe flung toga-like over the left shoulder. | 多羅究留 Uttarakuru, also | | | 拘樓; | | | 鳩婁; 郁 | | | |; | 怛 | | 璢; | 怛羅越; | 單越, etc. The northern of the four continents around Meru, square in shape, inhabited by square-faced people; explained by 高上作 superior to or higher than other continents, 勝 superior, 勝生 superior life, because human life there was supposed to last a thousand years and food was produced without human effort. Also, the dwelling of gods and saints in Brahmanic cosmology; one of the Indian "nine divisions of the world, the country of the northern Kurus, situated in the north of India, and described as the country of eternal beatitude". M. W. | 持 Uda; also | | 迦; 優陀伽; 烏娜迦 Udaka; water. | 瑟尼沙; | 失 | | v. 烏 10 Uṣṇīṣa. | 頭藍 (佛) Udra(ka) Rāmaputra; | | | 子; | 陀羅羅摩子 A Brahman ascetic, to whom miraculous powers are ascribed, for a time mentor of Śākyamuni after he left home. | 金 Kuṅkuma, saffron; a plant from which scent is made. | 鉢羅 v. 優 17 Utpala, blue lotus. | 陀 cf. 憂 15 and | 頭. | 陀那 v. 優 17 Udāna, voluntary addresses. | 鞞羅 Uruvilvā, the forest near Gaya where Śākyamuni was an ascetic for six years; also defined as a stream in that forest; cf. 優 17.

33. THIRTY-THREE STROKES

麤 Sthūla. Coarse, rough, crude, unrefined, immature. | 人 The immature man of Hīnayāna, who has a rough foundation, in contrast with the mature or refined 細人 man of Mahāyāna. T'ien-t'ai applied | to the 藏, 通, and 別 schools, reserving 細 for the 圓 school. | 惡苑 The rough and evil park, one of Indra's four parks, that of armaments and war. | 惡語 Coarse, evil, slanderous language. | 相 The six grosser or cruder forms of unenlightenment or ignorance mentioned in the 起信論 in contrast with its three finer forms. | 言 Coarse, crude, rough, immature words or talk; evil words. Rough, outline, preliminary words, e.g. Hīnayāna in contrast with Mahāyāna. The rough-and-ready, or cruder words and method of 誡 prohibitions from evil, in contrast with the more refined method of 勸 exhortation to good.

SANSKRIT AND PALI INDEX

The page numbers are followed by "a" indicating the left-hand column and "b" the right-hand column. Words sometimes occur more than once in the column indicated.

A, 3b, 211b, 285a, 362a, 377a, 426b
Ababa, 252a
Ābhāsvara, 85b, 179a, 202b, 220b, 289a, 403a
Ābhāsvara-vimāna, 202b, 289a
Abhāva, 295a
Abhaya, 68b, 381a
Abhayadāna, 303b
Abhayagiri, 292b, 381a
Abhayagiri-vāsinaḥ, 56a, 166a
Abhayaṁkara, 286b
Abhayandada, 303b
Abhayapradāna, 381a
Abhicāra(ka), 123b, 288b, 317b
Abhidhāna, 428b
Abhidharma, 44b, 84b, 288b, 306a, 315b, 386b, 395a, 423b, 444a, 467b
Abhidharma-hṛdaya-śāstra, 256a
Abhidharma-jñāna-prasthāna-śāstra, 315b
Abhidharma-kośa-śāstra, 256a
Abhidharma-mahāvibhāṣā-śāstra, 122b
Abhidharmāmṛta-śāstra, 466a
Abhidharma-piṭaka, 221b, 305b, 330a, 434a, 444a
Abhidharma-prakaraṇa-pāda-śāstra, 384b
Abhidheya, 410a
Abhijit, 22b, 288b
Abhijñā, 138b
Abhimāna, 238b
Abhimukham, 288b
Abhimukhī, 47b, 288b
Abhimukti, 288b
Abhirati, 104b, 290a, 293b, 378a, 394b, 487a
Abhisamaya, 359b
Abhisaṁbodha, 288b
Abhisaṁbuddha, 288b, 473b
Abhiṣecana, 125a, 413b, 483b
Abhiṣeka, 250a, 344a, 483b
Abhūta, 389b
Abhyudaya, 449b
Abhyudgata-rāja, 97a
Abrahmacariyā veramaṇī, 50a
Abrahmacarya, 177b
Abrahmacaryād vairamaṇī, 106a
Acala, 59a, 104a
Acalā, 47b, 52b, 378a
Acalacetā, 104b
Ācāra, 287b
Ācārya, 38b, 292b, 463b
Acchā-vāka, 169a
Acintya, 106b, 292b
Acintya-dhātu, 106b
Acintya-jñāna, 106b
Ādāna, 40b, 284b, 293b, 345a
Ādānavijñāna, 293b, 345a
Ādara, 294a
Ādarśa, 475a
Ādarśana-jñāna, 120a
Adattādāna, 109a
Adbhuta, 189a, 254a, 304a, 414a
Adbhuta-dharma, 44a, 189a, 236b
Adhigamāvabodha, 473b
Adhimāna, 238a
Adhimukti, 288a
Adhipati-phala, 361b, 431b
Adhipati-pratyaya, 260a
Adhiṣṭhāna, 167b
Adhyātma-vidyā, 119a, 131a
Ādi, 108a
Ādi-Buddha, 83b, 225a, 288a
Ādikarmika, 286b
Adinnādāna-veramaṇī, 50a
Āditya, 12b, 60b, 184b, 188b, 289a
Advaita, Advaya, 103a
Ādyanutpāda, *or* -panna, 288a
Agada, 225a, 285a
Agadaṁ, 292b
Āgam-, 249b
Āgama, 67b, 215a, 249b, 286a, 351b, 431a
Āgantuka, 289b
Āgantu-kleśa, 300a
Āgāra, 290b
Agaru, 241b
Agastya, 290a
Āgata, 249b
Agha, 292b, 371b
Aghana, 285a, 292b
Aghaniṣṭha, 220b
Agni, 3b, 184b, 290a, b, 330a, 372a
Agnidatta, 290b, 341a
Agni-dhātu samādhi, 161b
Aguru, 241b, 285a, 372a
Aḥ, Āḥ, 120b
Ahaha, 286a, 421b
Āhāra, 292a, 318b
Āhāra āharaṇam āyuḥ-saṁtāraṇe, 344a
Ahiṁsā, 106a
Āho, Āhu, 286a
Ahorātra, 6b, 216b
Ahrīka, 379a
Ahūṁ, 286a
Aicchantika, 71a
Aikāgrya, 1a
Aindrī, 12a
Aiṇeya, 290b, 205b
Aiṇeyajaṅgha, 200b
Airāvaṇa, 201a, 201b, 369b, 478b
Airāvata, 369b
Aiśvarikas, 292a
Ajātaśatru, 17b, 189a, 293b, 453b
Ajātaśatru-kaukṛtya, vinodana, 189a
Ajiravatī, 38a, 286b, 287b
Ajita, 49b, 286a, b, 290b, 292b, 378a, 382a
Ajita-keśakambali, 290b
Ajitaṁjaya, 291b
Ajitavatī, 203b, 285b
Ājīvika, 290b
Ajñānakarmatṛṣṇā, 380a
Ājñāta-Kauṇḍinya, 20b, 121b, 291a, 433a
Ājñātāvīndriya, 22a
Ājñendriya, 22a
Akaniṣṭha, 122a, 179b, 215b, 220b, 221a, 292b, 391a
Ākarṣaṇī, 114a, 123b
Ākāśa, 292b, 380b, 389b
Ākāśagarbha, 94b, 389b, 390a
Ākāśānantyāyatana, 17a, 180a, 278a, 382a
Ākāśapratiṣṭhita, 96a, 389b
Ākhu, 419b
Ākiñcanyāyatana, 17a, 18a, 379b, 382a
Ākrośa, 287b
Akṣa, 371b
Akṣamālā, 286a
Akṣapāda, 199a, 205b, 245a
Akṣara, 211b, 372a, 472a
Akṣayamati, 287a, 381a
Akṣobha, 378a
Akṣobhya 96a, 104a, 293b, 378a
Akṣobhya-tathāgatasya vyūha, 104b
Ākulakara, 294a
Alabhya, 105a
Alakavatī, 286a
Alakṣaṇa-buddha, 381b
Ālambana(-pratyaya), 62a, 259a, 361b, 392b
Alaṁkāraka, 363b
Alātacakra, 445a
Ālaya, 285b, 292a
Ālaya-vijñāna, 40b, 264b, 292a, 327a, 359b, 362a, 394a, 426b, 467b, 473b, 474a
Āliṅg-, 288a
Aṁ, 120b
Amala, 77a, 288a, 356b, 378a, 387a
Amalā, 387a
Āmalaka *v.* Āmra, 288a
Amalavijñāna, 357a
Āmantraṇa (-e), 35a
Amarāvatī, 188b, 228a
Ambā, 288a
Ambapāli, 387a
Ambarīṣa, 387a
Amida, 93b
Amita, 63a, 287a, 382b
Amitābha, 63a, 77b, 96a, 230b, 382b, 457a, 490a
Amitāyus, 77b, 287a, 382b, 490a
Āmla, Amlikā, 387a
Amogha, 108, 289b, 375b
Amoghadarśin, 108b
Amoghāṅkuśa, 108b
Amoghapāśa, 108b, 289b
Amoghasiddhi, 104a, 108b
Amogha Tripiṭaka, 108a
Amoghavajra, 108a, b, 289b, 333a
Āmra, 247b, 288a, 304b, 387a
Āmradārikā, 304b, 326b, 387a
Āmraka, 461a
Āmrapālī, 304b, 387a
Āmrāta(ka), 288a, 387a
Āmravana, 241a, 387a
Āmrāvatī, 387a
Amṛta, 195b, 287a
Amṛtakuṇḍalin, 195b, 463b
Amṛtodana, 195b, 287b
Aṁśuvarman, 454b
Amūḍha-vinaya, 13a
Āna, 293a
Anabhraka, 45b, 179b, 220b
Anāgamana-nirgama, 103b
Anāgāmin, 106b, 109b, 226b, 247b, 293a
Anāgata, 188b
Anājñātamājñāsyāmīndriya, 22a
Ānanda, 22b, 48b, 209b, 294a, 368b, 386b, 423b, 475a
Ānandabhadra, 294a
Ānandapura, 294a

Manoratha, 192a, 211a, 435b
Manorhita, 22b, 192a, 435b
Manovijñāna, 40a, 400b, 473b
Mantra, 80a, 252b, 256b, 333a, 335b, 352b
Manu, 152b
Mānuṣa, 435b
Mānuṣa-kṛtya, 31b
Manuṣya, 31b, 191b, 213b, 214a, 435b
Manuṣya-gati, 138b
Mānuṣi-Buddha, 63b
Māra, 485b
Māra-dhyāna, 486a
Marakata, 192a, 436a
Mārakāyikās, 486b
Maraṇa, 191a, 216a
Mardala, 216b
Mārga, 37b, 182a, 191a, 415b, 416b, 417a
Mārgaśīrṣa (*or* -śiras), 147a, 191a
Marica, 192a
Marīci, 23a, 405a, 435a
Markaṭa, 437b, 478b
Markaṭa-hrada, 192a
Marmacchid, 465a
Marman, 191b
Māṣa, 245a, 430b, 449a
Maskari-Gośālīputra, 184a, 191a
Maskarin, 134b
Masūra-Saṅghārāma, 245a, 435b
Mātā, 449a
Mātaṅga, 438a, 483b
Mātaṅga-araṅyaka, 291b, 436a
Mātaṅgī, 438a
Māthava, 436a
Mathurā, 46a, 335a, 430b, 435a
Mati, 191b, 213b, 435b
Matipura, *v.* Māthava, 148b, 335a
Matisiṁha, 191b
Mātṛ, 12a, 193b, 435a, b, 449a
Mātratā, 344a
Mātṛgrāma, 193b
Mātṛkā, 190a, 193b, 221b, 228a, 299a, 435b
Matsara, 191b, 423b
Matsya, 366b, 367b
Matta, 262a
Maṭutacaṇḍī, 395b
Maudgalīputra, 199a, 241b
Maudgalyāyana, 48a, 199a, 241b, 286b, 350b, 400b
Maurya, 148b
Māya, 339b
Māyā, 228a, 379b, 430b, 437b, 482b, 149a
Māyādṛṣṭi, 241b
Mayūra, 148b, 436a
Mayūrarāja, 23a
Megha, 394a, 456b
Megha-dundubhi-ṣvara-rāja, 394a
Meghasvara, 96a
Meghasvara-rāja, 96a, 394a
Mekā, 457a
Mekhalā, 457a
Meru, 457a
Merudhvaja, 394b
Merukalpa, 96a, 394b
Merukūṭa, 96a, 394b
Micchaka, 22b, 373a, 457a
Middha, 408a
Mihira, 44a
Mihirakula, 90a, 149a, 486b
Mikkaka, 457a
Milinda, 457a
Milindapañha, 247b, 455b
Mīmāṁsā, 301a
Mīmāṁsā-ṛddhi-pādaḥ, 174a
Miśrakāvana, 181a
Mithyā, 126b, 210a
Mithyāmāna, 246b
Miti, 457a
Mitraśānta, 457a
Mleccha, 251b, 428b, 443a, 457a
Moca, 313a
Moggaliputta Tissa, 117b
Moha, 241b, 364b, 371b, 400a, 432b, 468b
Mokṣa, 157b, 412b
Mokṣadeva, 157b, 194b, 413a
Mokṣagupta, 157b
Mokṣala, 378a
Mokṣa-mahā-pariṣad, 90a, 338a
Moṅgali, 245a, 422b, 435b
Mṛdaṅga, 216b
Mṛdu, 60b, 241b
Mṛga, 367a, 428b
Mṛgadāva, 166a, 367a, 428b
Mṛgānandi, 140b
Mṛgāṅka, 156a
Mṛga-rāja, 428b
Mṛgaśiras, 22b
Mṛgasthāpana, 428b
Mṛta, 216a
Mṛta-manuṣya, 193b
Mṛtyu, 241b
Mucilinda, 153a, 199a, 216b, 437a
Mucira, 157a
Mudga, 199a
Mudgalaputra, 159a
Mudgara, 199a
Mūḍha, 399b, 408a
Muditā, 178a
Mudrā, 89b, 157b, 193b, 203a, 299b, 391b, 432b
Muhūrta, 216b, 436a
Mukha, 82a, 199a
Mukhaproñchana, 157b
Mukta, 199a, 206b
Mukti, 157b, 412b
Mūla, 22b, 327a, 432b
Mūlabarhaṇī, 22b
Mūlagrantha, 189b
Mūlasarvāstivādāḥ, 3a, 215a, 432b
Mūlasthānapura, 313a
Muni, 153a, 216b, 313a, 482b
Muniśrī, 216b
Mūrdhābhiṣikta, 483b
Mūrdhajāta, 154a
Mūṣa, 419b
Musala, 184b
Musālagarbha, 384a
Musāragalva, 12a, 216b, 384a, 435a
Musāvādāveramaṇī, 50a

Ṇacca-gīta-vādita-visūkadassanā veramaṇī, 50b
Nāda, 226a
Nada, Nadī, 186b, 247a, b
Nadī-kāśyapa, 216b, 247b, 316b, 350a
Naga, 323a
Nāga, 247a, 390b, 454b
Nāgakanyā, 454b
Nāgakrośana, 247a
Nāgapuṣpa, 455a
Nagara, 247b, 486a
Nagarahāra, 247b, 486a
Nāgarāja, 455a
Nāgārjuna, 22b, 176b, 214a, 225a, 243b, 247a, 287b, 333a, 373a, 391b, 454a
Nāgasena, 247b, 455b
Nāgavajra, 184b
Nagna, 450a
Naiḥsargikāḥ pāyattikāḥ, 27a
Naiḥsargika-prāyaścittika, 185b
Nairañjanā, 185b, 197b, 236b, 364b, 460b
Nairātmya, 379b
Naivasaṁjñānāsaṁjñānāyatana, 17a, 180a, 295a, 382a
Nakṣatra, 22b, 348a, 396a
Nakṣatra-nātha, 156a
Nakṣatra-rāja-saṅkusumitābhijña, 348a
Nakṣatra-rāja-vikrīḍita, 348a
Nakṣatratārā-rājāditya, 155b
Nakula, 450a
Nālandā, 206b, 247b, 303b
Namaḥ, 248b, 298a, 336a
Namaḥ sarva-tathāgatebhyaḥ, 95b
Nāmamātra, 344a
Nāman, 204a, 247b
Nāmarūpa, 204a
Namo, 248b, 298a
Ñamo Amitābha, 55a
Nanda, 137b, 475a, 487a
Nandā, 457a
Nandanavana, 181a, 487a
Nanda Upananda, 475a
Nandi, 415a
Nandika, 198b, 475a
Nandikāvarta, Nandyāvarta, 475a
Nara, 248a
Narādhāra, 248a
Naraka, 35a, 207b, 248a, 350a
Nāraka, 350a
Nārakagati, 15a
Naramānava, 248a
Nara-nārī, 248a
Narasaṁghārāma, 31b
Nārāyaṇa, 91b, 184b, 204b, 248a
Nārāyaṇadeva, 248a
Narendrayaśas, 88b, 248b
Nārikela, 247b
Nārikeladvīpa, 247b
Narmadā, 311b
Narya, 248a
Naṭa, 102b, 247b, 248a
Nāṭya-gīta-vāditra-viśūkadarśanād vairamaṇī (virati), 107a, *also see* Śikṣāpada, 50a
Nava, Navan, 15b, 247b
Navadevakula, 336a
Navagraha, 18a
Navanīta, 115b
Navamālikā, 247b
Navasaṅghārāma, 336a
Naya, Nāya, 248a, 323a
Nāyaka, 143b, 447a
Nayuta, 247b, 299b
Nemiṁdhara, 17b, 185a, 303a
Nemindhara, 49a
Nepāla, 185b
Nidāna, 44a, 186a, 359b
Nidāna-mātṛkā, 186a
Nidhāpana, 329a
Nidhi, 185a
Nigamana, 119a
Nīla, 185b, 294a
Nīladaṇḍa, 50a
Nīlanetra, 146b
Nīlapiṭa, 185b
Nīla-udumbara, 185b
Nīla-utpala, 265b
Nīlavajra, 185b
Nīlotpala, 185b, 207b
Nimba, 385b
Nimindhara, 185a
Nimitta, 309b
Nirābhāsa, 379a, 381b
Nirarbuda, 36a, 184b, 207b
Niraya, 207b, 253b, 265b
Nirdahana, 329a
Nirdeśa (-e), 35a
Nirgrantha, 134b, 185b, 428b, 475b
Nirgranthajñātiputra, 184a, 185b
Nirgranthaputra, 185b
Nirlakṣaṇa-buddha, 381b
Nirmāṇa, 457b
Nirmāṇabuddha, 141a, 226a
Nirmāṇakāya, 63b, 77b, 142b, 269a, 381a, 457b, 458a, 488a

Prajāpati, 267b, 418a, 482b
Prājña, 387b
Prajñā, 97b, 195a, 337b, 374b, 375a, 433a, 475b
Prajñābala, 114b, 433a
Prajñā-bodhisattva, 338a
Prajñāgupta, 338a
Prajñākūṭa, 375b
Prajñā-pāramitā (sūtra), 84b, 215a, 228a, 262b, 275b, 337b, 338a, 374b, 482a
Prajñapti, 59a, 342b
Prajñapti-śāstra, 429a
Prajñapti-vādinaḥ, 95a, 429a
Prajñātāra, 22b, 337b
Prajñendriya, 22a
Prākāmya, 89b
Prākāra, 266b
Prakaraṇa, 417b
Prakṛti, 218b, 258b, 417b
Pramāṇa, 359b, 392b
Pramiti, 337a
Pramuditā, 47b, 487a
Prāṇa, 338b
Prāṇātipātād vairamaṇī (virati), *see also* Śikṣāpada, 107b
Praṇidhāna, 51b, 476a
Praṇihita, 476a
Prāṇyamūla-śāstra-ṭīkā, 76b, 111a, 182a
Prāp, 349b
Prapañca, 458b
Prāpta, 349b
Prāpti, 89b
Prāsāda, 345a, 391b
Praśaka, 418a
Praśākhā, 34b, 346b, 418a
Praśama, 348a
Prasenajit, 191a, 251b, 266a, 368a, 418a
Praśrabdhi-saṁbodhyaṅga, 14b
Prastha, 418b
Pratāpāditya, 102a
Pratāpana, 92b, 207b, 377a, 403a
Pratibhāna, 178a, 439a
Pratibimba, 432a
Pratideśanā, 418a
Prātideśanīya, 27a, 187a, 266b, 373b, 418a, 440a
Pratigha, 68a, 213b, 439b
Pratijñā, 66a, 223b, 392b
Pratijñākāraka vinaya, 13a
Pratikrānta, 417b
Pratimā, 226a, 236b
Pratimokṣa, 240a, 266b
Prātimokṣa, 266b, 418a
Prātipadika, 169a
Pratirūpa(ka), 420a
Pratisaṁkhyā-nirodha, 380b, 447b
Pratisaṁvid, 178a, 390b, 439a
Pratiśrut, 487b
Pratītya-samutpāda, 43a, 441b
Pratyakṣa, 359b
Pratyātmāryajñāna, 219b
Pratyavekṣaṇa-jñāna, 120a
Pratyaya, 205a, 418a, 440b
Pratyaya-bala, 440b
Pratyeka, 245a, 414a
Pratyeka-buddha, 361a, 414a, 441a, 448b
Pratyutpanna (samādhi), 337b
Pravacana, 351b
Pravāda, 308b
Pravara, 266a
Pravāraṇa, 219a, 224b, 417b
Pravari, 266a
Pravartana, 469b
Praveśa, 418a
Pravicaya, 490a
Pravraj, 166b
Pravṛtti-vijñāna, 469a
Prayāga, 418b
Prāyaścitta, 267b, 431a, 440a
Prāyaścittikāḥ, 27a
Prayoga, 167b
Prayuta, 418b
Preta, 320a, 341b, 361a, 454a, 462a
Pretagati, 138b
Prīti, 368b
Prīti-saṁbodhyaṅga, 14b
Priyadarśana, 368b
Priyavacana, 176a
Pṛkkā, 361a
Pṛthagjana, 188a, 361b
Pṛthak, 361a
Pṛthivī, 23a, 82b, 206b, 207a, 266b, 417b
Pudgala, 31b, 187b, 370b, 412a
Pūga, 465a
Puggala, 187b
Pūjā, 249b
Pukkaśa, 54b
Punar, 370b
Punarvasu, 22b, 137b, 370b
Puṇḍarīka, 36a, 140b, 189b, 198a, 254a, 280a, 443a
Puṇḍravardhana, 254a
Puṇya, 370b, 426a
Puṇyādarśa, 188a
Puṇyamitra, 22b, 106a
Puṇya-prasava, 45b, 179b, 220b, 426a
Puṇyaśālā, 254a
Puṇyatara, 167b, 174b, 188a
Puṇyavardhana, 47a
Puṇyayaśas, 22b, 370b
Puṇyopāya, 186b, 247b
Purāṇa, 370b
Pūraṇa-kāśyapa, 109a, 134b, 184a, 186b, 370b
Purandara, 370b
Pūrikā, 186b
Pūrṇa, 48a, 186b, 370a, b, 412a, 425a
Pūrṇabhadra, 186b, 370b
Pūrṇaghaṭa, 190a
Pūrṇaka, 140b
Pūrṇamaitrāyaṇīputra, 246b, 370a
Pūrṇeccha, 370b
Puruṣa, 31b, 187a, 219a, 248a, 334b, 370a, 412a
Puruṣa-damya-sārathi, 52b, 444a
Puruṣakāra-phala, 361b
Puruṣapura, 228a, 370a
Puruṣendriya, 22a
Pūrva, 263b, 297a, 412a
Pūrva-aṣāḍhā, 22b
Pūrva-dvitīya, 303a
Pūrva-phalgunī, 22b
Pūrvanivāsana, 348a
Pūrvanivāsānusmṛti-jñāna, 123a, 348a, 474a
Pūrvapraṇidhāna, 190b
Pūrva-proṣṭhapada, 22b
Pūrvaśaila (*or* -āḥ), 95a, 188a, 228a, 263b
Pūrvaśaila-saṅghārāma, 188a, 263b
Pūrvavideha, 34a, 178a, 186b, 187b, 225b, 227a, 263b, 365a, 367b, 412a
Puryamitra, 106a
Puṣpa, 187a, 280a, 387a, 412a
Puṣpadantī, 52b, 388b
Puṣpadeva, 188a
Puṣpāhara, 188a
Puṣpanāga, 254a
Puṣpapura, 388a
Puṣṭikarman, 484b
Puṣya, 22b, 188a, 297b, 370b, 374a, 412a
Puṣyamitra, 188a
Pūtana, 41a, 186b, 370a
Pūti-agada, 186b

Rāga, 290a, 364a, 400b, 472b
Rāgadveṣamoha, 364b
Rāhu, 18a, 472a
Rāhu-asura, 472a
Rāhula, 48b, 223a, 473a, 472a, 482b
Rāhulata, 22b, 472a
Raivata, 230b
Rāja, 163b, 263a, 290b, 472a
Rāja-dhātu, 290b
Rājagṛha, 91a, 164a, 205a, 304a, 472b
Rāja-haṁsa, 159a, 470b
Rājamahendrī, 87b
Rājan, 472a
Rājapura, 304a
Rajas, 297b, 355a
Rājñī, 486a
Rājyavardhana, 102a, 163b
Rakṣaḥ, 10b
Rakṣalevatā, 184b
Rakṣas, 471b
Rākṣasa, 291b, 471b
Rākṣasī, 4a, 291b, 471b
Rakta, 311b
Raktapadma, 418a
Rāma, 467a, 472a
Rāmacandra, 472a
Rāmagrāma, 467a
Rāmāyaṇa, 472a
Rasa, 252b, 328b
Raśmiprabhāsa, 202a
Raśmi-śata-sahasra-pari-pūrṇa-dhvaja, 311b
Rāṣṭrapāla, 451a
Rathakāya, 171a
Ratna, 297b, 472b, 476a
Ratnadhvaja, 477a
Ratnadvīpa, 477a
Ratnagarbha, 304a, 478a
Ratnākara, 297b
Ratnakaraṇḍaka, 477b
Ratnaketu, 176b, 476b, 477b
Ratnakūṭa, 477b
Ratnamati, 343b
Ratnamudra, 476b
Ratnapāṇi, 120b
Ratnapiṭaka, 477b
Ratnarāśi, 477b
Ratnasaṁbhava, 120b, 477b
Ratnaśikhin, 101b, 297b
Ratnatraya, 63b
Ratnāvabhāsa kalpa, 270b
Raudrī, 12a
Raurava, 35a, 169a, 207b, 233b, 252a, 412a, 464a
Rāvaṇa, 472a, b
Ravi, 201a
Ṛddhi, 211a
Ṛddhi-mantra, 334b
Ṛddhipāda, 61a, 173b, 211a, 335a
Ṛddhi-sākṣātkriyā, 123a, 335a
Ṛddhividhi-jñāna, 245b
Repa, Repha, 199b
Revata, 230b, 475b
Revatī, 22b, 300a
Riktamuṣṭi, 277a
Rocana, 449a
Rohiṇī, 22b
Rohitaka, 43b
Rohita-mukta, 12a, 448b
Ṛṣabha, 58b, 343a
Ṛṣi, 166a, 334b
Ṛṣigiri, 201a
Rucika, 438b
Ruciraketu, 234b
Rudhirāhāra, 254a
Rudra, 60b, 188b, 438b, 446b, 449a
Rudrākṣa, 281a, 371b, 396a
Rugṇa, 337b
Ruṇḍa, 123b, 337b
Ruṇṇapaṇḍaka, 330b

Veṣṭana (Veṣṭu), 231a, 233b
Vetāla, 101a, 307b, 339b, 421b
Vibhā, 236b
Vibhāga, 139b
Vibhajya, 139b
Vibhajyavādinaḥ, 3a, 140a, 305b
Vibhārakṣita, 399a
Vibhāṣā, 58a, 182a, 245a, 305b
Vibhāṣā-śāstra, 305b, 435b
Vibhāvana, 231a, 369a, 490a
Vicāra, 223a, 305b, 370b
Vichavapura, 307a
Vicikitsā, 425b
Vidagdhaka, 17b
Vidarśanā, 489a
Videha, 34a, 186b, 305b, 367b
Vidhu, 266a
Vidyā, 262a, 275a, 307a
Vidyācaraṇa-saṁpanna, 52b, 263a, 464a
Vidyādharapiṭaka, 408b
Vidyā-mātra-(siddhi)-śāstra, 237b
Vidyā-mātra-siddhi-tridaśa kārikā-śāstra, 344b
Vidyā-mātra-siddhi-viṁśakakārikā śāstra, 344b
Vigama, 453b
Vigata, 453b
Vigatāśoka, 318a
Vighna, 80a
Vighnāntaka, 50a
Vihāra, 212a, 307b, 396a
Vihāragrāma, 247b
Vihārapāla, 74a, 250a, 307b, 484b
Vihārasvāmin, 74a, 165b, 307b
Vihiṁsā, 323b
Vīja, v. Bīja, 426b
Vijaya, 113b, 376a, 399a
Vijaya-Saṁbhava, 90b
Vijitavat, 305b
Vijñāna, 40a, 42b, 126a, 275a, 307b, 398a, 473b
Vijñāna-dhātu, 474a
Vijñana-mātra, 344b
Vijñāna-mātra-siddhi-śāstra, 344b
Vijñānānantyāyatana, 17a, 180a, 382a
Vijñāna-skandha, 474a
Vijñānavāda, 77b, 407b
Vijñapti, 307a
Vijñapti-mātra, 307a, 344b
Vijñapti-mātra-tāsiddhi-śāstra, 212a
Vikāla-bhojanād vairamaṇī (virati), 109b, 110a
Vikālabhojanā veramaṇī, 50a
Vikalpa, 139b
Vikāra, 305a
Vikarāla, 44a
Vikhāditaka, 17b
Vikīrṇa, 113b
Vikrama, 391a
Vikramāditya, 307b, 391a, 430a
Vikrīḍita, 414b
Vikrītavana, 391a
Vikṣiptaka, 17b
Vilamba, 52b
Vilohitaka, 17b
Vimala, 47b, 306a, 357a, 378a
Vimalacitra, 233b, 306a
Vimaladattā, 202b
Vimalagarbha, 358b
Vimalakīrti, 154a, 234a, 306a, 427b, 454b
Vimalakīrti-nirdeśa sūtra, 84b, 427b
Vimalākṣa, 251b
Vimalanetra, 349b, 358a
Vimba, Bimba, 453b (Bot.)
Vimbara, 453b
Vimokṣa, 306b, 412b, 413a
Viṁśatikā vijñaptimātratāsiddhi śāstra, 84a
Vimuktaghoṣa, 306b
Vimukti, 306b, 412b, 413a
Vimuni, 216b
Vīṇā, 140b
Vinata, 159a
Vinataka, 17b, 307b
Vinaya, 48b, 239b, 240a, 301b, 306a, 408b, 467b
Vināyaka, 184b, 307b, 453b, 487a
Vinaya-piṭaka, 301b, 306a
Viṅgila, 360b
Vinīlaka, 17b
Vinītaprabha, 126b
Viṅkila, 36b
Vipaḍumaka, 17b
Vipāka, 306a, 361a
Vipākahetu, 133b, 361a
Vipākaphala, 361b
Viparyaya, 170b, 475b
Vipāśā, 306a
Vipaśyanā, 305b, 307b, 489a
Vipaśyin, 96b, 305b, 427b
Viprakṛ, 373b
Vipula, 305b, 432a
Vipulamati, Vipulaprajña, 432a
Vipūyaka, 17b
Vīra, 41b, 381a
Vīrabhadra, 50a
Vīradatta, 381a
Vīraṇakacchapa, 305a
Viruddha, 159a
Virūḍhaka, 23a, 145b, 236b, 266a, 306b, 356a, 425b, 431b
Virūpākṣa, 23a, 145b, 236b, 265b, 306b, 321b, 356a, 430b, 432a, 463a, 470b
Vīrya, 306a, 392a, 396a, 427a
Vīryabala, 114a
Vīrya-pāramitā, 41b
Vīrya-ṛddhi-pāda, 174a
Vīrya-saṁbodhyaṅga, 14b
Vīryasena, 307b
Vīryendriya, 22a
Viśākhā, 22b, 293a, 306b, 307a,
Viśāla, 307a
Visaṁyoga-phala, 361b
Viṣāṇa, 244b, 306a
Visarj, 140a
Viṣaya, 421b
Viśeṣa, 138b, 231b, 305b
Viśiṣṭa-cāritra-Bodhisattva, 57a, 173b
Viṣṇu, 63b, 231a, 318a, 399a
Viśuddha, 399a
Viśuddhacāritra, 173b
Viśuddhasiṁha, 159a
Viśuddhi, 357a
Viśva, 306b, 374a
Viśvabhadra, 69b, 280b, 374a
Viśvabhū, 3a, 307a
Viśvakarman, 43b, 307b
Viśvamitra, 305a, 451b
Viśvapāṇi, 120b
Vitarka, 305b, 314b, 370b
Vītāśoka, 305a, 318a
Vitasti, 424a
Vitatha, 389b
Vivarjana, 429b
Vivarta, 83a, 85b, 232b, 237b, 470b
Vivarta-siddha, 85b, 224a, 232b, 237b, 470b
Viveka, 139b, 305a
Vivikta, 348a
Vivṛj, 429b
Vrata, 241b
Vṛji, 58b, 168b, 188a, 232a, 392a
Vṛjisthāna, 228a, 484b
Vṛkṣa, 305a, 448a
Vṛtti, 469a
Vyādhmātaka, 17b
Vyāghra, 280a
Vyākāra, 351a
Vyākaraṇa, 19b, 44b, 253a, 305a, 339a, 351a
Vyākaraṇa-kauṇḍinya, 433a
Vyañjana, 296a
Vyāsa, 307a
Vyūharāja, 363b

Yācñā, 310b
Yadbhūyasikīya-vinaya, 13a
Yajñadatta, 424b
Yajurveda, 230a, 253b, 361b
Yakṣa, 41a, 253b, 363a
Yakṣa-kṛtya, 253b
Yakṣa-rāj, 46a
Yama, 37b, 184b, 187b, 216a. 233a, 253b, 452a, 453b
Yama(deva)loka, 253b, 377a, 383b
Yama-maṇḍala, 377a
Yamana, 452a
Yamāntaka, 49b, 317b, 452a
Yamarāja, 23a
Yamī, 452a
Yāmī, 419a
Yamunā, 383b, 452a, 489b
Yāna, 320a
Yaśas, 204b, 311b, 344a
Yaśaskāma, 241b
Yaśodā, 311b
Yaśodharā, 231b, 311b, 465b
Yaṣṭi, 250b, 297b
Yaṣṭivana, 197b, 213a, 241a, 308a
Yathā, 210a
Yathābhūtam, 211a
Yathāvat, 253b
Yava, 311b, 367b
Yavadvīpa, Yavana, 311b, 452a, 311b
Yāvat, 15b
Yoga, 50b, 310a, 347b, 407b
Yogācāra, 335a, b, 407b
Yogācārya, 89b, 285b, 289b
Yogācārya-bhūmi-śāstra, 89b, 399a, 407b
Yogin, 407b
Yojana, 2a, 197b
Yoni, 98a, 312a
Yuga, 164a
Yugaṁdhara, 17b, 49a, 303a, 342a, 407b
Yuktā, 278b
Yuktabodhi, 278b
Yukti, 278b

INDEX OF TERMS OTHER THAN SANSKRIT AND PALI